THE
NEW BOOK
OF
KNOWLEDGE

THE
NEW BOOK
OF
KNOWLEDGE

Grolier Incorporated, Danbury, Connecticut

VOLUME 15

P

ISBN 0-7172-0528-2 (set)

The publishers wish to thank the following for permission to use copyrighted material:
The Cresset Press Limited for "The Country Bedroom" from *Collected Poems* by Frances Cornford.
Holt, Rinehart and Winston, Inc., Laurence Pollinger Limited, and Jonathan Cape Limited for "The
    Runaway" from *Complete Poems of Robert Frost*, copyright 1923 by Holt, Rinehart and Winston,
    Inc., 1951 by Robert Frost.
Margot Johnson Agency for "Human Things" from *The Next Room of the Dream* by Howard Nemerov,
    published by University of Chicago Press, copyright 1962 by Howard Nemerov.
Little, Brown and Company and J. M. Dent & Sons Ltd. for "The Eel" from *Verses from 1929 On* by
    Ogden Nash, copyright 1942 by Ogden Nash.
McGraw-Hill Book Company for epigram from *Light Armour* by Richard Armour, copyright 1954 by
    Richard Armour.
The Macmillan Company for "The Dark Hills" from *Collected Poems* by E. A. Robinson, copyright 1920
    by E. A. Robinson, renewed 1948 by Ruth Nivison; and the Macmillan Company, Mrs. Iris Wise, the
    Macmillan Company of Canada Ltd., and Macmillan & Co. Ltd. for "Seumas Beg" from *Collected
    Poems* by James Stephens, copyright 1909 by the Macmillan Company.
Random House, Inc., for "Summer Holiday" from *The Selected Poetry of Robinson Jeffers*, copyright
    1925, renewed 1953 by Robinson Jeffers.
Charles Scribner's Sons and Hodder and Stoughton Ltd. for excerpt from *Peter Pan* by James Barrie,
    copyright 1911, renewed 1939 by Lady Cynthia Asquith and Peter L. Davies.
The Viking Press, Inc., for "The Circus" and "Firefly" from *Under the Tree* by Elizabeth Madox Roberts,
    copyright 1922 by B. W. Huebsch, Inc., 1950 by Ivor S. Roberts.
Penguin Books Ltd. for illustrations from *The Tale of Jemima Puddle-Duck* by Beatrix Potter. Copyright
    © 1908 by Frederick Warne and Co.

Trademark
THE BOOK OF KNOWLEDGE
registered in U.S. Patent Office

P, the 16th letter in the English alphabet, was the 17th letter in the ancient Hebrew and Phoenician alphabets and the 16th letter in the classical Greek alphabet. The Hebrews and Phoenicians called it *pe* (pronounced "pay"). The Greeks called it *pi* (pronounced like the word "pea").

Many language scholars believe that the Phoenician letter *pe* represented a mouth and that the word *pe* meant "mouth." The letter *pe* looked like this: ⟩

The Greeks based their alphabet on the Phoenician alphabet. The letter *pi* looked like this at first: Γ Later this form developed into the classical Greek letter *pi:* Π (pronounced "pie").

Before the Greek letter reached its final form, the Romans learned the earlier Greek form from the Etruscans (another ancient people, who lived in Italy). The Romans used the letter for the same sound as the Greeks, but they changed its form slightly to the P used in the English language today.

In English the sound of P is most often that of the words *pill* or *pen.* When P is followed by H, it is usually pronounced like F, as in the word *phonograph.* Before N and some other letters, P at the beginning of a word is silent. Many of the words in which P is silent, such as *psalm* and *pneumatic,* come from the Greek.

In chemistry, P is the symbol for the element phosphorus. In music, P stands for piano, which is an instruction to play in a soft or quiet manner.

The letter P is also found in many abbreviations. P.T.A. stands for Parent-Teacher Association, and p. stands for page. P.S. is written at the end of a letter when something left out of the letter is added. The initials come from the Latin *postscriptum,* which means "written afterward."

The Latin *post,* meaning "after," is also used in the abbreviation P.M., or *post meridiem,* which stands for "afternoon."

Reviewed by MARIO PEI
Author, *The Story of Language*

See also ALPHABET.

SOME WAYS TO REPRESENT P:

The **manuscript** or printed forms of the letter (left) are highly readable. The **cursive** letters (right) are formed from slanted flowing strokes joining one letter to the next.

The **Manual Alphabet** (left) enables a deaf person to communicate by forming letters with the fingers of one hand. **Braille** (right) is a system by which a blind person can use fingertips to "read" raised dots that stand for letters.

The **International Code of Signals** is a special group of flags used to send and receive messages at sea. Each letter is represented by a different flag.

International Morse Code is used to send messages by radio signals. Each letter is expressed as a combination of dots (•) and dashes (––).

Left: White sandy beaches, clear blue waters, and towering palms are typical of the coral islands of the Pacific. This is one of the numerous islands of Micronesia. *Above:* Kayangel, part of Palau in the western Carolines, shows the distinctive shape of an atoll, with coral formations enclosing a lagoon.

PACIFIC OCEAN AND ISLANDS

The Pacific is the largest and deepest of the world's oceans. With an area of some 70,000,000 square miles (180,000,000 square kilometers), including neighboring seas, the Pacific has nearly half of the earth's ocean surface and makes up more than one third of its total surface. It is more than twice the size of the Atlantic Ocean, the world's second largest body of water. Because of its enormous area, the Pacific Ocean is often considered the earth's principal physical feature.

The Pacific was given its name, which means "peaceful," by the Portuguese navigator Ferdinand Magellan. Magellan, who sailed across the Pacific in the 1520's, found its waters especially calm. But he may have been luckier than he realized. The Pacific, although it can be peaceful, is also subject to destructive typhoons, or storms similar to hurricanes.

Boundaries, Extent, and Depth. The Pacific extends from the Arctic Ocean on the north to Antarctica on the south, a distance of more than 9,000 miles (14,480 kilometers). The coastlines of North and South America make up its eastern boundary. The western boundary is more difficult to define, because of the numerous islands and seas found there, but it is broadly formed by the mainland of Asia, Indonesia, and Australia. The Pacific measures about 11,000 miles (17,700 kilometers) from east to west along the equator, which divides it into the North Pacific and South Pacific oceans.

The Pacific is linked to the Indian Ocean by the Strait of Malacca (between Malaysia and Indonesia). The two oceans also join south of Australia. The Bering Strait connects the Pacific with the Arctic Ocean, and at Cape Horn (at the southern tip of South America), the Pacific merges with the Atlantic Ocean.

The Pacific has an average depth of about 14,000 feet (about 4,270 meters). Its greatest known depth is in the Challenger Deep of the Marianas Trench, which is the deepest point on earth. Located near the island of Guam, the Challenger Deep plunges 36,198 feet (11,033 meters)—or more than 7 miles—below the ocean surface.

Pacific islanders often employ fine carvings in their art. This intricate shield is from the Solomon Islands.

Islands: Continental and Oceanic. The Pacific has an enormous number of islands, estimated at about 25,000, most of which are found in the southern ocean and particularly in its western reaches. Although they vary in size, most are relatively small in area. The islands fall into two main but very different groups—continental and oceanic.

The continental islands rise from the continental shelves, the underwater areas surrounding most continents. These islands are really partially submerged mountain chains. They belong to the long chain of mountains and volcanoes that border the Pacific Basin.

Two processes helped to form the Pacific's oceanic islands—volcanism and subsidence. In volcanism, lava (hot, melted rock) is extruded, or poured out, from the earth's interior and then cools. An island forms if enough lava is extruded to produce a mass rising above the ocean surface. Hawaii is the largest of the Pacific islands formed by volcanism.

In subsidence, the great weight of the volcanic mass forces the crust of the ocean basin to sink, or subside. The older an island is, the more it will have sunk and, therefore, the lower it appears in the water.

In 1993 oceanographers mapping the ocean floor discovered more than 1,000 volcanoes in an area of the South Pacific. It was considered to be the largest known concentration of active volcanoes on earth.

Coral Reefs, Islands, Atolls. As a volcanic island subsides, colonies of small organisms called corals, living just below the surface of the water, sometimes attach themselves to it.

In time the volcanic material may disappear beneath the ocean. But the corals go on building upward, forming reefs. If sand, formed by breakup of the coral rock, collects on top of the rock, a low sandy island results. If this sandy island is shaped like a ring, it is called an atoll. The water enclosed by an atoll is a lagoon. In some cases masses of coral rock have been lifted above the surface by upward movement of the earth's crust. Many islands of the Tonga group were formed in this way.

Oceania: Land of the Pacific. The islands of the Pacific are often called Oceania. Australia and the islands and island groups in the shallow waters off the Asian mainland (such as the Philippines and Japan) are generally not considered part of Oceania. New Zealand is sometimes included.

The islands of Oceania are divided into three main groups—Polynesia ("many islands"), Melanesia ("black islands"), and Micronesia ("small islands").

Polynesia, the largest division, is made up of a large triangle of islands in the central and southeastern Pacific. It includes French Polynesia; the Hawaiian Islands; Tonga; Tuvalu; American Samoa and Western Samoa; part of Kiri-

Below: Fiery lava pours from Hawaii's Kilauea volcano. Many of the Pacific islands were created by volcanic action. *Right:* A ceremonial mask from Vanuatu depicts the body of a man and the head of a woman.

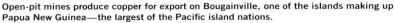
Yap islanders prepare copra, or dried coconut meat. Most of the low coral islands have little fertile soil, and copra is usually the main cash crop.

Melanesia, in the southwestern Pacific, includes Irian Jaya (the Indonesian half of the large island of New Guinea); New Caledonia; and the nations of Papua New Guinea, Vanuatu, the Solomon Islands, and Fiji. The larger Melanesian islands are mountainous, and many of them are densely forested.

The many small islands in northwestern Oceania are known as Micronesia. This region includes Nauru, Wake Island, part of Kiribati, the Marshall Islands, the Carolines (including the Federated States of Micronesia), and the Marianas. Most of the islands of Micronesia are low-lying coral atolls.

Peoples of the Pacific. The peoples of Oceania are often divided into three ethnic groups that parallel the geographic division of the islands. This is not strictly correct, as only the Polynesians form a distinct ethnic group. Melanesians and Micronesians include peoples of many different origins. Other groups include Americans, Japanese, and Chinese on the Hawaiian Islands and people of East Indian descent, who make up about half the population of Fiji. The native Fijians are a mixture of Melanesian and Polynesian ethnic groups.

Polynesians share the same basic language and have common physical and cultural characteristics. Before Europeans came to Oceania, Polynesians occupied almost all the

bati; Easter, Midway, and Niue islands; and the Tokelau, Cook, Pitcairn, and Wallis and Futuna island groups. The Maoris, who are the original inhabitants of the islands of New Zealand, are also Polynesian. Many of the Polynesian islands are the tops of submerged mountains. Others are atolls or coral islands.

Open-pit mines produce copper for export on Bougainville, one of the islands making up Papua New Guinea—the largest of the Pacific island nations.

What is the Great Barrier Reef?

The Great Barrier Reef is the world's longest coral formation. Situated in the Coral Sea, it stretches for some 1,250 miles (over 2,000 kilometers) between New Guinea and the northeastern coast of Australia. The great reef is actually a series of reefs and coral islands, extending between 10 and 100 miles (15 and 160 kilometers) off the Australian mainland. Over many millions of years, the hundreds of different types of corals have built up "gardens" of unusual and beautiful shapes in varied colors. These attract a wide variety of marine life, including brightly colored fish, sea birds, green turtles, and giant clams and other mollusks. The Great Barrier Reef is an Australian national park and an especially popular tourist attraction.

islands of the South Pacific, as well as Hawaii and New Zealand.

Most Melanesians live on New Guinea and nearby islands. Although generally dark-skinned, they differ in appearance, language, and customs. Many of them, especially in the remote, mountainous areas of New Guinea, had little contact with the outside world until fairly recent times. The Micronesians live mainly on the small islands scattered over a vast area of the northwestern Pacific. They, too, have different languages, customs, and physical characteristics.

Most islanders live in villages or small towns. There are few large cities, except on Hawaii and New Zealand.

Climate. Most of the islands of Oceania lie within the tropics, and the climate here is uniformly warm. Temperatures along the equator vary only from about 70 to 81°F (21 to 27°C) throughout the year. By contrast, in the far northern and southern waters, temperatures fall to less than 14°F (−10°C). The amount of rainfall varies considerably, with most of the islands having distinct wet and dry seasons. The most destructive typhoons occur in the western and southwestern Pacific.

Economic Activity. Agriculture remains the region's most important economic activity. Most Pacific islanders practice subsistence farming, growing food for their own use. On the low coral islands, which have little fertile soil and receive relatively light rainfall, copra (dried coconut meat) is the only cash crop. On the higher volcanic islands, which usually have more rainfall and better soil, such crops as pineapples, sugarcane, cacao, and bananas are grown for export. The surrounding waters teem with fish.

There is little industry, aside from the processing of copra and other agricultural products, although tourism is a major source of income on some of the Pacific islands. Mineral resources are limited. New Caledonia has important nickel deposits, and copper is found on Bougainville. New Guinea has oil and gold, and tiny Nauru is rich in phosphate rock, used in making fertilizer.

Early History. The first migration of peoples to the Pacific islands probably originated from Southeast Asia tens of thousands of years ago, when the largest islands were linked by a land bridge. Later, seafarers ventured farther out on the uncharted waters of the Pacific.

The Europeans and Americans. The first European known to have seen the Pacific was the Spanish explorer and adventurer Vasco Núñez de Balboa. After crossing the Isthmus of Panama in 1513, Balboa sighted the great ocean, which he called the South Sea. Magellan, a few years later, gave the ocean its present name during his attempt to sail around the world. Although Magellan himself was killed, his crew completed the epic voyage. Other Spanish and Portuguese navigators explored the islands in the 1500's and 1600's. The greatest of the Pacific explorers, the British captain James Cook, discovered Hawaii and mapped much of Oceania during the late 1760's and 1770's. American and British whaling ships also began to call at the islands. Europeans and

The art of the Marquesas Islands includes this stern-looking figure, carved from bone.

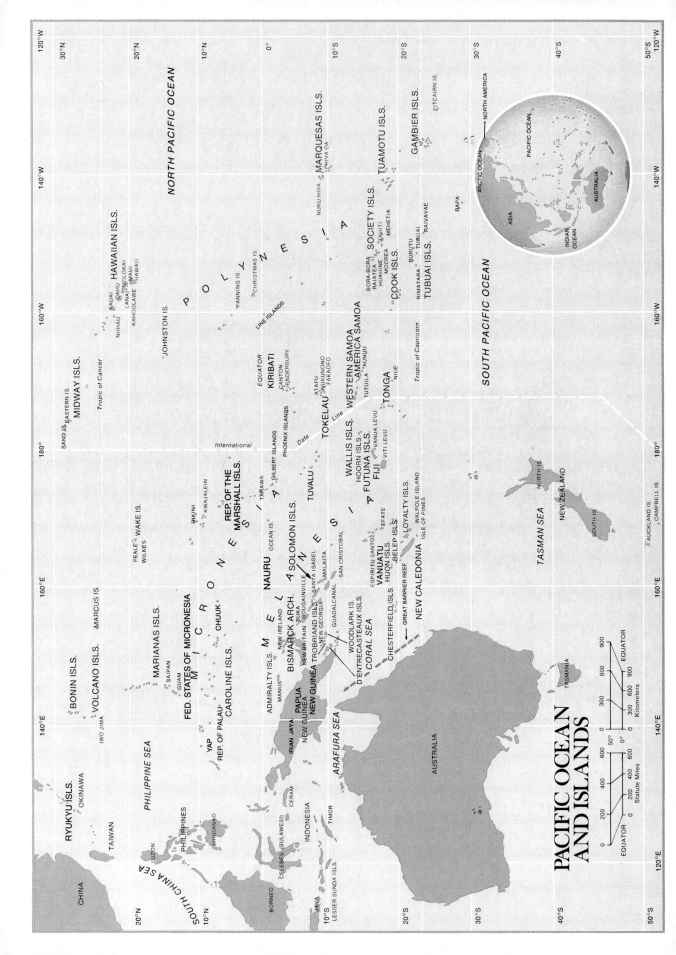

PACIFIC OCEAN AND ISLANDS

Left: The British navigator Captain James Cook is seen here landing at Tana, in the New Hebrides (now Vanuatu), in 1774. Tragically, Cook was killed in Hawaii, in 1779, after a misunderstanding with the islanders. *Below:* U.S. Marines wade ashore under Japanese attack on Saipan (in the Marianas) in 1944, during World War II. The Pacific was a major theater of operations in the war.

Americans settled here as planters and traders, and missionaries soon followed. A few of the islands became important as naval bases or as coaling stations in the days when ships were fueled by coal. By the end of the 1800's, Britain, France, Germany, and the United States all had established themselves as colonial powers in the Pacific.

See articles on Balboa, Cook, and Magellan in the appropriate volumes.

Two World Wars and After. Germany lost its Pacific colonies after its defeat, in 1918, in World War I. Japan received the German colonies in the Marianas, the Carolines, and the Marshalls under a mandate from the League of Nations. During World War II, many of the islands were battlegrounds in the Pacific war (1941–45). Its defeat in the war forced Japan to give up the islands, which then became a United Nations trust territory, administered by the United States. Since the 1960's, a number of Pacific islands have gained their independence. Hawaii became a state of the United States in 1959. The islands of the U.S. Trust Territory of the Pacific became independent in 1986 and 1994, in free association with the United States.

WARD BARRETT
University of Minnesota
Author, *Mission in the Marianas*

See also CORALS; ISLANDS; OCEANOGRAPHY; OCEANS AND SEAS OF THE WORLD.

Brief descriptions of some of the Pacific islands and island groups follow.

INDEPENDENT NATIONS OF OCEANIA

COUNTRY	CAPITAL	AREA[1]	
		(sq mi)	(km²)
Fiji	Suva	7,056	18,274
Kiribati	Tarawa	281	728
Marshall Islands, Rep. of[2]	Majuro	70	181
Micronesia, Fed. States of[2]	Colonia	271	702
Nauru	No formal capital	8	21
New Zealand[3]	Wellington	103,736	268,676
Palau, Rep. of[2]	Koror	192	497
Papua New Guinea	Port Moresby	178,260	461,691
Solomon Islands	Honiara	10,983	28,446
Tonga	Nuku'alofa	270	699
Tuvalu	Funafuti	10	26
Vanuatu	Vila	5,700	14,763
Western Samoa	Apia	1,097	2,842

[1] Land area.
[2] In free association with the United States, which is responsible for their defense.
[3] New Zealand is sometimes included in Oceania.

These children of the Cook Islands are Polynesians, one of the three main Pacific peoples. This native Fijian is a mixture of Polynesian and Melanesian groups.

PACIFIC ISLANDS AND ISLAND GROUPS

The following is an overview of many of the islands and island groups of Oceania. Cross-references to other articles are noted where appropriate. Areas given are land areas, with measurements in square miles (sq mi) and square kilometers (km²).

Admiralty Islands (Papua New Guinea) are part of the Bismarck Archipelago. (An archipelago is a chain of islands.) They are located in the southwestern Pacific and are volcanic in origin. Manus is the largest of the Admiralty group. Area: about 800 sq mi (2,072 km²).

American Samoa (U.S.A.) consists of seven islands in the eastern part of the Samoa group. The western part forms the independent country of Western Samoa. American Samoa is a U.S. territory. It has local self-government under an elected governor and legislature. Area: 75 sq mi (195 km²). See also TERRITORIAL EXPANSION OF THE UNITED STATES (American Samoa); and UNITED STATES (Outlying Areas of the United States).

Belau, Republic of. See entry **Palau**.

Bismarck Archipelago (Papua New Guinea) consists of New Britain, New Ireland, the Admiralty Islands, and other islands, making up part of Papua New Guinea. Most of the larger islands are volcanic. Area: 19,200 sq mi (49,730 km²).

Bonin Islands (Japan) are a group of small volcanic islands in the western Pacific. Area: 40 sq mi (104 km²).

Borneo, the world's third largest island, is shared by the nations of Indonesia, Malaysia, and Brunei. See BORNEO.

Bougainville (Papua New Guinea) is the largest island of the Solomon Islands chain. It has one of the world's largest copper mines. Area: 3,880 sq mi (10,049 km²).

Buka (Papua New Guinea) is one of the Solomon Islands. Area: 190 sq mi (492 km²).

Caroline Islands number nearly 1,000 coral and volcanic islands, spread over a vast area of the western Pacific but with a total land area of only about 450 sq mi (1,165 km²). At the end of World War II, they became part of the U.S. Trust Territory of the Pacific. They include the Republic of Palau and the Federated States of Micronesia.

Christmas Island (Kiribati), one of the Line Islands of the central Pacific, is the largest island of Kiribati. Area: 60 sq mi (155 km²).

Chuuk (formerly called **Truk**), in the Carolines, is the main island of Chuuk state in the Federated States of Micronesia. Area: 39 sq mi (100 km²).

Cook Islands (New Zealand) are a group of 15 small islands in the South Pacific. The largest is Rarotonga. The islands are internally self-governing. Area: 93 sq mi (240 km²).

Easter Island (Chile). See ISLANDS.

Ellice Islands. See TUVALU.

Fiji. See FIJI.

French Polynesia includes Clipperton Island, and the Society, Marquesas, Gambier, Tuamotu, and Austral islands. A French overseas territory, its people are citizens of France. The capital is Papeete, on the island of Tahiti. Extending over a large area of the Pacific, the islands have a land area of about 1,550 sq mi (4,000 km^2).

Gilbert Islands (Kiribati) are a group of coral atolls in the central Pacific. See KIRIBATI.

Guadalcanal (Solomon Islands) is the largest island of the nation of Solomon Islands. It was the site of one of the decisive battles of the Pacific in World War II. Area: 2,500 sq mi (6,500 km^2).

Guam (U.S.A.) is the largest and most populous of the Marianas Islands, in the west central Pacific. It was ceded by Spain to the United States in 1898. See UNITED STATES (Outlying Areas).

Hawaiian Islands (U.S.A.). See HAWAII.

Iwo Jima (see **Volcano Islands).**

Kiribati. See KIRIBATI.

Kosrae is the largest island of Kosrae state in the Federated States of Micronesia. Area: 42 sq mi (110 km^2).

Line Islands (Kiribati) are a group of small coral islands in the central Pacific. Area: 222 sq mi (576 km^2).

Marianas, Northern, Commonwealth of the, (U.S.A.) includes all the islands of the Marianas chain except Guam. The islands are internally self-governing. Saipan, the largest island, and Tinian were the scene of fierce fighting in the Pacific war. See UNITED STATES (Outlying Areas).

Marquesas Islands (France) are the northernmost islands of French Polynesia. They consist of twelve volcanic islands. Area: 492 sq mi (1,274 km^2).

Marshall Islands, Republic of. See MARSHALL ISLANDS.

Micronesia includes more than 2,000 islands scattered over a vast area in the northwestern Pacific Ocean. See MICRONESIA, FEDERATED STATES OF.

Midway (U.S.A.) consists of a coral atoll and two islets, lying in the north central Pacific. The islands are a naval base, as well as a national wildlife preserve. The U.S. victory at the Battle of Midway (1942) was a turning point in World War II. Area: 2 sq mi (5 km^2).

Nauru. See NAURU.

New Britain (Papua New Guinea) is the largest island of the Bismarck Archipelago. Rabaul is its largest town and chief port. The island is mountainous, with several active volcanoes. Area: 14,570 sq mi (37,736 km^2).

New Caledonia (France) is a large island in the southwest Pacific, with several smaller island dependencies. An overseas territory of France, its people are French citizens. The capital is Noumea. Nickel is the chief export. Area: 7,243 sq mi (18,760 km^2).

New Guinea, the world's second largest island, is divided between Indonesia and Papua New Guinea. See NEW GUINEA; PAPUA NEW GUINEA.

New Hebrides is the former name of the nation of **Vanuatu.** See VANUATU.

The boys are Melanesians from Papua New Guinea. The man with the sea turtle is from Chuuk and is a Micronesian, the third of the major Pacific peoples.

The beauty of the Polynesians can be seen in this Tahitian woman.

New Ireland (Papua New Guinea) is the second largest of the islands of the Bismarck Archipelago. Area: 3,700 sq mi (9,600 km²).

New Zealand is sometimes considered part of Oceania. See NEW ZEALAND.

Niue (New Zealand) is an island in the South Pacific Ocean. Its people have internal self-government and are New Zealand citizens. Area: 100 sq mi (259 km²).

Northern Marianas. (see **Marianas, Northern**).

Okinawa (Japan), in the western Pacific, is the largest of the Ryukyu Islands chain. It was the site of the last major battle between U.S. and Japanese forces in World War II. Area: 454 sq mi (1,176 km²).

Palau (formerly called **Belau**) includes numerous small islands in the western Carolines. The last of the U.S. trust territories of the Pacific, it gained independence, in free association with the United States, in 1994. See PALAU.

Papua New Guinea includes the eastern half of New Guinea, the Bismarck Archipelago, the northern Solomon Islands, and other islands. See PAPUA NEW GUINEA.

Pitcairn Island (U.K.) is a tiny British dependency in the South Pacific. Area: 2 sq mi (5 km²).

Pohnpei (formerly **Ponape**) is the largest island of Pohnpei state in the Federated States of Micronesia. Area: 129 sq mi (334 km²).

Samoa, an island group in the South Pacific, is divided, politically, into American Samoa and the independent nation of Western Samoa.

Society Islands (France) are a chain of 14 islands in French Polynesia. They are an overseas territory of France. Area: 650 sq mi (1,660 km²).

Solomon Islands are an archipelago in the southwestern Pacific. The northernmost islands, including Bougainville, Buka, and smaller islands, are part of Papua New Guinea. The remainder, including Guadalcanal and other islands, make up the nation of Solomon Islands. Total area: 15,130 sq mi (39,190 km²). See SOLOMON ISLANDS.

Tahiti (France), largest of the Society Islands, is the chief island of French Polynesia. Its scenic beauty and attractive people made it a byword for the ideal South Pacific island. The French artist Paul Gauguin painted some of his greatest works here in the 1890's. Area: 402 sq mi (1,042 km²).

Tokelau (New Zealand) is a small island group in the central Pacific. Area: 4 sq mi (10 km²).

Tonga. See TONGA.

Truk (see **Chuuk**).

Tuamotu Islands (France) are a chain of about 75 atolls spread over a large area of the South Pacific. Politically, it is part of French Polynesia. Area: 300 sq mi (775 km²).

Tuvalu. See TUVALU.

Vanuatu. See VANUATU.

Volcano Islands (Japan) are three small islands lying southeast of the Bonin Islands. Iwo Jima, the largest island, was the site of a major battle between U.S. and Japanese troops in World War II. Area: 11 sq mi (28 km²).

Wake Island (U.S.A.) consists mainly of a coral atoll in the central Pacific. See UNITED STATES (Outlying Areas).

Wallis and Futuna Islands (France) are two groups of islands in the southwestern Pacific, lying west of Samoa. They are a French overseas territory. Area: 106 sq mi (274 km²).

Western Samoa. See WESTERN SAMOA.

Yap is one of the Federated States of Micronesia. The island of Yap is the site of the capital, Colonia. Area of Yap state: 46 square miles (119 km²).

A woman of Vanuatu displays face markings of the Cargo cult, a religious movement founded in Melanesia.

PADDLE TENNIS

Paddle tennis was invented in 1898 by two boys, Frank and Charles Beal. They were permitted by their father, a professor at Albion College in Michigan, to watch the college students play tennis. But because of the high cost of tennis rackets and balls, the boys' father did not allow them to play.

However, the Beals were not to be denied. In their backyard Frank and his brother halved the dimensions of a tennis court and laid out a playing area 11.9 meters (39 feet) by 5.5 meters (18 feet). They set up a net of chicken wire and made paddles from pieces of maplewood 2.5 centimeters (1 inch) thick. At first they used "seconds"—inexpensive, imperfect tennis balls. Then the boys found that inflated 5-cent rubber balls were just as satisfactory.

The Beal brothers decided to call the game "paddle tennis." They kept all the rules of tennis, changing only the racket, the ball, and the court size. Soon they had an audience. Students and neighbors watched them from a raised sidewalk above the playing field. The game was later introduced in New York City and immediately became popular with children. The ball was easier to control with the paddle than with a tennis racket, the basic skills were easy to learn, the game required little space, and it was inexpensive to play.

In 1923, the American (now the United States) Paddle Tennis Association was formed. It standardized the sizes of the court, net, paddle, and ball and arranged for the equipment to be manufactured. The National Recreation Association helped introduce paddle tennis to municipal playgrounds.

Paddle tennis reached its height of popularity during the 1920's and 1930's. Then, interest in the sport declined. This was due mainly to the players' improvement in the overhead serve and the rush to the net. The game became one of constant slamming—that is, hitting hard, fast shots that are impossible to return. There were hardly any rallies.

Interest in paddle tennis was revived in 1959 when new rules, equipment, and court size were instituted.

▶ PLAYING THE GAME

The ball used today is a deadened tennis ball. The tennis ball is punctured, usually with a safety pin, so that it will not bounce so high. The net is 79 centimeters (31 inches) high and is pulled taut across the court. The paddle may be solid or perforated and not more than 44.5 centimeters (17½ inches) long and 21.6 centimeters (8½ inches) wide. The court is 15.2 meters (50 feet) long by 6.1 meters (20 feet) wide. It is the same size for singles and for doubles. The area is divided into four service courts. Each is 6.7 meters (22 feet) long by 3 meters (10 feet) wide. The surface may be asphalt, cement, clay, composition, or any other material used for tennis courts.

Paddle tennis is played in basically the same way as lawn tennis. But there are certain differences. Children under 14 years of age are permitted two overhand serves, as in lawn tennis, but only one underhand service is allowed for adults (players 14 years and older). To serve, the player stands behind the baseline, which is the end line of the paddle tennis court. The server may bounce, drop, or throw the ball into the air and then strike it with the paddle at a point not higher than the top of the net. A player must continue with one method of serving throughout the set.

To prevent slamming a return of a serve, there is a "one-bounce" rule that applies only to adult singles. The served ball must hit the ground once before the receiving player may return it. Then the server must let the returned ball bounce once before hitting it.

Tennis champion Althea Gibson's career started with the paddle tennis she played on the street in front of her home in Harlem, in New York City. Sidney Wood, Bill Talbert, Bobby Riggs, Jack Kramer, Pancho Gonzales, and other tennis champions became expert at paddle tennis and did much to increase its popularity.

Paddle tennis is still a great game for children, and the rule changes of 1959 have made it a popular sport for adults. Thousands of courts have been built in the United States, and participation in the sport is increasing. There is a National Open Men's Doubles Championship, held annually in New York City, in which players from throughout the United States play this exciting, fast-moving sport for prize money.

MURRAY GELLER
President, U.S. Paddle Tennis Association
See also TENNIS.

PAGEANTS

A pageant is a special kind of play in which large numbers of people take part. Usually it takes place outdoors before an audience, and its purpose is generally to celebrate some great event.

▶ RELIGIOUS PAGEANTS

During the Middle Ages pageants were usually held for religious reasons. Since this was a time when very few people could read or write, other means had to be found to teach religion. One way was the morality play, in which characters named Pride, Greed, Honesty, or Laziness represented human traits. The struggle in life between good and evil could be shown by the characters on stage, with good winning out over wickedness.

Another type of religious pageant is the Passion play, which tells the Passion (suffering and death) of Jesus. The people of Oberammergau, Germany, threatened by a terrible plague, made God a promise: if their town was spared, they would honor Him forever with a pageant every 10 years. And they have done so since 1634.

▶ HISTORICAL PAGEANTS

A historical pageant tells the story of a well-known event. At Roanoke Island, North Carolina, a pageant called *The Lost Colony* is held every year. It commemorates the ill-fated Virginia colony that left no survivors. The colony was founded on Roanoke Island by Sir Walter Raleigh in 1584, more than 20 years before the Jamestown colony was established.

A pageant held each year in Interlaken, Switzerland, is performed in the woods outside the town and retells the story of the legendary hero William Tell. More than 600 years ago, Tell was supposed to have refused to salute the cap of the Austrian imperial governor. The cap had been put in the marketplace by order of the governor, as a symbol of Austrian authority. For his disobedience Tell was ordered to shoot an apple from his son's head. Using a bow and arrow, Tell succeeded. Later on, he shot the governor, helping to free Switzerland from Austrian rule. Thus Tell became a symbol of national independence and freedom.

JAMES W. HOERGER
Great Neck Public Schools

PAINE, THOMAS (1737–1809)

A citizen of three countries and a champion of two great revolutions, Tom Paine has come down in history as a man with two sharply contrasting reputations. The most widely read author of his day, he aroused both admiration and hate. To many he was an unselfish idealist fighting for the cause of universal freedom. To others he was an immoral atheist and a vicious radical. In his own day Paine was admired by such men as Benjamin Franklin, Thomas Jefferson, and George Washington. He was attacked by such individuals as John Adams and the French revolutionary leader Robespierre.

Later writers have reflected some of these conflicting opinions. To one 19th-century historian Paine was "of all the human kind . . . the filthiest and the nastiest." To Theodore Roosevelt he was "a dirty little atheist." But to others Paine was "the greatest pamphleteer that the English race has produced, and one of its great idealists"; and "one of the noblest of our humanitarians."

The truth lies more with Paine's admirers than with his attackers. He was neither little nor an atheist. Quite the contrary. Paine was in many ways a great man and a passionate believer. But he was a troubled man, possibly as a result of a poor and humble background, and somewhat wayward in his personal behavior. Nevertheless, he was a courageous fighter for democracy as he saw it and a brilliant writer whose words can still arouse warm response. Paine's chief weakness was an inability to conform or to compromise. In addition, he had a compulsion to speak the truth bluntly, as he understood it. This helps to explain the hatred many felt toward him.

Early Years

Paine was born on January 29, 1737, at Thetford, England, the son of a poor corset maker. His father was a Quaker, but Paine never became a Quaker himself. He explained later that when, at the age of 8, he heard a sermon on the Redemption, he was repelled by the cruelty of Christianity. At the age of 13 Paine was apprenticed to a corset maker. He left home 6 years later and spent the next 17 years in various English towns, holding odd jobs. His two brief marriages ended in failure. He was depressed by a life of ugliness and monotony, relieved only by his avid reading.

By a stroke of luck, Paine met Benjamin Franklin in London. Franklin, impressed by the "ingenious, worthy young man," gave him letters of introduction to Americans. Paine emigrated to America, arriving in Philadelphia in 1774. He had never published a word before. But soon he was caught up in the political excitement of the time, especially the question of American independence from Great Britain. "It was the cause of America," he said, "that made me an author."

Common Sense

In 1776 Paine published a 2-shilling, 47-page pamphlet called *Common Sense*. The pamphlet became a sensational success and one of the most influential publications in history. It was read by nearly everybody.

Common Sense was a fighting book. It sparkled with unforgettable phrases. Those who favored reconciliation with Great Britain were described as "Interested men, who are not to be trusted, weak men who cannot see, prejudiced men who will not see." To those who said that America had flourished under British rule, Paine answered: "We may as well assert that because a child has thrived upon milk, that it is never to have meat."

The basic conclusion of *Common Sense* was a call for independence from Great Britain. "Everything that is right or reasonable," Paine wrote, "pleads for separation. The blood of the slain, the weeping voice of nature cries, 'TIS TIME TO PART.' " Such flaming words worked, in the words of George Washington, "a powerful change . . . in the minds of men." There is no doubt that *Common Sense* influenced the Declaration of Independence.

Paine joined Washington's army and was with it during the New Jersey retreat in the winter of 1776. "Writing at every place we stopped at," he composed No. 1 of *The Crisis* papers. It began with the stirring words "These are the times that try men's souls." The last of *The Crisis* papers came out in 1783. By then Paine could justly say: "The times that tried men's souls are over." The American Revolution was won.

In 1777 Congress appointed Paine secretary of its committee on foreign affairs in reward for his services. He resigned in 1779 and was made clerk of the Pennsylvania Assembly. In 1781 he was a member of an American diplomatic mission to France. From 1783 to 1787 he lived in Bordentown, New Jersey, and New York City, working on the invention of an iron bridge.

The French Revolution

In 1787 Paine went to France and then to England. After the outbreak of the French Revolution in 1789, he traveled between London and Paris, acting as a defender of the new revolutionary cause. In 1791 Paine published his *Rights of Man*. Outlawed in England because of his book, Paine fled to France. There he became an honorary French citizen and a member of the revolutionary Convention. In the struggle between the Jacobin and Girondist parties Paine was arrested and spent nearly a year in jail. He was released in November, 1794.

While in prison, he had begun his famous book *The Age of Reason*. The book brought widespread hostility upon him for its rejection of orthodox religion. In the first chapter Paine stated his beliefs: "I believe in one God, and no more; and I hope for happiness beyond this life. I believe in the equality of man; and I believe that religious duties consist in doing justice, loving mercy, and endeavoring to make our fellow creatures happy."

Paine returned to the United States in 1802. There he spent the last 7 years of his life, socially rejected and suffering from poverty and ill health. He died on June 8, 1809, and was buried in New Rochelle, New York. In 1819 his bones were removed to England.

Time is softening the undeserved hostility to Paine. He deserves to be remembered as a man whose motto was, "My country is the world, and my religion is to do good."

SAUL K. PADOVER
Author, *The Genius of America*

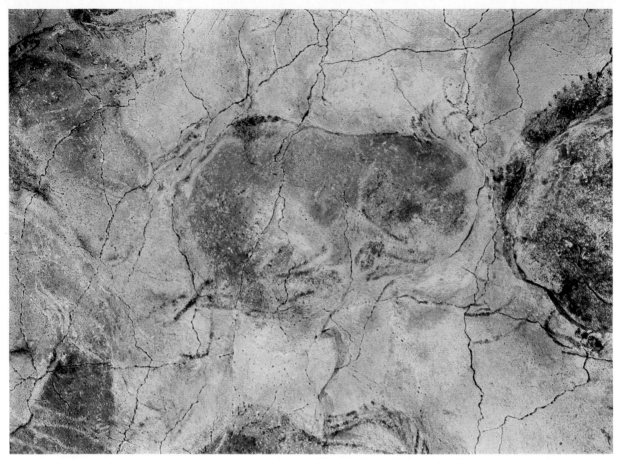

Wounded Bison. Cave painting, Altamira, Spain (15000 B.C.).

PAINTING

The history of painting is a never-ending chain that began with the very first pictures ever made. Each style grows out of the styles that came before it. Every great artist adds to the accomplishments of earlier painters and influences later painters.

We can enjoy a painting for its beauty alone. Its lines, forms, colors, and composition (arrangement of parts) may appeal to our senses and linger in our memories. But enjoyment of art increases as we learn when and why and how it was created.

A painting always describes something. It may describe the artist's impression of a scene or person. It also describes the artist's feelings about the art of painting itself. Suppose, for example, the artist paints a picture of the birth of Venus, the Roman goddess of love—a subject that has been used many times. The viewer may not learn anything new about the subject from the more recent version that could not have been learned from the older one. Why, then, do painters bother to depict the same scene again? The answer is that they want to tell us something new about the way the scene can be painted. In a way, the artist is saying, "I have painted the birth of Venus as no other artist before me has painted it." The artist not only depicts the birth of Venus but also makes a statement about the art of painting itself.

Many factors have influenced the history of painting. Geography, religion, national characterics, historic events, the development of new materials—all help to shape the artist's vision. Throughout history, painting has mirrored the changing world and our ideas about it. In turn, artists have provided some of the best records of the development of civilization, sometimes revealing more than the written word.

▶ PREHISTORIC PAINTING

Cave dwellers were the earliest artists. Colored drawings of animals, dating from about 30,000 to 10,000 B.C., have been found on the walls of caves in southern France and in Spain. Many of these drawings are amazingly well preserved because the caves were sealed up for many centuries. Early people drew the wild animals that they saw all around them. Very crude human figures, drawn in lifelike positions, have been found in Africa and eastern Spain.

The cave artists filled the cave walls with drawings in rich, bright colors. Some of the most beautiful paintings are in the Cave of Altamira, in Spain. One detail shows a wounded bison, no longer able to stand—probably the victim of a hunter. It is painted in reddish brown and outlined simply but skillfully in black. The pigments used by cave painters were earth **ochers** (iron oxides varying in color from light yellow to deep orange) and **manganese** (a metallic element). These were crushed into a fine powder, mixed with grease (perhaps animal fat), and put on with some sort of brush. Sometimes the pigments were used in sticks, like crayons. The grease mixed with the powdered pigments made the paint fluid and the pigment particles stick together. The cave dwellers must have made brushes out of animal hairs or plants, and sharp tools out of flint for drawing and scratching lines.

As far back as 30,000 years ago, people had invented the basic tools and materials for painting. Techniques and materials were refined and improved in the centuries following. But the discoveries of the cave dweller remain basic to painting.

▶ EGYPTIAN AND MESOPOTAMIAN PAINTING (3400–332 B.C.)

One of the first civilizations was developed in Egypt. From the written records and the art left by the Egyptians, much about their way of living is known. They believed that the body must be preserved so that the soul may live on after death. The great pyramids were elaborate tombs for rich and powerful Egyptian rulers. Much Egyptian art was created for the pyramids and tombs of kings and other important people. To make absolutely sure that the soul would continue to exist, artists made images of the dead person in stone. They also recorded scenes from the person's life in wall paintings in the burial chambers.

Egyptian techniques of painting remained the same for centuries. In one method watercolor paint was put on mud-plaster or limestone walls. In another process outlines were cut into stone walls, and the designs were painted with watercolor washes. A material called gum arabic probably was used to make the paint stick to a surface. Fortunately, the dry climate of the region and the sealed tombs have prevented some of these watercolor paintings from being destroyed by the dampness. A number of hunting scenes from the walls of tombs in Thebes of about 1450 B.C. are well preserved. They show hunters stalking birds or spearing fish of many varieties. These varieties can still be identified today because they were so accurately and carefully painted.

The Mesopotamian civilization, which lasted from 3200 to 332 B.C., was located in the valley between the Tigris and Euphrates rivers in the Near East. The Mesopotamians built mostly with clay. Because clay is softened by rain, their buildings have crumbled away to dust, destroying any wall paintings there may have been. What has been preserved are the decorated **ceramics** (painted and fired pottery) and colorful mosaics. Although mosaics should not be considered painting, they frequently influenced the forms of painting.

▶ THE AEGEAN CIVILIZATION (3000–1100 B.C.)

The third great early culture was the Aegean civilization, on the islands off the shores of Greece and in the peninsula of Asia Minor. The Aegeans lived around the same time as the ancient Egyptians and the Mesopotamians.

In 1900 archeologists began to excavate the palace of King Minos at Knossos on the island of Crete. The excavations turned up works of art painted around 1500 B.C. in an unusually free and graceful style for that time. Evidently the Cretans were a lighthearted, nature-loving people. Among their favorite themes in art were sea life, animals, flowers, athletic games, and processionals. At Knossos and other Aegean palaces, paintings were made on wet plaster walls with paints made of mineral substances, sand, and earth ochers. The paint soaked into the wet plaster and became a permanent part of the wall. This kind of painting was later called

Roman wall painting (50 B.C.) at the Villa of the Mysteries near Pompeii.

Justinian and His Court (A.D. 550?), a Byzantine mosaic. Church of San Vitale, Ravenna.

fresco, an Italian word meaning "fresh" or "new." The Cretans liked bright yellow, red, blue, and green.

▶ **GREEK AND ROMAN CLASSICAL PAINTING (1100 B.C.–A.D. 400)**

The ancient Greeks decorated their temples and palaces with mural (wall) paintings. We can tell from ancient literary sources and from Roman copies of Greek art that the Greeks painted small pictures and made mosaics. The names of the Greek master painters and something of their lives and works are also known, although very little Greek painting has survived the effects of time and wars. The Greeks did not paint much in tombs, so their works were not protected.

Painted vases are about all that remains of Greek painting. Pottery making was a large industry in Greece, especially in Athens. Containers were in great demand for exports, such as oil and honey, and for household purposes. The earliest style of vase painting was known as the **geometric style** (1100–700 B.C.). Vases were decorated with bands of geometric shapes and human figures in a brown glaze on light-colored clay. By the 6th century, vase painters were using the **black-figured style**, in which human figures were

painted in black on the natural red clay. The details were cut into the clay with a sharp instrument. This allowed the red beneath to show through.

The **red-figured style** eventually replaced the black. It is just the opposite; the figures are red and the background black. The advantage of this style was that the painter could use a brush to make the outlines. A brush gives a freer line than the metal tool used in black-figured vases.

Roman mural paintings were found chiefly in the villas (country homes) of Pompeii and Herculaneum. In A.D. 79 these two cities were completely buried by an eruption of the volcano Vesuvius. Archeologists who have excavated the area have been able to learn much about ancient Roman life from these cities. Almost every house and villa in Pompeii had paintings on its walls. Roman painters carefully prepared the wall surface by applying a mixture of marble dust and plaster. They put the mixture on in layers and polished it to a marblelike finish. Many of the pictures are copies of 4th-century B.C. Greek paintings. The graceful poses of the figures painted on the walls of the Villa of the Mysteries in Pompeii inspired artists of the 18th century when the city was excavated.

The Greeks and Romans also painted portraits. A small number of them, mostly mummy portraits done in the Greek style by Egyptian artists, have survived around Alexandria, in northern Egypt. Founded in the 4th century B.C. by Alexander the Great of Greece, Alexandria became a leading center of Greek and Roman culture. Mummy portraits were painted in the encaustic technique on wood and were fitted into mummy cases after the death of the person portrayed. Encaustic paintings, done in paint mixed with melted beeswax, last for a very long time. Indeed, the mummy portraits still look fresh, though they were done as long ago as the 2nd century B.C.

▶ EARLY CHRISTIAN AND BYZANTINE PAINTING (A.D. 300–1300)

The Roman Empire began to decline in the 4th century A.D. At the same time Christianity gained strength. In A.D. 313 the Roman Emperor Constantine gave the religion official recognition and became a Christian himself.

The rise of Christianity greatly affected the arts. Artists were commissioned to decorate the walls of churches with frescoes and mosaics. They made panel paintings in the church chapel and illustrated and decorated the books of the Church. Under the authority of the Church, artists had to communicate the teachings of Christianity as clearly as possible.

Early Christians and Byzantine artists continued the technique of **mosaic** that they had learned from the Greeks. Small, flat pieces of colored glass or stone were set into wet cement or plaster. Sometimes other hard materials, such as bits of baked clay or shells, were used. In Italian mosaics the colors are especially deep and full. The Italian artists made the background with pieces of gilded glass. They set the human figures in rich colors against the glittering gold. The general effect is flat and decorative, not realistic.

The mosaics of Byzantine artists often were less realistic and more decorative than those of the early Christians. "Byzantine" is the name given to a style of art that developed around the ancient city of Byzantium (now Istanbul, Turkey). The mosaic technique perfectly suited the Byzantine taste for splendidly decorated churches. The famous mosaics of Theodora and Justinian, made about A.D. 547, show the taste for rich display. The jewelry on the figures glitters, and the brilliantly colored court dresses are set against a shining gold background. Byzantine artists also used gold liberally in fresco and panel paintings. Gold and other precious materials were used throughout the Middle Ages to set spiritual subjects apart from the everyday world.

▶ MEDIEVAL PAINTING (500–1400)

The first part of the Middle Ages, from about the 6th to the 11th centuries A.D., is commonly called the Dark Ages. In this time of unrest, art was kept alive mainly in the monasteries. In the 5th century A.D. barbarian tribes from northern and central Europe roamed over the continent. For hundreds of years they dominated Western Europe. These people produced an art that has a strong emphasis on pattern. They were especially fond of designs of intertwining dragons and birds.

The best of Celtic and Saxon art is found in manuscripts of the 7th and 8th centuries. Book illumination and miniature painting, practiced since late Roman times, increased in the Middle Ages. **Illumination** is decoration of the text, the capital letters, and the margins. Gold, silver, and bright colors were used. A **miniature** is a small picture, often a portrait. Originally the term was used to describe the decorative block around the initial letters in a manuscript.

Charlemagne, who was crowned emperor of the Holy Roman Empire in the early 9th century, tried to revive the classical art of the late Roman and early Christian periods. During his reign painters of miniatures imitated classical art, but they also conveyed personal feelings about their subjects.

Very little wall painting survives from the Middle Ages. There were several great series of frescoes painted in churches built during the Romanesque period (11th–13th centuries), but most of them have disappeared. Churches of the Gothic period (12th–16th centuries) did not have enough wall space for mural paintings. Book illustration was the main job of the Gothic painter.

Among the finest illustrated manuscripts were the books of hours—collections of calendars, devotional prayers, and psalms. A page from an Italian manuscript shows elaborately decorated initials and a finely detailed marginal scene of Saint George slaying the dragon. The colors are brilliant and jewel-like, as in stained glass, and gold shimmers over the page. Exquisitely delicate leaf and flower designs border the text. Artists probably used magnifying glasses to do such intricate work.

▶ ITALY: CIMABUE AND GIOTTO

Italian painters at the close of the 13th century were still working in the Byzantine style. Human figures were made to appear flat and decorative. Faces rarely had any expression. Bodies were weightless and seemed to float rather than stand firmly on the ground. In Florence the painter Cimabue (1240?–1302?) tried to modernize some of the old Byzantine methods. The angels in his *Madonna Enthroned* are more active than is usual in paintings of that time. Their gestures and faces show a little more human feeling. Cimabue added a new sense of monumentality, or largeness, to his paintings. However, he continued to follow many Byzantine tradi-

tions, such as the gold background and patternlike arrangement of objects and figures.

It was the great Florentine painter Giotto (1267?–1337) who actually broke with the Byzantine tradition. His fresco series in the Arena Chapel in Padua leaves Byzantine art far behind. In these scenes from the lives of Mary and Christ, there is genuine emotion, tension, and naturalism. All the qualities of human warmth and sympathy are present. The people do not seem at all unreal or heavenly. Giotto shaded the contours of the figures, and he put deep shadows into the folds of their clothing to give a sense of roundness and solidity.

For his smaller panels Giotto used pure **egg tempera**, a medium that was perfected by the 14th-century Florentines. The clearness and brightness of his colors must have greatly affected people accustomed to the darker colors of Byzantine panels. Tempera paintings give the impression that soft daylight is falling over the scene. They have an almost flat appearance in contrast to the glossiness of oil paintings. Egg tempera remained the chief painting medium until oil almost completely replaced it in the 16th century.

▶ LATE MEDIEVAL PAINTING NORTH OF THE ALPS

Early in the 15th century, painters in northern Europe were working in a style quite different from Italian painting. Northern artists achieved realism by adding countless details to their pictures. Every hair was delicately outlined, and each detail of drapery or floor pattern was faithfully set down. The invention of oil painting made it easier to paint details.

The Flemish artist Jan van Eyck (1370?–1441) contributed to the development of oil painting. When tempera is used, the colors have to be put on separately. They cannot shade into one another very well because the paint dries quickly. With oil, which dries slowly, an artist can achieve more intricate effects. *The Moneylender and His Wife* by Quentin Massys (1466?–1530) was done in the Flemish oil technique. All details, and even the mirror reflection, are clear and precise. The color is strong and has a hard, enamel-like surface. The wood panel on which the painting was done was prepared in much the same way that Giotto prepared his panels for

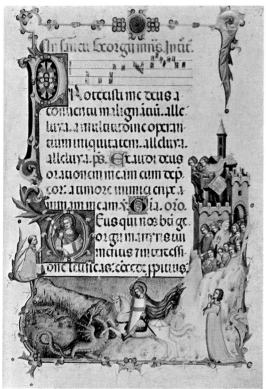

A page from a medieval illuminated manuscript. Vatican Library, Rome.

The Moneylender and His Wife (1514) by Quentin Massys. Louvre, Paris.

The Descent from the Cross (1306?), by Giotto. Arena Chapel, Padua.

19

Detail from *The Tribute Money* (1425?), a fresco by Masaccio. Church of Santa Maria del Carmine, Florence.

tempera. Van Eyck built up the painting in layers of thin color, called **glazes.** Tempera was probably used in the original underpainting and for highlights.

▶ ITALIAN RENAISSANCE PAINTING

At the same time that van Eyck was working in the North, the Italians were moving into a golden age of art and literature. This period is called the Renaissance, which means rebirth, or revival. Italian artists were inspired by the sculpture of the ancient Greeks and Romans. The Italians wanted to revive the spirit of classical art, which glorifies human independence and nobility. Renaissance artists continued to paint religious subjects. But they emphasized the earthly life and accomplishments of human beings.

Florence

Giotto's accomplishments in the early 14th century laid the foundation of the Renaissance. Fifteenth-century Italian artists continued the movement. Masaccio (1401–28) was one of the leaders of the first generation of Renaissance artists. He lived in Florence, the wealthy merchant city where Renaissance art began. By the time of his death in his late twenties, he had revolutionized painting. In his famous fresco *The Tribute Money* he puts solid sculptural figures into a landscape that seems to go far back into the distance. Masaccio may have learned perspective from the Florentine architect and sculptor Brunelleschi (1377?–1446).

The fresco technique was very popular during the Renaissance. It was particularly suitable for large mural paintings because the colors dry perfectly flat. The picture can be viewed from any angle without glare or reflections. Frescoes are also available. Usually the artists had several assistants to help them. Work was completed by sections because it had to be finished while the plaster was still wet.

Masaccio's full three-dimensional style was typical of the new progressive trend of the 15th century. The style of Fra Angelico (1400?–1455) represents the more traditional approach used by a number of early Renaissance painters. He was less concerned with perspective and more interested in decorative pattern. His *Coronation of the Virgin* is an example of tempera painting at its most beautiful. The gay, intense colors are set against a gold background and accented with touches of gold. The picture looks like a greatly enlarged miniature painting. The long, narrow figures have little in common with Masaccio's. The composition is organized in sweeping lines of movement circling about the central figures of Christ and Mary.

Another Florentine who worked in the traditional style was Sandro Botticelli (1444?–1510). Flowing, rhythmic lines link the sections of Botticelli's *Primavera*. The figure of Spring, carried by the West Wind, sweeps in from the right. The Three Graces dance in a circle, the fluttering folds of their dresses and graceful movements of their arms expressing the rhythms of the dance.

The famous artist Leonardo da Vinci (1452–1519) studied painting in Florence. He is known for his scientific studies and inventions, as well as for his paintings. Very few of his pictures have survived, partly because he often experimented with different ways of making and applying paint, rather than using tried and true methods. The *Last Supper* (painted between 1495 and 1498) was done in oil, but unfortunately Leonardo painted it on a damp wall, which caused the paint to crack. Even in its poor condition the painting has the power to stir emotions in all who see it.

One of the distinguishing characteristics of Leonardo's style was his method of painting lights and darks. The Italians called his half-dark lighting *sfumato,* which means smoky, or misty. The figures in the *Madonna of the Rocks* are veiled in a sfumato atmosphere. Their forms and features are softly shaded. Leonardo achieved these effects by using very fine gradations of light and dark tones.

Rome

The climax of Renaissance painting came in the 16th century. At the same time, the center of art and culture shifted from Florence to Rome. Under Pope Sixtus IV and his successor, Julius II, the city of Rome was gloriously decorated by Renaissance artists. Some of the most ambitious projects of the period were begun during the papacy of Julius II. Julius commissioned the great sculptor and painter Michelangelo (1475–1564) to paint the ceiling of the Sistine Chapel and to carve sculpture for the Pope's tomb. Julius also invited the painter Raphael (1483–1520) to help with the decoration of the Vatican. With assistants, Raphael frescoed four rooms of the Pope's apartments in the Vatican Palace.

Michelangelo, a Florentine by birth, developed a monumental style of painting. The figures in his painting are so solid and three-dimensional that they look like sculpture. The Sistine ceiling, which took Michelangelo 4 years to complete, is composed of hundreds of human figures from the Old Testament. To paint this tremendous fresco Michelangelo had to lie on his back on scaffolding. The brooding face of Jeremiah among the prophets that surround the ceiling is thought by some people to be his self-portrait.

Raphael came to Florence from Urbino as a very young man. In Florence he absorbed the ideas of Leonardo and Michelangelo. By the time Raphael went to Rome to work in the Vatican, his style had become one of great beauty. He is especially beloved for his beautiful paintings of the Madonna and Child. These have been reproduced by the thousands and can be seen everywhere. His *Madonna del Granduca* is successful because of its complete simplicity. Timeless in its peacefulness and purity, it is just as appealing to us as it was to the Italians of Raphael's time.

Venice

Venice was the chief northern Italian city of the Renaissance. It was visited by artists from Flanders and other regions who knew of Flemish experiments with oil paint. This stimulated an early use of the oil technique in the Italian city. The Venetians also painted on tightly stretched canvas, rather than on the wooden panels commonly used in Florence.

Giovanni Bellini (1430?–1516) was the greatest Venetian painter of the 15th century. He was also one of the first Italian painters to

Madonna of the Rocks (1485?), by Leonardo da Vinci. Louvre, Paris.

Above: *View of Toledo* (1604–14?), by El Greco. Metropolitan Museum of Art, New York. Below left: *Madonna with Saints and Members of the Pesaro Family* (1528), by Titian. Church of the Frari, Venice. Below right: *Prince Phillip Prosper of Spain* (1660), by Diego Velázquez. Kunsthistorisches Museum, Vienna.

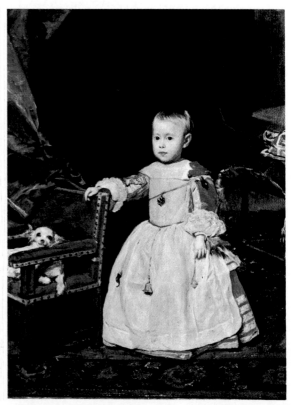

use oil on canvas. Giorgione (1478?–1511) and Titian (1488?–1576), who is the most famous of all Venetian painters, were students in Bellini's workshop.

A master of the oil technique, Titian painted huge canvases in warm, rich colors. In his mature paintings he sacrificed details to the sweeping effect of the whole painting, as in the *Pesaro Madonna*. He used large brushes to make broad strokes. His colors are especially rich because he patiently built up glazes of contrasting colors. Usually the glazes were put on over a brown tempera ground, which gave the painting a unified tone.

Another great 16th-century Venetian painter was Tintoretto (1518–94). Unlike Titian, he usually worked directly on the canvas without making preliminary sketches or underpaintings. He often distorted his forms (twisted them out of shape) for the sake of the composition and drama of the scene. His technique, which includes broad brushstrokes and dramatic contrasts of light and dark, seems very modern.

The painter Kyriakos Theotokopoulos (1541–1614) was known as El Greco ("the Greek"). Born on the island of Crete, which was occupied by the Venetian army, El Greco was trained by Italian artists. As a young adult he went to Venice to study. The combined influence of Byzantine art—which he saw all around him in Crete—and of Italian Renaissance art made El Greco's work outstanding.

In his paintings he distorted natural forms and used even stranger, more unearthly colors than Tintoretto, whom he admired. Later El Greco moved to Spain, where the grimness of Spanish art influenced his work. In his dramatic *View of Toledo* a storm rages above the deathlike stillness of the city. Cold blues, greens, and blue-whites cast a chill over the landscape.

▶ THE RENAISSANCE IN FLANDERS AND GERMANY

The golden age of painting in Flanders (now part of Belgium and northern France) was the 15th century, the time of van Eyck. In the 16th century many Flemish artists had taken up the discoveries of Italian Renaissance painters. Some Flemings, however, continued the Flemish tradition of realism. They painted **genre**—scenes from everyday life, which were often charming and sometimes fantastic. Hieronymus Bosch (1450?–1516), who preceded the genre painters, had an unusually vivid imagination. He invented all sorts of weird, grotesque creatures for *The Temptation of St. Anthony*. Pieter Brueghel the Elder (1525?–69) also worked in the Flemish tradition but added perspective and other Renaissance characteristics to his genre scenes.

Albrecht Dürer (1471–1528), Hans Holbein the Younger (1497?–1543), and Lucas Cranach the Elder (1472–1553) were the three most important German painters of the 16th century. They did much to soften the grim realism of earlier German painting. Dürer made at least one visit to Italy, where he was impressed with the paintings of Giovanni Bellini and other northern Italians. From this experience he brought to German painting a knowledge of perspective, a feeling for color and light, and a new understanding of composition. Holbein absorbed even more of the Italian achievements. His sensitive drawing and ability to select only the most important details made him a master portrait painter.

▶ BAROQUE PAINTING

The 17th century is generally known as the baroque period in art. In Italy the painters Caravaggio (1571–1610) and Annibale Carracci (1560–1609) represented two contrasting viewpoints. Caravaggio (whose real name was Michelangelo Merisi) always painted directly from life. One of his main concerns was to copy nature as faithfully as possible without glorifying it in any way. Carracci, on the other hand, followed the Renaissance ideal of beauty. He studied ancient sculpture and the works of Michelangelo, Raphael, and Titian. Caravaggio's style was admired by many painters, especially by the Spaniards Ribera and the young Velázquez. Carracci's painting inspired Nicolas Poussin (1594–1665), a major French painter of the 17th century.

Spain

Diego Velázquez (1599–1660), court painter to King Philip IV of Spain, was one of the greatest of all Spanish painters. An admirer of Titian's work, he was a master in the use of rich, harmonious color. No artist could better create the illusion of rich fabrics or human skin. The portrait of little Prince Phillip Prosper shows this skill to great advantage. His remarkable brushwork was much admired by the 19th-century French impressionists.

Flanders

The paintings of the Flemish artist Peter Paul Rubens (1577–1640) are representative of the full-blown baroque style. They are bursting with energy, color, and light. Rubens broke with the Flemish tradition of painting small, detailed pictures. His were huge canvases filled with human figures. He was given many more commissions for large pictures than he could possibly handle. Therefore he often painted only a small, colored sketch. Then his assistants transferred the sketch to a large canvas and completed the painting under Rubens' supervision.

Holland

The accomplishments of the Dutch painter Rembrandt (1606–69) are among the most outstanding in history. He had a remarkable gift for capturing human emotions. Like Titian, he worked long at building up a painting in many layers. Earth colors—yellow ocher, brown, and brown-red—were his favorites. His paintings are basically dark in tone and have many very dark areas. The rich values of these dark areas, created with many layers of color, make his technique unusual. Important sections of his paintings are dramatically illuminated by brilliant light.

Jan Vermeer (1632–75) was one of a group of Dutch artists who painted the humble scenes of daily life. He was a master at painting textures of every kind—satin, Persian rugs, bread crusts, metal. The overall impression of a Vermeer interior is that of a sunny, cheerful room filled with cherished household objects.

▶ 18TH-CENTURY PAINTING

In the 18th century, Venice produced several fine painters. The most famous was Giovanni Battista Tiepolo (1696–1770). He decorated the interiors of palaces and other buildings with tremendous, colorful frescoes representing scenes of wealth and pageantry

Francesco Guardi (1712–93) and Antonio Canaletto (1697–1768) painted scenic views, many of them recalling the past glories of Venice. Guardi was very skillful with a brush. With a few patches of color he could conjure up the idea of a tiny figure in a boat.

France: The Rococo Style

In France a taste for pastel colors and intricate decoration brought about the development of the rococo style in the early 18th century. Jean Antoine Watteau (1684–1721), a court painter to King Louis XV, and, later, François Boucher (1703–70) and Jean Honoré Fragonard (1732–1806), were associated with the rococo trend. Watteau painted visions of a dream life in which all is gaiety. There are picnics in the park or woodland parties where gallant gentlemen and elegant ladies amuse themselves.

Other 18th-century painters portrayed scenes of ordinary, middle-class life. Like the Dutch Vermeer, Jean Baptiste Simeon Chardin (1699–1779) valued simple domestic scenes and still-life arrangements. His colors are sober and calm compared to Watteau's.

England

In the 18th century the English, for the first time, developed a distinct school of painting. It consisted mainly of portrait painters who were influenced by Venetian Renaissance artists. Sir Joshua Reynolds (1723–92) and Thomas Gainsborough (1727–88) are the best-known. Reynolds, who had traveled in Italy, was devoted to reviving the Renaissance ideals of painting. His portraits, although charming and touching, are not particularly interesting in color or texture. Gainsborough, on the other hand, had a talent for brilliant brushwork. The surfaces of his paintings glow with shining color.

▶ 19TH-CENTURY PAINTING

The 19th century is sometimes regarded as the period during which modern art began to take shape. One important reason for the so-called revolution in the arts at this time was the invention of the camera, which forced artists to re-examine the purpose of painting.

A more important development resulted partly from the widespread use of manufactured paints. Before the 19th century, most

The Polish Rider (1655?), an oil painting by Rembrandt van Rijn. The Frick Collection, New York.

Marie de' Medici, Queen of France, Landing in Marseilles (1622–23), by Peter Paul Rubens. Pinakothek, Munich.

Embarkation for Cythera (1717), by Antoine Watteau. Louvre, Paris.

Above: *The Snow Storm* (1842), by J. M. W. Turner. National Gallery, London.
Below: *Madame Julie Récamier* (1800), by Jacques Louis David. Louvre, Paris.

artists or their assistants made their own paints by grinding pigment. Early commercial paints were inferior to handmade paints. Artists late in the 19th century found that the dark blues and browns of earlier paintings were turning black or gray within a few years. They began to use pure colors again. These artists used pure colors in order to preserve their work and sometimes because they were trying to capture the effects of sunlight in outdoor scenes more accurately.

England

Although France was the great center of art in the 1800's, the English landscapists John Constable (1776–1837) and Joseph Mallord William Turner (1775–1851) made valuable contributions to 19th-century painting. Both were interested in painting light and air, two aspects of nature that 19th-century artists explored fully. Constable used a method known as **divisionism,** or broken color. He put contrasting colors side by side in thick, short strokes or dots over a basic background color. He often used a palette knife to apply the color thickly. *The Hay Wain* made him famous when it was shown in Paris in 1824. It is a simple rural scene of a hay wagon (wain) crossing a river. Clouds drift over meadows dappled with patches of sunlight. Turner's paintings are more dramatic than Constable's. He painted the majestic sights of nature—storms, seascapes, glowing sunsets, high mountains. Often a golden haze partially conceals the objects in his pictures, making them appear to float in unlimited space.

Spain: Goya

Francisco Goya (1746–1828) was the first great Spanish painter to appear since the 17th century. As the favorite painter of the Spanish court, he made many portraits of the royal family. The royal personages are outfitted in elegant clothes and fine jewels, but in some of their faces all that is reflected is vanity and greed. Besides portraits, Goya painted dramatic scenes such as *The Third of May, 1808.* This picture shows the execution of a group of Spanish rebels by French soldiers. Bold contrasts of light and dark, and somber colors pierced by splashes of red, bring out the grim horror of the spectacle.

France

The period of Napoleon's reign and the French Revolution saw the rise of two opposing tendencies in French art—**classicism** and **romanticism.** Jacques Louis David

Self Portrait (1815), by Francisco Goya. San Fernando Academy, Madrid.

Orphan Girl at the Cemetery (1823), by Eugène Delacroix. Louvre, Paris.

Above: *Field of Yellow Corn* (1889), by Vincent van Gogh. National Gallery, London. Below: *Kitchen Table* (1888–90), by Paul Cézanne. Louvre, Paris.

(1748–1825) and Jean Auguste Dominique Ingres (1780–1867) were inspired by ancient Greek and Roman art and the Renaissance. They emphasized drawing and used color mainly to aid in creating solid forms. As the favorite artist of the revolutionary government, David often painted historical events of the period. In his portraits, such as that of Madame Récamier, he aimed at achieving classical simplicity.

Théodore Géricault (1791–1824) and the romanticist Eugène Delacroix (1798–1863) revolted against David's style. For Delacroix, color was the most important element in painting, and he had no patience for imitating classical statues. Instead, he admired Rubens and the Venetians. He chose colorful, exotic themes for his pictures, which sparkle with light and are full of movement.

The Barbizon painters were also part of the general romantic movement that lasted from about 1820 to 1850. They worked near the village of Barbizon on the edge of the Fontainebleau forest. They sketched out-of-doors and completed the paintings in their studios.

Other artists experimented with everyday, ordinary subject matter. The landscapes of Jean Baptiste Camille Corot (1796–1875) reflect his love of nature, and his figure studies show a kind of balanced calm. Gustave Courbet (1819–77) called himself a realist because he painted the world as he saw it—even its harsh, unpleasant side. He limited his palette to just a few somber colors, which he sometimes put on with a palette knife. Édouard Manet (1832–83) also took his subject matter from the world around him. People were shocked by his colorful contrasts and unusual techniques. The surfaces of his pictures often have a flat, patternlike texture of brushstrokes. Manet's techniques and methods of recording the effects of light on form influenced younger painters, especially the impressionists.

Working in the 1870's and 1880's, the group of artists known as the **impressionists** wanted to paint nature exactly as it was. They went much further than Constable, Turner, and Manet in studying the effects of light on color. Some of them worked out scientific theories of color. Claude Monet (1840–1926) often painted the same view at different times of day to show how its ap-

pearance changed under different conditions of light. Whatever the subject matter, his scenes are made up of hundreds of tiny brushstrokes laid side by side, often in contrasting colors. From a distance the strokes blend to give the impression of solid forms. Pierre Auguste Renoir (1841–1919) used the impressionist techniques to capture the festivity of Parisian life. In his *Dance at the Moulin de la Galette* people in vividly colored clothes mingle and dance gaily. Renoir painted the entire picture with small, even brushstrokes. The dots and dashes of paint create a texture on the surface of the painting that lends it a special kind of unity. The crowds of people seem to dissolve in sunlight and shimmering color.

▶ 20TH-CENTURY PAINTING

A number of artists soon became dissatisfied with impressionism. Artists such as Paul Cézanne (1839–1906) felt that impressionism did not describe the solidity of forms in nature. Cézanne liked to paint still lifes because they allowed him to concentrate on the shapes of fruits or other objects and their arrangements. Objects in his still lifes look solid because he reduced their forms to simple geometric shapes. His technique of placing patches of paint and short brushstrokes of rich color side by side shows that he learned much from the impressionists.

Vincent van Gogh (1853–90) and Paul Gauguin (1848–1903) reacted against the realism of the impressionists. Unlike the impressionists, who said that they were viewing nature objectively, Van Gogh cared little for accurate drawing. He frequently distorted objects in order to express his ideas more imaginatively. He used the impressionist device of putting contrasting colors next to each other. Sometimes he squeezed paint from the tubes right onto the canvas in thick ribbons, as in *Field of Yellow Corn.*

Gauguin did not care for the spotty color of the impressionists. He applied color smoothly in large flat areas, which he separated from one another by lines or dark edges. The colorful civilizations of the tropics provided much of his subject matter.

Cézanne's method of building up arrangements in space with simple geometric forms was further developed by Pablo Picasso

(1881–1973), Georges Braque (1882–1963), and others. Their style became known as **cubism**. The cubists painted objects as if they could be seen from several angles at once, or as if they had been taken apart and reassembled on a flat canvas. Often the objects barely resemble anything in nature. Sometimes the cubists cut out shapes from cloth, cardboard, wallpaper, or other materials and pasted them on the canvas to make a **collage**. Textures were also varied by adding sand or other substances to the paint. Since Manet, the trend has been to put less emphasis on subject and more emphasis on composition and technique.

▶ **PAINTING IN THE UNITED STATES**

American painting before the 20th century had mainly consisted of portraits and landscapes based on European styles. Many American artists, such as James Abbott McNeill Whistler (1834–1903) and John Singer Sargent (1856–1925), lived abroad and were influenced by European art. There was, however, an important group of American genre painters, the best of whom were Winslow Homer (1836–1910) and Thomas Eakins (1844–1916).

In the 1890's a group of young painters known as The Eight, led by Robert Henri (1865–1929), tried to create an art that was distinctly American. John Sloan (1871–1951) and George W. Bellows (1882–1925) painted life in the alleys, backyards, harbors, and slums. Members of The Eight helped organize the 1913 Armory Show of New York City. This exhibition, held in an armory, brought together modern art from the United States and Europe. At this show Americans saw the daring art of the cubists and other modern Europeans for the first time.

By the beginning of World War I, United States artists were aware of everything that was going on in modern European painting. But they did not make use of the new ideas until years later. Many painters in the 1930's were

THE ARTIST'S PAINTS

ACRYLIC—Also called plastic paint or acrylic-resin paint. Depending on how the painter handles it, acrylic paint may be as transparent as watercolor or as thick and pasty as some oil paints. It will stick to almost any surface. It will not yellow, and it is not affected by heat and humidity. All these qualities make it one of the most popular paints today.

DISTEMPER—Pigment and glue. This somewhat impermanent kind of paint is used in schools a great deal, for it is cheap and dries quickly.

EGG TEMPERA—Pigment ground into egg yolks and thinned with water. Tempera dries almost immediately. It is usually applied with short strokes of a soft, small brush. Most tempera paintings are done on wooden boards that have been prepared with several coats of gesso—white chalk mixed with glue. Tempera is transparent and is often applied in several layers.

ENCAUSTIC—Pigment and wax. In this ancient technique the color and vehicle are heated and applied, while still hot and liquid, to a wall or other surface.

FRESCO—Painting done with watercolors on moist plaster walls or ceiling.

GOUACHE—Opaque (it cannot be seen through) watercolor. Gouache (pronounced "gwash") is applied like watercolor, but white may be used to lighten colors.

OIL PAINT—Pigment ground into oil. For centuries after its invention, probably in the 15th century, oil painting dominated all other techniques until the development of acrylics. It dries slowly. It can be wiped off or painted over. It can be applied thickly or thinly. It can be transparent or opaque. The most common oil used for mixing is linseed oil, but for various effects, varnish, turpentine, beeswax, and other kinds of oils can be added. Until commercially made oil paints became available, the artist had to grind powdered pigment on a marble slab while adding oil little by little.

Oil paintings can be made on wood prepared in the same way as tempera boards. More frequently, however, stretched canvas is used. Most canvas is made of linen, which is available in a great variety of weights and weaves. Cotton sailcloth is much cheaper and less permanent, but it is also widely used. The canvas is tacked to a frame called a stretcher. Then it is coated with glue made from the hide of a rabbit or some other animal. This shrinks and sizes the canvas, which means that air can no longer pass through the spaces between the strands of linen. Then the tightly stretched canvas is primed with gesso, or white lead, a pasty paint that must be spread with a knife. Priming and sizing protects the canvas from rotting. Ideally, the oil paint should remain on top of the surface. It should be absorbed only slightly by the primer. The sizing prevents oil from touching the fabric itself.

Oil paint is applied with a variety of brushes, most of which are stiff and long-bristled. It can also be applied with a flexible knife (spatula) or even squeezed directly onto the surface from the tube.

PASTELS—Powdered pigment mixed with just enough glue to hold it together in ball or stick form. Working with pastels is as close as the artist can come to working with pure pigment. The stick or ball is stroked against a roughly textured piece of paper (some artists even use sandpaper). Since the vehicle is not liquid and cannot be absorbed, pastel paintings must be sprayed with varnish or lacquer (fixative) to prevent the pigment from coming off the paper.

PIGMENT—The material from which colors are made. Today some pigments can be chemically produced in laboratories. But all early paints were made from natural pigments found in such minerals as cobalt, cadmium, and lead.

VEHICLE, or MEDIUM—The substance with which pigment is mixed to make paint. The vehicle is usually liquid.

WATERCOLOR—Pigment ground into water. Regular water-color paints are transparent (you can see through them). Watercolors are usually applied to textured paper with a soft-bristle brush, such as sable hair. Since there is no such thing as white transparent paint, the artist must leave the white area of the paper unpainted. To lighten the colors, he adds more water.

Green Still Life (1914), by Pablo Picasso. Museum of Modern Art, New York.

Double Metamorphosis II (1964), by Vaacov Agam. Marlborough-Gerson Gallery, New York.

Green Coca-Cola Bottles (1962), by Andy Warhol. Whitney Museum of American Art, New York City.

regional artists like Grant Wood (1891–1942), who painted realistic scenes of life in the Middle West.

After World War II, the United States became the world center of painting. Arshile Gorky (1904–48) and Jackson Pollock (1912–56) were among the leaders who helped to create a new style called **action painting** or **abstract expressionism.** Instead of trying to represent specific objects, they were interested mainly in color, design, rhythm, and new ways of applying paint. Pollock experimented with flinging and dripping color on his canvases from sticks dipped into buckets of paint. Such a bold technique is just one example of the 20th-century artist's search for originality and freedom of expression.

Early in the 1960's a group of artists in the United States reacted against abstract expressionism. These artists went to the other extreme. In trying to produce an art that expresses the spirit of today, they began to paint realistic pictures of everyday things. Their subjects included dart boards, light bulbs, comic strips, and street signs. The innovators in this movement included Robert Rauschenberg (1925–) and Jasper Johns (1930–). Roy Lichtenstein (1923–), Claes Oldenburg (1929–), and Andy Warhol (1930?–87) were some of its leaders. Sometimes called ''pop'' (for popular) art, it represented a phase through which art passed. To many people, however, pop art presented an invitation to take a good look at the objects all around them. The design on a soup can or a bottle of cola might never have been noticed otherwise. Abstract expressionism opened people's minds; pop art opened their eyes.

In the mid-1960's, other types of art emerged. "Op," or optical art, was one. In op art, the tricks our eyesight can play become part of the artist's style. In Vaacov Agam's *Double Metamorphosis II,* the specially arranged patterns of line and color seem almost to vibrate.

Some abstract artists, such as Frank Stella (1936–   ) and Ellsworth Kelly (1923–   ), sometimes shape the canvas itself into circles, triangles, and other forms. Using bright colors, they often apply paint in hard-edged geometric shapes that conform to the shape of the canvas. So, it may be difficult to distinguish between painting and sculpture today, but we appreciate purity of color and relationships of shapes.

SARAH BRADFORD LANDAU
Department of Fine Arts
New York University

See also BAROQUE ART AND ARCHITECTURE; COLOR; DESIGN; MODERN ART; PREHISTORIC ART; RENAISSANCE ART AND ARCHITECTURE; names of individual artists, as REMBRANDT; and art of individual countries, as ITALY, ART AND ARCHITECTURE OF.

PAINTS AND PIGMENTS

High on the supports of a bridge a man brushes a shiny protective surface over a heavy metal beam. In a nursery school a child brushes streaks of color across a sheet of paper. Both the man and the child are painting. The man is using paint for one of its two main purposes: protection. The child is using paint for the other main purpose: decoration.

Paint can change the appearance of a surface by giving it a different gloss or texture. A coat of paint may cover a surface with a film only a few thousandths of an inch thick. Yet the protection and decoration it gives last for many years.

Paints usually are made up of a **pigment**, a **vehicle**, and a **thinner**.

The pigment of a paint gives the paint color and the ability to hide a surface. It also gives hardness and bulk. The texture and quantity of the pigment determine the gloss of a paint. Rough pigments or large quantities of pigment make dull paints. Finely ground pigments make glossy paints. White lead, iron oxide (rust), and carbon black (soot) are some examples of pigments.

The vehicle is the part of the paint that carries the pigment particles and holds the entire film to the surface. Vegetable oils and natural or synthetic resins are often used for paint vehicles. (Natural resins are gummy liquids that come from trees and other plants. Synthetic resins are completely man-made.)

The thinner usually evaporates after the paint is applied. Its job is to make the paint flow freely. The thinner does not affect the quality of the dry paint. Sometimes water is used as a thinner, and sometimes mineral spirit (a liquid made from petroleum) or turpentine is used.

▶ TYPES OF PAINTS

What kind of paint is best for a particular use? This depends upon many different things: the type of surface to be painted, the weather it will be exposed to, the wear it will receive, and the length of time the paint is expected to last. There are several hundred different types of paints available. The chief types are listed here.

Paints for Exterior Use

The commonest paint is exterior paint, or **outside house paint**. It is usually made with linseed oil, although other oils may be used. It is applied to the sides of wooden houses. These paints keep their color and appearance for long periods of time in spite of rain and sunlight. They are able to take the swelling and shrinking of wood.

Some house paints use **alkyd resins** (types of liquid plastics) or **latexes** (synthetic rubber materials) as vehicles. They may allow water vapor to pass through them fairly easily. This is very important in house paints—if water builds up in the wood under the paint, the paint will blister.

Exterior latex paints are especially useful for painting masonry because they can be put on before the masonry is completely dry. Also, latex paints are alkali-resistant. This is

Paints are exposed outdoors to test the effects of all kinds of weather.

important because nearly all masonry, such as concrete, brick, stone, or stucco, is either alkaline itself or is put together with an alkaline mortar.

Steps, decks, and similar surfaces are usually treated with floor and deck enamels made for taking a lot of wear. **Enamels** are glossy (shiny) paints that flow out into a hard, smooth coat when they are applied.

Metal exposed to dampness is usually given a coat of **anticorrosive primer**—a first coat of a paint that prevents rusting. On top of this are painted one or more coats of an exterior enamel. Because metal expands and contracts with changes of temperature, paints for metal must be flexible.

Interior House Paints

The walls of rooms are usually painted with **flat paints**. Flat paints are dull paints. Instead of being shiny, they diffuse, or spread out, light that shines on them. Either alkyd or latex paints are used. The alkyd is more washable and hides the wall surface better. The latex paint is easier to apply and gives brighter and stronger colors.

Bathrooms, kitchens, and trimming around doors and windows all need to be covered with a paint that will take a lot of wear and can easily be washed. For them a **gloss** or **semigloss enamel** is generally used. Enamels with a gloss are very shiny. Semigloss paints have a dull shine.

Floor enamels are made to wear well despite a lot of rubbing and walking. They

also dry rapidly, so that the floor can be used soon after it is painted.

Chemical Coatings

Paints that give special protective coatings are called chemical coatings. These coatings are used for manufactured articles, such as automobiles and refrigerators. The paints, applied while the articles are on a production line, dry rapidly. Even textiles and paper are often coated with this kind of paint.

Paints for Use in Industries

The walls, floors, and machines in industrial plants often require special paints. Chemical plants, for instance, need paints with very high resistance to acids or other chemicals. Usually the proper paint for an industrial job cannot be chosen until all the jobs that the paint must do are known.

Marine Finishes

A surface that is always underwater requires a very special paint. Not only do boats stay in either fresh or salt water a good part of the time, but they are likely to have barnacles, algae, and other plants and animals growing on them. Special **antifouling paints** are used to discourage this growth. Many antifouling paints have copper in them for a poison.

A boat may need to be painted with three different marine paints. One will be an antifouling paint for the bottom. Another will be for the area that is sometimes underwater and sometimes exposed. The third will be for the deck that is exposed to salt air and strong sunlight. Making marine paints is such a difficult job that many paint companies make nothing else.

Special Paints

There are hundreds of paints for special uses. The **highway paints** used for the center lines on highways, for example, are made for this one purpose and would be almost useless for anything else. Highways paints must dry rapidly so that their drying does not delay traffic. They must stay colorful and be easy to see in both daylight and dark. They must resist being worn out by tires, chains, salt, snow, rain, and sun. They must be suitable for either concrete or asphalt. All in all, this is a long set of requirements for a paint.

To slow down the spread of fire, **fire-retardant paints** are used. No paint can make a piece of wood fireproof. Paint film is only a few thousandths of an inch thick. But fire-retardant paint can slow down the spread of fire and in this way save both lives and property.

Another interesting special paint is **luminous paint**. Luminous paints may be either **fluorescent** or **phosphorescent**. Fluorescent paints glow brightly when they are exposed to ultraviolet light rays. These paints are used in signs, on instrument dials, and on parts of airplanes for extra safety in the dark. Phosphorescent paints glow for several hours after being exposed to sunlight. They are used for exit signs and other emergency guides. Unfortunately, few of them are bright enough to do more than point the way to safety.

▶ WAYS TO APPLY PAINT

The way paint is applied depends on the type of surface being painted and the thickness of the paint being used. Paints are usually applied by brush, roller, or spray. There are a number of other methods, like roll coating and dipping, but these are used only for factory-applied finishes.

Painting by Brush. The usual method of applying paint is by brush. Paintbrushes come in dozens of sizes and shapes, each with its special use. When furniture is painted, it is usually by brush.

Painting by Roller. When large flat areas, such as walls and ceilings, are to be coated, rollers are fast and do the job well. Special rollers are made for corners and other difficult places.

Spraying Paint. Spraying is often used for paints that dry too rapidly to be put on by brush or roller. Spraying is fast and gives a smooth surface with no brush marks. Spraying is often used in factories to paint cars, refrigerators, and other large items. When it is difficult to protect the surfaces that should not be painted, spray cannot be used. In homes spray paint is most useful for carved or wicker pieces where the surface cannot easily be given an even coat by brush. But it is difficult to use spray paints where there is poor ventilation or where the painting quarters are small.

FRANCIS SCOFIELD
National Paint and Coatings Association

See also PAINTING.

PAKISTAN

Pakistan, a country of South Asia, is a young nation in an ancient land. The region that is now Pakistan has a history going back thousands of years, to the Indus Valley civilization, the remains of which can still be seen. But the present-day nation of Pakistan was first established in 1947. It was created from areas of the British Indian empire that had a majority Muslim population.

When Pakistan won its independence, it consisted of two parts, West Pakistan and East Pakistan, which were separated by about 1,000 miles (1,600 kilometers) of territory belonging to India. In 1971, following a civil war and war between Pakistan and India, East Pakistan broke away from Pakistan and declared its independence as the nation of Bangladesh.

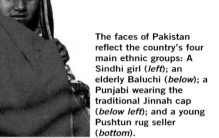

The faces of Pakistan reflect the country's four main ethnic groups: A Sindhi girl (*left*); an elderly Baluchi (*below*); a Punjabi wearing the traditional Jinnah cap (*below left*); and a young Pushtun rug seller (*bottom*).

▶ THE PEOPLE

Ethnic Groups. The Pakistanis are the descendants of the varied peoples who arrived in the land, either as conquerors or settlers, over the course of its long history. There are four main ethnic groups, who traditionally have inhabited the regions that now form the country's four provinces.

The largest group is the Punjabis, who make up nearly 60 percent of the population and live chiefly in the plains of the Punjab. The second largest, the Sindhis, occupy the southern province of Sind. The Pushtuns (or Pathans), who are related to a people of neighboring Afghanistan, are found mainly in the mountainous North-West Frontier Province. The Baluchi consist of numerous nomadic tribes who inhabit Baluchistan, the largest but most desolate of the four provinces, in the southwest.

Language and Religion. Pakistan's languages are as diverse as its people. The official language is Urdu, which is similar to the Hindi of northern India but includes words from Arabic and Persian and is written in a modified Arabic script. It is used as a primary language, however, only by a small minority of the people. Most Pakistanis speak their regional languages, chiefly Punjabi, Sindhi, Pushtu, and Baluchi. English, a reminder of

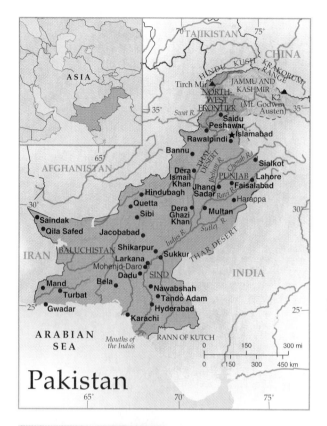

Pakistan

the centuries of British rule, is also used widely and has semiofficial status.

Nearly all Pakistanis are Muslims. The great majority belong to the Sunni branch of Islam, although there are numerous other sects.

Education. Primary education, for children between the ages of 5 and 10, is free but not compulsory by law. There are shortages of teachers and educational facilities, and only about half of the primary-age students actually attend school. Secondary school begins at age 10 and lasts for four or five years, depending on the course of study. Pakistan has more than 20 universities. The largest is the University of Peshawar. About 36 percent of the adult population is literate (that is, able to read and write).

▶ **WAY OF LIFE**

The Village. Although young Pakistanis are increasingly attracted to the growing cities, chiefly because of job opportunities, more than 70 percent of the people still live in rural areas, in villages of varying sizes.

Pakistani villages are built close together, usually around a well or irrigation canal. Almost every village has its mosque (the Muslim house of worship), from whose minaret, or tower, the faithful are called to prayer five times a day. Villagers grow most of their own

Villages like this one are home to the majority of Pakistanis. Houses are usually square in shape with flat roofs. Bread, baked in a clay oven, is a staple food.

food in the nearby fields, while other needs are supplied by local blacksmiths, potters, carpenters, barbers, and tailors.

Homes are made of local materials, such as mud, stone, or reed thatch. A typical house is square, with a flat mud roof covered by a layer of thatch and supported by wooden beams. Most homes have a veranda, or front porch, where guests are received. Sleeping rooms usually have cots of fiber woven on wooden frames. The main room is part living room and part kitchen, traditionally with a clay fireplace in the corner where meals are cooked. A farmer's house will have an outside enclosure, where cattle, farm implements, and grain are kept.

Foods. Bread, supplemented by vegetables and meat, is the staple food, while tea is the most commonly drunk beverage. Pilaf, or rice cooked with meat and broth, is traditionally served on ceremonial occasions. More sophisticated dishes include kebabs, or broiled meat usually cut into squares. Pakistani meat dishes consist mostly of lamb or beef. Chicken is also used. Pork is not eaten, however, because it is forbidden by Muslim religious law. A wide variety of spices are used in preparing foods.

Dress. Traditional dress for men in rural areas usually consists of the *pugri*, a long strip of cloth wound around the head as a turban, the *shalwar*, or baggy trousers, and a long shirt worn outside the trousers. More formal dress may include a fur hat known as a Jinnah cap (after the leader of Pakistan's independence movement, Mohammed Ali Jinnah), a long jacket called a *sherwani*, and *churidars*, or tight-fitting trousers.

Pakistani women traditionally wear the *shalwar*, together with a shirtlike garment called a *kurta* and a long scarf called a *dupatta*. Both men and women in the cities may also wear Western-style clothing.

Holidays and Festivals. Many holidays and festivals are religious in nature. Ramadan, the ninth month of the Muslim year, is a period of fasting and prayer. It is followed by Id-al-Fitr, a festival that breaks the fast. Id-al-Adha is a feast celebrating Abraham's offering of his son as a sacrifice to God. Those Muslims who can afford it buy a sheep to sacrifice at this time. Secular holidays include Independence Day, August 14th, and Pakistan Day, March 23rd.

▶ **THE LAND**

Overview. Pakistan shares borders with four other countries: Iran on the southwest, Afghanistan on the west and northwest, China on the northeast, and India on the east and southeast. The northeastern boundary includes the disputed territory of Jammu and Kashmir, claimed by both India and Pakistan, part of which is under Pakistani control.

Regions. Eastern Pakistan is made up largely of the great plains of the Punjab and Sind, which are drained by the Indus River and its tributaries. The Punjab and, to a lesser extent, Sind are the most heavily populated regions and, where irrigated, provide most of the country's fertile farmland. Baluchistan in the southwest is a vast, barren plateau. There are two desert areas, the Thar in the southeast and the Thal farther north. Most of the rest of Pakistan consists of rugged hills or mountains that culminate, in the far north, in the lofty, snowcapped ranges of the Hindu Kush and the Himalayas.

Climate. Pakistan's climate varies, depending on the season and elevation. Summers are generally quite hot, with temperatures of

FACTS and figures

ISLAMIC REPUBLIC OF PAKISTAN is the official name of the country.

LOCATION: South Asia.

AREA: 310,404 sq mi (803,943 km^2).

POPULATION: 123,000,000 (estimate).

CAPITAL: Islamabad.

LARGEST CITY: Karachi.

MAJOR LANGUAGES: Urdu (official), Punjabi, Sindhi, Pushtu, Baluchi, English.

MAJOR RELIGIOUS GROUP: Muslim.

GOVERNMENT: Republic. **Head of state**—president **Head of government**—prime minister. **Legislature**—National Assembly and Senate.

CHIEF PRODUCTS: Agricultural—wheat, cotton, rice, corn, millet, sugarcane, citrus fruits, livestock. **Manufactured**—cotton textiles and clothing, processed foods, chemicals, fertilizers, refined petroleum and petroleum products, machinery, iron and steel. **Mineral**—petroleum, natural gas, coal, limestone, gypsum, chromite.

MONETARY UNIT: Rupee (1 rupee = 100 paisa).

The lofty peaks of the Hindu Kush form part of Pakistan's northwestern border. Terraced farming is practiced in the mountain foothills to utilize all available land.

land is still forested, most of the valuable timber coming from the foothills of the Himalayas. There is a variety of wild animal life, including tigers, bears, and snow leopards, but many of these species are now endangered.

▶ THE ECONOMY

Agriculture. Agriculture has traditionally been the mainstay of the economy, although only about one-fifth of the land is under cultivation. Agriculture employs about half of Pakistan's workforce and provides about one-quarter of the national income. Most farms are relatively small. Their size is limited by the government, which has sought to distribute some of the larger holdings among landless peasants. The government has also encouraged farm mechanization, expanded irrigation, and the use of improved seeds in order to obtain larger crop yields.

Wheat is the basic food crop. Cotton is the main commercial crop. Rice, corn, millet, sugarcane, citrus fruits, and vegetables are also grown, with rice being an important export. Land unsuited to farming is used to graze livestock, including cattle, goats, sheep, and camels.

Manufacturing. The country's industry has increased greatly in recent decades, to where it now engages about one-fifth of the labor force and provides more than one-quarter of income. The chief industries are the manufacture of cotton textiles and clothing, along

120°F (49°C) not uncommon in the lower elevations, although the mountainous areas are much cooler. Winters are often cool and dry. Rainfall is limited, with most of it coming during the summer monsoon. The eastern plains receive only from 10 to 35 inches (250 to 900 millimeters) of rain a year and the northern mountains slightly more.

Natural Resources. Pakistan's most important mineral resources are petroleum and natural gas. It also has deposits of coal, limestone, gypsum, and chromite (chromium ore). The richest soils are in the eastern plains, but because of the arid climate, cultivation is dependent on irrigation from the Indus and its tributaries. Less than 5 percent of Pakistan's

A farmer in the North-West Frontier Province examines the remains of a sugarcane harvest. Sugarcane is one of the country's main crops.

This striking mosque, or Muslim house of worship, typifies the modern architecture of Islamabad, Pakistan's capital since 1967.

with the processing of foods and other agricultural products. Heavy industry includes the production of chemicals, fertilizers, refined petroleum and petroleum products, machinery, and iron and steel.

Mining and Fishing. Pakistan obtains close to half of its energy needs from its own deposits of natural gas (found chiefly in Baluchistan) and petroleum. It also exports some of its petroleum and petroleum products.

The country's long coastline on the Arabian Sea has made fishing an important economic activity. Shrimp, salmon, mullet, and mackerel are all caught in offshore waters. Some seafood is intended for domestic consumption, while the rest, shrimp in particular, is exported.

Transportation and Trade. Railroads linking the larger cities carry much of Pakistan's passenger and freight traffic. The national airline, Pakistan International Airlines (PIA), flies to cities within Pakistan and to countries abroad. Buses and trucks operate along Pakistan's network of highways and roads, but there are few private automobiles.

Pakistan has generally suffered from an unfavorable balance of trade, importing more than it exports. The United States is the chief market for its exports.

▶ **MAJOR CITIES**

While the great majority of the people still live in rural areas, Pakistan has a number of large cities. Several have populations of 1 million or more, and others are rapidly approaching that figure.

Karachi, Pakistan's largest city and former capital, is situated on the Arabian Sea. It is the country's chief port and the center of its commerce and industry. See the separate article on Karachi in Volume J-K.

Islamabad, Pakistan's capital since 1967, is a modern city that was designed to be the country's administrative center. It is situated in northern Pakistan, in the Himalayan foothills. **Lahore**, the second largest city and the capital of the province of Punjab, has many historical monuments, including the fort of the Emperor Akbar, the Badshahi Mosque, and the Shalimar Gardens. **Faisalabad** (formerly called Lyallpur), the third largest city, is an industrial and transportation hub. **Rawalpindi**, another major city of the Punjab and situated just a few miles south of Islamabad, served as Pakistan's interim capital until Islamabad was completed. **Hyderabad** is a principal city of the province of Sind. **Multan** is one of Pakistan's oldest cities and one of the first centers of Muslim culture in the region. **Peshawar**, capital of the North-West Frontier Province, lies

By contrast, Karachi, Pakistan's largest city, is a bustling metropolis where the old and the new exist side by side.

near the fabled Khyber Pass leading into Afghanistan. **Quetta** is the capital and largest city of Baluchistan.

▶ GOVERNMENT

Pakistan has had several changes of government since independence. The present government is based on a constitution adopted in 1973 and amended a number of times since. The head of state is the president, who is elected for a term of five years by an electoral college drawn from both the national and provincial legislatures. The national legislature consists of two houses—the National Assembly, which is elected directly by the people, and the Senate, elected mainly by the provincial legislatures.

The government is headed by a prime minister chosen by the president from the political party with the largest number of seats in the National Assembly. Each province has an elected legislature and a governor appointed by the president.

▶ HISTORY

Early History. The early history of the region dates back to the Indus Valley civilization, which flourished more than 4,000 years ago. The ruins of its chief cities, Mohenjo-Daro and Harappa, stand as a reminder of its past glories.

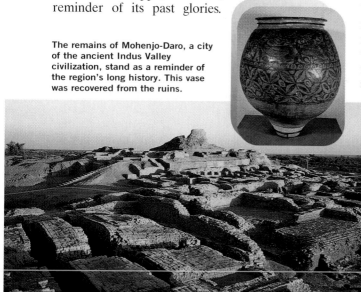

The remains of Mohenjo-Daro, a city of the ancient Indus Valley civilization, stand as a reminder of the region's long history. This vase was recovered from the ruins.

The two cities were first unearthed in the 1900's, revealing a civilization that has been compared to those of ancient Egypt and Mesopotamia. See ANCIENT CIVILIZATIONS (Indus Civilization) in Volume A.

In about 1500 B.C., a people known as Aryans, whose language was the ancestor of the Indo-European languages of India and Pakistan, entered the region from the north. In the centuries that followed, numerous other invaders—Persians, Greeks, Turks, Arabs, and Mongols among them—arrived in the land, leaving their mark on what would become the Pakistani people. At different times, various kingdoms and empires ruled over parts of what is now India and Pakistan.

From Islam to British Rule. Islam was introduced by Arab conquerors, who established themselves in Sind, in the south, in the A.D. 700's. By the early 900's, the north had also come under Muslim rule.

The last great native empire, that of the Moguls, lasted until the 1700's, when the empire came under the control of the British East India Company. In the 1850's the British government took over the Indian empire. Indian nationalism first manifested itself in the 1800's and grew into demands for complete independence from Britain in the 1900's.

Independence. When, after World War II ended in 1945, Britain announced its intention of withdrawing from its Indian empire, Muslims under the leadership of Mohammed Ali Jinnah (1876–1948) demanded a separate state of their own. The Muslims were fearful of Hindu domination under a united India and insisted that they constituted a separate nation with their own culture, language, and traditions.

Independence and the partition of the Indian subcontinent in 1947 saw a vast exchange of populations, as Muslims moved from their homes in India into Pakistan and Hindus living in Pakistan migrated to India. This large-scale movement of peoples created a host of problems for the new nation. Later, Muslim and Hindu religious riots further hindered the government's attempt to maintain order and improve living condi-

Mohammed Ali Jinnah (*left*, far right), the father of Pakistan's independence, is seen in 1947 with Britain's Lord Mountbatten (center) and India's Jawaharlal Nehru (far left). Benazir Bhutto (*below*) became prime minister of Pakistan in 1988 and again in 1993.

tions. The death of Mohammed Ali Jinnah in 1948 added to the government's woes.

A few months after independence, the shaky peace between India and Pakistan was broken by a dispute over the state of Jammu and Kashmir, which led to several wars between the two countries.

Political instability brought about a takeover of the government in 1958 by military officers led by General Mohammed Ayub Khan. A new constitution establishing a presidential form of government was adopted in 1962. But riots, caused by demands for a return to direct elections, brought about Ayub Khan's resignation in 1969. He was succeeded as head of government by General Agha Mohammed Yahya Khan.

Civil War. The two parts of Pakistan were unalike in several ways. West Pakistan was larger in area but East Pakistan had a larger population. They were also dissimilar in language and in their ethnic origin. Although they shared the Muslim religion, this proved insufficient to keep them together.

The breakup of the country had its beginnings in the 1970 elections for the National Assembly. Most of the seats allotted to East Pakistan were won by the Awami League, which favored local self-government. When the government postponed the opening of the National Assembly, strikes broke out in East Pakistan. Troops were sent from the West to put down what the government believed was a movement by the East to break away from Pakistan. In 1971 war broke out between India and Pakistan. The Pakistani forces were defeated, and East Pakistan be-

came the nation of Bangladesh. Yahya Khan resigned and was replaced by Zulfikar Ali Bhutto, who became prime minister of a new government in 1973.

Political turmoil and the breakdown of law and order led to a military coup in 1977. General Mohammed Zia ul-Haq took control of the government under martial law. Bhutto was tried and convicted of involvement in the murder of a political opponent and executed in 1979.

Recent History. Zia governed Pakistan as president from 1978 until his death in 1988. He lifted martial law in 1985, but a civilian government that took office was dismissed by him in 1988. Benazir Bhutto, daughter of the former prime minister, became prime minister herself in 1988. But she was removed from office in 1990 by President Ghulam Ishaq Khan on charges of corruption, and in elections that followed, Bhutto's Pakistan People's Party was defeated by the Islamic Democratic Alliance, led by Nawaz Sharif. In 1993 both President Ishaq Khan and Prime Minister Sharif resigned, and Bhutto and her party returned to power after their victory in new parliamentary elections.

Reviewed by KHALID BIN SAYEED
Queen's University (Ontario)
Author, *Politics in Pakistan*

See also BANGLADESH; INDIA (History); KASHMIR.

PALAU

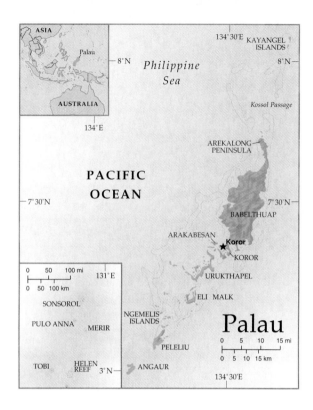

The Republic of Palau is an island nation situated in the northwestern Pacific Ocean. It consists of more than 200 islands and islets making up the western end of the Caroline Islands chain. Most of the islands are small, and only about eight of the larger ones are permanently inhabited. Palau was the last of the territories administered by the United States as part of the United Nations Trust Territory of the Pacific Islands. In 1994 it gained independence in free association with the United States.

The People. Palau has a population of about 16,000. The Palauans are chiefly Micronesians. Physically, they are generally of medium height, brown-skinned, with wavy or curly hair. Filipinos make up the largest ethnic minority. The official languages are Palauan and English. Most Palauans are Christians, primarily Roman Catholics.

The Land and Climate. Palau has a land area of about 192 square miles (497 square kilometers). Most of the islands are coral, while others are of volcanic origin. Nearly all the islands lie within an extensive barrier reef. Babelthuap, the largest and highest of the volcanic islands, makes up about three-quarters of Palau's total land area. The most populous island is Koror, which has about two-thirds of the country's people and is the site of the interim capital, Koror.

The climate is warm and humid. Monthly temperatures average about 80°F (27°C). Rainfall is heavy, with Koror receiving about 150 inches (3,800 millimeters) a year.

The Economy. The Palauans have traditionally relied on subsistence agriculture and fishing for their livelihood. The country's deposits of phosphates, its only mineral resource, have been exhausted. At present the government is the largest employer and depends on financial aid from the United States. Money sent home by Palauans living and working abroad is another important source of income. Hopes for the future rest on increasing tourism and the leasing of Palau's fishing grounds to other countries.

History and Government. The first Europeans to visit Palau were the Spanish, who arrived in the 1500's. The islands remained a possession of Spain until 1899, when they were sold to Germany. At the outbreak of World War I in 1914, they were occupied by Japan, which governed them after the war under a mandate from the League of Nations. The islands fell to the United States in 1944, during World War II. In 1947, Palau was made a U.S. trust territory by the United Nations. Negotiations for Palauan independence were complicated by a non-nuclear clause in its constitution, adopted in 1980. The United States' offer of a Compact of Free Association, which would allow nuclear materials to enter the country, was finally approved by Palauans in 1993. Independence took effect in 1994. Under the Compact, the United States provides financial aid to Palau and is responsible for its defense.

The government consists of a president and legislature, the National Congress, which is made up of the Senate and House of Delegates. The president and Congress are elected for 4-year terms.

WARD BARRETT
University of Minnesota

PALESTINE

Palestine is a historic region in southwestern Asia. It is situated at the eastern end of the Mediterranean Sea and forms part of the larger region known as the Middle East. Strategically located at a crossroads between East and West and near where Africa and Asia meet, Palestine has been the site of countless invasions and movements of peoples. It is, moreover, the land of the Bible and is considered holy by three major religions—Judaism, Christianity, and Islam. Few regions of such relatively small size have been so bitterly fought over through the centuries.

The word "Palestine" comes from "Philistine," the name for one of its early peoples. The Roman province in this region was known as Syria Palestina. Palestine's boundaries have varied widely over its long history. Although it once extended over a wider area, it is generally thought of today as the geographical region extending from the Sinai Peninsula on the south to Lebanon and Syria on the north and from the Mediterranean Sea on the west to the Jordan River and the Dead Sea on the east.

The article that follows provides a brief historical overview of Palestine.

▶ THE HEBREWS AND JUDAISM

Palestine has been inhabited since prehistoric times. In about 2000 B.C., the Hebrews, a nomadic people then living in Mesopotamia (modern Iraq), began their migration to the land of Canaan, as Palestine was then known. The twelve Hebrew tribes were united under their first king, Saul, to form the kingdom of Israel, and they eventually controlled most of the region. In about 1000 B.C., Saul's successor, David, made the city of Jerusalem his capital. Israel reached the height of its power under King Solomon, son of David, but after his death in 922 B.C., it was divided into two rival kingdoms—Israel in the north and Judah in the south. (The term "Jew," which

originally applied only to a Hebrew of Judah, eventually came to be used in referring to any Hebrew.)

Weakened by internal quarrels, the two kingdoms fell prey to stronger neighbors. In the 700's B.C., Israel was conquered by the Assyrians and its people were dispersed. Judah survived until the 500's B.C., when it fell to the Babylonians and many of its inhabitants were forced into exile. The Babylonians were succeeded by the Persians, under whom the Jews were allowed to return, and the Persians by the Greek and Macedonian armies of Alexander the Great. After Alexander's death in 323 B.C., his followers founded kingdoms in Egypt and Syria, which ruled Palestine in turn. Attempts by the Seleucid rulers of Syria to introduce Greek religious practices into the region in 167 B.C. provoked the Jews to revolt. After a long struggle led by Judah Maccabee and his brothers, they re-established an independent Jewish kingdom, which lasted until 63 B.C.

▶ ROME AND CHRISTIANITY

From 63 B.C. to about A.D. 630, Palestine was part of first the Roman and then the Byzantine empires. During the reign of Herod the Great, who ruled Judea (the Roman name for Judah) as a Roman protectorate, Jesus was born in the town of Bethlehem. It marked the humble beginning of what would become Christianity and eventually spread throughout the Roman world.

Roman rule over Palestine led to repeated Jewish revolts. The first, from 66 to 73, resulted in the destruction of the Temple in Jerusalem, the center of Jewish worship, along with much of the city itself. A second revolt broke out in 115 and a third in 132. The last, led by Simon Bar Cocheba (or Bar Kokhba), while at first successful, was eventually put down with great harshness. An independent Jewish nation would not appear again in the region for more than 1,800 years.

THE ARABS AND ISLAM

Shortly after 630, a powerful new force erupted out of the deserts of the Arabian Peninsula. The Arabs, united under the banner of Islam, the religion of the Muslims, swiftly conquered Palestine, along with most of the rest of the Middle East. Jews and Christians continued to live in Palestine, but Muslim Arabs became the dominant people of the region. Since Islam shared some of its traditions with the two earlier religions and Muslims believed that their prophet, Mohammed, had ascended to heaven from Jerusalem, Palestine became a holy land for them as well.

For most of the centuries that followed, Palestine remained under the rule of one or another Muslim dynasty. The exception was a period during the 1100's, when European Crusaders ruled Jerusalem and other small states in the region.

Palestine was the birthplace of three great religions—Judaism, Christianity, and Islam. An elderly Jew (*above*) prays at the Western Wall, the remnant of the ancient Temple in Jerusalem and Judaism's most sacred site. A cross is borne by a clergyman of the Greek Orthodox Church (*left*), one of the region's Christian denominations. Muslim women (*below left*) gather before Jerusalem's Dome of the Rock, an Islamic holy place.

In the 1500's, Palestine became part of the empire of the Ottoman Turks and remained so until the 1900's.

ZIONISM AND ARAB NATIONALISM

In the late 1800's and early 1900's, two nationalist movements—both involving Palestine—began to develop. The first was Zionism, which sought to re-establish a Jewish homeland in the region. From the 1880's on, considerable numbers of Jews from Europe settled in Palestine. A separate Arab nationalist movement, begun not long after, had as its aim independence from Ottoman rule. Arab nationalism was not focused specifically on Palestine, as Zionism was, but considered it part of the larger Arab community.

To this was added the role played by Britain, which sought the aid of both Arabs and Jews during World War I. In 1917, British forces occupied Palestine. That same year the British government issued the Balfour Declaration (named for Arthur J. Balfour, then the British foreign secretary). It pledged support for a Jewish homeland in Palestine while acknowledging the rights of its non-Jewish population. Arab leaders also claimed that Britain had promised to make Palestine part of an independent Arab state. These competing aspirations and claims set the stage for the clash between Jews and Arabs over the region that continues to the present day.

▶ THE BRITISH MANDATE

After World War I ended in 1918, the Ottoman Empire was broken apart, its core becoming the republic of Turkey. Palestine itself was placed under British administration in 1922 as a mandate of the League of Nations, the forerunner of the United Nations. The mandate also included land east of the Jordan River, where Britain established the state of Transjordan (now Jordan) in 1923.

Arab opposition to Zionist aims led to violent incidents in the 1920's. These grew worse during the 1930's, as increasing numbers of Jews, fleeing Nazi persecution in Europe, arrived in Palestine. Britain was increasingly hard-pressed to contain what had become an Arab rebellion. In 1939, just before the outbreak of World War II, the British government proposed the creation, within ten years, of an independent Palestine, composed of both Arabs and Jews but maintaining an Arab majority. Jewish immigration was to be limited and would end entirely within five years, unless approved by the Arabs. Both sides rejected the plan.

The murder of millions of European Jews by Nazi Germany during World War II intensified Zionist efforts to win a Palestinian homeland. After the war's end in 1945, the Jewish population swelled with the arrival of concentration camp survivors. Because of the immigration restrictions imposed by Britain, many of these refugees were smuggled into Palestine by Jewish underground groups, some of which used guerrilla warfare, sabotage, and terrorist tactics against the British forces.

▶ PARTITION

In 1947 the British, unable to find a solution acceptable to both sides, turned the issue of Palestine over to the United Nations, which voted to partition the region into separate Jewish and Arab states. Jerusalem was to be an international city, administered by the United Nations. The Jews of Palestine and Zionists elsewhere generally accepted this decision. Palestinian Arabs and Arab nationalists almost universally opposed it.

As the British prepared to depart, the new Jewish state of Israel was proclaimed on May 14, 1948. It was invaded almost immediately by armies of neighboring Arab countries, beginning the first Arab-Israeli war. When the war ended in 1949, Israel had not only

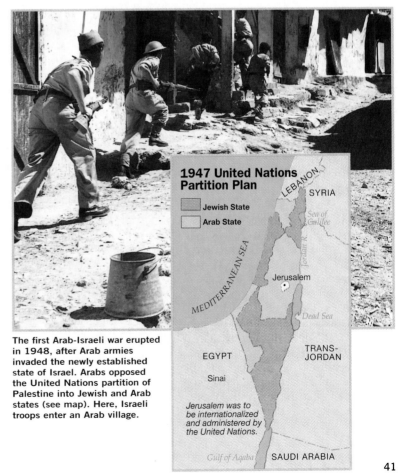

The first Arab-Israeli war erupted in 1948, after Arab armies invaded the newly established state of Israel. Arabs opposed the United Nations partition of Palestine into Jewish and Arab states (see map). Here, Israeli troops enter an Arab village.

1947 United Nations Partition Plan

■ Jewish State
□ Arab State

LEBANON
SYRIA
Sea of Galilee
MEDITERRANEAN SEA
Jordan R.
Jerusalem
Dead Sea
EGYPT
Sinai
TRANS-JORDAN

Jerusalem was to be internationalized and administered by the United Nations.

Gulf of Aqaba
SAUDI ARABIA

THE WEST BANK AND THE GAZA STRIP

The West Bank and the Gaza Strip are parts of the territory allotted to the Arabs by the United Nations when, in 1947, it partitioned Palestine into separate Arab and Jewish states.

The West Bank takes it name from its location on the western side of the Jordan River. It has an area of about 2,263 square miles (5,860 square kilometers) and a population of about 1.6 million. Most of the people are Palestinian Arabs, with a minority of Israeli settlers. It produces citrus fruits, vegetables, olives, and beef and dairy cattle. Historically, the region included ancient Samaria and Judea (Judah), and it has many sites of religious interest to Jews, Christians, and Muslims. Towns include Hebron, Nablus, Jericho, and Bethlehem.

The region was occupied by Transjordan (now Jordan) during the 1948–49 Arab-Israeli war. It came under Israeli control in the 1967 war. Since 1994–95, the Palestinian Authority (the Arab governing body) has had increasing self-rule in the region.

The Gaza Strip is a small, narrow territory, situated on the Mediterranean coast, north of the Sinai Peninsula. It has an area of about 147 square miles (380 square kilometers) and a population of more than 700,000, which is mainly Palestinian Arab. The economy is based largely on agriculture and livestock raising. Gaza is the main city. The region fell to Egypt during the 1948–49 war and was occupied by Israel in the 1967 war. It has been governed since 1994 by the Palestinian Authority.

successfully defended itself but had won additional territory as well. During the fighting, Transjordan occupied the West Bank, the region west of the Jordan River (subsequently changing its name to Jordan), and Egypt took over the Gaza Strip. Both were areas that had been allotted to a Palestinian Arab state. The war left Jerusalem divided between Israel and Jordan. Large numbers of Palestinian Arabs fled from Israeli to Arab territory, particularly the West Bank and the Gaza Strip.

▶ THE PALESTINIANS. EFFORTS TOWARD PEACE

The question of a Palestinian Arab state has remained one of the main causes of hostility between Israel and the Arab countries. Three more Arab-Israeli wars followed—in 1956, 1967, and 1973. During the 1967 war, Israel gained control of the West Bank, all of Jerusalem, the Gaza Strip, and the Sinai peninsula of Egypt, as well as Syria's Golan Heights. Israel's occupation of the West Bank and the Gaza Strip

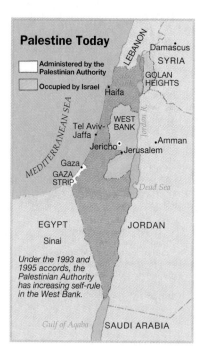

Palestine Today

□ Administered by the Palestinian Authority
□ Occupied by Israel

MEDITERRANEAN SEA

LEBANON
Damascus
SYRIA
GOLAN HEIGHTS
Haifa
WEST BANK
Tel Aviv-Jaffa
Jericho
Jerusalem
Amman
Gaza
GAZA STRIP
Dead Sea
EGYPT
JORDAN
Sinai

Under the 1993 and 1995 accords, the Palestinian Authority has increasing self-rule in the West Bank.

Gulf of Aqaba   SAUDI ARABIA

brought large numbers of Palestinian Arabs under its control. Israel returned the Sinai following a peace treaty with Egypt concluded in 1979. The treaty also discussed, in general terms, the possibility of a Palestinian Arab state in the West Bank and Gaza, but there was no agreement on how the state would be set up and governed.

Palestinian Arab nationalism, meanwhile, found expression in militant guerrilla organizations. Most were included in an overall body, the Palestine Liberation Organization (PLO), headed by Yasir Arafat. The PLO was eventually accepted by Arab countries as the "sole legitimate representative of the Palestinian people" and was granted observer status by the United Nations. Although the diverse groups had different aims, most shared the goal of replacing Israel with a predominantly Arab state. Their activities included widespread terrorism, often carried out far from Palestine itself, and raids against

Yasir Arafat (left), chairman of the Palestine Liberation Organization (PLO), and Israeli prime minister Yitzhak Rabin signed historic accords in 1993 and 1995 on Palestinian self-rule in Gaza and the West Bank. Rabin was later killed by an Israeli opposed to the peace plan.

Tensions between the Arabs and the Israeli government escalated in 1987. Violent demonstrations against the Israeli occupation spread from the Gaza Strip to the West Bank in 1988. A breakthrough in the long dispute came in 1993, when Israel and the PLO signed an accord giving Arabs self-rule in the Gaza Strip and the West Bank city of Jericho. In 1994, Jordan signed a peace treaty with Israel. A second accord, in 1995, provided for increasing self-rule in the West Bank by the Palestinian Authority. But the assassination of Israeli prime minister Yitzhak Rabin in 1995 and the election of a conservative Israeli government in 1996 slowed the peace process. This and Israel's opening of an archaeological tunnel in Jerusalem, near Muslim holy places, set off new violence later in 1996.

JAMES JANKOWSKI
University of Colorado
Coauthor, *The Middle East:*
A Social Geography

Israeli settlements. Israeli opinion on the Palestinian question has been mixed. Some Israelis have been willing to trade territory for peace; others have opposed a Palestinian Arab state, fearing that it would mean the elimination of Israel.

See also ARABS; ISRAEL; JERUSALEM; ZIONISM.

PALESTRINA, GIOVANNI PIERLUIGI DA (1525?–1594)

Giovanni Pierluigi, called Palestrina after the Italian town where he was born, was a great composer of Roman Catholic church music. He was born about 1525 and began his musical training in the choir of the cathedral of Palestrina. As a youth he was a choirboy at the Church of Santa Maria Maggiore in Rome.

In 1544, Palestrina was appointed organist and choirmaster at the cathedral in his hometown. In 1551, when the bishop there became Pope Julius III, he made the composer choir director of the Julian Chapel at St. Peter's Basilica. Several years later, Palestrina dedicated his first book of masses to Pope Julius. In appreciation, Julius made him a member of the papal choir, which sang in the Sistine Chapel. But in 1555 the new pope, Paul IV, declared that married men could no longer sing in the choir. Because Palestrina had married in 1547, he was dismissed.

During the next 16 years, Palestrina held several posts in Rome and published many masses and motets—sacred choral compositions based on Latin texts. In 1571 he re-

sumed his post as choirmaster of the Julian Chapel. Pope Gregory XIII gave him the title Master of Music at the Vatican Basilica.

All of Palestrina's music was written to be sung without instrumental accompaniment. One of his best-known works is the mass *Missa Papae Marcelli*, published in 1567.

In 1580, Palestrina's wife and several other family members died during a severe outbreak of disease in Italy. Upset by these tragedies, Palestrina thought of becoming a priest. But in 1581 he married a wealthy widow and took over his new wife's fur business. The income from the business enabled Palestrina to publish many compositions. His works include more than 100 masses, some 375 motets, and about 150 madrigals. (Madrigals are musical compositions for several voices, based on non-religious texts.)

Palestrina remained at St. Peter's until his death on February 2, 1594. He was buried in a side chapel of the old basilica. The inscription on his casket reads, "Prince of Music."

Reviewed by JON GILLOCK
The Juilliard School

PANAMA

Panama is a small nation of Central America. It occupies the narrowest part of Central America (known as the Isthmus of Panama), where it joins South America. The isthmus narrowly separates the Caribbean Sea, an arm of the Atlantic Ocean, from the Pacific Ocean.

Panama's shape and geographical location have played an important role in its history. For its earliest inhabitants, American Indians, Panama was a land bridge between North and South America. To Spanish colonists, who first arrived in the region in the 1500's, it was a short overland route between the Atlantic and Pacific oceans. The construction of the Panama Canal, linking the two oceans, in the early 1900's, greatly enhanced Panama's importance. (An article on the Panama Canal follows this article.)

▶THE PEOPLE

As a people, the Panamanians have been strongly affected by living in a country that is a crossroads of the world. Their character and culture, however, have been formed by a variety of influences.

Origins. Panamanians are descended from three main ethnic groups: American Indians, Europeans, and black Africans. Only a small minority of Indians remain. Most live in isolated regions—the Guaymí in the northwestern mountains, the Kuna (or Cuna) on the coastal islands of the northeast, and the Chocó in the rain forests of Darién.

Many of the Spaniards who settled in Panama intermarried with the Indians. Their mixed-race descendants (*mestizos*) now make up the country's largest ethnic group. Blacks originally were imported from Africa as slaves. Later, other blacks came from the West Indies to work on the Panama Canal. The building of the canal also brought smaller numbers of people from other European countries, from North America, and from the Middle East, India, and China. Racial harmony is the rule, although antagonisms exist.

Language and Religion. All Panamanians speak Spanish, the official language. English is also used widely, particularly by people of West Indian and North American origin. Panama has the largest share of English-speaking inhabitants in Latin America. Indians speak their native languages among themselves, but learn Spanish to deal with outsiders or when seeking work away from their own regions.

Roman Catholicism, brought by the Spaniards, is the religion of most of the people. Many other faiths, however, are practiced freely. Panamanians of West Indian origin are largely Protestant. Most Indians prefer to follow their traditional religions. There also are small Hindu, Buddhist, and Jewish communities. Religious freedom is guaranteed under the Panamanian constitution.

Education. Panamanians take pride in their school system. The government devotes a considerable part of its budget to education. As a result, the literacy rate (the number of people able to read and write) is about 90 percent. The University of Panama, founded in 1935, enrolls students from all over the country. Many Panamanians also study at universities abroad.

Way of Life. The Panamanian way of life is a mixture of several cultures. The centuries-old Spanish tradition prevails in language, architecture, family life, food, and in many

The Panama Railroad (*above*) crosses the narrow but rugged Isthmus of Panama. Much of the land is covered with dense rain forests. Indians, like this Kuna girl (*left*), were Panama's earliest inhabitants. *Mestizos*, or people of mixed Indian and European ancestry, such as these sidewalk vendors (*opposite page*), are the largest ethnic group.

leisure activities. As in other Latin American countries, the holidays of Carnival and Christmas dominate the calendar, and each town celebrates its saint's day in the Spanish manner. The traditional dress worn during these festivals comes from Spain, as does the music, particularly the *tamborito* ("little drum"), the national dance. It is performed by couples accompanied by drummers and a hand clapping audience. A relatively few Panamanians, often well-to-do, proudly trace their ancestry back to Spain.

Many other cultural influences can also be seen in Panamanian daily life. Baseball, introduced by Americans, draws as many fans as soccer. The large American community also contributed french fries, rock music, and miniskirts. The West Indians brought the calypso music of the African-American and Caribbean culture. The Indians gave Panama many of its handicrafts and certain foods, including plan-

tains (a kind of banana) and potatoes. Other immigrant groups brought elements of their own way of life, adding great variety to the country's life-style and outlook.

▶THE LAND

Panama is shaped roughly like the letter "S" laid on its side. It is bordered on the north by the Caribbean Sea, on the east by the South American nation of Colombia, on the south by the Pacific Ocean, and on the west by the Central American country of Costa Rica.

Overview. Mountain ranges form a backbone stretching nearly the entire length of the country. The highest point is Barú, an inactive volcano near the Costa Rican border, which rises to 11,401 feet (3,476 meters). At its narrowest point, just east of the canal, the isthmus measures only some 32 miles (51 kilometers) across. Its mountains divide Panama into distinctive Caribbean and Pacific regions. The plains and valleys have moderately fertile soil. Less than one quarter of the land, however, is suitable for farming.

Climate and Vegetation. Panama has a tropical climate, with generally warm, humid days and cool nights. Temperatures vary little throughout the year, averaging about 81° F (26° C) on the coasts, but less in the mountains. Rainfall is considerable but seasonal. It falls heaviest on the Caribbean coast, which

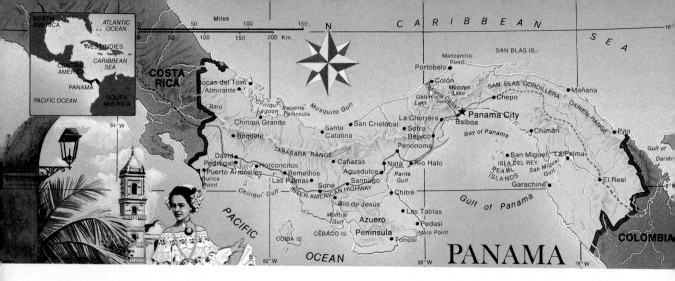

receives about 128 inches (3,250 millimeters) a year. The Pacific coastal region receives about half that amount.

Jungle and tropical rain forests cover much of Panama. The Caribbean area and Darién, the eastern region of Panama, are the most densely forested. They are sparsely inhabited, mainly by Indians. Parts of the Pacific region consist of savanna, or thinly wooded grassland. This was the chief area of settlement by the Spanish.

Natural Resources. Panama has large deposits of copper and smaller amounts of coal, manganese, zinc, gold, and silver, although its mineral resources are still largely undeveloped. The forests of Darién have been a source of mahogany and other hardwoods, and the surrounding waters abound in fish and other seafood. By far, however, the country's most important natural resource is its narrow shape, which favored the building of the Panama Canal.

▶**ECONOMY**

Panama's single largest economic enterprise is the canal itself. The fees Panama receives for the use of the canal help to offset its trade deficit. Farming is the country's oldest economic activity. Commerce, industry, and services dominate the economic life of the two largest cities—Panama City, the capital, and Colón.

Agriculture. About one quarter of the work force is engaged in farming. The majority of Panamanian farms are small. Farmers grow such basic food crops as rice, corn, beans, and potatoes for their own use and for sale in nearby towns or in cities. The main commer-

cial crops—bananas, sugarcane, and coffee—are grown on plantations. Bananas traditionally were the country's chief export. Panama is self-sufficient in some foods, but it must import others. Cattle are raised in the southwest.

Fishing and Forestry. Fishing plays an important role in the economy. Exports of shrimp, in particular, are a leading source of income. Much of the shrimp is now harvested in saltwater "farms."

Some logging is carried out in the Darién region. But the government has temporarily limited the felling of trees to allow the regrowth of valuable hardwoods.

Manufacturing and Services. Panama is too small a country to support large-scale industries. Its major industry is oil refining and the processing of petroleum products. Processed foods, construction materials, clothing, and shoes are other manufactured products.

FACTS AND FIGURES

REPUBLIC OF PANAMA (República de Panamá) is the official name of the country.

THE PEOPLE are known as Panamanians.

LOCATION: Central America.

AREA: 29,761 sq mi (77,082 km²).

POPULATION: 2,300,000 (estimate).

CAPITAL AND LARGEST CITY: Panama City.

MAJOR LANGUAGES: Spanish (official), English.

MAJOR RELIGION: Roman Catholic.

GOVERNMENT: Republic. **Head of state and government**—president. **Legislature**—Legislative Assembly.

CHIEF PRODUCTS: Agriculture—rice, sugarcane, bananas, corn, beans, coffee, cattle and other livestock. **Manufactured**—Refined petroleum and petroleum products, processed foods (including refined sugar, fish and shrimp), clothing, shoes, construction materials. **Mineral**—copper, gold, silver, manganese.

MONETARY UNIT: Balboa (1 balboa = 100 centésimos).

NATIONAL ANTHEM: *Himno Nacional* (First line: "Victory is ours at last").

The Colón Free Zone is one of the world's largest free-trade areas. Here, raw materials and partly finished goods can be imported and transformed into finished products for export without payment of duties (taxes).

Important service industries include banking, inexpensive ship registry, and other commercial activities. The Panama Canal, as one of the world's great engineering feats, also attracts tourists.

Transportation. Two main highways link Panama's cities. The Inter-American Highway runs from Costa Rica to Panama City and on to Chepo, where it has stopped due to the difficulty and cost of construction in the dense Darién rain forests. The Trans-Isthmian Highway runs parallel to the canal and links Panama City and Colón. The two cities are also joined by a railroad. Tocumen airport near Panama City is a center of air transportation between the Caribbean and South America.

▶**MAJOR CITIES**

Panama City is the commercial and cultural heart of the country as well as its capital and largest city. It is situated on the Bay of Panama, near the Pacific end of the Panama Canal. The population of the city proper is more than 400,000, with a much larger number of people living in its metropolitan area. Virtually all of the nation's business is conducted here. The city's architecture varies from Spanish colonial, in the old district, to modern high-rise in the newer areas.

The modern section of Panama City, Panama's capital and largest city, juts out into the Bay of Panama on the Pacific Ocean. The original city, or Old Panama, was founded by the Spanish in 1519. The present city dates from 1673. A statue of the Spanish explorer Vasco Núñez de Balboa stands in Panama City, overlooking the Pacific. Balboa crossed the Isthmus of Panama in 1513 and was the first European to see the Pacific Ocean.

The original city, or Old Panama, was founded by the Spanish in 1519, and soon became an important port. It was destroyed by pirates in 1671, and the present city was established, a few miles away, in 1673.

Colón, the second largest city, lies at the Caribbean end of the canal. It was founded in 1851 as the northern station of the Panama Railroad. Colón's docks and warehouses serve ships using the Panama Canal. The city grew in importance after a free-trade zone was established here in 1948.

Panama's provincial cities, such as David, Santiago, Penonomé, and La Chorrera, are quiet and attractive places rarely visited by tourists. They are situated in a part of the country that Panamanians call the interior.

GOVERNMENT

Panama is a republic. Its government is based on a 1972 constitution, amended in 1983. The president, who is head of state and government, is elected (together with two vice presidents) for a 5-year term. The law-making body is the Legislative Assembly, which is also elected for five years. The judiciary (court system) is headed by the Supreme Court, whose nine members are appointed by the president.

At various times in its history, the military has exercised considerable power in the government. The United States, because of its long operation of the canal, has also been a major influence in Panamanian affairs.

HISTORY

Colonial Era. The Indians who inhabited the region put up little resistance to the Spanish when they arrived in the isthmus in 1501. After Vasco Núñez de Balboa crossed Panama and reached the Pacific Ocean in 1513, ports were established on both coasts. (See the article on Balboa in Volume B.)

Panama enjoyed a golden age in the 1600's, as silver from Peru was transported across the isthmus for shipment to Spain. Panama declined in importance in the 1700's, and after 1740 it was governed as part of the Spanish colony of New Granada (which included modern Colombia).

Union with Colombia. When the wars of independence broke out in Latin America in the 1800's, Panama at first remained loyal to Spain. After Colombia won independence in 1821, however, Panama joined the Colombian union. For the next 82 years, Panama was Colombia's most troublesome province. Several times Panama broke away from Colombia. Each time it was brought back by military force.

In the 1880's a French company tried to build a canal across Panama. It failed, but in the 1890's interest grew in the United States for the construction of such a canal.

Independence and a Canal. Colombia at first encouraged purchase of the canal rights by the United States. But in 1903 it rejected the U.S. terms of a canal treaty as inadequate. At this point, on November 3, 1903, Panama declared its independence. U.S. President Theodore Roosevelt sent warships to the area to prevent Colombia from suppressing the revolt.

Soon after, the United States and Panama signed the Hay-Bunau-Varilla Treaty of 1903. Under its terms, the United States guaranteed Panama's independence in return for rights to build a canal. In 1904, Panama adopted its first constitution. Construction of the canal was begun that same year. The waterway was opened in 1914.

Modern History. Much of Panama's later history revolved around the struggle to gain more benefits for Panamanians from the canal. These years often were marked by political instability. One president, Arnulfo Arias, who first won office in 1940, was elected to the presidency several times. Each time he was deposed by the military. Arias was removed from office for the last time in 1968 by General Omar Torrijos, head of the National Guard, the Panamanian armed forces. Under Torrijos, Panama and the United States signed new canal treaties in 1977, under which ownership of the canal will pass to Panama at the end of 1999.

Recent Events. Torrijos died in 1981. In 1983, General Manuel Antonio Noriega became commander of the armed forces, giving him control over the government. Although several civilian presidents were elected, real power rested with Noriega. The United States cooperated with him at first but later used

U.S. troops deposed Panama's military ruler, General Manuel Noriega, in 1990. Many Panamanians welcomed Noriega's overthrow.

diplomatic and economic pressure in an effort to oust him. Finally captured by U.S. troops in 1989, he was taken to the United States and tried for drug trafficking. He was found guilty in 1992 and sentenced to prison. Meanwhile, a new Panamanian government had been sworn in, headed by Guillermo Endara, whose earlier election had been nullified by Noriega. Endara was succeeded as president by Ernesto Perez Balladares, elected in 1994.

MICHAEL L. CONNIFF
University of New Mexico

PANAMA CANAL

The Panama Canal is a waterway built across the Isthmus of Panama in Central America, connecting the Atlantic and Pacific oceans. Before the canal was opened in 1914, ships traveling between the two oceans had to make a long voyage around the southern tip of South America. The canal shortened the interocean journey by more than 7,000 miles (11,200 kilometers). Upon its completion, the canal was hailed as one of the world's engineering marvels.

The Panama Canal was built by the United States under a treaty signed with the Republic of Panama in 1903. Under the treaty, the United States operated the canal with little participation by Panama. New treaties were signed by the two countries in 1977. They provide for Panamanian cooperation in running the canal and for transfer of ownership to Panama at the end of 1999.

Description. The Panama Canal has a length of 51 miles (82 kilometers). It extends from the Caribbean Sea, a part of the Atlantic Ocean, on the northwest to the Pacific Ocean on the southeast. The canal follows an irregular path, taking advantage of natural features of the land.

Ships cross the canal through a system of locks. These are large open chambers, made of concrete, with a gate at each end. Each lock is 1,000 feet (305 meters) long and 110 feet (33 meters) wide. Their function is to raise and lower ships from one level of the canal to another. Ships are raised by flooding locks with water, and lowered by emptying them. The locks are built in pairs, so that ships can pass in both directions.

Route. A ship entering the canal on the Atlantic side crosses Limón Bay, near the town of Cristóbal and the city of Colón, and passes into a channel. It is then raised by locks 85 feet (26 meters) to the surface of Gatun Lake, a vast lake created by the damming of the

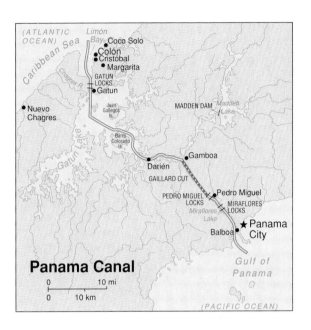

Panama Canal
0   10 mi
0   10 km

Chagres River. In addition to Gatun, two other artificial lakes, Madden and Miraflores, form part of the canal.

The ship follows the old Chagres River valley until it is about halfway across the canal. It then enters another channel, the Gaillard Cut, which takes it through the Continental Divide, the highest mountains on the canal route. Finally, the ship is lowered, by the Pedro Miguel and Miraflores locks, to the level of the Pacific Ocean. The town of Balboa marks the Pacific terminus of the canal. The crossing takes about eight hours.

Economic Importance. By reducing the cost of interocean shipping, the canal has long played a vital role in world commerce. On average, more than 12,000 ships pass through the canal each year. The United States uses the canal more than any other country. Under the 1977 treaties, Panama receives about $50–$60 million a year for use of the canal. Its economy also benefits from wages paid to Panamanians employed by the canal.

Ships cross the canal through locks, which raise and lower them from one level to another. The locks are in pairs, so that ships can pass in both directions.

Although the Panama Canal is still an important waterway, it can no longer handle the largest ships now in use. The United States and Panama have studied ways to improve service. Panama already has an oil pipeline, the Trans-Panamanian pipeline, which bypasses the canal altogether. This has reduced the need for oil tankers to use the canal. Other possible changes include a third set of locks and a new sea-level canal, which would make locks unnecessary. Any new canal project would need the approval of both countries.

The Dream of a Canal. The dream of building a canal across Panama dates from 1513, when the Spanish explorer Vasco Núñez de Balboa crossed the region from the Atlantic Ocean to the Pacific Ocean. The first European to see the Pacific, Balboa also discovered that only a narrow neck of land—the Isthmus of Panama—separated the two oceans.

The first important step toward the goal of creating a canal came in 1855, with the completion of the Panama Railroad. The railroad made it easier to cross the narrow but rugged isthmus.

In 1881 a French company headed by Ferdinand de Lesseps attempted to build a canal across Panama. De Lesseps, who earlier had built the Suez Canal, sought to construct a similar sea-level canal at Panama. He did not foresee the difficulty and cost that this would involve, and in 1889 De Lesseps' company went bankrupt.

(See the article on De Lesseps in Volume L, and the article on the Suez Canal in Volume S.)

U.S. Interest. The French failure renewed the interest of the United States in building a canal across Central America. Two sites were considered—Nicaragua and Panama. The Panama site eventually was chosen, and in 1902 the U.S. Congress approved purchase of the French canal rights. As Panama was then a part of Colombia, the United States negotiated a treaty with the Colombian government. The Hay-Herrán Treaty was signed in 1903, but it was rejected by the Colombian legislature as unfavorable to Colombia.

Panamanian Independence. Soon after Colombia's rejection of the treaty, Panama declared its independence on November 3, 1903. The independence movement was supported by U.S. President Theodore Roosevelt, who dispatched warships to Panamanian waters to prevent the landing of Colombian troops and soon recognized the new nation. Two weeks later, the United States and Panama signed the Hay-Bunau-Varilla Treaty.

The 1903 Treaty. The 1903 treaty permitted the United States to build a canal in Panama. It also gave the United States complete authority over a 10 mile- (16 kilometer-) wide strip of land across the isthmus, on which to build, operate, and defend the canal. The government of this territory, known as the Canal Zone, was headed by a governor appointed by the U.S. president. The United States also maintained military bases in the zone. The rights of the United States to the Canal Zone were to last "in perpetuity"—that is, forever.

In return, Panama received $10 million and a yearly rental fee of $250,000, beginning in 1913. This amount was increased two times. The United States also guaranteed Panama's independence.

Building the Canal. The canal took ten years to build and required the excavation of more than 232 million cubic yards (177 million cubic meters) of soil and rock. An average of 35,000 workers, the great majority of them blacks from the West Indies, labored on its construction.

Three men played especially important roles in the successful outcome. President Roosevelt guided the canal project. Colonel George W. Goethals, a U.S. Army engineer, supervised construction from 1907 to the canal's completion. Colonel William C. Gorgas, an

Army doctor, introduced health measures that greatly reduced cases of malaria and yellow fever, which had been one of the major causes of the failure of the French canal project.

The Panama Canal was opened to commercial traffic on August 14, 1914. It had cost some $380 million to build.

U.S.-Panamanian Relations. Although Panama's leaders had agreed to the 1903 canal treaty, most Panamanians never really accepted it. They increasingly came to resent U.S. control over what they considered Panamanian territory. Panama won some changes in the treaty, but these did not satisfy Panamanian hopes.

Panamanian discontent reached a climax in 1964, with the outbreak of riots in the Canal Zone and in several Panamanian cities. The outburst, which left dozens dead, convinced the two governments that a new basis for operating the canal had to be found. After years of negotiations, the United States and Panama concluded two new treaties in 1977. They went into effect in 1979.

The 1977 Treaties. The first treaty abolished the Canal Zone and gave most of the territory back to Panama. The remaining territory—necessary for the operation and defense of the canal—is called the Panama Canal Area. The United States has primary responsibility for the canal until December 31, 1999, but Panama is now a partner in most respects. Separate agreements reduced the number of U.S. military bases to four. The treaty also calls for a study by both countries of the possibility of a new sea-level canal. The second treaty guarantees the permanent neutrality of the canal.

Administration of the Canal. Until the treaty expires, the canal is operated by the Panama Canal Commission, a U.S. government agency. The commission is supervised by a board of directors made up of five Americans and four Panamanians. In 1990 a Panamanian became administrator, the chief operating official of the canal. About 85 percent of the canal's employees are Panamanians. Panama is also responsible for the police, sanitation, law courts, and mail service in the area.

MICHAEL L. CONNIFF
University of New Mexico
Author, *Black Labor on a White Canal: Panama—1904–1981*

See also PANAMA.

A political cartoon of 1903 depicts President Theodore Roosevelt digging the Panama Canal himself, after Colombia had rejected the terms of a treaty.

PANDAS

Pandas are extremely rare, bearlike animals that inhabit the snowy regions of central China. There are two kinds of pandas—the giant panda and the red panda, also called the lesser panda. The giant panda, with its distinctive black and white markings, is the more familiar of the two. Giant pandas and red pandas belong to their own separate animal family, the Ailuropodidea. Their closest living relatives are the bears.

Giant pandas start life at the surprisingly small weight of 4 ounces (104 grams), about the size of a stick of butter. This tiny infant grows into an adult weighing between 180 and 270 pounds (80 and 120 kilograms). Adult giant pandas have coarse black and white fur, small black ears, and large black eye patches that give them their unique appeal.

Giant pandas in the wild are found in only one place in the world: central China, mainly in Sichuan province. They are protected in forest reserves, but the growing human population, a decrease in their food supply, and illegal hunting threatens their existence. Fewer than 1,000 pandas live in the wild.

Diet. Giant pandas spend most of their time roaming the forest feeding on bamboo. Bamboo is the giant pandas' main food, although they sometimes eat other kinds of plants. In captivity pandas have remained healthy on a diet of cooked rice, apples, carrots, cooked sweet potato, and cooked meat in addition to bamboo. Pandas have dietary needs that are very similar to animals that regularly eat meat, so they must eat great quantities of bamboo to obtain the nourishment they need. One panda can eat up to 85 pounds (38 kilograms) of bamboo in a single day.

To help them eat such tough, fibrous food, pandas have extremely powerful jaws and large, flattened molars designed for crushing. They also have an unusually shaped wrist bone that sticks out like a small thumb. This bone helps pandas hold stalks of bamboo.

Reproduction. The giant panda is a solitary animal, but once a year, between March and May, males and females come together for the breeding season. They find each other in the thick forest by leaving scent markings on trees, bushes, logs, or other objects. Pandas communicate with each other using bleats, chirps, honks, moans, and growls.

Hunting and the destruction of its habitat has made the giant panda, which inhabits the bamboo forests of eastern China, one of the rarest animals on earth.

Zoos. In 1936 the first giant panda was exhibited in a zoo outside China. Today there are more than a dozen pandas in zoos in other countries. Pandas can be seen in Washington, D.C., Mexico City, London, Tokyo, Madrid, Paris, and Berlin. All pandas in captivity are given double names, following the Chinese custom, to indicate affection. Scientists study the zoo pandas in hopes of learning how to save wild pandas from extinction.

Red Pandas. The red panda lives in the bamboo forests of China, Tibet, and Nepal. The average adult is much smaller than the giant panda, weighing only 9 to 13 pounds (4 to 6 kilograms). The body and tail are covered with long, rust-brown fur. The tail has cream-colored bands on it.

Red pandas spend much of their time curled up like cats in the trees of their forest home. They come down to feed on bamboo and other grasses as well as on roots and fruit. Occasionally red pandas will eat meat. Like giant pandas, red pandas are generally solitary animals. During the breeding season male and female pairs travel together. The young remain dependent on their mothers for up to a year.

LISA M. STEVENS
Panda Collection Manager
National Zoological Park

PAPER

The paper on which these words are printed is made of millions of tiny fibers. The fibers are cellulose, a substance from the cell walls of plants. The average length of cellulose fibers is about 1/20 inch (1.3 millimeters). The fibers have been mixed in water and treated with chemicals, matted into a sheet, and dried to form paper.

Paper is one of the most important products ever invented. Widespread use of a written language would not have been possible without some affordable and practical material to write on. The invention of paper meant that more people could be educated because more books could be printed and distributed. Industry could grow because all the plans, blueprints, records, and formulas it uses could be written down and saved. Together with the printing press, paper provided a very important way to communicate knowledge.

Paper is important for other reasons. Paper and paperboard are made into cartons, wrappers, and containers for hundreds of products. Everything from washing machines to candy comes wrapped in paper or in paper cartons. Paper is made into many useful objects, such as plates, cups, and towels. New types of paper have been developed for use as clothes, bedsheets, and pillowcases.

The word "paper" comes from the word "papyrus." Papyrus was not really paper. It was a writing material made, originally by the ancient Egyptians, from the fibers of the papyrus plant. Papyrus was too brittle to be bound into books, so it was glued together in long strips and carefully rolled up on wooden or ivory rods.

▶ HOW PAPER IS MADE

All paper is made in basically the same way. A mixture of cellulose fibers, water, and chemicals is placed on a fine-meshed screen that lets the water drain off. As the fibers dry, they mat together to form a sheet. The sheet is removed from the screen, dried, and pressed smooth to form paper.

Heavy rolls of newsprint are unloaded from a delivery truck in London. Newsprint, used for newspapers, is one of many different types of paper.

Until about 150 years ago, all paper was made by hand. Today, paper is made by machine. Some of the large papermaking machines can produce more than 2 million pounds (900,000 kilograms) of paper in a single day.

Materials

The cellulose used in paper today comes from wood waste, fiber from recycled paper, and trees.

Fiber to make pulp comes directly or indirectly from the forest. Fast-growing species of trees, such as softwoods and some hardwoods, are grown on tree plantations specifically for use as wood pulp. After being cut, these logs are hauled to the pulp mill by truck or railroad, and the plantation is replanted with the next crop of trees. Sometimes logs are taken to the nearest river and floated down to the mill. In other cases, wood fiber comes from a sawmill in the form of bark, shavings, and other wood waste left over from the manufacture of lumber, plywood, and similar products. This way, virtually no part of a harvested tree is wasted.

Recycled paper, such as used boxes, computer paper, and old newspapers and magazines, comes from commercial and retail outlets, household curbside collection programs, and paper converting facilities.

Pulp, a material from which paper is made, comes from wood and recycled paper.
Above: At a paper plant in Maine, logs are lifted from a truck and placed on a huge pile.
Above right: A towering wall of wastepaper waits to be recycled.

Paper mills are built near water, because papermaking requires a large supply of water. The water must be pure, because any impurities will show up in the finished product. Paper mills have their own equipment for purifying water, and they use the same water over and over to keep consumption down.

Converting the Wood into Pulp

The first step is to prepare the wood for papermaking. Wood arrives at the mill in the form of pulpwood, chips, and sawdust. Pulping is done either by grinding up the pulpwood or by cooking the chips and sawdust with chemicals. Some pulping methods use both grinding and cooking.

The wood is ground up by being pressed against a large, rapidly turning grindstone. Water is sprayed over the wood and grindstone to cool the stone and carry away the pulp. Wood is ground into pulp when the paper does not have to be very strong or durable. One of the largest users of groundwood is newsprint, the paper on which newspapers are printed.

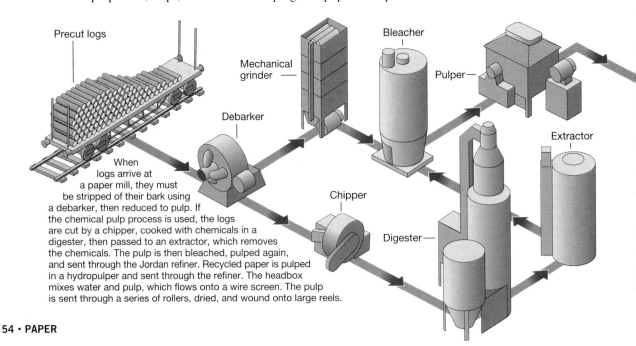

Precut logs
Mechanical grinder
Bleacher
Pulper
Debarker
Extractor
Chipper
Digester

When logs arrive at a paper mill, they must be stripped of their bark using a debarker, then reduced to pulp. If the chemical pulp process is used, the logs are cut by a chipper, cooked with chemicals in a digester, then passed to an extractor, which removes the chemicals. The pulp is then bleached, pulped again, and sent through the Jordan refiner. Recycled paper is pulped in a hydropulper and sent through the refiner. The headbox mixes water and pulp, which flows onto a wire screen. The pulp is sent through a series of rollers, dried, and wound onto large reels.

For chemical processes, the wood must be in the form of chips. The wood chips are cooked with several different chemicals to turn them into pulp. The sulfate process is the major chemical pulping method.

Other pulping processes include the semichemical process and the sulfite process. In the semichemical process, the wood is ground up as well as being cooked with chemicals. This pulp is most often used for making corrugated paperboard. The sulfite process results in nearly pure cellulose fibers, which are used to make high-quality paper for expensive stationery, maps, and photographs.

Another way of making pulp is by exploding the wood. Chips of wood are put under high pressure in a closed vessel. Then the pressure is suddenly released, causing an explosion. Pulp made in this way goes into the paper used in building construction.

Recycling wastepaper is another important way of making pulp. For more information, see the Wonder Question on page 57.

Preparing the Pulp

Wood pulp is screened and washed to clean out impurities and chemicals. If the pulp is to be bleached, the bleaching is done right after the cleaning. Bleaching removes impurities from paper. It also makes the paper whiter.

After cleaning and bleaching, the pulp is beaten in a large mixing machine and mixed with water. The beating frays the fibers, which helps them mat together. Starch, clay,

or other materials may be added to improve the surface of the paper for printing and writing. To make "wet-strength" paper, which is used for such things as paper towels, special additives are added to the pulp.

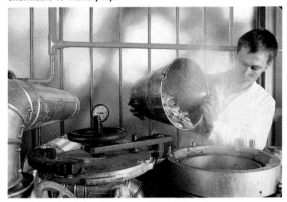

After wood is chipped into pieces, it is poured into a machine that will cook the wood along with different chemicals to make pulp.

The pulp then goes into a machine called a Jordan refiner, where the fibers are trimmed evenly. At this stage the pulp consists of 99 percent water and 1 percent fiber. It is now ready to go into the papermaking machine.

Sheet Formation

Most of the paper produced in the United States is made on Fourdrinier machines. The machine has a tank called a headbox, in which pulp and water are mixed. The pulp

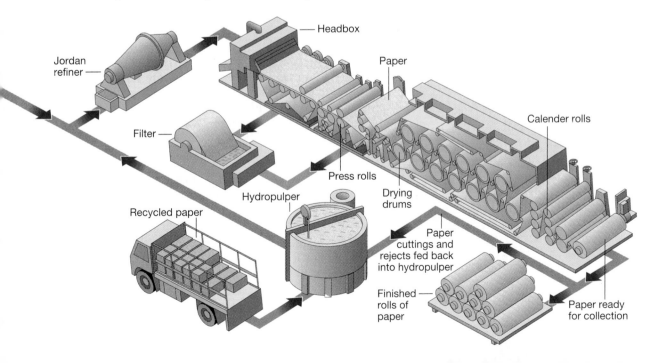

Headbox

Jordan refiner

Filter

Paper

Calender rolls

Press rolls

Drying drums

Hydropulper

Recycled paper

Paper cuttings and rejects fed back into hydropulper

Finished rolls of paper

Paper ready for collection

A layer of pulp moves along a Fourdrinier machine. Water drains out of the pulp and down through a wire screen. Suction pumps remove more water.

flows onto a wire screen that moves along like a conveyor belt. Water drains out of the pulp and down through the screen. Suction pumps underneath help remove more water. The screen vibrates to make the fibers interlock and mat together.

The wet mat passes under a metal roller, called a dandy roll, that presses it down into a smoother sheet. The dandy roll may contain a design that will be pressed into the sheet of fibers. This is the watermark, which can be seen when the paper is held to the light.

At the end of the trip on the screen, the sheet passes over a suction roller called a couch roll. By this time the pulp consists of about 80 percent water.

The sheet goes through a series of pressing rolls, which squeeze out water and make the paper dense and smooth. Until this point, the paper has been in the "wet end" of the machine. It now passes into the machine's "dry end," traveling through a series of heated drums called dryers. At this time, coatings can be applied to make the paper slick and shiny.

To give the paper a smooth, hard surface, it is threaded through a series of rollers called calenders. Then it is wound onto large reels and taken off the machine.

Another type of papermaking machine, the cylinder machine, is generally used for making paperboard and heavy building paper. In a cylinder machine, the pulp and water are mixed in a vat. A revolving wire-mesh cylinder turns in the vat. The cylinder picks up cellulose fibers and deposits them on a moving belt. The sheet is carried to rollers that press and dry it in the same way as the rollers of a Fourdrinier machine.

Cylinder machines can produce paper that is made of more than one layer of pulp. The surface of a sheet of paper may be made of expensive pulp, while the body of the paper is made of cheaper pulp. The different pulps can be mixed in different vats and laid onto one another and rolled into a single sheet.

Paper comes off the machines in large rolls. It is trimmed to take off the rough edges and cut to the desired width. Some kinds of paper, such as printing and writing paper, are cut into sheets. Paper used for printing newspapers and magazines and for wrapping is rewound onto rolls.

▶ TYPES OF PAPER PRODUCTS

There are many different types of paper. Each type is made to best serve a special purpose. **Newsprint**, the paper used for newspapers, does not have to be very durable. Therefore it is made of groundwood pulp. Other types of **groundwood papers** are used for directories and similar publications.

Paper for books and magazines must be of better quality. This **book paper** is also used for commercial printing. Magazines are usually printed on coated book paper.

The highest-quality paper, a type of fine paper, is made mostly from cotton fibers obtained from rags. Fine papers are also made from chemical pulp. They are used for bank checks, expensive stationery, photographic papers, and papers for computers.

Coarse papers are heavy-duty papers. They are used for grocery bags, brown and colored wrapping paper, and paper sacks such as those for cement and flour. Brown paper envelopes, gummed paper, and coin wrappers are also made of coarse paper.

Absorbent papers, a type of specialty paper, are made in such a way that they can absorb a certain amount of liquid or purify air without falling apart. They are used chiefly for blotters and filter papers.

Facial tissues, toilet paper, paper towels and napkins, and the soft paper used for wrapping gifts, fruits, and vegetables are made of **tissue paper**.

Paperboard is one of the most-used types of paper. An important variety of paperboard is called **containerboard**. It is made into boxes and containers. Corrugated containerboard is made by passing the paper through rollers that have ridges and grooves. This gives the board a wavy contour. Corrugated board is often covered on each side with smooth paperboard. This sandwich construction makes the paperboard very sturdy. It is used for making heavy shipping containers.

Boxboard is another type of paperboard. It is made into boxes to hold cereals, soap powder, toothpaste, and many other products. Sometimes a coating is applied to the surface to make it easier to print graphics.

Other special types of paperboard are used for milk and ice cream cartons, frozen-food packages, shoeboxes, candy boxes, and paper plates. Some of these paperboards are coated with wax or plastic to keep substances from seeping through. The material known as **cardboard**, used as a backing for writing tablets and picture frames, is a special type of paperboard. It should not be confused, as it often is, with containerboard.

Very thick paperboard is used for the bindings of books and as linings between the inner and outer soles of shoes. This paperboard is called **wet machine board**. It is too thick to go through drying rollers and must be taken from the papermaking machine while still wet and dried in an oven.

▶ HISTORY

Before paper was invented, people used a great variety of writing materials. Records were scratched and written on stone, wood, metal, ivory, wax tablets, leaves, papyrus, animal skins, and tree bark.

In the ancient Mediterranean world, the chief writing material was papyrus. It was made originally in Egypt, and eventually its use spread to Greece and Rome.

In the later Roman Empire and in the Middle Ages, writing was done mostly on parchment and vellum, made from animal skins. These materials were expensive and scarce. Paper was the first practical, inexpensive, and plentiful writing material.

Paper was first made about 2,000 years ago, when the first sheets of paper were produced in China. The materials used were pulp made from the bark of a mulberry tree and fibers from cloth and hemp. These were

WONDER QUESTION

How is paper recycled?

To obtain recycled fiber from wastepaper, one and sometimes two operations are needed.

Hydropulping involves mixing the recycled paper with water to form a slurry, or a mixture containing paper, water, and chemicals. The action that takes place is like that of a kitchen blender. Afterward, screens and cleaners are used to remove non-fibrous contaminants, such as tape, glue, metal, and plastic.

Following hydropulping, some pulp goes through a second process called de-inking. There are two types of de-inking processes, washing and flotation. The washing system uses strong countercurrent washers that literally wash ink from the pulp. In the flotation process, air is injected into the pulp, and ink and other non-fibrous particles collide with the air bubbles and become attached to them. The inky "foam" is then skimmed off the top.

mixed with water, spread on a piece of cloth, and allowed to dry to form a sheet of paper.

The knowledge of papermaking spread from China to Arabia and Europe by the 1100's. Papermaking in Europe may have been introduced by the Muslims who conquered Spain. In the 1200's, paper mills were set up in Italy. These were soon followed by mills in Germany, France, and the Netherlands. Papermaking started in England late in the 1400's. In 1690, the first paper mill in the United States was built by William Rittenhouse (1644–1708) and William Bradford (1663–1752) in Philadelphia.

Until about the mid-1800's, linen and cotton rags were almost the only source of papermaking fibers. Although early Chinese papermakers used both wood pulp and cloth fibers for their paper, later papermakers did not seem to realize that wood pulp could also be made into paper.

Early in the 1700's, the French naturalist René Antoine de Réaumur (1683–1757) pointed out that wood pulp might also be used for making paper. Réaumur had noticed that wasps build paper nests out of wood pulp by chewing off pieces of old timbers and logs and moistening them with saliva.

It was not until the middle of the 1800's, however, that wood pulp was used for papermaking on a large scale. A less expensive raw material was needed, because at about the same time, a papermaking machine was developed that could rapidly produce large quantities of paper. Until this time, all paper had been made by hand.

A machine for making paper in an endless sheet had been patented by Nicholas Louis Robert (1761–1828), a Frenchman, in 1798. The machine was later developed in England by two brothers, Henry (1766–1854) and Sealy (?–1847) Fourdrinier. At this time the machine did not have drying rollers. The paper had to be taken from the machine wet and hung up in lofts to dry. But the machine still could turn out as much paper as six hand-operated paper mills.

The first machine-made paper in the United States was made in 1817, not on a Fourdrinier, but on a cylinder machine. The first Fourdrinier machine in the United States was put into operation in 1827.

With abundant raw material and a machine for making paper, paper production increased greatly in the 1800's. In the United States between 1810 and 1840, paper production increased by about 10 times. It has been steadily increasing ever since. In 1810, 3,300 tons (3,000 metric tons) of paper were made in the United States. Today, more than 91 million tons (83 million metric tons) of paper are used each year in the United States.

The demand for paper has steadily increased with the spread of education and the growth of industry. To keep up with the demand, Fourdrinier machines have been improved to produce paper much faster. In the 1860's, a machine could turn out about 100 feet (30 meters) of paper a minute. Today's Fourdriniers can produce about 5,000 feet (1,500 meters) of paper a minute.

More paper than ever will be made and used in the future. One of the challenges in satisfying the growing demand for paper is to provide an adequate supply of cellulose fiber, the main raw material for making pulp. The world's forests are enormous, but they must serve many purposes, and not all are suitable for growing trees to harvest. In addition to wood pulp, forests supply the lumber used in building homes and making furniture.

Another challenge is finding new supplies of recycled paper, as more and more new paper is made wholly or partially with recycled fiber.

The paper industry has an interest in the use and care of forests. Along with other industries that use wood, it sponsors a tree-farming program designed to replant trees that were harvested. It also sponsors research to lead to faster-growing trees and to more efficient use of trees.

Methods have been developed to make pulp from almost every kind of tree and from the leftovers of lumber and plywood mills. More than one-fourth of the wood used for making paper comes from such leftovers. The industry helps conserve its resources by recycling paper to make new paper. More than one-third of the fiber used in making paper and paperboard comes from recycled paper.

Paper will continue to be one of the basic materials in our lives. In new forms and with new uses, paper may become even more important than ever before.

Reviewed by VIRGIL K. HORTON, JR.
American Forest and Paper Association

See also WOOD AND WOOD PRODUCTS.

PAPERBACK BOOKS

No development in book publication since the invention of movable type in the 1400's has brought about greater changes than the introduction of paperback books. Books bound with paper covers appeared in large numbers after 1945. In the years that followed, the publication of paperback books became a major industry all over the world. Paperbacks are now sold in bookstores, stationery stores, drugstores, airports, and supermarkets.

In a bookstore, a youngster tries to select from the many titles that are available in paperback.

▶ HISTORY

The ancestor of today's paperback was the chapbook. Chapbooks, small illustrated books or pamphlets, were sold from the 1500's to the 1700's by peddlers known as chapmen. Throughout the 1600's and 1700's, chapbooks were quite popular in England and the North American colonies. The contents of chapbooks covered a wide range of subjects. Some were almanacs; some narrated sensational tales. Many contained songs and ballads or stories for children. Produced to be sold quickly and inexpensively, they were of poor quality and design.

The day of the fine-quality paperback was a long way off. Although publishers were constantly seeking ways to provide good low-cost books for larger audiences, this advance depended on many factors. Paper that was made by machine rather than by hand had to be introduced, as well as mechanical typesetting machines and fast cylinder presses. It was not until the 1800's that most of these changes came about.

In the late 1800's, a new kind of paperback, the dime novel, gained popularity. As its name implies, this paperback often sold for 10 cents. These books were usually poorly written adventure tales. In spite of their great success, dime novels did little to advance the cause of the superior paperback.

During the late 1800's and early 1900's, several attempts were made to persuade the reading public to buy paperbound books. The movement had notable success in Europe, particularly with the Tauchnitz series published in Germany and with Penguin books in England. Travelers learned the advantages of buying the books at railway stations, reading them on their journey, and then discarding them if they wished to do so. However, most early attempts to interest people in buying paperbacks failed, since most readers considered them to be inferior.

After World War II (1939–45), publishers began to experiment with paperbacks on a large scale. Lists of titles were enlarged, and distribution methods were improved. The public was made aware of the many advantages, other than price, of buying books of this kind.

▶ PAPERBACK BOOKS TODAY

One of the earliest manufacturers of paperback books in the United States was Pocket Books. Other publishers, encouraged by their success, began to produce paperbacks. When paperbound books first appeared, most titles sold for as little as 25 cents. Today, although increases in paper and production costs have caused prices to rise, paperbacks continue to sell for less than hardcovers.

Readers have come to appreciate the many great advantages of paperbacks. Aside from their price, paperbacks are light in weight, can be carried easily, and take up less shelf space at home.

At one time, owning books was a privilege for only a few people who could afford to spend large sums of money on their collections. Today, thanks to good-quality paperbacks, the enjoyment of building a personal library is within the reach of countless numbers of people.

LAVINIA DOBLER
Head Librarian, Scholastic Book Services

PAPIER-MÂCHÉ

Papier-mâché is a French term that means "chewed paper." It was applied to a process used in Paris in the 18th century. Old posters were ripped from walls, converted into pulp, and mixed with size—a gummy preparation made by combining glue or paste with resin and drying oil. When the papier-mâché hardened, it was lacquered and decorated. Papier-mâché was used to make boxes, trays, decorative pieces, and statuettes.

This art has been practiced in Asia for centuries. Today it is used for such purposes as making store-window displays. It is fast to work with, light in weight, and easy to handle. Because papier-mâché is a strong material, objects made with it can be expected to last a long time.

▶ PREPARING THE MATERIALS

Other types of paper may be used, but newspaper is best because it tears easily and absorbs water and paste quickly. Its torn edges blend into one another and give an overall smooth surface.

Tear several sheets into strips 2 to 3 centimeters (about 1 inch) wide. Lay the strips flat in a dishpan and cover them with water. In another pan mix cold water with ½ cup of flour to form a heavy creamy texture. Slowly add boiling water. As the paste thickens add more water to return it to a creamlike state. You can also use wallpaper paste (an excellent adhesive), which comes as a powder. Put 2 cups of cold water into a bowl. Slowly stir in enough powder to form a smooth paste. Library paste is also good but more costly.

▶ DEVELOPING YOUR TALENTS

Besides bowls such as those pictured on this page, papier-mâché can be used to make masks, puppets, bracelets, and even furniture. Papier-mâché is a medium that offers great opportunities for developing creative talents. Your efforts may delight you.

CATHERINE ROBERTS
Author, *Real Book of Real Crafts*

Colorful bowls made of papier-mâché.

HOW TO MAKE A PAPIER-MÂCHÉ BOWL

(1) Equipment you will need includes flour and water (or ready-made paste), newspaper, and a wet bowl.

(2) Tear the newspaper into strips and soak the strips in water. Then fit the strips to the inside of the bowl.

(3) Rub paste over the first layer of paper and add more wet strips. Build five or six such layers.

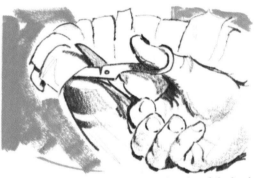

(4) Trim the outside edges to match the edge of the bowl. Place on a radiator or sunny windowsill for 2 days.

(5) After it has dried, the papier-mâché bowl will slip easily out of its mold.

(6) The beauty of the papier-mâché bowl will depend on how imaginatively you decorate it with paints.

PAPUA NEW GUINEA

Papua New Guinea lies in the southwest Pacific Ocean just north of Australia. It is a country made up of part of one very large island plus many smaller islands and island groups. The largest land area is the eastern half of the island of New Guinea (the western half belongs to Indonesia). To the east are New Britain, New Ireland, the Admiralty Islands, and other islands of the Bismarck Archipelago; Bougainville and Buka in the Solomons; Woodlark, and the Trobriand, D'Entrecasteaux, and Louisiade island groups. Formerly administered by Australia, Papua New Guinea became independent in 1975.

▶ THE PEOPLE

The people of Papua New Guinea generally show the physical characteristics of the Melanesians of the Pacific—short to medium height, brown to black skin, broad noses, and curly or frizzy hair. In fact, the word "papua," which comes from the Malay language, has been translated as "frizzy hair." Most of the people live in villages, which are often small and sometimes isolated from each other by the mountainous terrain. Most vil-

lagers are farmers, growing just enough food for their own needs. In recent years some of the people have migrated from the rural areas to the cities, especially to Port Moresby, the capital, and Lae, the second largest city.

Tribal and family relationships are important in everyday life. Families remain together, so that one house may shelter several brothers, their wives, their children, and their grandchildren. A typical village house is built on stilts to protect it against flooding in rainy weather. The ordinary houses show little decoration. But ceremonial buildings display painting and sculpture related to religious beliefs.

About half the people of Papua New Guinea belong to Christian churches. But in the isolated villages change comes slowly, and traditional religion holds sway. Ancestor and spirit worship is common and the people believe that their ancestors watch over them.

Papua New Guinea lacks a single common language. There are an estimated 750 different languages spoken, some by thousands of people, others by only a single village. However, Melanesian Pidgin, an altered and simplified form of English with some words from other languages, is widely understood. English is spoken by educated people and serves as the language of commerce and government.

▶ THE LAND

Papua New Guinea is 461,691 square kilometers, or 178,260 square miles, in area.

Port Moresby is the capital, the chief port, and the largest city of Papua New Guinea.

PAPUA NEW GUINEA

Towering mountain ranges, deep valleys, great swamps, swiftly flowing rivers, and vast forests make up the varied landscape of the mainland. Mountains in the Owen Stanley Range in the southeast rise to a height of over 3,900 meters, or over 13,000 feet. The chief rivers are the Fly in the south and the Sepik in the north. Many of the smaller islands are also mountainous, some of the peaks being active volcanoes. The climate is tropical, though temperatures vary with elevation. Rainfall is abundant.

▶ THE ECONOMY

Agriculture and mining are basic to the country's economic life. The most important mineral is copper, large deposits of which are found on Bougainville island. Other valuable minerals include gold, silver, and manganese. The chief commercial crops are coffee, tea, copra (dried coconut meat), rubber, and cacao. The forests provide an abundance of trees, and major industries center around wood and wood products. Fishing is important in the coastal areas.

▶ HISTORY AND GOVERNMENT

Seafaring people from Asia reached the islands of Papua New Guinea at least 10,000 years ago and probably even earlier. Spanish and Portuguese navigators arrived in the early 16th century, but many years passed before outsiders took a great interest in the region.

In the early 19th century the Dutch established themselves in the western half of New Guinea (now part of Indonesia). Later in the 19th century the Germans set up trading settlements on the northeast coast, and the British established a protectorate over the southeast. In 1906, Australia took over British New Guinea and governed it as the Territory of Papua. At the start of World War I, Australian troops occupied the German-held area in the northeast, and later administered it as the Territory of New Guinea under a mandate from the League of Nations. During World War II much of the region was occupied by the Japanese and saw some of the heaviest fighting of the Pacific war. After the war the Territory of New Guinea became a United Nations trust territory, again administered by Australia. In 1949 the administration of the two territories was unified.

Australia gradually led the region toward independence. In 1973 Papua New Guinea achieved self-government, and on September 16, 1975, it won full independence. The country has a parliamentary form of government with a prime minister and a single-chamber legislature, the House of Assembly. It is a member of the Commonwealth of Nations.

CHARLES PAUL MAY
Author, *Oceania: Polynesia, Melanesia, Micronesia*

See also NEW GUINEA.

A rectangular canopy parachute gives a much softer and more accurate landing than a round parachute.

PARACHUTES

If you throw a package out of an airplane, it falls rapidly toward the ground and lands with a crash that probably breaks everything in it. But if you attach a parachute to the package, it falls slowly and lands gently.

A parachute is an umbrella- or wing-shaped device. Its shape creates resistance to the air, which, in turn, slows the descent of a package or body so it falls to the ground safely.

As early as the 1100's, the Chinese amused themselves by jumping from high places with rigid umbrella-like structures. Some 300 years later the Italian artist and inventor Leonardo da Vinci designed a pyramid-shaped parachute. The first successful parachute jumps were made in the late 1700's from a tower and, later, from a balloon. The first jump from an airplane was made in 1912.

During the first and second world wars, parachutes were used to drop supplies and troops behind enemy lines and to drop flares for nighttime reconnaissance. It was not until after World War II that sport parachuting developed. Today, many people enjoy this sport. The military continues to use parachutes to deliver troops, foods, vehicles, and other loads. Parachutes are used as landing brakes on jet airplanes that land on aircraft carriers and for recovering instruments from missiles.

A parachute has five basic parts. The pilot chute is a small canopy used to pull out the larger canopy. The main canopy is most commonly made of nylon. Round canopies used in sport jumping vary in diameter from 6.7 to 9.8 meters (22 to 32 feet). Those used for cargo may be as much as 30 meters (100 feet) across. Suspension lines run from the canopy to the harness. The harness is a series of straps that fit around and support the person's body. Attached to the harness is the ripcord. When pulled, it causes the main canopy to inflate. The container, or pack, holds everything except the harness.

There are three ways of opening the parachute. It may be opened by hand, by pulling the ripcord. It may be opened automatically by a line, called the static line, that is hooked to the aircraft. This is used by military jumpers and beginning sport jumpers. The canopy may also be opened at a pre-set altitude by an automatic opening device.

In typical sport jumps, parachutists usually wear protective jumpsuits, helmets, gloves, and goggles. Besides the main parachute, jumpers always wear reserve parachutes for protection in case something goes wrong.

An airplane carries jumpers up into the sky. The higher they go, the longer they have for free-fall—the period before opening the main canopy. When the plane reaches the desired altitude, the jumpers leave the plane.

Free-fall feels more like flying than falling. Jumpers can reach speeds of more than 300 kilometers (187 miles) an hour during this period. They feel the air pressure against the body and learn to use this pressure to perform loops and rolls. Experienced jumpers may leave the aircraft together and, by maneuvering their bodies, join up to form a wide variety of formations.

Jumpers carry altimeters, which tell how high they are. At 760 meters (2,500 feet), they end their free-fall by pulling the ripcord. People who are jumping together must move apart before opening their parachutes.

The open canopy greatly slows the jumpers' speed. By pulling on steering lines that they hold in their hands, jumpers can control the forward speed and direction of the parachute. Experienced jumpers can steer precisely to a landing spot no larger than 10 centimeters (4 inches) in diameter.

ALAN T. KING
United States Parachute Association

A fife and drum band is an important part of many parades.

PARADES

There have been parades for almost as long as there have been crowds of people to enjoy them. Paintings on ancient Egyptian tombs and monuments show the pharaohs and their priests in many processions.

Roman victory parades were grand affairs. The procession, called the triumph, celebrated the return to Rome of a victorious general and his army. Flowers were scattered and incense was burned as the troops marched from the Campus Martius (a large grassy field where many military events took place) to the Capitol, where there was a temple dedicated to Jupiter. Behind the dignitaries paraded men carrying the spoils of war, important captives, priests with incense burners, and the general with his army.

▶ MILITARY AND PATRIOTIC PARADES

Today many parades are held for patriotic purposes and take place on national holidays. In the United States, soldiers and sailors parade on Memorial Day, Armed Forces Day, and Veterans' Day. In Canada, Dominion Day is marked with parades.

In many European countries parades are held to celebrate independence.

In France on Bastille Day, July 14, there are military parades down the Champs Élysées. In Moscow, military units, students, and workers march each year in Red Square to celebrate the October Revolution of 1917.

In the United States there are parades held by people of various national origins. March 17 is a great day for the Irish in New York. On that day thousands of real and would-be Irish march down Fifth Avenue in the St. Patrick's Day parade. Italian Americans feel that Columbus Day is their holiday, and they have a similar parade on that day.

JAMES W. HOERGER
Great Neck (New York) Public Schools

PARAGUAY

Paraguay is a small country in the heart of South America, completely surrounded by other countries—Brazil, Argentina, and Bolivia. The Spanish colonists who arrived in what is now eastern Paraguay in the early 1500's must have thought they had reached an earthly paradise. The Guaraní Indian people who lived there were friendly and helpful. Gaily colored birds flew in and out among the trees. Wild game was plentiful. The climate was pleasant, and the land was green and full of flowers and tropical fruits.

But when colonists crossed the broad Paraguay River, it was as if they had entered another world. In the western two thirds of Paraguay, known as the Chaco, they found a desolate, swampy plain covered with scrub forests and grasslands. During the dry season, it was a parched wasteland. When the rains came, it was flooded. To this day, eastern and western Paraguay are almost like two different countries.

▶ THE PEOPLE

Paraguay has a smaller population than most other South American countries, and nearly all the people live in the eastern section. Paraguayans today are chiefly of mixed Guaraní and Spanish origin. Paraguay is the only truly bilingual country in South America. Almost everyone speaks both Spanish and Guaraní. Spanish is taught in the schools, and Guaraní is learned at home. The people are very proud of their Guaraní heritage. Many literary works have been written in Guaraní.

Beginning in 1926, several thousand Mennonites (members of a Protestant sect) came to Paraguay from Germany, Canada, and the Soviet Union. Promised freedom to live and worship in their own way, they bought land in the Chaco and established their own farming communities. People in the Mennonite communities speak German.

The government has encouraged immigration. A number of people from Japan, Brazil, Argentina, and various parts of Europe have come to live in Paraguay.

Religion and Education

More than 95 percent of the people are Roman Catholic, and Roman Catholicism is the state religion. But freedom of worship is guaranteed by law.

Primary education is free and required by law. In recent years, many schools have been built, and large numbers of teachers have been trained. Today over 80 percent of the people are able to read and write. The country has two universities—the National University of Asunción and the Catholic University, which is also in Asunción.

Way of Life

Slightly less than half the people of Paraguay earn their living from the land. Some work on the large agricultural estates where most of the export crops are grown, or harvest timber and other forest products. A smaller number are gauchos (cowboys), who herd cattle. Most of the rural people, however, live on small farms, where they grow food for their own use and keep some livestock.

While the majority of Paraguayans still live in rural areas, an increasing number of the people are moving to urban areas. About 15 percent of the population now lives in Asunción, the capital.

The chief food of the country is *mandioca* (cassava). After it is boiled, the root of the

The Paraguay River divides Paraguay into two distinct parts. The area west of the river, known as the Chaco, is a vast swampy plain where few people live.

mandioca plant tastes somewhat like a potato. *Mandioca* is also dried and ground into flour to make bread, or *chipa*. Many delicious stews are made by mixing meat with *mandioca*, corn, or other vegetables.

Yerba maté, the national drink of Paraguay, is an herb tea made from the dried and ground leaves of a plant related to holly. The tea is sipped through a silver *bombilla*, or straw, from a small gourd that is often beautifully decorated with silver.

Popular pastimes include playing soccer and singing to the accompaniment of guitars and accordians. People also enjoy dancing the Santa Fe, or Paraguayan polka. There are many religious feasts and festivals. One of the most popular is held each December 8 at Caacupé, a resort near Lake Ypacaraí. It features fireworks, candlelight processions, and appearances by the famous Paraguayan bottledancers, who perform their intricate steps while balancing bottles on their heads.

▶ THE LAND

Paraguay is one of the smallest countries in South America. In area, it is about the size of the state of California in the United States. Paraguay has no seacoast, but the great Paraná-Paraguay river system provides a water route to the Atlantic Ocean, some 1,600 kilometers (1,000 miles) away. The Paraguay River divides the country into two parts—the Región Oriental in the east and the larger Chaco in the west.

In the eastern part of the Región Oriental, bordering the Paraná River, is the heavily forested Paraná Plateau. The highest point in the country—about 700 meters (2,300 feet) above sea level—is on this plateau near Villarico. Between the plateau and the Paraguay River is a fertile grassland with gently rolling hills. Citrus and other tropical fruit trees, coconut palms, and colorful jacaranda trees grow in this part of the Región Oriental, which also contains Lake Ypacaraí and Lake Ypoá.

The Paraguay River, which divides the country, is filled with floating islands in the wet summer season. These little islands, called *camalotes,* are torn from the riverbanks by the heavy rains. Still carrying shrubs and flowers (and sometimes animals seeking refuge from the floods), the *camalotes* drift downstream with the current.

The Chaco is a vast plain covered by dense scrub forests, palm trees, and marshes. It is also the place where the quebracho trees grow. (A substance used in tanning hides is extracted from these trees.) The Pilcomayo, the third major river of the country, flows along the southwestern edge of the Chaco. Many other slow-moving rivers flow across this region, and during the rainy season the broad river valleys are covered with lakes and streams. But in the winter the lakes dry up, and the streams are just trickles of water.

Climate

In general, Paraguay's climate is subtropical. But temperatures vary because there are no high mountains to provide protection against the cold winds from the south and the hot, humid winds from the north. The summer season—October to March—is hot and rainy. At times the north wind brings oppressive heat. The winter season, from April to September, is mild and comparatively dry. The heaviest rainfall is in the east.

Small farms such as this one are a common sight in eastern Paraguay, where the soil is fertile and rainfall abundant.

Natural Resources

Eastern Paraguay has fertile soils and valuable forests, and the land on either side of the Paraguay River is suitable for grazing large herds of cattle. The Paraná River has great potential for hydroelectric power. Stone, especially limestone, is the only important mineral.

Birds, animals, and reptiles of many kinds live in the forests of eastern Paraguay. Colorful parrots and parakeets, hummingbirds, toucans, and flamingos mingle with assorted waterfowl. Alligators, iguanas and other kinds of lizards, jaguars, tapirs, monkeys, and ant-eating bears—all make their homes in the dense woodlands of the Paraná Plateau. Huge boa constrictors encircle tree trunks like twining vines. The Chaco has swarms of mosquitoes, vampire bats, and other disease-carrying creatures.

▶ THE ECONOMY

The economy of Paraguay has long been based on agriculture and forestry. In recent times the country has developed a new export product—electricity. Dams have been built or are under construction along the Paraná River in joint ventures with Argentina and Brazil. The construction of dams provides work for thousands of people, and Paraguay expects to become one of the world's largest exporters of hydroelectric power.

The leading agricultural exports—cotton, soybeans, and frozen meat—are produced on large farms and cattle ranches that employ only a small part of the rural population. The Mennonite communities in the Chaco are known for their cattle, dairy products, and fine cotton.

A lack of good transportation limits development in most parts of the country. Away from the rivers and the few paved roads, people grow a variety of food crops for their own use. They may also plant one or more cash crops, such as cotton, sugarcane, or tobacco. Cattle graze on unfenced pastures in most parts of the country.

Much of the world's petitgrain oil (a fragrant oil used in perfumes, soaps, and cosmetics) comes from the leaves and twigs of citrus trees in the forests of Paraguay. Other forest products include timber, quebracho extract, and yerba maté.

Manufacturing is limited. It involves chiefly the processing of local raw materials such as cotton, timber, hides, and oils. The tourist industry is expanding, and Asunción has become an important regional banking center.

Asunción, on the Paraguay River, is the country's capital, principal port, and only large city. Founded in 1537, Asunción served briefly as the hub of the Spanish empire in southern South America. Today it is the center of Paraguay's government, commerce, industry, transportation, and culture.

Asunción contains many fine old Spanish homes and buildings, a national theater, and a government palace built to resemble the Louvre in Paris. Orange trees line the modern avenues and boulevards, and many new skyscrapers have been built in the downtown area. But streets on the outskirts of the city are often unpaved.

Timber, soybeans, yerba maté, tobacco, cotton, and hides are exported from the bustling port of Encarnación, on the Paraná River. Concepción, a port where goods are shipped to Brazil free of customs duties, is the trade hub of the northern part of the Región Oriental. The textile industry is centered on Pilar. Puerto Presidente Stroessner, the headquarters for the giant Itaipú Dam on the Paraná River, has been one of the fastest-growing cities in the country.

Many of the buildings in Asunción date from the mid-1800's, when the rulers of Paraguay tried to rebuild the city to make it look like a European capital.

FACTS AND FIGURES

REPUBLIC OF PARAGUAY is the official name of the country.

CAPITAL: Asunción.

LOCATION: Central South America. **Latitude**—19° 16′ S to 27° 35′ S. **Longitude**—54° 16′ W to 62° 37′ W.

PHYSICAL FEATURES: Area—406,752 km² (157,047 sq mi). **Highest point**—On Paraná Plateau, near Villarica, about 700 m (2,300 ft). **Lowest point**—60 m (200 ft). **Chief rivers**—Paraguay, Paraná, Pilcomayo. **Chief lakes**—Ypacaraí, Ypoá.

POPULATION: 3,300,000 (estimate).

LANGUAGE: Spanish (official), Guaraní.

RELIGION: Roman Catholic.

GOVERNMENT: Republic. **Head of government**—president. **International co-operation**—United Nations, Organization of American States (OAS), Latin American Free Trade Association (LAFTA).

NATIONAL ANTHEM: *Paraguayos, república o muerte* ("Paraguayans, republic or death").

ECONOMY: Agricultural products—livestock, *mandioca* (cassava), maize (corn), soybeans, yerba maté, coffee, tobacco, cotton, sugarcane, fruit, beans, cowpeas, peanuts, rice. **Industries and products**—meat products, vegetable oils, sugar refining, flour milling, leather goods, textiles, cement, timber, quebracho extract, petitgrain oil. **Chief mineral**—stone. **Chief exports**—raw cotton, soybeans, meats, vegetable oils, tobacco. **Chief imports**—machinery, petroleum, construction and manufacturing materials. **Monetary unit**—guaraní.

▶HISTORY AND GOVERNMENT

The earliest known inhabitants of what is now Paraguay were the Guaraní. By the time the Spanish arrived, the Guaraní were living in large communal houses and cultivating the fertile soil east of the Paraguay River.

From their base in Asunción (founded in 1537), the Spanish colonized much of southern South America, including large parts of Argentina and Bolivia. Jesuit missionaries came to Paraguay in 1609 to convert the Guaraní, and they carried out an experiment unique and famous in all the Americas. These missionaries gathered large groups of Guaraní into communities called *reducciones*. Here they were taught Christianity, learned various trades, and grew crops. The Jesuits were pleased with their success, and the Guaraní were content.

By the early 1700's, the Jesuit communities controlled most of the trade of the colony, selling large quantities of yerba maté to Argentina. But other Spanish settlers were eager to take control of the trade in yerba maté and use the Guaraní labor. They convinced the

Spanish king to drive the Jesuits from the colony in 1767.

Independence, Dictators, Wars. When Argentina revolted against Spanish rule in 1810, Paraguay refused to form a federation with Argentina. Instead, it declared its own independence in 1811. A republic headed by two consuls was established. One of these consuls, José Rodríguez Francia, assumed power in 1814 and ruled as a dictator until his death in 1840. Before the century ended, Paraguay had been ruled by two other dictators—Carlos Antonio López and his son Francisco Solano López. Solano López led Paraguay into a war with Brazil, Argentina, and Uruguay. Known as the War of the Triple Alliance (1864–70), it was a disaster for Paraguay. It cost the lives of more than half the total population.

The country had no sooner recovered from this tragedy than it went to war for a second time (1932–35) over the Chaco, which was claimed by both Paraguay and Bolivia. Paraguay was victorious. But the Chaco War left it exhausted and bankrupt, and it went through a long period of political instability.

The Stroessner Era. In 1954, General Alfredo Stroessner, the commander of the army, took control of the government. He became president that same year. With the support of the armed forces and the ruling Colorado Party, Stroessner governed Paraguay for nearly 35 years, until his overthrow in 1989. Under Stroessner, Paraguay had political stability and achieved considerable economic growth. But this was achieved at the expense of political freedom and individual rights.

A New Government. Stroessner was elected to an eighth term as president in 1988. But in early 1989, he was removed from power in a military coup led by General Andrés Rodríguez, who headed an anti-Stroessner group within the government. In elections held in 1989, Rodríguez won the presidency.

An elected constituent Assembly approved a new constitution in 1992, and in 1993, in the first truly free elections in the country's history, Juan Carlos Wasmosy of the ruling Colorado Party was chosen the new president.

Reviewed by MORTON D. WINSBERG
Florida State University

PARAMECIUM. See PROTOZOANS.

PARENT-TEACHER ASSOCIATIONS

A parent-teacher association is an organization that involves parents directly in the activities of their children's school. The idea behind such involvement is that children learn and develop best when the home and the school work closely together. Often school administrators and high school students are members, as well as parents and teachers.

Usually the association in each school decides what it wishes to do to provide better opportunities for children and youth. For instance, the association may buy equipment or books for the school, or it may sponsor health programs that provide medical and dental care. But some activities may extend beyond the school system to benefit the entire community. Programs that seek to obtain better housing and well-run juvenile courts are examples. Parent-teacher associations may support scholarship funds for training teachers and draw up guidelines for teenage groups in the community. They may form committees to study ways of improving television, radio, and movies for children or to study such subjects as family life and child development.

There are parents' groups in schools throughout the world. They are known by different names in different countries. In Britain and the United States, the school groups are called parent-teacher associations, or PTA's. Japan also uses this name. In Canada, local groups are called home and school associations or parent-teacher associations. In Denmark, committees of parents, known as parents' advisory councils, are appointed by town councils. They meet with teachers and administrators.

▶THE NATIONAL CONGRESS OF PARENTS AND TEACHERS (United States)

Most parent-teacher associations in the United States are connected with the National Congress of Parents and Teachers, known as the National PTA. It has nearly 6,000,000 members. The national organization has 52 branches, made up of PTA's from each state, the District of Columbia, and U.S. schools abroad, which are served by the European Congress of American Parents, Teachers, and Students. Many parents of parochial-school pupils belong to separate organizations called home-school associations. Private, or independent, schools generally have their own associations, such as parents' leagues.

The National PTA—called at first the National Congress of Mothers—was founded on February 17, 1897, in Washington, D.C., by Alice McLellan Birney and Phoebe Apperson Hearst, mothers of schoolchildren. Their purpose was to help children by teaching parents about child development. The mothers gradually became interested in schools and held their meetings there. Men and teachers joined the organization, and in 1924 the current name was adopted. In 1970 the National Congress of Colored Parents and Teachers—which existed in those states having segregated schools—and the National Congress of Parents and Teachers were united into one organization. Local units of the National PTA are called parent-teacher or parent-teacher-student associations.

In the early days, PTA's often raised money for needed school supplies and equipment. PTA's still raise funds for such purposes, but they are equally active in other areas. The activities sponsored by the National PTA are guided by these objectives:

To promote the welfare of children and youth in home, school, community, and place of worship.
To raise the standards of home life.
To secure adequate laws for the protection of children and youth.
To bring into closer relation the home and the school, that parents and teachers may co-operate intelligently in the education of children and youth.
To develop between educators and the general public such united efforts as will secure for all children and youth the highest advantages in physical, mental, social, and spiritual education.

One of the National PTA's first important projects was to encourage the formation of kindergartens in public schools. The National PTA has planned programs in such areas as health education and urban education, and it has helped provide volunteer workers in juve-nile courts. Through a special office in Washington, D.C., it actively supports federal legislation that will benefit public education. It encourages local PTA's to influence school policies by working with school administrators and boards of education.

The work of the National PTA is carried out largely by three commissions and certain special committees. There are commissions on education, health and welfare, and individual development. The National PTA publishes a number of pamphlets, a legislative newsletter, and a periodical, *PTA Today*. Headquarters are at 700 North Rush Street, Chicago, Illinois 60611.

▶ CANADIAN HOME AND SCHOOL AND PARENT-TEACHER FEDERATION

In Canada, local parents' groups belong to a national association called the Canadian Home and School and Parent-Teacher Federation. The national association is organized into ten provincial federations.

The first parents' group in Canada was formed in Baddeck, Nova Scotia, in 1895. Its founder was Mabel Hubbard Bell, the wife of the inventor Alexander Graham Bell. Other groups formed independently and became organized into provincial federations. The national organization was formed in 1927.

The objectives of the Canadian Home and School and Parent-Teacher Federation are similar to those of parent-teacher groups elsewhere. They include raising the standards of home life; obtaining the best for each child, according to the child's physical, mental, social, and spiritual needs; fostering high ideals of citizenship; and promoting international goodwill and peace.

Activities of the national federation have included studies of smoking habits among Canadian schoolchildren and of broadcasting aimed at children. Many of the national group's activities deal with needs expressed at local association meetings. Examples include the national group's support of vocational courses in high schools, preschool education programs, school lunch programs, and the elimination of commercial advertising directed at children. The headquarters are at 240 Eglinton Avenue East, Suite 204, Toronto, Ontario, M4P 1K8.

Reviewed by the NATIONAL PTA (U.S.)

The Cathedral of Notre Dame is built on Île de la Cité, an island in the Seine River.

PARIS

Paris is one of the most beautiful capital cities in the world. There are larger towns, but few have been better planned. The city of Paris proper has over 2,000,000 inhabitants. The Paris metropolitan area, including the suburbs, has a population of about 9,000,000, which increases every year.

No capital city is the heart and brain of a country as completely as is Paris. Most French railways start from Paris. Most major highways lead to Paris. Not only is Paris the seat of government; it is also the administrative, artistic, scientific, theatrical, and fashion center of France. More than one fourth of French industry has its seat in Paris. Many factories are located in the *faubourgs,* as the outlying sections and suburbs are known. French people dreaming of successful careers in any field sooner or later must live in Paris. Buyers come there in search of new fashions.

Theater managers seek authors and plays. Many country doctors spend 1 or 2 weeks in Paris every year to become acquainted with new discoveries and to keep in touch with the latest developments in their field. To sum up, nothing in France can be done without help and advice from Paris.

Many international institutions, including the United Nations Educational, Scientific, and Cultural Organization (UNESCO), have made Paris their home. This is partly because of the city's charm and partly because it is an intellectual and spiritual center. Paris was also the site of the World War I peace conference, which met in 1919. Paris is often called the City of Light because of the many lights on its wide streets and monuments and because it has been both a source of new ideas and a champion of freedom for 3 centuries.

One can become a Parisian without having been born in France. The city has such a rich past that at every step visitors will remember something they once read about. They will feel at home, for Paris is not only the capital of France but also one of the centers of western civilization.

A Boat Ride Through the City

If vistors want to become acquainted with the beauties of Paris, their first trip should be down the Seine in a pleasant boat called a *bateau mouche*. The river traces a fine curve right through the town. Along the banks on both sides of the river they will see monuments that tell the history of Paris. The Seine River is the natural center of a work of art. On the lower banks, sheltered by big trees, fishermen patiently wait to catch tiny fish. Up on the street level are the outdoor stands of the *bouquinistes* (secondhand booksellers). The custom of displaying books on the parapets goes back 300 or 400 years. Why do people take more pleasure in rummaging among books here than elsewhere? Perhaps because the booksellers, both men and women, with their worn-out coats, are picturesque. Perhaps it is also because above the boxes of books and engravings one sees the lovely sky of Paris, golden-blue, with small white clouds.

The boat will pass the Île Saint-Louis, a sister of the Île de la Cité, with its fine old mansions. Then comes the Cathedral of Notre Dame. Farther along, visitors will find themselves between the Louvre on the Right Bank and the Institut de France on the Left. In the center of that building is the famous cupola under which writers, scientists, and artists—who represent the five academies of the Institut—hold their solemn meetings. The Pont des Arts, a footbridge, connects the Louvre museum with the Institut. Then the boat will hug the Tuileries gardens and the Place de la Concorde. That is the place previously known as Place Louis XV and Place de la Révolution. When the time for reconciliation and forgiveness came, after the French Revolution, the word *concorde* ("harmony") seemed an appropriate term to encourage such sentiments. In the distance one will see the Obelisk of Luxor, brought from

All of Paris can be seen from the Eiffel Tower.

Interior of the Cathedral of Notre Dame. This glorious church was built in the Gothic style in the 13th century.

under another dome, that of the Panthéon, in the heart of the Latin Quarter.

The boat continues to glide along the Seine, and on the left is the Eiffel Tower. When this iron structure, over 1,000 feet tall, was erected in 1889, many Parisians claimed that it dishonored their city. Nowadays people have become used to the tower and would miss it greatly if it were to disappear. And what would the tourists say? One of their favorite pastimes is to climb to the top. From there one sees all of Paris and the hills that surround the city—from the famous Montmartre, crowned by the white basilica of the Sacred Heart (Sacré Coeur), to the hill of Sainte-Geneviève, dominated by the Panthéon. In front of the tower, on the Right Bank on another hill, stands the Palais de Chaillot. The Palais de Chaillot houses two modern museums and an immense auditorium. Then, on the Avenue du President Kennedy, one may admire the round tower that is the House of French Radio and Television. This is a very interesting building. From a huge, spiral structure devoted to offices rises an originally designed and powerful skyscraper.

▶ A WALK THROUGH PARIS

And now visitors should leave their boats. If the Seine permitted us to see some of the jewels among the monuments of Paris, there are important areas that can be reached only by foot. It is very pleasant to walk up the Champs-Élysées on a beautiful day at twilight time, just as the sun is setting under the Arc de Triomphe and the countless streetlights are suddenly turned on. Along the Grands Boulevards are the theaters that make it the Broadway of Paris.

The Comédie-Française, which occupies one wing of the Palais-Royal, is the home of traditional repertory plays and also of some modern experimental dramas. On Wednesdays and Sundays the schoolchildren of Paris fill the theater to see classical plays.

The children of Paris are lucky to have been born in a city that has such a rich accumulation of history. They can visit the places they have studied in their history courses. For their sports and games many lovely parks are available, including the Bois de Boulogne, the Bois de Vincennes, and the

Egypt and presented to Louis Philippe in 1831. At night one may admire the enchanting floodlighting on the white palaces.

On the Left Bank is the Quai d'Orsay, where the Ministry of Foreign Affairs and the Hôtel des Invalides are located. The Invalides may very well be the most beautiful building in Paris. Its long facade has all the majesty of the colonnaded side of the Louvre, but it has more grace and charm. The bronze and golden dome is covered with sculptures of lovely design.

It is in the chapel of the Invalides that France has buried her great soldier-heroes—not only Napoleon but Marshal Foch (1851–1929), Marshal Lyautey (1854–1934), and many others. The heroes of the mind—Voltaire (1694–1778), Victor Hugo (1802–85), and Émile Zola (1840–1902)—are buried

The broad, tree-lined Avenue Champs-Élysées leads to the Arc de Triomphe.
This huge monument was built by Napoleon in honor of the French Army.

Sidewalk cafés are among the charms of Paris.

A station in the Métro, the Paris subway.

The elaborately decorated Paris Opera House was built in the 19th century.

Parc des Buttes-Chaumont. They can launch their toy sailboats on the ponds of the Luxembourg or Tuileries gardens or on any little stream running down the streets of Montmartre. These children will remain attached to the Paris of their childhood. If someday they become painters, writers, or singers, they will probably devote their best works to Paris.

▶ TRANSPORTATION

What are the other means of moving about Paris? First, of course, there is the automobile, but the traffic in the city has become difficult. Paris was not built, as were many American cities, to accommodate car traffic. There are few wide avenues that intersect each other at right angles. Paris was built during the course of centuries, and its narrowest streets are its most charming ones. The *bateau mouche* is one escape from overly crowded streets. So is the Métro, the common name for the Métropolitain, the Paris subway. Trains follow each other in rapid succession. The system is well maintained, clean, and inexpensive. But during rush hours it is crowded.

The best way of all to move about Paris is on foot. On a walk through the old sections of the city, at nearly every step one will find an exquisitely sculptured door, a colorful sign outside a quaint shop, or an ancient courtyard to stop at and admire. This is also true of a walk down the Rue Saint-Honoré, where every shopwindow is a masterpiece. Under the arcades of the Rue de Rivoli are most of the souvenir shops, the English bookshops, and some famous tearooms. The visitor strolling along the Rue Bonaparte will enjoy browsing in the antique stores filled with ancient clocks, porcelain miniatures, old books bound in leather and gold, and other bric-a-brac.

▶ HISTORY

What are the historical causes that explain the unique character of this town? Paris began on a small island—the Île de la Cité—in the middle of the river Seine. Poor fishermen who belonged to a Gallic tribe—the Parisii—lived on the island. They built a small village there, called Lutetia Parisiorum, as a refuge against the invasions of Romans and barbarians. But the Romans succeeded in conquering the island and began building on both sides of the river. On the Left Bank, in the Cluny Museum grounds, are the remains of the Roman town—including baths, amphitheaters, and the palace of the Emperor Julian (331–363).

When the country became Christian, in the late 5th century, churches and monasteries were built. Later some of them gave their names to the parts of Paris in which they stand. Sainte-Geneviève became the Latin Quarter because students, who spoke Latin, lived there. Saint-Germain-des-Prés is now the center of attractive cafés and nightclubs. Saint-Germain l'Auxerrois is still tragically known because its bell gave the signal for a massacre of Protestants on Saint Bartholomew's Day, August 24, 1572. On the Île de la Cité, Parisians built the great cathedral Notre Dame de Paris, a Gothic church of the 13th and 14th centuries. Notre Dame was the setting of Victor Hugo's famous novel *The Hunchback of Notre Dame* and also the scene of many great events in French history. Napoleon I crowned himself emperor there in 1804, and on August 26, 1944, a service of national thanksgiving for the liberation of Paris from the Nazis was held there.

The rest of the Île de la Cité belongs to judges and lawyers. The Courts of Justice stand on the spot where the palace of the first kings stood. Parisians still call the place *le Palais.* Only the two black towers of the Conciergerie (the royal fortress) remain. These evoke memories of the Reign of Terror and the injustice of both royal and popular "justice." On the Right Bank the kings, in the course of many centuries, built a new palace, the Louvre. This was their residence and the seat of government until Louis XIV (1638–1715) moved the court to Versailles, 13 miles from Paris. Philip II (1165–1223) had built the first fortified tower of the Louvre as a medieval structure. Under Francis I (1494–1547) and Henry IV (1553–1610) the Louvre was transformed architecturally into a Greco-Roman-style building, with Renaissance decoration. Louis XIV added the famous colonnade. The Louvre was really more a town than a palace. Thousands of artists, courtiers, and craftsmen lived in it. Most of them later moved with the court to Versailles. Today the Louvre is an immense museum where one finds the *Vénus de Milo,* the *Mona Lisa,* the *Winged Victory,* and many other wonderful works of art.

By the 16th century there was already a great difference between the Left Bank and the Right Bank of the Seine. The Rive Gauche (Left Bank) was a center of learning. It is now the home of the Sorbonne (the University of Paris), with its large numbers of teachers and students. On the Rive Droite (Right Bank), beyond the Louvre, is a section called Le Marais. There the nobility who wished to live near the rulers built their mansions. Most of these fine houses still exist and may be visited. One may also visit the lovely Place Royale (today Place des Vosges), built by Henry IV. Later, when Le Marais was invaded by the bourgeoisie (middle class) and tradespeople, the aristocracy migrated to the Faubourg Saint Germain or to the Rue Saint-Honoré. But recently Le Marais has again become a fashionable place to live. The Left Bank has always been the capital of the mind. It is a publishing center, and many artists' studios are located there.

For the most part the Paris of the 17th century was a maze of narrow streets, which were very difficult to defend against rioters. However, many palaces and mansions were built during the first half of that century. Queen Marie de Médicis (1573–1642) erected the Palais du Luxembourg (now the home of the French Senate). Cardinal Richelieu (1585–1642) built the Palais-Cardinal (today Palais-Royal). Cardinal

Many famous people have lived on the Place des Vosges (formerly Place Royale), including writer Victor Hugo.

Mazarin (1602–61) built the Palais-Mazarin (now the Institut de France and seat of the French Academy).

Early in the reign of Louis XIV an uprising, called the Fronde, caused serious riots in Paris and frightened the boy-king. Later, as a young man, he made up his mind to leave Paris and to build a palace in nearby Versailles. From that time on, one spoke of the Court and the Town as two separate worlds. Yet the Town, Paris, remained the capital of ideas. In the 18th century it was the spirit of Paris—through its philosophers, artists, and political *salons* (gatherings of intellectuals) —that ruled European minds.

The great French Revolution of 1789 inflamed the town. Parisians stormed the old royal fortress, the Bastille. They took it and razed it to the ground. Today one can see the empty Place de la Bastille at the end of the Grands Boulevards and the Rue Saint-Antoine. Then came the bloody days of the Reign of Terror. Prisons were filled with the enemies of the Revolution. The guillotine did its grim work in the Place Louis XV (which was renamed Place de la Révolution) and Place du Trône (now Place de la Nation). General Napoleon Bonaparte restored public order. Because he was a great believer in centralized power, he even increased the authority of Paris over France. He proved as great a builder as the kings. Paris is indebted to Napoleon for the Arc de Triomphe, the Church of the Madeleine, the Rue de Rivoli. His tomb (in the church of the Invalides) remains a favorite shrine for both Frenchmen and foreign visitors. Even those who blame the conqueror respect the statesman.

During the first half of the 19th century Paris was shaken by a series of public disturbances. After the fall of Napoleon the Bourbon kings were restored to the throne. They chose as their residence the palace of the Tuileries near the Louvre. In 1830 the Parisians overthrew the Bourbons and called to the throne Louis Philippe (1773–1850), a cousin of the former king. During the Revolution of 1848 he was expelled by the people. Paris was now a town devoted to big business and to speculations in real estate. Honoré de Balzac described the period in his novels with genius and exactness. During the Second Empire, Napoleon III (1808–73) favored businessmen. He hired a great town-planner, Baron Haussmann (1809–91), to rid Paris of many slums, open large avenues, and build new residential quarters. Paris was moving west, toward La Plaine Monceau and the Champs-Élysées. That trend continued under the Third Republic (1871–1940). World's fairs (1878, 1889, 1900) left new buildings: the Eiffel Tower, the Grand Palais and the

The Madeleine (Church of St. Mary Magdalene) is noted for its Grecian-style architecture.

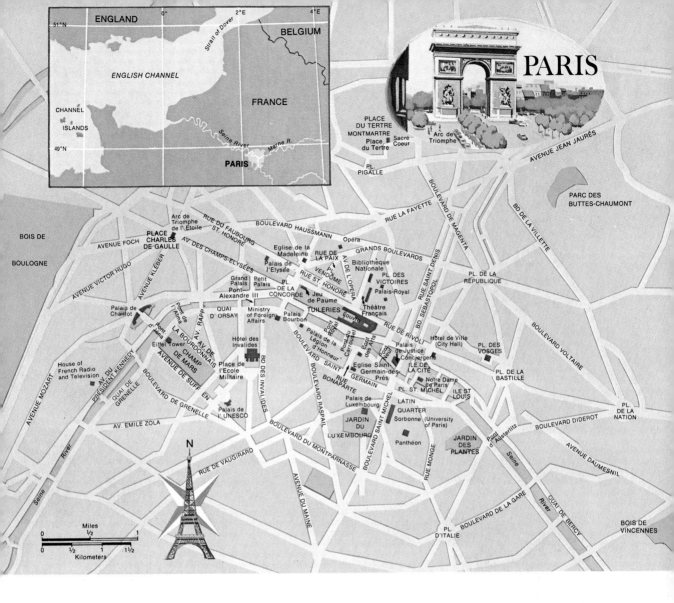

PARIS

Petit Palais, and the Pont Alexandre III, one of the many bridges that cross the Seine.

Three wars endangered the freedom and even the existence of Paris. In 1870 the town was besieged, bombarded, and captured by the Prussians during the Franco-Prussian War. In 1914, during World War I, Paris was saved by the victory of the Marne (in which the Paris taxi-drivers played a part). The city was declared an open city during World War II to prevent its destruction by bombing and was occupied by the Germans for more than three years. Adolf Hitler gave orders to blow up every monument and bridge in Paris if his troops had to withdraw. His plan misfired, thanks to the Paris resistance forces, Allied troops, and several officials—including a German general—who refused to carry out Hitler's orders. The city was liberated in 1944, and General Charles de Gaulle walked triumphantly down the Champs-Élysées.

Since the war, the landscape of Paris has undergone some changes, such as the renovation of the Louvre and the opening of the Bastille Opera House.

ANDRÉ MAUROIS
Late member, Académie Française
Reviewed by ANDRÉ BAEYENS
Director, Press and Information Division
French Embassy, New York City

See also FRANCE.

PARKER, ELY S. See INDIANS, AMERICAN (Profiles).
PARKS, ROSA. See AFRICAN AMERICANS; ALABAMA (Famous People); CIVIL RIGHTS MOVEMENT.

PARKS AND PLAYGROUNDS

The Palace of Versailles, France, was once the home of French kings. The palace grounds consist of magnificent gardens and a park, which are now open to the public.

Parks and playgrounds have a long history. The Hanging Gardens of Babylon, built about 600 B.C., was an early park that was considered one of the seven wonders of the ancient world. The outdoor gymnasiums of Greece, where young men trained for the Olympic Games, first held in 776 B.C., were the forerunners of our modern playgrounds.

▶ PARKS

Before the 18th century, parks were developed by the nobility and the wealthy for their private use. Some of these were landscaped hunting parks out in the country and were stocked with game animals. Other parks were spacious formal gardens surrounding palaces and villas. These gardens featured great lawns, trees, and shrubbery clipped into decorative shapes (topiary) or sheared to form dense arches over paths. Statuary, reflecting pools, elaborate fountains or water cascades, and outdoor stages for concerts and drama were all part of the formal parks.

In England and France, garden design was formal. Many private parks contained a maze (an intricate series of paths enclosed by high hedges) designed so that once you were inside, it was difficult to find the way out.

The development of European private parks was a blending of nature and art. Only on rare occasions were they open to the public. But social changes such as those brought about by the French Revolution opened private estates to public use. In addition, high property taxes and inheritance taxes often forced owners of large estates to turn them over to the community. Some parks were given to the public by generous owners. Thus many private parks eventually became public.

Former market squares and military drill grounds in large cities became public parks after they had outlived their original uses. Village greens, or commons, were widespread in Europe and were duplicated by settlers in the colonies.

Early in the 19th century in England, a totally new idea of park design developed. Regent's Park, created by an act of Parliament in 1812, was planned to be informal in design. Its landscaping was a reflection of nature. A lake was made for boating. Clumps of trees stood along the edges of large grassy meadows where people took part in the popular games of the day.

This park set a pattern for people's parks everywhere, though older parks, such as Kensington Gardens, kept much of their formal garden architecture long after they were opened to the public. France's famous parks of the 15th and 16th centuries also kept their formal appearance.

Development of Modern City Parks

The two factors that influenced the creation of public parks in large cities were the rapid increase in population and the construction of homes and industrial buildings. Meadows and woods that had been public recreation areas became sites for these buildings, and open land disappeared. The banks of rivers and bays were spoiled for recreational use by piers and docks. The waters were polluted by unrestricted dumping of industrial waste and refuse. In many cities, cemeteries were the only open spaces where working people could spend their few hours of leisure time.

On Manhattan Island, in New York City, the lack of open space was most acute. The need for a public park was recognized early in the 19th century. Influential and public-spirited citizens returning from European visits urged the creation of a large public park similar to those in London, Paris, and Berlin.

It was not until 1853 that public demand for such a park brought about the acquisition of the land for Central Park. The design for the park, drawn up by Frederick Law Olmsted and Calvert Vaux in 1857, kept the natural features of the land and was a milestone in park development. It included three playgrounds for children—a new concept in park planning.

Regional and National Parks

Larger parks, with recreational resources that city parks cannot provide, are becoming more and more important. To preserve these extensive lands from commercial development, large sections have been acquired by national governments for future park systems.

The first national park, Yellowstone Park, was established by the United States in 1872. It covers more than 800,000 hectares (2,000,000 acres) in the state of Wyoming and parts of Idaho and Montana.

Tall buildings form a backdrop for ice skaters in Central Park in New York City. City parks provide valuable space for city dwellers to enjoy the outdoors.

Regional (relating to a certain area) and national parks, together with state and national forests, preserve natural scenery and wildlife for present and future generations. You can read more about these parks and forests in the articles NATIONAL PARK SYSTEM and NATIONAL FOREST SYSTEM in Volume N.

▶PLAYGROUNDS

Playgrounds designed as recreational areas for children are a modern development. Playgrounds provide a wide variety of play and exercise equipment, courts for active games, numerous types of sports fields, rooms for indoor recreation, and wading pools.

Recently some countries have pioneered in creating "junk" playgrounds, where children may play on obsolete locomotives, boats, trucks, and airplanes. Highly imaginative sculptured forms for play and exercise are installed in some playgrounds. Others use natural materials such as cross sections of big trees in various lengths, which are placed to form climbing and balancing equipment. Nat-

Ropes, ladders, wooden beams and structures, and a sandy ground allow children to exercise freely and enjoy themselves in a city playground.

ural boulders have been used by some playground architects to form waterfalls and cascades for wading pools. These are meant to imitate nature's rocky streams.

Playground equipment is designed to satisfy the natural desire of children to climb, swing, jump, balance, and slide.

Usefulness and Value to Young People

The greatest benefit of playgrounds is that they provide a safe place for children to play. When the woods and fields were turned into cities, the children had to play on the city streets. First, horse-drawn, and later, motor, vehicles were a constant danger. Dirt in the streets was a health hazard.

Playground programs under the guidance of recreational leaders offer a great variety of activities for all age groups. These programs are planned to help children progress from games requiring only simple skills to those that demand greater co-ordination, speed, strength, and endurance. Physical activity on the playgrounds helps to make up for the inactivity of mechanized living. The more we use machines to lift, pull, and carry us, the more important playground games and sports become to our well-being.

The first consideration in designing a playground is to make sure that it will serve both the immediate and future needs of the community. When planning playgrounds, new residential communities (where most children are under 5 years of age) must consider the future recreational needs of these children. Sandpiles, kindergarten swings, simple exercise apparatus, and wading pools are needed by young children. But later, larger exercise equipment, ball fields, and basketball, volleyball, handball, and paddle-tennis courts, to name only a few, will be required, to provide adequate recreational resources for young people of all ages.

The design of the playground must make the best use of the available land. In crowded communities, playgrounds are designed like jigsaw puzzles because land is costly. Equipment and game areas are fitted together carefully, so as not to waste space or to sacrifice safety or attractiveness.

Safety factors must be provided. The play areas of young children should be set apart from those of older boys and girls so that little children will not be hurt by batted or thrown balls, or be pushed over by runners in active games. Backstops for baseball and softball fields and fences for tennis courts are necessary to protect spectators. Benches should be provided for parents supervising children.

The story of park and playground development illustrates how people have created the resources to meet their recreational needs.

VIENO RAUTIO
Department of Parks, City of New York

AMUSEMENT AND THEME PARKS

Amusement parks, sometimes called theme parks, specialize in rides, games, and entertainment. Unlike public parks these parks are owned by private businesses or individuals. They charge admission, and they usually also charge for all goods and services inside the park.

The oldest amusement park still operating is Bakken Amusement Park, in Copenhagen, Denmark. It was started more than 400 years ago. But Copenhagen has a more famous park —Tivoli Gardens, which is right in the middle of the city. This park combines rides and games with theaters, concert halls, restaurants, and beautiful gardens.

The first American amusement parks were built by streetcar companies in the mid-1850's. There were no automobiles then, and only wealthy people owned carriages. If average people wanted to go somewhere, they had to walk or ride the streetcars.

The streetcars were crowded six days a week, but no one rode them on Sundays. So streetcar owners decided to build places for people to go on that day. They built parks at the ends of streetcar lines, equipping them with swings, slides, pony rides, merry-go-rounds, picnic areas, and places to dance. Soon many people rode to these parks to have fun on Sundays.

Some early parks are still operating. Cedar Point, near Sandusky, Ohio, began in 1870 when Great Lakes steamboats stopped there to let passengers swim and picnic. In 1888 a dance pavilion was added, and in 1894 a roller coaster was built. Later the park added a diving platform, a water trapeze, and a parachute jump. Today Cedar Point is a popular midwestern amusement park.

Coney Island, on the Atlantic Ocean near New York City, began with a sandy beach that was popular with vacationers. In the late 1800's, 40 trained seals and a shoot-the-chute ride were added. The Switchback Railway ride made its debut in 1884, thrilling everyone with its speed of over 9.5 kilometers (6 miles) an hour. Other attractions were added as well.

Hersheypark, in Hershey, Pennsylvania, had its beginnings in 1907. Milton S. Hershey, the chocolate manufacturer who founded the town, built the park for factory workers and their families. Rides were soon added, and on the park's 20th anniversary, Hershey presented a roller coaster to the citizens.

When Walter and Cordelia Knott moved to Buena Park, California, in 1920, they began to grow boysenberries. Then they set up a roadside stand to sell the jams and jellies made from the berries. Soon they were serving chicken dinners to visitors in their home. By 1940 so many people were coming for dinner that long waiting lines formed. The Knotts built a replica of a ghost town to entertain the people. Today Knott's Berry Farm is a full-fledged amusement park that entertains millions of people—and still serves chicken dinners.

Amusement parks are popular for their exciting rides and spectacles. Left: Riders are thrilled by the ''Cyclone,'' the roller coaster at New York's Coney Island. Right: The lights of Copenhagen's Tivoli Gardens are dazzling at night.

The world's most famous mouse joins friends at Tokyo's Disneyland, which opened in 1983. In the background is a castle in Fantasyland. The original Disneyland theme park opened in Anaheim, California, in 1955.

Safety was not always a consideration in the early amusement parks. Rides sometimes collapsed, and fires were a frequent occurrence at some parks. Others were flooded out by spring rains. During the Great Depression of the 1930's, many parks were forced to close because people had little money to spend on entertainment. From 1939 to 1945, the world was involved in World War II, and there was little time for fun. Even after the war was over, many amusement parks had to struggle to stay open.

Then, in 1954, Walt Disney announced plans to build a 73-hectare (180-acre) park in Anaheim, California. A year later, Disneyland opened. This was the first theme park, in which rides, restaurants, shows, costumes, and other attractions were all related to a central idea. Disneyland was built in five theme areas—Fantasyland, Tomorrowland, Frontierland, Adventureland, and Main Street U.S.A. Two more theme areas were added subsequently: Bear Country and New Orleans Square.

Other theme parks followed. Kings Island, near Cincinnati, Ohio, uses cartoon characters as a theme. The Old South is the theme of Carowinds, in Charlotte, North Carolina. Parks that feature animal preserves, such as Busch Gardens in Florida, are also thought of as theme parks. The Six Flags over America parks focus on the history of U.S. settlers who came from other countries.

A second Disney theme park, Walt Disney World, opened near Orlando, Florida, in 1971. Disney's Experimental Prototype Community of Tomorrow (EPCOT), which features displays of the latest technology, opened there in 1982. Other Disneyland parks opened near Tokyo, Japan, in 1983, and near Paris, France, in 1992.

Today, in many countries of the world, amusement parks offer entertainment. All the major parks have at least one roller coaster and one carousel, along with rides that carry out the theme of the park. There is much greater concern for safety today than there was in the early days.

Live music and computer-animated shows are always park favorites. Midways, or "main streets," are lined with games of chance, gift shops, and restaurants. At some parks, animal preserves and white-water rides provide excitement. There is something for everyone in today's amusement park.

ELIZABETH VAN STEENWYK
Author, *Behind the Scenes at the
Amusement Park*

PARLIAMENTARY PROCEDURE

Parliamentary procedure is the method by which meetings are run in a fair and orderly manner. The British Parliament, the Congress of the United States, and other lawmaking bodies follow strict parliamentary procedure. In simpler form the rules are used by business and professional groups, church and school organizations, student councils, and social clubs. A basic principle of parliamentary procedure is to make certain of majority rule and minority rights.

Parliamentary procedure is known also as parliamentary law and, especially in the United States, as rules of order. *Robert's Rules of Order,* a book about parliamentary procedure, was published in 1876. It is still the book used by most organizations in the United States.

History

Most historians agree that the lawmaking bodies of ancient Greece and Rome must have used certain rules of order. But parliamentary procedure as it is known today was developed in the British Parliament.

The English settlers in the American colonies brought with them the basic rules of parliamentary procedure. They used the rules in colonial assemblies and later in state legislatures. Strict parliamentary procedure was followed in the formation of the first two-house Congress of the United States in 1789. During his term as vice president under John Adams, Thomas Jefferson drafted *A Manual of Parliamentary Practice,* which is still used in the Senate and the House of Representatives of the United States.

How an Organization is Set Up

When people meet to form a new organization, one of the first things they do is choose a temporary chairperson. A temporary secretary is then elected to keep the minutes (official records) of the meetings. Next, a temporary committee is formed to help the temporary chairperson draw up a constitution and a set of bylaws. The constitution describes the general structure, purpose, and principles of the organization. The **bylaws** state how the purpose and principles will be carried out. They describe qualifications for membership, procedure for selection of members, and the amount of dues each member must pay. The bylaws also explain how officers will be elected and what their duties will be. And they state how permanent (standing) committees will be formed and what their functions will be.

Officers

After the members have voted to accept the constitution and the bylaws, the officers of the organization are elected. Most officers are elected to serve for a specific period of time. An organization usually elects a chairperson or president, a vice president, a secretary, and a treasurer. Some groups also elect a sergeant at arms.

The president (or chairperson) heads the organization. The president occupies the place of authority at meetings and supervises the work of committees and other officers. The vice president helps the president and takes over when the president is absent. The secretary keeps the minutes and reads them aloud at the next meeting. The secretary's other duties include taking care of all correspondence and committee reports, making announcements, and notifying members of changes in schedule. The treasurer takes care of the organization's finances and prepares the financial reports and annual budget. The sergeant at arms keeps order during meetings.

How does an organization choose its officers? First, a member nominates another member. Usually after two or more people have been nominated, the voting takes place. The person receiving the majority vote is the elected officer. A majority vote is a vote of at least one more than half of all present.

Most organizations require that a quorum be present at elections and at meetings where important decisions are to be made. A **quorum** is a majority of the total membership (or a greater or lesser fraction if specified in the bylaws).

How Meetings Are Held

In parliamentary procedure, the president (or presiding officer) calls the meeting to order by rapping on a hard surface with a gavel and announcing, "The meeting will please come to order." The gavel, a small wooden hammer, is also rapped to quiet disturbances.

The secretary then calls the roll. The list of members present is included in the minutes to be read at the next meeting. The **minutes** are a record of everything that happens at a meeting. Following the roll call, the secretary reads the minutes of the previous meeting. The president asks if anyone would like to correct or add to the minutes. If so, members vote on each correction and addition. If not, the minutes are accepted as read.

The meeting then proceeds according to the agenda. An **agenda** is the list of items to be taken care of at a meeting.

As a rule, committee reports are first on the agenda of regular meetings. (Special meetings can be called for a particular purpose.) The chairperson of each committee gives the report. Members may ask questions, make suggestions, or approve the reports, or they may refer the report back to committee.

Unfinished business left over from earlier meetings is then given attention. If action must be taken, members vote on a decision. If action can be postponed, the matter may be **tabled** (set aside) for consideration at a later meeting or it may be given to a committee.

New business is then introduced. Before a member may introduce a new subject, he or she must stand up and be **recognized**—given permission to speak—by the president. After being recognized, the speaker **has the floor.** The speaker may discuss only one subject at a time, and no interruptions are allowed. If, however, the speaker changes the subject or speaks too long, a member may rise and claim that the speaker is **out of order.** If the president agrees, the speaker must either stop talking and sit down or return to the original subject. If members become disorderly, the president raps the gavel and calls for order. If members do not obey the call for order, they may be put out of the meeting by the sergeant at arms.

Motions

Often a member asks to be recognized in order to make a motion. A **motion** is a plan or suggestion that must either be approved or rejected by the other members. After one member makes a motion, it must be seconded by another member. If seconded, it must be approved or rejected. The motion is stated by the **chair** (the presiding officer). The group then debates (discusses) the motion. Debate continues until all members who wish to speak have had an opportunity to do so. All speakers for and against the motion must first be recognized by the presiding officer.

One of the ways to end debate is to make a specific motion to close the debate. If such a motion is made, seconded, and approved by a majority vote, the motion under discussion must then be put to a vote. All those who approve the motion say "Aye"; all those against the motion say "No." If the vote is very close, the presiding officer may call for a show of hands or a rising vote. With a rising vote, members stand up to indicate their vote. The presiding officer can vote to break a tie vote or vote to make a tie. A tie defeats a motion. If the majority of members present vote to accept the motion, it is approved. If the majority vote to reject the motion, it is dismissed.

Every motion must be taken care of in some way before the organization gives its attention to any other item.

After all action has been taken and matters needing further consideration have been tabled or otherwise disposed of, the business ends. A member moves that the meeting be closed, and another member seconds the motion. A vote is then taken; if a majority vote for adjournment, the presiding officer announces that the meeting is over.

Committees

Certain jobs are often handled better and more efficiently by small groups, or committees, than by the whole membership of an organization.

Permanent, or standing, committees are set up after the election of officers. Depending on the bylaws of the organization, standing committees may be either appointed by the president or elected by the membership.

Temporary, or special, committees (ad hoc committees) are formed whenever necessary to work on a particular job. For example, a special committee may be selected to organize an exhibit, to plan a picnic, or to draft a new constitution or set of bylaws. Special committees break up when their job is done. The president of the organization usually selects one member of the committee to be its chairperson. In some cases the committee members may elect a chairperson.

Reviewed by GEORGE R. HOUSTON
Former Assistant Librarian
Supreme Court of the United States

PARLIAMENTS

Many countries throughout the world are governed by legislative bodies called parliaments. These are broadly patterned on the government of Britain. Unwritten customs and traditions are an essential part of the British constitution. For this reason the parliamentary system is more difficult to understand than a system based on a written constitution like that of the United States.

▶HISTORY OF PARLIAMENTS

Originally the word "parliament" meant a "talk" in which the ruler discussed business with a group of advisers. The oldest parliament in existence is Iceland's Althing, which first met in A.D. 930. In the Middle Ages several European countries had parliaments. The Cortes, or assembly of states, developed in Spain. The Netherlands formed the States General of the Republics of the United Provinces.

During the late 1200's, elected bodies representing all the people began to meet in England to decide how the king should raise money. These early parliaments were not much like the British Parliament of today. But they marked the first time that a representative assembly became part of the English system of government.

The cabinet, the important ruling group within a parliament, developed and became strong because of several historical accidents. Early rulers of England had advisers called the Privy Council. But as government became more complicated, the rulers began to meet fairly regularly with only a few of the more important councillors. This small council was called the cabinet. As the role of the cabinet grew more important, it became an unwritten rule that all the members of the cabinet should sit in parliament to explain and defend government policies.

Modern parliamentary government by cabinets began in Britain in the 18th century. At that time the German-born king George I, who ruled Britain from 1714 to 1727, stopped attending cabinet meetings because he did not understand English. Left alone to make decisions, the cabinet gradually took over all the work and many of the powers of the king. Because they reported their decisions to the king as a group rather than as individuals, all cabinet members had to agree on those decisions. This agreement has become known as cabinet solidarity. Today any cabinet member who disagrees with a decision is expected to resign. Since the cabinet members had to cooperate, the ruler usually chose persons who shared the same political ideas. This led to the development of the modern system of political parties.

During the course of the growth of the parliamentary system in Britain, the House of Commons and the House of Lords were frequently involved in bitter power struggles. The House of Commons often showed its strength through the "power of the purse." Whenever British rulers or, later, cabinets wanted money, the House of Commons—by refusing to approve new taxes—could force rulers to change their policies or their councillors. Today this means that a cabinet must have the support of a majority of the House of Commons. Otherwise, it gets no money, and none of its policies will be approved. Over the centuries the House of Commons has become more powerful and the House of Lords has become less powerful in conducting the business of Parliament.

▶HOW A PARLIAMENT WORKS

A parliament has three parts—a chief of state, an upper chamber, and a lower chamber. In Britain the chief of state is the king or queen; the upper chamber is the House of Lords (nobles who inherit their right to a seat and others appointed for life); and the lower chamber is the House of Commons (democratically elected representatives). In other countries these names, and the means of appointing or electing, may differ. The head of state may be an elected president. The upper chamber may be called the senate or some other name. In Canada, for instance, the two houses are called the Senate and the House of Commons. But the part each plays in parliament is roughly the same. The lower house passes laws; the upper house examines these laws and, if necessary, revises them; and the head of state then approves the laws to make them official.

The power of the cabinet in parliamentary government is always present. The king or head of state reigns, but the prime minister and

Queen Elizabeth II presides at the opening session of the British Parliament.

the cabinet actually rule as long as a majority of the elected representatives support them. This means that the cabinet is "responsible to" parliament.

In a parliamentary system, governments can be defeated by a vote in parliament. However, a change of government usually comes at a general election. General elections must be held after a fixed number of years. But they can be held earlier if the party in power fails to get its policies approved. When an election is held, the voters can reject the government by electing more members from the opposition side. Or they can return the same government to power by electing more of its supporters. If the opposition party wins more than half the seats in the lower house, the head of state asks the leader of the majority party to serve as prime (first) minister and to choose a cabinet.

In the British parliamentary system, Parliament is all-powerful. The cabinet—the executive branch of government that shapes government policies—sits in Parliament and must answer to it. Parliament is the nation's chief legislative body. It not only makes new laws but also has the power to revise or repeal existing laws and to determine whether or not a law is constitutional.

Parts of Canada's Constitution Act of 1982 broke with British parliamentary tradition. The Constitution Act gave the Supreme Court of Canada, rather than Parliament, the power to interpret the constitution and the right to declare a law unconstitutional. It also made a bill of rights and freedoms a part of the written constitution.

The congressional system of the United States is not, strictly speaking, a parliamentary system. Presidents of the United States are both heads of state and heads of government. They appoint cabinet members and remove those members if they wish. Cabinet members do not sit in Congress, and the government can be changed only by the presidential elections held every four years. But the U.S. system grew out of the parliamentary system practiced in the American colonies at the time of the Revolutionary War.

▶THE INTER-PARLIAMENTARY UNION

In 1889, representatives of the parliaments of nine countries met in Paris. As a result of this meeting the Inter-Parliamentary Union was established. This union is an organization of countries having some form of parliamentary government. Its purpose is to unite the governments of these countries and to promote international peace and harmony.

Parliaments of countries all over the world send delegates to meetings of the union. Many of the countries represented, such as the United States, do not have parliaments in the strictest sense. But all of them have governments in which there is some form of general election. The union meets at least once a year. Its official headquarters are located in Geneva, Switzerland.

JOHN S. MOIR
University of Toronto

See also LEGISLATURES.

PAROCHIAL SCHOOLS. See EDUCATION; PREPARATORY SCHOOLS.

PARROTS

When you hear the word "parrot," you probably think of a colorful bird with a hooked beak that lives in a cage, kept as a pet. Parrots are fascinating as pets, but they are even more intriguing in the wild. More than 330 different species of parrots make up the order, or group, of birds known as Psittaciformes. Cockatoos, macaws, budgerigars, lorikeets, lovebirds, conures, and cockatiels are only some of the different types.

Most parrots are forest birds, dwelling in the Southern Hemisphere—in South America, Australia, sub-Saharan Africa, and Indonesia. Parrots are also found in the forests of India, Asia, and Central America. Some parrots have adapted to life in other habitats besides the forest. In Australia, New Zealand, and on other nearby islands, parrots live in the grasslands, in snowy mountains, and on rocky, seaside cliffs. Only a handful of species are native to the Northern Hemisphere.

Whether it is the nectar-collecting lory (*left inset*), the cockatoo with its crest of feathers, or the brightly colored macaw (*right inset*), a parrot can be recognized by its curved beak, large head, and reversed toes (two pointing forward, two pointing backward).

▶ THE CHARACTERISTICS OF PARROTS

Many, but not all, of the different parrot species have brightly colored feathers. Some parrots, including the few ground-dwelling or nocturnal species, have feathers that are dull, dark colors, which help conceal the birds in their environment. The bright plumage of many parrots also serves as camouflage. High up in flowering tropical trees, under the blazing sun, multicolored birds are not at all easy to spot.

Although parrots of different species have widely different colors, all parrots have the same kind of hooked beak. A parrot's beak is very strong and sharp, enabling the bird to crack and crush a variety of very tough seeds. Some of the larger parrots, such as macaws and cockatoos, have such powerful beaks, they can cut through fence wire. A parrot's beak is also extremely flexible, so the bird can use it as a third foot. It climbs across a web of high branches or up a tree trunk, clenching a branch or bark in its beak to steady itself while bringing one foot and then the other foot forward.

Parrots also have perfect feet for these jungle acrobatics. Most birds have four toes, three pointing forward and one pointing backward; parrots have two toes facing forward and two facing backward. This gives the bird a sure grip as it moves to the very tips of branches and feasts on fruits and flowers few other birds can reach.

Finally, unlike other birds, parrots use their beaks and claws together to manipulate food and other objects with ease. Just as people can be right- or left-handed, parrots can be right- or left-footed. Way up in the treetops, a parrot might hang upside down by one foot, bring a seed to its mouth with the other foot, and crack the seed with its beak. By such dizzying feats, the parrot gained its nickname: monkey of the bird world.

A parakeet's green color (*left*), the most common color of a parrot, keeps it well hidden as it perches on a tree branch. Parrots, such as these macaws dotting a cliff (*above*), tend to gather in large, noisy flocks.

▶ **THE LIFE OF PARROTS**

Parrots are social birds. Parrots that inhabit the forests tend to stick together in family groups. Those that inhabit more open areas tend to form huge flocks, sometimes made up of thousands of birds.

Most parrots nest in hollowed-out tree branches or trunks and mate for life. Small parrots lay up to eight eggs; large parrots lay one or two eggs. Usually the female broods the eggs, that is, she sits on them to protect them and keep them warm. Brooding may go on for a month or longer. During this time, the male usually brings food to the female, who stays on the nest.

When the young hatch, they are small, naked, blind, and completely helpless. They are fed food that their parents have partially digested. However, the female budgerigar, a parrot native to central Australia, feeds its young milk that it makes in its esophagus.

Young parrots remain in the nest for a long time, compared with most birds. Most cannot fly for at least a month; young macaws cannot fly until the end of their third month. Once they learn to fly, young parrots practice swooping and swerving through the forest and climbing through the uppermost branches of the trees. Most parrots stay with their parents for at least a few months after they have learned to fly. They leave their parents to join with flocks made up of other young parrots. The young parrots stay with their flock one to three years, until they have matured. Then they seek out a mate and start their own family.

▶ **PARROTS AND THEIR ENVIRONMENT**

Wild parrots face two major threats: They are popular as pets, so many people try to capture them for sale to pet dealers, and they live in forested areas, which are being cut down at alarming rates.

Because of these threats, more than one-fifth of all parrot species in the world are endangered. Some parrot species have such small populations that, despite strong efforts to save the birds, they are likely to become extinct. For instance, the imperial amazon—a parrot native to the Caribbean island of Dominica—has a population of less than 50.

With breeding programs carried out by zoos and other institutions that work to conserve different types of animals, some parrot species may be rescued from the brink of extinction. Efforts to save the rain forests and other parrot habitats are equally essential for the survival of many species. Just as important, the laws against capturing, selling, or buying endangered species must be enforced. Many types of parrots are bred in captivity for sale as pets. To help save the parrots, only these captive-bred birds should be brought into homes. Most wild parrots breed slowly; they will not survive if people continue capturing them to sell as pets.

ELIZABETH KAPLAN
Series Coauthor, *Ask Isaac Asimov*

See also BIRDS; BIRDS AS PETS.

PARTHIANS. See PERSIA, ANCIENT.

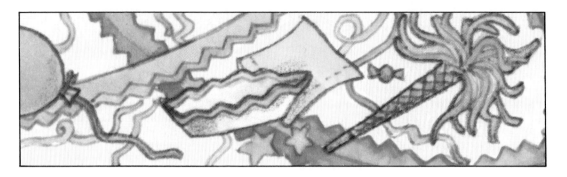

PARTIES

Everyone loves a party. It's fun to go to a party at a friend's house, and it can be even more fun to give one at your own house. Your fun can actually begin beforehand as you think of ideas to make your party a success. The key to a successful party is planning and preparing ahead of time.

There are many occasions throughout the year for giving a party. Birthdays, Halloween, Christmas, St. Valentine's Day, St. Patrick's Day, Easter, and patriotic holidays are some of those times. Do not feel that you must wait for a special day to justify having a party. Sometimes people have parties just because they want to, and that is fine, too.

▶ PLANNING THE PARTY

Before you begin the plans for your party, you must have one very important thing and that is permission from your family. It might not be possible for you to have a birthday party every year. Some years you might just have one special friend come over for dinner (your favorite dinner, of course) and birthday cake.

If this is your lucky year and it is all right for you to have a party, the first step is to sit down with an older member of your family and make plans. Decide, first, whom you would like to have at your party. The number of guests that you are able to invite will depend a great deal on the size of your house or apartment. Remember that overcrowding a party can take away from everyone's fun. Your age and the age of the children attending your party is another thing to consider when trying to decide how many guests to invite. A good rule to follow seems to be to invite as many guests as you are years old—for example, eight children at your eighth birthday.

If your home is simply too small to accommodate all of the children you were hoping to invite, your family might consider letting you have a party at a nearby restaurant. Many restaurants offer birthday party packages that include everything from the invitations to the hats and food at a very reasonable price. You might also consider taking a small group of friends to a special children's movie or to a bowling alley, a rollerskating rink, or a miniature golf course. A beach or a local park or playground are other possible places for a party.

Next you will need to pick out a theme for your party. Perhaps this could come from some special interest or hobby that you have, such as trains, cowboys, Indians, pirates, outer space, the circus, or dolls from many lands. The chart at the end of the article shows you how a theme can be carried out in all phases of your party.

You might prefer to choose a color scheme instead of a theme. You could choose two colors that you think go well together and use them for everything from the invitations to the favors and decorations.

▶ INVITATIONS

The invitations can carry out your theme or color scheme. You can make very simple ones by cutting colored construction paper to fit into a standard-size envelope and writing your party information on the cut paper with a crayon or marker. If you are using one of the party themes suggested on the chart in this article, you might want to follow the suggestion given for making special invitations to go along with that theme.

Whatever kind of invitation you decide to use, you must be sure to include on each one

all of the information your friends will need to attend the party. You should include the day, date, and the time the party begins and ends. You should also include your name and your address or the address of the place where the party is going to be. It is also a good idea to put the letters *RSVP* on your invitation with your phone number next to the letters. The letters stand for the French words *Répondez s'il vous plaît,* which means "Please reply." It is helpful to the planning of your party for you to know ahead of time who is able to come and who is not. If you have any special information your guests might need to know such as "wear play clothes"—if it is a picnic —this should be written on your invitation, too.

The invitations need to be in the mail or hand-delivered a week to ten days before your party. It is not a good idea to take your invitations to school to hand out. It is likely that those children you were not able to invite will notice that invitations were handed out to others and feel hurt because they have been left out.

▶ DECORATIONS AND FAVORS

Decorations for the house and table, favors (small gifts for each guest), and prizes all add to the fun of a party. Crepe paper streamers hung from the ceiling to the corners make any room look festive. Crepe paper needs to be hung with tape, so be sure it won't harm the paint or wallpaper in that room. Balloons also add to the gay atmosphere of a party. Blow them up an hour or so before your guests are scheduled to arrive and stick them to the walls of the room by first rubbing each one on your clothes. You might also want to tie several balloons together to hang from the ceiling in the middle of the room.

For your party table, paper cups and plates and a paper tablecloth in the theme or color scheme of your party look pretty and save work. You can also purchase plain paper plates and cups and decorate them yourself using stickers or markers. If the theme of your party is one mentioned on the party chart included with this article, you might want to try the special suggestions given under the "table setting" column of the party chart. A bedsheet makes an excellent tablecloth. Today's sheets are so gay and colorful that the pattern you need to set off your table might be found right in your linen closet.

The list of possible party favors is almost endless. Small cars, dolls and animals, stickers, marbles, and pipe bubbles are all popular favors. Find out how much your family would like to spend for favors, then go to the store with them to find something you would like to give your friends within the budget. You might also want to shop for some prizes to award to those children who win games. You need not have prizes for all your games, but it does add to the excitement.

If you are planning to hand out favors or game prizes, it would be helpful to your guests to provide each one with a lunch bag with his or her name on it.

▶ GAMES

Next you will need to plan the kinds of activities with which to entertain your guests once they arrive. It is a good idea to have more games planned than you think you will need. Your friends may tire of some of the games sooner than you expected, so be prepared with other games to play to keep your party going. Do not be upset if there is one boy or girl who does not wish to join in any of the games. Make an effort to include everyone, but do not try to force anyone to play. All the guests should feel comfortable and enjoy the party in their own way.

It is not unusual to feel a bit shy as your first guests start to arrive. It is helpful to have an older member of your family at the door with you to help you greet your guests and make them feel welcome. If you have access to an instant-photo camera, you might want to take a picture of each guest as he or she arrives. Everyone will crowd around eagerly to see the results. Another way to get your party off to a good start is by pinning the name of a famous person to the back of each guest as each one arrives. The only way they can discover who they are is by asking the other

guests questions. This is a great way to get your friends talking to each other quickly.

When you are planning your list of games, try to alternate active games with quieter games so that your guests are not worn out before the party is over. You might start your party off with a lively game such as ''musical chairs,'' then go to a word game where everyone will need to sit down and think about their answers. A good word game would be to ask your guests to see how many words they can make using only the letters of your first and last name. Give them about ten minutes to work on it, then award a prize to the person who has made the most words.

Another good resting game is to show your guests a tray with 20 objects on it for one minute. When the tray is taken away, ask your friends to write down as many of the objects as they can remember. The winner of the game is the person who is able to recall the most objects from the tray.

Charades, Simon Says, Pin the Tail on the Donkey, Bingo, hunts, relay races, and guessing games are all popular party activities. Many of these can be made to fit into the theme of your special party with just a little extra thought and work on your part. If you are having a Halloween party, you could play ''Pin the Nose on the Witch'' instead of ''Pin the Tail on the Donkey.'' For a picnic party, you could play ''Pin the Handle on the Picnic Basket.'' If you are having a hunt for candy, pennies, or small prizes, you could call that hunt something that fits in with your party theme. For example, if you were having a pirate party, it could be a ''treasure hunt''; or if you were having a circus party, it could be a ''peanut hunt.''

As you grow older, you will probably become interested in playing records and dancing at your parties. If you decide to include this in your list of activities, a Cinderella dance might be fun. Have all of the boys leave the room and have each girl remove one of her shoes and place it in the middle of the floor. When the boys come back, each boy must quickly grab a shoe from the pile and find his Cinderella, who is his partner for that dance.

▶REFRESHMENTS

After all of the fun and excitement of the games, your guests are sure to be hungry. Ice cream and cake are traditional party foods, especially if you are having a birthday party. But there are lots of other party foods to serve along with them if you would like to put some extra time and effort into the refreshments.

If you are thinking of serving lunch or dinner before having cake and ice cream, it is again time to go back to your party theme and see if you can make the food a part of your theme. Pizza, sandwiches, hamburgers, hot dogs, pasta, cut-up raw vegetables or fresh fruit, and ''munchies''—such as potato chips or popcorn—are all favorite party foods. If you are having a picnic, hamburgers and hot dogs on an outdoor grill would be perfect. For a Valentine's Day party, you might want to serve heart-shaped sandwiches filled with strawberry jelly. At Halloween time you could have individual pizzas with a jack-o'-lantern face, made of cheese, on each pizza.

Think about the kinds of foods you enjoy and would like to serve your friends at your party, then try to think of ways to make that food fit into the theme of your party. The extra thought and time you put into this will be well rewarded by the response from your guests. If you decide to serve ice cream and cake only, you can still be creative. Be sure that the cake in some way carries out the theme of your party if you have one. Or, as a special treat for your guests, you could set up a ''make your own sundae'' table with bowls of ice cream, different sauces, nuts, sprinkles, and fruit.

Time always goes by quickly at a party. Before you know it, you will be saying goodbye to your guests and thanking them for coming. Your party will be over except for the pleasure of remembering it.

Reviewed by KATHY ROSS
Director, Kenwood Nursery School

See also HALLOWEEN.

On the following pages is a party chart. It will give you lots of party ideas as well as show you how to carry out a party theme.

Valentine's Day

Heart Whale

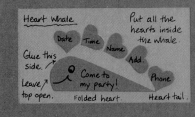

Put all the hearts inside the whale. Add.

Glue this side.
Leave top open.

Come to my party!

Folded heart.

Date Time Name Phone

Heart tail.

Heart Mouse

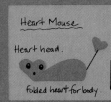

Heart head.

Folded heart for body.

Glue heart on end of flat lollypop and slip into folded hearts so stick forms mouse's tail.

Candy Heart Hunt

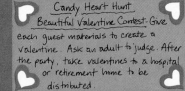

Beautiful Valentine Contest - Give each guest materials to create a valentine. Ask an adult to judge. After the party, take valentines to a hospital or retirement home to be distributed.

Teddy Bear Picnic

Circles Bear

Write party information on the bear's tummy. Tell each guest to "Bring a Bear."

Bag Bear Puppet

Use a brown lunch bag. Fill with prizes and candy. Staple shut.

Pom-Pom Bear Pin

Tie large pom-pom in center. Use tiny pom-poms for ears, nose, and paws. Add black felt eyes and glue a tiny pin to back.

Bear Judging - Judge the fattest, oldest, best dressed, etc. Make ribbons to pin on each bear.
Musical Bears - Sit guests in a circle. All but one have a bear. Each time music starts, pass bears to left. When music stops, guest with no bear is "out."

Easter

Chick-in-an-Egg

Decorate 2 egg halves and glue together around edges to form pocket. Write party information on back.

Use large sheet of construction paper.

Front of hat. Cut along each of four dotted lines.

Staple point 1 to point 2 on each side, tucking points A and B under front of hat. Add yarn ties.

• **Easter Egg Hunt.**
• Guess how many jelly beans in a jar.
• **Bunny Hop Relay** - Each person on a team must hop to a line and back with a basket of jelly beans. Racer must pick up any spilled ones before continuing.

Snow Party

Snowman Mobiles

Glue paper circles (6) to front and back of string. Decorate snowman's front. Write party information on back.

Felt Ear Warmers - Glue felt circles onto a ribbon. Add felt face or design.
Snowman Pins - Glue 3 cotton balls on a strip of felt. Add felt or paper details and a fabric-strip scarf. Glue safety pin to back.

• Make angels in the snow. Add faces and details with squeeze bottles full of colored water.
• See who can throw the most snowballs into a carton from a distance. Indoors, use styrofoam "snowballs."
• **Mitten race** - Mix guests' mittens in a carton. Guests must race to carton, find and put on their own mittens, and race back!

Space Party

Orbiting Invitation

Color a paper plate to look like the world. Write party information on the world in black marker.

Use paper fasteners to attach a paper rocket to one end of a cardboard strip and to attach the other end to the back of the plate.

Space Helmet

Cut away part of plastic jug. Turn over and cover with foil.

Space-Robot Finger Puppet

Glue half an egg shell on cardboard tube. Cover with tinfoil. Glue on nuts and bolts for face.

• Hang a decorated cardboard carton about a foot above guest's head. Have them make paper airplanes and fly them into the carton.
• Each guest must try to spoon as many cotton ball "clouds" as possible from one tray to another while blindfolded. 1 minute time limit.

Halloween

Pop-up Ghost

Cut long, sealed envelope in half.

Cut hole here.

Write party information on ghost stapled to a straw. Push and pull on straw to pop ghost in and out.

① **Ghostly Candy Cups** - ① Draw a ghost on a white styrofoam cup. ② Cut away just the top part of cup around the ghost.

Ghostly Lollypops - Tie a tissue around a lollypop. Draw a ghostly face on it.

Pumpkin Decorating Contest - Use permanent markers to draw with.
Drop the Clothes Pin in the Pumpkin - Use a real pumpkin.

Pumpkin Roll - Draw a pumpkin on the front of a box. Cut a hole for the mouth. See who can roll in the most tennis balls.

Row 1

• White or lace tablecloth.
• Large red paper heart placemats
• Cut rings from a cardboard tube and glue a red heart to each one, for napkin rings.
• Put valentine stickers on plain styrofoam cups and plates.

• Strawberry Sundaes.
• Heart-shaped red jello.
• Red jelly sandwiches cut with a heart-shaped cookie cutter.
• Drop red sour balls into each section of a filled ice tray. Freeze. Use in red punch.

Hearts and Flowers Cupcakes
Straws with paper hearts and flowers glued on one end. Chocolate frosting. For flower pots, bake cakes in ice cream cones.

Row 2

Staple round teddy bear ears to paper plates and have each guest draw a bear face on the plate while waiting to be served.
Fill a basket with teddy bears for a centerpiece.

• Pack each guest's lunch in a box or basket lined with a napkin.
• Let each guest toast a marshmallow and squeeze it between 2 graham crackers with half of a chocolate bar.

The cake is chocolate, of course.
Bake 2 round layers.
Make cupcake ears and paws.
Use chocolate icing and a candy face (try Necco wafers).

Row 3

Bunny Plates
Staple small white plate to large one. Add face, paper ears, and cotton tail.

Basket Cups
Glue pipe cleaner to white cup. Use ice with jelly beans frozen in center.

Marshmallow Bunnies
Use large and miniature marshmallows held together with toothpicks. Use scissors to cut ears from large marshmallow.

Boiled Egg Chicks
Use half of a hard-boiled egg with whole yolk. Make face with cloves or peppercorns.

2 round layers.
Frost white. Use candy for face and bow tie.
Cut on dotted line.

Row 4

• Let each guest cut a snowflake placemat from a large sheet of paper.
• Staple a paper hat to each plate. Leave a crayon at each place so guests may design snowman faces.

Marshmallow Snowman
Join with tooth pick. Add clove face. Float in hot chocolate.
Ice Cream Snowman
Flat-bottom cone hat. Vanilla ice cream (1 or 2 scoops) with M & M face.

Round layers – 2
White icing – sprinkle with coconut, if desired. Add candy details. Cut hat and scarf from "fruit leather" (fruit roll-ups).

Row 5

• Paint or cover cardboard paper-towel tubes with foil. Glue on paper cones and fins. Wrap silverware in napkins and slide into rockets. Write guest's name on tube.
• Make placemats by covering shirt cardboards with foil. Glue on paper stars.

• Space creature sandwiches. Cut funny faces out of dark bread so filling shows through.
• Drink like real space people do – serve punch in a twist-tied bag with straw.
• Rocket salad – stand half a banana in a pineapple slice. Place on a bed of shredded carrot.

Spaceship Cake
Wrap photo of you in plastic wrap. Put in spaceship "window."
Rectangular cake.

Row 6

Staple a green paper stem to the top of each orange paper plate. Carve out a large pumpkin for the center of the table — for a punch bowl.

Ice Cream Cone Witch
– Cone
– Cookie
– Ice Cream
Use candy for the face.

Jack-O'-Lantern Pizzas
Use English muffins with pizza sauce. Cut stem and face from cheese.

Jack-O'-Lantern Cake
Make an orange layer cake with orange frosting. Use licorice whips to outline features. Use candy corn teeth and jelly bean eyes.

PARTIES, POLITICAL.   See POLITICAL PARTIES.

PARTS OF SPEECH

The term "parts of speech" refers to the classification of words according to their common uses in sentences. Traditionally, words have been classified into eight parts of speech: noun, pronoun, verb, adjective, adverb, preposition, conjunction, and interjection. Sometimes a ninth part, the article, is added.

Many modern grammarians distinguish between four basic parts of speech, called **form classes** (nouns and pronouns, verbs, adjectives, and adverbs), and **function words.** Function words fall into groups such as prepositions (of, by, for, with, over, after, at, in, among, toward), various kinds of conjunctions (and, but, for, either . . . or, yet, still, when, while, as, since, because), and interjections (well, ouch! oh! hey!).

Usually a word cannot be classified until it is used in a sentence. Many words may be two parts of speech: A *whistle* shrilled (noun). Can you *whistle* the national anthem (verb)? Some words may be several parts of speech: I *long* for a glimpse of the ocean (verb). She worked *long* into the night (adverb). Vacations are never *long* enough (adjective). That's the *long* and the short of it (noun).

▶THE FOUR CLASSES

A sentence is built up from words in the four basic classes.

Noun

A noun is a word that refers to one or more persons, places, objects, or ideas. *Guitar, spinach, downtown, galaxy, infant,* and *soccer* are nouns. Most nouns indicate one or more than one by changing their form: *laser, lasers; werewolf, werewolves; child, children; peach, peaches.* A few nouns do not change their form to show number: *a sheep, a flock of sheep; an elk, a gang of elk; one fish, a school of fish (fishes* is sometimes used).

Nouns are usually classified as common or proper. Proper nouns are the names of particular persons and places: *Fred, Pac-Man, Uncle Sam, Oklahoma City, Nicaragua.* Proper nouns are always capitalized. All nouns that are not proper nouns are common nouns: *frog, celery, telephone, truth, beauty.* Common nouns are not capitalized.

In the list above it is easy to see that *truth* and *beauty* are different kinds of nouns from *frog, celery,* and *telephone.* The last three things you can see and touch. *Truth* and *beauty* name qualities or ideas. Such nouns are called abstract nouns. Nouns that refer to objects that can be touched are called concrete nouns. Some nouns may be either concrete or abstract, depending on the way they are used. The word "will" is concrete in this sentence: They found the old miser's will in his desk. But it is abstract in this sentence: Where there's a will, there's a way.

Pronoun.   A word used in place of a noun is called a pronoun. Many languages have developed pronouns in order to avoid repeating a noun. For example, "Pooh was sitting in his house one day, counting his pots of honey" is easier to read than "Pooh was sitting in Pooh's house one day, counting Pooh's pots of honey." When a pronoun is used in a sentence, it must agree in number, person, and gender with the noun it is replacing: Jennifer's violin was in *its* case on *her* desk. Mark took the socks back to the store, saying *they* didn't fit *him.* May I present *my* uncle to you and *your* aunt?

The case of a pronoun depends on its use in a sentence: *I* stayed home all day (subjective case, because "I" is the subject of "stayed"). Then Mom took my sister and *me* to a movie (objective case, because "me" is the object of "took"). I think I caught *my* cold walking there in the snow (possessive case, because "my" shows who possesses "cold").

Personal pronouns have many forms. Pronouns in the first person (I, my, mine, me; we, our, ours, us) indicate the speaker. Pronouns in the second person (you, your, yours) indicate the person spoken to. Pronouns in the third person (he, his, him; she, hers, her; it, its; they, their, theirs, them) indicate the person or thing spoken about. Older forms, such as *thou, thy, thine, thee,* and *ye,* survive in prayers and religious literature but are seldom used otherwise.

Demonstrative pronouns point out a particular person or thing: *This* is mine; *that* is yours. *These* look good enough to eat; *those* over there are even better.

Interrogative pronouns (who, whom, which, and why) ask questions. *Who* said that? *What* do you mean? To *whom* do you think you are speaking? *Which* dog did you say bit you?

The indefinite pronoun "it" is used in certain set expressions. For instance, we say, "It is raining." We do not say, "Rain is." In other expressions "it" postpones the subject to give it greater emphasis: "I could tell *it* was going to be a terrible, horrible, no-good, very bad day."

A relative pronoun joins an adjective clause or a noun clause to an independent clause. The most common relative pronouns are who, whose, whom, what, that, and which: That is the girl *who* ate my pizza. I wonder *whose* alligator that is. She disliked the boy *whom* you thought charming. Eat *what* you like from the buffet. The poodle *that* ran away was wearing her bracelet. Your nose isn't as nice as mine, *which* is perfect. Compound relative pronouns are made by adding *ever* to who, whom, what, or which: Do *whatever* you want with it. He will interview *whomever* you suggest to fill the position.

Verb

A verb is a word that expresses an action or a state of existence. In English grammar a sentence contains a subject (noun or pronoun) and a verb: Julia *cooks*. I *eat*. Charles *washes up*. Dinner *is* over.

Verbs may be identified by their forms. All verbs that are not special auxiliaries (such as *be, can, may, shall, will, ought, must*) add *s* to the present-tense form to make the third person singular: He *creeps*. The grass *rustles*. The deer *looks up*. The camera *clicks*. The other forms show whether the verb is regular or irregular.

Regular verbs add *d, ed,* or *t* to the present-tense form to make the past tense and the past participle. These three forms—the present tense, the past tense, and the past participle—are the principal parts of a verb. Here are the principal parts of some regular verbs:

Present	Past	Past Participle
smile	smiled	smiled
gaze	gazed	gazed
blush	blushed	blushed
sleep	slept	slept

In most cases, irregular verbs form the past tense and past participle by a change of vowel. Some irregular verbs have only one form for all three parts.

Present	Past	Past Participle
sing	sang	sung
set	set	set
sit	sat	sat
ride	rode	ridden
buy	bought	bought
lie	lay	lain

The verbs *go, do,* and *say* are also common irregular verbs. Some verbs that are usually regular may have an alternative irregular form: *prove, proved, proved* (or *proven*); *dive, dived* (or *dove*), *dived*.

When a verb expresses an action that is performed by the subject upon an object, the verb is called a transitive verb: Tom *grabbed* his hat. Sally *hailed* a taxi. When the verb expresses an action performed by the subject without an object or when it indicates a state of existence, it is called an intransitive verb: Johnny *jumped*. Spot *sits* in the street. The grass *grew* shoulder-high. Many verbs may be either transitive or intransitive: Sue *ate* elegantly (intransitive). Peter *ate* a pie (transitive).

Adjective

An adjective is a word, phrase, or clause that describes a noun or limits it in its meaning in some way. These are single-word adjectives: a *mighty* oak, a *funny* story, twelve *brave* men, only *one* slice each. If the adjective follows a linking verb (a form of "be") that joins the subject to the predicate, it is called a predicate adjective: The oak was *tall* and *mighty*. That's *funny!* They were *brave* to do that. These are adjectival phrases: The tree *on the hill* was struck by lightning. The people *at the party* had a good time. *Standing in the corner*, Sally watched what was happening. These are adjectival clauses: The man *who is climbing the flagpole* is my uncle. The package *that came this morning* is hidden under your desk.

Single-word adjectives usually come before the noun. Phrase and clause adjectives generally follow.

Adverb

An adverb is a word, phrase, or clause that modifies or qualifies the meaning of a verb. It sometimes modifies an adjective or another adverb. Many adverbs are formed by adding *ly* to an adjective, as in *curious, curiously*.

These are single-word adverbs modifying

verbs: I gazed *happily* around me. *Soon* the ball would begin. Pierre *eagerly* drank his champagne. These are adverbial phrases: The house stood *in the shadow of a volcano.* He borrowed a calculator *to balance his checkbook.* The rabbit was *in a hurry.* These are adverbial clauses: *When I reached the finish line,* the tortoise was already there. Alexander fell *because he could not balance himself on his skateboard.* The impatient audience left *before the play had even begun.*

These adverbs modify adjectives: This plum is *too* ripe. The breeze from the lagoon was *refreshingly* cool. These adverbs modify other adverbs: Please walk a *little* faster. The cat's grin vanished *quite* slowly. She was not *too* favorably impressed.

Some adverbs have two forms: *slow, slowly; quick, quickly; loud, loudly; soft, softly.* In modern English the short form is generally used in commands and exclamations, while the longer form is preferred for statements and questions: Drive *slow!* Susan cycled *slowly* down the street. Come *quick! Quickly* he explained his plan of escape. Not so *loud!* He had to speak *loudly* to be heard over the noise of the demonstrators. The wind whistled *softly* in the trees.

▶ **FUNCTION WORDS**

All the words that do not fit into the four basic classes are called function words, because their meaning comes from their use, or function, in a sentence. Prepositions, conjunctions, and interjections are function words.

Prepositions

Prepositions are words that come before a noun or pronoun and connect it to the rest of a sentence. The preposition, the noun, and the modifiers of the noun form a prepositional phrase. Prepositional phrases usually modify nouns or verbs. English has many prepositions. Some of the most common are *about, above, across, after, along, among, at, before, behind, beside, between, down, for, from, in, like, near, of, off, on, out, over, since, to, under, up,* and *with.*

These prepositional phrases modify nouns: The price *of each cassette* is clearly marked. The cat *behind you* is about to pounce. The tall blond man *with one black shoe* is here. These prepositional phrases modify verbs: But this letter is addressed *to me!* They divided the watermelon *into small pieces.* It all came out right *in the end.*

Prepositions are sometimes used in pairs or groups: His feet emerged *from under* the car. He ran *up along* the ridge and disappeared.

Conjunctions

Conjunctions are words that join together elements of a sentence, such as words, phrases, or clauses. When the elements joined together are of equal rank, the conjunction is called a co-ordinating conjunction. When one element is joined to another that is not of equal grammatical rank, the conjunction is called a subordinating conjunction.

And, but, yet, for, or, nor, and *so* are co-ordinating conjunctions: Snow *and* sleet fell all day *and* all night. I swam hard, *but* I could make no progress against it. Throw Paul that raincoat, *or* he will get wet, too. He won't wear it, *for* it is the wrong color. Jennifer had just washed her hair, *so* she didn't go out.

When co-ordinating conjunctions are used in pairs, they are called correlative conjunctions: *Either* we all contribute, *or* no one gets to go. *Neither* Jerry *nor* his brother would agree to that.

When, while, as, since, and *because* are examples of subordinating conjunctions. They connect a modifying clause to an independent clause: *Since* you came first, you may have the biggest piece of pie. You may go *when* you have finished it. Wait here *while* I put on my boots. The team began to smile *as* the crowd began to cheer. Geraldine picked Walter *because* he is tall and dances well.

Interjections

Interjections are exclamations that are used alone or inserted into a sentence. The word "interjection" means "something thrown in or into." Interjections generally express an emotion. *Hey! Ouch! Gosh! Oh my fur and whiskers!* are exclamations of this kind.

Interjections are sometimes filler words used to start sentences: *Well*, what next? *Now then*, let me get this straight. *Oh*, I don't care! These occur very frequently in speech, but they are usually omitted in writing. *Aha!* and *alas* are sometimes found in literature.

ROBERT C. POOLEY
Author, *Teaching English Grammar*

See also GRAMMAR.

PASCAL'S TRIANGLE. See NUMBER PATTERNS.

PASSOVER

Passover is the Jewish feast of freedom. It celebrates the Jews' deliverance from bondage in Egypt, described in the Bible as having happened about 3,000 years ago. It comes in March or April (the Hebrew month of *Nisan*), about the same time as Easter, and lasts for 8 days. It is a happy time, marked by synagogue services and a feast called the Seder.

The Story of Passover

In ancient days there was a time when Egypt was one of the mightiest nations in the world. It conquered smaller tribes and nations and made their people slaves. Among these people were the Hebrews, or Jews.

Pharaoh, the Egyptian king, forced the Hebrews to help build the great temples and pyramids. They had to pull heavy stones across the hot desert sands. They had little food. But worse, they were slaves. They had no freedom to live as they chose. They dreamed of escaping from Egypt to find a land of their own.

They found a great leader in Moses. The Bible tells us that Moses was a Hebrew baby whom Pharaoh's daughter found floating in the river in a basket. Moses grew up surrounded by luxury in Pharaoh's court. But he gave up all his riches to lead the Hebrews.

The Bible tells that Moses was commanded by God to lead the Hebrews out of slavery into the land of Canaan, which God had promised to the descendants of Abraham. Repeatedly, Moses asked Pharaoh to free the Hebrews. Each time Pharaoh refused, a plague fell upon the Egyptians. After the tenth plague, in which the firstborn in every Egyptian house died, Pharaoh agreed to let the Hebrews go. They wandered in exile for 40 years before they found their promised land. Moses died and never reached it at all.

The Hebrew flight from Egypt, called the Exodus, was the first known movement in the name of freedom. The Pilgrims, who came to America to escape oppression in England, compared their flight to the Exodus. In the American South, blacks in slavery sang about the flight out of Egypt while they dreamed of winning freedom for themselves.

The Observance of Passover Today

Jews everywhere gather every year to retell the Passover story. They eat *matzot*, the

At a Passover Seder, Jewish people read the *Haggadah*, which tells the story of the Jews' escape from slavery in Egypt. The foods served are symbolic of the story.

crisp, flat crackers that commemorate the unleavened dough that the Hebrews took with them in haste from Egypt. This *matzot* is the bread that Jesus broke with his disciples at the Last Supper, which was a Passover feast.

Passover is celebrated by worship services in the synagogue and gala feasts, or Seders, at home. The Seder is held on the first night of the holiday, and in Orthodox Jewish homes, it is also held on the second night.

The most important part of the Seder ceremony is the reading of the *Haggadah*, a book that tells the story of Passover. Each person at the table reads from the *Haggadah* in turn. All read the story as if they themselves had been slaves in Egypt and had been delivered from bondage by God. Prayers are said, and songs of thanksgiving are sung.

Children take part in the songs and reading. To the youngest goes the honor of asking the ceremonial four questions. The answers to these give the meaning of the Passover feast. A ceremonial Seder plate contains foods symbolic of Passover and of the ancient Jewish past. On the plate are a shank bone of lamb, an egg, bitter herbs, *charoset* (chopped apples, nuts, and wine), and parsley. The shank bone of lamb is a reminder of the time in the spring when Hebrew farmers sacrificed young lambs at the Temple in Jerusalem to celebrate the first harvest. The egg is the symbol of the renewal of life in the spring. The bitter herbs (usually horseradish) signify the bitterness of slavery in

Egypt. The *charoset* stands for the mortar that the Jews had to mix when they built pyramids for Pharaoh in Egypt. The parsley dipped in salt water marks both the salty tears of bondage and the green shoots of hope.

The *matzot* eaten during the eight days of Passover stands for the "bread of affliction" that the Hebrew slaves had to eat in Egypt. It also stands for the unleavened dough that the Hebrews brought with them from Egypt.

The Passover ceremony includes the drinking of wine. One cup of wine is set aside for the prophet Elijah. According to Jewish tradition, Elijah will appear on a Passover night to announce the Messiah and bring peace to the world. At a certain point in the ceremony, the door is opened to let the Prophet's spirit come in. This ceremony is also a reminder to Jews to have a special regard for strangers—because they themselves were once strangers in Egypt.

TOBY KARL KURZBAND
Co-author, *The Story of the Jewish Way of Life*
See also MOSES.

PASSPORTS AND VISAS

A passport is an official government document identifying a traveler as a citizen of the country that issued it. It also requests other governments to allow the bearer to travel freely. "Passport" comes from the two French words that mean "to pass" and "port."

A visa is an approval placed on the passport by a foreign government. "Visa" comes from the Latin word that means "to see." The visa indicates that the bearer has been granted permission to visit the country. Visa fees vary from country to country. Many are free. If a government does not wish a person to enter its country, it can refuse to grant a visa. Some governments require exit permits for residents leaving the country.

With a few exceptions, all U.S. citizens need passports to leave or enter the United States and to enter most foreign countries. U.S. citizens do not need passports for travel to Mexico and Canada. But these countries may require proof of citizenship.

The United States Government issues three types of passports. The diplomatic passport is for persons traveling on diplomatic missions for the government. The official passport is for persons traveling on official government business. The regular passport is for all other travelers.

A U.S. passport is valid for ten years from the date of issue. After that time, a new passport must be obtained. Passports are issued in the United States by the Passport Office of the Department of State. They are obtained through passport agencies in 13 major cities and through certain courts and some post offices. Previous passport holders may usually obtain a new passport by mail. While abroad, a U.S. citizen may obtain a new passport from a U.S. embassy or consulate. Canadian citizens obtain passports through the Department of External Affairs in Ottawa.

The United States requires visitors from most other countries to have both a passport (issued by their own country) and a visa (issued by the U.S. Foreign Service) to enter the United States. All persons wishing to immigrate permanently to the United States must obtain immigrant visas from consular officers of the U.S. Foreign Service.

Reviewed by EMIL W. KONTAK
Passport Office
United States Department of State
See also ALIENS; FOREIGN SERVICE; IMMIGRATION.
PASTE. See GLUE AND OTHER ADHESIVES.

A United States passport contains identification information and a color photograph of the bearer.

Pasteur helped prove that diseases are caused by harmful micro-organisms, or germs. His process for killing micro-organisms in food is now called pasteurization.

PASTEUR, LOUIS (1822–1895)

Louis Pasteur was a French chemist and microbiologist (someone who studies microscopic organisms) who contributed some of the most important ideas to modern science. He was one of the first people to discover that many diseases are caused by micro-organisms, or germs. The word ''pasteurize,'' usually used in reference to milk, comes from his name.

Louis was born on December 27, 1822, at Dôle, Jura, in eastern France. His father was a tanner. The family moved to Arbois when Louis was very young, and it was there that he grew up. One of his favorite hobbies as a boy was painting portraits.

In the fall of 1838, when he was 16 years old, Louis went to Paris to attend school. Homesickness drove him back to Arbois. The following year, Louis went to the college at Besançon, about 40 kilometers (25 miles) from Arbois. When he graduated in 1840, he became a teacher there.

Pasteur's Introduction to Chemistry

In 1842, Pasteur took the entrance examinations for the École Normale in Paris. This was a famous school established by Napoleon to train teachers for all of France. Pasteur passed the exams but decided his scores were not good enough. He studied and took the tests again a year later. He then entered the École Normale as the fourth-ranking student in his class.

Pasteur was fortunate in having excellent teachers, including three famous chemists of that time. All three chemists recognized that Pasteur had great ability in chemistry. From these men he learned of the latest discoveries in chemistry and the problems of greatest interest to chemists. One of these problems was that of the structure of crystals. While a student at the École Normale, Pasteur began research on crystal structure and other chemical problems.

In exchange for his education at the famous École Normale, Pasteur was required to serve as a schoolteacher for at least ten years. The leading French chemists were upset by this. They wanted Pasteur assigned to a research job, where they knew he held great promise. They pressured government officials. And as a result, Pasteur became a professor at the University of Strasbourg in 1848.

The next year he married Marie Laurent, the daughter of the rector, or head, of the university. They had five children (four girls and one boy). Only the boy and one of the girls survived early childhood.

At Strasbourg, Pasteur continued the research he had begun in Paris. Many of the crystals he studied were produced by the growth of mold and the spoiling of milk. This brought Pasteur to study the chemistry of living things. It was his introduction to **biochemistry,** the branch of science that deals with the chemical makeup and processes of living things.

Pasteur Helps the French Wine Industry

In 1854, Pasteur was appointed professor of chemistry and dean of science at the University of Lille. One important industry of the region was the production of alcohol from beet sugar. The beet sugar was fermented to produce alcohol. The producers of alcohol in Lille asked Pasteur to study fermentation, so that their product could be improved.

The producers of wine in eastern France learned of Pasteur's work on fermentation. Wine is produced by the fermentation of sugar in grapes. The wine producers were having serious trouble. The wine was turning sour instead of remaining sweet. The wine producers called upon Pasteur to investigate the source of the trouble.

At that time, most scientists thought that wine soured by itself because of some unknown action that took place in the wine. Pasteur doubted that wine could sour all by itself.

He went to eastern France and set up a laboratory there. After many experiments, he thought he had the answer to the problem. In 1857 he made a statement that was new to the world of science. He said that there were tiny micro-organisms (microscopic living things), floating in the air, that could cause chemical changes. When certain kinds of these micro-organisms got into wine, they caused the wine to sour. He said that some kinds of micro-organisms also caused milk to sour. Other kinds caused fermentation to take place.

Pasteur next showed that if the wine was heated to a certain temperature (about 57°C, or 135°F) and then cooled rapidly, many of the harmful micro-organisms were killed. This process, which is now called pasteurization in honor of Pasteur, kept the wine from spoiling.

Experiments with Milk

To show that micro-organisms from the air caused milk to spoil, Pasteur did another experiment. He heated some milk to kill many of the harmful micro-organisms in it. That is, he pasteurized the milk. Pasteur then showed that the milk soon spoiled when it was exposed to the air, because new micro-organisms were able to get into the milk. When he sealed pasteurized milk in a sterilized container, no new micro-organisms could get into the milk and it did not spoil so quickly.

In the 1850's many scientists thought that living things (such as micro-organisms) could arise from nonliving things. This idea was known as the **theory of spontaneous generation.** Pasteur's experiments helped prove this to be false. He believed that living things could only grow from other living things. A living micro-organism did not come from wine or milk. It appeared only when another micro-organism like itself reproduced.

The Germ Theory of Disease

Pasteur's reputation for solving practical problems spread rapidly. In 1865 the French Government asked him to study diseases of silkworms. By this time, Pasteur had come to think that diseases were caused by harmful micro-organisms called germs. This theory is called the germ theory of disease. Pasteur succeeded in finding the germs of two different silkworm diseases. He also found a way to prevent the spread of the diseases to healthy silkworms.

In 1877, Pasteur began an investigation of the disease called anthrax. This disease is found mainly in cattle and sheep. The animals that caught anthrax almost always died.

Pasteur found that he could inject healthy cows or sheep with weakened anthrax germs. That is, he **vaccinated** them against anthrax. The animals then did not get the disease.

But many scientists questioned Pasteur's results. To convince them, Pasteur conducted a public experiment with a herd of 50 sheep. He vaccinated half the herd against anthrax. A few days later he injected all the sheep with strong, live anthrax germs. He put the vaccinated sheep in one fenced-in field and the nonvaccinated sheep in another. Two days later the vaccinated sheep were healthy, but the others had all died of anthrax. Thus, Pasteur showed that vaccination against anthrax was effective.

Pasteur then developed other ways of making disease germs weak. He injected healthy persons with a small dose of weakened germs. These persons then became **immune** to the disease—they could not become sick from it.

Pasteur's most famous work in giving immunity to disease was with rabies. This disease is transmitted by the bite of a dog or other animal that carries the rabies virus. In 1885 he treated two boys who had been bitten by infected dogs and prevented the boys from getting rabies.

Pasteur's successful treatment for the prevention of rabies drew worldwide attention. People from all over the world contributed money for the establishment of a research institute in honor of Pasteur. This institute, located in Paris, was called the Pasteur Institute. Here Pasteur continued his research. Important research is still done there today.

Honors from many countries and scientific societies were showered upon Pasteur. Despite a stroke that partially paralyzed him, Pasteur continued his work for many years. He died in Villeneuve l'Éstang on September 28, 1895.

DUANE H. D. ROLLER
University of Oklahoma

PATENTS

Hundreds of years ago, English kings gave to some of their subjects papers known as **letters patent**. These papers gave to the person who received them some special privilege or favor. This might be the right to own a large tract of land or to explore a new territory. Or it might be the right to make and sell some product or article. In modern times the word **patent** has come to have a special meaning. It means the rights given by a government to a person who invented something. This includes the right to make and sell the invention or discovery or to profit from it by allowing another person or company to sell or use it.

The writers of the Constitution of the United States wanted to protect the rights of inventors. Article I, Section 8, says: "The Congress shall have Power . . . to promote the progress of Science and useful Arts, by securing for limited Times to . . . inventors the exclusive Right to their . . . Discoveries."

In 1790 the U.S. Congress passed the first patent law, and a Patent Office was set up soon afterward. The law provided that the inventor or discoverer has the right to own a patent for 17 years. After the 17-year period, anyone may use the patent without payment to, or permission from, the inventor.

The first U.S. federal patent was issued to Samuel Hopkins of Vermont for the ". . . making of Pot ash and Pearl ash by a new Apparatus, and Process." Since then, more than 5 million patents have been granted in the United States. Some 100,000 patents are issued and 50,000 trademarks are registered each year. In 1975 the Patent Office was renamed the Patent and Trademark Office. It is an agency of the U.S. Department of Commerce, and its offices are located in Arlington, Virginia.

The British Patent Office in its present form was created in 1883. British patent law is contained in the Patents Act of 1949. It gives an inventor the right to a patent for 16 years. After that the inventor may apply to have it extended for another five to ten years.

Most other countries have their own patent laws. Some countries, such as Russia, generally recognize inventors by awarding them inventors' certificates. Such papers do not give them ownership of their inventions. In some countries the invention must be produced within a certain period after the patent is granted. Otherwise the owner loses the right to the patent. In Canada, for example, this period is three years.

Many countries have signed international patent treaties that protect the rights of patent owners in countries other than the one granting the patent. An agreement called the Patent Co-operation Treaty took effect in 1978. It made it easier for an inventor to obtain protection in several countries.

Some Famous Patents. The patent granted in 1906 to the Wright brothers for their flying machine formed the basis of today's aircraft industry. The patented inventions of Samuel Morse and Alexander Graham Bell were the beginnings of the electronic communications industry. Edward H. Land's invention of a camera that could take, develop, and print pictures established a new field of photography. Thomas A. Edison, one of the most prolific inventors in history, obtained more than 1,000 patents.

How to Obtain a Patent. To be eligible for a patent, an invention must meet four legal requirements. The inventor must describe it in writing in enough detail for a person skilled in the art or technology to make and use it. The invention must be new. It must be useful. And it must be what is called "unobvious." An unobvious invention is one that is sufficiently different from earlier inventions that it does not appear obvious to a person of ordinary skill in that field.

When a patent application is submitted, it is assigned to an examiner. The examiner searches the files to be sure that the invention is new and unobvious. If the invention meets the four legal requirements, a patent is issued, and the inventor's rights come into effect. If the request for a patent is rejected, the inventor can attempt to convince the patent examiner that the invention should receive a patent. Or the inventor may alter the invention so that it meets the legal requirements. Inventors may file applications directly, but most inventors hire patent attorneys to obtain their patents for them. Patent law is a highly specialized field.

DONALD W. BANNER
U.S. Commissioner of Patents and Trademarks
See also INVENTIONS.

PATERSON. See NEW JERSEY (Cities).
PATERSON, WILLIAM. See NEW JERSEY (Famous People).

PATRICK, SAINT (389?–461?)

Saint Patrick is the most famous Irish saint. He was born in the late A.D. 300's, probably in Britain. His father, a Christian, was an official of the Roman Empire. When Patrick was about 16, he was captured by slave traders and taken to Ireland to be a shepherd.

Patrick led a life of hardship among the non-Christian Irish. One night he heard a voice telling him to return to his native land. He journeyed to the sea and in time made his way back to his people. Later, in another vision, he was told to return to Ireland as a missionary.

It is believed that Patrick studied for the priesthood in France and was made a bishop. He returned to Ireland around 430 with a group of missionary priests. For almost 30 years, Patrick worked among the Irish, establishing churches and baptizing thousands. He is also credited with founding a church and monastery at Armagh. Patrick resigned as bishop of Armagh in the late 450's and went to Saul in the north of Ireland, where it is believed he died in 461.

Many legends have grown up about Saint Patrick. One tells how he drove all the snakes of Ireland into the sea. Another relates how he explained the Trinity—the union of three persons in one God—by showing the people a shamrock, which has three leaves that grow from one stem. The shamrock became a national symbol of Ireland.

Saint Patrick's feast day is March 17.

KATHLEEN McGOWAN
Catholic Youth Encyclopedia

PATTON, GEORGE S. (1885–1945)

Outspoken, hot-headed, and strong-willed, General George S. Patton was one of the most controversial of the Allied commanders of World War II. Known as Old Blood and Guts, Patton was an inspired leader on the field of battle but lacked the diplomatic skills that would have made him one of the top-level commanders of the war.

Born in San Gabriel, California, on November 11, 1885, George Smith Patton, Jr., was descended from a long line of Virginia military officers. Upon graduation from the U.S. Military Academy at West Point in 1909, he was commissioned a second lieutenant in the cavalry. He served as an aide-de-camp to General John J. Pershing in Mexico (1916–17) and was the first man to lead a tank brigade in World War I, participating in the Saint-Mihiel and Meuse-Argonne offensives (1918).

When the United States entered World War II on December 8, 1941, Patton was a temporary major general and the commander of the Second Armored Division. In November 1942 he led the Western Task Force in the invasion of Morocco, in North Africa. He later took command of the Second Corps in Tunisia, and in July 1943 he was given command of the U.S. Seventh Army for the invasion of Sicily. After the Sicilian Campaign, Patton slapped two soldiers while visiting a hospital, believing the men were faking illness to avoid further combat. Patton, compelled to make a public apology, was called back to Britain in temporary disgrace.

On June 6, 1944, Patton led the Third Army in the invasion of Normandy, and in August he was promoted to major general. Advancing his troops through northern France, he assisted the Allied counterattack at the Battle of the Bulge, forcing the Germans to retreat from Bastogne. Patton later advanced across the Rhine River and relentlessly made his way through enemy territory.

When Germany collapsed in May 1945, Patton was made a full general and placed in charge of occupational forces in the American zone. But another controversial incident forced his removal to the inactive command of the Fifteenth Army. On December 9, 1945, Patton was severely injured in a car crash near Mannheim, Germany. He died on December 21 and was buried in Luxembourg.

Reviewed by JOHN KEEGAN
Author, *Who's Who in the Second World War*

PAUL, ALICE (1885–1977)

Alice Paul was a major figure during the final stages of the women's suffrage (right to vote) campaign and the author of the Equal Rights Amendment.

Born on January 11, 1885, in Moorestown, New Jersey, Paul was highly educated for a woman of her time. She earned a bachelor of arts degree (1905) from Swarthmore College; a masters (1907) and a doctoral degree (Ph.D.) (1912) from the University of Pennsylvania; and several law degrees, including one from Washington College of Law (1922).

While studying in England between 1907 and 1910, Paul took part in a number of militant demonstrations organized by Emmaline Pankhurst. She was arrested and imprisoned three times. In 1912, back in the States, Paul joined the National American Woman Suffrage Association (NAWSA) but quickly concluded that political speeches without militant action would not win the vote. Paul left NAWSA in 1913 and cofounded what be-

came the National Woman's Party (NWP).

On January 10, 1917, under Paul's leadership, the NWP began picketing the White House. That year, 500 women were arrested and 168, including Paul, were convicted of blocking a sidewalk. The women received sentences of up to seven months. In protest, Paul went on a hunger strike. She was force-fed and briefly transferred to a psychiatric hospital. A court of appeals later ruled that all the suffragists had been "illegally arrested, illegally convicted, and illegally imprisoned."

On August 26, 1920, the 19th Amendment to the U.S. Constitution was adopted, at last granting women the vote. Alice Paul drafted the Equal Rights Amendment in 1923 and campaigned tirelessly on its behalf until her death on July 9, 1977.

KATHRYN CULLEN-DUPONT
Author, *The Encyclopedia of Women's History in America*

See also WOMEN'S RIGHTS MOVEMENT.

PAUL, SAINT

Saint Paul was born at Tarsus in Asia Minor near the time of the birth of Jesus Christ. He was a Roman citizen as well as a Jew and was raised as a member of the strict sect called the Pharisees. His Jewish name was Saul, but outside the Jewish community, he was called Paul.

Paul became a leader in the persecution of the Christians. But on his way to Damascus to take action against the Christian community there, an event took place that changed the course of Christianity. The New Testament tells us that as Paul neared the city, a bright light blinded him. He heard a voice, which identified itself as Jesus, that commanded him to end his persecutions of the Christians. Paul was then taken to Damascus, where Ananias, a Christian, baptized him and his sight returned.

Paul spent the rest of his life establishing churches and spreading Jesus' teachings, often enduring abuse or imprisonment. Important to Paul's work were the epistles, or letters, that he wrote to various Christian communities. Known as the Pauline letters, they appear in the New Testament and teach much about the early Christian Church.

During Paul's last trip to Jerusalem, he was set upon by a mob accusing him of bringing non-Jews into the Temple. To protect him from the mob, the Romans arrested and later released him. It is believed he again took up his mission but was returned to Rome during the reign of Nero and executed about A.D. 67.

The Roman Catholic Church celebrates the feast of Saint Paul on June 29. It also honors his conversion with a feast day on January 25.

KATHLEEN McGOWAN
Catholic Youth Encyclopedia

PAUL VI, POPE (1897–1978)

Giovanni Battista Montini was born in Concesio in northern Italy on September 26, 1897. Montini was educated by the Jesuits at the seminary in Brescia. After ordination to the priesthood on May 29, 1920, he was sent to the Gregorian University in Rome for higher studies. A brilliant scholar, he also studied literature at the University of Rome.

In 1922, Montini entered the Academy of Noble Ecclesiastics, the training school for papal diplomats. While still a student, he was assigned to the nunciature, or papal embassy, of Poland. Poor health cut short this service, and he was recalled to Rome. In 1924, he entered the Vatican Secretariat of State.

From 1924 to 1933, Montini served as chaplain of the Federation of Italian Catholic University Students. In the growing struggle between church and state, Mussolini, the Fascist dictator, finally banned the federation. In 1937, Pope Pius XI made Montini Substitute Secretary of State of the Vatican.

Montini was appointed Archbishop of Milan in 1954. Four years later he became the first cardinal created by Pope John XXIII.

In 1963, after the death of Pope John, Montini was elected pope. He chose the name Paul and reconvened the Second Vatican Council, begun by Pope John, continuing the reform of the church and the efforts toward Christian unity. Pope Paul worked for world peace. In 1968 he issued an encyclical, "Humanae Vitae" ("Of Human Life"), maintaining the church's ban on artificial birth control.

Pope Paul was called the Pilgrim Pope because of his travels in many lands. He died at the Vatican on August 6, 1978.

Msgr. FLORENCE D. COHALAN
Cathedral College

PAULING, LINUS (1901–1994)

The American chemist Linus Carl Pauling was the only person to receive two unshared Nobel Prizes. Pauling's many other honors included the international Lenin Peace Prize (1972). His book *The Nature of the Chemical Bond* (1939) is considered a landmark of 20th-century science.

Pauling, who was born in Portland, Oregon, on February

26, 1901, had a searching and independent mind. He earned a bachelor's degree in chemical engineering from the Oregon Agricultural College. Pauling then attended the California Institute of Technology, earning a Ph.D. in physical chemistry in 1925. After studying in Europe for two years, Pauling returned to the California Institute of Technology to teach, becoming a full professor in 1931. He had a long and successful career there but left in 1963 to join the Center for the Study of Democratic Institutions in Santa Barbara, California. In 1969 Pauling joined Stanford University's faculty and helped to establish the Linus Pauling Institute of Science and Medicine.

His early work, for which Pauling received a Nobel Prize for chemistry in 1954, dealt with the structure of molecules. Through his studies, he was able to determine the physical properties of certain carbon compounds. It was also during the 1950's that Pauling became so concerned about nuclear bomb testing that he rallied other scientists to sign a petition against it. The petition, with more than 11,000 signatures, was presented to the United Nations. He also wrote *No More War!*, in which he presented his case against nuclear weapons. For this work he was awarded the Nobel Peace Prize in 1962.

Pauling's later work, which proved to be controversial, included the study of vitamin C and its role in preventing colds and cancer. He wrote *Vitamin C and the Common Cold* (1970) and coauthored *Vitamin C and Cancer* (1979). He died on August 19, 1994.

THOMAS H. METOS
Arizona State University

PAVLOV, IVAN (1849–1936)

Ivan Petrovich Pavlov was a famous Russian biologist. His studies of digestion in dogs led to new understandings about behavior in animals as well as in people. In 1904, he was awarded the Nobel Prize in physiology or medicine for his work.

Ivan was born on September 14, 1849, in the town of Ryazan, Russia. His father was a country priest in the Russian Orthodox Church. Because of ill health, Ivan did not enter school until he was 11. He attended a local seminary after finishing high school, but he was not enthusiastic about religious studies.

In 1870, Ivan entered the University of St. Petersburg. One of his teachers persuaded him to enter the field of physiology, which is the study of how the parts of living organisms function. He graduated in 1875 and went on to earn a degree in medicine from the Military Medical Academy in St. Petersburg. While still a student, Pavlov had already begun important research. His work focused on how the nervous system regulates blood circulation and digestion.

After studying in Germany for several years, Pavlov returned to St. Petersburg to study and teach. In 1895, he was appointed professor of physiology at the Military Medical Academy. While there, he also directed the Institute of Experimental Medicine, where he improved the standards of treatment and care for laboratory research animals.

Pavlov continued to be curious about digestion and how it was regulated by nerve impulses. He investigated the production of digestive juices, such as saliva, as a way to measure digestive processes. His best-known discovery concerned the flow of saliva in dogs. Pavlov was able to show that certain influences unrelated to food could start the flow of saliva.

In his now-famous experiments, Pavlov rang a bell every time one of his research dogs was fed. As the dog ate, saliva flowed in its mouth. After repeating this feeding routine many times, Pavlov then rang the bell without showing the dog any food. Even though no food was given to the dog, saliva still flowed from the dog's mouth. This happened each time the bell rang. Pavlov called this response, which was triggered by an external signal, a **conditioned reflex**. He believed it to be the basis for many kinds of animal behavior.

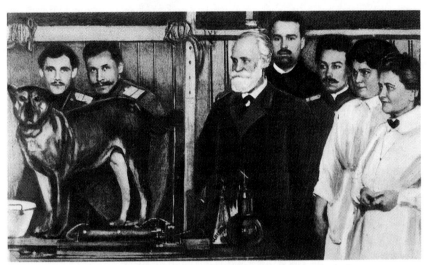

Before students of the Military Medical Academy, Ivan Pavlov (in center) demonstrates his famous experiment showing the conditioned reflex in a dog.

Pavlov later extended his theories to human psychology, stating that learned behavior is made up of many conditioned reflexes. He used these theories to develop treatments for mental illness, which he believed is caused by a breakdown in the brain's ability to process nerve impulses properly. He advocated quiet surroundings, hospitalization, and rest for people with mental illness.

Pavlov's work remains important because he showed that behavior—in both animals and humans—can be studied by examining small components of the behavior. He also showed that physiology can be used to understand problems of the mind. These ideas formed an important part of modern psychiatry. Pavlov died on February 27, 1936.

DUANE H. D. ROLLER
University of Oklahoma

See also LEARNING; PSYCHOLOGY.

A farmer in Belize works with a Peace Corps volunteer. Volunteers are trained in such fields as agriculture and health care and pass on their knowledge to their hosts.

PEACE CORPS

The Peace Corps is an organization of volunteers, sponsored by the United States Government. Its goal is to promote world peace, friendship, and understanding. To achieve this goal, members of the Peace Corps go to interested countries to help them meet their needs for trained workers.

President John F. Kennedy established the Peace Corps by executive order in March of 1961. Since 1971 it has been a part of ACTION, the U.S. Government agency for volunteer activities at home and abroad.

Peace Corps volunteers must be United States citizens and must be at least 18 years old. Many are over 60. In the early days most volunteers were teachers who staffed classrooms around the world. Today volunteers are also asked to help a country improve its health care, food production, or water supply, especially in rural areas.

Some volunteers come to the Peace Corps already trained in such fields as nursing, forestry, and agriculture. But most volunteers are trained by the Peace Corps. Host countries explain what they need, and volunteers are trained to do a specific job.

No matter what their jobs, all volunteers are still involved in teaching, although they are no longer mainly in classrooms. Their aim is to work themselves out of a job by training local people to take their place.

Volunteers for the Peace Corps are selected on merit. Candidates must first fill out a questionnaire. Those who have the needed skills are invited to train for a project in a certain country. They may accept or refuse the invitation, state a preference for another country, or ask to be invited for another project at a later date.

Volunteers must be dedicated to their jobs —whether they are teaching in a school, helping to improve local farming methods, working in a hospital, or surveying for mineral resources. They must be prepared to work hard, and they must always show understanding. Peace Corps members are a kind of ambassador for their country.

Training of Peace Corps volunteers is held at colleges and universities in the United States and at other sites. Extensive training within the host country gives trainees experience in the culture in which they will work. They spend 60 or more hours a week in study of the language, history, geography, economy, and customs of the host country.

The term of service is about 24 months, not including the training period. Volunteers are given allowances that cover clothing and living costs. When they leave the Peace Corps, they receive a payment for each month of satisfactory service, including the training period. All necessary transportation between a member's home, training station, and overseas post is provided.

Today Peace Corps volunteers serve in many countries in Africa, Asia, and Latin America. The number in each country varies widely. The success of the Peace Corps program can be measured by the fact that most countries where members are at work ask that more be sent.

For many members, service in the Peace Corps is a great adventure. This sense of adventure is heightened by the Peace Corps ideal of service to people in other nations of the world. Returning members have gained new understanding of the people, language, beliefs, and traditions of another country.

CAROLYN R. PAYTON
Former Director, Peace Corps

PEACE MOVEMENTS

The search for peace on earth is almost as old as human history. Most of the world's great religions preach the wickedness of war and hold forth the vision of peace and harmony among people. Since the days of ancient Egypt and Greece, practical efforts to set up organizations to guard the peace have been made in almost all parts of the world and in almost every century. They have been especially common in the 19th and 20th centuries.

In Western Europe, ideas for plans to promote peace date back many hundreds of years. In the 1300's, Pierre Dubois, a French jurist and politician, and Dante Alighieri, the famous Florentine poet, made definite suggestions for the establishment of universal peace. Similar plans were put forward by Desiderius Erasmus, a 16th-century Dutch scholar. In 1625, Hugo Grotius, a Dutch jurist, introduced the idea of international law in his book *De jure belli ac pacis (The Law of War and Peace)*. Also in the early 1600's, Henry IV of France and his minister, the Duc de Sully, proposed the so-called Great Design. This was a federation of Christian nations that aimed at enforcing the peace. Other plans were suggested by Pennsylvania's founder, William Penn, in the late 1600's and by the German philosopher Immanuel Kant a century later.

Organized peace movements became significant only in the early years of the 19th century. In 1815, three peace societies were formed in the United States—in New York, Massachusetts, and Ohio. Noah Worcester, founder of the Massachusetts society, wrote a book entitled *A Solemn Review of the Custom of War* (1814). He was one of the first to urge co-operation among peace societies.

In 1816 the British Society for the Promotion of Permanent and Universal Peace was established in London. Within the next five years, other societies were founded in France and Switzerland. In 1828 the American peace groups were united by William Ladd, one of the true pioneers of the peace movement. The united movement was given the name of the American Peace Society. Ladd's plan for a congress and a court of nations was approved by the society. The plan was also backed by the London Peace Society in England.

Between 1843 and 1851, peace societies in various Western countries sponsored five international peace conferences. A Universal Peace Congress was held in Brussels, Belgium, in 1848 to bring about "the entire abolishment of war." It supported the suggestion of an American, Elihu Burritt, for the creation of a congress of nations to prepare a code of international law. At a similar congress in Paris in 1849, the famous French writer Victor Hugo urged the formation of a United States of Europe. After the fifth congress, held in London in 1851, few efforts toward peace were made for 20 years. Three wars—the Crimean War (1854–55), the United States Civil War (1861–65), and the Franco-Prussian War (1870–71)—took place during these years.

Between the late 1800's and World War I, peace efforts were revived. They became more practical and more effective than earlier movements had been. Official and unofficial associations gave powerful support to the three basic aims of the peace movement: disarmament, use of peaceful methods (especially arbitration) of settling disputes between nations, and development of international law. A vast peace congress in Paris in 1878 endorsed these three aims. It also proposed an international federation of peace societies in various countries. Most of these societies took part in the Universal Peace Congress in 1889 and in similar congresses held almost every year thereafter. In 1892 an International Peace Bureau was formed in Bern, the capital of Switzerland. Over 400 peace societies were in existence in 1900.

The Hague conferences of 1899 and 1907, held in the Netherlands, were major international peace conferences. They attracted attention worldwide to the problems of disarmament and arbitration and to the principles of international law. They helped to prepare the way for the formation of the League of Nations after World War I and also for the United Nations after World War II.

Peace societies were especially numerous in the United States. Many Americans were prominently connected with peace movements. Many of the gifts of Scottish-born Andrew Carnegie, the famous American industrialist and philanthropist, went to further the cause of peace. The Carnegie Peace Palace at The Hague now houses the International Court of Justice. The Hague Academy of International Law, the Peace Palace, and the Carnegie Endowment for International Peace were all founded in 1910. They are living memorials to Andrew Carnegie's lifelong interest in peace.

Two other outstanding American peace workers were Jane Addams, the founder of Hull House in Chicago, and Nicholas Murray Butler, president of Columbia University from 1902 to 1945 and of the Carnegie Endowment for International Peace from 1925 to 1945. In 1931, Addams and Butler were joint winners of the Nobel peace prize. President Woodrow Wilson was, of course, a great champion of world peace. He was largely responsible for the founding of the League of Nations. The League's Covenant was incorporated into peace treaties ending World War I.

In the period between the two world wars, many of the peace movements supported the League of Nations and were associated with the International Federation of League of Nations Societies. These movements were in favor of the Briand Plan for European Union, proposed by Foreign Minister Aristide Briand of France in 1930. They also supported the Kellogg-Briand Pact (Pact of Paris) of 1928 and the ill-fated disarmament conference that lasted from 1932 to 1937. Some of the movements were in favor of suggestions for a federal union on a regional or global basis. One such plan was for a United States of Europe. Another was Union Now, in which the United States would join either with Britain or with all the leading democracies of the world. Similar approaches are now supported by world federalist organizations in many countries.

What Is a Pacifist?

A pacifist is a person who opposes war or violence as a means of settling disputes and who works for peace between nations. Pacifists believe that all wars are wrong—international wars as well as revolutions for national independence. They oppose defensive wars as well as wars of aggression.

Religion has played an important part in encouraging pacifism. The belief in nonviolence and nonresistance is characteristic of such Asian religions as Buddhism, Taoism, and Hinduism. There is also a strong element of pacifism in Christianity, especially among such sects as the Quakers (Society of Friends), Church of the Brethren, Moravians, Mennonites, and Doukhobors. Members of these sects oppose all forms of militarism. They are conscientious objectors and refuse to join the armed forces or to carry arms.

World War II was a great blow to hopes for peace. The horrors of that war and the even greater horrors of war in the nuclear age have given new life to movements to prevent war and to lay the foundations for real peace.

Peace conferences and organizations dedicated to peace are important features of present-day international life. The United Nations, whose Charter was drafted and approved even before the end of World War II, is a major peace organization. Its central purpose, as stated in Article 1 of its Charter, is "to maintain international peace and security." Many of the existing peace movements have been organized to support the United Nations.

In the 1960's, opponents of the Vietnam War formed many new peace groups, in the United States and elsewhere. These peace groups marched in parades and demonstrated against the war and the role the United States played in it. The peace groups also ran candidates for public office and issued statements explaining their antiwar stand. Some people in the United States have called for the establishment of a national peace academy—an institution devoted to the study of peace.

In recent years the antinuclear movement has grown large, especially in Western Europe and the United States. The antinuclear movement is supported by a wide variety of religious and nonreligious groups and organizations. The movement also has the sympathy, and occasionally the formal support, of political parties in several Western European countries. In West Germany a political party known as the Greens, formed in 1979, has made opposition to nuclear weapons a central feature of its platform. In national elections in 1983, the Greens won 27 seats in the West German parliament.

Peace movements, sincere or otherwise, exist in all parts of the world. They vary greatly in nature, size, and influence. They may be official or unofficial. Some are limited in their aims. Others have almost unlimited goals, such as general and complete disarmament, world government, or the complete abolition of war. All have given new dimensions to the search for peace in the nuclear age.

NORMAN D. PALMER
University of Pennsylvania

See also DISARMAMENT; INTERNATIONAL LAW; INTERNATIONAL RELATIONS; LEAGUE OF NATIONS; UNITED NATIONS.

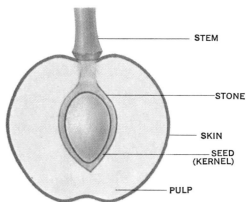

STEM

STONE

SKIN

SEED
(KERNEL)

PULP

PEACH, PLUM, AND CHERRY

Peaches, plums, and cherries are similar types of fruit. They have a thin outer skin, a soft juicy pulp, and a single seed in the center. The seed is covered with such a hard shell that these fruits are known as **stone fruits.** Stone fruits are also called **drupes.** Other drupes are apricots and nectarines.

▶**PEACH**

The peach was first grown in China thousands of years ago. It came to Europe by way of Persia (Iran) and was known for many years as the Persian apple. The Romans planted peaches in the sunny and mild parts of their empire. When the Spanish explorers set out for the New World, they, too, took the seeds of many plants, including peaches, with them. Peaches soon grew wild over the southern part of what is now the United States.

Peaches are grouped as **freestone** or **clingstone.** Freestone peaches have a pit that separates easily from the flesh. The pit in clingstone peaches is firmly attached.

Commercial peaches are carefully selected varieties that are bred from two groups—the so-called Persian peaches from Europe and other peaches brought from China. The Elberta peach, for example, is a cross between a Persian peach and a Chinese cling peach. Today more than 100 varieties of peaches— differing in season of ripening and color of skin and flesh—are grown commercially around the world.

The United States grows more peaches than any other country. California is the world's peach-canning center. Peach trees also thrive in parts of Canada, Europe, Asia, South Africa, Australia, and South America.

Nectarines. Nectarines are fuzzless, or smooth-skinned, peaches. They have been in existence as long as the ordinary peach, but they have never been as widely grown.

Apricots. Apricots look like fuzzless small peaches but have a slightly tart taste. In most temperate areas, apricots bloom so early that the blossoms are usually killed by frost. In warm, humid climates, the fruit cracks and decays. The warm, dry areas bordering on the Mediterranean Sea are well suited for apricots. California, where the climate also is warm and dry, is the center for apricot production in

Apricots are a stone fruit, like peaches, plums, and cherries. They look like small, smooth peaches.

These colorful Stanley prune plums are ready to be harvested. They will be dried and used as prunes.

The cherry trees most commonly grown today originated in Europe and western Asia. There are two main groups of cherries, sweet and sour (or tart). Sour cherries are mainly canned or frozen for later use in pies, preserves, and juice. Sweet cherries are eaten fresh, or they are canned or made into maraschino cherries. Maraschino cherries are colored bright red and are used as a decoration in drinks and desserts.

Cherries thrive in cool, temperate regions. But since they do not keep well, not many are exported fresh. In the United States, sour cherries are grown mostly near the Great Lakes. Most sweet cherries are grown in California, Oregon, and Washington.

►GROWING STONE FRUITS

Stone fruits are not grown straight from seed because the fruit of a tree grown from seed may be very different from the fruit of the parent tree. Instead the trees are budded onto a rootstock. A rootstock is usually a seedling of a variety of peach, plum, or cherry.

Stone-fruit trees grow best in a crumbly, fairly rich soil. Fruitgrowers cultivate the ground in spring and early summer, but they stop as the crop is beginning to ripen. In the fall a cover crop, such as rye or buckwheat, may be planted, or weeds are allowed to grow to keep the soil around the trees from eroding. The cover crops or weeds are turned under in the spring to enrich the soil. Fertilizing with nitrogen, and in some areas with potassium, also helps the trees.

Peach trees are more heavily pruned than other fruit trees. Because the color of the fruit improves with the amount of light that reaches it, young peach trees are usually pruned into the shape of a vase or a bowl. Young plum and cherry trees are trimmed to three to five branches on one main trunk. The trees must also be kept at a good picking height. Some varieties, such as Japanese plums, put out such a large crop of fruit that they must be as heavily pruned as peach trees.

Fruit trees are attacked by many insects, fungi, and viruses. New varieties of fruit trees, resistant to certain diseases, are being developed by plant geneticists. Various sprays have also been developed to combat insects and fungus diseases. Trees may be sprayed up to five or six times during the growing season.

the United States. Apricots are eaten fresh, canned, or dried, or they are made into juice, jams, and preserves.

►PLUM

There are three basic groups of plums—European, Japanese, and American.

European plums first grew in western Asia. Today eastern and central Europe are very important plum-producing areas. European plums were taken to North America by English and French colonists. The prune plum, which is meaty and suitable for drying, has done especially well in California. Today the United States is the largest producer of prunes.

Japanese plums actually had their beginning in China. They came to Japan at an unknown date. They were introduced to the United States about 1870. Luther Burbank helped to popularize them, and now they are extensively grown, mainly in California. The flesh is generally soft and juicy.

American plums have little commercial value today, but they were an important source of food in early America. Commonly called beach plums, American plums are very hardy and can be grown in colder climates than the Japanese and European varieties. They make very good jams and jellies.

Montmorency sour cherries are pulled from their stems and boxed for shipment to a cannery. Cherries that will be sold fresh are picked with their stems on.

▶ BLOOMING AND FRUIT BEARING

To bloom normally in the spring, peach, plum, and cherry trees need a period of a few weeks to several months of fairly cold temperatures in winter. The cold weather stops the growth of the trees and allows them to rest. But too severe a winter damages the fruit buds on the trees. Since peach trees bloom very early, they also are in danger from spring frosts. The hardiest stone fruits are the sour cherry and the American plum.

Most varieties of peach, sour cherry, and apricot trees are self-fruitful. This means that their blossoms can be fertilized by pollen from trees of the same variety.

The leading variety of sour cherry, the **Montmorency,** is self-fruitful, but sweet cherries are not. But if the fruitgrower plants the proper varieties of sweet cherry trees together, pollen is carried by honeybees and other insects from trees of one variety to another. Many varieties of plum trees can be fertilized only by pollen from certain other varieties of plum trees.

In some areas, peach trees may pass good producing condition in 10 years, but they may last 20 years or more in other sections. Plum trees and cherry trees last longer. Sour cherries generally do not give a good crop after 25 years nor do sweet cherries after 30 years.

▶ HARVESTING

Peaches become ripe from June to October, depending on their variety and location. Peaches are picked at different stages of ripeness, depending on how far they have to be shipped and whether they will be sold as fresh fruit or sent to canneries. Peaches soften rapidly at warm temperatures, but they can be held in storage about a month if they are kept a little above freezing temperatures. Peaches for canning are picked when they are firm but not quite table ripe.

Peaches are covered with a light fuzz. Those that are sent to fresh markets are passed through a brush machine that removes most of the fuzz from the fruit.

Plums ripen from June through October and are usually harvested several times as they ripen. Plums for canning can be picked all at one time. Prune plums are gathered in two ways. Some fall naturally from the trees. The others must be shaken off. Mechanical shakers are widely used for prune plums. Plums can be kept fresh for three to four weeks if they are stored at temperatures just above freezing.

Cherries are picked from June to August. The picker must wait until the cherries are fully ripe to get them at their best. But birds can often damage the crop. Rainy weather is also a threat to the crop because the rain soaks into the ripe cherries, and they crack open. Cherries are picked with their stems on when they are to be sold fresh. Cherries for canning are "pulled" (the stems are left on the tree).

To prevent sour cherries from spoiling, they are often hauled from the orchards to processing plants in trucks equipped with tanks of cold water. The water washes the cherries and prevents crushing. Sweet cherries can be left in cold storage for about three weeks.

▶ PROCESSING

Nearly half the peaches grown in the United States are canned. Plum, cherry, and apricot canning is a smaller part of the fruit-canning business. Stone fruits can also be dried or frozen fresh. Poorer grades of fruit are used to make jams, jellies, and pie fillings.

Reviewed by RODNEY W. DOW
State University of New York Agricultural
and Technical College at Farmingdale

See also AGRICULTURE; FOOD PRESERVATION; FRUITGROWING; RECIPES.

PEALE FAMILY

Peale is the name of a distinguished family of American painters who flourished in the 1700's and 1800's.

Charles Willson Peale (1741–1827), born in Queen Anne's County, Maryland, was a leading portrait painter. He taught himself to paint as a young man, after learning saddle making, clock repair, and several other trades. In 1766 he went to London to study with the American painter Benjamin West. During the Revolutionary War, Peale fought with the Philadelphia militia. Resuming his painting career after the war, he painted portraits of famous Americans of his day, notably George Washington. In 1782 he opened a portrait gallery next to his home.

Peale had many scientific interests, including archaeology, engineering, and taxidermy, and he patented several inventions. In 1786 he established a natural history museum, the first of its kind in the nation. He also helped found the Pennsylvania Academy of the Fine Arts (1805) and the Society of Artists (1810), which were among the first professional organizations in the United States to promote the development of the arts.

Peale had 17 children, some of whom were named for famous artists. He instructed them in painting, and several became artists in their own right. **Raphaelle Peale** (1774–1825) was a painter of still lifes—arrangements of fruits and flowers—which he depicted with a high degree of realism. But his masterpiece is a painting called *After the Bath* (1823), which showcases his ability to create a convincing illusion of reality. **Rembrandt Peale** (1778–1860) specialized in portraits of famous Americans, especially idealized images of George Washington. **Rubens Peale** (1784–1865) painted nature subjects and opened a museum in New York City. **Titian Ramsay Peale** (1799–1885) was a naturalist and scientific illustrator.

Charles Willson's brother **James Peale** (1749–1831) was also a painter. He was known particularly for his miniatures and still lifes. Three of James's daughters achieved success as painters. **Anna Claypoole Peale** (1791–1878) was a noted miniaturist; **Margaretta Angelica Peale** (1795–1882) painted still lifes; and **Sarah Miriam Peale** (1800–85) specialized in portraits of famous people.

Reviewed by KENNETH HALTMAN
New Britain Museum of American Art

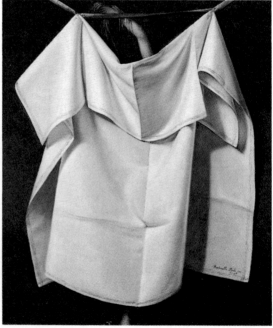

Left: In *The Artist in His Museum*, Charles Willson Peale painted himself at the entrance to his natural history museum. *Below: After the Bath* is considered the masterpiece of Charles Willson's son Raphaelle.

PEANUTS AND PEANUT PRODUCTS

The peanut is one of the important foods discovered in the New World. It has a pod that contains two or more nutlike seeds. In the United States the word "peanut" is used for these seeds and their pod. The same pods and seeds are called groundnuts in Britain because the pods develop underground. Both names suggest that the peanut is really a nut, which it is not. The peanut produces underground pods from above-ground flowers, making it a very unusual plant.

Peanuts can be used for many different products. George Washington Carver, who rose from slavery to become a great agricultural chemist, found many new uses for peanuts. He used them to make substitutes for milk, butter, cheese, coffee, and flour. He also used them to make nonfood products, such as ink, dye, soap, and insulation.

▶THE HISTORY OF PEANUTS

Peanuts probably originated in Bolivia or Brazil. Even now many varieties of wild peanuts grow in central South America. Cultivated peanuts, *Arachis hypogaea*, have been grown in both North America and South America for thousands of years.

Early in the 1500's, Portuguese traders carried peanuts to several places in Africa. The plants spread so quickly that a hundred years later they were as plentiful as native African plants. Portuguese and Spanish traders probably carried the plants to the East Indies and from there, it is believed, on to India and China.

Today India and China together grow about half the peanuts in the world. The plants are still grown in much of Africa and in Burma, Indonesia, and Brazil. Argentina and the United States also grow large quantities of peanuts.

▶WHAT IS THE PLANT LIKE?

There are different varieties of peanut plants, but all of them have an erect central stem that grows from 8 to 36 inches (20 to 90 centimeters) tall. There are three main types. Spanish varieties have a bunchy plant. Virginia varieties have many branches. Runner varieties have branches that stretch out into a mat that is about 3 feet (1 meter) or more in diameter.

The plant has flowers that look like yellow buttercups. They last only for a day. They develop during the night and open at sunup. The flowers are almost always self-pollinated, usually even before the blossoms open. During the afternoon the flowers wither. By midnight the process of fertilization is complete.

After a few days the fertilized part of the flower starts to grow toward the ground. It grows down 2 to 4 inches (5 to 10 centimeters) into the soil. In the soil, the peg, or stem, begins to enlarge at the end and form a pod with seeds. In about 65 days the seeds in the pod are fully grown.

SOME USES OF PEANUTS

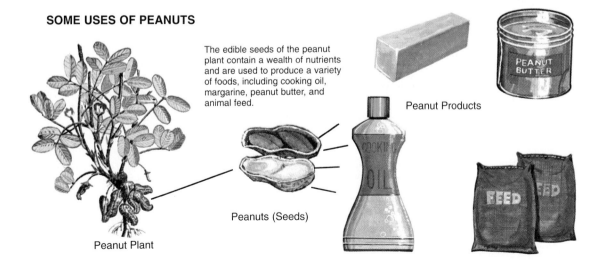

The edible seeds of the peanut plant contain a wealth of nutrients and are used to produce a variety of foods, including cooking oil, margarine, peanut butter, and animal feed.

Peanut Products

Peanuts (Seeds)

Peanut Plant

Different varieties produce different sizes of peanuts. Runner peanuts are the largest, averaging about 700 seeds per pound (1,500 per kilogram). Virginia peanuts are smaller, and Spanish peanuts the smallest of all.

▶ GROWING AND HARVESTING PEANUTS

Peanut plants need hot weather and plenty of moisture during the time they are blooming and forming pods. After this stage the plant does not need so much warmth and moisture for good growth. If it is rainy during the time just before harvest, the pegs weaken. Some of the peanuts break off and are left in the ground during harvest. Rain at this time may also cause the seeds of the Spanish varieties to start sprouting.

If the soil in which a peanut is planted is warm and moist, the roots grow rapidly. By the time leaves appear above ground, the roots may be more than 14 inches (35 centimeters) long. By the time the pods are fully grown and ready to harvest, the roots may reach a depth of 3 to 5 feet (1 to 1.5 meters). The deep roots enable the plant to reach moisture far down in the soil during a dry spell. A well-drained, loose sandy-loam soil is best for a peanut crop because roots grow more freely in such soil.

Because of its long roots the peanut plant can sometimes use nutrients that are too deep in the soil for other plants to use. Peanut plants use large quantities of nutrients, and fertilizer is applied regularly.

Before the seeds are sown, the soil is plowed and harrowed into a fine, smooth seedbed. Fertilizer is added. The seeds are shelled and are treated with a fungicide. They are planted soon after a rain so that they will sprout immediately.

In harvesting peanuts, a mechanical digger lifts the plants and shakes the soil off. It inverts them in long rows, where they dry for two days or more. Then the pods are threshed from the vines by harvesters.

When they are properly dried, peanuts contain only 7 to 10 percent moisture. They may then be stored for months if kept dry. They will keep much longer in cold storage. In the peanut industry, much of a year's crop is shelled and processed by spring.

▶ PEANUTS AS FOOD

Peanuts are among the most nutritious of all vegetable foods. Because about half the seed is oil, it has a very high energy value. There is more protein in peanuts than in the same weight of steak or ham. Peanuts have a low starch content and are rich in the vitamin B complex. Peanuts are eaten in many different ways. We may eat salted peanuts, peanut candy, peanut butter in sandwiches, or peanut oil in fried foods.

When salted peanuts are being prepared, they usually are blanched to remove the skins. This is done by heat or water treatments, which loosen the skins, and blowers, which remove them. Then the nuts are roasted in oil and salted. The nuts may also be dry-roasted (roasted without oil).

The peanuts used to make peanut butter are dry-roasted and blanched. Then they are ground very fine. Sometimes small amounts of other foods—such as salt, honey, vegetable oils, or yeast—are added to make the peanut butter tastier, easier to spread, and more nutritious.

A large part of the world production of peanuts is used to make peanut oil. Peanut oil is much like olive oil. In Europe it is used to make margarine. In North America it is used as a salad and cooking oil. It is an excellent oil for frying because it can become very hot without spattering.

Peanuts are also used in feed for animals. Peanut meal adds protein to the diet of livestock. The vines are used as forage for hogs and cattle.

ROBERT C. LEFFEL
United States Department of Agriculture

See also NUTS.

See For Yourself

HOW TO MAKE YOUR OWN PEANUT BUTTER

If you have a food grinder or an electric blender, you can easily make peanut butter. You need dry-roasted peanuts and peanut or vegetable oil.

Grind about ¼ cup of the peanuts at a time. Grind until the mixture is like paste. Add a teaspoon or less of oil to make it smoother. You may also wish to add a dash of salt. Mix thoroughly.

Store the peanut butter in a tightly covered container, and keep it in the refrigerator. Because your peanut butter has no chemical additives, it will separate on standing. Stir it before using.

PEAR

The pear is native to Asia and nearby Europe. Stone Age people discovered and ate the juicy fruit of the pear tree. As civilization developed, pear trees were improved by selecting and planting the best of the wild trees.

The Romans gave us the name for the group of fruits to which pears belong. The Roman word for fruits was *poma*, and **pome fruits** is the name now applied to apples, pears, and quinces. These fruits all have a thin outer skin, a fleshy pulp, and a core that has five parts in which the seeds are borne.

During the 1700's fruitgrowers in Europe, especially in Belgium and France, tried to improve the quality of pears by crossing different varieties. A Belgian priest, Nicolas Hardenpont (1705–74), developed the first of the pears having soft, juicy pulp that are now called butter pears. He and other pear breeders created many high-quality varieties. Some of these varieties are still grown.

The colonists brought European pears to America, and at first they did well. About the time of the Revolution, however, the trees began to die. The disease that killed them, called fire blight, was later found to be caused by bacteria that live in the bark. Although all high-quality European pears can be attacked by fire blight, the disease is less severe on the Pacific coast. For this reason 90 percent of the pears in the United States are grown in California, Oregon, and Washington.

Pears brought from eastern Asia were found to resist the fire blight disease. They were so hard and gritty, however, that they were called sand pears. Some of the sand pears and European pears growing nearby crossed naturally. Several of these crosses proved resistant to the blight and were also of better quality than the sand pears. The variety called Bosc is one of these. It is the most widely grown pear east of the Rocky Mountains. But it is very poor in quality compared to European varieties. Recently some high-quality varieties that resist fire blight have been developed by scientific breeding.

Fire blight has spread to Europe, but so far it has not been a serious problem there. The pear is an even more important crop in Western Europe than in North America.

All countries in the temperate zones, both north and south of the equator, produce pears. Commercially grown pears are not produced directly from seed because the fruit on trees grown from seed is usually poor. Instead, buds or shoots from the desired variety are grafted onto a young tree grown from seed. The new tree grown in this way will produce fruit like that of the parent.

Insects attack pears, and in rainy areas, fungus diseases must be controlled. The trees are sprayed several times a year to control these pests and diseases.

For the best quality, pears must be picked while still hard and still green in color. If they are to be kept for a long time, they are placed in cold storage immediately at a temperature set at freezing. If they are to be used soon, they are held at 65 to 70°F (18 to 21°C). At this temperature, they become ready for eating in one to two weeks.

The Bartlett variety, called Williams in Europe, is the most important in the United States and other pear-growing countries. It is used fresh or canned. Some pears are dried. In Europe, pears are also used for making perry, a fermented pear juice.

Reviewed by RODNEY W. DOW
State University of New York
Agricultural and Technical College
at Farmingdale

See also FRUITGROWING.

BARTLETT PEAR

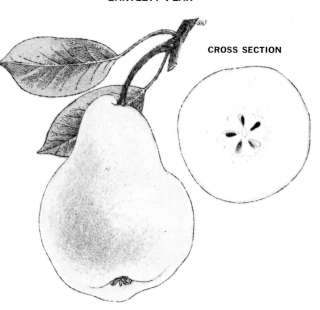

CROSS SECTION

A Japanese bay (*above*) is the site of an unusual kind of farm. Cages of oysters hang from rafts floating in the calm waters. Within the captive oysters, precious gems are forming. At harvest time, the oysters are gathered, and lustrous pearls (*shown in inset*) are plucked from the oysters.

PEARLS

The pearl is one of the most popular of all precious gems. It is the only one created by a living creature. Its softly shining beauty has made the word "pearl" mean almost the same thing to us as "beauty" and "great worth."

Pearls are made by certain kinds of oysters, clams, and mussels. All these animals are called **mollusks**, from a Latin word meaning "soft," because they have soft bodies inside their hard shells. The pearl is actually composed of the material with which a mollusk coats an irritating particle that it cannot get rid of. This irritant may be a piece of broken shell, a parasite that has bored through the shell, or even a tiny grain of sand. The material the mollusk keeps layering onto the piece to keep it from being an irritation is **nacre**, or **mother-of-pearl**. As many layers of mother-of-pearl are built up, a pearl is made.

What Makes a Pearl Valuable?

Natural pearls are found rarely, and large natural pearls even more rarely. The largest known natural pearl is one such rare find. Found in the shell of a giant clam and named the *Pearl of Lao-tze*, it weighs 14.06 pounds (6.38 kilograms)!

Only a few of the pearls found are considered valuable. A valuable pearl has a beautiful shimmering luster, which jewelers call the pearl's **orient**. The luster comes from below the surface of the gem. It is caused by light that is reflected and refracted (broken up) by the different layers of the pearl. Pearls that come from saltwater mollusks are the most sought after since they have a high degree of luster. Color, texture, and shape also determine a pearl's value.

Color is influenced by the type of oyster, the salt content of the water, the depth at which the oyster lives, and the temperature of the water. Pearls are usually white, cream, pink or rose, blue-gray, or black. White is generally the most popular color. Black pearls are especially treasured for their rarity.

The **round pearl** has the most desirable shape. It develops in the soft parts of the mollusk. A solid pearl in any irregular shape is called a **baroque pearl**. When a pearl becomes attached to the inside of the shell, it becomes a **button pearl**, rounded on one side and flat on the other. Sometimes a mollusk covers an injured spot on its shell with extra nacre, and then a **blister pearl** forms.

▶ NATURAL PEARLS

Not every pearl formed is valuable. Only those mollusks whose shells are coated on the inside with iridescent mother-of-pearl produce precious pearls. The most beautiful and costly pearls are almost all found in species of the *Pinctada*, a pearl oyster that lives in tropical seas. The pearls in edible clams and oysters are usually of poor quality and valueless.

Saltwater Pearls. Many of the finest natural pearls come from the Persian Gulf, especially the area off the coast of the island country Bahrain. In ancient times, Bahrain had a thriving pearling industry. However, Bahrain's economic activity now centers around the oil industry. Beautiful white and silvery pearls are found off the west coast of Sri Lanka. The pearl beds of Sri Lanka have been a source of pearls for more than 2,000 years, making them the oldest pearl fisheries. Fine black pearls are found off the west coast of Mexico and the United States. Natural saltwater pearls are also found near Australia and some islands of the South Pacific and of the Caribbean.

Freshwater Pearls. Pearls are also found in the mollusks inhabiting rivers and lakes of North and South America, Europe, and Asia. At one time, pearl-bearing mollusks were abundant in the rivers of the upper Mississippi Valley. But overfishing caused the population to fall so sharply that it was almost eliminated. Freshwater pearls from the Mississippi Valley are now rarely found.

▶ CULTURED PEARLS

Hundreds of years ago the Chinese discovered that objects would be covered with mother-of-pearl if they were placed inside the shells of clams and oysters. After experimentation

To produce a cultured pearl, the shell of a young oyster is opened, and a small bead made of mother-of-pearl is inserted (*above*).

Oysters with beads implanted are carefully tended in submerged cages (*above*). One to three years later, the oysters are gathered and the pearls nestled safely within (*below*) are harvested.

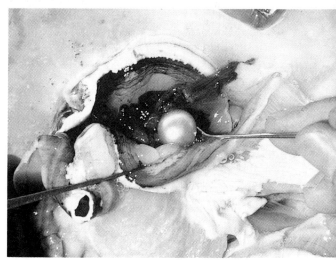

How are artificial pearls made?

Artificial, or simulated, pearls do not come from oysters at all. Instead they are manufactured from glass or plastic beads, which are covered with a nacrelike film. The film is made from fish scales. Artificial pearls may also be made by coating the inside of hollow glass beads with the nacre film.

that started in the late 1800's, some Japanese researchers learned how to treat oysters to produce "cultured" pearls at a fairly low cost. Cultured-pearl production is now a large industry in Japan.

To produce a cultured pearl, a smooth, round bead of mother-of-pearl is skillfully set into the living tissue of a pearl oyster. Then the oyster is returned to the water. The cultured pearls produced are less expensive than natural ones, but only an expert can tell the difference between them.

Most oysters used for making cultured pearls are gathered in special netting lowered from rafts. Others are gathered by divers. Once gathered, the oysters are taken to pearl "farms," where they are cleaned and graded according to age, size, and health. This sorting eliminates unsuitable oysters. The shells of suitable oysters are then cleaned of any sea growth and parasites. When the oysters open their shells, skilled workers cut into the **mantle** (the fleshy, glandular area) and insert the bead of mother-of-pearl covered with a bit of living tissue from another oyster. The treated oysters are then placed in cages suspended from rafts and anchored in sheltered water. Later the oysters are transferred to permanent rafts where they are protected against disease and natural enemies.

One to three years after treatment, the oysters are removed from the rafts, and their pearls are removed. The pearls are sorted according to shape, color, size, and luster. Only a very few are of truly fine quality. The pearls are then sent to manufacturers to be drilled and strung or set into pieces of jewelry. Pearls are selected carefully for each use. The pearls for necklaces, for example, must be of similar color and value and of the same size or of gradually increasing size.

MORTON R. SARETT
Jewelry Industry Council

See also GEMSTONES; JEWELRY.

PEARSON, LESTER B. (1897–1972)

Lester Bowles Pearson served as prime minister of Canada from 1963 until 1968. He was born in Toronto on April 23, 1897. After serving in the Canadian Army and Royal Flying Corps in World War I, he attended Oxford University and the University of Toronto, where he later taught history (1924–28).

Pearson became a career diplomat in 1928. He was appointed ambassador to the United States in 1945 and represented Canada at the United Nations Charter Conference. In 1948, Pearson entered the Canadian Parliament as secretary of state for external affairs. In this post he signed the North Atlantic Treaty Organization (NATO) agreement for Canada.

In 1957, the year after the Suez Crisis, Pearson was awarded the Nobel peace prize for his work in creating the United Nations Emergency Force, which kept peace between Israel and Egypt from 1956 to 1967. As leader of the Liberal Party (1958–68), Pearson stressed the need for programs to end unemployment and boost Canada's economy. He also promoted better foreign relations with the United States. In 1963 a crisis arose over the United States and Canada's joint defense policy, and a general election was held. The Liberals won enough seats to defeat the Conservatives under John G. Diefenbaker, and Pearson became prime minister.

Despite his weak position in Parliament and the threat to Canadian unity from separatists in the province of Quebec, Pearson's ministry was noteworthy for the establishment of the Canada Pension Plan, which became effective in 1966, and for the adoption of the Canadian flag in 1965.

On April 20, 1968, Pearson retired as prime minister and was succeeded by Pierre E. Trudeau. On December 27, 1972, after a long illness, Lester Pearson died at his home in Rockcliffe, a suburb of Ottawa, Canada.

JOHN S. MOIR
University of Toronto

PEARY, ROBERT E. (1856–1920)

Robert Edwin Peary is credited with leading the first successful expedition to the North Pole. Born on May 6, 1856, in Cresson, Pennsylvania, Peary was raised in Maine, where he spent much of his spare time hiking, collecting rocks and plants, writing poetry, and keeping a diary. He was an outstanding student and athlete, and in 1877 he graduated from Bowdoin College with top honors in civil engineering. In 1881 Peary became an engineer for the United States Navy in Washington, D.C.

One day in 1885, Peary found an old pamphlet written by a Swedish explorer, describing his journeys in Greenland. The pamphlet lured Peary to the Far North. In 1886 he explored Greenland's inland ice cap for several months. From 1891 to 1892 he again explored Greenland, this time with his young wife, Josephine. He went to Greenland five times in all. During each expedition, he made scientific findings about tides, polar seas, winds, temperatures, ice floes, plant and animal life, and the native people, the Eskimos (Inuit). He risked his life to cross northeastern Greenland —a distance of 1,200 miles (1,930 kilometers) —by dogsled. By charting the distance, he proved that Greenland was a huge island, not a continent as many had thought.

In the late 1890's Peary vowed that he would be the first man to visit the North Pole. His trips to the Arctic had taught him much about exploring on ice. He had his crew dress in light but warm clothes. He trained them to set up advance camps, carry few supplies, travel in small parties, hunt for food, and move quickly.

Peary first tried to reach the North Pole between 1898 and 1902 but failed. Early in this expedition his feet were so badly frostbitten that eight of his toes had to be amputated. Yet nothing could stop him. Once, while he was temporarily stranded in a deserted hut during a blizzard and in terrible pain, he wrote these words on a wall: *Inveniam viam aut faciam*— Latin for "I shall find a way or make one."

Peary headed for the North Pole again between 1905 and 1906 but failed once more to reach it. In 1908 he set out on his third polar expedition, sailing from New York City to Ellesmere Island in Canada. He built a base camp at Cape Columbia, about 450 miles (725 kilometers) from the North Pole.

Robert E. Peary once said, "The fame of Columbus will be equaled only by the man who stands at the top of the world —the discoverer of the North Pole." Seeking that place in history for himself, Peary conquered the North Pole on April 6, 1909.

In March 1909, he and his crew left by sledge for the Pole. For nearly a month they battled freezing cold, violent winds, and sudden openings in the ice. Many of his colleagues were sent back to the base camp, now 300 miles (480 kilometers) away.

By early April, only Peary, his aide and companion, Matthew Henson (1866–1955), and four Eskimo (Inuit) guides remained. The small band pushed forward another 133 miles (214 kilometers). On April 6, 1909, they made their final march and reached the Pole. Peary unwound the American flag he had worn under the furs around his waist and planted it at the Pole. The flag had been hand-sewn by his wife. Later he announced his discovery to the world with this cable message: "Stars and Stripes nailed to the Pole—Peary."

Five days before Peary cabled his message, explorer Frederick A. Cook announced that he had reached the Pole in 1908. His claim was generally dismissed, but for decades it clouded Peary's accomplishment. Nevertheless, Peary returned home to praise and honors. A U.S. warship was named after him, and Congress promoted him to rear admiral. The world's most northerly land area, in northern Greenland, was named Peary Land.

Peary died on February 20, 1920, and was buried with military honors in Arlington National Cemetery in Arlington, Virginia. In 1989 the National Geographic Society sponsored a study of his famous expedition. After extensive research, investigators concluded that Peary had come within at least 5 miles (8 kilometers) of the North Pole.

TONY SIMON
Author, *North Pole:
The Story of Robert E. Peary*

PEEL, SIR ROBERT (1788–1850)

Sir Robert Peel served three terms as prime minister of Great Britain and is considered the founder of that country's Conservative Party. He was born near Bury, England, on February 5, 1788. In 1809, at the age of 21, Peel entered Parliament as a member of the Tory Party. As chief secretary for Ireland (1812–18), he opposed seating Roman Catholics in Parliament. He later served as home secretary (1822–27) and as a leader in the House of Commons (1828–30).

In 1829, Peel modified his earlier views on the Catholics and sponsored the Catholic Emancipation Act, which removed many of the political and civil restrictions on Catholics in Britain and Ireland. He also reorganized the London police force with the Metropolitan Police Act. London's police have since been known as "Bobbies" in his honor.

During Peel's brief first term as prime minister (1834–35), he formed the Conservative Party in opposition to the Whigs and their Reform Act of 1832, which had extended the vote to 50 percent more people. During Peel's second (1841–45) and third (1845–46) terms, he reimposed an income tax, abolished import taxes on food and raw materials, and passed the Bank Charter Act (1844), which established many of Britain's most enduring financial policies.

After the potato famine struck Ireland in 1845, Peel pushed to repeal the Corn Laws, which had kept farm prices high due to tariffs on imported grain. This controversial action split the Conservative Party. Peel lost many of his supporters and was forced from office. He died on July 2, 1850, from injuries sustained after falling from his horse.

GEORGE CAREY
Georgetown University

PEI, I. M. (1917–   )

The Chinese-American architect Ieoh Ming Pei was born on April 26, 1917, in Guangzhou (Canton), China. He moved to the United States in 1935 to study architecture at the Massachusetts Institute of Technology (MIT) and at Harvard University. Pei became an American citizen in 1954. A year later he opened his own architectural firm in New York City.

Pei's buildings are noted for their bold geometric shapes and functional design. They also reflect his interest in designing small-scale units of space that work together as a whole. He succeeded in this approach with the design of the Everson Museum of Art (1968) in Syracuse, New York. A later example is the East Wing of the National Gallery of Art in Washington, D.C., completed in 1978. This structure was designed in the shape of two connecting triangles to conform to an awkward building site. Pei's firm also designed the immense Jacob K. Javits Convention Center in New York City, which opened in 1986.

One of Pei's most challenging commissions came in 1984, when President François Mitterand of France selected him to expand the Louvre Museum in Paris. Pei's plan included the construction of a glass pyramid 65 feet (20 meters) tall in the center of the old Louvre courtyard. This pyramid would serve as the new main entrance to the museum. Critics throughout France opposed the plan. Yet when the project was completed in 1989, it was found to be thoroughly functional and to lend unity to the entire architectural setting.

Pei's other works include the John F. Kennedy Library (1979) in Dorchester, Massachusetts, the Fragrant Hill Hotel (1983) in Peking, and the 70-story Bank of China headquarters (1989) in Hong Kong.

HOWARD E. WOODEN
Director Emeritus
The Wichita Art
Museum

The architect I. M. Pei sits in front of the giant glass pyramid he designed to serve as the new entrance to the Louvre, the national art museum of France.

PEKING. See BEIJING.

PELÉ (1940–   )

As a boy, Edson Arantes do Nascimento shined shoes and ran errands. But on days when his father played soccer, Edson forgot about earning money to help his family. He watched his father play and dreamed of being a player himself. Later, he became—in the opinion of many people—the greatest soccer player in the world.

Pelé, as Edson was nicknamed, was born on October 23, 1940, in Três Corações, Brazil. He left school after the fourth grade and was apprenticed to a shoemaker. But he continued to think of playing soccer.

When Pelé was 15, his coach took him to São Paulo to join a professional team. But the team there turned him down. Not discouraged, the coach took him to another team, in Santos. Pelé made a poor showing, but the Santos coach decided to accept him for the second team. In his first game, Pelé scored four goals. He soon moved to the first team and became a sports hero to all Brazil. He could kick with either foot, "head" the ball with accuracy, and put a curve on it as well.

In 1958, Pelé helped the Brazilian national team win the World Cup. He was already a legend in world play. Not surprisingly, he became a target for other players, and he began to lose some of his enthusiasm for the game. But before he stopped playing in international games in 1971, he led Brazilian teams to three World Cup, two World Club, and five South American championships.

Pelé in action.

Pelé continued to play for Santos until 1974. Partly because of him, people in the United States became enthusiastic about soccer. Pelé came out of retirement in 1975 to join the New York Cosmos. In 1977, he led them to the North American Soccer League title. He then retired from the game.

Reviewed by RICHARD B. ROTTKOV
United States Soccer Federation

PELICANS

"A wonderful bird is the pelican!" says the old rhyme. "Its bill will hold more than its belly can." And indeed, the bill of a pelican is remarkable. Attached to its bottom half is a large skin pouch. People sometimes think pelicans store food in their pouches, but they do not use the pouches in this way. Pelicans live on fish. When they catch fish, they use the pouch like a dip net. They scoop up the fish, let the water drain out, and then swallow the fish.

Pelicans are large water birds. Some kinds may be as long as 6 feet (180 centimeters) and have a wingspread of up to 10 feet (3 meters). Although they are large, they are good swimmers and graceful flyers. They form a family all of their own, with some six to eight species. Most are white or grayish, sometimes with pink tints or darker wing tips. One of the American species is brown or blackish gray. A variety of this species, the Eastern brown pelican, is the state bird

Pelicans are sociable birds. They band together in colonies to feed and build their nests.

of Louisiana. A few other families of water birds—such as the tropic birds, gannets, and cormorants—are like pelicans in certain ways. Together, they make up the bird order Pelecaniformes, meaning "pelican-shaped."

▶WHERE AND HOW PELICANS LIVE

Pelicans are found in lakes, swamps, lagoons, and coastal waters of all the continents except Antarctica. The American species range the farthest north. Those that live in cooler climates migrate to warmer areas in winter. In Europe, pelicans are now found only in the areas around the Black and Caspian seas and in the Balkans. The Danube delta is a favorite breeding ground.

The kinds of fish that pelicans eat are not eaten by people or caught for sport. And the droppings, called guano, of pelicans are used as fertilizer.

Pelicans are sociable birds. They feed and nest in large groups. Some species even engage in cooperative fishing. They form lines or semicircles and swim toward the shore, driving the fish before them. When the fish reach the shallower water near the shore, the pelicans scoop them up easily.

The American brown pelican has a fishing method unlike that of other pelicans. It flies above the water, then dives or spirals down, plunges under the water to seize a fish, and bobs back to the surface.

Pelicans build simple nests, always near water and sometimes floating on it. They lay one to four eggs and sit on them for four or five weeks. The young hatch naked and blind but are soon covered with down. They feed on predigested fish, which they take from the parents' pouches. The young leave the nest for good after about four months. But they do not get their adult plumage (feathers) for a couple of years and do not breed until a year or two later.

Pelicans are long-lived birds. They may live for over 30 years. The adults have few natural enemies. But they are easily disturbed when nesting and may then abandon their eggs or chicks. Many animals prey on young pelicans. And pelicans share two problems with many other birds and animals. Their habitats (the places where they live and breed, which for pelicans are wetlands) are being destroyed by human beings as they clear land for building projects and for agriculture. And pelicans are being poisoned by pesticides (weed- and insect-killing chemicals) in the environment.

▶PELICANS IN ART AND LEGEND

People once believed that if food was scarce, a mother pelican would stab her own breast with her beak and feed her young with the blood. At breeding time, some pelicans have a reddish spot on their breasts. Perhaps this spot helped give rise to the legend. Because of the legend, in the Middle Ages the pelican was considered a symbol of Christ, who, according to Christian belief, shed his blood for humankind. Pictures or carvings of "a pelican in her piety" (as depictions of this legendary behavior were called) are sometimes found in Christian churches. Following this tradition, a pelican "in the act of tearing its breast to feed its young" appears on the seal and flag of the state of Louisiana.

Reviewed by JOHN BULL
American Museum of Natural History

See also BIRDS.

PELOPONNESIAN WAR

The Peloponnesian War was one of the most important conflicts of ancient Greece, lasting, in its various phases, from 431 to 404 B.C. At a time when Greece was composed of many independent city-states, the war involved two of the most powerful, Athens and Sparta, and their allies. Much of what we know about the war has come down to us from the account written by the historian Thucydides, an Athenian, who took part in it.

Background. When the Persians invaded Greece in 480–479 B.C., during the conflict known as the Persian Wars, the Greek city-states had been defended by an alliance of Athenians and Spartans. Athens' superb fleet and Sparta's disciplined infantry had combined to drive off the invaders.

However, this wartime alliance soon disintegrated. The Athenians had used their navy to build a strong defensive league of island and coastal city-states against further Persian attack. Eventually they converted the league into an Athenian empire. The Spartans, suspicious of Athenian expansion, withdrew into their mountainous homeland in the Peloponnesus, the southern part of Greece, from which the war takes its name. There they strengthened their own alliances against threats from Athens.

Outbreak of War. Hostility between Athens and the city-state of Corinth, an ally of Sparta, finally led to the outbreak of war in 431 B.C. It was clear from the start that the Athenian navy would dominate the seas, while the Spartan army was virtually invincible on land. Therefore, as long as Athens, protected by its strong walls, retained access to the sea and avoided battle with the superior Spartan troops, it was safe.

This was the strategy adopted by Pericles, the Athenian leader, and it worked well. The Spartans regularly invaded Attica, the region around Athens. But the city itself held firm, in spite of a plague that struck in 430 B.C. and killed many of the inhabitants, including Pericles. After years of sporadic fighting, a truce—the Peace of Nicias—was signed in 421 B.C.

Sicilian Expedition. Although the Spartans were prepared to honor the peace, in 415 B.C. the Athenians launched a naval expedition against Syracuse, a city-state on the island of

GREECE IN THE PELOPONNESIAN WAR

Sparta and Allies   Athens and Allies

Sicily and a colony of Corinth. The Athenians also interfered in the affairs of some of Sparta's neighboring cities. The result was a resumption of the war. The undertaking of the Sicilian expedition, urged by the Athenian Alcibiades, ended in disaster. Nevertheless, the Athenian navy remained strong and the maritime empire it guarded provided continuing support for Athens. The Spartans realized that they would have to develop their own fleet in order to defeat the Athenians.

Fall of Athens. At just this moment, the Persians, who had never forgiven the Athenians for their role in the earlier Persian defeat, decided to intervene on the side of Sparta. They supplied money to construct and maintain a Spartan fleet. Although they were an inland people who lacked a seafaring tradition, the Spartans turned out to be excellent sailors. In a series of naval engagements in 406 and 405 B.C., they defeated the Athenian fleet that had protected the ships carrying grain to Athens from overseas Greek colonies. With its food supply cut off, Athens was starved into submission in 404 B.C. The defeat marked the end of the Golden Age of Athens and left Sparta as the leading Greek power.

EUGENE N. BORZA
The Pennsylvania State University
Author, *In the Shadow of Olympus*

See also PERICLES.

PENCILS. See PENS AND PENCILS.

A penguin travels over snow and ice by tobogganing.

PENGUINS

Penguins are birds, but they are unlike other birds in several ways. Their wings are flippers, and they cannot fly in the air. Penguins do, however, "fly" in the water, at speeds up to 30 miles (48 kilometers) an hour. While swimming, they can dive with a thrust of their flippers and travel 30 feet (9 meters) underwater before surfacing. They surface with such force that they may soar into the air, like porpoises. Some can leap out of the water onto a ledge 7 feet (2 meters) above the surface.

On land, penguins use their flippers for fighting and for balancing as they walk. Penguins waddle slowly along, standing up straight like a person. When traveling over snow and ice, they may flop on their bellies and "row" with their feet. They also use their flippers when in a great hurry. This way of traveling is called tobogganing.

Penguins differ from most other birds in that their feathers cover the body completely. Penguin feathers are so small they look like scales. They are tightly packed together and form a dense covering that sheds water and helps keep the birds warm.

Penguins spend most of their lives in water. They come on land to mate and to produce their young. Penguins are very social birds; tens of thousands live together in breeding grounds called **rookeries**.

There are 17 known species, or kinds; all live in the Southern Hemisphere. Though many people think of the Antarctic as the home of the penguins, only seven species nest there. The others breed on islands outside the Antarctic Circle and on the shores of South Africa, Australia, and New Zealand, as well as on the coasts of South America and on the Galápagos Islands of the Pacific.

▶ **MEMBERS OF THE PENGUIN FAMILY**

All 17 penguin species have white fronts and black or blue-gray backs. This coloring probably helps hide them from their main enemy in the sea—the leopard seal. To an enemy swimming below a penguin, the pale front may blend with the sky. From above, the dark back may blend with the sea.

The most obvious differences among species are in the colors and patterns around the face and across the chest. The macaroni and the rockhopper penguins have bright yellow feathers above their eyes. The emperor penguin is the most beautiful of all, with its purple bill and a golden sheen to its breast.

The coloring and markings of the chicks vary, too. The gray emperor penguin chick looks as if it were wearing a pair of big, black spectacles.

The emperor is the biggest member of the penguin family. It stands 4 feet (1.2 meters) tall and weighs about 60 pounds (27 kilograms). The Adelie penguin is one of the smaller species. It stands about 1½ feet (0.5 meter) tall when fully grown and weighs about 12 pounds (5 kilograms).

The Adelie penguin is one of the kinds that live in the Antarctic. It is the penguin that has been studied the most and is a good example of how the other species live.

The Adelie Penguin

During the Antarctic winter, February to October, the Adelies live at sea, hunting small shrimplike animals called krill. In October, which is early spring in the Antarctic, the Adelies pop out of the sea and start a long trek to their rookeries, or breeding grounds. The penguins may have to walk and slide, scramble and toboggan 60 miles (96.5 kilometers) across the sea ice to reach the rocky Antarctic coast. They arrive at their rookeries, singly or in groups, about the middle of October. Usually the males arrive first and go directly to their nests of the previous year. The nests are made of stones. The males seem to find the right nest even when it is covered by a foot or two of snow.

The male Adelie performs what is called the ecstatic display. The male stretches his neck, lifts his bill toward the sky, and slowly waves his flippers back and forth. He lets forth a raucous "caw." Like the songs of other birds, this call serves to warn other males to keep away from the nest territory. At the same time it attracts females to the nest.

When the female approaches the nest, the two birds face each other. They wave their heads and necks and make sounds to each other. This is called a mutual display.

The pair has to make a nest before the eggs are laid. One bird stays on the nest and guards it. The other goes back and forth, collecting stones from the outskirts of the colony or from unguarded colony piles. If a pair of penguins is so foolish as to leave the nest unguarded, the stones rapidly disappear. All the other penguins are also collecting stones. Penguins carry stones in their beaks. Both male and female collect stones and guard the nest in turn. The stones are dropped around the partner on the nest, who arranges them into a neat pile.

The Laying and Hatching of Eggs. In mid-November, about three weeks after arrival at the rookery, the female Adelie lays two bluish-white eggs. Then she leaves for the sea to feed. About two weeks later, the female returns to the nest. The penguins greet each other with very noisy and excited mutual displays. There is much of this display before the

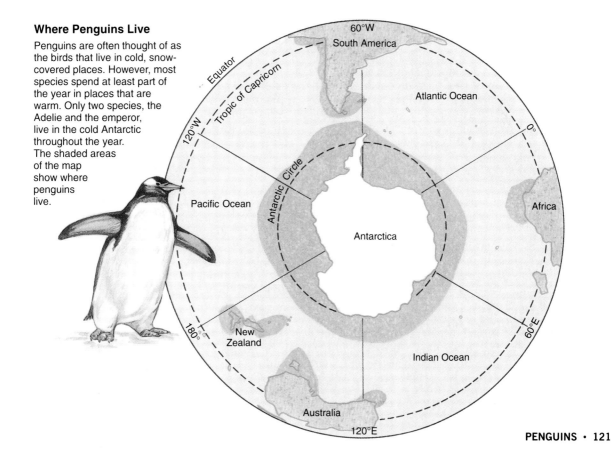

Where Penguins Live

Penguins are often thought of as the birds that live in cold, snow-covered places. However, most species spend at least part of the year in places that are warm. Only two species, the Adelie and the emperor, live in the cold Antarctic throughout the year. The shaded areas of the map show where penguins live.

Male and female penguins greet each other.

1½ pounds (0.7 kilograms) of food in one meal. While it is growing, the chick is fed about every two days.

When the chicks are about 4 weeks old, they leave the nest. By now their down is thick enough to protect them against the cold. Usually the parents manage to raise one chick to full growth. Sometimes harsh weather kills the eggs or chicks.

When the chicks are 4 or 5 weeks old, both parents are feeding at sea most of the time. They come back only for very short periods to feed their young. Left to themselves, the chicks gather together into large groups, called crèches, of 100 or 200 birds. This seems to protect them from the gull-like skua, which attacks and eats sick or starving chicks that become separated from the group. The crèche formation keeps the chicks warm, too.

Parents recognize their own chicks among the hundreds of others in the crèche, and feed only their own chicks. At 9 weeks the Adelie chicks are as big as their parents. They have shed their soft down for a coat of feathers. A young bird now looks like the parents, except that it has a white throat. In another year, the young Adelie sheds these feathers and gets adult feathers, including the black throat feathers. An Adelie changes its feathers every year. Sometimes Adelies molt on land, but most often they do so away from land, on floating pack ice.

The adult penguins desert their fully grown chicks. The chicks wander down to the beaches until large groups have gathered. After much excitement and noise, the birds plunge into the water in little groups. Adults do not give swimming lessons, and the first swimming movements of the chicks are clumsy bobbings up and down. Some of the young penguins are hurt or killed by leopard seals, which lurk in the water waiting to catch plump young penguins.

The remaining penguins head for the pack ice where the adults spend the winter. The young remain there for their first two or three years. They do not appear again at the rookeries until they are 3 or 4 years old.

The Emperor Penguins

The emperor penguin, unlike all other species, breeds during the dark and stormy polar winter. The emperors return in March to their breeding grounds on sea ice close to the Ant-

female changes place with the male. The male gets up stiffly. He looks thin and weary. He has fasted for about six weeks! A male Adelie starts off weighing about 13 pounds (6 kilograms), and at the end of the fast he weighs about 8 pounds (4 kilograms); he has lost about 40 percent of his weight.

The male collects a few more stones for the nest and then goes to the sea. The open sea may be right up to the coast by this time, because the summer is fast advancing. In two weeks the male Adelie has regained a good amount of the lost weight, and he again takes over the nest from the female. She now leaves for another feeding trip. By remarkable timing, when the female comes back to the nest with a full stomach, her chicks are coming out of the eggs and are ready for their first meal. It has taken the eggs 35 days to hatch.

Adelie Young. The fluffy down-covered chicks are closely guarded by their parents. One parent sits right on top of them while they are still small. The parents take turns guarding and going off to feed. They feed on small sea animals, which are partly digested and later forced up to the beak. A chick can eat about

Female penguin feeds her chicks.

Penguin chicks gather together for protection.

arctic shore. The birds pair off much as the Adelies do, except that they make no nest. In May the female lays one egg, which weighs about a pound. She gives the egg to her mate and goes off to sea to break her fast. The male keeps the egg warm until it hatches about 64 days later. He tucks the egg on top of his feet, between his legs. There it is kept warm by a flap on his belly. He can shuffle short distances without dropping the egg.

During all the time that he is incubating the egg, the male lives in continuous cold and darkness. During the gales and snowstorms of the Antarctic winter, the temperature may drop as low as $-70°F$ ($-57°C$). To protect themselves from the cold during this time, the males huddle close together.

The females return a few days before or after the egg is hatched. When the female returns, the male leaves for the sea. He has gone without food for three months. He feeds for several weeks before returning to the nest.

At birth the chick weighs about 11 ounces (312 grams) and is covered with gray down. Its parents take turns guarding it and keeping it warm beneath their bellies. When the chicks

A young emperor penguin, investigating the world, peers between the legs of its mother.

King penguins incubate eggs for about 54 days.

Strawlike plumes decorate head of the macaroni penguin.

are about half grown, they huddle together, like the Adelie chicks. In spite of this huddling, many chicks freeze in blizzards.

By early January the sea ice breaks up and spreads out into the oceans. The emperors go off with the ice. Their chicks are fully grown and ready for life in the sea.

The King and Macaroni Penguins

The king penguin nests on the islands off Antarctica. It lays one egg and raises a huge chick that eventually weighs about 30 pounds (14 kilograms). The parents take care of their chick for almost a year. Then when the chick is fully grown, the adults go off to the sea to grow fat again.

The king penguins lay their eggs between the beginning of summer and the beginning of winter. The parents incubate an egg for about 54 days. On this schedule a pair of kings can raise no more than two chicks in three years.

The macaroni penguin also breeds in the outlying Antarctic islands. It lays one big egg and one little one. The little one does not develop into a chick. This strange arrangement remains a puzzle for naturalists.

▶ PENGUINS IN CAPTIVITY

In the protection of zoos, king penguins have raised their young. The penguins in Edinburgh Zoo, Scotland, have done so most successfully. The African penguin adjusts well to captivity in the right surroundings.

However, it is difficult to keep captive penguins healthy. Penguins need a large fish supply. A male Humboldt penguin weighing about 9 pounds (4 kilograms) eats up to 3 pounds (1.4 kilograms) of fish every day. When he is about to molt, he will eat twice this amount. A penguin has to be taught to take a dead fish from someone's hand, or to eat it when the fish is thrown into the water. At first food may have to be forced into the penguin's mouth, so that the bird keeps a good weight while it learns this new way of feeding.

When penguins lose a lot of weight, they are almost certain to catch a lung disease that is usually fatal. This disease is caused by a fungus that grows in the lungs and in the airsacs that lead from the lungs. However, the disease can sometimes be cured.

Today most penguin rookeries are protected from too much interference by humans. Scientists of many different nations are working together to preserve the Antarctic penguins. To ensure the safety of penguins, some nations have made their penguin breeding grounds legally protected bird sanctuaries.

BRENDA SLADEN
WILLIAM J. L. SLADEN
The Johns Hopkins University

PENMANSHIP. See HANDWRITING.

PENN, WILLIAM (1644–1718)

William Penn was the founder of the colony of Pennsylvania in America. He is also important in English history. And the world remembers him because he worked for human liberty and co-operation among nations long before these ideas became popular.

Penn was born in London, England, on October 14, 1644. His father, also named William Penn, was an admiral on the side of the Parliamentary forces during the English Civil War (1642–46). But later he became involved in a dispute with Oliver Cromwell, the head of the government. Admiral Penn switched his allegiance to the exiled king, Charles II, and took his family to Ireland. There young William Penn continued the education he had begun in England. In 1660, when Charles II was restored as king, Penn was 16 and ready to enter Oxford University.

William Penn belonged to the ruling class. But he did not remain sympathetic to its ideals. Instead, he turned away from the pomp and worldliness of England at that time to the ideas of the Quakers. This was a new and radical religious group that had been founded in England in the 1650's by George Fox (1642–91). Penn was in Ireland in 1667 when he made the final decision to become a Quaker.

Penn lived at a time when religious toleration was almost unknown. As a member of the Quakers, a small and despised sect, he was persecuted and imprisoned. Penn worked for religious toleration and political liberty in England. He wrote and spoke out in defense of the fundamental rights of the people. He insisted that they have proper elected representation in the government.

In 1681, Penn obtained a charter from Charles II as founder of a new colony in North America. The King had owed Admiral Penn £16,000. When he granted the colony to William Penn in payment of the debt, Charles insisted that it be named Pennsylvania in honor of the naval hero. Penn recruited settlers, wrote a constitution for the colony, and prepared for the voyage to the New World. He arrived in Delaware Bay on the ship *Welcome* in late October, 1682.

Penn granted the colonists a great deal of self-government and guaranteed religious toleration to all. He signed treaties with the Indians and watched Pennsylvania's rapid economic growth with satisfaction. Penn was head of the colony in three different capacities. As governor, he was its political leader. As proprietor, he was landlord of all the inhabitants. In addition, he was the spiritual leader of the Quakers, who made up the vast majority of the colony's population.

Penn spent two years in Pennsylvania before returning to England. During his second and last visit, between 1699 and 1701, he granted the colony the Charter of Privileges of 1701. This remained the constitution of Pennsylvania until 1776. He also drew up a plan for uniting the English colonies under one government. But unification did not become a reality until after the Revolutionary War.

In the 1690's, Penn wrote his famous *Essay Towards the Present and Future Peace of Europe*. In it he proposed the establishment of a European parliament to settle international disputes. The League of Nations and the United Nations owe much to Penn's proposals. Penn published more than 150 works during his lifetime. His two other most famous works are *No Cross, No Crown* and *Some Fruits of Solitude*.

In 1672, Penn married Gulielma Springett, who was also a Quaker. They had eight children, but only two lived to maturity. After his first wife died in 1694, Penn married Hannah Callowhill, the daughter of a wealthy merchant. She accompanied Penn to America in 1699 and gave birth to a son called John the American. Seven other children were born, but only four of the eight survived.

William Penn suffered many setbacks and disappointments during his lifetime. A friend and a supporter of King James II, he was arrested several times after a revolution forced James into exile in 1688. He even lost control of Pennsylvania for two years. Because he placed too much trust in his business adviser, Penn had financial difficulties and spent a long period in debtors' prison.

Penn died on July 30, 1718. He was buried on the grounds of Jordans Meetinghouse, northwest of London.

EDWIN B. BRONNER
Author, *William Penn's Holy Experiment*
See also PENNSYLVANIA; QUAKERS.

PENNSYLVANIA

In 1681, England's King Charles II granted one of his subjects, William Penn, a large region in America west of the Delaware River. The new colony, named in honor of Penn's father, was called Pennsylvania, the Latin phrase for "Penn's Woods." William Penn established the colony as a "Holy Experiment," a safe haven for the Society of Friends, a religious sect whose members are more commonly known as Quakers. Pennsylvania thus became known as the Quaker State. Today it is known as the Keystone State because of its important central location within the original 13 colonies.

State flag

The Commonwealth of Pennsylvania, located in the northeastern United States, is a Middle Atlantic state with access to the Atlantic Ocean through Delaware Bay. Its pastoral landscape rises out of a low, level coastal plain in the east, to rolling hills and farmlands in its central region, to the Allegheny Mountains and Plateau in the west.

Pennsylvania's largest city, Philadelphia, is the fifth largest city in the nation. Since colonial days, it has served as the state's eastern hub of finance, manufacturing, and culture. Pennsylvania's western hub, Pittsburgh, was once the steel-making capital of the world. Approximately half of all Pennsylvanians live in either Philadelphia or Pittsburgh. Harrisburg is the state capital.

Once an industrial giant, Pennsylvania now has a service-driven economy. In some communities, school and medical centers have replaced iron and steel mills as the largest employers. However, Pennsylvania is still a leader in manufacturing, energy production, and mining. It is the only state still producing anthracite (hard coal) and is a leading supplier of electricity to the northeast. Pennsylvania, also an important agricultural state, is the nation's leading producer of mushrooms, plantation-grown Christmas trees, and hardwood lumber.

Every year millions of tourists visit Pennsylvania to enjoy its spectacular scenery, cultural attractions, and interesting historic sites. Most important among them are Independence Hall in Philadelphia, where the Declaration of Independence (1776) and the Constitution of the United States (1787) were signed; Valley Forge, where General George Washington and the Continental Army passed the cruel winter of 1777–78 during the Revolutionary War; and Gettysburg, the site of the most important battle (1863) of the Civil War.

Pennsylvanians have always played an important role in the nation's history. In addition to the industrialists who made their fortunes there, the state has brought forth an impressive array of world-renowned artists, writers, singers, composers, actors, entertainers, dancers, athletes, scientists, explorers, and statesmen.

▶ LAND

Pennsylvania is roughly rectangular in shape. It features a picturesque assortment of plains, wide and narrow valleys, hills and low mountains, rivers, lakes, and streams.

Land Regions

Pennsylvania spreads across four major land regions—the Coastal Plain, the Piedmont, the Appalachian Highlands, and the Great Lakes Plain.

The Coastal Plain covers the extreme southeastern corner of the state, where the city of Philadelphia is located. The portion of this region that lies within Pennsylvania's borders is a low-lying level, narrow strip of sand and gravel along the Delaware River.

Opposite page, clockwise from left: **Philadelphia is Pennsylvania's largest city. Its name comes from the Greek phrase meaning City of Brotherly Love. The Liberty Bell, in Philadelphia, is a cherished symbol of the nation's struggle for independence. Amish children walk to school in Lancaster County.**

State flower:
Mountain laurel

State tree:
Eastern hemlock

FACTS AND FIGURES

Location: Northeastern United States; bordered on the north by Lake Erie and New York, on the east by New York and New Jersey, on the south by Delaware, Maryland, and West Virginia, and on the west by West Virginia and Ohio.

Area: 45,308 sq mi (117,348 km^2); rank, 33rd.

Population: 11,924,710 (1990 census); rank, 5th.

Elevation: *Highest* — 3,213 ft (980 m) at Mount Davis; *lowest* — sea level, along the Delaware River.

Capital: Harrisburg.

Statehood: December 12, 1787; 2nd state.

State Motto: *Virtue, liberty, and independence.*

State Song: None.

Nicknames: Keystone State; Quaker State.

Abbreviations: PA; Penn.

State bird:
Ruffed grouse

Left: Raystown Lake in central Pennsylvania is just one of the hundreds of beautiful recreational spots that attract vacationers to the state.
Below: The fertile soils of the Piedmont and the Ridge and Valley regions support farms that raise crops and livestock.

The **Piedmont** consists of gradually rising hills that extend inland for about 100 miles (160 kilometers). This region contains some of the nation's most fertile farmland.

The **Appalachian Highlands** can be divided into four distinct sections. The **New England Upland**, also called the Reading Prong, is a small mountain range between Easton and Reading. The **Blue Ridge**, which Pennsylvanians call South Mountain, is the northernmost extension of the Blue Ridge Mountains. In the center of the state lies the **Ridge and Valley Region**. Its southeastern rim is a wide lowland known as the Great Valley, where well-kept farms from Chambersburg to Allentown raise much of Pennsylvania's crops and livestock. To the north and west of the Great Valley are wooded ridges, rising as high as 1,200 feet (370 meters). These ridges rise like accordion folds above wide and level valleys. The **Allegheny Plateau**, the northern portion of the Appalachian Plateau, covers almost all of northern and western Pennsylvania. It is a vast region of rolling highlands and deep ravines. Streams have chiseled cliffs and gorges out of soft sandstone and shale, making farming difficult. The Allegheny Mountains form the eastern border of this region and contain the state's highest point, Mount Davis, which rises 3,213 feet (980 meters) near the Maryland border.

The **Great Lakes Plain** covers a small strip of land in Pennsylvania's northwestern corner. Here the land levels out into a fertile plain as it slopes toward Lake Erie. The level land and moderate climate make this area suitable for agriculture.

Rivers and Lakes

Pennsylvania has three important river systems that drain 95 percent of the state—the Delaware, the Susquehanna, and the Ohio.

The Delaware River forms Pennsylvania's eastern border and flows south into Delaware Bay and the Atlantic Ocean. Its most important tributaries are the Schuylkill and Lehigh rivers. The Susquehanna River flows south through the center of the state and empties into Chesapeake Bay. Its main tributaries are the West Branch and Juniata rivers. The Delaware and the Susquehanna systems drain the eastern part of the state. The Ohio River is formed at Pittsburgh at the junction of the Allegheny River from the north and the Monongahela River from the south. These three rivers drain all of western Pennsylvania.

Pennsylvania has about 4,400 streams and about 300 lakes, both natural and artificial.

Lake Conneaut, in the northwest, is the largest natural lake lying entirely within the state. Lake Wallenpaupack, in the northeast, is the state's largest artificial lake. However, several of the lakes formed by dams on rivers are much larger. These include Pymatuning Reservoir on the Ohio border and the Allegheny Reservoir on the New York border. In addition to its many lakes and streams, the Pocono Mountain region is also graced with beautiful waterfalls.

Climate

Temperatures in Pennsylvania vary according to location and elevation. The average temperature in January ranges from 22° to 32°F (−6° to 0°C). In July the average temperature ranges from 66° to 76°F (19° to 24°C). Annual rainfall averages 41 inches (1,041 millimeters) across the state. Snowfall varies greatly, from 20 inches (51 centimeters) per year in the southeast to 90 inches (229 centimeters) in the north.

Southern Pennsylvania has the longest growing season, lasting about 200 days. The northern counties, except for the Great Lakes Plain, have the coldest weather and a growing season that lasts only about 130 days.

Plant and Animal Life

Forests once covered more than 95 percent of Pennsylvania but now cover only 60 percent due to clearing for farms and towns. The most plentiful varieties of trees include maple, beech, and hemlock in the north; ash, birch, cherry, hickory, locust, maple, oak, pine, poplar, sycamore, tulip, and black walnut in the south; and pine in the mountains. Flowering shrubs, including mountain laurel (the state flower), azaleas, and rhododendron abound. Common wildflowers are violets, honeysuckle, and black-eyed Susans.

Many kinds of mammals, birds, and fish thrive in Pennsylvania. Deer are abundant, even in some populated areas. Black bears can still be found in the mountains of the north and west. Smaller mammals, such as fox, beaver, otter, mink, raccoon, opossum, woodchuck, skunk, squirrel, and rabbit, survive in large numbers, as do wild turkeys, geese, ruffed

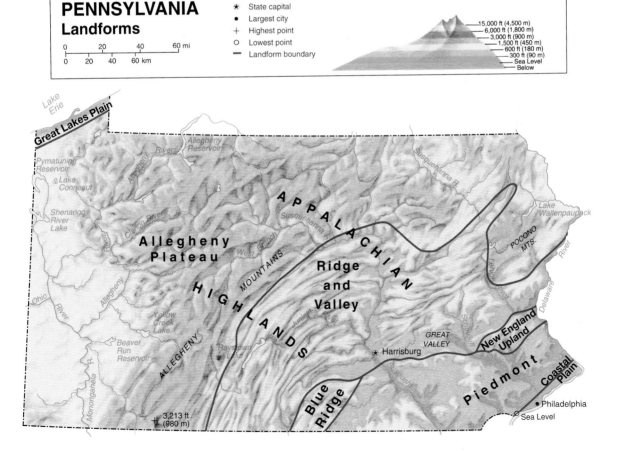

PENNSYLVANIA
Landforms

✳	State capital
•	Largest city
+	Highest point
O	Lowest point
—	Landform boundary

0   20   40   60 mi
0   20   40   60 km

15,000 ft (4,500 m)
6,000 ft (1,800 m)
3,000 ft (900 m)
1,500 ft (450 m)
600 ft (180 m)
300 ft (90 m)
Sea Level
Below

Left: Summer festivals and parades are common along Philadelphia's main boulevards. A statue of William Penn tops City Hall (background) at one end of Benjamin Franklin Parkway. *Above:* Field hockey is one of several popular collegiate sports in Pennsylvania.

grouse, quail, pheasant, and songbirds. The rivers, streams, and lakes contain a bounty of fish, including trout, pike, pickerel, bass, white carp, and catfish.

Natural Resources

The rich soil of Pennsylvania's Piedmont region, Great Valley, and Great Lakes Plain is one of the state's great natural assets. Coal is the most plentiful mineral. About 75 billion tons of bituminous (soft) coal, mostly in the southwest, and 23 billion tons of anthracite (hard coal), in the northeast, are yet available. Iron ore exists in the southern half of the state along with small quantities of copper, lead, zinc, nickel, and chromite. Petroleum and natural gas lie beneath the surface in the northwestern and western parts of the state.

▶PEOPLE

Pennsylvania is the fifth most populous of the fifty states. About 89 percent of its residents are of European ancestry. Approximately one third of this group are Pennsylvania Dutch, who are not Dutch at all, but German. (*Deutsch*, the German word for "German," long ago was mistaken for "Dutch.") Other ancestries include English, Welsh, French, Dutch, Irish, Scotch-Irish, and peoples from southern and eastern Europe, particularly Italians and Slavs. Approximately 9 percent of Pennsylvanians are of African origin. Hispanics, Asians, Native Americans, and other minorities make up the remaining 2 percent.

Education

Before public elementary and secondary schools were widely established, religious and ethnic groups provided education for their own members. Some of these schools still exist, most notably the William Penn Charter School, founded in 1689 by Quakers in Philadelphia. Since 1834 the state has provided public education; attendance is mandatory for those between the ages of 8 and 16.

Among the fifty states, Pennsylvania has one of the highest numbers of institutions for higher learning, both state-supported and private. The largest is the Pennsylvania State University, with campuses at University Park and more than twenty other locations. It is state-related, as are Temple University in Philadelphia and the University of Pittsburgh. Pennsylvania is also known for its many professional schools in medicine, law, and business.

The state's oldest private university is the University of Pennsylvania in Philadelphia.

Founded in the 1740's as a school for the poor, today it is the southernmost of the Ivy League schools. Among the dozens of private colleges and universities are Swarthmore in Swarthmore, Bryn Mawr in Bryn Mawr, Haverford in Haverford, Dickinson in Carlisle, Franklin and Marshall in Lancaster, Carnegie-Mellon in Pittsburgh, Villanova in Villanova, Lehigh in Bethlehem, Bucknell in Lewisburg, and Gettysburg College in Gettysburg.

Libraries, Museums, and the Arts

In 1731, Benjamin Franklin founded the Library Company of Philadelphia, the first circulating library in the United States. Today it is recognized for its outstanding collection of rare books. More than 500 public libraries are found throughout the state, as well as dozens of college and university libraries.

Pennsylvania has produced an impressive array of first-rate artists, many from the state's two major cultural centers, Philadelphia and Pittsburgh. Philadelphia boasts the Pennsylvania Academy of the Fine Arts, the Rodin Museum, the Philadelphia Museum of Art, and the Barnes Foundation collection in the suburb of Merion. Several Pittsburgh museums also contain priceless and varied collections, including the Carnegie and the Frick Museum. Other distinguished museums include Philadelphia's Academy of Natural Sciences, the oldest such institution in the country, and the Franklin Institute, which houses a science museum and a planetarium.

Pennsylvania is well established in the performing arts. Philadelphia and Pittsburgh have distinguished symphony orchestras; the Philadelphia Orchestra has made more classical music recordings than any other American orchestra. Philadelphia and Pittsburgh also support ballet and opera companies and numerous theater groups. Community drama groups are active throughout the state.

Philadelphia's Independence Hall is one of the nation's most important historic landmarks. The Declaration of Independence (1776) and the Constitution of the United States (1787) both were signed there.

Some of the nation's most outstanding architecture is located in Pennsylvania. Philadelphia's State House, now known as Independence Hall, is one of the finest examples of colonial architecture. Another of the state's most acclaimed buildings is a house called Fallingwater. Designed by Frank Lloyd Wright, it was built in the 1930's over a waterfall at Bear Run, near Pittsburgh.

Sports

Pennsylvanians are tremendous sports enthusiasts. South Williamsport hosts the annual Little League World Series. Collegiate highlights include the football rivalry of Penn State and Pittsburgh, the rowing regattas on the

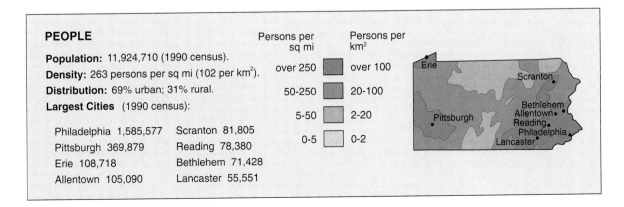

PEOPLE

Population: 11,924,710 (1990 census).
Density: 263 persons per sq mi (102 per km²).
Distribution: 69% urban; 31% rural.
Largest Cities (1990 census):

		Persons per sq mi	Persons per km²
		over 250	over 100
		50-250	20-100
		5-50	2-20
		0-5	0-2

Philadelphia 1,585,577	Scranton 81,805
Pittsburgh 369,879	Reading 78,380
Erie 108,718	Bethlehem 71,428
Allentown 105,090	Lancaster 55,551

From spring through late autumn, roadside stands display the bounty of Pennsylvania farms. Homemade jams, jellies, and baked goods are commonly sold along with the fresh produce.

Schuylkill River, and the Penn Relays, a major annual track meet sponsored by the University of Pennsylvania. Basketball, wrestling, and field hockey also are popular.

Pennsylvania has a full range of professional sports teams—the Philadelphia Eagles and the Pittsburgh Steelers of the National Football League; the Philadelphia 76ers of the National Basketball Association; the Philadelphia Flyers and the Pittsburgh Penguins of the National Hockey League; and the Philadelphia Phillies and the Pittsburgh Pirates of baseball's National League.

▶ECONOMY

Over the past several decades, Pennsylvania's economy has changed. Traditional heavy "smokestack" industries have declined while the service industries have grown. Transportation, communication, and utilities are also important income producers.

Services

Service-oriented businesses are the fastest-growing in Pennsylvania. They currently employ about 76 percent of the state's entire workforce. Services provided in areas such as business, law, medicine, tourism, and recreation as well as community and social services generate the most income, followed by financial services (banking, insurance, and real estate); wholesale and retail trade (the buying and selling of industrial and personal goods); transportation, communication, and utilities; and government services.

Manufacturing

Pennsylvania, once an industrial giant, remains one of the nation's leading manufacturing centers. Nineteen percent of the workforce is employed in the production of such items as primary and fabricated metals, processed foods, heavy machinery, machine tools, electrical machinery, transportation equipment, and paper and printed materials.

Agriculture

Farms cover more than 9 million acres (3.6 million hectares) in Pennsylvania, mostly in the southeast. Agriculture in the state is varied. Livestock, milk, eggs, and poultry are the state's most profitable agricultural products.

Pennsylvania leads the nation in the production of hardwood lumber and plantation-grown Christmas trees. It also leads the other states in mushrooms. Other principal products are corn, hay, apples, pears, and greenhouse plants. However, despite these many farm and forestry products, agriculture contributes only a small amount to the state's overall income.

Mining and Construction

Pennsylvania's coal mining industry was once one of the most important in North America. In 1917–18, its peak production

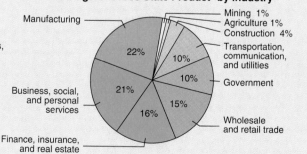

PRODUCTS AND INDUSTRIES

Manufacturing: Primary metals, fabricated metal products, food processing, nonelectrical machinery.

Agriculture: Cattle, hogs, sheep, dairy products, eggs, poultry, turkeys, corn, hay, Christmas trees, apples, pears, greenhouse and nursery products, wheat, soybeans, rye, oats, barley, tobacco, mushrooms, potatoes, tomatoes.

Minerals: Bituminous (soft) coal and anthracite (hard coal), natural gas, petroleum, iron, limestone, sand and gravel.

Services: Wholesale and retail trade; finance, insurance, and real estate; business, social, and personal services; transportation, communication, and utilities; government.

*Gross state product is the total value of goods and services produced in a year.

Percentage of Gross State Product* by Industry

Manufacturing — 22%
Mining 1%
Agriculture 1%
Construction 4%
Transportation, communication, and utilities — 10%
Government — 10%
Wholesale and retail trade — 15%
Finance, insurance, and real estate — 16%
Business, social, and personal services — 21%

Source: U.S. Bureau of Economic Analysis

Pennsylvania is one of the nation's leading producers of energy. *Right:* Three Mile Island, on the Susquehanna River near Harrisburg, is one of two nuclear power plants now operating within the state. *Below:* For many decades, Pennsylvania was the nation's leading producer of steel. Today it ranks third behind Indiana and Ohio.

year, the state produced 270 million tons. The industry declined dramatically through the century, and production reached only 65 million tons in 1991. Nevertheless, the state remains the nation's only producer of anthracite (hard coal) and among the top producers of bituminous (soft) coal. Pennsylvania also produces more stone and stone products than any other state; its limestone is used in the manufacture of agricultural lime, cement, and building stone. Today mining contributes a relatively small portion to the state's economy overall. However, the state's construction industry is a very profitable enterprise, especially in and around Philadelphia.

Energy

Pennsylvania is the nation's third largest producer of electricity; western Pennsylvania supplies 20 percent of the nation's natural gas. Dams on the Ohio and Susquehanna rivers provide hydroelectric power.

The nation's first atomic energy plant was built in Pennsylvania. Today nuclear energy is produced at Three Mile Island on the Susquehanna River and at Limerick on the Schuylkill River. All of these utilities contribute significantly to the state's income.

Transportation

Pennsylvania's waterways and port cities play a significant role in transportation. Philadelphia, on the Delaware River, is the state's busiest and the nation's fourth largest port. It receives more international freighters than any other port in the nation. Pittsburgh, at the head of the Ohio-Mississippi River route, is the nation's largest inland port. In addition to these is the port at Erie on the Great Lakes. Increasing amounts of freight have moved through since the St. Lawrence Seaway was opened to oceangoing vessels in 1959.

A number of interstate highways cross the state, including the Pennsylvania Turnpike, the nation's first superhighway. The state's 115,000 miles (185,000 kilometers) of highways make up the fourth largest state network in the nation. Pennsylvania's 44 railroads run on about 6,000 miles (9,700 kilometers) of track and carry one sixth of the nation's rail tonnage. Passenger travel and freight shipment by air are mostly done through the Philadelphia International and Greater Pittsburgh International airports. Smaller commercial airports service several other cities.

Places of Interest

Fallingwater, near Bear Run

Longwood Gardens, near Philadelphia

The Carnegie Museum of Natural History, in Pittsburgh

Gettysburg National Military Park, in Gettysburg

Delaware Water Gap National Recreation Area, shared with New Jersey, preserves a scenic gorge carved by the Delaware River. It provides a gateway to the Pocono Mountains, a popular winter and summer resort area.

Fallingwater, near Bear Run outside of Pittsburgh, is a spectacular home built over a natural stream and waterfall. Completed in 1936, it is considered a masterpiece of architect Frank Lloyd Wright.

Flagship *Niagara*, docked at Erie, is a reconstruction of the warship commanded by Oliver Hazard Perry during the War of 1812. He later became known as the Hero of the Battle of Lake Erie. (For more information, see the article PERRY, OLIVER HAZARD, in Volume P.)

Fort Necessity National Battlefield, in Farmington, marks the site of the opening battle of the French and Indian War (July 3, 1754). A 22-year-old George Washington, commanding the British colonial troops, was defeated there by the French.

Gettysburg National Military Park, in Gettysburg, commemorates the site of the Civil War's most decisive battle (July 1–3, 1863). Hundreds of monuments, erected in honor of both Union and Confederate forces, decorate the battlefield. The park features a visitors' center containing a museum and an electric map

that expertly explains the Union and Confederate troop movements over the course of the three-day battle. Tourists may also visit the National Cemetery where President Abraham Lincoln delivered the Gettysburg Address.

Hershey, near Harrisburg, is the site of the world's largest chocolate manufacturing plant, founded in 1903 by Milton S. Hershey. A visitors' tour through "Chocolate World" describes how chocolate is made. Nearby Hersheypark features rides, games, shows, and a zoo.

Little League International Headquarters, in Williamsport, is the home of all United States and foreign leagues as well as the Little League International Museum. Little League Baseball was founded in Williamsport in 1939.

Longwood Gardens, in suburban Philadelphia, is an internationally recognized horticultural site. Its beautiful formal gardens, greenhouses, decorative fountains, and seasonal exhibits cover several hundred acres.

Pennsylvania Dutch Country is a region that generally encompasses Lancaster and York counties in the southeastern part of the state. Of particular interest is its quaint population of Amish and Mennonites, members of small Protestant religious sects, who maintain their time-honored traditions by

rejecting modern ways. They are known for their plain dress, horse-drawn carriages, and beautifully kept farms.

Philadelphia is home to dozens of fine museums, performing arts centers, and important historical sites. Among the most frequently visited are Independence Hall, Carpenters' Hall, the Liberty Bell, Elfreth's Alley, and the U.S. Mint. For a detailed description of attractions, see the article PHILADELPHIA in this volume.

Pine Creek Gorge, near Wellsboro, is known as the Grand Canyon of Pennsylvania. The Pine Creek runs along the bottom of the gorge, which is more than 1,000 feet (300 meters) deep.

Pittsburgh, western Pennsylvania's cultural hub, features the Carnegie, a vast complex of museums. For a detailed description of attractions, see the article PITTSBURGH in this volume.

Valley Forge National Historical Park, in Valley Forge, preserves the site where General George Washington and his army camped during the winter of 1777–78.

State Recreation Areas. Pennsylvania has more than 100 state parks in addition to numerous scenic trails, state campgrounds, and picnic areas. To obtain more information, write to the Bureau of State Parks, P.O. Box 8551, Harrisburg, Pennsylvania 17105.

Communication

Pennsylvania has extensive communications systems that broadcast over more than 350 radio and 35 television stations. Pittsburgh's KDKA, the nation's first commercial radio station, began broadcasting in 1920. Radio and television have become increasingly important news sources as the number of newspapers printed in the state has declined. Among the state's major daily newspapers today are the Philadelphia *Inquirer*, the *Philadelphia Daily News*, the *Pittsburgh Post-Gazette*, and the *Allentown Morning Call*.

▶ CITIES

Pennsylvania has six cities with more than 75,000 residents. Harrisburg, the capital, is relatively small, with only about 52,000 residents. The largest cities are in the southeastern and southwestern corners of the state and are located on major waterways.

Harrisburg, located in south-central Pennsylvania, has been the state capital since 1812. It grew up in the early 1700's as a trading post and ferry station on the lower Susquehanna River. Today state government is the city's primary economic activity.

Philadelphia, Pennsylvania's largest city, is located on the Delaware River at the mouth of the Schuylkill River. Founded by William Penn in 1682, the city has always been a busy port. Today it is the financial, medical, educational, and cultural center of the state. An article on Philadelphia appears in this volume.

Pittsburgh, the state's second largest city, was founded as a fort in 1754 at the head of the Ohio River. It was named for William Pitt the Elder, a prime minister (1766–68) of England. No longer the "Smoky City" it was in the heyday of the steel industry, today Pittsburgh is the nation's leading inland port and the hub of business, culture, medicine, and education in southwestern Pennsylvania. An article on Pittsburgh appears in this volume.

Erie, the state's third largest city, is located on Lake Erie in the northwest. Its port lies at the westernmost end of the St. Lawrence Seaway, which connects it to the Atlantic Ocean. Founded in 1795, Erie today is an important transportation, commercial, and industrial city. It was named for the Erie Indians who once lived in the area.

Allentown, on the Lehigh River in eastern Pennsylvania, was founded in 1762. Along with its neighboring cities of Bethlehem and Easton, Allentown is important for its manufacturing industries and as a processing and shipping center for agricultural products. Six colleges are located within the tri-city area.

Scranton is located on the Lackawanna River in northeastern Pennsylvania. Together with the city of Wilkes-Barre, to the south, it is the center of one of the largest anthracite regions in the world. Although the coal industry has declined, Scranton remains an important manufacturing center. The United Mine Workers of America, a large labor union, was organized here in 1897.

The mighty city of Pittsburgh grew up at the site of Fort Duquesne, later Fort Pitt. Today it is the nation's leading inland port and a major center of culture and industry.

The state capitol in Harrisburg was completed in 1913. The main building contains floor-to-ceiling murals with scenes of Pennsylvania's history.

▶ GOVERNMENT

Pennsylvania is one of four states known officially as commonwealths. (The other three are Virginia, Massachusetts, and Kentucky.) Pennsylvania has had several constitutions. The present one was adopted in 1873, although it was revised extensively in 1968.

The governor, the head of the executive branch, serves a 4-year term and may be re-elected once. Other executive officers include the lieutenant governor, who presides over the state senate; an auditor general and an attorney general; and various commissioners, board members, and department heads.

The legislature, known as the General Assembly, consists of the Senate and the House of Representatives, whose members vote to pass the laws of the state. Pennsylvania's

GOVERNMENT

State Government
Governor: 4-year term
State senators: 50; 4-year terms
State representatives: 203;
  2-year terms
Number of counties: 67

Federal Government
U.S. senators: 2
U.S. representatives: 21
Number of electoral votes: 23

For the name of the current governor, see STATE GOVERNMENTS in Volume S. For the names of current U.S. senators and representatives, see UNITED STATES, CONGRESS OF THE in Volume U-V.

INDEX TO PENNSYLVANIA MAP

• County Seat   Counties in parentheses   ★ State Capital

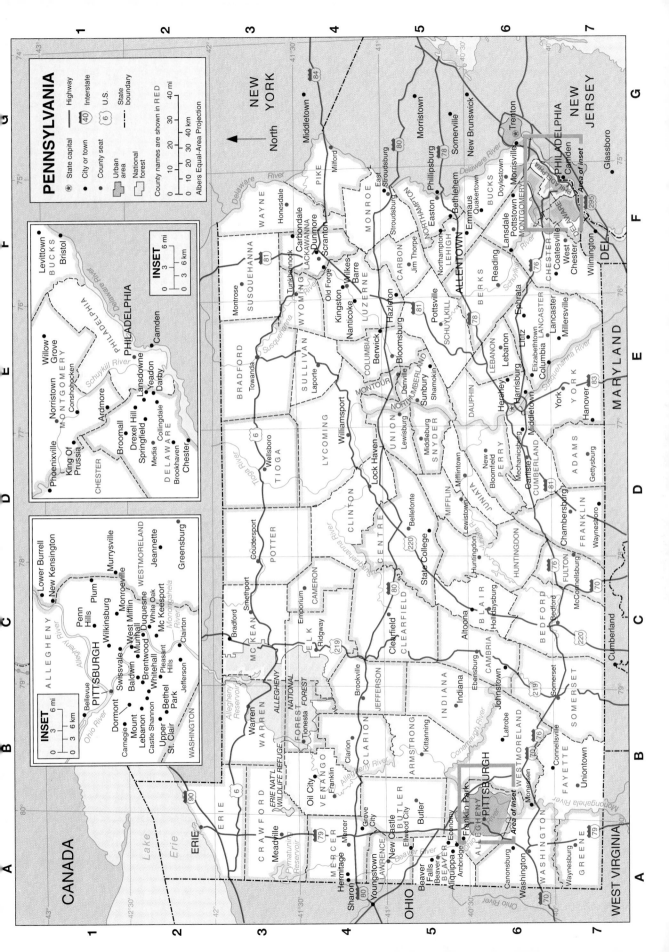

PENNSYLVANIA

Legend:
- ⊛ State capital
- • City or town
- • County seat
- Urban area
- National forest
- Highway
- 40 Interstate
- 6 U.S.
- State boundary

County names are shown in RED
City names are shown in RED

Albers Equal-Area Projection

0 10 20 30 40 km
0 10 20 30 40 mi

North

INSET (Pittsburgh area):
0 3 6 km
0 3 6 mi

INSET (Philadelphia area):
0 3 6 km
0 3 6 mi

CANADA

Lake Erie

NEW YORK

NEW JERSEY

OHIO

WEST VIRGINIA

MARYLAND

DEL.

Pittsburgh Inset
ALLEGHENY, PITTSBURGH, WASHINGTON, WESTMORELAND

Bellevue, Lower Burrell, New Kensington, Murrysville, Penn Hills, Plum, Monroeville, Wilkinsburg, Swissvale, Baldwin, Munhall, Duquesne, West Mifflin, Mc Keesport, White Oak, Brentwood, Whitehall, Pleasant Hills, Clairton, Jefferson, Bethel Park, Castle Shannon, Upper St. Clair, Mount Lebanon, Dormont, Carnegie, Greensburg, Jeannette

Ohio River, Allegheny River, Monongahela River

Philadelphia Inset
PHILADELPHIA, MONTGOMERY, CHESTER, DELAWARE, BUCKS

Levittown, Bristol, Willow Grove, Norristown, Conshohocken, King Of Prussia, Phoenixville, Ardmore, Broomall, Drexel Hill, Springfield, Media, Collingdale, Brookhaven, Chester, Yeadon, Darby, Lansdowne, Camden

Schuylkill River, Delaware River

Counties and cities
ERIE, CRAWFORD, WARREN, MCKEAN, POTTER, TIOGA, BRADFORD, SUSQUEHANNA, WAYNE, PIKE, ELK, CAMERON, CLINTON, LYCOMING, SULLIVAN, WYOMING, LACKAWANNA, MONROE, NORTHAMPTON, CARBON, LUZERNE, COLUMBIA, MONTOUR, UNION, SNYDER, NORTHUMBERLAND, SCHUYLKILL, LEHIGH, BERKS, MIFFLIN, JUNIATA, PERRY, DAUPHIN, LEBANON, LANCASTER, CUMBERLAND, YORK, ADAMS, FRANKLIN, FULTON, BEDFORD, SOMERSET, FAYETTE, GREENE, WASHINGTON, ALLEGHENY, BEAVER, LAWRENCE, MERCER, VENANGO, CLARION, FOREST, JEFFERSON, CLEARFIELD, CENTRE, BLAIR, HUNTINGDON, CAMBRIA, INDIANA, ARMSTRONG, BUTLER, WESTMORELAND

Erie, Meadville, Sharon, Hermitage, Youngstown, New Castle, Ellwood City, Grove City, Butler, Economy, Ambridge, Aliquippa, Beaver, Beaver Falls, Franklin Park, PITTSBURGH, Monessen, Canonsburg, Washington, Waynesburg, Uniontown, Connellsville, Latrobe, Somerset, Johnstown, Ebensburg, Indiana, Holidaysburg, Altoona, Bedford, McConnellsburg, Waynesboro, Gettysburg, Hanover, York, Chambersburg, Carlisle, Mechanicsburg, Middletown, Harrisburg, Hershey, Lebanon, Lititz, Elizabethtown, Columbia, Lancaster, Millersville, Ephrata, Reading, ALLEGHENY, Easton, Northampton, Bethlehem, Emmaus, ALLENTOWN, Quakertown, Pottstown, Lansdale, Doylestown, Morrisville, PHILADELPHIA, Camden, Trenton, Wilmington, West Chester, Coatesville, Glassboro, Jim Thorpe, Pottsville, Shamokin, Sunbury, Danville, Bloomsburg, Berwick, Hazleton, Nanticoke, Wilkes-Barre, Kingston, Old Forge, Scranton, Dunmore, Carbondale, Honesdale, Tunkhannock, Montrose, Towanda, Wellsboro, Coudersport, Smethport, Bradford, Ridgway, Emporium, Brookville, Kittanning, Clarion, Oil City, Clearfield, Bellefonte, State College, Lock Haven, Williamsport, Laporte, Lewisburg, Middleburg, Mifflintown, New Bloomfield, Lewistown, Huntingdon

Milford, East Stroudsburg, Stroudsburg, Phillipsburg, Somerville, New Brunswick, Morristown, Middletown

Allegheny River, Susquehanna River, West Branch Susquehanna River, Juniata River, Delaware River, Schuylkill River, Conemaugh River, Monongahela River, Ohio River, Tioga River, Beaver River

ALLEGHENY NATIONAL FOREST, ERIE NAT'L WILDLIFE REFUGE, Pymatuning Reservoir, Allegheny Reservoir, Tionesta

Interstate routes: 90, 79, 80, 81, 78, 76, 70, 83, 84, 219, 220, 295

U.S. routes: 6

General Assembly is one of the largest state legislatures in the country.

The judicial branch is headed by the state Supreme Court. This court judges the most important cases and administers the lower courts, including the superior court and the commonwealth court. Each of these courts has justices who are elected to 10-year terms and may be re-elected. There are sixty judicial districts, each with a court of common pleas. At the local level, community courts, justices of the peace, aldermen, and magistrates preside over the less important cases.

▶HISTORY

Archaeologists believe that the first Pennsylvanians were prehistoric hunters and gatherers, who settled the region about 12,000 years ago. It is estimated that their Native American descendants numbered about 15,000 when Europeans first came to Pennsylvania in the early 1600's. They belonged to a variety of tribes that included the Delaware (also called Lenni-Lenape or Lenape), Susquehannock, Shawnee, Monongahela, Erie, and Iroquois Seneca.

European Exploration and Settlement

Records show that Dutch explorers sailed up the Delaware River in 1614. French explorer Etienne Brulé traveled up the Susquehanna River the following year. Swedish fur traders moved into Delaware Bay in 1638. They established the first permanent European settlement in Pennsylvania, on Tinicum Island near Philadelphia in 1643. Johan Printz acted as governor of this colony that they called New Sweden.

In 1655 the Swedes were conquered by Dutch forces, who in turn were routed by the English in 1664. The English came to Pennsylvania by way of New Jersey and established themselves in the Delaware Valley.

This decorative Pennsylvania Dutch sign says "Welcome."

William Penn's Colony

In 1681, England's King Charles II granted a tract of land to William Penn, an English Quaker, in payment of a debt owed to Penn's father, Admiral Sir William Penn. Describing his colony as a "Holy Experiment," William Penn promised his settlers that there they would have freedom of worship, representative government, and economic opportunity. His promises were incorporated in the colony's first written constitution, called the Frame of Government. Penn also made peace treaties with the Native Americans and purchased settlement rights from them. His Charter of Privileges, granted in 1701, gave additional rights to the colonists.

The colony prospered almost from the very beginning. Large numbers of English, Welsh, Scotch-Irish, and German-speaking colonists of various religions, as well as a few African slaves, settled there. They cultivated the fertile soil, growing crops for food and for trade. Flour, bread, and biscuits were sent to the West Indies, although most of the colony's goods went to England. Iron ore and iron products, such as kettles, stoves, and plows, were widely produced. In Philadelphia and other towns, craftspeople made hats, furniture, silver and pewter utensils, and rifles. The Conestoga covered wagon originated in Lancaster County about 1725.

Peaceful development continued until 1754, when the French and Indian War began with a clash of French and British colonial forces near the French Fort Duquesne. In an attempt to gain full control of the Ohio Valley, the British sent two armies into Pennsylvania, one in 1755 and another in 1758, which forced the French to withdraw. When the Treaty of Paris concluded the war in 1763, the British took control over the North American continent.

The Revolutionary War and Statehood

After the French and Indian War ended, the British became more strict with their colonial policies. Resisting British authority, the American colonists established the First Continental Congress in Philadelphia in 1774. During the Revolutionary War that ensued, the Second Continental Congress met in Philadelphia and on July 4, 1776, issued the Declaration of Independence.

Philadelphia was by then the largest city in the colonies. It became the seat of the American government and the leading supplier of the

The Constitutional Convention took place in Philadelphia in 1787. George Washington (standing on platform) presided over 55 delegates from twelve states (Rhode Island declined to participate). The document they created was the Constitution of the United States. It was signed by 39 delegates on September 17, 1787, and ratified by a majority of states the following year. Since that time it has served as the framework of the United States government.

Continental Army. In 1777 the battles of Brandywine and Germantown were fought near Philadelphia, and during the harsh winter of 1777–78, General George Washington and his army made camp at Valley Forge on the banks of the Schuylkill River.

After declaring their independence, the American colonists developed their own system of government. The Second Continental Congress, while meeting in York in 1777, created the nation's first written constitution, the Articles of Confederation. This was replaced by the present Constitution of the United States, which was drawn up in Philadelphia in 1787. Benjamin Franklin, Robert Morris, and Gouverneur Morris were among the eight delegates who signed for Pennsylvania. Pennsylvania was the second state (after Delaware) to ratify the new Constitution on December 12, 1787, and for a short time (1790–1800), Philadelphia served as the nation's capital.

Pennsylvanians made numerous efforts to ensure democracy in their state. They formed America's first antislavery society (1775), and the Pennsylvania legislature was the first to move toward abolishing slavery. During the 1800's Lucretia Mott, Sarah and Angelina Grimké, Thaddeus Stevens, and many others based in Pennsylvania tried to persuade southern slave owners to free their slaves. Those slaves who escaped to Pennsylvania by way of the Underground Railroad often received help, especially from Quakers and free African-Americans, such as James Forten and William Still.

The Civil War (1861–65)

Largely because of the states' disagreement over slavery, the Civil War broke out in 1861. Over the next four years, Pennsylvania sent nearly 400,000 troops to fight for the Union. Its factories produced uniforms and weapons, and its railroads transported troops and supplies to the battlefronts. About 80 percent of all the pig iron used by the Union Army during the war came from Pennsylvania.

From July 1 through July 3, 1863, the war's most important battle was fought at Gettysburg, not far from the Maryland border. Union forces, led by Pennsylvania's own General George Gordon Meade, defeated the Confederates and for the first time turned the war to the Union's favor. On November 19, 1863, while visiting the town to dedicate a cemetery to the thousands of soldiers who lost their lives there, President Abraham Lincoln delivered his famous Gettysburg Address, which many consider to be the most stirring speech ever written. (The article GETTYSBURG ADDRESS appears in Volume G.)

Prosperity and a New Century

By the turn of the century, Pennsylvania was the nation's leading producer of steel and coal and was among the largest producers of oil and lumber. Small businesses combined to form vast corporations and trusts, controlled by some of the world's most powerful industrialists. Among them were Andrew Carnegie, who came to dominate the steel industry, and his partner, Henry Clay Frick, who controlled

Famous People

Richard Allen (1760–1831), born a slave in Philadelphia, founded and was first bishop of the African Methodist Episcopal (A.M.E.) Church. In 1787, following a racial incident at St. George's Methodist Church in Philadelphia, Allen organized the Free African Society to provide spiritual guidance to a black congregation in a nondiscriminatory environment. In 1799 he was ordained a deacon of the Methodist Church. In 1816 he founded the A.M.E., a national organization of black congregations. It is the oldest continuous organization of African Americans in the United States.

Andrew Carnegie (1835–1919), born in Dunfermline, Scotland, made a fortune developing the Pennsylvania steel industry. After he sold his Carnegie Steel Company to J. P. Morgan in 1901, he devoted himself to helping people and causes. He donated more than $350 million in support of museums, libraries, universities, and the international peace movement. A biography of Andrew Carnegie appears in Volume C.

Benjamin Franklin (1706–90) was born in Boston but spent much of his life in Pennsylvania. Considered one of the most important and remarkable people in all of history, Franklin was an accom-

Andrew Carnegie

plished scientist, inventor, printer, writer, diplomat, civic leader, and statesman. A biography of Benjamin Franklin appears in Volume F.

Martha Graham (1894–1991), born in Allegheny, was a major force in the evolution of modern dance. A brilliant dancer and choreographer, she pioneered extremely bold body movements to express a full range of human emotions. Her themes ranged from literary figures in ancient Greece to rituals of Native Americans. Among her most memorable works are *El Penitente* (1940), *Appalachian Spring* (1944), *Clytemnestra* (1958), and *Rite of Spring* (1984).

Andrew William Mellon (1855–1937), born in Pittsburgh, amassed a fortune in his family's banking business. He used his wealth to promote oil, steel, and other industries in the Pittsburgh area. The financier served as U.S. secretary of the treasury (1921–32) and later served as ambassador to Great Britain (1932–33). In 1937, Mellon donated his art collection, worth approximately $35 million, to the people of the United States. He also donated $15 million to build the National Gallery of Art in Washington, D.C., which now houses the collection.

Eugene Ormandy (Eugene Ormandy Blau) (1899–1985), born in Budapest, Hungary, conducted the Philadelphia Orchestra for more than forty years (1938–80). Trained as a violinist, he emigrated to the United States in 1921 and became a U.S. citizen in 1927. He led the Minneapolis Symphony (1931–36), then moved to Philadelphia where he served as associate conductor (1936–38) under the great Leopold Stokowski, whom he succeeded as music director and principal conductor in 1938. Ormandy remains one of the most recognized names in the history of symphony orchestra recording.

much of the coal and coke production. John D. Rockefeller dominated the state's oil business, and the Pennsylvania Railroad, led by J. Edgar Thompson and Thomas C. Scott, became the nation's leading freight carrier.

Labor Conflicts

While businesses grew enormously rich and powerful, most miners and laborers lived and worked in wretched conditions. To fight more effectively for higher wages, shorter hours, and safer working conditions, the workers joined together and formed some of the nation's first labor unions. Among the most notable founded in Pennsylvania were the Noble Order of the Knights of Labor (1869), the American Federation of Labor (1886), and the reorganized Congress of Industrial Organizations (1938).

Pennsylvania was the first oil-producing state. Edwin L. Drake (in top hat), a retired railroad conductor, drilled the nation's first oil well, near Titusville, in 1859.

William Penn (1644–1718), born in London, England, was a prominent English Quaker and reformer who founded the colony of Pennsylvania and the city of Philadelphia. A biography of William Penn appears in this volume.

John Hoyer Updike (1932–), born in Shillington, is a renowned author of American fiction. His carefully crafted novels and short stories are concerned mainly with small-town, middle-class American life. In novels such as *Rabbit Is Rich* (1981), which won the 1982 Pulitzer prize for fiction, the characters lead worldly lives but search for spiritual fulfillment. Updike's other works include *Rabbit Run* (1960), *Rabbit Redux* (1971), and *The Witches of Eastwick* (1984). In 1992 he won a second Pulitzer prize for *Rabbit at Rest* (1991).

August Wilson (1945–), born in Pittsburgh, is a prize-winning playwright, whose stories often take place in his hometown. Wilson's plays examine the issue of black indentity through the generations. His first theatrical breakthrough was *Ma Rainey's Black Bottom* (1984). He won his first Pulitzer prize for drama in 1987 with *Fences* (1985); a second was awarded in 1990 for *The Piano Lesson* (1987).

Martha Graham

Consult the Index to find more information on these and other famous Pennsylvanians:

ALCOTT, Louisa May	FIELDS, W. C.	MONTANA, Joe
ANDERSON, Marian	FORTEN, James	NAMATH, Joe
ANDERSON, Maxwell	FOSTER, Stephen	O'HARA, John
BARBER, Samuel	FRICK, Henry Clay	PALMER, Arnold
BARRYMORE Family	FULTON, Robert	PEARY, Robert E.
BOONE, Daniel	GRACE, Princess	ROGERS, Mister
BUCHANAN, James	GRANGE, Red	ROSS, Betsy
CALDER, Alexander	IACOCCA, Lee A.	RUSH, Benjamin
CAMPANELLA, Roy	JACKSON, Reggie	RUSTIN, Bayard
CARSON, Rachel	KAUFMAN, George S.	STEIN, Gertrude
CASSATT, Mary	KELLY, Gene	STEWART, James
CHAMBERLAIN, Wilt	MARSHALL, George C.	TARBELL, Ida
COMMAGER, Henry Steele	MCCLELLAN, George B.	WARHOL, Andy
COSBY, Bill	MCGUFFEY, William Holmes	WATERS, Ethel
DALLAS, George Mifflin	MEAD, Margaret	WEST, Benjamin
EAKINS, Thomas	MIFFLIN, Thomas	WYETH, Andrew

Workers often came into violent conflict with industrial leaders. Irish immigrant coal miners, who called themselves the Molly Maguires, terrorized Pennsylvania mine owners in the 1870's. Major conflicts included the Great Railroad Strike of 1877 and the Homestead steel strike in 1892. However, for half a century corporate giants were able to prevent the passage of most labor-reform laws due to their powerful influence over state politics.

Industrial Decline

By the 1920's, Pennsylvania's economy was beginning to decline, despite the boost that World War I had provided to its industries. Then came the Great Depression of the 1930's, when many industries, businesses, and banks failed. American participation (1941–45) in World War II restored prosperity to Pennsylvania's heavy industries due to the country's need for war supplies. But after the war, coal, steel, and textile production fell, and the railroad industries also declined. Between 1950 and 1962, Pennsylvania had the second highest percentage of jobless workers in the nation.

Recent Trends

Pennsylvania continues to face serious challenges, including unemployment and overcrowding in its cities. However, the state still ranks high in steel production, and statewide economic conditions have slowly improved due to the growth of other industries, particularly tourism. New technology has created jobs in the fields of telecommunications, biotechnology, and computer research and development. Nuclear power is also a strong industry, despite a disaster at the Three Mile Island plant near Harrisburg in 1979. Also expanding is the number of jobs in business, education, and health care services. In spite of its struggles, Pennsylvania has consistently remained one of the largest income-producing states in the nation.

JOHN B. FRANTZ
The Pennsylvania State University

See also PHILADELPHIA; PITTSBURGH.

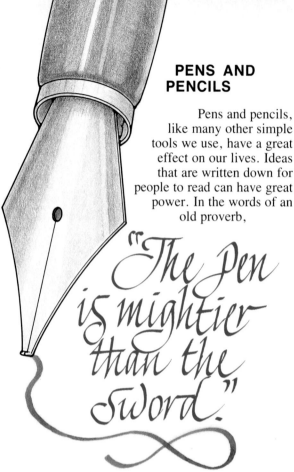

PENS AND PENCILS

Pens and pencils, like many other simple tools we use, have a great effect on our lives. Ideas that are written down for people to read can have great power. In the words of an old proverb,

"The Pen is mightier than the Sword."

▶PENS

A pen is a writing tool that uses ink. The first such tool was a swamp reed that had a writing end that was slightly frayed, like a brush. The swamp-reed pen was used about 2,000 years before the time of Christ. This reed pen was first used with ink to write on a sheet of **papyrus** (a paper-thin sheet of pressed papyrus plant) and later used on **parchment** (thin-scraped animal skin).

Quills were first made into pens early in the 600's. A **quill** is the hollow, hard part of a large feather, usually from a goose. The word "pen" comes from the Latin word *penna*, meaning "feather." Quill pens were usually used for writing on parchment. As a writer used a quill pen, he or she had to sharpen it several times. The little knife used for this was known as a **penknife**, a term still used today for a small knife.

Steel **pen nibs** (points) came into general use early in the 1800's. Since steel pens did not need sharpening, they were more efficient than quill pens. But like quill pens, they still needed to be dipped in ink after every few words were written.

Fountain Pens

The first practical fountain pen was manufactured in the United States in 1884. Like all fountain pens since, it had four basic parts: a

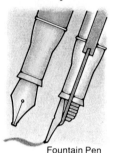

Fountain Pen

barrel to hold ink, a point for writing, a feed bar that supplied ink to the point, and a cap to protect the point and keep the ink from drying up when the pen was not in use. To fill the pen, the user had to unscrew the point and drop ink into the barrel with an eyedropper. This was a messy chore, but fountain pens held enough ink for a great deal of writing, so they did not need to be filled often.

Between the late 1800's and 1950, most pens were filled by the use of a lever on the side of the barrel. The lever squeezed a rubber ink sac inside the barrel. When the lever was released, the rubber sac expanded and sucked up ink. Some pens used a plunger instead of a lever.

Later two other methods of filling a fountain pen became common. In one an **ink cartridge** (a small plastic container of ink) is put into the ink barrel. In the other method the pen is filled with many tiny tubes, or channels. When the pen is set into ink, the channels suck up ink by capillary action, much as a sponge soaks up water. There is nothing to put into the barrel and nothing to squeeze.

Ballpoint Pens

A ballpoint pen has as its point a small rotating metal ball that continually inks itself as it turns. The ball is set into a tiny socket. In the center of the socket is a hole that feeds ink

Ballpoint Pen

to the socket from a long tube inside the pen. Small hairlike grooves run from the center hole almost to the edge of the socket. The grooves help to spread the ink over the inside of the socket. As the ball spins, it picks up a thin layer of ink and transfers it to the paper as a line.

The first practical ballpoint pen was made in South America in 1943 by a journalist and printer named Laszlo Biro. His first model had a roller instead of a ball at the tip. But this model could only write straight lines, and handwriting is full of curves. So Biro replaced the roller with a ball, which can revolve freely in any direction and therefore make the curves of handwriting.

Early ballpoint pens had ordinary ball bearings as writing tips. The small, smooth balls tended to skip over the paper instead of rolling. In 1957 a ball made of finely powdered metal was developed. The tiny particles of the metal powder fuse together when the ball is shaped under great pressure and heat. The powdered-metal ball has about 50,000 tiny ridges on its surface. The ridges grip the paper much as the tread of an automobile tire grips the road. They keep the ball from skipping and skidding. This type of ball or a synthetic jewel ball is now used in most ballpoint pens.

The ink used in ballpoint pens is different from the ink used in fountain pens. The free-flowing fountain-pen ink would run out of a ballpoint pen. Therefore, a thick, more flow-resistant ink is used.

A ballpoint pen looks simpler than a fountain pen, but it is very difficult to manufacture. Exceedingly fine work is needed to place a ball in a tiny socket so that it will spin freely yet not fall out. Ballpoint pen manufacturers work with measurements as precise as those used in spacecraft.

Soft-Tip and Rolling-Ball Pens

Since 1950 two other types of pens have been introduced. Soft-tip pens have a tip made

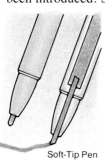

of felt or soft, absorbent plastic that is fed a free-flowing ink from a reservoir. Rolling-ball pens combine the tip of a ballpoint pen with the free-flowing ink of a soft-tip pen for smooth writing. The flow of ink between the reservoir and the tip is controlled by a wick that

Soft-Tip Pen

can only hold a certain amount of ink at a time.

Special-Purpose Pens. Some pens are designed for specific purposes. Technical pens come with changeable tips of different sizes. Artists use these pens to achieve special effects in their work.

ALFRED P. DIOTTE
The Parker Pen Company

▶**PENCILS**

The simple pencil we use today developed gradually over a long period of time. A pencil is a writing stick made of a slender rod of **graphite** (a soft, black, lustrous form of carbon) and clay surrounded by a wooden case. But it did not take this form until late in the 1600's.

Probably the first pencils—sticks of metallic lead that drew faint lines—were those used by the Greeks and Romans around the beginning of the Christian Era. Such lead pencils were still being used in the 1800's.

The use of graphite in pencils dates back to 1564. There is a story that at that time a hurricane roared across the British Isles. Wind uprooted a great tree near Borrowdale, England, and a strange black substance was turned up. A farmer discovered that the black stuff made marks that would not wash off. He and other farmers began to use it to mark sheep. The material was graphite.

Steps in Making a Pencil

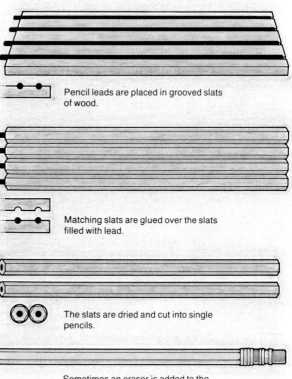

Pencil leads are placed in grooved slats of wood.

Matching slats are glued over the slats filled with lead.

The slats are dried and cut into single pencils.

Sometimes an eraser is added to the finished pencil.

Scientists who examined the graphite called it *plumbago*—Latin for a kind of lead ore. The name "lead" has stuck to this day.

The Borrowdale graphite was so solid that it could be cut into lengths to be peddled in London streets as writing sticks. At first the sticks were used without any covering. Then they were wrapped in string to keep the user's fingers from getting dirty. Metal cases were also used. Around 1686 a way of putting the graphite between strips of wood was discovered, and the pencil took its present form.

Although the Borrowdale graphite was mined very carefully, it began to run out near the end of the 1700's. About the same time, a French chemist, Jacques Conté, discovered that graphite could be mixed with other substances and still make marks. He mixed powdered graphite with powdered clay and water. Once this material was baked, it wrote as smoothly as Borrowdale graphite.

Around 1839 a German named Johann Lothar von Faber (1817–96) developed the idea of forcing graphite paste through a die, or mold. This made pencil leads all the same thickness. Von Faber also developed machinery to cut and groove the wood that surrounds a pencil.

Pencils are made in different degrees of hardness, which are usually identified by the numbers 1, 2, or 3. Variations in hardness depend on the use of different proportions of clay and graphite; the more clay a pencil has, the harder it is. A number 1 pencil is very soft and makes a heavy black mark with little pressure. A number 2 is an ordinary (medium-soft) writing pencil. A number 3 is a hard pencil, good for making light, fine lines.

Mechanical Pencils. A mechanical pencil has a metal or plastic body with a long, thin holder inside, into which one or more sticks of lead are set. There are two methods of bringing the lead out. In one, the lead is moved forward by turning the top of the pencil. In the other, a button on the pencil's cap or side is pressed to push the lead forward.

Special-Purpose Pencils. Pencils are made in a large variety of colors and in many types of leads. Colored pencils, often used by editors, are made with dyes in place of graphite. Grease or wax pencils are used to make marks on glass, plastic, and film. Charcoal pencils are used by artists.

For certain jobs, pencils may be specially shaped or colored. For example, a carpenter's pencil has a flat shape, so that it will not roll when set down. The outside is bright red, so that it will show up quickly in wood shavings.

ARTHUR VAN DER KAR
Venus Pen and Pencil Corporation

PEORIA. See ILLINOIS (Cities).

PEPPER. See HERBS, SPICES, AND CONDIMENTS.

PERCENTAGE

A percent is one-hundredth of something. The "something" can be almost anything—a sum of money, a group of people, or the number of games in a baseball season. Percentages are widely used in schools, businesses, sports, government, and many other fields.

The word "percent" comes from the Latin *per centum* and the Italian *per cento*, meaning "for each hundred" or "out of each hundred." Italian merchants in the 1400's were the first to use a symbol for percentage. When they computed how much waste or spoilage had occurred in shipping, they abbreviated *per cento* to *p cº*. Later this became *cº*, still later $\frac{o}{o}$, and finally the symbol we use today: %.

▶ UNDERSTANDING PERCENT

The total amount of something is always 100%. If a bag contains 25 golf balls, 100% of the total is 25 golf balls. If you answer all the questions on a test correctly, your score will be 100%, whether there are 15 or 150 questions on the test. If a candidate in an election wins 65% of the vote, 65 out of every 100 people voted for that candidate.

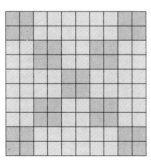

There are 100 squares in this blue and green grid. What percent of them are blue? Since 36 out of the 100 squares are blue, 36% of the squares are blue.

If everyone voted for the candidate, he or she would win 100% of the vote—100 out of every 100 votes.

▶ PERCENTS, FRACTIONS, AND DECIMALS

Since percents are hundredths of something, they can be written in the form of a common fraction or a decimal fraction. To write a percent as a common fraction, drop the percent sign and add a denominator of 100. You can then reduce the fraction.

$$75\% = \frac{75}{100} = \frac{3}{4}$$
$$20\% = \frac{20}{100} = \frac{1}{5}$$

To write a percent as a decimal, change the percent to a common fraction. Then change the common fraction to a decimal.

$$25\% = \frac{25}{100} = 0.25$$
$$80\% = \frac{80}{100} = 0.8$$

To change a decimal fraction to a percent, you simply move the decimal point two places to the right and add the symbol for percent. Thus 0.05 becomes 5%. To change a common fraction to a percent, first change it to a decimal fraction. To do this, divide the numerator by the denominator, then change the decimal to a percent.

$$\frac{2}{5} = 2 \div 5 = 0.4 = 40\%$$

▶ PERCENTAGE PROBLEMS

Since percents can be written as common fractions or as decimal fractions, percentage problems are solved in the same way as fraction or decimal problems.

Finding a Percentage of a Number. If a salesclerk receives a 15% commission on the price of goods sold, how much is the commission on a sale of $34? First change the percent to its equivalent decimal: 15% = 0.15. Then multiply the price of the item sold by the decimal fraction: 0.15 x $34 = $5.10. The commission is $5.10 on a sale of $34.

Usually you do not have to write this type of problem down on paper or use a calculator. You can often compute the answer in your head. For example, if you are making a $10 purchase for which there is a 10% discount, you can think of the percentage as a common fraction. Thus 10% is the same as $\frac{1}{10}$, and $\frac{1}{10}$ of $10 is $1. For every $10, the dis-

count is $1. If the price is $20, the discount is $2, and the purchase costs only $18.

In some situations you can also use estimation to determine the amount by rounding it off to the nearest ten. If the purchase price is $27, you would think $27 is close to $30, so the discount will be almost $3. The purchase will then cost $27 – $3, or about $24.

Finding What Percent One Number Is of Another. Suppose there are 15 questions on your science test. If you answer 12 correctly, what should your grade be if it is expressed as a percentage? To find out, first write your test score as the fraction $\frac{12}{15}$. Divide the numerator by the denominator to change the fraction to a decimal. Then change the decimal to a percentage.

$$\frac{12}{15} = 12 \div 15 = 0.8 = 80\%$$

You should receive a grade of 80% on the test.

Finding a Number When the Percent Is Known. Imagine that a baseball team wins 56% of its games. You know that the team won 14 games. How many games did the team play? The question "14 is 56% of what

$$
\begin{array}{r}
25 \\
0.56\overline{\smash{\big)}\,14.00} \\
\underline{112} \\
280 \\
\underline{280} \\
\end{array}
$$

number?" can be written 14 = 0.56 x ? To find the answer, divide 14 by 0.56.

Since 14 is 56% of 25, the team played 25 games.

▶ USES OF PERCENTS

There are many common uses of percents. You are probably most familiar with percents as grades—the percent of the correct answers on your test scores. Some test scores, however, are expressed as **percentile** scores. A percentile is a value based on a scale of 100. If you receive a percentile rank of 80 on a test, it means that you scored as well as or better than 80% of the people who took the test. It does not mean that you got 80% of the questions correct.

Making Comparisons. The standings of sports leagues or teams are often expressed as the percent of games won out of the total games played. Even though this is called a

there are laws regulating whether a discount or the sales tax is calculated first on a purchase? Why does it make a difference?

Suppose you want to buy a $25 shirt that is on sale for 20% off the original price. There is also a 5% sales tax. Does computing the sales tax before or after you take your 20% discount make any difference in the total amount you pay? Does it make any difference in how much money the store earns or the state gets in taxes?

If you take the 20% off first, you are actually paying 80% of $25, or $20. The sales tax is 5% of $20, or $1. Your total bill is $21. The store gets $20 for the purchase and the state gets $1 in taxes.

If you compute the tax first, 5% of $25 is $1.25. The total price becomes $26.25. The result of the discount of 20% on $26.25 is $21. You still pay $21, but since the state gets $1.25 in taxes, the store gets only $19.75 for the purchase of the shirt. State laws often

specify that stores need only collect sales tax on the money they actually receive. As a result, they can compute the discount before the tax and keep more of the amount you pay for a product.

percent, it is actually written as a decimal to the thousandths place. Percents make it easy to compare one team or one player against another, even though both may not have played the same number of games. Percents are used for comparisons in other fields, too.

In Business. Stores and other businesses use percents to show price discounts and to state the commissions earned by salespeople. Profits, or the income left after subtracting the costs of doing business, are also usually expressed as a percent of total income. Packaged foods are labeled to show the percent of vitamins and minerals they contain. Clothing labels list what percent of different fibers make up the fabric.

Interest. Banks charge interest on money they lend, and they pay interest on money that is deposited in the bank. The interest on a loan is sometimes figured as a percentage of the total amount of the loan. Interest on savings deposits is also a percentage, and it is usually compounded. This means that the bank calculates interest on the total amount of money in an account, including previous interest payments. Credit card companies also charge interest on balances left unpaid at the end of a month.

Taxes. Taxes are often figured as percentages. For example, the sales tax on an item is usually a percentage of the item's selling price, and income taxes are usually a percentage of a person's earnings.

Inflation. The rate of inflation—how much prices rise over a certain time—is shown in percents. If something that cost $1 one year costs $1.25 the following year, it costs 25% more, and the rate of inflation is 25%. The new price is 125% (100% + 25%) of the old price.

Probability. Percents are also widely used to express probability, the chance that something will happen. A weather forecaster may tell you that there is a 40% chance of rain today. Experience has shown the forecaster that on 40 out of every 100 days with weather conditions like those shaping that day's weather, it rains.

There are many other situations in which percents are used. Knowing about them will be useful often.

JESSICA DAVIDSON
Author, *Using the Cuisenaire Rods*
Reviewed and updated by ERICA DAKIN VOOLICH
Solomon Schechter Day School

See also INTEREST.

PERCUSSION INSTRUMENTS

Almost anything that gives off a sound when struck can be used in music as a percussion instrument. The word "percussion" comes from a Latin word meaning "to beat." When primitive people danced, they stamped on the ground with their feet. The thudding sound they made became a rhythm. Planks laid across a hollow pit in the earth made a more satisfactory sound because the air in the pit resonated. Hollow trees struck with the hands had even greater resonance. Before long, drums were invented.

How Drums Are Made and Played

Drums are found all over the world. They are hollowed out from solid wood or built up from thin strips. Pottery or metal bowls and empty gasoline cans are turned into drums.

Drums are usually made by stretching a membrane across one end or both ends of an open cylinder. The membrane is usually thin parchment (skin or vellum). The drum is sounded by making this membrane vibrate. The vibrations, passing through the air, reach our ears as sound.

Vibrations are set up in the drum by striking the membrane. It may be struck with the fin-gers, the flat of the hand, a drumstick, or a pair of drumsticks.

Very delicate tappings may be made with the fingers. As the fingers move from the edge of the membrane toward the center, the sound grows stronger and more resonant. If the flat of the hand is used, there is more of a dull boom. Asian drummers are especially clever at making contrasts in the sound.

Drumsticks, too, can be used in different ways: sometimes lightly, sometimes violently; sometimes near the edge of the membrane, sometimes near the center. When the stick is light and hard, the sound is dry. A heavier stick will make a more booming sound, especially when it is covered at the end with a soft material, such as felt. A wire brush is often used by jazz drummers to make a swishing sound.

Sometimes the drummer chooses to strike the rim of the drum or another part of the cylinder. This, too, makes the drum vibrate. But it gives off a much harsher sound than striking the membrane.

In Asian orchestras, the chief drummer may squat on the ground with the drums set out in a half circle, so that they can all be reached with equal ease. Using only fingers and the flat of the hand, the drummer plays on the

Two street musicians at an outdoor concert in New York City play percussion instruments: drums, cymbals, and a xylophone.

drums like a virtuoso pianist. The sounds vary from very soft to rather loud. A good drummer does not use any great violence but makes a sort of shading and tone coloring. And each drum in turn gives a note of different pitch.

Many drums can give a distinct note that is perfectly in tune. The drum is tuned by altering the tightness of the membrane. The tighter the membrane, the higher the note. Little drums sound higher than big drums when the tightness is the same.

Not all drums can give a distinct note. There are big drums that thunder in the orchestra. They sound powerful but have no distinct note of their own. There are smaller drums that clatter excitingly but, again, give no special note. The big drums are bass drums. The smaller ones may be tenor drums or side drums. Side drums have a special feaure: The end that is not struck has cords stretched lightly across it. These rattle when the drum is played. The cords are called snares, so this kind of drum is called a snare drum.

In the symphony orchestra, bass drums and side drums are not so common as kettledrums, or timpani as they are sometimes called. The kettledrum has a deep, bowl-shaped body that looks rather like half of an enormous eggshell. The top is covered by a large parchment of the finest quality. The shape of the kettledrum affects its tone. The rounded bottom reflects back sound as evenly as possible. Since kettledrums are made of brightly polished metal—usually brass or copper—they stand out in the orchestra.

A kettledrum is played with two padded drumsticks.

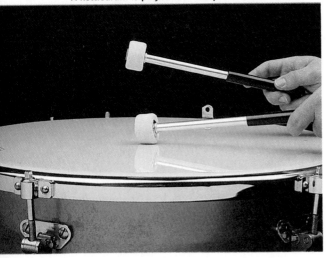

The kettledrum gives a beautifully distinct note. It can be tuned exactly. The kettledrummer turns thumbscrews or operates a pedal mechanism to tighten or slacken the parchment until the note is tuned exactly right. The note of a drum may have to be changed in the middle of a piece. A skilled drummer does this quickly and carefully.

Like the Asian drummer, the kettledrummer sets the drums out in a half-circle. But the kettledrums are larger and not so numerous. There are usually from three to five kettledrums. They are played not with the hands or fingers but with two drumsticks, one in either hand.

The heads of the sticks are covered with felt. The drummer has a choice of sticks, some covered with thick, soft felt and some with thin, hard felt. By using different sticks and by playing sometimes near the edge and sometimes near the center, the drummer can vary the sound.

For a soft sound, the sticks hardly need to be lifted. For a loud sound, they are raised high. A special technique is the roll. Instead of separate sounds, we hear a continuous sound. When very soft, it is like a murmuring wind. But when it is louder, it is like the roar of a great waterfall. The roll is done by rapidly striking two sticks close to the parchment. Because the sticks strike so rapidly, the sound has no time to die away between strokes.

Drums in the Orchestra

Drums are often very important in Asian orchestras. Sometimes there are no other instruments at all. Sometimes there are other percussion instruments like bowls, bars, and clappers. An orchestra of drums and percussion instruments makes powerful music. The sound can be both subtle and exciting.

In Western symphony orchestras the drums are rarely as important. But they add a range of sounds all their own, from the deep bass drum and the snarling side drum to the mellow kettledrums. The kettledrums are the aristocrats of the percussion section. Their clear notes are so finely outlined that they are occasionally given solo passages to play.

The drums also set the rhythm. Music is full of varying rhythms. The drums and other percussion instruments mark these rhythms with the utmost sharpness. Rhythm is especially prominent in dance music.

Other Percussion Instruments

In the 1700's, Europeans became fascinated with the marching bands of the Turkish Army. These bands used an assortment of instruments that made clashing sounds. One instrument was the Turkish crescent. This was a tall stick mounted with metal plates. It was played simply by shaking it in rhythm with the music. This instrument and other Turkish noisemakers became very fashionable.

Two Turkish instruments, the cymbals and the triangle, became permanent members of the Western orchestra. The cymbals are a pair of brass plates. They come in all sizes, but in the orchestra they are usually large and resonant. The player can jingle them together softly or clash them loudly. A jazz percussion player usually has them set on a stand, so that they can be played with a foot pedal. The player's hands are then free for the drums and other percussion instruments.

The triangle is nothing but a bent rod of steel. One corner of it is left open so that the rod can vibrate freely, giving a ringing sound. The triangle is played with another rod of steel. It can be struck powerfully, or it can be made to give a continuous trill by rattling the rod in one corner of the triangle.

A Turkish crescent, also called a "Jingling Johnnie," is topped by a crescent and an ornament shaped like a Chinese hat, from which another crescent, bells, jingles, and two horsehair tails are suspended.

There is one instrument, used occasionally in the orchestra, that is half drum and half cymbals. This is the tambourine. It is about the size of a dinner plate, and the frame is only about 3 inches (7 centimeters) deep. Parchment covers one end, and the other end is left open. Pairs of tiny cymbals are set around the outside. The players can strike the parchment with the hand or rub it with the fingers to produce a throbbing sound. Or they can shake the tambourine at rhythmic intervals. Whatever they do, the cymbals jingle together.

Castanets are a pair of wooden clappers, held in one hand. They have a dry, brittle sound when clapped together in rhythm with the music. Dancers in Spain use castanets.

Bells of all sizes have been used in the orchestra. But since large bells take up much room and are very expensive, the sound of bells is usually produced on long, hollow tubes of steel. A row of tubes of different lengths is mounted on a frame, making it easy to play different notes.

Another bell-like instrument is the glockenspiel. (The word is German for "bell play.") It is a row of metal bars played with hammers held like drumsticks. An instrument very much like the glockenspiel is the celesta. It has a keyboard for working the hammers. The sound of these two instruments in the orchestra is light and ringing. The xylophone ("wood sound," from the Greek) has bars made of wood instead of metal. The playing sticks are hard, and the tone crisp and hollow. The xylophone is the sort of instrument that can be used only occasionally, for a special effect.

Strange instruments sometimes find their way into the percussion section. Gongs are close relatives of cymbals, but they are played with soft, heavy drumsticks. Anvils are heard in the "Anvil Chorus" of Verdi's *Il Trovatore*, and in Wagner's opera *Das Rheingold* to create the sound of dwarfs hammering away at their work. In one famous passage of Schoenberg's *Gurre-Lieder*, heavy iron chains have to be lifted and dropped. The effect of the passage is meant to be exceedingly gloomy, and that is how it sounds.

It is no wonder that orchestral players sometimes call the percussion section the kitchen of the orchestra.

ROBERT DONINGTON
Author, *The Instruments of Music*

See also DRUM.

PERFUMES

Perfume is a delightful fragrance. It may come from a woodland after rain, an apple tree in bloom, a freshly cut orange, or a liquid in a pretty bottle.

The fragrances of natural materials are caused by oils within them. These oils are used to make perfumes in either a liquid or a solid form. The liquid perfumes are those usually found in bottles, aerosol sprays, and bath oils. Liquid perfumes are also used to add a pleasant scent to soap, hand cream, and other toilet preparations. Perfume sticks, incense, and perfumed candles are examples of perfume in solid form.

Usually we think of perfumes as flowery or fruit-scented substances used to make a person or a room smell pleasant. But it is also possible to make scents that smell like popcorn, new cars, or a seashore.

▶HISTORY OF PERFUME

The use of perfumes goes far back in time. Some of the first perfumes were fragrant woods and spices that were burned as incense in religious ceremonies. In fact, the word "perfume" comes from the Latin *per* ("through") and *fumus* ("smoke"). Later it was discovered that some perfumes helped to prevent decay. People came to believe that scent had magical properties. For these reasons perfumes were used in treating the sick and embalming the dead.

The people of ancient Egypt used fragrant oils and ointments when bathing. Cleopatra is famous for her use of perfumes. She is said to have perfumed not only herself but also the sails of her boat. Flower perfumes were first used in Greece. Both the Greeks and the Romans used perfumes very freely. At that time people probably made their fragrances by dipping flowers and herbs into hot oils or wines. Or they may have spread petals out on trays of fat until the fat absorbed the odor of the petals. The Persians learned to boil off and collect the fragrance of petals.

After 1500 the habit of wearing perfumes became especially fashionable in Europe. Men and women hung from their waists ornamental pomanders (a mixture of fragrant dried leaves, blossoms, and other substances enclosed in a perforated bag or box). Wealthy households contained a room called a still, where the family's perfumes were made. Italy and France began to grow flowers especially for perfumes.

▶WHAT GOES INTO A PERFUME?

The materials with which perfumes are made come from all over the world—rich spices from Asian lands, rare blossoms from jungles, musk from the musk deer that roam the Himalayan mountains of Tibet. As many as 300 different materials may be used to make one perfume. Three types of materials are used—fragrant essential oils, fixatives, and synthetic aromatic chemicals.

The fragrant essential oils once were available only from natural materials, such as flowers, leaves, fruits, roots, and seeds. These oils are still used. But chemists now can make identical or very similar oils in laboratories. Today most perfumes contain a combination of natural and synthetic oils.

The natural oils provide a large number of different odors. Some of the most familiar ones are listed in the chart. Others that are also used are clove, heliotrope, lilac, bay, eucalyptus, wintergreen, angelica, orris, bergamot, and lime. Synthetic perfume oils have been created that smell like lemon verbena, hyacinth, rose, gardenia, orange blossom, hawthorn, and wintergreen.

Most perfumes contain fixatives that keep the fragrance from evaporating quickly. The fixatives do not spoil the odor of the perfume

WONDER QUESTION

What are toilet water and cologne?

Cologne is a perfumed liquid that is used in or after a bath and for a skin freshener. It is largely alcohol. Traditionally, cologne has been based on the fragrance of citrus, and this fragrance has distinguished cologne from toilet water. But few companies today make toilet water and cologne in the traditional way. Now the words "cologne" and "toilet water" refer to different concentrations of perfume oils. Toilet water is usually the stronger of the two. Both are intended to be splashed freely over the body or sprayed in the hair. Because they contain a great deal of alcohol, toilet water and cologne are much less expensive than perfume. Because they are more diluted, their fragrance does not last nearly so long as the fragrance of perfume.

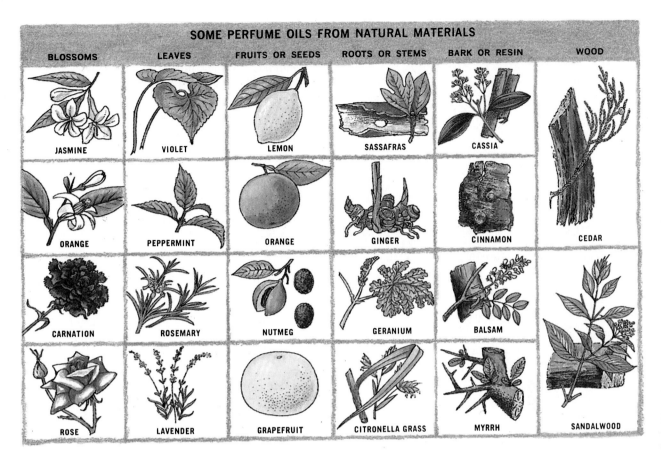

SOME PERFUME OILS FROM NATURAL MATERIALS

BLOSSOMS	LEAVES	FRUITS OR SEEDS	ROOTS OR STEMS	BARK OR RESIN	WOOD
JASMINE	VIOLET	LEMON	SASSAFRAS	CASSIA	
ORANGE	PEPPERMINT	ORANGE	GINGER	CINNAMON	CEDAR
CARNATION	ROSEMARY	NUTMEG	GERANIUM	BALSAM	
ROSE	LAVENDER	GRAPEFRUIT	CITRONELLA GRASS	MYRRH	SANDALWOOD

even though they may be, themselves, unpleasant. Some fixatives have a pleasant odor that can be blended with that of the essential oils. The most valuable fixative is **ambergris**—a waxy material that is formed in the stomachs of sperm whales and is found floating on oceans. Other valuable fixatives are animal products that come from the scent glands of the civet cat, the male musk deer, and the beaver. Only a very small amount of fixative is needed in a perfume.

▶ **HOW ARE PERFUMES MADE?**

The first step in making perfume is to obtain the essential fragrance oils. This is done in many different ways. The oils may be dissolved out of flowers and leaves by solvents such as alcohol. Another method is to squeeze the oils out by pressure from heavy rollers. In some cases the petals are placed in great tanks that are heated gently. As the petals become hot, the vapors from them rise. As they cool, the vapors are collected on overhead trays.

In still other cases, flat trays are covered with thin layers of pork or beef fat, and the petals are spread over them. The fat absorbs the fragrance from the petals. The old petals are picked off, and new ones are put on until the fat is saturated with the perfume oils. Petals may also be soaked in hot, melted fats. The fragrant fat that is made by these two methods is called a **pomade**. It is usually further treated to remove the perfume oils.

Perfumers are specialists who blend raw materials to create fragrances. They must have an especially sensitive sense of smell. An expert perfumer can recognize the odors of a thousand perfume ingredients and knows how they will interact with one another.

The raw materials for a perfume and its method of manufacture are often well-kept trade secrets. Typically, the raw materials are dissolved in pure grain alcohol and are aged in darkness for perhaps a year until a smooth perfume is formed. The mixture is chilled to freeze out unwanted solids, and then it is filtered. The final perfume is sparkling clear.

RICHARD K. LEHNE
Contributor, *Cosmetics: Science and Technology*

See also COSMETICS.

PERICLES (495?–429 B.C.)

Pericles, the greatest statesman of ancient Athens, was born about 495 B.C. Though of a noble family, he was always on the side of the common people. When he entered politics, the government of Athens was still partly controlled by the Areopagus, a permanent council of former magistrates. In 461 Pericles and his friends took away most of its power. From then on Athens was governed by an assembly of all male citizens. Pericles usually led it, partly because he was known to be honest and patriotic and partly because he was a powerful speaker. He created an overseas empire by planting Athenian colonies on the coasts of the Aegean Sea, along the Dardanelles, and even in southern Italy. Also, he took over control of a Greek league. He used the league's treasury to strengthen the Athenian fleet and erect public buildings.

Pericles was an able general and a highly intelligent man. It was Pericles who promoted the building of the magnificent temple called the Parthenon, which still stands in Athens.

Pericles' life ended sadly. Jealous of the growing power of Athens, the Greek states of the Peloponnesus (the southern peninsula), headed by Sparta, declared war on the Athenians (the Peloponnesian Wars). Through its navy Athens controlled the sea. But the refugees from the Spartan invasion were packed miserably into the city, and a terrible epidemic broke out. Pericles was blamed for the invasion and the epidemic. He was publicly disgraced, and he died soon afterward.

None of Pericles' speeches have been preserved. But the historian Thucydides (455?–400?) describes a memorial service for the Athenians killed in the first year's fighting and reports a speech made at it by Pericles. It is full of the noble spirit of patriotism that inspired him, and it is one of the finest statements of the ideals of democracy.

GILBERT HIGHET
Columbia University

PERIODICALS. See MAGAZINES; NEWSPAPERS.

PERIODIC TABLE. See ELEMENTS, CHEMICAL; CHEMISTRY.

PERIODONTAL DISEASE. See DISEASES (Descriptions of Some Diseases).

PERRY, MATTHEW C. (1794–1858)

Matthew C. Perry, like his brother Oliver Hazard Perry, was a famous American naval commander. Matthew Perry, however, gained fame not in battle but through diplomacy.

Matthew Calbraith Perry was born in Newport, Rhode Island, on April 10, 1794. He entered the Navy as a midshipman when he was 14, serving first under his brother. In 1814 he married Jane Slidell. They had 10 children.

In 1820, Perry went to Africa to help American blacks establish themselves in Liberia. He fought pirates in the West Indies and visited Turkey and Greece. In 1830, commanding the *Concord,* he brought the new American minister to Russia, John Randolph, to St. Petersburg. Czar Nicholas I urged Perry to join the Russian Navy, but he refused.

Perry spent the 10 years following 1833 in New York City, where he made his home. He pioneered in the construction of steam vessels and the development of naval weapons. He also helped found the United States Naval Academy. In 1843 he returned to Africa in command of a squadron to eliminate slave trading. During the Mexican War (1846–48) Perry took part in the capture of Veracruz.

Perry's greatest service came almost at the end of his career. In 1852 he was given command of the East India Squadron and sent to Japan. His task was to persuade the Japanese rulers to open diplomatic and trade relations with the United States. In July, 1853, he arrived in Tokyo Bay—previously closed to foreigners—carrying a letter from President Millard Fillmore to the Japanese Emperor. The Japanese, reluctant at first, were impressed by Perry's determination and his naval force. The Treaty of Kanagawa, signed in March, 1854, gave the United States trading rights in two ports. This was soon followed by similar treaties between Japan and other nations.

Perry spent most of his remaining years writing a book on his expedition to Japan. He died in New York City on March 4, 1858.

JOHN D. HAYES
Rear Admiral, United States Navy (Ret.)

PERRY, OLIVER HAZARD (1785–1819)

Oliver Hazard Perry gained his place in American history by his victory over the British on Lake Erie in the War of 1812.

Perry was born in South Kingston, Rhode Island, on August 20, 1785. At the age of 14 he was appointed a midshipman. His father was a captain in the Navy, and young Perry first served aboard his father's ship, the *General Greene*, in the West Indies and then took part in the Tripolitan War (1801–05). In 1811 he married Elizabeth Champlin Mason, who bore him five children.

Early in the War of 1812, Perry, then a lieutenant, was given command of the American squadron on Lake Erie. Perry had ten vessels. However, he could not get his largest ships, the *Lawrence* and the *Niagara*, across the sandbar at Presque Isle without first removing their heavy guns. This could not be done while the British squadron blockaded the harbor. Unwisely, the British commander abandoned the blockade for several days. This gave Perry his chance.

On September 10, 1813, Perry met the British in battle near Put-in-Bay. Perry's battle flag on the *Lawrence* was inscribed with the motto "Don't give up the ship." These had been the dying words of Captain James Lawrence, whose ship the *Chesapeake* had been defeated by the British some months earlier.

After two hours of fighting, the *Lawrence* was almost a wreck, and Perry transferred to the *Niagara*. The enemy had also suffered heavily, and when Perry brought the undamaged *Niagara* into action, the British ships were forced to surrender. "We have met the enemy and they are ours," wrote Perry to General William Henry Harrison. Perry then ferried Harrison's soldiers across Lake Erie, where they defeated the British at the Battle of the Thames.

Perry survived his victory by only six years. In 1819, while on a naval diplomatic mission to Venezuela, he fell ill with yellow fever. The hero of the Battle of Lake Erie died on board ship on August 23, 1819.

JOHN D. HAYES
Rear Admiral, United States Navy (Ret.)

PERSHING, JOHN J. (1860–1948)

John Joseph Pershing, commander in chief of the American Expeditionary Force (A.E.F.) in World War I, was born on September 13, 1860, near Laclede, Missouri. He attended the teacher-training school at Kirksville and later entered the United States Military Academy at West Point, New York. He graduated as president of his class in 1886.

Pershing began his active service as a cavalry officer, fighting in campaigns against American Indians. He then taught military science and mathematics at the University of Nebraska while earning a law degree. In 1897 he returned to West Point as an instructor.

During the Spanish-American War in 1898, Pershing requested active duty and was sent to Cuba. The following year he was sent to the Philippines. His assignment was to subdue the Moro tribes, who had rebelled against the new American government of the Philippines. By hard fighting and wise diplomacy, Pershing persuaded the Moros to make peace. For this and other accomplishments, President Theodore Roosevelt promoted him from captain to brigadier general.

Pershing married Helen Warren in 1905. He then returned to the Philippines for eight years as military governor. In 1916, Pershing was ordered to capture the Mexican bandit and revolutionary Pancho Villa, who had raided U.S. border towns. Though unable to catch Villa, Pershing scattered the bandit forces.

In 1917, when the United States entered World War I, Pershing was given command of the A.E.F. At his insistence, the 2 million men of the A.E.F. fought in Europe as an independent unit instead of simply filling in the ranks of the Allied armies. They played an important role in defeating Germany.

In 1919, Pershing was made general of the armies—a rank previously conferred only on George Washington. Pershing retired in 1924. His book *My Experiences in the World War* won the Pulitzer prize for history in 1932. He died on July 15, 1948.

Reviewed by STUART ROCHESTER
Historian, U.S. Department of Defense

PERSIA. See PERSIA, ANCIENT.

The walls of Persepolis, one of the two capitals of the Achaemenid Empire, were adorned with relief sculptures. The guards are Persians (in fluted hats) and Medes (in round hats).

PERSIA, ANCIENT

In the ancient Middle East, centered in what is now Iran, the Persians created a universal empire, which was made up of varied peoples and was a model for the later Roman Empire. At its height, in the 500's B.C., the Persian Achaemenid Empire stretched from the Indus River (now in Pakistan) to the Mediterranean Sea and northern Africa, encompassing much of what was then the known world. The empire was distinguished by its code of laws, roads and postal system, new methods of government administration, and for its tolerance of many religions. The Achaemenid Empire lasted for some 220 years and was succeeded in the region by later empires, both Persian and non-Persian, that ruled for nearly a thousand years more.

Origins. The Persians were one tribe of a group of peoples who called themselves Aryans and who migrated to the Iranian plateau from the north sometime about 1000 B.C. A related tribe, the Medes, settled to their north. At some unknown time during the Persians' migration, a prophet, Zoroaster, appeared among the eastern tribes. He preached a new faith, called Zoroastrianism or Mazdaism, after its god, Ahura Mazda, which became the religion of Persian kings and later of the em-

pire itself. This religion still exists but now mainly in India. (See the article on Zoroastrianism in Volume W-X-Y-Z).

In the 600's B.C., the Medes united and formed their own state. Allying themselves with the Babylonians, they overthrew the empire of the Assyrians. The Median Empire that resulted lasted until about 549 B.C., when Cyrus, leader of the Persians, defeated Astyages, the last ruler of the Medes, and inherited their empire.

The Achaemenid Empire. Cyrus, known as the Great, was the founder of the Achaemenid Empire. He extended his domain, conquering the kingdom of Lydia (in what is now Turkey) and absorbing the Babylonian lands. His reign was noted for its mildness toward subject peoples, including the Jews, whom he freed from Babylonian captivity and allowed to return to their homeland. Cyrus was preparing for an invasion of Egypt, when, in 530 B.C., he was killed fighting in Central Asia. He was succeeded by his son Cambyses II, who conquered Egypt but died in an accident in 522 B.C. After a period of turmoil and revolt, Darius I, who belonged to another branch of the Achaemenid dynasty, became ruler.

Organization of the Empire. The empire was divided into satrapies, or provinces, ruled by satraps, or governors, appointed by the king.

The army was organized into units of tens, hundreds, and thousands, and a military intelligence service was developed. A postal system was established, which much impressed the Greek historian Herodotus, who wrote that "neither snow nor rain nor heat nor darkness stays these couriers from their appointed rounds." (This description was to be adopted as part of the motto of the U.S. postal service.)

The policy of tolerance for all religions, begun by Cyrus, was continued. A system of laws was established for the entire empire, although local laws and customs were retained. A network of roads (the Royal Road) connected the far-flung parts of the empire. The imperial bureaucracy, or government administration, used a single language, Aramaic (a Semitic tongue then in common use), everywhere in the empire, and it became the model for later governments of the region.

Taxes, Trade, and Arts. Taxes and trade were mostly in goods, such as grain, cattle, and precious stones and metals, rather than money, until 490 B.C., when gold and silver coins were introduced. Their use was important both for the growth of trade and for the financial stability of the empire. Taxation was based mainly on land but was also imposed on caravans of merchants traveling from area to area. There were also fees on ships using harbors and many other taxes. Military service was often rewarded with grants of land, and the empire gradually came to depend on foreign mercenaries, or professional soldiers.

Achaemenid art and architecture was influenced by Egyptian, Assyrian, and other styles. Workers from all over the empire were brought to build the royal palaces at Susa and Persepolis, whose imposing columns and beautifully carved relief sculptures still stand amid their ruins. The Achaemenids, in turn, strongly influenced the art and architecture of India and Central Asia.

Decline of the Empire. The revolt of Greek city-states in Ionia (western Turkey) had prompted an unsuccessful expedition by Darius I against Greece in 490 B.C. Other revolts after his death detached lands from the empire for periods of time, but the empire survived in spite of weak rulers. Darius I's successor, his son Xerxes I, launched a full-scale invasion of Greece in 480 B.C., but it, too, was repulsed.

Alexander and His Successors. In 334 B.C., Alexander III of Macedon (or Macedonia), the Great, invaded the empire. His defeat of Darius III in 331 B.C. at the Battle of Gaugamela and the burning of Persepolis marked the end of the Achaemenid dynasty and the rise of a new, Greek empire.

Alexander's early death, in 323 B.C., led to years of fighting between his generals, until one of them, Seleucus, established his rule over Alexander's old empire, minus Greece and Egypt, in about 301 B.C. Greek became the official language, but Aramaic remained in use in government administration. In less than a century, however, the Seleucid rulers lost control over the eastern part of the empire, although Hellenic, or Greek, culture remained very strong there. The first to break away from the Seleucids were the Greeks of Bactria (in present-day Afghanistan). They were followed, in about 247 B.C. by the Parthians.

Alexander the Great of Macedon invaded the Persian lands in 334 B.C. His defeat of King Darius III at the Battle of Gaugamela (331) and the burning of Persepolis marked the end of the Achaemenid dynasty, or ruling family, and the rise to power of a Macedonian-Greek empire. The Greeks were succeeded, in turn, by the empire of the Parthians.

This formidable-looking bronze figure depicts a Parthian prince. An Iranian people, like the Achaemenids, the Parthians ruled Persia for nearly 500 years.

The Parthians. Like the Persians, the Parthians were an Iranian people and Zoroastrians. But although they followed Achaemenid traditions, the early Parthian rulers were patrons of Greek culture. They used the Greek language on their coins and in their government, which became a union of many local rulers rather than a centralized empire. By the A.D. 100's, however, local culture and the Parthian language had replaced Greek in the Parthian domains.

For more than 300 years, the Parthians were formidable enemies of the Romans. Expert horsemen and archers, they had employed hit-and-run cavalry tactics to destroy a Roman army at the Battle of Carrhae in 53 B.C. Thereafter, Rome's rule ended at the Parthians' western borders, although warfare continued between them. In spite of this, trade and commerce flourished in the Parthian subject kingdoms, most of which were located in Mesopotamia (modern Iraq).

Confronted in the west by the Romans, in the east the Parthians faced nomadic invaders from Central Asia, among them the Kushans, who established a wealthy kingdom in the eastern part of the Iranian plateau. This was to be a historical pattern for the Persians—situated between a strong settled state to their west and nomadic conquerors to their east. A lack of unity among the Parthian rulers led to their decline and to the rise of a new dynasty, that of the Sassanians.

The Sassanians. The first great ruler of the Sassanians (or Sasanians) was Ardashir I, who defeated his Parthian overlord, Artabanus, in about A.D. 224, and within a few years had conquered the Parthian lands. His rise to power in the historical homeland of the Persians, Persis (the present Fars province of Iran), parallels that of Cyrus the Great. The Sassanians claimed descent from the Achaemenids, even though they knew about the earlier empire only from legends. They adopted the title of *shahinshah* ("king of kings") for their rulers and re-established a centralized empire, with Zoroastrianism as its official religion.

Ardashir had begun a campaign against the Romans in Mesopotamia. War with Rome continued under his son and successor, Shapur I, who captured the emperor Valerian in battle in A.D. 259. Many of the Roman prisoners were settled in Persia, where they became the nucleus of a Christian community in the empire. The Sassanians fought the Romans many times, and the borders between the two great empires were constantly changing. The eastern part of the empire was also threatened by new invasions from the east.

Persian Society. Persian society under the Sassanians was strictly organized into a system of four castes, or classes. At the top were the warriors, or nobility. Below them were the priests; and below the priests were the scribes, or clerks. The fourth and lowest caste was that of the common people, the peasant farmers and workers. This organization of society was the heritage of the ancient Aryan social divisions. Castes later disappeared in Persia but long remained in India, where a related Aryan people had invaded and settled.

SOME NOTABLE PERSIAN RULERS
(and their reign dates)

Achaemenids
Cyrus the Great (549–530 B.C.)
Darius I (522–486 B.C.)
Xerxes I (486–465 B.C.)
Artaxerxes III (359–338 B.C.)
Darius III (336–330 B.C.)
Parthians
Arsaces I (247 B.C.–?)
Mithradates I (171–138 B.C.)
Artabanus V (A.D. 213–224)
Sassanians
Ardashir I (A.D. 224–239)
Shapur I (A.D. 239–272)
Shapur II (A.D. 309–379)
Chosroes I (A.D. 531–579)
Yazdegird III (A.D. 632–651)

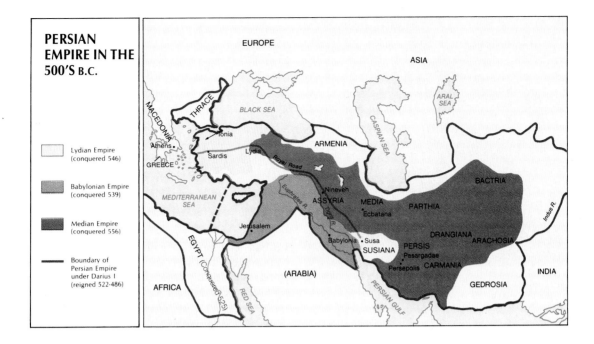

PERSIAN EMPIRE IN THE 500'S B.C.

Lydian Empire (conquered 546)

Babylonian Empire (conquered 539)

Median Empire (conquered 556)

Boundary of Persian Empire under Darius I (reigned 522-486)

EUROPE
ASIA
MACEDONIA
THRACE
BLACK SEA
ARAL SEA
IONIA
ARMENIA
CASPIAN SEA
Athens
Sardis
Lydia
GREECE
Royal Road
BACTRIA
MEDITERRANEAN SEA
Euphrates R.
Nineveh
ASSYRIA
MEDIA
Ecbatana
PARTHIA
Indus R.
Jerusalem
DRANGIANA
ARACHOSIA
Babylonia • Susa
PERSIS
EGYPT (Conquered 525)
SUSIANA
Pasargadae
Persepolis
CARMANIA
INDIA
AFRICA
(ARABIA)
PERSIAN GULF
GEDROSIA
RED SEA

Art and Commerce. The Sassanians followed the style of their time by building in brick, which was more flexible than stone. As a result, intricate decoration became a hallmark of Sassanian architecture, which also included domed roofs. Late Sassanian art was dominated by stylized flowers and geometric designs, while representation of human and animal forms, typical of the Achaemenids, almost vanished. This style continued into the Islamic period, which followed the Sassanians.

During the A.D. 500's, the Sassanians increased their trade with India, exchanging Persian textiles and carpets for Indian spices. The "Silk Road" to China also became more important as the demand for luxury goods increased. Hostilities with their neighbors made commerce profitable only in the most expensive goods.

Expansion and Decline. During the long reign of Shapur II, from 309 to 379, the borders of the empire were expanded in the east and west. Under Kavad I, who reigned from 488 to 531, a social and religious revolt led by a priest, Mazdak, threatened the stability of the Sassanian state. The revolt was crushed by Chosroes (or Khosrow) I, who ruled from 531 to 579 and under whom many reforms of government and society were made and the power of the nobility checked.

Meanwhile, wars continued with the Byzantine Empire, successor to the Romans, in the west, while the east was overrun by new invaders, the Turks. The constant hostility and fighting between the Byzantines and Sassanians eventually so weakened both empires that they fell prey to a new threat from the south—the Arabs. Infused with the new religion of Islam, the Arabs defeated the Sassanians at the final battle, at Nihavend, in 642. The last Sassanian ruler, Yazdegird III, died in 651. Persia became part of a wider Islamic Empire, and, culturally, one of its most important parts.

RICHARD N. FRYE
Harvard University
Author, *The Heritage of Persia*

See also ALEXANDER THE GREAT; ANCIENT CIVILIZATIONS (Assyrian and Persian Civilizations); ANCIENT WORLD, ART OF THE (Persian Empire); BABYLONIA; IRAN; ISLAMIC ART AND ARCHITECTURE.

A decorated bowl and plate made of silver and gold are part of the Sassanian artistic heritage.

Allied tanks, part of an international coalition of forces led by the United States, liberated Kuwait from Iraqi occupation in the 1991 Persian Gulf War.

PERSIAN GULF WAR

The Persian Gulf War was a brief but decisive conflict that took place from January to March of 1991. It was fought between Iraq on one side and a large coalition, or alliance, of nations on the other. The anti-Iraqi forces were led and directed by the United States, which provided by far the largest number of troops, aircraft, ships, and arms. The cause of the war was the invasion and occupation by Iraq of Kuwait, its small but wealthy neighbor. The conflict took its name from the location of the two countries on the northwestern shore of the Persian Gulf.

Background. Iraq had often been ambitious and aggressive in its relations with neighboring states. An unprovoked attack against Iran in 1980 led to a costly eight-year war. Iraq had made threats against Kuwait on a number of occasions—in 1961, 1973, and in the 1980's. Iraq's claim was that Kuwait should properly be a part of Iraq. This argument was weak, however, since Kuwait has been ruled by the Sabah family since the 1750's, when it was nominally a part of the Ottoman (Turkish) Empire. Iraq, by contrast, had never existed before the 1920's. When the Ottoman Empire, defeated in World War I, broke up, Iraq was created by Britain out of three of its former administrative divisions. Oil, discovered just before the outbreak of World War II, made Kuwait very rich and a tempting prize.

Invasion and Crisis. In the spring of 1990, Iraq's leader, Saddam Hussein, began voicing various grievances against Kuwait, mostly connected with the overproduction and price of oil, which threatened Iraq's own oil-based economy. On August 2, 1990, the day after walking out on negotiations, Iraq invaded and quickly overran Kuwait.

Six months of crisis and intense diplomatic activity followed. To counter a possible Iraqi advance southward into oil-rich Saudi Arabia, U.S. forces were dispatched to the region under Operation Desert Shield. International reaction against Iraq's aggression was strong and included most Arab countries. Skillful diplomacy by the United States made possible the passing of resolutions by the United Nations Security Council that condemned Iraq, imposed economic sanctions against it, and finally authorized the use of force. When Iraq ignored the United Nations deadline of January 15, 1991, for withdrawal, the war, codenamed Operation Desert Storm, began.

Course of the War. The Allied forces were commanded by U.S. General H. Norman Schwarzkopf. The first phase of the war, from January 16 to February 22, consisted entirely of air bombardment of Iraqi military facilities. While destructive, this did not produce any willingness by Iraq to withdraw. In fact, on January 17, Iraq began launching long-range Scud missiles against Israel. The second phase, which began on February 25, was a large-scale ground offensive against Iraqi troops. Dramatically successful, it resulted in the complete liberation of Kuwait by February 27. Hostilities were formally ended on March 2, 1991.

ARTHUR CAMPBELL TURNER
University of California, Riverside
Author, *Ideology and Power in the Middle East*
See also KUWAIT.

PERSIAN WARS. See GREECE, ANCIENT.

PERU

The third largest country in South America (after Brazil and Argentina), Peru is located on the western, or Pacific Ocean, coast of the continent. Much of Peru lies in the towering, snowcapped Andes, the great mountain range that runs the length of South America.

Peru was once the center of the vast Indian Inca Empire. Conquered by the Spanish in the 1500's, Peru was a source of great wealth for Spain, which ruled it as part of its own South American colonial empire for almost 300 years.

▶THE PEOPLE

Most Peruvians are either descendants of the Incas and other Indian people or are mestizos, persons of mixed Indian and Spanish ancestry. About 10 to 15 percent of the people are of pure Spanish origin. The remainder of the population includes descendants of black African slaves who intermarried with Peruvians, and immigrants from China, Japan, Italy, Germany, and Britain.

The most widely spoken languages in Peru are Spanish and the Indian languages Quechua and Aymará. Spanish and Quechua are the country's official languages. Mestizos generally speak Spanish, though they may speak Indian languages as well. Most of the people are Roman Catholics.

Education is compulsory for all Peruvian children between the ages of 7 and 16. Almost all towns and villages have primary schools, but high schools and colleges are found mainly in the large cities. The National University of San Marcos in Lima, the capital, was founded in 1551 and is one of the oldest universities in the Americas.

Way of Life

Life in Peru varies widely from region to region. The geography of the country divides it into several distinct regions, and the different cultural backgrounds of the people often determine where and how they live. The whites and some mestizos live in the coastal cities. Most of the Indians inhabit the highlands of the Andes and the rain forests of the Amazon River basin in the interior.

Life in the Coastal Cities. City life in Peru generally follows the customs handed down by the early Spanish settlers. In Lima and other cities, people may take two hours for a noontime meal at home with the family, which includes grandparents and other relatives. Fiestas, or festivals, are held on birthdays and other special occasions, such as saints' days, and feature singing and dancing.

Traditional foods include soups, spicy chicken and fish dishes, and caramel custard for dessert. The most popular restaurants are the *chifas*, which serve Chinese-Peruvian style food. Also popular are *anticuchos*—bits of

Colorful Indian textiles help create a festive atmosphere on market day in the Andean highland town of Pisac, not far from the ancient Inca capital of Cusco.

beef heart on bamboo sticks—barbecued by street vendors over charcoal grills.

Some wealthy urban families live in colonial-style mansions with large patios, balconies, and fancy iron window grilles. But modern-style houses and tall apartment buildings are found in many residential areas. Most of the people live in older apartments and row houses. Walls around the yard enclose most houses, which usually have small lawns and flower gardens. So many people have moved to the cities in recent years that huge squatter settlements have grown up around all the large coastal cities. The houses of these settlements are often made of bamboo mats. They are slowly being replaced by permanent dwellings as the migrants struggle to improve their lives.

Coastal people enjoy the beaches along the Pacific Ocean during the summer months. Boys start playing soccer (called *futbol*) as soon as they can run, and girls play volleyball (called *voli*) just as enthusiastically. Peru's professional soccer teams and the national women's volleyball team are very well known.

Life in the Andean Highlands. Closely-knit families are the basic work and social groups of the highland people, who are called *serranos*. Farm families work together in the fields, and children take care of the animals. Children in highland towns also often help their parents. Almost all highlanders raise chickens, ducks, turkeys, and *cuyes* (guinea pigs) in their backyards. And *picante de cuy* (guinea pig with potatoes and pepper sauce) is a favorite highland food. Other popular dishes include thick vegetable and cereal soups, mutton, potatoes, and home-baked bread.

The Indian people of the highlands live in small villages. They grow a variety of crops for their own use and raise livestock. The native Andean llamas, animals belonging to the camel family, are used for meat and as beasts of burden in southern Peru. A related animal, the alpaca, is also bred at high altitudes. The Indians spin and weave sheep and alpaca wool into beautiful ponchos and other clothing. The hard-working Indian farmers have chewed coca leaves for thousands of years. It was long thought that this was a bad habit. But recent studies show that chewing this leaf aids digestion and helps people adapt to high altitudes.

Mestizo highlanders live in the towns, where they work as storekeepers, teachers, government officials, and technicians. They tend to be wealthier than the Indians, and they often employ Indians as servants or laborers. The Indians who work in the towns often learn Spanish and begin to adopt mestizo ways. They may stop chewing coca leaves, for example, or cease wearing traditional homespun wool clothing. People who alter their Indian culture in this way are usually called *cholos*.

Houses and other buildings in the highlands are usually made of adobe (sun-dried mud bricks) and have red tile roofs. Houses in the towns are often coated with white plaster. All highland towns have a central plaza around which the town offices and the Catholic church are located. These plazas often have gardens and fountains in the middle and serve as centers for community activities such as parades and religious processions. Each town has its patron saint, whose day is celebrated with elaborate fiestas. The highland fiestas differ from those of the coast. Indians and mestizos don colorful costumes to act out historic events. Lively songs and dances called *waynos*, which are based on ancient Indian music, are very popular at these fiestas.

Highland life has many problems. Most of the people are poor, and the Indians have often been exploited. But education and increased contact with the outside world are bringing change to the highlands.

Life in the Amazon Region. The eastern slopes of the Andes and the interior lowland are part of the huge basin of the Amazon River. Only 12 percent of the people live in this vast area. About 50 different Indian tribes —such as the Campas, the Shipibos, and the Aguarunas—live in small villages near the rivers and lakes. There they farm, hunt, and catch fish. The Indian peoples of this region have lived in this way for thousands of years. The government has built airports and roads to encourage the development of the remote Amazon frontier. The Indian way of life is changing rapidly as the Indians come into closer contact with other Peruvians. For most Indians, change has created serious economic and social problems.

▶ **THE LAND**

Peru spans the central part of the rugged Andes. The Andes are so high—second only to the Himalayas in altitude—that Peru has many ecological and climatic zones. Each of these zones has its own special plant and animal life and possibilities for development.

The Pacific Coast

The Pacific coastal area is a long, narrow strip of land between the Pacific Ocean and the western slopes of the Andes. This area may have rain only once or twice in ten years. But rivers flowing down from the Andes have deposited fertile soil that has been intensively irrigated for 7,000 years. Most of Peru's large cities and the huge farms where crops are grown for export are located in the coastal valleys. The climate of this region is hot and dry in the north and cool and humid farther south. During the cool winters (June to September), the sun rarely shines, and there are heavy fogs and mists.

Indian boys on Lake Titicaca, the largest lake in South America. Their boat is woven from reeds. Their cargo of miniature reed boats will probably be sold to tourists.

The Andean Highlands

The lower slopes of the Andes have little irrigated land and are generally sparsely populated. Most highlanders live in the *quechua* zone, which begins at 8,000 feet (2,400 meters) above sea level and extends to 11,500 feet (3,500 meters). This is an area of beautiful valleys that can be farmed. The climate is temperate, with bright sunshine. Rains fall only in the summer months.

The region just above the *quechua* is rugged and sparsely populated, except around Lake Titicaca, the highest navigable lake in the world. Half of this lake is in Bolivia. The Aymará and Quechua peoples who live along its shore sail the lake in reed boats, called *balsas*, to fish. Abundant water plants provide food for their cattle.

Between 13,000 and 15,700 feet (4,000 and 4,800 meters) is a region of vast grassy plains, the *altiplano*. This region is used extensively for grazing cattle and sheep, but there are few permanent residents. The climate at this altitude is cold, with freezing temperatures and some light snows in the winter months and heavy, unpredictable rains in summer. Above these plains rise great mountain peaks that are permanently covered with snow and glaciers.

FACTS
and figures

REPUBLIC OF PERU (República del Perú) is the official name of the country.

LOCATION: Western coast of South America.

AREA: 496,222 sq mi (1,285,216 km²).

POPULATION: 23,000,000 (estimate).

CAPITAL AND LARGEST CITY: Lima.

MAJOR LANGUAGES: Spanish and Quechua (both official).

MAJOR RELIGIOUS GROUP: Roman Catholic.

GOVERNMENT: Republic. **Head of state and government**—president. **Legislature**—a single-chamber Congress.

CHIEF PRODUCTS: Agricultural—cotton, sugarcane, potatoes, rice, wheat, corn, beans, barley, coca, coffee, livestock, fruits and vegetables.
Manufactured—paper, textiles, steel, leather goods, processed foods, rubber, petroleum products.
Mineral—copper, lead, zinc, silver, iron ore, gold, vanadium.

MONETARY UNIT: Nuevo sol (new sol): (1 nuevo sol = 100 céntimos).

Among these peaks is Huascarán, the highest point in Peru.

The Amazon Region

The lower eastern slopes of the Andes, known as the Montaña, and densely forested interior plains form part of the Amazon Basin. The climate is hot and humid, and rainfall is heavy throughout the year. This region covers more than half the area of Peru, but it is sparsely populated. Few roads cross the Andes to link the Montaña with the coast. The unfavorable climate and dense jungle growth also discourage settlement. Many small groups of Indians live along the lakes and rivers throughout the jungle. Peru's chief rivers—the Marañón and the Ucayali—flow north and east before joining to form the Amazon. Rivers are the roads and highways of the Amazon Basin, and most settlements are built along the riverbanks.

The Earthquake Threat

Geological faults, or deep fractures in the layers of rock, run the entire length of the Andean mountain range. These faults have produced many earthquakes in Peru. In 1970 north central Peru suffered the Western Hemisphere's worst known earthquake. About 70,000 people were killed, and another 500,000 lost their homes. Other earthquakes have caused extensive damage in Lima, Cuzco, Trujillo, and Arequipa.

Because the Andean slopes are very unstable, there are many landslides. Building and maintaining highways is therefore difficult and costly.

Natural Resources

Water is a precious commodity in the highlands and along the coast. Special irrigation councils control its use for agriculture in many areas, but there are still frequent conflicts between users. In the highlands the Mantaro, Santa, and Urubamba rivers are sources of hydroelectric power for the entire country. Many of the exotic tropical fish sold in pet shops come from the great rivers of the Amazon Basin. The dense forests of this region contain a variety of valuable trees. The Amazon jungles are also home to a wide variety of plant and animal life.

Peru is rich in minerals. There are large deposits of copper, lead, zinc, silver, iron ore, gold, and vanadium. Oil is found in Piura and in the Amazon jungle near the border with Ecuador.

The Peru, or Humboldt, Current surges north from Antarctica and creates one of the world's richest fishing grounds off the coast of Peru. For thousands of years, cormorants, gulls, and pelicans have caught fish in this current and deposited their bird droppings, a rich fertilizer known as guano, on the coastal islands off Peru.

▶THE ECONOMY

Many Peruvians are very poor. And one of the government's main challenges is finding a way to distribute the country's wealth and resources more equally.

Agriculture

Traditionally a few wealthy families owned most of the land—including the cotton, sugarcane, and rice plantations on the coast and the grazing lands in the highlands that produced agricultural exports. Indian and mestizo farmers worked on the large estates or grew food crops for their own use. After 150 years of conflict over land ownership, the government passed a land reform act in 1969. This historic act ended the system of estates called haciendas. The serfs who had worked on the haciendas for 20 cents a day suddenly became the owners of the fields their families had worked for generations. Indian and mestizo farmers now operate many former estates as cooperatives. But the amount of cotton, sugar, and rice produced for export has fallen under the new system.

Many attempts have been made to expand the irrigated areas along the coast. The fertility of the soil in the coastal valleys makes such projects attractive, but they are very costly. The government has also tried to open the Amazon jungle for farming and logging. But enormous costs and many environmental problems continue to delay the work.

Mining and Other Industries

Mining has long been an important part of the Peruvian economy. A variety of metallic minerals are mined, and oil from the Amazon jungle is transported to the coast along a pipeline completed in 1977.

Peru has exported textiles since colonial times. Manufacturing plants that produce a wide range of goods have been built in the coastal cities since 1950. They turn out steel, paper, textiles, leather goods, processed foods, rubber, and petroleum products.

Tourists are drawn to Peru by its splendid scenery, fascinating pre-Columbian ruins, and interesting peoples. The major attractions are the former Inca capital of Cuzco and the nearby "lost city" of the Incas, Machu Picchu. A paved highway completed in 1976 opened the spectacular highland valley of the upper Santa River and the snow-capped peaks of the Cordillera Blanca to visitors.

For many years, guano from islands off the coast of Peru was sold around the world as fertilizer. The guano industry has declined in importance. Since 1950 the country has developed a major fishing industry. But recent changes in the ocean currents and overfishing have threatened this industry.

Few highland farmers use modern equipment, fertilizer, or improved seed varieties. These Indian women are weeding a vegetable field by hand.

Lima, the capital, is the most important city in Peru. It is the industrial, commercial, artistic, and literary center of the country, and it offers the greatest opportunities for employment. Greater Lima is the home of almost 30 percent of all Peru's people. An article on Lima appears in Volume L.

Near Lima is Callao, the country's leading port. Other major cities include Chiclayo and Trujillo in the north, Arequipa in the south, and Iquitos in the Amazon Basin.

All cities in Peru have grown rapidly in recent years. Mestizos and *cholos* have moved to the coastal cities from the small highland towns in search of a better life, and more people now live in the coastal valleys than in the highlands.

▶HISTORY AND GOVERNMENT

The first people came to what is now Peru at least 10,000 years ago. Since that time, many civilizations have come and gone.

Pre-Columbian Peru

People in the Andes learned to domesticate plants and animals by 5500 B.C. They also discovered how to weave the intricate textiles of cotton and wool for which Peru is famous

The ancient fortress city of Machu Picchu, high in the Andes, was abandoned by the Incas in the 1500's. It was discovered by an American explorer in 1911.

today. By about 3800 B.C., people in Peru had begun to irrigate their crops. A large political and religious cult called Chavín emerged in the highlands around 1500 B.C. and lasted for hundreds of years. The Moche people irrigated large areas around modern Trujillo about 500 B.C. They also built enormous temples. And they made beautiful pottery and gold and silver objects, which are highly prized by museums today. The Huari and Tiahuanaco empires controlled much of highland Peru and Bolivia by about A.D. 500. These states lasted for about 500 years.

In the 1200's the Quechua-speaking Inca tribe of Cuzco began its conquest of the region. Beginning in 1438 the armies of the Inca emperor Pachacuti and his son Topa conquered much of the Andean area. The Inca Empire became one of the largest in the world. It stretched from northern Ecuador to central Chile and ruled about 16 million people.

The Incas were famous for their efficient government. They were skilled engineers who built cities, roads, forts, irrigation systems, religious centers, and large suspension bridges to span the Andean chasms. The vast Sacsahuamán fortress, the Coricancha (Sun Temple), and other Inca buildings made of large, beautifully carved stones can still be seen in Cuzco, the Inca capital.

A smallpox epidemic swept the Inca Empire in 1524. It killed millions of people, including the emperor. This led to a government crisis and civil war. The empire was thus disorganized when a small group of Spaniards led by Francisco Pizarro arrived in Peru. Pizarro managed to capture the Inca leader Atahualpa in 1532. Atahualpa was executed in 1533. Later that year the Spanish reached Cuzco, and the largest native American Indian nation came to an end.

Colonial Peru

After the Spanish conquest, the Inca Empire became the Viceroyalty of El Peru, owned by the kings of Spain. Lima, founded by Pizarro in 1535, became the first important Spanish colonial outpost in South America.

During the 289 years of colonial rule, Peruvian society and culture were greatly changed. Spanish became the official language, and Catholicism the state religion. Land ownership fell into the hands of a few powerful families. The Indians were afflicted by European diseases and harsh working conditions, and many of them died. There were several Indian rebellions. The most famous was that of Tupac Amaru II, in 1780.

The Peruvian Republic

International forces commanded by José de San Martín, of Argentina, declared Peru's independence at Lima on July 28, 1821. And the Venezuelan general Antonio José de Sucre led rebel troops to victory over the Spanish forces at Ayacucho in December, 1824. Mestizos and Peruvians of Spanish descent then took charge of the new government and the economy. One unstable regime followed another as military *caudillos* (strong leaders) fought for control. In the 1830's an attempt was made to join Peru and Bolivia into one nation. But the attempt failed, and General Ramón Castilla emerged as the leader of the country. He speeded the development of the guano industry, and freed the slaves in 1854.

Peru's first civilian president, Manuel Pardo, involved Peru in Bolivia's quarrel with Chile over valuable nitrate deposits in the Atacama Desert. The War of the Pacific (1879–83) ended with the occupation of Peru by Chile. Peru lost substantial portions of its territory to Chile and was left bankrupt.

The economy improved, in the late 1800's and early 1900's, under Nicolás de Piérola and Augusto Leguía. Leguía also re-established Indian community rights over ancient lands. But his dictatorship provoked open rebellion. A new political party, the American Popular Revolutionary Alliance (APRA), was formed in 1924. Its leader, Víctor Raúl Haya de la Torre, played a major role in Peruvian politics until his death in 1979.

Continued demands for modernization and social justice led to the election of Fernando Belaúnde Terry as president of Peru in 1963. Belaúnde began some reforms, but he was overthrown by the military in 1968. Peru's military rulers carried out wide-ranging economic and social reforms. The system that bound landless workers to the landowners on whose estates they worked was abolished, as was tenant farming. New taxes were imposed and Indian communities were re-organized. The government also nationalized many industries. But these reforms did not have the desired results. The economy suffered and increased inflation brought social unrest.

A statue of the liberator José de San Martín dominates the Plaza San Martín in downtown Lima, the capital and largest city of Peru.

Recent History. Public demand forced Peru's military leaders to accept a new constitution and a return to civilian rule. Belaúnde again won the presidency in 1980. He was succeeded by Alan García Pérez, elected in 1985. Alberto Fujimori, the son of Japanese immigrants, won election in 1990. Faced with Peru's enormous foreign debt, spiraling inflation and unemployment, and a spreading Communist guerrilla movement called Shining Path, Fujimori temporarily suspended the constitution in 1992 and ruled with the aid of the army. The leader of Shining Path was captured and Fujimori was able to make inroads on the country's economic problems. In 1993 a new constitution was approved, which made the president eligible for re-election. In 1995, Fujimori easily won election to a second term.

PAUL L. DOUGHTY
University of Florida
Author, *Peru: A Cultural History*

See also INCAS.

PETER, SAINT

The Roman Catholic Church honors Saint Peter, the Prince of the Apostles, as the first pope. According to the New Testament, he was born in Bethsaida. His original name was Simon, and he was the son of John and the brother of Saint Andrew the Apostle. Matthew's gospel tells how Jesus named Peter. "You are Peter," Jesus said, "and on this rock I will build my church. . . ." The name Peter comes from the Greek *petra*, whose meaning is "rock."

Before he became an Apostle, Peter was a fisherman and lived with his wife in the city of Capernaum. Jesus promised to make Peter and his brother Andrew fishers of men, which meant that, like Jesus, they would try to save men's souls. The two brothers answered Jesus' call to follow him. Peter became the leader of the Apostles and witnessed Jesus' most important miracles.

The New Testament tells how Peter declared his undying love for Jesus at the Last Supper. But Jesus predicted that before the following day Peter would deny him three times. Later that evening Jesus allowed himself to be arrested. Peter fled with the other Apostles and then went to the house where Jesus had been taken. Under questioning, Peter three times denied knowing Jesus. Thus the prophecy was fulfilled.

The New Testament records Peter's great sorrow and repentance for denying Christ. After Jesus' death, Peter's authority as leader of the Apostles continued, and he made many important decisions.

Peter's later life is somewhat obscure. He is known to have visited Antioch and may have made a trip to Corinth. An early and widely believed tradition tells us that Peter made his way to Rome. There he is said to have been crucified during the reign of the emperor Nero, about A.D. 64.

The Catholic Church celebrates two feast days in honor of Saint Peter—his martyrdom on June 29 and the Feast of the Chair of Saint Peter on February 22.

KATHLEEN MCGOWAN
Catholic Youth Encyclopedia

PETER PAN.   See BARRIE, SIR JAMES MATTHEW.

PETER THE GREAT (1672–1725)

Peter I is known as Peter the Great because of his accomplishments as czar, or ruler, of Russia. He introduced new ideas to his country and made Russia an accepted European power. His reign was marked by great change and by struggle for and against his reforms.

Peter was born in Moscow on May 30, 1672. In 1682 he became joint czar of Russia with his half brother Ivan. Because they were so young, their sister Sophia governed for a time as regent. The young Peter was left to himself during these childhood years, and his formal education was neglected. While still young, he developed a fondness for military life that never left him. In 1696, Ivan died and Peter became sole ruler of Russia.

He was a remarkable young man—6½ feet (200 centimeters) tall, handsome, intelligent, and possessing great physical strength. In 1697 he toured western Europe to learn all he could of its ways. On his return he set about transforming his country. He forced Russians to adopt western European styles of dress and culture. The sons of the nobility were sent abroad to be educated. Peter moved his capital from Moscow westward, where he built the new city of St. Petersburg. He established a regular army, strengthened the navy, encouraged industry, and started the country's first newspaper. He introduced reforms in government and education.

But Peter could also be cruel and tyrannical. He persecuted members of the clergy who objected to his changes in the church and who wanted to maintain the old customs. His son and heir, Alexis, was killed for opposing him.

Peter fought a series of wars that greatly enlarged Russian territory. His victory over Sweden in the Great Northern War (1700–21) allowed Russia to expand to the west and acquire lands on the eastern coast of the Baltic Sea. Peter's military successes brought Russia recognition as an important power, and in 1721 he was given the title of emperor. He died in his new capital of St. Petersburg on January 28, 1725.

Reviewed by ROBERT K. MASSIE
Author, *Peter the Great: His Life and World*

PETROLEUM AND PETROLEUM REFINING

After you have been awakened by the ringing of your plastic alarm clock, you put on clothes made of synthetic fibers. At breakfast, you drink milk that comes from a container coated with wax and you eat an orange that was wrapped in a plastic package. You then ride to school on a bicycle with synthetic rubber tires or in a gasoline-powered car. Although it is still early in the day, petroleum already has played a big part in your life.

Petroleum, or crude oil, is one of the world's most important natural resources. Plastics, synthetic fibers, and many chemicals are produced from petroleum. It is also used to make lubricants and waxes. However, its most important use is as a fuel for heating, for generating electricity, and especially for powering vehicles.

The word "petroleum" comes from the Latin words *petra*, meaning "rock," and *oleum*, meaning "oil." The word is appropriate since petroleum is found in rock formations under the ground. The petroleum found in different areas can vary in appearance, from a thin, clear liquid to a black substance as thick as molasses. It can range in color from reddish to greenish yellow to brown or black. It can also vary in density and in chemical composition. These various characteristics affect the refining process by which petroleum is turned into valuable products, such as gasoline.

▶ THE ORIGIN OF PETROLEUM

Petroleum is a fossil fuel that was formed over millions of years by the accumulation and compression of organic, or plant and animal, material. Many of today's land areas were under water millions of years ago. The living things in the water stored the sun's energy in their bodies. When these plants and animals died, their remains sank to the bottom and were covered by sediments, which are tiny particles of rock and mineral. As plant and animal remains settled under layers of sediment, chemicals and bacteria began to break them down. Meanwhile, new sediments continued to accumulate, burying older sediments to great depths. Heat and pressure slowly changed these deep sediments into layers of sandstone, limestone, and other

A derrick on an offshore platform drills for oil in deep reservoirs under the Gulf of Mexico, one of the most important oil exploration areas in the world.

types of sedimentary rock. The tremendous temperatures and pressures also changed the organic materials into petroleum.

Some of the layers of sedimentary rock contained many tiny holes, or pores, which made the rock porous. Over time, oil seeped into the porous rocks and was held there just as water is held in a sponge. These porous rocks are known as reservoir rocks because they contain reservoirs of oil. The oil is trapped in the reservoirs by surrounding layers of clay, salt, or other nonporous materials.

While oil was being formed, the Earth's crust was shifting. Over millions of years, great movements changed the location of old ocean floors and the oil beneath them. Some ocean floors were pushed deeper beneath the sea. Others were raised above the ocean surface and became land areas. Continents gradually changed in size, shape, and appearance. As a result of these changes, oil-bearing layers of rock are now found in various areas, including some that are inland and far from present ocean shorelines. Other oil deposits lie offshore on the continental shelf—the relatively shallow, gently sloping ocean bottom lying between the shorelines and the deeper areas of the oceans.

▶ EARLY USES AND EXPLORATIONS

Even in ancient times, petroleum and tar seeped to the Earth's surface at certain places. These seepages, known as oil springs, were easy to locate. People used the oil and tar as medicine, as waterproofing for baskets, and as caulking for ships. They also burned oil in lamps and torches. For the most part, however, petroleum was a curiosity. The richest oil deposits lay deep underground, and there were few clues to their existence on the Earth's surface. The real history of the oil industry began during the 1800's when better lamp fuels were needed to light factories created by the Industrial Revolution.

In the early 1800's, people who were drilling for brine, or salt water, often struck oil, much to their disgust. Such wells were abandoned because at that time there was no demand for the sticky, smelly substance they called "rock oil." Then, in the mid-1800's, George Bissell, a New York lawyer, sent a sample of crude oil to Benjamin Silliman, a chemist at Yale University. Silliman analyzed the substance and reported that petroleum could yield many useful products, including lamp oils, lubricating oils, and wax. Silliman's report, published in 1855, was a milestone in the history of petroleum because it convinced people that profitable businesses could be developed with oil.

In 1857, Bissell and his partner, Jonathan Eveleth, hired Edwin Drake, a retired railroad conductor, to take charge of oil properties they owned near Titusville, Pennsylvania. Drake began to bore a hole near the site of a well-known oil spring there. On August 28, 1859, "Uncle Billy" Smith, a veteran well digger working at the site, saw a dark fluid down in the hole. It turned out to be oil. News of the oil well spread rapidly, and people raced to the area to buy or lease land where oil might be found. The world's first oil rush had begun.

▶ LOCATING OIL DEPOSITS

Since the 1800's, scientists have learned much about searching for oil, and technological advancements have made the search easier. The chances of finding oil are now better than ever because new ways to locate oil deposits and new methods of drilling into those deposits have been developed. Scientists first gather information about potential oil deposits. While all oil deposits occur in sedimentary rock, not all sedimentary rock contains oil; only certain sedimentary rock formations offer good conditions for oil accumulation. These types of formations, called **traps**, have an arrangement of rock layers that holds the oil in a limited space and prevents it from further movement (Figure 1).

The most common traps are anticlines, fault traps, and stratigraphic traps. An **anticline** is an arch or dome formed by an upward fold in rock layers. A **fault trap** is a formation caused by a shearing movement in the rock layers, resulting in a porous layer being cut off by a nonporous layer. A **stratigraphic trap** is a rock formation in which porous layers are pinched between nonporous layers. Traps also occur near **salt domes**, which are gigantic underground columns of rock salt forced up from deeply buried salt beds by the weight of overlying rocks. Since oil cannot pass through salt, it is often trapped near rock salt domes.

Aerial photographs are commonly used to speed the search for oil. Taken from airplanes

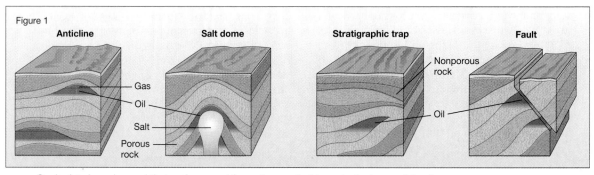

Figure 1

Anticline   **Salt dome**   **Stratigraphic trap**   **Fault**

Gas
Oil
Salt
Porous rock

Nonporous rock

Oil

Geologists have learned that underground formations called traps indicate possible oil accumulation. In each case, porous rock is surrounded by layers of nonporous rock.

in the past, aerial photographs now usually are taken by Earth-orbiting satellites. After examining the photographs, surveyors and geologists make detailed surface maps and collect rocks and fossils in land areas that look promising. By studying fossils, scientists can estimate the age of rocks. They compare this data to what they know about the geologic periods in which oil was formed and add this evidence to data already collected.

Geologists also gather clues to underground rock layers and oil traps by using three basic measuring instruments. The **seismograph**, which measures vibrations of the Earth, is the most widely used device. Geoscientists—scientists who study the Earth—explode dynamite just below the surface or use special trucks that "thump" the surface with heavy weights to create small artificial earthquakes. Large air guns are shot toward the bottom of the ocean to produce a similar effect on the ocean floor. The shock waves from these "earthquakes" move through the Earth and bounce back from the different rock layers. The waves are received by devices called geophones. As each geophone receives the reflected shock waves, it relays an electric current to the seismograph. By collecting a number of such seismic records, scientists are able to map the depth and position of underground rock layers and, possibly, oil traps within them.

The **magnetometer** measures differences in the Earth's magnetism. This information discloses the character of the rock surface on which the layered rocks rest. Fortunately, large magnetic surveys can be made quickly over a wide area by trailing the magnetometer from an airplane.

The **gravity meter** measures differences in gravitational pull in different places on the Earth's surface. Heavy, dense rocks have a greater gravitational pull than lighter, less dense rocks. Thus a salt dome will register a weaker gravitational pull than surrounding sedimentary rocks. Rocks near the surface have a greater pull than the same kinds of rocks at greater depths. Different gravity measurements give further clues to the nature and depth of rock beneath the surface.

Computers have revolutionized the search for oil by making it easier for scientists to process complex seismic data and other information. Computers have also helped them

An oil worker checks the dials of a giant wheel on an oil well's Christmas tree, a collection of steel valves and gauges used to divert crude oil coming out of the ground into a storage tank.

develop more-sophisticated testing techniques. In the past, scientists could create only two-dimensional maps using seismic surveys. With computers, they can create highly detailed three-dimensional maps, improving their ability to locate oil successfully.

After data is gathered and analyzed, scientists can pinpoint places where oil is likely to be found, but only the drilling process can actually locate oil. If the evidence indicates that a site is promising, a decision may be made to drill a "wildcat," or exploratory, well.

▶ DRILLING FOR OIL

When you think about oil drilling, you may picture a tall steel structure—an oil derrick—with black oil gushing out the top. Gushers are a thing of the past. Modern drilling techniques generally prevent oil from "gushing" from a well, thus improving production and protecting the environment around the well.

Today's oil derricks have also been adapted to particular jobs and locations. Some are as tall as a 20-story building. Others are small enough to be attached to trucks that bring them to drilling sites. Some oil derricks are placed on large platforms and barges and used for drilling offshore on the continental shelf.

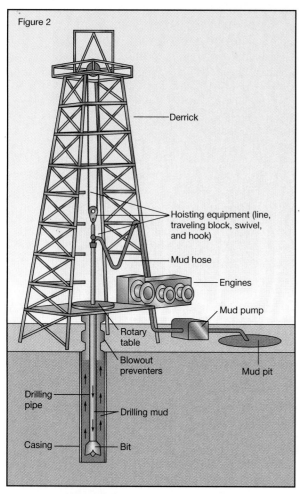

Figure 2

- Derrick
- Hoisting equipment (line, traveling block, swivel, and hook)
- Mud hose
- Engines
- Mud pump
- Rotary table
- Blowout preventers
- Mud pit
- Drilling pipe
- Drilling mud
- Casing
- Bit

A rotary rig uses a rotating bit to cut and crush rock as it drills a hole in the ground.

There are two methods of drilling for oil: cable-tool and rotary. Cable-tool drilling is an older method. In this type of drilling, a heavy, button- or chisel-shaped bit on a cable is raised and then dropped suddenly. When it strikes the ground, the heavy bit literally punches its way through dirt and rock. From time to time, the bit is pulled out of the hole, and the crushed rock is removed. It is used now primarily for drilling shallow wells.

Most modern drilling is done by the rotary method (Figure 2). Rotary drilling utilizes a rapidly turning bit that bores into the Earth. Different bits are used, depending on the type of rock. Most bits have small carbon steel buttons with artificial diamonds on them. Others have three rotating cones. Attached to the drill bit is drilling pipe in 30-foot (9-meter) sections called joints.

In the middle of the derrick is the **rotary table**, a round, flat, steel turntable turned by a powerful motor. This rotates the drilling pipe. When the pipe turns, the bit attached to it cuts into the Earth. As the drill chews its way down, more pipe is attached. Joint after joint is added, and the combined length and weight of the sections make the heavy steel pipe behave like a thin, flexible rod. It takes skill to control the pipe and keep the hole going straight down. The workers who handle this equipment are known as roughnecks.

During "mud-rotary" drilling, a special mixture of water, clay, and chemicals that is called **drilling mud** is pumped down inside the pipe. The mud flows through holes in the bit, cooling and lubricating it. The mud then comes back to the surface between the drill hole and the pipe, carrying chips of broken rock with it. As the hole deepens, the crew adds **casing**, a steel pipe large enough to let the drilling pipe pass through it. After drilling with the first string of casing in place, a second string of casing may be slipped inside the first one. Each string of casing, sometimes several hundred feet long, must be a little smaller than the previous one.

Instead of using drilling mud, some rotary drilling rigs rely on high-pressure air to cool, lubricate, and bring cuttings to the surface. The bit in such an "air-rotary" unit turns and vibrates vertically like a jackhammer. Like cable-tool drilling, this method is most useful for drilling shallow holes less than 3,000 feet (1,000 meters) deep.

Horizontal drilling has become popular for reaching certain oil formations. In this method, drillers steer the drill bit into an oil-bearing formation so that it enters horizontally. This bores a larger hole in the formation, allowing oil to drain more easily than in a vertical well. The use of horizontal drilling also helps recover oil from some difficult-to-reach oil reservoirs.

Along the seacoast, drillers may use a technique called **whipstocking**, or directional drilling, in which workers bend a hole in a wide curve from shore to under the seafloor by changing the angle of the bit at intervals. This allows them to reach offshore oil fields from land.

New technology has allowed drillers to overcome a number of challenges in their work in offshore oil fields. For instance, drilling platforms at sea can now drill for oil in water over 1/2 mile (0.8 kilometer) deep, and they will soon be able to drill in water over 1 mile (1.6 kilometers) deep. These oil rigs are floating platforms anchored to the seafloor on huge cables. Some offshore platforms also have undersea pipeline systems that link them to other offshore wells. Oil from the various wells is sent to one undersea collection point and is then pumped through a pipeline to shore.

Cutting through rock dulls the drill bits, making it necessary to replace them frequently. Rotary bits generally need to be replaced about every 1,850 to 3,600 feet (564 to 1,097 meters). Very hard rock, however, may require new bits as often as every 5 feet (1.5 meters).

After a well has been drilled to a desired depth, engineers evaluate whether there is evidence of enough petroleum to make the well worthwhile to complete. Many times, though, despite promising signs that led to the decision to drill, the hole is dry.

▶ **PRODUCING OIL**

The most exciting part of oil drilling is bringing in the well, or preparing it to produce oil. The bit and drilling pipe are pulled out of the hole. Casing is run to the bottom of the well and filled with chemical mud. A specialized gun is lowered into the hole to shoot holes through the casing into oil deposits in order to open passages through which oil may flow. Generally, however, nothing happens because the heavy column of mud acts like a liquid cork, preventing entry of oil into the drill hole.

The derrick is then removed and a collection of steel valves and gauges, called a **Christmas tree**, is lowered into place and bolted to the top of the casing. Water is pumped in to thin the heavier mud, which is then pushed out of the hole by natural pressures. When crude oil without water or mud appears, another valve on the Christmas tree is turned, diverting the oil to a pipe connected to a storage tank. Natural gas and brine usually are produced along with crude oil when the well is brought in and are separated from the oil before it leaves the oil field for processing.

In the best wells, oil will flow upward from the oil reservoir as a result of underground pressure. However, as a well ages, this pressure lessens and a pumping mechanism must be installed to produce artificial lift in order to get the oil to the surface.

In the past, oil was allowed to flow at its natural rate or was pumped at the maximum rate possible. Today oil producers try to produce as much oil as they can over the longest period of time. To do this, they hold down production from a well when it begins operating. This helps slow the reduction in natural pressure and generally results in greater long-term production. It was once thought that drilling more wells in an area would increase oil production. Now it is known that drilling fewer wells produces better results. Most modern oil fields have one well for every 40 acres (16 hectares) or more.

Experts estimate that there is between 1.4 and 2 trillion barrels (a barrel is 42 gallons, or 159 liters) of recoverable oil in the world. Recoverable oil is oil that can be brought to the surface economically. Additional oil deposits may exist, but they await discovery or the technology needed to reduce the costs of production. Until recently, only about 30 percent of the oil in a reservoir was recoverable, but new methods now capture more oil from known reservoirs.

When natural production is no longer economical, other methods may be used. One such method involves drilling special wells called service wells into an oil reservoir and injecting natural gas. The pressure of the gas forces more oil into the producing wells. In another method known as water flooding, large quantities of water are injected into the oil reservoir. The water displaces the oil and pushes it toward the producing well. A third method is to inject steam into the reservoir, which causes the heavy oil to flow more freely. Another technique, called fire flooding, injects air into the rock, making it possible to ignite some of the heavy oil. This leaves the remaining oil thin enough for water flooding. Although expensive now, these methods may become more affordable in the future.

In the United States, the largest oil and gas companies not only search for and produce oil, they also transport and refine oil and market petroleum products. Many other companies are also involved in the American oil industry. These independents concentrate on only one segment of the industry, such as oil exploration and production. In most of the rest of the world, large companies, often government owned, control the oil industry. In countries where governments have established their own oil companies, such as in Saudi Arabia, Mexico, and Venezuela, foreign companies are often not allowed to operate.

▶ REFINING PETROLEUM

Crude oil is made into useful products through a process called **refining**. A modern oil refinery is a large maze of tanks, spheres, and towers connected by as much as 300 miles (500 kilometers) of pipe. After crude oil is brought to the refinery by truck, tanker, or pipeline, it is changed into other products by a process that involves heating, cooling, chemicals, and pressure.

Petroleum is a mixture of hundreds of different chemicals called hydrocarbons—combinations of hydrogen and carbon atoms—and various impurities. Some hydrocarbons consist of only two or three carbon atoms, while others have thousands strung together in long chains. The hydrogen atoms are arranged in various patterns around these carbon atoms. The more carbon atoms in a hydrocarbon molecule, the thicker and heavier the hydrocarbon. Gasoline consists of a mixture of lighter hydrocarbons. Slightly heavier hydrocarbons make up kerosene and distillate fuel oil. Asphalt, which is often used for paving streets, is composed of very heavy hydrocarbons.

Different hydrocarbons boil at different temperatures, making it possible to separate hydrocarbons by a process called **fractional distillation** (Figure 3). This process involves several steps. First, pipes carry crude oil into a furnace, where it is heated to about 800°F (425°C). The heat causes most of the hydrocarbons in the oil to change into hot vapors. These vapors then pass into a cooling tower, called a fractionating tower, that is hotter at the base than at the top. The tower is divided into a series of trays arranged one above the other. The various hydrocarbon vapors change back into liquids at different temperatures, with each collecting on a separate tray in the tower. The liquids are then drawn off through pipes for further processing.

Although the original crude oil mixture is now separated, further refining is required to obtain different petroleum products. During the distillation process, for example, only 20 percent of each barrel of oil can be made into gasoline. To create more gasoline, the natural proportions of the hydrocarbons in crude oil must be changed. This is done by using **catalysts**, special chemicals that increase the speed of chemical reactions. Together with heat and pressure, catalysts are able to make one kind of hydrocarbon change into another. For example, in a process called **catalytic cracking**, one type of catalyst helps split large hydrocarbons into smaller ones. In a process called **polymerization**, other catalysts transform smaller hydrocarbons into larger ones. It is estimated that more than 500,000 different materials can be made from crude oil. What is actually made, however, depends on what consumers want.

▶ TRANSPORTING PETROLEUM PRODUCTS

A vast transportation system exists to transport crude oil to refineries and refined petroleum products to customers. In the United States, for example, about 200,000 miles (322,000 kilometers) of pipelines carry petroleum to refineries and refined products to distribution centers around the country. Most pipelines are underground. One exception is the Alaskan pipeline, an 800-mile (1,288-kilometer) pipeline that carries petroleum from oil fields in northern Alaska to the port of Valdez in southern Alaska. The Alaskan pipeline is above ground in order to prevent damage to the **permafrost**, which is a layer of permanently frozen ground that is found in far northern areas near the Arctic Circle.

Pipelines are the most important means of transporting oil in the United States. One reason for their importance is that they often carry oil long distances. Some oil is also transported by tankers or barges along the coast or up rivers. Trucks transport all the gasoline within the country, but they transport it only for short distances, usually between a distribution center and local gasoline stations.

▶ HOW PETROLEUM IS USED

In industrialized societies such as the United States and Canada, there is a great demand for petroleum products. While most often used to produce fuel, petroleum is also used to make lubricants and greases, asphalt and waxes, and various petrochemicals.

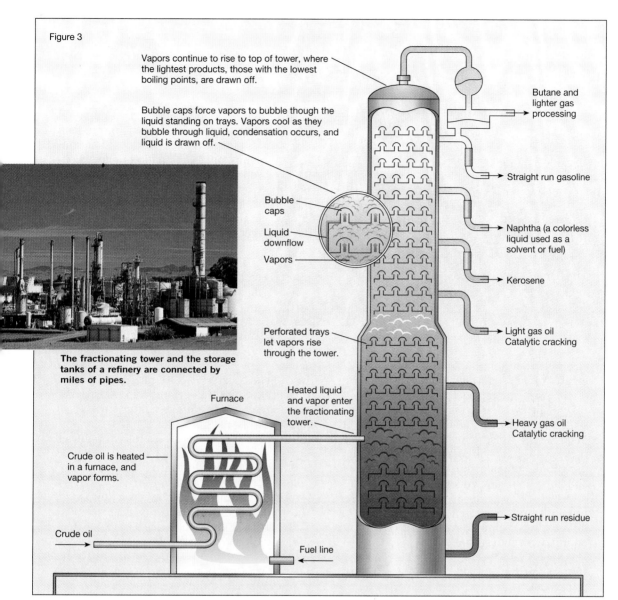

Vapors continue to rise to top of tower, where the lightest products, those with the lowest boiling points, are drawn off.

Bubble caps force vapors to bubble though the liquid standing on trays. Vapors cool as they bubble through liquid, condensation occurs, and liquid is drawn off.

Bubble caps

Liquid downflow

Vapors

Butane and lighter gas processing

Straight run gasoline

Naphtha (a colorless liquid used as a solvent or fuel)

Kerosene

Perforated trays let vapors rise through the tower.

Light gas oil Catalytic cracking

The fractionating tower and the storage tanks of a refinery are connected by miles of pipes.

Furnace

Heated liquid and vapor enter the fractionating tower.

Heavy gas oil Catalytic cracking

Crude oil is heated in a furnace, and vapor forms.

Crude oil

Fuel line

Straight run residue

At an oil refinery, crude oil is heated in a furnace, and the resulting vapors are turned back into different liquids at different temperatures in the fractionating tower.

The major fuels derived from petroleum are gasoline, diesel fuels, fuel oils, jet fuels, kerosene, and liquefied petroleum gas, also called bottled gas. The most important of these are transportation fuels used to power cars, trucks, buses, planes, ships, trains, and farm machines. Petroleum-based fuels are also burned for heating, for running industrial machinery, and for generating electricity.

Automobiles use the largest share of the petroleum consumed for transportation. Some kinds of vehicles, such as jet planes and supertankers, consume tremendous quantities of these fuels. A jumbo-sized jet plane, for example, may burn as much as 3,500 gallons (13,248 liters) of fuel during each hour of flight. A supertanker may consume 25,000 gallons (94,625 liters) of fuel oil for each day of operation. On a long voyage, a single ship might consume over 1 million gallons (3.8 million liters) of fuel.

Many different kinds of lubricants and greases are made from petroleum. Some of these products are used for lubricating delicate watch and machine parts. Others are used as lubricants for locomotives and giant

At a modern refinery, crude oil is changed into many useful products by processes that involve heating, cooling, the use of chemicals, and pressure.

electric generators. Different lubricants and greases often are formulated to withstand different types of climates.

Asphalt is a dark, solid or semisolid substance that turns to liquid when heated. Its major use is as a paving material for roads, parking lots, and airport runways. It is also used in the manufacture of roofing materials and in automobile undercoatings.

Waxes obtained from petroleum are used primarily to waterproof packaging, such as milk cartons. Some petroleum-derived waxes are used in making candles.

Petrochemicals are chemicals obtained from petroleum or natural gas that can serve as raw materials to make other products. For example, when the petrochemicals benzene and ethylene are reacted together, they produce styrene, a material used to make synthetic rubber, plastic, and latex paint. Although only a small percentage of petroleum ends up as petrochemicals, these chemicals are used to make thousands of different products, including plastics, synthetic rubber, synthetic fibers, paints, and fertilizers.

▶ PETROLEUM PRODUCERS AND CONSUMERS

Petroleum is produced in many areas of the world. Yet about half of all this oil must be shipped from where it is produced to where it is needed. As a result, most countries around the world are either oil exporters or oil importers.

The United States uses more oil than any other country, more than 25 percent of the world's total consumption. The nation once consumed an even greater share of the world's oil, but in recent years, petroleum use has grown more slowly in the United States and in other industrialized nations than it has in developing countries around the world.

The United States was one of the first producers of oil, and its oil production grew steadily until 1970. At that time, the nation produced about 20 percent of the world's oil. Since 1970, however, oil production in the United States has fallen. The country remains one of the top oil producers in the world, but because it consumes more than it produces, it must import oil from other countries. Many industrialized nations must also import oil. Japan, for instance, imports almost all the oil it consumes, as do many countries in Europe.

Much of the world's oil is found in undeveloped areas of nonindustrialized countries. Among these are a number of countries in the Middle East, where about 65 percent of the world's known oil reserves are located. These nations produce much more oil than they consume. As a result, they have become major exporters of oil. In 1960 a group of oil exporters formed the Organization of Petroleum Exporting Countries (OPEC). Its members include Algeria, Indonesia, Iran, Iraq, Kuwait, Libya, Nigeria, Qatar, Saudi Arabia, the United Arab Emirates, and Venezuela. Since the early 1980's, OPEC has controlled the price and supply of much of the oil used around the world.

▶ PETROLEUM FOR TODAY AND TOMORROW

There is only so much petroleum in the Earth. Once the supply is used up, there will be no more. Several times in the past, people have thought that the supply of oil was about to run out. To everyone's surprise, new oil reserves were discovered and scientists found ways to recover more oil from old oil fields. Such developments have led to increased supplies of oil and better prospects for finding more.

Another important development has been the discovery of new ways to obtain liquid fuels that could substitute for petroleum. These methods include getting liquid fuels from oil shales and tar sands. **Oil shale** is a slatelike rock containing organic matter called kerogen. When oil shale is crushed and heated to about 900°F (480°C), the kerogen changes to a thick liquid, from which crude oil can be extracted. **Tar sands** are sandstones that contain a thick hydrocarbon residue called bitumen. Treating the sands with steam or hot water releases the bitumen. When hydrogen is added to the bitumen, crude oil is produced.

Venezuela has large deposits of bitumen in its Orinoco region and has looked for ways to exploit this vast resource for decades. Recently, Venezuela has begun processing the bitumen into a special heavy fuel oil mixed with water. Known as **Orimulsion**, this fuel is burned in power plants to produce electricity.

Despite Venezuela's success in producing Orimulsion, few attempts to exploit oil shales and tar sands have been able to compete with conventional oil supplies. Until oil prices rise substantially and remain high, the potential of these resources will be limited.

▶ PETROLEUM AND POLLUTION

The quality of our environment is a major concern in today's world. Many efforts are being made to prevent damage to the environment by petroleum and its refined prod-

ucts. Some causes of pollution that were common decades ago have been eliminated. In the early days of the petroleum industry, for example, oil wells often had "blowouts," which were sudden and uncontrollable escapes of gas and oil from wells caused by high pressures within the underground oil reservoirs. This no longer happens. Instead, special devices that prevent blowouts save oil from being wasted and prevent the pollution of surrounding areas.

During recent decades, environmental rules and practices have helped prevent pollution in two ways: by controlling how oil is produced, refined, transported, and stored; and by controlling the quality of the refined product that is burned as a fuel.

Environmental rules also dictate how to prevent pollution from an oil well after it is no longer producing and how far apart oil wells should be. The disposal of by-products of drilling, including drilling mud and brine, are also carefully controlled.

Oil refineries once produced great amounts of air and water pollution. However, now they must obey many regulations that prevent or greatly reduce the output of pollutants during the refining process. For example, before water used in refining can be returned to waterways, it must be purified and cooled.

Serious environmental problems can result if oil is spilled into the sea by oil tankers. Oil spills can injure or kill fish, marine animals, and aquatic birds. They can also foul beaches and damage microscopic organisms living in

A tanker takes on some of the unspilled oil from the *Exxon Valdez*, which ran aground in Alaska's Prince William Sound in 1989. The oil spill that resulted was the largest ever to occur in U.S. waters.

Oil pollution is a serious problem. Onshore workers use hoses to clean up oil and other debris from an oil spill (*left*). Medical workers treat a duck that was injured during an oil spill at a refinery in Fidalgo Bay, Washington (*below*).

tidal basins. Such damage can be overcome in time, but the speed of recovery depends on various factors, including the type of oil spilled, the depth of the water, and the action of the waves. Oil spills can affect not only the environment, but also industries, such as fishing and tourism, that depend on the sea.

Rules to prevent pollution from oil spills have become stricter since a tanker spilled 11 million gallons, or 258,000 barrels, of oil into Alaska's Prince William Sound in 1989. Companies must now pay heavy penalties for spills or careless practices that can lead to spills. Shipowners must replace existing tankers with ships that have double hulls. If a hole is poked in the outer hull by running aground or by hitting an obstacle, the inner hull helps prevent oil from leaking out. Since these rules have gone into effect, pollution from oil spills has declined in the United States.

Because burning petroleum products can also cause pollution, the quality of fuels is also controlled. For example, environmental rules require gasoline to evaporate more slowly in the summer to prevent smog and other forms of air pollution. In some areas, gasoline must contain more oxygen in winter in order to prevent carbon monoxide pollution. Beginning in the mid-1970's, pollution-preventing devices that run only on unleaded gasoline were installed on many cars in the United States. Since then, new knowledge about the dangers of lead have resulted in the banning of leaded gasoline. In 1995 some regions of the United States also began using a new kind of low-pollution fuel known as reformulated gasoline.

Other petroleum products must also meet stricter environmental standards. Many rules, for example, limit the amount of sulfur that petroleum products can contain. To produce low-sulfur products, refiners must use more expensive low-sulfur crude oils that are low in natural sulfur, or they must remove the sulfur with special processes. Sometimes they must do both. These strict environmental rules allow people to continue using petroleum products and protect the environment at the same time. Other less-polluting fuels may become widely available in the future. For now, such fuels would be too expensive to compete effectively with petroleum.

CHERYL J. TRENCH
Executive Vice President
Petroleum Industry Research Foundation, Inc.

SCOTT ESPENSHADE
Independent Petroleum Association of America

See also DISTILLATION; ENERGY SUPPLY; FUELS; GASOLINE; KEROSENE; ORGANIZATION OF PETROLEUM EXPORTING COUNTRIES (OPEC).

PETS

If a creature is four-footed or two-footed, or if it flies, swims, crawls, or hops, you can be sure that someone at some time has made a pet of it. Interesting pets from all over the world have won places in the homes and hearts of people who keep animals for pleasure.

Of all the animals, the domestic cat and dog continue to hold the preferred places around the family hearth. The dog is still the favorite animal out-of-doors.

▶MAMMALS AS PETS

Mammals are animals that have backbones and nourish their young with milk. They include domestic and wild animals. Among the small domestic mammals are dogs, cats, rabbits, guinea pigs, mice, and hamsters.

There are over 100 breeds of dogs from which to choose. Your choice of a dog should depend upon whether you live in the city or in the country. If you live in the city, you will be wise to have one of the smaller breeds, such as a pug, cocker spaniel, or Pekingese or a small mixed breed if you do not wish to buy a purebred dog. If you live in the country, you may enjoy one of the hounds, a sporting dog, a terrier, or maybe one of the working dogs, such as a Newfoundland or a boxer. These dogs require considerable exercise, which they can have easily in the country.

Most dogs are easy to feed and to train. They are naturally meat eaters but will thrive on good-quality prepared dog foods, which can be bought in any market.

All dogs should be inoculated against distemper, hepatitis, leptospirosis, and parvovirus when they are puppies. They should receive boosters every year.

There are many kinds of domestic cats, and most of them are easy to care for. Feeding has been simplified by commercial cat foods. Consider the several breeds—long-haired and short-haired—and pick the one that appeals most to you. But remember that long-haired cats, such as the Persian, must be combed frequently. All cats should be inoculated against cat distemper.

Rabbits breed readily in cages and eat a simple diet of hay, greens, and rabbit pellets, which are small bits of compressed food, ob-

Above: Puppies of almost any breed are firm favorites with children. Below: Short-haired Siamese cats are very popular pets.

A green Amazon parrot. Parrots and parakeets, if properly trained, can often repeat phrases that they hear.

flower seeds, apples, and carrots. Both hamsters and gerbils reproduce very rapidly.

Mice, in their great variety of colors, make particularly interesting pets. There are many sizes, and some are fat and some are thin. These pets should be kept in a cage and should have an exercise wheel. They breed rapidly and tame easily. If you decide to have mice as pets, clean the cage frequently, or the odor will be very unpleasant. Feed your mice hamster food and let them drink from a tube attached to a bottle.

▶ FEATHERED PETS

If you are thinking of a bird as a pet, you will find an interesting variety from which to choose. Domestic bird pets are parakeets, canaries, pigeons, finches, chickens, parrots, mynas, ducks, and geese.

Chickens, ducks, and geese are often tamed, but bantam chickens are those usually kept for pets. They range from tiny to larger varieties, and there are long-legged, short-legged, bare-legged, and feather-legged breeds.

Pigeons are fun to own if you have the space. They are raised outdoors in lofts or pigeon houses. There are dozens of fancy varieties with differing features. These varieties include tipplers, which fly high in kits, or schools, for hours at a time; tumblers, which fly up and do somersaults in the air; parlor tumblers, which somersault close to the ground; and racing homers, which return home from distances as great as 1,600 kilometers (1,000 miles) and are used in sport.

Parakeets are little birds that talk, if properly trained. They are simple to care for and can be permitted freedom of the house. They eat a standard seed diet, which is available even in grocery stores, and they enjoy some greens, too. Many thousands are bred for sale and for show, and new varieties in size and color are being produced.

Like parakeets, parrots make entertaining pets because of their ability to mimic human speech. But parrots need much more care and attention than parakeets do. A parrot's living quarters must be larger, and its seed diet must be supplemented with protein foods, fruits, and greens.

It should be pointed out that pigeons, parakeets, and parrots can pass on to people a

tainable at pet stores. Since they stand cold weather well, they can be kept outdoors. Rabbits can be housebroken and make fine indoor pets. Their soft fur makes them particularly endearing.

Guinea pigs (cavies) are fascinating creatures, although some people object to the sharp, loud whistling sound that they make. They come in many colors, with short, wiry or very long hair, depending upon the breed. The young of the guinea pig look quite mature directly after birth. They nurse, but they also eat adult food almost immediately. In the wintertime guinea pigs need some artificial heat. Thousands of guinea pigs are bred and exhibited for prizes at pet shows. If you don't mind their whistling, you can have great enjoyment from raising guinea pigs.

Hamsters and gerbils are also popular pets. Hamsters can be fed prepared food, some raw vegetables, nuts, and grains. Gerbils originated in the dry, sandy regions of Africa and southwestern Asia. They need water. But because of their desert background, they need relatively little. Their diet may include sun-

serious disease. This disease, called psittacosis, or ornithosis, is an infection like pneumonia. Anyone who handles sick birds or cleans their cages is in danger of catching it. Sometimes an infected bird will not appear to be very sick. For this reason a bird with any sign of illness should be checked immediately by a veterinarian. The bird should be cared for by the veterinarian until it is well. People who catch the disease are treated with antibiotics.

Canaries are pleasant pets, and many of the males are lovely songbirds. The females are not singers. There are many breeds and colors. Some are yellow, some green, some shaded with red. Canaries are easy to keep. They, too, eat seeds and greens. Cages can be bought at pet stores.

Myna birds, which are natives of India, make interesting pets. The hill myna is the most satisfactory. With patient training they can become wonderful talkers. Some have considerable vocabularies, and some whistle tunes. Their favorite diet is fruit, but they also eat meat, insects, eggs, and bread.

▶ WATER PETS

Among the many fish of the world, only four kinds are domestic pets. These four are goldfish, Roman eel, carp, and paradise fish. The goldfish bred under domestic conditions has been greatly changed into many forms by selection. All the other fish kept in aquariums (glass tanks) are natural wild species but are adaptable and easily tamed. Fish fall into two classifications—warm-water and cold-water species. This fact should guide the choice and treatment of fish.

Goldfish are carp that are not always gold. Some are silver, some black, some mixtures of colors. They are best kept in water with a temperature of about 15°C (60°F). If there is enough aeration, they will live in ponds that freeze over in winter. They eat aquarium plants, as well as worms, daphnia (water fleas), chopped beef, and liver.

Of all aquarium fish the tiny guppy is the most popular. The guppy comes in a great variety of colors and shapes. Guppies bear live young instead of producing eggs.

You can net some wild fish and make pets of them. Baby bullheads, minnows, and several other species will live in captivity if you

Fish kept as pets range from ordinary goldfish to tropical fish in brilliant colors.

simulate (copy) their natural habitat. The food and the temperature of the water must be the same as in nature.

Turtles, especially box turtles, can be kept in backyards. They will thrive on worms, slugs, and other garden pests. They learn to know their owner and will come for food, which may be bread, meat, angleworms, or mealworms. They will drink from a pan sunk in the ground and filled with water. If a male and a female are kept, the female will lay eggs from which baby turtles will hatch.

▶ HOW TO CARE FOR PETS

A pet is not a plaything but a living creature that depends on its owner for its very life. There are different requirements for the care of various kinds of pets. Here is a list of general suggestions that can be applied to the care of almost any pet:

(1) It should have fresh water every day, always within easy reach.

(2) The pet must have regular feeding times but must never be overfed. It must be housed in clean living quarters.

(3) Above all, each pet owner should learn how to take care of the pet's special needs and to handle it gently.

LEON F. WHITNEY
Author, *Complete Book of Home Pet Care*

See also BIRDS AS PETS; CATS; CATS, WILD; DOGS; FISH AS PETS; GUINEA PIGS, HAMSTERS, AND GERBILS.

PEWTER. See TIN.

PHENYLKETONURIA (PKU). See DISEASES (Descriptions of Some Diseases).

PHILADELPHIA

In 1682, William Penn founded a city on the Delaware River in southeastern Pennsylvania. Penn, a Quaker from England, wanted the city to be a place of religious freedom. He named it Philadelphia, which means "brotherly love" in Greek. It became known as the City of Brotherly Love and was the largest city in colonial America.

Although Philadelphia was settled 75 years after Jamestown, Virginia, and 62 years after Plymouth, Massachusetts, it was in Philadelphia that the United States was truly born. In Philadelphia, Thomas Jefferson, Benjamin Franklin, and other patriots wrote the words

Elfreth's Alley, one of the oldest streets in the United States, was opened in 1703. Old Philadelphia has many narrow lanes with beautifully preserved houses.

"When in the course of Human Events . . . ," introducing the Declaration of Independence. In Philadelphia, colonial patriots developed the ideas behind the American Revolution. In Philadelphia, the nation's founders wrote "We, the people of the United States, in order to form a more perfect union . . . ," which began the Preamble to the United States Constitution.

Independence Hall, where the Declaration of Independence was signed, where the Constitution was written, and where the Liberty Bell first rang out, still stands as a monument to the nation's beginnings. Congress Hall, where Congress met from 1790 to 1800, when Philadelphia was the nation's capital, stands on Independence Square. Other historic sites include Carpenters' Hall, where the first Continental Congress met; Christ Church and Burial Ground, where Benjamin Franklin is buried; and Library Hall, which is the library of the American Philosophical Society. These buildings and many others make up Independence National Historical Park.

Nearby are the Betsy Ross House, where the first American flag may have been made, and Elfreth's Alley, one of the oldest streets in the United States.

Independence Square and its nearby buildings are only a part of the story of Philadelphia. This "greene countrie towne," as William Penn called it, also became a center of culture. It was the home of the first American hospital, the first American medical college, the first women's medical college, the first paper mill, the first bank, the first daily newspaper, the first United States Mint, and the first public school for black children.

▶THE CITY TODAY

The population of Philadelphia is approximately 1.58 million and the metropolitan area has about 4.8 million people. The city has more than 4,000 industrial establishments that produce electrical machinery, radios and television sets, automobile and truck bodies, railroad cars, buses, textiles, clothing, chemicals, drugs, tobacco products, and leather goods. Other industries include oil refining, printing and publishing, banking, and food processing and distribution.

The Philadelphia Naval Shipyard has been building and repairing ships for the United States Navy, although not continuously, since

A statue of William Penn atop Philadelphia's City Hall overlooks the plaza and modern office buildings of Penn Center, a part of the city's urban renewal program.

1867. The Delaware River connects the city to the Atlantic Ocean, and the port of Philadelphia is one of the largest in the world. It is one of the best-equipped ports in the United States and ranks among the busiest American ports in the amount of tonnage handled. The waterfront, Penn's Landing, is undergoing a vast renovation.

Philadelphia's skyline has changed dramatically since the early 1970's, with the addition of many modern buildings. The city's downtown area includes tall, glass-covered skyscrapers; the Gallery, a large shopping mall; and Society Hill, the largest concentration of restored residences from the 1700's in the United States.

The city is the home of fine cultural institutions. The Philadelphia Orchestra is internationally famous. The Pennsylvania Academy of the Fine Arts, the nation's oldest art institution, has exhibits of painting, sculpture, and graphic arts. The Philadelphia Museum of Art and the Rodin Museum are among the finest in the world. The Franklin Institute Science Museum and Planetarium is one of the leading museums of its kind. The American Philosophical Society, founded by Benjamin Franklin in 1743, is the oldest learned society in the United States. The Academy of Natural Sciences, the first natural history museum in the United States, has nature exhibits, live-animal shows, and a children's museum. The Philadelphia Zoo is the oldest in the country.

Philadelphia is an educational center. The University of Pennsylvania and Temple University are among many well-known institutions. The city is also an important medical center, known for several excellent hospitals and medical schools.

Many sports events take place in Philadelphia, including the Army-Navy football game. The Penn Relays, a track-and-field meet sponsored by the University of Pennsylvania, are held at Franklin Field. The city is also the home of several professional sports teams: The Philadelphia Phillies baseball team and the Philadelphia Eagles football team play in Veterans Stadium, and the Philadelphia Flyers hockey team and the Philadelphia 76ers basketball team play in the Spectrum. Fairmount Park, one of the world's largest city parks, has golf courses, trails for riding and hiking, and ice-skating areas during the winter.

Philadelphia, originally about 2 miles square (5 kilometers square), is today a great metropolis covering about 130 square miles (340 square kilometers). Yet even as Philadelphia has grown and developed, it has retained a sense of history that can be found in few other American cities.

Reviewed by REBECCA M. RIDGWAY
Greater Philadelphia Chamber of Commerce

PHILIPPINES

The Philippines is an island nation lying off the southeastern coast of Asia. It is made up of more than 7,000 islands, which form an archipelago, or chain of islands, extending for about 1,100 miles (1,800 kilometers) along the western edge of the Pacific Ocean. Most of the islands are small and uninhabited. The vast majority of the people of the Philippines live on the eleven largest islands.

Situated at a crossroads between East and West, the Philippines has been influenced by both Asian and Western cultures. An Asian land, it was ruled for centuries by Spain, which brought European traditions and the Christian religion to the islands. At the end of the 19th century, the Philippines came under the control of the United States, which governed it for many years. After a long struggle for self-determination, the people of the Philippines gained complete independence in 1946 and began the building of their own distinctive nation.

▶THE PEOPLE

Most Filipinos, as the people are called, are of Malay stock, closely related to the people of Malaysia and Indonesia. In appearance, they are usually of medium height, with brown skin and straight black hair. Their ancestors migrated to the Philippines by boat in ancient times. The earliest known inhabitants of the islands are the Negritos. They are believed to have crossed into the Philippines over land bridges that connected some of the islands to the mainland of Asia many thousands of years ago. Some Negritos still live in remote areas of the islands.

A number of Filipinos have some Spanish, American, or Chinese ancestry. Chinese settled on the islands as merchants and traders over the centuries. Today, they make up a small but distinct minority. Some Spaniards and Americans also live in the Philippines.

The Philippines has a fairly large and fast-growing population, with many people concentrated on a small number of islands. About half the people live on Luzon, the largest island. The majority of Filipinos live in rural areas, though in recent years many people have moved to the cities, especially to the large metropolitan area of Manila, the capital, on Luzon island.

Language. The ancestors of the Filipinos settled in different parts of the islands, where they were often isolated from each other by the mountainous terrain. As a result, many different languages developed. More than 80 languages are spoken in the Philippines, though most people speak one of about ten major languages. In order to create a common language for all Filipinos, the government adopted Pilipino, which is based on Tagalog, as the national language. Pilipino is spoken by many Filipinos and is a required language of instruction for children in primary schools. English is also spoken widely throughout the islands. It is taught in some school classes, and a

---

FACTS AND FIGURES

REPUBLIC OF THE PHILIPPINES (Republika ng Pilipinas) is the official name of the country.

THE PEOPLE are known as Filipinos.

LOCATION: Southeast Asia.

AREA: 115,830 sq mi (300,000 km^2).

POPULATION: 59,000,000 (estimate).

CAPITAL AND LARGEST CITY: Manila.

OFFICIAL LANGUAGES: Pilipino (national language), English.

MAJOR RELIGIONS: Christian, Muslim.

GOVERNMENT: Republic. **Head of state and government**—president. **Legislature**—Congress (consisting of the Senate and the House of Representatives).

CHIEF PRODUCTS: Agricultural—rice, corn, coconut products, sugarcane, bananas, tobacco, peanuts, livestock. **Manufactured**—processed food, textiles, chemicals, wood products, assembled automobiles, electronics equipment, glass, rubber and steel products. **Mineral**—chromite (chromium ore), copper, manganese, iron ore, gold.

MONETARY UNIT: Peso (1 peso = 100 centavos).

NATIONAL ANTHEM: ''Beloved Land.''

---

knowledge of English is required for entrance into colleges and universities. Both Pilipino and English are official languages of the Philippines. Spanish, which was formerly an official language, is now spoken by relatively few Filipinos.

Religion. The Philippines is the only country in Asia with a predominantly Christian population. The development of Christianity resulted from Spanish rule of the islands from the 16th to the end of the 19th century. More than 90 percent of the people are Christian. Most of them are Roman Catholics. Other Filipinos belong to the Philippine Independent Church (Aglipayan), founded in 1902 as part of a movement of Filipino nationalism. Another Philippine church is the Iglesia ni Kristo, or Church of Christ, which was founded in 1914 as a popular religion.

Spanish missionaries were unable to convert the Filipinos living in the southern part of the country to Christianity. They had been converted to Islam (the religion of the Muslims) before the arrival of the Spaniards and refused to abandon their religion. These Muslim Filipinos, sometimes called *Moros* by the Christians, make up about 5 percent of the population. Most Muslim Filipinos live on Mindanao and the Sulu islands. There are also a small number of Buddhists in the Philippines. Freedom of religion and separation of church and state are guaranteed by the constitution.

Education. Public education is based on a three-level system—four years of primary school, two years of intermediate school, and four years of high school. Under Spanish rule, public education was not greatly encouraged. Education was encouraged by the United States during its governing of the Philippines, and public school attendance is now compulsory through the first four grades.

Filipinos place a high value on education. The Philippines has one of the highest literacy rates in Asia, with almost 90 percent of the people able to read and write. Besides the millions of students enrolled in public schools, many others attend private elementary and secondary schools, colleges, and universities. These private schools are often church-sponsored. There are many universities and colleges in the Philippines. The oldest, the University of Santo Tomás, founded in 1611, is in Manila. Other large universities include

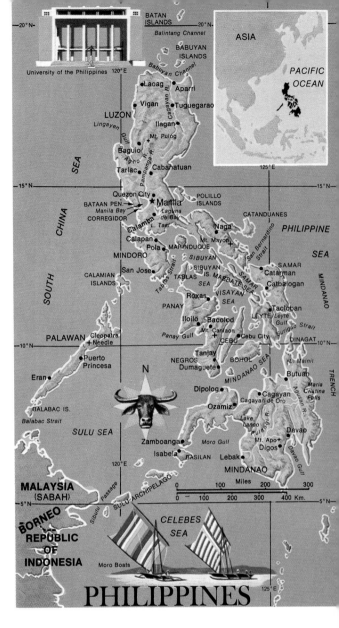

PHILIPPINES

Feati University, the University of the East, and Far Eastern University, all in Manila; the University of the Philippines in Quezon City, the University of the Visayas, in Cebu City; and the University of Mindanao, in Davao.

The Arts. Filipinos are an artistic people. They have a rich body of folklore, including epics that take many nights to recite. On rainy days children are amused by folktales about princes and princesses or supernatural beings. Filipino music includes ancient melodies played on cleverly made bamboo flutes or on century-old bronze gongs. Filipino music also includes concerts by symphonies or rock music by local bands. Many lively songs and dances, accompanied by guitars, reflect a Spanish influence. Many Filipinos in the cities and in the provinces are very fond of movies. There are hundreds of theaters in many parts of the country.

Paintings and sculpture by Filipino artists have won prizes in international art exhibits. They often represent styles that are a unique blend of Asian and Western influences. Novels and short stories by such Filipino authors as José Rizal, N. V. M. González, and Benvenido Santos have been translated into many languages. Filipino artistic talent is also seen in delicately woven fabrics that combine silk and pineapple fibers or in baskets of intricate design woven from rattan.

Way of Life. In the big cities of the Philippines, such as Manila, many Filipinos live much like people in the United States. They attend good schools and live in modern houses, with electricity, running water, and often air-conditioning. They go to the latest movies and participate in many sports. Their children become Girl Scouts and Boy Scouts. Basketball and baseball are the most popular games. These Filipinos speak English and dress in Western-style clothes.

But the great majority of Filipinos live in small towns (*poblaciones*) or villages (*barrios*). Their houses, often built on bamboo stilts, have nipa and bamboo walls. The roofs are thatched with nipa palm leaves. Most houses lack electricity and running water. Most of these people earn their living by fishing and farming. Children help grow rice, corn, and other crops in the fields and work on nets and other fishing gear. Although rural Filipinos know some English, they usually speak in their native tongue. They rarely see a movie and often do not travel beyond their province. The children amuse themselves with such outdoor activities as flying kites and swimming. Once a year the community honors its patron saint with a fiesta. Dances and processions are held in honor of the saint. There are also contests for the children, such as a race to catch and hold a greased pig. There may be fireworks in the evening. In the rural areas meat is rarely served except on festive occasions, such as the annual fiesta, or for a special event, such as a wedding. In coastal areas most people eat locally-caught fish every day.

▶ **THE LAND**

The Republic of the Philippines is located in the Pacific Ocean, northeast of Borneo and south of Taiwan (Formosa). The island group has a total land area slightly smaller than that of the British Isles. Many of the numerous small islands in the Philippines have not been named.

There are three main island groups in the archipelago. The Luzon group in the north contains the islands of Luzon and Mindoro. In the central Philippines are Palawan Island and the Visayan Islands, with Bohol, Cebu, Leyte, Masbate, Negros, Panay, and Samar islands. Mindanao and the Sulu Archipelago compose the Mindanao group in the southern part of the Philippines.

The largest island is Luzon. In the northern part of this island are high mountains. Central Luzon is a wide plain, where rice and sugarcane are grown. Southern Luzon has many active volcanoes. One of the most famous is Mount Mayon.

The second largest island in the archipelago is Mindanao. Mount Apo, the highest peak in the Philippines, is located here. Mindanao has some good ports, such as Zamboanga in the western part of the island and Davao in the eastern part. The island has many resources that are not yet fully developed. South of Mindanao is the Sulu Archipelago, which nearly touches Sabah, Malaysia.

Corn is grown on many of the islands of the Visayan group. Negros Island is known as the sugar bowl of the Philippines. There are vast sugarcane fields in the western plains of the island. Cebu City is the major port of the Visayas.

Rivers. The Cagayan River in northeastern Luzon is the longest river in the Philippines. The Pampanga and Agno rivers on Luzon and the Agusan and Pulangi (Rio Grande) rivers on Mindanao are also important as sources of waterpower. For the most part, these rivers are too short or turbulent to be used for commercial navigation.

Climate. The annual rainfall of the Philippines averages over 2,000 millimeters (80 inches). Typhoons (called *bagyós* by Filipinos) happen most commonly between July and November. The strong winds and heavy rains of these *bagyós* often do great damage to property in Luzon and other islands. Earthquakes also occur. Annual temperatures average 24 to 29°C (75 to 85°F). Midafternoon is the warmest part of the day.

Natural Resources. Like soils in other tropic regions, most soils in the Philippines are not very fertile. The richest soils are found in the central plain and Cagayan River valley of Luzon and in parts of Mindanao. Because of heavy rainfall and improper use of the land, erosion is a serious problem. About 60 percent of the Philippines suffers from soil erosion.

The Philippines has many valuable minerals. There are large deposits of chromite, copper, manganese, iron ore, and gold. Most of these are being mined.

More than half the Philippines is covered by forests. Vegetation reflects elevation and climate. Nipa palm and mangrove swamps are found in the coastal region. In the lowland areas are tropical rain forests. Many of the trees found there are of great commercial value. Higher up on the mountain slopes are the moss forests, often with hanging mosses and dwarf trees.

Many wild animals—such as the civet, mongoose, Malayan badger, porcupine, wild tamarau, and long-tailed monkey—live in the Philippines. There are about 1,000 varieties of birds, including brightly colored parrots. Lizards abound in the country, but crocodiles are not numerous. Over 2,000 species of fish inhabit the Philippine waters. Fish is an important part of the diet.

▶ THE ECONOMY

The Philippines is mainly an agricultural nation, although it is developing industries of various kinds. About two thirds of all working people are engaged in agriculture or the processing of agricultural products.

Agriculture. Rice, the most important food crop, is grown in many of the islands. But the Central Luzon Plain is known as the nation's "rice bowl."

Corn is another important food crop, especially for the many people living in the Visayas. These Filipinos eat corn daily instead of rice. Dried corn is shelled, milled to the size of rice, and boiled. Cebu, Bohol, eastern Negros, and Mindanao are major corn-growing areas.

Copra (dried coconut meat), sugarcane, and abaca are the chief cash crops. Copra is produced mainly in southern Luzon, Mindanao, and the Visayas. It is processed to make a fine oil for the manufacture of many items, particularly soap. In the Philippines the coconut tree is called the tree of life. The leaves are woven into fans and baskets, the trunk is used for soft lumber, and household utensils are made from the hard coconut shell. The fibrous coconut husk is used to polish house floors and is a firewood substitute. Nearly three fourths of the abaca, or Manila hemp, is raised in the southeastern part of Luzon and in the Davao area of southern Mindanao. The production and sale of sugar

Rice is grown on terraces in mountainous northern Luzon.

is an important source of government revenue. Tobacco, bananas, sweet potatoes, and peanuts are also grown.

Livestock raising is important to the economy. Cattle, hogs, goats, sheep, chickens, ducks, and turkeys are raised. The water buffalo (carabao) is used to pull the plow.

Industries and Products. Philippine industry has made its greatest advance in the years since World War II. Manufacturing is still dominated by the processing of agricultural products. But Filipinos are manufacturing more consumer goods and expanding their light industries. Industry remains concentrated in the area around Manila, including the nearby provinces of Rizal, Bulacan, and Laguna. Cebu City also has a growing number of industries. A large industrial complex has been built in northern Mindanao, using electric power generated by the nearby Maria Cristina Falls. Factories assemble automobiles and produce chemicals, plastics, rubber and steel goods, glass, plywood, and radios.

Handicraft workers make many articles for local use. Baskets and mats are made from palm and bamboo. Handwoven cloth from western Luzon, hats from Luzon and Bohol, and metalwork from the Sulu islands are well known throughout the archipelago.

Transportation. In a nation of islands, water transportation is very important. Nearly a dozen inter-island shipping lines operate out of Manila to hundreds of Philippine ports. These shipping lines often carry both passengers and freight. Many Filipinos use small homemade boats when they want to travel from one part of an island to another or to nearby islands.

Many roads in the Philippines are unpaved and often difficult to use during the rainy season. Buses and trucks are the most common vehicles for travel on the islands.

The most important railway in the Philippines is the one that connects Manila with western and southern Luzon. In addition to passengers, this railroad transports sugar, rice, logs, and copra. There is a shorter railroad on the island of Panay. But most of the islands in the republic are too small to justify the expense of building railroads.

The main islands of the country are connected by domestic air service. There is an international airport in Manila.

▶CITIES
Manila, the largest city of the Philippines, is located on Luzon Island. In the middle of the 19th century, Manila was an old Spanish city surrounded by high stone walls. Today it is a modern city and the nation's capital. Manila is the leading port and the commercial and industrial center of the Philippines. Much

Once a small city surrounded by stone walls, Manila has become a modern metropolis. It is the capital, chief port, and commercial and industrial center of the Philippines.

of Manila was destroyed during World War II, and the city was largely rebuilt after the war. A greater Manila, called Metro Manila, was created in 1975. It includes many neighboring cities and towns.

The second largest city in the Philippines is Quezon City. It was the official capital of the nation until 1976. The next largest city is Davao, a major port on Mindanao. The oldest city, and next in size, is Cebu City, on the east coast of Cebu Island. The first permanent Spanish settlement in the Philippines was founded there in 1565.

▶ HISTORY AND GOVERNMENT

It is believed that people were living in the Philippines more than 250,000 years ago. Some of their stone tools have been found on Luzon. In 1542–43, the Spanish explorer Ruy López de Villalobos (1500–44) named the islands Las Filipinas (the Philippines) in honor of Prince Philip of Asturias, who later became King Philip II of Spain. Miguel López de Legazpe (1510?–72) founded the first permanent Spanish settlement at what is now Cebu City. Six years later he moved his headquarters to Manila.

The Philippines and Spain. For more than 300 years the Philippines was a crown colony of Spain. Spanish influence was to make it the only Christian nation in Asia. The colonization of the Philippines was, to a great extent, a missionary endeavor by Catholic religious orders. By the 17th century a great many of the Filipinos living in the lowlands (excluding Mindanao) were baptized Catholics.

Spain's contributions to the Philippines were numerous. The Western alphabet, Spanish language, and Gregorian calendar were introduced. Encouragement was given to the arts, especially for the decoration of churches. A lasting scientific legacy of Spain is the famous observatory of Manila, founded in 1865 by the Jesuits. The Spaniards opened private schools and colleges, in which the courses of study were religion-oriented. Most students came from well-to-do families. The Spanish brought many of the benefits of European civilization to the Philippines. But the Filipinos were denied freedom and individual dignity. Their economic life, dominated by the Spanish, brought the Filipinos only hard work and high taxes. Many Filipinos were forced to work on public projects. The growing wealth of some Spanish religious orders also created ill will among many Filipinos.

Many educated Filipinos, such as José Rizal (1861–96), wrote novels, essays, and newspaper articles urging equality before the law for both Filipinos and Spaniards. From this struggle José Rizal emerged as a brilliant political leader. He was finally arrested by the Spaniards in 1896. He was accused of inciting rebellion and was shot. This injustice increased the anger of Filipinos. (Today José Rizal is the national hero of the Philippines. His statue is found throughout the country.) By 1898 the Filipinos were waging a full-scale revolt against Spain. Then the United States appeared on the scene.

At the start of the Spanish-American War, President William McKinley sent the fleet under Commodore George Dewey (1837–1917) to Manila. Dewey defeated the Spanish warships in Manila Bay on May 1, 1898. With the help of Filipino troops, Manila was captured four months later. Under the 1898 Treaty of Paris, Spain ceded the Philippines, Guam, and Puerto Rico to the United States.

The Philippines and the United States. Before the surrender of Spain, the leader of the Filipino revolt, General Emilio Aguinaldo (1869–1964), had declared the Philippines an independent country. In 1899 the first Philippine republic was proclaimed. But the United States claimed the right to rule the Philippines as the successor to Spain. Disputes between the American and Filipino military forces finally led to war. Two years later General Aguinaldo was captured, and a year later the Filipinos surrendered.

For half a century the Philippines remained an American colony in Southeast Asia. The United States announced that its objective was to retain the Philippines only until the country was ready for self-rule. Gradually, more and more Filipinos were given posts in the government. In 1916 the Filipinos elected a senate and a house of representatives. Executive power remained with an American governor-general, appointed by the president of the United States. The governor-general lived in Manila in the Malacañang, the present "White House" of Filipino presidents.

The United States developed Philippine agriculture, particularly sugar, copra, and abaca. Most of these crops were sold to the United States. Free trade between the United States and the Philippines was established in 1913. Freedom of worship was guaranteed, and the principle of the separation of church and state was upheld. Protestant missionaries were then able to enter the country. Nationwide vaccination and inoculation programs ended the many terrible epidemics of the past. One of the greatest contributions of the United States was the founding of a national system of public education. The state-supported University of the Philippines was established in 1908. Since the Filipinos were to be trained for self-government, their education for democracy was essential.

Commonwealth and World War II. In 1935 the Filipinos attained self-government, and the Philippine Commonwealth was inaugurated. A constitution, written by Filipinos and accepted by the people in a plebiscite, was approved by the United States. The constitution of 1935 was modeled after the Constitution of the United States. As in the United States, the president served as head of state and government. The legislature consisted of a congress made up of the Senate and House of Representatives. Manuel Quezon (1878–1944) became president of the Philippine Commonwealth, and Sergio Osmeña (1878–1961) became vice-president. But complete independence was delayed until 1946.

The Japanese cut short the life of the Philippine Commonwealth when they attacked the archipelago on December 8, 1941. The Filipinos fought bravely against the Japanese. On May 6, 1942, after heroic battles at Bataan and Corregidor, the Filipino and United States troops in the Philippines surrendered to the Japanese. Quezon and Osmeña later escaped to Australia. A Commonwealth government-in-exile was established in Washington, D.C.

The Japanese surrendered the Philippines on September 3, 1945. In April, 1946, Manuel A. Roxas (1892–1948) was elected president of the Commonwealth. On July 4 of the same year he became the first president of the Republic of the Philippines.

Independence. The newly independent republic faced many problems. Cities had been bombed and burned and roads and bridges destroyed during the war. Industry and commerce were at a standstill. In rebuilding the nation, United States funds played a vital role. In 1948, Roxas died in office. The vice-president, Elpidio Quirino (1890–1956), became president. Quirino faced a rebellion by the Communist Huk guerrillas. Under Ramón Magsaysay (1907–57), the secretary of defense, the army put down the Huk rebellion. Magsaysay became president in 1953. He died in an airplane crash in 1957 and was succeeded by Vice-President Carlos P. Garcia (1896–1971). Diosdado Macapagal served as president from 1961 to 1965, when Ferdinand E. Marcos was elected to the presidency.

The Marcos Years. Marcos held power longer than any president of the Philippines. During his first term, more roads and schools were built and rice production increased. But his second term, following his re-election in 1969, was marked by civil unrest and economic problems. A new Communist rebellion broke out, and a Muslim separatist movement re-emerged in the south. In 1972, Marcos declared martial law. The legislature was suspended, and some opposition political leaders were arrested. A new constitution in 1973 provided for a president as head of state and a prime minister as head of government. Marcos held power as both president and prime minister. Martial law was lifted in 1981. That same year Marcos won election as president with greatly strengthened executive powers.

The Aquino Presidency. Opposition to Marcos, already strong, became widespread after the assassination of his chief political opponent, Benigno S. Aquino, in 1983. In presidential elections held in 1986, Marcos was defeated by Corazon Aquino, Benigno's widow. Marcos left the country and died in Hawaii in 1989. Surviving several coup attempts, Aquino retired after the completion of her term, with the presidency passing peacefully to her successor, Fidel V. Ramos, in 1992.

Under a new constitution approved in 1987, the president, who is both head of state and government, is elected for six years. The legislature, the Congress, consists of an elected Senate and House of Representatives.

DONN V. HART
Northern Illinois University

Reviewed by MARIO D. ZAMORA
College of William and Mary

See also AQUINO, CORAZON.

PHILOSOPHY

Philosophy, science, art, and religion are the four major achievements of the human mind. Like science, philosophy calls for careful reasoning and exact language. Like art, it expresses one's feeling about life. Like religion, it offers a vision of the universe and humanity's place in it. There is no sharp difference between philosophy and the other three branches of culture. The writings of great artists, scientists, and religious leaders have often been classified as philosophy.

At one time all fields of study were accepted as parts of philosophy. Religion and science were particularly important in every philosophic system. But with the rapid advance of knowledge the sciences and the humanities separated from philosophy. They developed their own ways of investigation and their own vocabularies. Philosophers now tend to concentrate on general ideas common to various fields.

Philosophy can be understood in either a popular way or a technical way. In the popular sense any set of deeply held beliefs about human beings, nature, society, and God is called a philosophy. Everyone who has wondered about the meaning of life and found an answer that is satisfying has a philosophy. In its more technical sense philosophy means a highly disciplined and rational method of criticizing fundamental beliefs to make them more clear and reliable. This method was first developed by the ancient Greeks in the 6th century B.C. Thales, Anaximander, Anaximenes, Pythagoras, and other learned people began to speculate about the underlying causes of natural phenomena like birth and death, rainfall and drought, the perfectly regular motions of the planets, the reach of fire toward the sky, and the fall of heavy objects toward the earth.

▶ANALYTICAL METHOD

The ancient Greeks formed the word "philosophy" from *philos* ("lover") and *sophia* ("wisdom"). A philospher to them was a person who was devoted to the pursuit of knowledge for its own sake without regard for its practical uses. The kind of knowledge that interested Thales and other philosophers of the 6th century B.C. was knowledge of nature and its laws. Socrates (470?–399 B.C.) turned at-

tention away from nature toward human beings and society. His motto was "Know thyself." He placed knowledge of right conduct above natural science as deserving of the name wisdom. Socrates was the first to use the analytical method of reasoning. This method searches for clear definitions of central ideas like virtue, justice, and knowledge. It explores the reasons for beliefs so common that people tend to accept them without question, such as the belief that physical objects are more real than ideas or that pleasure, wealth, and power are the best things in life.

Socrates challenged his fellow Athenians to justify their assumptions and usually showed that their reasons were unsound. His refusal to accept established principles without question disturbed many people. Some of his enemies accused him of corrupting the youth and introducing new gods to Athens. In 399 B.C. Socrates was sentenced to death. He accepted his punishment philosophically—calmly and without complaint. He reassured his friends that death should not be feared, since the soul is immortal. Socrates' teaching inspired his disciple Plato (427?–347 B.C.) to write his dialogues, the first masterpieces of philosophical writing to come from the Western world. Their influence on Western civilization has been second only to that of the Bible.

▶SYNTHETIC METHOD

Plato founded a school known as the Academy. Its most gifted pupil was Aristotle (384–322 B.C.). Aristotle combined a concern for pre-Socratic speculations about nature with the Socratic concern for social and moral problems. He continued the task begun by Plato of organizing all the fields of human knowledge into a unified view of nature and humankind. This is called synthetic philosophy. Aristotle set down in a clear and systematic form the general principles of most of the sciences and humanities. He established logic, metaphysics (the study of the nature of reality), and art criticism as fields of rational study.

The synthetic method of philosophizing developed by Plato and Aristotle is better known to the public than the analytical method of Socrates. Philosophers who have excelled at building new world views have deeply influenced the beliefs and attitudes of later generations. The great synthetic philoso-

Left: Plato and Aristotle (standing beneath the arch). Below: Saint Augustine.

Old Testament Prophets
Zoroaster (7th century B.C.)
Thales (640–546 B.C.)
Anaximander (611?–547? B.C.)
Lao-tzu (604?–531 B.C.)
Pythagoras (582?–500? B.C.)
Gautama Buddha (563?–483? B.C.)
Confucius (551–479 B.C.)
Socrates (470?–399 B.C.)
Plato (427?–347 B.C.)
Diogenes the Cynic (412?–323 B.C.)
Aristotle (384–322 B.C.)
Chuang Tzu (365?–290 B.C.)
Zeno of Citium (4th–3rd century B.C.)
Epicurus (341?–270 B.C.)

The Early Christians

Saint Augustine (354–430)

The Early Muslims

phers, or system builders—Plato, Aristotle, Saint Augustine (354–430), Saint Thomas Aquinas (1225?–74), René Descartes (1596–1650), Thomas Hobbes (1588–1679), Baruch Spinoza (1632–77), Immanuel Kant (1724–1804, and G. W. F. Hegel (1770–1831)—created new ways of thinking that have guided people ever since. The most remarkable achievement of a philosopher is to develop a new system of ideas that can be used to fit together pieces of knowledge in different fields in order to form a single picture of nature.

Plato believed that ideas were more real than things. He developed a vision of two worlds—a world of unchanging ideas and a world of changing physical objects. Aristotle did not believe in a separate world of ideas. He provided a vision of nature as a single system of things that can be classified by genus and species. He said that each natural object contains its destiny within it, as an acorn contains a tendency to grow into an oak tree. Saint Augustine fashioned a view of life as a stage on which creatures of God act out a drama of good and evil. Aquinas combined the thought of Augustine and Aristotle. His philosophy later became the official doctrine of the Roman Catholic Church.

Hobbes and Spinoza developed a mechanistic vision of the world in which all events are governed by strict mathematical laws. They said that with sufficient scientific knowledge events would be as predictable as clockwork. Descartes set God and the human mind apart from the world machine and created the view known as Cartesian dualism. Kant deepened the division between mind and matter by separating moral laws from laws of science. But he drew mind back into nature by claiming that the mind organizes natural events into a logical structure the way pudding is given form by the container into which it is poured. Hegel worked out a vision of the world produced by the evolution of mind through many stages, the highest of which are nature, society, and philosophy.

900   1100   1300   1500   1700   1900   2000

Above: René Descartes.
Left: Jean Jacques Rousseau.
Below: Jean-Paul Sartre.

Shankara (788?–820)
Avicenna (980–1037)
Averroës (1126–1198)
Moses Maimonides (1135–1204)
Saint Thomas Aquinas (1225?–1274)
Niccolò Machiavelli (1469–1527)
Thomas Hobbes (1588–1679)
René Descartes (1596–1650)
Baruch Spinoza (1632–1677)
John Locke (1632–1704)
G. W. von Leibniz (1646–1716)
Jean Jacques Rousseau (1712–1778)
Immanuel Kant (1724–1804)
G. W. F. Hegel (1770–1831)
John Stuart Mill (1806–1873)
Søren Kierkegaard (1813–1855)
Karl Marx (1818–1883)
William James (1842–1910)
Friedrich Nietzsche (1844–1900)
Bertrand Russell (1872–1970)
Martin Buber (1878–1965)
Paul Tillich (1886–1965)
Jean-Paul Sartre (1905–1980)
Albert Camus (1913–1960)

▶ BRANCHES OF PHILOSOPHY

The synthetic type of philosophy that organizes knowledge into a single picture of the world has become more difficult to carry out as human knowledge has grown in scope and detail. It is hardly possible today for one person to master all the fields of specialized knowledge. Philosophers now set themselves more limited goals. They connect psychology with biology in explaining the relation between the mind and the body. Or they relate science to religion in order to try to explain how the world began and how life grew out of inanimate matter. Philosophy today is analyti-

Information about the philosophers listed on this chart may be found in this encyclopedia. Use the index as a guide for finding this information.

cal in the Socratic style, rather than synthetic in the Aristotelian manner.

The advance of philosophical understanding has made it necessary to divide philosophy itself into smaller areas according to the type of problems investigated.

Ethics is the study of the standards for judging whether things are good or bad, and the analysis of terms like justice, virtue, morality, and responsibility.

Epistemology deals with the problems of defining knowledge, truth, logic, and perception. It investigates the ways in which knowledge is acquired.

Metaphysics deals with the nature of reality: What is real, and what only appears to be real? One branch of metaphysics, called ontology, searches for the standards by which we can judge the reality of different types of things, such as material objects, mental states, numbers, and relations. Cosmology, another branch of metaphysics, interprets the findings of physics and astronomy, attempting to decide whether the world was created by God or evolved by chance and whether the world is finite or infinite in space and time.

Aesthetics is concerned with the definition of art and beauty, and with discovering general standards of art criticism.

In addition to these wide areas of philosophical study, each field of scholarship faces philosophical problems in defining its subject matter and methods of procedure. Thus, for example, we have the philosophy of physics, the philosophy of religion, the philosophy of history, and the philosophy of law.

In brief, philosophy is disciplined thinking about basic principles and common beliefs. Whenever a person is not satisfied with specific answers and tries to understand how all his or her information fits together and what it adds up to, that person is philosophizing.

RAZIEL A. ABELSON
New York University

PHOENIX

Phoenix, the capital and largest city in Arizona, is the ninth most populous city in the United States. It has a population of about 980,000, and the metropolitan area includes more than 2 million people. Known for its clear, dry air, Phoenix is located on flat desert terrain in south central Arizona, on the Salt River.

A popular resort and retirement spot, Phoenix has sunny weather nearly every day, except during the months of July and August, when light rain falls. Most of the year the average temperature is 72°F (22°C), but during the summer months the temperature can rise to 100°F (38°C) or more. Swimming, boating, horseback riding, tennis, and golf are year-round activities.

Phoenix is a major industrial, commercial, and agricultural center of the Southwest. Important industries include tourism and the manufacture of chemicals, electronics, aircraft, textiles, and leather goods. The surrounding agricultural area grows lettuce, melons, vegetables, cotton, and citrus fruit—most of which are processed and packaged in Phoenix. Dams constructed in the surrounding mountains collect rain and hold the water until needed for crop irrigation, industrial uses, and domestic consumption.

Phoenix offers many places of interest to visitors and residents alike. The Heard Museum of Anthropology and Primitive Art features collections of primitive and Indian artifacts, including Senator Barry Goldwater's famous Hopi Indian kachina doll collection. The museum holds an Indian Arts and Crafts Fair every spring. The Phoenix Art Museum exhibits examples of Southwestern art and also houses the Arizona Costume Institute. The Arizona Mineral Museum has outstanding rock specimens, and the Hall of Flame Museum

displays antique firefighting equipment dating as far back as 1725.

The Pioneer Outdoor Living History Museum recreates an early historical settlement. Papago Park houses the Phoenix Zoo and the Desert Botanical Garden, with its collection of plants that grow in dry climates. The Pueblo Grande Museum, maintained by the city of Phoenix, features relics of the Hohokam Indians and a small archeological dig.

The old State Capitol, constructed of native stone, includes a museum of Arizona historical memorabilia and exhibits of prehistoric Indian cultures and modern Indian crafts. Modern additions to the building were completed in 1960 and 1974.

Institutions of higher learning in Phoenix include Grand Canyon College and the DeVry Institute of Technology. Nearby, in Tempe, is Arizona State University.

Special events occur mostly during the winter tourist season, December through March. Some of these events are the Phoenix Open Golf Tournament, the Jaycees Rodeo of Rodeos, Fiesta Bowl football game, Desert Botanical Garden Cactus Show, and the Arizona Boat Show. Phoenix also celebrates the Mexican holiday El Cinco de Mayo (the fifth of May). A sizable percentage of the city's residents are of Mexican ancestry.

Phoenix was first inhabited about 300 B.C. by the Hohokam Indians, who built irrigation ditches that used water from the Salt River to irrigate their crops. By A.D. 1450, however, the Indians had mysteriously disappeared.

In 1864 the first white settlers established a hay camp on the former Indian site to supply feed for the horses at the nearby army outpost, Camp McDowell. In 1867 a soldier-prospector, Jack Swilling, and an Englishman, Darrell Duppa, began to rebuild the ancient irrigation canals used by the Hohokams. Duppa named the site Phoenix after the legendary sun-bird that rose from its own ashes. He hoped that a city would rise from the ruins of the old Indian settlement.

The town grew as a commercial center and was incorporated in 1881. It became the capital of the Arizona Territory in 1889, two years after the arrival of the railroad. In 1911 the U.S. Reclamation Bureau built the Theodore Roosevelt Dam on the Salt River east of Phoenix. The dam controlled floods, produced electricity, and provided water for agriculture.

Phoenix is a major industrial, commercial, and agricultural center of the Southwest. This "bird's eye" view shows the capitol dome and the downtown area.

In 1912, when Arizona became a state, Phoenix remained the capital.

During World War II the U.S. armed forces took advantage of the year-round warm climate for aviation and desert warfare training. Many military people returned to the Phoenix area after the war.

In the 1950's the cost of air conditioning became low enough for most homes and businesses to be cooled in the hot summer. The widespread use of air conditioning has stimulated several decades of growth. The population of Phoenix increased almost 25 percent between 1980 and 1990.

The continued growth of the city depends, to a great extent, on the availability of water. In 1985 the $3.5 billion Central Arizona Water Project began pumping water to Phoenix from the Colorado River, 190 miles (306 kilometers) away. The water is actually pumped uphill through specially built canals and tunnels and allows for the continued growth of industry and agriculture.

JEANNETTE BRUSH
Phoenix Public Library

See also ARIZONA.

PHONICS

Phonics is the study of relationships between written letters and speech sounds. These relationships can be used to help figure out the pronunciations of written words. Phonics is a part of reading instruction in schools throughout the world.

In the teaching of phonics, a big problem is that in many cases a single letter can represent different sounds. For example, the letter *a* stands for different sounds in the words *ate, cat,* and *about.* Even with this problem, however, phonics is a useful way of helping pupils figure out words on their own.

Before pupils learn to read, they are prepared for phonics instruction. They learn to hear differences in the pronunciation of sounds. They learn the letters of the alphabet and how to tell one letter from another. They learn to listen for likenesses and differences in the pronunciation of words.

Then formal phonics instruction starts. The exact order of instruction varies. Usually the letters that are always pronounced the same are presented first. These include consonants such as *b, d, f, k, l, m, n, r,* and *t.* Then the letters that can stand for a variety of sounds are taught. These include the vowels and some consonants, such as *c, g,* and *w.* Finally, combinations of letters and the sounds they represent are taught—*ch, sh,* and *th,* for example.

Much attention is given to learning the letter-sound relationships in the early grades. In the later grades, pupils learn how to divide words into syllables, how to pronounce the syllables, and how to blend the sounds together to form the words. They also learn how to stress, or accent, the proper syllable.

Since phonics was first introduced as a part of reading instruction, its popularity has risen and fallen many times. Today teachers recognize the importance of phonics, and it is taught in schools throughout the world. But teachers know that reading involves more than just using phonics. Phonics is taught as one of a number of ways to help readers understand what they read.

NICHOLAS DIOBILDA
Glassboro State College (New Jersey)

PHONOGRAPH

Thomas A. Edison, who invented the first practical phonograph, was a bit deaf. He found he could not trust his ears to tell him how much sound was coming out of the telephone receiver. But he noticed that a small disc inside the receiver vibrated as the person on the other end of the line spoke. Edison thought to attach a tiny needle to the center of the disc. The force of the needle on his finger told him the amount of sound—loud or soft— that was being sent out.

A few months later a second discovery showed Edison something else about sound. This time he was working on a device to improve the telegraph. He was running a paper tape covered with Morse code dots and dashes through an instrument at high speed. Each time the dots and dashes passed over the end of a steel spring, Edison heard strange soft sounds that were very much like the sound of people talking. Edison had found out that a human voice could make a needle move. Why, he wondered, couldn't that same needle prick the pattern of the sound waves on paper tape?

The inventor lost no time in rigging up an experiment. A disc with a needle in it was set vibrating by the human voice, while paper coated with paraffin was moved under the needle at a fairly high speed. The needle pricked the paper just as Edison thought it would. But the gadget needed work before it could store up any kind of sound that was recognizable.

The first thing Edison did was to replace the paraffin paper with a metal cylinder. Edison wrapped tinfoil around the cylinder and attached two disc-and-needle units. One was to speak into. The other was for sound to come out of.

When the "in" disc vibrated, Edison hoped the needle would make little indentations in the tinfoil as the cylinder turned. When the "out" needle traveled over these same marks, its disc should vibrate, too, re-creating the sound. It was a memorable day in 1877 when Edison put on the first cylinder, leaned close to the in disc, and shouted, "Mary had a little lamb." He then set the out needle in the same groove and turned the crank of the cylinder.

Back came his voice. He admitted later, "I was never so taken aback in my life."

There was a great deal of excitement over this spectacular device. Edison manufactured about 500 sets, which he sent around the country to be displayed to curious audiences. People were glad to pay admission to hear the machine play back "Yankee Doodle" and other songs. Some of the machines made as much as $1,800 in a single week.

An important development occurred when Emile Berliner put the first phonograph record on the market in 1895. His record, or disc, was made of zinc coated with wax. When the in needle vibrated to the sound of a voice, it scratched a pattern in the wax. He plunged the record into an acid bath. The acid ate into the zinc where the needle had cut its path through the wax. Berliner proudly announced that he had etched the human voice.

In 1901, Berliner and a former watchmaker, Eldridge Johnson, created the Victor Talking Machine Company. Berliner had found an effective way to make hundreds of records from one master. Up to this time, singers had to sing the same song over and over again because only a few copies could be made of each recording. But with Berliner's new method of stamping out copies from a master, great singers were eager to record their voices. The marches of the famous United States Marine Band, directed by John Philip Sousa, were also very popular.

Singers made most of the first records because the voice was easier to record than a musical instrument. The hardest sound of all to capture was that of an orchestra. It was difficult for a large group of musicians to get close enough to the recording horn to be heard properly. And a single record side, turning at the standard speed of 78 rotations a minute, could hold only 4½ minutes of music. Symphonies, of course, were much longer.

Victor was the most successful company in the competition to make good records as fast as possible. A white fox terrier listening to "His Master's Voice" coming out of the brass horn of a phonograph was a famous Victor trademark. The dog, known as Nipper, came from a portrait painted by Francis Barraud in 1900. Today Nipper's grave in London is marked by a brass plaque.

By 1925, electric microphones began to replace the old brass recording horn. The micro-

Nipper listening to "His Master's Voice" was the symbol of the Victor Talking Machine Company, an early manufacturer of phonographs.

phone changed the sound vibrations of the voice or musical instrument into electrical energy. This energy, in turn, was used to drive the recording needle, or cutter, as it cut grooves into the wax of the master disc. One sensitive microphone could pick up with fair accuracy a whole roomful of sounds.

In 1948 came the long-playing microgroove record. The record was made of smooth vinyl plastic, which was very quiet in playback. It turned at a speed of 33⅓ rotations a minute. Twenty-five minutes or more of music could be heard on each side. New equipment—sensitive needles, wide-range speakers, powerful amplifiers—was developed to make the records sound even better. This equipment was known as high-fidelity, or hi-fi, because of the accurate, clear sound it produced.

A new dimension was added to high fidelity in 1957, when it was found that two separate tracks could be cut into the groove of a record. The two tracks were then played back through separate speakers. This system, which produced stereophonic sound, created a broad spread of sound very much like the live sound heard in a concert hall.

The complexities of magnetic tape, electric microphones, vinyl microgroove records, expensive stereo equipment, and digital recording are a far cry from Edison's tinfoil-wrapped cylinder. It is safe to predict that the "talking machine" has not stopped changing.

SHIRLEY FLEMING
High Fidelity magazine

See also HIGH-FIDELITY SYSTEMS; RECORDS AND RECORD COLLECTING.

PHOTOELECTRICITY

Have you ever noticed how streetlights go on by themselves at dusk? Or how the doors of some buildings open by themselves as you approach? Devices that turn lights on and off and open and close doors operate as the result of a phenomenon called the **photoelectric effect**, or **photoelectricity**. Electronic components that take advantage of this effect are called **photoelectric cells**.

▶ HOW PHOTOELECTRICITY WORKS

Light is a form of energy. When light, in the form of visible light, infrared rays, or ultraviolet rays, strikes certain chemical substances, it interacts with the atoms in the material. If the light energy is strong enough, it causes the electrons in the atoms to break free and either escape from the substance into the surrounding space or move to another substance touching it. This flow of electrons—in fact, any flow of electrons—is called an **electric current**.

Photoelectricity takes two basic forms: the photovoltaic effect and the photoconductive effect. In the **photovoltaic effect**, an electric current is generated and flows between two different substances when light falls upon them. In the **photoconductive effect**, the ability of a material to conduct electricity is changed as light falls upon it. The photoelectric devices that utilize these effects are known specifically as photovoltaic cells and photoconductive cells.

Photovoltaic Cell

A photovoltaic cell generates electricity by itself when light shines on it. Silicon is one substance often used to produce the electric current in a photovoltaic cell, which is made up of two thin wafers, or slabs, of silicon to which impurities have been added. These impurities might include such substances as boron, arsenic, selenium, platinum, or copper oxide. One wafer in the cell is mixed with an impurity that easily gives up its electrons; the other is mixed with an impurity that attracts electrons. The resulting materials are known as **semiconductors** because they are able to conduct an electrical current under certain conditions. A junction is formed along the boundary where the two semiconductor wafers meet. It is called the p-n junction.

Thousands of photovoltaic cells connected together within solar panels (*above*) are at the heart of large solar energy systems that can produce electricity for remote communities. A small floating lighthouse (*right*) also has solar panels that produce electrical energy in daylight. That energy is then stored in a battery used to keep its lights on after dark.

When light strikes the p-n junction at the heart of a photovoltaic cell, the atoms in one semiconductor wafer release some of their electrons, and the atoms in the other wafer attract electrons. This causes a shortage of electrons in one wafer and an excess of electrons in the other. If a wire or some type of electric circuit or device is connected between the two wafers, electrons will move from one wafer to the other in an attempt to restore the atoms to equilibrium, or a state of balance. This movement of electrons is an electric current.

Did you know that...

the photovoltaic effect was discovered in 1839 by French physicist Antoine-César Becquerel? Thirty-four years later, in 1873, English scientist Willoughby Smith became the first person to observe the photoconductive effect. The first practical application of these effects occurred around 1895, when German physicists Julius Elster and Hans Geitel invented the photoelectric cell. But it was not until the early 1900's that the photoelectric effect was fully understood and played an important role in Albert Einstein's and Max Planck's development of quantum theory. Photoelectric cells were not produced commercially, however, until the 1950's.

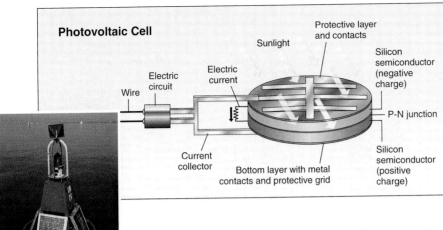

Photovoltaic Cell

Sunlight

Wire

Electric circuit

Electric current

Protective layer and contacts

Silicon semiconductor (negative charge)

P-N junction

Current collector

Bottom layer with metal contacts and protective grid

Silicon semiconductor (positive charge)

When sunlight strikes the p-n junction inside a photovoltaic cell, it causes electrons in the atoms of the cell's two semiconductor layers to move between them, creating an excess of electrons in one layer (treated to attract electrons) and a shortage in the other (treated to give up electrons). When a wire, electric circuit, or other device connects the layers, the motion of the electrons, called an electric current, continues in an attempt to restore the atoms in each layer to a state of balance. This current can be collected and used as a power source to operate many different and useful objects.

A photovoltaic cell will produce electricity as long as light continues to strike it. If the light becomes brighter or the light energy greater, the photovoltaic cell will generate more electrical current up to a certain maximum. This maximum, known as the **saturation current**, depends on the surface area of the p-n junction and the types of semiconductors used in the photovoltaic cell.

Photoconductive Cell

A photoconductive cell does not generate electricity by itself when light shines on it. Instead, it strengthens an electric current that is already flowing. A photoconductive cell is similar in structure to a photovoltaic cell, except that it is connected to a battery or some other power source. It is this power source that generates the electrical current.

A **photodiode**, one of the most common types of photoconductive cells, is a semiconductor device that is a good conductor of electricity in one direction, but not as good a conductor in the other direction. This difference in conductivity is caused by the behavior of the atoms at and near the p-n junction of the cell.

A photodiode is connected to a power source so that the electrical current flows in the same direction in which the diode conducts poorly. This is called **reverse bias**. When a photodiode is reverse biased, very little current flows in the circuit when no light is striking the p-n junction. When light strikes the junction, the photodiode conducts the electric current much better, allowing it to increase dramatically. The brighter the light, the better the photodiode conducts electricity up to a certain maximum.

Another type of photoconductive cell, a **phototransistor**, is similar to a photodiode. It allows an electrical current to be amplified as well as switched on or off. The ability of a phototransistor to conduct electricity also depends on the level of light striking the cell.

A third type of photoconductive cell is the **phototube**, which consists of a metal plate coated with a light-sensitive chemical and a metal rod placed near it. These two parts are enclosed in an airtight glass tube and connected to a battery outside the tube. When light strikes the metal plate, electrons are pushed out into the surrounding space. The electrons are then attracted to the metal rod. The flow of electrons from the plate to the rod constitutes an electric current. The amount of the electric current depends on the amount of light that strikes the phototube. Today, phototubes have largely been replaced by photodiodes for many applications.

▶ USES OF PHOTOELECTRICITY

Photoelectric cells are used in many ways. Solar panels made up of many photovoltaic cells connected together can be used to catch light from the sun and generate electricity for homes and buildings on Earth as well as for satellites in space. Photoelectric cells can act as switches to turn many devices on or off. For example, they are used to set off burglar alarms, to operate bar-code readers in stores, and to activate the exposure meters of cameras. These and many other uses of photoelectricity help make our lives easier and more productive.

STANLEY GIBILISCO
Editor, *Illustrated Dictionary of Electronics*

See also ELECTRONICS; FIBER OPTICS; LIGHT; MATERIALS SCIENCE; SOLAR ENERGY; TRANSISTORS, DIODES, AND INTEGRATED CIRCUITS.

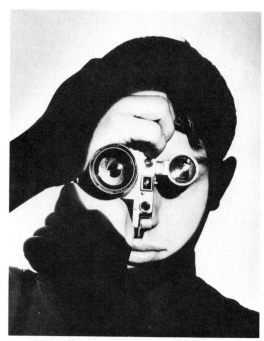

This famous picture of a photojournalist was taken by Andreas Feininger.

PHOTOGRAPHY

It is hard to imagine what the world would be like without photography. It is used in almost every activity that is of interest to people.

Photography records events that make world history. It shows you faraway places and people you have never met. It also records your personal history. Photography preserves yesterday's documents and today's findings. It illustrates schoolbooks, magazines, and every other kind of publication. It sells products through advertising and catalogs.

Photography also enables us to see things that we cannot normally see. Cameras carried by satellites spot the beginning of a tropical storm from far above the earth. Cameras carried by spacecraft have photographed several of the planets. Photography looks closely at microbes and molecules that are too small to be seen with the naked eye—and at vast galaxies that are too far away.

Skilled and imaginative photographers have made photography an art form. The beautiful pictures they take increase our appreciation and understanding of the world.

Photography is so much a part of your daily life that you may take it for granted. But it was not developed until the 1800's. Before that time, people had to rely on drawings and paintings. The accuracy of these pictures depended on how well a person could draw. Today, anyone can take good photographs.

▶ **HOW ARE PHOTOGRAPHS MADE?**

A photograph is a picture made through the action of light. The word "photography" comes from Greek words meaning "light" and "writing."

To take a photograph of a subject, you need only three things—light, film, and a camera. The film is made of transparent plastic, coated with crystals of a silver compound that are sensitive to light. The camera is a tool. Its job is to produce an image on the film.

When you take a picture, light rays reflected from your subject enter the camera through the lens, which focuses them on the film. The light rays form a latent (unseen) image of the subject on the film. The film has now been "exposed."

To make the latent image visible, the film must be developed, or treated with chemicals. The ways in which exposed film is processed to produce photographs are described later in this article.

▶ **PHOTOGRAPHIC EQUIPMENT**

The most important pieces of photographic equipment are, of course, the camera and the film. Without these, you would not be able to take photographs. But there are many other pieces of equipment that help photographers take good pictures. These include special lenses, filters, lighting equipment, attachments for taking close-ups, and tripods.

Cameras

There are many different kinds of cameras. Some are very simple. Others are quite complex. But all of them can be used to take good photographs.

Consult the Index of this encyclopedia to find biographies of the photography pioneer Louis Daguerre, the inventors George Eastman and Edwin Land, and the photographers Ansel Adams, Diane Arbus, Richard Avedon, Cecil Beaton, Henri Cartier-Bresson, Yousuf Karsh, Gordon Parks, Eliot Porter, and Edward Steichen.

A distinguished nature photographer for over 40 years, Eliot Porter took pictures with rich texture and detail. Note how the autumn colors of the dying leaves contrast with the pine needles.

Photography, like painting or drawing, is an art. Photographic artists use form, color, light, and shadow for the best possible effect. A photograph can show motion. It can tell a story or make a social comment. A well-made photograph can be a masterpiece.

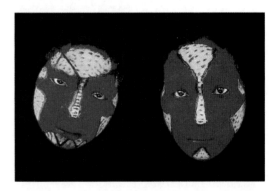

Pete Turner took this photograph in New Guinea. At first, the strange, bright colors make you think of two masks. But when you look closely at the eyes, you know you are looking at two painted human faces.

Ernst Haas created the sensation of motion in this image of a rodeo rider.

The popular single-lens reflex (SLR) camera is simple to use but highly sensitive and efficient.

The Parts of a Camera. No matter how simple or how complex a camera is, it has five basic parts—the body, lens, shutter, film holder, and viewfinder. Many cameras also have special features that help you in such steps as counting exposures and focusing.

The **body** of a camera is a lightproof framework, or box. It keeps out all light except the light that passes through the lens.

In the simplest cameras, the **lens** is a piece of glass or plastic with curved surfaces. The lens concentrates the light rays as they enter the camera to make a sharp image of the photographed object on the film.

The subjects you photograph will be at different distances from you. It is important that you focus on a subject before shooting the picture. Otherwise, the picture may be out of focus, or blurry. When a picture is in focus, it is sharp and clear.

Some cameras have a fixed-focus lens. You cannot change the focus. Such a lens is set to focus on most objects beyond 150 or 180 centimeters (5 or 6 feet) fairly well.

A lens that you can focus will provide a greater variety of pictures. It can be set to focus sharply on subjects at almost any distance. You do not have to compromise as you must with a fixed-focus lens.

In many cameras, you focus by turning the lens. The lens mount contains spiral threads. You turn the lens along these threads to focus the image on the film.

The **shutter** is a mechanical device behind the lens. It opens and closes to let the light in.

The photographer opens the shutter by pressing the shutter release, a button on the outside of the camera. In many cameras, you can change the speed at which the shutter opens and closes. If the shutter opens and closes quickly, little light enters the camera. If the shutter is set to stay open longer, more light enters.

In bright sunlight, the photographer can set the shutter at a fast speed, since there is plenty of light to make an image on the film. On gloomy days or in dim light, the shutter can be set at a slower speed. This gives time for more light to enter the camera.

A fast shutter speed lets you take pictures of moving subjects without blurring. Even if the subject is one that does not move, such as a landscape, a fast exposure cuts down the chances of getting a blurred picture. This could happen at a slower speed if you moved the camera.

A simple camera has only one shutter speed. A more costly camera will have many shutter speeds, ranging from as slow as 30 seconds to 1/1000 of a second or even less.

Another device that controls the amount of light entering through the lens is the **diaphragm.** All but the simplest cameras have a diaphragm. With it you make the lens opening larger or smaller to admit more or less light.

Lens openings are scaled in **f-numbers.** The smallest f-numbers, such as f/1.4 and f/2, are for the widest openings. They transmit the most light to the film. The largest f-numbers, such as f/11 and f/16, are for small lens openings. They transmit the least light to the film.

Lens openings are scaled in f-numbers. The smaller the f-number, the larger the lens opening.

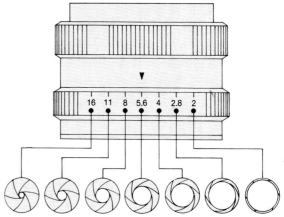

THE BASIC PARTS OF A CAMERA

The body of a camera is a lightproof framework, or box. It keeps out all light except the light that passes through the lens when the shutter is open.

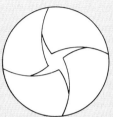

The diaphragm helps control the amount of light entering through the lens. With it you make the lens opening larger or smaller to admit more light or less light.

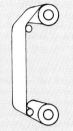

The film holder keeps the film flat and in position for the light from an image to hit it properly. After taking a photograph, you wind the film so that the next picture can be taken.

The shutter is a mechanical device behind the lens. It opens and closes to let the light in. In many cameras, you can change the speed at which the shutter opens and closes.

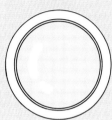

The lens is a piece of glass or plastic with a curved surface. The lens concentrates light rays as they enter the camera to make a sharp image on the film.

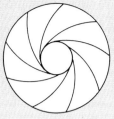

The viewfinder shows you the scene that the lens will focus on the film. Some viewfinders are glass windows, some make use of lenses, and some are reflecting prisms.

The diaphragm also controls the **depth of field** of a photograph. The depth of field is the amount of space in front of and behind the subject that is in focus. Sometimes photographers want great depth of field. That is, they want everything in a photograph to be in focus. At other times, they want a shallow depth of field. The subject is in focus, but the foreground or background is blurred. Making the diaphragm opening smaller increases the depth of field. If you make the opening larger, the depth of field becomes shallower.

The **film holder** keeps the film flat so that the image can be accurately focused on the film. It is usually in the back of the camera. You drop the metal or plastic cassette that carries the film into it. After taking a photograph, you wind the film so that the next blank spot, or frame, on the roll is in line to make the next picture.

Most popular cameras use rolls or cartridges of film that produce from 8 to 36 pictures. Such cameras need a way to keep track of the exposed pictures. In simple cameras, you can see the frame number on a paper strip that covers the back of the film. In most complex cameras, a dial outside the camera shows how many frames have been exposed.

A **viewfinder** of some kind is a part of all cameras. It shows you the scene that the lens will focus on the film. Some viewfinders are glass windows. Some make use of lenses. And some are reflecting prisms that show the actual image coming through the lens.

In a complex camera, the viewfinder may be combined with a device to aid in focusing. One such system is the **range finder.** It is a device on the camera that splits the image of the subject. When you look through the viewfinder, you see two images. To focus, you turn the focusing ring until the two images come together.

Another system that combines viewfinding and focusing is the **reflex finder.** In this you see the subject by looking directly through the lens. When you do, you will see a small circle in the center of the finder. This circle is usually filled with wiggly lines. To focus, just turn the lens until the wiggly lines disappear.

Many cameras contain a self-timer. With this, the camera delays taking the picture after you have pressed the shutter release. This allows you several seconds to hurry into the scene and be included in the photograph.

All but the simplest cameras include circuits that measure the amount of light reaching the camera from the subject. This is more accurate than having to guess how much light is entering the camera. In many cameras the proper exposure settings are shown in the viewfinder as the user sets the shutter speed and diaphragm opening. Or the camera may set the exposure automatically.

Types of Still Cameras. Still cameras (as opposed to movie cameras) range from tiny units that fit in your pocket to giant cameras used in professional studios.

Viewfinder cameras are the simplest cameras to operate. They are small and easy to carry. Generally, they have a small window through which you can ''find'' the view. The lens cannot be changed, and it often has a fixed focus. You just aim the camera and shoot the picture. These cameras are used mostly for taking small snapshots.

As you become more expert, you may want to use an **adjustable camera.** With its range of lens openings and shutter speeds, you will be able to shoot even in dim light. The fast shutter speeds will let you ''stop'' the action even of fast-moving subjects. Some of these cameras measure the light and show you the correct lens opening. Others have a built-in electronic eye that measures the light and sets the lens opening automatically. This type of camera makes shooting fast, easy, and sure under almost all lighting conditions. With this camera you can take good, sharp pictures of subjects only 60 centimeters (2 feet) away as easily as subjects at a great distance.

The **single-lens reflex** (SLR) is by far the most popular type of camera for serious photography.

In the SLR camera, a mirror behind the lens reflects the image upward onto a viewing screen. You can then see your picture and also focus it. When you shoot the picture, the mirror automatically swings up out of the light path. The image is focused on the film as the shutter opens, and the exposure is made.

The most widely used SLR's take pictures on 35mm (millimeter) film, but some use larger roll film. Up to 36 pictures can be taken on a roll of 35mm film.

An SLR is a small, all-around camera. You can fit different lenses on it. With a telephoto lens, you can photograph a distant scene or even the moon. And with a close-up lens you can photograph a flower or insect. An SLR can easily be held in your hand. For long exposures or exacting work, you can mount it on a tripod.

The **rangefinder camera** is another important style of camera. It, too, is a 35mm camera. It has a separate, built-in viewfinder. Visible in it is a range finder. The range finder shows when the lens is focused. Such cameras are smaller than SLR's. But in most rangefinder cameras you cannot change the lens.

The **compact 35** is another popular camera, especially with hobbyists. It is highly automatic. It may have a lens-coupled range finder for focusing. It produces a full-sized 35mm picture. Yet it is small enough to fit in a coat pocket. This type of camera sometimes has a built-in electronic flash.

View cameras are often used by photographers who make portraits and pictures for advertisements.

Instant-photo cameras produce a fully developed print shortly after the photograph is snapped.

Even more compact are the so-called **pocket 110 cameras.** Some of these are fixed-focus cameras, and some are complex rangefinder and even SLR types. All use tiny 110-format (13 by 17 mm) cartridge-loading film, which is best suited for wallet-size and photo album pictures.

The **disc camera** is a new type of camera that arrived on the market in the early 1980's. The film for this camera is mounted around the edge of a small plastic disc. The disc camera is very simple to use. It is almost completely automatic. You aim the camera and press the button. The camera looks over the scene. It sets the right exposure. It decides whether the built-in flash is needed. It takes the picture. It advances the film to the next frame. And it recharges the flash as needed. All this happens in about a second.

View cameras are most common in professional studios. They use individual sheets of film that may be as large as this page or even larger. They are used mostly by photographers who make portraits, pictures of products for advertising, or other types of pictures that call for precise control of the image.

Large pictures need little or no enlargement in printing. Thus the picture quality is excellent. But the cameras are big and heavy. They must be used on a tripod. This is a three-legged stand that supports the camera. View-camera lenses and shutters are large and expensive. Large film is also expensive.

Cameras used in commercial studios focus the image on a sheet of ground glass. The glass is at the rear of the camera. The photographer replaces the glass with film before the exposure is made.

Instant-photo cameras produce a fully developed print shortly after the picture is snapped. This is possible because the film includes the developing chemicals. After an image is exposed, the film comes in contact with the developers. It is then automatically processed as either a black-and-white or a color print, depending on the film.

Filmless cameras are a new development. In this type of camera, photographic images are recorded on a magnetic disc instead of on film. The pictures can be shown immediately on a television screen. They can also be sent long-distance with a special telephone hookup.

Disc cameras were introduced in the early 1980's. The film is mounted on the edge of a small plastic disc.

Special-use cameras include many special kinds of cameras used in industry, science, and technology. These include underwater cameras, heat-imaging cameras, and cameras used with telescopes for astronomical pictures. They are designed to do one or two types of photography very well. Generally they are not used for the more common types of pictures.

Lenses

For SLR and view cameras, extra lenses are major accessories. They can be used to give images of different sizes and to take pictures far away or very close up.

Every lens has a certain **focal length.** Lenses come in normal, short, and long focal lengths. A **normal lens** shows about what your eye sees when looking at the scene. In 35mm cameras, this is a lens with about a 50mm focal length. A 50mm lens provides about a 45-degree angle of view.

Lenses with very short focal lengths are called **wide-angle lenses.** They take in a very large area of the scene. But they produce a small image of any given object in the scene. One of the most interesting wide-angle lenses is the **fish-eye lens.** An 8mm fish-eye has a 180-degree angle of view. There are even special lenses that take in everything around the photographer. That is, they produce a 360-degree angle of view.

Telephoto lenses—lenses with long focal lengths—''see'' less of the scene from a given spot. But they enlarge part of the scene on the film. A lens with a long focal length makes a larger image.

Simple lenses can be added to the front of the normal lens to allow close focusing. These are called **close-up lenses.** With them, you can photograph flowers and other small objects.

These photos were taken from the same position but with different lenses. Above left: A wide-angle lens includes a large area and gives a great sense of depth. Above right: A normal lens gives a typical view and a normal sense of depth. Below left: A short telephoto lens narrows the view. Below right: A long telephoto concentrates the view and gives little sense of depth.

Lenses with a focal length that can be changed to make a larger or smaller image are called **zoom lenses.**

Film

There are three main types of photographic film for general use. Each produces a different kind of photograph. **Black-and-white negative film** is used to make black-and-white photographs, or prints. **Color negative film** is used to make color prints. And **color reversal film** is used to make color slides, or transparencies.

All film has a plastic base thinly coated with crystals of a silver-bromide compound. The crystals are mixed in a transparent gelatin. This mixture is called an **emulsion.** In black-and-white film, there is usually only a single layer of emulsion. In color film, there are three layers of emulsion. Each layer is sensitive to one of the three additive primary colors of light—blue, green, and red.

When choosing a film of any one of these types, there are three factors to be considered —film speed, graininess, and contrast.

Films vary in their sensitivity to light. This sensitivity is commonly known as **film speed. Graininess** is the degree of visibility of the silver crystals, or grains, in the photographic image. Graininess is especially noticeable when a photograph is enlarged. **Contrast** is the degree of difference between the light and dark areas of the subject. Generally, the faster the film, the grainier the photograph will be and the less contrast it will have. Photographs with too high contrast lack fine detail.

When choosing a color film, a fourth factor —**color balance**—must be considered. Most color films are balanced to give accurate color reproduction when used in daylight. Others are balanced to give accurate color reproduction when used with different types of artificial light.

Film speed is measured on a scale called the American Standards Association (ASA) film-speed index. Each film is given an ASA number that indicates its speed. Fast films have high numbers. Slow films have low numbers. The faster a film is, the more sensitive it is to light.

Films rated ASA 64 or lower are slow films. The silver compound on slow films contains fine silver grains. These grains need a relatively long exposure to light. They produce images with good contrast and very fine detail. Use slow films when you want strong contrast and detail in your pictures or when there is a great deal of light.

Films rated ASA 250 or higher are fast films. The silver compound on these films contains coarse silver grains, so the photographic image may be visibly grainy. It will not have as much detail or contrast as slower films. But fast films need far less exposure than slow films. Use them when the light is poor or when fast action must be "stopped."

Films between ASA 80 and ASA 200 are medium-speed films. They are a compromise between the speed of fast films and the detail-capturing ability and high contrast of slow films. They have adequate speed for most situations. And they have good contrast. Medium-speed films are the most commonly used outdoor films.

Cameras that accept a variety of films have a film-speed dial. This dial must be set at the ASA number of the film being used. Do this before you take the first picture. If you forget, all your pictures will be too dark or too light.

Lighting Equipment

How can you tell whether the light is bright enough to take a picture? You use an exposure meter. It measures the light and gives the proper exposure settings for the film speed you are using.

Some cameras have exposure meters built into them. You can also buy a separate, hand-held exposure meter. Some of these meters are sensitive enough to use by moonlight.

With a flash, you can take pictures even when the other light is not bright enough. Some cameras have flash units that use flash-bulbs. Each flashbulb flashes just once. Flash-cubes and flash bars permit several pictures to be taken before a change is needed. There are also electronic flash units that can be used over and over. Even many simple cameras have flash units built into them.

The flash attachment must be the right distance from your subject. With most cameras this is about 2 to 3 meters (6 to 10 feet). In complex cameras, exposure settings should be adjusted for the flash. There are electronic flash units that automatically provide the correct exposure.

Filters

Filters are transparent pieces of glass or plastic that are placed over the lens. They change the light that hits the film. When used with black-and-white film, they change the tones of gray. The filters you use with color film usually change the actual colors. In some cases, filters improve the light reaching the camera. For example, a polarizing filter gets rid of reflections, so that pictures can be taken through windows. In other cases, filters are used for special effects. For example, by darkening a blue sky, filters make white clouds stand out more clearly.

Other Accessories

There are dozens of other accessories. Tripods, handgrips, and other devices steady the camera. Remote releases work the shutter release from a distance. Detachable motors advance the film and cock the shutter for the next exposure as you press the shutter release.

▶TAKING GOOD PHOTOGRAPHS

Photography is a favorite pastime because people of all ages can operate a camera—and operate it easily and well. It is not hard to snap a picture.

Taking outdoor pictures on bright days is the easiest way to begin. Suppose you have a fixed-focus camera. All you need to do is wind your film until the first frame is in place behind the lens. Then look into the viewfinder to locate the subject you wish to photograph.

The viewfinder on your camera is your best guide to good pictures. It shows you in advance what the picture will be. When you are satisfied with what you see in the viewfinder, you are ready to take the picture. Hold the camera steady and press the shutter release. When the shutter clicks, you know that the film has been exposed. Advance the film so that the next frame is in position behind the lens. You are now ready to take your next picture.

But creating good photographs does require more than just pushing a button. You should understand how your camera operates. Every camera comes with an instruction booklet. You should read it carefully before you begin to use the camera. The more you know about your camera, the more fun you will have using it. Check the instruction booklet also for the kinds of films to use for the best results with your camera.

You should also learn some simple rules that may mean the difference between really good photographs and ordinary or even bad photographs.

Light

Always keep in mind the position of the source of light when you are taking pictures. Light from different directions—from above, below, behind, or in front or to the side of the subject—produces entirely different shadow effects.

Outside, there are short, dark shadows at noon. There are long, slanting shadows in the early morning and late afternoon. These different shadows may completely change the appearance of a scene.

The sun should never shine on the lens. When it does, light reflects inside the camera and causes streaks and glare spots on the picture. And people should not be photographed as they face the sun. They will look pale, or washed-out—and they may be squinting. Instead, photograph people in the open shade. This is much more flattering. In open shade you have plenty of clear, bright sky above your subject.

Suppose you want to photograph someone who is under a leafy shade tree. There will be much less available light. If your camera shows that there is not enough natural light, you can still take a picture with a flash unit.

Professionals use lighting, contrast, and composition techniques to produce dramatic photographs. Left: *Man in White/Woman in Black, Morocco,* by Irving Penn (1971). Right: *Migrant Mother, Nipomo, California,* by Dorothea Lange (1930's).

(1) Use of one light, the "key" light, gives a harsh effect. The subject's hair looks lifeless.

(2) A second light, or spotlight, is placed behind the subject. This adds life, but the effect is harsh.

(3) Key light, spotlight, and a "fill" light in front of the subject give a soft effect and bring out detail.

STANDARD LIGHTING FOR PORTRAITS

(4) Daylight from a window gives good but somewhat dramatic lighting for portraits.

(5) A reflector opposite the window acts as a fill light. Shadows are softened, and details brought out.

(6) Outdoors, light from the sky acts as the key light. The sun takes the place of the spotlight.

(7) A camera flash can be used as a fill light outdoors, to soften shadows and add sparkle to the picture.

Shadows that would appear too dark, especially in a picture of a person, can be softened. Simply place a reflector near the subject. Use a sheet of white cardboard, newspaper, or anything that will catch light and throw it back toward the subject. Or have the subject stand near a white wall in such a position that light is reflected to the subject's shaded side.

Above: A slow shutter speed produces a blurred picture. Below: The cyclist's motion is stopped when the picture is taken with a fast shutter speed.

Focusing

To produce a sharp image, the camera must be properly focused. Focusing depends on matching the distance from the camera to the subject with the correct distance from the lens to the film.

In fixed-focus cameras, the focus cannot be changed. You must take the picture from the correct distance, usually at least 150 centimeters (5 feet) from the subject. If pictures taken with a fixed-focus camera look blurred or fuzzy, you may have been too close to the subject. On the other hand, stay close enough to people so that they are not too small in the picture and lost in the background.

In adjustable cameras, the focusing mechanism changes the distance between the lens and the film. Most of these cameras have a device of one kind or another that tells you when the camera is properly focused. A blurred picture may mean that the distance was not properly set.

Blurred pictures can also occur if the subject moves too quickly or if you fail to hold the camera steady. A dirty lens will spoil the sharpness of your photographs. Clean the lens gently with a camel's-hair brush or special lens paper.

With an adjustable camera, you can bring the subject into sharp focus but allow the background to be blurred. Do this by increasing the lens opening to produce a shallow depth of field.

Exposure

Exposure is that amount of light that falls on the film. If a picture has no detail in the shadows, it is underexposed. This means that the light was too weak. If there is no detail in the bright parts, the picture is overexposed. This means that the light was too strong.

Even simple cameras often have an arrow or some other device at the side of the viewfinder that shows whether there is enough light to take a picture. With the proper combination of shutter speed and lens opening, an adjustable camera can take pictures under a wide range of light conditions. In bright light, use a large opening with a fast shutter speed. Or use a small opening with a slow shutter speed. In dim light, use a large opening with a slow shutter speed. This lets as much light as possible reach the film.

Composition

Composition refers to the way the parts of a picture—the main subject, background, and other elements—are arranged. Usually you cannot arrange all the elements of a photograph the way an artist composes a painting. But you can do many things to improve the composition of your pictures.

The simplest pictures are often the best. They present one main subject. When you take a picture, try moving the camera to the left or right or up and down, to eliminate confusing elements and present the subject in the best way.

As a rule, it is better not to have a person or other subject exactly in the center of a picture. The subject should be a bit away from the center, and other things in the picture should guide the eye toward the subject. Avoid a cluttered background. If this is not possible and you are using a camera that has different lens openings, open the lens wide. This will blur the background. Or move closer to the subject. In a close-up shot, the subject will fill most of the picture, and less of the background will be seen.

If you are taking pictures of lakes, parks, or other scenic spots, put people in the foreground. Doing so increases the feeling of depth and size in the picture.

Many subjects can be photographed either horizontally or vertically. Before pressing the shutter button, hold the camera in both positions. See which position provides a better picture.

If trees, buildings, or people seem to lean backward or sideways, it means you tilted the camera. Sometimes a photographer will tilt the camera purposely to get an unusual effect. Unless you are trying to do this, keep your camera as level as possible.

Try to have each picture tell a story. For a picture to tell a story, the subject should be doing something. For example, take a picture of a small child. Show the child playing with a toy. Your picture will be more interesting than one in which the child is simply looking at the camera. When you take pictures, ask your subjects not to look at you. If possible, catch them before they know that you are taking pictures. These pictures look more natural than posed pictures. They are often called candid pictures.

Left: The car in the background spoils this picture. Right: The photographer solved the problem by moving the subject to a less distracting background.

Left: Again, a car provides a distracting background. Right: A wide lens opening throws the car out of focus and makes it less noticeable.

Left: Steps in the background and handlebars in the foreground clutter this picture. Right: Moving the camera closer to the subject improves the picture.

DEVELOPING THE FILM

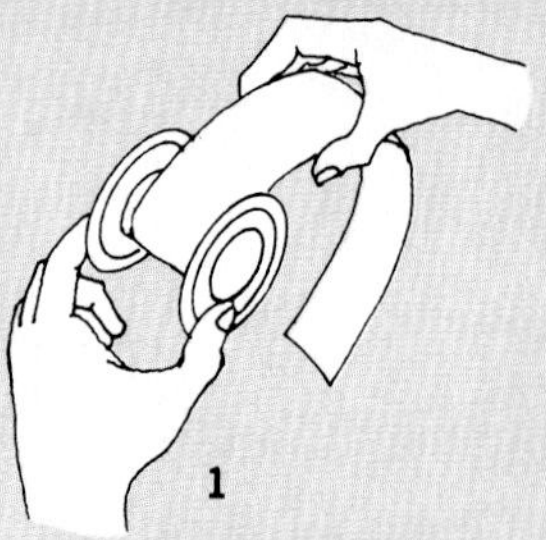

1

In complete darkness, load the exposed film onto the developing reel and place it in the developing tank.

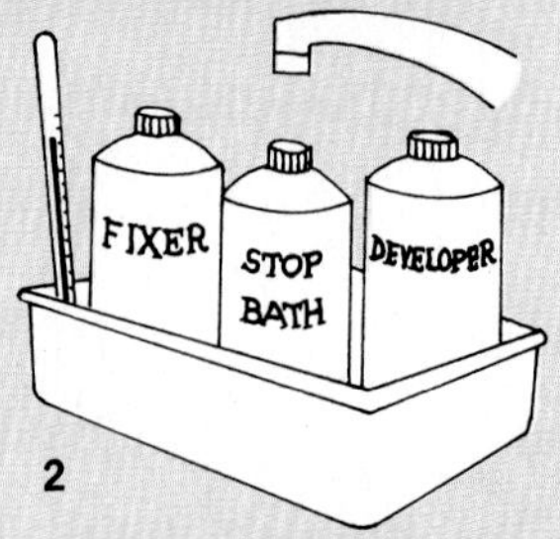

2

Put the developer, stop bath, and fixer in a water bath and bring it to the required temperature—20°C (68°F). Use a thermometer.

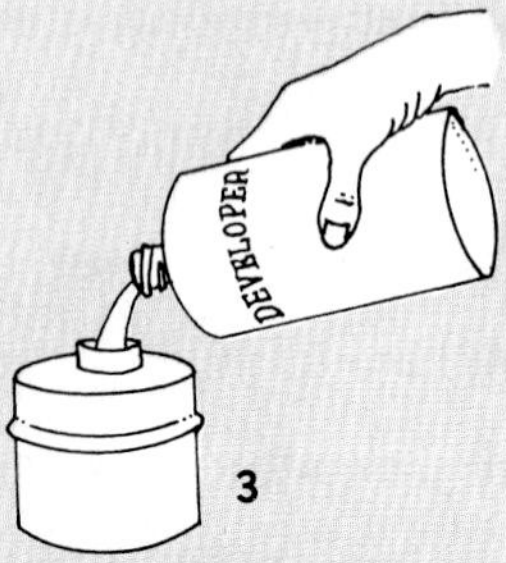

3

Pour enough developer into the developing tank to cover the film. Keep the tank in the 20°C water bath.

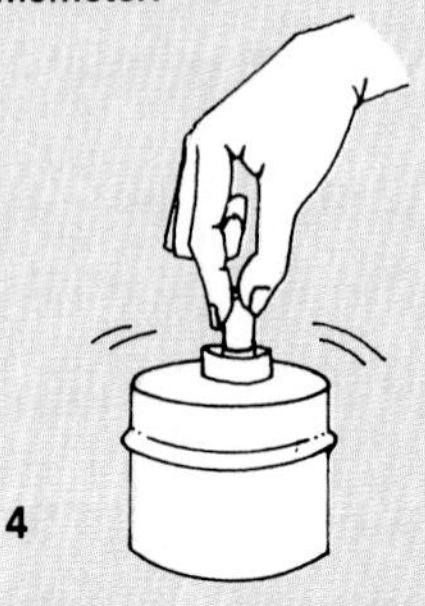

4

Leave the developer in the tank for the exact time listed on the developer package. Shake or stir the liquid every half minute.

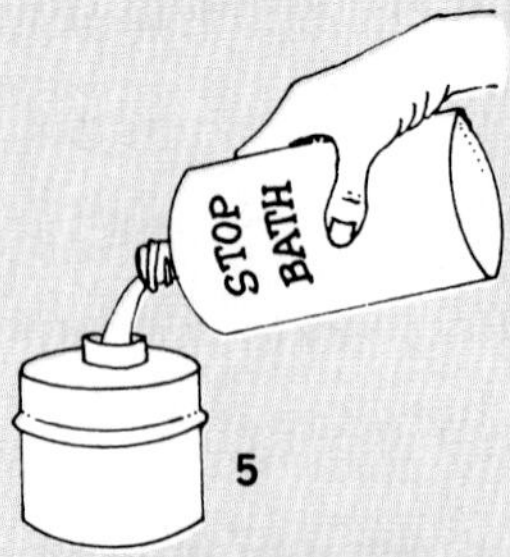

5

Without removing the tank cover, pour the developer out of the hole in the top. Pour in the stop bath. Shake or stir the stop bath.

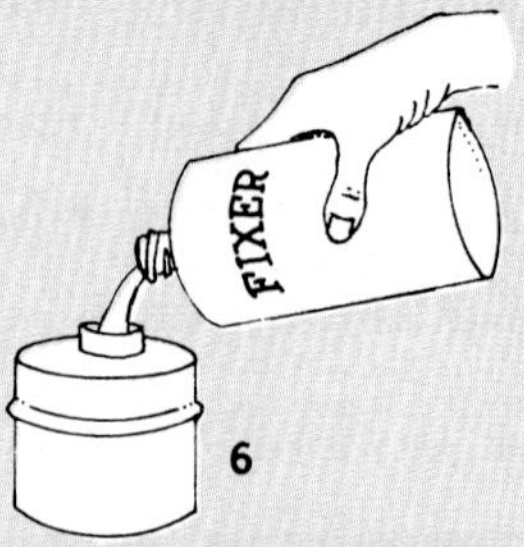

6

Without removing the cover, pour out the stop bath and pour in the fixer. Shake or stir. The fixing time is on the fixer package.

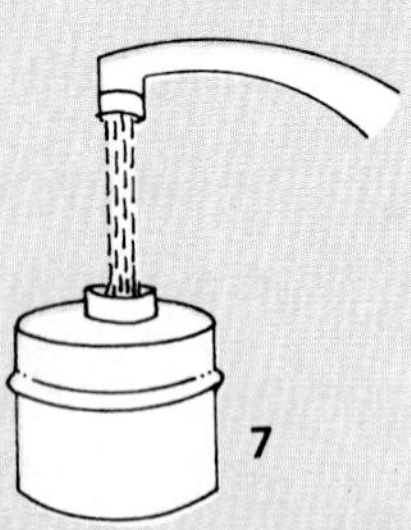

7

Pour out the fixer. Light cannot now ruin the film. Wash the film for 30 minutes in slowly running water kept at 20°C.

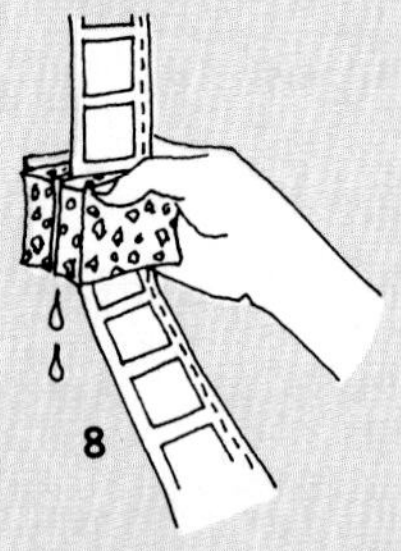

8

Hang the film with a film clip and pull it taut. Wipe both sides with a sponge. Let the film hang until it is totally dry.

▶DEVELOPING AND PRINTING

Many people prefer to let a photofinisher develop and print their film. But you may want to try your hand at doing this yourself. Or you may let a photofinisher develop your film, and then make your own prints or enlargements. From the beginning, photographers have developed and printed film themselves. It is a rewarding part of the skill of photography. It lets you control how the final picture will look.

Black-and-white film is relatively simple to process and print. Color film is more difficult to process because the temperature and time must be precisely controlled.

Black-and-White Film

When light is reflected from a face, a flower, or a landscape, it has many levels of brightness. Light-colored areas are the brightest. They reflect the most light. Shadow areas, dark skin, or dark clothing reflect less light.

When the reflected light reaches the film, it hits a thin coating that covers the film. The coating is called an emulsion. The emulsion contains crystals of a compound of silver and bromine, called silver bromide. The light causes the silver bromide to change. How much it changes depends on how much light hits it. The stronger the light and the longer it falls on the film, the more the silver bromide will change. The changes in the silver compound form an image of whatever the camera is pointed at. This image cannot be seen by the human eye. It is invisible. It can be made visible by processing the film in chemicals called **developers.**

Developers set the bromine free from the silver bromide. This leaves behind a speck of black metallic silver. The black silver appears wherever light has hit the film. Since the brightest parts of the subject reflect the most light, these parts will be blackest in the developed image. In other words, light and dark areas are reversed on the photographic image. As a result, this image is called a **negative.** Dark clothing, for example, will appear white in a negative. A white house will be black.

Because photographic films are sensitive to light, they must be handled in a completely dark place. Total darkness is needed only while you are loading the film into the developing tank. Loading the film into the tank is a

PRINTING THE PHOTOGRAPHS

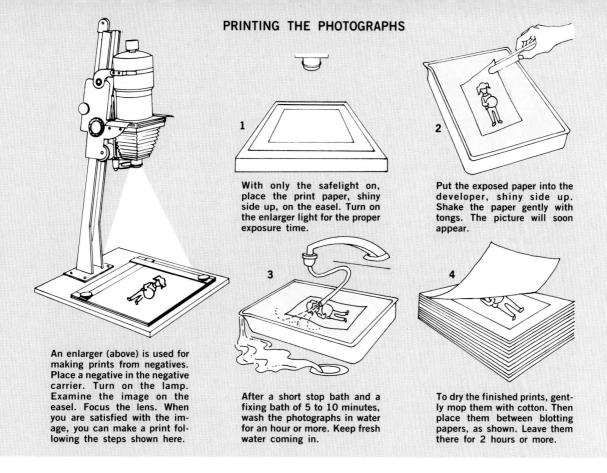

An enlarger (above) is used for making prints from negatives. Place a negative in the negative carrier. Turn on the lamp. Examine the image on the easel. Focus the lens. When you are satisfied with the image, you can make a print following the steps shown here.

1 With only the safelight on, place the print paper, shiny side up, on the easel. Turn on the enlarger light for the proper exposure time.

2 Put the exposed paper into the developer, shiny side up. Shake the paper gently with tongs. The picture will soon appear.

3 After a short stop bath and a fixing bath of 5 to 10 minutes, wash the photographs in water for an hour or more. Keep fresh water coming in.

4 To dry the finished prints, gently mop them with cotton. Then place them between blotting papers, as shown. Leave them there for 2 hours or more.

dry operation. It may even be done in a closet, which is fairly easy to darken. Use some rags or newspapers to shut out completely any light that may come through the crack under the door.

After the film has been developed, it is rinsed in water or in a chemical solution called a **stop bath.** This stops the action of the developers. Next, the film is put into a liquid called a **fixer.** This chemical gets rid of the undeveloped silver-bromide crystals. If this were not done, the crystals would react to light and cause the negatives to fade. After the film is fixed, it undergoes a final washing.

One or more prints can be made from the negative after it has been developed, rinsed, fixed, washed, and dried. A print is made on special photographic printing paper. When a light is shone through the negative onto the paper, an invisible image of the negative is made on the paper. The paper is then developed, fixed, washed, and dried. The result is a positive image of the original subject.

A print that is the same size as the negative is called a **contact print.** It is made by pressing the printing paper tightly against the negative in a glass frame. Light is shone through the negative onto the printing paper for a few seconds. Contact prints generally are used to help the photographer decide which exposures are worth enlarging.

The most commonly used cameras today produce small negatives. To make big prints from little negatives, an **enlarger** is used.

It is possible to project only part of the negative onto the paper. Suppose, for example, the negative shows two houses located next to each other. The printing paper can be moved so that only the house on the right side of the negative will be printed. This procedure is called **cropping.** It is one way in which you can control the final look of a print.

Printing or enlarging does not need total darkness. But be sure that the only light in the room comes from a safelight. This is a lamp especially designed for darkroom use. A corner of the kitchen makes an ideal temporary printing darkroom. It provides three important aids—running water, an electric outlet, and a working surface. The tops of counters should be covered with plastic sheets to protect them from splashed or spilled solutions.

Storing Negatives and Prints

Whether you do your own developing and printing or have a photofinisher do it, you should take good care of your negatives and prints. Never touch the negative emulsion with your fingers. Hold the negatives by the edges only. A negative file book or a heavy accordion-fold envelope (one that expands) is the safest place for your negatives. These should be kept in a cool, dry place. An album or a large scrapbook keeps prints from loss or damage. It also is a good idea to label each picture according to subject, date, and place as you mount it in your album. In that way, you will not forget when and where the picture was taken.

▶MOTION PICTURE PHOTOGRAPHY

Movies are actually long strips of film. The film has one still picture after another on it. In a motion picture camera, the film is moved forward one frame at a time. As each frame moves into position behind the lens, it stops still for a fraction of a second. The camera's shutter quickly opens and closes to take a picture. Then the next frame moves into position, and another exposure is made.

All this happens very fast. Most movie cameras take 16 pictures every second. Many allow the moviemaker to take 12, 24, 32, 48, or 64 pictures a second. The result is a series of still pictures. The subject is in a slightly different position in each picture. The figures seem to move because the eye still sees each of the pictures for a fraction of a second after it is taken away.

In some systems, you can record sound as you shoot the movie. In other systems, sound can be added later. In making movies, you use most of the devices and techniques that you use for making good photographs—filters, lenses of different focal lengths, different exposures for special effects, and so on.

▶HISTORY OF PHOTOGRAPHY

Long ago, people were using a cameralike device to make pictures. This was the **camera obscura.** *Camera* is the Latin word for "chamber." *Obscura* means "dark." This early ancestor of today's camera was actually a dark room with a tiny hole in one wall. Light came through the hole. It produced an image, on the opposite wall, of people or objects outside the hole.

For about 500 years, the camera obscura was used mostly for watching eclipses of the sun. Using it, people did not have to look directly at the sun. Then artists and mapmakers realized that the camera obscura could be very useful to them. Portable versions—tents and small wooden huts that could be carried from place to place—were developed.

In time, the camera obscura was reduced to a small box much like a modern camera. A lens was placed in the hole where the light entered. The lens helped to concentrate the light rays. There also was a diaphragm to control the amount of light coming in. The back of the box was a translucent screen. (Something translucent lets light pass through, but we cannot see through it.) A sheet of paper could be placed over the screen and the image traced on the paper.

By the late 1600's, the development of the camera obscura was well advanced. But it was more than a century before people learned how to capture the image made by the camera. A German doctor, Johann Schulze, made the

This drawing from the 1600's shows a camera obscura, which was a dark room with a tiny hole in one wall.

This picture, taken by Louis Daguerre in 1837, is the earliest daguerreotype in existence.

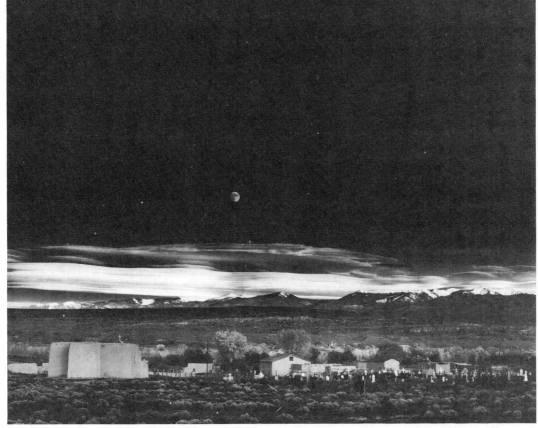

Moonrise, Hernandez, New Mexico, 1941, by Ansel Adams, a famed photographer of the West.

discovery that finally led to the film used today. In 1727, Schulze found that sunlight would blacken chalk that had been treated with a solution of silver nitrate. Modern photography is based on Schulze's discovery that light affects certain silver compounds.

The first successful photographs were made by a French inventor, Joseph Nicéphore Niepce, about 1826. He succeeded in capturing an image that did not immediately fade when light struck it. He placed the exposed metal plate (coated with an asphalt compound) in a solution that brought out the picture. The solution also washed away all the compound that had not yet been exposed to light. In other words, he fixed the picture.

In 1829, Niepce became a partner of Louis Daguerre, a French theatrical designer. Before they had finished improving a developing process, Niepce died. Daguerre continued work on the process. In 1839, he revealed what became the first widely successful system of photography. His pictures were called daguerreotypes. Each was unique—one of a kind.

There was no negative, and no prints could be made.

At about the same time, in England, William Henry Fox Talbot invented the first practical process that produced a negative from which prints could be made. The process—called the calotype—began with a negative image on paper. It was then printed on another sensitized piece of paper to produce a positive print.

Paper negatives had a drawback. The natural grain of the paper made the details of the picture somewhat unclear. To avoid this, people began experimenting with glass plates. Unfortunately, photographic chemicals would not stay on the glass. In 1847, Abel Niepce de Saint-Victor, the nephew of Joseph Niepce, tried something new. He coated a glass plate with albumen (the white of an egg). This sticky coating held the chemical fast.

In 1851, Frederick Scott Archer, an English chemist, introduced the wet collodion process. This process uses a syrupy, transparent liquid called collodion to hold the silver compounds

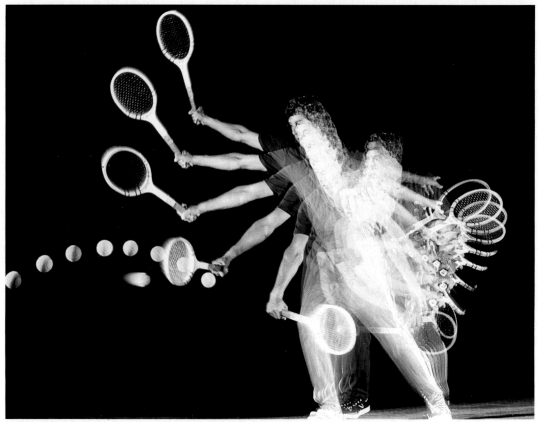

Using high-speed photography, continuous motion can be shown by rapidly making a number of exposures on one piece of film. The flowing motion of a tennis stroke is caught in this picture.

on glass. The response of collodion plates to light was much faster than in other processes. But the photographer still had to coat the glass plate and load it into the camera. Then the plate had to be exposed, and the image developed, before the collodion dried. By the 1870's, gelatin-based dry emulsion began to replace the wet collodion plates.

In the 1880's, two developments changed photography. First, flexible, roll-up film was introduced by George Eastman, founder of the Eastman Kodak Company in Rochester, New York. A few years later, Eastman brought out a hand-held roll-film camera. This camera was easy to carry and use. Eastman's company even processed the film, so amateur photographers no longer had to do their own developing. This marked the beginning of photography's popularity as a hobby.

Along with its increasing popularity, photography began to be recognized as an art. Some photographers of the early 1900's experimented with new printing techniques to make their photographs look more like paint-

ings. Later photographers produced abstract compositions through darkroom techniques and multiple exposures. Others continued to use the shapes and textures of the natural world to create beautiful photographs.

In the 1920's and 1930's, more technical advances affected amateur and professional photographers alike. In 1924, the Leica camera was introduced in Germany. This miniature 35mm camera came with a wide range of accessories and attachments. The Leica gave photographers new flexibility, allowing them to take sharp, detailed pictures under many conditions. It was the forerunner of the many 35mm cameras available today. The range of photography was further extended with the development of convenient flash equipment in the late 1920's and early 1930's.

Many photographers used this new flexibility to dramatize social issues, such as poverty, with moving candid shots. This became known as documentary photography. Other photographers concentrated on recording news events. With advances in printing, newspapers

Children playing in war-torn Seville, Spain, during the 1930's, by Henri Cartier-Bresson.

In *Louisville Flood Victims* (1937), by Margaret Bourke-White, photography makes a social comment.

Photographer Philip Hyde took this picture of Coyote Gulch, in Utah. Such photographs have helped draw attention to unspoiled areas that are threatened by development.

and magazines were demanding more and more photographs for illustration.

Meanwhile, color photography had been developing since the early 1900's. In 1935, Kodachrome film was introduced. It became the first popular, affordable color film, and it is still widely used. "Instant" film, which develops within seconds, appeared in 1947. It was produced by the American scientist and inventor Edwin H. Land for use in his Polaroid Land Camera. The first instant film was black-and-white. Full-color instant film came in the 1960's.

Also introduced in the 1960's was the film cartridge, which simplified loading the camera. Other advances—in-camera exposure meters, automatic exposure setting, improved films and processing—have made it easier to take good pictures. And new developments, such as the filmless camera, promise to increase the popularity and usefulness of photography.

▶ SPECIAL USES OF PHOTOGRAPHY

With special cameras, films, and other equipment, photography has been adapted to a wide range of uses in science and industry.

Photomicrography is extremely useful to scientists and engineers. It combines a camera with a microscope. Pictures can then be taken of things too small to be seen with the naked eye. These pictures are called photomicrographs. They enable us to study the cells of living tissue. We can see the crystal structure of a piece of metal or study parts of ancient plants discovered in a thin slice of coal.

X-ray photography is widely used in medicine, industry, and science. It is quite different from ordinary photography. X rays are invisible electromagnetic waves. They behave much like visible light. But they can pass through things such as wood, cardboard, and flesh, which light cannot penetrate. X rays cannot be focused by a lens, so no camera is used. The subject is placed between an X-ray tube and the film. A special film that is sensitive to X rays is used. The photograph obtained is a life-size shadow picture.

In medicine, X rays are used to locate where a bone is broken and to examine internal organs such as the lungs. In an X-ray picture, the bones and denser tissues of the body show up as dark shadows. Healthy muscle shows as a light shadow.

X-ray photographs are used in industry to test and inspect materials and parts. A hidden flaw in a welded joint, for example, shows up in an X-ray photograph. The flaw cannot be detected by the eye. Today, welded joints of pipelines, steel beams, and many other objects are routinely checked by X-ray photography.

Aerial photography has many uses. Photographs taken from the air are of great value to mapmakers and surveyors. These photographs reveal many things that cannot be seen by an observer on the ground. Aerial photographs also help locate mineral deposits. The different landforms and kinds of vegetation that show up in the photograph give clues to the rock formations beneath the surface. Traffic studies are another important use of aerial photography. Even archeologists make use of aerial photographs. The boundary lines of ancient fields and the sites of long-forgotten, ancient cities and settlements show up clearly in photographs that have been taken from a great height.

One of the chief uses of aerial photography is in military intelligence—the gathering of information about the military strength of other countries. Military specialists study photographs taken from a great height to learn about airfields, fortifications, missile bases, and other military installations.

Spacecraft and satellites are often used to carry cameras that photograph the earth's surface. The Apollo astronauts took many spectacular photographs of the earth. Some satellites—such as Landsat D, launched in 1982—take very detailed pictures. But Landsat does not use a regular camera. It uses a special device called a scanner.

Infrared photography uses special films that are sensitive to infrared radiation. Infrared rays, which are invisible, have a longer wavelength than visible light. They can penetrate haze that scatters the waves of visible light. For this reason, infrared photographs often are much clearer than ordinary photographs. Pictures can be taken with infrared rays even at night or in complete darkness.

Infrared photography is used in medicine to inspect damage to veins and healing beneath scabs. Faults in the weaving of textiles show up in infrared photography. Even crossed-out words or writings on a charred piece of paper can be read if photographs of them are taken

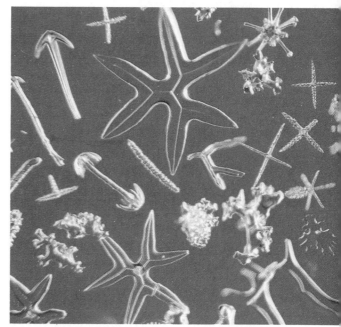

Above: Photomicrography combines a camera with a microscope. Impurities in mica show up as colored flecks in this photomicrograph (magnified 100 times). Below: This aerial photograph of Los Angeles, California, was taken through a fish-eye lens. Part of the city's vast freeway system can be seen. Aerial photography has often been used to study traffic patterns.

This young woman is holding a hologram of the Italian film star Marcello Mastroianni.

with infrared rays. Astronomers use infrared photography to study stars that are covered with a haze.

Spectrography combines a camera with a spectroscope. This is an instrument that breaks up light into its different wavelengths. Using spectrography, scientists can analyze the light given off by the stars and the sun. Spectrographs of the planets reveal which gases are present in their atmospheres. Spectrographs can be used to analyze materials such as metal alloys. A small piece of the material is heated until it melts, then turns to gas. The pattern of lines in the spectrum identifies each element that is present in the material.

Holography is three-dimensional photography. A laser beam, which consists of only a very narrow range of light waves, is used. Part of the beam is directed at the object. This is reflected from the object to the photographic plate. The other part of the beam is focused directly on the photographic plate. The two parts of the beam interfere with each other. This interference is recorded in the silver compound on the photographic plate. To view the hologram, the plate is exposed to a laser beam. This beam usually has the same frequency as the one that recorded the image.

Holography can be used to test materials without harming them. It can reveal very small changes of size and shape when an object is subjected to pressure, heat, or other forces.

There are even ways to make three-dimensional pictures using sound, rather than light, as the energy source. These are called acoustic holograms. They are used in medicine, underwater studies, and other fields.

▶ CAREERS IN PHOTOGRAPHY

Photography is an interesting and challenging profession. One of the best ways to enter the profession is to take courses in photography. Some high schools, technical schools, and art schools offer such courses. So do many colleges and universities. Some of them have programs leading to degrees in photography. You will find courses in basic photography, black-and-white photography, color photography, basic and advanced darkroom techniques, and portrait photography. You can also take courses in such special subjects as nature and wildlife, travel, and underwater photography.

Many people compete for the jobs available. Because competition is keen, most professionals are specialists in one or two kinds of pictures. Some specialize in advertising work. Much of this kind of photography is done in studios equipped with large cameras and a great deal of lighting equipment. Some photographs are used to present people or products at their most appealing. The idea in advertising work is, of course, to sell the advertiser's product or service.

Portrait photographers specialize in family and individual pictures. These photographers are skilled at posing subjects, lighting, and retouching photographs.

Scientific, medical, and police photographers work in hospitals and laboratories. They must know photography as well as the field in which they work.

Photojournalists concentrate on news stories that are told more through pictures than through words. They usually work for newspapers and magazines.

Free-lance photographers work independently instead of working for any one employer. They usually have to do many different kinds of assignments.

People who do not make photography their career also benefit by learning this skill. In many careers a knowledge of photography can help people do their jobs better. And knowing how to take photographs can add great pleasure to our personal lives. Few things are more satisfying than creating a beautiful, exciting, or unique photograph.

KENNETH POLI
Editor, *Popular Photography* magazine

See also LENSES; LIGHT.

PHOTOSYNTHESIS

Green plants can make their own food. They take water from the soil and carbon dioxide from the air to make sugar. In doing so the plants give off oxygen. This process is called photosynthesis.

The energy for this process comes from sunlight. If plants are kept in the dark, photosynthesis stops. That is the reason for the name of the process. "Photosynthesis" comes from two Greek words meaning "putting together with light."

When a plant has formed sugar, using the energy of sunlight, it then can form starch and all the other complicated food substances it needs for life. For this reason we say that plant life is made possible by using energy from the sun.

Photosynthesis occurs only in the plant kingdom. But animal life as well as plant life depends on the sun. Animals cannot use the sun's energy directly. Since they cannot make their own food, animals must get food from plants or from other animals that eat plants.

Animals that just eat plants are called herbivorous (plant-eating) animals. Carnivorous (flesh-eating) animals do not eat plants. Instead they eat other animals. Usually they eat herbivorous animals, which get their energy from the plants they eat. And the plants, of course, produce food by photosynthesis. In the long run, then, nearly all life depends on the sun.

▶ HOW DO PLANTS GET ENERGY FROM SUNLIGHT?

Plants can make use of the sun's energy if their leaves possess a green chemical substance called **chlorophyll.** Chlorophyll particles are contained in **chloroplasts,** which are small disk-shaped bodies located in many plant cells.

Plant leaves and often plant stems are green because of their chlorophyll content. The word "chlorophyll" comes from Greek words meaning "green leaf." Chloroplast means "green shape."

The leaves of some plants may have a dark reddish color. They contain colored substances that hide the green chlorophyll. But since the leaves do have chlorophyll, they still carry on photosynthesis.

Unlike the green plants, mushrooms have

When chlorophyll breaks down, a leaf loses its green color and its ability to carry on photosynthesis. This happens in the fall as many leaves change color and die.

no chlorophyll. They cannot obtain energy from sunlight. They obtain it from dead and decaying plants.

When chlorophyll absorbs sunlight, it gains energy through a series of chemical reactions. That energy is used to carry out other chemical changes needed to make food.

A single particle of chlorophyll absorbs and passes on many bits of energy from sunlight. It provides energy for much chemical change, while remaining basically unchanged itself. Chemists call any substance that behaves in this way a **catalyst.** It helps a chemical process along, but it is not part of the chemical change that takes place.

▶ HOW DO PLANTS USE THE SUN'S ENERGY?

Chlorophyll, using the energy of sunlight, chemically changes water molecules in the plant. (Water is absorbed by the plant from the soil.) The chemical change is the splitting apart of water molecules.

Water molecules consist of atoms of hydrogen and oxygen bound tightly together. A lot of energy must be added to water before its molecules split apart. Sunlight supplies this energy. The water molecules are split apart, and hydrogen and oxygen are formed.

Once this happens, some of the hydrogen and oxygen atoms recombine into water. The energy given off when this happens is used to form a certain compound called **adenosine triphosphate.** This is a long name even for chemists, and it is usually abbreviated **ATP.** Molecules of ATP are stored in the plant until they are needed as a source of energy. Then the ATP is broken down in another chemical process and the energy used.

Not all the hydrogen and oxygen formed by the splitting of water molecules recombines. The rest is used for other purposes, which will be explained later.

Carbon Dioxide Traps

The carbon dioxide used by plants is absorbed from the air. The carbon dioxide molecules, once absorbed, are held fast by certain sugarlike molecules that are already present in plant cells. These sugarlike molecules are often called carbon dioxide traps.

Water, carbon dioxide, and sunlight combine during photosynthesis to produce food. A by-product of this process is oxygen, which is released into the air.

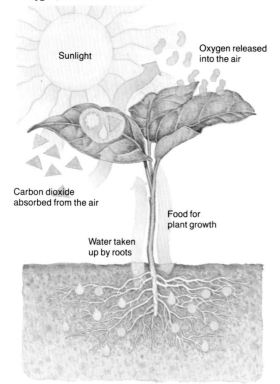

Sunlight

Oxygen released into the air

Carbon dioxide absorbed from the air

Food for plant growth

Water taken up by roots

Six trapped carbon dioxide molecules are used in forming one molecule of glucose. Glucose is an important sugar present in all living things. It is always present, for instance, in the blood of animals with spinal columns, including human beings.

The molecules of glucose can be put together to form large molecules of starch or even larger molecules of cellulose (the main substance of wood). Moreover, the plants absorb certain minerals from the soil. If these are added to the glucose molecules, complicated molecules of protein can be formed.

Carbon dioxide molecules cannot be built up into glucose without help. Hydrogen and energy must be added. The hydrogen comes from the water molecules that split and did not recombine. The energy comes from ATP. When hydrogen and energy are added to the carbon dioxide, glucose is formed.

You may wonder how photosynthesis can work if the carbon dioxide traps must be present in the plant tissues to begin with. How did those sugarlike molecules come to be there in the first place?

Most green plants produce new plants through spores or seeds. When a spore or seed is fully formed, it contains a supply of starch or other foodstuff. If you cut open a bean seed, for example, you will see the light-colored food supply beneath the seed's coat.

As the seed develops, it breaks down the food for energy. The seed uses that energy to build up compounds such as chlorophyll and carbon dioxide traps. A green shoot appears aboveground, and by the time the young plant has used up the original food supply, photosynthesis can take over.

These magnified plant cells contain the small, round chloroplasts where chlorophyll is found. The photosynthesis process, shown at left, takes place here.

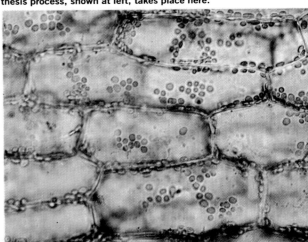

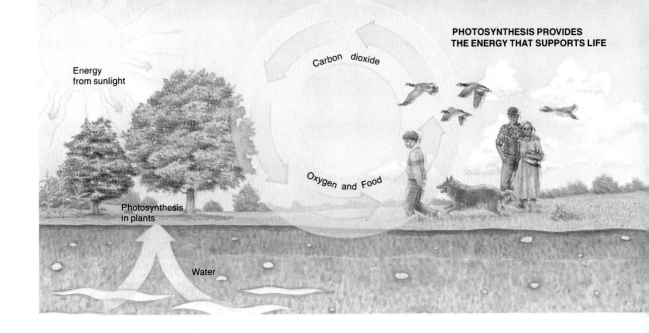

Energy
from sunlight

Carbon dioxide

Oxygen and Food

Photosynthesis
in plants

Water

▶ WHAT HAPPENS TO THE LEFTOVER OXYGEN?

Let us return to those water molecules that split up into hydrogen and oxygen and did not recombine into water. The hydrogen was used up. It combined with carbon dioxide, forming glucose. But what happened to the oxygen?

The plant uses only a part of it. The rest of it escapes into the air. That is another reason that photosynthesis is important. It supplies us with oxygen.

In order to get energy, animals combine the food they eat with the oxygen they inhale. In this process, water and carbon dioxide are formed. Animals then give off these unused compounds. You might think that after many, many years of animal life, all the oxygen in the atmosphere would have been used up and carbon dioxide would exist in its place.

Because of green plants, this has not happened. During photosynthesis, green plants combine carbon dioxide and water to form food and oxygen again.

Plants and animals working together keep the atmosphere in balance. There is enough oxygen for animal life and enough carbon dioxide for plant life. What is more, as plant food is eaten up by animals, more plant food is formed by plants through photosynthesis.

▶ HOW CAN PLANTS PRODUCE MORE FOOD?

As the world's population increases, new sources of food must be found. People are farming more efficiently by using better fertilizers and quick-growing varieties of plants with high food value. There is better control of insect pests. Researchers also are learning to make more use of food from the sea.

However, there will always be a limit to the total amount of food available. The amount of food depends on how efficiently the energy of sunlight can be turned into food by the chlorophyll of plants. Perhaps researchers will have to search for plants that make better use of sunlight than the plants now used for food.

For instance, there are microscopic one-celled seaweeds called **algae**. Unlike plants they have no roots, wood, flowers, fruit, or other parts that lack chlorophyll. Their entire structure can work at photosynthesis. For this reason and others, algae are more efficient at changing sunlight into food. Perhaps, scientists will learn how to grow algae and make tasty and nourishing food from them. Then the Earth's food supply would be vastly increased. (Even now, people in Asia and other parts of the world eat seaweed, a form of algae.)

Algae may be essential for space travel. If a spaceship is to go from Earth to Mars, for instance, it will have to spend many months in space. Astronauts will find it difficult to store enough food and oxygen on board ship for such a long journey. Instead, supplies of algae may be taken. Algae grow quickly under sunlamps. And algae would keep the air fresh by restoring the oxygen astronauts use up in breathing.

ISAAC ASIMOV
Boston University School of Medicine

See also ALGAE; CELLS; FLOWERS; LEAVES; LIFE; PLANTS.

Swimming is one of the many sports included in physical education programs. Students may receive instruction in competitive swimming and in water safety and lifesaving.

PHYSICAL EDUCATION

Physical fitness has always been one of the major goals of physical education. At one time the normal demands of everyday living provided enough exercise to keep people physically fit. Today machines do more and more of the work that our muscles used to do. As a result the body development of many modern people is far below what it should be. Most schools all over the world today stress the development of physical fitness. Students are helped to improve strength, balance, agility, posture, endurance, speed, and accuracy.

It is true that physical fitness depends greatly on exercise, but nutrition, sleep, rest, and good health habits are also important. Physical education programs in schools, therefore, emphasize the learning of good health habits as well as provide opportunities for physical activities.

Many physical education programs also include leisure-time activities or sports. Games such as tennis and bowling give people the opportunity to play a game regardless of age.

In North American schools, physical education activities may include the following.

Individual Sports

Badminton	Racquetball
Bowling	Skating
Boxing	Swimming
Golf	Table tennis
Gymnastics	Tennis
Handball	Track and field
Jogging	Wrestling

Team Sports	Rhythmical Activities
Baseball	Calisthenics
Basketball	Dance
Football	Gymnastics
Hockey (ice and field)	Marching
Soccer	
Volleyball	

Elementary School Programs. Most elementary school programs include rhythms, dancing, exercises, and instruction in simple game and athletic skills. The programs help children develop their bodies and learn the basic concepts of good conduct and fair play.

Secondary School Programs. These programs include dance, calisthenics, tumbling, apparatus work, and team sports. Body growth is very rapid during the junior and senior high school years. Therefore, activities that promote balanced development are offered at this time. Current programs emphasize instruction in skills needed for team sports and encourage the development of teamwork, leadership, and a sense of responsibility.

College Programs. These programs continue the development of general athletic ability, as well as skills in various sports. In addition, fitness programs are receiving emphasis in colleges today. Many college programs include intramural and interscholastic competition in team and individual sports. Special programs are also available for students interested in professional physical education—who seek careers as trainers, teachers, coaches, and so on.

▶HISTORY OF PHYSICAL EDUCATION

Physical education goes back to the first parents who taught their children to jump, throw, wrestle, climb, and swim. Early people needed these skills for survival.

The people of the ancient world needed soldiers who could fight well and who were able to take care of themselves on long marches. Young boys in ancient countries were trained in such skills as running, jumping, riding, and javelin throwing. The Spartans of southern Greece considered physical education important for both boys and girls. Boys were trained in running, wrestling, throwing weights, and other skills that would make strong, rugged soldiers. Physical education for the girls of Sparta included gymnastics, dancing, swimming, discus throwing, running, and wrestling. The same activities were developed in Athens, but body development, beauty, grace, and sportsmanship were stressed.

The Romans also stressed activities related to military training and added gladiatorial (fighting) contests, ball games, chariot races, and exercises with dumbbells.

For about 1,000 years after the decline of the Roman Empire in the 5th century A.D., there was little or no interest in formal physical education.

During the 15th and 16th centuries, there were important changes in general education and physical education. Vittorino da Feltre of Italy believed that physical training and mental training should be combined. He established a school in Mantua in 1423 in which special teachers taught dancing, riding, fencing, swimming, wrestling, jumping, running, archery, hunting, and fishing. In addition, students were taught academic subjects. Some other educators during this period emphasized the place of exercise and physical activity in the general curriculum.

Between 1750 and 1850, the countries of Europe developed somewhat distinctive styles of physical education. In Germany, Johann Basedow established a school in 1774 in which physical education was given a place in the daily program. He introduced high jumping, long jumping, and the use of such equipment as hoops and seesaws. Physical education in Germany was furthered in the early 1800's by Guts Muths, who wrote several books about gymnastics and games, and Friedrich Jahn, who established a formal sys-

Gymnastics has been an important part of physical education since the early 1800's. The sport helps students develop strength, agility, flexibility, and balance.

tem of gymnastics that involved exercises on such apparatus as the horizontal bar, vaulting horse, and parallel bars. Adolph Spiess (1810–58) used Jahn's methods and introduced physical education to schools in Germany.

During the same period, Per Henrik Ling was changing physical education in Sweden. His system of gymnastics included simple exercises that required little or no apparatus and were designed to promote body development.

In Denmark, under the leadership of Franz Nachtegall (1777–1847), the physical education program emphasized movements that would increase flexibility and grace.

The French in this period developed physical education by following the programs of other countries and selecting those activities they thought best.

Czarist Russia gave little thought to physical education, and it was given no importance until the development of the socialist state, after 1918.

In Britain the emphasis was on games and sports until the 1850's, when gymnastic exercises were added to school programs.

In the United States, gymnastics dominated the early physical education programs. But in the second half of the 19th century, intercollegiate sports started becoming popular—especially rowing, baseball, track and field, and football. The emphasis on team sports grew in the 20th century, but present trends in physical education also stress personal fitness.

LAWRENCE S. FINKEL
Chester Township, New Jersey, Public Schools

As part of a physical fitness program, aerobic activities such as bicycling, rope skipping, and cross-country skiing help keep the body fit and healthy.

PHYSICAL FITNESS

Do you have it? We all need it. It is very valuable, but we are often careless about it. It is easy to lose and difficult to get back. What is it? Physical fitness.

For a long time, most people did not realize how important physical fitness was. Today, however, we know that staying in good physical condition not only makes life more enjoyable but also quite possibly helps us live longer. That is why millions of people today participate in some sort of strenuous exercise several times each week.

There are four foundations to physical fitness.

First, you must eat in an intelligent way, based on principles of good nutrition.

Second, you must get plenty of rest and sleep. This is vital when you are growing, and it is important at all times of your life.

Third, you must practice good hygiene and health habits, and you should avoid dangerous substances such as tobacco and narcotics.

Fourth, you must get plenty of exercise. Exercise keeps your muscles, heart, and lungs in good working order. There are many different exercises, but just three basic kinds are necessary for physical fitness. They are aerobic exercises, stretchers, and strengtheners.

▶AEROBIC EXERCISES

It used to be that doctors would recommend rest for their patients with heart problems. This has changed. Now exercise is often recommended to help strengthen weak hearts. Even normal, healthy hearts benefit greatly from exercise. Doctors have discovered that the heart is like any other muscle. Making it work strengthens it. The heart is working hard when it is pumping hard.

Exercises that strengthen the heart and lungs are called **aerobic** exercises. The word "aerobic" means "with oxygen." Muscles need oxygen in order to produce heat and energy. Our lungs collect oxygen and feed it into our blood. Our hearts pump the blood through the arteries and veins of our circulatory systems, delivering oxygen to every muscle in the body.

The blood also carries food to the muscles and takes away wastes produced as the food and oxygen are used. When muscles have too much waste, they do not work well. Your muscles become fatigued (tired). They also become sore or develop cramps.

With an efficient heart and a strong pair of lungs, however, you can work your muscles hard for a long time without getting fatigued.

Left: Even though they prefer different forms of aerobic exercise, a jogging father and his cycling daughter enjoy each other's company during a workout. Right: Aerobic dancing—continuous rhythmic movement accompanied by music—is a popular exercise.

And you can be sure that every organ and tissue in your body is receiving a healthy supply of food and oxygen.

What exercises will strengthen your heart and lungs? Running, jogging, bicycling, swimming, rope skipping, cross-country skiing, basketball, soccer, and hockey are all aerobic activities. Some people enjoy dancing as an aerobic exercise. Continuous body movements, such as running in place, hopping in place, or different exercises done without pauses between them may all be aerobic. Even walking long distances has aerobic benefits. Anything that raises your pulse and makes you breathe hard steadily for 15 minutes or more is aerobic. If you do aerobic exercises daily, or at least three or four times a week, you will keep your heart and lungs in good condition. If your goal is to take part in athletic competition, then you will want to devote much more time than 15 minutes daily to aerobic exercises.

Many sports, such as baseball and football, require only short bursts of energy. These sports do not produce aerobic benefits. But you need good aerobic conditioning to perform at your best when those bursts of energy are needed. That is why baseball and football players make aerobic exercises a major part of their conditioning programs.

Some sports, such as bowling or billiards, will not keep you fit. But being fit will improve your performance in all sports.

How hard you work at aerobic exercise determines the amount of benefit you get from it. If your bicycle riding is nothing more than downhill coasting, you will gain little benefit. You must exercise hard for maximum benefit.

But suppose you do not enjoy exercising hard for 15 minutes or more. You can also benefit from slower activities such as walking or easy swimming, but you must do them for longer periods. An hour of brisk walking, for example, will do as much good for most people as 15 minutes of jogging.

If you are not in condition, you should ease into aerobic exercises slowly. This is especially important if you are overweight. At first, just five minutes of jogging may tire you out. Lengthen your workouts slowly. The chances are that within two weeks you will notice a difference. You will be able to jog further and faster. And if you have been careful about eating, you will probably be getting slimmer. Aerobic exercises combined with dieting will help you get rid of excess fat.

Left: For all-around physical fitness, swimming is perhaps the most favored aerobic activity. It is relaxing, and it exercises many of the body's large muscle groups.

A related type of exercise is **anaerobic** exercise. The word "anaerobic" means "without oxygen." When doing anaerobic exercises, such as sprinting, you very quickly become out of breath. It is impossible to sprint for long periods of time. You must soon stop to catch your breath. Anaerobic exercises are used by top athletes to build up their speed. But in an ordinary physical fitness program, anaerobic exercises are not recommended. Instead you should concentrate on aerobic exercises.

▶ STRETCHERS

All muscles tend to tighten up when idle, particularly the long muscles in your legs, back, and the sides of your body between your hips and your armpits. Sitting for a long time in the same position at a desk or bench will often stiffen neck or shoulder muscles. Such stiffness creates tension in the body and can even influence your state of mind. But the most common danger of stiff muscles is that sudden movement of them may cause damage. Pulled muscles and torn tissues are often caused by failure to stretch before vigorous exercise.

Make stretching exercises the first part of your daily workout. You might also do them in the morning to help you wake up or during the day to break the monotony of desk work.

Along with making you feel good, stretching exercises, done regularly, help improve posture, muscle tone, and overall fitness while reducing muscle tension and stiffness. Yoga exercises, which were developed in Asia over many centuries, are excellent examples of good stretchers.

You can design your own stretchers for your special needs. But whatever the stretcher, it should be done slowly and gently. A gradual stretcher through a muscle's full range of movement is much better for your muscles than stretchers that include quick, repetitive, bouncing movements. Sudden movements increase the risk of muscle soreness and injury.

The following are some popular stretchers.

Bend and Sway. With your feet apart and your hands on your hips, bend the upper body to the left; then bend back as far as you can go, then to the right, and then forward. Bend to the left again and repeat. After several bends, reverse direction and do several more. You should feel the muscles stretching on both sides of your body. Clasping your hands behind your neck or above your head will increase the stretching benefit.

From the same starting position as above, sway, do not rotate, from one side to the other. Extending the arms high above the head will give you maximum benefit.

Wing Flaps. To loosen the shoulder muscles, stand with your elbows out and your fists together in front of you about neck high. Your forearms should be parallel to the floor. Slowly pull your fists apart, and bring your elbows back as far as they will go. Do several smooth repetitions. Raising or lowering the level of your arms will spread the stretch up and down your shoulders.

It is a good idea to do stretching exercises both before and after sports activity. This re-

Center: Aerobic exercises at health clubs include riding exercycles and jogging on treadmills. Right: Stretching is recommended both before and after strenuous activity.

duces the chance of injury, and it also allows the muscles to recover sooner from fatigue.

▶ STRENGTHENERS

There are hundreds of good exercises that build muscle, and you can do them anyplace and anytime. You do not need cables, pulleys, or weights. In fact, when your body is growing, you should not lift weights without expert coaching.

Sit-ups, push-ups, and other strengtheners put a different demand on muscles than the stretchers. You will feel the difference. At first do not expect to repeat these exercises as often as the stretchers. Never work to the point of pain. Usually the more slowly you move, the greater the benefit.

Pull-ups are another kind of strengthener. An overhead bar is necessary for this exercise. Grip the bar in overhand fashion and pull yourself up until your chin touches the bar. Let your body down slowly. Repeat as often as you are able to without pain. Changing from an overhand to an underhand grip will bring different arm and shoulder muscles into play. Pull-ups strengthen the arms, shoulders, hands, and wrists.

▶ YOUR PROGRAM

Experiment with all these exercises and any others you may learn about. Decide what your aerobic activity will be. It does not have to be the same thing every day. Two days of basketball, three days of swimming, and two days of bicycling can be more fun than jogging seven days per week.

No matter what you choose, do not begin until you have done your stretchers. Most should be repeated at least ten times, but you should not be a slave to numbers. If you are warming up for soccer, tennis, or some other sport that has a lot of quick starts, stops, and turns, then 20 groin stretchers might be just enough. Stretchers like the propeller are excellent for cooling off gradually after an aerobic workout.

You might also do strengtheners to cool off. Select them to fit your needs. Tennis players, for example, should do plenty of push-ups and pull-ups to assure equal muscle development in both arms. Runners, whose legs get plenty of exercise, should also do push-ups and pull-ups in order to develop their upper bodies. Sit-ups are recommended for everyone. Do them daily for the rest of your life and you will not be likely to grow a pot belly.

People who are very inactive or who may have health problems should always consult with a physician before planning a fitness program.

One final point: Once you have started a fitness program, stay with it. It is all right to miss a day or two, and you should not force yourself to exercise if you are not feeling well. But to maintain fitness, you should exercise regularly. A daily exercise routine will soon become an important and enjoyable part of your life. And you will look better and feel better.

RICHARD B. LYTTLE
Author, *The New Physical Fitness*

See also HEALTH; NUTRITION.

PHYSICS

Physics is the study of matter and energy. Matter is the basic substance of which everything consists; energy is what makes matter move and change. By studying matter and energy, physicists try to understand the universe. Thus physics is the science behind such things as gravity, motion, magnetism, electricity, atomic energy, and black holes.

Unlike biologists, who study living things, physicists investigate nonliving things, from the smallest and simplest atoms up to vast and complex galaxies. Chemists and geologists also study nonliving matter, such as water, rocks, and plastics. But physicists study the basic elements of matter before they join together to form compound things like rocks or trees. Physicists want to know what forces hold atoms together, how gases change to liquids, why metals conduct electricity, and how stars and galaxies evolve.

The science of physics can be loosely divided into two traditional categories: classical physics and modern physics. Within each category are various branches of study.

Physicists study images of the collisions of highly charged subatomic particles sent racing through a bubble chamber by particle accelerators to help them analyze certain theories about the creation of the universe. One such theory, the Big Bang theory, begins with the explosion of a minute particle of matter.

▶ CLASSICAL PHYSICS

Classical physics deals with several fields of study that were quite well developed before the 1900's. These branches include mechanics, heat, sound, light, and electromagnetism.

Mechanics

The science of **mechanics** is concerned with the effects of forces on bodies at rest or in motion. These effects are described by mathematical equations called **laws of motion**, which were introduced in 1687 by the English scientist Isaac Newton to explain why the planets orbit the sun. Newton demonstrated that a gravitational force of attraction acting between the sun and a planet causes the planet to move around the sun in an elliptical path.

Newton was able to apply his laws to the motion of all bodies, not just planets. According to Newton's laws, when no force acts on an object, it moves uniformly, that is, along a straight line at a constant speed. This is called the **law of inertia**. But planets and most bodies do not move uniformly. Newton discovered that their motion is changed or accelerated by pushes or pulls, which he called **forces**. For example, the motion of a baseball traveling through the air is determined by forces exerted on the ball by the air and gravity. An iron nail slides across a table toward a magnet because of the attractive force of magnetism. When a gas is heated, forces resulting from its molecules colliding with one another cause the gas to expand.

Everything from the activity of the electrons in an atom (electrons are tiny particles of matter that travel around the nucleus of an atom) to the rotation of a galaxy can be understood using Newton's laws of motion. The explanation of an object's motion in terms of the forces acting on it is the central idea in Newton's science of mechanics, which remained the foundation of physics until the 1900's.

Heat

Closely related to motion is the idea of energy, which describes the activity of objects and their ability to do work. Since objects often generate heat as they do work, there is also a relationship between energy and heat. In fact, heat is a form of energy. For example, chemical energy stored in a battery supplies electrical energy to run a motor, which does mechanical work such as pulling or lifting. This transformation of energy may also produce heat, but no energy is created or destroyed in the process. The transformation of one form of energy into another without loss or gain is called the **conservation of energy**. It is one of the fundamental laws of science.

The idea that heat is a form of energy is essential to understanding how engines operate, why your hands heat up when you rub them together, how an atomic bomb works, and how the universe has evolved. The science of heat, which is known as **thermodynamics**, is the study of all energy transformations in matter. It is another fundamental branch of physics.

Sound

All sounds result from the motion produced when the molecules making up a substance are made to vibrate, or move back and forth, very rapidly. Sound is caused by the vibrating motion of molecules in a medium such as air, water, or a solid such as wood. Sound travels as waves, which are vibrating disturbances that move through air or any other medium like ripples traveling on a lake. Since sound is caused by motion, the science of mechanics, with its laws of motion, explains how sound is generated and then travels through matter to reach our ears. The study of sound and its effects on objects is known as **acoustics**.

Light

The study of light, how it is produced and how it behaves, is known as **optics**. In the 1600's and 1700's, many scientists thought that light consisted of tiny particles given off

A rainbow is formed by the reflection of sunlight off millions of raindrops. Each raindrop acts like a tiny prism, splitting the light into an array of colors called a spectrum. Sometimes a secondary rainbow, with the color sequence reversed, is produced when the sun's rays are reflected twice off each drop.

by shining objects. Then experiments in the 1800's indicated that light was a wave. In 1865 James Clerk Maxwell, a Scottish physicist, proved mathematically that light was a wave traveling in an electromagnetic field—a force in space that is both electrical and magnetic. The process in which energy is emitted, or given off, is called radiation. Light is only one form of electromagnetic radiation. Other forms include radar and X rays.

The wave theory of light helps explain how light moves through different materials and how it is reflected by some materials and refracted, or bent, when it passes from one material to another. It also explains many optical effects, such as the appearance of narrow light and dark bands at the edge of a shadow,

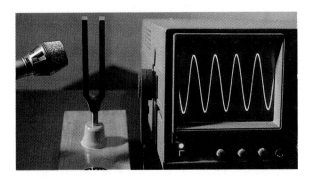

An oscilloscope can convert sound waves, which cannot be seen ordinarily, into electric signals and display them as wave patterns on its phosphorescent screen. Patterns formed by a vibrating tuning fork, shown here, are one example.

or the rainbow that appears on an oil slick on a wet street. The colors of light that can be seen when a beam of sunlight passes through a prism can also be understood in terms of light waves. Light waves of different frequencies (a frequency is the number of times per second that a wave vibrates) are associated with different colors, just as the different frequencies of a sound wave are associated with different pitches of sounds.

The wave theory does not, however, explain how light is emitted or absorbed. Nor does it answer the question of how a light wave can travel through empty space, as it does from the sun to the Earth. Even without knowing the exact nature of light, in the 1800's scientists were able to investigate how light rays are deflected by a mirror or a lens to form an image of an object. These studies led to the invention of many important optical instruments, such as the telescope, the microscope, and the camera.

Electromagnetism

The study of electricity and magnetism and the relationship between these two forces is called **electromagnetism**. The effects of electrical and magnetic forces have been observed and used since ancient times. But it was not until the 1800's that the close relationship between electricity and magnetism was discovered and the laws of electromagnetism were stated. At that time, Michael Faraday, an English chemist and physicist, and Hans Christian Oersted, a Danish physicist, demonstrated the connection and introduced the idea of electric and magnetic fields. Oersted showed that when an electric current is passed through a wire, a magnetic field forms around the wire. This is the principle of the electromagnet. Faraday found that when he moved a loop of wire through a magnetic field, an electric current was produced in the wire. This is the principle behind generators and transformers.

James Clerk Maxwell summarized and combined all of the known effects of electricity and magnetism into a few mathematical equations. These equations demonstrated the unity of electric and magnetic fields as two aspects of the same force, which he called electromagnetism. His calculations also led

An electromagnet turned on by an electric current attracts iron, steel, and certain other metals and is commonly used in scrap yards and recycling centers to separate these metals from other materials.

him to the idea that the electromagnetic force moved through space in waves at the speed of light (186,000 miles per second), proving that light must be a form of electromagnetic radiation.

By the late 1800's, Isaac Newton's science of mechanics, together with James Maxwell's work on electromagnetism, could explain the motion of atoms, planets, and projectiles (objects that are propelled forward, like an arrow shot from a bow). Newton's and Maxwell's work also explained the basic principles behind what was then known about optical, acoustic, electric, and magnetic phenomena. Some problems concerning light and radiation remained, but at that time, it seemed that there was not much left to do in physics. At the turn of the century, however, scientists began to observe phenomena that could not be explained by classical physics, and modern physics was born.

▶ MODERN PHYSICS

Modern physics is concerned with the basic structure and behavior of matter and energy on a very large or very small scale—from distant stars and galaxies to the tiniest particles of matter. Three of the main areas of study in modern physics are relativity, quantum theory, and cosmology.

Relativity

James Clerk Maxwell's theory of electromagnetic radiation predicted that light will always travel at the same speed regardless of the motion of the source or the observer. At first this prediction was unbelievable to most scientists because the measured speed of all objects, from trains to planets, depends on their relative motion—their motion in relation to the observer. Then, experiments performed between 1880 and 1920 proved that the speed of light is not relative, just as Maxwell predicted.

Special Theory of Relativity. In 1905, the German scientist Albert Einstein published a paper that assumed the truth of Maxwell's prediction and explored its consequences. Einstein formulated a special theory of relativity, which revolutionized physics. According to this theory, space and time are relative—the measurement of space and time depends on relative motion, or the observer's frame of reference—but the speed of light is not. He further stated that when an object travels at a high speed relative to an observer, the length of the object shrinks in the direction of travel, the mass of the object increases, and the object's clock appears slow to the observer. Although these effects seem impossible, they have all been verified by experiments. We are not aware of them because they are noticeable only if you travel at high speeds approaching the speed of light.

The special theory also examined mass and energy, proposing that mass and energy are equivalent (stated by Einstein's famous formula $E = mc^2$, in which E represents energy, m represents mass, and c stands for the speed of light). Because they are equivalent, under certain circumstances they can change from one form to the other. Discovering how to produce such changes subsequently led to the development of the atomic bomb and many uses of nuclear energy.

General Theory of Relativity. In 1915, Einstein published a paper describing what he called the general theory of relativity, which revolutionized ideas about gravity. According to this theory, not only are space and time different for moving observers, but also they are warped or curved, like the surface of a sphere or an hourglass. According to Einstein, matter curves or distorts space, and it is this distortion that causes objects near one another to "gravitate" toward one another. With these ideas, Einstein was able to describe planetary motion more accurately than Isaac Newton had.

Quantum Theory

If the discovery of the motion of light sparked the relativity revolution in physics, then theories about the emission and absorption of light started the quantum revolution. One of the things Maxwell's theory of light could not explain was the absorption of light waves that occurs in the **photoelectric effect**, in which electrons are emitted from certain metals when ultraviolet light falls on their surfaces, producing a current of electricity.

Albert Einstein and Max Planck, another German scientist, explained the emission and absorption of light by introducing the quantum hypothesis. **Quantization** means there is a grainy, or discontinuous, structure to matter and energy. According to this idea, atoms can vibrate only at certain quantized, or discrete (separate and distinct), frequencies. Also, energy such as light is emitted and absorbed only in tiny, discrete amounts. These discrete amounts of energy act like particles of matter rather than waves and help to explain the photoelectric effect.

Quantum Theory and Atoms. Danish scientist Niels Bohr applied the quantum idea to atoms. Bohr modified the picture of an atom as a tiny solar system with electrons moving in orbits around a nucleus. He assumed that the radius of each orbit and the energies of the electrons in an atom could have only certain quantized values. He then proved that when an atom is stimulated by electricity or heat, electrons may change their orbits, producing energy that leaves the atom in the form of photons of light. The atomic spectrum, or spread of color, of that light consists of separate, distinct lines of specific colors. Atomic spectra are discrete, not continuous, or unbroken, like the spectrum of sunlight. Only the quantized atom could explain this. This was one of the early applications of the theory of quantization.

The idea that electrons and light can act like either waves or particles depending on the circumstances demonstrated the dual nature of matter and energy that characterized the quantum hypothesis. These discoveries relating to the quantization of light, electrons, and atoms subsequently led to a new **quantum theory of matter and motion**, discovered by the European scientists Erwin Schrödinger and Werner Heisenberg.

The ideas of Newton were unable to explain the nature and behavior of atoms or the molecules they form. The quantum theory was refined by the American physicist Richard Feynman and others to explain the forms of matter and radiation and their behavior. Its explanations of electrical conductivity have led to the development of semiconductors, transistors, and microchips, and its use in optics has led to the development of lasers and fiber optics.

Atoms and Subatomic Particles. Quantum theory has enabled scientists to make discoveries about atomic forces. This work was pioneered by the German-American scientist Maria Goeppert-Mayer, among others. They have found that the nucleus of an atom is made of positively charged protons and uncharged neutrons. These are all held together by a **strong nuclear force**, which overpowers the electrical force of repulsion among the protons. This powerful force is responsible for the hydrogen bomb. Another atomic force, the **weak nuclear force**, is responsible for a form of radioactivity called beta decay, which causes atoms in certain elements to break down or disintegrate.

Within this Hubble Space Telescope image of a small region of the Orion constellation is an area where new stars have formed (*inset*). The gas and dust orbiting these stars could be protoplanetary disks that may someday evolve into planets. By studying such images, cosmologists hope to learn more about the evolution of the universe.

Quantum physics also has led to the discovery of a whole new world of subatomic particles. These particles, known as elementary particles, are thought to be the most basic components of the universe. Scientists now know that protons, neutrons, and many strange particles associated with the strong nuclear force are made of simpler particles called **quarks**. Another group of particles, the **leptons**, are governed by the weak nuclear force. The explanation of matter in terms of quarks and leptons and their interactions is called the **standard model**, which is used to investigate how matter, stars, and galaxies originally formed.

Physicists hope someday to find an explanation of all particles and their interactions that is even simpler than the standard model. They think the four basic forces of nature—gravity, electromagnetism, the strong nuclear force, and the weak nuclear force—may be different versions of one unified force that split apart as the universe evolved.

Cosmology

A third area of modern physics is cosmology, the study of the structure and evolution of the universe. The universe that scientists can observe today is far more vast than had ever been imagined. The stars visible in the night sky are just a fraction of the hundreds of billions of stars in our Milky Way galaxy, and the universe contains about a trillion other galaxies. Furthermore, the universe is not static, or unchanging, as scientists in the past assumed, but is thought to be expanding in all directions because of a cataclysmic explosion—the Big Bang—that scientists think occurred between 10 and 20 billion years ago. This is the view of contemporary cosmology: a universe that began with the explosion of an infinitesimally small, compact "particle" of matter, energy, space, and time, and has been expanding ever since.

Cosmologists are unsure of the universe's ultimate fate. Will the universe continue to expand forever? Or will the expansion someday reach a maximum, and will the universe then collapse in a "big crunch"? Most cosmologists today think that the answer may lie between these two extremes—that the universe will expand forever, but at an ever-decreasing rate. Proving this will depend on future discoveries in physics. If these discoveries force physicists to change their ideas, it will not be the first time.

ROGER S. JONES
Associate Professor of Physics
University of Minnesota
Author, *Physics for the Rest of Us*

See also ATOMS; ELECTRICITY; ENERGY; FISSION; FORCES; HEAT; LIGHT; MAGNETS AND MAGNETISM; MATTER; MOTION; NUCLEAR ENERGY; PHYSICS, HISTORY OF; RADIATION; RELATIVITY; SOUND AND ULTRASONICS; STARS; UNIVERSE.

PHYSICS, HISTORY OF

Physics is an old science. Its roots reach back about 2,600 years to when the Greek philosopher and mathematician Pythagoras discovered the mathematical rules of musical harmony. He found that the strings of a lyre, an ancient harp, were in tune when their lengths followed the ratios of simple whole numbers, such as 1:2 or 2:3. This discovery, that simple numerical ratios could explain the beauty of musical harmony, led Pythagoras to believe that the cosmos, or universe, was also governed by simple mathematical rules or natural laws that were themselves orderly and harmonious. This belief in the mathematical order of the cosmos has remained the guiding principle of physics to the present day.

▶ THE ANCIENT GREEKS

The Greek philosopher Plato expanded on the ideas of Pythagoras. Plato saw great order and harmony in the celestial realm of the stars and planets. The stars followed circles around the Earth in their nightly motions, thus demonstrating heavenly order to the Greeks who considered the circle to be the perfect geometrical form. Yet there were some objects in the sky—the sun, the moon, and the planets—that did not follow this orderly rule of circular motion. They lagged a little behind the stars every night; and now and then, the planets would even reverse direction and move ahead of the stars, only to return later to their normal motion. This reverse motion, called retrograde motion, disturbed Plato and his student Aristotle, who sought to find the perfect harmony of circular motion in the skies.

For 500 years after Aristotle, Greek astronomers tried to explain the apparent irregular motion of the planets in terms of perfect circular paths. The astronomer Ptolemy devised a complex system in which the planets moved on circles within circles, and this became the standard description of the motion of the planets for the next thousand years. Yet, as astronomical observations improved, it became clear that Ptolemy's system was not accurate.

▶ THE MODERN ERA OF PHYSICS

In 1543, *On the Revolutions of the Heavenly Spheres* by the Polish astronomer Nicolaus Copernicus was published in Europe.

Isaac Newton, known for his laws of gravity and motion, also made contributions to the science of optics. In a famous experiment, he guided sunlight through a glass prism, proving that ordinary white light is made up of many colors.

This book altered the course of history because it described a fundamental change Copernicus made in the celestial system devised by Aristotle and Ptolemy. In his book, Copernicus described a **heliocentric system** in which the sun (*helios* in Greek) rather than the Earth was at the center of the cosmos. According to Copernicus, the planets all revolve around the sun, and as the Earth moves around the sun, it passes and is passed by the other planets. This explained the reverse, or retrograde, motion of the planets as seen from the Earth. Copernicus, however, still assumed that the planets moved in circular orbits. As a result, his new heliocentric system still did not provide a completely accurate description of planetary motion.

In the early 1600's, the German astronomer Johannes Kepler spent many years studying the latest and most accurate data on planetary motion. Kepler realized that the orbit of the planet Mars could not possibly be a circle but, instead, was an oval curve called an ellipse. Based on this insight, Kepler devised three simple mathematical laws that ac-

Johannes Kepler spent many years formulating his three laws of planetary motion. Kepler also made important discoveries in optics and designed and built a new type of telescope.

curately described the orbits, orbital speeds, and times of revolution of all the planets. The stage was now set for the era of modern physics.

While Kepler was developing his laws of planetary motion, Galileo Galilei, an Italian astronomer, physicist, and mathematician, and René Descartes, a French philosopher and mathematician, had been studying motion in general. They realized that any material body free from other influences or forces has a natural tendency to move uniformly—that is, to move along a straight line at a constant speed. This **law of inertia** became the foundation of the laws of motion developed by the English scientist Isaac Newton.

Why do the planets move in elliptical orbits around the sun if their natural tendency, according to the law of inertia, is to move uniformly along straight lines? Newton realized that there must be a force of attraction acting between the sun and a planet that deflects the planet from its uniform path and bends it into a curved ellipse. Newton called this force of attraction the **force of gravity**. With this explanation for planetary motion, Newton devised a new method to explain motion in general. According to Newton, any material body departs from uniform motion if a force acts on it. In the case of the planets, their elliptical paths were caused by the universal force of gravity. But there is always some force—a push or pull, friction or air resistance, electrical attraction or repulsion—that causes the nonuniform motion of material bodies. Thus Newton's ideas became the basis for the science of **mechanics**, the study of the motion of objects as a result of forces acting on them. Mechanics became the basis of all of physics.

▶ INVESTIGATION OF MATTER AND ENERGY

As scientists began to understand the laws of motion, efforts were made to understand the nature and behavior of matter. The ancient Greeks were divided in their ideas about matter. Leucippus and Democritus believed that matter was "grainy," that it was made up of tiny indivisible particles called *atomos*. Aristotle, on the other hand, thought that matter was "smooth," or continuous. Aristotle's idea dominated scientific thinking about matter until the Renaissance.

In the 1500's and 1600's, new techniques of science were developed that involved careful observation and measurement and controlled experimentation. At that time, the Irish physicist Robert Boyle, the English chemist John Dalton, and the Italian scientist Amedeo Avogadro carefully weighed materials before and after they underwent a chemical reaction, and they observed how gases behaved when heated, cooled, and put under pressure. As a result of their separate studies, these scientists concluded that matter must be composed of tiny indivisible units, which we now call atoms.

Boyle discovered that as a gas is heated, its atoms move faster and faster, causing an increase in the temperature and pressure of the gas. This explanation of the behavior of a gas in terms of the motion of its atoms is known as the **kinetic theory of gases**. It was a remarkable new application of Isaac Newton's science of mechanics—this time applied to tiny atoms rather than to immense planets.

Included within kinetic theory was the idea that heat is a form of energy. Earlier, it had been thought that heat was a fluid contained within matter, and when matter was heated or burned, this fluid was released. But American scientist Benjamin Thompson and English physicist James Prescott Joule demonstrated in experiments that heat is

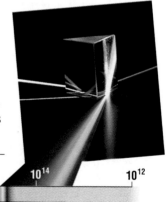

The Electromagnetic Spectrum

10^{24}	10^{22}	10^{20}	10^{18}	10^{16}	10^{14}	10^{12}
	Gamma rays		X rays	Ultraviolet	Visible light	Infrared

The electromagnetic spectrum includes all forms of electromagnetic radiation. Although they all travel through space as waves at the speed of light, each has its own frequency. Wave frequency values are shown here in hertz (cycles per second).

one of several forms of energy. Other forms of energy include electrical, chemical, and nuclear energy and the kinetic energy of motion. Through experimentation it was later demonstrated that these different forms of energy can be transformed into one another, but they can never be created or destroyed. This principle is known as the **conservation of energy**. It has been a cornerstone of physical science ever since it was stated clearly by the German physicist Hermann von Helmholtz in 1847.

The notion of atoms also reinforced evolving ideas about electricity and magnetism. The ancient Greeks were aware of the electrical and magnetic properties of certain materials, and early civilizations used magnetic compasses for navigation. Very little about these phenomena was understood, however, until the 1600's and 1700's. At that time, several people including English scientist Stephen Gray, American scientist and inventor Benjamin Franklin, French engineer and physicist Charles Augustin de Coulomb, and Italian physicist and chemist Allessandro Volta explored the basic properties and laws of electrical phenomena. They discovered that there are two kinds of electricity, or electrical charge—positive and negative. Both kinds exert attractive and repulsive forces. It was also found that metals are conductors of electricity—that is, they allow electrical charge to pass freely through them—while other nonmetallic minerals are insulators that block the flow of electric charge. These discoveries could be understood by assuming that electric charge was a property of the atoms contained in all matter. Chemical reactions also could be explained on the basis of the electrical attractions between atoms, which result in the formation of molecules.

▶ THE 1800'S

During the 1800's, ideas and theories about atoms were gradually improved and refined in an effort to explain the structure and behavior of matter. During this period, the mystery of light, which scientists had not yet explained, was also further clarified.

In ancient Greece, Pythagoras had thought that light consisted of particles emitted by shining objects. Aristotle believed that light was not a substance but a quality or action traveling through a medium. The Greeks also were able to apply some simple laws of light to their use of mirrors and lenses, which were very crude at that time.

In the 1600's, Isaac Newton demonstrated that when white light passes through a glass prism, it is separated into different colors to form a spectrum. Newton thought that this dispersion of light, as well as the transmission of light, could be explained by assuming that light consisted of particles. Other scientists, such as Dutch physicist Christiaan Huygens, believed that light was a wave similar to water waves on a lake or sound waves in the air. But Newton's great authority and prestige influenced many to accept his particle theory of light.

In the 1800's, scientific thinking began to turn against the particle theory of light. English physicist Thomas Young investigated the interference of light, in which two light beams cancel each other to produce darkness. Young explained this phenomena by assuming that light consists of waves rather than particles. Augustin Fresnel, a French physicist, also developed a wave theory of light to explain many optical phenomena.

Finally, in 1865, Scottish physicist James Clerk Maxwell developed his comprehensive theory of electromagnetism, proving that light was a wave. As Newton had done with mechanics and gravity 200 years earlier, Maxwell provided a unified explanation of all known electric and magnetic phenomena. But Maxwell went much further. He predicted the existence of electromagnetic waves traveling through space. Most remarkable of all was his discovery that these waves travel at the speed of light, thus demonstrating convincingly that light was a wave. In fact, light is only one of various electromagnetic waves. Others include radio, television, microwaves, radar, infrared, ultraviolet, X rays, and gamma rays. In 1886, German physicist Heinrich Hertz was able to demonstrate the existence

10^{12}	10^{10}	10^8	10^6	10^4	10^2	1

| Infrared | Microwave | Radar | TV FM | Short wave | AM | Long wave | Induction heating | AC power |

Biographies of the following physicists and scientists who played important roles in the history of physics are included elsewhere in *The New Book of Knowledge*: Antoine Henri Becquerel, Niels Bohr, Robert Boyle, Marie and Pierre Curie, Albert Einstein, Michael Faraday, Enrico Fermi, Galileo Galilei, Robert Goddard, Robert Hooke, Robert Milliken, Isaac Newton, Ernest Rutherford, and Benjamin Thompson.

Richard P. Feynman

Maria Goeppert-Mayer

Richard P. Feynman (1918–88), born in New York City, received the Nobel Prize in 1965 for work leading to the development of the theory of quantum elec-

trodynamics, the fundamental theory of electromagnetic radiation. He introduced Feynman diagrams — symbolic graphics that greatly simplify our understanding of the complicated interactions between charged particles and the electromagnetic field. During World War II,

Feynman worked on the Manhattan Project, which developed the atomic bomb. A great teacher, Feynman was very popular with his students, and his introductory physics textbook has become a classic. Feynman also helped discover that a frozen gasket was responsible for the tragic disaster of the space shuttle *Challenger*.

Maria Goeppert-Mayer (1906–72) was born in Kattowitz, Germany (now Katowice, Poland), and migrated to America in 1930. After arriving in America, her husband, Joseph Mayer, was hired as a professor of chemistry at Johns Hopkins University. The university did not offer her a position, however, since she was a woman. Nevertheless, Goeppert-Mayer did research in nuclear physics while raising a family. In 1940, she became an associate professor without pay at the University of Chicago. Goeppert-Mayer developed a theory of nuclear structure in terms of shells, or levels, occupied by the neutrons and protons in the atomic

---

of Maxwell's electromagnetic waves, making possible the electronics and telecommunication of the 20th century.

In the late 1800's, it seemed as though there was nothing new to be learned in physics and that no new discoveries would be made. Newton's science of mechanics, together with the new theories of heat and energy, explained the motion of atoms as well as of planets. The atomic theory of matter described the behavior of gases, and the electrical properties of atoms explained chemical reactions. Maxwell's theory of electromagnetism explained not only electricity and magnetism but also light. What was there left to do? It was time for engineers and technicians to work out marvelous applications based on what was known.

Nothing, however, could have been further from the truth. Toward the end of the 1800's, several significant discoveries occurred that challenged what physicists already knew. In 1887, Hertz would discover the photoelectric effect. In 1895, German physicist William Röntgen would detect X rays, and in 1897, J. J. Thomson, an English physicist, would discover electrons. Polish chemist Marie Curie would isolate radium in 1898. In 1900, German physicist Max Planck would apply a new

concept, called quantization, to explain radiation, and in 1905, another German physicist, Albert Einstein, would propose a new particle theory of light and would also introduce the theory of relativity. Physics was on a new threshold.

▶ **PHYSICS IN THE 1900'S**

During the first three decades of the 1900's, the physics of Newton, which had dominated the study of physics for more than 200 years, was upset by two revolutionary ideas—relativity and quantum theory—and by new thinking in the field of cosmology.

Relativity

In 1905 Einstein published a paper on the **special theory of relativity** in which he developed completely new ideas about space and time. He proposed that space and time are relative—that their measurement depends on the observer's frame of reference. Ten years later, he introduced his **general theory of relativity**, which enlarged his original theory to include gravity. In this second theory, Einstein demonstrated that space and time were warped and bent as well as relative. He replaced Newton's idea of a gravitational field with the idea of curved space to explain

nucleus. She was able to explain the great stability of certain nuclei, which had a specific "magic number" of both neutrons and protons. Goeppert-Mayer received the Nobel Prize in 1963 for her work.

James Clerk Maxwell (1831–79), born in Edinburgh, Scotland, showed great mathematical talent at an early age. After graduating from Cambridge University, he studied the rings of Saturn and showed that they could not be solid, but must consist of countless small bodies called planetoids forming a belt around the planet. Maxwell developed the kinetic theory of gases, which explained changes in the temperature and pressure of a gas by applying statistical methods to the motion of the gas molecules. During the 1860's, while at King's College in London, Maxwell developed the equations that completely summarized all electromagnetic phenomena and predicted the existence of electromagnetic waves traveling at the speed of light. Maxwell

James Clerk Maxwell

thus demonstrated the electromagnetic nature of light.

Max Planck (1858–1947) was born in Kiel, Germany. Although thoroughly trained in the classical physics of Isaac Newton and other early physicists, Planck went on to revolutionize the field with his quantum theory of

Max Planck

radiation. Planck and other scientists wondered why an iron poker changes in color from red to yellow to white when it is heated in a fire. Earlier theories could not explain the spectrum, or color, of this light radiation. By assuming that energy could be absorbed and emitted only in quantized, or discrete (separate and distinct) amounts, Planck was able to derive the correct spectrum. In the process, he initiated the quantum era in physics. Planck's quantization became the basis for Albert Einstein's idea of photons to explain the photoelectric effect and for Niels Bohr's atomic model. Planck won the Nobel Prize in 1918 for his contribution to quantum theory.

---

the curved motion of the planets. Furthermore, his idea of relativity correctly predicted other astronomical effects that could not be explained by Newton's theory of gravity.

Quantum Theory

As the idea of relativity was developing, a new theory of matter was evolving as well. This new theory became known as the **quantum theory of matter**.

In 1900, German physicist Max Planck developed a new concept to explain radiation called quantization. Einstein then proposed that radiant energy such as light is released in small bursts, which were later called **quanta**, and not in a smooth, or continuous, stream as was previously thought. Einstein applied the idea of quantization to light in order to explain the **photoelectric effect**, in which electrons are released from the surface of a metal that is illuminated by ultraviolet light. Einstein assumed that light was quantized into tiny discrete (separate and distinct) bundles of energy or particles called **photons**. This

idea reopened the debate over whether light was a wave or a particle. We now know that light exhibits both characteristics—sometimes acting like waves, sometimes like particles.

Danish physicist Niels Bohr applied quantum ideas to the atom in 1913. When atoms

The theories of Nobel Laureates Albert Einstein and Niels Bohr contributed to the revolutionary thinking in physics that led to new paths of investigation and discovery at the beginning of the 1900's.

Erwin Schrödinger (1887–1961), born in Vienna, Austria, was one of the creators of the fully developed mathematical quantum theory. In 1926, Schrödinger applied the idea of electron waves, first developed by French physicist Louis-Victor de Broglie, to Niels Bohr's model of the hydrogen atom. He developed a

Erwin Schrödinger

wave equation that treats electrons in the atom like standing wave patterns rather than orbiting particles. The standing electron waves can resonate only at certain quantized frequencies or energies, like the waves on a guitar string. Schrödinger thus was able to explain the quantized nature of the atom and of atomic spectra naturally, without requir-

ing an arbitrary quantum hypothesis. Schrödinger was awarded the Nobel Prize in 1933 for his work in wave mechanics.

Sir Joseph John Thomson (1856–1940), born in Cheetham, England, is regarded as one of the pioneers of atomic physics. In 1884, Thomson became head of the illustrious Cavendish laboratory at Cambridge University, where he trained a whole generation of physicists in applying the new quantum ideas to matter and radiation. Thomson was the first scientist to identify the electron as a tiny charged particle circling the nucleus of the atom. By identifying a basic component of the atom, Thomson inaugurated a revolution in physics and opened the field of subatomic physics. He also helped to develop Maxwell's mathematical theory

Sir Joseph John Thomson

of electricity and magnetism and did pioneering work on the electrical conductivity of gases. In 1906, Thomson received the Nobel Prize for his work with electrons. Seven of his assistants went on to receive Nobel Prizes of their own.

---

are stimulated by electrical energy or heat, they emit spectra of light called atomic spectra. But an atomic spectrum is not a continuous band of colors like the spectrum of white light. Instead, atomic spectra consist of distinct color lines. Bohr explained this by assuming that electrons in the atom could have

only certain specific quantized energies. When an excited electron drops from a high energy state into a lower one, the difference in energy is emitted in the form of a photon of light. Since the energies of each electron state have quantized, or separate and distinct, values, the energy differences are also quantized, and so are the frequencies of the light which determine their colors. Thus only certain specific color lines appear in the atomic spectra.

In 1923, French physicist Louis-Victor de Broglie argued that if light could sometimes act like a particle, then perhaps an electron could sometimes act like a wave. When this conjecture was verified, it became apparent that the concept of quantization was essential to any theory of matter and motion. A new mathematical theory known as quantum mechanics was developed by the work of several physicists, including Austrians Erwin Schrödinger and Wolfgang Pauli, Germans Werner Heisenberg and Max Born, and Englishman Paul Dirac. Quantum mechanics,

In the Linear Accelerator at Stanford University, high-energy electrons streak along a 2-mile-long tube at close to the speed of light, then collide with other elementary particles. Physicists study the effects of these collisions to learn more about the structure of matter.

which replaced classical mechanics, has since remained the principle theory of matter and motion and has led to many remarkable discoveries such as the laser and the microchip.

Elementary Particle Physics and Cosmology

In 1932, British physicist James Chadwick discovered the neutron, a particle in the nucleus of an atom. This discovery was an important step in the study of elementary particle physics, which explores the components of the atomic nucleus. Probing nuclei and their subparticles at ever-higher energies in particle accelerators has been one of the main areas of physics research in the 1900's. This high-energy research has resulted in the development of what is called the **standard model**, an explanation of atomic and subatomic particles and their interactions. According to the standard model, elementary particles known as **quarks** and **leptons** are assumed to be the simplest and most basic components of all other atomic and nuclear particles.

The standard model has given rise to new theories of unification, in which physicists attempt to combine the four basic forces of nature—gravity, electromagnetism, the strong nuclear force, and the weak nuclear force—into one unified force.

Research in elementary particle physics is closely tied to the latest theories in cosmology, the study of the origin, structure, and evolution of the universe. In the 1920's, American astronomer Edwin Hubble and others discovered that the universe was expanding. They determined that there were great galaxies far beyond our own Milky Way galaxy and that these other galaxies were moving away from the Milky Way at great speeds.

If the universe is growing larger, then it must have been smaller in the past. This idea led to the **big bang theory**, which assumes that the universe originated in a great cosmic explosion some 10 or 20 billion years ago. Originally proposed by American physicist George Gamow in the 1940's, the big bang theory has since been refined and strengthened by astronomical observations.

As the universe expands, it is also cooling. The cooling of the expanding universe is a crucial concept for understanding how matter

The movements of spiral galaxies such as these beyond the constellation Fornax have led astrophysicists to conclude that there is more mass in the universe than has been seen. Sometimes called "missing mass" or "dark matter," it may represent most of the total mass in the universe.

and energy evolved and ultimately produced the stars and galaxies. In the earliest instants after the big bang, the cosmos was so hot and active that only the most exotic forms of matter could exist. This was presumably the era of quarks and the unified force. As the universe cooled, the individual forces of nature and the more familiar particles of matter separated out and began to interact, ultimately forming galaxies and stars. Today some physicists think that we may be getting close to a "theory of everything" that will explain all the forces of nature and everything about matter and energy. Whether this represents another "end" of physics or a new beginning is a matter for scientists of the 21st century to decide.

ROGER S. JONES
Associate Professor of Physics
University of Minnesota
Author, *Physics for the Rest of Us*

See also ATOMS; ENERGY; FORCES; MATTER; MOTION; PHYSICS; RADIATION; RELATIVITY; STARS; UNIVERSE.

PHYSIOLOGY. See BODY, HUMAN.

PI. See GEOMETRY.

Concert grand piano made by Steinway & Sons.

PIANO

The piano is a stringed keyboard instrument whose strings are struck by felt-covered hammers. "Piano" is short for "pianoforte," which comes from the Italian words *piano* ("soft") and *forte* ("loud"). The piano's wide tonal range, from very soft to very loud, is one of its most important features.

Piano Action

The tone of any stringed keyboard instrument is determined by its **action**, the mechanism that makes the strings vibrate. Strings are made to vibrate by being plucked or struck.

The piano has a hammer action. The hammers are attached to the keys by levers. When a key is pressed down, its hammer jumps up and strikes a string. The string needs freedom to vibrate and also needs dampers to stop the vibrations. Therefore, dampers made of felt rest on the strings. When a key is pressed, the damper rises to free the string. The hammer strikes and falls back into position. When the key is released,

the damper falls back onto the string and stops the sound. Most of the notes have two strings. The highest notes have three strings, and a few of the very lowest notes have only one. (The highest notes have the shortest strings and therefore need additional strings for resonance.)

All the dampers may be raised off the strings by pressing down the piano's sustaining pedal. As long as this pedal is held down, all

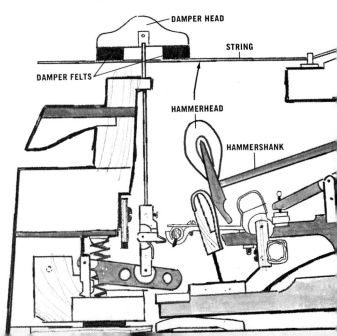

the notes played will continue to sound. The abbreviation "ped." is used in piano music to indicate the use of the sustaining pedal.

The piano also has a soft pedal. When it is pressed down, the keyboard and hammers move to one side so that only one string (or sometimes two) is struck by each hammer. This makes the sound softer. *Una corda,* meaning "one string," is an Italian term used in piano music to indicate the soft pedal.

Most modern pianos have a third pedal between the sustaining and soft pedals. Called the sostenuto pedal, it is another type of sustaining pedal. Instead of holding all the notes, it lets the player sustain only certain notes he wishes held. It is used for special effects, such as sustaining bass notes while other notes are played.

Construction

The essential parts of the piano are the frame, soundboard, strings, and action. The frame is made of iron or steel in order to withstand the enormous pulling force of the strings. The soundboard is a sheet of wood set into the frame. The strings, made of steel wire, are stretched over the soundboard and fastened to the frame. The soundboard serves as a resonator to amplify the sound. The frame, soundboard, and keyboard are attached to a strong wooden case.

The standard number of keys for the piano is 88. They are made of wood. The white keys are covered with ivory, and the black keys with ebony. Today ivory is being replaced more and more by plastic.

Temperature and humidity affect the tuning of the piano. A piano should never be placed directly in front of a radiator or other heating device. In climates where each season brings an extreme change in temperature and humidity, the piano should be tuned when the seasons change. Piano tuners, who acquire their art by long practice, are needed to adjust the tuning.

▶ HISTORY OF THE PIANO

The earliest known piano was built in 1709 by Bartolommeo Cristofori (1655–1731), a maker of harpsichords for Prince Ferdinand de' Medici in Florence, Italy. A harpsichord is a stringed keyboard instrument whose strings are plucked by quills or leather points. In place of the plucking quills, Cristofori put small hammers that struck the strings from below. He called the new instrument a harpsichord with *piano e forte*. Its advantage over the harpsichord was that the player could control the loudness of each note. The harder a key was struck, the harder the hammer hit the string and the louder the sound. Even so, the first pianos had a weak and fragile sound. To produce a louder, richer sound, the strings were made thicker, giving the string greater strength to take the stroke of the hammer.

About 1730 Gottfried Silbermann (1683–1753) built the first pianos in Germany. In 1747 Johann Sebastian Bach played a Silbermann piano at the palace of Frederick the Great and praised the instrument. Johann Andreas Stein (1728–92) was the first great piano maker in Vienna. Wolfgang Amadeus Mozart played a Stein piano in 1777. After 1794 Johann Andreas Streicher (1761–

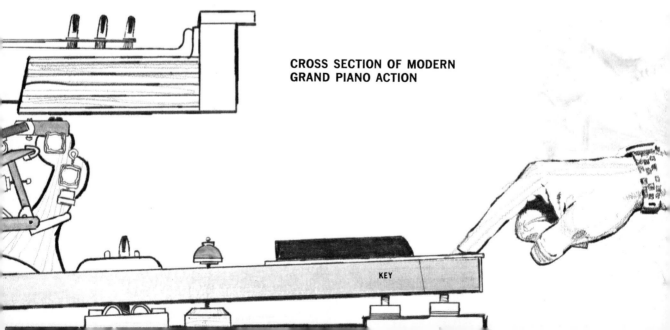

CROSS SECTION OF MODERN GRAND PIANO ACTION

KEY

The spinet, a modern type of upright piano, is used in many homes.

1833), Stein's son-in-law, succeeded Stein as the leading Viennese piano builder.

The earliest pianos were wing-shaped, like the larger harpsichords. The first known upright piano was made by Christian Friederici, a pupil of Silbermann's, in Gera, a city in Saxony. The first square piano dates from about 1760. It was made by Johannes Zumpe, a German living in England.

Americus Backers, a London instrument maker, and Robert Stodart, a young apprentice working for the London firm of John Broadwood (1732–1812), developed the action for the first grand pianos. It was patented in 1776. Broadwood invented sustaining and soft pedals for the piano in 1783.

The frames of early pianos were usually made of wood. As the strings became thicker, their pulling force became too great for the wooden frames. After about 1788 the frames were reinforced with bars of iron or steel. Metal was used very cautiously in piano building until 1827, when metal frames were adopted by Broadwood.

The United States led in the development of an iron or steel frame cast in a single piece. In 1825 Alpheus Babcock of Boston patented a cast-iron frame for a square piano. Jonas Chickering (1798–1853) of Boston improved the single casting in 1827.

In 1855 Steinway and Sons of New York City and Hamburg, Germany, produced a grand piano that became the model for the best piano makers. In 1881 Mason and Hamlin, organ builders of Boston, made their first pianos. They later became the Steinways' closest rivals. Other great piano makers of the 19th and 20th centuries include Blüthner and Bechstein in Germany, Bösendorfer in Vienna, and Pleyel and Gaveau in Paris.

Piano Virtuosos

During the 1830's and 1840's, piano virtuosos (artists) took Europe by storm. Franz Liszt was one of the first to be idolized. Others were Frédéric Chopin, Sigismond Thalberg (1812–71), and Louis Gottschalk (1829–69).

During the 1850's the virtuosos began to show more concern for the interpretation of the music than for the display of technical ability. Clara Schumann (1819–96), the wife of Robert Schumann, led the way. Anton Rubinstein (1829–94), Hans von Bülow (1830–94), and Ferrucio Busoni (1866–1924) soon followed.

Great 20th-century pianists include Sergei Rachmaninoff (1873–1943), Josef Hofmann (1876–1957), Artur Schnabel (1882–1951), Wilhelm Backhaus (1884–1969), Artur Rubinstein (1889–1982), Dame Myra Hess (1890–1965), Walter Gieseking (1895–1956), Robert Casadesus (1899–1972), Rudolf Serkin (1903–   ), Vladimir Horowitz (1904–   ), Sviatoslav Richter (1914–   ), Emil Gilels (1916–   ), Van Cliburn (1934–   ), Daniel Barenboim (1942–   ), and André Watts (1946–   ).

Composers for the Piano

The first great composer for the piano was Mozart. Since Mozart's time, the most important composers for the piano have been Ludwig van Beethoven, Franz Schubert, Chopin, Liszt, Schumann, Peter Ilyich Tchaikovsky, and Claude Debussy. Outstanding 20th-century composers for the piano include Alexander Scriabin, Sergei Prokofiev, Rachmaninoff, Béla Bartók, Igor Stravinsky, Arnold Schoenberg, and Aaron Copland.

ROSALYN TURECK
Concert pianist; author, *Introduction to the Performance of Bach*

See also KEYBOARD INSTRUMENTS.

PICASSO, PABLO (1881–1973)

Pablo Ruiz y Picasso—the most famous artist of the 20th century—was born on October 25, 1881, in Málaga, Spain. When Pablo was very young, his family moved to Barcelona. At an early age Picasso showed great talent. He especially liked to paint pictures of the city life around him. In 1896 he entered the School of Fine Arts, where his father was a professor.

Around the turn of the century, Paris was the world center of art and literature. Picasso visited the city in 1900 and fell under the spell of the artistic atmosphere. He returned a year later, and he settled on the Left Bank in 1904. He was very poor, but his studio became a meeting place for many artists, writers, and composers.

In Paris, Picasso still painted scenes of the day-to-day life of poor people in his neighborhood. He was also fascinated by circus life and painted a series of circus pictures. Early in the century his works were painted in varieties of gray-blues. The figures were long, thin, and sad. These paintings belong to what is called Picasso's blue period.

Like many other young artists in Paris at that time, Picasso was influenced by the work of Paul Cézanne. Cézanne had tried to show

Picasso's cubist *Three Musicians* (1921). Can you see the fourth head? It is imposed on the central figure.

the geometric forms that he saw in nature. Picasso and his friend the painter Georges Braque attempted to portray the many different geometric planes of an object all at once. For example, they might paint a full face with one eye and with the nose in profile (a side view). This style became known as **cubism** because in the paintings objects were composed of geometric forms such as cubes and cones. Picasso and Braque were also among the first to make **collages** by pasting various scraps of materials onto flat surfaces.

In 1917, Picasso went to Rome to design scenery and costumes for the Russian Ballet's production of *Parade*. He married Olga Koklova, one of the ballerinas, and they had a son, Paulo. Picasso did not care for the social world in which he found himself. But Olga enjoyed it. He became unhappy, and the distorted, sad figures in his paintings of this period reflect his unhappiness.

Civil war broke out in Spain in 1936. The following year, the ancient city of Guernica was destroyed by bombs. Picasso was enraged at this inhuman act. All his bitterness was released in his brilliant mural *Guernica*. Picasso worked at such a furious pace that the mural was completed within a few weeks and was shown at the Paris Exhibition in 1937.

Child with a Dove (1901) belongs to Picasso's blue period. During this time, his works were painted in gray-blues.

The mural shows the terrified people of the town, their mouths open wide in screams. Images from bullfighting are used to symbolize the brutality of war. While some artists might have painted the scene in bloody reds and other vivid colors, Picasso painted *Guernica* entirely in black, white, and shades of gray.

During World War II, Picasso lived in Paris, which was at that time under Nazi occupation. Because the Nazis did not approve of modern art, Picasso had to hide his paintings in a secret vault in the Bank of France. His work during this period included a play, *Desire Caught by the Tail* (1941).

After the war Picasso moved to a huge house in the south of France. There he continued to experiment with painting as well as sculpture, printmaking, ceramics, and collage. In 1958 he painted a large mural for a United Nations building in Paris. His marriage to Jacqueline Roque, a Frenchwoman,

took place in 1961. In 1962, he was awarded the Lenin peace prize.

Picasso's moods were known to change as often as his styles. He was thoughtful and distant at times, but he also displayed a fine sense of humor. His art was extremely valuable even in his own lifetime because of the great variety of his styles. He used elements from the work of Toulouse-Lautrec, the ancient Greeks, El Greco, and African sculptors. The large number of his fine works during any one period would have satisfied another artist. But Picasso never stopped experimenting. His great imagination and outstanding skill earned for him the name El Maestro ("the master") of modern art.

Picasso died at his home in southern France on April 8, 1973, at the age of 91.

Reviewed by ARIANE RUSKIN BATTERBERRY
Author, *The Pantheon Story of Art for Young People*

PICCARD, AUGUSTE (1884–1962)

Auguste Piccard was a Swiss scientist, inventor, and explorer. He is famous for his work in exploring both the high atmosphere and the ocean depths.

Piccard was born in Basel, Switzerland, on January 28, 1884. He attended the Swiss Institute of Technology in Zurich, where he obtained a degree in mechanical engineering and a doctorate in natural science.

In 1913 Piccard made a balloon trip with his twin brother, Jean, who later became a famous aeronautical engineer. For 16 hours they drifted across Germany and France, taking measurements of the atmosphere.

Piccard married Marianne Denis, and they had five children. In 1922 he became a professor at the University of Brussels, Belgium.

One of Piccard's early inventions was an airtight aluminum cabin, called a gondola, that was attached to a balloon. On May 27, 1931, Piccard ascended to a height of nearly 10 miles (more than 15 kilometers), into that part of the atmosphere called the stratosphere. Piccard had made 28 balloon flights into the stratosphere by 1937. He then began to concentrate on inventing a vehicle that would take him to great depths in the ocean.

Piccard designed an underwater ship called a bathyscaphe ("deep ship") in 1946. Seven years later, he and his son, Jacques, also a deep-sea explorer, descended in a bathyscaphe to a depth of 2 miles (3 kilometers) beneath the sea's surface. In 1960 Jacques Piccard and Lieutenant Don Walsh of the U.S. Navy descended nearly 7 miles (11 kilometers) under the surface of the Pacific Ocean in the bathyscaphe *Trieste*. This set a world record as the greatest depth reached in a deep-sea diving machine.

Auguste Piccard ascended higher into the air and descended deeper into the sea than any person before him. His studies of cosmic rays and electricity in the atmosphere helped in the planning of spaceflights in later years. His bathyscaphe made deep-sea exploration and research possible.

Piccard remained an active inventor until his death at the age of 78. He died in Lausanne, Switzerland, on March 24, 1962.

DUANE H. D. ROLLER
University of Oklahoma

PICKFORD, MARY. See MOTION PICTURES (Profiles: Movie Stars).

PICNICS. See OUTDOOR COOKING AND PICNICS.

FRANKLIN PIERCE (1804–1869)

14TH PRESIDENT OF THE UNITED STATES

PIERCE, FRANKLIN. When Franklin Pierce was inaugurated president of the United States in 1853, he was 48 years old. Young Hickory of the Granite Hills, as he was called (Andrew Jackson was called Old Hickory), had been a general in the Mexican War, a successful lawyer, a congressman, and a senator. As president he was faced with a crisis over slavery that brought on a war in Kansas and gave the territory the name "bleeding Kansas."

▶ EARLY YEARS

Pierce was born in a log cabin in Hillsborough County, New Hampshire, on November 23, 1804. He was one of the eight children born to Benjamin and Anna Kendrick Pierce. Benjamin Pierce was a rough frontier farmer. He had served during the Revolutionary War, became a general of the state militia, and was twice elected governor of New Hampshire. As a boy Franklin Pierce heard so much about the military exploits of his father in the Revolutionary War and of his older brother in the War of 1812 that at first he wanted to become a soldier.

Pierce attended school at Hillsborough Center and later went to Hancock Academy. Disliking the stern discipline there, he ran away from school and came home. His father surprised him by saying nothing about his truancy. But after lunch he hitched up the carriage and told young Frank to get in. Halfway back to Hancock his father told him to jump out and walk to school. He had to hike the rest of the way in a rainstorm. Later, Pierce wrote that this lesson in discipline marked a turning point in his life.

In 1820 Pierce entered Bowdoin College in Brunswick, Maine. There he began a lifelong friendship with one of his classmates, Nathaniel Hawthorne, who was later to become a famous author. Pierce's carefree and irresponsible attitude toward his studies soon carried him to the bottom of his class, though he became a favorite among the students. However, after applying himself to his studies, he graduated fifth from the top of his class in 1824. He then studied law and in 1827 was admitted to the bar.

That same year his father became governor of New Hampshire. Pierce now began to take an active part in state politics as a member of the Jacksonian (later the Democratic) Party. He entered the state legislature in 1829. In 1833 he was elected to Congress. He remained in Congress for 4 years, loyally supporting President Andrew Jackson's political program. In 1837 New Hampshire sent Pierce to the United States Senate. At the age of 33 he was the youngest member of the Senate.

Jane Pierce

On November 19, 1834, Pierce married Jane Means Appleton (1806–63), daughter of a former president of Bowdoin College. The Appletons, an aristocratic New England family, did not approve of Jane's match with the young Democrat from the backcountry. Mrs. Pierce found life in Washington, D.C., so distasteful that her husband agreed to abandon his political career. He resigned his Senate seat in 1842 and returned to Concord to practice law.

The early years of the Pierces' marriage were saddened by the loss of two of their three sons. Franklin, Jr., the first child, lived only a few days after his birth. The second son, Frank R., died at the age of 4. Only Benjamin, the youngest, born in 1841, was left to them.

The Mexican War

When the Mexican War broke out in 1846, Pierce enlisted as a private in the Concord Light Infantry. He was soon appointed a colonel and then a brigadier general of volunteers. In June, 1847, he arrived in Mexico and led his 2,500 men inland. At the battle of Churubusco, Pierce suffered a painful leg injury when his horse reared and fell. The next day, while again advancing into battle, he wrenched the injured leg so sharply that he fainted from the pain and was unable to take an active part in the fighting. In later years his political enemies twisted this incident into a charge that he had been cowardly under fire.

Pierce remained in the field until the capture of Mexico City in September, 1847. Then he returned to his law practice at Concord.

Presidential Candidate

In the years that followed, Pierce's friendliness, kindness, and concern for people gained him increasing political popularity. His growing law practice brought him wealth. And his military career, though rather frustrating to him because of his accident on the Churubusco battlefield, had made him a local hero.

Thus, in 1851 many New England Democrats turned to Pierce as a presidential prospect. Few expected that he could be nominated. But some thought that he might have a chance if the Democratic convention came to a deadlock between the more prominent leaders—Lewis Cass, William L. Marcy, Stephen A. Douglas, and James Buchanan. When such a deadlock did arise, Pierce's friends introduced his name, and the tired delegates nominated him on the 49th ballot. William R. D. King (1786–1853) of Alabama became Pierce's running mate. Mrs. Pierce, horrified that she might have to return to Washington, fainted upon hearing the news. Pierce's son, Benjamin, now 11 years old, said: "I hope he won't be elected."

In the campaign of 1852 Pierce ran against his former army commander, General Winfield Scott, the Whig Party candidate. Pierce promised, if elected, to respect the rights of the states and to conduct a vigorous foreign policy. His friendliness, simplicity, and ease in meeting people gained him many votes. He had the knack of remembering the name and face of nearly everyone he met. But his desire to please led him to make promises he could not always fulfill.

Pierce as a brigadier general in the Mexican War.

Jane Appleton Pierce.

PRESIDENT

Pierce won the election, carrying all but four states. He received 1,601,117 popular votes to 1,385,453 for Scott and 254 electoral votes to Scott's 42.

But a personal tragedy soon dimmed Pierce's joy over his victory. On January 6, 1853, during a family trip, the Pierces were in a train wreck. President-elect and Mrs. Pierce were uninjured, but Benjamin was killed. It was a terrible blow to the parents. Mrs. Pierce, completely overcome, lived in seclusion at the White House. She came to believe that her son's life had been the price of her husband's victory. Pierce had to bear his wife's bitter accusations, as well as his own grief, at the very moment when he most needed strength and confidence.

Pierce invited into his Cabinet well-meaning men without much experience. The only prominent Democrats to serve were William L. Marcy (1786–1857), as secretary of state, and Jefferson Davis, as secretary of war. These men held different political views, and people predicted that the Cabinet would soon break up. But Pierce's Cabinet proved to be the first in U.S. history to remain unchanged throughout an entire 4-year term.

The Kansas-Nebraska Bill

Pierce's term was marked by bitter debate over the expansion of slavery. His hopes to quiet this debate received a setback when the Kansas-Nebraska bill was introduced in January, 1854. The bill proposed to create two new territories, Kansas and Nebraska, and to allow settlers there to decide whether or not to allow slavery. Pierce was not enthusiastic. But he promised to support the bill in return for Senate support of his political appointments and foreign policy. The bill brought on a violent debate about slavery. The prospect of slavery in Kansas split the Democratic Party into Northern and Southern wings and gave birth to the Republican Party. The bill became law later in 1854, and supporters and opponents of slavery rushed to Kansas. They fought for control of the territory throughout Pierce's administration.

Foreign Affairs

In 1853, Pierce acquired from Mexico the region known as the Gadsden Purchase. This

---

IMPORTANT DATES IN THE LIFE OF FRANKLIN PIERCE

1804	Born in Hillsborough County, New Hampshire, November 23.
1824	Graduated from Bowdoin College.
1827	Admitted to the bar.
1829–1833	Member of New Hampshire legislature.
1834	Married Jane Means Appleton.
1833–1837	Served in United States House of Representatives.
1837–1842	United States senator.
1847	Brigadier general of volunteers in Mexican War.
1853–1857	14th president of the United States.
1869	Died at Concord, New Hampshire, October 8.

---

included parts of present-day Arizona and New Mexico. This following year he signed a treaty with Britain by which the United States gave trade privileges to Canada in exchange for certain fishing rights.

Pierce hoped that the United States would acquire Cuba from Spain. He told the U.S. ministers in Europe to draft a plan for obtaining the island. Their proposal was called the Ostend Manifesto, after the city in Belgium where they met. The ministers recommended purchasing Cuba but hinted that if Spain refused to sell, the United States might be justified in seizing the island.

The premature publication of the manifesto caused an uproar. Northerners objected strongly to adding any new slave territory. And Spain was insulted and refused to sell the island. Pierce later tried to acquire Hawaii and Alaska, also without success.

The most far-reaching diplomatic event of Pierce's term was the opening of Japan to Western trade. In 1853 a U.S. naval squadron under Commodore Matthew C. Perry arrived in Japan. The Treaty of Kanagawa, signed in 1854, opened two Japanese ports to U.S. ships. Treaties between Japan and other Western nations soon followed.

Pierce hoped for renomination in 1856. But largely because of the difficulties in Kansas, the Democrats instead chose James Buchanan. After leaving the White House, the Pierces toured Europe. Franklin Pierce died in Concord on October 8, 1869. He is buried there.

PHILIP S. KLEIN
Author, *President James Buchanan,
A Biography*

See also KANSAS-NEBRASKA ACT.
PIGMENTS. See PAINTS AND PIGMENTS.

A sow with baby pigs.

PIGS

A pig has a snout for a nose. Its eyes are small, and its tail is a little corkscrew. Its voice is either a grunt or a squeal. It has a thick body and short, rather thin legs. There are four toes on each foot. But only the longer, middle two are used in walking.

The pig has only a few thin bristles on its skin, instead of a thick coat of hair. It likes to wallow in mud. This keeps flies off and helps it to stay cool.

The pig's snout is long and tapered. It ends in a flat, leathery disk. The pig pushes the disk of its nose along the ground like a little plow, to dig up roots.

People have been raising pigs for as long as 5,000 years, but many kinds of pigs also live in the wild. The farm pig is raised in many countries for pork, ham, bacon, sausage, and lard. The male farm pig is called a **boar,** and the female a **sow**. In North America pigs are kept in pens or special houses and are fed corn, other grains, and specially prepared feed. They do not often need their plowing nose. The nose comes from their ancestors of millions of years ago. The ancestors of pigs had to root out tough plants that grew in swamps and along rivers. These ancestors were animals like the wild pigs of today that are called **wild boars**.

A pig eats almost anything. It eats roots and weeds, grass and grasshoppers, snails, mice, and lizards. It will also eat meat and bones, although pigs seldom kill for food.

Pigs belong to the **swine family**. They are also called **hogs**. Wild pigs also belong to the swine family. Some wild pigs are the wild boar, the warthog, the forest hog, the river hog, and the babirusa. The nearest relatives of the swine family are the peccaries and hippopotamuses.

Wild pigs are quite different from tame pigs. The wild boar of Europe and Asia is fast and fierce. When it is cornered, the wild boar is dangerous. It defends itself with long tusks that curve up from both the upper and lower jaws. The wild boar was once fairly common and was often hunted. Now it has disappeared in many areas. But it can still be found in various forested regions of Europe and Asia.

Some wild boars live in North America. They were brought in from other countries and turned loose for hunting. They live wild in the Great Smoky Mountains of Tennessee and North Carolina.

There are three kinds of African wild hogs. The giant forest hog lives in the forests. The bushpig, or river hog, lives in the jungle, too, but around water. It has long, pointed ears that end in tufts of hair.

The African warthog lives on the open plains of Africa along with antelopes and zebras. It has a mane of coarse hair, but the rest of its body is nearly naked. It has a gristly growth, or wart, the size of a golf ball, under each eye. Tusks grow out of its upper jaw, like the horns growing out of a cow's head. The warthog is often seen in zoos. It and other members of the pig family may live 15 years or so in captivity.

The babirusa of the East Indies is another unusual-looking wild pig. The male babirusa's upper tusks grow out of the snout and sweep backward in a curve. The babirusa is a good swimmer.

The only piglike animals native to the Americas are the peccaries. But peccaries are not true pigs. They are placed in a separate family.

Reviewed by Robert M. McClung
Author, science books for children

See also Hoofed Mammals.

PILGRIMS. See Thirteen American Colonies; Mayflower; Plymouth Colony.

PINEAPPLE

The pineapple is one of the best-known and most delicious fruits of the tropics. Of all the tropical fruits only bananas and mangoes are grown in greater quantity. The pineapple has the scientific name *Ananas*. It was given the common name "pineapple" because it looks much like a large pinecone.

The pineapple is native to the Americas. Columbus found it being eaten by Indians on the West Indies island of Guadeloupe during his second voyage to America. The pineapple had probably been taken there from Brazil and Paraguay by Indian traders. Columbus and other explorers carried the plants to other areas of the world. The pineapple is now grown widely in tropical zones. Hawaii, Asia, and Latin America produce the most fruit.

▶THE PLANT

The pineapple plant has a short stem and shallow roots. The leaves are stiff and slender and are 60 to 120 centimeters (2 to 4 feet) long. They are specially adapted for holding moisture. For this reason, the plants can live through long periods of dry weather.

In some varieties, the leaves have sharp spines along the edges. A fully grown pineapple plant is about 1 meter tall.

Pineapple plants produce fruit one to two years after planting. The central stem grows from a small shoot into a flower spike topped by a crown of leaves. The flowers are blue-violet in color. The fruit develops in one piece from the flower spike, but it is made up of 100 or more fruitlets. You can see the outline of each on the surface.

Each stalk bears one pineapple. While this fruit is developing, the plant produces new shoots called suckers from the stem near or beneath the soil. Each sucker will grow into a full-size plant and will bear a fruit the following year. This second crop is called a ratoon crop. New plants are started by planting suckers, crowns of older plants, or shoots called slips that grow from the fruit stalks. Suckers are the largest, and they will bear fruit sooner than slips or crowns.

There are many varieties of pineapple. They vary greatly in the size, shape, and color of their fruit. Depending on the variety, fruits may weigh from 1 to 7 kilograms (2 to 15 pounds). The most common outside colors are yellow and orange, but some varieties show some green and red. The flesh may be whitish or golden yellow. It is fibrous and remains firm after ripening and canning. The fruit has a strong aroma, and the flavor is a mixture of tartness and sweetness.

▶GROWING NEEDS

Pineapples will grow in many different types of soil, but sandy loam is best. Most

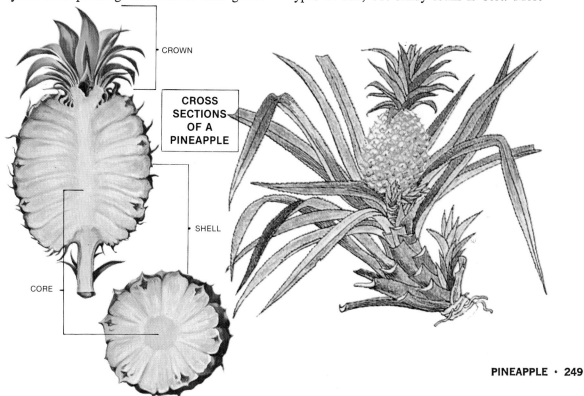

CROWN

CROSS SECTIONS OF A PINEAPPLE

SHELL

CORE

soil must be heavily fertilized for good growth. Since the plant can withstand dry weather, it will grow well in semi-arid conditions.

The soil in which pineapples are to grow is prepared carefully. Usually the soil is plowed and harrowed by tractor. In some places the planting, too, is done by machine. In Hawaii asphalt-coated paper or plastic strips are laid along the pineapple rows before the shoots are planted. This paper keeps down weed growth. It keeps the moisture, heat, and plant food in the soil. The shoots are planted through holes in the paper.

Fertilizer is usually added to the soil when it is prepared for planting. In most areas more fertilizer is added about three months after planting and, after that, at least once or twice a year. The fertilizer may be sprayed on the leaves in a weak solution, for the leaves of the pineapple absorb moisture and nutrients.

▶ **DISEASES**

The pineapple is subject to a number of diseases and insects. Most of them can be kept under control if healthy shoots are planted in clean soil. Insecticides are sometimes used to control mealybugs and mites. Nematodes (eelworms so small that they can be seen only with a microscope) are especially troublesome. Nematodes live in the soil and attack roots. They can be checked by treating the soil with special gases.

▶ **HARVESTING**

Ripe pineapples are removed from the plants by breaking or cutting the stem just below the fruit. Harvesting is done by hand. It cannot be mechanized completely because all the pineapples do not ripen at one time. In Hawaii conveyor belts mounted on tractors move the fruit to central bins, which are hauled from the fields by trucks.

After the pineapples are harvested, some of the suckers are left in the field to produce fruit (the ratoon crop) the following year. Pineapple plants that are very carefully cultivated and fertilized may keep producing for 25 to 30 years. But the fruits get somewhat smaller every year. Commercial growers do not keep plants producing for many years. Usually the fields are replanted after two or three fruiting seasons to keep the yield and quality of the fruit as high as possible.

▶ **MARKETING**

Pineapples are best if they are picked when they are ripe and eaten when they are fresh. The sugar content of the fruit increases a great deal during ripening.

To provide fresh fruit for distant markets, the fruit is harvested before it is fully ripe. The less ripe fruit can tolerate long-distance transportation, but it has poorer quality than ripe fruit.

Canned Pineapple

Pineapples for canning are picked when fully ripe. They are taken by truck immediately from the fields to a canning factory. When the fruit is unloaded, it is graded by machine according to size.

Once it is graded, each pineapple goes to a machine adjusted to its diameter. The machine cuts off both ends and removes the shell and the core. The flesh left on the shell may be scraped by machine and used for crushed pineapple and juice.

The fruit is carefully inspected, sliced by machine, and placed in cans. Broken pieces are sent to the shredder to be crushed.

Every part of a pineapple is used in the canning process. The flesh is canned in slices or cubes or in crushed form. The juice also is canned. The shells and other trimmings are shredded, pressed, and dried to make pineapple bran to feed livestock. Other by-products of the canning process are sugar, alcohol, and vinegar.

▶ **THE PINEAPPLE AS FOOD**

Pineapple, canned or fresh, is a source of vitamins A and C. It is a good source of potassium and contains a few other minerals. The fruit is rich in sugar. Fresh pineapple is often considered an aid to digestion.

The fruit may be served by itself, or it may be used in pies, ice cream, puddings, sauces, and salads. It may also be served with meats. The flavor blends well with other flavors. Fresh pineapple cannot be used in molded gelatin because it contains a substance that digests and softens gelatin. This substance is destroyed by heating.

F. W. LIU
Cornell University

PING-PONG. See TABLE TENNIS.
PINWORMS. See DISEASES.

Pioneers journey westward in search of new homes in the wilderness.

PIONEER LIFE

Pioneer life has a special meaning in America, where in less than 3 centuries civilization spread across a vast continental wilderness. From the first landings in Virginia and Massachusetts, American settlement kept pushing westward behind an ever moving frontier. Into wild country went hunters, trappers, fur traders, miners, frontier soldiers, surveyors, and pioneer farmers. The farmers tamed the land and made it productive. Every part of America had its pioneers.

Kinds of Pioneers

Pioneer people were as varied as human nature. Some were adventurous and independent. Some were irresponsible and shiftless, like the Indiana squatter who moved eight times without ever clearing timber or fencing a field. "To move," he said, "all I have to do is put out the fire and call the dog." Others were determined and industrious, like Silas Garber, who settled in a sod-roofed dugout on a prairie creek bank. Four years later he had succeeded in becoming the governor of Nebraska.

Most pioneers were willing to face toil and hardship for the sake of opportunity. They meant to carve homes out of the wilderness. Yankee farmers went west from the stony fields of New England, and Piedmont families went west from the crowded lands of Virginia and the Carolinas. Still other pioneers were immigrants newly arrived from Europe. English, Scotch, Welsh, and German pioneers went into the Ohio valley. Scandinavian colonists settled in the upper Mississippi valley and on the Great Plains beyond the Missouri.

Pioneer Motives. All the pioneers hoped to find something better over the horizon. New England families, tired of farming rocky valleys, were attracted to broad and fertile lands beyond the Appalachian Mountains. Southern farmers, suffering from bad luck or bad management, sought a new life in the West. To European immigrants the American frontier offered political freedom and economic opportunity. In the western wilds a man could own his own land and work for his own future. The West meant a new chance.

In the "Great Migration" after the War of 1812, multitudes of people went to the American interior. Population was growing in the

Dinner is prepared outside a lean-to in the wilderness.

Cabin in the Clearing

On every new frontier the pioneers made homes for themselves, using what the wild land provided. In the great forests of the Ohio and Mississippi valleys the land provided timber. Here the pioneers' essential tool was the ax. The ax would clear the forest for the plow. But its first task was to shape a pioneer shelter.

When he got to the spot where he planned to make his home, a settler began chopping saplings and trimming poles to build a lean-to. Between two forked trees he laid a crosspole. With the help of his oxen or horses he rolled up a log, which was banked with earth to form a low back wall. Then he laid poles, slanted upward, from the back log to the crosspole. The sloping roof was covered with bark and branches. The ends of the lean-to were walled with shorter poles and pickets. This was the pioneer's "half-faced camp." It always faced south, away from wind and rain. Before the open side he dug a fire pit. Logs smoldered there day and night, giving warmth and protection.

This temporary home served while a pioneer family prepared ground for their first crop. A real clearing took months of work, but a "deadening" was made quickly. A few ax cuts girdled the trees so that sap could not flow up to the branches. Soon the leaves withered and sunlight found the damp earth. Seed corn was dropped into ax-cuts in the ground. The crop from that crude planting provided food for the first winter.

Before winter came, the pioneer family hoped to have a small clearing and a snug cabin. The forest was the settler's enemy—it had to be destroyed to create his fields. At the same time, it was his friend—it gave him logs for his cabin, fuel for his fire, rails for his fences, wheels for his wagon, a frame for his plow. It even gave him a helve, or handle, for the ax blade with which he brought the forest down.

Notched logs formed the cabin walls. A ridgepole at the peak supported lighter roof poles, and a bark thatching made the roof complete. Logs split into flat-faced "puncheons" made the cabin floor. Two openings, a window and a door, were sawed out with patient labor. The first doorway covering was an old quilt weighted with a log; later a board

Eastern states. Families were large, and only one child could inherit the homeplace. The rest went to the growing cities or to the frontier. During hard seasons, when crops failed or when farm prices fell, many movers headed for a new beginning in the West. Most Americans had no rooted family tradition, no ancestral home. Land, they felt, was to possess, not to be possessed by. Pioneer people had more than their share of American restlessness and optimism. To them the best land lay to the west.

Many went almost empty-handed to the frontier. They traveled light and arrived with only an ax and a rifle. Others carried heirlooms and implements. Some took seed corn and orchard shoots, cattle, hogs, and poultry. But how does one prepare for sickness and danger, for accident and misfortune? Some settlers failed, and many died early. A few returned to the land of steady habits and small expectations. Most new countries are made by unprepared people, and the American vanguard survived. They turned a wilderness into a civilization, and they gave America such men as Daniel Boone, Andrew Jackson, and Abraham Lincoln.

door would be hung on leather hinges. The first window covering was greased paper, which turned away wind and water and admitted a dim light. Pioneers used any paper they had. One settler greased his wedding certificate with bear fat and put it in his window frame.

Opposite the cabin doorway was the yawning chimney mouth. Clay from the creek bank, mixed with dried grass, was formed into clumsy bricks, which hardened in the sun. Laid against the cabin wall, the bricks formed a "cat and clay" chimney with a broad opening. The fire that smoldered there gave heat for cooking and light and warmth to the cabin.

Outside, the ax thudded and the smoke of brush fires hazed the air. Slowly the field was widened; a few new acres were cultivated every year. The cabin in the clearing was the pioneer homestead. When it gave way to a frame house, with a traveled road going past, the pioneer life had ended.

Home on Wheels

In the 1840's and 1850's thousands of pioneers made the long trek west to new frontiers in Oregon and California. For months they lived in covered wagons. These settlers traveled in caravans, with 30 or more wagons rocking westward on the Overland Trail. On fine days a wagon train covered 20 miles; in

A pioneer woman tends her first crop of corn.

rain and mud they were satisfied with 10. When the caravan was large, it was divided into two groups. Behind the line of wagons came the "cow column," milk cows and spare oxen driven by men and boys on horseback. At night the wagons drew into a circle and the oxen were turned loose to graze. Men took turns at guard duty under the western stars.

A wagon train on the Overland Trail to California.

The wagon train stops on Sunday, and the pioneers do their washing and other chores.

In the first daylight the guards went around the circle shouting "Arise! Arise!" Cows were milked while breakfast sizzled on the fire. The oxen were yoked and the wagons pulled into line. As the long bullwhips cracked, another day's travel began. At noon the captain called a halt on a prairie ridge or beside a creek bank. While lunch was laid out, children ran over the prairie, gathering buffalo chips for the evening fire. After an hour's rest the march started again. The sun beat down, and heat waves shimmered on the horizon. When the shadows lengthened behind them, the captain began looking for a camping place. Supper was a happy meal while sunset flamed in the west. Children ran from one campfire to another. Men talked about the next day's travel, and women talked about the homes they would have at the end of the journey. After a fiddler played a few tunes, the people went to bed, some in the wagons, others on the ground. When the fires winked out, the night wind brought the quavering call of coyotes.

Sunday was commonly a day of rest. However, even on Sundays the women washed clothes and baked bread and the men repaired harnesses and greased the wagon wheels. While dinner was cooking, the whole company gathered in the shade of the circled wagons as the captain read a chapter from the Bible. Most often he turned to the Book of Exodus, which told of people wandering in the wilderness, seeking a promised land.

Sod Houses

On the Great Plains, which were settled soon after the Civil War, the pioneers built their first dwellings with the deeply rooted grass. Here the farmer plowed up building material while breaking his first field. With a spade he cut the furrows into 3-foot lengths. These he piled up like bricks, leaving openings for a door and window. Roof poles came from willow thickets along the infrequent prairie creeks. When a layer of sod covered the crisscrossed poles, the house was completed. It was cool in summer, warm in winter, windproof, fire-proof. But it did not keep out water. Spring rains seeped through the sod roof long after the sky had cleared. Sometimes a pioneer woman had to hold an umbrella over the stove while she turned the pancakes in the morning.

Outside the sod shanty a settler chopped into the broken ground and dropped seed corn into each cut. A year of wind and weather would soften the field for cultivation. But the first crop was sod corn, growing in the matted grass roots. On the prairie lay buffalo bones left by the hide hunters. Pioneer settlers hauled wagonloads of bones to the nearest railroad town, trading them for a wooden door, a glass-paned window, or some joints of stovepipe. The bones were ground up for fertilizer.

Near the first sod hut other pioneers marked their claims with a "straddlebug"— three boards nailed in a flimsy pyramid. New "soddies" appeared on the prairie, with new breakings beside them. These small fields, almost lost in the blowing grasslands, were the beginning of a changed country. In a few years roads were graded along the section lines, settlements sprang up at the township corners, wheat and corn grew where the buffalo grass had been. Then the farmers built frame houses with imported lumber, and the pioneer life was past.

▶ PIONEER WAY OF LIFE

Whatever his surroundings, the pioneer had to depend upon himself and upon his land. Self-reliance was a frontier requirement. Game provided food and leather clothing.

Meals were prepared in open fireplaces with this equipment. Meat was grilled on the iron rack; soup was simmered in the iron pot (which was hung over the fire); food was kept warm in the covered iron pan with legs. The frying pan had a long handle to keep the cook from getting burned. The cooking utensils were made of tin.

New settlers gathered wild grapes and fruits, nuts and berries. For salt they boiled the water of saline springs. Maple sugar was made by tapping maple trees in early spring and boiling the sap until it thickened to a tasty sweetening. Substitutes for tea and coffee were provided by boiling sassafras root and brewing parched corn and barley. With an ax and adze the pioneer made beds, tables, benches, and stools. He split logs into rails to make the zigzag fence that enclosed his clearing.

A busy pioneer housewife (left) cooks over an open fire. The settler (right) builds his own furniture from trees he has chopped down in the wilderness.

WILD HONEY

BEAVER PELT

WATER BUCKET AND DIPPER MADE OF GOURDS

LOGS

HERBS FOR MEDICINES AND COOKING

BEARS FOR FOOD, GREASE, AND SKINS

H.B.V.

Pioneers made use of what they found in the wilderness.

months there was no fresh fruit or vegetables. In early spring, women looked eagerly for the first wild mustard and dandelion plants, which would be boiled into a dish of "greens."

With health and strength people could stand hardship, but every family had frequent bouts of illness. The most common frontier ailment was chills and fever. Young and old suffered from "the shakes," shuddering with cold and then breaking into a drenching sweat. This disease came at the end of summer and lasted until frost. Since it was most common in marshy districts, the settlers thought it came from breathing damp air. Actually it was malaria, carried by mosquitoes. When swamps were drained, there were fewer mosquitoes and fewer people with "the shakes."

For medicines the pioneers had, again, to provide for themselves. Women soon learned the use of herbs for healing—boneset for fever, pennyroyal to purify the blood, horehound for coughs, ginseng for tonic. Syrups and salves were made from cherry root, horseradish, and witch hazel. Wild mustard, poplar root, and red-sumac root went into teas, poultices, and powders. The standard cure for a chest cold was to rub the chest with goose grease and apply a mustard plaster. Some frontier remedies contained more superstition than science—potions of walnut bark "peeled upward," boiled nettles, and "nanny tea," made from sheep dung.

Pioneer families were large. Every cabin had a cradle, hollowed from a poplar or cottonwood log, and the cradle was rarely empty. Children were helpful in new lands. Girls soon learned the primitive household tasks—gardening, cooking, spinning, weaving, mending, sewing, making soap and candles. Boys worked in the woods and fields with their fathers. They learned to fell timber, to grub out brush, to split rails and build fences. A rail fence would keep hogs and sheep out of the corn, but deer could leap that barrier. It was the children's job to chase deer out of the fields and to keep squirrels from devouring the growing crop. Children pounded cornmeal in a hollow stone. When gristmills came into the neighborhood, it was a boy's chore to ride to the millstream with a bag of grain behind his saddle. He came back with a dusty bag of meal.

Pioneer women learned to supply their own household goods. Gourds served as pails and dippers. Wood ash was sifted to make soap. Tallow was molded into candles. Every cabin had two spinning wheels—a big wheel for wool and a smaller wheel for flax. With her own home-woven "linsey-woolsey," a coarse cloth of mixed linen and wool, the pioneer woman made the family's clothing. Clothes were also made from animal skins, which the pioneers tanned.

Winter was a hard season on the frontier. In bitter weather the family huddled around the fire. When there was no leather, some people went barefoot and suffered frostbite. Food was scanty and monotonous. For

CHORES FOR PIONEER CHILDREN

MENDING

SPLITTING LOGS
FOR THE FIRE

POUNDING DRIED CORN
TO MAKE CORNMEAL

BAKING

CHASING SQUIRRELS
FROM THE CORNFIELD

FETCHING WATER
FROM THE STREAM

HOEING IN THE FIELDS

H.B.V.

On the frontier everyone helped a newcomer build his first log house.

Although pioneer families were resourceful and nearly self-sufficient, neighbors were highly valued on the frontier. When her fire went out, a woman took the trail to the nearest cabin and borrowed a pan of glowing coals. Neighbors from miles around helped a newcomer with logrolling, house-raising, and barn raising. Entire communities joined in hunts for wolves, foxes, squirrels, and rabbits.

These common tasks, shared by pioneer neighbors, provided the amusement of the frontier. A house-raising was also a picnic, with women spreading a dinner on the grass while children swung from grapevines and the men laid up the roof poles on a new cabin. Neighbors gathered for "husking bees," competing to see who was fastest at stripping the husks from ears of corn. The cornstalks were kept for fodder, while the husked corn was stored in a crib. Pioneer women held "quilting bees," exchanging family news while they sewed patchwork together. One amusement that did not involve household tasks was the barn dance. With a local fiddler playing "Skip-to-my-Lou" and "Way Down in the Pawpaw Patch," men, women, and children joined in square and circle dances by lantern light on a rough barn floor.

Pioneer Schools and Churches

To pioneer people "book l'arnin'" was less important than learning to use an ax and a plow, a loom and a spinning wheel. But as settlements grew, parents wanted their children to know the "three R's"—reading, writing, and 'rithmetic. In the crude log schoolhouse, shelves fastened to the wall served for desks and the scholars sat on three-legged stools. They used charcoal to write on hand-smoothed writing boards. Later came slates and slate pencils. A slate, wiped clean after each lesson, could be used for years.

In front of the schoolroom sat the schoolmaster or schoolmistress at a rough plank table. In the corner he kept a bundle of hickory switches, because frontier boys were often unruly. The master "boarded round," a week at a time, in the homes of pioneer families. Often he slept in cabin lofts. Schoolmasters

In a frontier schoolroom a girl reads aloud from her copy of McGuffey's Reader.

were paid according to the number of children they taught. All grades sat in the same room. Twenty scholars made a typical school, and a schoolmaster's common rate of pay was between $1 and $2 a term for each scholar. In wooded regions children walked as far as 5 miles on forest trails to the schoolhouse. On the prairie frontier they often went to school on horseback. They ate their lunch in the schoolyard in good weather and around the stove on winter days.

In frontier schools all over America the most common textbooks were McGuffey's Readers. Their pages were full of references to rural and pioneer America. In the McGuffey Primer the first lesson was "A is for ax." After *ax* came *box, cat, dog*—all homely and familiar things. The readings described children at work and play in barnyard, field, and forest. These schoolbooks brought learning close to pioneer life.

Before the first churches were built, religion was carried to the frontier by the circuit rider. A preacher on horseback, the circuit rider visited pioneer families in their own cab-ins. He carried a Bible and a hymnbook in his saddlebag. He preached at crossroad settlements, standing on a stump or a wagon bed. He read from the Bible, prayed, and "lined out" hymns, reading one line at a time, which the people sang after him. In remote cabins he performed baptisms and marriages. He prayed over the graves of the dead.

As settlements grew, communities organized congregations and built churches at the crossroads. The church became a social as well as a religious center. It was a place of community socials and suppers, of Christmas entertainments, of Sunday school parties and neighborhood gatherings. The frontier church provided the first strong social bond in new communities.

Pioneer Government and Law

The first political organization on the frontier was the territorial government, with officials appointed by the President of the United States. Statehood could be sought when a region had enough population; 60,000 was the original requirement. With statehood the pioneers elected their own legislators and sent representatives to the federal Congress.

But pioneers went into new lands ahead of the law. Therefore, in its first years every frontier had its own unwritten laws, which were enforced by common consent. Some of the unwritten rules were remembered from older regions. Others were evolved on the frontier to meet frontier needs. It was generally agreed that a stray horse became the property of the first man who could catch it. A horse thief, the worst of criminals, deserved to die. Anyone involved in a quarrel had a right to defend himself. Killing another man in self-defense was not regarded as a crime, but it was criminal to shoot an unarmed man or to strike anyone in the back.

In Western communities bands of self-appointed vigilantes enforced their own ideas of justice. At its worst this action became mob violence. At its best it was a temporary assertion of community judgment. Though it was a necessity on the frontier, this lawless judgment had to give way to a legal system. In the process some vigilantes became officers of the law. Still, the pioneer districts had no trained officials. In west Texas a weathered justice of the peace was called Old Necessity because he knew no law. On his bench he kept a mail-order catalog, which he always consulted before making a judgment. Once, considering a man charged with a misdemeanor, he put on his spectacles, flipped open the catalog, looked at it a moment, and announced, "I fine you $4.88." When the man jumped up to protest, a friend yanked him back. "Sit down," he said. "You're lucky he opened it at 'pants' instead of at 'pianos.' "

Pioneer Roads

In the interior of America the first roads were rivers. The great rivers, notably the Ohio and the Mississippi, became frontier highways, carrying the population and the produce of the new West. The tributary streams were only a little less important. Settlers paddled and poled up the side rivers, finding their way into a trackless land. On flatboats they took corn, wheat, pork, lard, and apples to market. Settlers and town builders alike chose sites on running water.

Through the forest the pioneers cut primitive "traces." Boone's Trace was a pioneer path in Kentucky. The historic Natchez Trace led north from Natchez, Mississippi, to Nashville, Tennessee. Zane's Trace ran through the Ohio woods; it began and ended at landings on the Ohio River.

The first improved highway, straight, wide, and smooth, was the National Road, begun at Cumberland, Maryland, in 1815. It eventually ran through the frontier capitals of Columbus, Indianapolis, and Vandalia. Multitudes of pioneer settlers traveled the National Road, as later emigrants to the far West traveled the Overland Trail to Oregon and California. Canals between the Great Lakes and the Ohio and Mississippi rivers hastened the settlement of the Midwest.

▶ LAND LAWS

After the Revolutionary War the United States had a spacious domain extending to the Mississippi River. The Louisiana Purchase in 1803 extended it to the Rocky Mountains, and the annexation of Oregon and California carried it to the Pacific by 1850. The western regions were sparsely occupied by Indians. A piece at a time, by treaty and purchase, the tribes ceded vast lands to the United States. So the public domain was offered to settlers, at first by purchase and finally as free homesteads.

Before land could be sold and legally settled, it had to be surveyed. Government surveyors mapped it into mile-square sections and 6-mile-square townships. By this system any tract of land could be precisely located and its bounds determined. With chain and compass the surveyors went into wild country. They left a numbered post at each mile and a marked cone of earth at the township corners.

After it was surveyed, the land was open to sale and settlement. The first federal land law offered a minimum tract of 640 acres at $2 an acre, half the price to be paid within 30 days and the remainder within a year. Many settlers did not have that much money. They became "squatters," living on the public land without legal ownership.

In a series of reforms the land laws were made more democratic. The Harrison Land Act of 1800 allowed sales of 320 acres at

A pioneer family could travel downriver on a keelboat and carry their livestock with them. They often used the lumber of the keelboat to build their new house.

$2 an acre and allowed 4 years to pay. In 1820 the revised law offered 80-acre tracts at $1.25 an acre. This enabled a pioneer with but $100 to buy a small farm. At last, in 1862, President Lincoln signed the Homestead Act, which offered land free to any adult who would live on it and improve it. People then sang a popular song: "Uncle Sam is rich enough to give us all a farm." The Homestead Act helped to fill up the Great Plains frontier.

On a stump-studded street in a raw new town stood the government land office, with survey maps on the wall and a big open ledger on a table. Steubenville, Marietta, Chillicothe, and Cincinnati had the first land offices in the Northwest Territory. As new districts were surveyed, land offices were opened at Zanesville, Vincennes, Shawneetown, and Kaskaskia. By 1820 they were extended to Detroit and St. Louis. In all these places a familiar scene was repeated. While a woman and her children waited outside in a wagon, a pioneer settler studied the survey maps in the land office. At last he counted out his ad-

vance payment and signed his name or made his mark in the ledger. He got a certificate that he could exchange for a deed of ownership when payment was completed. Then the wagon creaked on to the township and section numbered on his claim. So another pioneer family found their land.

▶ END OF THE FRONTIER

In 1889 central Oklahoma was opened to homeseekers. Thousands of people, on horseback, in wagons, and on foot, raced into the area to mark out homesteads. In this dramatic land rush, settlement came to the last large tract of public domain. In 1890 the U.S. Census Director declared, "There can hardly be said to be a frontier line." After more than 2 centuries the moving frontier had come to an end. Vast stretches of wilderness remained in the Western mountains and deserts. Much of it would become national forest land. But an era of American history had closed, an era shaped by the hope, the hardship, and the toil and accomplishment of pioneer people.

Modern pioneers in Alaska can use airplanes to reach their houses in the wilderness.

▶ PRESENT-DAY PIONEERS

Crisscrossed as it is with railroads and highways, the United States still has remote and primitive areas. Resourceful, self-reliant people can still go beyond the reach of civilization. In the mountains of Montana, Idaho, and Oregon there are huge counties with only a small population. Some of the people live in the wilderness. They have to be self-sufficient and independent.

The new state of Alaska is sometimes called the last frontier. With large areas of uninhabited land it attracts pioneer people as the American interior did a century and a half ago. Most Alaskan settlers have come from the older states. They went to Alaska, like all pioneers, for independence and opportunity.

Alaskan districts like the Matanuska Valley have deep, rich soil, where crops grow quickly in the long northern summer sunlight. Here, amid magnificent forests and mountains, Alaskan pioneers build cabins, clear fields, and plow virgin land. Unlike the settlers on earlier frontiers, they have radios in their cabins and they work together to clear an airstrip. They are the first pioneers to hear the news of the world as it happens and to fly their crops to market.

▶ PIONEERING AND THE AMERICAN CHARACTER

To all pioneers, from Virginia to Alaska, the frontier life gave common traits of resourcefulness, individualism, and belief in the future. Men were free and equal on the frontier, and democracy was strengthened by the pioneer experience. New country stimulated initiative, energy, and determination.

With many urgent tasks to do—clearing forests, building roads, erecting towns and cities—the pioneers emphasized practical values to the neglect of the mind and spirit. For its material success America owes much to the pioneering tradition. But material success alone is empty. When the last frontier was crossed, a new pioneering was needed—in realms of social justice, education, public health, religion, the arts, and the sciences. Wrote the American poet Walt Whitman:

We take up the task eternal, and the burden and
     the lesson,
          Pioneers! O Pioneers!
This pioneering is endless.

WALTER HAVIGHURST
Author, *First Book of Pioneers, First
Book of the Oregon Trail*
See also OVERLAND TRAILS.

PIRATES AND PIRACY

No character in literature is more romantic or colorful than the roaring, swaggering pirate, and his adventures have been popular with generations of readers. Many authors (among them Robert Louis Stevenson, Sir Walter Scott, and James Fenimore Cooper) have written exciting tales about pirates sailing under the skull-and-crossbones flag, searching for buried treasure, and making their prisoners walk the plank. James M. Barrie created the comic, cowardly Captain Hook in *Peter Pan,* and Gilbert and Sullivan poked fun at sea robbers in their operetta *The Pirates of Penzance.*

Although many of the familiar tales are exaggerated and fanciful (there is no proof, for example, that anyone was ever forced to walk the plank), real pirates did roam the seas for thousands of years. Until as recently as the last century, peaceful sailing ships were often at the mercy of ruthless pirates who captured helpless crews and stole precious cargoes. Now considered a crime in all countries, piracy was once accepted as a common hazard of sea travel.

▶ HISTORY

The real story of piracy, or robbery on the high seas, is as old as the history of seafaring. The ancient Phoenicians, Greeks, and Romans who sailed the Aegean and Mediterranean seas often ran the risk of having their cargoes stolen. Pirates became so powerful in the ancient world that they established their own seacoast settlements, from which they attacked trading vessels. In 78 B.C., while crossing the Aegean Sea to Greece, Julius Caesar was captured by a band of pirates and held until ransom was paid. Attacks by pirate ships became so frequent that the Romans sent a naval expedition under Pompey the Great to force them from the Mediterranean area. Although the Roman Navy succeeded in conquering a large settlement at Cilicia in Asia Minor (67 B.C.), piracy was not completely wiped out and sea robbers were soon roaming the waters once again. Later, as shipping in northern waters increased, Viking pirates attacked ships in the Baltic Sea and English Channel.

The pirate and his Jolly Roger terrified merchantmen.

In the 1300's bands of ruthless seafaring criminals established settlements along the North African coast. These barbarous robbers were called corsairs, and the lands they inhabited (parts of present-day Morocco, Algeria, Tunisia, and Libya) were known as the Barbary States. For hundreds of years Barbary corsairs attacked European and American trading vessels. Cargoes were looted, and crews were held for ransom or sold into slavery. In order to safeguard their shipping, many nations paid tribute, or protection money, to the corsair rulers in return for guaranteed passage.

During the 16th century several governments gave privately owned vessels the right to carry arms and attack the shipping of enemy nations. These armed vessels, as well as their commanders and crew, were called privateers; and privateering, a kind of legalized piracy, became a respected occupation. Some of the most famous privateers were the English "sea dogs" Sir Francis Drake, Sir John Hawkins, and Sir Walter Raleigh.

Protected seas, with many islands and irregular coastlines, offered excellent hideouts for pirates. The Caribbean Sea and the Spanish Main (or the mainland of South America), offered just such advantages. Soon after the first settlements in the New World began to flourish, pirates began their plundering. The pirates of the Spanish Main came to be known as buccaneers from the *boucan,* or wooden grill, on which they cured their meat. From well-concealed hiding places on the islands of the West Indies, buccaneers

Pirates often buried their stolen gold, silver, and jewels in secret hiding places. Captain William Kidd buried treasure on Gardiners Island, near Long Island, New York. When Kidd was jailed, this booty was recovered by the British and sent to London.

Captain Edward Teach (?–1718), the notorious Blackbeard, is said to have buried vast amounts of gold and silver near Ocracoke Inlet, North Carolina. Many expeditions have searched on Cocos Island, off the coast of Costa Rica, for the "Lost Loot of Lima (Peru)." This treasure of the pirate "Benito Bonito of the Bloody Sword" is supposed to be worth $65,000,000. Other pirate treasures are said to be buried all along the Gulf Coast from Florida to Texas.

A pamphlet, "Descriptive List of Treasure Maps and Charts in the Library of Congress," is sold for a small fee by the U.S. Government Printing Office, Washington, D.C. 20402.

attacked not only the Spanish galleons that traveled between Spain and her colonies, but also the colonies themselves. For over 200 years buccaneers captured cargoes of jewels, gold, and silver and plundered island cities and coastal settlements on the continent of South America.

As the hazards to shipping and colonies increased, many efforts were made to clear the seas of pirates. In 1718 an important stronghold on New Providence Island in the Bahamas was destroyed by British men-of-war. Pirate leaders were offered pardons if they would surrender their ships and give up their attacks. It was not until about the middle of the 19th century, however, that the combined efforts of the navies of the United States and several European countries succeeded in ridding the Mediterranean and Caribbean seas of pirates.

▶ PIRATE LIFE

From old diaries, letters, ships' logs, and memoirs, a great deal has been learned about the way pirates lived. Most of the men who became pirates, buccaneers, or corsairs were cruel and lawless. The capture of treasure was their chief aim, and human life was cheap. But there were laws of the sea, both written and unwritten, that even the most ruthless pirates observed.

Most pirate crews worked together and shared captured booty. Pirates displayed great loyalty to one another and always took good care of sick and wounded shipmates. Many crews practiced a strict democracy, whereby captains were elected by a majority vote and shares of treasure were agreed on in writing before a voyage.

The life stories of many pirates have been told and retold so many times that it is often difficult to distinguish between fact and fiction. This is particularly true of the career of the famous Sir William Kidd, who abandoned privateering to become a pirate in the Caribbean Sea. Many cruel exploits have been attributed to Captain Kidd, and for years the mention of his name struck terror in the hearts of honest sea captains. Captain Kidd was finally captured, convicted of murder, and hanged in London in 1701.

One of the cruelest and most notorious of all the English buccaneers was Sir Henry Morgan (1635?–1688). Morgan's greatest exploit was the sacking of Panama City (1671) and the seizure of its stores of gold and jewels. Although Morgan's acts were clearly against the law, tales of his exploits captured people's imagination and he became a romantic hero during his lifetime. Knighted by King Charles II, Morgan was eventually made lieutenant governor of Jamaica.

It seems strange that piracy, so often a ruthless and bloodthirsty game, should have appealed to any but the toughest men. And yet, not all pirates were completely evil. Captain Bartholomew Roberts (1682–1722), for example, was supposed to have been so proper and gentlemanly that he forbade all swearing, drinking, and gambling aboard his ship. Roberts had a great sense of fair play and showed every mercy toward his victims. Jean Laffite, for years a plunderer and smuggler, became a pirate-turned-patriot. During the war of 1812, Laffite offered his aid to the United States and was largely responsible for winning the battle of New Orleans. Stranger still is the case of the notorious pirates Anne Bonny (lived about 1720) and Mary Read (?–1720). For many years these two women successfully plundered countless ships in the Caribbean area. Both were finally convicted of piracy and imprisoned.

Reviewed by HAMILTON COCHRAN
Author, *Pirates of the Spanish Main*
See also KIDD, CAPTAIN WILLIAM; LAFFITE, JEAN.

PITT, WILLIAM, EARL OF CHATHAM (1708–1778)

William Pitt, Earl of Chatham, was a great British statesman. His leadership in a war with France enabled Britain to win control of Canada and opened up the Ohio Valley to settlement by American colonists.

Born in London on November 15, 1708, Pitt was educated at Oxford University and then spent four years in the Army. In 1735 he was elected to Parliament. An eloquent speaker, he aroused the hostility of King George II by attacking government policies. The King so disliked Pitt that he refused to appoint him to office, in spite of his ability. It was not until 1746 that the King was persuaded to make Pitt paymaster general.

When the French and Indian War broke out in 1754, Pitt became increasingly critical of the way the government was handling the war. George II was furious and dismissed Pitt. By 1756 the war in America had spread to Europe as the Seven Years' War. Things went so badly for Britain that the King was forced to take Pitt back into the government, where he directed the war against France. Pitt was so successful that the French were defeated in Canada and Europe and driven from their territory in the Ohio Valley. Fort Duquesne, which had been captured from the French, was renamed Pittsburgh in his honor. In 1760, George III came to the throne. The King and Pitt disagreed on how the war should be fought, so Pitt resigned the following year.

Much of the latter part of Pitt's life was spent in opposition to the policies of George III and his ministers. In 1766 he was made Earl of Chatham and became prime minister. But he suffered a severe nervous breakdown and resigned in 1768. For the rest of his life Pitt championed the cause of the American colonists in their struggle against the British Government. He died on May 11, 1778.

DOROTHY MARSHALL
Author, *Eighteenth Century England*

PITT, WILLIAM, THE YOUNGER (1759–1806)

William Pitt the Younger, the second son of William Pitt, Earl of Chatham, was born in Hayes, in Kent, England, on May 28, 1759. Though sickly as a boy, he was determined to follow his famous father's example—to enter Parliament and become prime minister. After graduating from Cambridge University, Pitt studied law and in 1781 was elected to Parliament. His abilities, especially as a brilliant speaker in parliamentary debates, were soon recognized. When he was only 23 he became chancellor of the exchequer, the minister in charge of finance. In 1783, at the age of 24, he was asked by King George III to become prime minister. Pitt's opponents laughed at the idea of so young a man becoming prime minister. They thought he would last only a short time. They were wrong. Except for the period between 1801 and 1804, Pitt was prime minister until his death in 1806.

Pitt held what were then very modern ideas. He realized that the way the government collected taxes and raised loans was old-fashioned. Pitt succeeded in carrying out a number of financial reforms that increased Britain's commercial prosperity. He also united the separate Irish and British parliaments in 1801. This Act of Union created the United Kingdom of Great Britain and Ireland. Pitt also wished to pass a Catholic emancipation act, to end discrimination against Catholics. But George III was so strongly opposed to the measure that Pitt resigned in 1801.

Since 1793, Britain had been almost continuously at war with France. When Pitt returned as prime minister in 1804, Europe had long been dominated by the French under Napoleon. Pitt allied Britain with France's enemies, providing them with money to equip their armies. But they were no match for Napoleon, who crushed the British alliances. However, the British fleet ruled the seas, and Pitt used it to blockade French ports, seize French colonies, and protect Britain against invasion.

Pitt did not live to see the end of the war with France. He died on January 23, 1806. A lonely man, Pitt never married and had only a few close friends. His life was devoted almost entirely to politics. He is remembered today as one of Britain's great prime ministers.

DOROTHY MARSHALL
Author, *Eighteenth Century England*

PITTSBURGH

Pittsburgh is the second largest city in Pennsylvania. Located in the southwestern part of the state, it is strategically situated at the point where two rivers, the Monongahela and the Allegheny, flow together to form the headwaters of a third river, the mighty Ohio. The jut of land that lies where the three rivers converge is aptly called the Point.

Pittsburgh's landscape of hills and valleys covers approximately 55 square miles (142 square kilometers), and the city's abundant waterways are spanned by more than 700 bridges, more than are found in any other city in the world except Venice, Italy. Pittsburgh's climate is temperate, averaging 30°F (−1°C) in midwinter and 72°F (22°C) in the summer. Normal annual rainfall is about 36 inches (914 millimeters); annual snowfall is about 43 inches (109 centimeters).

Approximately 375,000 live within the city, but about 2 million people live in its greater metropolitan area, which covers parts of four counties, making Pittsburgh the 18th largest metropolitan area in the United States. The city has more than 100 neighborhoods, many of which are traditionally associated with a particular ethnic group or nationality.

Education and Communications

Education is one of Pittsburgh's largest industries. More than 100,000 students attend 31 regional colleges and universities. Chief among these is the University of Pittsburgh, which is also the city's single largest employer. One of its special points of interest is its Cathedral of Learning, the world's second tallest classroom building. Other notable educational institutions include Carnegie Mellon University, Duquesne University, Robert Morris College, Chatham College, Carlow College, and Point Park College.

Pittsburgh is served by one major newspaper, the *Pittsburgh Post-Gazette*, six local television stations, and more than forty local radio stations.

Culture and Recreation

Pittsburgh's largest museum complex is called the Carnegie, named for the steel baron Andrew Carnegie (1835–1919), one of Pittsburgh's greatest benefactors. The complex boasts the world-class Carnegie Museum of Art; the Carnegie Museum of Natural History, which displays one of the best dinosaur collections in the country; the Carnegie Science Center, containing an actual submarine; the Carnegie Music Hall; and the Library of Pittsburgh. Other notable local museums include the Frick Art Museum, the Fort Pitt Museum, the Stephen Foster Memorial, and the Pittsburgh Children's Museum.

Major arts groups in the city include the Pittsburgh Symphony Orchestra, the Pittsburgh Ballet Theatre, the Pittsburgh Opera, Pittsburgh Public Theater, and the City Theatre Company. Also, the emerging Cultural

Pittsburgh, Pennsylvania, is located at the junction of three rivers—the Allegheny (top), the Monongahela (right), and the Ohio (left). At the fork lies a triangular plot of land called the Point. Traditionally regarded as a major steelmaking center, today Pittsburgh is also renowned for its cultural and educational institutions and its advanced technology industries.

District downtown features two spectacularly renovated halls for the performing arts, the Benedum Center and Heinz Hall.

Despite its smoky reputation, Pittsburgh, with an extensive parks system, is actually one of the greenest cities in the United States. Major city parks include Shenley, Frick, Highland, and Mellon. In addition, one of the country's oldest and grandest amusement parks—Kennywood Park—lies just east of the city.

Pittsburgh has been called the City of Champions due to the achievements of its professional sports teams—the Pittsburgh Pirates of baseball's National League, the Pittsburgh Steelers of the National Football League, and the Pittsburgh Penguins of the National Hockey League. The Steelers and Pirates play at the modern Three Rivers Stadium and the Penguins play at the Pittsburgh Civic Arena, known as the Igloo because of its domed shape.

History

Because of its easy river access from three directions, Pittsburgh was a strategic trading site for the Shawnee, Delaware, and Iroquois Indians who originally inhabited the area. Later the land became an important military site for both French and British colonists, who competed for control of the territory. The British built the first fort there in 1754 and called it Fort Prince George. It was destroyed four months later by the French, who replaced it with Fort Duquesne. In 1758, the British, in turn, destroyed Fort Duquesne and built the last fort to stand at this site—Fort Pitt, named after then prime minister William Pitt.

Because many travelers heading west on the Ohio River started their long journey from Fort Pitt, a town quickly grew up near the fort. The town was officially incorporated as Pittsburgh in 1816. The land around the city was rich in natural resources—especially coal and iron—and Pittsburgh quickly grew into a center of industry. By the mid-1800's, Pittsburgh's economy was booming. Glassmaking and ironworks became its principal industries, and by the latter part of the century, its factories were producing half of the world's glass and iron and two thirds of the nation's steel. Pittsburgh became a magnet for immigrants from many countries, who came to labor in the mills.

During the first half of the 1900's, Pittsburgh's industrial growth continued to skyrocket, and when the United States took part in World War II (1941–45), Pittsburgh factories supplied the steel for America's war machines. The city became known worldwide as the Iron City and Steeltown. But there was a negative side to this explosive growth—pollution. Pittsburgh also came to be known by such nicknames as Hell With the Lid Off and the Smoky City. So thick was the soot in the air, businessmen had to change their white shirts at midday, and at times the smoke was so dense, street lights had to be turned on during the day so people could see. Something had to be done to make the city livable again.

In the late 1940's, Mayor David Lawrence joined forces with many of the city's business and civic leaders, including financier Richard King Mellon, and launched one of the country's first urban renewal projects. Called Renaissance I, the project encompassed flood control, air pollution control, and highway development. Several new buildings were erected in a once-blighted downtown area. Another urban renewal project, Renaissance II, was begun in the 1970's, under the leadership of Mayor Richard Caliguiri.

However, on the heels of Renaissance II, Pittsburgh faced a new challenge—the collapse of America's steel industry. One after another, the area's steel mills were shut down, and by 1983, unemployment had reached almost 15 percent. Nevertheless, Pittsburgh bounced back. By supporting the development of advanced technology, medical research, and its educational resources, the city reduced its unemployment to 5 percent by 1990.

Pittsburgh was once rated "the most livable city in the nation." Today it continues to boast a relatively low crime rate, low housing costs, and a top-rated public education system.

BRUCE VANWYNGARDEN
Contributing Editor, *Pittsburgh Magazine*

PIUS XII, POPE (1876–1958)

Eugenio Pacelli, the future Pope Pius XII, was born in Rome, Italy, on March 2, 1876. A distinguished diplomat and expert on both church and civil law, he led the Roman Catholic Church during World War II and in the difficult years that followed the war.

Young Pacelli decided to become a priest while in his teens. He was educated at the Capranica seminary and Gregorian University in Rome. He later received doctoral degrees in theology, philosophy, and canon (church) and civil law. He was ordained a priest in 1899. Pacelli's scholarly achievements brought him to the attention of the church government at the Vatican, and in 1901 he began a long and brilliant career in the papal secretariat of state. He taught law, assisted in reforms made in the code of canon law, and served on diplomatic missions abroad. In 1917 he was made an archbishop and sent as nuncio, or papal ambassador, to Germany. Pacelli served there until 1929, when he was elevated to the rank of cardinal. The following year he was appointed papal secretary of state. In this post he represented Pope Pius XI and traveled to many countries on church matters. He visited the United States in 1936.

Pacelli was elected pope after the death of Pius XI in 1939, six months before the outbreak of World War II. As the "Pope of Peace," Pius XII worked tirelessly to try to prevent the war. When war came, he sought to lessen its spread. Through his efforts, many Jews were saved from death. Later, critics of Pius claimed that more lives might have been saved if he had spoken out more strongly against Nazi Germany. But many believe that if he had done so it would have led to even greater persecution of the Jews.

Pius strongly opposed the spread of Communism in the years after the war. But he felt deeply about social justice and supported the rights of workers.

Pius wrote many encyclicals, or letters to bishops on subjects concerning the church. He made Holy Communion more easily available to the people by modifying the rules of fasting and encouraging evening Mass.

Pius XII died on October 9, 1958. He was succeeded by Pope John XXIII.

Reviewed by THADDEUS HORGAN, S.A.
Director, Graymoor Christian Unity Center

PIZARRO, FRANCISCO (1475?–1541)

Francisco Pizarro, the conqueror of the Inca Empire of Peru, was born about 1475 in Trujillo, Spain. In 1502, seeking fame and fortune, he sailed for the recently discovered new world of America.

Pizarro served with the explorer Vasco Balboa in 1513. (An article on Balboa appears in Volume B.) They were the first Europeans to cross the narrow strip of land in Central America known as Panama and reach the Pacific Ocean. Pizarro settled in Panama, where he heard of a wealthy land to the south—Peru, the heart of the Inca Empira. He formed a partnership with Diego de Almagro and Hernando de Luque to try to find this rich land. Their first attempt ended in failure. In 1526, Pizarro and Almagro set out again. Almagro returned to Panama, but Pizarro continued on. After much hardship, he reached Tumbres, a town rich in gold and silver. With this evidence of the wealth of the Incas, Pizarro received permission to conquer Peru.

Pizarro began with only about 180 men, a few cannons, and some horses. But the Incas had been weakened by civil war. At Cajamarca he trapped the much larger force of the Inca ruler, Atahualpa, took him prisoner, and demanded a huge ransom for him. But after it was paid, Pizarro had him killed.

In 1533, Pizarro entered Cuzco, the Inca capital, completing, in effect, the conquest of Peru. In 1535 he founded the city of Lima, now the capital of Peru. His partner Luque had died. But Almagro, feeling cheated of his share of the gold and power, gathered his own army and in 1538 marched against Pizarro. Almagro was defeated in battle and killed. His followers waited for a chance to gain revenge, and on June 26, 1541, they assassinated Pizarro in his palace in Lima.

SANFORD G. BEDERMAN
Georgia State College

PLANCK, MAX. See LIGHT (The Quantum Theory); PHYSICS, HISTORY OF (Profiles).

Visitors to planetariums can attend exciting shows where dazzling views of objects and events in space are projected onto the domed ceilings of theaters.

PLANETARIUMS AND SPACE MUSEUMS

Planetariums are wonderful places to learn about astronomy and space. In them you can go to shows on different topics in astronomy and see realistic images of stars, planets, galaxies, and other objects in space projected onto the domed ceiling of a theater. Planetariums are often part of science parks or museums that specialize in science or space-related topics. Planetariums may also be part of astronomical observatories, libraries, and universities.

▶ EARLY PLANETARIUMS

The word "planetarium" was originally used to refer to a small model of the planets or the solar system. The first such model planetarium was designed in 1682 by the Dutch astronomer Christian Huygens (1629–95). Over the next 150 years, many other model planetariums were built. In early planetariums, models of the solar system usually consisted of a series of balls that represented the sun and the planets. These balls were attached to rods that were connected to gears. When a handle was turned, the gears would move the rods so that the "planets" circled the "sun." A small model like

this, called an **orrery**, demonstrated the motions of the solar system.

The first planetarium that people could walk into was built in 1654 in Germany. It was a hollow copper ball more than 11 feet (3 meters) in diameter and it weighed more than 3 tons. Painted on the outside of the ball was a map of the Earth, and the stars and constellations were painted on the inside. To the ten people who could sit inside on benches set on a platform, the painted stars seemed to rise and set in the sky as the globe was rotated.

Several similar planetariums were built in Germany shortly after this one was completed. Then, nearly 100 years later, one was built in Cambridge, England. In the United States, a globe planetarium was built at the Chicago Academy of Sciences and opened in 1913.

The first modern planetarium, which used a dome and a projector to display objects in space, was built in Germany in 1924. Today, modern planetariums can be found throughout the world. Some of the well-known planetariums in the United States are the Hayden Planetarium in New York, the Adler Planetarium in Chicago, and the Griffith Planetarium in Los Angeles.

This orrery—a small model of the sun and planets—was made in England around 1800.

▶ MODERN PLANETARIUMS

Today's modern planetariums are much different from the early model planetariums. Most are built in rather large buildings and include planetarium theaters where people can attend shows about space and related topics. In addition to these shows, many planetariums also offer lectures and educational programs, live or recorded music concerts, and even live theatrical performances.

The Planetarium Theater

Not all planetarium theaters look alike. While almost all the theaters are round, some are less than 15 feet (4.6 meters) in diameter and can seat only a few dozen people. Others are 75 feet (23 meters) or more in diameter with room for hundreds of people. Some theaters have flat floors with all seats facing the middle of the room. In others, the seats may all face one side of the room. Still other planetarium theaters have tilted floors. Despite such differences, a common feature of all planetarium theaters is a domed ceiling.

The Planetarium Dome

The domed ceiling in a planetarium acts as a projection screen similar to those in movie theaters. Unlike the screen in a movie theater, however, the domed ceiling of a planetarium is usually made of sheets of thin metal with millions of tiny holes. These holes help reduce the weight of the dome and let air circulate through. The whole ceiling may be coated with a vinyl-like material, or it may be painted white or light gray, which allows it to reflect images like a movie screen.

In most planetariums, large speakers are located behind the metal sheets of the dome. This makes it seem as though the words, music, and sound effects for the planetarium shows come from the dome. Sounds may even

The mechanical star projector (*below* and *right*) is a key instrument in planetarium shows. It can show how the night sky would look from anywhere on Earth and project how the stars would change position in the sky over hundreds or thousands of years.

appear to move around the theater as the projected images move across the dome.

Star Projectors

One of the most common and spectacular images projected on the planetarium dome is a clear night sky with thousands of stars. A special "star projector," usually located at the center of the planetarium theater, is able to show the sky as seen from anywhere on the Earth at any hour of the day or night. It can also show the sky as it would appear for any date within several thousand years of the present. The two most typical types of star projectors are mechanical star projectors and digital video star projectors.

Mechanical Star Projectors. The most common type of star projector is the mechanical star projector. Some of these projectors are shaped like large dumbbells with one or two spheres on each end. Others have single large spheres. Within a sphere is a powerful lamp and glass or metal plates with pinpoint openings. As the light from the lamp passes through these tiny openings, it is focused onto the planetarium dome by lenses that are on the surface of the sphere. These projections of light create an artificial sky with images of the stars. The process is similar to what happens in an ordinary slide projector when light shines through a slide to project an image on a screen.

Gears and motors on the star projector allow it to be turned in different directions, which makes the images of the stars move. Sometimes the stars move across the artificial sky of the planetarium dome as they do in the real sky at night. This type of motion, called **diurnal motion**, imitates the motion of the stars as seen from the Earth as it rotates on its axis. The planetarium theater, however, is like a time machine. Its star projector can make this happen in only seconds rather than the hours it would take in the real night sky. The star projector can also change the latitude from which the sky is observed. This type of motion allows the audience to see the sky as it appears from anywhere on Earth. The projector can also show how the sky changes as the Earth revolves around the sun or slowly wobbles on its axis. This latter motion, called **precession**, shows how the North Star would slowly change over the course of thousands of years.

Attached to the star projector, or located nearby, are other projectors used to display images of the sun, the moon, and the five planets that can be seen in the sky by the naked

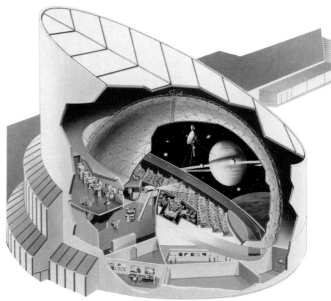

This diagram of a planetarium with a tilted floor shows the location of the projectors and computers and the spectacular view the audience has of the objects projected on the domed ceiling of the theater.

eye—Mercury, Venus, Mars, Jupiter, and Saturn. These projectors can be timed so that the stars, planets, sun, and moon move through the sky in harmony with each other. Changes in position that might take months or years in the real sky can be demonstrated in only seconds in the planetarium sky. Other projection devices are also used. They can create such things as the outlines of constellations and the faint glow of the Milky Way galaxy.

Digital Video Star Projectors. Mechanical star projectors date back to the 1920's, but the digital video star projector is a more recent

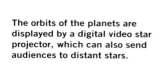

The orbits of the planets are displayed by a digital video star projector, which can also send audiences to distant stars.

development. This projector is a special kind of television set connected to a powerful computer. The computer stores information about the planets and stars and their positions in space. It can then generate images of these objects on a circular television screen about 9 inches (23 centimeters) in diameter located at the center of the planetarium theater. A special lens then projects these images onto the planetarium dome.

While the mechanical star projector can only show the sky from on or near the Earth's surface, the digital video star projector can take an audience on imaginary flights to the stars. It can also move the audience forward or backward millions of years to show how the positions of the stars and the shapes of constellations change over time. The projector's computer can also create and project images of the sun, the moon, space stations, and spacecraft, and it can present information about these objects.

Other Projectors

In the modern planetarium theater, the star projector is only one of dozens, or even hundreds, of computer-controlled projection devices. These projectors use slides, film, videotape, optical laser disks, and other media to create a wide variety of objects or scenes on the planetarium dome. Among the images they can create are moving clouds, shooting stars, rotating planets, galaxies, black holes, and landscapes of the surface of the moon or of planets in our solar system. With such images, the audience can experience trips to other planets or to the far corners of the universe, and they can see and learn about the latest discoveries in astronomy and space science. Some planetariums have devices in each seat that let audience members control the computers operating these projectors. In this way, audiences can decide for themselves what they wish to see and learn.

Laser Systems

Many modern planetariums have powerful laser systems that can create colorful patterns or moving pictures or words in the planetarium sky. These images are generated by computer and can be used to help illustrate a wide variety of planetarium shows. They can also be used in combination with music during live or recorded concerts in the planetarium theater. Sometimes special machines that create a fine mist are used to generate an artificial fog inside the theater. As lasers pass through this fog they create colorful beams or patterns of light that move in the air above the heads of the audience. Recently, special glasses have been developed that give people the illusion of seeing these three-dimensional laser images move in mid-air without the use of the fog-generating machines.

This museum display of the solar system (*left*) is made up of scale models of the planets. Each model rotates on its axis as dots of light show its orbit. A designer (*above*) completes a scale model of the Hubble Space Telescope that will be used in a planetarium show.

CREATING A PLANETARIUM SHOW

The shows seen in planetarium theaters are often created by people whose work is similar to making movies for theaters or television.

A planetarium show is created in several stages. After a subject is chosen, someone must research the information about it that is to be used in the show to be sure it is correct and up to date. When all of the information is gathered and checked, a script is written. This script is usually written by an astronomer and it contains all the words the audience will hear during the show. It also indicates what the audience will see on the planetarium dome as the words are being spoken.

While working on a script, the scriptwriter must work with others who create the visual images that will appear on the dome. These visual images are created by artists using paints and brushes or perhaps computers. Sometimes an artist will also build models of spacecraft because they often look more realistic than paintings. When the paintings and models are finished, they are recorded on film, videotape, or optical laser disks for projection onto the planetarium dome during the show. Computer images may also be stored on film, videotape, or laser disks.

Creating special effects for a planetarium show requires the help of skilled technicians who build special projectors that can project moving images, such as planets or spacecraft, across the planetarium dome. Motion is sometimes created by moving a piece of film or a slide within a projector. Sometimes images from projectors are reflected from moving mirrors, which causes the images to move in the artificial sky of the dome.

After the script for a planetarium show is finished, it is read by one or more narrators and recorded on tape. Music and sound effects to generate excitement and build suspense are recorded on tape as well. The music and sound effects must work well with the script and images, and they must be just the right length to accompany the different parts of the show.

Finally, the planetarium show is put together. All slides, film, videotape, laser disks, and other visual materials are placed in projectors or other playback devices. This may require dozens or even hundreds of different projectors, all being turned on and off at various times during the program. Controlling all these projectors and timing their action with

Visitors to the National Air and Space Museum in Washington, D.C., can see full-scale models of the many kinds of spacecraft used to explore outer space.

narration and music can be very complicated. To do it manually would be almost impossible. Today, however, it is possible to control and time everything with a computer, and a special computer program is written for each planetarium show.

SPACE MUSEUMS

Many planetariums are part of science-technology centers or space museums that feature exciting exhibits on space and space-related topics. A well-known space museum is the National Air and Space Museum at the Smithsonian Institution in Washington, D.C.

The National Air and Space Museum is a particularly exciting place to visit. Its exhibits show how far people have progressed in the areas of flight and space exploration. These exhibits trace the development of flight from early hot air balloons to the first airplanes to more advanced aircraft and different types of spacecraft. Among the exhibits is a large col-

In the *Challenger* shuttle area of the Space Center in Iowa, you can experience some of the activities astronauts have in flight. Here students are using a computer to send messages to mission control.

lection of spacecraft replicas, including various weather and communication satellites, the *Mariner 10* and *Voyager* spacecraft sent to study other planets, the *Mercury* space capsule that carried the first American astronauts into space, and the *Apollo* lunar lander. There is even a replica of the Skylab Space Station that visitors to the museum can walk through. With its planetarium theater and hundreds of exhibits, slide shows, movies, replicas, and actual aircraft, the National Air and Space Museum provides a comprehensive look at space and space exploration.

Types of Exhibits. Space museums typically have a variety of exhibits. Many of these exhibits are interactive. This means that visitors can touch or manipulate (operate) parts of the exhibit. In some interactive exhibits, computers that can store large amounts of information and images are used to help explain the exhibit or to answer visitors' questions.

Museum exhibits often include real meteorites and models of planets, stars, and galaxies. They help visitors understand what these objects are made of and how they relate to each other in terms of size and distance. Other exhibits may include astronomical instruments and dioramas (three-dimensional scenes) of different objects or activities with explanations of how they work. Some space museums even have small observatories with working telescopes. When fitted with special filters, these telescopes can be used to look at the sun during the day and see explosive storms on its surface or huge glowing clouds of hot gas stretching far out into space. At night, the tele-scopes allow visitors to see the moon, planets, galaxies, nebulae, and stars. Images from such telescopes can also be projected onto television monitors or movie screens located elsewhere in the museum.

Other Activities. Many space museums, as well as planetariums, also have classrooms where people can take courses in astronomy or related subjects. They may also have lecture halls where experts speak about different topics related to space and astronomy. Some museums have libraries or research facilities where people can get information about topics in which they are interested. Many offer educational programs for students of all ages.

At some space museums, including the Houston Museum of Science and Natural History, and Discovery Place in Charlotte, North Carolina, young people can go on simulated missions to a space station or to the planet Mars. Working in teams, they learn what it is like to perform tasks similar to those done by astronauts. They also learn what it is like to be the engineers and scientists on the Earth who work with astronauts to solve problems that arise during space missions.

Space museums and planetariums are fascinating places. With their many shows, exhibits, and programs, they allow everyone who visits them to learn about and experience some of the wonders of space.

WILLIAM A. GUTSCH, JR.
Chairman, American Museum–
Hayden Planetarium

See also SPACE AGENCIES AND CENTERS; SPACE RESEARCH AND TECHNOLOGY.

PLANETS

In ancient times, sky watchers observed that there were five special points of light in the night sky. All the other points of light always kept their same positions relative to one another. These were the stars, and the constellations that they formed remained the same year after year, lifetime after lifetime. The five points of light were different because, from week to week and month to month, they slowly moved among the stars as if they had special powers. The ancient Greeks called these points of light the *planétai*, a word that means "wandering stars," and named them after their gods: Hermes, Aphrodite, Ares, Zeus, and Chronos.

Today we know that these points of light, which we call planets, wander slowly in the sky because they are other "worlds" in our solar system that are traveling at different speeds around our sun. Instead of using the names of the Greek gods, we call these planets by the names of the equivalent Roman gods: Mercury, Venus, Mars, Jupiter, and Saturn.

A planet is very different from a star. A star is a huge ball of fiery gases that gives off light. A planet shines by reflected light. The planets in our solar system are captives of our star, the sun. They travel around the sun in paths called orbits.

Our own Earth is one of these planets. If you could observe the Earth from outer space, you would see that it, too, seems always to be moving among the stars. Part of it would appear bright and part would appear dark. The bright part is where sunlight is striking it. Like the other planets, the Earth gives off no light of its own. When a planet shines brightly in the night sky, it is reflecting the sun's light.

In addition to the five planets known since ancient times, three more—Uranus, Neptune, and Pluto—have been discovered since the invention of the telescope. Counting our Earth, there are nine known planets in our solar system. Some of the planets have one or more satellites, or moons, that revolve around them. Our moon is one of these satellites. The planets with their satellites, and all of the asteroids and comets that orbit the sun, make up our solar system.

In this article, you will travel outward from the sun and visit the planets one at a time. Your first stop is Mercury.

On a voyage to Jupiter, you will be met by violent winds and frigid temperatures in its upper atmosphere and a boiling liquid ocean in its interior.

▶MERCURY

Mercury is the closest planet to the sun. Its average distance from the sun is about 35.9 million miles (57.8 million kilometers). The orbits of all the planets are ellipses, or flattened circles, but Mercury's orbit is particularly flattened. As a result, Mercury can come as close as 29 million miles (46.7 million kilometers) to the sun, and at other times it is about 44 million miles (70.8 million kilometers) away. It takes 88 Earth days for Mercury to complete one trip around the sun. In other words, one Earth year of 365 days is longer than four Mercury years. Radar waves bounced off Mercury from Earth show that it rotates on its axis once every 59 Earth days. The diameter of Mercury is 3,032 miles (4,880 kilometers).

Mercury appears tiny and almost without features, even when observed with powerful telescopes. Little was known about this planet until *Mariner 10* flew past it and sent back hundreds of images, showing thousands of craters, long cliffs called scarps, and a giant impact basin about 800 miles (1,280 kilometers) across.

An extremely thin veil of helium gas has been detected around Mercury. These atoms, which are actually given off by the sun, flow around the planet as it orbits the sun. In addition to this veil, a very thin atmosphere of sodium, potassium, and oxygen gases, which probably escapes from Mercury's surface, has also been detected. The magnetic field that surrounds Mercury is much weaker than the Earth's magnetic field. Its gravitational pull is also much weaker than that of the Earth.

THE SOLAR SYSTEM

Someday you may be able to plan an adventurous trip from Earth to the eight other planets in our solar system. You will certainly have to pack a variety of things to meet the different climates and circumstances you will encounter along the way. In addition, you will find that your weight differs after you arrive at each planet. When the gravitational pull on a planet is weaker than that of Earth, you will weigh less than you do on Earth. If the gravitational pull is stronger, you will weigh more. If you weigh 100 pounds on Earth, you will weigh 38 pounds on Mercury, 91 pounds on Venus, 38 pounds on Mars, 254 pounds on Jupiter, 108 pounds on Saturn, 91 pounds at the top of Uranus' clouds, 119 pounds on Neptune, and 6 pounds on Pluto!

Because Mercury is so close to the sun, temperatures can reach about 800°F (420°C) during the day. However, Mercury has practically no atmosphere to retain this heat, so during its long nights the temperature can plunge to −280°F (−171°C). Mercury has no known satellites.

▶ VENUS

Your next stop is Venus. This planet travels around the sun in a nearly circular orbit, and its average distance from the sun is about 67.2 million miles (108.2 million kilometers). Venus takes 224.7 Earth days to make one trip around the sun. It is nearly the same size as the Earth, and its diameter is 7,519 miles (12,100 kilometers). Its gravitational pull is almost the same as that of the Earth.

Venus comes closer to the Earth than any other planet—it is only about 26 million miles

(41.9 million kilometers) away. Even so, we can see virtually no details in a telescope because Venus is completely covered by thick clouds. These clouds reflect the sun's light, and at times Venus is the brightest object in the sky except for the sun and the moon.

Venus' atmosphere is about 90 times as dense as that of the Earth, and its chief component is carbon dioxide. The carbon dioxide traps the sun's heat and creates a very strong greenhouse effect, driving the surface temperature of Venus to more than 800°F (420°C). Venus has no magnetic field and, like Mercury, this planet has no known satellites.

By using radar to penetrate the clouds of Venus, scientists have learned that while Venus' clouds can circle the planet in as little time as four Earth days, its surface spins very slowly, completing one rotation in 243 Earth days. Another discovery was that Venus

Pluto

Neptune

Saturn

Asteroids

Jupiter

rotates from east to west like Uranus and Pluto. All of the other planets rotate from west to east.

Radar waves bounced off Venus from Earth as well as from spacecraft have allowed scientists to map the surface of this planet in great detail. Such maps show that about 60 percent of its surface is covered by flat, gently rolling plains and a few craters. Two large areas, the size of small continents on Earth, consist of mountainous terrain. Radar maps suggest that, unlike Earth, Venus is made of only one continental plate. There is nothing that resembles the Earth's mid-ocean ridges or similar features.

▶EARTH

Beyond the orbit of Venus is Earth, the next planet. The Earth's orbit is almost as circular as that of Venus. The Earth travels around the sun at an average distance of 93 million miles (149.7 million kilometers). It completes one orbit around the sun in 365.25 days, and it takes 23 hours and 56 minutes for the Earth to rotate on its axis.

The Earth is a ball of rock and metal. Its diameter is 7,923 miles (12,751 kilometers) at the equator. Surrounding the Earth, like a great blanket of gases, is an atmosphere that is made up mainly of nitrogen and oxygen. As seen from space, however, the Earth's atmosphere appears very thin. If the Earth were the size of an apple, its atmosphere would be thinner than the apple's skin.

Unlike Mercury and Venus, the Earth has a natural satellite, the moon. It orbits the Earth at an average distance of 240,000 miles (386,400 kilometers). Because the moon rotates on its axis in the same period of time as it revolves around the Earth, it always keeps the same face toward the Earth. The moon is 2,160 miles (3,478 kilometers) in diameter, which is more than one fourth the diameter of the Earth.

▶MARS

After leaving Earth, your next stop is Mars, a planet that shines in the sky with a reddish color and is sometimes called the Red Planet. The orbit of Mars is more oval shaped than that of the Earth. As a result, the distance between Mars and the sun may be as little as 128.4 million miles (206.7 million kilometers) or as much as 154.8 million miles (249.2 million kilometers). The average distance between Mars and the sun is about 142 million miles (228 million kilometers). It takes Mars 687 Earth days to travel once around the sun, and it rotates once on its axis in 24 hours and 37 minutes.

Mars is a small, rocky world that is very dry. Its diameter is 4,200 miles (6,760 kilometers), only a little more than half that of the Earth, and its gravitational pull is weaker.

Mars has two small satellites. Phobos, the larger one, measures 8.5 miles (13.7 kilometers) in its longest dimension, and it circles its planet at a distance of 2,462 miles (3,964 kilometers). Phobos completes its orbit in about 7.5 hours, which is less time than it takes Mars to turn once on its axis. Therefore, to a visitor on Mars, Phobos would seem to rise in the west and set in the east. Deimos is smaller than Phobos. It circles Mars at a distance of 14,700 miles (23,600 kilometers).

The *Mariner* and *Viking* space probes provided scientists with a great deal of information about Mars. They learned that Mars has no magnetic field and that there is very little atmosphere surrounding it. The atmospheric pressure on its surface is 1/600 of the atmospheric pressure on the Earth's surface. Its thin atmosphere is made up almost entirely of carbon dioxide. Temperatures at the planet's equator may occasionally reach 60°F (16°C), but nighttime polar temperatures can plunge to nearly $-202°F$ ($-130°C$).

The surface of Mars has a variety of features, including craters, giant extinct volcanoes, and a canyon system almost as long as the width of the United States. No evidence of life was found at the two points where the *Viking* landers touched down on its surface.

▶ASTEROIDS

On your journey from Mars to Jupiter, you will encounter a gap of more than 340 million miles (547.4 million kilometers) between the orbits of these two planets. However, the gap, known as the main belt, is not empty—there are thousands of small objects called asteroids in it. The largest asteroid, named Ceres, is about 480 miles (770 kilometers) in diameter. Some of the smallest asteroids are less than a mile (1.6 kilometers) across.

At least 1,700 asteroids have been named or numbered, and as many as 100,000 may exist. Most stay in the main belt while traveling around the sun. Some make a complete orbit in 1.5 Earth years, and others may take as long as 6 years to complete one orbit.

▶JUPITER

The next stop on your planetary journey is Jupiter, which is more than five times farther from the sun than Earth. The planet travels around the sun at an average distance of 483 million miles (778 million kilometers), taking 11.9 Earth years to complete one orbit.

Jupiter, the largest planet, is one of the four gas giants in our solar system. Its diameter is 89,000 miles (143,000 kilometers)—more than 11 times greater than that of Earth.

Through a telescope Jupiter appears to be a whitish globe with darker bands of color crossing it. It is wider at its equator than at its poles because it spins quickly, taking 9 hours and 55 minutes to rotate once on its axis.

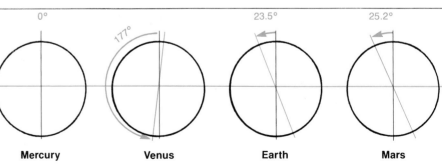

The Tilt of Each Planet on its Axis

Except for Mercury, each planet tilts as it rotates on its axis. In the art at right, the green line shows the plane of each planet's orbit. The red lines shown perpendicular to that plane are used to calculate the degree to which each planet tilts on its axis. The degree of that tilt is shown by the blue lines and numbers.

| 0° | 177° | 23.5° | 25.2° |
| Mercury | Venus | Earth | Mars |

What appears to be Jupiter's surface is really the top of a thick, cloudy atmosphere. Nearly 82 percent of it is hydrogen, and most of the remaining 18 percent is helium. There are also very small amounts of methane, ammonia, and some other substances that give Jupiter's clouds their beautiful colors.

The instruments in the *Pioneer* and *Voyager* space probes confirmed that at the top of Jupiter's atmosphere it is very cold, about −186°F (−121°C). Deeper down in the clouds, however, temperatures climb to thousands of degrees. The tremendous heat rising through the atmosphere combines with Jupiter's rapid rotation to produce large and violent weather systems. Cloud belts on Jupiter are driven by powerful winds that move at speeds of up to 350 miles (560 kilometers) per hour. The most amazing feature in Jupiter's clouds is an enormous orange-red area known as the Great Red Spot, which is more than twice the size of our planet.

Deep below the clouds there is no solid surface. Instead, astronomers think there is probably a planet-wide ocean that consists mostly of hydrogen compressed under such great pressure that it forms a liquid with metallic properties. At the center of Jupiter there is probably a core, consisting of iron and silicates, about twenty times the total mass of the Earth. The molten metallic materials in the core create a strong magnetic field that extends far out into space. At the top of Jupiter's clouds, this magnetic field is about ten times stronger than that of the Earth. Jupiter's gravitational pull is about two and one-half times stronger than the Earth's.

Jupiter has 16 known satellites. The largest, Ganymede, is 3,200 miles (5,200 kilometers) in diameter. Callisto is slightly smaller, with a diameter of about 3,000 miles (4,800 kilometers). Each of these satellites has an icy surface covered with craters. Another satellite, Europa, which is about 1,900 miles (3,100 kilo-

LOOK AT THE PLANETS

Observing Mercury and Venus

Because Venus and Mercury are closer to the sun than the Earth is, we see them go through phases like those of the moon. You can observe these phases if you have a telescope.

When either planet is almost between the Earth and the sun, it is difficult to see. This is because the sunlit side of the planet is facing away from us, and the planet lies close to the sun in our sky. Over a period of days as Mercury or Venus moves from this position, we are gradually able to see more and more of its sunlit side. During these times, a thin crescent of Venus or Mercury can be seen in a telescope. As the planet gradually moves on around the sun, the crescent fills in. The planet also appears to be growing smaller during this time because its distance from the Earth is increasing. When the planet goes around the far side of the sun, it is near full phase, looking quite round but also very small because it is so distant. During such times it is also difficult to see because it is very close to the sun in the sky and the sun's glare blocks our view. Finally, as the planet again swings close to the Earth, it again appears to grow larger, but we see less and less of its sunlit face.

Because of this motion, Mercury and Venus alternately appear to the right or left of the sun in our sky. When they are to the left of the sun, they set after sunset and are visible for a while in the western sky during early evening. When they lie to the right of the sun, they rise shortly before sunrise and can be seen in the eastern sky a little before dawn. That is why the names "Morning Star" and "Evening Star" have been used for both planets, although they are not stars at all.

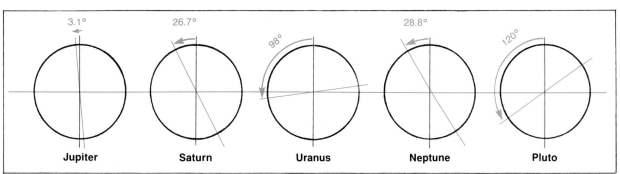

Jupiter 3.1° Saturn 26.7° Uranus 98° Neptune 28.8° Pluto 120°

Mercury

Venus

Earth

Mars

Jupiter

Saturn

Pluto

Uranus

Neptune

The Sizes of the Planets
This drawing gives you an idea of the sizes of the planets compared to one another. Basic facts about the planets are given in the chart at right.

meters) across, is also covered with a layer of ice. Io has a diameter of about 2,200 miles (3,500 kilometers), and its surface is covered with volcanoes and lava flows. There are 12 more known satellites, ranging from 50 to 100 miles (80 to 160 kilometers) in diameter. Before the *Voyagers*, little was known about Jupiter's satellites because they appear only as dots when seen through even the largest telescopes. *Voyager 1* also discovered a thin, delicate ring of fine particles circling Jupiter.

▶SATURN

The next stop on your journey is Saturn, another gas giant. It orbits the sun at an average distance of 885.5 million miles (1.4 billion kilometers) and takes nearly 29.5 Earth years to make one trip around the sun.

Saturn, which is not quite as large as Jupiter, has a diameter of about 74,500 miles (120,000 kilometers). Like Jupiter, Saturn rotates very quickly; it takes 10 hours and 40 minutes for it to turn once on its axis. Saturn bulges even more at its equator than Jupiter.

Saturn has a very deep atmosphere, which is made up mainly of hydrogen and helium, with some methane and ammonia. At the top of its atmosphere, the temperature is about −300°F (−185°C). This low temperature causes ammonia in the outer atmosphere to freeze, forming high-altitude haze. This gives Saturn a softer appearance than Jupiter. There are also spots similar to Jupiter's Great Red Spot in Saturn's atmosphere, but they are smaller. The largest is about the size of Earth.

The largest of Saturn's 18 known satellites

THE PLANETS	MERCURY	VENUS	EARTH	MARS	JUPITER	SATURN	URANUS	NEPTUNE	PLUTO
Average Distance from Sun (in miles) (in kilometers)	35,900,000 57,800,000	67,200,000 108,200,000	93,000,000 150,000,000	142,000,000 228,000,000	483,000,000 778,000,000	885,500,000 1,400,000,000	1,800,000,000 2,900,000,000	2,800,000,000 4,500,000,000	3,700,000,000 5,900,000,000
Length of Year (in Earth days and years)	88.0d	224.7d	365.25d	687.0d	11.9y	29.5y	84.0y	165y	247.7y
Period of Rotation (in Earth minutes, hours, and days)	59d	243d	23h 56m	24h 37m	9h 55m	10h 40m	17h	16h 5m	6d 9h
Diameter at Equator (in miles) (in kilometers)	3,032 4,880	7,519 12,100	7,923 12,751	4,200 6,760	89,000 143,000	74,500 120,000	32,000 51,500	30,800 49,600	1,400 2,253
Number of Known Satellites	0	0	1	2	16	18	15	8	1

is Titan. The diameter of Titan, including its atmosphere, is 3,400 miles (5,470 kilometers). This is the only satellite in the solar system that has a thick atmosphere—it is about two and one-half times as dense as that of the Earth. This atmosphere is mostly nitrogen, with small amounts of methane and other hydrogen compounds. Phoebe, the most distant satellite, is 8 million miles (13 million kilometers) from Saturn. It moves in the opposite direction from the other 17 satellites.

Saturn is one of the most beautiful objects in the sky because of the rings that circle the planet at its equator. The entire ring system is more than 170,000 miles (274,000 kilometers) in diameter, but it is only about 66 feet (20 meters) thick. As Saturn orbits the sun, astronomers can see the rings from different angles. Sometimes the rings are viewed edge-on and almost disappear from sight because they are so thin. The rings may have formed at the same time as the solar system, or they may be the remains of a nearby satellite that was broken up by Saturn's gravitational pull, which is almost the same as that of the Earth.

▶URANUS

Leaving Saturn and traveling even farther from the sun, you come to Uranus. Uranus is 32,000 miles (51,500 kilometers) in diameter. It orbits the sun at an average distance of 1.8 billion miles (2.9 billion kilometers), and it takes 84 Earth years to complete one orbit. Uranus rotates once on its axis in an east-to-west direction in approximately 17 hours—the rate at which both its magnetic field, which is anchored in the planet's interior, and its interior rotate. Uranus' magnetic field is about 50 times stronger than that of the Earth.

Determining how fast Uranus' clouds rotate is difficult because a deep layer of haze makes the planet's atmosphere almost featureless. Like Jupiter and Saturn, Uranus has a very thick atmosphere. A system of thin, very dark rings encircles the planet.

The blue-green color of Uranus is caused by methane in its atmosphere. The temperature at the tops of the thick clouds in the atmosphere is $-355°F$ ($-215°C$). Scientists think that the atmosphere surrounds a rocky and metallic core. At the tops of Uranus' clouds, the gravitational pull is somewhat weaker than that of the Earth.

Most of the planets spin in a more or less straight up-and-down position as they orbit the sun, although some are tilted a little more than others. If the solar system could be placed on a gigantic table, the planets would look like spinning tops as they moved around the sun. Uranus, however, tilts at the extreme angle of 98 degrees. You could almost say that the planet lies on its side as it travels around the sun. This means that the north and south polar regions of Uranus experience alternate periods of day and night (and summer and winter), each of which is up to 42 Earth years long. If Uranus were much closer to the sun, this could result in very extreme seasons. Because of its distance from the sun and the odd wind patterns in its atmosphere, Uranus has rather even global temperatures, and the north and south polar regions are actually a little warmer than the regions around its equator.

Uranus has 15 known satellites. The largest is Titania, with a diameter of about 1,000 miles (1,600 kilometers). The ten smallest satellites range in size from about 19 to 96 miles (31 to 155 kilometers) in diameter.

NEPTUNE

Traveling even farther away from the sun, you come to Neptune. This planet was discovered when astronomers observed that the movement of the planet Uranus appeared to be influenced by the gravity of an unknown planet. In 1846, using calculations that indicated where the other planet should be, German astronomers discovered the new planet, which is now called Neptune.

Neptune's average distance from the sun is about 2.8 billion miles (4.5 billion kilometers), and it takes nearly 165 Earth years to complete one orbit. Its diameter is 30,800 miles (49,600 kilometers).

Like Jupiter, Saturn, and Uranus, Neptune is a gas giant with a thick atmosphere. This atmosphere, which is mostly hydrogen and helium along with traces of methane gas, is wrapped around an ocean of water, methane, and ammonia. The temperature at the ocean's surface may be 4500°F (2500°C), while the temperature in Neptune's upper atmosphere is about −355°F (−215°C).

The upper atmosphere includes the Great Dark Spot, which is dark blue in color. There are also several smaller dark spots and an unusual white cloud, which is named Scooter because it moves at a speed different from the speeds of the rest of Neptune's cloud cover.

Neptune's magnetic field rotates once in about 16 hours. The rate of rotation of the features visible in its atmosphere varies greatly and depends on the latitude of the features.

A system of dark, thin rings encircles Neptune, and the planet has eight known satellites. Triton, its largest satellite, has a thin atmosphere, consisting mostly of nitrogen gas.

PLUTO

You complete your planetary trip as you near Pluto, the smallest planet in our solar system. After discovering Uranus and Neptune, astronomers observed that these two planets were being pulled a little bit away from their expected paths around the sun. This indicated that there must be another planet beyond Neptune. In 1930, the American astronomer Clyde Tombaugh (1906–   ) discovered the new planet, which was named Pluto.

Pluto has a diameter of about 1,400 miles (2,253 kilometers), and its average distance from the sun is 3.7 billion miles (5.9 billion kilometers). Its trip around the sun takes 247.7 Earth years, and it takes 6 Earth days and 9 hours for Pluto to rotate once on its axis. Like Venus and Uranus, Pluto rotates from east to west. Its orbit is a long ellipse, bringing it as close to the sun as 2.8 billion miles (4.4 billion kilometers) and as far away as 4.6 billion miles (7.4 billion kilometers). At times, its orbit brings Pluto closer to the sun than Neptune ever gets.

Temperatures on Pluto probably never rise above −382°F (−230°C). Pluto consists of a mix of rocky materials and ice, and it has a thin atmosphere of methane gas. Its gravitational pull is very weak. Charon, Pluto's one known satellite, is about 746 miles (1,200 kilometers) across and is close to the planet.

WILLIAM S. GUTSCH, JR.
Chairman, American Museum–
Hayden Planetarium

See also ASTRONOMY; COMETS, METEORITES, AND ASTEROIDS; SATELLITES; SOLAR SYSTEM; SPACE PROBES; SPACE SATELLITES; and articles on individual planets.

WONDER QUESTION

Do planets exist beyond the solar system?

Astronomers studying radio signals from a pulsar—the dense, rapidly spinning, collapsed core of a star that exploded millions of years ago —have detected two planet-sized objects orbiting it. The pulsar, PSR B1257+12, is about 1,500 light-years away, in the constellation Virgo.

Unusual but regular variations in the radio signals coming from the pulsar indicated to the astronomers that something must be having enough of a gravitational influence on it to affect the way it was spinning. By examining the pattern of those variations, they were able to detect objects orbiting the pulsar. These objects may be planets. One of the objects is 3.4 times the mass of the Earth; the other is 2.8 times the Earth's mass.

In examining the pulsar's radio signals, which are received and recorded by the radio telescope near Arecibo, Puerto Rico, astronomers have also detected the presence of a smaller object about the size of our moon. Additional evidence suggests that there may also be a more distant object the size of Jupiter.

The Hubble Space Telescope has detected evidence that many newly evolving stars are surrounded by the raw materials that could form into planets. This discovery is an important addition to the growing evidence that planets may orbit stars other than the sun.

PLANKTON

Life all over the world depends on the billions upon billions of tiny living things that drift like a pale mist in the waters of the world. This drifting mass of organisms is called plankton. Plankton is the cornerstone of the ocean's food chain and the major supplier of the Earth's oxygen.

Plankton is made up of many kinds of organisms, most of them so small they can only be seen with a microscope. All of these organisms are very different from one another. But in one respect they are all alike—they share a drifting way of life. In fact, the term "plankton" comes from a Greek word for "wandering" or "drifting."

Although a wide variety of organisms make up plankton, scientists generally separate it into two groups: phytoplankton and zooplankton. Phytoplankton includes single-celled plants and plantlike organisms, such as algae. Zooplankton includes minute protozoans and sea animals. Some organisms, such as diatoms, always remain plankton. Others, such as fish and lobsters, are plankton only while they are in the egg or larva stages of their development.

Plankton is not found at all depths in water. While phytoplankton gathers in the sunlit surface waters less than 500 feet (153 meters) deep, zooplankton avoids the light. It spends the daytime gathered in the darkness of deep water, hundreds to thousands of feet down. At dusk, the dense swarm of zooplankton comes to the surface to graze on the rich phytoplankton food source. Before daybreak it descends, sinking back to the depths beyond the sunlight.

▶ PHYTOPLANKTON

The smallest, and most plentiful, plankton organisms now known are microscopic phytoplankton called diatoms and dinoflagellates. These small algae, especially diatoms, exist in huge numbers. Just 1 gallon of seawater can contain between 1 million and 2 million diatoms.

The name "diatom"comes from Greek words meaning "cut through, " for a diatom looks as though it has been cut in two and then fitted back together again. It has a glasslike shell with one half overlapping the other. Diatoms come in a marvelous variety of shapes, such as stars, needles, and pillboxes, and with intricate markings.

The dinoflagellates are equally small, but they have no shells. Most dinoflagellates move by lashing the water with two threadlike whips called flagella. The name "dinofla-

Some Common Kinds of Plankton

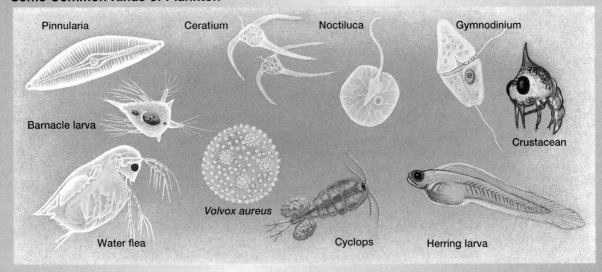

Pinnularia
Ceratium
Noctiluca
Gymnodinium
Barnacle larva
Crustacean
Volvox aureus
Water flea
Cyclops
Herring larva

the largest animal on Earth depends on some of the smallest living things for its survival? The blue whale, which can weigh up to 209 tons (190 metric tons), eats almost nothing but tiny shrimplike crustaceans called krill, some of which are only 3/10 inch (8 millimeters) in length. Krill are part of the zooplankton inhabiting the world's oceans. They can be found from the surface to depths of about 6,500 feet (2,000 meters).

The blue whale, along with other whales such as fin and humpback whales, uses a special structure to feed on the krill. Instead of teeth, the blue whale has fringed plates called baleen, that hang from its upper jaw. The baleen have brushlike fibers on the inside edges. When the whale takes in seawater, the fibers trap the frill inside the whale's mouth and filter out all the water. Whales that feed using this method are often referred to as baleen whales.

Sometimes whales have to strain thousands of tons of seawater to get enough krill. But there are species of krill that live in huge swarms, covering an area of 450 square feet (42 square meters) or more. Most often the whales feed on these concentrated masses of krill, sometimes consuming 5,000 pounds (2,300 kilograms) at one feeding! Whales are not the only animals that feed on these floating masses so do seals, fish, and squids.

gellate" comes from Greek words meaning "whirling whips."

In one way, dinoflagellates, diatoms, and other algae are like green plants that grow on land—they contain the green pigment called chlorophyll. Through the action of chlorophyll, in the presence of sunlight, these organisms combine water and carbon dioxide to make their own food in a process called photosynthesis.

Diatoms and dinoflagellates are found in both fresh and salt waters. Their numbers depend on the amount of light and on the supplies of raw materials available. In some places the light and raw materials remain almost the same throughout the year, while in other parts of the world there are seasonal changes. During the North Atlantic winter, for example, diatoms grow and multiply slowly. Days are short, and there is little light for food production. However, spring brings longer days. Raw materials that have washed in from the land and welled up from the water's bottom during the winter are plentiful. During this time, diatoms may double their numbers every 24 hours. Such rapid growth is called a bloom. A bloom may make water look yellow, green, red, or brown, depending on what creature is blooming.

▶ **ZOOPLANKTON**

Drifting with and feeding on the phytoplankton are the countless small animals that make up zooplankton. These animals provide food for larger animals, which may in turn become food for people.

Among the smallest and most numerous organisms found in zooplankton are the pearshaped crustaceans called copepods. The name "copepod" comes from Greek words meaning "oar feet." A copepod swims by jerky, oarlike movements of its tiny limbs. The largest copepod is less than 1/2 inch (1.3 centimeters) long. Most are very much smaller. Yet copepods are an important food of many fish.

Crustaceans of many kinds spend the early stages of their lives as part of the drifting plankton mass. Saltwater varieties include shrimps, krill, crabs, lobsters, and barnacles, and freshwater, fairy shrimp and water fleas. The larvae of these crustaceans are tiny or even microscopic. They usually do not look very much like their parents. They are too small and weak to move off on their own.

This is true also of the young mollusks, such as snails, clams, and mussels, that are found in both fresh and salt waters. When they are fully grown, their drifting lifestyles end, and they take up life on the water's bottom. Plankton may also include the eggs and larvae of many kinds of fish. They swim off on their own when they reach adulthood. They may feed on plankton, but they are no longer part of the drifting mass of life.

In freshwater, animal plankton often includes developing insects. Mayflies, dragonflies, mosquitoes, water beetles, and many other insects lay their eggs in water. When the larvae hatch out, they live and feed on other plankton.

Rotifers, or wheelworms, are also commonly found in freshwater plankton. If the ponds they live in dry up, rotifers and their eggs may be blown about by winds for months. When at last they land in water—whether lake or puddle—they start growing and feeding again.

In saltwater plankton, small, finned arrowworms dart about, capturing diatoms and larvae in bristling "jaws." Because its body is as clear as glass, this animal is sometimes called a glassworm. If you put one under a microscope, you would probably see some small plankton organisms passing down the worm's digestive tube.

Other saltwater plankton includes young starfishes, sea urchins, sea cucumbers, comb jellies, and jellyfishes. When fully grown, all but the comb jellies and jellyfishes leave their plankton nursery to live and feed on the ocean bottom.

Sea squirts belong to a group of animals known as tunicates because of the tough, clear tunic (cloak) of flesh that covers the bodies of these animals. Their larvae look like tiny frog tadpoles and drift about as plankton. The larvae swim by bending their tails from side to side. Their bodies, which are clear enough to see through, are stiffened by a sort of spine, called a notochord. The notochord disappears as the animals develops. This saltwater group includes a number of organisms, such as salps and pyrosomes, that remain plankton all their lives.

▶ THE IMPORTANCE OF PLANKTON

Directly or indirectly, every living thing owes its existence to plankton. More than a billion years ago, plankton first started putting oxygen into the atmosphere, making life possible for land plants and animals, including people. All the living things in the

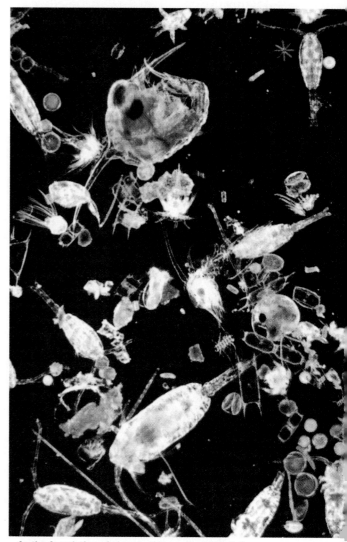

As the foundation of almost all the major food chains, the tiny organisms making up plankton support huge populations of creatures in oceans and large lakes.

oceans, seas, and other bodies of water depend on plankton for food as well as oxygen. The flow of food energy begins with phytoplankton, which are eaten by zooplankton, which are eaten by small fish, which are in turn eaten by larger fish, and so on. If we change the waters of the world, we risk destroying the plankton. This is dangerous because the health of our waters, and of our planet, depends on plankton.

Reviewed by N. J. BERRILL
McGill University

See also ALGAE; CRUSTACEANS; MICROBIOLOGY; OCEAN; OCEANOGRAPHY.

An attack by pine beetles, which feed on the bark of trees and on the wood inside, has left injured and dying trees throughout this Montana forest.

PLANT PESTS

People depend on plants for many reasons. They provide food, wood, fibers for clothing, even oxygen for us to breathe. We grow plants for these and many more useful products as well as for the beauty of a world filled with trees, flowers and other greenery. Living things that eat or damage the plants we grow are called pests.

Throughout human history, crop failures due to pests have caused tremendous suffering. In 1845, the potato crop in Ireland was suddenly destroyed by a fungus disease. One day the potatoes looked fine; a few days later, the leaves had turned black and the potatoes were rotten! The disease destroyed most of the potato crop in Ireland for the next several years, causing the Potato Famine of 1847. It is estimated that in only a few years, as many

as 2 million people died of starvation in Ireland because of this one plant disease. Several million more people fled to the United States to escape the famine.

The appearance of vast destructive swarms of locusts, a type of grasshopper, are described in the Bible and still happen today. The locusts gather together in huge groups and fly hundreds of miles seeking food. A single locust swarm may contain millions of insects and darken the sky as it flies over! When the locusts land, they rapidly eat everything, stripping the area of all crops, tree leaves, and grass.

Dramatic pest disasters such as the Irish potato famine and locust plagues are unusual. Most of the time pests exist in smaller numbers, causing damage to crops and plants, but not total destruction. People also create pest problems, such as when they grow large fields of the same crop, providing pests with huge food supplies, or when they transport crops with hidden pests from one area to another. Plants may also be damaged by air pollution and toxic wastes produced by people.

▶ THE ENEMIES OF PLANTS

There are many kinds of plant pests. Insects, mites, birds, and animals sometimes eat crops before people can harvest them. Plant diseases can cause crops to suddenly die, or make the crop rot before it can reach market.

Imported Pests

In its native land, a pest has many enemies, such as parasites (a living thing that feeds and grows on another living thing), predators, and diseases, that keep its numbers small. However, in places where none of the pest's usual enemies exist, a pest problem can develop quickly.

The Japanese beetle is a shiny green and gold insect. It lays its eggs in grassy areas, and the young, called grubs, eat grass roots for a year until they emerge as adults in midsummer. The adult Japanese beetle eats a wide variety of plants, including many cultivated plants. In Japan, this insect is not a pest because there are many other insects that eat the beetle. There are also many diseases that kill most of the grubs. In the United States, however, the Japanese beetle became a serious pest. The grubs damaged lawns, and the adult beetles ate just about everything in the garden!

The number of beetles in many areas was astounding. Now this beetle is controlled with a combination of chemical sprays and a disease called milky spore. The milky spore disease, which is grown in laboratories, is made into a powder and sprinkled on lawns, killing most of the grubs without harming the grass.

The gypsy moth was brought into the United States by a scientist who wanted to use it to produce a hardy silkworm. In Europe, its native land, the gypsy moth is not a serious pest. Unfortunately, it escaped from the laboratory and established itself in the forests of Massachusetts. The gypsy moth caterpillars eat the leaves of most trees. In the absence of the European parasites, diseases, and predators that kill the gypsy moth, its population exploded in the United States. Without control measures, the caterpillars are capable of eating the leaves off of every tree in the forest—making it look like winter in June! The gypsy moth is spreading slowly southward along the East Coast of the United States. Over time, parasites will appear and diseases will develop that affect the gypsy moth in the United States. But left to nature, this process could take hundreds of years. Scientists are therefore developing diseases, parasites, and other enemies to control the gypsy moth.

Many other exotic pests have caused large amounts of damage. The chestnut blight, a fungus disease, has killed the American chestnut tree throughout its entire natural range. Another fungus disease, Dutch elm disease, has killed many elm trees. The Mediterranean fruit fly, or Med fly, became a major pest after its arrival in California. The bacterial disease citrus canker caused similar problems in Florida when it was found in some nurseries.

While holding its plant prey in a dense tangle of vines, the parasitic dodder feeds off the plant's tissues.

Weeds

Farmers are always working to protect their crops from all kinds of enemies. They probably spend the largest share of their time and energy controlling weeds—any plant that is growing where it is not wanted. Weeds compete with the plant crop for water, sunlight,

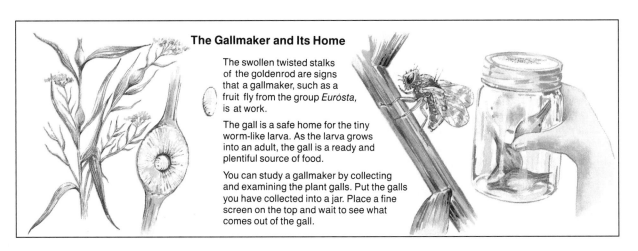

The Gallmaker and Its Home

The swollen twisted stalks of the goldenrod are signs that a gallmaker, such as a fruit fly from the group *Eurósta*, is at work.

The gall is a safe home for the tiny worm-like larva. As the larva grows into an adult, the gall is a ready and plentiful source of food.

You can study a gallmaker by collecting and examining the plant galls. Put the galls you have collected into a jar. Place a fine screen on the top and wait to see what comes out of the gall.

and soil nutrients. In addition, some weeds actually harm the crop. The witchweed is a parasitic plant that grows next to the crop plant. The witchweed attaches its roots to the crop roots, taking the food that the crop plant is making for itself. In fields with witchweed, the crop ends up stunted (smaller than normal). Dodder is another common parasitic plant. It looks like yellow or orange spaghetti. It twines around the stems of the crop, and sends plant shoots, or suckers, into the stem to take water and food from the crop.

The boll weevil is the most destructive insect to attack cotton, feeding on its tender shoots and blossom buds.

Insects and Mites

Insect pests come in many shapes and sizes. Caterpillars, beetles, beetle grubs, grasshoppers, and locusts are all **chewing** pests. They damage the plant as they bite off and eat pieces of leaves, fruits, or roots.

You can tell that a chewing insect is at work when you see the holes made in leaves and fruit. Some chewing insects are hidden from sight. They bore into the stems and twigs of the plant. Once inside, the insects feed on the plant. The plant, or part of the plant, wilts as the insect tunnels through it.

Other chewing insects dig into the soil to get at the plant roots. The adult corn rootworm is a beetle that eats corn leaves and lays its eggs in the soil. When the grubs hatch from the eggs, they eat the corn roots. Because of

the damage to the roots, the plants wilt and are smaller than normal; sometimes they even fall over when the wind blows.

Aphids, thrips, mealybugs, leafhoppers, scale insects, spider mites and many others are called **sucking** pests. Their mouths are specially formed for piercing plants and sucking the juices. When sucking pests feed on plants, they often stunt the plant's growth. The leaves of the plant curl and twist and develop blotches of yellow or brown.

Some pests live in close co-operation within the plant. The pest causes the plant to grow an elaborate swelling called a gall. **Gall** pests do this by making chemicals similar to the plant's own growth hormones. These chemicals cause the plant to form the gall. Then the gall-producing insect or mite lives and feeds inside the gall. Tiny wasps cause lots of different galls on the leaves and twigs of oak trees.

Diseases

Plants get diseases just as people do. Diseases can stop plants from growing or make them grow in unnatural ways. Often diseases will kill plants. Plant diseases are caused by organisms so small they can only be seen with a microscope.

Viruses, viroids, fungi, bacteria, and microscopic worms called nematodes can all cause plant diseases. But organisms that cause plant diseases do not ever cause human or animal diseases. They are specialized to attack only plants and usually only certain plants.

When a wheat plant has a disease called wheat stem rust, you can see rusty-colored spots and streaks on the stems. If you rub the spots, a very fine red-brown powder comes off. The powder is made up of the microscopic spores of the wheat stem rust fungus. These tiny spores are easily carried long distances on wind currents to unaffected areas. Entire fields of wheat can be infected with wheat stem rust; if the disease is severe enough, no grain will be produced.

When plants are infected with powdery mildew fungus, white moldy spots suddenly appear on the leaves and stems of the plants. The white spots are made up of fungal strands and tiny chains of spores. Plant leaves curl and eventually die when attacked by powdery mildew. If the leaves die, they can't make the food needed to produce the crop. Powdery mildews are serious pests of grain crops, such

Corn smut, a fungus disease producing sooty black masses, gradually destroys infected corn plants.

caused by a fungus. Tiny insects called elm bark beetles carry the fungus from sick trees to healthy trees. When this beetle emerges as an adult from under the bark, it carries many of the fungus spores on its body. The newly emerged adult beetles fly to healthy elms to feed on the sap. When the beetle chews a small hole in the elm twigs in order to feed, it puts the spores of the Dutch elm disease fungus into the tree. Within a few weeks the fungus will grow in the tree's feeding network. Parts of the tree will wilt as the system becomes clogged and is no longer able to spread nourishment throughout the tree.

Sucking pests such as aphids can transfer plant diseases. If an aphid feeds on a plant with a virus disease and then flies to a healthy plant, it can carry the virus to the healthy plant. Vegetable plants are often infected with virus diseases originally found in weeds. The aphids feed on the virus-infected weeds, then fly into the crop and transfer the disease to the crop. Cucumber and squash plants produce very odd looking lumpy fruit if they are infected with a virus.

▶ CONTROLLING PLANT PESTS

Over the long history of agriculture many methods and strategies have been developed to protect crops from pests. It is necessary to understand the pests so that methods can be developed to keep them from increasing in number—to the point where they damage the crop. When pests are few in number, they are usually not a problem. In fact, a few pests are needed so the population of a pest's enemies, which help control the pest, can be maintained. The basic rules of pest control are: Grow a plant that is not susceptible to pests or diseases; grow the plant when or where the pests are not present; and if the pest appears, destroy it.

Many of the basic practices used in agriculture play a role in controlling pests and diseases. Farmers plan to use seeds from the best plants for future crops. Often the best plants are those with pest resistance. Deep plowing buries weeds and any pests or diseases remaining from the previous crop. Burning the field before planting has long been used to destroy weeds and pests. Simply cutting the weeds on a regular basis is also a form of pest control.

The farmer can grow a mixture of many varieties of the crop, so even if a pest or dis-

as wheat, and of many vegetables and fruits. They also can be found on trees and flowers and even on grass. Like the rust spores, these mildew spores are easily carried on wind currents to infect new plants.

Some bacteria, fungi, and nematodes grow inside the plant, clogging it up so water and nutrients can't flow from the roots to the leaves. When this happens the plant wilts, the leaves may turn yellow, and the entire plant may die. Trees, flowers, vegetables and other crops can all have wilt diseases.

In other cases, a plant may wilt because its roots become diseased. Many nematodes and fungi also damage plant roots. Plants invaded by the root-knot nematode have lumpy knotted-looking roots. The tiny nematodes live inside the roots. Like the gall insects and mites, the root-knot nematode is able to make the plant produce these root-knot homes. When a plant has a lot of nematodes living in the roots, it may not have enough food left to grow normally after feeding all of the hungry nematodes.

Sometimes insect pests will carry a fungus, virus, bacterium, or nematode from a sick plant and put it into a healthy plant. The Dutch elm disease is a wilt disease of elm trees

Agricultural methods to control pests include (*left*) burning fields, then deep plowing the burnt stubble to bury any remaining weeds and pests, and (*above*) spraying pesticides to coat plants with a thin layer of chemical protection.

ease destroys some varieties, some will survive. Growing a different crop each year, a process called **crop rotation**, helps control pest populations. The pests and diseases do not build up in the field as they might if the same crop were grown year after year.

Using the natural enemies of pests is called **biological control**. The milky spore disease, which was used to fight the Japanese beetle, was discovered by scientists of the United States Department of Agriculture. It has been used successfully for more than forty years to control Japanese beetles. While the Japanese beetle was considered a pest, another beetle, called a lady beetle, or ladybug, was used as a biological control of a pest. More than one hundred years ago, ladybugs were imported into California to control a serious new pest of citrus plants, the cottony cushion scale insect. Within a few years, the ladybugs had spread throughout the entire state and had nearly eliminated the cottony cushion scale insect as a pest. Even today we think of the red and black ladybug as our friend.

Insects and plant diseases can also be used as control agents for weeds. One of the first examples of using an insect to control a weed was the case of the prickly pear cactus in Australia. In the late 1800's, the cactus was introduced to Australia, where it thrived and grew into dense, impenetrable thickets covering millions of acres of land. A variety of insects and mites that feed only on the cactus were introduced to Australia to control the cactus. Scientists are very careful to test a potential weed-control insect or mite to make sure it does not like to eat any crop plants.

Chemical controls, or pesticides, are relatively new in the long history of agriculture. The use of pesticides allows us to produce more food than ever before on less land. You can tell which insect or disease a pesticide is used to control by the pesticide's name. The first part refers to the pest, and the last part, "cide," is from the Latin word for "killer." **Insecticides** kill insects; **miticides** kill mites; **herbicides** kill plants (the word "herb" is from the Latin word herba for "plant"); a **fungicide** kills fungi. Like any rule, however, this one also has an exception: Chemicals used to kill bacteria are usually called **antibiotics**, not bacteriacides.

Pesticides work in a variety of ways. Some pesticides poison the pest and stop basic life processes, such as the ability to breathe. Other pesticides stop the pest from growing normally. Insecticides that are similar to an insect's natural hormones cause the insect to grow abnormally. The insect may never grow into an adult, so it would never reproduce. There are also herbicides similar to plant hormones that cause the weed to grow in a twisted, abnormal way that prevents the plant from producing seeds.

Some pesticides must be applied before the pest attacks the plant. Other pesticides, called systemics, are absorbed into the plant where they remain active inside the plant's system. Systemic insecticides are especially useful for the control of sucking insects. Some systemic fungicides can be applied to the leaves of the plant, and move into the roots where they control root rots. Other systemic fungicides are able to stop the growth of the fungus after it has invaded the plant.

A wide variety of herbicides exist to control weeds. Often several kinds of herbicides are used throughout the growing season of a crop. Some kill any plant they contact; other herbicides only kill certain kinds of plants. Many herbicides are applied to the soil before the weeds even begin to grow. As soon as the weeds start to grow, the poison takes effect and kills them.

Pesticides have been a tremendous benefit to people. Pesticides are used to perform some of the work that in the past was performed by the crop growers; so with the use of pesticides, fewer people are needed to cultivate the same amount of land. Chemical fungicides allow the farmer to grow fruit free of any spots and rot. Fruit and vegetables can be shipped long distances to cities without spoiling. The skillful use of pesticides can prevent the terrible disasters and crop failures that in the past have caused such great human suffering.

After any pesticide has been used in the same place over a long period of time, the pest may become resistant to the pesticide—that is, the insect is no longer harmed by the pesticide. Resistance develops because the pest population is composed of many individuals with slightly different survival abilities. Within every pest population there are a few individuals that can tolerate a particular pesticide. When most of the pests that cannot tolerate the pesticide are killed, only the few tolerant individuals are left to reproduce, thus creating a population of resistant pests. Insects and mites were the first pests noticed to develop pesticide resistance. Now weeds and fungi are also known to have resistance to specific chemical pesticides. Great care must be taken to use pesticides wisely to avoid creating pesticide-resistant pests. Different kinds of pesticides should be used in rotation rather than always using the same pesticide many years in a row.

Most pesticides will also harm people if large enough amounts are eaten, inhaled, or gotten on the skin. Pesticides can also kill the enemies of the pests, allowing the pest population to continue growing and creating a greater pest problem. This is why there is so much interest in combining a variety of pest control strategies for pest control.

▶ FUTURE TECHNOLOGY

The control of plant pests remains a difficult task requiring clever solutions to old and new pest problems. The search for better plants continues. Equally important is the preservation of populations of insects that may include important potential pest- or weed-control agents. Many wild plants of no known use may contain traits that could be used to make crop plants better.

It is now possible to add specific traits to plants using **biotechnology**. In agricultural biotechnology, a new product is created by transferring genetic material. One idea currently being tested uses a bacteria that can live inside a corn plant without damaging the plant. The bacteria produces a substance, called a **toxin,** that is poisonous to the corn borer caterpillar. When the corn borer caterpillar eats a corn plant that has the new bacteria, it gets sick and dies from the poison. The toxin is not dangerous to people, however.

Experts estimate that weeds, pests, and plant diseases may destroy or damage as much as one third of the world's food. The number of people in the world increases every year, but the amount of land stays the same. It is important to understand pests and how to control them in order to allow our crops to make the most food possible.

Many other ideas for new forms of pest control are being developed. New ideas and a better understanding of how pests harm plants and how plants defend themselves can all be used in the future to improve agriculture for all of the people in the world.

ETHEL M. DUTKY
Director, Plant Diagnostic Laboratory
University of Maryland

See also BACTERIA; FUNGI; INSECTS; VECTORS.

PLANTS

Without plants, nearly all life on earth would cease. Directly or indirectly, most living things depend on plants for food. But more than that, we depend on plants for the very air we breathe. As plants perform their necessary life processes, they produce oxygen as a by-product. Human beings and other land animals breathe the oxygen in the atmosphere; fish and other water life breathe the oxygen that is dissolved in water. So it is the abundance and diversity of plants that determine how much animal life, including human life, can survive on earth.

It is difficult to imagine a landscape that does not have some kind of plant, whether it is a kind of tree, shrub, flower, or grass. Plants inhabit some part of every continent. They are found over most of the earth, wherever there is soil—unless it is too dry, too cold, or too hot. They are also found in the sea and in freshwater lakes, rivers, and ponds.

Each green plant, whether it is a delicate meadow flower bursting with colorful blooms or a massive tree towering high above the forest floor, possesses an amazing ability that sets it apart from every other type of living thing—it can capture the light energy of the sun and convert it to chemical energy. There is not another kind of organism that is able to do this. This unique ability has made green plants the essential link that transfers the sun's energy to all other organisms. Without green plants, we simply could not survive.

Scientists estimate that there are more than 300,000 species, or kinds, of plants. The greatest number of different kinds of plants can be found in the humid tropics. In fact, there are so many different kinds of plants in the tropics that have not yet been identified that scientists can only estimate how many species of plants inhabit the earth. Regrettably, many plant species will become extinct before they have even been seen. The fewest different plant species are found in the cold and barren areas of the Arctic and Antarctic.

People and other animals are able to capture the energy that is trapped and stored by plants. Some people receive the energy when they eat plants. Others receive the energy when they eat plant-eating animals. The string of events that occurs when energy is transferred as a herbivore (plant eater) eats a plant and in turn is eaten by a carnivore (meat eater) is called a food chain.

The sizes of plants range from the microscopic flowering duckweed, which is only about ³⁄₁₂₅ inch (0.61 millimeter) long and weighs ¹⁄₁₅ ounce (2 milligrams), to the giant sequoia tree of California, which can grow to over 270 feet (82 meters) tall and weigh 6,167 tons (5,594 metric tons).

There is an amazing variety in the size and appearance of plants; however, there are basic characteristics that all plants share: Plants are made up of many cells. Each cell is surrounded by a solid cell wall made of the substance **cellulose**. Each plant cell has a **nucleus**, or "control center." Each cell also has organ-like structures called **plastids**, where many of the biochemical reactions of energy use and energy storage occur. Most plants make their own food during the process of **photosynthesis**. Plants also produce **embryos**—young plants that develop from an egg, or **ovum**. Plants are nonmotile; that is, they do not move about like animals do.

▶PLANTS AND THE CYCLE OF NATURE

All things on earth are linked, one to another, in the cycle of nature. Within the cycle there are complex relationships between living things and the elements in their environments. As the cycle progresses, many different processes work to create, exchange, and recycle the earth's chemicals.

Each living thing and element fulfills a role or function that helps keep the cycle intact. Plants are an essential part of the cycle. Plants could not survive without the energy they receive from the sun, the original source of all energy. Without the food and oxygen that plants supply, we could not live. The plants, with all their life-giving materials, return to the earth as waste matter when animals, including human beings, die. The waste matter provides food for other living organisms that break down, or decompose, the material. As the material is broken down, the chemicals are released and return to the air, water, and soil where they are once again available to growing plants. Humans and other living things use the plants as food, and the cycle continues.

This article presents an overview of the living things we call plants. The discussion focuses on the importance of plants; their evolution, diversity, and classification; their life cycle, including plant characteristics and processes; and in the final pages, the distribution of plants throughout the world and the impact of human activity on that plant life.

The New Book of Knowledge also contains many articles that provide in-depth material on plants. BIOMES; DESERTS; PRAIRIES; and RAIN FOREST examine plant communities. Information on plant features, traits, and destruction is supplied in articles such as LEAVES; PHOTOSYNTHESIS; and PLANT PESTS. Plant groups are covered in several articles, including GRASSES and TREES. Additional projects and activities can be found in GARDENS AND GARDENING; HOUSEPLANTS; and TERRARIUMS.

▶PLANTS AND SOCIETY

Plants are a familiar part of the environment. We use plants every day, in every field of life to fulfill the need for foods, products, and raw materials.

Rather than rely just on plants that are native to one country or area, human settlers have carried plants with them from place to place whenever they have wandered. Early writings document plant travelers in the time of the ancient Romans and Greeks. Plant journeys also are revealed by comparing domesticated plants—plants that have been adapted so that they are useful to human beings—with their wild relatives.

Food plants were the first plant travelers. At first, plant material was carried by travelers as food to eat on their journeys. Later, travelers carried plants and seeds around the world in an attempt to extend the range of specific plants.

A sometimes unnoticed, but very important, function of plants is the role they play in soil renewal and conservation. The roots of plants secrete small amounts of organic acids that help break down mineral particles, adding nutrients to the soil. Matter from decaying plants also adds to the soil's nutrient stores. Soil is held in place by plant roots, thus slowing down the natural processes of wind and water erosion. Plants are also a source of recreation and enjoyment. The natural beauty of plants growing in parks and gardens provides enjoyment to all who view them. People grow many thousands of species and varieties of ornamental plants just because they are pleasing to look at.

Plants contribute to the celebrations, rituals, and artistic expressions of many cultures. Pollen from plants is used in an Apache Sunrise Ceremony (*above*), while a garden surrounding a Portuguese church (*right*) offers visitors a beautiful and tranquil setting for reflection.

Food from Plants

A surprisingly small number of plant families supply most of the plant food used by people. Foodstuffs from the grass, legume (pea), potato, rose, citrus, crucifer (brassica), and palm families dominate the worldwide menu. Within the major plant families, only about 20 plant species supply 90 percent of the world's food.

Human beings have used every part of the plant as food. We eat seeds, fruits, leaves, stems, roots, even the flowers of some plants.

The seeds of grasses are the most important food source for much of the world's population. Wheat, rice, and corn supply the seeds that are most often used for food. Rice is the main food for the most people, especially in Asia. Wheat, which is the cereal produced in the greatest abundance, is used as a main food by slightly fewer people than rice is. Corn, or maize, is the main food in Latin America and parts of Africa. Barley, oats, sorghum, and millet also supply important seeds.

Although the fruit of the legume family is sometimes eaten, it is the seeds that are most often consumed. Beans, peas, lentils, and chickpeas are all legume seeds. The soybean, another important legume seed, is the most valuable crop in the United States.

Foods from the roots of plants are staples for much of the world, especially in areas where grasses do not grow well, such as tropical regions. Important root crops include yams, sweet potatoes, and cassavas. Carrots, parsnips, turnips, and beets also are important root foods in cooler climates.

An incredible array of plants have been used as food, beverages, and flavorings. As many as 10,000 species have been recorded as having been tried, and certainly, many more have been tried but not documented. Modern crops, such as cranberries (*right*), pineapples (*below*), and wheat (*below right*), evolved as plants were selected based on those that were hardy, provided the most useful food, and could supply seeds for future crops.

The fruit of a plant contains its seeds. Apples, pears, melons, peaches, plums, and oranges are all fruits. So are tomatoes, peppers, cucumbers, squashes, and nuts. Many fruits have been part of some peoples' diets for a long time. Dates, coconuts, olives, figs, and pineapples are all mentioned in writings and pictured in art from ancient times.

The stems, flowers, and leaves of a variety of plants are used as food. Edible stems include the potato, which is an enlarged portion of an underground stem, and celery and asparagus, which are stems that grow above the ground. The flowers of cauliflower and broccoli are regularly eaten, while the flowers of artichokes are eaten as a delicacy. The leaves of many different plants are eaten as food. While the leaves of plants such as brussels sprouts, spinach, and cabbage are the only part of the plant that is used as food, the leaves as well as other parts of turnips and beets are used as food. Although it is easy to recognize that it is the leaves of the spinach, cabbage, and lettuce plants that are being eaten, it is not so easy to recognize that it is the tightly wrapped, fleshly leaves of the garlic and onion plants that are eaten.

Medicines from Plants

Thousands of medicinal compounds have been found in plants, many of commercial importance. The pain relievers morphine and codeine come from the opium poppy; quinine, the most effective agent against malaria, comes from the cinchona tree; digitalis, which comes from foxglove, is used to treat heart disease; and reserpine, which comes from rauwolfia, is used to treat high blood pressure.

In ancient and medieval times, almost all medicines came from plants. Plants were used to ease pain, heal wounds, and cure fever. Today some areas of the world still rely on plant medicines to meet the medical needs of the population. People who are often called healers practice traditional, folk, or herbal medicine, using plants as their main source of medicine. It is estimated that at least 25,000 plants are used by traditional practitioners.

Although the making of medicines now depends less on plants and more on antibiotics made by fungi and on synthetic chemicals made from petroleum, there is a renewed interest in exploring the potential of plants. Many synthetic medicines are patterned on the

Chinese herbalists are among the traditional practitioners who have developed a great botanical knowledge of local plants, their uses and properties.

substances found in plants, so the development of medicines still depends on a supply of newly discovered plant compounds. One recent example is a substance called taxol. Taxol, which is taken from yew trees, is being tested for use in treating stubborn tumors.

There is a renewed interest in exploring the potential of plant species in tropical areas where up to this time only 1 percent of the plants have been examined for use as medicines. Scientists believe that one out of ten plant species may contain compounds with ingredients that are active against cancer.

Did you know that . . .

the most widely used pain reliever, aspirin, was named after Spiraea, a genus of flowering shrubs in the rose family? For thousands of years, soothing teas were brewed from the flowers of the meadowsweet plant (*right*), one of the spiraeas. The plant contained salicin—a naturally occurring pain reliever. When aspirin was developed, its activity was based on the properties of salicin.

Raw Materials from Plants

Plants supply many of the raw materials that are used to provide people with fuel, shelter, and clothing. In the same manner as food products, raw materials can come from the leaves, stems, fruits, or roots of plants. Sometimes a material, such as coal, is formed from the entire plant. Other materials, such as cotton cloth and cooking oils, come from just one part of a plant.

Coal is a product of plants that died hundreds of millions of years ago. As the dead plants accumulated, they became compressed into coal. Peat, another fuel, is the product of plant remains that accumulate in a type of wetland called bogs in cold regions.

We depend heavily on plants for our shelter. Trees provide wood to make lumber for homes. Wood is also used in making many small and more specialized products, such as furniture, tool handles, and musical instruments. Whatever the product, the characteristics of its wood need to be matched to its use. For instance, soft balsa wood is used to make airplane models that can fly because it is lightweight and easy to shape.

Wood fibers are used to make paper, an indispensable tool of civilization. Fibrous stems are split into long, thin pieces to make baskets, matting, and wicker furniture. Plants with soft fibers, such as cotton, are used to make thread that is then woven into cloth. The fabric linen is made from long stem fibers of the flax plant. The coarse fibers of jute stems are useful for items such as carpet backing and cloth sacks. Other fibers are used to make nets, sailcloth, brushes, and as filler for mattresses and furniture.

Substances that are taken from plants are made into many different products. We cook with oils extracted from plants. Oils are also processed to produce cosmetics, fine lubricants, perfumes, and plastics. Animal hides are softened and preserved with tannins, chemical substances obtained from bark. Other chemical compounds are used as thickeners and gelling agents for food products, for making medicine tablets, and for stiffening fine papers and textiles.

Because plants are a part of the everyday landscape, it is easy to forget how much we depend on them for a wealth of goods. Raw materials from plants were used to produce these giant rolls of paper (*above*), the sturdy frames for these buildings in a housing development (*left*), and the peat being gathered from a bog in Ireland (*far left*).

Using plants, Gregor Johann Mendel (*above left*) discovered the basic principles of heredity. Mendel, who was an Austrian monk, began his breeding experiments in a monastery garden. There he used garden peas to examine characteristics such as plant height and seed color. His findings, published in 1866, laid the foundation for the science of genetics. The research work that Barbara McClintock (*above right*) conducted with corn plants led to a new understanding of how genes, the units of heredity, behave. She described how some genes can change their positions on the chromosomes and so change the traits that are inherited.

▶THE PLANT KINGDOM

Scientists who study organisms name them and classify them into groups according to the natural similarities they share. Along with aiding in the identification of an organism, the name and classification help reveal how the organism has evolved and its relationship to other living things.

Before the invention of the microscope, scientists classified organisms based on characteristics that were easily observed. It was generally accepted that there were two kinds of organisms: plants and animals. Plants were green and did not move about; animals moved about, ate food, and had complex behavior. When microscopic organisms were first described, they were classified as either plant or animal. But there are many organisms that do not fit neatly in either of these two large groups, called kingdoms.

Since the 1950's, biologists have divided all living organisms into five kingdoms. Plants make up one kingdom. Animals make up another. Certain one-celled organisms, some of which have characteristics of both plants and animals, belong to yet another kingdom called Protista.

Bacteria and fungi each have their own kingdoms, too. Living things in the same kingdom share more characteristics than living things in different kingdoms.

The First Plants

The evolution of plants began more than 3.5 billion years ago with the earliest forms of life. Scientists believe the first organisms were bacteria known as cyanobacteria (formerly called blue-green algae). The ability to produce energy through photosynthesis probably developed in these simple water-dwelling organisms. However, it was not until about 1 billion years ago that ancient organisms developed into life-forms that released oxygen into the atmosphere during photosynthesis. This was first accomplished by green algae. Once there was oxygen in the atmosphere, life on land became a possibility.

The way living things are classified changes as botanists, the scientists who study plants, and other biologists learn more about them. When all living things were considered to be part of either the animal kingdom or plant kingdom, then organisms such as mushrooms (*left*) were considered to be plants, as were bacteria and algae.

Millions of years passed before there was enough oxygen in the atmosphere to support life out of water. The first organisms to come from the sea were green algae. They acquired the ability to survive in the newly oxygenated atmosphere and began to populate the earth's land surfaces about 600 million years ago. Many varieties of green algae developed. These early plant ancestors, with their simple, sticklike bodies, bear little resemblance to the plants we see today.

The first land plants, which appeared more than 400 million years ago, probably evolved from the land-dwelling green algae. The early land plants did not have complex structures or life cycles. They were multicelled organisms without roots, leaves, and flowers. Even though these early plants were primitive, they spread over the earth's surface and carpeted the ancient continents.

Plants evolved and the new generations became more complex. Plants with numerous stems and branches developed, followed by plants with leaves and roots and then, about 300 million years ago, plants with seeds. Finally, more than 200 million years ago, the most important plant group appeared: flowering plants.

Botanists have long sought the origin of the first flowering plant. Many scientists believe that the first flower resembled today's magnolias. Magnolias have many characteristics that are considered primitive, features that are similar to some extinct and very ancient nonflowering plants. The strongest connection to early plants are some fossil flowers from around 110 million years ago that look like magnolias. Other scientists suggest that magnolias are too complex a plant to be the first flower. They point to the simpler water lily, hornwort, or black pepper as the early ancestor of all flowering plants.

Ancient magnolia leaves, preserved for 18 million years in an Idaho bog, were found to have DNA that was identical to present-day magnolias (*above*).

One way to trace the evolution of plants is to compare the features of existing plants to determine their relationships with each other. Another is to examine plant fossils. Fossils are the remains of organisms that have been preserved in rock. There are problems in identifying plants from fossils. Usually only a part of a plant is discovered, and it is difficult to match up a fossil leaf with a fossil stem of the same species.

Plant fossils have been found all over the world. A great array of extinct plants has been identified from the fossils that have been discovered. Scientists use fossils not only to identify the kinds of plants and the length of their existences, but also to study ancient environments. In comparing fossils, paleobotanists (the botanists who study plant fossils) have found that many fossil remains are the same as existing plant species. The California redwood, which today grows only along the fog-bound coast of northern California, is a good example. Fossils of redwoods have been found throughout areas of North America that have a moderate climate. The redwood fossils were an indication to scientists that in ancient

How Plant Communities Change

Plant communities change in an orderly process called **plant succession**. Over a period of time, mineral and organic matter accumulate and soil becomes deeper and richer, creating a more favorable environment for additional life-forms. With each stage, the population of living things — plants and animals — changes as each generation adapts to the new environment. Soon one kind of plant community is replaced with another kind. The example below is the transformation of an abandoned field to a forest. The bare landscape of a field gradually fills with grasses and weeds. As more time passes, shrubs begin to dot the grassy habitat. Finally, trees start to emerge among the shrubs until the predominant plants are large trees — the field has gradually evolved into a forest. Natural events, such as volcanic eruptions and erosion, can interrupt or even reverse the process of plant succession. Human-produced events, such as agriculture and settlement development, can also disrupt the process.

Abandoned field

Grasses (1 to 10 years)

Grasses and shrubs (10 to 25 years)

times there must have been widespread cool, moist habitats like that of the present-day northern California coast.

The newest tool in the study of the evolution of plants is the comparison of plant genes, the basic hereditary units that carry the characteristics of a plant from one generation to the next. Researchers attempt to recover a chemical substance called **DNA** (*d*eoxyribo-*n*ucleic *a*cid) from plant genes. The DNA of different plants is then studied to determine if there are any similarities that could be used to show the relationship between the plants or the evolution of one kind of plant to another.

Vascular plants share one basic characteristic: They all have specialized tissues for transporting materials from one part of the plant to another. The large group includes ancient plants, such as the whisk ferns, horsetails, and club mosses, that lack roots and leaves or possess simple, primitive structures. It also includes those that are the most complex and evolved, that is, flowering plants.

▶ KINDS OF PLANTS

When scientists classify the many different species of plants, they separate them into groups, depending on the characteristics the plants share. Major groups, called divisions, include plants that share one or more characteristics. Plants within each division are separated into groups called classes according to certain differences between the plants. The classes are further divided into orders, the orders into families, the families into genera, and the genera into species.

With each subdivision, the relationship between the plants becomes stronger, and the members of the group share more characteristics of appearance, body structure, and development. With the final separation into species, the plants share so many of the same basic characteristics that they look almost alike.

Along with scientific classification, plants can be separated in another way. Plants can be put into two basic groups: vascular and nonvascular plants. Vascular plants are those plants that have specialized tissues to transport materials from one part of the plant to another. Tissue composed of **xylem** conducts water throughout the plant, and tissue composed of

phloem conducts food. Seed plants, ferns, whisk ferns, horsetails, and club mosses are the main types of vascular plants. Nonvascular plants are those plants that do not have specialized tissues to transport materials. Bryophytes, which include liverworts, hornworts, and mosses, are nonvascular plants.

Vascular Plants. Seed plants are vascular plants that, along with their specialized tissues, have an additional unique structure—the seed. Seed plants are separated into two groups: **gymnosperms**, plants with naked seeds, and **angiosperms**, plants with seeds enclosed in fruit. The principal gymnosperms are the conifers, trees that bear seeds on a female cone; the male cones produce pollen. Conifers are very important ecologically, forming the dominant vegetation in cold, moist regions. The cycads, a minor group of gymnosperms, bear one male or female cone at the top of the stem, surrounded by leaves. They are often mistaken for palms. Another unique gymnosperm is the ginkgo, or maidenhair tree, which bears naked seeds but no cones.

**Emerging forest
(25 to 100 years)**

**Mature forest
(More than 100 years)**

The angiosperms, or flowering plants, are the most successful group of plants if the amount of landscape they cover and the number of species are measured. They can be divided into groups based on the number of leaves, called **cotyledons**, contained within their seeds. **Monocotyledons** (monocots) have one seed leaf, or cotyledon; **dicotyledons** (dicots) have two cotyledons.

Ferns are the oldest living vascular plants. Like the seed plants, ferns have true leaves, stems, and roots. All species of fern have two distinct reproductive forms. With each reproduction cycle the form alternates, so that one generation is the product of wind-borne spores, and the next generation is the product of a sperm and an egg. Ferns are usually found on the forest floor.

Whisk ferns, **horsetails**, and **club mosses** represent the primitive plant groups that are sometimes referred to as fern allies. They are among the first plants to have grown on land. Some, such as the whisk ferns, lack roots and leaves. Horsetails have hollow jointed stems with a rough-textured outer covering. The presence of the mineral silica, which is deposited in the walls of the stems' outer cells, makes the stems very coarse. Club mosses have true stems but primitive needlelike or scalelike leaves and no true roots.

Nonvascular Plants. The **bryophytes** are a division of ancient and rather simple plants. The plant groups that make up the bryophytes are the mosses, liverworts, and hornworts. None of them have true leaves, stems, or roots, as vascular plants have, but they do have structures that resemble them externally.

The bryophytes are fairly small plants that grow close to the ground. They are distributed all over the world. Although most bryophytes are found growing in moist, shaded areas, some of the mosses do live in deserts.

Nonvascular plants are small, multicellular plants with a simple system for transporting water and food through plant cells. Members of this ancient plant group, called bryophytes, include mosses, liverworts, and hornworts. Although bryophytes have structures that are stemlike and leaflike, they do not have true roots, stems, or leaves.

▶**PARTS OF A PLANT**

All plants, whether vascular or nonvascular, flowering or nonflowering, are made up of cells. Within the plant, groups of cells form tissues that perform specific functions, including transporting substances, respiration, and photosynthesis. The number of different tissues that make up a plant depends on the kind of plant. Not all plants have the same amount or kinds of tissues.

Plants also vary in their structures. Because there are many more flowering plants than any other kind, the flowering plant can be considered the typical plant. The basic parts, or organs, of such a typical plant include the roots, stems, leaves, and flowers. The roots, stems, and leaves of a plant are the vegetative organs, which function in photosynthesis and provide support for the plant. The flowers, along with the seeds and fruits, of a plant are the reproductive organs, which provide new young plants.

WONDER QUESTION

How big can a plant grow?

Plants are some of the smallest and the largest living things on earth. The duckweed (*below*) is less than an inch in length and under an ounce in weight, while a giant sequoia tree named General Sherman (*right*) stands almost 275 feet (84 meters) tall and is estimated to weigh 2,756 tons (2,500 metric tons).

Roots

Roots are underground organs that support and anchor the aboveground parts of the plant, absorb water and dissolved minerals from the soil, and store food. They grow down into the soil, often branching again and again, sometimes forming miles of roots and penetrating deep into the earth. A single winter rye plant was shown to have produced an amazing 387 miles (623 kilometers) of roots, while the roots of a wild fig tree in South Africa were reported to have penetrated an estimated 400 feet (122 meters) deep into the soil.

There are three major types of roots. Some plants have only one kind of root system; however, many have a combination of the different types of roots. Dicots have a **taproot**, or primary root, extending from the bottom of the stem into the soil. Smaller lateral, or secondary, roots extend from the sides of the taproot. The taproot, which is a storage root, can be quite large and fleshy. The cells of the taproot are filled with starch grains, the plant's food reserve during a cold or dry season. Carrots, beets, and manioc are taproots widely used by humans for food.

Monocots have **fibrous** roots. Although a taproot first emerges from the seed, it dies and is replaced by a group of smaller roots extending from the bottom of the stem. The fibrous root system grows close to the soil's surface, collecting moisture before it sinks deep into the ground. Plants such as grasses and rushes have fibrous roots.

Some plants, such as ivies and mature corn plants, have **adventitious** roots. These roots grow from the side of a stem or leaf rather than as part of the main root system. Adventitious roots help to anchor a plant and keep it

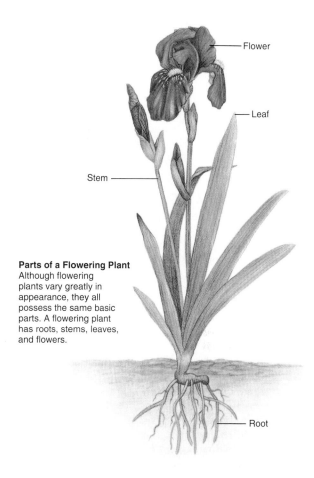

Parts of a Flowering Plant
Although flowering plants vary greatly in appearance, they all possess the same basic parts. A flowering plant has roots, stems, leaves, and flowers.

from being moved by the wind. In the mature corn plant, a ring of adventitious roots called prop roots extends from the stem to just above the soil to anchor the plant. In ivies, adventitious roots extend along the trailing stem to help stabilize the ivy as it climbs.

In addition to the primary and secondary roots, there are many tiny root hairs near the

Types of Roots
The roots of a plant anchor and support the plant, absorb water and nutrients from the soil, and store food. The major types of roots are taproots, fibrous roots, and adventitious roots. A plant's root system may be made up of just one kind of root or a combination of different kinds of roots.

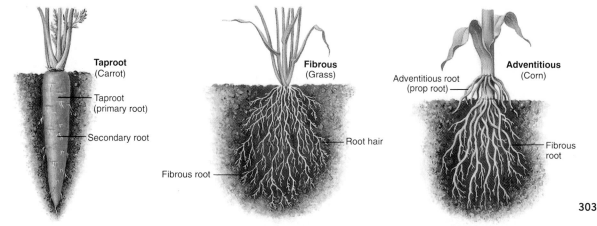

303

tip of each root. These are distinct from the other kinds of roots. Root hairs are specialized for absorbing water and dissolved minerals. They greatly increase the exposed surface of the root system, which in turn increases the plant's ability to absorb moisture and nutrients. Root hairs live for only a few days and "mine" water and minerals from a small zone of soil near the tip of the root. As the root grows in length, new root hairs appear nearer the tip.

At the very tip of each root is a root cap, a specialized structure of slimy cells that protects the newly produced root cells. The cells of the root cap secrete a lubricant that eases the way for the root and prevents the root from being worn away as it pushes down through the soil. The cells, which are constantly damaged and scraped off as they come into contact with soil particles, are rapidly replaced.

Stems

The stem has a variety of functions: It supports the plant, houses a transport system, and provides storage for food. In some plants the stem is also the main location of photosynthesis, and the leaves are either very small or modified for some other function. There are also modified stems that perform special functions. Some modified stems store water or other plant materials, aid in the spread of new plants, or protect the plant from pests.

The leaves of a plant are attached to the stem at a **node**. The part of the stem between two nodes is called the **internode**. Just above each leaf, in the angle formed by the leaf and the stem, is a **lateral bud**. This bud, which is usually dormant, can grow into a branch, leaf, or flower.

The stem is usually the strongest part of a plant. Its strength comes from a material called lignin that is deposited in the stem's cell walls. Plants are either **woody** or **herbaceous** depending on the amount of lignin in the plant. If a stem is relatively soft and green, as in a tulip, the plant is herbaceous; if the stem is strong and hard, as in an oak tree, the plant is woody.

Whether a plant is herbaceous or woody, the stem's most important job is to support the plant. The stem holds the leaves and flowers up in the air so that they are in the best position to receive the sunlight that the plant needs to perform life-sustaining functions.

The transport system within the stem is made up of the tissues xylem and phloem, which conduct water, minerals, and other nutrients to various parts of the plant. The conducting cells of xylem tissue carry water and dissolved minerals upward from the roots of a plant. In the spring, these cells also carry dissolved food materials that have been stored in the roots during the winter. This is why sugar maples are tapped for their sweet sap in the spring. The cells of phloem tissue move material both up and down through the stem of the plant. Dissolved foods are transported from the leaves to the roots and stem for storage or to the growing parts of the plant for immediate use.

In some plants, photosynthesis takes place in the stem rather than in the leaves. Such plants, which include the asparagus and the cactus, have leaves that are either very small or that are modified for some other function. The stems of asparagus are branched so much

Types of Stems
The stem of a plant supports the plant, houses a transport system, acts as a food storehouse, and sometimes is a center for photosynthesis. Stems are either woody or herbaceous.

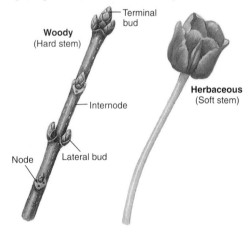

that they resemble feathers, but the leaves are small. The cactus has a large leafless stem, the site of photosynthesis as well as water storage. The needlelike spines covering the cactus take the place of leaves.

Modified Stems. There are several kinds of modified stems. Some modified stems contain only stem tissue; others contain stem tissue and tissues from other parts of the plant. Each kind of modified stem has its own special function. **Rhizomes**, **tubers**, **corms**, and **bulbs**

are underground stems that are thickened for storage. The rhizome stores food and often serves as the main stem of a plant, so only the leaves protrude from the soil. Gingerroot, which is often used in cooking, is a rhizome. Most ferns growing in moderate climates have rhizomes as their main stem. So do some common ornamental flowering plants, such as the iris. Tubers are thickened underground stems, but not the main stem. The most common example of a food-storing tuber is the potato.

Corms and bulbs are storage structures that contain a dormant shoot, which when active will produce the stem and leaves. Corms are mostly stem tissue, while bulbs have very little stem tissue. They are mostly leaf tissue. The gladiolus forms a corm. Onions, garlic, and tulips form bulbs.

Tendrils can be a modification of a stem. The grape plant produces tendrils. The tendrils extend out from the plant to twist around and clasp another plant or an object for support.

Many herbaceous plants have modified stem structures called **stolons,** or runners. These thin green horizontal stems grow along the ground. When a stolon reaches a location that is suitable for growth, it may send out roots and produce leaves. Strawberries, grasses, and many weeds have stolons and spread in this way.

The sharp **thorns** and **spines** of some plants, such as roses, are protective structures that arise from stem tissue. These modified stems can help protect a plant from being eaten by insects and other animals.

Leaves

Leaves produce food, in the form of sugar, for the plant. They are able to do this through the process of photosynthesis. Any green part of a plant has the ability to carry on photosynthesis; however, leaves are the primary site of food production. During photosynthesis, light energy from the sun is captured by **chloro-**

Types of Leaves

The leaves of a plant are responsible for producing most of a plant's food. A leaf's size, appearance, and arrangement vary according to the kind of plant. However, most kinds of leaves have two basic parts: a blade and a petiole. Some leaves also have stipules.

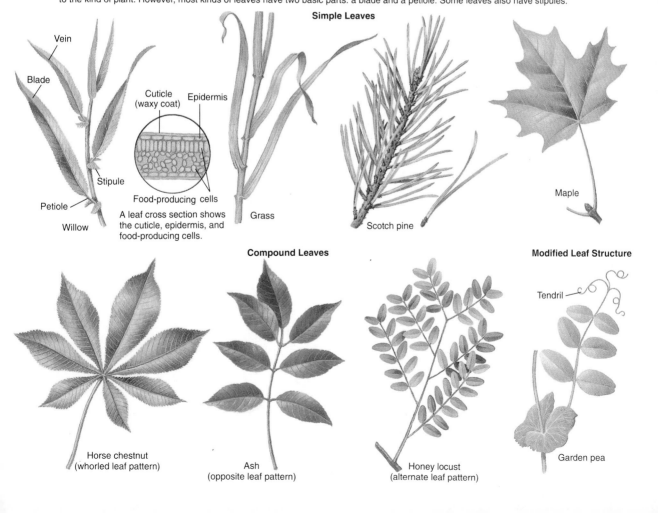

Simple Leaves

Vein

Blade

Cuticle (waxy coat)   Epidermis

Stipule

Food-producing cells

Petiole

Willow

A leaf cross section shows the cuticle, epidermis, and food-producing cells.

Grass

Scotch pine

Maple

Compound Leaves

Modified Leaf Structure

Tendril

Horse chestnut (whorled leaf pattern)

Ash (opposite leaf pattern)

Honey locust (alternate leaf pattern)

Garden pea

Why do leaves change color in the autumn?

The leaves of deciduous trees contain groups of different colored pigments. During most of the year, there is more chlorophyll, or green pigment, within leaf cells. Environmental changes, such as decreasing day length, trigger changes in the plant, including a decrease in the chlorophyll. As the chlorophyll diminishes, other pigments are exposed and a riot of color results.

phyll, the green substance in leaves, and turned into chemical energy that powers the plant's life processes.

A thin, tough layer of cells, the **epidermis**, covers the outside of a leaf. The epidermis secretes a thin waxy film, or **cuticle**, on the surface of the leaf, protecting the inside from injury and from losing moisture. Along with epidermal cells, a leaf has special cells called **guard cells** that control the flow of gases through the leaf. Two guard cells work as a pair, each changing shape to open or close the tiny pore, or **stoma**, between them. Carbon dioxide enters through the **stomata** (plural of stoma), and oxygen and water vapor exit.

There is great variety in the size and appearance of leaves. Generally they grow in a broad, flat shape that exposes the largest amount of their surface area to the sun's rays. But plants also produce leaves that are small and spinelike, needlelike, or scalelike. In addition, modified structures such as tendrils may form from leaf tissue.

Most kinds of leaves have two main parts: the **blade**, which is the flat part of the leaf, and the **petiole**, which is the thin stalk that grows from the node on the stem to the blade. Some kinds of leaves also have **stipules**, tiny leaflike structures that grow at the base of the petiole. A leaf that has only one blade is called a simple leaf; a leaf that has two or more blades is called a compound leaf.

Leaves grow along the stem in a particular arrangement. They may grow in an alternate pattern, with one leaf at each node; in an opposite pattern, with two leaves growing from opposite sides of the same node; or in a whorled pattern, with three or more leaves growing from one node.

Flowers

Flowers vary widely in size, shape, and color. Each kind of plant grows a characteristic number of flowers. Some plants have only one flower, while others have many flowers grouped in clusters. A typical flower is made up of four kinds of organs at the end of a stem. At the base of the flower are the small, leaflike **sepals**. The sepals form an overlapping cover for the unopened flower bud. As the **petals** grow, these protective structures are pushed

Types of Flowers
Flowers contain a plant's reproductive organs. A flower with both male and female organs is called a perfect flower; a flower that has only male or female parts is called an imperfect flower.

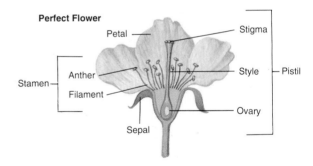

Perfect Flower

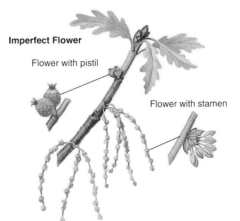

Imperfect Flower

apart. The petals are usually the largest and most brightly colored part of the plant and serve to attract insects, birds, and other animal pollinators to the flower.

The petals surround the reproductive organs of the flower. The male organs are the **stamens**. A stamen is made up of a long, stalklike **filament** that ends in an enlarged part called the **anther**. The anther produces the pollen grains that develop sperm, the male sex cells. The bottle-shaped **pistil**, the female reproductive organ, is made up of three parts: The flattened top is called the **stigma**, the slender neck is the **style**, and the large base is the **ovary**. The ovary contains one or more **ovules**. Each ovule contains an **egg cell**, which is the female sex cell. Stalks attach the ovules to the inside wall of the ovary.

A flower that contains both male and female parts is said to be a perfect flower. Other flowers, however, may have stamens or pistils, but not both. Such flowers are said to be imperfect flowers. The male and female flowers may be on separate plants, as they are in willows, cottonwoods, and holly. Or the two kinds of flowers may be present on the same plant, as in walnuts, oaks, and corn.

Fruits and Seeds

When a pollen grain unites with an ovule, the ovule develops into a seed. Each seed is like a very small package of plant life. It contains a tiny new plant and food to nourish it. The seed's main parts include an embryo, food storage tissue, and a seed coat. The embryo contains the basic parts from which the new plant will develop. It is protected by the seed coat, or outer skin. The seed grows using food from food storage tissues, such as the **endosperm** in flowering plants.

As the seed develops, the ovary develops into a fruit around the seeds. The fruit may be fleshy and moist like that of melons, grapes, and pears, or hard and dry like that of nuts and bean pods. The fruit protects the seeds.

Types of Seeds
A seed contains the new plant and the food to nourish it. The two main types of seeds are naked (uncovered) and enclosed (enclosed by an ovary).

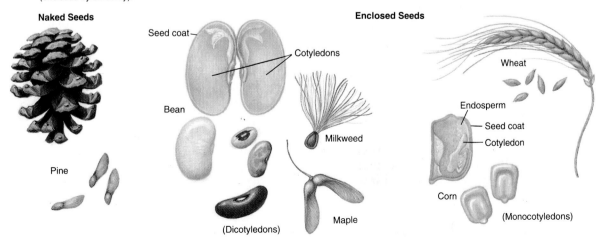

Naked Seeds

Seed coat

Cotyledons

Bean

Pine

Milkweed

Maple

(Dicotyledons)

Enclosed Seeds

Wheat

Endosperm

Seed coat

Cotyledon

Corn

(Monocotyledons)

▶A NEW PLANT IS BORN

Plants produce new plants by sexual reproduction or asexual reproduction. In sexual reproduction, a male sex cell (sperm) and a female sex cell (egg) join to produce a seed that develops into a new plant, or seedling. In asexual reproduction, a new plant forms from some part of the old plant.

Butterflies and other animal pollinators are lured to their task by a flower's distinctive color combinations, bold markings, or rich fragrance.

Sexual Reproduction

For seeds to be produced, two things must occur. Pollen must reach the stigmas. Then it must reach and unite with the ovules. Pollination is the first step; the second is called fertilization. When sexual reproduction is complete, the result is a new, individual plant that has some combination of characteristics from both the male and female parents.

Pollination. Pollination consists of a pollen grain landing on the stigma at the top of the pistil. There are two types of pollination: **self-pollination** and **cross-pollination**.

Some plants are able to pollinate themselves, in the process called self-pollination. No help is needed from any outside source. For example, in a perfect flower, which contains both male and female parts, the flower's pollen often spills onto the stigma of the same flower. This can happen before the flower even opens.

Most plants rely on cross-pollination, the process in which pollen from one flower lands on the stigma of another flower of the same species. Cross-pollination occurs in many ways. Pollen may be deposited by an insect or other animal as it searches for food. As it forages for pollen or the sweet nectar it eats, the insect rubs the anthers and dumps pollen on itself. This pollen is then spread to the stigma of the next flower it visits. Most flowers are pollinated by flying insects, such as bees, wasps, butterflies, and moths. A few flowers are pollinated by birds, such as hummingbirds, and ants and other small animals.

Flowers and their animal pollinators are adapted to each other. Adaptations in the color, shape, and smell of flowers make them attractive to the insects and other animals and also put pollen within their reach. Bees collect pollen from plants that produce great amounts of it. The bees' ability to see specific colors—white, yellow, and blue—enables them to find the flowers that produce the greatest amounts of pollen. Color also aids the moths that fly at night. Many night-blooming flowers are white, a color that makes them more easily visible in the dark.

Butterflies and moths have long tongues that allow them to gather nectar from flowers with long, tubular shapes. Flowers pollinated by flies often give off an odor like that of decaying meat, a smell that is attractive to flies that lay their eggs on rotting animal flesh.

Pollen is also scattered by the wind. Many trees and grasses are adapted to this method of pollination. The flowers do not have showy petals, sweet nectar, or pleasing aromas to attract animal pollinators. Instead, the flowers produce amazingly large amounts of pollen and vast numbers of female flowers. There may be so much pollen that the area around the plant looks as if it is coated with a yellow dust. Many wind-pollinated trees tend to have flowers of one sex, either on the same plant or on different plants.

A shower of light, dry pollen grains is produced by yew tree flowers. Air currents carry the pollen to other yew flowers, sometimes over great distances.

Sexual Reproduction in a Flowering Plant

After a pollen grain reaches the stigma of a pistil (1), it sprouts, sending a slender pollen tube down to the ovule (2). The sperm nuclei travel down the pollen tube to the ovule (3). One nucleus unites with an egg cell to form the embryo (4); another unites with the polar nuclei to form the endosperm (5). The seed develops from the fertilized egg (6). Once the seed falls to the ground, it germinates in the soil and a seedling emerges (7).

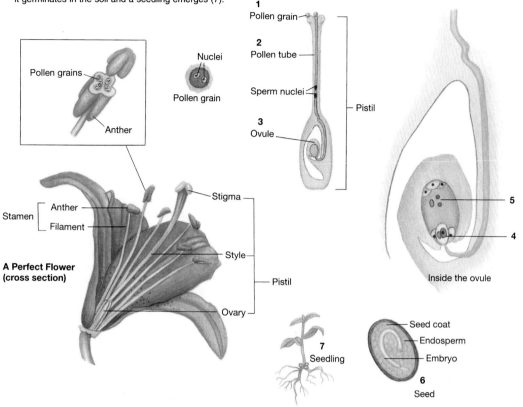

Sexual Reproduction in a Conifer

Pollen grains from the male cone are carried by the wind to the female cone (1). The pollen grains attach to the cone scale and enter the pollen chamber (2). A pollen tube grows from the pollen grain into the ovule. Sperm travels through the tube to the egg cell. Fertilization occurs when a sperm cell and an egg cell unite (3). The fertilized egg develops into a seed containing an embryo and an endosperm (4). Once the cone matures, it opens and the wind scatters the winged seeds (5). The fallen seeds germinate, and a new plant begins to grow (6).

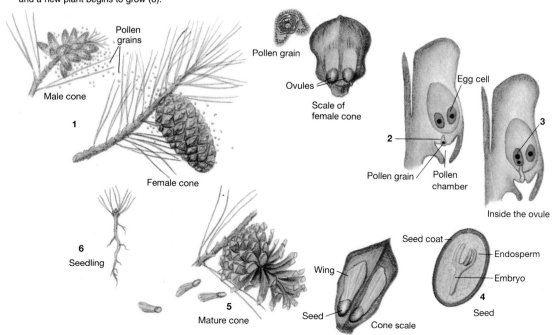

For cross-pollination to take place in corn plants, rows of male plants (with pollen-laden tassels at the top) are alternated with rows of female plants.

How Propagation Works

Propagation is the method of asexual reproduction that many plant growers use to produce new plants. Rather than using seeds, a gardener uses some part of the plant, such as the root or a leaf. By taking a part of the parent plant, the plant grower can be sure that the new plants will be genetically identical to the parent plant. This is important when the grower wants plants to have the specific features of another plant, such as a particular color.

This simple experiment using a potato will let you be the gardener and see how propagation works. Select a potato that has "eyes," or buds, and a small container that the potato will fit in. Place the potato, with several toothpicks in it as shown at right, in the container and fill it with water. You do not have to use a whole potato; just the part with an eye can be used.

Place the container in a sunny spot, adding water when necessary to keep the level constant. Soon the eyes will form shoots that will grow into plants that are identical to the parent plant.

Fertilization. After pollen lands or is deposited on the stigma, it must reach the ovule if a seed is to form. The pollen grain sprouts and soon sends a slender pollen tube down through the style into the ovary. The pollen tube enters an ovule and deposits sperm into the egg cell. With the joining of the egg nucleus and the sperm nucleus, the ovule is fertilized. Part of the ovule becomes food for the new plant, and part becomes the new plant itself.

A plant may have one, several, or even hundreds of ovules to be fertilized. Pollen tubes grow down to each one. In some flowers, it takes a long time for the pollen tube to grow down to the ovule. In witch hazel, for instance, it may take up to seven months. In others, such as barley, it takes about an hour.

Both the male and female sex nuclei contain genes, the basic units of heredity. The genes determine the characteristics of a plant. During fertilization, a new plant receives genes from each parent plant, making it a unique plant with a set of characteristics different from that of each parent plant.

Asexual Reproduction

In addition to sexual reproduction, most plants are capable of asexual reproduction—that is, reproducing without seeds. When new, independent plants grow away from the rest of the plant or from a part that is physically separated from the rest of the plant, it is called asexual, or vegetative, reproduction.

Most of the non-cereal food plants you eat are grown from roots, stems, or leaves—not seeds. When gardeners and fruit tree growers use asexual re-

production to produce new plants, it is called **propagation**. The advantage of asexual reproduction is that the new plant is genetically identical to the parent plant, which means that the new plant will have all the same characteristics as the parent plant.

Even one single plant cell can be used to grow a new plant. In a process called **micropropagation**, plants are produced by placing plant cells in prepared nutrients, or cultures. Micropropagation is an efficient, inexpensive way to produce many plants at one time.

Vegetative Reproduction
Many plants can reproduce by vegetative reproduction. Strawberry stems, or stolons, take root and, when they are separated from the parent plant, grow into new plants.

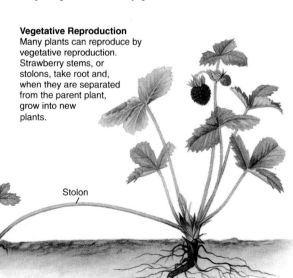

Stolon

▶THE LIFE CYCLE OF A PLANT

All flowering plants go through similar stages as they grow and develop. During its life, a plant will germinate, flower, scatter its seed, and die. The life span of a plant varies with each different kind of plant. Life spans can range from months to years to centuries!

Plants that grow, produce seeds, and die all in one growing season are called **annuals**. Some plants live two or three years but usually do not flower until the second year of growth. These plants are called **biennials**. **Perennials** are plants that produce flowers and seeds year after year for many years.

Growth and Development

Plants, unlike animals, tend to grow throughout their lives. As they grow, they develop new cells and increase in size. Growth also gives plants the ability to change their environment. By growing, plants can obtain a place or position that puts them closer to light, food, and substances such as water.

Germination. Seeds **germinate**, or sprout, at different times depending on the species of plant. Some seeds sprout as soon as they fall from the plant. Seeds enclosed in fleshy fruits, such as apples and tomatoes, do not sprout until they have been removed from the fruit. This is because the fruit contains substances that prevent sprouting. The seeds of certain desert plants do not sprout until heavy rains fall. Most seeds need a resting period before they will sprout. The seed can remain in this inactive, or dormant, state for several weeks, months, or even years.

When the proper amounts of water, oxygen, and warmth are

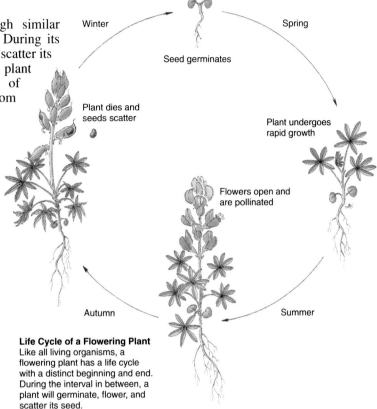

Winter   Spring

Seed germinates

Plant dies and seeds scatter

Plant undergoes rapid growth

Flowers open and are pollinated

Autumn   Summer

Life Cycle of a Flowering Plant
Like all living organisms, a flowering plant has a life cycle with a distinct beginning and end. During the interval in between, a plant will germinate, flower, and scatter its seed.

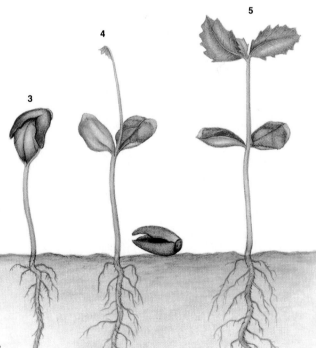

Germination of a Seed
A seed is in an inactive state (1) before it begins to germinate. When conditions are favorable, the seed starts to germinate. The embryo uses stored food to grow. The root emerges from the seed first (2), followed by the shoot with its cotyledons, or seed leaves (3). For the first few days, the plant lives on stored food. As its growth continues, leaves begin to develop (4). Once the plant has a few green leaves (5), it can begin the process of photosynthesis.

available, the seed begins to germinate. The dry dormant seed quickly swells as it soaks up moisture from the ground. Inside the seed, the embryo uses water, oxygen, and the food stored in the endosperm or the cotyledons (special seed leaves) to fuel its growth processes. As it absorbs water, the seed swells and its coat softens. Soon the seed coat breaks open and the root emerges from the seed. The root grows downward into the soil, anchoring the seedling. The root system, which will supply water and minerals to the growing plant, develops from this first root.

The shoot emerges next with its one or two cotyledons. For the first few days, as the shoot grows toward the surface, the new plant lives on stored food. Once it reaches the surface, the plant's first green leaves appear. With the appearance of green leaves, the plant is able to manufacture its own food through the process of photosynthesis.

Patterns of Growth. Once germination is complete, the plant grows quickly. Roots and stems grow in length near their tips only. The new growth takes place in three distinct zones, or areas, one behind the other. At the tip there is a zone of intense cell division. Just behind it is a zone of newly divided cells. Within this second zone, the cells expand to their final size by absorbing water. If there is not enough water, growth cannot occur. In the third zone, cells mature into the cell types that make up the different tissues of the plant.

The growth rings of a woody stem can be used to calculate a tree's age. They can also reveal when events, such as drought or injury, have altered a tree's growth.

Plant Hormones

Plant hormones, which were first discovered in the 1920's, travel throughout a plant and coordinate its activities. Sometimes only one hormone is responsible for regulating an activity, but usually it is the interaction of several hormones that guides a process. Below are the known plant hormones and the roles they play in a plant's growth and development.

Abscisic acid is most abundant during stress responses to factors such as dryness. It sets in motion activities that prevent water loss and guard against wilting and other injury.

Auxins affect many changes in plants, including the elongation of young stem and root cells, leaf fall, and the development of fruit.

Cytokinins, which are present and working in seeds, are the major hormones affecting the process of cell division. They are also involved in the development of new buds and stems.

Ethylene triggers the many changes that occur during fruit ripening. It is also a stress hormone that activates the plant's response to stress or injury.

Gibberellins are a group of growth hormones that are especially involved in stem growth, the production of flowers, and the digestion of stored food in germinating seeds.

In plants that also grow in thickness, such as trees, growth takes place in the **cambium** cells. The cambium cells form new layers of growth between the bark and wood. These layers form the rings that are visible when a cross section of a tree trunk is exposed.

Plant growth is finely controlled through the use of **hormones**. Hormones are chemical substances that act as messengers traveling throughout the plant, coordinating activities between cells. Depending on what tissue they enter, plant hormones trigger different patterns of growth or development. Hormones, which are present in very tiny amounts, generally are made in one tissue and transported to another tissue, where they perform their work.

Early in the life cycle of a plant, all the growth is vegetative; that is, the plant produces leaf, stem, and root tissue. Unlike animals, plants can keep growing as long as environmental conditions are favorable. Their growth is only limited by the nature of each kind of plant and by conditions around it. A plant that is tree-sized in one place may be only a shrub someplace else where growing conditions are less favorable.

Vegetative growth stops when reproductive growth begins. Age or an environmental condition can trigger the start of reproductive growth. Then, instead of making leaves, stems, and roots, the plant makes flowers. Following pollination and fertilization, the flower withers and reproductive growth includes the production and growth of the fruit and seeds.

Spreading Seeds. The last phase of a plant's life cycle—the scattering of its fruit or seeds—ensures that new plants will develop. Many plants have developed special adaptations to spread their seeds. Small, light seeds are often dispersed by the wind. The dry seeds of tobacco plants are as small as dust particles. They are swept into the air and carried by the wind over thousands of miles. Other larger, heavier seeds have special structures that allow them to be carried by the wind, too. Milkweed and dandelion seeds have small, silky parachutes. Maple seeds have a sturdy, flat wing that propels them short distances.

Some seeds are carried by water. The coconut is a large seed surrounded by a fibrous husk with a hard outer shell. The outer shell traps air inside, so that the entire fruit floats. Safe within its shell, the seed can float in the ocean for hundreds of miles.

Birds and other animals also help spread plant seeds. When they eat sweet fleshy fruits, the seeds pass through their digestive tracts unharmed. Those that land in suitable places sprout and grow. Some seeds have hooks or

A seed is more likely to germinate successfully if it does not have to compete with the parent plant for nutrients. Seeds can be carried to suitable new locations in several ways, including by animals (*above*) or air currents (*right*).

barbs that can catch onto an animal's fur. The hooked seeds of both the beggar's tick and the cocklebur can cling to an animal for several days and over many miles.

Once the seeds have been scattered about, they will remain dormant until conditions are right for germination. Then, the seeds will come alive, setting the cycle in motion again.

Plant Processes

Throughout the phases of its life, a plant must obtain and transport food, move water, and perform photosynthesis and respiration.

Obtaining and Transporting Food. Plants cannot live, grow, and reproduce unless they have all they need of certain nutrients. The substances needed by plants are taken from the air, water, soil, and other living organisms.

Plants get carbon and oxygen from the air, hydrogen from water, and the other necessary nutrients, which include substances such as nitrogen, phosphorous, iron, and magnesium, from the water in soil.

Many plants live in a symbiotic association with fungi in or around their roots. This means that both the plant and the fungi benefit from their association with each other. These fungi are called mycorrhizal fungi. The fungi get their food, mainly sugar, from the plant. In turn, the fungi absorb minerals from the soil and pass them on to the plant. Plants grown without their normal mycorrhizal fungi will grow slowly.

How Plants Move

Plants are affected by their environment. In fact, plants perform a variety of movements in response to environmental stimuli. These movements are called tropisms. Try the experiments below and see how plants move in response to light (phototropism), gravity (geotropism), and touch (thigmotropism).

Put a plant near a light source, such as a window, noting the positions of the stem and leaves. After the plant has been in the same place for several days, you will be able to see how the stem bends toward the light and the leaves turn to face the light.

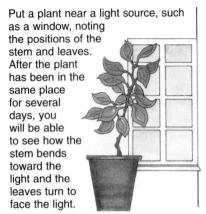

Plant two seeds in the same pot of dirt, but place one seed in the pot upside down. When the new plants start growing, you will see that in response to gravity the shoots from both plants reach up out of the soil and their roots grow downward.

Place a ruler or short pole in the soil near a climbing plant, such as a garden pea or an ivy. When the plant grows and touches the anchored object, you will see the tendrils wrap tightly around it.

There are a small number of colorless plants that cannot perform photosynthesis and must absorb their food from organic matter in the soil like fungi do. A common example in the woodlands of the eastern United States is the Indian pipe.

There are several special methods that some plants use to obtain nitrogen, needed for making proteins and nucleic acids. Nitrogen in the air is abundant, but it is unavailable directly to plants. However, some bacteria can use nitrogen from the air, in the process of nitrogen fixation. Plants in several families, but especially the pea family, have little lumps on their roots called nodules that are full of these bacteria. The bacteria are fed carbohydrates by the plant and in turn secrete ammonia, a useful form of nitrogen, for the plant.

Another way in which some plants, called carnivores, obtain nitrogen

The ghostly looking Indian pipe, which cannot make its own food, gets its nourishment from dead and decaying matter. Plants that survive in this manner—by absorbing nutrients from the breakdown products of once-living organisms—are called saprophytes.

is by eating animals. Pitcher plants have pitcher-shaped leaves that trap insects. Hairs pointing downward grow inside the pitcher and prevent the insects from crawling out. They are digested by digestive juices in a pool at the bottom of the pitcher. Other carnivorous plants trap insects by quickly closing a leaf, as in the Venus's-flytrap, or by trapping the insect in a sticky secretion, as in the sundew.

Parasitic plants live on other plants and get their food from them. Mistletoe is a common example, growing on the trunks and branches of trees. It is green and therefore can perform photosynthesis to make some of its food, but it gets most food from its host.

Food is transported through phloem tissue from wherever the food becomes available to wherever it is needed. Food travels either up or down by way of the **sieve tubes**. In a seedling, food is transported from the seed to the growing shoot tip and root tip. In a young plant, it is transported from the leaves to the growing points. In a mature plant, it is transported from leaves to a storage area, either fruit, seed, bulb, or root.

Water Movement. Water moves constantly from the soil through the plant and into the air. It moves through the cells of the plant by **osmosis**—the movement of water through cell membranes. The direction in which the water moves depends on the concentration of substances inside and outside the cell. Water moves through the membrane to the area with the highest concentration of certain particles or molecules.

Water travels through the system of hollow tubes making up the xylem tissue. The tubes, which run the length of the plant, allow water to move in an upward direction through the plant. The energy for most water movement is supplied by sunlight.

Turgor movements are the fairly rapid movements of various parts of the plant that occur because of the rapid gain or loss of water in certain cells. Water is gained or lost because the concentration of potassium salts in the cell changes and, because of osmosis, so does the amount of water. The movement of the plant does not involve growth. Some examples are the opening and closing of stomata, the folding of leaves at night, the rapid closing of leaves of the sensitive plant when they are touched, the rapid twisting around of some tendrils, and the closing of the Venus's-flytrap leaf when it is touched. The movements can be performed over and over, as long as the in-and-out flow of water occurs.

Many plants can move some of their parts in response to touch or other stimuli. One of the most familiar examples is the sensitive plant (*above*), a tropical shrub. The fernlike leaves of the plant quickly fold together (*below*) if the plant is touched or shaken.

Photosynthesis. During photosynthesis, light energy is converted into chemical energy by the plant. In plants, this process takes place in special organs of the cell called **chloroplasts**. Within the chloroplast, chlorophyll converts the light energy to a chemical energy called **ATP** (*a*denosine *tri*phosphate) and stores it until it is needed.

ATP is the high-energy compound all cells use to drive chemical reactions within the cell. When the trapped energy is freed, one of the reactions it powers combines carbon dioxide from the air and water and minerals from the soil to produce the plant's food. In addition to the food substances produced during photosynthesis, oxygen is produced as a by-product. The oxygen is released into the environment surrounding the plant.

The plant also makes compounds to transport and store energy. The most common form of transported energy is sucrose, or table sugar. The most common form of stored energy is

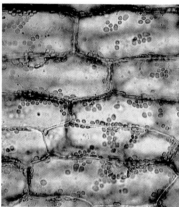

Chloroplasts are the pigment-containing structures that give plants their green color. The number of chloroplasts in a plant cell varies; there may be as many as 300 or as few as 1.

starch. Both of these can be converted to the simple sugar glucose, which can then be used in respiration.

Respiration. The function of respiration is the same as photosynthesis: to provide usable energy to the cell in the form of ATP. Respiration occurs in cell organs known as **mitochondria** (plural of **mitochondrion**).

During aerobic respiration, food molecules are broken down and combined with oxygen to form carbon dioxide and water. Another form of respiration takes place without using oxygen. Called anaerobic respiration, this process occurs when plants are unable to get enough or any oxygen, such as plants that are flooded with water or plants that have roots buried in mud. It yields a much smaller amount of ATP for the cell than does aerobic respiration. While it also produces carbon dioxide, it yields ethanol as its by-product.

Plant Defenses

Plants have many enemies. They are eaten by large animals, such as cattle and deer, and by small animals, such as rabbits and raccoons. And they are eaten by still smaller animals, such as insects, snails, and worms. They are attacked by diseases and destroyed by frost, fire, and high winds.

Some plants ward off attacks by releasing poisons. However, they keep these weapons in reserve until predators actually start munching.

Plants, however, have defenses against these environmental extremes, diseases, and insects and other animals that feed on them. Their weapons include poisons, bad-tasting juices, unpleasant odors, thorns and burrs, deep roots, and thick seed coverings. Many defense mechanisms protect the plant against several threats.

Structural Defenses. Barbs, burrs, spines, and thorns are structures that protect many plants. They are not poisonous, but they can injure an animal's eyes and mouth or pierce its skin. Blackberries, many kinds of roses, honey locusts, cacti, cockleburs, and other plants have these prickly defenses.

Other plant structures also protect against extreme environmental conditions. Many desert plants have very thick stems and small leaves. Most cacti have no leaves at all. Since plants lose water as it evaporates through their leaves, small leaves help desert plants hold water. Water is stored in their thick stems.

The thick bark of many trees forms a good barrier against cold, as well as disease and insect invasion. The bark of the huge sequoias of California is sometimes more than a foot thick. Such thick bark also helps trees resist the heat of forest fires.

Many mountain plants, such as evergreens, must be able to survive the cold temperatures that would kill most other plants. They have gradually become suited to the cold climate of the high regions in which they grow. By growing close to the ground, some small mountain plants are able to find shelter and protection among rocks.

Poisons and Other Chemicals. Many plants contain poisonous substances that can and do kill. Poisons are one of the most effective plant defenses. A small piece of water hemlock root, for example, contains enough poison to kill a cow. The leaves of the death camas, which is part of the lily family, often kill cattle in the western United States. People have been poisoned by eating the bulbs of this plant.

Mountain laurel is a shrub that grows in parts of the eastern United States. The poison in its tough leaves can make sheep and other grazing animals sick. Soon these animals learn to leave the plant alone.

Many familiar plants contain poisons. These include lily of the valley, larkspur, foxglove, English ivy, and dumbcane. The nightshade family, to which tomatoes and white potatoes belong, has many poisonous members, including henbane, belladonna, mandrake, and jimsonweed.

The effects of some plant poisons from oils or saps can be felt by just touching some plants. When any part of the poison oak, poison ivy, or poison sumac plant is touched,

Plants have evolved an arsenal of strategies to defend themselves. For example, the thick stem of a cactus (*below left*) protects it from water loss, while poisons in the deadly nightshade (*below right*) protect it from being eaten by animals.

blisters, rashes, and other skin irritations can result. Similar problems are caused by members of the spurge family and the leaves and stems of lady's slippers.

Some plants are protected by nonpoisonous chemical substances that can injure or even kill the animal that dares to eat them. One example is the taro plant. The leaves and other parts of the taro contain sharp, slender crystals. When a leaf is chewed, these crystals pierce the lining of the animal's mouth, causing great pain. Although it is a dangerous plant, humans use the taro root for food. When the root is thoroughly cooked, the crystals are destroyed.

Protective Relationships. Special relationships exist between some plants and animals that provide benefits to both groups. This helpful, or protective, kind of relationship is called **mutualism**. The acacia plant has this most unusual defense. This tall, branching shrub is armed with heavy, hollow spines. It is not these spines, however, that protect the shrub. It is the stinging ants that live inside the spines. Sweet nectar is produced near the bases of the spines. The ants feed on this nectar and also on fruitlike bodies that grow at the tips of the leaves. In return for food and shelter, the ants patrol all parts of the shrub, driving off any leaf-eating insects.

▶ **SAVING OUR PLANTS**

Earth's original vegetation has been greatly altered where people have settled. Much of the temperate forests worldwide have been cut down and the land converted into farmland or second-growth forests. Original grasslands have been largely converted to cropland. Even semidesert grassland has been converted to scrub shrubland by overgrazing of cattle, sheep, or goats. Cropland has far fewer plant species—sometimes it only has one!—than the vegetation it replaces. Also, human intervention has greatly increased soil erosion by wind and water, resulting in less fertile land and, at times, gullies and eroded land. Significant areas of tropical rain forest are destroyed when all the plants are burned to make way for agriculture. The cleared land can only be farmed for a few years before soil fertility is severely depleted. In many poor countries, the forests have been harvested for firewood, leaving bare, eroded hillsides that are completely unproductive.

Each hour, close to 6,000 acres (2,428 hectares) of tropical forest are destroyed. Thousands of plant species vanish as forests fall to land developers.

Human activity and population growth are making many plant (and animal) species extinct, especially in the humid tropics. The long-term danger is that humans will destroy so many plant species that we will depend on only a few to supply our needs. These few would be vulnerable to plant diseases or insects. The most famous example of this was the potato famine in Ireland in the 1800's, when a fungal disease, called late blight, killed the entire potato crop. The potato was the main food for the population. Without the potato crop, many people starved and many more left the country.

There are various conservation organizations that are actively saving endangered plants. For instance, the Nature Conservancy buys land in threatened habitats for conservation purposes. Originally, land was bought only in the United States, but now it is also bought in other countries. The Wilderness Society is active in trying to save unique federal lands as wilderness areas. Saving a habitat with sufficient undisturbed land ensures the survival of all of the plants and animals in it. This method is much more efficient than trying to save one species at a time with heroic efforts. In the end these methods will succeed only if we learn to value the wealth of our green inheritance.

NEAL M. BARNETT
Department of Botany
University of Maryland

A description of plants and the biomes they occupy is presented on the following pages.

PLANT DISTRIBUTION

Plants have successfully adapted to almost all of the earth's environments. Only the driest deserts, deepest oceans, coldest polar regions, and highest mountains are without some kind of plant life. The plants, animals, and other organisms that live and grow together in the same environment form a **community**.

Each community has its own specific kinds of plants

The yellow poppy displays the great adaptability of plants. It thrives despite the harsh conditions of its tundra home, among them cold temperatures, scarce water, and frozen soil.

Climate is the major characteristic that scientists use to divide the earth's land surfaces into biomes. Important biomes include grasslands, deserts, chaparral, deciduous forests, coniferous forests, tundra, and tropical rain forests. There are also aquatic biomes in rivers, lakes, ponds, and oceans. Because similar communities occur in different parts of the world, there are similar biomes throughout the world. For example,

and animals. When a community of living things covers a large area of the earth's surface, it is called a **biome**. Along with its own unique life-forms, each biome has distinctive conditions and physical factors, such as climate, type of soil, and amount of moisture. grasslands exist in North America as well as in Asia and Africa. The map below identifies the major biomes of the world. The chart on the following page identifies some of the plants that are commonly found in the world's major biomes.

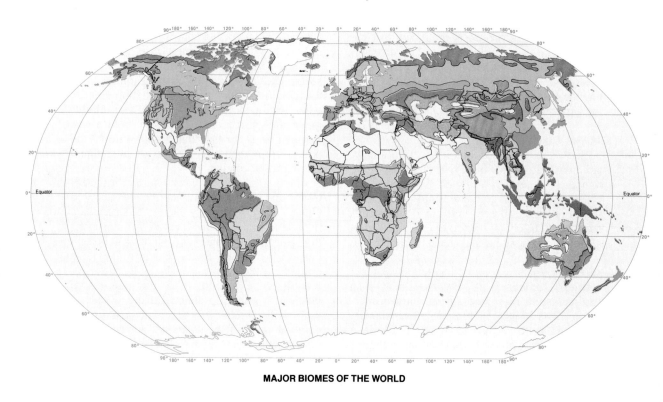

MAJOR BIOMES OF THE WORLD

Tropical Rain Forest

Temperate Coniferous Forest

Deciduous Forest

Northern Coniferous Forest (Boreal Forest)

Chaparral

Tropical Grassland (Savanna)

Temperate Grassland (Prairie, Steppe, Pampa)

Semidesert

Desert

Tundra

Alpine Tundra (Mountains)

Ice Sheet

PLANTS AND THEIR BIOMES

Plants of the Forest

Deciduous Forest

Black cherry
Black locust
Blue violet
Deerberry
Dutchman's-breeches
Great laurel
Green ash
Harebell
Hickory
Indian pipe
Jack-in-the-pulpit
Lady fern
Pincushion moss
Primrose
Quaking aspen
Red maple
Royal fern

Shortleaf pine
Spicebush
Starflower
Teaberry
Tree club moss
Tulip tree
White oak
Wood anemone

Hawthorn

Coniferous Forest

Balsam fir
Black spruce
Bloodroot
Bracken fern
Elderberry
Fireweed
Goldthread
Harebell
Horsetail
Mountain maple
Nodding trillium
Quaking aspen
Red baneberry
Red pine
Sheep laurel
Sphagnum moss

Starflower
Tamarack
White pine
Wood sorrel

Pink lady's slipper

Rain Forest

Antarctic beech
Brazilwoods
Broadleaf evergreens
Bromeliads
Cassia
Epiphytes
Eucalyptus
Lianas
Mangosteen
Orchids
Redwood
Sapodilla
Shell seed
Sitka spruce
Strangler fig

Plants of the Grassland

Temperate Grassland (including prairies, steppes, pampas)

Bluestems
Bromegrass
Buffalo grass
Chokecherry
Crazyweed
Death camas
Evening primrose
Feather grass
Fescue
Foxtail barley
Green ash
Hackberry

Indian grass
Ironweed
Mexican hat
Milkweed
Needle-and-thread
Needle grass
Prairie acacia
Prairie alfalfa
Purple prairie clover
Smooth sumac
Snow-on-the-mountain

Solidago
Sunflower
Switchgrass
Timothy
Wild tulips
Wormwood

Indian paintbrush

Tropical Grassland
(including savannas)

Acacias
Baobab
Bermuda grass
Bluestem
Candelabra tree
Dropseed
Elephant grass
Spurges
Palms
Red oat grass
Umbrella thorn
Whistling thorn

Plants of the Tundra
(including alpine tundra)

Alpine bearberry
Bear grass
Bog bilberry
Bristlecone pine
Cotton grass
Dwarf clover
Englemann spruce
Fairy primrose
Fescue
Fireweed
Forget-me-not
Glacier lily
Goldenbush
King's crown
Moss campion
Mountain avens
Mountain heath
Mountain sorrel
Saxifrage
Sedges
Sheep laurel
White phlox
Willow

Plants of the Desert

Agaves
Artemisia
Barrel cactus
Brittle bush
Creosote bush
Desert holly
Desert marigold
Desert paintbrush
Desert peach
Devil's claw
Giant wild rye
Gold poppy
Indian blanket
Indian rice grass
Joshua tree
Jumping cholla
Mesquite
Needle grass
Ocotillo
Organ pipe cactus
Paloverde
Prickly pear cactus
Pygmy cedar

Saguaro
Seep willow
Spurges
Tamarisk
Yuccas

Sagebrush

Plants of the Chaparral

Black sage
Buckthorn
California buckwheat
Chamiso shrub
Coyote brush
Deerweed
Heath
Manzanita
Mountain lilac
Mountain mahogany
Oak
Prickly pear cactus
Scrub oak
Sugarbush
Sumac
White sage

Each biome has characteristic plants that are adapted to the environment of that particular biome. A desert biome (*above*) has succulent plants—plants with fleshy tissues that conserve water—and tough small-leafed shrubs. After an infrequent rain, many desert annuals will germinate, mature, flower, set seed, and die, all in a few days. The plants in an aquatic biome (*below*) are either floating plants or plants that root at the water's edge or in the shallow portions of the body of water. In the high altitudes of mountain tundra (*left*), the summers are short. The small, compact plants have to flower and produce seeds quickly before winter comes around again.

Forest biomes are dominated by trees, but they also include shrubs, vines, and herbs. The pine, spruce, and fir trees found within a coniferous forest (*above left*) keep it green throughout the year. The leaves of trees in a deciduous forest (*above*) turn colors and are shed every autumn. Woody shrubs and succulents cover the rocky landscape of a dry chaparral (*below*). A mixture of shrubs, colorful wildflowers, and grasses of various heights populate the grassland biome (*below left*).

PLASTICS

Plastics are very popular materials because they are colorful, lightweight, strong, easy to clean, and inexpensive. Most important of all, there are so many different types of plastics available that one of them can be found to suit almost any purpose. There are at least 40 different types of plastics in everyday use. Chemists are still discovering new plastics.

Plastics are not found in nature, as are coal, iron ore, wood, and diamonds. But some of the earth's most abundant natural resources are used in making plastics. The discovery of plastics led to the development of a whole new family of materials. Thousands of things that we see and use every day are made of plastics. Buttons, toys, floor and wall coverings, automobile parts, telephones, and clothing are just a few examples. In addition, plastics have thousands of uses in industry.

The word "plastic" comes from the Greek word *plastikos,* meaning "fit for molding." In English the word "plastic" is sometimes used in the same way. For example, we say that clay or wax are plastic, meaning that they can be molded, or shaped, easily. Sometimes easily shaped materials such as clay, wax, glass, or rubber are called plastics. Usually, however, the word "plastics" refers only to man-made materials.

▶ HISTORY OF PLASTICS

Shortly after the Civil War the high cost of ivory led people who made billiard balls and other items from ivory to search for a substitute. A New York billiard ball company offered a $10,000 prize to anyone who could invent such a substitute. John Wesley Hyatt (1837–1920), a printer and inventor in Albany, New York, heard about the prize and began experimenting with materials he thought might work. In 1868 he came up with a good billiard ball material. It was cellulose nitrate, and Hyatt named it Celluloid. It was the first plastic made in the United States. Hyatt discovered that the addition of camphor made the cellulose nitrate easy to mold.

Celluloid quickly became a very important material. Handles, combs, buttons, buckles, false teeth, shirt collars, and photographic film were just a few of the products made from this plastic. Celluloid is still used today to make Ping-Pong balls.

For many years, Celluloid, or cellulose nitrate, was the only plastic man could make. Then in 1909 the Belgian-American chemist Leo Hendrik Baekeland (1863–1944) discovered phenol-formaldehyde. This was the first of a type of plastics called thermosetting plastics. Baekeland was actually trying to invent a substitute for shellac. Instead he produced a dark syrup that would harden when heated. The new material had many valuable properties. It was not dissolved by ordinary solvents, it could be molded into any shape, it did not conduct electricity, and it was inexpensive. An early use of phenol-formaldehyde was in making insulators for wireless sets. Baekeland named the new material Bakelite, after himself.

After the introduction of Bakelite in 1909, the plastics industry grew steadily. Some new plastics were discovered, and more and more uses were found for them. The shortage of metals during World War II and the need for new types of materials gave plastics a chance to show their usefulness.

▶ CHEMISTRY OF PLASTICS

All plastics are organic chemicals. That is, they contain the element carbon. Carbon atoms can link together to form a "backbone" for a chainlike molecule. Polyethylene is a well-known plastic that has very simple, though very long, molecules made of carbon and hydrogen.

The molecules of plastics are long chains that are made up of smaller units. The two middle diagrams on page 325 show, for example, how a long polyethylene chain is made by putting together molecules of ethylene, which have only two atoms of carbon and four of hydrogen.

Long-chain molecules like those of polyethylene are called polymers. The word "polymer" comes from the Greek *poly,* "many," and *meros,* "part." The name "polyethylene" means that the molecules of that particular plastic are made up of many ethylene molecules. Each of the ethylene molecules is a monomer. The word "monomer" means "one part." The names of many plastics are made up in the same way. For example, polystyrene molecules are made up of styrene monomers. Polymers can be made using more than one type of monomer. These are called copolymers.

Many products are made entirely or partly of plastic.

▶ BASIC INGREDIENTS OF PLASTICS

A plastic may be made of six basic ingredients: resin, filler, pigment or dye, lubricant, accelerator or inhibitor, and plasticizer.

Resin. The resin, which is also called the binder or base, is the most important part of the plastic. The resin gives the plastic its main properties. There are many kinds of resins and therefore many kinds of plastics. The resin in a plastic is something like the flour in bread. Without flour a baker cannot make bread. The kind of flour he uses determines whether the bread will be whole wheat, rye, pumpernickel, or white.

The words "resin" and "plastic" are often used as though they had the same meaning, but there is a big difference between the two. The resin is the plastic before it is made into a finished article. In general, a resin is mixed with other ingredients to form a molding compound. Sometimes this molding compound is changed chemically when the plastic is

Left: Plastics sometimes are stored in pellet form and later processed into finished goods.
Right: A technician matches colors from a "color library" of more than 39,000 polyethylene chips.

Freshly extruded plastic filaments are wound on spools.

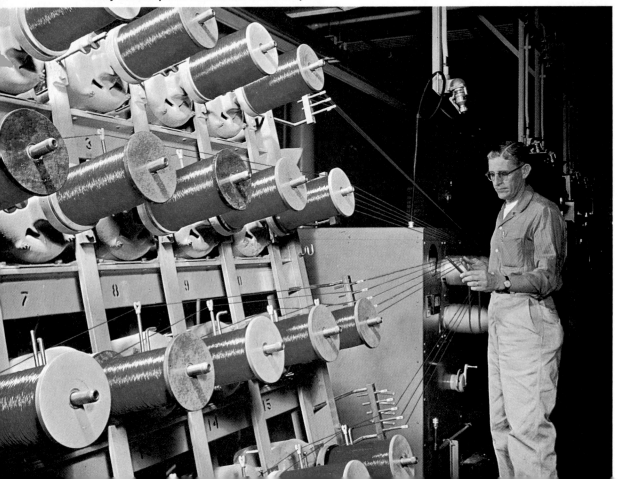

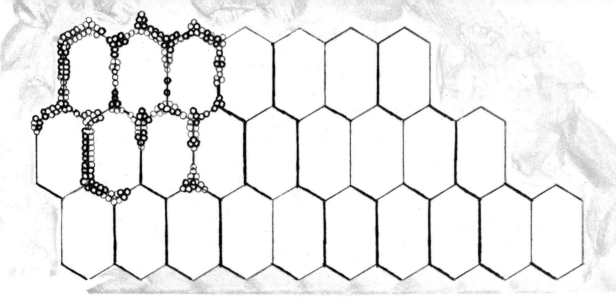

NETLIKE LINKAGE OF MOLECULES IN A THERMOSETTING PLASTIC

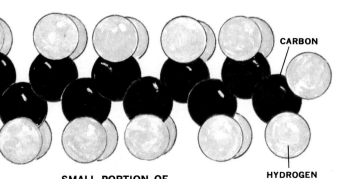

SMALL PORTION OF
A POLYETHYLENE MOLECULE

CARBON

HYDROGEN

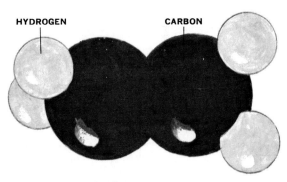

HYDROGEN   CARBON

ETHYLENE MOLECULE, BASIC BUILDING
BLOCK OF POLYETHYLENE

formed. In a few cases nothing is added to the resin, and it is not changed chemically. In these cases the resin and the plastic are the same thing.

Filler. Fillers are usually cheap materials that are added to a product to make it less expensive. In plastics, however, fillers are usually used to improve the qualities of the plastic. For example, ground asbestos is used to make a plastic that resists burning. Ground quartz or mica may be added to a plastic to make it hard. Glass fiber is often used to strengthen plastics.

Pigment or Dye. A great advantage of plastic is that it can be made in many colors. Pigments or dyes are used to color plastics.

Lubricant. Lubricants are used to prevent the resin or molding compound from sticking to the equipment in which it is made or molded. Lubricants are melted out of the plastic by the heat of manufacturing. Therefore they are not part of the final plastic.

Accelerators and Inhibitors. These are chemicals that control the speed at which monomers join to form polymers. If a resin takes too long to harden, an accelerator is added to speed up the process. If a resin hardens too quickly, an inhibitor is used.

Plasticizer. A plasticizer keeps the resin from being gummy and in that way makes it easier to handle during molding.

Often one ingredient or another is not needed. For example, if the resin is naturally slippery, no lubricant is needed. If the plastic is to be clear and colorless, no dye or pigment is needed.

TYPES OF PLASTICS

There are two main types of plastics— thermoplastics and thermosetting plastics. **Thermoplastics** can be softened or melted by heating and cast into a new shape as often as desired. **Thermosetting plastics** are just the opposite. They become hard when heated. Once a thermosetting plastic, also called a thermoset, has set, its shape cannot be changed.

The words "thermoplastic" and "thermoset" come from the way these materials behave. "Thermo-" means heat. "Thermoplastic," therefore, means a material that becomes plastic, or moldable, when heated. "Thermoset" means a material that sets, or becomes permanently hard, when heated.

Some nonplastic materials behave in a similar fashion. For example, a piece of lead or solder, like a thermoplastic, can be melted down and cast into some shape. If a new shape is wanted, the lead is simply remelted and recast. Plaster of paris is a good example of a material that behaves like a thermoset. When powdered plaster of paris is mixed with water and poured into a mold, the mixture soon becomes very hard. If the hardened material is ground up into a powder again and mixed with water, the mixture does not become solid and rocklike. This is because a chemical reaction took place after the first mixing. The reground material is chemically different from the original powdered plaster of paris.

Curing is the process that makes thermosetting plastics hard. During this process the molecules of the resin change. They link together to form a netlike arrangement instead

SOME IMPORTANT PLASTICS

PLASTIC	YEAR INTRODUCED COMMERCIALLY	PROPERTIES	USES
THERMOPLASTICS			
ABS Plastics	1948	Strong; tough; resist heavy blows and hard wear.	Construction workers' helmets; football helmets and face guards; luggage; tool handles; pipes.
Acetals	1956	Lighter and less expensive than metal; stiff; strong; not affected by changes in temperature or humidity; acetal parts need no lubrication.	Moving parts in automobiles, electrical appliances, and business machines; gears.
Acrylics	1936	Strong; weather resistant; not affected by high or low temperatures; can be made transparent, translucent, or opaque; can be clear or colored.	Store counters and display racks; television screens; safety goggles; skylights; automobile taillight lenses; trays and bowls; outdoor signs; paints; fabrics; furniture.
Cellulosics **Cellulose acetate**	1927	Strong; clear; easily colored; moisture resistant.	Eyeglass frames; toys; recording tapes; photographic film; combs; tool handles.
Cellulose acetate butyrate	1938	Tough; transparent; weather resistant.	Pipe used to carry natural gas; tool handles; steering wheels; boat lights; streetlight globes; outdoor signs; fountain pens; toys; irrigation pipe.
Cellulose acetate propionate	1945	Tough; shock resistant; weather resistant; easily colored; cellulose acetate propionate parts have smooth, shiny surfaces.	Telephones; packagings; steering wheels; tool handles; toys; pens; mechanical pencils.
Cellulose nitrate	1868	Strong; clear; easily colored; explosive.	Has been replaced for most uses by nonexplosive plastics, particularly cellulose acetate.
Ethyl cellulose	1935	Strong; tough; shock resistant; slightly yellow in color.	Flashlight cases; bowling-pin bases; floor-sweeper parts; paper coatings; toys; football helmets.
Chlorinated polyethers	1959	Great resistance to strong chemicals.	Linings for metal pipes, tanks, and other chemical equipment; valves and fittings.
Fluorocarbons	1943	Very strong; do not conduct electricity; can withstand very high and very low temperatures; chemically resistant; have a very low-friction surface.	Laboratory and industrial equipment; insulation for high-voltage wire and cable; self-lubricating bearings; nonstick cookware.
Nylon (polyamide)	1938	One of the toughest and most durable plastics; can be boiled and sterilized in steam without losing shape; nylon parts need no lubrication.	Fabrics; surgical instruments; gears; heat-sealing adhesives.

of simply lying side by side in long chains, as do the molecules of thermoplastics. It is this netlike linking that keeps thermosets from softening and melting when they are heated again.

▶ PLASTIC FORMING

The first synthetic resin was discovered more than a century ago. The methods used to mold the resin into finished products at that time were very crude compared to the methods used today. As new plastics were developed, new methods of forming them were also developed. Plastics are now formed by several methods. Molding is still the most important.

Molding. There are several methods of molding plastics. The method used depends on the plastic used and the product desired.

In molding thermoplastics, the mold is kept relatively cool. When the hot, melted plastic is fed into the mold, it cools and becomes solid. In molding thermosets, however, the mold is kept hot, so that the plastic will cure. High pressure is usually needed for curing both thermoplastics and thermosets.

Extrusion. Thermoplastics may be formed by extrusion. The soft plastic is pushed through a shaping tool called a die. This die is a metal plate with a hole in it. The shape of the hole determines the shape of the plastic. In this way sheet, film, rods, tubes, and various other shapes can be formed. Filaments, such as those of Saran and nylon, are also made by extrusion. Filaments are long, thin strands of man-made fibers, used to make such things as textiles, webbing, upholstery material, and industrial filter fabrics.

PLASTIC	YEAR INTRODUCED COMMERCIALLY	PROPERTIES	USES
Polycarbonates	1957	Shock resistant.	Business-machine casings; battery bases; special aircraft and automobile parts.
Polyethylene	1942	Strong; tough; flexible; easy to clean; inexpensive; not harmed by most household chemicals. Nearly 6,000,000,000 (billion) pounds produced every year—more than any other plastic.	Toys; ice-cube trays; squeeze bottles; raincoats; buckets; storage bags; pipe; weather balloons; telephone-cable covering.
Polypropylene	1957	Lightest plastic known; can be sterilized by steam; has "living hinge" property—can be bent back and forth over 2,000,000 times without wearing out.	Toolboxes; lunch boxes; automobile accelerator pedals; baby bottles; hospital trays; pans, tumblers, etc.
Polystyrene	1938	Inexpensive; easy to clean.	Hair curlers; knife handles; toys; television and radio cabinets.
Vinyls (polyvinyl chloride)	1927	Tough; strong.	Chair coverings; tablecloths; shower curtains; wall coverings; floor coverings; raincoats; toys; garden hoses; phonograph records; piping; bottles.
THERMOSETTING PLASTICS			
Alkyds	1926	Do not conduct electricity; may be molded at low pressure.	Paints; lacquers; electrical insulators.
Epoxies	1947	Extremely strong adhesives; often used with fiber glass to make reinforced plastic.	Adhesives; battery cases; electronic devices; laboratory equipment; boat hulls.
Melamine-formaldehyde	1939	Very hard; colors do not wash out or fade; does not conduct electricity; not burned or scratched easily; not harmed by soaps, detergents, bleaches, oils, or greases.	High-quality plastic dinnerware; laminated tabletops and counter tops.
Phenolics	1909	Strong; hard; rigid; poor conductors of heat; do not burn easily; made only in dark brown or black because resin tends to darken.	Camera cases; washing machine agitators; radio and television cabinets; knobs; handles for cooking utensils.
Polyurethanes	1954	First foamed plastics; can be flexible or rigid.	Mattresses; pillows; car seats; topcoat linings; luggage; sound and shock absorbers; heat insulators in refrigerators, railroad cars, storage tanks, and homes.
Urea-formaldehyde	1929	Very hard; colors do not fade or wash out; does not conduct electricity; not harmed by soaps, detergents, bleaches, oils, or greases.	Bottle caps; electric switches; electrical appliances; stove knobs; handles.

Plastic films may be extruded in the form of a tube. In one method the tube is inflated with air, which stretches the hot plastic until it is a thin film. Plastic bags are often made by this method.

Calendering. Calendering is an important method of making film and sheeting from thermoplastic resins. This is done by squeezing the plastic between several pairs of large heated rollers, which are called calenders. By adjusting the space between the last pair of rollers, almost any thickness of plastic film or sheeting can be made. If the last pair of rollers is textured—given a rough pattern—the plastic film or sheet will come out textured. Calendering is also used to coat materials such as paper, cloth, aluminum foil, and wood veneer with plastic.

Laminating. The word "laminate" comes from the Latin *lamina,* which means "a thin plate or layer." In laminating, the resin is used to bind together layers of cloth, paper, wood, or glass fiber. The material is soaked with resin and then placed in a hydraulic press. The heat and pressure of the press cures the resin, forming thick sheets. Products made by this method are very strong because they have the combined strength of the reinforcing material and the resin.

Laminated materials used for tabletops and counter tops use paper as the reinforcing material. The top layer of paper is printed with the design that is to appear on the finished material. Plywood is another important laminated product. In plywood the amount of resin used is very small compared to the amount of reinforcing material.

Some plastics may be formed by laminating at low pressure. The resin, which is in liquid form, is simply brushed or sprayed onto the reinforcing material. Sports-car bodies, boat hulls, luggage, and truck bodies can be made in this way.

Coating. Plastics are used to coat all kinds of materials: paper, metal, wood, fabric, leather, glass, concrete, and ceramics. Plastic

Steps in making a plastic bottle: (1) Machine extrudes a cylinder of heat-softened plastic. (2) Cylinder is dropped over an air nozzle, which will inflate it inside a heated mold. (3) Mold surrounds plastic while bottle is formed. (4) Completed bottle is ready for trimming.

Scores of familiar things, from fresh-baked bread to nylon stockings, come wrapped in plastic.

coatings can make materials resistant to heat, fire, stains, tarnish, or moisture.

Paints and lacquers are common coating materials. Before the invention of plastics, natural materials such as linseed oil were used as bases for paints and lacquers. Now many paints and lacquers have plastic bases.

Plastic coating may be rolled or spread on paper, fabric, and similar materials. Or the material may be coated by dipping it into a tank of liquid resin.

WONDER QUESTION

What is cellophane?

Cellophane is a smooth, shiny, transparent material produced in the form of a thin sheet, or film. Cellophane is naturally colorless, but it can be made in many different colors. Most cellophane is treated to make it waterproof. Cellophane is used chiefly for wrapping food and cigarette packs. Some cellophane is used in pressure-sensitive tapes, drinking straws, and party decorations.

Although cellophane looks very much like a plastic wrapping material, it is not a plastic itself. Cellophane is actually composed of cellulose, a common natural material found in plants.

There are many uses for plastic-coated fabrics—as wall coverings, raincoats, and imitation leather, for example. The cover of this book is made of plastic-coated cloth.

▶ **PLASTICS TODAY**

Plastics are everywhere. The United States, the world's largest producer and consumer of plastics, produces an estimated 67 billion pounds (30 billion kilograms) of plastics a year. This heavy use of plastic leads to a vast amount of plastic waste. Because most plastics do not break down easily, plastic waste poses a serious threat to the environment. The recycling of plastic items and the use of biodegradable plastics that will break down over time are two possible solutions to the problem of plastic waste disposal.

PATRICIA E. LESLIE
Basford, Inc.
Reviewed by RALPH L. HARDING, JR.
Executive Vice-President
Society of the Plastics Industry, Inc.

See also NYLON AND OTHER SYNTHETIC FIBERS.

PLATH, SYLVIA. See MASSACHUSETTS (Famous People).

Plato, from a painting by Raphael.

PLATO (427?–347 B.C.)

Plato, one of the greatest Greek philosophers, was born in Athens about 427 B.C. and died there in 347. He belonged to a rich and noble family. In his youth he met the philosopher Socrates, who molded his whole life. Plato admired Socrates for his strong character and was fascinated by his brilliant ideas.

In 399 B.C. Socrates was accused of not believing in the gods of Athens and of corrupting young men's minds. He was found guilty and put to death. Plato's friends urged him to enter politics, but he despised the Athenians who had condemned Socrates. He left home and stayed abroad for 12 years. All through his life he took no part in the political struggles of Athens.

Plato was determined to keep the teaching of Socrates alive. He himself had a quick and fertile mind. He returned to Athens and opened a school. It was called the Academy because it was in a grove sacred to the hero Academus. This was the first university in the world. It remained active for nearly 1,000 years. Plato and his friends taught science, law, and philosophical thinking to carefully picked students. His most famous pupil was Aristotle, who worked in the Academy for 20 years.

Plato wrote at least 25 books, some quite short, others long and complicated. These are truly wonderful works, for Plato has a clear and graceful style, and the ideas he discusses are most important. One strange thing about them is that they do not read like ordinary books. They are conversations. As we read them we hear Socrates talking with his friends, his pupils, and even his enemies. In each conversation a problem is raised, and then the talkers, usually guided by Socrates, try to find a solution on which all can agree.

Another strange thing is that Plato himself never appears or speaks. In many hundreds of pages his name is mentioned only twice. His brothers, his kinsmen, and his friends come in, but never Plato. Plato wanted his readers to know that the thoughts worked out in the books were originally the thoughts of Socrates, even if Plato wrote them down and carried them further.

The chief thoughts in the books are these: (1) There are two worlds—this world, in which everything keeps changing, nothing is perfect, and truth is almost impossible to reach; and another world where everything is perfect and permanent, and truth can be found. Our world is a poor copy of the other world. (2) Our bodies belong to this world and die. Our souls come from the other world, return to it, and never die. (3) We understand important truths, such as the laws of mathematics, because our souls bring knowledge of them from the other world. (4) Many important truths cannot be written down because books cannot explain them fully. They can be grasped only by a few men or women engaged in free discussion. (5) Virtue is knowledge. If you know what is good, you naturally do it. Therefore no one does wrong willingly. But most people do not know the truth, so they act stupidly and wrongly. (6) Democratic government is disorderly, inefficient, and corrupt because most people do not know what is best for them. They will vote for anyone who flatters them and promises them they can have everything they want. The only safe and sensible type of government is government by a few trained thinkers—a king who is a philosopher, with wise advisers, or a group of tightly disciplined philosophers.

The most important of Plato's books are *The Defense of Socrates,* Plato's version of the speeches Socrates made at his trial (this is the only book not set out as a conversation); *Phaedo,* the last discussion of Socrates with his friends in the condemned cell; *The Republic,* a dialogue about the meaning of justice and a plan for the ideal government; *Gorgias,* a keen argument about truth and lies in politics; and *Phaedrus* and *The Symposium,* talks on the meaning of love as an ideal that can bring our souls closer to perfection.

GILBERT HIGHET
Formerly, Columbia University

PLATYPUS AND SPINY ANTEATERS

The platypus and the spiny anteaters live in Australia and a few nearby islands. They are among the most unusual animals in the world. The platypus has webbed feet and a flat, leathery bill somewhat like a duck's bill. A spiny anteater, or echidna, has long claws, a tube-like snout, and a covering of short, stiff spines like that of a hedgehog or porcupine.

The platypus and spiny anteaters are mammals—the females produce milk and nurse their young. But one of the strangest things about them is that they lay eggs, as birds and most reptiles do. They are the only mammals in the world that do this. Like birds and reptiles, they have only one body opening, which serves both for the elimination of all body wastes and for laying eggs. For this reason, platypuses and spiny anteaters are known by the group name **monotreme,** which means "single hole, or opening."

▶ **THE DISCOVERY OF MONOTREMES**

Australia has always been noted for its unusual animal life. Kangaroos and many other marsupials, or pouched mammals, live there. They were known before the platypus and spiny anteater were discovered. One of the first reports about a spiny anteater was written in 1792.

The platypus was first recorded in 1797, when colonists saw it in the Hawkesbury River in eastern Australia. They called the odd little creature a water mole. When the first platypus skin was sent to England, scientists thought it was a joke—that parts of different animals had been sewn together.

When scientists studied later specimens, they found that the platypus was not a joke. But just what was it? It had fur, and it was soon shown to have milk glands. It had to be a mammal. Yet it had a bill. And it was said to lay eggs—which seemed unbelievable. Finally, in 1884, two scientists, working separately, proved that the platypus and spiny anteater are mammals that lay eggs. They observed these animals and their eggs in the wild and reported what they had seen.

▶ **THE PLATYPUS, OR DUCKBILL**

The platypus lives in eastern Australia and Tasmania. It always lives near streams, lakes,

The platypus has a long, skin-covered bill and heavily webbed feet.

or ponds, and it gathers its food in the water. The male measures as much as 60 centimeters (2 feet) in length and may weigh about 2 kilograms (4½ pounds). The female is smaller. Both sexes have thick coats of soft, dark brown fur. Platypuses were once widely hunted for their fur. Today, hunting these animals is against the law.

All four feet of the platypus are webbed. The webs of the front feet extend some distance beyond the claws. These outer portions are folded under when the platypus walks about on land. The tail is broad and rather thick. The adult male has sharp spurs on his hind legs. The spurs are connected to poison glands and can give painful wounds to an attacker.

The broad, flattened bill is covered with soft, flexible skin. In this skin are sensitive nerves that help the animal locate food. Adult platypuses have no teeth. Hard ridges on their bills help to crush and grind up their food.

Platypuses live in burrows that they dig in the banks of streams. They sleep in their burrows during the day but come out at dusk to hunt for food. Their appetites are enormous. Swimming along stream bottoms, they nuzzle through the mud and pebbles, gobbling worms, insects, crayfish, and other small freshwater animals.

Baby Platypuses

The platypus breeds during September and October. Those are spring months in the Southern Hemisphere. At this time the female prepares a breeding burrow, which may vary in length from 5 to 18 meters (15 to 60 feet). In this burrow she prepares a special nesting chamber and lines it with leaves and grass. After she has mated, the female goes into her burrow and plugs it up with earth. Then she retires to her nest and lays her eggs—usually two but sometimes one or three. The eggs are almost round and are about 2 centimeters (¾ inch) in diameter. They are white and have wrinkled, leathery shells. The mother platypus curls around the eggs and incubates them for about ten days. Then the babies hatch.

Newborn platypuses are blind, naked, helpless, and little more than 2.5 centimeters (1 inch) long. They nurse by drinking milk that oozes from pores on the underside of the mother's body and dribbles onto her fur. The young platypuses develop quite slowly. They finally leave the nest when they are about 17 weeks old.

Mother platypus and babies at feeding time.

THE SPINY ANTEATER, OR ECHIDNA

The platypus is equipped for a life in the water. The spiny anteaters are equipped for digging and for gathering ants and other insects as their principal food. Spiny anteaters live in the same areas as the platypus and in New Guinea as well. They usually inhabit open woodlands or rocky areas.

A spiny anteater is perhaps even more unusual looking than a platypus. The stout body is covered with hair and also with a great many short, thick spines on the back and sides. The short, powerful legs have long,

The spiny anteater, or echidna.

curved claws for digging. The snout is long and narrow—shaped somewhat like a tube. The sticky, wormlike tongue can be thrust out like the tongue of any anteater.

During the day, the spiny anteater sleeps in a cavity under roots or rocks or perhaps in a hollow log. At dusk it goes out to search under stones and in the ground for ants, termites, and other insects. These are picked up with the long tongue. During cold weather, spiny anteaters may hibernate. This means that they are inactive or dormant (asleep).

At breeding time, the female develops a pouch on her underside. The pouch opens to the rear. Almost always, she lays just one egg into the pouch. It is not certain exactly how the egg gets there. But the female probably curls her body so that the egg is laid directly into the pouch. She carries the egg until it hatches. The baby lives in the pouch until it becomes too big for the mother's comfort. Then the mother leaves it in the burrow or some other hiding place.

If it is threatened, a spiny anteater may roll itself into a ball or dig straight down, feet first; into the ground. Only its sharp spines can then be seen or felt by its enemies.

There are several different species of spiny anteaters. The largest is native to New Guinea. It may measure 75 centimeters (30 inches) in length.

ROBERT M. McCLUNG
Author, science books for children

See also ANTEATERS; MAMMALS.

PLAYGROUNDS. See PARKS AND PLAYGROUNDS.

PLAYS

Putting on a play is fun for everybody. It is fun for the actors and the director, for the stage crew, the set designers, and the audience. A successful play takes a great deal of time from the first "let's-have-a-play" meeting through the rehearsals to opening night. It takes careful thinking and planning, good organization, and a lot of hard work. But it is probably the most satisfying kind of entertainment there is.

▶ CHOOSING A PLAY

The first step, of course, is choosing the play you want to put on. There are a number of things you have to think about before you decide.

How many people do you want in the cast? Do you need parts for just a few or for a whole club or a whole class?

How much real talent is there in the group, and what kind of talent? You can't do a musical without good singers or a serious drama without good actors. Be sure that the play you choose is right for the age, skill, and number of actors in the cast.

What kind of audience will you be playing to? A talky, worldly play is a poor choice for a young audience. Be sure to choose a play that everyone can understand and enjoy.

How much money do you have for the production? Elaborate scenery and costumes can be expensive, even if you make them yourselves. If your play is to be a fundraiser, be sure your expenses don't amount to more than your ticket sales.

Where can you have your play? Consider the size of the stage you will be working on. A huge cast cannot be squeezed onto a small stage. Don't choose a play with problem scenery, lighting, or special effects. Keep it simple. Fifteen scenes might be exciting to the audience but hard on the stage crew.

▶ KINDS OF PLAYS

Maybe you will want to write an original play. Maybe you will want to dramatize (adjust for stage production) a special story or poem. (If you are going to dramatize a published work, you will have to ask the publisher's permission to use it.) Maybe you will want to use a play that is all written out, complete with dialogue and stage instructions.

Your librarian can be very helpful in suggesting books in which you will find all kinds of printed plays. But watch for one thing. Every printed play states whether you have to pay royalties on it or not. (A royalty is the money an author gets when his play is performed.) It is particularly important to check on royalties if your are charging admission to your play.

▶ ORGANIZING A PLAY

Good organization is very important, especially in an undertaking as complicated as putting on a play. Everything is simpler when the work is divided. Every person in the production should know exactly what he is responsible for, whether it is handing the hero his sword, turning on the right spotlight at the right moment, or closing the curtains at the end of a scene.

The Director

The director is in charge of the production. He chooses the actors and assigns the nonacting jobs. He sees that everyone knows his job and does it. The director may have assistance and advice, but he is the captain of the team and should have the final word.

COSTS

ROYALTY FEE . . . . . . _____

RENTAL OF SPACE . . . . . _____

PROFESSIONAL ASSISTANCE . . . _____
    (electricians, carpenters, etc.)

MANUSCRIPTS FOR PLAYERS . . . . _____

SUPPLIES . . . . _____
    Scenery
      (lumber, paint, material, etc.)
    Electrical equipment
      (bulbs, wire, etc.)
    Props
    Sound effects
    Costume material
      (include safety pins, elastic, etc.)
    Makeup
      (include tissues, cold cream, etc.)
    Music or other records

CLEANING OF COSTUMES . . . . _____

PRINTING COSTS . . . . . . _____
    Tickets
    Programs

POSTERS . . . . _____
    (paper, paint, etc.)

PUBLICITY . . . . _____

JANITOR . . . . _____

INCIDENTAL COSTS . . . . . _____
    (phone calls, pickups, stamps, etc.)

                TOTAL _____

The Stage Manager

The director chooses the stage manager, who is his chief assistant. The stage manager co-ordinates the work of the cast and the crew.

The Actors

Every actor must want his part, be able to act his part, and learn his part. He is expected to come to all rehearsals. Members of the group who have activities that would interfere with rehearsals should not try out for parts or sign up for other jobs that involve rehearsals. When a rehearsal schedule is set up, it should be understood that those who do not attend rehearsals give up their parts.

The Stage Crew and Other Workers

The stage crew and other workers are as necessary to the success of the play as the actors are. The scenery movers are very important members of the backstage crew. So is the propman, who is responsible for all objects that are not scenery or costumes. Usually he is responsible for obtaining them, taking care of them, seeing that they are on stage at the proper time, and returning them in good condition after the performance.

Each stage crew has an electrician in charge of the lights and a man for sound and other special effects. There is a prompter (for children's plays there may be two), who stands in the wings and holds the script of the show. He follows the action of the play from the script and is ready to remind the actors when they forget their lines or words. Others who help run the show are the curtain men, who open and close the stage curtain to mark the beginning and the end of the scenes and acts, and the runners, who call the members of the cast to make their entrances on time. The actors and the stage crew are responsible to the stage manager.

The Art Director

In children's productions an art director sees to scenery, costumes, and makeup. The members of his committee design and build the scenery and borrow, rent, or make the costumes. They make the actors up before the performance and have enough dressers on hand that costume changes may be made quickly and smoothly. The art committee also makes the posters advertising the show.

The Business Manager

The business manager is in charge of all money matters. His committee is responsible for finances, tickets, a place to put on the show, programs, publicity, ushers, and cleanup.

Almost every show costs something. The business manager should make a list of all possible expenses, find out what each item will cost, and then figure out how many tickets he will have to sell to make a profit.

▶ REHEARSALS

A play needs a great deal of rehearsing. The first rehearsal should be spent in explaining the play or idea, so the actors will understand the story and the characters that they are going to try to portray.

Next come walk-through rehearsals. The actors speak their lines without acting out the part and learn entrances and exits and positions on the stage.

Next come rehearsals with lines. The director may call special rehearsals for those scenes that need more work than others. The way an actor moves, talks, and listens should be in character every minute he is on the stage. An audience will lose interest in the play if the actors cannot be heard and understood. Occasionally during rehearsals someone not too familiar with the lines should sit in the back and listen.

SOUND EFFECTS

Crowd noises—People backstage muttering loudly.

Distant gunfire—Drumbeats.

Doorbell—Battery, bell, and push unit rigged up where bell is supposed to be heard.

Doorknocker—Real doorknocker mounted on a board and put against a wall, door, or the floor offstage.

Gravel path—Mark time on gravel in a large wooden tray.

Hoofbeats—A person—one for each horse—slapping his open palms against his thighs.

Machine gun fire—Bird-scaring rattle turned by hand.

Pistol shot—Starting pistol; or strike leather chair with bamboo cane.

Rain—Rice dropped in an open shoebox; or a shallow tin pan filled with dried peas or rice and rotated.

Surf and waves—Large round tray filled with small lead pellets, swished around in circular movement.

Thunder—Padded wooden spoon banged on a tin pan backstage.

Trains—Sandpaper blocks rubbed together.

FLATS, LIGHTING, TREE PROPS

FLAT

BRACE

WOODEN FRAME

STAND

MUSLIN STRETCHED OVER FRAME

PAINT WITH SIZING

SUNLIGHT EFFECT

WINDOW CUTOUT

FLASHLIGHTS

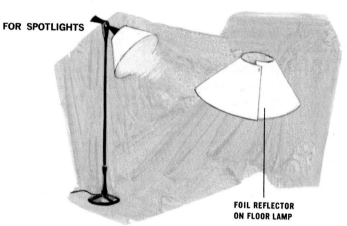

FOR SPOTLIGHTS

FOIL REFLECTOR ON FLOOR LAMP

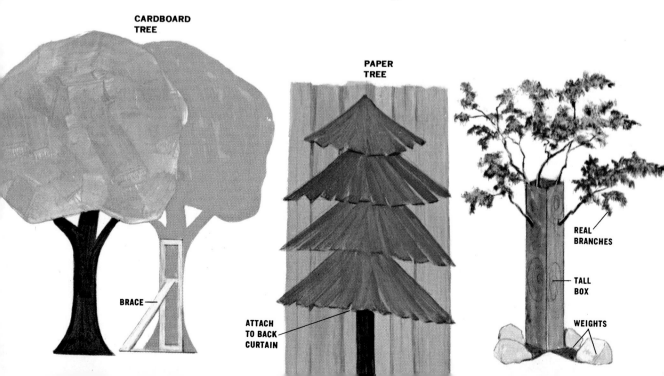

CARDBOARD TREE

BRACE

PAPER TREE

ATTACH TO BACK CURTAIN

REAL BRANCHES

TALL BOX

WEIGHTS

SETS

SKY AND BEACH PAINTED ON SHEET AS BACKDROP

BEACH

PAINT FLATS

OFFICE

CARDBOARD OR WOODEN SLATS

PAPER FLOWERS

GARDEN

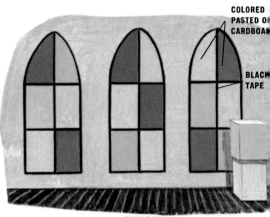

COLORED PASTED O CARDBOA

BLACK TAPE

CHURCH

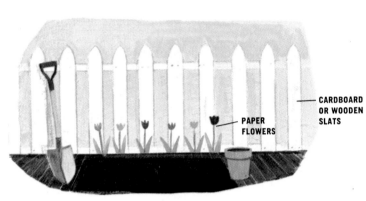

PAINTED BACKDROP

TENT ON FOUR STICKS

INDIAN TEPEE

APPLES 10¢

ORANGES 15¢

PEACHES 10¢

WOO CRA

STORE

PEDESTAL AS BIRDBATH

PARK

SPACESHIP

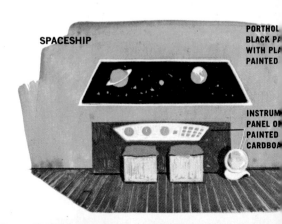

PORTHOL BLACK PA WITH PLA PAINTED

INSTRUM PANEL ON PAINTED CARDBOA

COSTUMES

SHAPE IS MOST IMPORTANT IN PLANNING THE PERIOD OF A COSTUME. TRY TO WORK FROM A TRUE HISTORICAL PICTURE TO GET THE CORRECT SILHOUETTE, OR SHAPE. HAIRSTYLES SHOULD BE AUTHENTIC.

19TH-CENTURY LADY

LONG, FULL SKIRT AND FLAT HAT SET THE PERIOD

FAIRY-TALE PRINCESS AND PRINCE

ON HER HEAD THE PRINCESS WEARS A CUFFED WIMPLE (CARDBOARD CONE), WITH TASSEL OR VEIL HANGING FROM IT

TRAMP

A TOO-LARGE JACKET, BAGGY PANTS, AND A BATTERED HAT MAKE A PROPER TRAMP

Sceneshifters need a special rehearsal to practice working together quickly and quietly.

The first dress rehearsal should be the last time for making any changes.

The final dress rehearsal should be a complete performance. Everything, both on and off stage, should be done just as though it were opening night. Any problems or discussions should be saved until the end of the rehearsal. Before going home, every member of the production should know exactly what to do on opening night—what time to come, where to dress and to be made up, where to wait for cues. In fact, he must know everything he is responsible for.

▶ **SCENERY AND LIGHTING**

Scenery may be real furniture, painted backdrops, or only large props. The scenery may be simple, for it is supposed only to suggest the scene. The imagination of the audience will complete the picture.

Proper lighting can add a great deal to the realism of the play. Consider brightness, color, and direction in lighting your play. Does the action take place in the bright light of morning, or in the dull gray of evening?

Is your scene gay or mysterious? White, yellow, amber, and pink lights brighten the stage and are happy colors. Blue and green dull the scene and produce a cold effect. Red and purple are exciting or mysterious.

Think of the direction from which your light is supposed to be coming. Outdoor sunlight shines from the top of the stage. Light coming through a window must appear to come through the window. Unless the light is coming from a lamp that is part of the scenery, lighting should be placed where the audience can't see it.

Stage lighting is always electrical. **Never use an open flame, such as a candle or a lantern, on the stage.** Only the assigned person should touch the electrical equipment.

MAKEUP

OLD PERSON
- GREY SMUDGES UNDER EYES
- LINES WITH GREY EYEBROW PENCIL
- LIPS PALE

PIRATE
- HOOP EARRING
- PATCH OVER EYE
- DARK FOUNDATION

WITCH
- ATTACH STRING HAIR TO HAT
- BLACKEN TOOTH WITH BLACK CHEWING GUM

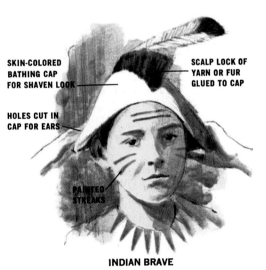

INDIAN BRAVE
- SKIN-COLORED BATHING CAP FOR SHAVEN LOOK
- SCALP LOCK OF YARN OR FUR GLUED TO CAP
- HOLES CUT IN CAP FOR EARS
- PAINTED STREAKS

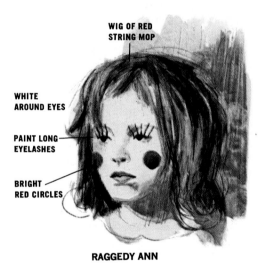

RAGGEDY ANN
- WIG OF RED STRING MOP
- WHITE AROUND EYES
- PAINT LONG EYELASHES
- BRIGHT RED CIRCLES

▶**COSTUMES AND MAKEUP**

Every costume should be comfortable and securely put together so the actor does not have to worry about it once it is on. Before the dress rehearsal all the parts of each costume should be hung together and tagged. A dressing crew from the costume committee should be on hand to assist the actors at dress rehearsals and final performances.

The makeup crew should allow plenty of time to do their work after each actor is dressed. Everything in the makeup box should have its own place and be covered when not in use. Makeup pencils should be sharp, sponges should be clean, and when grease paint and other materials are running low, they should be replaced before they are needed.

Putting on a show is called staging it, and this does not just happen! All the pieces that make up a play must be planned and fitted together. This means everything from learning lines and painting scenery to being sure that the curtain opens and closes on cue.

JEANNE BENDICK
Coauthor, *How To Have A Show*

PLEDGE OF ALLEGIANCE. See FLAGS (Saluting the Flag).

PLUM. See PEACH, PLUM, AND CHERRY.

PLUMBING

When you fill a glass with water from the faucet in your kitchen sink, do you wonder how water reaches the faucet? If you pour the water down the drain, do you wonder where it goes? One system of pipes inside the walls of the building brings water to the faucet, and another system of pipes carries away waste. These pipes are the plumbing of the building.

The source of water that comes from your faucet is an underground well or a lake, reservoir, or river that may be far from your home. The water is brought to the people who use it in huge concrete pipes that are something like underground rivers. Such pipes are called **aqueducts.** If you live in a rural area, water may be pumped from a small well on your property directly into your home.

From the aqueducts water enters large metal pipes called **water mains.** Water mains are buried beneath city and suburban streets. From the mains, water is carried by smaller metal or plastic pipes into each building along the main.

Water that goes down the drain in your sink is carried away by a system of pipes called **drains.** The drains join a larger pipe called a **sewer** located under the building. The sewer runs out to the street where it joins a still larger pipe, a **sewer main,** buried beneath the street. The sewer main carries wastes to a sewer treatment plant. In rural areas, the sewer pipe empties into an underground **septic tank** where the wastes are broken down by bacteria.

Fixtures are also a part of the plumbing system. They are connected to both water and drain pipes. Sinks are fixtures. Other fixtures are drinking fountains, bathtubs, toilets, water heaters, and washing machines.

Fittings are small parts used to connect pipes together, to turn corners, and to attach pipes to fixtures. There are many hundreds of kinds of fittings, each for a particular size of pipe and a particular use.

Water that goes to a kitchen faucet or to any other fixture is under constant pressure—enough pressure to force the water up through the pipes in tall buildings. In order to let water out of the pipes when it is needed, **valves** are

The plumbing system in a two-story house is made up of pipes to supply fresh water and drains to carry away waste. Vents prevent unhealthy fumes from entering the house.

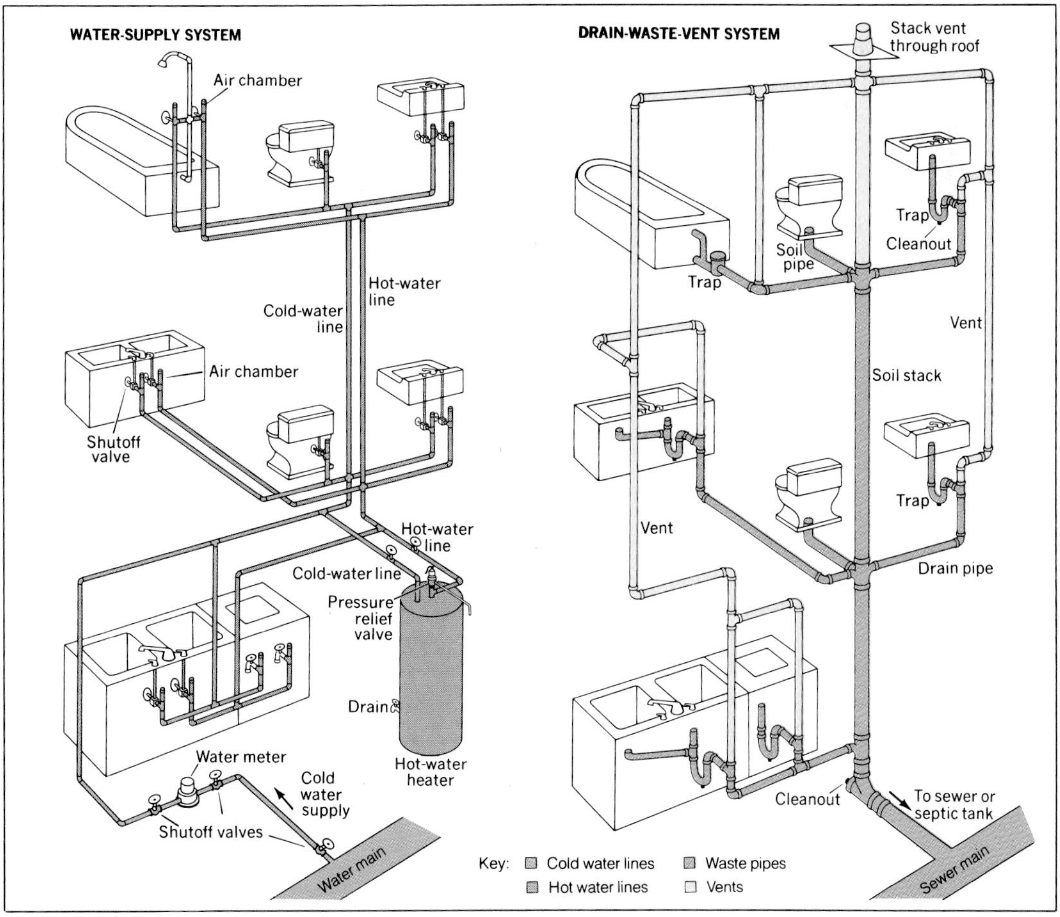

WATER-SUPPLY SYSTEM

- Air chamber
- Cold-water line
- Hot-water line
- Air chamber
- Shutoff valve
- Hot-water line
- Cold-water line
- Pressure relief valve
- Drain
- Water meter
- Cold water supply
- Hot-water heater
- Shutoff valves
- Water main

DRAIN-WASTE-VENT SYSTEM

- Stack vent through roof
- Trap
- Cleanout
- Soil pipe
- Trap
- Vent
- Soil stack
- Vent
- Trap
- Drain pipe
- Cleanout
- To sewer or septic tank
- Sewer main

Key: ☐ Cold water lines ▨ Waste pipes
     ▨ Hot water lines ☐ Vents

339

placed in the pipes. Valves control the flow of water in plumbing systems. The most familiar valves are those found at sinks, bathtubs, and fire hydrants. Larger valves control the flow of water in water mains and in the piping systems of large buidings.

Someone in your family should know about the valve that turns off all the water in your house or apartment. If a pipe inside the wall breaks or the toilet runs over, someone must turn off the water supply until the repairs can be made.

In the sewer system, there are no valves because there is no pressure in the pipes. Drains and sewers work by gravity. Water flows to a lower level because of its weight.

Sewers contain unpleasant fumes, so **stack pipes,** which are open at the top, run up through the roof to vent the drain pipes and to keep pressure from growing inside the system.

To keep unpleasant sewer fumes from entering your house, **traps** are used in each drain. A trap is an S-shaped pipe that stays filled with water, even when water is not running from the faucet. If you look under a sink you will see the trap just below the place where the drain pipe connects to the sink.

Plumbers

While plumbing is the term for all the pipes, fittings, and fixtures in a building, it also refers to the work of installing and repairing the pipes and fixtures connected to them. The men and women who do this work are called plumbers.

Plumbers do two main kinds of work, installing and repairing. If you have a broken pipe or a leaking water heater, you need a plumber right away. If your sink is worn out or the faucet is beyond fixing, a plumber will install a new one.

Plumbers also work in construction. They know how to cut and join pipes so there are no leaks. They know how to work with steel, iron, copper, plastic, and glass pipes. They must be able to read engineers' drawings so they can install pipes and valves properly in new buildings. Plumbers also install gas pipes and heating and air conditioning pipes where they are needed.

Plumbers learn their trade in two ways. They serve an **apprenticeship** under a master plumber, and they also complete a technical training program offered by a trade school or a plumbers' union. A plumber who has completed this training is called a **journeyman** plumber.

Extra training is needed for plumbers who work on the special plumbing systems in ships, hospitals, refineries, and power plants. Another special plumbing field is pipe welding. Pipe welders join pipes and fittings by using gas or electric welding techniques.

History of Plumbing

For thousands of years people have controlled the flow of water in order to grow crops or to save water in wet seasons so they would have it during drought. But the simple channels dug in the ground or the mud dams built to reserve water cannot be called plumbing systems.

The first plumbing system that we know of in a building was in the palace of King Minos of Crete. It was built about 4,000 years ago, and much of it remains today. Water was carried in clay ducts in the walls of the palace to the places where it was used. There was even a bathroom with running water. A sewer carried away unused water and wastes.

By Roman times, a thousand or more years ago, above-ground stone aqueducts moved water for many miles to bring it to populated areas. The water was piped into cities in buried clay pipes.

The Romans also used metal pipes, which they made by hammering a thin sheet of lead around a wooden rod. (The Latin word for lead is *plumbum,* which is where the words plumbing and plumber originated.) The Romans devised ways to keep the metal pipe from leaking by folding the edges together and hammering them flat. The person making the pipe had to mark the pipe with a special mark, because pipes were taxed by the Roman Government. From the marks we know that some of the pipe makers were women.

For centuries, most small pipes in home plumbing systems were made of lead like those in ancient Rome. In the 1960's and 1970's, scientists determined that by drinking water from lead pipes, people could absorb enough lead into their bodies to suffer from lead poisoning. Today, most small pipes in home plumbing systems are made of copper, iron, or plastic.

JAMES R. SKELLY
Co-author, *Pipes and Plumbing Systems*

PLUTO

Cold, dark, and icy—these words describe the planet Pluto, a tiny world orbiting the sun at the distant outer edge of the solar system. At an average distance of about 3.7 billion miles (5.9 billion kilometers) from the sun, the planet receives 1,000 times less light and heat from the sun than does Earth. In addition to being the outermost planet, Pluto is also the smallest planet in the solar system—so small that some astronomers think Pluto should not even be called a planet.

Yellow arrows mark the spot of light identified by Clyde Tombaugh as a planet. When he compared these two photographs of the same area of the sky, he found the one spot that had changed position among the stars. It was later named Pluto.

The Discovery of Pluto

Because Pluto is so far away, it remained undiscovered by astronomers until 1930. Long before its discovery, however, astronomers suspected that there was another planet beyond Neptune. They had noticed that Neptune deviated slightly from the orbit predicted for it. After taking into account the gravitational pulls from all the known planets, they concluded that this orbital deviation was caused by the gravitational pull of an unknown planet.

An astronomer named Percival Lowell was particularly fascinated by the idea that there might be another planet in the solar system. In the early 1900's he made extensive studies of the skies, hoping to learn where this "planet X" was hiding. Lowell even built an observatory in Arizona where for many years astronomers searched for planet X.

Astronomers looked for planet X by taking photographs of the sky at intervals several nights apart. Since the positions of the stars appear fixed in the sky but planets change position among them, astronomers compared photographs taken at different times, searching for a tiny dot of light that had changed position. This would be the mystery planet.

When Lowell grew too old to continue his work, the astronomers at his observatory continued the search. In 1929 they hired Clyde Tombaugh, a young amateur astronomer, to take photographs and to study them. A skilled observer, Tombaugh discovered planet X within a year of starting his search. As astronomers learned more about this planet, they named it Pluto after the god of the underworld, a mythical place of cold and darkness —a fitting name for such a dim and distant world.

A Strange and Unusual Planet

Astronomers were astonished by some of the characteristics of this newly discovered planet. Because Pluto was so dim, astronomers determined that it was smaller than Lowell had predicted. They were also very surprised by the planet's peculiar orbit. During Pluto's 247.7-year trip around the sun, its distance from the sun varies from about 2.8 billion miles (4.4 billion kilometers) to as far away as 4.6 billion miles (7.4 billion kilometers). Although all the planets travel in elliptical (oval-shaped) orbits, Pluto's orbit is more elliptical than that of any other planet. At its **aphelion**, the point in orbit at which a planet is farthest from the sun, Pluto is the ninth planet, orbiting far beyond Neptune. But at its

WONDER QUESTION

Is Pluto really a planet?

Ever since the discovery of Pluto, astronomers have wondered whether it is really a planet. Pluto's small mass, its unusual orbit, and its tilted orbital plane make it very different from any other planet. Even some of the satellites, or moons, of the other planets are more massive than Pluto.

Some astronomers think that Pluto resembles an asteroid more than a planet. The largest known asteroid, Ceres, has a diameter that is almost half that of Pluto, and Ceres has nearly one eighth of Pluto's mass. Like Pluto, many asteroids also have orbits that are elliptical and tilted. Most astronomers, however, still choose to classify Pluto as a planet, even though it is not a typical one. Whatever it is, Pluto is certainly a unique member of the solar system.

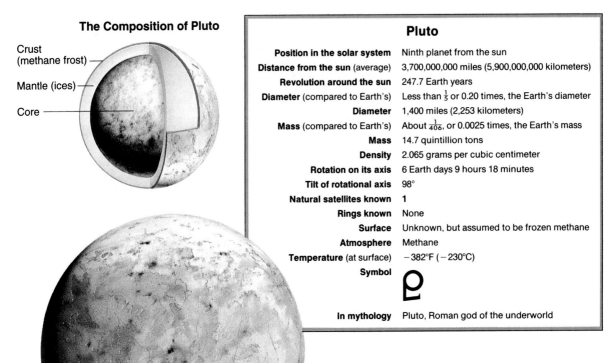

The Composition of Pluto

Crust
(methane frost)

Mantle (ices)

Core

Pluto

Position in the solar system	Ninth planet from the sun
Distance from the sun (average)	3,700,000,000 miles (5,900,000,000 kilometers)
Revolution around the sun	247.7 Earth years
Diameter (compared to Earth's)	Less than $\frac{1}{5}$ or 0.20 times, the Earth's diameter
Diameter	1,400 miles (2,253 kilometers)
Mass (compared to Earth's)	About $\frac{1}{406}$, or 0.0025 times, the Earth's mass
Mass	14.7 quintillion tons
Density	2.065 grams per cubic centimeter
Rotation on its axis	6 Earth days 9 hours 18 minutes
Tilt of rotational axis	98°
Natural satellites known	1
Rings known	None
Surface	Unknown, but assumed to be frozen methane
Atmosphere	Methane
Temperature (at surface)	−382°F (−230°C)
Symbol	♇
In mythology	Pluto, Roman god of the underworld

perihelion, the point in orbit at which a planet is closest to the sun, the planet is actually closer to the sun than Neptune.

Another strange characteristic of the planet is its orbital plane—the tilt of its orbit in relation to the orbits of other planets. While the orbital planes of the other planets are tilted only slightly from each other, Pluto's is tilted at a 17 degree angle.

Since Pluto was too far away for even the largest telescope to reveal any of its details, astronomers did not learn much about Pluto for many years. A few astronomers measured the planet's position and brightness from time to time and learned that it takes the small planet a little more than six days to rotate once on its axis. This fact was determined by observing the small variations in Pluto's brightness that are visible from Earth. Most astronomers, however, ignored Pluto until new discoveries about it were made in the late 1970's.

The Discovery of Charon

In 1978, while measuring Pluto's position in a photograph, an astronomer named James Christy noticed an unusual bump on one side of the planet's image. He looked at other photographs and soon realized that the bump went around Pluto every six days, which is the same amount of time that Pluto takes to rotate on its axis. James Christy had discovered Pluto's only known satellite. He named it Charon after the ferryman of the underworld in Greek mythology. A few weeks after discovering Charon, Christy realized that Pluto and its satellite would each soon undergo a series of eclipses of one another. For astronomers this became a tremendous opportunity. By measuring how much the light given off by Pluto and Charon decreased during these eclipses and timing when the eclipses began and ended, they could determine the size and surface features of both the planet and its satellite. While these events occurred during the years 1987 through 1990, astronomers discovered most of what they now know about Pluto and Charon.

New Findings About Pluto and Charon

Astronomers have discovered that Charon is a large moon in relation to Pluto. Its diameter of 746 miles (1,200 kilometers) is more than half the diameter of Pluto. Also, Charon is only 12,200 miles (19,640 kilometers) away

The diagram (*far right*) illustrates Pluto's moon Charon orbiting the planet. The photographs show that an image of the two taken by an Earth-based telescope (*right*) is not as clear as one taken outside the Earth's atmosphere by the Hubble Space Telescope (*middle*), which can see them as two distinct objects.

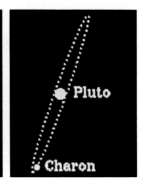

from Pluto. No other satellite in the solar system is as large in relation to its planet or as close in distance to its planet.

Pluto is brighter than Charon and has bright regions at both its north and south poles. Fifty percent of the light that strikes the planet from the sun is reflected back into space, and the planet's surface has large bright and dark spots. Charon is a bit darker than Pluto; its surface reflects only about 40 percent of the light that strikes it.

Recent studies have determined that Pluto consists of a mix of rocky materials and ice and has a thin atmosphere of methane gas. Pluto may have only a part-time atmosphere, however. In 1989, Pluto was at its closest point to the sun and warm enough so that the methane on the planet was in a gaseous state. However, as Pluto moves farther away from the sun it will become colder. By the year 2020, Pluto will be so cold that all the methane in its atmosphere will freeze and form a layer of methane ice on the planet's surface. During its 247.7-year orbit around the sun, Pluto may have an atmosphere for only about 60 years.

The Origin of Pluto

When astronomers compared the orbital periods of Neptune and Pluto (the time it takes the planets to travel around the sun), they noticed something odd. Neptune travels once around the sun in 165 Earth years. Pluto travels once around the sun in 247.7 Earth years. What is odd about this is that three orbital periods of Neptune are very nearly equal to two orbital periods of Pluto. Astronomers say that these planets are locked in **orbital resonance**, which means that the orbital period of one planet is almost an exact fraction of that of another planet of larger mass. In this case, their orbital resonance is 3:2, or 3 to 2.

Orbital resonance results in a series of gravitational pulls by the larger planet on the smaller one. This means that if Pluto slows down a bit, Neptune's gravity causes it to speed up again. If Pluto speeds up, Neptune's gravity causes it to slow down. The result of the orbital resonance of Pluto and Neptune is that the two planets will never collide.

Orbital resonance may also help explain what Pluto is and why it exists. Astronomers think that Pluto may be the sole survivor of

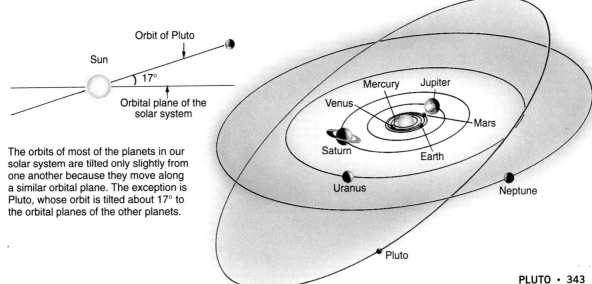

The orbits of most of the planets in our solar system are tilted only slightly from one another because they move along a similar orbital plane. The exception is Pluto, whose orbit is tilted about 17° to the orbital planes of the other planets.

the time early in the history of the solar system when the planets were forming. When the sun condensed from a large cloud of interstellar gas, the matter that was left over formed a thin disk circling the sun. Solid materials formed as tiny grains of rock and ice in this disk stuck together in larger and larger clumps. Over the course of millions of years, these growing clumps of matter became the planets.

Astronomers think that during this period of planet formation, thousands of icy bodies about the size and shape of Pluto formed in space beyond Jupiter and Saturn. As these mini-planets orbited the sun, they collided with one another and formed the planets Uranus and Neptune. Eventually every Pluto-like body, except Pluto itself, had disappeared.

Why did Pluto never collide with Neptune even though its orbit takes it close to the larger planet? The answer may lie in the 3:2 orbital resonance between the two planets. Even though their orbits cross, Neptune and Pluto never move through the intersection at the same time. Therefore, Pluto was the one body out of thousands that escaped the larger planet's gravitational pull.

Learning More About Pluto

Astronomers are anxious to learn much more about Pluto. If they are correct in their assumption that Uranus and Neptune formed from thousands of Pluto-like bodies, then Pluto may help to reveal more about the nature of the early solar system. Unfortunately, since Pluto is so far away, it is difficult to send space probes to observe and explore the planet. A flight to Pluto would take from ten to thirty years, depending on the size of the spacecraft and the power of the rockets used to launch and propel it through space. Sooner or later, however, probes will probably be sent to explore the planet. Until then, Pluto orbits the sun but holds its secrets in cold storage.

RICHARD BERRY
Author, *Discover the Stars*

See also PLANETS; SOLAR SYSTEM.

PLYMOUTH COLONY

The colony of Plymouth in Massachusetts was founded in 1620 by a group of English settlers, who were known as Pilgrims because they traveled to the New World. It was the second permanent colony in the New World to be settled by the English (the first was Jamestown, Virginia, founded in 1607). About one third of Plymouth's original settlers were Puritans, who came to the New World in search of religious freedom. But most of the Pilgrims who journeyed to the New World were simply hoping to find a better life than they had known in England.

The Puritans

The Puritans' search for religious freedom began in England in the 1500's. King Henry VIII (1491–1547) and later his daughter, Queen Elizabeth I (1533–1603), had tried to force all of the English people to practice Protestantism according to the ways of the newly formed Church of England. However, some of the English objected to the rituals of the new church, believing they too closely resembled the Roman Catholic form of worship. Because these objectors wanted to "purify" the church, they became known as Puritans. Some of these Puritans eventually broke away from the church. They were called Separatists.

King James I (1566–1625) made it a crime for anyone to hold privately organized religious services. Books and pamphlets that contained Separatist beliefs were seized. Many Separatist leaders were thrown in jail or condemned to death.

To escape this persecution, Separatists began to flee from England. About 100 of them settled in a small university town called Leyden in the Netherlands in 1609. Here they could worship as they pleased, but they found it difficult to earn a good living. They also worried that their children would forget their English heritage. As time passed, they longed to return to the English way of life.

Because they could not safely worship as they pleased in England, the Leyden Separatists decided to go instead to the English lands in North America. After long efforts their representatives persuaded the English Government to let them settle there. Expecting that the King would soon fix his seal on their charter, the representatives set about raising

The Pilgrims who settled Plymouth Colony came to the New World in search of a better life. Many were Puritans, who sought religious freedom from the Church of England.

money for the venture. A group of about 70 Merchant Adventurers formed a joint-stock company for this purpose. It was decided that the Separatists would settle on land granted to the Second (Plymouth) Virginia Company and earn their living by fishing.

In July, 1620, a small group of about 46 men, women, and children sailed for England aboard the leaky little *Speedwell*. There they were joined by another group of about the same size. Its members had been recruited by the venture's merchant backers, and most of them belonged to the Church of England. The Separatists called themselves Saints. The others they called Strangers. A third group included 5 artisans (people with special work skills) and 18 servants, most of whom had pledged to work for their masters in return for their passage. Three of the best-remembered Pilgrims—Captain Myles Standish (1584?–1656), John Alden (1599?–1687), and Priscilla Mullins—were not Saints, but Strangers. When the *Speedwell* proved to be unseaworthy, the Saints and Strangers all crowded aboard the larger *Mayflower* in the port of Plymouth.

According to the Old Style calendar, the *Mayflower* set sail for Plymouth on September 6, 1620 (which would be September 16 by the calendar we now use).

The Founding of Plymouth

After 65 long days at sea, the *Mayflower* dropped anchor on November 11 (or Novem-

ber 21) in the sheltered harbor of what is now Provincetown at the tip of Cape Cod, Massachusetts. Because they were far away from an established system of law and order and had begun to argue among themselves, the Pilgrim leaders decided they must create a governing authority. The drew up an agreement called the Mayflower Compact, which became the first agreement for self-government signed in America. This document was signed by the 41 men aboard the *Mayflower,* who pledged to obey its laws. After the signing, John Carver (1576?–1621) was chosen to be the colony's first governor.

THE MAYFLOWER COMPACT

In ye name of God Amen. We whose names are underwriten, the loyall subjects of our dread soveraigne Lord King James, by ye grace of God, of great Britaine, franc, & Ireland king, defender of ye faith, &c. Haveing undertaken, for ye glorie of God, and advancements of ye Christian faith and honour of our king & countrie, a voyage to plant ye first Colonie in ye Northerne parts of Virginia [land granted to the Virginia Company]. Doe by these presents solemnly & mutualy in ye presence of God, and one of another, covenant, & combine our selves togeather into a civill body politick; for our better ordering, & preservation & furtherance of ye ends aforesaid; and by vertue hereof to enacte, constitute, and frame such just & equall Lawes, ordinances, Acts, constitutions, & offices, from time to time, as shall be thought most meete & convenient for ye generall good of ye Colonie: Unto which we promise all due submission and obedience. In witnes wherof we have hereunder subscribed our names at Cap-Codd ye · 11 · of November, in ye year of ye raigne of our soveraigne Lord King James of England, france, and Ireland ye eighteenth, and of Scotland the fiftie fourth. Ano: Dom · 1620 ·

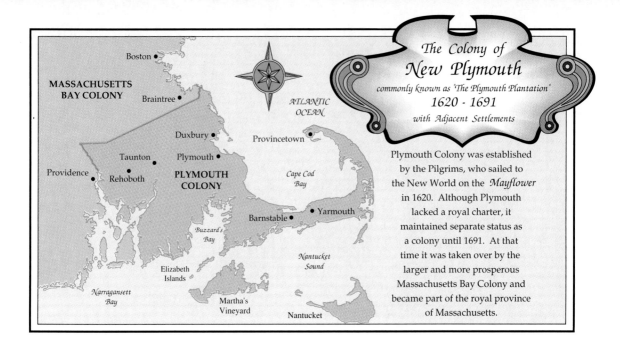

After exploring the coast along Massachusetts Bay, the Pilgrims on December 11 (December 21) chose Plymouth as the site of their colony. Plymouth had been named by Captain John Smith on his trip to New England in 1614. According to legend the Pilgrims stepped ashore onto a large boulder, the famous Plymouth Rock. Cannons were dragged to the top of a nearby hill and set in place for protection. The first building to rise was the Common House. Then rough huts began to go up. Soon, however, sickness struck the Pilgrims. By the end of their first winter half the group were dead.

Toward the end of winter an Indian brave suddenly appeared among them. To their amazement he greeted them in English. His name was Samoset, and he had been in contact with English traders on the coast of Maine several years before. From him the Pilgrims learned that they had nothing to fear from the Indians of the region, as most of them had died in a smallpox epidemic a few years before. Later Samoset brought his friend Squanto (?–1622), who had once been captured and sold as a slave to Spain, but had later escaped to England and returned to America in 1619. Squanto became a trusted friend of the Pilgrims, acting as their guide and interpreter for the rest of his life.

Through Samoset, the Pilgrims had also met Massasoit (?–1661), chief of the Wampanoag Indians of what is now eastern Massachusetts. The Englishmen and the Indian chief made a peace treaty that remained in force for many years. Under this treaty Plymouth Colony prospered. Its population grew with new arrivals from England.

Life in Plymouth Colony

At first the colony had only a single street. On either side stood low wooden houses with small gardens in back. Larger homes were built in the neighboring countryside when each settler was granted land there in 1627. From the beginning, however, one building was more important than any of the others. This was the meetinghouse. On Sunday mornings the whole colony gathered there for religious services. They remained, sitting on hard wooden benches, all morning. After going home for midday dinner, they came back to spend the rest of the day praying, singing hymns, and listening to sermons that went on for hours.

The Indians taught the colonists how to plant maize (corn) in rows and how to use fish traps to catch herring for fertilizer. Corn and other vegetables as well as berries, wildfowl, game, and fish soon gave an ample and varied diet. To celebrate the first bountiful harvest, in 1621, the Pilgrims held a thanksgiving feast and invited their Indian friends.

To fulfill their contract with the London merchants, the Pilgrims had to contribute their labor for seven years in return for funds and supplies. They were not allowed to work for their own gain. Everything had to go into a common store, from which food and other necessities were drawn. Sometimes the London backers were slow in sending supplies, and the colonists did not have enough food to go around. The main source of the colony's wealth was beaver furs received in trade with the Indians in exchange for cheap trinkets. In 1627, profits from the beaver trade enabled the colony to buy out its London backers and to get their permission to continue trade with the Indians. The colonists built trading posts in the Connecticut Valley to the west and along the Kennebec and Penobscot rivers to the north, in what is now Maine.

Religion and Government. Religion remained the driving force in the affairs of Plymouth. Although the Pilgrims were victims of religious persecution themselves, they often were intolerant toward members of other persecuted religious groups. Thus, the Quakers, who had fled to the New World for the same reasons as the Pilgrims, were driven out of Plymouth Colony.

Although the governors of the colony were not ministers, they were devout churchgoers and frequently were called on for advice in church matters. The governors were elected, but only certain members of the community (called freemen) had the right to vote. The most notable governor was William Bradford, who headed the colony for 30 of the years between 1621 and 1656. Bradford was also Plymouth's leading historian. In his history, *Of Plymouth Plantation,* he wrote a long account of its founding and early years.

With the aid of his council the governor issued laws ruling the lives of the colonists. These laws were strict but not severe by the standards of the time. Only seven crimes, including witchcraft, were punishable by death. In England, on the other hand, hundreds of petty crimes could send a man to the gallows. In the entire history of Plymouth Colony only two men were hanged for their crimes. Lesser offenders usually had to pay fines. Sometimes, however, judges sentenced an offender to the stocks in order to make a public example of him. He would have to sit or stand for hours in the town square—his ankles, his wrists, and sometimes his neck locked in a wooden frame. The stocks were uncomfortable enough, but the stares and jeers of the passersby must have been even harder to bear for some offenders.

Later Years

As time went on, other English settlements sprang up along the shore of Massachusetts Bay. One, Mount Wollaston, proved a troublesome neighbor. In 1628 its leader, Thomas Morton (?–1647?), renamed the settlement Merry Mount. He gave jolly parties for white men and Indians at which generous amounts of liquor were drunk. The Pilgrims were angered as much by Morton's success at trade with the Indians as by his high living. They sent after him a small group of armed men commanded by Captain Myles Standish. Morton was arrested and sent back to England.

The Pilgrims' most important neighbor was the Puritan colony of Massachusetts Bay, in the area of Boston and Salem. Many Puritans came there from England during the 1630's, and the colony grew rapidly. Thereafter, it overshadowed the colony at Plymouth more and more. Neither King James nor his successors ever fixed the royal seal to Plymouth Colony's charter. As a result, the Pilgrims' right to their land was never clearly established. In 1691, Massachusetts Bay Colony was granted a royal charter that included much of the area it had asked for, including Plymouth. Seventy-two years after the Pilgrims first stepped ashore, the Old Colony, as it had come to be called, was no more.

The Pilgrims proved beyond doubt that ordinary English people could support and govern themselves in the New World. Governor Bradford wrote, ". . . as one small candle may light a thousand, so the light here kindled hath shone unto many, yea, in some sort, to our whole nation."

Today the Pilgrim village has been rebuilt at Plymouth, Massachusetts, under its original name, Plimoth Plantation. In addition to seeing Plymouth Rock, visitors may go aboard *Mayflower II* (a replica of the original ship), and tour the First House, 1627 House, Fort Meetinghouse, Pilgrim Hall, and Burial Hill.

MARY LEE SETTLE
Author, *O Beulah Land*

See also COLONIAL LIFE IN AMERICA; MAYFLOWER; REFORMATION; THANKSGIVING DAY; THIRTEEN AMERICAN COLONIES.

PNEUMATIC DEVICES. See HYDRAULIC AND PNEUMATIC SYSTEMS.

PNEUMONIA. See DISEASES.

POCAHONTAS. See INDIANS, AMERICAN (Profiles); SMITH, JOHN.

Poe's contribution to the development of the modern short story was significant. His tales are filled with strange events, but Poe insisted that they were expressions of reality. He believed that a story should work toward a single effect. Among his best-known stories are *The Fall of the House of Usher, The Gold Bug, The Masque of the Red Death*, and *The Black Cat*. In *The Purloined Letter* and *Murders in the Rue Morgue*, Poe invented the detective story. The character of the brilliant Auguste Dupin, who solved mysteries by his intellectual genius, was a model for later fictional detectives.

Poe's last volume of poetry, *The Raven and Other Poems*, appeared in 1845. He continued to write, but in 1847 his wife's death from tuberculosis was a severe blow. The cause of his own death, on October 7, 1849, is unknown.

Reviewed by ERWIN HESTER
East Carolina University

POE, EDGAR ALLAN (1809–1849)

Edgar Allan Poe, who became one of America's most famous poets and short-story writers, was born in Boston, Massachusetts, on January 19, 1809. His parents were actors. Edgar's father deserted his family, and his mother died in 1811. John and Frances Allan of Richmond, Virginia, took Edgar into their home.

Edgar received his early schooling in Richmond. In 1815 he went to England with the Allans and attended boarding schools there before returning to Richmond in 1820. In 1826 he entered the University of Virginia. He was an honors student, but gambling debts forced him to drop out in less than a year.

Penniless, Poe enlisted in the army. He was discharged in 1829 so that he could enter West Point Military Academy. His first volume of poetry, *Tamerlane and Other Poems*, had been published in 1827. Two years later, *Al Aaraaf, Tamerlane, and Minor Poems* was issued. Unable to persuade John Allan to agree to his resignation from West Point so that he could pursue a literary career, Poe deliberately neglected his duties and was dismissed in 1831.

Poe married his cousin, Virginia Clemm, in 1836. He worked as an editor and critic for the *Southern Literary Messenger* in Richmond, and increased the magazine's circulation from 500 to 3,500. He later worked for magazines in Philadelphia and New York City.

In ''Eldorado,'' Poe is saying that hope and something to strive for prevent despair.

ELDORADO

Gayly bedight,
A gallant knight,
In sunshine and in shadow,
Had journeyed long,
Singing a song,
In search of Eldorado.

But he grew old,
This knight so bold,
And o'er his heart a shadow
Fell as he found
No spot of ground
That looked like Eldorado.

And, as his strength
Failed him at length,
He met a pilgrim shadow:
''Shadow,'' said he,
''Where can it be,
This land of Eldorado?''

''Over the Mountains
Of the Moon,
Down the Valley of the Shadow,
Ride, boldly ride,''
The shade replied,
''If you seek for Eldorado!''

POETRY

"Poetry sometimes crowns the search for happiness. It is itself a search for happiness."

Wallace Stevens

How Did Poetry Begin?

The beginning of poetry is lost with the early history of man on earth. But we may guess at the beginning. We may guess because we know something of the way primitive people acted. Doubtless the man who lived thousands of years ago produced some sort of rhythmic dance even before he created the first words of the first language. Grunts, gestures, cries, and body action combined themselves into a performance. Both the performer and his audience felt a kind of poetic pleasure, although neither had a name for it. Before the hunt, before a battle, the performance was a rousing call to action.

Then man made the drum by stretching a hairless skin over the end of a hollow log. His noisy little ceremony took on new rhythms and perhaps new purposes. He could beat on his drum in endless ways. His joyous or warlike efforts must soon have led him into incantations, magic words to his gods. Perhaps the medicine man, in his doctoring, used the sounds and added new ones.

We may further guess that the dance of primitive man progressed. It grew more complicated, perhaps with more and more performers taking part. But as man developed a language his drum no doubt became quieter. The words of the chant to the gods could be clearly understood. And given thousands of years for further change and refinement, the leading performer at some point took on the role of bard, or poet.

During all this time there were other influences at work, influences one can still see in the current poetry of every nation, from Scotland to China, from Russia to Brazil. There was surely something poetic in the moving tongues of flame, once man had learned to produce and find a use for fire. There was always rhythm, even music, in the sound of water flowing over stones. There was the rumble of thunder, the sound of great winds in the forest, the wide, soaring circles of the gulls and hawks. There was the deep mystery of the night sky full of stars. And always there was the earth's own rhythm of the ocean tides and the changing seasons.

There were lesser influences as well. Butterflies and other insects often seem to dance in couples or in swarms to a rhythm all their own. We know now, as primitive man did not, that honeybees have a special dance inside the hive. With this dance the finder of a field of flowers gives the news in detail to his fellows. Animals like the deer and antelope run and bound into the air with pure poetic motion. In the deep snows of winter, then as now, rabbits would gather suddenly in moonlight in a clearing and play a curious leaping game that few people have the luck to see. In a world of endless grace and related movement it is unthinkable that a speechless man did not begin in some way to imitate it. And this imitation was surely part of the beginning of poetic imagination.

Centuries ago these dances, chants, and incantations had reached a point where men kept a record of them. They were handed down to us. We know, for example, something of the chants of the poet-priest, or shaman, as he was called by the American Indian. The shaman chanted and prayed that the growing corn might continue to thrive. He chanted that rain might end the withering drought. We know that the Eskimo did much the same to speed the hunter in his kayak. And we know also that in many lands the singer, the chanter, the poet, began to take on a certain power in the community. Ceremonies for the sun and rain gods grew into stories of heroic deeds and tribal triumphs. In time the dance mattered less than the dance of words.

We have come a long way from those chants and drumbeats. We have come a long way, too, from the old Norse sagas, from Chaucer and *The Canterbury Tales,* from Dante's *Divine Comedy,* from Milton's *Paradise Lost.*

What Is Poetry?

Then, as now, poetry meant deeply felt, deeply moving language, written or spoken in a special form. The rhythm of a poem is what sets it apart from prose, which usually has a tempo slower and more varied. Rhythm is what gives poetry a fistful of life. Although some poems are divided into parts, the rhythm is not destroyed. It is the over-all rhythm that the poet wishes us to hear.

Every good poem comes to the reader as a surprise. Robert Frost called it "the surprise of remembering something I didn't know I knew." The English poet A. E. Housman said that he could not think about poetry while shaving, because his skin would bristle and the razor refuse to act. Ralph Waldo Emerson, American poet-essayist, made the important observation that "every word was once a poem."

Not all words are or ever were poems, of course. "From," "we," "has," "the," and so on, have their places in poems. The right choice of such prepositions, pronouns, verbs, articles, and the like is important to the reader's ear and to the poems as well. But in themselves they are simply words. Look at some other words, however, and we do find poems:

sky	grass	spring	snow	share
star	wind	meadow	sea	home
fire	wave	dawn	green	plow
tree	river	apple	cry	fly
cloud	summer	corn	tongue	seek

There are thousands more. The words listed above are all simple words, largely of Anglo-Saxon origin. They are words we use every day. One could choose longer words— "happiness," "consideration," "miraculous" —but the simple words suffice. Each of the simple words listed will likely suggest not one thing but many things, according to the reader's imagination. Say "corn," and you see a field of it or a dish of it or the cob from which you are eating the kernels, or even a corncob pipe. "Dawn" suggests the sky, songbirds awakening, having to get up, a new day of excitement—many things. How can one possibly read that list and not be struck by the particular music that each word gives off in the saying of it? Who does not sense the warmth in "fire," the feel of "snow," the very breath of idleness in "summer"?

Before we look at whole poems, let us consider some lines lifted out of certain poems. "Over the hills and far away" is thought by many to be one of the most beautiful lines of poetry in the English language. It comes from a nursery rhyme, and we do not know who wrote it. Yet a number of fine poets, including Tennyson, Burns, and Stevenson, have used it as their own. What is

so magic about "Over the hills and far away"? Practically everything, since it expresses distance, travel, longing, scenery, escape, happiness, desire, a new land, or almost any idea in between.

Look next at William Wordsworth's

> For old, unhappy far-off things,
> And battles long ago.

There is a sadness to these lines, a sadness beyond expression, because it has been completely expressed. Or take the opening lines of a poem by the English poet James Elroy Flecker:

> I have seen old ships sail like swans asleep
> Beyond the village which men still call
> Tyre. . . .

These are clearly great sailing ships, of whiteness equal to a swan's, and Tyre is a dead seaside city of the ancient world. Most of the great sailing ships and all of Tyre have vanished; only the swans remain. But can anyone possibly fail to see what the poet saw or fail to be haunted by what we in turn shall never see?

For the wonder of life itself, take the beginning lines of a brief poem by Housman:

> From far, from eve and morning
> And yon twelve-winded sky,
> The stuff of life to knit me
> Blew hither: here am I.

We need not know why the sky should have twelve winds. We need only to read, and the wonder is upon us. Poets often use the colon at the close of a general statement, as Housman does after "hither" in the lines above. The colon introduces the conclusion, or summary.

For the stretch of time, for the feeling of everlastingness, there is this by Walter de la Mare:

> Oh, no man knows
> Through what wild centuries
> Roves back the rose.

Who but a poet would have used the verb "roves," which so perfectly suggests timeless wandering? We feel the wind across the land, across the centuries, scattering the seed. In short, these three lines really describe the history of the poet in man. They say in 12

simple words most of what was guessed at in the beginning of this article.

A poem that runs a shiver down your back will always seem to have been written just for you.

> When all the world is young, lad,
> And all the trees are green;
> And every goose a swan, lad,
> And every lass a queen;
> Then hey for boot and horse, lad,
> And round the world away:
> Young blood must have its course, lad,
> And every dog his day.

The English author Charles Kingsley, who wrote these lines from *The Water Babies,* took the last line from *Hamlet;* but what a poem it is, and how well it sticks in the mind!

Suppose we say, "I saw a firefly. He flew up and turned his light on and off." Nothing is wrong with these words; they are simply dull.

Here is what Elizabeth Madox Roberts says in "Firefly":

> A little light is going by,
> Is going up to see the sky,
> A little light with wings.
>
> I never could have thought of it,
> To have a little bug all lit
> And made to go on wings.

Anyone can see that the whole poem has wings and light. It is also unforgettable. Miss Roberts' complete mastery of form and her ability, not to imitate, but to be, a child speaking, amounts to genius.

In "The Circus," note Miss Roberts' choice of "going" in the last stanza. Lesser poets would have said "sliding" or "writhing over his feet." A very small child would say "going." Note, too, how the whole poem comes smartly—not limply—to an end.

The Circus

Friday came and the circus was there,
And Mother said that the twins and I
And Charles and Clarence and all of us
Could go out and see the parade go by.

And there were wagons with pictures on,
And you never could guess what they had inside,
Nobody could guess, for the doors were shut,
And there was a dog that a monkey could ride.

A man on the top of a sort of cart
Was clapping his hands and making a talk.
And the elephant came—he can step pretty
    far—
It made us laugh to see him walk.

Three beautiful ladies came riding by,
And each one had on a golden dress,
And each one had a golden whip.
They were queens of Sheba, I guess.

A big wild man was in a cage,
And he had some snakes going over his feet
And somebody said "He eats them alive!"
But I didn't see him eat.

Poetry in Everyday Life

Millions of people go through life with
scarcely a line of poetry in their heads. One
can tell in 5 minutes of casual talk with them
that this is so. For the love and understanding
of poetry has a great deal to do with the way in
which a person speaks. A feeling for poetry
also influences the style and excitement of
letters and other writing. We do not expect
people to spout poetry. But if they read poetry
and have even a few splinters and chips of
good verse by heart, they will show at once—
without quoting a single line of what they have
read—a strength and grace in their speech.
Country people, living close to nature, usually
have more flavor in their talk than people
living in a city. The influences of nature (the
rhythm of nature) that worked on primitive
man are still at work on them.

Here and there in the business world, in
advertising, in newspapers, you will find some
small influence of poetry. Even the names of
business and law firms are ordered and arranged, when possible, with care for the best
rhythm and sound of the names involved.
Poetry is not only the right way but the fresh
way, the perfect way, of saying something.
Good English—to speak well, to write well—
is one of the golden assets in this world. A
knowledge and love of poetry is the best
guarantee for acquiring it.

The Techniques of Poetry

To enjoy poetry, one need not know the
craft of the poet. Yet some knowledge of
techniques helps the reader understand how
poetry takes on different forms and moods.

Rhyme and Pattern. A rhyme is a word
or a line that has the same last sound as

note of the doves and the faint buzzing of bees:

> The moan of doves in immemorial elms,
> And murmuring of innumerable bees.

A single line of poetry is called a **verse**. A number of verses grouped together, usually following a certain rhyme scheme, form a **stanza**. Poets use stanzas the way prose writers use paragraphs, to give the reader a pause. Stanzas vary in length, but in general they have three, four, six, eight, or nine lines.

Poets arrange rhymes in a number of patterns. The pair of Blake rhymes above is a **couplet**. A **quatrain** is four lines, usually rhymed in one of four ways: *aaaa, abab, aabb, abba*. Here is a famous quatrain from Stevenson's *Child's Garden of Verses*. Its rhyme scheme is *aabb*.

When I am grown to man's estate	*a*
I shall be very proud and great,	*a*
And tell the other girls and boys	*b*
Not to meddle with my toys.	*b*

In an *abab* rhyme scheme, then, the first and third lines rhyme, and so do the second and fourth.

Spenserian stanza is one of the many other interesting verse patterns. This nine-line stanza has a rhyme scheme of *ababbcbcc*. It was named for the 16th-century English poet Edmund Spenser. There are two principal kinds of **sonnets** in the English language, Italian (Petrarchan) and Shakespearean. Their rhyme schemes differ, but each has 14 lines. The **ballade** is a tricky form of three eight-line stanzas plus an envoi of four concluding lines. In each stanza the eighth line, the refrain, is the same. The envoi carries the refrain as the final line. Poets often use unrhymed verse called **blank verse**, and thus avoid the restriction of rhyme schemes. **Free verse**, also, is unrhymed.

Meter. Meter measures the rhythm of a line of poetry. ("Meter" comes from the Greek word *metron,* which means "measure.") Each line is made up of a number of small sections, called "feet." Within each foot syllables are accented or unaccented, and when they are read aloud, the voice stresses or does not stress them. To find out where the accents fall, one **scans** a line of poetry. A straight line (—) indicates an accented, or

another word or line. The simplest rhymes have only one syllable, as in "just-must." An example of a line rhyme is William Blake's

> I was angry with my friend:
> I told my wrath, my wrath did end.

Of course, many poets use rhymes of more than one syllable:

mountain—fountain   terrible—bearable

Alliteration and **assonance** are the names of two kinds of rhyme. Alliteration is the repetition of a certain first letter or sound in a group of words. Note the recurring B sound in this line from Shakespeare's *Henry IV,* Part I, Act V, Scene 4:

> I *b*etter *b*rook the loss of *b*rittle life . . .

Assonance is vowel rhyme. For example, a poet may decide to use the vowel O for an effect of rhyme, as Thomas Gray did in the second line of "Elegy Written in a Country Churchyard":

> The l*o*wing herd wind sl*o*wly *o*'er the lea . . .

Onomatopoeia is neither rhyme nor pattern, but many poets employ this device to create a certain effect. Onomatopoeia is the use of words with sounds that suggest the subject. Here, in two lines from "The Princess," Tennyson suggests both the mournful

long, syllable. A curved line (⌄) indicates an unaccented, or short, syllable.

In English-language poetry five kinds of feet are most often used. Their names come from the Greek. An **iamb** (usually called iambic) is a two-syllable foot: one short syllable followed by a long syllable:

Wĕ went̄/ tŏ town̄/ tŏdāy.

A **trochee** is made up of one long syllable followed by a short syllable:

Mār̆y,/ Mār̆y,/ quīte cŏn/trār̆y . . .

Dactyls have one long syllable followed by two short ones:

Mēr cĭ fŭl/ hēav ĕns, Īm/ blūnd ĕr ĭng.

Anapests—dactyls in reverse—have three syllables: two short ones followed by a long one:

Thĕ Ăssȳr/iăn cămē down̄/likĕ ă wōlf/
on̆ thĕ fōld . . .

Two long syllables of equal stress form a **spondee**:

Stānd stīll,/ dōn't mōve,/ dōn't tālk.

These, then, are some of the types of feet, or measures, found in lines of poetry. Lines differ in length. A line having one foot is called monometer; a two-foot line is dimeter. Some other meters are:

trimeter	three feet	**hexameter**	six feet
tetrameter	four feet	**heptameter**	seven feet
pentameter	five feet	**octameter**	eight feet

A line with five iambic feet is called **iambic pentameter**. (Most sonnets and most blank verse poems are written in iambic pentameter.) Five trochees in one line form **trochaic pentameter**, and so on.

Kinds of Poetry. The mood and pattern of a poem tell us what kind of poem it is. A **lyric** is a short, musical poem expressing personal emotion. **Epics** are long and deal with heroic action. **Narrative poems** can be either long or short; they tell a story. A **ballad** is a kind of narrative poem, often tragic. **Didactic poetry** teaches, and **odes** are stately poems of noble sentiment. An **elegy** expresses sorrow, usually for a dead person.

Metaphor and Simile. Every reader of poetry should recognize the differences between metaphor and simile. A simile likens a person, object, action, or idea to something else:

Then felt I like some watcher of the skies

said Keats. What is a metaphor? A metaphor is a figure of speech in which a word or a phrase that usually denotes one object or idea is used to suggest something else. Dawn is not a ship until Housman makes it a ship:

And up from India glances
The silver sail of dawn. . . .

Wit in Poetry. Finally, there is the matter of wit in poetry. Milton has none, while Shakespeare has a great deal. Frost had wit and used it with power in a number of his poems. W. H. Auden, Marianne Moore, John Ciardi, and Howard Nemerov have it. Ogden Nash, Morris Bishop, and Phyllis McGinley largely depend on their very special gifts of wit and humor. The short poems called **epigrams** are often witty. Here is a funny one by Richard Armour, a master of light verse:

The hand is quicker than the eye is,
But somewhat slower than the fly is.

The Range of Poetry. A good poem shows the poet in control of rhythm, meter, and (if he uses it) rhyme. In the most successful poems words are in their most exact and delightful order. The words make music. The music touches the spirit and has a kind of second meaning, which is part of the mystery and wonder of a poem. The range of poetry is vast, capturing many moods, reflecting many moods. The following poems support this truth. There is the charm and lyric mastery of Edwin Arlington Robinson. Then come the bright fooling and feeling of Ogden Nash, the quiet beauty of the lines by Howard Nemerov. There is the narrative power, the strong, simple language, of Robert Frost. You will also note a poet's distinctive voice in the poems by Frances Cornford, James Stephens, and Robinson Jeffers.

DAVID McCORD
Poet and essayist

See also FIGURES OF SPEECH; NONSENSE RHYMES; NURSERY RHYMES; ODES.

POISONS AND ANTIDOTES

A poison might cause sickness or death when it is taken into the body. Poisons may be swallowed, inhaled, or absorbed through the skin. Some poisons harm the tissues of the body that they touch. Other poisons enter the bloodstream and are carried throughout the body, harming organs in different parts of the body. The brain and spinal cord may be affected.

Poisons found in the home are grouped into five categories:

(1) Pesticides and chemicals that are used to kill insects, rodents, and some plants.

(2) Drugs or medicines that are safe when used properly but dangerous when taken in large amounts.

(3) Caustic, or burning, chemicals. These are acids or alkalis. Substances in the home that commonly have a high acid content are rust removers, metal polishes, and toilet bowl cleaners. Substances containing large amounts of alkali are lye, drain cleaners, ammonia water, and many kinds of soaps and detergents.

(4) Petroleum products, such as gasoline, turpentine, paint thinner, furniture polish, and kerosene.

(5) Poisonous leaves or berries of plants, such as English ivy, mistletoe, philodendron, dieffenbachia, holly, and poinsettia.

Young children will often eat or drink substances that they find in kitchen cabinets and on bathroom shelves. And more accidental poisonings occur between the ages of 1 and 2 than at any other ages. Medicines taken by mouth are the single largest cause of poisoning in children. Aspirin causes more poisonings than any other drug.

▶ TREATMENT OF POISONING

There are drugs and medications that can overcome the harmful effects of a few poisons. These substances are called antidotes. In many cases, antidotes are printed on the labels of poisonous substances. But this information is not always reliable. It is best to get medical advice about the proper antidote.

There are some first aid measures that will help the poisoning victim. If the victim is conscious and is not having convulsions, he or she should be given half a glass of milk or water to drink. Next, the kind of poison taken should be determined. If the poison is a drug, a pesticide, or a poisonous plant, the victim should be made to vomit. Giving syrup of ipecac will make the person vomit. Salt water or mustard should not be used to induce vomiting.

But the person who has swallowed a petroleum product or a caustic product should not be made to vomit. These two kinds of poisons will cause more problems as they are vomited. Petroleum products may get into the lungs and cause chemical pneumonia. Caustic poisons that burn the throat and stomach as they go down may cause more burning as they come back up during vomiting.

A person who has inhaled a poison such as the cleaning fluid carbon tetrachloride should be taken to an open window immediately. This enables the person to inhale fresh air and exhale the carbon tetrachloride. If a person has spilled a liquid poison such as cleaning fluid or insecticide on the skin, it should be washed away with water.

To prevent deaths from accidental poisoning, there are over 550 poison control centers throughout the United States. Canada, England, France, and Denmark have similar centers. Poison control centers are open day and night to give information about the poisonous substances in various products and about the symptoms and treatment of poisoning.

In all cases of poisoning, the poison control center or a doctor should be called immediately. If it is at all possible, the medical expert should be told what poison has been taken. Good medical treatment is important, but prevention of poisoning is more important. No accidental poisoning need ever occur.

These two rules should be observed in every home:

(1) Poisonous substances as well as medicines should be kept in their original, labeled containers. In this way they will not be mistaken for harmless substances.

(2) Drugs and household chemical products—bleaches, detergents, lye, cleaning fluids, furniture polishes, insect killers, cosmetics, sleeping pills, tranquilizers, cough medicines, and vitamins—should be stored out of the reach of children.

Reviewed by G. RICHARD BRAEN, M.D.
University of Kentucky

▶CARBON MONOXIDE POISONING

Carbon monoxide is an unseen killer. Nobody can smell it. Nobody can see it, but it is one of the deadliest of gases. It has killed people in their cars, sailors in submarines, pilots in airplanes, and families in their houses. When a fuel such as coal, gasoline, or oil is burned and the fire does not get enough oxygen, carbon monoxide is formed.

Carbon Monoxide from Cars

Carbon monoxide is always found in the exhaust of an internal-combustion engine. This is the engine that makes a truck, car, ship, or an airplane go. A person who warms up a car with the garage door shut is in danger of carbon monoxide poisoning. If there are no doors open so that fresh air can come in and stale air can go out, carbon monoxide collects and can cause poisoning.

If there is a leak in a car's exhaust system, carbon monoxide can find its way into a car parked out-of-doors. Anyone who sits in a parked car with the windows shut and the motor running is in danger. When the car is moving, fresh air comes in through the air vents. If a car with its heater turned on parks behind a car with its motor running, there is danger of carbon monoxide poisoning. The heater fan may suck in the exhaust of the car ahead.

To guard against carbon monoxide poisoning, families who own cars should have an automobile mechanic test the exhaust system. When a car is parked, the engine should be shut off unless the windows are kept open.

Carbon Monoxide from Stoves

A family gathered around a leaky gas stove or room heater on a cold winter day, when all the windows are shut, could be poisoned by carbon monoxide. So might a family living in a house with a poorly installed furnace or a badly adjusted water heater.

To be safe from carbon monoxide in the home, a family must make sure that furnaces, stoves, fireplaces, and all appliances that burn fuel are installed in the right way and are kept in good working order. A stove or a furnace should have an airtight flue, or passageway, leading to the outside air. This flue helps oxygen reach the fire in the furnace so that the fuel can burn properly. It also lets smoke and gases escape into the outside air.

How Carbon Monoxide Poisons

How does carbon monoxide kill? In 1799 the English chemist Sir Humphry Davy tried to learn the secret. He breathed a mixture of air and gas from a silk bag. As he breathed the gas he felt his own pulse. He wrote that he felt sick and numb. His pulse became weak. He had just enough strength left to drop the bag. His experiment taught him how it felt to be poisoned by carbon monoxide gas, but he could not learn how the gas killed.

Today we know the secret. When carbon monoxide is breathed into the lungs, red blood cells absorb it 250 times as fast as oxygen. The gas captures the red blood cells and keeps them from carrying life-giving oxygen to all the parts of the body. Starved for oxygen, the victim dies.

Carbon monoxide gas kills quickly. In Fayetteville, North Carolina, two mechanics were repairing a truck. Three friends dropped in to keep them company. The men closed the garage doors to keep out the cold night air and turned on the truck engine. Suddenly one man realized something was wrong. He staggered to his feet and flung his hand through the window to let in fresh air. But it was too late. The fresh air could not change the effect of the gas on the men in time to save them from death.

Signs of Danger

How can you tell if carbon monoxide gas is making you sick? At first there may be a tightness around the forehead. Your head aches. You feel dizzy and tired. Your eyes blur. Then you feel nauseated. Finally your heart flutters and throbs. You lose consciousness. If you ever feel these symptoms, go into the fresh air. Don't go back into a room that might have carbon monoxide in it.

Breathing pure oxygen is one emergency treatment for carbon monoxide poisoning. Artificial respiration is another.

Carbon monoxide lurks wherever a fire is lighted or an internal combustion motor is turned on. It is an unseen killer that strikes when people grow careless.

RICHARD DUNLOP
Contributor, *Today's Health*

See also FIRST AID.

POITIER, SIDNEY. See MOTION PICTURES (Profiles: Movie Stars).

POLAND

The nation of Poland takes its name from the Slavic word *pole*, meaning "field." The name is fitting, for Poland covers part of a vast plain that extends across much of east central Europe. Poland lies between Germany in the west and the Soviet Union in the east. This location and a lack of natural barriers has greatly affected Polish history. Through most of its existence, Poland has fought to be independent of its powerful neighbors.

Poland was once one of the largest kingdoms in Europe. In later centuries, however, it was often conquered and occupied by other countries. Between the late 1700's and early 1900's, Poland disappeared from the map of Europe, its territory having been partitioned (divided) among its neighbors.

During this period, patriotism held the people of Poland together. Poland regained its independence in 1918, at the end of World War I. But it was invaded by German armies in 1939, at the outbreak of World War II. Much of Poland was destroyed during the fighting, and after the war's end in 1945, the Poles had to rebuild their country from ruins.

A Communist government was established in Poland following World War II, under the direction of the Soviet Union, backed by Soviet troops. The Communists held all power until 1989, when Poles, after the first free and open elections in more than fifty years, formed a government of their own choosing.

▶THE PEOPLE

After World War II, Poland lost a large part of its eastern territory, which had an ethnically mixed population, to the Soviet Union. In return, Poland received part of defeated Germany. Poles, mostly from the eastern region of Poland taken over by the Soviet Union, settled in these former German lands, known as the Western Territories. The Germans, who were expelled from the region, were resettled in present-day Germany. Almost all of the population of Poland is now Polish.

Language. Polish is a Slavic (or Slavonic) language. It belongs to the Western Slavic group, which also includes Czech and Slovak. Polish is written in the Latin alphabet, which was introduced into Poland in the 900's and

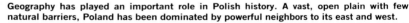

Geography has played an important role in Polish history. A vast, open plain with few natural barriers, Poland has been dominated by powerful neighbors to its east and west.

1000's by Christian missionaries from Western Europe.

Education. Polish children usually attend nursery school and kindergarten before beginning primary school at the age of 7. Eight years of primary education are compulsory, after which students may attend from two to four years of vocational school or general secondary school (high school). Secondary school graduates may go to a polytechnic (engineering) school or a university. Agricultural students spend some time working on farms. Industrial students work part-time in factories.

Most of Poland's colleges and universities are located in the large cities. The oldest, the Jagiellonian University in Cracow, was founded in 1364. All universities are state-controlled, except for the Catholic University in Lublin, which is operated by the Roman Catholic Church.

Religion. The great majority of the Polish people are Roman Catholic. Most Poles historically have associated their religious faith with their national identity. During the years of Communist rule, they strongly resisted any attempts by the government to discourage religious observance.

Poland's most famous religious shrine is at the monastery of Jasna Góra in Częstochowa. It is the site of the Black Madonna, an ancient painting of the Virgin Mary. The shrine celebrates an event in 1655, when the Virgin Mary is said to have appeared in the sky above the monastery, where monks and Polish soldiers withstood a siege by a powerful Swedish army. Each year in May hundreds of thousands of Polish Catholics make a pilgrimage to Jasna Góra.

The first Polish-born pope, John Paul II (the former Karol Cardinal Wojtyla), was elected in 1978. An article on Pope John Paul II appears in Volume J-K.

A small number of Poles belong to the Eastern Orthodox and Protestant churches. Only a few Jews remain of the more than 3 million who lived in Poland before World War II. Most Polish Jews were killed by the Germans during the war. Many of the remainder have emigrated to Israel and the United States.

▶**THE LAND**

Most of Poland consists of a low, rolling plain dotted with many small lakes and forests. The land rises toward the south, reaching its greatest height in the Carpathian Mountains, along the border with Czechoslovakia. The highest part of the Carpathian range is the Tatra Mountains. In the north, Poland borders on the Baltic Sea.

Lakes and Forests. The Masurian region in the northeast is an area of countless lakes and majestic forests. It is especially popular with tourists, who come here to enjoy water sports, hunting, and fishing. The Bialowieza Forest in eastern Poland is the site of a national park, where large herds of bison live in their natural state.

Rivers. Poland's longest river, the Vistula, flows north from its source in the Carpathians,

Poles long have linked their Roman Catholic faith with their nation's identity. John Paul II (*left*), the first Polish-born pope, received wide acclaim on his visits to Poland. The Black Madonna (*right*) is Poland's most venerated religious symbol.

past Cracow and Warsaw, Poland's capital, to Gdańsk on the Baltic Sea. West of the Vistula are the Oder and Neisse rivers, which mark Poland's border with Germany. In the east are the San and Bug rivers, both tributaries of the Vistula. The Bug forms part of the border with Belarus and Ukraine.

Climate. Winters in Poland are cold and frequently snowy. Summers are cool. The average January temperature near the German border is about 30°F (-1°C). In the east it is colder. The average annual precipitation (rain and snow) is 24 inches (600 millimeters).

Natural Resources. Poland has a variety of natural resources, including coal, copper, salt, lead, zinc, sulphur, and natural gas, as well as fertile soil. Its large deposits of coal have made Poland one of the world's leading producers of this fuel. The coal deposits are largely in western Poland, near the German-Polish border. The rich black soil of the Lublin plateau makes this one of Poland's most important agricultural regions.

▶**THE ECONOMY**

Agriculture. Before World War II, Poland's economy was predominantly agricultural. Today less than one third of the work force is engaged in agriculture. Most Polish farms are small, 12.4 acres (5 hectares) or less in size.

POLAND

The principal crops are rye, potatoes, wheat, sugar beets, oats, and barley. The raising of livestock, including pigs, sheep, and cattle, represents an important part of Polish agriculture. Meat products, particularly hams and sausages, are a leading export.

Industry. Industry is now the most important sector of the Polish economy. The chief industries involve the production of iron and steel and other metal products, engineering equipment and machinery, chemicals, processed foods, and textiles. Poland is also an important shipbuilding country, with shipyards located at Gdańsk and other port cities on the Baltic Sea.

Other manufactures include electrical and electronic appliances, transportation equipment, plastics, wood pulp, paper and paper products, leather goods, and fertilizers.

The mining industry is also of importance. Because Poland has almost no petroleum, it relies on coal and imported petroleum for most of its energy needs. Coal and other minerals, such as copper and sulfur, also are exported.

FACTS AND FIGURES

POLISH REPUBLIC (Rzeczpospolita Polska) is the official name of the country.

THE PEOPLE are known as Poles.

LOCATION: East central Europe.

AREA: 120,725 sq mi (312,677 km^2).

POPULATION: 38,000,000 (estimate).

CAPITAL AND LARGEST CITY: Warsaw.

MAJOR LANGUAGE: Polish.

MAJOR RELIGION: Roman Catholic.

GOVERNMENT: Republic. **Head of state**—president. **Head of government**—prime minister. **Legislature**—National Assembly (consisting of the Senate and the Sejm).

CHIEF PRODUCTS: Agricultural—rye, potatoes, wheat, sugar beets, oats, barley, livestock. **Manufactured**—iron and steel and other metal products, engineering equipment and machinery, chemicals, processed foods, textiles, ships, electrical and electronic appliances, transportation equipment, plastics, wood pulp, paper and paper products, leather goods, fertilizers. **Mineral**—coal, copper, salt, lead, zinc, sulphur, natural gas.

MONETARY UNIT: Zloty (1 zloty = 100 groszy).

NATIONAL ANTHEM: *Jeszcze Polska nie zginela* ("Poland is not yet lost").

Trade. Before its breakup, the Soviet Union had been Poland's chief supplier of raw materials, including iron ore, cotton, and petroleum. For many years, Poland traded largely with the Soviet Union and other Communist nations of Eastern Europe. However, after Polish workers rioted in the 1970's over living conditions and high food prices, the government began to change its trade patterns. Grain was imported, and machinery was purchased from Western European countries and the United States in order to produce high-quality manufactured goods for export beyond the Soviet bloc. As a result, Poland's foreign debt grew enormously, and further imports were severely restricted. The government's economic policies led to shortages of consumer goods and higher prices, which brought about further worker protests in 1980. These protests eventually brought about the downfall of the old Communist regime in 1989.

Cracow, once the capital of the Polish kings, is an important cultural center. The Castle of Wawel, built between the 900's and 1300's, was the royal palace. Each day at noon from one of the towers of the church of the Virgin Mary, a trumpeter plays a tune that breaks off in the middle. This custom dates from the 1200's, when Cracow was threatened with an invasion by Tatar armies from the east. The guard in the tower had the task of warning the people of the enemy's approach by playing a certain melody on his trumpet. As the Tatars drew near, the guard began to play the warning notes, but he was killed by a Tatar arrow before he could finish.

Wroclaw (formerly Breslau), in the old German Western Territories, like many other cities that had once been part of Germany, was also largely destroyed during World War II and had to be rebuilt and resettled. In addition, the Poles had to construct new factories and

Left: Warsaw is Poland's capital and largest city and an important industrial center. Much of the city had to be rebuilt after the destruction caused by World War II.
Below: The church of the Virgin Mary overlooks a square in the old city of Cracow. Once the capital of Polish kings, Cracow remains a center of Poland's cultural life.

▶CITIES

Warsaw is the capital and the largest city of Poland and the center of its intellectual life. During World War II, about 75 percent of the city was destroyed. After the war, the Poles completely reconstructed the Old Town of Warsaw based on old plans and maps. Modern offices and apartment houses have been built in much of the rest of the city. See the article on Warsaw in Volume W-X-Y-Z.

shipyards in the Baltic port cities of Gdańsk, Gdynia, and Szczecin.

Other leading cities include Lódź, Poland's second largest city, Poznan, and Katowice.

► GOVERNMENT

From 1947 to 1989, Poland was a Communist state dominated by the Polish United Workers' Party, a Communist party. A few smaller political parties were allowed to function, but they supported the Communists. Amendments to the constitution in 1989 and 1990 paved the way for a return to representative government. An interim (temporary) constitution went into effect in 1992.

The parliament, or legislature, is the National Assembly, which is elected for four years. It is composed of two houses—the Senate, with 100 members, and the Sejm, with 460 members. The Sejm is the chief lawmaking body. The Senate reviews laws passed by the Sejm. A president, elected for five years, serves as head of state. The president appoints the Council of Ministers, led by a prime minister, who handles the day-to-day operations of the government. The appointment requires approval by the Sejm.

► HISTORY

Early History. Poland's recorded history dates from 966, when Prince Mieszko, leader of the united Polish tribes, was converted to Christianity. Mieszko claimed descent from Piast, the legendary founder of the first dynasty of Polish kings. By the 1000's, the kingdom of Poland had expanded to almost the borders of Poland today.

Over the next few centuries, however, Poland was a fragmented country, divided among petty princes. It was frequently at war with more powerful states and was devastated by invasions of the Tatars, descendants of conquerors from Asia. Casimir III (the Great), the last of the Piast kings, reunited Poland in the 1300's. He encouraged trade and industry, founded the University of Cracow (now the Jagiellonian University), and made Poland a center of learning.

The Jagiellonian Era. The marriage of Jadwiga of Poland to Grand Duke Jagiello of Lithuania in 1386 marked the beginning of the Jagiellonian dynasty, which lasted until 1572. Under King Jagiello and his successors, Poland, united with Lithuania, reached its greatest territorial expansion, extending deep into Russia.

The Jagiellonian era was a golden age of prosperity and culture for Poland. One of the famous people of the time was the Pole Nicolaus Copernicus, who is considered the founder of modern astronomy. (An article on Copernicus appears in Volume C.)

Decline and Partition. After the Jagiellonian dynasty, the Polish monarchy declined in power, while the Polish nobility became predominant. The nobles elected the kings of Poland, many of whom were foreigners. The last great Polish king was John III Sobieski. He is best remembered for leading the Polish army that in 1683 defeated the Turks at the siege of Vienna, the capital of Austria, thus halting Turkish expansion in Europe.

As rival nobles struggled for power, Poland grew weaker politically and became a prey for the territorial ambitions of its neighbors. Russia, Austria, and Prussia (now part of Germany) partitioned Poland among themselves three times—in 1772, 1793, and 1795. After the last partition Poland virtually ceased to exist as an independent state.

The Poles revolted against foreign rule a number of times. One of the heroes in the struggle for independence was Thaddeus Kościuszko, who had served with George Washington's army during the American Revolution. But after each uprising the Poles were defeated, and for many years the Polish nation existed only in the minds and hearts of its people.

The Polish Republic. In 1918, at the end of World War I, the victorious Allied powers, Britain, France, and the United States, restored the Polish state. The 1919 Treaty of Versailles with defeated Germany gave Poland a strip of land at the mouth of the Vistula River, in order to provide the country with access to the Baltic Sea at the port of Danzig (now Gdańsk). Polish territory separated East Prussia from the rest of Germany. Danzig was established as a free city under the supervision of the League of Nations, the forerunner of the United Nations. In 1920, Poland fought a short war with the Soviet Union over disputed territory in the east.

The famous pianist Ignace (Ignacy) Jan Paderewski served briefly as prime minister of Poland. The dominant figure of the time, however, was Marshal Józef Pilsudski, a military leader during World War I and a hero of the 1920 war with the Soviet Union. Pilsudski became provisional president of Poland and commander of the Army. Pilsudski retired in 1922, but in 1926, following a period of economic and political difficulty, he overthrew the government and ruled Poland virtually as a dictator until his death in 1935.

World War II. On September 1, 1939, Germany suddenly invaded Poland, setting off World War II. On September 17, the Soviet Union also invaded Poland, occupying its eastern part. When Germany attacked the Soviet Union in 1941, all of Poland fell under German control. During the five years of occupation, some 6 million Poles, half of them Polish Jews, lost their lives.

Soviet armies, pursuing retreating German forces, re-entered Poland in August 1944. They advanced almost to Warsaw before halting. Poles rose up against the German troops in the capital, but the uprising was crushed by the Germans and Warsaw was left in ruins. The Soviet armies finally entered the city in January 1945. At the Yalta Conference in 1945, the Soviet Union, the United States, and Britain agreed that Poland would have free elections after the war. Only Communists and their allies, however, were allowed to run for office in elections held in 1947.

Recent History. The Communist government of Poland generally was a loyal ally of the Soviet Union. But the Polish people often were at odds with their government over political and economic conditions. In 1980, Polish workers, led by Lech Walesa, won the right to form a union. Called Solidarity, it was the first free labor union permitted in a Communist country. But when Solidarity leaders in 1981 called for a vote by the people on whether the Communist party should continue to rule Poland, the government declared martial law, or rule by the army. Martial law was lifted in 1983, but Solidarity was banned.

Renewed labor unrest in the late 1980's eventually forced the government to compromise. An agreement in 1989 provided for legalized labor unions and democratic political reforms. In elections that followed, Solidarity's candidates won an overwhelming victory. Wojciech Jaruzelski, the former Communist party head, became president, but Tadeusz Mazowiecki, a Solidarity supporter, was named prime minister. In 1990, Lech Walesa

As head of the trade union Solidarity, Lech Walesa (center) led a revolt against Communist rule in Poland. He served as Polish president from 1990 to 1995.

was elected president by popular vote. See the article on Walesa in Volume W-X-Y-Z.

In 1992, Hanna Suchocka, leader of the Democratic Union, a centrist party, was named prime minister, becoming the first Polish woman to hold the office. In 1993 parliamentary elections, however, the largest number of seats was won by the Democratic Left Alliance, made up of former Communists. The swing to the left was blamed largely on problems arising from Poland's rapid changeover to a free-market economy. The former Communists solidified their victory in the 1995 presidential election, when the anti-Communist Walesa was defeated by the candidate of the Democratic Left Alliance, Aleksander Kwasniewski.

JAMES CHACE
Former Managing Editor, *East Europe*
Updated by M. K. DZIEWANOWSKI
Author, *Poland in the 20th Century*

POLAR REGIONS. See ANTARCTICA; ARCTIC.

POLICE

Uniformed police officers are a visible part of every community. Popular television programs portray police officers using weapons to prevent crime and protect the public. However, while enforcing the law and protecting people's lives and property are the main responsibilities of police, only about 15 percent of their time is devoted to the kinds of activities shown on television. The remaining 85 percent is devoted to more routine services to the community, which over the years have become police duties. These include responding to emergencies, settling disputes, regulating traffic, taking care of sick and injured people, and responding to complaints. The police are on duty seven days a week, 24 hours a day, to provide these services.

▶POLICE IN MODERN SOCIETY

Police responsibilities are divided into three general areas: patrol operations, crime detection, and traffic control.

Patrol

Uniformed patrol officers are assigned **beats** (areas or routes), which they patrol (survey), alone or with a partner, on foot, in squad cars, on motorcycles, and sometimes on horseback or by boat or helicopter.

Officers on patrol are responsible for preventing crime, apprehending criminals, and maintaining order. They keep alert for suspicious persons or circumstances, and they try to maintain peace on the beat assigned to them. Patrol officers keep in touch with one another and with their headquarters by means of walkie-talkies or two-way car radios. Sometimes they need to call for help to handle an accident, control a large crowd, or settle a family argument. Officers in patrol cars receive directions from headquarters telling them where to go and what to do next.

Detection

When a community's police department becomes large enough to maintain special units, the first to be formed is usually a detective squad. A detective is a member of the uniformed force who has been selected to work out of uniform (usually in a business suit), and whose special assignment is solving and preventing crimes. These **plainclothes officers** re-

Police gather at their precinct for a daily briefing. The familiar blue uniforms will be a welcome sight to local citizens as the officers head out on their beats.

ceive special training for their jobs. They often work long hours because they must be prepared to devote whatever time is necessary to solve crimes as quickly as possible.

In many detective units in large cities, there are even more specialized units within the detective division to handle certain types of crimes. For example, members of the narcotics squad devote all their time and effort to eliminating drug traffic.

When certain crimes are committed so often that the entire community is concerned, the solution, as in the case of narcotics squads, is for the police to form a specialized detective unit. Many cities have squads trained to deal with such specific types of crime as burglary, robbery, vice (gambling and other activities considered to be "victimless" crimes), fraud, and homicide (murder). Many police departments also have special divisions to deal specifically with juvenile problems. An article on juvenile crime appears in Volume J.

1

2

6

Traffic Control

In many towns and cities a special unit of uniformed officers is designated to control the flow of traffic, investigate traffic accidents, and issue traffic summonses to those who violate traffic laws.

Drunk driving is a major concern in the United States today. When a person is suspected of driving while intoxicated (under the influence of alcohol), it is the duty of the police to test the suspected driver and, if the driver fails the test or refuses to take it, to place the driver under arrest.

Accident investigation is another function of the traffic unit. Such investigations are particularly important in hit-and-run accidents, in which a driver who has hit another vehicle or even a person does not stop at the scene, as required by law. Skilled police investigators often can determine the color, make, and model of the car that left the scene.

Police officers often use radar guns to measure the speed of moving vehicles. They then relay a description of the speeding auto to another police car by radio so the speeder will be caught. This system is more accurate, and safer, for police officers than high-speed chases. Helicopters are also used to observe traffic conditions and to assist in emergencies.

Special Forces

Other special units within a large community police department may include a search and rescue team, a bomb squad, a hostage

Uniformed officers protect and assist people (1)—but police personnel provide many other community services as well. They develop ways to prevent crime by sponsoring activities such as the recent program to fingerprint children (2). Police monitor and control traffic (3). They form special highly skilled teams, such as bomb squads, to deal with community emergencies (4). They work to solve crimes in a variety of ways—often working "under cover" (5). And, of course, they pursue and arrest criminals (6).

negotiating team, and a special weapons and tactics (SWAT) team.

Search and rescue teams look for people lost in remote areas. Bomb squads respond to bomb threats. They look for the bomb, and if there really is one they try to defuse it (prevent it from exploding) or to remove it in specially built trucks. Both search teams and bomb squads sometimes use specially trained police dogs, which can find both people and bombs by their acute sense of smell. Dogs can also be trained to "sniff out" drugs.

Hostage negotiating teams handle cases in which criminals hold innocent people captive. The negotiating unit tries to persuade the criminals to release the hostages unharmed. Special weapons units handle especially dangerous situations involving armed criminals. Members of these units are trained to carry out their missions without endangering innocent bystanders.

Community Relations

Many police departments have special units to promote good relations between the police and the community. Officers assigned to such units have often had special training in psychology and community relations.

These units develop a variety of programs to encourage positive attitudes toward the police. One of the best known is the Police Athletic League (PAL). Open to boys and girls from ages 7 to 21, PAL programs emphasize sports as a way to prevent juvenile crime.

POLICE ORGANIZATION IN THE UNITED STATES

In the United States there are more than 40,000 independently operating national, state, metropolitan, and rural police departments.

Federal Police Forces

The largest and best-known federal (national) law enforcement agency is the Federal Bureau of Investigation (FBI), which is a part of the U.S. Department of Justice. The FBI's crime laboratory, in Washington, D.C., is one of the most famous in the world. The FBI investigates federal crimes and handles robbery, kidnapping, hijacking, and other cases that may not remain confined to one state. Because FBI agents may operate across state lines, state and local police may call on them for assistance. An article on the FBI appears in Volume F.

Another federal agency within the Department of Justice is the U.S. Marshals Service. U.S. marshals have the same powers to enforce federal laws in their districts as sheriffs have to enforce state laws in their smaller districts.

Some of the many other federal law enforcement agencies include the Bureau of Alcohol, Tobacco, and Firearms; the Secret Service, which is responsible for protecting the president of the United States; the Border Patrol of the Immigration and Naturalization Service, which prevents people from entering the United States illegally; and the U.S. Customs Service, which is responsible for protecting U.S. points of entry against persons who try to bring illegal goods into the country.

State and Local Police

Most states of the United States have their own police forces with full power to enforce state laws. By custom, state troopers (so called because in the past they were often on horseback) are mainly concerned with highway patrol and traffic regulation. But they may also assist local police in the investigation of major crimes. In some small towns, which may not have their own police force, the state police also serve as the local police department.

County police departments are usually called sheriff's departments. Sheriffs are generally elected to office and have the power to appoint individual officers (or deputies). A sheriff may perform such duties as running the county jail, delivering summonses, patrolling the county, and investigating accidents. The sheriff is usually the highest-ranking police officer in the county.

Metropolitan Police

A metropolitan, or city, police department is responsible for enforcing state, criminal, and vehicular laws, as well as local laws, within the city. The department may have thousands of officers if the city is a large one, or only one or two if it is a small town. The department head may be known as the chief of police, commissioner, or superintendent and is appointed by the mayor or city manager.

Some large metropolitan police forces have special units to deal separately with housing, parks, transit, and youths.

CAREERS IN THE POLICE

Police work is an excellent way to serve the community. Police officers work long hours and sometimes face danger, but an officer's job is secure and seldom boring, and there are many opportunities for advancement.

Young men and women interested in careers as police officers should have at least a high school diploma. Some police departments require a college degree as well. Applicants must pass a Civil Service test and a rigorous physical examination.

Those who are accepted as new members of a police force generally attend police training schools, where they learn necessary skills. Many colleges offer degrees in law enforcement and criminal justice that may also lead to a career in the police.

Police Careers for Civilians

In addition to sworn officers, there are other job opportunities for those who would like to be part of a police department.

Laboratory Technicians. Also called forensic scientists, these technicians examine evidence such as illegal drugs, blood, bullets, or guns to try to determine who committed a crime. These scientists may also appear in court as expert witnesses to explain their findings to the jury.

Photographers. Police photographers take pictures at accident and crime scenes, as well as pictures of suspects under surveillance (close observation). Often their photographs are used as evidence in court. Sometimes a review of such photographs will disclose evidence overlooked by visual inspection.

Artists. Police artists must be able to sketch profiles of suspects from the verbal descriptions of witnesses. These sketches are photocopied and distributed to patrol forces, often leading to the arrest of a suspect.

Computer Programmers and Analysts. The use of computers in police work is increasing. Computers are used to store records, compare fingerprints, keep track of the activities of suspects, and for a variety of other uses.

Radio Dispatchers. The radio dispatcher is often the citizen's first contact with police. How the dispatcher performs the job can make the difference between life and death, catching a criminal or not, or the success or failure of any police mission.

Secretaries and Clerks. Police departments of all sizes must have competent and efficient help with the record keeping that is an essential part of police organization.

▶ **POLICE AROUND THE WORLD**

The International Criminal Police Organization (INTERPOL) was established in 1923. Headquartered in Paris, Interpol keeps current files of information gathered from the police of its more than 125 member nations about criminals involved in international counterfeiting, kidnapping, smuggling, and drug cases. This information is given to any member nation requesting it.

The police systems of individual countries fall roughly into three types. In some countries the central government exercises almost complete control over all levels of the police department. In other countries the central government exercises a limited control only, and in still others the central government has very little control.

In countries where the police are tightly controlled by the central government, the police protect the government rather than the people. The people often fear the police instead of respecting them. The Gestapo in Nazi Germany was an extreme example of a police system tightly controlled by the central government.

The police system of Great Britain is an example of an organization that is partly government controlled. The London Metropolitan Police are under the authority of the Home

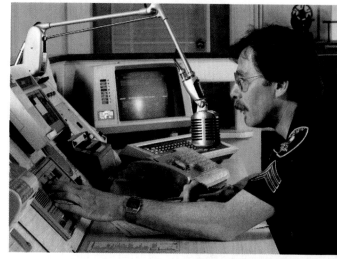

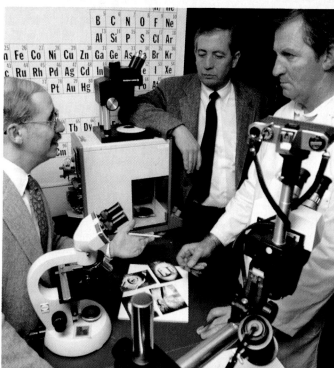

Top: Members of special police forces, such as this anti-terrorist squad, receive special training in handling weapons. *Middle:* The police radio dispatcher is often the first officer with whom a citizen comes in contact. *Bottom:* Forensic scientists work in crime labs examining evidence to determine who committed a crime.

Office, a national government agency. Local police departments outside London are governed by a separate police authority, with the Home Office retaining the right to inspect local departments and make recommendations.

The police system of Canada is an example of an organization, much like that of the United States, that is run largely without central government control. The Royal Canadian Mounted Police is empowered to enforce all national laws, but the "Mounties" assist provincial police departments only at the request of the provinces. Individual provincial departments are not under the direct control of the national government.

In democratic societies people expect the police to help them in time of trouble. In the United States, for example, anyone who is sick, injured, lost, or the victim of a crime should know that the police are there to help.

Citizens in democratic societies also have the right to complain to the government—and to the press—about police abuse of authority, police brutality, and other misconduct.

▶ HISTORY OF POLICE ORGANIZATION

Little is known about the origins of police. Ancient armies had military police to control conquered nations. Imperial Rome, in the 1st century A.D., apparently had some civil police. But no evidence of an organized civil police force appears until many centuries later.

In 1754, Sir Henry Fielding, a well-known London lawyer and writer, and his brother, John Fielding, organized a private system of patrol in London. It was a voluntary system, paid for out of private funds and the money collected from fines. John Fielding believed that, along with men on foot patrol, there should be police officers able to rush to the scene of a crime. This group became known, therefore, as the Bow Street Runners. The Fielding system lasted 50 years, but as London grew, the Runners could no longer control crime.

In 1829, Sir Robert Peel organized the first modern police system. The London Metropolitan Police, with headquarters at Scotland Yard, began with 1,000 men spread over 17 districts. The officers were carefully selected and trained. From Sir Robert Peel's name come the familiar nicknames "bobby" and "peeler" for British police officers.

In the United States in the 19th century, large urban areas such as New York, Boston, and Philadelphia supported separate day and night "watches" (patrols). In 1845, New York combined its dual forces to form a single citywide police force modeled on the London Metropolitan Police. Other cities soon followed New York's lead.

Many of the new police first recruited in New York were Irish, and they refused to wear uniforms that reminded them of the political troubles they had left behind in Ireland. But after ten years, they accepted the idea of blue uniforms with copper buttons. It is said to be from those copper buttons that they got the nickname "coppers," which in modern times has been shortened to "cops."

Early police departments in the United States were often under the control of politicians. Police officers were poorly equipped and usually poorly paid. They often abused their authority. About 1900, commissions of investigation began recommending new procedures for choosing police officers. Gradually Civil Service examinations replaced political appointment as a method of choosing police officers.

Early police forces in the United States were made up only of men. Of the approximately 500,000 police officers in the United States today, about 3 percent are women. They are assigned interchangeably with male officers and perform the entire range of police duties.

▶ POLICING IN THE FUTURE

It is predicted that policing in the future will be much different than it is today. Advances in technology—particularly in computers, television, and communication—will assist the police in solving and preventing crimes. Advances in forensic science should make evidence more reliable and meaningful. All of these changes will be for the better if they help to improve the quality of police service.

LEO C. LOUGHREY
Chairman, Department of Law
and Police Science
John Jay College of Criminal Justice

See also CRIME AND CRIMINOLOGY; FEDERAL BUREAU OF INVESTIGATION; FINGERPRINTING; JUVENILE CRIME; LAW AND LAW ENFORCEMENT; LIE DETECTION.

POLIO. See DISEASES.

POLISHING. See GRINDING AND POLISHING.

POLITICAL PARTIES

A political party is a group organized to support certain policies on questions of public interest. The aim of a political party is to elect officials who will try to carry out the party's policies. The questions may range from issues of peace, war, and taxes to how people should earn a living. A large political party usually has millions of members and supporters. When people in a democracy disagree about what the government should do, each voter expresses his opinion by voting for the candidate that supports his side of the argument.

▶ HOW PARTIES BEGAN

Although parties began long ago, they have not always existed. The ancient Greeks, who were pioneers in political affairs, had no organized political parties in the modern sense. In ancient Athens all native, free, male Athenians belonged to the Assembly, the governing body of the city. Each man voted as he thought best. The Council of Five Hundred, renewed each year, carried out the wishes of the Assembly and proposed measures for their consideration. Groups in the Assembly sometimes acted together to pass a law. But they did not organize into lasting political parties.

The Roman senate had two groups that were somewhat like modern political parties— the Patricians and the Plebeians. The Patricians represented noble families. The Plebeians represented the wealthy merchants and the middle class. Although these two groups often mingled, at times they voted as factions, or parties, on particular issues that were important to the groups they represented.

For many centuries after the fall of Rome (A.D. 476), the people of Europe had little voice in politics. But in the 14th and 15th centuries a fierce struggle developed among the young republics of the Italian peninsula. During this struggle the modern idea of a political party began to take shape. Most Italian city-states were split into two warring parties, the Guelphs and Ghibellines. Both of these groups had their origins in Germany. The Guelph party represented merchants and businessmen. The Ghibelline party represented nobles, professional soldiers, and other people who favored feudalism. Throughout Italy, the Guelphs and the Ghibellines fought for control. About 1500 the struggle began to die down, with the Ghibellines gaining the advantage in most places. So the city-states gradually came under the rule of powerful men and leading families.

English Political Parties. English political parties were born after what was called the Popish Plot of 1678. Although there was no real plot, a rumor spread through England that Roman Catholics were plotting to kill King Charles II. According to the rumor, Catholics planned to give the throne to Charles's brother, James, Duke of York (who was a Roman Catholic), and take over the country. Parliament was alarmed and shut out all Roman Catholics from public office. Parliament also tried to take away the Duke of York's right to inherit the throne. Although King Charles II was head of the Church of England, he sympathized with his brother and with the Catholic cause. By its acts Parliament seemed to be challenging royal authority, so King Charles struck back by dissolving Parliament.

All over England people were either for or against the King's act. Those who urged the King to call a new Parliament were called Petitioners. Those who backed the King's deed were called Abhorrers because they abhorred any attempt to control the King's actions. Soon the Petitioners were called Whigs, and the Abhorrers were called Tories. "Whig" was an old word for Scottish Presbyterians who opposed the government. "Tory" was the name given the Irish Roman Catholics who had their homes and farms taken from them when the Puritans under Oliver Cromwell ruled both England and Ireland. But now the two old names took on new meanings.

The basic difference between 17th-century Whigs and Tories was their view of what government should do and how strong it should be. Tories wanted rule by a strong king. Whigs wanted ordinary people to have more rights and gain more control of their government. A hundred years later many Whigs sided with the American Revolutionists of 1776. Most Tories supported King George III's policy of crushing the rebellion.

After the peaceful English revolution of

PROGRESSIVE
("BULL MOOSE") PARTY
(FOUNDED 1912)

WHIG PARTY
(1840 CAMPAIGN)

DEMOCRATIC PARTY
(1844 CAMPAIGN)

DEMOCRATIC-REPUBLICAN PARTY
(1816 CAMPAIGN)

1688 brought William and Mary to the throne, Parliament became the real ruler of England. The Whigs and Tories became large, loosely knit groups, usually led by men of wealth and noble family. Later the major parties were the Liberals and the Tories (also called Conservatives). In the 20th century the Liberals grew weaker, while the young Labour Party rose to challenge the Conservatives for control of the government.

Parties in France. Before the French Revolution of 1789 there were three classes (called estates) in France: the nobility, the clergy, and the middle-class merchants and businessmen (the Third Estate). The estates chose representatives, who met in a group called the Estates General. In some ways the estates were like political parties. However, they had no real political power until 1789, for the king of France was an absolute monarch.

In 1789 there was a great crisis in France. King Louis XVI did not have enough money to run the government, and so he had to call the Estates General together to find ways of raising new taxes. Before 1789 the nobility and the clergy had not been taxed. The Third Estate was taxed. The representatives of the Third Estate were determined to institute reforms at the meeting of the Estates General. One of the reforms was to be the payment of taxes by the other two estates. Since the representatives of the nobles and the clergy could join together and outvote the Third Estate, the Third Estate decided to rebel. They invited all interested members of the Estates General to join them in a new reform assembly. Some nobles and clergy with democratic ideals did join them, and the National Assembly was formed. It was the conflict between the National Assembly and the king that triggered the Revolution and eventually ended absolute monarchy in France. Several political parties were formed in the National Assembly: the Jacobins, Cordeliers, Girondists, and others. The most radical reformers,

the Jacobins, sat on the left side of the Assembly chamber, while the most conservative delegates sat on the right side. Some scholars think the terms "left" for radical and "right" for conservative began at this time.

Political Parties in Colonial America. In the French and Indian War the American colonists and English Army fought side by side against the French. The French were defeated and pushed out of North America in 1763. Then England began trying to control the colonies more strictly. The Americans, through the Committees of Correspondence and the Sons of Liberty, voiced their anger against England's new colonial policies.

Each of the 13 colonies had its own assembly. Americans who wanted close ties with England were called Tories. Those who wanted more freedom for the colonies were called Whigs. Again these two names took on new meanings in a new country.

When the colonies declared their independence from England in 1776, Americans divided into two groups. The Revolutionists called themselves Patriots. American supporters of England were called Loyalists or Tories. The American Patriots in turn were divided between the leaders, who were wealthy and educated, and the followers—farmers, laborers, and small shopkeepers. But all Patriots were united to win the Revolution, so parties did not form until later.

▶**PARTIES BEGIN IN THE UNITED STATES**

The leaders of the American Revolution did not like the idea of parties and political battles between parties. George Washington, in his Farewell Address, warned Americans against "faction" (parties). James Madison thought parties were probably necessary, although he did not entirely approve of them. Alexander Hamilton thought that faction was a vice to be guarded against at all times. Thomas Jefferson declared in 1789, "If I could not go to heaven but with a party, I would not go there at all." Yet the men who held these views founded the first two great American political parties.

Hamilton and other leaders who wanted a strong central government banded together to put over their policies. In 1787 they began calling themselves the Federalists. This was the first United States political party. In 1796, anti-Federalists gathered around Jefferson. Members of Jefferson's group called themselves Democratic-Republicans. Northern businessmen, bankers, and merchants supported the Federalists. They believed in a strong national (or federal) government. Federalists held that capital and industry were the basis of a healthy republic and that the federal government should act to protect the country's infant industries. The Democratic-Republican Party drew its followers from farmers and people with little property. These people wanted government to leave them alone as much as possible. They wanted to limit the federal government's power and leave the most power in the hands of state and local governments. In foreign affairs the Federalists leaned toward England, while the

Democratic-Republicans sympathized with Revolutionary France.

Early leaders, such as John Adams (second president), had Federalist sympathies. But the Federalists lost control of the government to Jefferson and his party in 1800. The Federalists lingered on as a minority party, especially in New England, for 20 years.

By 1820 American political life was being influenced by sharp differences of opinion between sections of the country. In time these quarrels led to the Civil War. The agrarian South, the frontier West, and the industrial North each wanted the government to follow a different course of action.

In 1828 the first president from what was then called the West was elected—Andrew Jackson, a Democratic-Republican from Tennessee. His party had great support in the South and the West. Jackson changed the party's name to Democrats. People who had once been Federalists joined with anti-Jackson Democrats to form the Whig Party. Between 1836 and 1852 the Whigs gave the Democrats strong opposition. One of the major issues was the western expansion of the nation, favored by Jacksonian Democrats.

By 1854 the issue of Negro slavery overshadowed all political debate. Another related issue was states' rights. If a state government was in conflict with the national government, which government had the final authority? Northern Abolitionists—people who wanted to abolish slavery—were leaving the Whigs. The Whigs lost voters also to the Know-Nothings. This was a new party that supported the interests of native-born Protestants and violently opposed Roman Catholics and foreigners. The Whig Party began to go to pieces. At the same time, the issues of slavery and states' rights divided Democrats into Northern and Southern branches. Southern Democrats strongly favored slavery and states' rights. Extremists among them believed that a state had a right to secede (leave the Union) if the national government tried to interfere with slavery.

In 1854 antislavery forces and Free Soil forces (a group founded in Buffalo, New York) formed the Republican Party. It attracted ex-Whig Abolitionists. The Republicans ran their first presidential candidate, John C. Frémont, in 1856. By 1860 the vot-

A campaign poster for the U.S. election of 1864.

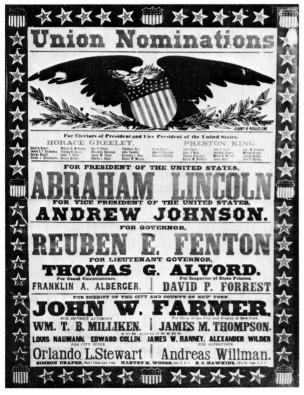

ers had a choice of four major parties—the Northern Democrats, the Southern Democrats, the Republicans, and the Constitutional-Union Party, which drew some ex-Whigs. Antislavery feeling was so strong that Republicans were helped enormously in capturing the presidency for Abraham Lincoln. In 1861 the Southern states seceded and the Civil War began.

After the Civil War. The defeat of the Confederacy weakened the Democrats, who were associated in voters' minds with the Southern cause. For many years the Republicans were the major party. They favored business interests and high tariffs. The Democrats supported free trade. They attracted farmers and the immigrants who poured into the country between the Civil War and the turn of the century.

With slavery no longer an issue, the two major parties were not so deeply divided again until the 1930's. At that time the Depression struck the country. The election of 1932 brought in Franklin D. Roosevelt and his New Deal. Roosevelt Democrats thought that the federal government must act strongly to help people who had been hurt by the Depression. Under the New Deal the government passed relief measures, social security, laws helping unions, and other bills. Republicans thought the government was taking too much power and moving the country toward a welfare state. They fought against governmental interference with business.

Today both parties agree in general on social security, unemployment insurance, basic foreign policy, and civil rights. The issues on which they disagree now are not goals so much as means: how best to cure the nation's economic ills (inflation and unemployment), how best to conserve dwindling energy supplies, and how best to protect an environment constantly threatened by industrial pollution. In solving these and other problems, most Republicans tend to disapprove of government spending and government regulation. But most Democrats believe that government spending and regulation can produce results that are good.

Third Parties

Unlike many other countries, the United States has a two-party system. Third parties have developed, but a balance of more than two strong parties has never lasted.

In the 19th century the Populists were an active third party. They favored free silver, cheap money, and an end to monopolies. By 1900, extra parties were forming, including the Farmer-Labor Party, the Socialist Party, and the Socialist Labor Party. Such parties, often small, were formed by people who felt the major parties did not express their views. Sometimes a third party has gained part of its goals by supporting a major party that promised to act on the third party's views. The Socialists, who reached their height in the 1930's, never won a national election. But many of their ideas were adopted by the major parties.

In the United States and Canada strong third parties sometimes exist at the state or provincial level. Among these are the Liberal and Conservative parties in New York State. The Parti Québécois, in the Canadian Province of Quebec, favors Quebec's separation from Canada. The Social Credit Party is important in the Canadian provinces of British Columbia and Alberta.

Third parties develop also when a major party is violently split on an issue. The progressive wing of the U.S. Republican Party broke away in 1912. It formed a third party, the Progressive, or "Bull Moose," Party. Theodore Roosevelt was the party's presidential candidate. The Progressives lasted into the 1920's under the leadership of the La Follette family of Wisconsin. They elected senators but no presidents. The Progressives opposed big business monopolies and favored the interests of farmers and workers.

After World War II the issues of states' rights and Negro civil rights again caused a party split. The Dixiecrat Party of the South broke from the Democratic Party in 1948, running Strom Thurmond for president. In the same year a new Progressive Party was formed that favored wider social welfare measures. Its candidate was Henry Wallace. President Harry Truman, a Democrat, won the election in spite of the split. Once more, in 1968, the Democratic Party split over the civil rights issue, and Alabama's George Wallace formed the American Independent Party.

Usually both major parties manage to keep members who differ on some issues within the

The donkey represents the Democratic Party in the United States; the elephant, the Republican Party. The above symbols are modern versions of those created by the political cartoonist Thomas Nast in the 1870's.

party. Therefore both parties have lively arguments within their ranks. A party that persists in following an extreme position held by only part of its membership is likely to lose the election.

How Parties Work in the United States

American political parties are organized on both national and local levels. Every four years, parties hold national conventions. Delegates are chosen in primaries, by state conventions, or at closed local party gatherings called precinct caucuses. These delegates gather at the conventions to nominate a presidential and a vice-presidential candidate.

Each party at its convention drafts a platform. The platform is a statement of what the party stands for. If the party wins, the platform is supposed to guide the actions of the elected officials.

American parties are run by county and state committees. Committee members may be elected at primaries, chosen at state conventions, or appointed by party officers. The two major parties also have national committees, made up of one man and one woman from each of the 50 states and the territories. State and federal laws control the ways political parties can raise and handle money.

Parties today use computers to draw up lists of possible supporters and take public opinion polls to explore the views of voters on certain issues. Special-interest groups able to raise money and turn out voters for candidates they favor have grown in influence.

Newspapers, radio, and television have strongly influenced modern elections. Political parties use advertising to mold public opinion and compete for favorable media coverage for their candidates. Candidates, some say, are now packaged and sold as a business sells its products. Televised debates have enabled candidates to present themselves and their views to large audiences. Recently there has been widespread criticism of the prediction of election results by television before all voters have gone to the polls.

▶POLITICAL PARTIES IN OTHER COUNTRIES

Political parties are often a standard by which a country's political freedom can be measured. Some countries have only one political party, while others may have two or more, giving their voters a choice of candidates. In Communist countries such as China (and the former Soviet Union), there is only one legal political party—the Communist Party. Under such a system, people who do not agree with the party in power cannot express their objections by voting for another party. In some one-party countries, the ruling party holds power with the support of the army. In developing countries with many different and sometimes competing ethnic groups, supporters of a one-party state claim that a single party helps unify the country.

The countries where two or more parties have the right to compete with each other in elections are the democracies. Democracies usually operate under either a two-party or a multi-party system. Like the United States, Britain operates under a two-party system. The major parties are the Labour Party and the Conservative Party, though there are active third parties such as the Liberal Party and the Social Democratic Party. Canada also has two major parties, the Progressive Conservatives and the Liberals.

Many European countries have multi-party systems. Three countries in Asia—India, Israel, and Japan—are also multi-party democracies. Countries such as these may have many parties representing a wide range of political views. Because of the number of competing parties, however, it is sometimes difficult for any one party to get a clear majority of the votes. In such cases, leading parties that can agree on general policies form a coalition (a combination of parties) to run the country. Frequently, of course, even in a multi-party system, one party may sometimes win by a clear majority.

STEPHEN FLANDERS
Correspondent, Columbia Broadcasting System
See also ELECTIONS; GOVERNMENT, FORMS OF.

JAMES K. POLK (1795–1849)

11TH PRESIDENT OF THE UNITED STATES

POLK, JAMES KNOX. James K. Polk became the first "dark horse," or little-known candidate, to win the presidency when he unexpectedly defeated Henry Clay in the election of 1844. At 49 years of age, he was also the youngest president the United States had yet had. During his term of office Polk added to the United States a vast region stretching from the Rocky Mountains to the Pacific Ocean. Antislavery men of his own day condemned him, for they believed that he desired only to extend the area of slavery. But modern scholars deny this and generally rank Polk as one of the 10 greatest American presidents.

▶ EARLY YEARS

James K. Polk was born in Mecklenburg County, North Carolina, on November 2, 1795. The future president was the eldest of 10 children born to Samuel and Jane Knox Polk. In 1806 the Polk family moved from North Carolina to Duck River, Tennessee. There Samuel Polk became a successful frontier farmer. James never developed the physical strength needed for farming. His parents therefore trained his mind. They provided tutors for him and sent him to several preparatory schools. In 1815 he entered the University of North Carolina. He applied himself diligently to his studies, graduating in 1818 with honors in mathematics and the classics.

Polk then studied law and in 1820 was admitted to the bar. He began his practice in Columbia, Tennessee, and soon became a well-known lawyer. In 1823 he was elected to the state legislature. As a young politician he became friendly with Tennessee's new United States senator, Andrew Jackson.

On January 1, 1824, Polk married Sarah Childress, the daughter of a prosperous family from Murfreesboro, Tennessee. She was a tall, handsome woman with a queenly bearing and remarkable cultural refinement.

▶ CONGRESSMAN

In 1825 Polk was elected to the United States House of Representatives. There he championed Andrew Jackson, who had just lost the contest for the presidency to John Quincy Adams. Polk proved a courageous and able debater and blunted the effect of the worst attacks against Jackson. When Jackson was elected president in 1828, Polk became one of his most trusted lieutenants, serving without expecting political reward. In 1833

<table>
<tr><td colspan="2" align="center">IMPORTANT DATES IN THE LIFE OF
JAMES K. POLK</td></tr>
<tr><td>1795</td><td>Born in Mecklenburg County, North Carolina, November 2.</td></tr>
<tr><td>1818</td><td>Graduated from the University of North Carolina.</td></tr>
<tr><td>1820</td><td>Admitted to the bar; began practicing law in Columbia, Tennessee.</td></tr>
<tr><td>1823</td><td>Elected to the Tennessee Legislature.</td></tr>
<tr><td>1824</td><td>Married Sarah Childress.</td></tr>
<tr><td>1825–
1839</td><td>Served in the United States House of Representatives.</td></tr>
<tr><td>1839–
1841</td><td>Governor of Tennessee.</td></tr>
<tr><td>1845–
1849</td><td>11th president of the United States.</td></tr>
<tr><td>1849</td><td>Died in Nashville, Tennessee, June 15.</td></tr>
</table>

Polk became chairman of the Committee on Ways and Means. Two years later he was elected Speaker of the House of Representatives. He was re-elected Speaker in 1837.

During these years Polk had to preside over some of the stormiest sessions ever known in the House of Representatives. He was heckled unmercifully from the floor of the House and hounded by enemies, some of whom tried to goad him into a duel. Nevertheless, Polk served efficiently if unhappily.

▶ GOVERNOR

In 1839 the Tennessee Democrats, hoping to capture control of the state from the Whig Party, nominated Polk for the governorship. Although he would have preferred to remain in Congress, Polk consented to run for the good of the party. He was elected and served a 2-year term, from 1839 to 1841. His success proved more a personal than a party victory, for in the presidential election of 1840 Tennessee cast its vote for the Whig candidate, William Henry Harrison. Polk ran for re-election as governor in 1841 and 1843 but suffered defeat.

▶ THE ROAD TO THE WHITE HOUSE

President Harrison's death in 1841 put Vice-President John Tyler in the White House. Tyler, however, was soon ousted from the Whig Party for vetoing their favorite measures. This immediately raised the question of who would become president in 1844. Senator Henry Clay of Kentucky proposed to take charge of the Whig Party and become its candidate. Former president Martin Van Buren was expected to be the Democratic candidate.

Meanwhile, President Tyler concentrated his efforts upon achieving the annexation of Texas. On April 22, 1844, he submitted a Texas annexation treaty to the Senate. The proposed treaty immediately started a national controversy. The entry of Texas into the Union was popular in the South and Southwest. But many people, in the North and elsewhere, objected because it would add a new slave state to the United States. In addition, they felt that annexation would almost certainly lead to war with Mexico.

On April 27 both Clay and Van Buren published letters opposing statehood for Texas. The Whigs nominated Clay for the presidency shortly thereafter, but all politicians agree that his letter had weakened his hold on the voters of the Southwest. Van Buren's letter, appearing just a month before the Democratic nominating convention, ruined his chances. The aged but still influential Andrew Jackson informed his friends that the Democratic Party and its candidate would have to support annexation. Furthermore, Jackson believed, the Democratic candidate ought to come from the Southwest, to capture Whigs who would refuse to vote for Clay. Jackson suggested James K. Polk—who had been mentioned as a possible vice-presidential candidate—as a man who could lead the Democrats to victory.

"Who Is James K. Polk?"

The Democratic National Convention met in Baltimore, Maryland, in May, 1844. The delegates took Andrew Jackson's advice and nominated Polk on the ninth ballot. George M. Dallas (1792–1864) of Pennsylvania became the vice-presidential candidate. Polk's success against men much better known prompted the Whigs to ask mockingly: "Who is James K. Polk?"

The Democrats adopted a platform calling for the annexation of Texas and the "reoccupation" of the whole of Oregon. The vast Oregon Territory included present-day Washington, Oregon, and Idaho; parts of Montana and Wyoming; and a large area of western Canada. Since 1818 it had been occupied by both Great Britain and the United States.

The Democratic platform emphasized Polk's own devotion to Manifest Destiny—the concept that the United States must continue to expand across the North American continent.

President Tyler, who had accepted renomination, withdrew from the campaign and threw his support to Polk. In return, Polk promised to support the immediate annexation of Texas. On December 3, 1844, Tyler recommended annexation by a joint resolution of Congress. The next day, December 4, Polk won the presidency over Clay by an electoral vote of 170 to 105. Polk received 1,337,243 popular votes to Clay's 1,299,062. James G. Birney (1792–1857) of the Liberty Party, an antislavery party, received 62,300 votes. The vote for Birney's party in New York cost Clay the electors of that state and gave the victory to Polk. Tennessee, Polk's home state, gave its electoral votes to Clay by a margin of only 113 popular votes. The election was one of the closest in American history.

On March 1, 1845, just before Polk's inauguration, President Tyler signed the joint resolution authorizing the annexation of Texas. Polk had thus redeemed half of his party's platform pledge 3 days before entering the White House.

▶ PRESIDENT

Polk was keenly aware that many leading Democrats doubted his qualifications for the presidency and expected to control his administration. He therefore felt a special compulsion to act firmly and with independence. His determination to exercise all his powers as president made him excessively suspicious of advice. Although he early decided to serve only one term, Polk asked all his cabinet members to pledge not to seek the presidential nomination in 1848. He hoped by this means to prevent conflicts of private ambition from interfering with public business. But his efforts weakened party leadership.

At the beginning of his administration, Polk told his Secretary of the Navy, George Bancroft (1800–91), "There are four great measures which are to be the measures of my administration: one, a reduction of the tariff; another, the independent treasury; a third, the settlement of the Oregon boundary question; and lastly, the acquisition of California."

Polk quickly accomplished the first two measures. In 1846 he signed into law the Walker-McKay Tariff, which greatly reduced import taxes. That same year he signed the act restoring the independent treasury system. Under this system the federal government kept its own funds instead of depositing them in state and private banks. The Independent Treasury Act remained in effect until 1913, when the Federal Reserve System was established.

Oregon

Foreign policy, however, dominated Polk's administration. A major problem was the Oregon boundary, which had long involved the United States and Great Britain in controversy. During the presidential campaign of 1844 the Democrats had demanded American occupation of all of Oregon up to 54° 40′ north latitude. This included a large part of what is now British Columbia. A favorite Democratic slogan was "Fifty-four forty or fight." Polk offered to compromise by setting the disputed boundary at the 49th parallel (its present boundary). But when the British minister curtly refused, the President withdrew the offer and declared his intention to press American claims to the entire region up to 54° 40′ Influenced by Andrew Jackson's dislike of

Polk's inauguration on March 4, 1845, was marred by rain.

President Polk in a daguerreotype (early photograph).

Great Britain, Polk wrote: "The only way to treat John Bull is to look him straight in the eye." War over Oregon was avoided, however, and on June 15, 1846, the United States and Great Britain signed a treaty setting the boundary at the 49th parallel.

The Mexican War

Polk had determined to acquire California, which was then a part of Mexico. On March 6, 1845, Mexico broke relations with the United States in protest against the annexation of Texas. At this time two Mexican governments were struggling for control, and the distracted nation had failed to pay an installment on some $3,000,000 in claims owed to American citizens. Polk tried to use these circumstances to persuade the government of President José Herrera (1792–1854) to accept the Rio Grande as the southern boundary of Texas and to sell California.

Polk sent Senator John Slidell (1793–1871) to offer Mexico $25,000,000 plus the $3,000,000 in claims for the territory. The effort failed. Polk then decided to recommend war. In May, 1846, he learned that Mexican troops had attacked General Zachary Taylor's forces along the Rio Grande, in territory claimed by both Mexico and Texas. Polk told Congress that Mexico had shed American blood on American soil, and he called for war. Congress declared war on May 13, 1846. The conflict caused great resentment in the north-eastern states. Many Northerners felt that the war was unjustified and motivated by a Southern desire to expand the area of slavery.

The fighting lasted about a year and a half. General Taylor seized northern Mexico, and American forces occupied California. In September, 1847, General Winfield Scott (1786–1866) captured Mexico City. The treaty of Guadalupe Hidalgo, ending the war, was ratified by the Senate on March 10, 1848. By its terms the United States acquired California and New Mexico (including parts of present-day Nevada, Arizona, Utah, and Colorado). The United States paid Mexico $15,000,000 and assumed the $3,000,000 owed to American citizens.

The Polk Doctrine

In his first annual message to Congress in 1845, Polk set forth the Polk Doctrine, an extension of the Monroe Doctrine. Polk declared that the United States opposed "any European interference" in any country in the Americas. In addition, the United States would resist even the voluntary transfer of such a country or territory to a European power. In 1848 Polk applied this doctrine to prevent Yucatan, a rebellious province of Mexico, from uniting itself to Spain or Great Britain. Latin-American nations, now fearful of the United States, challenged the Polk Doctrine as an invasion of their sovereignty. Polk defended it on the ground that only a firm stand by the United States would prevent European control of weak American nations.

Polk's administration represents the point when the United States began to regard itself as the equal of Europe. In his last annual message to Congress, Polk proudly announced that with the addition of the new territories "the United States are now estimated to be nearly as large as the whole of Europe."

Other Events

Many other events occurred during Polk's administration. The Department of the Interior was established. Wisconsin and Iowa as well as Texas became states, while Minnesota and Oregon became federal territories. Congressman David Wilmot (1814–68) introduced the Wilmot Proviso to prohibit slavery in any territory acquired from Mexico.

Though Wilmot's measure did not pass the Senate, it became the basis of the antislavery Free Soil Party and later of the Republican Party.

▶ LIFE IN THE WHITE HOUSE

Polk showed little imagination or humor. He organized his life methodically, seeking workable answers to practical problems. He labored harder and longer than perhaps any other president of the United States. During his 4 years as president Polk spent only 37 days away from his desk. He arose at daybreak and applied himself to state business usually until midnight. Before going to bed, he carefully recorded in a diary the details of the day's activities.

Sarah Polk greatly aided her husband. She maintained social life at the White House on a dignified and formal level, permitting no cardplaying, liquor, or dancing. She had political intelligence and social grace, and she was able to give her husband some protection from the constant pressure of office-seekers. The Polks had no children.

Polk was succeeded as president by General Zachary Taylor, a hero of the Mexican War. Worn out by his unceasing labor, Polk died on June 15, 1849, scarcely 3 months after leaving office. He was buried at his home, Polk Place, in Nashville, Tennessee. In 1893 his body was moved to the state capitol grounds at Nashville.

PHILIP S. KLEIN
The Pennsylvania State University

See also MEXICAN WAR.

POLLOCK, JACKSON (1912–1956)

After World War II the center of artistic activity shifted from Europe to the United States. One important reason for this shift was the work of Jackson Pollock—probably the first painter in American history whose influence was worldwide.

Pollock was born on January 28, 1912, on a farm near Cody, Wyoming. He first studied painting at the Manual Arts High School in Los Angeles. In 1929 he moved to New York and became a pupil of Thomas Hart Benton (1889–1975), a well-known painter of dramatic scenes from the old American West. Following Benton's lead, Pollock traveled across the country during the 1930's, sketching American scenes. From 1938 until 1942 he worked on the Federal Arts Project, painting pictures in New York.

Early in the 1940's Pollock experimented with modern European styles. But gradually he began to work without subject matter. He developed a new style that was at first shocking and then greatly influential. In 1945, he married Lee Krasner, who was also a painter.

Pollock believed that an artist should be part of his paintings. He unrolled huge lengths of canvas on his studio floor. Walking all around and over the canvas, he dripped or poured paint on it. Sometimes he added sand or broken glass to the paint. The result was a work that showed the energy and emotion of the painter. The swirling mazes of color also had rhythms and orderly patterns. Pollock's technique was named action painting.

Within a few years, Pollock began to receive recognition from around the world. He died in an automobile accident near East Hampton, New York, on August 11, 1956.

Reviewed by HAROLD SPENCER
University of Connecticut

In paintings such as *Reflection of the Big Dipper* (1947), Jackson Pollock poured and dripped paint on the canvas.

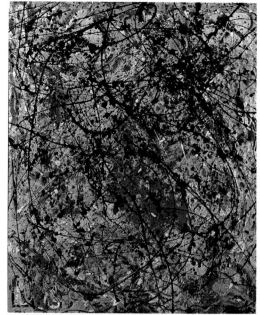

POLLUTION. See AIR POLLUTION; WATER POLLUTION.

POLO

Polo is a game played by two teams on horseback. The riders, using long-handled mallets, attempt to drive a ball down the field and through their opponents' goal.

Modern polo originated in India, where it had been played since 1862. British army officers took the game to England in 1869. Polo was introduced into the United States in 1876. Today polo is played in North and South America, Europe, Australia, New Zealand, India, and many other places.

Outdoors, polo is played by two teams made up of four players each. The field is 300 yards (274 meters) long and 160 yards (146 meters) wide. It is bounded on each side by sideboards 11 inches (28 centimeters) high. A white line extends across each end of the field. Goalposts are placed on these lines 24 feet (7.3 meters) apart and equal distances from the sideboards.

Indoor polo is played by two teams of three players each. The field is 100 yards (91.4 meters) long by 50 yards (45.7 meters) wide.

Mounts. The term "polo pony" stems from the early days of the game, when a height limit allowed only ponies to be used. There is no height limit today. Because of the demands of speed, polo ponies are sometimes Thoroughbreds. They are trained for the game, usually for at least a year.

The Game. Today the game consists of six or eight periods, called "chukkers," of seven minutes each. There are time-outs between chukkers during which the players change to fresh ponies.

Two mounted umpires are on the field, and one referee, unmounted, is on the sidelines. Rules to protect players from dangerous plays or unfair use of the mallet are enforced by the umpires. Violations of rules are called fouls and are penalized. The team that is fouled is given a free shot at its opponents' goal from a distance of 30, 40, or 60 yards (27, 37, or 55 meters) from the goal, depending on how severe the foul is.

The team that scores the most goals wins. If the score is tied at the end of the last period of play, extra periods are played until a goal is scored and the game is ended.

When the ball goes over the sideboards, it is returned to play by the umpire. It is thrown in between the players, who line up facing the umpire side by side where the ball went out of play. After a goal has been scored, the umpire throws the ball in from the center of the field. When the ball is knocked over the back line, it is returned to play by the defending team from the point where it went out of play.

The players play positions designated as No. 1, No. 2, No. 3, and No. 4. No. 1 spearheads the attack and stays at the front of the game, playing directly against defensive No. 4. No. 1 is the scoring position. The No. 2 position demands a player who rides hard and remains constantly on the attack. No. 3 is the key member of a team and usually the strongest player, whose work is divided between offense and defense. The No. 4 player, also known as the back, is almost entirely a defensive player.

Polo players are rated on a scale from 0 to 10, according to their individual experience and abilities. This rating is called a handicap. When a game is played on a handicap basis, the difference between the total handicaps of the teams is given in goals to the team of lesser total handicap.

CYRIL R. HARRISON
Official Polo Instructor
United States Polo Association

A polo player and his mount race to the attack. Polo is a fast, often dangerous sport that requires quick reflexes on the part of both riders and horses.

Marco Polo and his father and uncle traveled for 24 years on their 15,000-mile journey through Asia. A miniature from the 1300's shows them near the Yellow River in China.

POLO, MARCO (1254–1324)

Marco Polo, the greatest of all travelers of the Middle Ages, was born in 1254 in Venice, then an independent city-state in northern Italy. His father and uncle, who were merchants, journeyed deep into Asia until they finally came to China and the court of Kublai Khan. This was the first contact in many centuries between Europe and China.

Kublai Khan, grandson of the conqueror Genghis Khan, was a man of intelligence and great energy. He was delighted with the Venetian gentlemen and eager to hear all they could tell him of far-off Christian Europe.

Marco was 15 when his father returned home. He was 17 when, in 1271, he left Venice to accompany his father and uncle on the long return journey across Asia to Cambaluc, the capital of China and the court of Kublai Khan. It was a very difficult journey and took three and a half years.

Because of his outspoken frankness and honesty, Marco at once became a favorite of the Khan, who often employed him as his special envoy to distant parts of his vast empire.

After an absence of 24 years, the Polos returned home to Venice. They brought with them a great fortune in jewels and other valuable things.

Some time after his return, Marco Polo commanded a Venetian war galley in a naval battle with Genoa. He was taken prisoner by the Genoese. While waiting to be ransomed by his family, Marco Polo dictated the story of his astonishing experiences to a fellow prisoner. This manuscript soon became the sensation of Europe. And after the invention of printing in the 1400's, the story of Marco Polo's travels appeared in many languages. Today the work is regarded as one of the greatest travel narratives in all literature.

Marco Polo was the first traveler to journey across the entire width of Asia, naming each kingdom along the route and describing the lands and their people. He described China under the rule of Kublai Khan: its great wealth; its trade, roads, long canals, and fast couriers; its government and postal system—and its paper money. But no one in Europe then would believe that paper could substitute for metal coins as money. Nor could they believe that China had black stones that burned, because coal was still unknown in Europe. And so, many of the wonders described by Marco Polo were considered lies.

In 1299, Marco Polo was released from prison. He returned to Venice, where he died in 1324. For many years afterward, he was regarded as Europe's greatest liar. Yet his work influenced the early map makers. Christopher Columbus possessed a Latin version of Marco Polo's travels, which inspired him to seek a westward sea route to Asia. It was on this voyage that Columbus reached America.

MANUEL KOMBROFF
Editor, *The Travels of Marco Polo*

POLYGONS. See GEOMETRY.

POLYHEDRA. See GEOMETRY.

POMPEII

Pompeii was an ancient city on the southwestern coast of Italy, on the Bay of Naples. It was founded in the 7th century B.C. by a tribe called the Oscans. Later other peoples—Etruscans, Samnites, and Greeks—settled there. In the 1st century B.C., Pompeii was taken over by the Romans.

On August 24 in the year A.D. 79 the volcano Vesuvius, located about 5 miles (8 kilometers) north of Pompeii, suddenly came alive. Dark clouds, hot cinders and ash, and poisonous gases poured from its cone. The terrifying eruption buried Pompeii beneath 10 to 20 feet (3 to 6 meters) of cinders and volcanic ash. At least 2,000 of the city's 20,000 inhabitants were killed, and possibly many more. The layers of ash sealed up the people's homes with the furniture and other belongings inside. The nearby towns of Herculaneum and Stabiae were also destroyed in the eruption. In a matter of two days the once flourishing seaside city, where many wealthy Romans had their country homes, disappeared.

Most ancient cities either died gradually or were robbed and destroyed by conquerors. Pompeii was struck down in one swift blow by a natural disaster. It lay buried nearly 2,000 years.

In 1748, Charles III, King of Naples and Sicily, ordered the digging out of Pompeii to begin. He hoped that this excavation would uncover treasure to enrich his archaeological collection. Since then, almost all the city has come to light.

Today, when you go to Pompeii, you see not a heap of ruins but streets with paving stones worn by chariot wheels, well-preserved public buildings, wine shops, and restaurants. Some walls are scratched with Latin phrases praising or criticizing the wine and food or advertising fights between gladiators.

Many of the rich country homes and their gardens with ornamental pools can still be seen. The gateways were often guarded by dogs. One unfortunate beast was left tied to a gatepost by a master so anxious to escape that the dog was forgotten. In another house an unfinished meal was left on a table when guests fled for their lives. Citizens had little time to remove their valuables. In the crush near the city gates many inhabitants were choked to death by the poisonous gases. The imprint of their bodies remains in the hardened volcanic ash.

Most of the art treasures, cooking utensils, household furnishings, and implements from Pompeii and Herculaneum are now on view in the Naples National Museum. All these articles have been so well preserved that archaeologists are able to piece together in a remarkable way what everyday life was like in Roman times 2,000 years ago.

LEONARD COTTRELL
Author, *Lost Worlds*

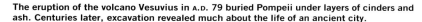

The eruption of the volcano Vesuvius in A.D. 79 buried Pompeii under layers of cinders and ash. Centuries later, excavation revealed much about the life of an ancient city.

PONCE DE LEÓN, JUAN (1460?–1521)

Juan Ponce de León discovered Florida while searching in vain for the legendary Fountain of Youth—a magic spring that would restore youth to the aged.

Ponce de León was born about 1460 to a noble family in Tierra de Campos, Spain. He was raised at the court of King Ferdinand II of Aragon and as a youth fought against the Moors in Granada. In 1493 he accompanied Christopher Columbus on his second voyage to the New World. There Ponce de León took part in the conquest of Hispaniola (now Haiti and the Dominican Republic). He established the first Spanish settlement in Puerto Rico and in 1509 became its governor.

While serving as governor, Ponce de León amassed a fortune in gold and slaves. At the same time, he learned of an island the Indians called Bimini, where the Fountain of Youth was supposedly to be found. Now in his 50's, Ponce de León was intrigued by the legend. In March, 1513, he set out to discover Bimini.

About 175 miles south of present-day St. Augustine, Ponce de León sighted a strange coastline and went ashore. Because of the many flowers he found there and because it was the Easter season, he named the new land Florida (from *Pascua florida,* Spanish for "flowery Easter"). He claimed it for Ferdinand (then king of Spain) but spent only a short time on land, most of it fighting the Indians.

Still searching for Bimini, he sailed past Miami Bay and the Florida Keys and back to Puerto Rico. He returned to Spain to report his discovery. The King commissioned him to settle the "island" of Florida (as it was then thought to be) and to continue the search for Bimini. In 1521 Ponce de León began his second voyage, with two ships and about 200 men as colonists. Soon after landing on the western coast of Florida, the expedition was attacked by Indians. Ponce de León was severely wounded and taken to Cuba, where he died a few days later. The rest of the expedition abandoned Florida.

SANFORD H. BEDERMAN
Georgia State College

PONTIAC (1720?–1769)

Pontiac was a chief of the Ottawa. There are so many legends about him that it is difficult to separate fact from fiction. Some historians say he was a wise and courageous leader; others say he was really a cruel coward whose dream of uniting many Indian tribes never came about.

Pontiac was born about 1720, probably in Ohio. His father was an Ottawa chief. During his youth he saw increasing numbers of British colonists settle in Indian territory. Pontiac feared that the Indians would be forced to give up more of the land that belonged to them. During the last French and Indian War (1754–63) the Ottawa, under Pontiac, joined the French against the British. It is possible that Pontiac led his tribesmen in the defeat of General Edward Braddock (1695–1755) near Fort Duquesne in 1755.

According to the most widely accepted stories of Pontiac's life, he began to organize his Indian confederacy early in the 1760's. The union included tribes living in the Ohio Valley and Great Lakes regions. Pontiac believed that by banding together, the Indians would become strong enough to drive out the British settlers. He sent messengers to leaders of many tribes and told them of his plans. At a council near Fort Detroit in 1763, Pontiac addressed the chiefs. He spoke of the wrongs the British had inflicted on the Indians.

Pontiac planned to capture the British forts from Pennsylvania to Lake Superior. In May, 1763, the Indians attacked a dozen different forts and captured most of them. Pontiac led the attack on Fort Detroit. But he failed to capture the settlement and laid siege to it instead. The siege lasted several months and finally ended in failure. A peace treaty was signed at Detroit on August 17, 1765.

Pontiac died in 1769. According to some reports he was killed in a quarrel during a wild celebration. Other accounts say that the British bribed an Indian to murder him.

Reviewed by DANIEL JACOBSON
Montclair State College

A Pony Express rider leaves his weary horse at a relay station and makes a swift departure on a fresh mount in *Coming and Going of the Pony Express*, by Frederic Remington.

PONY EXPRESS

The Pony Express, which carried mail between Missouri and California, is a famous chapter in the winning of the West. It operated for just 18 months—from April, 1860, to October, 1861—but it will never be forgotten.

When California became a state in 1850, about 3,200 kilometers (2,000 miles) of empty country separated it from the frontier states along the Missouri River. Stagecoaches carried passengers and mail over this great distance. It took them three weeks, traveling day and night, to make the journey. As the population grew in the 1850's, a faster mail service was needed.

In 1860, Senator William M. Gwin of California persuaded the freighting company of Russell, Majors, and Waddell to organize the Pony Express. They established a route of about 3,000 kilometers (1,900 miles) from St. Joseph, Missouri, to Sacramento, California. It was about 160 kilometers (100 miles) shorter than the stage route.

For most of the route, the Pony Express used the California Trail, which had been traveled by wagon trains since the 1840's. From St. Joseph this trail followed the Platte River over the Nebraska prairie. It passed famous posts and landmarks—Fort Kearny, Scott's Bluff, Fort Laramie, Independence Rock. It crossed the Rocky Mountains at South Pass, Wyoming. Beyond Fort Bridger the Pony Express route rounded the southern shore of the Great Salt Lake and crossed the vast desert of Utah Territory. At Carson City it climbed the Sierra Nevada and came down to Sacramento, California. From there the mail was hurried to San Francisco by steamboat on the Sacramento River.

Along the route, relay stations were established at intervals of about 24 kilometers (15 miles). Some stations were ranch houses or stagecoach depots; others were newly built for the Pony Express. Some were remote posts in hostile Indian country. Fast, wiry horses were kept at these stations. They galloped at full speed from one station to the next.

About 100 riders were hired for the express. They were young men—lean, hardy, and daring. One of the first riders was Buffalo Bill. All were expert riders who could break and train wild broncos. Riding day and night, they faced many dangers. Sandstorms and blizzards, wild animals, bandits, and hostile Indians all brought risk and adventure.

The Pony Express riders were paid $100 a month, a good salary at that time. They had to be trustworthy, loyal, and courageous. Every rider signed a pledge of good behavior.

In the first weeks of the service, each rider carried a Bible, a sheath knife, a horn, a cavalry rifle, and a pair of Colt revolvers. But the weight of these objects slowed the horses, and soon this equipment was reduced to a single revolver. The original postage charge was $5 for 14 grams (½ ounce); the fee was later reduced to $1. In his mochila a rider carried 9 kilograms (20 pounds) of mail.

The Pony Express crossed the plains and deserts at breakneck speed. Mark Twain in his book *Roughing It* gives an eyewitness account of a rider racing in from the trail. The rider "came crashing up to the station where stood two men holding a fresh, impatient steed [horse], the transfer of rider and mail-bag was made in the twinkling of an eye, and away flew the eager pair."

Each rider used five horses to cover a daily (or nightly) run of 120 kilometers (75 miles). If his replacement was not ready, he would dash on to the next relay station.

The Pony Express riders carried the mail about 3,200 kilometers in eight or nine days. This was less than half the time required by stagecoach. The Pony Express covered 400 kilometers (250 miles) a day—twice as far as a day's travel by stage.

While the express riders were racing across the West, workers were erecting poles and stringing wires from Missouri and eastward from California. When the two lines met, the East and West were linked by telegraph. On October 24, 1861, the Pony Express made its last run. Then the staccato chatter of telegraph keys replaced the clatter of horses' hooves, and the Pony Express became another frontier memory.

Reviewed by WALTER HAVIGHURST
Author, *First Book of the Oregon Trail*

POPE. See ROMAN CATHOLIC CHURCH; VATICAN CITY.

POPE, ALEXANDER (1688–1744)

The English poet Alexander Pope was born into a Roman Catholic family in London on May 21, 1688. His father was a prosperous linen merchant. About 1700 the family moved to an estate at Binfield, in Windsor Forest.

As a boy, Alexander was bright and tiny. (He had a deformed spine and grew to only 4 feet 6 inches as an adult.) He liked to display his independence and was sometimes hard to get along with. His parents hired priests to tutor him in Latin and Greek. At 15, he insisted on going to London to master French and Italian. But he worked so hard that he became ill and soon returned home.

English laws prohibited Catholics from attending a university, and Pope learned to content himself at home. He rode in the forest, continued his studies, and wrote poetry imitating his favorite authors. His own poetry was almost all in couplets (two rhyming lines containing a complete thought). Some of Pope's lines—such as "to err is human, to forgive, divine"—are often quoted.

Several days a week, Pope rode with his neighbor, Sir William Trumball, a retired diplomat who encouraged Pope in his writing. By the time Pope was 21, some of his poetry had been published, and he was becoming known.

In his twenties, Pope began to write satirical verse. In *The Rape of the Lock* (1712; expanded, 1714), he made fun of a silly quarrel between two prominent families. In other poems he mocked established writers. But he made his living by serious writing. Pope's translation of Homer's *Iliad* (1715–20) brought him great success. He considered his *Essay on Man* (1733–34) his finest work.

In 1719, Pope and his mother moved into a villa on the Thames River at Twickenham. He enjoyed working in his garden and building an underground study. Occasionally he took a boat ride up to London. Jonathan Swift visited him in 1726 and brought along his manuscript of *Gulliver's Travels*. Pope dedicated his next major work to Swift. This was *The Dunciad*, a mock-heroic poem attacking writers whom Pope considered to be dull scribblers, or dunces. He kept revising this work and brought out an expanded *New Dunciad* in 1743. Pope died on May 30, 1744.

Reviewed by DAYTON HASKIN
Boston College

POPULATION

Few things are more important to a country than to know how many people live there and whether the number is growing or declining. Information about population—the total number of people living in a country or region—is important in many ways.

How well a government serves its people depends partly on how many there are to be served and how large an area they live in. It is also important to know how many people are in each age group. Younger people will need schools, while health care and social security may be more important to older people. Business prospects, opportunities for jobs, and even crime rates are influenced by the size of the population.

Changes in population are caused by births, deaths, and the movement of people into and out of a country. The number of children born, called the fertility of a population, increases the size of the population. The number of deaths, called mortality, decreases the population. Migration—the number of people entering or leaving a country—can cause either an increase or a decrease. A natural increase in population of a country comes from a greater number of births than deaths.

The three factors that cause changes in population are talked about in terms of rates. Rates show how often an event happens, or how common it is. In the United States in 1990, for example, the number of births per 1,000 people (the birth rate) was 16.7. Scientists who study population changes and the results of these changes are called demographers. The study of population and population changes is called demography.

▶WORLD POPULATION

Human beings have lived on earth for many thousands of years, and during most of that time their numbers were relatively small. Before agriculture was developed about 10,000 years ago, the death rate was high, partly because of a limited food supply. Probably no more than 8,000,000 people were alive at any one time. But after people began to grow crops and raise animals for food, the death rate fell. And the population of the world slowly grew.

At the beginning of the Christian era (the year A.D. 1), about 250,000,000 people inhab-

POPULATION OF THE WORLD BY REGION	
Region	**Estimated Population**
Asia [1]	3,200,000,000
Europe [2]	710,000,000
Africa	700,000,000
North America	432,000,000
South America	302,000,000
Oceania, Australia, and New Zealand	27,000,000

[1] Including Russia in Asia.
[2] Including Russia in Europe and European Turkey.

ited the earth. This number increased to about 800,000,000 by 1750. In the next century industrialization and scientific knowledge about the cause of disease began to spread quickly. There was a further increase in food supplies, as well as a decrease in deaths caused by diseases. The human population began to grow at an enormous rate. Although it had taken many thousands of years for the world to reach a population of 800,000,000 (in 1750), it has taken less than 250 years to reach its present number of more than 5 billion.

Population Density. The population of the world is not spread evenly over the earth. The average number of people who live in an area is called the population density. The most densely populated continents are Asia and Europe. Cities, where people live in apartment houses or other crowded multiple-family dwellings, are more densely populated than rural areas, where most people live in single-family homes.

Age Differences. The countries of the world fall into two broad groups—those with young

THE TEN MOST POPULOUS COUNTRIES	
COUNTRY	**POPULATION**
China, People's Republic of	1,140,000,000
India	844,000,000
United States	249,632,692*
Indonesia	180,500,000
Brazil	150,500,000
Russia	148,000,000
Japan	123,500,000
Bangladesh	115,600,000
Pakistan	112,500,000
Nigeria	108,500,000

* 1990 census.

populations and those with large numbers of older people. Countries where many babies are born and most of them survive have youthful populations. In Africa, Latin America, southern Asia, and the Middle East, about two persons in five are children under 15 years of age.

Countries where the birth rate has been low for several decades have not produced many children. This is the case in Western Europe, the United States, and Japan, where only about one person in five is under the age of 15. Because there are fewer children in countries with low birth rates, the proportion of older persons is high. In a number of European nations, including Sweden, Germany, and the United Kingdom among others, more than one in seven persons is over 64 years of age.

Countries with the Largest Populations. Over 60 percent of the world's people live in just ten countries. The country with the largest population is China. More than one fifth of the world's people live in China. However, the rate of growth of the Chinese population has slowed dramatically in recent years. The Chinese government has tried to get people to marry at a later age and to have only one child per family. In spite of great opposition to this plan at first, it seems to have had significant results.

Of the other nine countries, three—the United States, Russia, and Japan—are indus-

COUNTRIES WITH HIGHEST AND LOWEST BIRTH RATES (NUMBER OF BIRTHS PER 1,000 PERSONS)			
HIGHEST		LOWEST	
Kenya	54	Denmark	10
Rwanda	53	Germany	10
Malawi	52	Italy	11
Benin	51	Sweden	11
Niger	51	Switzerland	11

trial nations with slow-growing populations. Six are developing countries with rapidly growing populations—India, Indonesia, Brazil, Bangladesh, Pakistan, and Nigeria. Of these six, three—India, Indonesia, and Brazil—have lowered their birth rates in recent years.

▶POPULATION GROWTH

Because of recent developments in medicine, many diseases from which people used to die can now be cured. This has brought a decrease in mortality rates. And babies who once might have died at birth, or shortly after, now live. As a result, the world's population has been growing rapidly. At its present rate of growth, the total population of the world will double in about 40 years.

Growth Rates. The most rapidly growing populations in the world are in Africa, which is doubling in population every 24 years. The

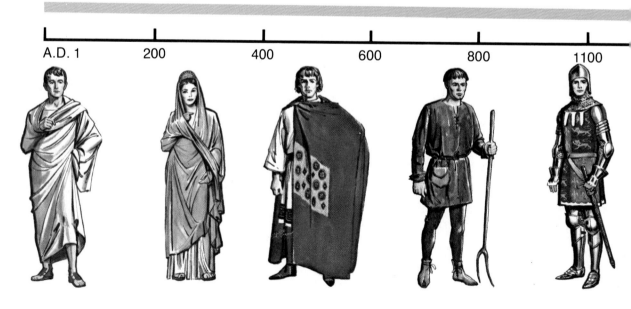

A.D. 1	200	400	600	800	1100

COUNTRIES WITH HIGHEST AND LOWEST INFANT MORTALITY RATES*

HIGHEST		LOWEST	
Afghanistan	20.5	Finland	0.6
Sierra Leone	20.0	Japan	0.6
Gambia	19.3	Sweden	0.7
Malawi	16.5	Iceland	0.7
Kampuchea	16.0	Switzerland	0.8
Guinea	15.5	Norway	0.8
Yemen (Sana)	15.4	Denmark	0.8

* Deaths of infants under one year of age per 100 live births.

continent with the slowest growth rate is Europe, where the population doubles only every 240 years.

Comparing projected figures of individual countries may be even more helpful. For example, the population of Nigeria, the most populous nation in Africa, is doubling every 22 years. At that rate, there would be about 156,000,000 Nigerians by the year 2000, and about 258,000,000 in 2020. In contrast, the present population of the United Kingdom, 56,000,000, will be about the same in the future if birth and death rates continue to equal. This would mean that by the year 2020, if population growth rates continue, Nigeria could have more than four times as many people as the United Kingdom.

The growth rate is affected by a country's mortality, or death, rate. For example, in some developing nations, about one in every five infants dies in its first year. This can be compared with about one or less in every hundred in industrialized nations. With improvements in medical care in developing nations, death rates, both in infants and adults, can be expected to drop. Therefore, if overpopulation is to be controlled, birth rates must drop even faster.

Concern About Overpopulation. The rapid population growth now taking place is sometimes called a population explosion. Many persons fear that population will grow faster than the resources—such as food, fuel, and housing—needed to support all the people. If this should happen, the first result would be lower standards of living. Then, as living standards fell below what was needed to keep the poorest people alive, the death rate would rise. If living standards were reduced to a point where dangerous diseases could not be controlled, death rates would rise among the wealthy as well as the poor.

Concern with overpopulation is not new. Almost two centuries ago, the English economist Thomas R. Malthus (1766–1834) argued that the growth of human population eventually takes away any gains made in living standards. He wrote at the beginning of the industrial age. He did not foresee the increase in material wealth that industry has produced or the safe, reliable ways to control fertility that have been developed.

6 Billion

5 Billion

4 Billion

3 Billion

2 Billion

1 Billion

1400   1600   1800   1900   2000

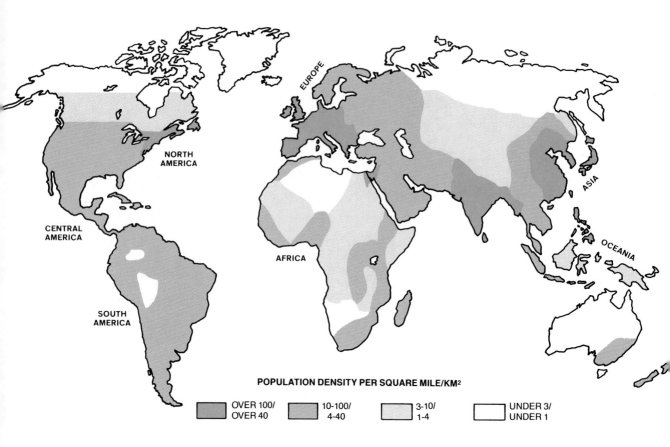

POPULATION DENSITY PER SQUARE MILE/KM²

■ OVER 100/ OVER 40	■ 10-100/ 4-40
▫ 3-10/ 1-4	□ UNDER 3/ UNDER 1

Will Population Growth Stop? Is there truth in Malthus' view of the world as a place of limited resources? This remains an important question. If Malthus was right, then the growth of human population must stop sometime. The only questions are how and when. Will population growth be stopped by low birth rates or by a return to the high death rates of the pre-industrial past? Will this happen soon or not for several decades?

Answers to such questions can be given only for specific countries. In several countries of Western Europe, the population has already stopped growing, because of balanced birth and death rates. But these countries do not have all the resources they need. They must import metallic minerals, fuels, and food from other regions of the world. In fact, very few countries have the right combinations of resources to support their present populations— to say nothing of populations two or three times larger. In less developed regions of the world the situation is even more ominous.

Future Trends. In recent years famine has struck a number of African countries south of the Sahara desert. Death rates in several African nations were higher in the 1980's than they had been previously. Nevertheless, Africa remains the continent with the most rapidly growing population. Even with major improvements in agricultural practices, by the year 2000 several African countries may be unable to support their populations. The next ten years probably will show if, because of rising mortality or falling fertility, the population growth of Africa has slowed.

ROBERT E. KENNEDY, JR.
University of Minnesota
Author, *The Irish:
Emigration, Marriage, and Fertility*

See also CENSUS.

COUNTRIES WITH HIGHEST AND LOWEST LIFE EXPECTANCIES (IN YEARS)

HIGHEST		LOWEST	
Iceland	77	Sierra Leone	34
Japan	77	Gambia	35
Netherlands	76	Afghanistan	37
Norway	76	Guinea	40
Sweden	76	Angola	42
Switzerland	76	Mali	42

PORCUPINES

Most people have never seen a real porcupine, but practically everyone knows about its long, needle-sharp quills. These quills are the porcupine's most distinguishing feature and provide this large rodent with a prickly and very effective form of self-defense.

The porcupine's short legs and heavy body make it a somewhat slow and clumsy animal. But its quills and spiny tail protect it from almost all predators. If threatened or attacked, the porcupine will turn its back and raise its back and neck quills—some of which measure up to 4 inches (10 centimeters) long.

If this threat does not deter an attack, the porcupine will swish its tail back and forth. This causes some quills, which are loosely attached to the porcupine's body, to shake out and stick to the face or body of the attacker. Each quill has a needle-sharp tip. Just below the end are tiny barbs, or hooks, that are directed backward. When a quill comes in contact with the skin of an animal, the barbs hold it in place.

Contrary to popular belief, a porcupine cannot shoot its quills. The quills just shake loose, but because they are light they may seem to fly through the air. Quills can also be lost as the porcupine walks or climbs through the woods. Like fingernails or hair, quills grow back after they are lost.

In addition to its stiff quills, the porcupine's 3-foot (1-meter) body is covered with brownish black hairs and a wooly underfur that keeps the animal warm in winter. (The porcupine does not hibernate but will seek shelter in holes or rock crevices.) It is also well equipped for climbing trees, with heavy claws on each foot. Long, orange-colored front teeth enable it to peel and eat the bark. Porcupines are especially fond of smooth-barked trees such as aspen and birch. They also eat tender buds, evergreen needles, fruits, and leaves.

The porcupine is well known for its habit of visiting cabins and lumber camps to find salt. Sweat-stained ax handles, tires that still have traces of road salt, door knobs, and old wooden chairs all attract porcupines.

Many porcupines, however, never come in contact with people. This is because they are usually nocturnal and live solitary lives in wilderness areas. The North American porcupine inhabits wooded regions from Alaska and

Long, needle-sharp quills distinguish the porcupine from all other rodents. These animals eat bark and will often spend several days in one tree.

Canada southward to the western United States and Texas. It is absent only from the southeastern United States. Other New World porcupines live in forest habitats in Mexico and Central and South America. Their Old World relatives live in Africa, southeastern Europe, and Asia.

Porcupines mate in the fall, and usually a single baby is born in May or June. A porcupine at birth weighs just over a pound (0.5 kilogram). It has a soft fur coat and half-inch (1-centimeter) quills. Six hours after birth it is able to waddle about and by the second day can already climb a tree. It continues to grow for about three years, up to a weight of about 30 pounds (14 kilograms).

The only predators that have learned to kill and eat porcupines are the mountain lion and the fisher, a weasel-like animal now absent from most of the porcupine's range. These animals flip the porcupine on its back to attack its soft belly. All other predators, however, know that a porcupine's sharp quills mean they must look elsewhere for a meal.

THOMAS D. FEGELY
Author, *Focus on Nature*

PORPOISES. See DOLPHINS AND PORPOISES.
PORTLAND (Maine). See MAINE (Cities).

PORTLAND (OREGON)

The rugged beauty of northern Oregon provides a splendid setting for Portland, the state's largest city. Rich farmlands and forests surround the metropolitan area. The snow-capped peak of Mount Hood rises from the Cascade Range about 50 miles (80 kilometers) east of Portland. The city itself lies on the banks of the Willamette River, near its junction with the Columbia River.

Portland is considered a pleasant and comfortable place in which to live. The climate is moderate. Some 437,000 people live in the city, which covers about 105 square miles (272 square kilometers). The metropolitan area has a population of about 1.24 million, which represents well over one-third of Oregon's total population.

The city is the economic center of Oregon and southern Washington. Oceangoing ships travel along the Willamette and Columbia rivers, making Portland a major Pacific port. Portland's industries run on hydroelectric power provided by the Bonneville Dam on the Columbia River. The most important part of

The Downtown Program helped Portland rebuild while solving pollution and traffic problems as well. A clean-up of the Willamette River was also successful.

the city's economy is manufacturing. Metal-working, food processing, and the manufacture of chemicals, paper, lumber, furniture, and other timber products are especially important. The 1980's brought the expansion of various high-technology industries.

Institutions of higher education include Portland State University, the Oregon Health Sciences University, Lewis and Clark College, the University of Portland, and Reed College.

Recreational as well as cultural opportunities abound in and near Portland. The Pacific Ocean is a one-hour drive to the west, and the mountains are a one-hour drive to the east. The city has many parks, including Forest Park, the nation's largest wilderness totally within a city's limits. Washington Park includes the Portland Zoological Gardens, the Oregon Museum of Science and Industry, the Japanese Gardens, the Western Forestry Center, and the International Rose Test Gardens. The city's moderate, moist climate is particularly suitable for growing roses, and Portland is nicknamed the City of Roses. A week-long Rose Festival in June is a popular event. Performing arts attractions include the Oregon Symphony Orchestra and the Portland Opera Association. The Memorial Coliseum is the home of the Portland Trail Blazers of the National Basketball Association.

The Portland area was settled by Indian peoples long before white settlers arrived. In 1842 an Englishman built a cabin where South Portland now stands. Three years later two settlers, one from Boston and one from Portland, Maine, tossed a coin to see who should name the town. The Portland man won. By 1850, Portland had a sawmill, stores, churches, a school, and about 800 citizens.

Portland was a trading town from the beginning. Portlanders soon did a brisk business selling salmon. Then lumbering became the major industry. Later the city became a leading Pacific Coast livestock market and wheat shipping port. During World War II, vast shipbuilding yards brought boom times.

During the 1970's and 1980's, a major redevelopment project helped to preserve and restore Portland's downtown area. Thanks to the Downtown Program, Portland today is a vital and modern city.

VANESSA E. BLAKE
Portland Chamber of Commerce

PORTSMOUTH. See NEW HAMPSHIRE (Cities).

PORTUGAL

Portugal is the westernmost country on the European continent. It is situated on the Iberian Peninsula, at the southwestern edge of Europe, directly facing the Atlantic Ocean. From this location, Portuguese navigators, in the 1400's and 1500's, set sail to map the coasts of Africa, Asia, and South America and to open new trade routes with these continents. The discoveries of these bold explorers helped make Portugal the center of a vast and wealthy empire, many times greater than the country itself. Large areas of its former empire remained under Portuguese rule until recent times.

▶ THE PEOPLE

Ethnicity, Language, and Religion. The Portuguese are a mixture of the many different peoples who have occupied the Iberian Peninsula. These included the ancient Iberians, Celts, Phoenicians, Greeks, Carthaginians, Romans, Germanic tribes, and Moors from North Africa. In appearance, most Portuguese today are of medium height with dark hair and eyes, although some, particularly in the north, have the light hair and blue eyes inherited from their Germanic ancestors.

Portuguese belongs to the Romance group of languages, as do Spanish, Italian, and French. It is closely related to the Galician dialect of northern Spain. In religion, the people are mostly Roman Catholics.

Way of Life. Some aspects of Portuguese life vary from region to region, but there are many similarities throughout the country. Although Portugal has a number of cities of considerable size, the majority of the people live in rural areas or in small towns and villages, where life usually follows familiar patterns. Most rural Portuguese are farmers. Others make their living from the sea as fishermen. The average income is relatively small.

The high points of the year are the various religious festivals and pilgrimages that are celebrated in many of the towns and villages. Soccer is the favorite sport. In the larger towns, bullfights are also a major attraction,

With its long Atlantic Ocean coastline, Portugal historically has been a nation of seafarers, who once ruled a vast empire. These fishing boats lie beached at the town of Albufeira.

although in Portugal, unlike Spain, the bull is not killed. Dancing and folksinging are popular pastimes, and the sad, haunting melody of the fado, a traditional type of Portuguese song, often can be heard in cafés.

Education. Nine years of primary education is required by law for all children between the ages of 6 and 15. Secondary

Portugal

REPUBLIC OF PORTUGAL (República Portuguesa) is the official name of the country.

LOCATION: Iberian Peninsula in southwestern Europe.

AREA: 35,553 sq mi (92,082 km²).

POPULATION: 10,300,000 (estimate).

CAPITAL AND LARGEST CITY: Lisbon.

MAJOR LANGUAGE: Portuguese (official).

MAJOR RELIGIOUS GROUP: Roman Catholic.

GOVERNMENT: Republic. **Head of state**—president. **Head of government**—prime minister. **Legislature**—Assembly of the Republic.

CHIEF PRODUCTS: Agricultural—wheat, corn, rice, potatoes, tomatoes, oranges, olives, grapes. **Manufactured**—textiles, clothing, shoes, glass and ceramics, wine, forestry products (cork, resin, turpentine, paper, wood pulp), processed fish (particularly sardines) and other foods, electrical appliances. **Mineral**—tungsten ore, copper, coal, iron, tin.

MONETARY UNIT: Escudo (1 escudo = 100 centavos).

The Tagus River divides Portugal into two quite different halves. To the north the country is mountainous. The major mountain range is the Serra da Estrela, whose highest peak, Malhão da Estrela, reaches 6,532 feet (1,991 meters). South of the river the land consists chiefly of rolling plains and plateaus. The majority of the people live in the region north of the Tagus, with the coastal areas and the valley of the Douro River the most densely populated areas.

Climate. Northern Portugal has a generally cooler climate than the south, with heavier rainfall. About 60 inches (1,500 millimeters) of rain falls in the northern mountains each year, compared to some 20 inches (500 millimeters) in the south. Temperatures are mild over most of Portugal during the winter, except in the mountains of the northern interior, where it is cold and snowy. Summers are warm in the northern valleys and coastal districts and hot in the dry plains of the south.

Natural Resources. Portugal has limited natural resources. Its soils are not especially fertile, except in the larger river valleys, and much of the land is suitable only for grazing

schooling, which is not compulsory, lasts for three years. In the final year, students take courses that will prepare them for either a university or for vocational training. Portugal's oldest university, the University of Coimbra, was founded in 1290.

▶ **THE LAND**

Characteristics. Portugal shares the Iberian Peninsula with its much larger neighbor, Spain. Several large rivers rise on the Spanish plateau and wind their way westward through Portugal to the sea. The largest and most important of these are the Douro, in the north, and the Tagus, which runs diagonally across the center of the country.

Northern Portugal has a hilly and often mountainous landscape, with high plateaus cut by deep valleys. Much of the land in the north is planted with vineyards.

livestock. Forests cover nearly one-third of the land. Of the varieties of trees found, the cork oak is the most valuable, economically. Tungsten ore, copper, tin, and coal are the most important minerals. The coastal waters are rich in a variety of fish, and the swift rivers of the north are an important source of hydroelectric power.

▶ MAJOR CITIES

Lisbon is Portugal's capital, largest city, chief port, and commercial center. The city is built on a series of hills rising from the Tagus River, near where it flows into the Atlantic Ocean. See the separate article on Lisbon in Volume L.

Oporto (or Porto) is Portugal's second largest city. Like Lisbon a city of hills, it is located in the northern part of the country, on the Douro River. It occupies the site of an ancient seaport known as Portus Cale, from which Portugal takes its name. Its most famed export is port wine, but it also produces textiles and clothing.

The only other Portuguese cities of any great size are Braga, Coimbra, and Setúbal. Braga, the most northerly of the major cities, is a historic religious center. Coimbra is famed for its an-

cient university, while Setúbal, situated to the south of Lisbon, is a fishing port as well as a shipbuilding center.

▶ MADEIRA, THE AZORES, AND MACAO

Madeira and the Azores are autonomous regions of Portugal, each with its own elected legislature. The Madeira Islands cover a land area of about 305 square miles (790 square kilometers), located in the Atlantic Ocean off the northwestern coast of Africa. Madeira is a popular resort noted for its lush semitropical plant life and mild climate. Its best-known product is Madeira wine.

The Azores are a chain of nine small islands in the Atlantic Ocean, lying about 1,000 miles (1,600 kilometers) west of Lisbon and covering an area of about 893 square miles (2,314 square kilometers). For centuries the islands have served as stopping places for ships and planes crossing the Atlantic. Farming and fishing are the most important economic activities.

Fishing and wine making are traditional Portuguese industries. The man at left carries grapes for the country's famed port wine. The woman above processes sardines, one of its chief exports.

Macao (or Macau) is an overseas territory of Portugal and the remnant of its once-vast empire. Situated on the South China coast, it occupies less than 7 1/2 square miles (about 19 square kilometers) and includes a mainland area and two small islands. Tourism and textile manufacturing are the main industries. Macao's government is headed by a governor appointed by the president of Portugal with the approval of the territory's legislature. Macao is due to be returned to China in 1999.

▶ THE ECONOMY

Agriculture and fishing were long the mainstay of the Portuguese economy. In recent years, however, the emphasis has been on industrial development. Agriculture, fishing, and forestry now employ less than 12 percent of the workforce; about 33 percent is engaged in manufacturing, mining, and construction; and the remainder in service industries and other occupations. Tourism has traditionally been an important source of income.

Agriculture. In spite of its declining percentage of the labor force, agriculture remains a vital economic activity. Wheat is grown extensively on large estates in the drier southern plains, while rice thrives in the moist northern lowlands. Grapes, corn, olives, potatoes, and tomatoes are other chief crops. The main forms of livestock are cattle, grazed mainly in the north, and sheep, pigs, and goats, raised chiefly in the south.

Fishing and Forestry. Fishing remains an important industry. Portugal's offshore waters are a source of sardines, one of its major exports. Larger fishing vessels journey to the Grand Banks off Newfoundland to catch cod and other fish. Portugal's forests produce about half of the world's supply of cork. Other forestry products include resin and turpentine, which are also important exports, and paper, wood pulp, and timber.

Manufacturing and Trade. Textiles and clothing are the chief manufactured products,

Prince Henry the Navigator (1394–1460) encouraged the explorations that led to Portugal's great age of discovery.

with clothing accounting for about 20 percent of Portugal's export earnings. Other manufactured goods include shoes, electrical appliances, ceramics and glass, wood pulp, cork, and other forestry products. Lisbon and Porto are the major manufacturing cities. Portugal's trade is primarily with other members of the European Union. Its chief imports are petroleum, iron and steel, motor vehicles, sugar, and cotton.

▶ GOVERNMENT

Portugal is a republic governed under a constitution adopted in 1976 and revised in 1982 and 1989. The head of state is the president, elected for five years, who appoints a prime minister to lead the government. The legislature is the Assembly of the Republic, whose members are elected for four years. There is, in addition, an advisory body, the Council of State, which is headed by the president. The judiciary consists of the Supreme Court and various other courts.

▶ HISTORY

Early History. The earliest inhabitants of what is now Portugal (and Spain) were the Iberians. Celtic peoples settled in the north around 1000 B.C., while Phoenicians, and later Greeks and Carthaginians, founded cities and colonies in the south. The Romans conquered the region in the 1st century A.D., after a long and stubborn resistance by a warlike people they called the *Lusitani*. With the collapse of the Roman Empire in the A.D. 400's, Visigoths and Suevi, two Germanic tribes, fought for control of the region. In the 700's, the Muslim Moors invaded the peninsula, conquering most of Spain and more than half of Portugal and adding a new element to the population.

The first independent Portuguese state came into being in 1143, when Afonso Henriques took the title of king as Afonso I. During the 1200's, his successors completed the reconquest of Portugal from the Moors.

The Age of Discovery. In 1385, John I founded the royal house of Avis, which ruled

Portugal until 1580. His son Prince Henry, known as Henry the Navigator, encouraged the explorations that led to the great Portuguese age of discovery of the 1400's and 1500's. There were several famous Portuguese explorer-navigators of the period.

Bartholomeu Dias discovered the Cape of Good Hope at the southern tip of Africa, opening up a sea route to Asia. Vasco da Gama, following Dias, reached India and brought back evidence of its great wealth. Pedro Cabral discovered Brazil, claiming it for Portugal. Ferdinand Magellan's expedition, sponsored by the king of Spain, was the first to sail around the earth, although he did not live to complete the voyage. See the article on Vasco da Gama in Volume G and the one on Ferdinand Magellan in Volume M. Also see EXPLORATION AND DISCOVERY in Volume E.

By the mid-1500's, Portuguese possessions stretched halfway around the world. But it was trade more than colonization that brought wealth to Portugal.

Spanish Rule and Loss of Brazil. In 1580, Portugal was annexed by Spain. The Portuguese successfully revolted against Spanish rule in 1640, when John IV, of the house of Bragança (Braganza), the last line of Portuguese kings, came to the throne. A period of renewed prosperity followed, but good fortune did not smile on Portugal for long.

In 1755 an earthquake almost destroyed Lisbon. During the Napoleonic Wars in the early 1800's, the country was a battleground for both British and French armies. The royal family fled to Brazil, where Rio de Janeiro temporarily became the capital of the Portuguese empire. In 1821, King John VI returned to Portugal, but his son Dom Pedro I remained in Brazil as its ruler. In 1822 he declared Brazil's independence.

The Portuguese Republic. During the 1800's, Portugal was torn by civil wars. In 1910 the last king, Manuel II, was overthrown and Portugal became a republic. The freely elected government did not last long, however. General António Óscar de Fragoso Carmona seized power in a military revolt in 1926. He was elected president in 1928 and held the office until his death in 1951. António de Oliveira Salazar, the minister of finance under Carmona, became prime minister in 1932. Over the years, Salazar's

Paraders in Lisbon commemorate the revolution of April 25, 1974, which overthrew the old authoritarian regime and brought democratic government to Portugal.

powers increased greatly, and he ruled Portugal virtually as a dictator until 1968.

Colonial Wars in Africa. Portugal held on to its African territories—Portuguese Guinea (now Guinea-Bissau), Sao Tome and Principe, Cape Verde, Angola, and Mozambique—longer than other colonial powers. The long and costly wars that Portugal fought to keep them divided the nation and resulted in a military coup, led by General António de Spínola, in 1974. The country's new leaders recognized the right of the territories to independence and promised to restore democratic government to Portugal.

Recent History. Although conflicts between right and left about what kind of government Portugal would have threatened to lead to civil war, a stable, democratic government finally emerged. One of the country's leading political figures of this period was Mário Soares, who served as both prime minister and president, holding office as president until 1996, when he was succeeded by Jorge Sampaio. Portugal officially became a member of the European Community (now the European Union) in 1986.

VINCENT MALMSTROM
Dartmouth College

All United States mail was sorted by hand until 1970 (*left*). Each person could sort about 850 letters per hour. A Letter Sorting Machine (LSM) (*right*) came into use in 1970, allowing each postal worker to sort about 1,250 letters per hour. Then, in 1982, postal workers began using Optical Character Reader (OCR) machines (*far right*). These speedy machines allowed one postal worker to sort as many as 10,000 letters in an hour.

POSTAL SERVICE

The mailbox can be a doorway to the world. Through it you can reach into nearly every country on earth. Each postage stamp becomes a gaily colored personal messenger.

The postal service is the government agency that handles the mail. The job of the postal service is to deliver letters and packages to people and businesses all over the world. Its goal is to see that your mail gets to its destination as quickly as possible. People rely on the postal service to deliver important letters and even valuables, on time and to the right person.

Much of the world's business depends on the postal service. That is why most countries co-operate closely on postal matters. The mail always "goes through." A flood in South America or an earthquake in Asia may cause a delay, but new routes are quickly found and mail is delivered. A letter mailed from Alaska, in North America, may travel to Kenya, in Africa, by boat, plane, train, truck, and even horseback.

In a country as large as the United States, the operation of the postal service is big business. The United States Postal Service is responsible for delivering mail, printing stamps, and handling various related duties. There are hundreds of thousands of postal workers, and the budget runs into billions of dollars a year. In many countries the post office also operates the telephone and telegraph systems.

▶ HOW THE MAIL TRAVELS

Basically, mail is handled in the same way in almost every country. A stamped letter is mailed at the post office or dropped in a mailbox. The mail is collected from mailboxes on a regular schedule. All letters, postcards, and small parcels are taken to a central post office, where many people work. The sacks of mail are emptied onto a long conveyor belt. As the belt moves along, mail handlers separate large envelopes, books, magazines, and parcels from letters and postcards. This is called culling.

The large pieces are postmarked and canceled by hand. Letters and postcards are turned in the same direction and placed in trays by hand or by machines. The machines also cancel the mail by printing lines and sometimes a slogan over the stamp. They postmark the envelopes by stamping the name of the city where the letter was mailed, the time of day (A.M. or P.M.), and the date. In small post offices, letters are postmarked by hand.

After the mail is postmarked, it is separated according to sections of the country. Modern post offices have machines, called Optical Character Readers (OCR's) that separate letters according to their destinations. An OCR reads the typed address, then translates the address into a special code, which is sprayed onto the envelope with special ink. The OCR then reads the code and sends the letter into a bin, depending on its destination. At the des-

tination post office, a machine reads the coded address and sorts the letter into another bin. The mail is then sent, usually by truck, to a local post office. There it is sorted once again, this time for individual mail routes. All the mail for one route is given to the mail carrier, who delivers it to each mailbox.

Some countries have unique methods of postal delivery. Mail in London, England, speeds under the city in an automatic subway railroad running across the center of the city. The trains run from a railway station to a post office, with stops along the way at several other post offices. The subway, which opened in 1923, is completely automated.

Some cities in Europe use pneumatic-tube systems to send mail under the streets. Compressed air sucks the mail through a tube system to carry it quickly to its destination. In Sweden the postal service uses skis in addition to the usual methods of delivering mail. Until 1963 dogsled routes were used in Alaska. But the huskies have been replaced by the airplane.

▶HISTORY OF MAIL SERVICE

The world's first known mail carriers hauled the inscribed clay tablets of Babylon more than 4,000 years ago. The young men were said to be fleet of foot and staunch of courage. They must have been strong of back, too. Their burden was much heavier than the maximum of 35 pounds (16 kilograms) that can be carried today by a United States letter carrier.

In time the clay tablets were replaced by tablets of bronze. And the messenger on foot began to give way to the courier on horseback. In Persia in the 6th century B.C., mail was carried by riders. Relay posts, where a courier either mounted a fresh horse or turned over the message to another courier, were used by the Chinese more than 2,000 years ago.

Postal services were an important means of communication during the time of Augustus, emperor of Rome, and of Charlemagne, emperor of the Roman Empire. When the Spanish explorers arrived in the Western Hemisphere, they found that postal systems were in use among the Aztecs of Mexico and the Incas of Peru.

The word "post" comes from the French word *poste*, a station where couriers would stop. In France the postal service was started in the 1400's by Louis XI. But it was for the use of high court officials only. To delay a courier's journey was to invite extreme punishment, even death. The first public French postal service began in 1506. The route expanded to include Flanders, Vienna, Castile, Paris, and Rome. But its cost was so high that it was used only by the rich.

England's first successful postal system, for the use of the royal family, was started in 1516. During the reign of Queen Elizabeth I (1558–1603), the warning phrase "Haste, Post, Haste, For Thy Lyfe, For Thy Lyfe, Haste" was often written on letters to remind postboys of their duty. The postboys carried the mail for about 200 years. They were required to blow the post horn frequently and to ride, at 7 miles (11 kilometers) per hour in the summer. Winter speed was 5 miles (8 kilometers) an hour.

In 1639 the General Court of Massachusetts authorized that all mail arriving from abroad be delivered to Richard Fairbanks of Boston, who, for a penny, forwarded each letter to its destination. In 1672 a monthly post was begun between Boston and New York. Philadelphia's first post office was established in 1683. A postal route extending from Maine to Georgia was established over the routes that became the main highways of the eastern seaboard.

In 1692 the British Crown put Thomas Neale in charge of postal service in the American colonies. Neale appointed Andrew Hamilton, the governor of New Jersey, to organize and administer a colonial postal system. In 1737, Benjamin Franklin was appointed postmaster at Philadelphia. Franklin became joint deputy postmaster general for the northern British colonies in 1753. He served until 1774, when he was fired for being sympathetic to the cause of the colonists. Franklin was appointed head of the American postal system by the Continental Congress on July 26, 1775, at a salary of $1,000 a year. He served until November 7, 1776. The establishment of a dependable postal service in the United States was largely the work of Franklin.

After the U.S. Constitution was officially approved and the present form of government took shape, Samuel Osgood of Massachusetts was appointed postmaster general under President George Washington. The postal service was then a part of the Treasury Department. It remained so until 1829, when the postmaster general became a member of the president's cabinet. In 1872 a separate Post Office Department was established.

The postal service was an early user of the railroads (in the 1830's). Its support was partly responsible for the rapid growth of railway transportation in the United States.

The discovery of gold in California in 1849 hastened the rush westward, and the mails followed close behind. Mail from the east at first reached the west by ship. It was sent by steamer from South Carolina to Panama, where it was carried to the Pacific. The mail was then shipped to the Columbia River in the northwestern United States. In 1858 the first transcontinental overland mail was sent by stagecoach from St. Louis to San Francisco. The exciting and glamorous Pony Express began in 1860. You will find a separate article on the Pony Express in this volume.

Great dogsled teams traveled throughout northern Alaska to deliver mail in the late 1800's and early 1900's. The sleds could carry 700 pounds (318 kilograms) of mail. Sometimes two sleds were coupled together, and as many as 24 dogs were used. A typical dogsled route, over the bleak and dangerous trail between Kotzebue and Barrow, was 650 miles (1,046 kilometers) long.

Mail was carried by plane experimentally as early as 1911. Scheduled airmail service began in 1918. The first airmail pilots were postal employees. Among them was Charles A. Lindbergh, the "lone eagle." By demonstrating that airplanes could carry a payload, the Post Office Department played a vital role in the development of commercial aviation.

▶**UNITED STATES POSTAL SERVICE**

In 1970 the Postal Reorganization Act was adopted. It provided that within one year the Post Office would be converted into the U.S. Postal Service, an independent establishment within the executive branch of government. On July 1, 1971, the postmaster general left the president's cabinet.

The Postal Service is run by an eleven-member board of governors. Nine of the members are appointed by the president, with the approval of the Senate. These nine select a postmaster general, and this group of ten then chooses a deputy postmaster general. Postal rates are suggested by a Postal Rate Commission. The commission has five members, appointed by the president with the Senate's approval.

On an average day, more than 480,000,000 pieces of mail move across the country—the equivalent of two letters a day for every man, woman, and child in the country. The United States Postal Service handles more mail than any other postal department in the world—more than 138,000,000,000 (billion) pieces a year. This includes more than 900,000,000 pieces of foreign mail, arriving from all over the world and written in many languages.

There are about 30,000 post offices, one in almost every city and small town in the nation, and about 9,500 stations, branch post offices, and other installations. Because of this, the Postal Service comes into close contact each day with more people than any other branch of the federal government.

The Postal Service owns and leases thousands of cars and trucks. Among these are specially designed vehicles that have the steering wheel on the right side, so that mail carriers do not have to get out to place mail in roadside mailboxes.

The department also uses thousands of vehicles for ''star'' routes, or highway contract routes. Star carriers are not Postal Service employees but are under contract to handle transportation and delivery in many areas. Usually star routes link a large post office to a post office in a rural section not served by airplanes, trains, or trucks. But many star routes serve cities. The longest one runs from Seattle, Washington, to Dallas, Texas—a distance of about 2,522 miles (4,058 kilometers).

Many mail carriers travel on foot, carrying the mail in pouches or wheeling it in carts. They separate their mail into two or more pouches when the load for the full route is too heavy to carry all at once. When the mail from the first pouch is delivered, the carrier picks up the next pouch from one of the storage bins located on many street corners. These boxes are marked ''Not for Deposit of Mail.''

U.S. mail carriers wear bluish gray uniforms with the emblem of the Postal Service —a blue eagle poised in flight—on the sleeve. In other countries, too, letter carriers wear distinctive uniforms to make them easily recognizable.

Post Office Services

The U.S. Postal Service offers many different services. A description of some of them follows.

Free delivery of mail to homes and places of business is available to nearly every community of 2,500 or more people. In rural areas, service is provided by **Rural Free Delivery.** Mail is usually delivered once a day, six days a week. In some business districts, commercial firms receive two deliveries a day.

There are four classes of mail, with different postage rates. **First-class mail** consists of letters, postcards, and similar items. **Second-class mail** is made up of magazines and newspapers. **Third-class mail** consists mostly of

The U.S. Postal Service, with more than 650,000 employees, is one of the world's largest organizations. Its seal is an eagle poised for flight.

advertisements and catalogs. Books and other parcels are sent by **fourth-class mail.** Bulk rates are available for large commercial mailings.

Parcel post provides for the mailing of packages. Fees depend on size, weight, distance sent, and form of transportation. **Special handling** is available for an additional fee, to provide special care and speedier service. **Insurance** up to $200 can be obtained for parcel post.

Dead mail is mail that cannot be delivered or returned to its sender. This may happen if it is addressed incorrectly and does not have a return address. Such mail goes to the deadmail, or dead-letter, office. The mail is opened to try to determine the sender or addressee. If this is unsuccessful, the mail is destroyed, and any valuables are sold.

Money orders are like bank checks and are a safe way to send money by mail. They can be bought at post offices and cashed at post offices or banks.

Stamps are sold in various denominations (values) for postal use and for collecting. Commemorative stamps are issued throughout the year. They usually honor important individuals or events and are often highly prized by collectors. Postal cards, stamped envelopes, and stamp collecting kits and guides are also sold.

Metered postage is often used by businesses. Mail is stamped by a machine. A specific amount of postage is purchased from the post office, which sets the machine for that amount.

Registered mail offers extra safety for valuable mail at an additional fee. The post office insures such mail and keeps a careful record of it. The addressee must sign a receipt for it. **Certified mail** is similar but less expensive, and does not provide insurance.

HOW A LETTER TRAVELS

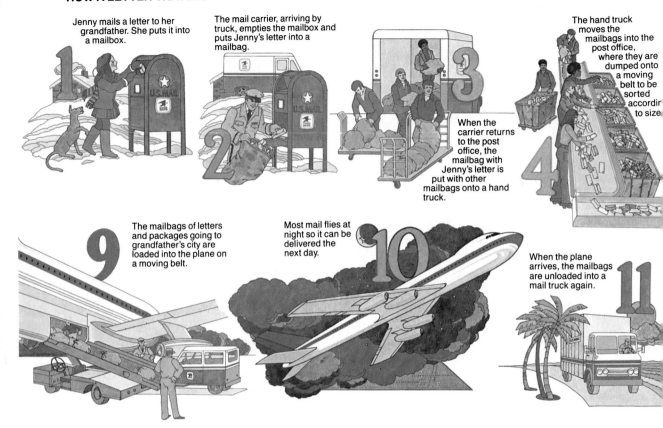

Jenny mails a letter to her grandfather. She puts it into a mailbox.

The mail carrier, arriving by truck, empties the mailbox and puts Jenny's letter into a mailbag.

When the carrier returns to the post office, the mailbag with Jenny's letter is put with other mailbags onto a hand truck.

The hand truck moves the mailbags into the post office, where they are dumped onto a moving belt to be sorted according to size.

The mailbags of letters and packages going to grandfather's city are loaded into the plane on a moving belt.

Most mail flies at night so it can be delivered the next day.

When the plane arrives, the mailbags are unloaded into a mail truck again.

Special Delivery provides for delivery on Sundays, holidays, and after post office hours. **Express mail** service guarantees quick delivery in most metropolitan areas. There are several kinds of express service—next day delivery, same day delivery to airports, custom-designed service for frequent users, and international service.

Collect on Delivery (C.O.D.) allows a person to pay for something when it is delivered rather than in advance. The post office collects the money (plus postage) from the recipient and transmits it to the sender.

Post office boxes are locked mailboxes inside the post office. They are rented by people who find them more convenient or more private than regular service.

General Delivery is a service for people without permanent addresses. Mail sent to a post office care of General Delivery is picked up by the addressee.

A **Mailgram,** a combination letter-telegram, can be sent by wire and delivered by a letter carrier. Mailgrams were first transmitted by satellite in 1974.

Postal inspectors are the Postal Service's detectives. They police the postal system and investigate theft of mail and postal equipment. They track down people who have used the mails to send bombs, poisons, or extortion letters or who have forged money orders. They guard against mail fraud, the mailing of obscene literature, and the use of the mails to preach the overthrow of the government by force.

Other duties of the U.S. Postal Service include the following: sale of U.S. savings bonds in places where banking facilities are not available; assisting the Bureau of the Census in the decennial census; helping to obtain passports for individuals in places without State Department facilities; sale of migratory bird hunting stamps; distribution of federal income tax forms; and Selective Service registration.

The Postal Service co-operates with other federal agencies in obtaining statistical information. Rural letter carriers survey wildfowl populations, report forest fires, and distribute livestock and crop acreage survey cards. The

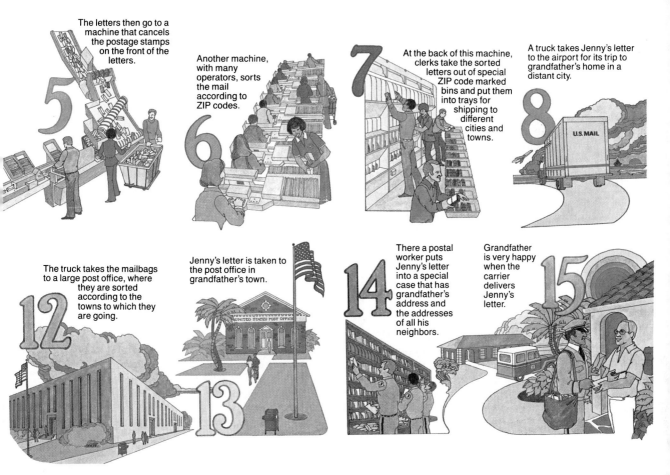

The letters then go to a machine that cancels the postage stamps on the front of the letters.

Another machine, with many operators, sorts the mail according to ZIP codes.

At the back of this machine, clerks take the sorted letters out of special ZIP code marked bins and put them into trays for shipping to different cities and towns.

A truck takes Jenny's letter to the airport for its trip to grandfather's home in a distant city.

The truck takes the mailbags to a large post office, where they are sorted according to the towns to which they are going.

Jenny's letter is taken to the post office in grandfather's town.

There a postal worker puts Jenny's letter into a special case that has grandfather's address and the addresses of all his neighbors.

Grandfather is very happy when the carrier delivers Jenny's letter.

department also locates relatives of deceased personnel for the armed forces.

ZIP Codes and Abbreviations

A familiar figure in the United States is the cartoon character Mr. ZIP. He is the symbol of a modern method of moving the mail called Zoning Improvement Plan (ZIP). ZIP codes are five-number codes that appear at the end of addresses. They originated from the postal-zone system introduced in the 1940's. For about 20 years the areas serviced by branch post offices in major cities had zone numbers. These numbers helped speed mail sorting.

ZIP codes go a step further in helping to direct the mail. The five-digit ZIP code was first introduced in 1963. The first three digits of this code represent a delivery area of the country; the last two a post office within this delivery area.

POSTAL SERVICE ABBREVIATIONS FOR STATES AND OTHER AREAS

AL	Alabama	HI	Hawaii	MO	Missouri	PR	Puerto Rico
AK	Alaska	ID	Idaho	MT	Montana	RI	Rhode Island
AZ	Arizona	IL	Illinois	NE	Nebraska	SC	South Carolina
AR	Arkansas	IN	Indiana	NV	Nevada	SD	South Dakota
CA	California	IA	Iowa	NH	New Hampshire	TN	Tennessee
CZ	Canal Zone	KS	Kansas	NJ	New Jersey	TX	Texas
CO	Colorado	KY	Kentucky	NM	New Mexico	UT	Utah
CT	Connecticut	LA	Louisiana	NY	New York	VT	Vermont
DE	Delaware	ME	Maine	NC	North Carolina	VA	Virginia
DC	District of	MD	Maryland	ND	North Dakota	VI	Virgin Islands
	Columbia	MA	Massachusetts	OH	Ohio	WA	Washington
FL	Florida	MI	Michigan	OK	Oklahoma	WV	West Virginia
GA	Georgia	MN	Minnesota	OR	Oregon	WI	Wisconsin
GU	Guam	MS	Mississippi	PA	Pennsylvania	WY	Wyoming

In 1983 the Postal Service expanded the ZIP code to nine digits. The new code is called a ZIP + 4 code. The four new numbers help to make automated machine-sorting of first-class mail easier. The first two new digits indicate a large delivery unit, such as a city block or group of blocks. The remaining two new digits indicate a small delivery unit, such as a large building or group of post office boxes.

In addressing mail many companies use mechanized systems. These systems allow only a limited amount of space for each line of an address. The Postal Service therefore devised special two-letter abbreviations for the states and some other areas. By using these abbreviations, mechanized systems can show city, state, and ZIP code all on one line. The general public also uses these abbreviations, which are listed in the box on the previous page.

A quotation from the ancient Greek writer Herodotus is carved on the General Post Office building in New York City: "Neither snow nor rain nor heat nor gloom of night stays these couriers from the swift completion of their appointed rounds." This is not the official motto of the U.S. Postal Service. But it does seem to sum up the round-the-clock work of many post offices around the world.

UNITED STATES POSTAL SERVICE

POSTERS

Posters are signs displayed in public places to inform or instruct people about events or products or about services available. Billboards, safety campaign signs, advertisements on buses—all are posters. To be effective, all good posters must deliver clearly understandable messages that can be grasped at a glance.

An effective poster, such as this one urging people to use libraries, combines a short, written message with the use of attractive graphics, or artwork.

The history of posters is unclear. Leaflets, handbills, and posted notices informed and persuaded people whenever and wherever there was written language. From these the poster gradually developed. Posters as we know them were probably first used by theater companies to advertise their plays.

Modern posters—with the fewest possible words and greatest visual effect—came into widespread use late in the 19th century. The Industrial Revolution brought about an age in which competing companies wanted to advertise consumer products. These companies were able to make wide use of the poster because of the invention of color lithography, a method of printing. The French artist Henri de Toulouse-Lautrec (1864–1901), in his beautiful posters for Paris cafés, demonstrated how effective printed posters could be.

Most commercial posters are printed in great quantity. Schools and clubs, however, display handmade posters to advertise plays, athletic events, or dances. Handmade posters are much more economical than printed ones, and they can be just as effective.

To make a poster, first decide on your text and how to match it with an effective and expressive picture. The colors and lettering should fit the purpose. Whatever design you use, remember that good posters must make people stop and look.

Reviewed by RAFAEL FERNANDEZ
Sterling and Francine Clark Art Institute

POSTURE.   See PHYSICAL EDUCATION.

POTATOES

Fried potatoes, whipped potatoes, baked potatoes—potatoes in their many forms are such a common food that they are taken for granted. Yet the white, or Irish, potato is the most important vegetable grown. It is a basic food for millions of people. Potatoes are grown in at least 80 countries.

▶THE USES OF POTATOES

In European countries potatoes are used not only for food but also for livestock feed. Large quantities are manufactured into starch, flour, alcohol, and distilled liquors.

In the United States most of the potato crop is used for food. Only the extra potatoes and those too poor to use for food are turned into manufactured products. In Canada the crop is used mostly for food and for seed potatoes that are exported. Large quantities are also manufactured into starch, while still other potatoes are used for food for livestock.

Most potatoes used as food are sold fresh. But many potatoes are treated in some way before they are eaten. At least 53 different food products are made from potatoes. These include potato chips, frozen french fried potatoes, and dehydrated, pre-peeled, and canned potatoes.

Food Value. The potato has excellent food value. The main value of the potato is its starch (carbohydrate) content, which provides energy. It contains little protein and almost no fat. Potatoes also contain ascorbic acid (vitamin C) and some minerals, particularly potassium. One medium-sized, boiled, unpeeled potato provides 120 Calories.

The food value of potatoes differs in different varieties. It also varies with different conditions of soils, climate, fertilization, and temperature. The amount of vitamin C decreases as potatoes remain in storage. For the most nutrition, potatoes should be cooked with the skins on, as most of the vitamins and minerals are found in the skin.

The taste and texture of potatoes depend in part on the variety. People prefer mealy potatoes, which contain a high percentage of dry matter. Soggy potatoes are less desirable.

▶THE POTATO PLANT

The potato plant is a member of the nightshade family. Other plants of the nightshade family are tomatoes and eggplant, as well as some narcotic-containing plants, such as tobacco, henbane, and belladonna.

The potato plant is an annual plant; that is, it goes through its entire life cycle within a year's time. It has a stout, erect stem that grows from 12 to 24 inches (30 to 60 centimeters) high. The flowers are white, rose, lilac, purple or blue. Under certain conditions, the plants may produce a smooth, round green or yellow berry (fruit). Each fruit may contain 100 to 200 seeds.

Soon after the potato stems appear above ground, slight growths develop on the underground portion of the stems. These growths lengthen for a time and then swell at their tips

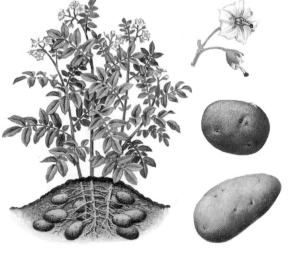

The aboveground part of a potato plant has dark green leaves and small flowers. The edible parts are the thin-skinned tubers that grow underground. After being harvested by machine, the potatoes are sorted and graded.

to form tubers. The tuber, which is the part we call the potato, is a shortened, thickened stem.

The tubers differ according to the variety of potato. They may be oblong or oval, have a somewhat rough or a smooth skin, and have a light yellowish-brown or red skin color. With good growing conditions, certain varieties of potato plant will produce large tubers within 2½ or 3 months of planting.

GROWING AND HARVESTING POTATOES

When new varieties are produced, potato plants are raised from seed. But in commercial potato growing, seeds are not used. The plants are grown from the potato itself. A whole small potato is planted, or a large potato is cut into pieces, each containing an **eye.** An eye is really the bud of an underground stem. Each potato piece, called a **seed piece,** has at least one eye and as much potato flesh as possible. The flesh around the eye provides the food for the new plant's first growth. Generally the seed pieces are planted in hills about 4 inches (10 centimeters) deep and 10 inches (25 centimeters) apart. The rows are about 34 inches (85 centimeters) apart.

Most garden soils are suitable for growing potatoes. Somewhat acid soil is preferable, as this prevents the potato from contracting a bacterial disease known as potato scab. Special fertilizers are used for potatoes. The fertilizer must be applied so that it does not touch the seed pieces. In addition, the growing plants must be thoroughly sprayed or dusted. No crop has been more troubled by diseases than the potato. Even the seed pieces are treated to prevent diseases. Potatoes can be badly affected by potato late blight, a fungus that infects the stems, leaves, and tubers of the plant. Potatoes also must be protected against the potato beetle, the blister beetle, and the potato leafhopper.

Potatoes are dug up in various stages of maturity. Varieties of potatoes that are grown early in the season may be left in the ground for a short while if the weather is not too warm and wet. In some warm locations it is safe to leave varieties of potatoes that are grown late in the season in the ground for 4 to 6 weeks after maturity.

Potato combines are used to harvest large potato crops. The digger of the combine brings potatoes out of the ground, shakes off the dirt and vines, and puts the potatoes into a truck. From here they are delivered to storage or to grading stations.

Storage. Potatoes should be stored in a cool, dry place. Too much exposure to light causes the skin of the potato to turn green. A bitter-tasting substance called solanin accumulates in green potatoes, making them unfit for eating.

POTATO PRODUCTION

Russia is by far the world's leading potato-producing country, accounting for about 25 percent of the world's total production in the 1990's. China, with about 15 percent, is the second largest producer. Poland (with about 12 percent) and the United States (with about 6 percent) are next in importance. The chief U.S. potato-growing states, in order of production, are Idaho, Washington, Maine, Oregon, and Colorado.

HISTORY

When the Spanish invaded South America in the middle of the 1500's, they found the white potato being grown by people of the Andes. Potatoes were brought back to Spain and by the end of the 1500's, they were common in Spain and Italy. The potato grew well in Europe and soon became important in Germany, Poland, and Russia.

There are legends that Sir Walter Raleigh or Sir Francis Drake introduced the potato into Britain at some time between 1585 and 1587. Soon afterward it was taken to Ireland, where it grew well and became the staple food of the country. In 1845 and 1846 there was a terrible potato blight in Ireland. The blight killed off practically all the potato crop. About 1,500,000 people in Ireland died of starvation and many others were forced to emigrate.

The potato was first grown in the United States in 1621, when it was brought to Virginia from Bermuda. In 1719, potatoes were brought from Ireland to New Hampshire. The potatoes that grew from those brought from Ireland were known as Irish potatoes.

The spread of the potato throughout the world is one of the miracles of agriculture. Today it is the world's second most important food crop, exceeded only by grains.

Reviewed by RODNEY W. DOW
State University of New York
Agricultural and Technical College
at Farmingdale

POTTER, HELEN BEATRIX (1866–1943)

Helen Beatrix Potter was born in London on July 28, 1866. Unlike her younger brother, who was sent off to school, Beatrix was educated at home by governesses. She had no playmates her own age, so she turned for friendship to the stuffed animals she played with in the nursery of her family's large house.

In the summer her parents took Beatrix and her brother to Scotland. These vacations opened her eyes to the wonders of the countryside. She made sketches of the animals, birds, and insects that she saw. Back in London she would entertain herself with her pet snails, mice, rabbits, and a hedgehog named Mrs. Tiggy-Winkle, which drank out of a doll's teacup.

As Beatrix grew older, she wrote many letters to her younger friends. These letters were filled with drawings and stories she made up to entertain them. One series of letters to the sick child of her former governess tells the original tale of the naughty Peter Rabbit. Her stories became so popular among her friends that, in 1900, she decided to publish *The Tale of Peter Rabbit* in a private edition. Her publisher was soon bringing out her stories as quickly as she could write and illustrate them.

The following years saw the publication of *The Tailor of Gloucester* (1902), *the Tale of Squirrel Nutkin* (1903), and *The Tale of Benjamin Bunny* (1904). Beatrix Potter believed that a small child's book should be small itself, so all of her tales appeared in little books, with only one or two sentences and a watercolor illustration on each page.

In 1905 she purchased Hill Top Farm in the village of Sawrey in northern England and began to raise sheep. Many of the scenes and animals in her most famous books were drawn from Hill Top Farm. The next eight years were Beatrix Potter's most creative period. She published her finest work, including the tales of Jeremy Fisher, Jemima Puddle-duck, Tom Kitten, the Flopsy Bunnies, Mrs. Tittlemouse, and Pigling Bland.

In 1913, Beatrix Potter married William Heelis, a lawyer. In her later years she dedicated herself to buying tracts of land in the Lake District in order to preserve the area from commercial development. In her will she turned over her vast holdings to the National Trust for future preservation.

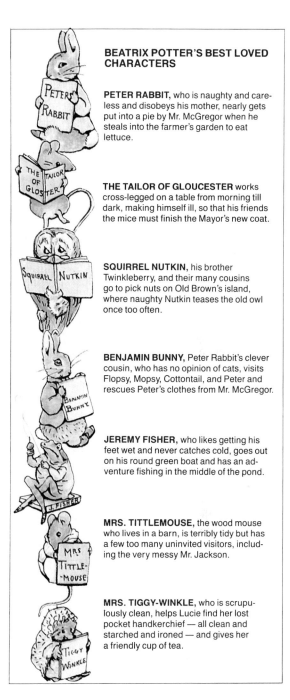

BEATRIX POTTER'S BEST LOVED CHARACTERS

PETER RABBIT, who is naughty and careless and disobeys his mother, nearly gets put into a pie by Mr. McGregor when he steals into the farmer's garden to eat lettuce.

THE TAILOR OF GLOUCESTER works cross-legged on a table from morning till dark, making himself ill, so that his friends the mice must finish the Mayor's new coat.

SQUIRREL NUTKIN, his brother Twinkleberry, and their many cousins go to pick nuts on Old Brown's island, where naughty Nutkin teases the old owl once too often.

BENJAMIN BUNNY, Peter Rabbit's clever cousin, who has no opinion of cats, visits Flopsy, Mopsy, Cottontail, and Peter and rescues Peter's clothes from Mr. McGregor.

JEREMY FISHER, who likes getting his feet wet and never catches cold, goes out on his round green boat and has an adventure fishing in the middle of the pond.

MRS. TITTLEMOUSE, the wood mouse who lives in a barn, is terribly tidy but has a few too many uninvited visitors, including the very messy Mr. Jackson.

MRS. TIGGY-WINKLE, who is scrupulously clean, helps Lucie find her lost pocket handkerchief — all clean and starched and ironed — and gives her a friendly cup of tea.

Beatrix Potter died in Sawrey on December 22, 1943. Her home, now part of the National Trust, is open to the public.

RICHARD KELLY
University of Tennessee

An excerpt from Potter's *The Tale of Jemima Puddle-duck* appears on the following page.

THE TALE OF JEMIMA PUDDLE-DUCK

Jemima Puddle-duck sets off to find a secret place to hatch her eggs. She meets an elegant gentleman with black ears and a long bushy tail, who offers her the use of his cozy wood-shed. But Jemima is such a foolish duck that she does not recognize her benefactor as—a fox!

He was so polite, that he seemed almost sorry to let Jemima go home for the night. He promised to take great care of her nest until she came back again the next day.

He said he loved eggs and ducklings; he should be proud to see a fine nestful in his wood-shed.

Jemima Puddle-duck came every afternoon; she laid nine eggs in the nest. They were greeny white and very large. The foxy gentleman admired them immensely. He used to turn them over and count them when Jemima was not there.

At last Jemima told him that she intended to begin to sit next day—"and I will bring a bag of corn with me, so that I need never leave my nest until the eggs are hatched. They might catch cold," said the conscientious Jemima.

"Madam, I beg you not to trouble yourself with a bag; I will provide oats. But before you commence your tedious sitting, I intend to give you a treat. Let us have a dinner-party all to ourselves!

"May I ask you to bring up some herbs from the farm-garden to make a savoury omelette? Sage and thyme, and mint and two onions, and some parsley. I will provide lard for the stuff—lard for the omelette," said the hospitable gentleman with sandy whiskers.

Jemima Puddle-duck was a simpleton: not even the mention of sage and onions made her suspicious.

She went round the farm-garden, nibbling off snippets of all the different sorts of herbs that are used for stuffing roast duck.

And she waddled into the kitchen, and got two onions out of the basket.

The collie-dog Kep met her coming out, "What are you doing with those onions? Where do you go every afternoon by yourself, Jemima Puddle-duck?"

Jemima was rather in awe of the collie; she told him the whole story.

The collie listened, with his wise head on one side; he grinned when she described the polite gentleman with sandy whiskers.

He asked several questions about the wood, and about the exact position of the house and shed.

Then he went out, and trotted down the village. He went to look for two fox-hound puppies who were out at walk with the butcher.

Jemima Puddle-duck went up the cart-road for the last time, on a sunny afternoon. She was rather burdened with bunches of herbs and two onions in a bag.

She flew over the wood, and alighted opposite the house of the bushy long-tailed gentleman.

He was sitting on a log; he sniffed the air, and kept glancing uneasily round the wood. When Jemima alighted he quite jumped.

"Come into the house as soon as you have looked at your eggs. Give me the herbs for the omelette. Be sharp!"

He was rather abrupt. Jemima Puddle-duck had never heard him speak like that.

She felt surprised, and uncomfortable.

While she was inside she heard pattering feet round the back of the shed. Some one with a black nose sniffed at the bottom of the door, and then locked it.

Jemima became much alarmed.

A moment afterwards there were most awful noises—barking, baying, growls and howls, squealing and groans.

And nothing more was ever seen of that foxy-whiskered gentleman.

POTTERY

Wet clay can be modeled into almost any shape. After a few days the clay becomes dry and hard. But putting it into water will make it soft again. If the clay is baked, or **fired**, the nature of the clay changes. It can no longer be made soft and workable. Objects made of baked clay are called **ceramics**, after the Greek word *keramos,* which means "potter's earth." Ceramic **vessels** (containers) are called pottery.

The first pottery was made about 10,000 years ago. At that time water was kept in bags made of animal skins, and food was kept in woven reed baskets. To keep grain from spilling through the holes in the baskets, the insides were smeared with wet clay. Perhaps one day a basket of this kind fell unnoticed on a campfire. The reeds burned away, and the first piece of pottery had been made.

Old pottery is treasured for many reasons. Pieces of pottery made very long ago are often dug up today, and they tell us much about the people who made them. Archeologists use these ceramic scraps to find out about life in ancient civilizations.

▶ KINDS OF POTTERY

There are three kinds of pottery—earthenware, stoneware, and porcelain.

Earthenware. The simplest kind of pottery is made from clay and then fired. It is called earthenware. Water will slowly leak out of an earthenware pot because it is porous—full of holes too small to be seen by the eye. After glass was discovered, potters found that covering the surface of the pot with a thin layer of glass would fill up these holes. This layer of glass is called a **glaze**.

Stoneware. At first pottery was made from clay just as it was dug from the earth. As time passed, people learned that certain rocks could be melted into a kind of glass. The rocks were crushed to a fine powder and mixed with clay. The pottery made from this clay is called stoneware. It is fired in a closed oven (**kiln**) with a very hot fire. Stoneware does not leak even when it is not covered with a glaze. Stoneware pots could also be used over a fire for cooking. Today stoneware is often used for casseroles—covered cooking pots that can be put into the oven.

A vase being shaped on a motor-driven potter's wheel.

Porcelain. During the T'ang dynasty (A.D. 618–906) the Chinese began to make another kind of pottery. It was made from a special white clay mixed with powdered rock. This pottery, called porcelain, was fired in a kiln almost hot enough to melt iron. The porcelain is translucent (light can be seen through it) and hard. When porcelain was first brought to the West, merchants called it China ware. The name became popular, and porcelain is often called china. It is used today for the finest tableware and ornamental objects.

▶ EARLY POTTERY

The earliest method of making pots took a long time. A new basket had to be woven for each new clay pot. But potters soon found faster ways. They made long rolls of clay and coiled them around until they had a roughly shaped hollow pot. The sides of the pot were smoothed with a scraper.

Then, about 3300 B.C. the **potter's wheel** came into use. This round table is still used,

Greek black-figure vase (570? B.C.) known as the François vase. Museo Archeologico, Florence.

even in big factories. The potter puts a ball of wet clay onto the center of the wheel. As the wheel spins, the potter shapes the clay by pressing it with his fingers. Making a pot on a wheel is called **throwing**. Pots made on wheels are always round. Square or oval shapes and figurines are made in other ways.

When the baskets around the early pots were burned off, the marks made by the woven reeds remained on the clay. The people who made pots by coiling clay often imitated the pattern of the basket weave by making marks with a pointed stick. Later they drew other simple patterns for decoration.

Clay taken from different places usually turns different colors when fired. It may turn red, yellow, almost black, or nearly white. Early potters often made a bowl of common red clay and then dipped it into a mixture of rarer white clay. The white clay had been mixed with water until it was as thin as cream. This liquid clay is known as **slip**. Often patterns were scratched through the thin layer of white clay into the red clay underneath. This kind of decoration is called by an Italian name, **sgraffito**, meaning "scratched."

▶ EGYPTIAN AND MESOPOTAMIAN POTTERY

The Egyptians and the Persians were outstanding potters. The potter's wheel was probably first used in the Middle East. Glaze may have been an Egyptian invention. The Egyptians used glazes on ceramic beads and figurines of animals and birds. By 1540 B.C. the Egyptians had developed many different-colored glazes, although blue was their favorite.

Like the Egyptians, the Persians had been painting on their pottery since 4000 B.C. Their earliest pottery was decorated with black and red designs. Later, they developed a brilliant cobalt blue that could be put in the hottest fire without losing its color. The Persians also discovered how to paint on top of a glaze with colors called **enamels**, or **overglaze**. Enamels are made of ground glass. They cannot stand as hot a fire as cobalt, but they give us many colors—red, green, yellow, and greenish blue.

The Mesopotamians also discovered several different kinds of glaze. By 600 B.C. they had found that if they added tin oxide to a clear glaze while it was being made, it became milky-white and translucent. They covered their pottery with this **tin-enamel glaze**. It produced a white surface on which they could paint in colors. Mesopotamian vases and dishes painted by hand were so popular that their method was carried to many other countries.

▶ GREEK AND ROMAN POTTERY

The Greeks did not use glazes. Instead, their polished red earthenware was frequently covered with black slip. As early as the 9th century B.C. the Greeks made very large vases—some of them 5 feet tall. These were ornamented with geometric patterns—patterns formed from squares, circles, or diamond shapes. Later, when figures of men and animals were used, they were drawn with geometric outlines.

In the 6th and 5th centuries B.C. potters began to paint figures and scenes in a lifelike way. They used black slip on the red earthenware vases. This style is called **black-figure**. The subjects of the paintings were scenes from Greek daily life, history, and mythology (stories of the gods). After about 500 B.C. **red-figure** vases were made. The background is painted with black slip around the red figure. The Romans, who copied all kinds of Greek art, also made vases in this style. Roman vases became too complicated, however, and often lacked the good taste of their Greek models.

▶ CHINESE PORCELAIN

The Chinese were the world's cleverest potters. They first used glazes on pottery

Majolica dish, Italy, early 16th century.
Metropolitan Museum of Art, New York.

Above: Detail of a 17th-century German tankard. Left: Hawthorn vase of Chinese porcelain, made during the K'ang-Hsi period (1662–1772). Below: Earthenware jug (16th century), from the workshop of Paul Preuning, Nuremberg, Germany. All three pieces are in the Metropolitan Museum of Art, New York.

English Delftware lion (18th century).

Staffordshire urn (18th century). Metropolitan Museum of Art, New York.

Left: Sèvres vase (18th century) with portraits of King Louis XVI and Marie Antoinette. Below left: Group of Meissen porcelain (18th century). Metropolitan Museum of Art, New York.

during the Han dynasty (206 B.C.–A.D. 220). In the T'ang dynasty (A.D. 618–906) the Chinese made earthenware figurines—of men, horses, and camels—as well as dishes. Glazes of several colors were dabbed on with a sponge. The discovery of porcelain was made during the T'ang dynasty, and for a long time only the Chinese knew how to make it.

During the Sung dynasty (960–1279) white pottery was replaced by hard porcelain and stoneware. Potters made fine bowls and dishes covered with pale monochrome (one color) glazes and carved decoration. Somewhat later, potters painted bowls with cobalt blue before adding the glaze. Color added before the glaze is called **underglaze**.

It was the porcelain of the Ming dynasty (1368–1644) that was first known in Europe and imported in quantity. Ming porcelain was decorated in underglaze blue and colored enamels. European potters copied the colorful Ming patterns on their pottery and porcelain.

▶ EUROPEAN POTTERY AND PORCELAIN

The people of Europe traded with China and the Near East in very early times. Chinese pottery was exported to India from about the 9th century A.D. Pieces of Chinese porcelain began arriving in Europe toward the end of the Middle Ages and were greatly valued. Kings and princes mounted porcelain pieces in silver and gave them as presents to other kings. From the 16th century on, more and more Chinese wares were brought to Europe.

The Europeans greatly admired porcelain, and they tried to copy it. They thought it was some kind of precious stone. But potters could see that it had been made on a potter's wheel—just like their own wares. Today we would have a piece of porcelain studied by a chemist to find out what it was made of. But the European potters of the 16th and 17th centuries did not know how to do this. In trying to imitate china, the Europeans developed many different kinds of pottery. But none was really porcelain.

▶ TIN-ENAMELWARE AND FAIENCE

Earthenware pottery covered with a tin-enamel glaze was copied from that of the ancient Persians. These glazes were known in Italy at the end of the 14th century. Italian potters often copied the works of painters on the fine white glaze of their dishes and vases. Raphael's pictures were copied so often that Italian dishes were once called Raphael ware. They are now called **majolica**. Scenes from mythology and history were painted in many colors. Occasionally dishes were covered with **lustre**—a shiny metallic glaze.

In France and Germany, tin-enamelware was called **faience** because the first wares of this kind brought into France, about 1525, came from the Italian potteries of Faenza. By the end of the 17th century all but the poorest people in France and Germany had gaily colored tin-enamel dishes.

▶ DELFT WARE

The first cargoes of Chinese porcelain were brought to Holland in the 17th century. At this time the Dutch were also making pottery with a white tin-enamel glaze. They soon began to copy the flower and figure patterns of Chinese blue-and-white porcelain. Toward the end of the 17th century another style, called gilded delft, copied Japanese and Chinese designs in blue, green, red, and gold.

This Dutch pottery is called **delft** because much of it was made in the town of Delft. The Dutch exported it to England, where potters made similar pottery, called English delft. Like all faience, delft ware is much thicker than porcelain.

▶ MEDICI PORCELAIN

In the late 1500's, over a century ahead of the rest of Europe, potters in Florence, Italy, tried to make porcelain. Because Chinese porcelain was translucent, these potters decided it must have some glass in it. Therefore, they mixed powdered glass with their clay before firing it. They finally made an artificial, or **soft**, porcelain. The potters were paid by a member of the wealthy Medici family, and their pieces were called **Medici** porcelain.

Because the potters were experimenting, Medici porcelain often had bubbles, cracks, and other defects. It was thick and often lost its shape. Some pieces were decorated in the style of majolica ware. Others copied the flower motifs of Chinese and Near Eastern pottery. Most Medici ware was white, with the decoration painted in blue or blue and purple.

DRESDEN PORCELAIN

Porcelain made with clay and ground glass is called soft porcelain to distinguish it from the true, or **hard**, porcelain made by the Chinese. True porcelain was made in Europe for the first time in 1708 by J. F. Bottger (1682–1719). His factory was housed in a fortress at Meissen, near Dresden. Dresden porcelain is world-famous for its beautiful decoration. Birds, flowers, and landscapes were painted on the white porcelain in brilliant colors. Figurines and figure groups were also made and painted in gay colors.

SÈVRES PORCELAIN

Soft porcelain was still made in the 18th century. About 1738 a large factory was founded in France with the help of King Louis XV. First located in Vincennes, the factory was moved in 1756 to Sèvres, just outside Paris. Practically all Sèvres porcelain was made for the king and his court. Unlike Dresden porcelain, which had mostly white backgrounds, Sèvres pieces were usually painted in rich greens, blues, and reds. Landscapes and stories from mythology were painted on the porcelain. Much gold paint was used, and many pieces were mounted in gilded bronze (bronze coated with gold).

The Sèvres potters knew, however, that they were not making true porcelain, and they tried hard to discover the secret of the Chinese. They finally discovered it in 1768. In the late 18th and 19th centuries, figures were made in "biscuit" porcelain—unglazed porcelain that looks like marble.

ENGLISH PORCELAIN

Soft porcelain was also made in England at several factories. But English potters tried to find the kind of clay needed to make true porcelain. William Cookworthy (1705–80) of Plymouth, England, found large quantities of white clay in southern England. He also found a rock similar to the one used by the Chinese. He opened small factories to produce true porcelain. But competition from stoneware factories forced Cookworthy to close his Plymouth factory after a few years. He sold his Bristol factory, which still produces china.

Around 1800 Josiah Spode II (1754–1827) found a way of making another kind of porcelain. By adding powdered animal bone to hard porcelain, he produced a translucent and strong porcelain, which he called **bone china**. This is the kind of porcelain that most English factories make today. But porcelain factories in Europe, the United States, China, and Japan continue to produce conventional hard porcelain.

EUROPEAN STONEWARE

Before porcelain and bone china were made in England, potters made tin-enamelware and other kinds of pottery. About 1650 tea was brought to Europe from China. The merchants who sent the tea to Europe put small red Chinese pots into the chests. Soon there were not enough of these teapots for everyone who wanted them. Potters in England imitated them very successfully in red clay. They called their pots red porcelain, although they were actually a kind of stoneware.

About 1550 the Germans had begun to make stoneware beer mugs, which they exported in large quantities to England. In the 1670's John Dwight (1637–1703) also discovered a way of making them. By 1750 the potters of Staffordshire, where most English pottery is still made, produced cream-colored stoneware. Many people used it instead of imported porcelain. One Englishman decorated it with speckled colored glazes like those of the ancient Chinese.

Wedgwood. The large modern ceramic industry in Staffordshire was largely created by one man, Josiah Wedgwood (1730–95). Around 1760 he began to make a cream-colored earthenware, which he covered with a transparent glaze. It was very popular because it was both cheap and strong. Queen Charlotte allowed Wedgwood to call his new earthenware queensware.

Wedgwood was a good businessman. He was the first to make pottery cheaply by mass production. Since his pottery was cheaper than tin-enamelware, potters in other countries were forced to copy him. Those who did not often went out of business.

Wedgwood was also the leader of a new fashion in design. He copied the shapes and ornamentation of old Greek and Roman pottery. It was almost impossible to copy this style in porcelain. Wedgwood pottery became extremely popular. The demand for European porcelain declined, and many factories closed.

Modern stoneware from the American Craftsmen's Council. (1) Three vases by D. C. Herring. (2) Teapot by Michael Cohen. (3) Casserole by Harriet Cohen. (4) Vase by F. C. Ball.

Wedgwood invented new kinds of ornamental pottery and stoneware. One was a black ware, **basalt**, which was often decorated with enamel colors. Another was the famous stoneware known as **jasper**, which imitated antique colored glass or polished stone. Jasper ware usually has white ornamentation raised from a blue or green background. These different kinds of pottery are still made by the Wedgwood factory in Staffordshire.

▶ POTTERY TODAY

During the 19th century many pottery factories were established in the United States and Europe. The mass-production methods invented by Wedgwood were improved, and very little porcelain was imported from China. Hand-painted wares were replaced by pottery that could be decorated on an assembly line. Pottery and porcelain were made in such large quantities that they became very cheap, and almost everyone could afford some. Only a few factories, such as Worcester, still made the old, expensive wares.

Today artists have again become interested in creating individual pieces of fine pottery. Working in their own studios instead of in factories, they are using stoneware and earthenware.

Many countries nowadays have successful pottery industries. Fine porcelain is still made and decorated in many traditional designs. Such factories as Rosenthal in Germany and Lenox in the United States manufacture china of good quality, decorated with simple patterns in keeping with modern tastes. Japan has become well-known for its cheap pottery, but it also produces very fine, glazed stoneware. Heavy stoneware is made by hand on the potter's wheel in Sweden and Holland. It is unglazed, and the toolmarks are not removed. This rugged-looking ware is especially interesting because every piece is different. The Italians make a similar kind of pottery, but they frequently hand-glaze it in rich, bold patterns.

Making pottery is one of the oldest arts. Pottery has been made everywhere and at all times, and many great artists have helped to produce it. It is perhaps the best example of our common desire to make beautiful the useful objects of everyday life.

GEORGE SAVAGE
Author, *Pottery Through the Ages*

See also CERAMICS; DECORATIVE ARTS; GREECE, ART AND ARCHITECTURE OF.

POUCHED MAMMALS. See KANGAROOS; KOALAS; MARSUPIALS.

POULTRY

Think about the foods you have eaten today. Perhaps you had eggs for breakfast and a bowl of noodle soup and a piece of cake at lunchtime. Chicken may be on the menu for dinner. All of these foods come from the products of the poultry industry.

Birds that are domesticated (tamed) to serve the purposes of people are called poultry. These birds are most often used to produce meat or eggs; but they may be bred as show stock or fighting cocks. Swans, guinea fowl, pea fowl, and ostriches may be listed as poultry. But the most important poultry in terms of numbers and commerce are chickens, ducks, turkeys, and geese.

▶ **CHICKENS**

The chicken is the most widely raised kind of poultry. Chicken meat and eggs are enjoyed as food all over the world. Famous chicken recipes have come from many places: southern fried chicken from the United States; chicken in wine, or *coq au vin,* from France; barbecued chicken from China; chicken curry from India; and so on. Chicken eggs are nutritious and delicious when fried, boiled, poached, or scrambled. Eggs also are an important ingredient in many other foods, such as baked goods, noodles, and casseroles.

Female chickens are called ''hens''; males are called ''cocks'' or ''roosters.'' Young females—those less than one year of age—are known as ''pullets.''

The present domestic chicken breeds and varieties came from the jungle fowl found in Southeast Asia. Many small, brightly colored Red Jungle Fowl still run wild in the jungles of India. From this small, timid, but scrappy fowl, hundreds of breeds and varieties have been developed. In the past, chickens often were bred for their feather coloring, body shape or size, or ability to fight. Although this type of breeding is still practiced, most chickens are bred only for their ability to lay eggs or produce meat.

Many present breeds carry the name of the country or area in which they were domesticated and developed—for example, the Polish breed, from Poland; the Sussex, from the county of Sussex, England; the Rhode Island Red from the state of Rhode Island in the United States.

Chickens are developed with different characteristics for meat or for egg farming. Here a White Rock hen has been bred to produce an ideal broiler chick.

Many standard breeds and varieties have miniature look-alikes called bantams. They look just like the standard breed except for their smaller size. They are kept mainly for pleasure and hobby.

Chicken fanciers—people who raise chickens only for their appearance—get much pleasure and satisfaction from improving the recognized breeds and varieties for use in poultry shows. Chicken fanciers are interested only slightly in the chicken's ability to lay large numbers of eggs or to produce meat. The commercial chicken farmer, on the other hand, does not care what the chickens look like as long as they lay many dozens of premium eggs or produce many pounds of high-quality meat.

Commercial chicken farming is of two types—meat, or broiler, farming and egg farming. A breed that is good for one type of farming will not be satisfactory for the other. The broiler farmer wants a fast-growing, tender, meaty chicken that can be marketed at a young age. The egg farmer demands a small-bodied hen that lays many large, high-quality eggs and eats a minimum amount of feed. These two sets of traits have not yet been found in the same breed.

Chicken farms are always faced with the threat of a disease outbreak that can kill or make useless large numbers of chickens. Common chicken diseases are Marek's disease, infectious bronchitis, coccidiosis, Newcastle disease, and avian influenza. Constant attention is given to disease control programs designed to prevent outbreaks. When disease outbreaks do occur, proper diagnosis and treatment are essential.

Broiler Farming

A broiler is a young chicken that is grown for its meat. Large specialized farms raise three or four flocks of broiler chicks each year, some flocks numbering 100,000 or more. The most popular size broiler weighs 4 to 5 pounds (1.8 to 2.3 kilograms) when 6 weeks of age. The size of the broiler may be varied by marketing a flock earlier or later, depending on what the market calls for. For example, a ''roaster'' weighing 6 or 7 pounds (2.7 to 3.2 kilograms) can be grown by keeping the broilers until they are 12 weeks of age; or a ''squab broiler'' weighing 2 pounds (0.9 kilogram) can be obtained at 4 weeks of age.

The broiler farmer may buy chicks from a hatchery specializing in hatching broiler chicks; buy scientifically mixed feeds from another company; and sell the live broilers to a company that prepares them for stores to sell. However, most broilers today are produced by companies that own farms, broiler houses, hatcheries, feed mills, and processing plants —integrating all the means necessary to market the ready-to-cook broiler. These ''integrated'' companies exist because they can produce broilers at less cost than can other types of farming.

Some companies specialize in the genetic improvement of broiler chicks. These companies breed male and female chickens that will produce chicks that grow faster on less feed. Crossbred chicks (chicks with parents from different breeds) grow faster and use less feed than purebred chicks (chicks with parents of the same breed). Most specialized breeding farms spend much of their time improving breeds that, when mated together, will make quality broilers.

The most popular broiler is crossbred from White Rock hens and white-feathered roosters, one of whose ancestors is the White Cornish male noted for its broad breast. This crossbred broiler carries the desirable traits of white feathers, yellow skin, fast growth, good feed conversion, and a broad breast.

Broiler chicks are fed a dry mash, scientifically formulated and nutritionally balanced, consisting mainly of ground corn, soybean meal, minerals, and vitamins. With 8 pounds (3.6 kilograms) of this feed, a broiler weighing 4 pounds (1.8 kilograms) can be grown in six weeks. No other animal is as efficient in converting feed into meat.

Egg Farming

An egg is one of the marvels of nature. It is a nutritionally complete food providing all the carbohydrates, fats, proteins, vitamins, and minerals necessary for life.

Reproduction is nature's primary purpose in forming an egg. But humans recognized the egg as a good source of food and developed hens whose primary purpose is to lay large numbers of eggs for use as food.

Above: Broiler chicks are usually raised in large pens where they are fed a high-energy diet to make them grow rapidly. *Below:* Layers are most often raised in wire cages. Their eggs are collected on a belt that runs below the cages. On a well-automated egg farm, one worker can care for as many as 100,000 laying hens.

People's preference for smaller white turkeys led to the development of the 8- to 10-pound Beltsville Small White (*far left*). Geese are an important commercial species in Europe, but in North America they are usually raised only in small flocks on small farms (*left*). Chinese in origin, the Pekin duck is a popular breed because of its rapid growth. By 7 weeks of age, a Pekin may weigh 7 pounds and be ready for market (*below*).

A good egg-producing hen will lay 270 to 280 eggs per year. She weighs 4 pounds (1.8 kilograms) and uses 4 pounds of feed to produce a dozen large eggs. There are several crossbreeds that are good egg layers. The choice of which to use may depend on the color of the shell of the egg that it lays. A type of hen known as the White Leghorn strain cross hen lays a white-shelled egg and is very popular in some parts of the world.

Some people prefer a brown-shelled egg. A very popular brown-egg layer is the black pullet resulting from the mating of Barred Plymouth Rock hens with Rhode Island Red roosters. Brown eggs are not more nutritious than white ones. The color of the shell has nothing to do with the food value of the egg.

Egg farms are growing larger and more mechanized and automated each year. Layer houses are equipped with long rows of small wire cages, each cage housing several hens with their own water and feed. All the chores that the hired worker used to do are now mechanized—feeding, watering, ventilating, cooling, heating, manure handling, egg gathering, egg grading, and packaging.

The various stages in the egg-production cycle take place on different farms. A specialized farm handles the breeding improvement, another handles the hatching of chicks, another the growing of the pullets, another the manufacture of feed, and another the keeping of the egg layers. All the phases of the cycle often will be owned by one company.

TURKEYS

The strutting turkey with its tail feathers fanned out is a symbol of Thanksgiving. Traditionally from the time of the Pilgrims, turkey has graced the Thanksgiving table.

America is the native home of the turkey. Although they were found roaming wild over most of North America, the present domestic turkeys probably were developed from those originally found in Mexico.

Today, turkeys are an important source of meat in many parts of the world. Many of the turkeys produced in the United States are roasted as whole birds for holiday feasts. But turkey is also being eaten more in everyday diets as turkey steaks and ground turkey, as well as turkey bologna, turkey salami, turkey rolls, and other processed items.

One of the first varieties developed for commercial farming was the Broad-Breasted Bronze turkey. Tom (male) turkeys of this variety weigh 24 to 26 pounds (10.9 to 11.8 kilograms) at 22 weeks of age.

A dressed turkey is one that is ready for roasting. Cooks like dressed turkeys to be free of skin blemishes or marks. Many Broad-Breasted Bronze turkeys carried black marks under the skin left by immature feathers called pinfeathers. These marks made the finished turkey look unappetizing. Therefore the Broad-Breasted Large White turkey was developed, because white pinfeathers leave no marks. Today this variety is used almost exclusively in commercial production.

Turkey farming is big business. Flocks of 5,000 to 10,000 birds are common. Hens and toms are separated at hatching and raised separately. The hens, which mature at 16 to 18 weeks of age, are marketed earlier than the toms, which may be ready at 22 to 24 weeks of age. The trend is to produce turkeys during all seasons of the year. To do this, many turkey flocks are kept in enclosed sheds, where they can be protected from the weather.

GEESE

Goose traditionally was eaten in Europe during holiday celebrations. But it has never become very popular in North America.

The goose is valued for its size, flavor, feathers and down, and long productive life. A goose may reproduce for 25 years or more. Geese are sturdy, generally easygoing birds, but at times they may be quite disagreeable.

The goose is an excellent forager for food. It can live, and even grow fat, on green pasture. This is important in areas of the world where little grain is available to feed animals.

Nearly all domesticated geese in North America are kept in small flocks. Only a few farms specialize in raising geese. Geese are important on some farms as weeders of cotton, strawberries, or other cultivated crops.

Domestic geese are believed to have come from the greylag goose. The greylag goose can be found wild in Europe but once was scattered over the world. The names of some of the common domestic breeds—the Toulouse, Embden, African, Chinese, Canadian, and Egyptian—tell in which part of the world the breeds were domesticated.

DUCKS

The domestication of ducks began long ago. The ancient Chinese were known as duck raisers as far back as their records date. The modern Pekin breed is of Chinese origin.

Young Pekin ducklings grow very rapidly. As with other types of poultry used for meat, a white-feathered, fast-growing breed is used exclusively.

Until the 1970's, more ducks were grown on Long Island, New York, than in any other place in the United States, probably because of the closeness to the water and proximity to the duck market in New York City. But ducklings do not need to swim in a pond or river in order to thrive and grow. Now, many ducklings are grown in windowless, climate-controlled houses.

Ducks are also raised to lay eggs. In the United States, duck eggs are not popular, but in Europe and England they are considered a delicacy and are widely eaten.

Ducks, in general, are very good layers. Even the Pekin duck, bred principally for meat production, has been known to lay 100 eggs in 100 days. Average egg production in duck flocks often exceeds that for chicken hen flocks. Many egg-producing duck breeds have been developed, including the Khaki Campbell, Indian Runner, Aylesbury, Rouen, Cayuga, and Muscovy. Each is different in size, shape, carriage, and economic use.

JAMES R. CARSON
School of Agriculture, Purdue University
See also DUCKS, GEESE, AND SWANS; TURKEYS.

POUND, EZRA. See IDAHO (Famous People).

POVERTY

Poverty is the word used to describe the conditions under which poor people live. A poor person is someone who does not have as adequate a supply of food and clothing or as good housing as the average person in his own neighborhood, region, or country. Poverty does not mean the same thing every place. Nor does it mean that a poor person is someone who fails to measure up to some general, world-wide standard. Poverty—being poor—means something different in each region and country, depending on the general standards of that country or region. Looking at the condition of the world's people is very much like looking into a kaleidoscope in which the shape of the pattern or design changes with each turn of the cylinder.

Taking the widest possible view of poverty, most of the people living in the industrialized countries of the world know almost nothing of poverty by comparison with people in the developing nations of the world. The United States, the countries of Western Europe, and Japan are examples of prosperous, industrialized nations without widespread poverty. The developing nations of Asia, Africa, and Latin America, which have large populations and are just beginning to develop modern technology, are examples of countries where real and often widespread poverty exists. On a much smaller scale, city people in most countries, as far as the amount of money they earn or possess is concerned, are rich in comparison with most country people or farmers. And yet the farmer's ability to live off the products of his land and to grow the raw material to make his own clothing can make an important difference in his economic life. He may be able to have a way of life comparable or even better than his city cousin's life—even though his city cousin may earn more money. In other words, the farmer may be poor in terms of income and what his income could buy if he moved to the city, but he is well-off at home in the country.

The idea of what poverty is also changes

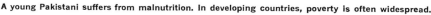

A young Pakistani suffers from malnutrition. In developing countries, poverty is often widespread.

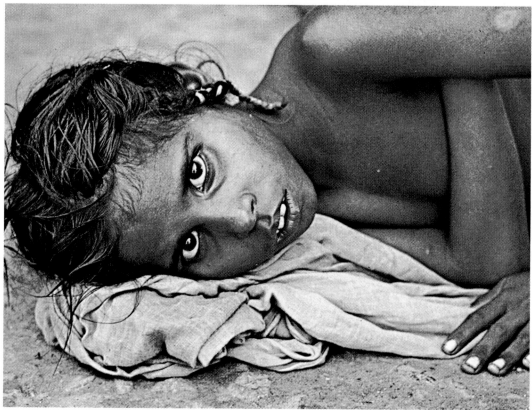

with the passage of time. For instance, a person in the United States in 1900 might have been considered quite well-off if he earned $2,000 a year. If a person earned that same amount of money in the second half of the 20th century, he would be considered poverty-stricken. The increased cost of living and the general changes in economic standards of all kinds have helped bring about this situation in the United States and in many of the other countries of the world.

▶ WHY PEOPLE ARE POOR

Most of the governments of the world want to destroy poverty. They also want to provide a better, happier, and more worthwhile life for their people. The first step in doing this is to provide people with good food, good housing, and adequate clothing. However, the task of eliminating poverty is an enormous and complicated matter. This is because poverty, when it occurs in a country, rarely exists for just one simple reason.

In India and Pakistan, the vast countries of the Indian subcontinent, there is great poverty despite the efforts of the governments involved (and agencies of the United Nations) to improve the situation. In some areas, traditional social and ethnic groups or castes were formerly restricted to specific jobs. These jobs sometimes failed to provide the workers with adequate means of supporting life. In some cases modern advances eliminated the need for certain skills or jobs to exist at all. And yet the people trained in these skills might well know no other means of making a living. In some cases they are retrained by their governments or by UN agencies, but the huge population of these countries makes retraining an almost insurmountable task.

It is also true in India and Pakistan, as well as in many other Asian and African countries and in some Latin American countries, that vast numbers of people depend closely on the land and what they can grow to feed themselves. A famine that brings about the failure of crops, a drought, a plague of insects, or a devastating flood could mean abject poverty or death for thousands of people.

In the history of the world, poverty has often been caused by political problems. A people displaced from their homes—from their farms, shops, or businesses—by war,

Extreme poverty still exists in the United States—one of the richest nations in the world.

revolution, or other political conflicts, may frequently become poverty-stricken. In many cases, these same displaced people formerly enjoyed a good or even prosperous way of life.

The United States currently has the highest standard of living in the world. But the United States also has pockets, or areas, of poverty both in the cities and in some rural areas as well.

In cities, extreme poverty sometimes occurs in urban ghettos where some minority groups have not had the opportunity to learn skills that will help them to earn a living in a rapidly changing modern world. People trapped in this kind of situation often have inadequate housing and, living in normally more expensive urban situations, must pay higher prices for what little food they can obtain.

In the Appalachian areas of West Virginia, southern Pennsylvania, western Virginia, and Kentucky there are pockets of great poverty of an especially complex kind. In these regions, coal mining was once a thriving industry. The land in the area was frequently hilly and rocky and not good for anything but the most primitive subsistence farming (farming in which the farmer and his family are barely

In some Indian cities, many people are homeless and forced to sleep in the streets.

able to feed themselves from their land). Therefore, most men went into mining to make a living. In recent years, however, mining has become increasingly automated and fewer men are needed to produce coal. The result is that the miners are thrown out of work and are unable to make a living off the land. Programs now in operation are attempting to retrain miners to do new jobs that will raise them and their families above the poverty level. But it is a long, slow process.

In most countries faced with the problem of poverty, the single most important fight is the fight to break the cycle of poverty in which a family remains poor for generations because they know no other way of life and no means of escape. Governments are working hard to make sure that the children of poor parents

will have the chance of a different and better way of life for themselves.

▶CURES FOR POVERTY

Most of the nations of the world have tried many ways to destroy the great ill of poverty. The United Nations, through its specialized agencies, has tried to offer assistance to those countries with specific emergencies, such as natural disasters, war, famine, and revolution. However, the most important problem is to overcome long-standing patterns or traditions of poverty.

In India, with its vast population and the economic restrictions remaining from the caste systems of the past, there have been many new approaches. Farmers have been taught new skills in farming, workers and craftsmen have been taught new industrial skills that were either unknown in the past or limited to certain groups in society. In India, as well as in other densely populated countries in Asia, Africa, and Latin America, there have been attempts to help people plan smaller families. Smaller families would then place less pressure on the economies of individual countries for there would be fewer people to feed.

The socialist countries have tried to conquer poverty by controlling all phases of their economies and attempting to provide every individual and family with an assured annual income. This has worked with varying degrees of success depending on social and economic conditions within the countries involved. Countries with free-enterprise economies have tried attacking poverty by establishing special agencies to meet emergency situations as they occur and by supplying government subsidies in times of crisis. This has also worked with varying degrees of success.

However, in most of the countries of the world, no matter what their political or economic system is, there is one vital weapon that is being used against poverty: education. The world-wide hope is to educate young people in professions and skills that will allow them to escape the economic and social problems of their parents and their nations.

Reviewed by STEPHAN THERNSTROM
University of California, Los Angeles

POWELL, ADAM CLAYTON, JR. See UNITED STATES, CONGRESS OF THE (House Representatives).

POWELL, COLIN (1937–)

Colin Luther Powell served as assistant to the president for national security affairs (1987–89) and chairman of the Joint Chiefs of Staff (1989–93). He was the first African American to fill either post.

Powell was born to Jamaican parents on April 5, 1937, in the Bronx, New York. While attending City College, he joined the Reserve Officers Training Corps (ROTC) and entered the United States Army as a second lieutenant on his graduation in 1958. In the early 1960's, Powell was one of the first American military advisers sent to Vietnam. On a second tour of duty (1968–69), his heroism earned him eleven medals, including a Purple Heart and two Bronze Stars. After Vietnam, Powell rose steadily in rank and responsibility, and in 1981 he was promoted to brigadier general. In 1987 he was named national security assistant by President Ronald Reagan, who also awarded Powell his fourth general's star.

In 1989, President George Bush selected Powell to head up the Joint Chiefs of Staff, the nation's highest military position. As

Colin Powell, the popular chairman of the Joint Chiefs of Staff under President Bush, was urged to run for president in 1996.

chairman, Powell sent American troops to the Philippines to avert a military coup against President Corazon Aquino; he oversaw the 1989 invasion of Panama, which resulted in the surrender of Panamanian dictator Manuel Noriega; and he was greatly responsible for the stunning success of the 1991 Persian Gulf War against Iraq, which made Powell a modern-day hero. That year the National Association for the Advancement of Colored People (NAACP) awarded Powell the Spingarn Medal, the organization's highest honor.

Powell retired in 1993 to devote time to his family and to a new career as a writer and public speaker. In 1994 he was called on by President Bill Clinton to help negotiate the return to power of Haiti's exiled president, Jean Bertrand Aristide.

Perceived as a man of immense personal integrity, Powell has been suggested as a strong candidate for president or vice president. His autobiography, *My American Journey*, was published in 1995.

JIM HASKINS
Author, *Colin Powell*

POWER PLANTS

There are many forms of energy—the energy of heat from the sun, moving air and water, burning fuels, and chemical reactions. Power plants convert these various forms of energy into electricity, which can then be used to provide lighting, heat, and power.

The two main types of power plants are hydroelectric and thermal. Hydroelectric plants use waterpower to produce electricity; thermal plants burn fuels, such as coal, oil, and natural gas. Hydroelectric power is the most important source of electricity in countries where waterpower is plentiful, such as Italy, Norway, Sweden, Switzerland, and Spain. Countries with abundant sources of fuel, such as the United States, Russia, Great Britain, Germany, France, and Japan, use thermal power to produce electricity.

▶ HYDROELECTRIC POWER PLANTS

In hydroelectric power plants, flowing water is used to turn turbines. These turbines run generators that produce electric power. The most convenient source of waterpower is a high waterfall. Since there are not enough natural waterfalls, artificial ones are created by building dams on rivers and lakes. Large dams can store water up to a height of several hundred feet (100 feet is equal to about 30 meters). Such dams, however, cannot be built on rivers in flat regions. A low-level dam on a river such as the Mississippi, for example, can provide a waterfall of only about 50 feet (15 meters). But the tremendous amount of water rushing down a river like the Mississippi can provide ample power to turn turbines that run electric generators.

Located in Foz do Iguazu, Brazil, the Itaipu hydroelectric power plant was completed in the early 1990's. It supplies 12,600 megawatts of electrical power to Brazil and Paraguay.

▶ THERMAL POWER PLANTS

In thermal power plants, a fuel such as coal or oil is burned to boil water and produce steam. The pressure of the steam turns the turbines that run the generators. These power plants generally use the most abundant fuel available in an area; power plants frequently are built near coal fields. It is easier to build power lines to transmit the electricity from the plants to the places where it is needed than it is to haul coal or other fuels over long distances to the power plants.

Heat for thermal power plants can also be obtained from solar energy and nuclear energy. In a solar thermal power plant, sunlight is converted to heat energy, which is then used to generate electricity. In a nuclear thermal power plant, heat is obtained from a nuclear reaction rather than from the burning of a fuel. For more information about thermal power plants, see SOLAR ENERGY in Volume S and NUCLEAR ENERGY in Volume N.

A problem with thermal power plants is that only about one-third of the energy used by the average plant is actually delivered as electricity. The rest is discharged as heat into the air or into cooling water. If the heat is discharged directly into a lake or river, the temperature of the water will rise, harming fish and other water life. This is known as **thermal (heat) pollution**. When fossil fuels such as coal and oil are burned, they can pollute the air unless special antipollution steps are taken. Another problem is that someday the supply of coal, oil, and natural gas will be depleted.

▶ CONTROL AND AUTOMATION IN POWER PLANTS

Controls are used in power plants in order to make equipment work efficiently and safely. In a hydroelectric plant, there are controls for opening and closing water valves, for regulating the speed of turbine generators, and for operating circuit breakers and switches that connect generators to transmission lines. In a thermal power plant, controls regulate the flow of fuel to boilers, the burning of fuel, and the speed of its turbine generators. Controls are important because the electricity generated by a power plant cannot be stored for later use. Each time electricity is needed, the plant must generate the added power necessary to produce it.

The accuracy required for controlling and operating complicated equipment in power plants created the need for automating the process, and computers and automatic regulators now coordinate the production of electric power in most large plants.

▶ ALTERNATIVE METHODS OF ELECTRIC POWER GENERATION

Alternative methods of generating electric power are being tested, and some of these methods have been used to generate electricity in space satellites and other spacecraft.

Thermoelectric power generation is based on a scientific principle called the Seebeck effect for its founder, Thomas Seebeck, a German physicist. In 1821, Seebeck found that if two different metals were joined at both of their ends and each junction was heated to a different temperature, an electric current would flow through the metals. Small thermoelectric generators have been used for limited jobs such as charging radio batteries.

A **thermionic generator**, which produces electricity from heat, consists of two electrodes inside a gas-filled chamber or a vacuum. If one of these electrodes, called the cathode, is heated to a higher temperature than the other electrode, called the anode, an electric current will flow between them.

A **fuel cell** converts the chemical energy of a fuel directly into electricity without going through the process of combustion. The first fuel cells were used to supply portable power for electronic equipment used by the military. The Consolidated Edison Company of New York constructed the first fuel-cell power plant for commercial purposes.

In a **magnetohydrodynamic (MHD) generator**, a very hot gas is forced through a magnetic field, and the energy in the hot moving gas is converted into electricity. In an MHD generator, however, the temperatures are extremely high—thousands of degrees Fahrenheit. New materials that can withstand this extreme heat must be developed, therefore, before MHD generators will be practical.

J. J. WILLIAM BROWN
General Electric Company
Reviewed by STANLEY W. ANGRIST
Author, *Direct Energy Conversion*

See also ELECTRIC GENERATORS; ELECTRICITY; NUCLEAR ENERGY; SOLAR ENERGY; WATERPOWER.

POWERS, FRANCIS GARY. See SPIES (Profiles).

PRADO

The Museo del Prado in Madrid is the national museum of Spain. Although the building was not opened until November 19, 1819, the history of its collection goes back at least 400 years before that date.

The kings of Spain had always loved good art. Each monarch supported outstanding artists of his own time and collected the works of older masters. King Ferdinand and his wife, Queen Isabella, who sponsored the 1492 journey of Christopher Columbus, are usually credited with having founded the royal collection. Isabella was especially fond of the work of the painters of Flanders—*Flamencos*, as they are called in Spain.

Later rulers added works of Italian, French, Dutch, and German artists to the collection. Some of these foreign artists accepted invitations to live and paint at the Spanish court. Gifts from foreign monarchs and careful purchases further enriched the collection. Some of the Prado's greatest treasures were bought from the estate of Charles I of England.

Although the Prado is a showplace of international art, it is best known for its Spanish collection. Every major Spanish artist from the Middle Ages to the 1800's is

The Prado Museum in Madrid, Spain, houses an important collection of international art. The building itself, designed by Juan de Villanueva, is an outstanding example of Spanish neoclassical architecture.

Museum visitors view *Las Meninas* (1656), a famous painting of members of the Spanish royal court by Diego Velázquez. The Prado has an especially fine collection of works by Spanish artists.

As the collection grew, its fame spread throughout Europe. Finally, in 1816, Ferdinand VII and his Portuguese wife, Isabella de Braganza, decided to put many of the marvelous works on public display. They moved part of the collection from the royal palace to the abandoned Palace of Science. The Palace of Science had been designed by the well-known architect Juan de Villanueva (1739–1811). It was originally intended to house laboratories and exhibits of natural science. But foreign invasions and lack of funds stopped work on the project. During the French occupation of 1808, Napoleon's troops stabled their horses in the building. Ferdinand VII and Isabella used their own money to have the neglected science building converted into an art museum. When it opened, the museum already owned more than 2,000 works of art.

The building, located in a shady parklike area, or *prado*, is three stories high and has 97 rooms. It is considered one of the most important Spanish buildings in the neoclassic style. The dry air of Madrid has kept the paintings in beautiful condition, and there has been a minimum of handling and cleaning. The works are well hung, and the galleries are well lighted.

The Prado has been remodeled several times in a constant attempt to improve conditions for photographing and copying works and for study. The exhibition space has been enlarged, and the building has been fireproofed and made quieter. But even during remodeling, the museum has remained open every day without exception.

Ferdinand VII had wanted the Prado to serve teachers, students, artists, and those foreigners with a "proper curiosity." The museum was so popular in the early 1800's that it was difficult to keep a Sunday's crowd moving.

In the spirit of Velázquez—who advised the king on art and bought paintings for him—the Prado traditionally appoints working artists as directors. Under their expert supervision the museum has continued to be an important influence on artists who come to Madrid. Great masters and casual tourists alike cannot help but be inspired by the glorious treasures of the Prado.

Reviewed by DON FRANCISCO SÁNCHEZ CANTÓN
Director, Museo del Prado

represented. The collection includes 50 paintings by the court painter Diego Velázquez (1599–1660). An entire room is devoted to his most famous work, *Las Meninas*. The painting gives the impression that the artist was looking into a mirror and copying the scene in his studio. To make viewers feel as though they, too, were in the room, a real mirror has been placed on the wall opposite the painting. When visitors look into the mirror, they appear to be part of the activity in the studio.

Francisco Goya (1746–1828) also painted at court. He did many portraits of the family of Charles IV. Sometimes Goya's portraits show his scorn for the silly and cruel rulers who supported him. Today, 115 of his paintings and several hundred of his drawings are in the Prado.

PRAGUE

Prague (Praha in Czech) is the capital and largest city of the Czech Republic, with a population of more than 1.2 million. It is the country's commercial, financial, and cultural center and a major industrial city. Its manufactured goods range from electronic equipment, metal products, machinery, and chemicals to textiles, beer, and processed foods.

Culturally, Prague was famed for its vibrant artistic, literary, and musical life. Today it still draws many foreign artists and art lovers, particularly to the historical center of the city, which dates from the Middle Ages.

The City. Prague is situated among low, scenic hills on both banks of the Vltava River. The two parts of the city are connected by a number of bridges. The oldest and best known of these, the Charles Bridge, was built in the 1300's and is adorned by many statues of the saints. Most of the city is located on the river's east bank. Its most famous district is Staré Město (Old Town), in the heart of which lies Old Town Square. Old Town Square has two particularly striking buildings—Old Town Hall, with its astronomical clock from the 1400's, and Týn Church, a Gothic structure built in the 1300's. Part of Charles University is also located here. Founded in 1348, it is the oldest university in

Prague, capital and largest city of the Czech Republic, lies on the Vltava River. The Charles Bridge is the oldest of the bridges linking both parts of the city.

Central Europe. Nearby is the former Jewish ghetto, with its old synagogue and cemetery.

Farther north, in the district of Nové Město (New Town), is Wenceslas Square. One of the busiest parts of the city, the square has traditionally been the scene of celebrations and demonstrations.

Prague's west bank includes the historic districts of Hradčany and Malá Strana (Lesser Quarter). The majestic Hradčany Castle, once the home of the kings of Bohemia, is now the official residence of the president of the republic. The most impressive of its many buildings is the medieval St. Vitus Cathedral. The palaces and mansions of the old nobility can be found along the winding cobblestoned streets of Malá Strana.

History. Prague was founded in the late 800's. It reached heights of prosperity in the late 1300's, when the Bohemian king Charles I was crowned Holy Roman emperor, as Charles IV, and made Prague the imperial capital. When the Austrian Habsburgs became Bohemia's rulers in 1526, however, the city's status began to deteriorate. An unsuccessful revolt against Habsburg rule erupted in Prague in 1618, setting off the Thirty Years' War. A second revolt, in 1848, also failed.

Prague became the capital of Czechoslovakia after its creation in 1918. It suffered through the Nazi German occupation of World War II (1939–45) and the Communist regime of the postwar years. In 1968, in the brief period known as the "Prague Spring," reformers sought to liberalize the system, but they were crushed by the Soviet Union. Democracy was restored in 1989. But it was followed by the breakup of Czechoslovakia in 1993, with Prague becoming the capital of the new Czech Republic.

EDWARD TABORSKY
University of Texas at Austin

PRAIRIES

Prairies are broad expanses of grassland on the plains of the middle latitudes (between the polar and tropical regions). The name "prairie" (the French word for meadow) is often given to any large area of flat land that has a natural grass cover. True prairie grasses are tall and have deep root systems. They grow in regions that have a subhumid climate—about 20 to 30 inches of rainfall annually. Drier (semiarid) plains with less than 20 inches of rain have shorter grasses and are known as steppes. "Steppe" comes from the Russian word for "treeless plain."

Where Are the Prairies?

All of the continents except Antarctica have vast grassy plains in the middle latitudes. In North America the prairies lie in mid-continent and extend from Canada to Mexico. Before settlers plowed the eastern Great Plains and upper Mississippi Valley, the natural vegetation was tall grasses with strips of forest along the rivers. Small "wet" prairies are found in the states along the Gulf of Mexico. Short-grass steppes cover the higher plains between the Rocky Mountains and the tall-grass prairies.

The humid eastern Pampa of Argentina and the grasslands of nearby Uruguay form the major prairie lands of South America. There are small areas of steppe in the drier western Pampa and along the Andes in Patagonia. A broad belt of grassland extends from Hungary in Europe to Manchuria in Asia. It is broken in places by mountain ranges and forests. The northern part of this grassy belt is tall-grass prairie. The drier southern portion includes the famous steppes of Russia. The grasslands of the High Veld in South Africa are similar to the prairies of the midwestern United States. *Veld* is a South African term for "open grassland." Australia's prairie lands lie in the Murray-Darling river basin, west of the Eastern Highlands. Large areas of steppe land, with shrubs as well as grasses, fringe the Australian deserts.

Environment of the Prairies

The climates of the middle latitude grasslands vary from subhumid to semiarid. Rainfall averages 20 to 30 inches a year in most of the tall-grass prairies. More moisture is necessary for grass growth in hot climates than in cold. The prairie and steppe lands produce excellent crops when there is enough moisture. Where there is not enough rain to support tall prairie grasses, only short grasses or bunch grasses can grow. Under still drier conditions the vegetation is limited to scattered grasses and desert shrubs. Most of the precipitation in the middle latitude grasslands comes in summer. The amount varies greatly from year to year. Sometimes there are long periods of drought.

Winters are cold and summers are hot on the prairies and steppes. In the northern grasslands of Europe, Asia, and North America temperatures drop far below zero in winter, yet they climb above 100 degrees Fahrenheit in summer. There are storms with windblown snow in the Northern Hemisphere prairies in winter. In summer there are thunderstorms. The Great Plains of the United States have frequent hailstorms, and tornadoes sometimes cause great damage. Winters in the Southern Hemisphere grasslands are not as cold as those in the Northern Hemisphere.

Soil and Plant Life of the Prairies

The soils of the prairies and steppes are among the most fertile in the world. Because of the light rainfall, minerals that nourish plant life have not been leached (carried downward by water) from the topsoil. The dead stems and roots of the grasses provide organic matter. Many grassland soils also have a high lime content, which increases their fertility.

Although grasses are the main kind of vegetation in the prairies and steppes, there are many other kinds of plants. Strips of trees, known as gallery forests, grow along streams. In the United States cottonwoods and willows are common along the streams of the short-grass steppe. Sagebrush grows among the grasses of the drier high plains of North America. In Texas grasses are mixed with thorny mesquite shrubs. The Pampa of Argentina has scattered scrub forests known as *monte*. Acacias and eucalypts are scrub trees of the Australian grasslands. The prairies also have many flowering plants.

Native animal life was abundant on the North American prairies before they were settled by farmers. Grazing animals such as the bison and antelope provided food for Native Americans on the Great Plains.

Grazing on the Prairies

On the grassy plains, early human beings depended upon hunting wild animals and gathering berries and roots for food. When grazing animals were domesticated, the grasslands became vast pasturelands. People on the steppes of Russia and Central Asia have made their living for centuries by herding sheep, goats, and cattle. Many of these people are semi-nomads who move their animals frequently to better pastures.

Most of the grazing regions on the plains of North and South America, South Africa, and Australia were not settled until the 1800's. In North America the Native Americans were replaced by cattlemen, who developed huge ranches. On the Edwards Plateau of Texas, goats have become an important source of Angora wool. The grasslands of Argentina and Uruguay are the leading livestock regions of South America. Both nations export wool, and Argentina is one of the world's leading beef exporters. Sheep, goats, and cattle are grazed on the High Veld of South Africa.

Australia's grasslands are noted for Merino sheep, which produce fine wool. Australia leads the world in wool exports.

Grazing is an extensive form of land use. Some ranches have many thousands of acres of land and large numbers of sheep or cattle. In the drier grasslands several acres of land are needed to provide enough feed for one animal. For this reason, the population of grazing regions is usually sparse. The small towns and villages are widely scattered, and there are few large cities. Ranchers live many miles from their nearest neighbors.

Farming on the Prairies

Before the invention of steel plows and heavy machinery, farmers could not cultivate the grasslands easily. It was easier to cut and burn forests to obtain farmland than to dig the thick, grassy sod with their simple tools. When it became possible to use more advanced implements, the prairies became the world's major grain-growing regions. The only grasslands developed for cultivation before the invention of the steel plow were the Russian steppes.

After the introduction of machinery, settlement spread rapidly into Siberia. Rye and wheat are the main crops of the Russian steppes today. Corn, flax, and hay are also grown. In southwestern Siberia irrigated

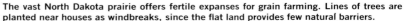

The vast North Dakota prairie offers fertile expanses for grain farming. Lines of trees are planted near houses as windbreaks, since the flat land provides few natural barriers.

farms produce cotton and fruits. The farmers of the steppes keep dairy cows and meat animals.

On the wetter eastern prairies, North American farmers developed general farms for the production of grain crops, hay, and livestock. Corn, oats, soybeans, and hay are the main feeds for hogs and cattle. The productive corn-hog belt of the upper Mississippi Valley extends westward into the prairies. Farther south, cotton is an important crop. During periods of high grain prices and favorable rainfall, farmers have cultivated land still farther west in the short-grass steppes. Spring wheat has been the leading crop of the Prairie Provinces of Canada and of the northern plains of the United States. In the central and southern plains states winter wheat is grown.

Because rainfall is not dependable in the drier grasslands, drought has brought disaster to grain farms in the past. Many farmers left the Great Plains as a result of crop failures and dust storms in the 1930's. Modern farmers have learned how to overcome drought problems to some extent by better cultivation methods. Grasses and forage crops have been planted to protect the soil against erosion and to help conserve moisture. Many thousands of acres of land have been returned to livestock grazing. In some places where water is available, irrigation projects have been developed. On irrigated land in the valleys of the Missouri River and its tributaries, farmers grow sugar beets, potatoes, alfalfa, and vegetables.

The cultivated lands on Argentina's Pampa grow corn, wheat, flaxseed, and alfalfa—an important cattle feed. Like the rest of the world's cultivated grasslands, those in Australia have become important for wheat growing. Much of the wheat is grown on farms where sheep are also raised. The main wheat-sheep zone lies west of the Eastern Highlands. Drought has been a serious problem for Australian wheat farmers.

In South Africa the wetter parts of the High Veld have farms that grow corn and other grain crops for livestock feed. Beef cattle, dairy cows, and sheep are the principal farm animals. The farmsteads are widely spaced in the drier areas. Windmills are used to pump water from deep wells.

Other Activities in the Prairie Lands

Mining has not been as important in the middle latitude grasslands as in mountainous regions. However, the North American Great Plains have huge deposits of lignite coal. Esterhazy, in Saskatchewan, has the world's largest deposit of potash. Oil fields have been widely developed in the Prairie Provinces of Canada and in North Dakota, Oklahoma, and Texas in the United States. Few minerals are known in the prairie regions of Uruguay and Argentina or in the tall grass region of Australia. Coal and oil are produced in the steppe regions of Russia. The High Veld of South Africa is noted for its gold and diamond mines. The Witwatersrand, in the vicinity of Johannesburg, is the world's leading gold mining area.

The prairies and steppes do not have many large manufacturing cities. Except in the few places where there is local coal or petroleum, power supplies are poor. Hydroelectric stations are also uncommon because rivers flow too slowly over flat plains to generate enough waterpower. The most important factories are those which process livestock products and farm crops. These include meat-packing plants and flour mills. In irrigated regions there may be beet sugar refineries and vegetable canneries. Ore crushing plants or smelters are found in the mining areas. The major oil fields have oil refineries.

Because most of the world's grassy plains are located in the interiors of the continents, good transportation networks are needed to carry products to the ports. In North America the railway systems focus on cities at the eastern edge of the prairies, such as Chicago or Winnipeg. In the southern plains, products move to ports on the Gulf of Mexico. The Mississippi River is an important waterway for products like wheat and cotton.

The railway network of Argentina radiates from Buenos Aires and other ports on the Río de la Plata to farmlands on the Pampa. In Uruguay, Montevideo is the port that receives cattle wool from the grazing lands. Both waterways and railroads serve the steppes in Russia, and major ports for handling agricultural products are on the Black Sea. The High Veld of South Africa and the interior prairies of Australia are more isolated than the other major grassland

Steppes (treeless plains) in Russia.

regions, but railroads reach from these areas to seaports.

The Future of the Prairies

Most of the world's grasslands were settled late in history. The humid prairies have become highly productive farmlands and are more densely populated than the steppes. Many parts of the semiarid steppes are still pioneer regions. In spite of the uncertainty of rainfall, farmers are finding better ways to manage pastures and cultivate croplands. Irrigation and soil conservation methods are helping to increase food production. As population increases in the wetter regions, more people will settle in the open spaces of the world's grassy plains to develop their agricultural and mineral resources.

HOWARD J. CRITCHFIELD
Western Washington State College

Oil refinery on the Canadian prairie.

Sheep ranch in Patagonia, Argentina.

PRAYER

One definition of prayer is that it is a person's response to a higher power—God. Prayer can be a personal response made by a person alone or it can be a response made in the company of other people. From earliest times, people have prayed together in a group. American Indians, for example, gathered to sing and dance before a hunt or a battle. Afterwards perhaps they enjoyed a feast in thanksgiving to the Great Spirit for a successful hunt or for a victory.

There is a similarity between prayers of all religions. The Bible and other holy books record many prayers. Two familiar examples often used in public worship are the *Shema,* "Hear, O Israel; the Lord our God, the Lord is One." (Deut. 6:4), and the Lord's Prayer, which begins, "Our Father who art in Heaven, hallowed be thy name," (Matt. 6:9–13 and Luke 11:2–4). Most written prayers are collected into prayer books. Some prayer books are intended for public worship, and others are for personal devotion.

But not all prayers are written in books. Some are spoken only and may deal with anything of concern to the person praying. The services of some Protestant churches have a special prayer called the pastoral prayer. In this prayer the minister uses his own words to pray on behalf of his congregation.

Whether a person sits, stands, bows, kneels, or prostrates himself while praying is generally determined more by his cultural background than by religious belief. The position he takes during prayer is likely to follow the pattern set by his spiritual ancestors. Some people even dance to show the joy they feel while they are praying.

▶ TYPES OF PRAYER

The Calling Prayer. Since the beginning of time, man has used some means to attract God's attention. He may have shouted loudly or rung a gong. A prayer of calling is usually called an invocation. People today often use a traditional phrase such as "O Lord, hear our prayer."

The Prayer of Adoration. In this prayer, a person expresses his love and praise of God.

The "Thank-You" Prayer. People have al-

A SELECTION OF PRAYERS

Lord, make me an instrument of thy peace,
Where there is hatred let me sow love;
Where there is injury, pardon;
Where there is doubt, faith;
Where there is despair, hope;
Where there is darkness, light;
And where there is sadness, joy.
O Divine Master, grant that I may not so much seek to be consoled as to console; to be understood as to understand; to be loved as to love; for it is in giving that we receive; it is in pardoning that we are pardoned; and it is in dying that we are born to eternal life. Amen.

St. Francis of Assisi

O Lord, support us all the day long, until the shadows lengthen and the evening comes, and the busy world is hushed, and the fever of life is over, and our work is done. Then in Thy mercy grant us a safe lodging, and a holy rest, and peace at the last. Amen.

From the *Book of Common Prayer*

For health and food,
For love and friends,
For everything
Thy goodness sends,
Father in Heaven,
We thank Thee.

Ralph Waldo
Emerson

We thank Thee for all Thy mercies unto us during the past week, for the preservation of our lives, of our health and our strength, for the blessings of home, of love, of friendship, and for all other good influences which support us in the hour of trial and temptation.

From the Jewish liturgy

Give me a sense of humor, Lord,
Give me the grace to see a joke,
To get some happiness from life
And pass it on to other folk.

Found in Chester
Cathedral, England

---

ways given thanks to God for the blessings and favors they have received. We call such a "thank-you" prayer thanksgiving.

The "I'm Sorry" Prayer. People say "I'm sorry" to God when they have done something they know to be wrong. The "I'm sorry" prayer is called a confession. It is often said in churches and synagogues. In some churches confession is made in the presence

God grant me the serenity to accept the things
I cannot change, courage to change the things
I can, and wisdom to know the difference.

> Attributed to Friedrich Oetinger
> 18th-century German evangelist

Dear God, be good to me. The sea is so wide and
my boat is so small.

> Prayer of the Breton fishermen, France

23rd Psalm

The Lord is my shepherd; I shall not want.
He maketh me to lie down in green pastures;
He leadeth me beside the still waters.
He restoreth my soul;
He guideth me in straight paths for His name's sake.
Yea, though I walk through the valley of the shadow
  of death,
I will fear no evil,
For Thou art with me;
Thy rod and Thy staff, they comfort me.
Thou preparest a table before me in the presence
  of mine enemies;
Thou hast anointed my head with oil; my cup run-
  neth over.
Surely goodness and mercy shall follow me all the
  days of my life;
And I shall dwell in the house of the Lord for ever.

> Old Testament

Glory to God in the highest, and on
earth peace, good will toward men.

> New Testament

May the road rise with you
And the wind be ever at your back,
And may the Lord hold you in the hollow
  of his hand.

> Ancient Irish blessing

Grant, O Lord, peace in our days. Peace to souls,
peace to families, peace to our country, peace
among nations. May all men realize that they are
brothers, and that the nations are members of one
family. And on this family may the sun of a universal and sincere peace shine. Amen.

> Based on prayers of Pope Pius XII

The Lord bless us and keep us. The Lord make his
face to shine upon us, and be gracious unto us. The
Lord lift up his countenance upon us, and give us
peace, both now and evermore. Amen.

> From the *Book of Common Prayer*

O Lord, Thou knowest how busy I must be this day;
if I forget Thee, do not Thou forget me.

> Sir Jacob Astley, 17th century

From ghoulies and ghosties and long-leggity beast-
ies, and things that go bump in the night, good
Lord, deliver us.

> Ancient Scottish prayer

In the name of God, Most Gracious, Most Merciful.
Praise be to God,
The Cherisher and Sustainer of the Worlds;
Most Gracious, Most Merciful;
Master of the Day of Judgment
Thee do we worship,
And Thine did we seek.
Show us the straight way,
The way of those on whom
Thou has bestowed thy Grace.
Those whose portion
Is not wrath,
And who go not astray.

> Islamic prayer from the Koran

The Lord's Prayer

Our Father who art in heaven,
  Hallowed be Thy name.
Thy kingdom come,
Thy will be done,
  on earth as it is in heaven.
Give us this day our daily bread;
  And forgive us our debts,
As we also have forgiven our debtors;
And lead us not into temptation,
  But deliver us from evil. Amen.

> Matthew 6:9–13
> (Revised Standard Version
> of the Bible)

(The phrase, "For Thine is the kingdom
and the power and the glory forever" is
frequently added.)

---

of a priest. The priest delivers God's forgiveness, which is called absolution. In other
churches confession is said by all the people
together. This is called general confession.

The Prayer for Others. A prayer that a person offers for others is called intercession.

The Asking Prayer. Asking prayers, in which
people tell God of their needs and ask for
help, are called petitions.

The Listening Prayer. Sometimes prayer is
silent. The person who is praying does not
speak. He feels that he is in the presence of
God. This kind of prayer is called meditation.
When meditating, the person does not talk to
God so much as he listens to Him speak.

> THE REV. SMITH L. LAIN
> Editor, *Findings*

PRECIOUS STONES. See GEMSTONES.

During the first part of the Paleozoic era, the seas were the home of all plant and animal life. A great variety of invertebrates (animals without backbones) appeared. Later in the Paleozoic, the amphibians evolved, and life began to develop on land.

PREHISTORIC ANIMALS

Long before the beginning of written history there were saber-toothed tigers and woolly mammoths. Millions of years before that, huge dinosaurs walked on earth and flying reptiles soared through the sky. These animals have long since become extinct, or died out. Such animals are called prehistoric animals.

Most of what we know of prehistoric animals we know through the study of fossils—the remains of animals preserved in the earth. Some animals have bodies with hard parts. When these animals die, their hard parts may be preserved in rock. Other animals are soft-bodied. We know of these animals through imprints of their shapes left in rocks. Such imprints are rare, and so our knowledge of these animals is limited.

▶EARLY LIFE FORMS

The earth is some 5,000,000,000 (billion) years old. Scientists think that the first life forms appeared some 3,000,000,000 years after the earth was formed. They think that the first life forms were probably single-celled plants, for only plants can manufacture food—using the energy of sunlight together with certain raw materials. Animals cannot do this and must depend on plants for food. And so, probably, plant life came before animal life.

The first animals, like the first plants, were probably made up of a single cell. From these creatures, over millions of years, many different life forms developed. Some of the first animals to be found in the fossil record are worms, jellyfish, and arthropods (arthropods are represented by today's insects, spiders, and crustaceans). Although they are rare, traces of these animals have been found in rocks more than 600,000,000 years old.

Scientists have divided earth's history into spans of time called geologic eras. These eras are named the Paleozoic (meaning "oldest life"), the Mesozoic ("middle life"), and the Cenozoic ("recent life"). The end of an era marks a time when great changes occurred in the surface of the earth and in earth's climate. Following these changes some life forms disappeared and new ones emerged.

▶THE PALEOZOIC ERA

The Paleozoic era began approximately 600,000,000 years ago. During much of this era the seas covered the continents as we know them today. Many forms of sea-dwelling life appeared. The first clams, snails, and corals appeared during this era. They branched out along many different lines. Many other invertebrates (animals without backbones) also developed. Toward the end of the Paleozoic the first ammonites appeared. These creatures, like today's chambered nautilus, had coiled shells with chambers separated by walls.

Vertebrates (animals with backbones) made their first appearance early in the Paleozoic. These were the first fish, which also developed along many different lines. Some fish were the ancestors of those that are living on earth today. Others flourished for a time and then died out. Still others gradually developed footlike fins. From these creatures a new kind of animal developed. This animal—an amphibian—had legs and lungs and could spend most of its life on land. Amphibians, too, flourished. Some led to present-day amphibians such as the frogs and toads. Others gave rise to the reptiles—represented today by snakes, turtles, and their relatives. Reptiles first appeared toward the end of the Paleozoic. At that time many kinds of animals became extinct.

Scientists think that there were probably many reasons for the extinction of so many kinds of animals at the end of the Paleozoic. For one thing, the seas, which had covered the continents during much of the era, gradually withdrew from the land. The ancient sea was very shallow and was teeming with life. When the seas withdrew from the land there was only a narrow strip of shallow water left between the land and the deep water. Many creatures living in the shallow water died out, for there was room for only a few kinds of animals.

▶THE MESOZOIC ERA

The Mesozoic era began approximately 230,000,000 years ago. New forms of sea-dwelling life developed. Creatures called ammonites were the dominant form of life. Fish, too, were abundant in Mesozoic waters.

The Mesozoic era is also known as the Age of Reptiles. Dinosaurs thrived during the era—a period of almost 165,000,000 years—but all of them died before the Mesozoic was over. Animals such as the *Kannemeyeria* (left) and the fierce *Cynognathus* (right) lived in what is now Africa during the early part of the Mesozoic.

During the Mesozoic era the reptiles were the ruling creatures on land. There were dinosaurs, large sea-dwelling reptiles, and flying reptiles. While many kinds of reptiles developed and flourished, certain other reptiles began to change. Some developed coats of hair and became the first mammals. Another branch of reptiles gave rise to the first birds.

At the end of the Mesozoic era, great changes occurred in climate and the surface of the land. The ammonites, dinosaurs, and many other kinds of animals became extinct. Birds and mammals, however, continued their development into the Cenozoic era.

▶THE CENOZOIC ERA

The Cenozoic era began approximately 70,000,000 years ago. During this era most of the animals we know today developed. New and different animals appeared in the seas. There were many kinds of fish. Ammonites were replaced by the squids and their relatives, and the snails and clams reached the peak of their development.

Birds developed into the many different forms we know today. Mammals, small and insignificant during the Mesozoic era, developed along many different lines and became the dominant creatures on earth. Some mammals began to live in the trees. Monkeys, apes, and the ancestors of human beings descended from these tree-dwelling mammals.

The earth and the life upon it are still changing. If we were to take a cross section of the animals living today we would find some groups just beginning to become varied, some at the peak of their expansion, and some about to become extinct.

In general, the changes that are occurring are going on so slowly that we cannot see them. Some changes, however, take place very rapidly—many as a result of human beings' actions. Humankind has been responsible for the extinction of many animals—the passenger pigeon, for example—and threatens the extinction of many others, such as the blue whale.

ROGER L. BATTEN
Curator
American Museum of Natural History

See also DINOSAURS; EVOLUTION; FOSSILS.

Mammals became the ruling creatures during the Cenozoic era. Many animals similar to those we know today first appeared. These include the bison (foreground), large cats (left), wolves (right), small birds, and vultures. Fossil remains of these and other animals have been found in what is now the city of Los Angeles, California.

PREHISTORIC ART

There have been men, women, and children on earth for many thousands of years. In the beginning, people lived very differently from the way we do today. Before the development of cattle herding and farming, people obtained food by gathering nuts, berries, and other plants. They hunted animals that they learned were good to eat. There were no villages, shops, hospitals, or schools. No one could read or write. The word "prehistoric" refers to the time before there were any written records of what was taking place.

▶ HOW DO WE KNOW ABOUT PREHISTORIC ART?

Between 14,000 and 24,000 years ago the entire earth was as cold as the Arctic region is today. The world was passing through what is called the Ice Age.

People of the Ice Age lived in the mouths of caves or under overhanging cliffs on the sunny sides of valleys. Life must have been fierce and hard. It was a constant struggle to get enough to eat and to keep warm and safe. There were few of the comforts we expect today. People had not yet learned to make bowls and cups.

People lived roughly, hunting and wearing only animal skins. But they were not completely savage. In western Europe they made beautiful carvings, engravings, and paintings on pieces of bone, antler, or stone. They decorated the walls of deep caves. It would require a fine artist of our time to create art as beautiful as theirs.

All this has been found out by digging up the homesites of prehistoric people. Let us suppose that a family lived in the mouth of a cave. They never cleaned out their room, and the ashes from the fire were never removed. Animals were cooked and eaten. The bones were thrown to one side. Broken tools and pebbles from children's games were also discarded and left on the cave floor. Several generations of families lived in the same room. Finally, the room would be completely filled with layers of rubbish, and the latest family would have to look for a new home.

If nothing has disturbed the layers, we assume that the bones and tools of any lower level are older than the things in the layers

A deer, drawn with a brush. Niaux Cave, France.

above. This is how we begin to date layers. Next, we examine the objects themselves and find that sometimes they differ according to different cultures.

If we look at the bones carefully, we sometimes find on them beautiful little carvings or engraved drawings of animals. These engravings and carvings must have been made with the very fine, specially pointed flint tools and knives found in the same layers. The way the engravings were made changed from time to time in the different levels. In this way we note the growth of art throughout long periods of time.

Usually figures of animals were made. But there were also signs, patterns, and simplified drawings of natural things. Many of the animals that lived in the Ice Age no longer exist. But we know that they usually had long hair to help them keep warm. In the drawings we can see the great woolly elephant, the woolly rhinoceros, the cave bear, and the cave lion. Some of the cave dwellers' animals, such as the reindeer, still flourish. But nowadays these lovely animals are found in regions much colder than southern Europe, where the cave drawings were made.

▶ CAVE ART

Caves are found in limestone areas. Today many caves are dry because the water that

Bison, scratched into cave wall and painted. Altamira Cave, Spain.

formed them has sunk to lower levels. Some caves are very long and have many complicated passages.

An outstanding cave called Niaux is in the French Pyrenees. The opening is halfway up a hillside, above a mountain stream. After several hundred meters, you can see on the right-hand side a series of red painted dots, dashes, and lines just where a narrow passage leads off to the right. At the end of a wide passageway, there are dozens of paintings of bison, ibex, and other creatures. These paintings have lasted so long because weather conditions never change in deep caves. Variations of dampness, temperature, and light quickly destroy paint.

The artists painted with natural lumps of **ocher,** a material easily found in the earth. Crushed ochers give a red, orange, or yellow color. Charcoal black was also used. It has often survived despite the fact that it rubs off easily. The colors were put on the walls in

Little horses and a jumping cow, a famous painting from the Lascaux Cave in France.

These four animal heads were carved on an antler found in Gourdan Cave, France.

various ways, sometimes with a brush. A small bone, snapped off at the end, may have been used as a brush handle. To make bristles, the artist may have taken hairs from a horse's mane, bent them double and inserted them into the bone, and then chopped off the ends to a suitable length. The colored, powdered ochers were probably mixed with warmed suet, or fat. Perhaps an ox's shoulder blade served as a palette. It was dark in the caves, and the artist had to have a small fire for working and for melting the fat. Indeed, small stone lamps have been found in the caves. A twist of moss could have been used to make a wick. A helper probably aided the cave artist in all these operations.

The pictures of animals were often painted and engraved over each other. Like the layers of homesite rubbish, the figures underneath must be older than those that cover them. One can see, too, that not all the drawings and paintings were made in the same way. Certain styles of work can be made out. We know that some styles are older than others because they are always found underneath.

Cave dwellers never lived in the depths of caves. It is pitch-dark inside a deep cave. For this reason, we know that cave pictures were not made for fun or because they were nice to look at. Group pictures or scenes are rare, and figures of human beings are even more unusual. Cave dwellers drew queer figures of lines and strokes that may stand for huts or traps. Perhaps they represent holes dug in the ground and covered with branches. Animals might fall into these holes and be killed easily. The pictures are mostly of single animals— usually animals that are good to eat. We know this by a comparison with the bones from the homesite. Reindeer and bison abound, but rhinoceroses and lions are rare.

The only suitable explanation of why these pictures were made as they were is that this cave art was part of a kind of magic called **sympathetic magic**. We know that some peoples today act out what they want. For example, during a drought, when rain is badly needed, a group may dance around a flowerpot, which is then solemnly watered from a watering can.

The cave folk we have been talking about were artistic. They expressed themselves by drawing or painting. Perhaps, instead of dancing or imitating what they wanted, they were led by an artist–sorcerer (one who could control evil spirits) into the dark and frightening depths of a nearby cave. There they would be shown the animals they were going to hunt. Sometimes arrows would be painted in the sides of the animals. Because meat is difficult to store, the very lives of the cave dwellers depended on the success of each hunt. Perhaps this ceremony was successful because it put confidence into the heart of the hunter.

In the cave in France called Les Trois Frères (after the three brothers who found it), there is a large chamber with walls that are covered with engravings. At the end of this chamber there is a small tunnel, also decorated with engravings. Passing through and around this tunnel, we re-enter the main chamber at a higher level, standing on a sort of platform. This natural "pulpit" overlooks and dominates any group of people who might be present. Beside the platform is the painted figure of a sorcerer. It is a male figure with the face of an owl, the antlers of a reindeer, and the tail of a horse. If you could visit this chamber, you would surely imagine yourself taking part in a magic ceremony of more than 14,000 years ago.

MILES C. BURKITT
Author, *Our Early Ancestors*

PREHISTORIC PEOPLE

The people known as prehistoric people lived on earth "before history"—that is, before writing was invented and the recording of human history began. Scientists believe that humans first inhabited the earth over 2,000,000 years ago. At first, there were very few human beings. They lived together in small bands of related families, or tribes. These groups moved from place to place hunting wild animals and gathering seeds, nuts, and plants. As they struggled to obtain food, clothing, and shelter, they were constantly learning new things and adapting the old ways to new conditions.

▶ **UNWRITTEN RECORDS OF THE PAST**

Scientists who study how prehistoric people lived are called prehistoric archaeologists. To find out how and where prehistoric people lived, scientists have studied records that tell them about the land and the weather in prehistoric times. They have discovered that at least six times in the past 3,000,000 years, great polar ice sheets, or glaciers, moved slowly southward from the North Pole to cover the northern part of Europe, Asia, and North America. During this period of time, called the Pleistocene Ice Age, the weather south of these masses of ice was very cold. Cold weather animals such as reindeer, woolly elephants (mammoths), and hairy rhinoceroses lived in these areas. Even in Africa and South America, the weather was cooler than it is now. In between glacial periods, the weather grew warmer, and the glaciers melted back. Then warm weather plants and animals increased and thrived.

Prehistoric people left no written records. But without really meaning to do so, they left many clues to their ways of life. Bones and teeth, seeds and nuts collected for food, and stone, bone, and metal tools provide these clues. The settling of dust and the shifting surface of the earth buried these prehistoric

items. Many of these materials have been preserved for millions of years, buried in the ground. Scientists dig them up, study them carefully, and learn much about the life of prehistoric people.

Among the most important discoveries of archaeologists have been tools made of durable materials such as stone and metal. As a result, scientists classify prehistoric people according to the main materials they used for making tools. At first, stone was by far the most common material for this purpose.

▶ **THE OLD STONE AGE**

The Old Stone Age refers to the time when people obtained their food by hunting, fishing, and gathering plants. The Old Stone Age began during the Ice Age, more than 2,000,000 years ago. It ended about 10,000 years ago, when the climate warmed up. This long period is divided into the Lower Paleolithic, Middle Paleolithic, and Upper Paleolithic periods. By the end of the Lower Paleolithic period, human beings were living in Europe, Africa, and Asia. At the end of the Ice Age, people were living in Australia and the Americas.

The Earliest Humans

Human beings are distinguished from other animals by their upright posture, the size of their brains, their intelligence, the ability to speak, and the ability to invent tools. The oldest humanlike bones were found in East Africa and southern Asia by several different scientists. These remains are usually classified as being those of a creature called *Australopithecus* (meaning "southern ape"). These small creatures stood upright and had apelike faces. Their brains were much smaller than modern human brains but slightly larger than those of apes. They had small teeth resembling human teeth.

The first Australopithecines did not leave behind any recognizable tools. They may have used sticks and stones, without changing their shapes. Later Australopithecines were somewhat larger in size. Then, about 2,300,000 years ago, they began to make crude tools of stone. They broke up large stones until they were a convenient size for holding. These were **choppers**, which resembled knives and were used for cutting, hacking, scraping, and digging.

THE STONE AGE

The Stone Age is normally divided into three main periods—**Old Stone Age (Paleolithic), Middle Stone Age (Mesolithic),** and **New Stone Age (Neolithic).** "Lithic" comes from a Greek word meaning "of stone" and refers to the material of which most prehistoric tools and weapons were made.

By this time, human beings had begun to hunt animals extensively. Because their equipment was limited, it is clear that most of the animals they caught must have been very old, very young, or very slow.

Simple clues can reveal a great deal. Three spots of burned earth were found at Lake Turkana (Lake Rudolf) in Kenya. These three spots reveal that fires once burned there—and that the tool-making people who lived there knew something about the use of fire. No one knows whether they could make fire when they wanted it or whether they depended on chance occurrences of nature, such as lightning flashes. In any case, fire warmed them in damp weather and frightened off large animals.

During the Mindel period—the coldest of the glacial periods—people living in regions such as northern China (Choukoutien Cave near Peking), Hungary (Verteszöllos Spring), and Heidelberg, Germany, had to endure very cold weather. The use of fire must have been important to these people. Humankind had now advanced to a step beyond the australopithecines and had become *Homo erectus,* or "erect human." Remains of *Homo erectus* have also been found in the tropics—at Olduvai in eastern Africa and in Java. These people of 500,000 to 700,000 years ago had bodies like short modern humans. But their heads were different. They had long sloping foreheads and brows that extended out over their eyes. They had large teeth and receding chins. *Homo erectus* knew how to control and use fire.

Hunters and Gatherers

Half a million years ago people lived mainly by hunting large and fast animals like reindeer, bison, mammoths, and woolly rhinoceroses. They also gathered seeds and berries and dug for edible roots. Families lived in small bands of closely related people.

These people were accomplished toolmakers. Choppers were still in use. But by the end of the Mindel period, the **hand ax** had been invented. This tool was quite different from naturally broken stone choppers. One end of the hand ax was chipped to form a rounded or pointed tip. The other end was shaped for holding. Hand axes were used for cutting meat, skinning, and digging up roots and clams.

Very few remains of the people who devised hand axes have been found. Besides several small bone fragments, the skulls of two women, dating from about 250,000 years ago, were recovered from riverside excavations at Swanscombe, England, in 1935 and Steinheim, Germany, in 1933. In 1971, the skull of a male of this period was dug out of the Arago Cave in southern France. These slim human beings had brains larger than those of *Homo erectus* but smaller than those of people today. They have been labeled *Homo sapiens steinheimensis.* (*Homo sapiens*—meaning "wise, or intelligent, human"—is the name given to all modern human beings.) Their faces were very rugged, with low foreheads and receding chins, but they looked more like modern humans.

Bluff Dwellers

Neanderthals were a kind of *Homo sapiens* about which a great deal is known. This is because they buried their dead. Hundreds of Neanderthal skeletons have been recovered. Many have been found under overhanging cliffs, or bluffs, which formed natural rock shelters. The name Neanderthal comes from the Neander Valley in Germany, where the first skeleton was found.

The first known Neanderthals, *Homo sapiens neanderthalensis,* were short. They had strong, powerful bodies. Their skulls were flat, with heavy jaws and jutting brows and small chins and foreheads. But their heads were very long, and their brains were larger than those of humans today.

In addition to small hand axes, Neanderthals made and used **flake tools**. These were easily and skillfully made of thin flakes of flint with razor-sharp edges. These pointed, triangular tools were probably used as knives for skinning and cutting up game animals. Another kind of flake tool was a side scraper, which had a blunt, curved edge. This seems to have been used to scrape animal skins so that they could be made into clothing.

About 45,000 years ago, the weather warmed up slightly. This warm period lasted nearly 10,000 years. During this time, the Neanderthals invented flint knives with blunt backs, wood engravers, and other tools. For some reason, most of the Neanderthal humans died out about this time. Other kinds of *Homo sapiens* developed into modern humans.

PREHISTORIC PEOPLE AND THEIR TOOLS

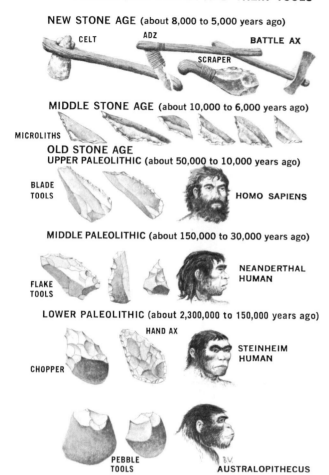

NEW STONE AGE (about 8,000 to 5,000 years ago)

CELT ADZ BATTLE AX
SCRAPER

MIDDLE STONE AGE (about 10,000 to 6,000 years ago)

MICROLITHS

OLD STONE AGE
UPPER PALEOLITHIC (about 50,000 to 10,000 years ago)

BLADE TOOLS HOMO SAPIENS

MIDDLE PALEOLITHIC (about 150,000 to 30,000 years ago)

NEANDERTHAL HUMAN
FLAKE TOOLS

LOWER PALEOLITHIC (about 2,300,000 to 150,000 years ago)

HAND AX
CHOPPER STEINHEIM HUMAN

PEBBLE TOOLS AUSTRALOPITHECUS

Burial of the dead was practiced by many tribes of *Homo sapiens*. Nearly complete skeletons have been found in rock shelters in France, Africa, and Australia.

The first people to arrive in Australia probably traveled aboard some kind of raft. Hunters in Siberia, following prey, traveled across a strip of land (land bridge) that once connected Siberia and Alaska. These hunters were the first to live on the North American continent. They were the ancestors of the North American Indians.

By the last part of the Ice Age (Upper Paleolithic), there were many groups of people living in different parts of the world. Although they lived in different ways, they still had much in common. The effort to invent and make better tools continued. **Blade tools**— long, narrow, sharp chips—were made from the cores of flint. These blades were shaped into knives, scrapers, engraving tools, drills, and spear points. Bone and antlers were used

to make spear points, fish hooks, and needles.

People had time to devote to making jewelry and decorating clothes. Shells, teeth, and ivory were used to make necklaces and to decorate belts, caps, and loincloths. These precious belongings were carried from campsite to campsite. Up to this time, most things had been left behind when a new campsite was chosen. Now people began to accumulate and conserve possessions.

Upper Paleolithic people created art as well, decorating the roofs and walls of caves with skillful paintings of animals. The beauty of these prehistoric paintings came as a surprise when they were first discovered in Spain in the late 19th century.

The caves were seldom inhabited. For homes, the Upper Paleolithic hunting bands preferred rock shelters, under which they pitched tents. Where there were no rock shelters, the hunters built half-buried houses with roofs made of a framework of poles covered with skins.

▶ THE MIDDLE STONE AGE

By 8000 B.C., the glaciers had begun to melt away, opening up new lands in northern Europe, Asia, and North America. Hunters followed reindeer and musk-ox into these new lands. As forests grew up in southern areas, game animals became harder to find.

People had to devise new hunting tools. One new hunting tool was the **microlith**. Microliths were tiny flint blades glued onto wood to form barbed arrows, spears, knives, and sickles. The bow and arrow became another common weapon. Traps and nets were used to catch fish. Shellfish were gathered and eaten.

With the new ways of hunting came new ways of living. In Japan, a clay pot was invented for cooking clams. People made boats and sleighs to use for hunting. Dogs joined the hunt and were tamed to become the first domesticated animals. People found that they could now get from other people materials that they could not find on their own camping and hunting grounds. This was the beginning of trade. Warring tribes became friendly in order to engage in trade.

▶ THE NEW STONE AGE

The taming of animals grew to include animals that could be used for food. Farming began with the planting and harvesting of edible plants. The New Stone Age began.

Farming and trading with other groups made it easier for people to remain in one place. This meant that they could accumulate more belongings. People discovered how to make and sharpen tools by grinding and rubbing them. This new method was especially useful for making axes and hoes. It was a distinct invention of the New Stone Age, but farming was by far the most important development of this period.

Farmers, Herders, and Villagers

The first farming was done across a wide area of southern Asia, from the Middle East to the northern Indochina peninsula. Soon after 8000 B.C., people in this area began to grow wheat and barley. They also began to keep sheep, goats, and pigs. Rice and bananas were grown in Southeast Asia, and cattle raising began in northeastern Africa and Europe.

Crops and domesticated animals ensured a more regular food supply, and the number of people living in a group grew larger. Instead of roaming, they stayed in one place to tend their gardens. They began building houses of reeds and dried mud, woven branches plastered with clay, logs, or stone. Tiny villages appeared. The people started to make simple rules for living and working together.

A more settled way of life gave them more time to think and experiment. They invented a way of making fired clay containers for cooking and storing the grains they grew. They learned to spin flax fibers and to weave the fibers into fabric on looms. From village to village there was a good deal of trading of such things as flint, amber, seashells, and semiprecious stones. Small clay symbols were used to keep track of trading records. For example, a tiny clay cone represented a conical loaf of bread.

From southern Asia, farming spread slowly across Asia into northern Africa and Europe. When populations became too large for local hunting or farming, people moved on.

The time between 5000 and 3000 B.C. was a period of great invention and discovery in the Near and Middle East. People learned how to grow new crops. They used donkeys and oxen as beasts of burden. They molded and

Middle Stone Age people used traps woven of reeds to catch fish.

baked mud and straw into bricks. They dug irrigation ditches linking rivers with garden plots so they could cultivate crops in dry places.

They learned that the position of the sun and stars changed with the seasons. Huge stones, or megaliths, arranged in circles or parallel rows were used as devices for sighting objects in the sky and plotting the positions of these objects. This information about the seasons helped the farmers to decide when to plant crops and when to bring livestock down from mountain pastures to warm shelter.

Most important of all, the New Stone Age people discovered how to use metal. They first experimented with copper. In the beginning, they treated metal as though it were stone, pounding it into various shapes. Then they learned how to melt and cast it. Copper was used to make jewelry and other decorative items. About 3000 B.C., people discovered that copper could be melted with tin to make

New Stone Age villagers at work. Left to right: Pounding grain, grinding the grain into meal, shaping a clay pot on a potter's wheel, and lighting a fire by striking a flint stone against a stone containing iron.

axes and other tools that were even stronger than stone. This strong metal is called bronze.

▶HISTORIC TIME BEGINS

Metalworking brought many important changes. The need for copper and tin made trade more important because the ores for these metals were found in only a few places. As trade increased, villages grew into cities. The old clay symbols used to keep records were discarded for drawings. Drawings were lighter and took up less room. From these first drawings, writing was developed shortly before 3000 B.C. Writing was bound to be useful not only for trading but also for keeping records of events. In this way, the recording of human history began.

The Bronze Age

The development of bronze, which is a mixture of copper and tin, made many changes in human life. Bronze was used to make many different objects, including tools and strong weapons. People who had bronze weapons and armor easily defeated their primitive neighbors. The first empires were formed in southern Asia and the Middle East.

Knowledge of how to make bronze spread from the Middle East to Greece and other parts of the world. In Europe and central Asia, villages united under tribal chiefs. The chiefs supervised the distribution of bronze weapons and farming tools.

The difficulty of obtaining scarce copper and tin made bronze an expensive metal. Then glassmakers in ancient Turkey discovered that a strong metal could be made from iron. Some iron ore is found in most parts of the world. Word of this strong, cheap metal—even better than bronze—spread rapidly. From 1000 to 750 B.C., most of Europe and Asia began to use iron for making weapons and tools.

The Iron Age

During the Iron Age, steel was developed. The blacksmith found that when carbon, or soot, from the forge was hammered into iron, the iron became a metal called steel. Steel was even stronger than iron. The use of steel made it possible to improve old tools and invent new ones. Steel supports were used to make strong wagons and ships.

Inexpensive steel made it possible for every person to carry a weapon for protection. Now tribal chiefs of Europe and Asia could defend their villages against city empires. The use of metal coins and improvements in transportation encouraged the expansion of trade. And where trade spread, large cities grew up.

RALPH M. ROWLETT
University of Missouri—Columbia

See also ANTHROPOLOGY; ARCHAEOLOGY; FIRE; FOSSILS; ICE AGES; PREHISTORIC ART; TOOLS.

PREPOSITION. See PARTS OF SPEECH.
PRESERVATION OF FOOD. See FOOD PRESERVATION.

Some high school—age students attend private, independent secondary schools that are known as preparatory schools. Although these schools vary greatly in size, setting, and academic programs, all of them stress sound preparation for college.

PREPARATORY SCHOOLS

Preparatory schools are independent secondary schools that prepare students for college. While the majority of today's secondary school students attend free public high schools, a smaller number attend nonpublic, or independent, schools. Because independent schools are not run by a city, county, state, or province, they are not supported by taxes and must charge fees, or tuition.

Independent schools are of many different types. In some independent schools, students live at home and commute to school each day. These schools are known as day schools. At other schools, called boarding schools, students live at the school and go home only on vacations. Some independent schools are run by religious groups, and others are organized as military academies. Some teach only boys, others only girls. The term "preparatory school," frequently shortened to "prep" school, generally refers to a particular type of independent school that developed in America shortly after the Civil War.

▶ **HISTORY**

During much of early American history, few young people attended college. Those who did usually were prepared at home by private tutors or in schools known as grammar schools and academies. These schools charged small fees to teach subjects, such as Latin and Greek, that were required for admission to college.

Free public high schools, open to all, were not common until after the Civil War. The growth of industry and cities and the establishment of many new public colleges and universities led to the creation of more and more public high schools. By 1900 the public high school was the most common type of secondary school in America.

However, some parents, especially those from families who traditionally sent their children to college, felt that the public high schools tried to do too much. As a result, college preparation seemed neglected. For this and a number of other reasons, a type of secondary school new to America developed. These schools, because they were specially designed to prepare students for college, became known as preparatory schools.

Some preparatory schools were entirely new, while others were remodeled grammar schools or academies. They were greatly influenced by the famous British boarding schools, such as Eton, Harrow, and Rugby, and adopted many of their traditions.

While continuing to emphasize the subjects required for college admission, the new preparatory schools did more. Like the British schools, they provided dormitories in which students lived together under the supervision of a teacher who lived in the same building. They encouraged organized athletics as a way of teaching healthy competition, team work, school spirit, and sportsmanship. They sought to teach good manners, character, and proper behavior as well as academics. Most required attendance at frequent religious services, and many were run by the clergy.

Many of the new schools were located in the country or in small towns, because the growing cities were thought to be difficult places to raise children. Boys and girls almost always attended separate schools.

▶ PREPARATORY SCHOOLS TODAY

While traditional features remain, preparatory schools have changed over the years. Although in the United States the largest number are still located in the Northeast, where they originated, examples are now found throughout the country. Latin (and in some cases even Greek) is still taught, but students have a wider choice of subjects to study. Schools also actively seek students from a wide variety of backgrounds, and financial aid is available to qualified students. Student life in most schools is less formal than it once was, but perhaps the greatest change of all has been coeducation—the education of boys and girls in the same school.

Because preparatory schools educate a small percentage of high school–age children, they are not always well known or understood. Why do some students prefer to attend such a school? The main reason is sound preparation for college. Classes are usually smaller than in public school, and students receive a great deal of individual attention.

The programs offered by nearby schools do not always fit a student's personal or academic needs and interests. Students may wish to attend school in another part of the country or the world and meet people different from those they would meet at home.

While most preparatory schools have common features, they also differ in important ways. Some are quite small, while others enroll more than 1,000 students. Some offer religious instruction, which public schools are not allowed to teach. Preparatory schools also vary greatly in the levels of academic and athletic competition they provide. This variety makes it possible to find a school to fit a particular student.

▶ CHOOSING A SCHOOL

Where can students and their families turn for information on preparatory schools? Local educators and professional counselors can offer advice, and most public libraries contain guides and directories of independent schools.

A general investigation should reveal several schools that seem appropriate. Write or telephone these schools for catalogs and other information and study this material carefully. At first, many schools may seem to be quite similar. Differences begin to appear when courses offered, graduation requirements, and special activities or athletics available are compared. The geographical distribution of students and the colleges and universities a school's graduates attend also provide important information about a school's reputation and the strength of its academic program.

After studying each school's materials, visits should be arranged to those schools that seem best suited to the prospective student's needs. A visit, which should be arranged in advance, will normally include at least one formal interview. Part of this interview will be with the student alone so the school can get an accurate sense of the prospective student's personality. The student should come prepared to ask questions about dress requirements, financial aid, arts programs, dormitory life, and other concerns.

The more each side knows about the other, the better the "fit" between student and school. Try to meet the head of the school and talk with faculty members or a coach if a particular sport is of interest. Visit a class and a dormitory and, if possible, attend an athletic or extracurricular event. Ask for copies of the school newspaper and other publications. Make it a point to talk with students.

If a campus visit leads to positive impressions, a formal application for admission should be submitted. Most applications require the prospective student to write at least one essay and to submit test scores from a national examination. Applications should be made to schools of differing degrees of competitiveness. If a candidate is accepted at several schools, a second visit to some or all may be necessary to obtain more information.

The Editors of Bunting and Lyon, Inc.
Publishers of the Directory *Private
Independent Schools*

See also EDUCATION.

George
Washington
1789-97

John
Adams
1797-1801

Thomas
Jefferson
1801-09

James
Madison
1809-17

James
Monroe
1817-25

John
Quincy
Adams
1825-29

PRESIDENCY OF
THE UNITED STATES

Every four years, on the first Tuesday after the first Monday of November, millions of Americans go to the polls to choose a new leader in a free and open election. The candidates, nominated during the preceding summer at the conventions of their respective political parties, have waged vigorous campaigns. Through the media of radio, television, newspapers, and magazines, they have made known their views on both national and international affairs and have become familiar faces to the people of the nation.

On Inauguration Day, January 20, the successful candidate for the high office of president of the United States takes this oath of office:

> "I do solemnly swear (or affirm) that I will faithfully execute the Office of President of the United States, and will to the best of my Ability, preserve, protect and defend the Constitution of the United States."

This is the same oath that has been taken by every American president since George Washington. And yet, in the two centuries since the first president was inaugurated, the obligations and duties implied in the oath have changed. The key to the changes lies in the words, "the Office of the President." Exactly what is the office of the president? What was it originally intended to be? And what has it become?

▶THE GROWTH OF THE PRESIDENCY

The men who wrote the Constitution of the United States were opposed to the idea of an all-powerful head of state. America's Founding Fathers thought of the presidency as an office of great honor and dignity, but one with little real power. The American colonists in general favored the parliamentary system of government but did not believe that all governmental powers should rest within any one body. So, in framing the Constitution, they provided for three separate branches—legislative, executive, and judicial.

Article I of the Constitution deals with the functions of the House of Representatives and the Senate. Not until Article II is any mention made of the president. This article states

Andrew
Jackson
1829-37

Martin
Van Buren
1837-41

William
Henry
Harrison
1841

John
Tyler
1841-45

James K.
Polk
1845-49

Zachary
Taylor
1849-50

that the president shall be the head of the executive branch of the government. But to limit and restrict the office, the Constitution provides Congress with checks against any president who may try to assume too much authority.

The framers of the Constitution believed that in the presidency they had created an office of prestige but little power. They would be astounded if they knew the changes that have occurred. The powers and responsibilities of the president have grown enormously. The president has become the leader of his country in fact as well as in name. His words and deeds affect the course of history not only in the United States but in every country throughout the world.

The men who were presidents early in the history of the republic were able to carry on the duties of their office with little assistance. When George Washington served as first president of the United States, his staff consisted of a secretary, one or two clerks, and household servants who acted as messengers. But with the enormous growth in presidential power and responsibilities, the office of the presidency now must be run by a large staff.

Today the president of the United States requires the assistance of over 1,500 people.

The employees assigned to jobs directly relating to the office of the presidency are staff members of the Executive Office of the President. The Executive Office was created by Congress, but it can be reorganized by the president through executive orders.

The Cabinet

The president's cabinet is one of the most important parts of the executive branch of the government. The cabinet was not provided for by the Constitution, nor was it created by an act of Congress. It developed through necessity. The cabinet traces its beginnings to George Washington's assembling his department heads in 1793 to discuss U.S. neutrality in the French Revolutionary wars.

The cabinet is made up of the heads of the 14 departments of the government. Its function is to advise the president on matters of the greatest importance. One of the first tasks of a new president is to select a cabinet. You can read more about this presidential advisory group in the CABINET OF THE UNITED STATES article in Volume C.

Millard Fillmore 1850-53

Franklin Pierce 1853-57

James Buchanan 1857-61

Abraham Lincoln 1861-65

Andrew Johnson 1865-69

Ulysses S. Grant 1869-77

The first executive posts, which became the president's cabinet, were created in 1789. They were the following:

Secretary of Foreign Affairs (State)
Secretary of War
Secretary of the Treasury
Attorney General

The present-day cabinet includes the following heads of executive departments:

Secretary of State
Secretary of the Treasury
Secretary of Defense
Attorney General (Justice Department)
Secretary of the Interior
Secretary of Agriculture
Secretary of Commerce
Secretary of Labor
Secretary of Health and Human Services
Secretary of Education
Secretary of Housing and Urban Development
Secretary of Transportation
Secretary of Energy
Secretary of Veterans Affairs

The president may also choose other members of government to serve in the cabinet; the vice president, the White House chief of staff, and the director of the Office of Management and Budget may all join the cabinet at the president's discretion.

▶ PRESIDENTIAL LEADERSHIP

The vast and complicated structure needed to run today's government has brought many changes to the office of the presidency. With each new president, the machinery of government becomes more complex.

The rise of presidential power did not come about all at once. Nor did the growth of leadership follow a fixed and steady course. Some presidents have strongly exercised the power of leadership. Others have been relatively weak leaders.

Since the time of George Washington many presidents have contributed to changing the powers of the office. People often have different views as to whether a president has acted wisely and exercised his power for the general good of the entire nation. Leadership takes many forms, and all leaders cannot appeal to all people. The leadership qualities of a few presidents, however, will serve to show how some have used the power of their office.

Thomas Jefferson was the nation's third president. Even though he served so early in the history of the office, he understood that in order to gain the results he desired, he would have to exercise a great deal of political power. Jefferson skillfully organized his sympathizers in Congress into a strong political group. These men worked together so well that they often were able to defeat their opponents in many important matters. This plan of Jefferson's was the start of the system of political parties as we know it today.

Andrew Jackson, seventh president of the United States, was another strong leader. Jackson was the first man of the people to be elected to the presidency. Many of the men in the government were not friendly to the new president or to his views. But Jackson was determined to overcome his opponents. In critical issues he relied on the support of the people and removed cabinet members who disagreed with his policies. By the skillful use of his leadership qualities, he was able to carry out many of his programs.

The strongest desire of President Abraham Lincoln was to preserve the Union. At the outbreak of the Civil War, Lincoln did not have the power to call up troops or to take certain other actions. But he knew that in order to protect the Union he would have to assume wartime powers. Many people disapproved of his actions. But Lincoln seized the power he felt he must have. By exercising leadership in a time of crisis, he succeeded in preserving the Union.

Woodrow Wilson, during whose term the bitter battles of World War I were fought, had one great dream. The dream was for the creation of a League of Nations that would help to prevent future wars. The League of Nations finally was established at the close of the war. But in spite of Wilson's strength, his own country refused to join. Wilson died a disappointed man. But under his leadership the office of the presidency outgrew the bounds of the United States and became an office with international responsibilities.

In another period of serious trouble for the United States, Franklin D. Roosevelt served as president. During the Depression of the 1930's Roosevelt sought tremendous powers. He recommended to Congress legislation that would create jobs for those who could find no work, in order to get the country back on its

FACTS ABOUT THE PRESIDENCY

Qualifications: (1) Natural-born citizen of the United States. (2) At least 35 years old. (3) At least 14 years a resident of the United States. Candidates are usually nominated at national party conventions held in the summer of the election year. Although only men have served as president, women are eligible to hold the office.

Election: By a majority vote of the Electoral College.

Term: 4 years. A president may not serve more than 2 terms (plus 2 years of an unexpired term).

Salary: (1) $200,000 plus allowances for expenses, travel, and official entertainment totaling $170,000. (2) Provided with White House, household help, transportation, health care. (3) Lifetime pension of $60,000 annually.

Removal: May be impeached (accused of serious wrongdoing) by a majority of the House of Representatives; must then be tried by the Senate and convicted by a two-thirds vote.

Succession: If the president dies or is disabled in office, the line of succession is as follows:

(1) Vice President of the United States
(2) Speaker of the House
(3) President Pro Tempore of the Senate
(4) Secretary of State
(5) Secretary of the Treasury
(6) Secretary of Defense
(7) Attorney General
(8) Secretary of the Interior
(9) Secretary of Agriculture
(10) Secretary of Commerce
(11) Secretary of Labor
(12) Secretary of Health and Human Services
(13) Secretary of Housing and Urban Development
(14) Secretary of Transportation
(15) Secretary of Energy
(16) Secretary of Education
(17) Secretary of Veterans Affairs

ASSASSINATIONS AND ATTEMPTS

1835	January 30: Andrew Jackson escaped assassination by Richard Lawrence in Washington, D.C.
1865	April 14: Abraham Lincoln shot by John Wilkes Booth in Washington, D.C. Died April 15.
1881	July 2: James A. Garfield shot by Charles J. Guiteau in Washington, D.C. Died September 19.
1901	September 6: William McKinley shot by Leon Czolgosz in Buffalo, New York. Died September 14.
1933	February 15: Franklin D. Roosevelt escaped assassination by Giuseppe Zangara in Miami, Florida.
1950	November 1: Harry S. Truman escaped assassination by two Puerto Rican nationalists in Washington, D.C.
1963	November 22: John F. Kennedy shot and killed in Dallas, Texas.
1975	September 5 and 22: President Gerald R. Ford twice escaped assassination in California.
1981	March 30: Ronald W. Reagan was wounded in an assassination attempt in Washington, D.C.

INTERESTING FACTS ABOUT PRESIDENTS

JOHN QUINCY ADAMS and **ANDREW JOHNSON** were the only men to serve in Congress after being president.

MARTIN VAN BUREN was the first president born after the signing of the Declaration of Independence.

WILLIAM HENRY HARRISON was president for the shortest time. He died of pneumonia 31 days after his inauguration.

JAMES BUCHANAN was the only president who never married.

ABRAHAM LINCOLN, at 6 feet 4 inches, was the tallest president.

THEODORE ROOSEVELT was the youngest person to become president (at age 42, following the assassination of McKinley) and the first to win the Nobel Peace Prize.

WILLIAM HOWARD TAFT was the only president who also served as Chief Justice of the Supreme Court.

HERBERT HOOVER was the first president born west of the Mississippi River.

FRANKLIN D. ROOSEVELT was the only president to be elected to more than two terms.

JOHN F. KENNEDY was the first Roman Catholic president and the youngest person to be *elected* president (at age 43; compare with T. Roosevelt).

RICHARD M. NIXON was the only president to resign from office.

GERALD R. FORD was the first president who had not been elected to the presidency or vice presidency.

RONALD REAGAN was the oldest person (69) to be elected president and the first ever to be divorced.

Eight vice presidents became presidents when their predecessors died. They were:

JOHN TYLER (succeeded William Henry Harrison).

MILLARD FILLMORE (succeeded Zachary Taylor).

ANDREW JOHNSON (succeeded Abraham Lincoln).

CHESTER ARTHUR (succeeded James A. Garfield).

THEODORE ROOSEVELT (succeeded William McKinley).

CALVIN COOLIDGE (succeeded Warren G. Harding).

HARRY S. TRUMAN (succeeded Franklin D. Roosevelt).

LYNDON B. JOHNSON (succeeded John F. Kennedy).

Seven presidents won fame as soldier-heroes. They were:

GEORGE WASHINGTON in the American Revolutionary War.

ANDREW JACKSON in the War of 1812.

WILLIAM HENRY HARRISON in the War of 1812.

ZACHARY TAYLOR in the Mexican War.

ULYSSES S. GRANT in the Civil War.

THEODORE ROOSEVELT in the Spanish-American War.

DWIGHT D. EISENHOWER in World War II.

Some presidents were related to other presidents. They were:

JOHN ADAMS and **JOHN QUINCY ADAMS** (father and son).

THEODORE ROOSEVELT and **FRANKLIN D. ROOSEVELT** (distant cousins).

WILLIAM HENRY HARRISON and **BENJAMIN HARRISON** (grandfather and grandson).

feet. He even attempted to change the structure of the Supreme Court by increasing the number of justices. During World War II he extended United States influence in the field of international relations.

Even though the president of the United States is today one of the most important individuals in the world, he is not all-powerful. There is an authority that is higher than that of the president. It is the will of the people of the United States, who have reserved to themselves the final authority that is called sovereignty.

▶ **DUTIES AND POWERS OF THE PRESIDENT**

"The executive Power shall be vested in a President of the United States of America. He shall hold his Office during the Term of four Years. . . ."

These words form the opening of Article II of the Constitution, outlining the powers and duties of the president. The four sections of the article also state how the president shall be elected and paid, and who shall succeed him if he is unable to serve out his term. This Article, written in a careful and straightforward manner, suggests that the document's framers were on their guard against the possibility of a too ambitious president. It gives little hint, however, that they had any idea of how enormous and important the office of the presidency would one day become.

To the average citizen it often seems that the power of the president is unlimited. But that is far from the truth. What acts is the president permitted to perform without restrictions of any kind? What is he prohibited from doing? The answers to these questions give some idea of the powers of the president and of the system of checks and balances provided by the Constitution.

Article II states that the president shall be commander in chief of the Army and the Navy. He shall have the power to make treaties—provided two-thirds of the Senate agrees. He shall appoint ambassadors, Supreme Court justices, and other officials—"by and with the Advice and Consent of the Senate." Section 3 of the Article provides that he shall address Congress on the state of the Union, see that laws are carefully carried out, and receive foreign ambassadors and ministers. Basically, all these provisions of the Constitution are still in force today.

Rutherford
B. Hayes
1877-81

James A.
Garfield
1881

Chester
Alan
Arthur
1881-85

Grover
Cleveland
1885-89
1893-97

Benjamin
Harrison
1889-93

William
McKinley
1897-1901

Even within the framework of the Constitution the duties and powers of the president have become highly complex. The best way to understand them is to examine the various branches of the government and see how the president functions in each.

Executive and Administrative Powers

The president stands at the head of the executive branch of the government. He is elected by the entire nation and is responsible for carrying out and administering the laws approved by the legislative branch—Congress. The Constitution outlined these powers only in the most general terms. Most presidential authority, therefore, has been granted by acts of Congress.

Power of Appointment and Removal. The president has the power to appoint important officials. The list of these officials includes ambassadors, members of the cabinet and their assistants, federal judges, military and naval officers, heads of agencies, and United States attorneys and marshals. In almost all cases Senate approval is assured. The president does, therefore, exercise a great deal of power in the choice of the people named for

key government posts. In 1926 the Supreme Court ruled that since the president has the power to appoint officers, the president also should have the power to remove them.

Executive Ordinances. Administration of policies outlined by Congress usually is left to the executive branch. The president (or subordinates acting for him) spells out the details in the form of executive orders that have the force of law.

Legislative Powers

The president is given certain legislative powers that make it possible for him to exert considerable influence over Congress.

Power to Recommend Legislation. At the beginning of each session of Congress the president delivers his "State of the Union" message. In his address he recommends a legislative program. This is followed by a proposed budget and economic report. The president also may submit special messages from time to time on particular subjects. In this way he makes known to Congress the laws he considers necessary.

Veto Power. Every bill or joint resolution passed by Congress must be sent to the presi-

Theodore
Roosevelt
1901-09

William
Howard
Taft
1909-13

Woodrow
Wilson
1913-21

Warren G.
Harding
1921-23

Calvin
Coolidge
1923-29

EXECUTIVE OFFICE OF THE PRESIDENT

The White House Office
Office of the Vice President
Office of the First Lady
Office of Management and Budget
Council of Economic Advisers
National Security Council
Office of Policy Development
Office of the United States Trade Representative
Council on Environmental Quality
Office of Science and Technology Policy
Office of Administration
Office of National Drug Control Policy
President's Foreign Intelligence Advisory Board
President's Intelligence Oversight Board

dent for action. If he signs it, it becomes law. If he vetoes it, he must send it back with the reasons for his veto. The veto power enables the president to act as a check on Congress.

Judicial Powers

The chief executive can exercise his judicial power in several ways. He recommends to the Senate his choices for Attorney General and Supreme Court justices. In every district of the country he appoints federal court judges and the United States district attorneys.

Pardoning Power. The president has the power to pardon a citizen of an offense. He may also grant a reprieve, or postponement of punishment. He cannot exercise this power in impeachment cases, where a pardon can never be granted.

Powers in Foreign Affairs

The president has enormous powers in the field of foreign affairs. He is the nation's chief diplomat. He receives diplomatic representatives, ambassadors, and ministers from foreign countries, and sometimes attends special international conferences.

Herbert
Hoover
1929-33

Franklin D.
Roosevelt
1933-45

Harry S.
Truman
1945-53

Dwight D.
Eisenhower
1953-61

John F.
Kennedy
1961-63

Lyndon
Baines
Johnson
1963-69

Power of Recognition. The president has the power of recognition—the formal approval of the government of a foreign country. Without recognition, normal trade and diplomatic relations cannot exist between two countries.

Treaty Power. If the United States wants to enter into commercial pacts, define its boundaries, make peace, or enter into any other international agreement, the president may negotiate a treaty with the country or countries concerned. The president shares this power with the Senate. Two-thirds of that body must ratify, or approve, a treaty before it goes into effect.

Executive Agreements. Agreements between the president and the chief executive (rather than the official government) of a foreign country are not subject to Senate approval.

Military Powers

As stated in the Constitution, the president is commander in chief of the armed forces. This position guarantees that the people always shall control the Army through their elected civilian leaders. Here, too, the president's powers are shared with Congress. Congress makes rules for the armed forces, sets

---

PRESIDENTIAL DISABILITY

The Constitution made no clear provisions for what would happen if a president became disabled in office. In 1965, Congress approved a projected 25th constitutional amendment that deals with this problem. The amendment became part of the Constitution in 1967, when it received the approval of three-fourths of the states.

The main provisions of the amendment are:

(1) If the president is disabled, he informs the vice president and the congressional officers—the president pro tempore of the Senate and the speaker of the House of Representatives. The vice president then takes over as acting president.

(2) If the disabled president fails to inform the congressional officers, then the vice president, with the written approval of a majority of the cabinet "or of such other body as Congress may by law provide," so informs the congressional officers. The vice president then takes over as acting president.

(3) When the president has recovered, he informs the congressional officers. However, if the vice president and a majority of the cabinet or of the "other body" do not agree that the president has recovered, it is up to Congress to decide. A two-thirds vote of both houses would be needed to continue the vice president as acting president.

Richard M.
Nixon
1969-74

Gerald R.
Ford
1974-77

James Earl
Carter, Jr.
1977-81

Ronald W.
Reagan
1981-89

George H.W.
Bush
1989–93

William J.B.
Clinton
1993–

apart funds for defense, and has the power to declare war. Appointments or commissions of military officers must be confirmed by the Senate. But in many emergencies the president can act without the consent of either house of Congress. He may use armed forces in combat abroad without a formal declaration of war. He may send troops to protect the mails and interstate commerce. At the request of a governor or state legislature, he may send troops into a state in case of domestic violence which is beyond the control of state and local police.

Political Party Leader

The president is the leader of his party. In this role he influences party policy in national and international affairs. He makes wide use of his patronage power—the power to appoint members of his own party to government posts. He also has the power to grant favors of many kinds to officials of either party.

The Presidency Today

The United States and its position in the world have changed greatly since the president's duties were outlined in the Constitution.

The role of the president has grown from that of a largely honorary officer to a powerful leader in national and international affairs. He is the single, unifying force in a political system in which power is highly dispersed. Probably no other person exercises as much influence in today's world as the president of the United States. What the president does cannot fail to affect the course of history.

But no matter how popular or powerful a president may be, his term of office is limited. At the end of four years he must submit his record to the people. If they do not re-elect him, he must surrender his power. The 22nd Amendment to the Constitution provides that no president can be elected more than twice. As long as these safeguards exist, complete sovereignty will remain subject to the will of the people.

GERALD W. JOHNSON
Author, *The Presidency*
Reviewed by DAVID C. WHITNEY
Author, *The American Presidents*

See also CABINET OF THE UNITED STATES; ELECTORAL COLLEGE; IMPEACHMENT; VICE PRESIDENCY OF THE UNITED STATES.

PRESIDENTS' WIVES. See FIRST LADIES.

PRIESTLEY, JOSEPH (1733–1804)

Joseph Priestley, a great scientist, was also a minister and a schoolteacher. He spoke out fearlessly in defense of liberty and of his religious, social, political, and scientific ideas. He wrote and preached tirelessly on many subjects, but he is best known for his scientific discoveries.

Priestley discovered a number of gases, then known as "airs." They include oxygen, nitrous oxide (laughing gas), sulfur dioxide, ammonia, and carbon monoxide. He also invented reliable ways of testing and making each gas.

Priestley was born in Birstal Fieldhead near Leeds in England on March 13, 1733. His family was poor, so at a young age Joseph was sent to live with an aunt. His education was directed toward the ministry though he often had to interrupt his studies in order to earn money. In 1761 he became a teacher at a religious academy. There he taught science by encouraging his pupils to do experiments. This was unusual because laboratory teaching was almost unknown in England at that time.

Priestley, who was deeply committed to his religious beliefs, became a minister in 1762. He was also married the same year. Though his duties as a minister took up much of his time, he continued with his scientific studies. In 1767 he wrote the still-famous book, *History of Electricity*, with the help of Benjamin Franklin, who loaned him books and supported his studies.

In 1773, Priestley became librarian to the Earl of Shelburne. He still found time for laboratory work and wrote five of his six great books on gases as well as several books on religion.

Priestley's greatest scientific triumph came in 1774. In that year he heated a red powder —mercury oxide—and noticed that it produced an "air" that differed in many ways from ordinary air. The French scientist Antoine Lavoisier later combined two Greek words to give this "air" the name it is known by today—oxygen, meaning "acid producer."

Although he was respected as a scientist, Priestley was often unpopular as a minister. He wrote and spoke frequently on religious and political matters and stated views that made him many enemies. For example, he openly sided with the Americans in their

The discovery of oxygen is just one of Joseph Priestley's many accomplishments. In addition to being a scientist, he was also a minister, a schoolteacher, and an author.

grievances against the British, and he sympathized with the French revolutionaries. These views were extremely unpopular in England at the time.

In 1791, Priestley's opposition to the Church of England along with his other ideas made him so unpopular that a mob burned his house and chapel in Birmingham. The fire destroyed his scientific apparatus, laboratory notebooks, and other important papers. In 1794, Priestley and his wife left England for the United States, settling permanently in Northumberland, Pennsylvania, where their two sons lived.

Joseph Priestley died on February 6, 1804, in Northumberland. He was honored then as he is today as one of the most accomplished scientists of his time. To the very last, Priestley continued his writing and preaching and experimenting. And in a tribute to this devoted scientist, Thomas Jefferson, who knew him well, said that his life was "one of the few lives precious to mankind."

LOUIS I. KUSLAN
Southern Connecticut State University

PRIMARY SCHOOLS. See EDUCATION; SCHOOLS.

PRIMATES

More than 70 million years ago, in the shadow of *Tyrannosaurus rex*, lived tiny mammals, probably smaller than squirrels. Their world, ruled by the fearsome dinosaurs, was a dangerous place. But these hardy creatures survived and evolved into a group of animals known as primates, the order of mammals that includes monkeys, apes, and humans.

There are 233 species, or kinds, of primates. Typically scientists separate primates into two major groups: **anthropoids**, which include human beings, apes, and monkeys, and **prosimians**,

which include aye-ayes, galagos, lemurs, lorises, pottos, and tarsiers. Most primates live in the tropics and subtropics of Africa, Asia, and the Americas, although a few, such as the Japanese macaque, live in temperate areas. Human beings are the only primates that populate almost every environment throughout the world.

▶ CHARACTERISTICS OF PRIMATES

As a group, primates have many traits in common, although not every primate has every trait. When you pick up an object with your hand, you demonstrate one of the most important characteristics of primates: Almost all primates have five digits on each limb. Primates have fingers and, in some cases, toes that can grasp and lock on to objects of many different shapes. Scientists believe that the early primates survived by living in the trees, away from large animals, where the ability to grasp branches is an important advantage. Most primates have flat nails on their fingers

and toes, rather than long claws, which get in the way of grasping.

All primates are able to climb trees, and most of them still spend most of their lives above the ground. Those that dwell primarily on the ground include some of the larger monkeys, such as baboons and macaques, the gorilla, and, of course, humans. The anthropoids are diurnal, or active in the day, while most prosimians are nocturnal, or active at night.

Primates have a keen sense of vision, the most important of their five senses. Unlike many mammals, most primates have large eyes set in the head so that they look straight forward.

Primates have developed from a common ancestor into a wide array of animals, such as the mandrill (*below*), human beings (*far left*), and ring-tailed lemurs (*left*), each with its own distinct features.

The anthropoids can focus both eyes on the same object. This ability helps them judge how far away an object is. The placement of the eyes also enables primates to see in three dimensions, while many other mammals see things as flat. For animals that must jump from branch to branch and judge distances in a split second, seeing in three dimensions is a big advantage. The primates with the best

Long, powerful upper limbs allow the gibbon (*above*) to swing quickly and gracefully from branch to branch. With its large staring eyes, the tarsier (*inset*) is well adapted to its nocturnal way of life.

lemur species and monkeys will eat insects, while pottos will kill young birds. For most primates, plants are the main food source. Humans are the primates most likely to eat meat. Baboons and chimpanzees also include the meat of larger animals, such as gazelles and monkeys, in their diets.

▶ THE LIFE OF PRIMATES

The vast majority of primates are social animals; that is, they live in groups and interact regularly with one another. Among the exceptions are the weasel lemurs and the aye-ayes of Madagascar, which live mostly solitary lives. Prosimians tend to form much smaller groups than those of the higher primates, the largest groups of which are the baboons and macaques. These social groups, which often consist of several hundred individuals, can have complicated structures and relationships among their members.

Chimpanzees live in loose groups called **communities** and share a particular area of a habitat. All members of the community do not gather or travel together at the same time within this territory, but they remain neighbors and communicate with one another. The chimpanzees in a community keep a stern watch over their territory, guarding its boundaries from other neighboring groups and attacking those that invade it. Sometimes wars occur between two communities. The wars can be so fierce that one of the communities is completely destroyed.

Not all primate communities have large populations or defend their territories. Squirrel monkeys form groups with a few dozen members and do not seem to defend their territories. Each group of squirrel monkeys is made up of smaller groups—pregnant females form their own group, as do females with young, and adult males. Some primates, including indri lemurs, marmosets, and tamarins, form small family units consisting of adult pairs and their offspring.

The reproductive cycles of primates vary. Most primates, except for lemurs and lorises, have no definite times of the year that they mate. While most males are capable of breed-

eyesight also see colors. Anthropoids have color vision. Most prosimians do not, but colors are not very visible at night, so they are not at a disadvantage. Moreover, prosimian eyes are very large and can gather whatever light is available from the moon and stars.

Most primates have large, well-developed brains and are among the most intelligent of mammals. Certain parts of their brains are particularly well developed. Among these are the parts used in seeing and in controlling movement. However, primates do not depend much on their sense of smell, and that part of the brain is smaller than in many mammals.

A wide variety of foods are consumed by primates, including fruits, buds, roots, leaves, and small animals, such as lizards. Some

Both of these marmosets benefit from a friendly act of grooming (*right*). Many primates, such as the orangutan (*far right*), are attentive parents.

ing at any time, most females have a reproductive cycle that allows them to breed only at specific times. Fewer offspring are born to primates than most other mammals. A mother bears only one or two young at a time. Another difference between primates and other mammals is that the young stay with the mother for a longer period. The long time that primate offspring stay with their mothers allows for learning. In many other mammal groups, the young strike out on their own early in life, and so their behavior is based mostly on instinct. Young primates have instincts, too, but they also learn behavior patterns from their mothers and from the group they live in. Generally, the father primate does not care for the young, although he will protect them and defend them from enemies.

▶ PRIMATES AND THEIR ENVIRONMENT

What separates primates from all other animals is that one of them, the human species, is causing worldwide environmental change that endangers some primates and many other creatures as well. Several primates are threatened with extinction, including some of the smallest, such as the golden lion tamarin, and the largest, the mountain gorilla.

The greatest threat to primates is the destruction of their habitats, particularly the great tropical rain forests. Primate habitats are disappearing because of human activities, such as the clearing of land for agriculture and development and the unrestricted cutting of trees

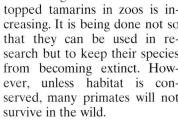

The golden lion tamarin stands at the brink of extinction due to disappearing habitat and its capture for use as a pet and in zoo exhibits.

for timber. Some primates, especially baboons, are killed as pests because they sometimes raid farmers' crops. In some parts of the world, such as West Africa and South America, monkeys are considered a human food source. Hunting endangered few primate populations in the past, but today, because their numbers are dwindling, it is an ever-increasing threat.

Another threat to the primate population exists because some primates are very similar to human beings. Vast numbers of monkeys and apes have been removed from the wild for use in medical research and testing. Although this practice has helped create surgical techniques and medicines that have saved countless human lives, it is the subject of heated debate. Some people believe it is wrong to use primates—or any other animal—in research. Others believe such research is necessary but that it should be more tightly controlled.

The breeding of rare primates such as gorillas and cotton-topped tamarins in zoos is increasing. It is being done not so that they can be used in research but to keep their species from becoming extinct. However, unless habitat is conserved, many primates will not survive in the wild.

EDWARD R. RICCIUTI
Coauthor, *The Audubon Society Book of Wild Animals*
See also MAMMALS.

PRIME MINISTER

In many countries of the world the head of government is called a prime minister or premier. Both "prime" and "premier" mean "first." The prime minister or premier, therefore, is literally the first, or chief, minister of the government.

Appointment and Function. The prime minister usually is appointed by a country's official head of state—who may be a king or queen in a monarchy or a president in a republic. (In the United States and a number of other countries a president serves as both head of state and head of government.) Generally, the head of state appoints as prime minister the leader of the political party that wins a majority (more than half) of the seats in the legislature in an election. If no party wins a majority, the prime minister may be the leader of a coalition government—one based on a combination of political parties. The prime minister chooses a number of other ministers to serve as heads of the various departments of the government. These ministers form an advisory group, usually known as the cabinet.

In many countries, such as Great Britain, where the office of prime minister originated, the prime minister is an especially powerful figure. With the help of the cabinet, the prime minister has the major responsibility for government policy. In fact, the prime minister and cabinet are known as the government. The prime minister and cabinet in turn are responsible to the legislature, of which they must be members. In Great Britain the legislature is called the Parliament, and the prime minister and cabinet are members of its elected chamber, the House of Commons. The cabinet system is sometimes called the parliamentary system of government.

Limits on the Prime Minister's Power. The election system works to prevent a prime minister from misusing the powers of office. If the legislature defeats one of the government's important measures, this is called a "vote of no confidence." After such a vote, an election must be held. If the prime minister's party loses the election, the party with the most votes forms a new government. And the leader of that party becomes prime minister.

The prime minister may also call for elections at other times, to find out whether the voters support the government's policies. In any case, an election must be held after a certain number of years—usually about five.

The power of the prime minister varies from country to country. A prime minister's actual power depends partly on the country's constitution and the powers it gives the head of state. In many countries the role of the head of state, whether monarch or president, is mostly ceremonial. The prime minister is usually the real executive head of the government. There are exceptions, however. The constitution of France, for example, gives more power to the president than to the premier. This is true also in some other countries, where the prime minister may handle the day-to-day operations of the government under the leadership of the president.

The terms "prime minister" and "president" were sometimes used when referring to the governments of Communist countries. But this was often misleading, since real political power rested with Communist party leaders. Most of the former Communist countries of Eastern Europe now have governments that are truly led by presidents or prime ministers who govern at the will of the people.

Origin of the Prime Minister's Office. The office of prime minister evolved from the British cabinet and parliamentary system of government. Sir Robert Walpole (1676–1745) is usually regarded as Great Britain's first prime minister. The development of the modern office of prime minister, however, is generally considered to date from the 1800's, and the title of prime minister itself was not formally adopted in Great Britain until the early 1900's. The British system of parliamentary government spread around the world as lands that once had been part of the British empire gained independence and adopted the British system.

Parliamentary forms of government, headed by prime ministers, developed as well in other European countries. (In Germany the head of government is called the chancellor.) These countries also brought their systems of government to territories that once were their colonies but are now independent nations. As a result, many of the world's people today are governed under parliamentary systems of one kind or another headed by prime ministers.

JOHN S. MOIR
University of Toronto

See also PARLIAMENTS.

SOME FAMOUS PRIME MINISTERS

William Pitt, the Younger
(1759–1806), Great Britain

William Ewart Gladstone
(1809–98), Great Britain

Winston Churchill
(1874–1965), Great Britain

Georges Clemenceau,
(1841–1929), France

Otto von Bismarck
(1815–98), Germany

Jawaharlal Nehru
(1889–1964), India

Indira Gandhi
(1917–84), India

Eamon de Valera
(1882–1975), Ireland

David Ben-Gurion
(1886–1973), Israel

John A. Macdonald
(1815–91), Canada

Wilfrid Laurier
(1841–1919), Canada

William Lyon Mackenzie King
(1874–1950), Canada

Margaret Thatcher
(1925–   ), Great Britain

Golda Meir
(1898–1978), Israel

PRIME MINISTERS WITH BIOGRAPHIES IN *THE NEW BOOK OF KNOWLEDGE*

Asquith, Herbert Henry
Attlee, Clement
Balfour, Arthur James
Begin, Menahem
Ben-Gurion, David
Bhutto, Benazir
Bhutto, Zulfikar Ali
Bismarck, Otto von
Brown, George
Campbell, Kim
Chamberlain, Neville
Chrétien, Jean
Churchill, Sir Winston
Clark, Charles Joseph
Clemenceau, Georges
Diefenbaker, John George
Disraeli, Benjamin
Gandhi, Indira
Gandhi, Rajiv

Gladstone, William Ewart
King, William Lyon Mackenzie
Laurier, Sir Wilfrid
Lloyd George, David
Macdonald, Sir John A.
Macmillan, Harold
Major, John
Meir, Golda
Mulroney, Martin Brian
Nehru, Jawaharlal
Pearson, Lester
Peel, Sir Robert
Pitt, William, Earl of Chatham
Pitt, William, the Younger
Thatcher, Margaret
Trudeau, Pierre Elliott
Turner, John Napier
Walpole, Sir Robert
Wellington, Duke of

PRINCE EDWARD ISLAND

Prince Edward Island's flag (above) and coat of arms (opposite page) recall its historical ties with England. The three oak saplings, representing the province's three counties, grow near the large oak, which stands for England. The British lion tops the design. P.E.I.'s provincial bird is the blue jay (right); its flower, the lady's slipper (opposite page).

Prince Edward Island is one of the four Atlantic Provinces of Canada. The other three are Nova Scotia, New Brunswick, and Newfoundland. Because of its location in the Gulf of St. Lawrence, its fertile soil, favorable climate, and many farms, Prince Edward Island is often called the Garden of the Gulf. It is the smallest of the Canadian provinces and the only island province. (Newfoundland is an island, but mainland Labrador is included in its territory.)

The original inhabitants of Prince Edward Island, the Micmac Indians, called it *Abegweit,* which means "home cradled on the waves." The first European settlers, the French, named it Ile Saint Jean (Saint John's Island). In 1799 the province was named for Prince Edward, Duke of Kent, the fourth son of King George III of Great Britain. Today Prince Edward Island is usually referred to simply by its initials—P.E.I.

▶THE LAND

Prince Edward Island is shaped roughly like a crescent, or a half-moon. It is nearly 120 miles (190 kilometers) long but varies greatly in width because of the many inlets of the sea. In some places, the island is as little as 3 miles (5 kilometers) wide. In others, it is almost 40 miles (65 kilometers) wide.

To the north of the province lies the Gulf of St. Lawrence; to the south, the Northumberland Strait. The neighboring provinces of Nova Scotia and New Brunswick lie only a few miles away, across the Northumberland Strait. The town of Borden in Prince Edward Island is only 9 miles (14 kilometers) from Cape Tormentine in New Brunswick. The eastern end of Prince Edward Island is only 14 miles (23 kilometers) from Nova Scotia.

The soft sandstone of Prince Edward Island has been worn down over the centuries by erosion, and the island now has a gentle, rolling landscape. There are a few hilly areas, and the highest point, which lies in the southeastern part of the island, is only 465 feet (142 meters) above sea level. The province has only one lake and a few real rivers. Most of the valleys are formed by tidal inlets of the sea.

The coastline of Prince Edward Island is very irregular, with many bays and inlets that jut far inland. On the north coast of the province, sandbars run across the mouths of the bays. Long stretches of beautiful, sandy beaches line this coast. The coastal waters are shallow, and the island has few good ports. To keep some of the ports open, channels have to be dredged, or cleared of sediment.

Climate

Prince Edward Island has the most favorable climate of all the Atlantic Provinces. It is free of fog in winter, and in summer it benefits from the warm waters of the Gulf of St. Lawrence. In summer, the weather is usually warm and sunny. The average July temperature is over 67°F (19°C). For this reason, the province is a popular summer resort area.

In winter the climate is not much different from that of the neighboring coastal areas. Cold air masses from inland Canada sometimes bring temperatures of 0°F (−18°C).

But the average January temperature is 19°F (−7°C). This is warmer than inland New Brunswick but colder than southern Nova Scotia. The Gulf of St. Lawrence and the Northumberland Strait are covered with ice in the winter. Winds blowing across the ice to Prince Edward Island also keep temperatures low.

Natural Resources

The island's rich red soil, or loam, is one of Prince Edward Island's most valuable natural resources. This loam is usually quite fertile. The many streams and coastal waters are filled with different fish and shellfish. The most valuable mineral resource is sand and gravel. Other important resources include a sparkling shoreline and a countryside of unusual natural beauty.

The forests of Prince Edward Island were once important for shipbuilding and lumbering. But most of the forests have been cleared for farming. The remaining forests are a mixture of deciduous and coniferous trees. The chief deciduous trees found on the island are maple, birch, beech, ash, elm, and oak. The coniferous trees include red and black spruce, fir, pine, hemlock, and cedar.

▶THE PEOPLE AND THEIR WORK

Prince Edward Island is the most densely populated of all the Canadian provinces, and the population is fairly evenly distributed throughout the island.

Farming long has been the main occupation. Improved transportation systems and mechanization in the 20th century made modern farming possible. But modern methods required fewer people. The same was true of the fishing industry. A number of small industries have recently located on the island. But it is still necessary for many islanders to seek employment outside the province.

Most of the people are of British, Scottish, or Irish origin. About one sixth of the people are of French descent, and French is still spoken in some areas. There are also some islanders of Dutch, Lebanese, and German stock and a few hundred members of the Micmac tribe. Nearly half the people are Catholics. The rest belong mainly to the United Church and to the Presbyterian, Anglican, and Baptist churches.

Industries and Products

Although farming is the basic activity, fishing, logging, manufacturing, and the tourist industry add to the economy of the province.

Agriculture. More than half of the land is farmed. Because of the fertile soil, the gently rolling land, and the favorable summer climate, a variety of crops can be grown successfully. The province is famous for potatoes—its principal crop. Very large quantities are marketed each year in Canada, the United States, and other parts of the world. Many of the potatoes are sold as seed potatoes.

Dairy farming and cattle raising are also important. Prince Edward Island exports large amounts of cheese, butter, and other dairy products. Other farm products include turnips, grains, fruits, beef, poultry, and eggs. There

are also some fox and mink ranches, where the animals are bred for their pelts.

Fishing. Cod, herring, halibut, and other fish are found in various parts of the Gulf of St. Lawrence. The lack of convenient harbors for large ships limits this type of fishing, and it is not as important here as in the other Atlantic Provinces. But the lobster and oyster fisheries are very valuable. The island has a large annual lobster catch, and it is noted for its excellent oysters. Mussels are also a valuable industry.

Forest Industries. Logging is of some importance on the island. The trees provide wood for fuel, railway ties, and lumber and for export as wood pulp.

Manufacturing. Small plants throughout the island process farm products and fish. Other manufacturing industries include printing and publishing and the building of ships and boats. But manufacturing is limited by problems of transportation and lack of raw materials and by the high cost of power. Since there are few rivers, hydroelectric power cannot be produced, and electricity must be generated by a more costly means—diesel engines.

Tourism. The tourist industry is one of the major sources of revenue for the province. Each summer large numbers of visitors come to Prince Edward Island to enjoy the sunshine, the sandy beaches, golfing, swimming, and other sports and, most of all, the beautiful countryside and shoreline. In addition to hotels and motels, many farms take in guests during the tourist season.

Transportation and Communication

A railway system connects many of the communities in Prince Edward Island. The island has many good paved roads. The main road, which runs the length of the island, is considered part of the Trans-Canada Highway. Air service is provided by Air Canada, Canadian Pacific Air, and Atlantic Air.

There is ferry service all year round between Borden and Cape Tormentine in New Brunswick. The ferries carry people, automobiles, and railway cars and are also used as icebreakers in winter. During the ice-free season, ferries operate between Wood Islands and Caribou in Nova Scotia.

The province has three daily newspapers— the *Guardian* and the *Patriot,* published in Charlottetown, and the *Journal-Pioneer,* published in Summerside. A weekly journal, *The Eastern Graphic,* enjoys a large circulation. It is published in Montague. Several radio and television stations serve the island.

Opposite page: The distinctive red soil of Prince Edward Island is very fertile, and more than half of the land is farmed. *Right:* Potatoes are the principal crop of the province. *Below:* Fishing also contributes to the island's economy, and lobster traps and fishing boats are a common sight in the small coastal villages. *Bottom:* A third important industry is tourism. Sandy beaches such as this one at Cavendish draw large numbers of visitors.

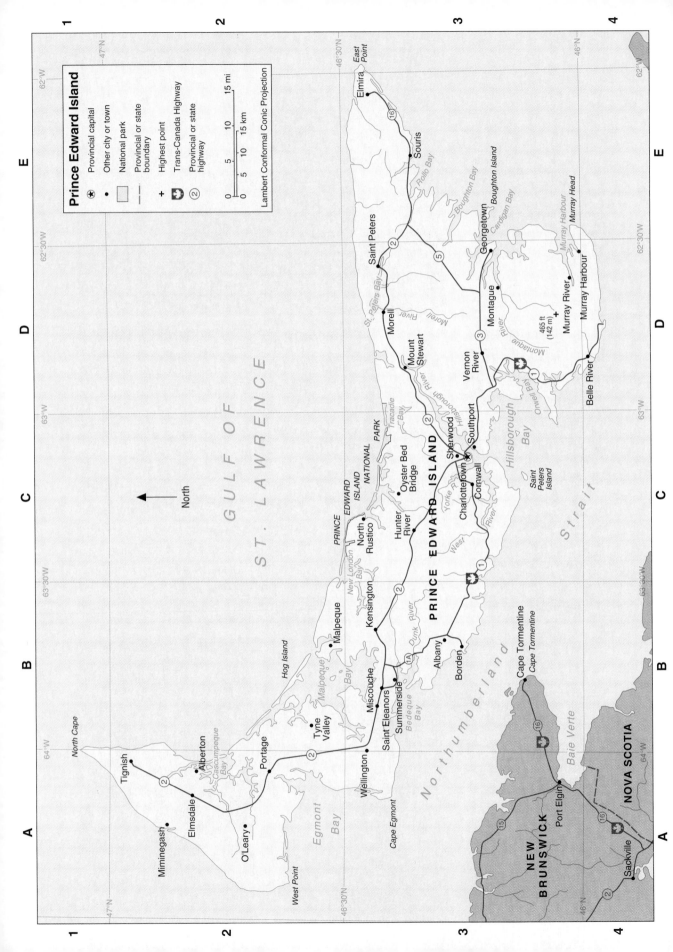

Prince Edward Island

- ⊛ Provincial capital
- • Other city or town
- ☐ National park
- ╎ Provincial or state boundary
- + Highest point
- 🛥 Trans-Canada Highway
- ② Provincial or state highway

Scale:
0 5 10 15 mi
0 5 10 15 km

Lambert Conformal Conic Projection

North

GULF OF ST. LAWRENCE

North Cape

Tignish
Elmsdale
Miminegash
O'Leary
Alberton

West Point

Cascumpeque Bay
Portage
Egmont Bay
Cape Egmont

Hog Island
Malpeque
Malpeque Bay

Tyne Valley
Wellington
Saint Eleanors
Summerside
Miscouche
Kensington

Bedeque Bay
Dunk River
New London Bay
North Rustico
Hunter River

PRINCE EDWARD ISLAND NATIONAL PARK

Oyster Bed Bridge
Yorke R.
West River
Charlottetown
Cornwall
Sherwood
Southport
Mount Stewart
Hillsborough River

Tracadie Bay
Morell
Morell River
Saint Peters
St. Peters Bay

PRINCE EDWARD ISLAND

Albany
Borden
Cape Tormentine

Northumberland Strait

Hillsborough Bay
Saint Peters Island
Orwell Bay
Belle River
Vernon River
Montague
Montague River
465 ft (142 m) +
Murray River
Murray Harbour
Murray Head
Murray Harbour

Cardigan Bay
Boughton Island
Boughton Bay
Georgetown

Souris
Rollo Bay
Elmira
East Point

NEW BRUNSWICK
Port Elgin
Baie Verte
Sackville
NOVA SCOTIA

INDEX TO PRINCE EDWARD ISLAND MAP

▶ EDUCATION

Primary education is free, and school attendance is compulsory for all children up to age 15. The school system is paid for by the provincial government and by local school boards. The province has one university, the University of Prince Edward Island at Charlottetown. In addition, vocational schools are located in Charlottetown and Summerside.

Libraries. The main public library of Prince Edward Island is located in Charlottetown. Many branch libraries are located throughout the province.

▶ PLACES OF INTEREST

The island abounds in places for recreation, as well as historic and scenic places.

Confederation Centre of the Arts, in Charlottetown, is Canada's national memorial to the Founders of the Confederation. It is the major center of cultural activity on Prince Edward Island. Built in 1964, the center houses a memorial hall, a library, an art gallery, a museum, and a theater.

Confederation Chamber, in the Provincial Building at Charlottetown, is known as the Cradle of Confederation and the Birthplace of Canada. In this room, in 1864, the Founders of Confederation met and planned the Confederation of Canada.

EPTEK Centre, in Summerside, houses the Prince Edward Island Sports Hall of Fame and various cultural exhibitions.

Fort Amherst National Historic Park, near Charlottetown, is the site of an old British fort and an earlier French settlement. The park has a visitors' center that includes a small theater.

Garden of the Gulf Museum, at Montague, displays historical objects from pioneer days.

Prince Edward Island National Park, between Cavendish and Tracadie on the north coast, is a favorite seashore resort. In the park near Cavendish is the farmhouse that served as the setting for the novel *Anne of Green Gables*, by Lucy Maud Montgomery.

Green Gables, in Prince Edward Island National Park, is a popular tourist attraction. It was the setting for *Anne of Green Gables*, a well-loved novel by the Canadian writer Lucy Maud Montgomery.

Robert Harris Memorial Art Gallery, in Charlottetown, has exhibits of paintings and sculpture.

St. Peter's Anglican Church, in Charlottetown, is famous for its murals, painted by the Canadian artist Robert Harris.

Souris, Malpeque, and **Murray Harbor** are fishing villages. Souris is noted for its deep-sea fishing and Malpeque for its oysters.

Strathgartney Park, between Borden and Charlottetown, is a recreation area on the island's south shore.

Charlottetown, the provincial capital, is a center of government, higher education, and cultural activity.

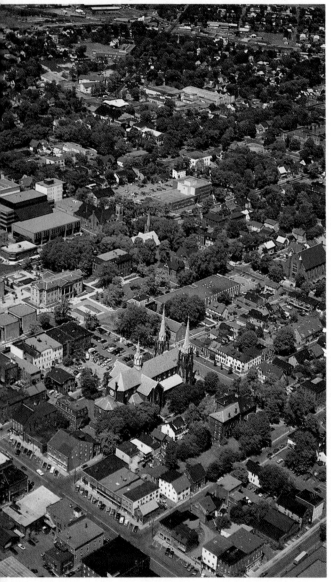

CITIES

Charlottetown, the capital, is the only city and the largest settlement on the island. It is situated on the south shore of a long estuary, or inlet, that nearly cuts the island in two. The town of Summerside has a population of about 10,000. It is located farther west, in the best farmlands on the island. Summerside is also situated on Bedeque Bay, which is noted for its oysters. Other important towns are Montague, Souris, Georgetown, Borden, Kensington, and Alberton.

GOVERNMENT

The government of Prince Edward Island is composed of the lieutenant governor, the Executive Council, and the Legislative Assembly. There is also a judiciary made up of the Supreme Court and the Provincial Court. The lieutenant governor, who is appointed by the governor-general of Canada on the advice of the prime minister, serves as the honorary head of the province. The real head of government is the premier. The premier is the leader of the majority party in the Legislative Assembly and chairman of the Executive Council, which acts as the premier's Cabinet. The Legislative Assembly makes the laws of the province. It is composed of 32 members who are elected for terms of up to five years. Elections must be held every five years, although they may be held more often.

HISTORY

The first European to sight Prince Edward Island was the French explorer Jacques Cartier. He landed on the island in 1534. Samuel de Champlain claimed the territory, which he called Ile Saint Jean, for France in 1603. But European colonization of the island did not begin until more than 100 years later. The first permanent settlement, Port La Joie, was established in 1719.

French settlement progressed very slowly and was followed by a struggle with Britain for control of the region. The British took the island in 1745, after capturing the fortress of Louisbourg on nearby Cape Breton Island. The French regained Prince Edward Island in 1748 but lost it for good in 1763 under the Treaty of Paris, which ended the Seven Years War. Under the British, the island became part of the colony of Nova Scotia. Charlottetown was established as the new capital.

Province House, in Charlottetown, was the site of the 1864 conference that led to the Confederation of Canada.

Saint John's Island—as the British called it —was divided into 67 lots. The lots were given to people in England who were supposed to colonize and develop the land. But few people did this, and the problem of ownership of the land by absentee landlords caused bitter disputes for many years.

In 1769 the island was separated from Nova Scotia and became a colony on its own. In 1799 it was renamed Prince Edward Island. Responsible government (self-government) was granted by Britain in 1851.

The first part of the 19th century was a period of prosperity for Prince Edward Island. Shipbuilding was a thriving industry. It remained so until the middle of the century, when steamships began to replace the old wooden sailing ships.

In 1864, delegates from Prince Edward Island, Nova Scotia, and New Brunswick met at Charlottetown to discuss a union of the three provinces. Representatives from what are now Ontario and Quebec joined them and suggested a union of all the provinces. This led to the Confederation of Canada in 1867. Prince Edward Island, however, did not join the other provinces in 1867 but waited until 1873 before becoming part of Canada.

In 1875, under the Land Purchase Act, money was provided to buy out the absentee British landlords who had held back the economic growth of the province. The islanders were thus able to purchase their own land and clear it for farming.

Today Prince Edward Island, like all the other Canadian provinces, receives a considerable amount of assistance from the federal government. Tourism has also been on the increase, as millions of Canadian and American vacationers come to enjoy the quiet pleasures of this friendly, rural island.

FRANCIS W. P. BOLGER
University of Prince Edward Island

PRINTING

Printing is the art and technology of rapidly reproducing multiple copies of images, such as words and pictures, on paper, cloth, or other surfaces. Every day billions of printed items are produced, including books, magazines, newspapers, posters, food packages, stamps, wallpapers, and fabrics. Because printed materials can quickly communicate ideas and information to millions of people, printing is considered one of the most important and influential inventions in history.

From the mid-1400's until the beginning of the 1900's, printing was the only form of mass communication. Education depended on the availability of reading materials. Even after the inventions of radio, television, and motion pictures, printed materials remained the world's primary source of information. Today, printing is an important industry in every advanced country in the world.

▶THE PRINTING PROCESS

Before a printed product is ready for market or display, it must go through a series of steps that include typesetting, artwork preparation, image assembly, platemaking, printing, and finishing operations.

Typesetting

Every character printed is created from **type.** Each type character represents one letter, number, or punctuation mark. Setting the type (typesetting) is the first step in the printing process. It is the method by which words (called copy) are converted into a style suitable for printing.

Today, most type is set by computers. Modern typesetting is called **phototypesetting** or computer composition. Computers have revolutionized the typesetting industry. Whereas newspaper printers once had to set each character by hand with individual pieces of type,

Left: Film negatives are stripped into flats for platemaking. *Below left:* Computerized systems make color corrections and remove blemishes from photographs. *Below right:* Automatic platemaking machines use photographic negatives to make image-carrying plates. *Opposite page:* A fully equipped press room contains machinery for all printing stages, including finishing and binding operations. *Inset:* As it passes through the yellow printing unit of a web offset press, paper picks up images from a lithographic plate.

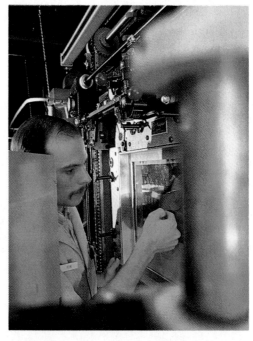

THE PRINTING PROCESS

All printed products must go through a series of procedures before they are ready for market. These steps include:

(1) typesetting text material, or putting words (called text copy) into type;

(2) preparing artwork (such as illustrations and photographs) for reproduction;

(3) assembling images (or designing layouts) by combining and arranging the typeset copy and artwork;

(4) preparing an image-carrying surface (called a plate) that, when mounted on a press, will transfer the image of the typeset copy and artwork onto the paper or other material;

(5) printing the image on a printing press, which inks the plate and brings it into contact with the paper or other material;

(6) and, in the case of most printed items, finishing the product by cutting, folding, binding, or other means.

today a reporter can type a story on a computer keyboard and send it electronically to an automatic typesetting machine. These machines are capable of setting type at rates of more than 10,000 characters per second.

In phototypesetting, each typeset character is created from a master image of that character. Master images are stored either photographically or as digital information in a computer. (You can read more about this in the article TYPE in Volume T.)

Image Assembly

Once type has been set, it is combined with illustrations and put into position on the page. This process is called **layout.** Film of the type is combined with film of the illustrations in a process called **stripping.** This final combined film of each page is used for platemaking.

One printing plate usually carries the images of many different pages. The final films of all the pages are positioned on the plate so that the pages will be in the correct sequence after a sheet is printed and folded. This process is called **imposition stripping.**

Platemaking

After all the films of typeset copy and artwork have been assembled into layouts, **proofs** are made to make sure all of the pieces and colors are in the proper place. "Pulling" a proof gives the customer a chance to check the work for errors and to see what the printed job will look like.

The final, corrected layouts (or flats) are used to make the **plate,** from which the images will be printed. Plates are made of hard substances, such as metals, rubber, or plastics. The images to be printed are transferred to the plate in one of a number of different ways. Images are printed when an inked plate is pressed against paper or other material. (Since each printing method has different requirements for platemaking, platemaking procedures are covered in the sections on Letterpress Printing, Lithography, and Gravure Printing in this article.)

Printing Presses

Once the printing plates are made, they are mounted on machines called **presses** to be used to print on paper or other materials. Presses perform a number of automatic functions: They apply ink to the plates; feed the

paper or other material to the plates; print the images by transferring the ink from the plate to the paper or other material; and stack the printed pieces. Some presses, called **perfecting presses,** can print both sides of the paper at the same time.

Presses are either **sheet-fed** (using one sheet at a time) or **web-fed** (using a continuous roll, or web, of paper or other material.) They can print one color or a number of colors. On a multicolor press, each color requires a separate printing unit, each with its own plate and ink.

There are many different kinds of presses, but each kind falls into one of three basic categories: platen (or flat-bed) presses; cylinder

---

▶**PREPARING ARTWORK FOR PRINTING**

Modern typesetting machines produce copy that is easily prepared for printing. However, artwork must be specially photographed before it can be reproduced. Photography for printing is called **process photography.** Special cameras, lights, lenses, high-contrast films, and developing systems are used to produce films from which printing plates are made.

There are two basic categories of artwork in terms of preparation for printing: line illustrations and continuous tone illustrations. **Line illustrations** are the simplest to prepare for printing. They are usually printed in one color (black is used most often). Shading can be accomplished with heavy concentrations of lines or dots, for example. However, line illustrations contain no gray tones. Examples include pen-and-ink drawings and etchings.

The process of preparing line illustrations for printing begins with photographically enlarging or reducing the illustration to the desired size. A photographic negative is made and used to create the image on the plate.

Continuous tone illustrations are black-and-white or color illustrations that have a range of gray tones between black and white or that have varying shades of color. Examples include black-and-white or color photographs and artwork.

Halftone Photography

Continuous tone illustrations are prepared for printing using a process called halftone

presses; and rotary presses. Of the three categories the rotary press is the kind used most often today. Each kind of press is more fully discussed in the section on Letterpress Presses in this article.

Finishing and Binding

After materials are printed, they must usually undergo final operations to become finished products. Some singly printed sheets, such as posters or stationery, can be shipped without further processing. However, most products are printed on large sheets containing a number of separate images. After these sheets are printed and folded, they are called **signatures.** Signatures are assembled into the proper sequence, bound, and trimmed. The work required to fold and cut signatures, or to make a variety of special packaging and advertising materials, is called **finishing.** The procedure of sewing, stapling, or gluing pages together along a spine (to create materials such as books, magazines, and catalogs) is called **binding.**

There are many different printing methods, but there are three kinds most commonly used. Their differences lie for the most part in the type of plates, or printing surfaces, they use: **letterpress** printing is done from a raised printing surface; **lithography** is done from a flat printing surface; and **gravure** is done from a sunken printing surface.

photography. The continuous tone illustration is photographed with a **process camera** using a **halftone screen.** The screen, which consists of a grid of dots, is in contact with the film during exposure.

The halftone screen breaks down the continuous tone illustration into a pattern of dots. At a normal reading distance of 10 to 12 inches (25 to 30 centimeters), for example, two dots separated by ¹⁄₂₅₀ inch (.01 centimeter) look like one dot. A screen that produces more than 125 dots per inch (50 dots per centimeter) produces an illustration that looks like continuous tone because the eye cannot distinguish the individual dots. Therefore, a halftone is really an optical illusion. Because the dots generally cannot be seen without the aid of a magnifying glass, the human eye interprets them as continuous tone.

The number of lines of dots in a halftone screen determines the quality of the reproduction. Screens range from 60 lines per inch (24 lines per centimeter) in low quality printing, such as newspaper printing, to 150 lines per

Simple line illustrations, such as the pen-and-ink drawing on the left, contain no gray tones. Shading is accomplished with a pattern of lines or dots. Gray tones in continuous-tone illustrations, such as in the photographs on the right, are created by dots of varying size that are produced by a halftone screen.

Fine halftone reproductions are made with halftone screens containing more than 100 lines per inch (40 lines per centimeter). The photograph on the left was made with a screen containing 133 lines per inch (53 lines per centimeter); the coarser reproduction below was made with a screen containing only 63 lines per inch (25 lines per centimeter).

▶LETTERPRESS PRINTING

Letterpress, or relief, printing is the oldest printing method. A simple example of the letterpress principle is a rubber stamp. The image to be printed is carved out of a flat piece of rubber, leaving the images raised above the surface. When ink is applied to this raised surface, then pressed against paper or some other material, the image is printed.

The Chinese used the relief method when they created the *Diamond Sutra* (A.D. 868), which was possibly the first book ever printed. It was made by carving Chinese word characters in relief out of wood blocks. Ink was applied to the raised characters, which were then pressed by hand against mulberry-bark paper.

Most historians credit Johann Gutenberg of Mainz, Germany, with the invention of letterpress printing as we know it today. Gutenberg did not use the hand and block method. About 1440, he invented a hand-held mold to make individual pieces of type out of molten (melted) lead, tin, and other metals. This mold could make many identical copies of the same character, and all characters could be made from molds in the same size, which allowed them to line up and fit together accurately. Because these pieces of metal type could be re-used and moved around, the invention was called **movable type.** This method of printing was called letterpress because it printed individual letters on a press.

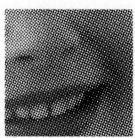

Color reproductions, such as the photograph at left, are printed from four separate plates inked with four different colors (*right*): yellow, magenta, cyan, and black. Magnification (*above*) shows how the dot patterns from each of the plates combine to create the appearance of all colors.

inch (60 lines per centimeter) in high quality printing. Therefore, the highest quality halftone reproductions contain the most dots.

Once line illustrations and halftones have been photographed, plates are made from the resulting films. The process of preparing plates of artwork for letterpress printing is called **photoengraving;** the process for lithography is called **photolithography;** and the process for gravure is called **gravure-photo-engraving.**

Color Reproduction

All continuous tone artwork must be converted to halftones. Black-and-white artwork

is photographed once, and only one plate—which prints with black ink—needs to be made. Color artwork, however, requires four separate plates for printing.

Before a color illustration can be reproduced, its colors must be separated into the three primary colors—red, green, and blue. This process is called **color separation.** Traditionally, separation negatives have been created by photographing the artwork three times, each time through a different primary-colored filter. Each of the separation negatives is used to create a plate for printing: The separation negative made with the red filter is used to create the plate that will print the blue and

Letterpress Plates

Most of the plates used for letterpress printing are actually **duplicate plates,** or copies of an original plate. Original plates are made from flat sheets of zinc, magnesium, or copper that have been coated with light-sensitive chemicals. After being exposed to light through a film negative, chemicals eat away at the unexposed non-image areas, leaving the images to be printed raised above the surface. These original plates, called **engravings,** are used to make the duplicate plates.

There are four types of duplicate plates most commonly used for letterpress printing. They are electrotypes, stereotypes, plastic plates, and rubber plates.

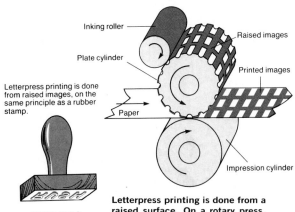

Letterpress printing is done from raised images, on the same principle as a rubber stamp.

Letterpress printing is done from a raised surface. On a rotary press, printing occurs when a sheet of paper passes between the inked plate, which is mounted on a rotating plate cylinder, and the impression cylinder.

green images in the artwork. This plate is printed in **cyan** (bluish green)-colored ink. The separation negative made with the green filter is used to create the plate that will print the blue and red images in the artwork. This plate is printed in **magenta** (bluish red)-colored ink. The separation negative made with the blue filter is used to create the plate that will print the red and green images in the artwork. This plate is printed in **yellow** ink. (For more information on how colors combine to create other colors, see the article COLOR in Volume C.)

A fourth separation negative is also made to create a plate that will print in **black** ink. This negative is made by exposing film through all three primary-colored filters or through a special filter. The addition of black extends the range, or contrast, of the artwork. Black also combines with other colors to produce neutral shades of gray.

Each separation negative must then be screened to create the dot patterns that will give the appearance of continuous tone. The screen is placed at a slightly different angle when photographing each of the four colors so that, when the artwork is reproduced, the different color dots will print next to or overlap each other. The combined use of cyan, magenta, yellow, and black inks to produce color prints is called **four-color process printing.**

Today, most color separations are made on electronic scanners that can read colors and produce screened separation negatives without using photographic equipment.

Electronic scanners have revolutionized color reproduction. They automatically read, separate, and correct colors and create separation negatives for platemaking.

Until the 1800's, all printing was done manually. Typesetters would create separate lines of text by arranging individual pieces of type. Early printing was done on screw presses, similar to those built to crush grapes for making wine.

The Gutenberg Bible, published in 1455, was the first book printed on a press using movable type. It is also known as the 42-line Bible because each column contains 42 lines. Each page was set by hand using approximately 2,500 individual pieces of type. Fewer than 50 copies are still in existence.

Letterpress Presses

Gutenberg used what is called a **platen press** to print his famous Bible. A platen press has two flat surfaces; one is called the **bed** and the other is called the **platen.** The bed holds the printing plate; the platen holds the paper. The plate is inked by inking rollers. Paper or other materials are sheet fed manually or automatically to the platen. The platen and the bed open and close like a clam shell.

A **cylinder press** also has a flat bed that holds the printing plate. However, a rotating cylinder provides the pressure for printing. Paper or other material is picked up by the cylinder and held by steel clamps called grippers. The plate on the flat bed moves in sideways to meet the cylinder. The paper is passed over the inked plate. The cylinder completes its rotation and delivers the printed piece as the flat bed moves back to its original position. The manufacture of flat-bed cylinder presses was discontinued in the United States in 1962 when the more productive rotary press came into widespread use.

Today, most letterpress printing is done on web-fed rotary presses. A rotary press has no flat beds. Instead it uses a plate cylinder and an impression cylinder. The plate is curved to fit the plate cylinder; the impression cylinder provides the pressure. The paper or other material is printed as it passes between the rotating plate cylinder and impression cylinder.

When phototypesetting was invented in the late 1940's, the use of cast-metal type and letterpress printing began to decline. Today, letterpress has been replaced in popularity by flexography (relief printing using rubber or plastic plates), lithography, and gravure.

▶LITHOGRAPHY (OFFSET PRINTING)

In lithography, images are printed from a flat, rather than a raised, surface. The process is based on the principle that oil (grease) and water do not mix. When lithography was discovered in 1798 by Aloys Senefelder in Munich, Germany, it was the first significant printing development in more than 350 years. Today more items are printed by lithography than by any other method.

The term lithography comes from two Greek words, *lithos* and *graphos,* which together mean "writing on stone." Senefelder used a greasy crayon or liquid to draw an illustration on a flat stone. Then he dampened the entire stone with water. The greasy illustration (the image) repelled the water (the water would not cling to the grease). However, the rest of the stone, containing the non-image areas, accepted the water and remained wet. When Senefelder put oil-based ink on the stone, it stuck to the greasy drawing, but not to any wet areas. When he pressed a piece of paper against the stone, Senefelder printed the first lithograph.

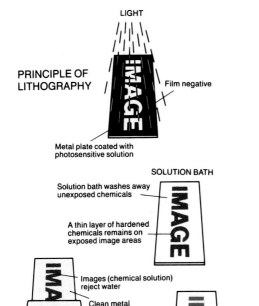

PRINCIPLE OF LITHOGRAPHY

LIGHT

IMAGE

Film negative

Metal plate coated with photosensitive solution

SOLUTION BATH

Solution bath washes away unexposed chemicals

IMAGE

A thin layer of hardened chemicals remains on exposed image areas

Images (chemical solution) reject water

Clean metal accepts water

Inking roller

Damp metal rejects greasy ink

Dampening roller moistens plate

Images (chemical solution) accept greasy ink

Lithographic plates are coated with light-sensitive solutions. Image areas are on the same plane, or level, as non-image areas. Coated plates are exposed to light through film negatives, making just the image areas receptive to ink.

Lithographic Plates

Today, practically all lithographic plates are made with finely grained sheets of aluminum, most of which have been specially treated to make the non-image areas more receptive to water. Then the plates are coated with a photosensitive (light-sensitive) solution.

A photographic negative of the image areas (the laid-out typeset copy and artwork) is used to make a lithographic plate. A strong light is passed through the negative, exposing the image areas on the plate. When the exposed plate is developed, the photosensitive solution hardens only on the exposed image areas. These are the only areas to which ink will cling; the unexposed non-image areas, when dampened, will repel ink.

Lithographic Presses

Throughout the 1800's, all lithographic printing was done on flat-bed presses, using stone plates. About 1900, a rotary press for lithographic printing was invented. Stone plates could not be mounted on the cylinders, so metal plates were substituted.

The most important improvement in lithographic printing was the invention of the **offset**

Most lithographic printing is done on offset presses. Instead of printing directly from the plate onto the paper or other material, inked images are first transferred, or "offset," onto a rubber blanket. The images are printed when a rotating impression cylinder presses the paper against the rotating blanket. *Inset:* The yellow printing unit of a web offset press prints only yellow images and is used for four-color process printing. Inking rollers transfer yellow ink to the lithographic plate. (Only the image areas on the plate will accept the ink.) The images are then offset from the plate onto the blanket, and finally, onto the paper (*bottom*).

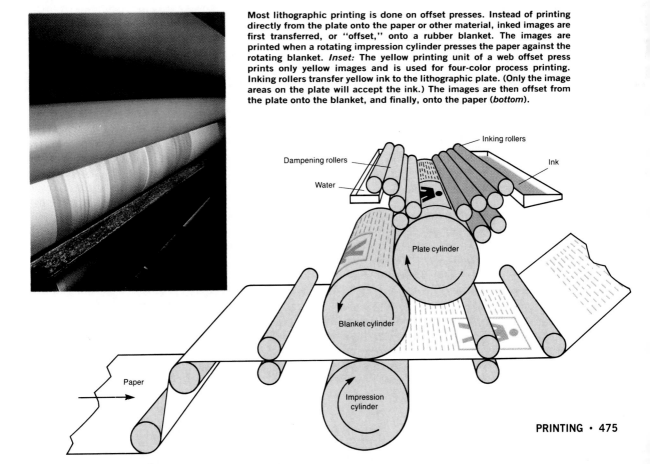

Inking rollers

Dampening rollers

Ink

Water

Plate cylinder

Blanket cylinder

Paper

Impression cylinder

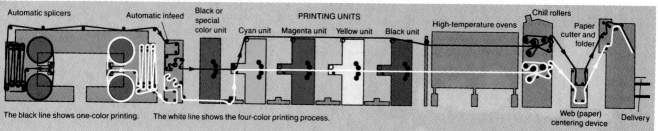

Automatic splicers   Automatic infeed   Black or special color unit   **PRINTING UNITS**   Cyan unit   Magenta unit   Yellow unit   Black unit   High-temperature ovens   Chill rollers   Paper cutter and folder

The black line shows one-color printing.   The white line shows the four-color printing process.   Web (paper) centering device   Delivery

The web offset press prints from enormous rolls of paper. This side-view diagram shows the press operations: Splicers join the end of one roll of paper to the beginning of another; the infeed adjusts the paper flow to each of the color printing units; ovens drive solvents from the ink; chill rollers set and dry the ink; and special devices cut or fold the paper into sheets or signatures.

press in 1906. On an offset press, the images are not printed directly from the plate to the paper or other material. Instead, the images are transferred from the plate cylinder to a rotating rubber blanket cylinder. (The images are ''offset'' onto a rubber blanket.) When the impression cylinder, carrying the paper or other material, presses against the rubber blanket cylinder, the images are printed.

Another type of offset printing press commonly used today is the **perfecting blanket-to-blanket press.** This type does not use impression cylinders. Instead it uses two rubber blanket cylinders. A perfecting press prints both sides of the paper on one pass through the press. Each side's rubber blanket cylinder serves as the impression cylinder for the other side. The paper is printed on both sides, or perfected, as it passes between the two rubber blanket cylinders.

The offset principle gives lithography several advantages over letterpress printing. Offsetting gives lithography the ability to print on rough surfaces, which the letterpress method cannot do well. And because lithographic plates only come into contact with soft rubber blankets, plate life is lengthened considerably.

▶GRAVURE PRINTING

Gravure is an intaglio process. The word *intaglio* comes from the Italian, meaning to carve or engrave. In gravure printing, images are printed from a sunken, rather than a flat or raised, surface. Gravure evolved from the art of engraving, a method of printing illustrations that was invented in Germany about 1476.

An engraving is made by hand carving images into a flat metal plate, using sharp instruments. The plate is covered with ink. When the engraver wipes the surface of the plate clean, the ink remains trapped in the sunken images. Then paper is forced against the plate and picks up the ink remaining beneath the surface of the plate, thus printing the images.

Gravure printing works on the principle of engraving; however, the plates are made photomechanically, rather than carved by hand. The process was developed in 1878 by Karl Klič, a Czech artist who used the process to make multiple high-quality reproductions of works of art.

Gravure Plates and Cylinders

Gravure plates and cylinders used to be made from continuous-tone film positives of page layouts exposed onto specially coated paper called carbon tissue. After exposure and processing, the tissue was transferred to a copper-plated cylinder, and the image was etched into the copper with chemicals. This was a long and tiresome process that required considerable time and extremely skilled operators. This process is still used for some short and specialized print runs; however, in most cases, it has been replaced by halftone gravure.

Although most rotogravure cylinders today are engraved by electromechanical machines, highly skilled workers are still required to make touch-ups and corrections.

Halftone gravure uses halftone positives and electromechanical engraving machines. These machines "read" the image electronically. Computer-controlled engraving heads carve about 4,000 "cells" per second on the cylinder. Lasers are also now being used to engrave plastic coatings on gravure cylinders.

Gravure Presses

Although some gravure printing is done on sheet-fed presses that use gravure plates, most is done on rotary web-fed presses that use gravure cylinders. This method is called **rotogravure.** A printing unit on a rotogravure press consists of a gravure cylinder, an impression cylinder, an inking system, a sharp scraper called a doctor blade, and an ink dryer. There are as many units on the press as colors to be printed. As the gravure cylinder rotates, it is inked by rollers or by spray, filling the sunken images with ink. Then a doctor blade scrapes the excess ink from the surface of the gravure cylinder. The impression cylinder squeezes the paper or other material against the gravure cylinder, thus printing the images.

In rotogravure printing, images are engraved into the printing plate. As the plate cylinder rotates, it is inked. The plate's surface is then scraped clean, but ink remains trapped in the sunken cells. Images are printed when the rotating impression cylinder presses the paper against the cells in the rotating plate cylinder.

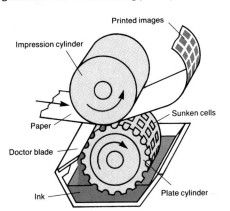

Printed images

Impression cylinder

Paper

Doctor blade

Ink

Sunken cells

Plate cylinder

OTHER PRINTING METHODS

Letterpress, lithography, and gravure traditionally have been the most commonly used printing methods. However, advanced technology and equipment have recently popularized several other methods, including screen printing, flexography, heat transfer printing, and photocopying.

Screen Printing

Also called **silk screening** or **serigraphy,** screen printing is done with a fine screen, usually made of wire or nylon, that is mounted on a frame. A stencil is produced on the screen to cover up the non-image areas. (The images to be printed are cut out of or exposed onto the stencil.) Ink is squeezed through the stencil and screen onto fabric, paper, or other material.

Because more ink is used in screen printing than in other printing methods, screen prints usually must be passed through an ink dryer before they are stacked. The process is often used to make art prints, decal stickers, greeting cards, clothing, and many other products.

Flexography

Flexography is a form of letterpress printing done on a web-fed rotary press. The process uses flexible rubber or plastic plates and inks that do not smear easily. Flexography is one of the simplest methods of printing and is being used increasingly for newspaper printing. Eventually it is expected to completely replace letterpress in newspaper printing.

Heat Transfer Printing

In heat transfer printing, images are first printed on paper with special inks. The inked images are then transferred to fabric or some other surface by heat and pressure (usually an iron is used). T-shirts are frequently printed by the heat transfer method.

Photocopying

Photocopying is also known as **xerography.** It is a fast and economical printing method used in businesses for quick copies of letters and office memorandums.

Photocopying works on static electricity. A rotating cylinder, coated with selenium (a nonmetallic element) and charged with static electricity, serves as the printing plate. Selenium discharges in non-image areas when exposed to light. Images, light-projected through a lens onto the cylinder, retain the charge. Negatively charged black powder is attracted to the positively charged image areas on the cylinder. When paper is passed over the cylinder, it picks up the black-powdered images. Then the powdered paper is slightly heated to make the powder stick to the paper.

HISTORY

The history of recorded information dates from the cave drawings of more than 30,000 years ago. By 2500 B.C., Egyptians were carving hieroglyphics in stone. But printing as we know it today was not invented until relatively recently—little more than 500 years ago.

The Chinese made many discoveries. They invented paper in the 1st century and movable type made out of clay by the 11th century. The Koreans first made movable type out of bronze in the mid-13th century. But there is no known connection between these early Asian inventions and the discovery of printing in Europe in the 15th century.

In Europe, before printing was invented, all recorded information was hand written. Books were carefully copied by **scribes** who would often take years to complete a single volume. This method was slow and expensive, and few people had the opportunity, or the ability, to read the finished works.

Johann Gutenberg's inventions in the 1440's—movable type and the printing press —played a significant role in bringing Europe out of the ''dark ages.'' Printing made books and other reading materials available to the general public. People learned to read. As they became educated, they started exchanging ideas and information that led to new discoveries and inventions. Europe entered into a period of growth and exploration, known as the Renaissance.

There were few developments in printing between 1440 and the start of the Industrial Revolution about 1800. However, in the 1800's tremendous advancements were made in printing methods and machinery. Industrialization made possible the inventions of the steam-powered cylinder press, the rotary press, paper-making machines, and automated typesetting machines. Machines reduced the cost of printed materials and made them more readily accessible. In addition, photography, photoengraving, and coal-tar dyes to make colored inks also were discovered.

IMPORTANT DATES IN THE HISTORY OF PRINTING

105	Paper invented by Ts'ai Lun in China.
868	Oldest known book created from wood blocks, the *Diamond Sutra,* printed in China.
1045?	Movable type made from hardened clay invented by Pi Sheng in China.
1250?	Movable type made from bronze invented in Korea.
1440	Movable metal type and first wooden printing press invented in Europe by Johann Gutenberg in Germany.
1455	Gutenberg Bible, the first book printed on a press using movable type, published in Germany.
1460?	Woodcuts first used to illustrate books in Europe.
1475	*The Recuyell of the Histories of Troy,* the first book printed in the English language, published by William Caxton in England.
1476	Copperplate engravings for reproducing illustrations introduced in Germany.
1487	Printing presses began operating in Rome, Venice, Paris, and other European cities.
1539	First printing press in North America began operating in Mexico City.
1638	First printing press in the American colonies began operating at Harvard College in Cambridge, Massachusetts.
1798	Lithography invented by Aloys Senefelder in Germany.
1811	First steam-powered cylinder press invented by Friedrich König in Germany.
1814	Steam-powered press first used to print a newspaper, the *Times* of London.
1826	Photographic process invented by Joseph Nicéphore Niépce in France.
1829	Wet mat process using papier mâché for duplicate platemaking patented by Claude Gennouz in France.
1837	Photographic process perfected by Louis Daguerre in France.
1846	First rotary press using two cylinders invented by Richard Hoe in the United States.
1849	Curved stereotype plates invented by Jacob Warms in France.
1852	Photoengraving process patented by William Fox Talbot in England.
1855	Photolithography invented by Alphonse Louis Poitevin in France.
1865	First perfecting web-fed rotary press invented by William Bullock in the United States.
1872	Photoengraving process for making letterpress plates first used by Charles Gillot in France.
1878	First illustrations printed using gravure method invented by Karl Klič, in Austria.
1884	First typesetting machine, the Linotype, invented by Ottmar Merganthaler in the United States.
1885	Halftone screen for photography perfected by Frederick Ives in the United States.
1887	Monotype typesetting machine patented by Tolbert Lanston in the United States.
1893	Color photoengraving process for making letterpress plates introduced in the United States.
1905	Offset printing accidentally discovered by Ira Rubel in the United States.
1907	Screen process for printing developed by Samuel Simon in England.
1920's	Teletypesetter (TTS) automated typesetting, using perforated tape, invented.
1947	First phototypesetting machine, the Fotosetter, invented.
1948	Reprography (photocopying) invented.
1950	Electronic scanners for color printing invented.
1954	First practical phototypesetting machine, the Photon, invented.
1969	Introduction of electronic magnification in scanners.
1970's	Introduction of microcomputers simplified pre-press operations.
1970	Introduction of video display terminals (VDT) made cast-metal type almost obsolete.
1972	Introduction of electronic dot generation (EDG) in scanners.
1979	First electronic color pre-press system, the Scitex, invented.
1980	Introduction of automatic toning systems (ATM) for off-press color proofing.
1987	Digital Data Exchange Specification (DDES) adopted, allowing interfacing of scanners and pre-press systems.

Modern Printing Developments

Throughout the 20th century, advanced technology and electronics have continued to change the printing industry. By the year 2000, letterpress will be used only in a few large daily newspapers and for some label and packaging printing, business forms, and job printing.

Flexography will eventually replace letterpress in newspaper printing. It will continue to grow in commercial packaging and book publishing. In addition, reprography is becoming more and more available, and the widespread use of word processors and electronic scanners are reducing printing costs.

Recently developed methods of gravure, using electromechanical and laser engraving of plastic-coated cylinders as well as electron-beam etching and photosensitive plates, are lowering the costs of cylinder making. New electronic systems have made it possible to make printing cylinders directly from original copy without films or manual operations. The future development of satisfactory water-based inks will further limit costs and pollution problems. This will assure gravure an even larger share of the printing market.

The rate of technological progress will continue to accelerate. Now that the world is in the midst of an information explosion, the printing industry will also progress and continue to record and distribute that information as we move toward a new century.

MICHAEL H. BRUNO
Editor, *Pocket Pal: A Graphic Arts Production Handbook*

See also BOOKS; COLOR; GRAPHIC ARTS; GUTENBERG, JOHANN; PHOTOGRAPHY; TYPE.

Prisons are designed to isolate criminals from society. Maximum-security prisons (*left*) hold dangerous criminals and are secured by thick walls and barbed-wire fences. Minimum-security prisons (*right*) hold minor offenders and are less closely guarded.

PRISONS

A prison is a place of confinement. People who commit crimes are removed from society and placed in prisons as punishment for their offenses. There are many different types of institutions that hold people accused of a crime: jails, detention centers, work camps, police lockups, and federal and state prisons. But only convicted criminals who have been sentenced to a year or more are imprisoned.

In the United States today there are more than half a million adults and children under the age of 18 serving time in prison. Most prisoners are male high-school dropouts between the ages of 18 and 29. Most of them have committed violent crimes against other people (such as murder or assault with a deadly weapon), property crimes (such as theft or burglary), or "white collar" crimes (such as tax evasion or embezzlement). Less than 5 percent of the convicted criminals in the United States are women.

▶TYPES OF PRISONS

There are many different types of prisons, or correctional facilities, in the United States. The facility chosen for confinement usually depends on the offender's age and the crime.

Jails. Municipal and county jails and detention centers are institutions maintained to hold people who have been accused of a crime and are awaiting a court trial. People are also sent to jails as punishment for a minor offense, such as disorderly conduct. These facilities are meant to serve as temporary places of confinement. However, if an accused offender is sentenced by the court to serve one year or longer, then he or she will be sent to a federal or state prison.

Federal Prisons. Criminals convicted of federal crimes, such as smuggling drugs across state lines or not paying income taxes, are sent to federal prisons. Federal prisons in the United States are administered by the Bureau of Prisons, a division of the Justice Department. Perhaps the best-known federal prison in operation today is the United States Penitentiary in Leavenworth, Kansas.

State Prisons. Each state has its own prison system to punish criminals convicted of crimes committed in that state. Some famous state prisons include San Quentin, a maximum-security prison in California; Sing-Sing (Ossining Correctional Facility) in New York; and the Michigan state prison in Jackson, which is the largest walled prison in the United States, having approximately 4,000 inmates.

PRISON LIFE

While prisons can be quite different from one another, the life of a prisoner tends to be the same: Prisoners lose their freedom to come and go as they please; all of their activities are supervised; and they live in a small cell with little more than a bed, a wash basin, and a toilet.

A typical day in prison begins early in the morning. Prison guards unlock each prisoner's cell to take a head count. When all of the prisoners have been accounted for, they file into the dining room for breakfast. After breakfast, they take part in various activities: Some have chores; others go to school; and still others go to prison workshops to make products for sale, such as license plates. Many others simply go back to their cell areas to read or watch television. After lunch, another head count is taken, followed by recreational activities. Dinner is usually served around 5 P.M. By 9 P.M., the prisoners are locked up in their cells for the night.

When prisoners misbehave, special measures are taken to punish them. Their recreation time may be suspended, or days may be added to their sentence. However, the most common form of punishment is placing a prisoner in isolation. He or she is kept apart from the others and is unable to receive visitors.

Rehabilitation Programs

Many prisons provide rehabilitation programs to prepare prisoners for their return to society. Programs are available to help those with drug and alcohol problems. Educational programs enable prisoners to earn a high-school or even a college degree. Other programs teach job skills to prepare prisoners for work after they are released. Some minimum-security facilities even permit some prisoners to work outside the prison, although they must return for the night. However, this is a privilege granted only to model prisoners who are well behaved and close to completing their sentence.

Parole and Probation

Prisons are very expensive to build and maintain, and they are severely overcrowded. This situation has led to the increased use of parole and probation to handle the criminal population. Parole means releasing a prisoner before the whole sentence is served. The person, however, remains under the public supervision of a parole officer until the sentence is completed. Probation means attempting to reform convicted criminals outside prison walls. Supervised by trained probation officers, criminals on probation are able to escape the harsh effects of prison life and the disgrace of having served a prison sentence.

HISTORY

Until the 1500's, when the first workhouses, or houses of correction, were built in England and the Netherlands, criminals were not punished by being put in prison. The only persons punished in this way were those who could not pay their debts or who were out of favor for political or religious reasons. Persons accused of a crime usually were imprisoned only while they were waiting to be tried. If found guilty, they were generally punished by various forms of corporal punishment (inflicting pain on the body of the offender). Some were executed or sent into exile. During the 1500's European countries began transporting criminals in work gangs to their colonies in the New World. England sent thousands out to its American colonies before the beginning of the Revolutionary War. Between 1787 and 1875 thousands more were sent to the British penal colonies in Australia. France exiled its criminals to colonies in Africa, New Caledonia, and French Guiana for many years. Labor camps in Siberia have received prisoners transported by both the czarist and Soviet governments.

England's American colonies inherited the methods of punishment of the mother country. In Pennsylvania the Quakers, or members of the Society of Friends, were determined to do away with corporal punishment. After the American Revolution the criminal code of Pennsylvania was changed. Imprisonment was made the chief form of punishment. By 1826 the other states had followed this example.

The first prisons did not have separate cells for convicts. Men and women waiting to be tried, as well as those already convicted, were herded together into large rooms. However, Quakers and other prison reformers were greatly influenced by the ideas set forth in 1777 by an Englishman, John Howard in his book, *The State of the Prisons*. Howard had been particularly impressed by his visits to the Hospice of San Michele in Rome and to the workhouse in Ghent, Belgium. Both institutions provided for the separation of different classes of inmates, medical care, the housing of inmates in individual cells, and their employment at useful labor.

Authorities at the Hospice of San Michele believed that prisoners could be made to feel penitent (sorry) for their crimes if they were confined and treated well. This idea appealed to Howard, and from it developed the penitentiary system. In England the Penitentiary Act was passed by Parliament in 1779, but construction of the first English penitentiary did not begin until about 1812.

In 1790 a section of separate cells for the worst criminals was provided in the Walnut Street Jail in Philadelphia, as a result of reforms urged by Pennsylvania Quakers. It thus became America's first penitentiary.

The Auburn and Pennsylvania Systems

The first prison to be built entirely with separate cells was opened in Auburn, New York, in 1819. In the Auburn system of punishment, convicts were allowed to leave their cells, eat in the prison dining room, and work in silence in the prison shops. This came to be known as the **silent** or **congregate system**.

The first separate-cell prison in Pennsylvania, the Western Penitentiary, was built in Pittsburgh in 1826. In the Pennsylvania system, each convict had a cell in which to eat, sleep, and work when ordered to do so. Attached to each cell was a small exercise yard. Inmates were not allowed to speak to anyone other than prison officials, nor could they leave their cells. This came to be known as the **separate system**.

The Auburn system was cheaper to run and easier to administer than the Pennsylvania system and became the model for state prisons in the United States. Most of the prisons built in Europe during the 1800's, however, were of the Pennsylvania type.

The Development of Reformatories

Programs geared to reforming prisoners to make them fit to return to society were first introduced in Ireland in the late 1850's by Sir Walter Crofton, one of the greatest of all prison reformers. He provided work and education for prisoners and encouraged them to reform by allowing them to gain early release through good behavior and hard work.

Crofton's Irish system attracted the attention of American reformers, who used the system to set up prisons for young offenders. These came to be known as reformatories. The first reformatory was opened in Elmira, New York, in 1876. In the United States the Irish system became known as the **Elmira system**.

Reform programs for adult prisoners were not introduced until the 1930's. Reformers tried to change the prisoner's ways of thinking and acting. Experts provided better prison schools and workshops where the prisoners could learn a trade. But in spite of these advances, few prisons even today are able to successfully reform many prisoners. This has led to the greater use of parole, probation, and other alternatives.

Punishment of Women and Children

In London during the 1800's, Elizabeth Fry organized the Association for the Improvement of Female Prisoners in Newgate Prison. Among the reforms she advocated was the separation of women and men prisoners.

In the United States, women were kept in the same prisons as men, although in different sections. In 1873 Indiana built a separate prison just for women, and today most states have separate institutions for women prisoners.

For many years young people convicted of crimes were put in prison with adult convicts. The first prison for children in the United States opened in New York City in 1825.

In the 1800's, reformers in Europe began to build small cottages for young convicts in order to give them more homelike surroundings. The first cottage system in the United States was for girls. It was opened in Lancaster, Massachusetts, in 1856. The following year one was opened for boys in Lancaster, Ohio. These institutions were later called **reform schools**. Today they are called training schools and are administered by the states. Aftercare programs also have been established to help young offenders return to society once their sentences are over.

HARRY ELMER BARNES
Coauthor, *New Horizons in Criminology*
Updated by ANNA KOSOF
Author, *Prison Life in America*

See also COURTS; CRIME AND CRIMINOLOGY; LAW AND LAW ENFORCEMENT.

PROBABILITY. See MATHEMATICS; MATHEMATICS, HISTORY OF.

PROGRAMMED INSTRUCTION

Programmed instruction, also referred to as programmed learning, is a way of individualizing instruction. Programmed teaching materials or programs are self-instructional and are made up of many small units, or steps, arranged so that each one leads logically to the next. Students work independently and advance in their units of study at their own pace.

Each program has a set of goals for a particular unit of study. These goals are called **behavioral objectives**. A behavioral objective is a statement of what skills and abilities students are expected to acquire as a result of their exposure to the program. For example, a behavioral objective for a mathematics program may be the following: "The student will be able to add decimal numbers." The program also contains instructional materials considered essential to achieving each stated objective.

Students usually work through the objectives in a program by following these steps:

1. Students are given information to read or a visual image to look at. They are asked questions about what they read or observe. They respond by writing an answer or drawing a picture or a diagram.
2. Students get immediate feedback by checking their answer against the correct answer.
3. If their answer is incorrect, students are guided to additional instructional material. When they are able to demonstrate that they have learned the objective, they proceed to the next one.
4. At regular intervals, students are tested to determine if they remember and understand what they are being taught.

In the early days of programmed instruction, students used programmed textbooks or worked on special machines called teaching machines that combined instruction and testing. Programmed instruction today is most often presented on a computer or on an interactive multimedia system that uses a computer linked to a videodisc or to a CD-ROM device.

Reviewed by Ibrahim M. Hefzallah
Fairfield University

See also EDUCATION.

PROHIBITION

The term prohibition refers to laws that prohibit, or forbid, the manufacture, sale, and transportation of alcoholic beverages. It is most commonly used in reference to an era in American history (1920–33) when all alcoholic beverages, including beer and wine, were illegal under the terms of the 18th Amendment to the Constitution. The federal ban on alcohol was lifted in 1933 with the passage of the 21st Amendment, which repealed (canceled) the 18th Amendment.

The Temperance and Prohibition Movements

The passage of the 18th Amendment was the result of a century-long reform movement to restrain people from drinking alcohol. The movement was joined by people who recognized that alcoholic beverages can be a dangerous drug when drunk too often or in large quantities.

During the prohibition years, federal agents seized and disposed of illegal alcoholic beverages under the authority of the Volstead Act.

Judith Ellen Horton Foster (1840–1910), born in Lowell, Mass., was an attorney who wrote the constitution of the Woman's Christian Temperance Union (WCTU). A close associate of Frances Willard (*see right*), Foster eventually came to disagree with Willard's plan for the WCTU. Foster believed that the WCTU should concentrate exclusively on the issue of prohibition and do so by influencing the Democratic and Republican political parties, not through a separate prohibition party. She continued her efforts toward temperance reform by establishing a nonpartisan branch of the WCTU. Foster later helped formulate the strategy of the Anti-Saloon League.

Carry Amelia Moore Nation (1846–1911), born Garrard County, Ky., became notorious for her destructive campaigns against illegal saloons. Nation, a former teacher, settled in Kansas with her second husband in 1889. Prohibition was

Carry Nation

enacted in Kansas in 1880, but the law was widely violated. Nation, whose first husband died an alcoholic, took it upon herself to attack saloons that openly violated the law, and her actions were dramatic. She used a hatchet to destroy whiskey bottles and beer barrels, and she threw rocks. Her violent actions, which she said were justified because her victims were criminals, gained her an international reputation as a fanatic supporter of prohibition. The WCTU rejected what were known as her "hatchetation" campaigns. Nation's actions helped promote public support in Kansas for enforcement of the prohibition law. Her notoriety on the lecture circuit also earned her large sums of money, which she donated to charity.

Wayne Bidwell Wheeler (1869–1927), born near Brookfield, Ohio, spent his entire career working for the Anti-Saloon League. He became active in the league while attending Oberlin College in Ohio, where the Anti-Saloon League was founded in 1893. After receiving a law degree (1898) from Western Reserve Uni-

versity, Wheeler became an attorney for the league in Washington, D.C., serving as its superintendent (1904–15) and general counsel (1915–27). Wheeler was known as a dedicated politician capable of engineering successful campaigns against the league's opponents. Although he was not the organization's most important leader, Wheeler sought publicity and became the best-known advocate of prohibition in the United States. He played a key role in the adoption of the 18th Amendment and advocated a policy of strict enforcement of the law.

Frances Elizabeth Caroline Willard (1839–98), born in Churchville, N.Y., was an educator and leading organizer of the temperance movement in the United States. Well educated for a woman of her day, she worked as a teacher and later served as dean of the Woman's College of Northwestern University in Evanston, Ill. Willard was a popular speaker who expressed a vision of a better world. She focused her energies on several causes, including women's rights. In 1879, the Woman's Christian Temperance Union (WCTU) elected her president, and she served in that position until her death. In 1883, Willard founded a world temperance union. Thereafter she was considered the best-known woman in the English-speaking world after Queen Victoria.

The roots of the prohibition movement were found in religion, especially in the Protestant churches. In the 1800's, many Protestants believed that after slavery, drunkenness was the nation's greatest evil. At first the reformers tried to persuade people to stop drinking on their own—or at least to drink less, or be "temperate." Organizations such as the American Temperance Society, founded in 1826, tried to get people to pledge to stop drinking. But many eventually decided that the only way to help people resist the temptation to drink was to outlaw the businesses that made and sold alcohol. To achieve this end, the prohibition movement had to become a political as well as a social movement, and in 1869 the Prohibition Party was established.

Prohibition was one of the first large political movements in the United States in which women played an important role. The Woman's Christian Temperance Union (WCTU), founded in 1874, was especially influential in the fight against alcohol abuse, but the orga-

nization focused on other causes as well, notably obtaining for women the right to vote. The prohibition movement gained momentum after 1893, when the Anti-Saloon League was founded. Unlike the WCTU, the league focused only on the issue of prohibition and supported candidates of any political party who would vote for prohibition laws.

Several state and local governments passed prohibition laws, especially where Protestant voters were numerous. By 1916 prohibition reformers were so successful in the U.S. congressional elections that they were confident of achieving national prohibition. Congress proposed the 18th Amendment to the Constitution the following year, and it was ratified by two thirds of the states on January 16, 1919. Before the 18th Amendment went into effect in January 1920, Congress passed the Volstead Act to make provisions for the government to enforce prohibition. This act was named for the U.S. representative who proposed it—Andrew J. Volstead of Minnesota.

The Dry Years (1920–33)

In the 1920's, many Americans stopped drinking, and alcohol-related diseases and accidents declined. However, many people continued to crave alcohol and were willing to obtain it illegally. This demand gave rise to a huge black-market business controlled primarily by gangsters, such as the notorious Al Capone. Those who smuggled liquor into the United States from other countries or made illegal alcohol for sale were called bootleggers; the saloons where people went to drink in secret were called speakeasies.

As time wore on, prohibition became increasingly unpopular. Leading the opposition were wealthy men and women who believed they could relieve their tax burden if the government would legalize alcohol and tax alcohol-related businesses. In addition, many Americans objected to the bootleggers and gangsters, who seemed to be the main beneficiaries of prohibition.

The End of Prohibition

When the Great Depression began in 1929, prohibition lost many supporters. Those in favor of repealing the 18th Amendment argued that legalizing alcoholic beverages would create badly needed jobs in related businesses. In addition, the taxes imposed on the manufacture and sale of alcoholic beverages would raise money for the benefit of local, state, and federal governments.

In 1933 the opponents of prohibition were successful in persuading two thirds of the states to ratify the 21st Amendment, and prohibition was repealed. The Amendment went into effect on December 6, 1933, and the making and selling of alcoholic beverages once again became legal in the United States, although some state and local laws continue to restrict their use.

K. AUSTIN KERR
Author, *Organized for Reform: A New History of the Anti-Saloon League*

PROJECTS, SCIENCE. See EXPERIMENTS AND OTHER SCIENCE ACTIVITIES.

PROKOFIEV, SERGEI (1891–1953)

Sergei Prokofiev, an outstanding Russian composer of the 20th century, was born in Sontzovka, Ukraine, on April 23, 1891. His mother, an amateur pianist, gave him his first music lessons. He showed unusual talent in both piano and composition, and by the age of 9 he had written a complete opera.

When he was 13, Sergei was sent to the conservatory in St. Petersburg, where he studied piano and composition with the finest teachers of the day, including Nikolai Rimsky-Korsakov (1844–1908). On his graduation in 1914, he was awarded the Anton Rubinstein prize for his performance of his First Piano Concerto. Three years later he wrote one of his most popular orchestral works, the *Classical Symphony*.

In 1918, Prokofiev left Russia on a concert tour of the world. He traveled first through Siberia and Japan and then to the United States. In 1921 his opera *Love for Three Oranges* was produced in Chicago. The following year he settled in Paris. Here he renewed his acquaintance with the director of the famous Russian Ballet, Sergei Diaghilev (1872–1929), who produced several of Prokofiev's ballets.

In 1934, Prokofiev returned to the Soviet Union, where he wrote some of his most famous works. These include the *Lieutenant Kijé* suite (1933), the ballet *Romeo and Juliet* (1935–36), the cantata *Alexander Nevsky* (1938), and the opera *War and Peace* (1941–43). Prokofiev's Fifth Symphony (1944) is considered by many people to be one of the greatest works of his generation. His piano music is also popular.

Beginning in 1948, Prokofiev was severely criticized by the Soviet government for allegedly composing music that was inappropriate for the Soviet people. The government later changed its position, and he was returned to favor.

Except for this short period, Prokofiev enjoyed success in the Soviet Union, and in 1951 he was awarded the Stalin prize. When he died in Moscow on March 5, 1953, his works had become familiar to audiences around the world. Perhaps the most beloved is *Peter and the Wolf* (1936), a fairy tale told in both words and music.

Reviewed by RONALD L. BYRNSIDE
Author, *Music: Sound and Sense*

PRONOUN. See PARTS OF SPEECH.

PRONUNCIATION

Where there is a language there is pronunciation. Pronunciation is language being spoken.

Pronouncing by Ear. As children grow up they learn to understand and speak, just by living with other people. They copy the pronunciation of those about them. The Australians pronounce the word "late" so that most Americans would hear "light." In England, London cockneys drop the *h* at the beginning of words, so that "he" becomes " 'e." In all countries people of certain regions have special oddities of pronunciation.

Pronouncing Written Words. We sometimes see new words for the first time in print. The pronunciation of such new words may be difficult because one letter may stand for different sounds in different words. The letter *o,* for example, stands for completely different sounds in t*o*p, s*o,* d*o,* c*o*rn, m*o*ther, and w*o*men. O is one of the five vowel letters in the Roman alphabet, used for writing English. The other vowel letters are *a, e, i,* and *u.* The remaining 21 letters of the alphabet are all consonants, although *y* is sometimes used as a vowel. Most of the consonant letters have the same pronunciation every time they are used.

Some dictionaries, encyclopedias, and other reference books have pronunciation keys, or guides. Pronunciation guides differ. The following list shows one way of writing the consonant sounds of English, with one or more of the common ways to spell each sound:

b	as in *b*ill	**r**	as in *r*ow
ch	as in *ch*ill, wa*tch*	**s**	as in *s*o, *c*ent
f	as in *ph*one, *f*an, lau*gh*	**sh**	as in ma*ch*ine, na*ti*on, so*ci*al, *sh*one, ti*ss*ue
g	as in *g*et, *gh*ost	**t**	as in cook*ed,* *Th*omas, *t*ill
h	as in *h*and, *wh*o		
j	as in *J*ill, ju*dge, George*	**th**	as in *th*in
		th̶	as in *th*an
k	as in *k*ill, *c*at, si*ck,* a*ch*e, *q*uick	**v**	as in *v*an, o*f*
		w	as in *w*e, q*u*ick
l	as in *l*ow	**y**	as in *y*es, on*i*on
m	as in ra*m*	**z**	as in *z*one, ea*s*y
n	as in ra*n*	**zh**	as in plea*s*ure, a*z*ure, divi*si*on
ng	as in ra*ng,* i*n*k		
p	as in *p*ill		

The letters *c, q,* and *x* are not listed. C sounds are represented by **k** as in *c*at and **s** as in *c*ent. The **k** also stands for *q,* as in *q*uick, and **ks** supplies the *x* sound found in ta*x*i.

Some written words contain consonant letters that are silent. Pronunciation guides omit these silent letters when spelling out words to show how they are pronounced: **det** (de*b*t), **lim** (lim*b*), **not** (*k*not), **rist** (*w*rist).

Vowel sounds are harder to show than consonant sounds because five vowel letters (and sometimes *y*) have to show 14 basic sounds. So we use some double letters and special marks. There are two kinds of vowels: simple vowels and diphthongs. The simple vowels that most Americans use are **a** as in b*a*t; **e** as in b*e*t; **i** as in b*i*t; **o** as in c*o*t; **ô** as in c*au*ght; **oo** as in p*u*t, g*oo*d; **u** as in b*u*t.

The most common unaccented vowel sound in English is called a **schwa**, for which the symbol is an upside-down *e,* that is: ə. A pronunciation guide might use the schwa in words like stanza (stanzə), sister (sistər), and so on. It is almost the same sound that is stressed in b*u*t, and sometimes the schwa is used instead of *u:* bət.

The diphthongs are really two vowels pronounced together. The pronunciation slides from one to the other. The diphthongs most used by Americans are:

ā	as in f*a*te, b*ai*t, *eigh*t, pl*ay*	**ō**	as in v*o*te, b*oa*t, sh*ow,* th*ough*
ē	as in *e*ve, f*ee*t, b*ea*t, k*e*y, w*e,* mach*i*ne	**oi**	as in b*oy,* s*oi*l
		o͞o	as in fl*u*te, b*oo*t, thr*ough*
ī	as in b*i*te, fl*y, figh*t	**ou**	as in b*ou*t, f*ow*l

Syllables and Accents. Words are made up of one or more syllables. A syllable is a speech sound or group of speech sounds pronounced as a unit. It may be a whole word or part of a word. "Go" is a syllable and a whole word. In "going" it is the first of two syllables. In words of more than one syllable, one syllable is stressed. To show which syllable is stressed, a mark called an accent is placed after the syllable (go'ing) or over the vowel (góing).

Diacritical Marks. Other aids in pronunciation are the diacritical marks put on letters, such as the lines over *ô* and *ē.* Standard dictionaries list these marks and illustrate how they are used.

J. DONALD BOWEN
University of California at Los Angeles

See also ALPHABET; LANGUAGES; articles on individual letters of the alphabet.

PROOFREADING

The word "manuscript" originally meant "written by hand." Today manuscripts (material for articles, newspapers, magazines, books) are typed before being sent to the printer. In the printshop the typesetter sets this material into lines of type. Since this is done with great speed, errors are sometimes made. For this reason proofs are made. Proof reproduces the type exactly as it has been set by the printer. By reading proof, a proofreader discovers the errors.

Galleys. First proofs, called galleys, are long sheets that contain print for about three pages of a regular-size book. The margins are wide so that the proofreader can make his corrections in them. When the proofs are returned to the printer he does not read all of the print. He merely makes the corrections indicated in the margin. This is why all corrections should be clearly and carefully indicated—so that the final printed pages will be perfect. In most instances the author also reads proof and indicates changes.

Page Proof. Because the typesetter has the type for each galley proof in a heavy metal tray (called a galley), making corrections is a slow, hard task. It often means moving the lines of type about. The printer makes all the corrections indicated on the returned galleys. Then he divides the type into pages and submits page proof to the proofreader. This is the last proof before the presses roll. It is important to have "clean" typewritten copy in the beginning in order to avoid errors and added expense at this stage. Every writer—the professional author and the student alike—should proofread his own written work before handing it in to a publisher or a teacher.

Proofreaders' Marks. So that all printers can understand the changes or corrections made in the copy they are printing from, a code of proofreaders' marks has been devised. These marks cover corrections in spelling, capitalization, punctuation, kind of type to be used, spacing, paragraphing, and so on. Corrections must be neatly made. It is best to draw a light line from the correction indicated in the margin to the precise spot for the correction.

Proofreading Schoolwork. Although few stu-

	PROOFREADERS' MARKS
∧	Insert a word or phrase.
⩘	Insert comma.
⩗	Insert apostrophe.
⩗⩗	Insert quotation marks.
;/	Insert semicolon.
:/	Insert colon.
⊙	Insert period.
?/	Insert question mark.
-/	Insert hyphen.
⅋	Delete.
¶	Begin a new paragraph.
No ¶	Do not begin a new paragraph.
Tr	Transpose.
Sp	Spell out.
Cap	Use CAPITAL.
⌣	Close up.
#	Space.
[	Move to left.
]	Move to right.
x	Broken letter.
stet	Restore word crossed out (place dots under word to be kept).
bf	Set in **boldface**, type that has thick, heavy lines and is used for headings and emphasis.
ital	Set in *italic* type, a style in which letters usually slant to the right.

dents see their work in print, every student prepares some written material. In language and literature classes, particularly, the teacher often corrects student-written paragraphs and compositions and indicates in the margin where errors have been made. To avoid writing an individual note to each student about his mistakes, the teacher frequently uses proofreaders' marks.

Some proofreaders' marks are boxed on this page. The first 14—through "Sp"—are marks commonly used in correction of both written and typewritten work. The marks following "Sp" are more technical marks used in correcting material prepared for printing. All the marks listed above are necessary, of course, in correcting proof for final printing.

Most dictionaries give a complete list of proofreaders' marks.

MARY C. FOLEY
Author, *Language for Daily Use*

PROPAGANDA

Propaganda is any effort to spread an idea. It can take many forms. It may be talk between people or words on the printed page. It may be films flashed on a screen or sounds transmitted over the air. It may be pictures at an exhibition or songs in a show.

The word "propaganda" comes from the Latin verb *propagare,* "to propagate." Originally "propagate" meant "to reproduce" or "to spread." It came to mean also "to transmit" and "to spread from person to person."

In the classic sense, propaganda is the art of communicating a message. But it goes beyond communicating. It reaches the point of persuading others. In the international sense, it means the attempt to persuade others of the rightness of one's cause.

Because propaganda at times has helped stir people to violent action, it is often thought to be bad. But propaganda can be good or bad, depending on its aims.

History

Ever since people began to live together, they have tried to influence one another. In some cultures, witch doctors performed tricks and wove spells to show they were in touch with the gods. Their magic helped them control the people. In early Babylonian, Egyptian, and Roman times, priests played on popular superstitions to keep themselves in power. They used auguries (omens) and sacrifices to hold people's attention. Later, military leaders advertised their might by taking part in magnificent processions, in which they showed off the slaves and treasure they had captured.

The word "propaganda" may well have been first used in its present meaning when Pope Gregory XV set up the Sacred Congregation of Propaganda in 1622. This was a committee appointed to study ways of spreading the Christian faith through the world.

Before the American Revolutionary War, Samuel Adams wrote pamphlets against the British to spur the revolt of the colonies. Patrick Henry made his famous "Give me liberty or give me death" speech. Benjamin Franklin and George Washington both expressed views that stirred the already seething settlers. Every effort was made to play on long-standing resentments.

By this time, propaganda was no longer only

Forms of propaganda were used by both sides in World War II. Left: This poster urged people of the Allied countries to unite to win the war. Right: Adolf Hitler used his powers as a speaker to win support in Germany.

488

a matter of the spoken word. Organizations produced pamphlets to air their views. Newspapers and periodicals published editorials.

By the 20th century, hundreds of organizations of all types had begun to spread their own doctrines. Some were political, some economic. Some were frankly commercial, advertising products for the public to buy.

Beginning about 1915, motion pictures became a forceful means of influencing people. Radio reached its full development in the 1920's, and television followed on its heels. Each offered propagandists a wider platform.

Methods

There are many means of propaganda. The oldest, and still one of the most effective, is person-to-person. In this regard, most governments are aware that their citizens overseas can play a critical role as messengers of goodwill. Information may be provided in many other ways, but a personal link may prove vital in making any message meaningful.

Printing is perhaps the most popular way to reach large numbers of people. Any person or group can print pamphlets, write articles, or place advertisements in newspapers to express a political view, promote a cause, or sell a product. Every daily newspaper has an editorial page, where the publisher's views and comments on the news appear.

The arts can also be used for purposes of propaganda. Playwrights present their views on stage, screen, and television. In both fiction and nonfiction, authors may plead for a special cause. Artists paint pictures and posters to arouse the public. With just a few strokes of the pen, cartoonists can ridicule people and events.

Press agents and public relations firms try to build prestige or increase business for their clients. Advertising agencies influence people to buy certain products. They conduct market research studies to find out which method of propaganda brings the best results for their clients.

Governments

In this century, propaganda is most often thought of as a tool of governments. It is a key weapon in dictatorships, which seek to direct the will of the people. Dictatorships control all media (means) of communication.

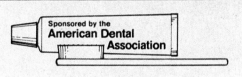

National Children's Dental Health Week

© 1979 American Dental Association

Propaganda can be good or bad, depending on its aims. This poster promotes better dental care for children.

They thereby control what people see, hear, read, and learn. Propaganda surrounds the people in their homes, their schools, and their communities.

Democracies use, but do not monopolize, the various media of communication. They try to offer a choice of viewpoints. They encourage debate. More than one political party vies for public favor. As times change, the parties in power change. When this happens, the official propaganda of the government may change as well.

In the collision of political beliefs among nations, propaganda has taken on new dimensions. Opposing governments use many of the same words but mean different things. Each government tries to express itself in ways that will make people think well of it. In so doing, it may have to deal with contrary ideas spread by hostile forces.

Today most governments make use of propaganda. The United States Government engages in propaganda to try to win support for its foreign policies. This is done through the United States Information Agency (USIA). The agency is best known through its broadcast division, the Voice of America.

CARL T. ROWAN
Former Director
U.S. Information Agency

Monument in Geneva showing important figures of the Reformation, among them Calvin and Knox.

PROTESTANTISM

Protestantism is the general term for the religious faith and practice within the Christian Church that resulted from the Reformation in Europe in the 16th century. During the early Middle Ages, Christianity in Europe was united by a common way of thinking and by a strong system of church government. But in the later Middle Ages this unity was broken by new kinds of political, social, and religious ideas. Old ways of living and thinking were being questioned as the Western world began to break out of its traditional boundaries.

Many religious leaders felt that the medieval (Middle Ages) form of the Christian Church had become too unbending. Others thought that the beliefs of the Church were out of touch with the simple teachings of Jesus Christ. The machinery of the Church's government was criticized by many as being too complicated and too far removed from the simple faith of New Testament times. The beginning of the 16th century marked a turning point in European history. With the passing of the Middle Ages the problems of life, society, politics, and religion became more complicated and difficult.

Protest and Reform

Those who felt strongly that something ought to be done about bringing the Church up to date were called Protestants or sometimes simply Reformers. Both names are correct, for they describe two different but related features of Protestantism. First, there was a protest against many of the beliefs and practices of the Roman Catholic Church as it had developed during the Middle Ages. Second, there was a deep desire to reform the principles, worship, and government of the Church so that they would be nearer to the New Testament ideal. In its earliest forms, and often in later years, Protestantism showed itself as both a negative (protesting) and a positive (reforming) religious movement.

The date for the birth of the Protestant Reformation is usually given as 1517. In that year Martin Luther, a German monk, first spoke out officially against the Roman Catholic Church and some of its beliefs. Luther did not want to leave the Roman Catholic Church or to begin a new church. His protest was so strong, however, that in a few years he became the recognized leader of the whole of Protestantism. He was followed by other leaders in other places in Europe. Among them were John Calvin (1509–64) in Geneva, John Knox (1505–72) in Scotland, and later, in the 18th century, John Wesley (1703–91) in England and the colonies of the New World.

Protestants believed that Roman Catholics did not make the Bible central enough in their teaching. So Protestants began a fresh study of the Old and New Testaments. One of Luther's first tasks was to translate the Bible from Greek and Hebrew into German, the common language of his people. This put the basic document of Christianity into the hands of the people. Now they were no longer completely dependent on priestly interpreters but could be encouraged to interpret the Scriptures for themselves. Protestants also objected to the supreme authority and power of the pope. They urged that the Church be organized on a freer and more democratic basis.

At first, Protestants defined their doctrines

and beliefs in terms of their opposition to Roman Catholicism. This suggested that, generally speaking, Protestants believed in salvation "by faith" (in Jesus Christ) rather than "by works" (of righteous living); the authority of the Bible rather than the authority of the pope; the divinity of Jesus Christ but with less emphasis on devotion to the Virgin Mary; a "priesthood of believers" (private interpretation of the Scriptures) rather than several different ranks of priests (hierarchy); the Church as the community of believers rather than the divine institution of the clergy, as stated by Rome; and the two essential sacraments of Baptism and Communion (Eucharist, or the Lord's Supper) rather than the seven sacraments of the Roman Catholic Church (Baptism, Confirmation, Holy Communion, Penance, Sacrament of the Sick, Holy Orders, and Marriage).

Major Groups

Three major types of Protestantism emerged from the 16th-century European Reformation. (1) The Lutheran and Calvinistic (sometimes called Reformed or Presbyterian) churches spread through Germany, the Netherlands, the Scandinavian countries, and Britain and later to North America. There were differences between Lutherans and Calvinists, mostly on interpretation (what the sacraments meant) and how the church should be governed. But they formed the main movement of Protestantism in Europe and America.

As the name suggests, the various branches of the Lutheran Church adopted the doctrinal views of Martin Luther. A common creed among Lutherans is the Augsburg Confession (1530). It emphasizes salvation by faith in Jesus Christ. This creed also recognizes two sacraments—Baptism and the Lord's Supper. Calvinists (Reformed and Presbyterians) look to John Calvin as their spiritual ancestor. They stress the primary authority of the Bible in matters of belief and worship. Their church organization is based on a democratic system of lower and higher courts, much like that of the United States federal government.

(2) In England, under Henry VIII, the Protestant Reformation resulted in a church tradition often called Anglican (or Protestant Episcopal—although some groups have dropped the word "protestant" from their

Protests by the German monk Martin Luther sparked the Protestant Reformation.

The Protestant leader John Calvin exercised strict control over his followers.

A Congregational church in Groton, Massachusetts.

churches. Baptists believe that Christians as adults (not infants) should receive the sacrament of Baptism by total immersion in water, rather than by mere sprinkling, and that they should make a public confession of their faith before the congregation. Another type of Baptist church, whose members are known as Disciples of Christ, developed its own church organization and is now known as the Christian Church. They are sometimes called Campbellites, after the founder, Alexander Campbell (1788–1866).

Especially in the United States, where churches and denominations multiplied, split apart, and reunited, it is difficult to keep the lines of history clear. For example, in 1957 four originally separate Protestant churches (Evangelical Synod, Reformed Church, Congregational Church, and Christian Church) came together to form the United Church of Christ. A generation earlier in Canada, the United Church of Canada was formed (1925) by the merger of Methodists, Congregationalists, and Presbyterians.

Two interesting and well-known denominations are the Church of Christ, Scientist (Christian Scientists) and the Church of Jesus Christ of Latter-Day Saints (Mormons). Christian Science is based on a combination of truths from the Bible and from *Science and Health, with Key to the Scriptures* (1875), by Mary Baker Eddy (1821–1910). Believing in the healing of bodily ills through faith, Christian Scientists emphasize spiritual rather than physical reality. The Mormons, too, combine Biblical truth with a more modern interpretation—*The Book of Mormon* (1830), by Joseph Smith (1805–44). Their most famous leader was Brigham Young, who settled Salt Lake City, which became the Mormon headquarters.

Growth and Variety

The chief forms of early Protestantism spread quickly as explorers discovered new lands and as the German, Dutch, English, Swedish and other colonies in North America were settled. Before the Revolutionary War, Anglicans and Episcopalians had settled in New England and the South. Reformed (Calvinistic) churches were established by the Dutch in New York and New Jersey. Puritans came from England, Presbyterians from

title). The English Reformation was not so critical of Roman Catholic doctrine or forms of worship as the Lutheran or Calvinistic churches. The Church of England is sometimes called a bridge church because it combines and brings together elements from both Catholic and Protestant traditions.

(3) A third group of churches, mostly in Switzerland, Germany, and the Netherlands, tried to carry the reform of the Church much further than either Luther or Calvin had. These smaller and usually unorganized churches became known as the Radical Reformation or "left-wing" Protestantism. They were highly independent as to church government, interpretation of the Scriptures, and doctrinal beliefs. These radical reforming movements had a great influence on the development of such churches as the Baptist. This type of Protestantism was never very strong in Europe or England. In America it grew rapidly into many different kinds of independent

The minister leads the congregation in hymns at a Sunday service in Connecticut.

Scotland, Lutherans from Germany and Scandinavia, and Mennonites and Moravians from Germany. Methodists looked to John Wesley as their spiritual father. Baptists remembered the courage and independence of Roger Williams.

With the opening up of the western frontier, and especially in the 19th century, the church traditions from Europe lost some of their original traits as they became more adapted to the freer American situation. As the country itself developed, not only did the churches become more numerous, but more kinds and varieties of churches emerged.

By the first half of the 20th century, there were more than 200 different Protestant church bodies in America. Most of these came from the Lutheran, Calvinistic, Anglican, and "radical" traditions. In each case there were divisions and regroupings according to language, custom, or belief. Many new churches arose as the population moved westward. The existence of many forms of Protestantism in the United States (called sectarianism or denominationalism) caused bitterness and prejudice both inside and outside church circles. But the American tradition of free enterprise in politics and economics encouraged individualism and differences of opinion in religious matters as well.

American Protestantism has always been less organized and more open to variety than European or British churches. But with variety there has also been growth. In the United States in 1850, only 16 percent of the population were members of Christian churches. One hundred years later the figure was nearly 60 percent—almost twice as much as the rate of growth for the total population. Today Protestant churches in the United States have over 73,000,000 members, more than any other group of churches.

Renewal and Reunion

Much of the 19th-century competition among the various Protestant churches gave way after World War II to a new spirit of cooperation and unity. Many actual reunions and mergers of Protestant churches took place, notably in the Presbyterian, Methodist, and Congregationalist traditions. New agencies (such as the National Council of Churches of Christ in the U.S.A. and the World Council of Churches, with headquarters in Geneva, Switzerland), arose for the encouragement of church union.

In the midst of a divided world in search of unity, Protestant churches were challenged to renew their beliefs and traditions. The development of the United Nations in the polit-

The new Jerusalem Lutheran Church, built on the site of the first Protestant mission in India.

PROTESTANT CHURCHES

The official or accepted names of the major Protestant denominations are given here. In many instances there are several kinds of church bodies using the same name in some form.*

Adventist
Baptist
Brethren
Christian Churches (Disciples of Christ)
Church of Christ, Scientist (Christian Scientists)
Church of England (Anglican)
Church of God
Church of the Nazarene
Friends, Society of (Quakers)
Jehovah's Witnesses

Latter-Day Saints (Mormons)
Lutheran
Mennonite
Methodist
Moravian
Pentecostal
Presbyterian
Protestant Episcopal
Reformed
Unitarian-Universalist
United Church of Canada
United Church of Christ

* Source: *Yearbook of American and Canadian Churches,* edited by Constant H. Jacquet, Jr., National Council of Churches, 475 Riverside Drive, New York, N.Y. 10027, and published by Abingdon Press.

ical field found a parallel in the development of the **ecumenical**, or unity, movement among the churches. This search for unity within Protestantism grew out of the missionary work of the churches and the early formation of the International Missionary Council (1910). The World Council of Churches (organized in 1948) joined forces with the International Missionary Council at New Delhi, India, in 1961. The joining together of these organizations emphasized the quest for unity.

Several developments in Protestant churches have taken place in recent years. Some large denominations (Episcopal, Presbyterian, Methodist, United Church of Christ) have declined in total membership. Other denominations (Baptist, Missouri Synod Lutherans, Seventh-Day Adventists, Church of the Nazarene, Jehovah's Witnesses, Christian Reformed) have grown in influence and membership. Television has brought the teachings of some groups to millions of people. Some Protestants have taken an active role in politics through such groups as the Moral Majority. And churches involved in the earlier ecumenical movement have shifted their main attention from the World Council of Churches (WCC) and the National Council of Churches (NCC). They have concentrated more on local grass-roots experiments in church unity and co-operation.

The growing interest of the Roman Catholic Church in the ecumenical movement was of great importance, not only for Protestantism but for all branches of Christianity throughout the world. In 1962, Pope John XXIII called for a new Catholic ecumenical gathering, known as the second Vatican Council. In so doing, Pope John helped to foster understanding of problems that have separated Catholics and Protestants since the time of the Protestant Reformation more than 400 years ago. Many Catholic and Protestant church leaders were encouraged by this move. It is believed that closer co-operation and better understanding are the paths that Christianity must take to relate its message to the new problems of a space-age world.

HUGH T. KERR
Princeton Theological Seminary

See also CALVIN, JOHN; LUTHER, MARTIN; MORMONS; QUAKERS; REFORMATION; ROMAN CATHOLIC CHURCH.

PROTOZOANS

Protozoans are one-celled organisms with animal-like characteristics. The tens of thousands of species, or kinds, of protozoans have survived for millions of years. By slowly evolving and changing, they have adapted to many different environments. They are found wherever there is water or moisture—in hot springs, in the ice of the Arctic, in deserts, in air, even inside the bodies of animals.

These adaptable creatures have fascinated humans from the time they were first seen in the 1600's. It was then that Dutch scientist Anton van Leeuwenhoek examined a drop of pond water using simple microscopes he had built. The water teemed with activity! Creatures of all different shapes and sizes moved through the water, feeding and multiplying. He called these tiny organisms "animalcules."

Based on their characteristics, the water creatures were originally classified as animals and placed in the animal kingdom within the phylum, or group, Protozoa. However, as the microscopic organisms were studied, some were seen to resemble animals, while others were seen to more closely resemble plants. Today, some scientists suggest that protozoans are neither animals nor plants, so they should be classified with other simple organisms in the kingdom Protista.

▶CHARACTERISTICS OF PROTOZOANS

Protozoans have many features that are common to multicellular organisms, such as human beings. But all of these complex features are designed so that the protozoan can live independently with just one cell.

Size and Shape. There is considerable variety in the size and shape of protozoans. A few are large enough to see with the naked eye, but most protozoans can be seen only with a microscope. In fact, they are so small they are measured in micrometers. A micrometer is about 1/25,000 inch. Protozoans range from 1 micrometer to 2,000 micrometers in length, with most protozoans measuring about 600 micrometers.

The bodies of some types of protozoans, like the amoeba, are formless. They gently flow from one shape into another as they

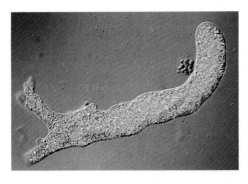

A sarcodine, such as the amoeba (*left*), uses flowing cell extensions to capture food. It slowly reaches out and surrounds the food, then takes it into the cell to digest it (*below*).

move. Other kinds have bodies shaped like barrels, cups, and radiating suns.

Structure. While protozoans can appear quite different, they all have similar basic structures. Like other kinds of cells, protozoans have a thin outer covering called a cell membrane. Inside their cells, protozoans have specialized structures surrounded by membranes called organelles, or little organs. Essential functions take place within the organelles that help protozoans move, feed, and reproduce.

The nucleus is an organelle that contains the cell's genes—the basic units of heredity. Genes, which are made of a chemical called DNA (*d*eoxyribo*n*ucleic *a*cid), ensure that every new generation of cells will have characteristics similar to its parents. Because the cell of a protozoan has a distinct nucleus that is separated from other cell parts, protozoans are considered to be more sophisticated organisms than other one-celled creatures, such as bacteria. In fact, **protozoologists**, scientists who study protozoans, have found that the protozoan cell has the same main features as the cells of higher, more advanced animals.

Along with the nucleus, protozoans have a variety of organelles called vacuoles. Vacuoles may help digest food or hold extra water. For example, a specialized water vacuole, called a contractile vacuole, helps some protozoans get rid of extra water. When too much water collects in the cell, the vacuole moves to the outer surface of the cell and squeezes out the water. This helps keep the cell from swelling up and bursting.

Feeding Habits. Protozoans hunt, digest, and store food. Most are heterotrophs, that is, they feed on others to get the organic sub-

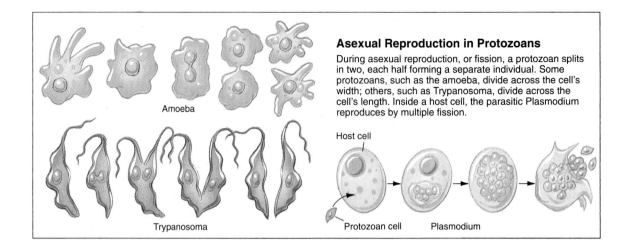

Asexual Reproduction in Protozoans

During asexual reproduction, or fission, a protozoan splits in two, each half forming a separate individual. Some protozoans, such as the amoeba, divide across the cell's width; others, such as Trypanosoma, divide across the cell's length. Inside a host cell, the parasitic Plasmodium reproduces by multiple fission.

Amoeba

Trypanosoma

Host cell

Protozoan cell   Plasmodium

stances, such as nitrogen and carbon, they need to live. Protozoans actively seek out bacteria and other living creatures as food. They also can control the amounts of water, wastes, and gases in their cell that result from the digestive process.

Reproduction. The ability to rapidly multiply and form new cells has played a major role in the long survival of protozoans. They can grow and reproduce using both sexual and asexual reproduction. All protozoans multiply by simple asexual reproduction, or fission. During fission, one cell splits into two similar daughter cells. Some divide across the length of the cell, while others divide across the width. Certain parasitic protozoans—those that live and reproduce only within the cells of other organisms—form many new cells by multiple fission, or division, within the host.

Sexual reproduction also occurs during the life of some protozoans. Sometimes two protozoan cells, each carrying half their normal genetic material, fuse to form a new cell. Other protozoans can exchange some of their genes during mating. The exchange and mixing of genetic material help protozoans evolve and adapt to new conditions.

▶**TYPES OF PROTOZOANS**

As the methods used to study protozoans have improved, many more species have been identified. Today, about 40,000 species are known. The addition of newly discovered kinds of protozoans has altered how they are grouped,

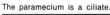
The paramecium is a ciliate.

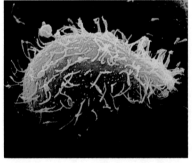

or classified. Some protozoologists have classified them according to how they reproduce or the stages of their life cycles. However, the most common method is to group them according to how they move. Based on locomotion, there are four groups: sarcodines, ciliates, flagellates, and sporozoans.

Sarcodines

Sarcodines have constantly changing shapes. They move by sending out fingerlike extensions of their cell membranes called pseudopods, or "false feet." These organisms use their pseudopods to find, trap, and eat food. Pseudopods slowly reach out, surround the food, and form a food vacuole around it. Once the food is inside the cell, it is digested.

The amoeba, whose name comes from the Greek word for "change," is an example of a sarcodine. Most amoebas are found in fresh or salt water. Some ocean-living amoebas can make a hard external shell. Through holes in their shells, they send out long, thin pseudopods to trap their food. Shells from these protozoans accumulate on the ocean floor forming chalk deposits. A few types of amoebas produce disease in humans; for example, the protozoan Entamoeba causes intestinal illness and diarrhea.

Ciliates

Some of the most beautiful and interesting protozoans to watch in pond water are those that are covered with many short hairs, called **cilia**. Some of these protozoans, or ciliates, have clumps of cilia, while others are completely covered with thousands of cilia. The motion of the cilia helps the protozoans move about and capture food.

A colony of flagellates (*Leishmania tropica*).

The paramecium is a well-known member of the ciliates. It is also called the "slipper animal" because of its long, footlike shape. Cilia cover the paramecium's body. They move like waves beating down and across its body. The short hairs move the paramecium by turning, rotating, and propelling the cell forward. The cilia also sweep food and water into a funnel-like mouth. A membrane at the end of the groove surrounds the food to form a vacuole. The food is digested and waste material is released from a small opening at the end of the cell.

This group of protozoans can also have different sizes of nuclei. The large nucleus is called a macronucleus and the many smaller ones are called micronuclei. Some protozoans exchange their micronuclei during sexual mating. Helpful genetic variations can occur because of this exchange.

Most ciliates can change into tough-walled forms called cysts. They can hide inside these shells when food is scarce or when it is too cold, hot, or dry. These cysts awaken and become active when conditions become better.

Flagellates

A third group of protozoans move by using long, thin structures called **flagella**. Flagella are like flexible whips that can bend in many directions. Most of these protozoans, known as flagellates, have one or two flagella sticking out of one end of the cell. But some have several.

Although there are flagellates that live free in water, most live in the bodies of plants and animals. They get nutrients by eating other organisms or by absorbing food molecules through their cell membrane. Some flagellates help the organisms they invade. For example, those found in the gut of termites help to digest the wood that the termites eat. Other flagellates may harm the host. Several human diseases, including African sleeping sickness, are caused by parasitic flagellates.

Sporozoans

Most of these protozoans cannot move. They do not have any specialized structures for movement. A few, which have flagella or pseudopods, are able to move.

All sporozoans are parasites. This small-celled protozoan has special organelles that allow it to invade a host cell. Some sporozoans have to live in two or more hosts to survive and multiply. They reproduce sexually in one host and then reproduce asexually in a second host. The parasite can damage the cells of the host during reproduction. Plasmodium, the organism that causes malaria, is an example. It needs both a human or other vertebrate and a mosquito to complete its life cycle.

▶ IMPORTANCE OF PROTOZOANS

While we have concern for the diseases that protozoans can cause, we must remember that most protozoans are harmless and some are helpful. Protozoans contribute to the natural balance that exists in our world.

Enormous numbers of protozoans are important as a source of food for larger animals. Protozoans also help in the exploration for oil. Scientists looking for oil deposits search for certain kinds of protozoan fossils, knowing that oil will be found nearby.

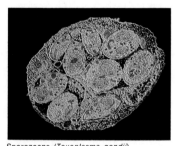
Sporozoans (*Toxoplasma gondii*) infecting a cell.

Characteristics that make protozoans deadly make them useful, too. They reproduce rapidly and are easily maintained in the laboratory. Because they reproduce asexually, a large pool of cells with the same genetic makeup can be developed and studied over time. Researchers can use this pool of genetically constant cells to study the hereditary mechanisms of living organisms.

CYNTHIA V. SOMMER
University of Wisconsin at Milwaukee

See also CELLS; DISEASES; MICROBIOLOGY.

PROVERBS

A proverb is a traditional saying that sums up a situation, passes judgment on a past matter, or recommends a course of action for the future. Some proverbs state a fact, such as "Honesty is the best policy." But most proverbs are metaphorical. When someone says, "Don't cry over spilled milk," he is not referring to milk. He is using a metaphor to tell another person not to worry about something that cannot be undone.

Proverbs consist of at least one topic and one comment about that topic. They can have as few as two words: "Money talks"; "Time flies." Many proverbs fall into one of several traditional patterns. They may present an alternative ("Sink or swim"; "Do or die") or an equation ("Seeing is believing"; "Enough is enough"). Proverbs often make use of contrast: "A good beginning makes a good ending"; "One man's meat is another man's poison." Sometimes the contrast is emphasized by parallel structure: "Out of sight, out of mind"; "Waste not, want not." Still another characteristic is the use of rhyme: "An apple a day keeps the doctor away"; "Haste makes waste."

Proverbs are one of the oldest forms of folklore. The earliest writings of ancient civilizations all contain numerous examples. An entire book of the Old Testament is devoted to proverbs. Many proverbs in common use can be traced back to the Bible: "A soft answer turneth away wrath"; "Money is the root of all evil"; "Pride goeth before a fall." Other proverbs can be traced to ancient Latin and Greek literature: "Love is blind"; "Two heads are better than one." Sometimes poets borrow from folklore. Shakespeare used a proverb as the title for one of his plays: "All's well that ends well." Sometimes a poet's proverb is borrowed by the folk. An example is Alexander Pope's "A little learning is a dangerous thing."

Proverbs are found among most of the peoples of the world, but very few have been reported from among the Indians of North and South America. Nowhere is the proverb more common than among the peoples of Africa. Most Africans use proverbs in their normal, everyday conversation. Proverbs are especially important in the conduct of African trials. An accused person will seek a lawyer who knows many proverbs and knows how to apply them. Just as lawyers in Western cultures cite previous cases and decisions to convince a judge and jury that their client's plea is just, Africans cite appropriate proverbs.

It is often supposed that proverbs are full of wisdom. In fact, a proverb has been defined as "the wisdom of many and the wit of one." However, a proverb may be found to support almost any view. "Look before you leap" urges caution, but "He who hesitates is lost" urges immediate action. Proverbs fit certain situations. They are not always true for all time.

Many proverbs, like certain folktales and folk songs, are truly international. The American proverb "A bird in the hand is worth two in the bush" has parallels in most European countries. Typical examples are the Rumanian "Better a bird in the hand than a thousand in the garden" and the Portuguese "Better a sparrow in the hand than two flying."

Proverbs often come from stories. "Don't count your chickens before they hatch" is from a folktale in which a girl, daydreaming about what she will do with the money from selling soon-to-be-hatched chickens, drops her basket and breaks all the eggs. Someone who does not know the story behind a proverb may fail to understand the proverb. It is impossible to guess the meaning of the Burmese proverb "I am not angry, but the buffalo's tail is shorter" without knowing its story. The story is about a farmer plowing his field with a water buffalo. At noon he is hungry, but his wife fails to appear with his lunch. After a few more hours he is so hungry that he cuts the tail off the buffalo, cooks it, and eats it. Finally his wife comes with his lunch. She asks him whether he is angry with her. His reply is the proverb.

Proverbs are frequently used by older people to educate the young. In school, proverbs may be the subjects of themes and essays. They also appear on standard aptitude and reasoning tests. The student must be able to explain their meaning.

ALAN DUNDES
University of California

PSYCHIATRY. See MENTAL HEALTH; MENTAL ILLNESS.

PSYCHOLOGY

If you have ever seen the Washington Monument, you can probably remember what it looks like. But your memory may not be wholly accurate. You may forget the windows at the top or the circle of flags at the bottom. Still, with certain changes that depend on the way your brain is working, you can see the monument in your mind's eye.

You can also imagine what you have never seen. You can imagine a purple elephant lying on its back with its legs in the air and a monkey dancing a jig on each of its feet. That image, too, is in your mind's eye.

If you look at the real Washington Monument, if you listen to a band playing 'Yankee Doodle," if you feel a cold piece of liver with your hand in the dark, you are **perceiving**. That is, you are getting information about outside objects and events by means of your senses, and you are putting this information together into images or patterns that have some meaning. This process of assembling information is called **perception**.

Perception is but one of the many activities that go on in the mind. The study of these activities and also the behavior of human beings and other animals is called **psychology**.

Psychology and Mental Illness

When people hear the word "psychology," many of them think of mental illness. But the study of mental illness is only part of psychology. The relation between psychology and mental illness is like the relation between biology and medicine. Biology deals with the basic processes of life, not just with disease. In the same way, psychology deals with the basic processes of the mind, not just with disorders of the mind. Psychologists who do basic scientific experiments in order to find out how the mind works are called **experimental psychologists**. Psychologists who use their knowledge to help people who are upset by mental disorders or adjustment problems are called **clinical psychologists**.

▶PERCEPTION AND ILLUSION

The earliest studies in the field of psychology concerned perception. A perception may be very different from the outside event that starts it up. And so, such studies seemed to offer the best way of finding out how the mind differs from outside events. The studies also seemed useful in trying to find out how what goes on in the mind is different from events in the brain.

Let us start with an inaccurate perception, or **illusion**, in order to understand better what the mind is like. Study the spirals in Figure 1. There seem to be about a dozen of them centering on the dot. Place your finger lightly at the spot marked A and trace the spiral around the broken line. Your finger comes back to A. What looks like a spiral is really a circle. The

Figure 1.

Figure 2.

Figure 3. Do you see a young lady or an old lady in this drawing?

Figure 4 *(left)* emphasizes young lady, Figure 5 *(right)*, old lady.

spiral is an illusion. Figure 2 proves this. It is exactly the same as Figure 1 except that it shows the circle your finger traces.

In Figure 1 true perception fell short of telling you what the outside world is like.

Psychologists explain what happens in this way: Sensory nerve cells in your eyes receive information about the twisted-looking circles and deliver that information to your brain. The brain selects and interprets the information received. For the circle you experience an illusion that is a spiral. You do not have accurate information about the actual drawing.

Now look at Figure 3. You can see either a young lady or an old lady. You cannot see both ladies at once; you cannot see just black and white. The brain insists on picking out the bits of black and white that let you see the young lady or the old lady. Since you cannot see both ladies together, try to see first one and then the other. That black ribbon around the young lady's neck becomes the old lady's mouth; the young lady's left ear becomes the old lady's left eye. If you can perceive only one of the two, study Figures 4 and 5. These are nearly the same drawing, but one emphasizes the young lady and the other brings out the old lady. Perception always involves se-

lecting—generally the brain selects what it is most important for the person perceiving to know.

Perception of Space

This kind of brain action is also very useful when you are perceiving objects in space. The eyes in the human face are about 2½ inches (6.35 centimeters) apart; thus they get slightly different views of the same nearby object. The right eye sees more around the right side of an object than does the left eye, and the left eye sees more around the left side. This kind of vision is called stereoscopic. The word "stereoscopic" comes from two Greek words meaning "solid" and "viewing."

Suppose you are looking with both eyes at a small cube held in front of your face. Figure 6 shows what the different images for the right and left eyes would be like. If you were to put one image on top of the other, you would not be able to fit the lines of one image on top of the lines of the other image. Still, you do not see double lines when looking at the cube with both eyes. Your brain has turned two flat images seen by two eyes into one three-dimensional cube. The front of the cube is near you, and the top and sides extend back from the front; the cube appears as a solid object in space.

Notice also that in Figure 6 the girl can see all along the wall from one side to the other in back of the cube, almost as though the cube were not there. What one eye cannot see, the other eye can. The right eye can see from B to C on the wall behind the cube. The cube hides this part of the wall from the left eye. The left eye can see from D to E, which the cube hides from the right eye. The two eyes working together see all of the wall from A to F.

If you drew the two images of the cube side by side on a card and put the card in a stereoscope, you would perceive a solid cube standing out from the card. A stereoscope has two lenses separated by a nosepiece. The viewer looks at the card through the stereoscope. Although each eye sees one cube, the viewer perceives a solid cube.

Perception of Size

Now look at Figure 7. You can see two women seated in a hallway at different distances from the camera. The far one is three times as far away as the near one. The sensory cells form an image of the near person that is three times as large as the image of the far one.

In the photograph the far person looks just a little smaller than the near person, because in a photograph, which is flat on paper, the hall does not look as long as it would if you were standing in it. If you were standing in the hall with the real women, the far woman

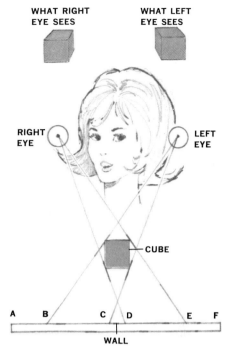

Figure 6. How the left eye and right eye view an object in space.

Woman at rear seems larger in Figure 7 than she seems in Figure 8. If you measure, you find that the woman is exactly the same size in both pictures.

FIGURE 7

FIGURE 8

would appear the same size as the near woman. Your brain would take into account the information about the distances seen by your eyes. It would then correct for the differences in the size of the images in your eyes. The mind tells you that the women are about the same size: One is not three times as large as the other. Similarly, the size of people walking away from you a short distance does not seem to change. Their size remains almost constant in your perception of them as they walk away.

You can see what the brain does if you look at Figure 8. The photograph of the far woman has been cut out and pasted in at what appears

to be the same distance from the camera as the near one. See how much smaller she becomes when the two women appear to be side by side. Yet, if you measure, you will find the picture of the far person is just the same size in both figures. However, in Figure 8 the brain does not try to correct for a difference in distance. The relative sizes of the two women are the same as the relative sizes of the images of them in the eyes.

The brain does all this interpreting of size in relation to distance instantly and without your being aware of it. You do not guess the distance and then try to calculate the sizes. You just see what you see.

▶ **WHAT THE MIND IS**

A spiral is perceived although there are only twisted rope circles. The perception of the spiral is the mind. The mind is the perception of the young lady or the old lady that appears out of the black and white splotches. It is the perception of the two women as being about the same size in Figure 7, while the images in the eyes differ greatly in size.

The mind is the experience of an event just as it comes to you without your having worked over it consciously. The brain works over the events instantly, but you know about the brain's action only if you have been told about what the brain can do. In other words the mind is **immediate experience**.

Many other things come to you as immediate experience. If you hear a band playing "Yankee Doodle" or see a clown juggling plates and there is nothing there to produce the perception, you may be imagining a concert or a circus performance or perhaps remembering one. If you plan something with your eyes shut and without talking to yourself, you may be thinking. The mind is the immediate experience of perceiving, remembering, imagining, and thinking.

▶ **THE DEVELOPMENT OF EXPERIMENTAL PSYCHOLOGY**

When you dream, some part of you seems to go far away while your body stays at home. Some such experience may have given ancient peoples the notion that there was some inner self, an essential and active part, that was separate from the body. This inner self perceived, thought, felt, decided, and remembered things. It was in the body until the body died,

---

TESTING THE WAY PEOPLE THINK AND REMEMBER

Here is a test used by psychologists to study the way people think and remember. You may want to try it on yourself and on some of your friends.

Using a stopwatch, give everyone 40 seconds to carefully study this picture. Then close the book. Ask everyone to write down all the details of the picture that they can remember.

Do you find you remember in visual images or in words? Does anyone remember the scene perfectly? What parts of the scene do most people remember?

Young people usually form more vivid images than grown-ups and remember the scene better. You can test this statement by using your parents as subjects for the experiment.

and it lived on afterward. Yet although this self was in the body, it took up no space there. It was something like light as it passes through glass. Light takes up no room in the glass and leaves no hole after it has gone.

When people began to know more about the insides of the body, they began to think the inner self was a distinct organ, or part, to wonder where it was located, and how it received information and acted on it. One very old idea was that the inner self was located in the heart. Eventually it was discovered that the nerves are lines of communication between the brain and the outside world. With this information, scholars decided that the inner self, the mind, must be in the brain or at any rate must use the brain as its communication center.

Then, in the 1600's a Frenchman got the idea that in human beings, mind and brain are different, but they act on each other. The mind gets the information that the nerves bring to the brain, this thinker said, and the mind may then make decisions. These decisions shape the commands that the brain sends back along the nerves to the muscles that move the body.

The man who stated all these things was René Descartes. He is often called the father of modern psychology. Although his ideas were later revised, they led in time to the first truly scientific study of the mind and of human and animal behavior.

The first experiments concerning such matters got under way in Germany in the mid-1800's. They were performed by philosophers, physiologists, and physicists. But toward the end of the century, psychology came to be recognized as an independent science, and in western Europe and North America some of these scientists began to call themselves psychologists. For example, in 1885 a German scholar, Hermann Ebbinghaus (1850–1909), developed a way of measuring learning and memory. This made it possible to study learning experimentally.

Hermann Ebbinghaus: Experiments in Learning

Ebbinghaus' work was based on an observation made by the Greek philosopher Aristotle more than 2,000 years earlier. Aristotle had stated a fundamental law about memory. If two objects are next to each other at the same time or are similar to each other, Aristotle said, then the remembering or thinking of one object will tend to bring up the memory

---

WONDER QUESTION

What is personality?

The word "personality" means the behavioral characteristics of a person. These characteristics include ways of perceiving, thinking, feeling, and acting. When people say that someone has "lots of personality," they may mean that he or she does things in an outgoing, warm, or charming manner. One person does not actually have more personality than another, but different people do have different personality traits. These traits include shyness, sociability, generosity, hostility, aggressiveness, and a sense of humor.

Some psychologists describe people's behavior in terms of personality types. For example, the Swiss psychologist Carl Jung defined **extroverts** as people whose interests are directed toward the world around them and toward other people and **introverts** as people whose interests are directed toward their own thoughts and feelings. An extrovert might prefer to spend the day meeting lots of new people, while an introvert might prefer to spend the day reading, writing, or listening to music. No one, however, is completely one personality type or the other.

---

of the other. The two objects are associated (linked) in the viewer's mind. This is the **law of association**.

Here is an example of how it works. The memory of a certain house brings up the memory of its garden because the two things are next to each other. They are associated in your mind. In a similar way the name of Tom Sawyer suggests that of Huckleberry Finn because the two boys appear in books by Mark Twain.

Earlier, scholars working with Aristotle's law of association decided that the association of one thing with another was actually based on the fact that the things are next to each other in time. You see the house and its garden during the same period of time. Ideas that occur to a person one right after the other or at the same time become associated. After that, the memory of one brings about the memory of the other.

This is where Ebbinghaus started. It was clear to him that there was not enough room in the mind for all the associated ideas to get in. For example, if you think of Abraham Lincoln, some—but not all—of the hundreds of ideas that have ever been associated in your mind with Lincoln come up. Only the strongest associations get through.

This thought led Ebbinghaus to ask what makes associations strong. The answer seemed clear to him: Association is strengthened by repetition. To test this, Ebbinghaus repeated aloud to himself poems and paragraphs of prose, and he counted the number of times he had to repeat them before he had them learned. Then he wrote down the number of repetitions.

Since forgetting always starts as soon as learning stops, it was possible to measure the strength of memory. Ebbinghaus did this by relearning the paragraph or poem he had learned the day before or the month before. He counted and recorded the number of repetitions needed to do so. It did not take as many

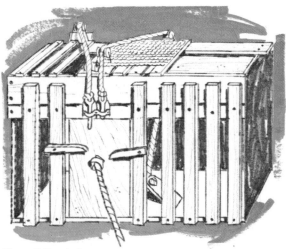

Figure 9. Puzzle box.

repetitions to relearn the piece as it first took to learn it; the strength of the memory is the number of repetitions saved. You may want to try this memory test on yourself.

Among other things, Ebbinghaus discovered that since a paragraph of prose has a meaning, it is already partly learned. Similarly, the rhythm and rhyme of poetry gives learning a head start. So for his experiments he invented series of nonsense syllables, which have neither meaning nor rhyme to help the learner. A nonsense syllable results when any vowel is placed between two consonants without forming a word—*kag*, *buv*, *wix*, *zep*, but not *bag* or *zip*. Hundreds of thousands of nonsense syllables have been learned since then by students acting as what psychologists call subjects in psychological experiments.

Ebbinghaus thought of the nonsense syllables as ideas in the mind. But what the experimenter actually observes is not so much the ideas in the subject's mind as the subject's ability to say what is remembered. Without knowing it, Ebbinghaus was shifting psychology from the study of the mind to the study of behavior. It is really behavior that is observed: what the subject says, how many syllables the subject gets right, and how soon. Once they had realized this, psychologists saw that they could use animals instead of human beings.

Edward L. Thorndike: the Puzzle Box

In 1898 an American psychologist, Edward L. Thorndike (1874–1949), designed a puzzle box with which to study animal learning. This box is shown in Figure 9. It has a system of bolts and catches that have to be used in a given order to open the door.

When Thorndike shut a cat inside the box, the cat wanted to get out. A desire to get out gave the cat its reason for trying. Getting out was both its motive and its reward. (For human subjects motives are often much more complicated. Sometimes pleasing the experimenter is all the reward a person needs to do a lot of hard work.)

Restless at being shut in, the cat tried first one bolt, then another. Finally it hit upon the right things to do. The cat did not learn the system of bolts and catches as a result of its first success. It needed more tries. But after repeated tests it learned the system perfectly.

Thorndike decided that the cat never perceived how the bolt mechanisms worked. It learned to get out by trial and error. A trial that led to an error made little impression on the learning, but a trial that led to success—to the reward of escape from the box—reinforced, or strengthened, learning very much indeed.

Today psychologists realize that in learning, such reinforcement is more important than repetition. Repeating the same problem over and over again simply gives the learner more chance of success—and so means that reinforcement has extra chances to work.

The Maze

Shortly after Thorndike reported on the learning behavior of cats and dogs in the puzzle box, another way of studying learning was introduced— the maze. The first one was patterned after a famous maze of hedges in the gardens of Hampton Court Palace in England. Rats,

which like to run through tunnels and alleyways, make excellent subjects for maze experiments that are used to study learning.

With your finger trace the correct route through the maze in Figure 10. You will find many blind alleys: They are the errors in the trial-and-error learning of the rat. At last, when the rat learns the correct route, it can dart through to the goal at full speed.

Ivan Pavlov: The Conditioned Reflex

Meanwhile, a Russian physiologist named Ivan Pavlov had found a new method for studying behavior in concrete physiological terms. He discovered this as a result of certain studies of digestive juices.

If a dog sees food that it likes and wants, its mouth will water. That is, its saliva will flow. The flowing of the saliva is a reflex action. The saliva flows automatically, without any conscious intent on the part of the dog to have it flow. Pavlov called this an **unconditioned reflex**. The event that sets off the action is called a stimulus, and the resulting action is called a response.

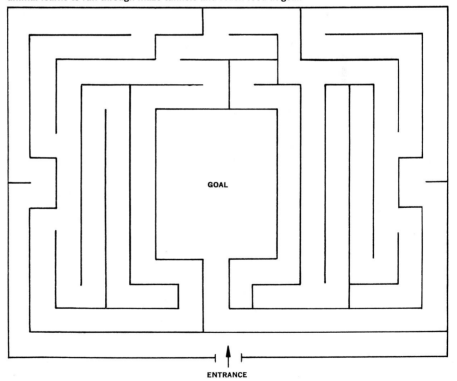

Figure 10. Mazes are often used in studies of animal learning. By trial and error an animal learns to run through maze tunnels and reach food at goal.

GOAL

ENTRANCE

What is instinct?

"Instinct" is the name most psychologists give to behavior that is unlearned. It is set off by some event inside or outside an animal's body and continues even after the original stimulus has disappeared.

Often instinctive behavior involves a complicated series of acts. This is true, for example, of the way stickleback fish act before and after they produce their eggs. Changes in the length of the day and the temperature of the water set off certain changes in the bodies of the fish. The fish then move to warm shallow water, where each male builds a nest. He chases off other males but leads females to his nest. After mating, male stickleback fish help care for the eggs by fanning them with their fins. No other sticklebacks have shown the males what to do, although their behavior is typical of all other sticklebacks.

Many other kinds of animals do things instinctively. In human beings, however, it is almost impossible to find examples of behavior that is completely instinctive. Though people sometimes say that boys have an instinct for fighting or that girls have an instinct for mothering dolls, such behavior is learned from observing other people.

Then Pavlov wondered whether a stimulus other than food would produce the same response. Just before offering the dog food, he rang a bell. After many repetitions he found that ringing the bell caused the saliva to flow. The bell had become the dinner bell. When the dog heard the bell, its mouth watered. Pavlov called this a **conditioned reflex**. A new stimulus—the bell—had become associated with the old stimulus—the food. The flow of saliva had become conditioned upon the new stimulus.

Finally, saliva flowed simply when the bell rang, without the presence of food. The new stimulus had taken over the job of the old.

Psychologists found that most of the learning and forgetting behavior observed in the experiments with nonsense syllables also held for the conditioned reflex. The conditioned reflex, however, can be used for many other kinds of observation. For instance, a psychologist can find out if a dog or some other animal can tell the difference between two notes on the piano. The animal is conditioned so that saliva flows for the note C. Then the psychologist tests the animal to see if saliva flows for D. The psychologist uses a similar method to see whether an animal can tell the difference between a triangle and a square or between a big square and a little square.

The Russians made great use of the conditioned reflex method of studying such behavior, and very soon psychologists in the United States took it up. More and more psychologists began concentrating only on the stimulus and the animal's response to it. This contributed to the development of a new kind of psychology, called behaviorism. Psychologists who work in this field study only behavior. They think they can get at the same facts that were originally discovered by studying immediate experience.

B. F. Skinner: Operant Conditioning

An American psychologist, B. F. Skinner (1904–90), made the next important discovery. He found that he could "shape the behavior," as he put it, of the animals used in his experiments.

Skinner waited for the animal to make the movement he wanted it to make. Then he rewarded the animal, usually with a pellet of food. After a while the animal would begin making the desired movement in order—it would seem—to get the pellet. Skinner called this response **operant behavior** and his method **operant conditioning**.

Rats shut in Skinner's box learned to get a pellet of food by pressing a bar with their forepaws. Pigeons learned to get a food pellet by pecking a button that dropped the pellet out of a bin. A pigeon's life is largely made up of pecking around for food, and if it is having fair success, it may make over 100,000 pecks in 12 hours. So although Skinner began his work with rats, he soon changed over to the patiently pecking pigeons. Figure 11 shows a pigeon pecking the button, and Figure 12 shows it getting its reward. (Learning is reinforced by the pellet.)

Skinner found he could change the way the pigeon pecked for its pellet. By operant conditioning he taught a pigeon to turn its bill counterclockwise before pecking the button for food. He did this by giving the pigeon no reward when it pecked the button. Then, when the pigeon accidentally made a turn partway to the left, Skinner rewarded its peck with a pellet. This reinforced the left turn. Very soon the pigeon was so well conditioned that it almost never tried to peck a pellet out of the machine without first making the magic turn. The pigeon becomes, in a sense, superstitious. Before pecking for food, it performs an act that is unrelated to the task of getting food. Its magic turn is like a child's stepping over the cracks between paving stones in order to get good luck.

Experimenters can use pigeons to study the effects of different ways of rewarding work done. If they let a pigeon get a pellet every time it pecks the button, then it works along at this pleasant job in a leisurely fashion. This activity is like reading an interesting book—the activity is its own reward.

An experimenter can, however, put the pigeon on a timed schedule. A clock is attached to the pellet bin so that the pigeon's pecks are rewarded only at intervals of 5 minutes. After getting a pellet, the pigeon soon loafs along with slow pecking; as the time for reward approaches, it speeds up its pecking to get the food as early as possible. Similarly, human beings do not work vigorously for rewards far in the future. Often students do not begin to study hard until just before a test. It is more difficult to start saving money for a bicycle than it is to save when you have almost enough to buy it.

Teaching Tricks by Operant Conditioning

It was very easy for Skinner to find a way to make the pigeon peck at the button in the first place. All he had to do was put the pigeon in the box and wait. Most pigeons naturally peck at round objects. So, after a moment or two, the pigeon pecked at the button and got its food. After that, the pigeon pecked at the button more often.

But suppose someone wanted to teach a pigeon to do something more complicated, like turning around in a circle counterclockwise. The experimenter could not just sit and wait for the pigeon to do that. In a normal hour in the life of an ordinary pigeon, it probably would not turn around in a circle counterclockwise. But the pigeon could be trained to do it by a method known as the **method of successive approximations**.

The method works in the following way: First the experimenter waits for the pigeon to make any turn part way to the left. The pigeon gets a food pellet as soon as it makes the turn. As a result, the pigeon turns to the left more often, and each time it is rewarded.

Pigeon learns to peck button (Fig. 11) before he receives food from cup (Fig. 12).

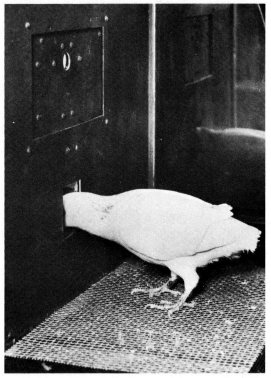

Sometimes the pigeon makes a little turn to the left. Sometimes the turn is as big as a quarter circle. Once the pigeon is turning to the left regularly, the experimenter can reward it when it makes a quarter circle turn, and not when it makes a smaller turn. The pigeon is soon making mainly quarter circle turns. Gradually the pigeon is rewarded for making bigger and bigger turns. Finally, it is rewarded only for turning around in a circle, and that is what it does.

This method of successive approximations is used by animal trainers to teach all kinds of animals how to do tricks. The trainers start with a simple action the animal naturally makes that is related to the trick. They reward that action and then make the animal do something more complicated for the next series of rewards. Dogs, parrots, monkeys, and porpoises have learned complex tricks this way.

Learning Without Repetition

In puzzle boxes, mazes, and conditioning experiments, the successes that occur as a result of trial and error are strengthened by repetition. However, learning can be very rapid with but little repetition. An ape, for instance, tries first one stick then another to reach a banana beyond the bars of its cage. Each of the two sticks is too short to reach the banana. So the ape fails. Later, playing with the sticks at the other side of the cage, the ape finds that the sticks fit together to make one long pole. The ape pauses, rushes across the cage, and fishes the banana in. The animal seems to have had a sudden insight, or understanding. Once it has learned what the two poles will do, the ape does not forget.

Important events can be remembered after only a single experience. You may look up a phone number and forget it before you have written it down. But suppose some night you were to open your closet door and find a dead mouse on the floor. You might shut the door at once; yet you would not forget what was inside. No phone number or nonsense syllable was ever so memorable. There is no need to keep opening the door to make sure what is in the closet.

Learning Rules

People and animals like monkeys and apes often learn rules, as well as specific actions or specific right answers to problems. After a series of problems of the same kind, a person or an animal may learn the rules for solving this kind of problem.

Psychologists demonstrate the learning of rules by presenting monkeys with a series of problems. In the first problem a monkey is given a tray holding two objects, such as a square block and a triangular block. There is a raisin under the square block. By trial and error the monkey finds the raisin.

On the next trial, the same two objects are on the tray and the raisin is still under the square block. But the positions of the two blocks are reversed. The monkey usually looks in the same place for the raisin, instead of under the same object. But when the monkey is presented with the tray again and again, finally it learns to pick up the correct object in order to find the raisin, regardless of the position of the object.

In the second problem, the monkey is given a tray holding two different objects, such as a circular block and a stick. Again, the raisin is always under the same block, regardless of its position. It takes fewer trials for the monkey to solve this second problem correctly every time. If the monkey is given many similar problems to solve, eventually it will learn to solve new problems in one trial.

A good example of the way people learn rules is the way young children learn grammar. A child may be taught to say, "Here is one shoe. Here are two shoes." The child has learned to add an S sound to the word "shoe" when he or she wants to talk about more than one. After learning to say *shoes*, *books*, *cars*, *apples*, *umbrellas*, and *dinosaurs*, the child has also learned a general rule: how to make a plural.

Of course, the child could not tell you the rule he or she is using. A 4-year-old does not say, "In order to make a noun plural, add the sound of S." But when talking, the child follows that rule. People often act on the basis of rules they cannot put into words.

▶THINKING

A great deal of learning is involved with solving problems. In the laboratory these problems are relatively simple: how to get out of a puzzle box; how to get a pellet of food; how to get the banana when the stick is too short. Outside the laboratory, problems are usually more complicated. But the problems are solved in the same ways. The solving of problems is what psychologists call thinking.

Images

Most people take it as a matter of course that thinking goes on in images that one is conscious, or aware, of. This is partly right. When you are solving a problem, you may see images in your "mind's eye," hear images with your "mind's ear," and feel others with your "mind's muscles." You can even have images of tastes and smells, although usually these are only parts of memories.

If you are tired after a day of exhausting work, you may be haunted by vivid images of the work you have just done. For instance, if you picked blueberries in the sun all day, then for long minutes in bed at night you may keep seeing hundreds of great big berries. Such vivid images are **hallucinations**. Dreams are a kind of hallucination. Almost everyone is bothered now and then by a tune in the "mind's ear" that will not go away. In most dreams, people have visual images, although they may also hear sounds and experience muscular tension in a dreamed fright. Usually the visual images are the ones people remember best.

People use images in many different ways. The composer Beethoven could hear his symphonies in his mind as he wrote them, even though he was stone deaf. More often people have visual images. If you were caught in a field with an angry bull, for example, you would quickly picture the different ways of escaping and then choose one. You could probably not afford the trial-and-error method of solving the problem. You would not have time to learn by error!

Words. Thinking goes on in another, very common kind of image—words. A very great deal of thinking is all in words. You may hear their sound without speaking them aloud, and you may feel your lips, tongue, and throat pronouncing them. Some people get the voice feel without the sound. Some people see the words. Then, too, they may be thinking in words with only the muscular sensations. The thought of a shovel or broom may be simply the way it feels to use it.

A person who is blind and deaf might think entirely in muscular sensations. Helen Keller was one such person. She believed she could feel music by putting her hand on the piano as

5	3	9	1	4
2	7	3	9	8
4	2	6	5	9
3	5	2	8	1
8	3	4	7	2

Figure 13.

it was played. At any rate, there seemed to be no kind of thought that was impossible for her to manage in muscular images.

Most people in their thinking can use all these kinds of images—sometimes one kind, sometimes another.

Using Images. The quickest way to read is to read visually—that is, without pronouncing or hearing the words. But if you are reading beautiful prose or poetry, it is well to slow down to let the sound come in.

The most common and slowest way to read is to pronounce the words separately. This is also the slowest way to do arithmetic. In adding, for example, you should be able to see at once that 8 and 5 are 13, without having to say it to yourself. You see the 8 and the 5, and the sight of the 13 adds itself instantly to your visual image, without your having to mutter anything.

Many children and some grown-ups see the letters of the alphabet as colored: A may be blue; B, pink; C, light yellow. Other people see different colors for the different notes on the piano. Children usually have more vivid imagery than adults, but once in a while this kind of imagery is found in a grown-up, perhaps in exaggerated form. Some mathematical geniuses can remember a page like Figure 13, which has 25 1-digit numbers. Without looking at the numbers a second time, they can repeat the numbers in rows, in columns, or in diagonals. It is said that the historian T. B. Macaulay was able to read whole pages of print from his imaged memory of the page.

Brain Habits

Images are, however, only the obvious, conscious part of thinking. The greater part is done by the brain without our knowing just what goes on. Knowledge already in the brain makes thinking easier. If the ape had not known how to get a banana with a stick, its discovery that two short sticks could make one long stick would not have solved its problem. Most often the brain draws on habits acquired from past learning. But sometimes it uses habits that are inherited, such as the sense of space that the brain uses in stereoscopic perception.

To see how brain habits work in solving a problem, try the ring puzzle shown in Figure 14. The cord is securely fastened at each end of the board, and there is a ring on each loop. The problem is to get both rings on the same loop. This seems impossible, since the rings are bigger than the hole in the board and cannot pass through it. You want to move one right along the cord through the hole, around the loop below the hole, and then back through the hole again. But the ring will not go through the hole.

Figure 14. The rings are too large to fit through the hole in the board. Can you see another way to get both rings on the same loop?

After perhaps hours of fussing over this contraption, a sudden insight comes to you. You see that although the ring will not go through the hole to pass around the loop, the loop will come up through the hole, where the ring can be passed around it. Then, when you push the loop down again through the hole, the ring comes down on the other loop just where you want it.

This insight is helped by knowledge. If you have done many rope tricks, you may have the insight sooner. The brain uses the unconscious memory of past tricks. In any case, most of the work was done by the brain. You were helpless until the needed insight suddenly popped up ready for use.

Playing Games with Unusual Possibilities

Sometimes the solution (or solutions) to a puzzle lies in the ability to think creatively by imagining unusual possibilities. Some psychologists think that people spend too much time learning facts and answers that are already known, instead of learning how to go about solving new problems. Getting practice in thinking of unusual possibilities may make problem solving easier.

Psychologists have invented some unusual possibilities games to give you a chance to exercise your imagination. The interesting thing about the games is that there is no one right answer. The more answers you can think of and the more unusual the answers, the more fun the games are.

Here are some of the games:

1. Name things you can use to make a noise.
2. Give different titles to a drawing of two curved lines, one lying above the other.
3. Tell the ways in which a blueberry and a cherry are alike.
4. Tell the ways you can use a chair.

Here are just a few of the possible answers:

1. You can jingle keys to make a noise, turn on the television set very loud, or shake a pot with spoons in it.
2. The drawing of two curved lines can be called An Arch or A Little Hill in Front of a Big Hill.
3. A blueberry and a cherry are both fruits. Both stain your fingers if you squeeze them, and both can be used as substitutes for marbles.
4. A chair can be used to sit in, to block a doorway, or it can be chopped up for firewood.

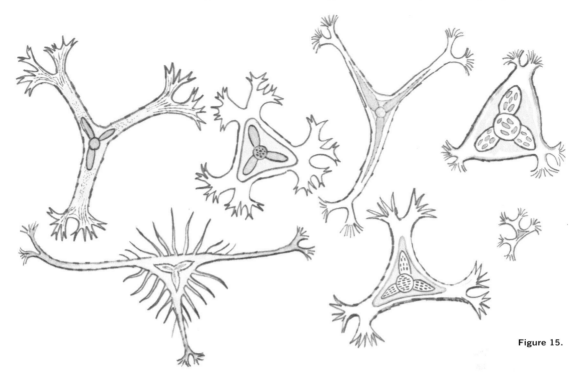

Figure 15.

Another good example of how brain habits can take over and control what the mind thinks is shown in the arithmetic test. You are given a sheet filled with pairs of numbers like these:

5	8	3	7	6
2	4	1	5	3

You are told to add each pair. You go automatically down the sheets, adding. When you come to the numbers 6 and 3, you say 9 without any trouble.

Later you may be given the same sheet, although you do not know it is the same, and be asked to subtract. Then 6 and 3 gives you 3, the difference. If you had been told to multiply, you would have come up with 18. Why did you once get one number—3—and then another—9 or 18? You are working under different brain habits. You do not consciously remember that you are adding and not subtracting or multiplying. The brain is remembering for you. This is the unconscious part of thinking.

Now look at Figure 15. These nonsense figures have a nonsense name. They are called Zalofs. After examining the lot, can you make up a definition of a Zalof, as if you were defining a starfish or a horse? You need a definition that will apply to every figure. You can define a Zalof, but you cannot quite see how you do it.

Your brain catches the similarities and skips over the differences. Presently it has formed a definition for you.

In humorous talk and writing you can get the point of a witty statement without having to explain it to yourself. Mark Twain described "an oyster so large that it took two men to swallow it." That is silly. Yet it must have been a big oyster. The point of any joke can be made conscious by explaining it, but the important thing in terms of psychology is that the joke is amusing without ever being explained at all.

All the while you are talking, your brain is working for you, too, without your realizing it. A person who speaks readily just thinks thoughts and opens his or her mouth. Then the brain puts the right words together, and they come tumbling out. The words get said before the speaker is consciously aware of what they are going to be. But the brain knows.

EDWIN G. BORING
Edgar Pierce Professor of Psychology Emeritus
Harvard University
Additional material by
CHARLOTTE LACKNER DOYLE
Sarah Lawrence College

See also ANIMALS; BODY, HUMAN; BRAIN; CHILD DEVELOPMENT; INTELLIGENCE; LEARNING; TESTS AND TEST TAKING.

PSORIASIS. See DISEASES (Descriptions of Some Diseases).

PUBLIC HEALTH

Public health is the measurement, improvement, and maintenance of a community's health by people who use specialized scientific methods, skills, and beliefs to control and prevent disease. Public health programs are usually funded and administered by government agencies. These agencies develop special programs for people at high risk for disease, such as the elderly, persons with chronic disease, disability, or addiction, and those living in poverty.

In a manner similar to how a medical doctor diagnoses and treats a patient, a public health agency also diagnoses and treats a community. First, an agency performs an assessment by asking careful questions of and about those people possibly affected by a particular disease. After deciding which people or groups may be at risk, the agency makes estimates of how much actual risk of disease or disability there is. The agency uses this information to design and implement preventive solutions tailored to each unique community. For example, during an infectious disease outbreak, a public health agency responds by investigating its cause and the likelihood of further spread of disease. It then develops and coordinates a program to treat all infected people as well as protect those not infected. After the emergency is over, the agency formulates a plan to prevent future outbreaks.

Testing runoff for pollutants is one of the ways a local health department makes sure a community's water supplies remain clean.

▶ THE HISTORY OF PUBLIC HEALTH

Early in civilization, people began to realize that some members of the community who lived in less crowded spaces with clean air, clean water, and clean food were often healthier than others less fortunate. These observations motivated many societies to develop ways to improve their people's health.

Examples of this include the Jewish laws of hygiene, the Greek belief in the link between human disease and the character of the air, water, and dwelling, and the Romans' construction of sewage systems and aqueducts.

These lessons were forgotten, though, during the Middle Ages. Many people lived with their cattle and other livestock crowded into walled cities. These conditions resulted in water polluted with animal and human excrement and streets teeming with rats and other vermin. Many diseases, like the plague, spread freely among the people who lived there.

During the 1800's, scientific studies called attention to the relationship between an unclean environment and disease and led to new ideas about public health. In 1798, an English doctor named Edward Jenner used careful observation and analysis to develop and test an effective vaccine to prevent smallpox. In the mid-1800's, another British doctor, John Snow, scientifically studied epidemics of diseases to understand a deadly outbreak of disease in London and was able to identify its cause. Using meticulous observation, Dr. Snow linked the cholera outbreaks with certain community water pumps and reported his findings to the city's leaders.

It was not long before governments began to take on the responsibility of protecting the public's health. The rapidly growing population in the United States began to cause serious problems in cities. Citizen pressure caused many city governments to begin to improve health conditions of their inhabitants. The first city to establish a board of health was New York City in 1866.

▶ THE FUNCTIONS OF PUBLIC HEALTH

The basic functions of public health are the study, surveillance, control, and prevention of diseases. These functions are carried out by public health care workers and agencies when they are dealing with a variety of problems. For example, when dealing with a communicable disease such as AIDS, the result of their work includes

The prevention of communicable diseases is one of the major concerns of public health agencies. Organized efforts to combat contagious diseases include vaccinating people at risk (*left*) and publishing educational materials (*below*).

understanding how the AIDS virus makes people ill, developing systems to report when a person is diagnosed with AIDS, creating consensus among doctors about the most effective way to treat patients infected with the AIDS virus, and inspecting the national supply of donated blood to ensure that it is not contaminated. Other types of public health issues for which these functions are used include chronic illnesses, special high risk populations, behavioral public health issues, and environmental concerns.

The public health system has a special function during an outbreak of disease that affects a large number of people, also called an epidemic. The public health system works to protect the community by ensuring that nurses, doctors, and public health officials report all cases of certain diseases to the health department, including whooping cough, diphtheria, hepatitis, measles, poliomyelitis, tetanus, and AIDS. Rapid reporting helps identify new outbreaks of disease in the community. All local cases are reported to the state and eventually to the United States Public Health Service (PHS). During an epidemic, the local health department can ask the state and in turn the PHS for extra help with the problem.

▶ **THE UNITED STATES PUBLIC HEALTH SERVICE (PHS)**

The PHS supervises all federal public health programs and collaborates with state and local public health departments, voluntary agencies, and private health foundations. In addition to helping coordinate various services, the PHS also promotes research, provides aid to medical education programs, and controls the spread of communicable diseases on a national level. The PHS pays for scientists to perform research in their laboratories and at medical schools, universities, and pharmaceutical companies. The PHS coordinates

research efforts. For example, one of its divisions, the Food and Drug Administration, sponsors a nationwide program to improve communication and cooperation among scientists and physicians who test new cancer drugs. PHS makes the education of physicians, dentists, nurses, and other health workers possible by supplying schools and colleges with grants to build laboratories and classrooms and improve training. Loans to help students pay for their education also come from PHS. PHS studies the country's future

Scientists at the U.S. Centers for Disease Control work as "disease detectives" to identify the dangerous viruses that cause deadly outbreaks around the world.

The United States Public Health Service

The United States Public Health Service (PHS) was first established as the Marine Hospital Service in 1798. PHS is a division of the Department of Health and Human Services and has eight divisions and eleven service program offices.

PHS DIVISIONS	FUNCTIONS
Agency for Health Care Policy and Research (AHCPR)	Produces and distributes information on the quality of health care, its effectiveness, and cost.
Agency for Toxic Substances and Disease Registry (ATSDR)	Reduces or eliminates illness, disability, and death from toxic substances.
Centers for Disease Control and Prevention (CDC)	Prevents disease, disability, and premature death, while promoting healthy lifestyles.
Food and Drug Administration (FDA)	Studies, regulates, and monitors products such as foods, drugs, cosmetics, and medical devices and the industries that produce them.
Health Resources and Services Administration (HRSA)	Guides health services; acts as a resource to improve access, distribution, quality, and cost of care.
Indian Health Service (IHS)	Provides health services for Native Americans, including the Inuit (Eskimos) of Alaska.
National Institutes of Health (NIH)	Performs biomedical research.
Substance Abuse and Mental Health Services Administration (SAMHSA)	Reduces the occurrence of mental health disorders and substance addictions; improves treatment methods for them.

SERVICE PROGRAM OFFICES	FUNCTIONS
Commissioned Corps of the Public Health Service	Acts as a mobile health corps.
Disease Prevention, Health Promotion, Health Planning and Evaluation	Improves disease prevention and health promotion efforts.
Emergency Preparedness	Coordinates emergency preparedness, response to emergencies, and recovery activities.
HIV/AIDS Policy	Assists the HIV/AIDS policy planning process.
International and Refugee Health	Creates and administers the health policy for refugee and alien health care.
Minority Health	Supplies technical assistance to minority health projects; improves public awareness of them.
Population Affairs	Acts as a resource on population and reproductive health issues; supplies policy advice on issues.
President's Council on Physical Fitness and Sports	Promotes exercise and sports to improve physical fitness and health.
Research Integrity	Investigates and resolves allegations of research misconduct in PHS-funded research programs.
Surgeon General	Manages the PHS Commissioned Corps.
Women's Health	Strives to improve the health of women.

needs for health care workers so that resources for institutions and individuals can be made available.

The PHS prevents many diseases from entering the country by checking for animals or people infected with diseases such as smallpox, yellow fever, cholera, and plague. Quarantine officers do this by examining potential visitors before arrival in the United States as well as at all United States ports of entry.

THE METHODS AND TECHNIQUES OF PUBLIC HEALTH

Public health workers use many different methods and techniques to identify, monitor, understand, treat, and prevent health problems. To provide public health care, health workers use such sciences as biostatistics, epidemiology, and nutrition. Public health care also includes the use of policy and management methods to improve the system of health care delivery and to decrease public health risks. All of these methods are used to develop areas of service such as nutrition, which helps the community as a whole, and maternal and child health, which helps a particular part of the population. Below are some methods and techniques and areas of service with descriptions of how they are used to provide public health care to a community.

Biostatistics—an essential tool that scientists and public health workers use to understand subtle relationships between the causes and outcomes of health problems.

Environmental Health—works to detect and prevent adverse health effects from chemical and physical factors in work and community settings.

Epidemiology—studies the frequency and distribution of disease to understand what causes it.

Maternal and Child Health—concentrates on ways to improve the health of mothers and children.

Molecular and Cellular Toxicology—examines the effects of environmental chemicals on the health of human beings.

Nutrition—works to improve nutrition and therefore health by understanding the influence of diet on health and works to educate researchers, practitioners, and the public.

Population and International Health—develops methods to help poor countries improve the health of their people despite few resources.

Social and Behavioral Sciences—attempts to understand challenges to the health of populations and to develop programs to improve health and quality of life.

Tropical Public Health—performs research on the biological aspects of diseases caused by tuberculosis and parasites such as protozoans and helminths (worms). It also works to develop vaccines and improve tools for diagnosis and disease control.

Doctors and inspectors check all travelers for proof of proper vaccination and signs of communicable disease. They inspect imported animals and animal products and have the authority to quarantine any person, animal, or product considered infected.

▶ THE WORLD HEALTH ORGANIZATION (WHO)

The international relief effort initiated after World War II ultimately led to the formation of the World Health Organization (WHO) of the United Nations in 1948. Today, the WHO is the largest coordinating international health agency and continues to work on health problems common to many countries. For example, the WHO regularly sets up large-scale campaigns to eradicate the mosquitoes in tropical areas that carry diseases such as malaria, yellow fever, and yaws. The global eradication of small-pox, the last case of which was diagnosed in Somalia in 1977, is the greatest success of the international programs of this sort.

Insecticides are sprayed on nesting sites to rid tropical areas of disease-carrying mosquitoes.

The WHO continues to monitor new epidemics by warning all the world's governments about outbreaks of serious diseases such as plague, cholera, typhus, influenza, poliomyelitis, Ebola, and the human immuno-deficiency virus (HIV). Lastly, the WHO also conducts health care worker education and research programs and helps many countries solve sanitation, nutritional, and other health problems in their communities.

▶ PUBLIC HEALTH IS PREVENTION

Many people do not realize the importance and scope of public health services because the outcomes are often hidden. Public health services prevent major disasters: epidemics, polluted waters, and unsafe food, to name a few. Ignoring the importance of good health is costly. The AIDS epidemic emerged as a major public health threat to all people in the

1980's, as did the re-emergence of syphilis and tuberculosis.

Good health is not just the responsibility of the public health system, a network of hardworking and dedicated professionals including physicians, dentists, nurses, and public health workers. Good health is the responsibility of all individuals. By keeping public health recommendations in mind, now more than ever, people can protect their health and the health of others in their community.

Christopher W. Shanahan M.D., M.P.H.
Assistant Professor of Medicine
School of Medicine, Boston University

PUBLICITY. See Public Relations.

PUBLIC LANDS

In 1780 the Second Continental Congress recommended that certain states give up their western lands to the national government. Massachusetts, Connecticut, New York, North and South Carolina, Virginia, and Georgia all claimed vast stretches of land between the Appalachian Mountains and the Mississippi River. Most of them required, as a condition for giving up their claims, that the lands be sold to pay off the Revolutionary War debt.

In this way, between 1781 and 1802, the "public domain" was created. It originally included nearly four-fifths of the nation's area. These public lands were added to as the years went by. Some were added by treaties of purchase or by treaties ending wars, others by annexation or territorial division. Finally, they reached to the Pacific Coast and Alaska. Today the federal government owns about 771 million acres (312 million hectares) of public lands, including those that have been set aside for national parks and forests, for recreation, and for other special purposes.

Early Methods of Sale and Survey

The western lands were needed to produce revenue. Also, many veterans of the Revolutionary War looked to these lands for settlement. To meet these pressures, the national government passed the Ordinance of 1785. This ordinance established a system of rectangular survey that later was used in Canada and in many other countries. Townships 6 miles square were divided into 36 sections, each 1 mile square, or 640 acres, in area.

The ordinance required that all Native American claims to the lands be settled before they were surveyed. Lands were sold chiefly by auction to the highest bidder. This type of sale tended to attract speculators with ready cash, who hoped to make a profit by reselling small tracts of land. But this type of public land sale was not very successful.

Not until the passage of the Harrison Act in 1800 were actual settlers favored. By this act, local land offices were set up, purchases could be made on liberal credit payments, and half-sections (320 acres) were to be surveyed and sold. However, by an act of 1820 the credit system was abolished. From this time on, lands were to be surveyed in parcels as small as half-quarter sections (80 acres). These "eighties" sold at the minimum price of $1.25 per acre.

Cheap Land for Settlers

In the 1830's President Andrew Jackson's administration ushered in an even cheaper land program. At last settlers were given a preference (or pre-emption) in buying a quarter-section before the auction and at the minimum price. This system was made permanent in 1841 and was a decided victory for settlers. In 1832 Congress agreed to survey and sell parcels as small as 40 acres. These were known as "forties" or "quarter-quarters." Swamplands, lands in distant territories, lands that had been on the market for some time, and other special lands were sold for even less than the minimum price. Some lands were even given to settlers who agreed to settle and improve them.

Free Land and Land Grants

Not until the Homestead Act of 1862 was the system of free land realized. Under its terms any settler was given title to the land who agreed to live on a tract not larger than a quarter-section and to improve it for a period of five years. This act has been called one of history's great democratic measures. Nevertheless, settlers had a difficult time establishing homesteads on the Great Plains.

The government aided the building of western communities in many other ways. The Ordinance of 1785 established the system of giving land grants for aiding public schools and universities. Section 16 of every township was set aside for public schools. In 1848 this amount was doubled. Beginning in 1850 many western railroads were given land grants. The railroads then resold this land to settlers. Under the Morrill Act of 1862 public lands for the founding of agricultural and mechanical arts colleges (known as land-grant colleges) were given to each state according to its population.

Exploitation

After the Civil War the public lands were actually thrown wide open to exploitation. The Mining Act of 1866 opened all of the mining country to development, subject only to the local mining laws and regulations. In much the same way, Texas cattlemen were allowed to drive their herds northward and graze the lands of the Great Plains. This brought about a clash with the homesteaders who were trying to settle that region. Elsewhere, on the public domain of Wisconsin, Minnesota, and the Far West, lumber companies were cutting down valuable timber.

Gradually public opinion became aroused. In 1891 Congress passed the General Revision Act. It did away with the sale of lands by auction and with the pre-emption laws. Only the Homestead Act remained as the means of obtaining public lands.

Conservation and a Permanent Public Domain

From 1891 to the present day a national program of conserving the public lands has been developed. Many millions of acres of lands have actually been bought back by the government for the purpose of saving the nation's valuable forests and park lands, for developing electric power, for flood control, and for recreation.

Finally, in 1934 and 1935, the remaining public lands (except in Alaska) were closed to homesteading by executive order of President Franklin D. Roosevelt. They remained open to the staking of mining claims and for public hunting, fishing, camping, and other recreation. These lands are known as the national land reserve.

The United States has been singularly generous in encouraging the private enterprise of its citizens by grants of cheap or free lands. In the public domain as well, there still exists a rich heritage for the future.

ROY M. ROBBINS
Municipal University of Omaha

See also TERRITORIAL EXPANSION OF THE UNITED STATES; WESTWARD MOVEMENT.

PUBLIC OPINION POLLS. See OPINION POLLS.

PUBLIC RELATIONS

When the founders of the United States wrote the Declaration of Independence, they said that a "decent respect" for the opinion of people everywhere required the American colonies to tell the world why they were freeing themselves of British rule. The American leaders believed that their cause could not win unless they had the confidence of the people of other countries.

Public relations, too, tries to win the confidence and goodwill of people. No company, government agency, school, hospital, or other institution can flourish if it pays no attention to what the people think of it. Public relations is the activity of giving a business or other organization information about how its actions might affect public opinion—or how

public opinion might affect its actions. It is also the job of the public relations officer to tell the public about a company's activities, plans, or ideas. This is necessary because people are likely to have more confidence in a company if they know something about it.

There is not just one big public whose opinion a company has to worry about if it is to survive and grow. Only a few organizations, such as a national government, are so

What is the difference between public relations and advertising?

Advertising tries to gain public confidence and goodwill so that people will buy a company's products or services. Public relations aims at getting the public to understand and approve of a company and its actions. In a sense, public relations may be thought of as a type of advertising—institutional advertising—which tries to make an important point about a company rather than about a product.

large that all the public has some opinion about their actions. Most companies and organizations have to think about the opinions of smaller groups—their customers, for instance, or their workers or their shareholders. A company must also have the trust and goodwill of its neighbors in the places where it has factories and offices. The company must be on good terms with the government, because every business can be seriously affected by government laws or regulations.

Gaining the confidence of others requires, first of all, thoughtfulness about other people's beliefs, interests, and feelings. Public relations begins by planning one's actions so as to respect the rights and beliefs of other people. Unless a public relations program takes these things into account, it can do little to help a company. Not all the money in the world, nor the most skillful writers or speakers, can make a company look as if it cares about other people if the company really does not care. Most companies, therefore, consider how any action, such as moving to a new location or buying another business, will affect public opinion. Having made a decision, the company wants everyone to understand the decision and the reasons it was made.

Most large companies have a public relations department, which tells the public about the company's plans and activities. The department is made up of writers, editors, photographic and picture experts, and researchers.

There are many ways to reveal a company's activities and character. A very effective one is through speeches by officials of the company before organizations such as the local chamber of commerce and various clubs. The speeches are usually reported in the newspapers and are often reprinted for distribution to government officials, educators, journalists, and others who might be interested in the company's views. Printed pamphlets and booklets, including the company magazine and the annual report of the management to the shareholders, also help inform the public about a company. Motion-picture films are often used to show people something about a company. A company may also, as a public service, undertake projects not directly connected with its business, to help make society better.

Besides using their own public relations staffs, many companies hire independent public relations firms, which work for several clients at once. Specially trained outsiders often see trends or problems that people inside a company might miss because they are too close to the situation.

Anyone who plans to do public relations work should get as broad an education as possible. In addition to a college education, work in some area of the communications field—on a newspaper or with a broadcasting station—is useful for the future public relations officer.

ARTHUR B. TOURTELLOT
Formerly, Earl Newsom & Company

See also ADVERTISING.

PUBLIC SCHOOLS. See SCHOOLS; EDUCATION.

PUBLIC SPEAKING

The term "public speaking" defines itself. It is the act of making a speech in public. The purpose of good public speaking is to add to the information and knowledge of listeners or to lead them to think or do as the speaker advises. Speechmaking is vital to the work of such people as the clergy, lawyers, and public officials. Public speaking also is important for many others. Business people, club members, schoolteachers, and boys and girls— these are but a few of those who use public speaking more and more each year.

Public speaking used to be called oratory.

Oratory, which dates back to ancient Greece and Rome, is one of the oldest regular studies in Western civilization. Since those early times almost every generation of civilized people has given time to the study of the rules, methods, and practice of public speaking. For many centuries in Europe and then in the United States, pupils learned to make speeches in Latin. It was thought that if they could make good speeches in Latin, they certainly could do so in their native tongue.

Through the ages, teachers and writers of books on speaking have agreed that to be a good speaker, a person needs natural ability, teaching, and practice. Some people are naturally better speakers than others. But most people can become fairly good speakers. They can improve their ability by studying and practicing the principles of good speechmaking and by intelligently following the example of good speakers.

People who make public speeches believe that they have a message. They have something worth saying, and there is a group of people who ought to hear the message and take the advice. That means that public speakers must know three basic things: (1) They must know (better than most people do) the subject on which they will speak. (2) They must know, as nearly as possible, their audience's needs, habits, wishes, and ways of thinking. (3) They must know how to build their speeches so that the speeches will have the greatest effect on the audience.

Public speakers will not think of themselves, therefore, as putting on shows of which they are authors, heroes, and leading actors. They should think of themselves, instead, as bringing people and valuable ideas together so that the people will grasp useful ideas correctly.

▶ **PREPARING A SPEECH**

In building their speeches, good speakers keep three very important matters in mind. First, they make their ideas as easy as possible for the audience to understand. Second, they make themselves seem like persons whose advice can be trusted. Third, they make their listeners want to understand, believe, or do what they propose.

If the ideas are going to be clear and understandable, a speech must be orderly. To make the speech orderly, a speaker usually sees that it has a real beginning, middle, and end. More formally, the parts of a speech are the **introduction, body,** and **conclusion**.

A lively, friendly introduction gets the attention and interest of listeners and leads to the **main idea**. The body of a speech gives the main ideas in good, clear, declarative sentences. Each idea is filled out with various kinds of **explaining and supporting material**. The most useful kinds of material with which to explain or support ideas are (1) facts and information, (2) examples, (3) comparisons and contrasts, and (4) opinions of authorities. The conclusion restates the main ideas and urges listeners to follow a certain line of action or thought.

To keep the plans of speeches clearly in mind, speakers find it useful to sketch out the body of each speech in a kind of outline. This usually consists of writing the main idea out in a declarative sentence and then noting the explaining and supporting material under the main idea. Here is an example of a plan:

Main idea:	The gymnasium in our school is too small.
Facts:	It was intended for 50 students per period. Each class now has almost 100. At basketball games only half the fans can get seats.
Example:	In my class yesterday half of us had to sit doing nothing while the others tumbled on the mats.
Comparison and Contrast:	It is like buses at rush hour—standing room only. East Junior High has fewer students than our school but twice as much gymnasium space.
Opinion of authority:	Our physical training teacher says that in our gymnasium he cannot give us the work we ought to have.

If speeches are to be clear, they must be orderly. And the ideas must be expressed in language that is familiar to the listeners and is full of meaning for them. Speakers choose definite words instead of vague words, lively words instead of weak words. They make their sentences simple and straightforward, not fancy. They pay attention to their listeners' needs, not to their own performance.

▶ **DELIVERING A SPEECH**

Giving a speech aloud before an audience is called delivery. Good speakers are easy to hear. Their pronunciation is sharp and correct. Their voices are pleasant and lively.

Speakers can prepare for one of three main kinds of delivery: (1) In speaking from memory, speakers may have learned their speeches by heart. This kind of delivery can be good for formal occasions, but it often sounds mechanical. (2) Many speakers read their speeches from typewritten copy or from a teleprompter. Reading is preferred by many government officials, television performers, and business people without time to prepare carefully for delivery. (3) The best all-round method of delivery is called **extemporaneous**. This means that speakers have prepared their material well, planned and outlined their speeches, and possibly practiced out loud. They have the plan firmly in mind but use the words as the words come to them. This kind of speaking seems more natural than speeches read or memorized.

A fourth kind of delivery is called **impromptu**. The speaker makes no preparation but speaks on the spur of the moment.

▶ PUBLIC SPEAKING TODAY

Public speaking has always taken many forms. Fashions and means of communication constantly change. Public speaking today is usually less formal and more conversational than it used to be. One possible reason for the change is that it is no longer the fashion—as it was in ancient Greece and later in Europe and America—to think of public speaking as a fine art, a means of creating beauty. Today it is thought of, for the most part, as a very practical kind of public communication. Speakers wish to appear as natural as possible to live audiences and to audiences that see them on television or hear them on radio. Modern life has become less formal—in clothes, social customs, language, and the like. Public speaking also has become informal.

DONALD C. BRYANT
Co-author, *Fundamentals of Public Speaking*
See also DEBATES AND DISCUSSIONS; ORATORY.

PUBLIC UTILITIES

A public utility is an industry or commercial enterprise that supplies services or products that people need for health and convenience. Water, electricity, gas, telephone, and telegraph companies are public utilities.

Generally, a public utility (or public service) company is the only one in an area that supplies a certain product or service. A company is said to hold a monopoly when it is the only one that supplies and sells a product. Businesses that are best run as monopolies are called natural monopolies.

Economists believe that public utilities are run most successfully as natural monopolies for these two reasons: First, one public utility company in an area is usually more practical than several companies that would have to compete for room under city streets—or on poles—for different sets of gas or water pipes and power lines. Second, one large plant can provide a public service, such as electricity or telephone service, more cheaply than can several small plants competing with one another.

But when any product is made and sold as a monopoly, the users, or consumers, of the product face a problem. Often they must have the product or service, and they cannot go elsewhere for it. They must pay the price the company sets and accept the quality given.

In the case of public utilities, consumers are protected in one of two ways. Either the national or local government operates the public utility or the government regulates the companies that operate utilities owned by private investors.

In the United States a public utility company owned by individuals must receive a special franchise from the community in which it operates. The franchise gives the company the right to install equipment under or along the city streets. Federal, state, and local commissions regulate the activities of public utility companies to make sure they give good service and charge fair prices.

In other countries, private companies may be licensed by the government or supervised by a particular government bureau. In the Soviet Union and other Communist countries, public utilities are run by the state. Elsewhere, the amount of ownership by governments varies from country to country. In Britain, the telephone system and electric power and gas utilities are all government-owned. But most of the water companies are privately owned. In general, throughout the world there is a combination of government and private ownership of public utilities.

In the United States most gas and electric utilities are run by private (investor-owned) companies. More water companies are owned and operated by the local government than by private companies. Government-owned electric plants produce about 20 percent of the country's electric power.

▶ FOUR MAJOR PUBLIC UTILITIES

Electric power, gas, waterworks, and the telephone all contribute to the industrial development of nations and to the health and comfort of individuals.

Public rail, bus, and air transportation systems are also public utilities in a broad sense because they provide service to the public. But people pay for these services on the basis of individual use, and they are provided outside the home. For these reasons, transportation services are generally not considered public utilities. Cable television is not regulated by public utility commissions. But it is under the control of the Federal Communications Commission. It does offer a service to the public and may therefore be considered a public utility in the broad sense.

Electric Power

Electricity is a form of energy. It supplies light, heat, and power. But it cannot be stored in large amounts for use as it is needed. It must constantly be produced or generated so that it is available whenever anyone flips on a light switch or plugs in an appliance.

Electricity is produced in a generating plant or power plant, which may be far from the place in which electricity is needed. From the power plant, electric current is sent with nearly the speed of light through wires that lead into homes, factories, schools, and other places.

Most of the world's electricity is produced in plants that are run by steam. These are called steam, or thermal, power stations. In conventional thermal power stations, the heat that creates the steam is produced by burning a fuel such as coal or oil. Nuclear power plants may also be considered thermal stations. They run on steam that is produced by nuclear fuels. The first nuclear power station in the United States was built in 1957. More and more electricity has been generated by nuclear power plants. But the possibility of accidents has caused public opposition to nuclear power, and in some areas the number of future nuclear power plants may be restricted.

The force of flowing water is used to run another type of power plant, the hydroelectric plant. In Sweden, there is not enough fuel to run steam plants. But there is a great deal of waterpower, and hydroelectric plants produce a large share of the electricity. The United States and Canada also have many hydroelectric plants.

The first electric generating plant in the United States was started by Thomas Edison in 1882. It transmitted, or sent, power only about 1,500 meters (5,000 feet) and served only 59 customers. Today the power system of the United States is the largest in the world. The Soviet Union has the second-largest power system.

In many countries today, large power companies connect their lines, forming a network of power systems. In this way the power com-

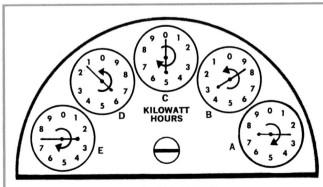

ELECTRIC METER

The size of your electric bill varies with the amount of electricity you use. This amount is measured in units called **kilowatt-hours** (KWH) by a device called a **kilowatt-hour meter.**

For example, a small electric oven may use 1,000 watts, or one kilowatt, in one hour. Ten light bulbs of 100 watts each would also use one kilowatt in one hour.

In the meter, a small motor turns the pointer of dial A. The more electricity you use, the faster the pointer turns. When the pointer has gone a whole space (for example, from 2 to 3), one KWH has been used. Each pointer is connected by gears (toothed wheels) with the next pointer. As pointer A makes a full *turn* clockwise, showing that 10 KWH have been used, it turns pointer B one *space* counterclockwise (for example, from 8 to 9). Thus, pointer A measures single KWH's, B measures tens, C measures hundreds, and so on.

The reading shown here is 71,082 kilowatt-hours.

pany for a certain area can draw on other companies to help meet the demand in time of trouble.

Gas

Gas is used to cook food, dry clothes, heat water, burn refuse, and heat and cool homes, factories, and public buildings. Gas that is used for these purposes is called fuel gas.

There are two kinds of fuel gas—natural and manufactured. The most important fuel gas of the 20th century is natural gas. Natural gas is found in many parts of the world. Large natural gas fields exist in the United States, Canada, Mexico, and the Soviet Union.

Wells must be drilled to find natural gas in the pores, or small spaces, of certain kinds of rock. The wells may be as little as a few hundred meters or as much as 8 kilometers (5 miles) deep. From the wells the gas is piped great distances to the cities in which it is to be used.

When gas from the pipeline reaches a city, it is measured, or metered, so that the company that piped the gas will know how much has been sold to the gas company in a particular city.

The gas is then delivered through the pipes, or mains, of the city's gas company to smaller pipes that lead into people's houses and other buildings. In these buildings the gas again passes through a meter that measures the amount of gas used. At regular times, a gas company employee checks the meter, which tells how much gas has been used. The company then sends the user a bill.

Most of the gas used in the 1800's was manufactured from coal, coke, or oil. Today manufactured gas is still in use where natural gas is not available through the large pipelines that cross the United States. Limited supplies of natural fuels have led researchers to improve or develop ways of producing synthetic natural gas, gasoline, and fuel oil from coal.

Water Supply

Water is one of the necessities of life. People cannot live much more than a few days without liquids. At one time people got the water they needed by carrying it from wells or streams or by storing rainwater in cisterns (underground tanks). In the developing countries people still use these methods to obtain water.

Where industry developed and cities grew up, supplying people with water became a community problem. In cities, potable (drinkable) water must be distributed to factories, schools, stores, office buildings, individual homes, and apartment buildings. Water is needed for fighting fires and other public uses.

A city's water usually comes from a central source. It may be either an underground or a surface source. Often surface water is stored in a reservoir formed by damming a river. If the source of a city's water is far from the city, the water is sent in closed pipes or in canals from the source to the city.

In a modern community a water treatment plant takes water from the central source and treats it, if necessary, to make it safe for people to drink. The plant stores enough for periods of great demand and distributes the rest.

Most water obtained from surface sources must be purified. First, the water is treated in tanks with chemicals, to help remove harmful bacteria, fine particles of matter that are suspended in it, and undesirable tastes, odors, and color. The chemicals used include chlorine, aluminum sulfate (alum), and powdered activated carbon.

Next, the water is filtered through beds of sand to remove the last traces of bacteria and suspended matter. Then it is disinfected again. Water from underground wells usually requires no treatment except a small amount of disinfectant, usually chlorine.

After treatment the water is ready for distribution. In many cities water is pumped from the treatment plant into elevated storage tanks to ensure that there is always water on hand to meet periods of great demand. From the storage tanks the water is delivered into the city's water mains and then into smaller pipes to each point of use. In most cities the water is metered in homes, and the customer is billed for the amount used.

The Telephone

Each day millions of people use the telephone for business and social purposes. In emergencies, it is used to call the police, the fire department, or a doctor.

Wires from each telephone lead to a central office. From there, local, long-distance, and overseas telephone connections are made. These connections are made by automatic equipment or by operators.

Most calls are transmitted through wires. The wires may be strung on poles. Or a protected bundle of wires, called a cable, may be buried under city streets or under a lake or river. Cables on the ocean floor are used in making calls from continent to continent. Some intercontinental calls are carried by radio waves and may be relayed by communications satellites. New methods of transmission include light waves, sent through microscopic glass fibers, and microwaves.

In the United States, most telephone systems are privately owned. In other countries, telephone systems are government-owned. In the United States the Bell system (American Telephone and Telegraph) was by far the largest phone company. But in 1983, Bell was broken up into a number of smaller independent companies to increase competition.

In Canada a very large percentage of the telephones are operated by Bell Canada, a private company, and by a number of small, independent companies. The remainder of the telephones are operated by the provinces.

The government has controlling interest in the telephone system in Denmark. But three private companies are licensed by the government. Several co-operative telephone companies are operating in the Danish islands.

When a telephone is installed in the United States, a fee is charged for installation. After that a monthly bill is sent to the user of the telephone. In some countries people receive their telephone bills every six months.

In Japan, where the government owns the telephones, a person must buy a government bond before the telephone is installed. Then regular bills for service are sent.

Today, telephones are found almost everywhere. People can make calls from their homes and from telephone booths in stores and railroad stations, on city streets, and along busy highways.

Reviewed by GEORGE E. SYMONS
Engineering Editor/Consultant

See also ELECTRICITY; NATURAL GAS; POWER PLANTS; TELEPHONE; WATER.

PUBLISHING

Publishing is the business of bringing the printed word to the public in books, magazines, and newspapers. Thousands of men and women work in publishing. Some are writers, some are editors, who adapt the writers' works, and others are in charge of putting the publication together. Still others handle the publicity and advertising that bring the publication to the attention of the reading public.

Books, magazines, and newspapers are the three basic fields of publishing. These three fields operate in different ways, although they have some characteristics in common.

In book publishing an author submits his manuscript to a publishing house. Some publishing houses, particularly those that publish encyclopedias, have their own teams of staff writers who are assigned articles on different subjects. Newspapers are almost completely staff written by writers and reporters who are experts in different areas of the news. Newspapers have their own printing presses so that they can print the news almost as soon as it happens.

Magazine publishing has some of the characteristics of both book and newspaper publishing. Weekly news magazines are published in much the same way as newspapers, although they are printed by an outside printing press. The monthly or biweekly magazines assign articles in advance, just as publishers of encyclopedias and other reference works do.

Over the past few years publishing firms with different specialties have begun to join together. Many magazine publishing companies now put out books and even encyclopedias. Newspaper publishing still remains, for the most part, completely separate.

▶ KINDS OF PUBLISHING

Book publishing is divided into several categories. **Trade book publishing** includes fiction, biography, history, poetry, and **juveniles** (children's books). To find out what a publisher is going to put out, booksellers consult the publisher's list. The list is an announcement of all the books the publisher is offering. Lists of new books can be found in advertisements in literary magazines and special booklets sent out by the publishers. Publishers issue their lists in the spring and the fall. Some publishers also send out a summer list.

Textbook publishing covers the many fields studied in schools. Textbook publishers work with experts in education to make sure their textbooks meet educational standards. Many textbooks are written at the suggestion of teachers who feel a present textbook is not adequate. Folders describing textbooks are sent out to teachers to keep them informed about new publications.

Scientific and technical publishing provides information on the many new developments in these fields and is generally aimed at people with a scientific or technical background. **Medical, law, and religious publishing** also have their special audiences. Many of their publications are sold mainly by advertising leaflets mailed out to buyers the publishers think would be interested.

Reference books, dictionaries, and atlases are usually put out by companies that specialize in compiling information. Other specialized areas of publishing produce **art books, music,** and **maps**.

Subscription book publishing produces encyclopedias, sets of classics, and similar books that are sold by salesmen directly to buyers.

A **university press** is a publishing house attached to a university. University presses publish scholarly works, textbooks for the university, and trade books they feel have special merit. The first university presses were officially established at the English universities of Oxford and Cambridge in the 16th century.

When a person publishes with a **vanity press**, he pays for the publishing himself instead of being paid by the publisher. He is said to be publishing out of vanity because commercial publishers do not think his book would have a wide enough market for them to publish it. Vanity presses are very useful for volumes of poetry and collections of family letters. Usually a limited number of copies are printed.

Governments publish a large number of pamphlets and books every year. These pub-

lications provide information on farming, various trades, new technical developments, and many other areas.

Paperbacks. A very important development in American book publishing is the rise of paperbacks. Although paperbacks have been published in the United States since the 1830's, their real success did not come until a hundred years later. At first, paperbacks were limited to detective stories, westerns, and other tales of adventure. Today almost all the classics and works of major poets, playwrights, historians, scientists, philosophers, and recent novelists are being reprinted in paperback. Usually, as soon as a new hard-cover book proves itself successful, it is issued as a paperback. Some titles appear originally as paperbacks.

Books reach their readers in various ways—through bookstores, libraries, mail order, house-to-house salesmen, and book clubs. Book club members agree to buy a certain number of books a year. Each month a folder describing the books chosen for that month is mailed to every member. The books are selected by specialists in various fields.

Authors' and publishers' profits depend on the number of books sold on the market. For each book that is sold, the author receives part of the book price. This is a fixed sum and is known as a **royalty**. The publisher uses the rest of the sales price to cover his operating costs and make his own profit. When a publisher accepts a book, he decides how many copies he should have printed. The number depends on the kind of book and the demand for it. Sometimes as many as 250,000 copies of a school textbook are printed, while a book of Renaissance drawings might be limited to 2,000 copies. For a trade book to pay its own way, it must sell between 7,500 and 10,000 copies. Publishers also sometimes sell different kinds of **rights** to help make a trade book profitable. These rights include the right to use the book as a book club selection, publish it in paperback, or adapt it for the screen or for television. These rights are called **subsidiary rights**, and the money made by their sale is shared with the author.

Many publishing firms employ a special person to handle these subsidiary rights, which have become an important source of revenue for both publisher and author. Literary agents represents authors frequently in such business arrangements, usually on a commission basis of 10 percent of the sum received. Some agents also act for publishers in arranging paperback reprint rights.

The book publishing industry is not one of the giant industries, but its importance and influence greatly outweigh its size in dollars. It is very difficult to compare book production in different countries because not all countries count their books in the same way. In the United States and many European countries, books are counted as **titles.** The United States publishes over 40,000 titles each year.

When a U.S. publishing company announces it has 50 titles, it means it has 50 different books. A best-seller, for instance, counts as one title even though thousands of copies of it are made and it may represent a major share of the publisher's profit for the year. To qualify as a title in the United States, a book must have at least 49 pages. Government publications are not counted.

Every year, publishers from all over the world attend the Frankfurt Book Fair in Germany. During the Middle Ages, Frankfurt was the center for another kind of fair, a merchant's fair. But instead of filling stalls with cloth or spices, the publishers bring their own special wares, books. These exhibits fill over five enormous buildings.

The fair is a busy place for publishers. Not only do they want to see what books each country is putting out, but they get together to plan for future books. Many books that come out simultaneously in different countries were first planned at the Frankfurt Fair. The publishers also arrange for translations or the use of illustrations by artists from different countries. A book may come out today that was written by an author of one country, translated by a writer of a second country, illustrated by an artist of a third, and finally published in yet another country.

ANNE J. RICHTER
R. R. Bowker Company

See also BOOKS; JOURNALISM; MAGAZINES; NEWSPAPERS; PRINTING.

PUCCINI, GIACOMO (1858–1924)

Giacomo Puccini, a famous opera composer, was born in Lucca, Italy, on December 22, 1858. From the time of his great-great-grandfather, the Puccinis had been musicians. As a boy, Giacomo showed no great talent or liking for music. But his mother insisted that he go to music school. There he learned to love music, and he soon became a church organist and choirmaster.

When he was 17, Puccini attended a performance of Verdi's opera *Aïda*. He was so excited by this opera that he decided to become an opera composer. With the help of a scholarship, he studied for three years at the Milan Conservatory (1880–83).

Puccini's first operas, written after he left the conservatory, were only moderately successful. His first triumph, *Manon Lescaut*, was produced in 1893. Three years later came *La Bohème*, a sad love story of Bohemian life in Paris. These operas made Puccini world-famous. They were followed in 1900 by another great success, *Tosca*.

Puccini married Elvira Gemignani in January 1904. A month later his new opera *Madama Butterfly* was first performed at La Scala opera house in Milan. The audience did not like this Japanese love story and hissed the performance. After making some minor changes in the work, he produced it a few months later in Brescia, with great success.

In 1907, Puccini went to New York City for the first performance at the Metropolitan Opera of *Madama Butterfly*. While he was there he wrote an opera on an American subject, *The Girl of the Golden West*, which was first performed in December, 1910. Puccini's next major work, after he had returned to Europe, was *Il Trittico* ("The Triptych"), a group of three one-act operas—*Il Tabarro* ("The Cloak"), *Gianni Schicchi*, and *Suor Angelica* ("Sister Angelica").

Puccini was at work on the last act of his opera *Turandot* when he died on November 29, 1924, in Brussels. At the first performance of *Turandot* in 1926, the conductor Arturo Toscanini stopped with the last notes Puccini wrote.

Reviewed by WILLIAM ASHBROOK
Philadelphia College of the Performing Arts

PUERTO RICO

Puerto Rico has long been known as one of the most beautiful islands in the Caribbean. Its rugged mountains, colorful tropical plant life, and scenic coastlines have impressed visitors since Columbus first visited the island in 1493.

Puerto Rico, a commonwealth associated with the United States, lies about 1,600 kilometers (1,000 miles) southeast of Florida. Once chiefly a farming area, Puerto Rico is now crisscrossed by modern highways, with factories, shopping centers, and fine hotels. "Puerto Rico" means "rich port" in Spanish. The island still has many poor people. But great social and economic progress has been made in the past 40 years, and Puerto Rico now has one of the highest standards of living in the Caribbean and in Latin America.

▶THE PEOPLE

Puerto Rico is densely populated. Two thirds of Puerto Rico is mountainous or dry, and the population is concentrated in the re-maining third of the island. A great many people live on the northern coast—in the San Juan metropolitan district.

The original inhabitants of Puerto Rico were Taínos, a branch of the Arawak Indian civilization. Perhaps as many as 30,000 were there when the Spanish first established colonies. But most of the Taínos soon died of disease or were sent to other islands as slaves. Some Taínos married Spanish colonists. Their descendants make up a very small part of the present population of the island. Indian words for everyday things, such as *bohío* ("house"), *conuco* ("plot of land"), *batey* ("yard"), and *hamaca* ("hammock"), possibly a Taíno invention, enliven the islanders' Spanish.

During the 18th and 19th centuries, African slaves were brought in to work on coffee and sugar plantations. After 1803, when the United States bought the Louisiana Territory from France, many French people left Louisiana and moved to Puerto Rico. At the same time, other French people arrived from Haiti

The fortress of El Morro guards the old city of San Juan. El Morro was built by the Spanish when they ruled Puerto Rico, and parts of it date from the 16th century.

COMMONWEALTH OF PUERTO RICO is the official name of the country. ''Puerto Rico'' means ''rich port.''

LOCATION: Greater Antilles, Caribbean Sea.

AREA: 3,435 sq mi (8,897 km²).

POPULATION: 3,522,037 (1990 census).

CAPITAL AND LARGEST CITY: San Juan.

MAJOR LANGUAGES: Spanish, English (both official).

MAJOR RELIGIOUS GROUP: Roman Catholic.

GOVERNMENT: Self-governing commonwealth, associated with the United States. **Head of government**—governor. **Legislature**—Senate and House of Representatives.

CHIEF PRODUCTS: Agricultural—sugarcane, livestock, dairy products, tobacco, coffee, poultry, pineapples, timber, citrus fruits, melons, bananas. **Manufactured**—processed foods, textiles and apparel, electronic equipment, pharmaceuticals, petrochemicals, metal products, stone, marble, clay and glass products, tourism, tobacco, rum, sugar processing. **Mineral**—limestone, clay, sand and gravel, gold, silver, copper, iron ore, platinum. **Chief exports**—sugar, tobacco, coffee, rum, textiles and apparel, pharmaceutical products. **Chief imports**—foodstuffs, wheat, building materials, fuel oils, shoes, automobiles.

MONETARY UNIT: U.S. dollar.

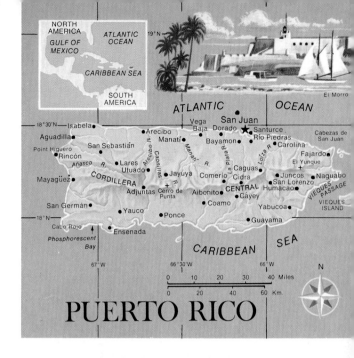

PUERTO RICO

schools and many Puerto Ricans speak it. In 1991, Spanish was made the official language, but in 1993, English also was designated as an official language.

Children are required by law to attend school between the ages of 6 and 16. Tens of thousands of students also are enrolled at the University of Puerto Rico, Inter-American University, and several small colleges. The government devotes a large part of its budget to education.

Sports and Culture

Puerto Ricans enjoy a wide variety of sports and games. Cockfights, horse races, boxing matches, basketball, and baseball are popular. Baseball is particularly enjoyed, and Puerto Ricans helped to popularize the game throughout the Caribbean. Many Puerto Ricans have played in the major leagues, including Roberto Clemente, the first Puerto Rican to be elected to the Baseball Hall of Fame. Angel Cordero, Jr., has been rated one of the finest jockeys in the history of horse racing. In boxing, Puerto Rico has produced several world champions.

Puerto Rico also has a vital cultural life. San Juan, the capital, has a symphony orchestra and is the home of the annual Casals Festival, named after Pablo Casals, the famous Spanish cellist whose home was in Puerto Rico. Works by island artists such as Lorenzo Homar, Rafael Tufiño, and Francisco Rodón are in major American and European mu-

following a revolt of Haitian slaves. But regardless of national or racial backgrounds, the language, religion (Roman Catholicism), and customs of a Puerto Rican are mainly Spanish.

Puerto Rican culture has also been influenced by the island's relationship, since 1898, with the United States. Many American customs have been adopted, but ties to Spanish traditions remain strong.

At Christmas and New Year, *parrandas* (strolling musicians) sing *aguinaldos,* ballad-like songs that are often witty and always cheerful. The singers are invited into the homes of friends to eat *lechón asado* (''roast pig'') or *morcillas* (''sausages'') and rice pudding, three of the country's festive dishes. A typical everyday dish is rice with plantain, beans, and beef.

Although Spanish remains the traditional language of the island, English is taught in the

The mountainous areas of Puerto Rico receive abundant rainfall, and lush vegetation abounds. Many homes are built on stilts to protect them during the rainy season.

seums. Well-known Puerto Rican actors include José Ferrer, Rául Julía, Rita Moreno, and Chita Rivera.

▶ THE LAND

Puerto Rico is the smallest island in a group of islands called the Greater Antilles. It is about 160 kilometers (100 miles) long and averages 56 kilometers (35 miles) in width. The interior of the island is mountainous, with peaks over 1,200 meters (4,000 feet) above sea level. The highest mountain is Cerro de Punta. The central mountain range is bounded on the north and south by flat coastal plains. These have been irrigated and are now among the richest farming areas in Puerto Rico.

Climate. Puerto Rico lies in the tropics, where the climate is warm the year round. Average temperatures along the coast range between 24 and 27°C (75 and 80°F). The climate is cooler in the mountains.

The island is located in the belt of the northeast trade winds. The winds cause heavy rains in the mountains. Sudden and brief showers are common, although more rain falls in summer than at other times. The southern coastal plain is dry, for the mountains prevent the rain from reaching it. The plain must be irrigated for crops to grow.

Like other islands in the Caribbean, Puerto Rico is subject to hurricanes during the late summer and early fall. These destructive storms are not frequent. But they have caused great damage to crops and buildings. In 1928 the San Felipe hurricane destroyed most of the coffee plantations and citrus groves. It took many years to restore the coffee plantations. The citrus orchards never completely recovered. Earthquakes are rare but have occurred in the past.

Natural Resources. Puerto Rico's climate, beaches, rich tropical vegetation, and farmlands are among its greatest natural assets. The chief minerals include limestone, marble, clay, and sand and gravel. There are large deposits of copper that have not yet been mined and small amounts of gold, silver, iron ore, and platinum.

Plant life in Puerto Rico is plentiful and varied. Palm trees and mangrove swamps are found along the seacoast. In the humid mountains, there are dense tropical rain forests. Desert-type plants grow in the southwestern coastal area.

Puerto Rico's generally beautiful environment has been marred by the modernization of its society. Some factories have polluted rivers and seashores with chemicals. The government has not installed sewage and garbage treatment facilities fast enough to keep pace with the growth of new suburban housing. Traffic jams on major roads generate noise, smelly fumes, and frayed nerves.

▶ THE ECONOMY

Until the 1940's, Puerto Rico's economy was based largely on farming. Then the island government took an active role in modernizing the society and attracting industrial investors. Public utilities were expanded to supply water, electricity, sanitation, and transportation. Under a program called Operation Bootstrap, the government of Puerto Rico invited investors from the United States and other countries to open factories on the island, and to provide jobs for the people.

Puerto Rico's economic growth attracted observers from distant corners of the world. Representatives from less economically developed countries in Africa, Latin America, and Asia, as well as from the United Nations, came to see the practices and policies that led to this remarkable economic progress in Puerto Rico.

The rapid economic change resulted in social progress as well. Health standards were raised considerably. Life expectancy has risen to over 70 years, about the same as in the United States and Europe.

But the island's economy has not been able to generate enough jobs for its people. Since the 1950's many Puerto Ricans have migrated to the United States. There are now about 2,000,000 Puerto Ricans in the United States, half of whom were born there. Puerto Ricans live in all 50 states. But most are concentrated in New York, New Jersey, Pennsylvania, Illinois, and New England. In recent years, however, some Puerto Ricans have been returning to the island, seeking economic opportunities at home.

Agriculture. Until the 1940's, sugarcane was the main crop. It accounted for over half the value of all agricultural products.

Above: Pineapples, one of Puerto Rico's important crops, are both grown and canned on the island. Below: Operation Bootstrap changed the economy of Puerto Rico by attracting new industry. Pharmaceuticals (medicinal drugs) are one of the products now being manufactured in Puerto Rican laboratories and plants.

Tourism has long been one of Puerto Rico's important industries. San Juan's Condado Beach is typical of the many beautiful beaches on the island.

More than half the people were employed in harvesting sugarcane or in processing and shipping the crop. Sugarcane plantations were developed mainly with money from the United States. The sugar industry thrived because Puerto Rico was included within the United States tariff (import tax) system. Tobacco and coffee were the second and third leading crops.

In recent years, agriculture has not only declined in importance but also changed in nature. Sugarcane, tobacco, and coffee are no longer dominant. The production of food products—meat, dairy products, and poultry —now accounts for over half of all agricultural income.

Sugarcane is grown on the flat lands, which are irrigated in some areas. Tobacco is cultivated mainly in the eastern highlands. Today coffee is grown in the central and western highlands. Pineapples are grown and canned on the island. Efforts have been made to pro-

duce larger amounts of melons, citrus fruits, mangoes, avocados, vegetables, pepper, and cherries. Bananas remain an important crop.

Manufacturing. As a result of mechanization, the number of farmers has decreased greatly. At the same time, jobs have become available in the hundreds of factories established since Operation Bootstrap. Many different kinds of products are manufactured in Puerto Rico. Among the most important are clothing, textiles, shoes, processed food, electric and electronic equipment, plastics, chemicals, and petrochemicals.

A number of Puerto Rican industries are based on the processing of agricultural products. Sugar is sold semi-refined to the United States. Some sugar is also made into rum, which is a very profitable export. High-grade Puerto Rican tobacco is used to make fine cigars.

Mineral resources are absolutely necessary for some of the island's industries. Limestone is used to make cement, and clay is used to make bricks and tiles. All these products are important to the construction industry. Sand provides the raw material necessary to the making of glass for bottles—which, in turn, are used in the rum and beer industry.

To supply power for industry and electricity for homes, hydroelectric power sites have been developed. New thermal plants based on the earth's own hot springs were built in an attempt to meet present and future demands for electric power.

Tourism. One of the most important developments in the island's economy has been the increase in the number of tourists and vacationers. Money spent by tourists in Puerto Rico has increased greatly since the 1950's. The island can be reached from most parts of the United States in a few hours by jet. The tropical climate, sandy beaches, and sparkling sea attract bathers, skin divers, and other water-sport enthusiasts all year-round. Historical monuments and colorful local customs are other attractions. Many hotels have been built to accommodate the growing number of vacationers.

▶CITIES

In the large cities new ways of life have emerged. New jobs in industry and business have created a way of life similar to that in the cities of the United States.

San Juan is the capital and the largest city of Puerto Rico. It was the site of the first Spanish fortresses built in the New World. Parts of the old city still stand, including El Morro, a fortress. The tomb of the Spanish explorer and first colonial governor, Juan Ponce de León, is in the Cathedral of San Juan Bautista (patron saint of the island). La Fortaleza has been the residence of the governors since colonial times. In the old part of the city, there are narrow, crooked cobblestone streets and fine old Spanish buildings. Modern stores and many new housing developments are found in the newer parts of the city. The modern airport near San Juan is the busiest terminal in the Caribbean. Most of the government buildings, as well as the main campus of the University of Puerto Rico, are within greater San Juan. Bayamón, the second largest city, is located within the San Juan metropolitan area. San Juan and its suburbs serve as the cultural, political, and educational center of the island.

Ponce is Puerto Rico's third largest city. It was named after Juan Ponce de León and is one of the oldest European settlements in the Western Hemisphere. The city still preserves its old Spanish atmosphere. It is a busy industrial center and an important port.

The leading inland city is Caguas. It is located south of San Juan in the center of a rich farming region. Many of its factories process sugar and other agricultural products. It also manufactures cigars and paper products.

Mayagüez, on the western coast, serves as the port for the coffee-producing region. It was once noted as the center of the island's needlework industry. Today it has a number of fish-processing plants. Much of the tuna fish consumed in the United States is processed and canned in Mayagüez. The gardens of the Mayagüez Institute of Tropical Agriculture contain what is thought to be the largest collection of tropical plants in the Americas.

Many smaller cities and towns throughout the island serve as resorts and marketplaces where people bring farm products and fish and in turn buy their food, clothes, and other goods.

▶GOVERNMENT

In 1898, following the Spanish-American War, Puerto Rico, till then a Spanish colony, became part of the United States.

Above: A waterfall in El Verde rain forest in eastern Puerto Rico. Below: The Fountain of Lions in Ponce, Puerto Rico's third largest city. One of the oldest cities in the Western Hemisphere, Ponce was founded by the Spanish in the 16th century. In the background is the city's Roman Catholic cathedral.

Between 1900 and 1917, the island was a territory. In 1917, when Puerto Ricans were granted United States citizenship, the island was governed by a two-house elected legislature and a governor appointed by the United States president. The cabinet (except the attorney general and the commissioner of education) and the judges (except in the Supreme Court) were appointed by the governor and the Puerto Rican Senate. The attorney general, the commissioner of education, and the Supreme Court judges continued to be appointed by the president of the United States and the United States Senate.

Since 1948 the governor has been elected directly by the Puerto Rican people for a 4-year term. The governor now appoints all members of the cabinet as well as the judges of the Supreme Court. The legislature, composed of the Senate and the House of Representatives, is also elected directly by the people for 4-year terms.

PUERTO RICO AND THE UNITED STATES

Puerto Rico is a self-governing commonwealth associated with the United States. The Spanish name for Puerto Rico's government is *estado libre asociado,* which means "free associated state." The United States and Puerto Rico share a common defense, economic market, currency, and postal service. As U.S. citizens, Puerto Ricans travel easily back and forth between the island and the mainland. Products are also shipped easily back and forth, without tariffs or import taxes. However, Puerto Rico is allowed to impose a special tax on imported coffee. Puerto Ricans do not vote in U.S. elections, and are represented in Congress solely by a resident commissioner. The commissioner has a voice but no vote in the House of Representatives.

Puerto Ricans do not pay most federal taxes, except those, such as social security taxes, that are imposed by the consent of both governments. Federal excise taxes on shipments of alcoholic beverages (mainly rum) and tobacco products between Puerto Rico and the United States are collected. The money, however, is then rebated (returned) to the commonwealth treasury. American social welfare programs such as food stamps, Medicare, Medicaid, aid to dependent children, welfare, and unemployment insurance are extended to Puerto Rico. But in some cases the payments are lower than in the United States.

Puerto Ricans are subject to service in the U.S. Armed Forces, and have fought in all American wars since World War I. The most important link between Puerto Rico and the United States is people. Puerto Ricans live in all the states of the Union, where they have the rights as well as the obligations of other American citizens.

▶ **HISTORY**

Early History. Puerto Rico was discovered in 1493 by Christopher Columbus on his second voyage to the New World. In 1508 a Spanish settlement was established by Ponce de León. For many years, Puerto Rico was an important seaport and military post, linking Spain with its colonies in Central and South America.

In the 19th century, most of Spain's colonies in the Americas became independent republics. A brief revolt for Puerto Rican independence, in 1868, was crushed by the Spanish military. In 1897, Puerto Rico was granted autonomy, or local self-government, but it was still controlled by Spain.

U.S. Territory. In 1898, Puerto Rico became a part of the United States as a result of war with Spain. See the article on the Spanish-American War in Volume S.

Since then, the United States Congress has granted Puerto Rico an increasing degree of self-government. Puerto Ricans became American citizens in 1917. In 1948 they elected their first governor, Luis Muñoz Marín (1898–1980), a writer who had lived in the United States. His father, Luis Muñoz Rivera (1886–1916), had led the autonomous government of Puerto Rico under Spain. Muñoz Marín was head of the Popular Democratic Party, which he had founded. In 1952, under Muñoz Marín's leadership, Puerto Rico became a self-governing commonwealth "freely associated" with the United States. In a referendum, or vote, held in 1967, Puerto Rican voters chose to continue the commonwealth status.

Recent Events. However, the question of Puerto Rico's political future continues to be debated. While the Popular Democratic Party wishes to maintain the commonwealth status, the New Progressive Party favors statehood for Puerto Rico. Two smaller parties seek complete independence. A bill authorizing a new referendum was rejected by a U.S. Senate committee in 1991, but in 1993, Governor Pedro Rossello of the New Progressive Party authorized a new vote on the island's political status. The result was a victory for commonwealth supporters.

JOHN F. LOUNSBURY
Arizona State University

Revised by KAL WAGENHEIM
Author, *Puerto Rico: A Profile*

PULITZER PRIZES

The Pulitzer Prizes are annual awards for excellence in American journalism, literature, and music. First awarded in 1917, the prizes are given each spring by the trustees of Columbia University on the recommendation of an advisory board. The board acts on the reports of juries appointed by the university in each of the categories. Each prize is $1,000.

The journalism prizes are awarded for work that appears in U.S. newspapers during the previous year. The categories are public service, general news reporting, investigative reporting, explanatory journalism, specialized reporting, national reporting, international reporting, feature writing, commentary, criticism, editorial writing, editorial cartooning, spot news photography, and feature photography.

Six awards in literature and one in music are given. The literature awards are for fiction, history, biography, drama, poetry, and general nonfiction.

The prizes were established by Joseph Pulitzer, an American newspaper publisher. He was born on April 10, 1847, in Mako, Hun-

Joseph Pulitzer, an American newspaper publisher, founded the Pulitzer Prizes, awarded annually for outstanding achievement in American journalism, literature, and music.

gary. When he was 17 he went to the United States and fought in the Union Army during the U.S. Civil War. He became a U.S. citizen in 1867.

The following year, he began reporting for the *Westliche Post*, a German-language newspaper in St. Louis, Missouri. In 1878 he bought the St. Louis *Dispatch*. He joined it with another paper, the St. Louis *Post*, to form the St. Louis *Post-Dispatch*. Pulitzer's crusades in the public interest made the *Post-Dispatch* one of the most influential papers in the United States. He went on to found the New York *World* and other newspapers.

Pulitzer believed in encouraging excellence in the arts and journalism. In his will, he gave $2 million to Columbia University. Part of it was to found the Columbia School of Journalism, which opened in 1912, and part was to create the Pulitzer Prizes. Pulitzer died on October 29, 1911.

JOHN HOHENBERG
Author, *The Pulitzer Prizes*

The following lists give the winners of the Pulitzer Prizes for fiction, history, biography, drama, poetry, and general nonfiction. No awards were given in the years not listed.

▶ **FICTION**

For distinguished fiction in book form by an American author, preferably dealing with American life.

1918 Ernest Poole, *His Family*.
1919 Booth Tarkington, *The Magnificent Ambersons*.
1921 Edith Wharton, *The Age of Innocence*.
1922 Booth Tarkington, *Alice Adams*.
1923 Willa Cather, *One of Ours*.
1924 Margaret Wilson, *The Able McLaughlins*.
1925 Edna Ferber, *So Big*.
1926 Sinclair Lewis, *Arrowsmith*.
1927 Louis Bromfield, *Early Autumn*.
1928 Thornton Wilder, *The Bridge of San Luis Rey*.
1929 Julia M. Peterkin, *Scarlet Sister Mary*.
1930 Oliver La Farge, *Laughing Boy*.
1931 Margaret Ayer Barnes, *Years of Grace*.
1932 Pearl S. Buck, *The Good Earth*.
1933 T. S. Stribling, *The Store*.
1934 Caroline Miller, *Lamb in His Bosom*.

1935 Josephine W. Johnson, *Now in November*.
1936 Harold L. Davis, *Honey in the Horn*.
1937 Margaret Mitchell, *Gone With the Wind*.
1938 John P. Marquand, *The Late George Apley*.
1939 Marjorie Kinnan Rawlings, *The Yearling*.
1940 John Steinbeck, *The Grapes of Wrath*.
1942 Ellen Glasgow, *In This Our Life*.
1943 Upton Sinclair, *Dragon's Teeth*.
1944 Martin Flavin, *Journey in the Dark*.
1945 John Hersey, *A Bell for Adano*.
1947 Robert Penn Warren, *All the King's Men*.
1948 James A. Michener, *Tales of the South Pacific*.
1949 James Gould Cozzens, *Guard of Honor*.
1950 A. B. Guthrie, Jr., *The Way West*.
1951 Conrad Richter, *The Town*.
1952 Herman Wouk, *The Caine Mutiny*.
1953 Ernest Hemingway, *The Old Man and the Sea*.
1955 William Faulkner, *A Fable*.
1956 MacKinlay Kantor, *Andersonville*.
1958 James Agee, *A Death in the Family*.

1959	Robert Lewis Taylor, *The Travels of Jaimie McPheeters.*
1960	Allen Drury, *Advise and Consent.*
1961	Harper Lee, *To Kill a Mockingbird.*
1962	Edwin O'Connor, *The Edge of Sadness.*
1963	William Faulkner, *The Reivers.*
1965	Shirley Ann Grau, *The Keepers of the House.*
1966	Katherine Anne Porter, *Collected Stories of Katherine Anne Porter.*
1967	Bernard Malamud, *The Fixer.*
1968	William Styron, *The Confessions of Nat Turner.*
1969	N. Scott Momaday, *House Made of Dawn.*
1970	Jean Stafford, *Collected Stories.*
1972	Wallace Stegner, *Angle of Repose.*
1973	Eudora Welty, *The Optimist's Daughter.*
1975	Michael Shaara, *The Killer Angels.*
1976	Saul Bellow, *Humboldt's Gift.*
1978	James Alan McPherson, *Elbow Room.*
1979	John Cheever, *The Stories of John Cheever.*
1980	Norman Mailer, *The Executioner's Song.*
1981	John Kennedy Toole, *A Confederacy of Dunces.*
1982	John Updike, *Rabbit Is Rich.*
1983	Alice Walker, *The Color Purple.*
1984	William Kennedy, *Ironweed.*
1985	Alison Lurie, *Foreign Affairs.*
1986	Larry McMurtry, *Lonesome Dove.*
1987	Peter Taylor, *A Summons to Memphis.*
1988	Toni Morrison, *Beloved.*
1989	Anne Tyler, *Breathing Lessons.*
1990	Oscar Hijuelos, *The Mambo Kings Play Songs of Love.*
1991	John Updike, *Rabbit at Rest.*
1992	Jane Smiley, *A Thousand Acres.*
1993	Robert Olen Butler, *A Good Scent From a Strange Mountain.*
1994	E. Annie Proulx, *The Shipping News.*
1995	Carol Shields, *The Stone Diaries.*
1996	Richard Ford, *Independence Day.*

▶ HISTORY

For a distinguished book on the history of the United States.

1917	J. J. Jusserand, *With Americans of Past and Present Days.*
1918	James Ford Rhodes, *History of the Civil War.*
1920	Justin H. Smith, *The War with Mexico.*
1921	William Sowden Sims, *The Victory at Sea.*
1922	James Truslow Adams, *The Founding of New England.*
1923	Charles Warren, *The Supreme Court in United States History.*
1924	Charles Howard McIlwain, *The American Revolution: A Constitutional Interpretation.*
1925	Frederick L. Paxton, *A History of the American Frontier.*
1926	Edward Channing, *History of the United States,* Vol. VI.
1927	Samuel Flagg Bemis, *Pinckney's Treaty.*
1928	Vernon Louis Parrington, *Main Currents in American Thought.*
1929	Fred A. Shannon, *The Organization and Administration of the Union Army, 1861–65.*
1930	Claude H. Van Tyne, *The War of Independence.*
1931	Bernadotte E. Schmitt, *The Coming of the War, 1914.*
1932	Gen. John J. Pershing, *My Experiences in the World War.*

1933	Frederick J. Turner, *The Significance of Sections in American History.*
1934	Herbert Agar, *The People's Choice.*
1935	Charles McLean Andrews, *The Colonial Period of American History.*
1936	Andrew C. McLaughlin, *A Constitutional History of the United States.*
1937	Van Wyck Brooks, *The Flowering of New England.*
1938	Paul Herman Buck, *The Road to Reunion.*
1939	Frank Luther Mott, *A History of American Magazines.*
1940	Carl Sandburg, *Abraham Lincoln: The War Years.*
1941	Marcus Lee Hansen, *The Atlantic Migration.*
1942	Margaret Leech, *Reveille in Washington.*
1943	Esther Forbes, *Paul Revere and the World He Lived In.*
1944	Merle Curti, *The Growth of American Thought.*
1945	Stephen Bonsal, *Unfinished Business.*
1946	Arthur M. Schlesinger, Jr., *The Age of Jackson.*
1947	Dr. James Phinney Baxter, 3rd, *Scientists Against Time.*
1948	Bernard De Voto, *Across the Wide Missouri.*
1949	Roy F. Nichols, *The Disruption of American Democracy.*
1950	O. W. Larkin, *Art and Life in America.*
1951	R. Carlyle Buley, *The Old Northwest, Pioneer Period 1815–1840.*
1952	Oscar Handlin, *The Uprooted.*
1953	George Dangerfield, *The Era of Good Feelings.*
1954	Bruce Catton, *A Stillness at Appomattox.*
1955	Paul Horgan, *Great River: The Rio Grande in North American History.*
1956	Richard Hofstadter, *The Age of Reform.*
1957	George F. Kennan, *Russia Leaves the War.*
1958	Bray Hammond, *Banks and Politics in America—From the Revolution to the Civil War.*
1959	Leonard D. White and Jean Schneider, *The Republican Era: 1869–1901.*
1960	Margaret Leech, *In the Days of McKinley.*
1961	Herbert Feis, *Between War and Peace: The Potsdam Conference.*
1962	Lawrence H. Gipson, *The Triumphant Empire, Thunder-Clouds Gather in the West.*
1963	Constance McLaughlin Green, *Washington, Village and Capital, 1800–1878.*
1964	Sumner Chilton Powell, *Puritan Village: The Formation of a New England Town.*
1965	Irwin Unger, *The Greenback Era.*
1966	Perry Miller, *The Life of the Mind in America: From the Revolution to the Civil War.*
1967	William H. Goetzmann, *Exploration and Empire: The Explorer and Scientist in the Winning of the American West.*
1968	Bernard Bailyn, *The Ideological Origins of the American Revolution.*
1969	Leonard Levy, *Origins of the Fifth Amendment.*
1970	Dean Acheson, *Present at the Creation: My Years in the State Department.*
1971	James MacGregor Burns, *Roosevelt: The Soldier of Freedom.*
1972	Carl N. Degler, *Neither Black Nor White.*
1973	Michael Kammen, *People of Paradox: An Inquiry Concerning the Origins of American Civilization.*
1974	Daniel J. Boorstin, *The Americans: The Democratic Experience,* Vol. III.
1975	Dumas Malone, *Jefferson and His Time,* Vols. I–V.
1976	Paul Horgan, *Lamy of Santa Fe.*

1977 David M. Potter, *The Impending Crisis.*
1978 Alfred D. Chandler, Jr., *The Visible Hand: The Managerial Revolution in American Business.*
1979 Don E. Fehrenbacher, *The Dred Scott Case.*
1980 Leon F. Litwack, *Been in the Storm So Long: The Aftermath of Slavery.*
1981 Lawrence A. Cremin, *American Education: The National Experience 1783–1876.*
1982 C. Vann Woodward (editor), *Mary Chesnut's Civil War.*
1983 L. Isaac Rhys, *The Transformation of Virginia, 1740–1790.*
1985 Thomas K. McCraw, *The Prophets of Regulation.*
1986 Walter A. McDougall, *. . . the Heavens and the Earth: A Political History of the Space Age.*
1987 Bernard Bailyn, *Voyagers to the West: A Passage in the Peopling of America on the Eve of the Revolution.*
1988 Robert V. Bruce, *The Launching of Modern American Science 1846–1876.*
1989 Taylor Branch, *Parting the Waters.*
James M. McPherson, *Battle Cry of Freedom.*
1990 Stanley Karnow, *In Our Image: America's Empire in the Philippines.*
1991 Laurel Thatcher Ulrich, *A Midwife's Tale: The Life of Martha Ballard, Based on Her Diary 1785–1812.*
1992 Mark E. Neely, Jr., *The Fate of Liberty: Abraham Lincoln and Civil Liberties.*
1993 Gordon S. Wood, *The Radicalism of the American Revolution.*
1995 Doris Kearns Goodwin, *No Ordinary Time: Franklin and Eleanor Roosevelt: The Home Front in World War II.*
1996 Alan Taylor, *William Cooper's Town: Power and Persuasion on the Frontier of the Early American Republic.*

▶ **BIOGRAPHY OR AUTOBIOGRAPHY**

For a distinguished biography or autobiography by an American author.

1917 Laura E. Richards and Maude Howe Elliott, assisted by Florence Howe Hall, *Julia Ward Howe.*
1918 William Cabell Bruce, *Benjamin Franklin, Self-Revealed.*
1919 Henry Adams, *The Education of Henry Adams.*
1920 Albert J. Beveridge, *The Life of John Marshall.*
1921 Edward Bok, *The Americanization of Edward Bok.*
1922 Hamlin Garland, *A Daughter of the Middle Border.*
1923 Burton J. Hendrick, *The Life and Letters of Walter H. Page.*
1924 Michael Pupin, *From Immigrant to Inventor.*
1925 M. A. DeWolfe Howe, *Barrett Wendell and His Letters.*
1926 Harvey Cushing, *Life of Sir William Osler.*
1927 Emory Holloway, *Whitman, An Interpretation in Narrative.*
1928 Charles Edward Russell, *The American Orchestra and Theodore Thomas.*
1929 Burton J. Hendrick, *The Training of an American: The Earlier Life and Letters of Walter H. Page.*
1930 Marquis James, *The Raven* (Sam Houston).
1931 Henry James, *Charles W. Eliot.*

1932 Henry F. Pringle, *Theodore Roosevelt.*
1933 Allan Nevins, *Grover Cleveland.*
1934 Tyler Dennett, *John Hay.*
1935 Douglas Southall Freeman, *R. E. Lee.*
1936 Ralph Barton Perry, *The Thought and Character of William James.*
1937 Allan Nevins, *Hamilton Fish, the Inner History of the Grant Administration.*
1938 Odell Shepard, *Pedlar's Progress* (Bronson Alcott).
Marquis James, *Andrew Jackson.*
1939 Carl Van Doren, *Benjamin Franklin.*
1940 Ray Stannard Baker, *Woodrow Wilson, Life and Letters.*
1941 Ola Elizabeth Winslow, *Jonathan Edwards.*
1942 Forrest Wilson, *Crusader in Crinoline* (Harriet Beecher Stowe).
1943 Samuel Eliot Morison, *Admiral of the Ocean Sea* (Columbus).
1944 Carleton Mabee, *The American Leonardo: The Life of Samuel F. B. Morse.*
1945 Russel Blaine Nye, *George Bancroft: Brahmin Rebel.*
1946 Linnie Marsh Wolfe, *Son of the Wilderness* (John Muir).
1947 William Allen White, *The Autobiography of William Allen White.*
1948 Margaret Clapp, *Forgotten First Citizen: John Bigelow.*
1949 Robert E. Sherwood, *Roosevelt and Hopkins.*
1950 Samuel Flagg Bemis, *John Quincy Adams and the Foundations of American Foreign Policy.*
1951 Margaret Louise Coit, *John C. Calhoun: American Portrait.*
1952 Merlo J. Pusey, *Charles Evans Hughes.*
1953 David J. Mays, *Edmund Pendleton 1721–1803.*
1954 Charles A. Lindbergh, *The Spirit of St. Louis.*
1955 William S. White, *The Taft Story.*
1956 Talbot F. Hamlin, *Benjamin Henry Latrobe.*
1957 John F. Kennedy, *Profiles in Courage.*
1958 Douglas Southall Freeman, *George Washington*, Vols. I–VI; John Alexander Carroll and Mary Wells Ashworth, Vol. VII.
1959 Arthur Walworth, *Woodrow Wilson, American Prophet.*
1960 Samuel Eliot Morison, *John Paul Jones.*
1961 David Herbert Donald, *Charles Sumner and the Coming of the Civil War.*
1963 Leon Edel, *Henry James:* Vol. II, *The Conquest of London, 1870–1881;* Vol. III, *The Middle Years, 1881–1895.*
1964 Walter Jackson Bate, *John Keats.*
1965 Ernest Samuels, *Henry Adams.*
1966 Arthur M. Schlesinger, Jr., *A Thousand Days.*
1967 Justin Kaplan, *Mr. Clemens and Mark Twain.*
1968 George F. Kennan, *Memoirs (1925–1950).*
1969 Benjamin Lawrence Reid, *The Man from New York: John Quinn and His Friends.*
1970 T. Harry Williams, *Huey Long.*
1971 Lawrence R. Thompson, *Robert Frost: The Years of Triumph, 1915–1938.*
1972 Joseph P. Lash, *Eleanor and Franklin.*
1973 William A. Swanberg, *Luce and His Empire.*
1974 Louis Sheaffer, *O'Neill, Son and Artist,* Vol. II (Eugene O'Neill).
1975 Robert A. Caro, *The Power Broker: Robert Moses and the Fall of New York.*
1976 Richard W. B. Lewis, *Edith Wharton.*
1977 John E. Mack, *A Prince of Our Disorder* (T. E. Lawrence).

1978	Walter Jackson Bate, *Samuel Johnson*.
1979	Leonard Baker, *Days of Sorrow and Pain: Leo Baeck and the Berlin Jews*.
1980	Edmund Morris, *The Rise of Theodore Roosevelt*.
1981	Robert K. Massie, *Peter the Great*.
1982	William S. McFeely, *Grant: A Biography*.
1983	Russell Baker, *Growing Up*.
1984	Louis R. Harlan, *Booker T. Washington: The Wizard of Tuskegee, 1901–1915*.
1985	Kenneth Silverman, *The Life and Times of Cotton Mather*.
1986	Elizabeth Frank, *Louise Bogan: A Portrait*.
1987	David Garrow, *Bearing the Cross: Martin Luther King Jr. and the Southern Christian Leadership Conference*.
1988	David Herbert Donald, *Look Homeward: A Life of Thomas Wolfe*.
1989	Richard Ellmann, *Oscar Wilde*.
1990	Sebastian de Grazia, *Machiavelli in Hell*.
1991	Steven Naifeh and Gregory White Smith, *Jackson Pollock: An American Saga*.
1992	Lewis B. Puller, Jr., *Fortunate Son: The Healing of a Vietnam Vet*.
1993	David McCullough, *Truman*.
1994	David L. Lewis, *W. E. B. Du Bois: Biography of a Race, 1868–1919*.
1995	Joan D. Hedrick, *Harriet Beecher Stowe: A Life*.
1996	Jack Miles, *God: A Biography*.

► **DRAMA**

For a distinguished play by an American author, preferably original in its source and dealing with American life.

1918	Jesse Lynch Williams, *Why Marry?*
1920	Eugene O'Neill, *Beyond the Horizon*.
1921	Zona Gale, *Miss Lulu Bett*.
1922	Eugene O'Neill, *Anna Christie*.
1923	Owen Davis, *Icebound*.
1924	Hatcher Hughes, *Hell-Bent fer Heaven*.
1925	Sidney Howard, *They Knew What They Wanted*.
1926	George Kelly, *Craig's Wife*.
1927	Paul Green, *In Abraham's Bosom*.
1928	Eugene O'Neill, *Strange Interlude*.
1929	Elmer Rice, *Street Scene*.
1930	Marc Connelly, *The Green Pastures*.
1931	Susan Glaspell, *Alison's House*.
1932	George S. Kaufman, Morrie Ryskind, and Ira Gershwin, *Of Thee I Sing*.
1933	Maxwell Anderson, *Both Your Houses*.
1934	Sidney Kingsley, *Men in White*.
1935	Zoë Akins, *The Old Maid*.
1936	Robert E. Sherwood, *Idiot's Delight*.
1937	George S. Kaufman and Moss Hart, *You Can't Take It with You*.
1938	Thornton Wilder, *Our Town*.
1939	Robert E. Sherwood, *Abe Lincoln in Illinois*.
1940	William Saroyan, *The Time of Your Life*.
1941	Robert E. Sherwood, *There Shall Be No Night*.
1943	Thornton Wilder, *The Skin of Our Teeth*.
1945	Mary Chase, *Harvey*.
1946	Russel Crouse and Howard Lindsay, *State of the Union*.
1948	Tennessee Williams, *A Streetcar Named Desire*.
1949	Arthur Miller, *Death of a Salesman*.
1950	Richard Rodgers, Oscar Hammerstein II, and Joshua Logan, *South Pacific*, based on James A. Michener's 1948 prize-winning book, *Tales of the South Pacific*.
1952	Joseph Kramm, *The Shrike*.

1953	William Inge, *Picnic*.
1954	John Patrick, *Teahouse of the August Moon*.
1955	Tennessee Williams, *Cat on a Hot Tin Roof*.
1956	Frances Goodrich and Albert Hackett, *The Diary of Anne Frank*.
1957	Eugene O'Neill, *Long Day's Journey into Night*.
1958	Ketti Frings, *Look Homeward, Angel*.
1959	Archibald MacLeish, *J. B.*
1960	George Abbott, Jerome Weidman, Sheldon Harnick, and Jerry Bock, *Fiorello!*
1961	Tad Mosel, *All the Way Home*, based on James Agee's 1958 prize-winning book, *A Death in the Family*.
1962	Frank Loesser and Abe Burrows, *How to Succeed in Business Without Really Trying*.
1965	Frank D. Gilroy, *The Subject Was Roses*.
1967	Edward Albee, *A Delicate Balance*.
1969	Howard Sackler, *The Great White Hope*.
1970	Charles Gordone, *No Place to Be Somebody*.
1971	Paul Zindel, *The Effect of Gamma Rays on Man-in-the-Moon Marigolds*.
1973	Jason Miller, *That Championship Season*.
1975	Edward Albee, *Seascape*.
1976	Michael Bennett, James Kirkwood, Nicholas Dante, Marvin Hamlisch, Edward Kleban, *A Chorus Line*.
1977	Michael Cristofer, *The Shadow Box*.
1978	Donald L. Coburn, *The Gin Game*.
1979	Sam Shepard, *Buried Child*.
1980	Lanford Wilson, *Talley's Folly*.
1981	Beth Henley, *Crimes of the Heart*.
1982	Charles Fuller, *A Soldier's Play*.
1983	Marsha Norman, *'night, Mother*.
1984	David Mamet, *Glengarry Glen Ross*.
1985	Stephen Sondheim and James Lapine, *Sunday in the Park with George*.
1987	August Wilson, *Fences*.
1988	Alfred Uhry, *Driving Miss Daisy*.
1989	Wendy Wasserstein, *The Heidi Chronicles*.
1990	August Wilson, *The Piano Lesson*.
1991	Neil Simon, *Lost in Yonkers*.
1992	Robert Schenkkan, *The Kentucky Cycle*.
1993	Tony Kushner, *Angels in America: Millennium Approaches*.
1994	Edward Albee, *Three Tall Women*.
1995	Horton Foote, *The Young Man From Atlanta*.
1996	Jonathan Larson, *Rent*.

► **POETRY**

For a distinguished volume of verse by an American author. Before this prize was established in 1922, awards were provided by the Poetry Society. Prize-winning works were *Love Songs* by Sara Teasdale (1918) and *Old Road to Paradise* by Margaret Widdemer and *Corn Huskers* by Carl Sandburg (1919).

1922	Edwin Arlington Robinson, *Collected Poems*.
1923	Edna St. Vincent Millay, *The Ballad of the Harp-Weaver; A Few Figs from Thistles; Eight Sonnets in American Poetry, 1922; A Miscellany*.
1924	Robert Frost, *New Hampshire: A Poem with Notes and Grace Notes*.
1925	Edwin Arlington Robinson, *The Man Who Died Twice*.
1926	Amy Lowell, *What's O'Clock*.

1927	Leonora Speyer, *Fiddler's Farewell.*
1928	Edwin Arlington Robinson, *Tristram.*
1929	Stephen Vincent Benét, *John Brown's Body.*
1930	Conrad Aiken, *Selected Poems.*
1931	Robert Frost, *Collected Poems.*
1932	George Dillon, *The Flowering Stone.*
1933	Archibald MacLeish, *Conquistador.*
1934	Robert Hillyer, *Collected Verse.*
1935	Audrey Wurdemann, *Bright Ambush.*
1936	Robert P. Tristram Coffin, *Strange Holiness.*
1937	Robert Frost, *A Further Range.*
1938	Marya Zaturenska, *Cold Morning Sky.*
1939	John Gould Fletcher, *Selected Poems.*
1940	Mark Van Doren, *Collected Poems.*
1941	Leonard Bacon, *Sunderland Capture.*
1942	William Rose Benét, *The Dust Which Is God.*
1943	Robert Frost, *A Witness Tree.*
1944	Stephen Vincent Benét, *Western Star.*
1945	Karl Shapiro, *V-Letter and Other Poems.*
1947	Robert Lowell, *Lord Weary's Castle.*
1948	W. H. Auden, *The Age of Anxiety.*
1949	Peter Viereck, *Terror and Decorum.*
1950	Gwendolyn Brooks, *Annie Allen.*
1951	Carl Sandburg, *Complete Poems.*
1952	Marianne Moore, *Collected Poems.*
1953	Archibald MacLeish, *Collected Poems.*
1954	Theodore Roethke, *The Waking.*
1955	Wallace Stevens, *Collected Poems.*
1956	Elizabeth Bishop, *Poems, North and South.*
1957	Richard Wilbur, *Things of This World.*
1958	Robert Penn Warren, *Promises: Poems 1954–1956.*
1959	Stanley Kunitz, *Selected Poems 1928–1958.*
1960	W. D. Snodgrass, *Heart's Needle.*
1961	Phyllis McGinley, *Times Three: Selected Verse from Three Decades.*
1962	Alan Dugan, *Poems.*
1963	William Carlos Williams, *Pictures from Brueghel.*
1964	Louis Simpson, *At the End of the Open Road.*
1965	John Berryman, *77 Dream Songs.*
1966	Richard Eberhart, *Selected Poems (1930–1965).*
1967	Anne Sexton, *Live or Die.*
1968	Anthony Hecht, *The Hard Hours.*
1969	George Oppen, *Of Being Numerous.*
1970	Richard Howard, *Untitled Subjects.*
1971	William S. Merwin, *The Carrier of Ladders.*
1972	James Wright, *Collected Poems.*
1973	Maxine Winokur Kumin, *Up Country.*
1974	Robert Lowell, *The Dolphin.*
1975	Gary Snyder, *Turtle Island.*
1976	John Ashbery, *Self-Portrait in a Convex Mirror.*
1977	James Merrill, *Divine Comedies.*
1978	Howard Nemerov, *Collected Poems.*
1979	Robert Penn Warren, *Now and Then.*
1980	Donald R. Justice, *Selected Poems.*
1981	James Schuyler, *The Morning of the Poem.*
1982	Sylvia Plath, *The Collected Poems.*
1983	Galway Kinnell, *Selected Poems.*
1984	Mary Oliver, *American Primitive.*
1985	Carolyn Kizer, *Yin.*
1986	Henry Taylor, *The Flying Change.*
1987	Rita Dove, *Thomas and Beulah.*
1988	William Meredith, *Partial Accounts: New and Selected Poems.*
1989	Richard Wilbur, *New and Collected Poems.*
1990	Charles Simic, *The World Doesn't End.*
1991	Mona Van Duyn, *Near Changes.*
1992	James Tate, *Selected Poems.*

1993	Louise Gluck, *The Wild Iris.*
1994	Yusef Komunyakaa, *Neon Vernacular.*
1995	Philip Levine, *The Simple Truth.*
1996	Jorie Graham, *The Dream of the Unified Field.*

▶ GENERAL NONFICTION

For a distinguished book not eligible for consideration in any other existing category.

1962	Theodore H. White, *The Making of the President, 1960.*
1963	Barbara W. Tuchman, *The Guns of August.*
1964	Richard Hofstadter, *Anti-intellectualism in American Life.*
1965	Howard M. Jones, *O Strange New World.*
1966	Edwin Way Teale, *Wandering Through Winter.*
1967	David Brion Davis, *The Problem of Slavery in Western Culture.*
1968	Will and Ariel Durant, *Rousseau and Revolution.*
1969	Norman Mailer, *Armies of the Night.* René Jules Dubos, *So Human an Animal.*
1970	Eric Erikson, *Gandhi's Truth.*
1971	John Toland, *The Rising Sun.*
1972	Barbara W. Tuchman, *Stillwell and the American Experience in China.*
1973	Frances FitzGerald, *Fire in the Lake.* Robert M. Coles, *Children of Crisis,* Vols. II and III.
1974	Ernest Becker, *The Denial of Death.*
1975	Annie Dillard, *Pilgrim at Tinker Creek.*
1976	Robert N. Butler, *Why Survive? Being Old in America.*
1977	William W. Warner, *Beautiful Swimmers: Watermen, Crabs and the Chesapeake Bay.*
1978	Carl Sagan, *The Dragons of Eden.*
1979	Edward O. Wilson, *On Human Nature.*
1980	Douglas R. Hofstadter, *Gödel, Escher, Bach: An Eternal Golden Braid.*
1981	Carl E. Schorske, *Fin-de-Siècle Vienna: Politics and Culture.*
1982	Tracy Kidder, *The Soul of a New Machine.*
1983	Susan Sheehan, *Is There No Place on Earth for Me?*
1984	Paul Starr, *The Social Transformation of American Medicine.*
1985	Studs Terkel, *The Good War: An Oral History of World War II.*
1986	Joseph Lelyveld, *Move Your Shadow: South Africa, Black and White.* J. Anthony Lukas, *Common Ground: A Turbulent Decade in the Lives of Three American Families.*
1987	David Shipler, *Arab and Jew: Wounded Spirits in a Promised Land.*
1988	Richard Rhodes, *The Making of the Atomic Bomb.*
1989	Neil Sheehan, *A Bright Shining Lie.*
1990	Dale Maharidge and Michael Williamson, *And Their Children After Them.*
1991	Bert Holldobler and Edward O. Wilson, *The Ants.*
1992	Daniel Yergin, *The Prize: The Epic Quest for Oil, Money and Power.*
1993	Garry Wills, *Lincoln at Gettysburg: The Words That Remade America.*
1994	David Remnick, *Lenin's Tomb: The Last Days of the Soviet Empire.*
1995	Jonathan Weiner, *The Beak of the Finch: A Story of Evolution in Our Time.*
1996	Tina Rosenberg, *The Haunted Land: Facing Europe's Ghosts After Communism.*

The Crab Nebula

Off On

X-ray images of the core of the Crab Nebula reveal the pulsar that appears to blink on and off (*above*) as its constant short bursts of radiation reach observers on Earth.

PULSARS

In 1967, radio astronomers at Cambridge, England, were astounded to find strange radio signals coming from certain places in space. The signals came in short rapid bursts, or pulses, each lasting only a few hundredths of a second but repeated with extraordinary regularity. No star had ever been known to emit signals as bizarre as these. The signals seemed almost like a Morse code, and some astronomers actually referred to their source as LGM's, for Little Green Men. But it soon became evident that these radio signals were coming from objects sending streams of radiation into space. From Earth, this radiation is seen as short bursts, or pulses, and these objects became known as **pulsars**.

The pulses that astronomers receive from these objects are very sharp, so they conclude that pulsars are very tiny and have a radius of only about 10 miles (16 kilometers). Astronomers base this conclusion on a simple fact. When an object emits a burst of radio-wave radiation, the waves from different parts of the object arrive at the Earth at different times. This causes the original burst of radiation to become blurred. The smaller the object, however, the sharper the burst, or pulse.

After discovering pulsars, astronomers tried to determine what they were. Only one other object in the universe—a **neutron star**—is known to have such a small size yet is able to emit such bursts of radiation. Neutron stars mark the final stage in the life of many giant stars. When a giant star has used up most of its fuel and its nuclear reactions begin to lessen, the star collapses. As it collapses, gases and other materials are compressed tightly together. Then, the hot, compressed gases explode outward violently, creating what is known as a **supernova**. The remaining materials in the dying star continue collapsing inward, producing enormous pressures that crush the nuclei of atoms together, forming particles called neutrons. The resulting ball of neutrons, called a neutron star, is very small and dense. The density of matter in a neutron star is about one billion tons per cubic inch.

If pulsars are actually neutron stars, it would help explain why they emit short bursts of radio-wave radiation. A neutron star spins rapidly and has a strong magnetic field because of its great density. This strong magnetic field acts like a radio transmitter, beaming a narrow radio wave into space. As a neutron star spins, this radio wave sweeps through space like the light from a revolving lighthouse beacon. Astronomers on Earth can only detect the radio wave when it is pointed directly at our planet, appearing to blink on and off as it arrives as a series of short pulses.

Astronomers searched for evidence that would link neutron stars and pulsars by studying the Crab Nebula—a cloud of gas produced by a supernova explosion that occurred in A.D. 1054. They reasoned that if neutron stars are the remains of supernova explosions and pulsars are the same as neutron stars, then they should find a pulsar in the remains of a supernova explosion. In 1968, astronomers found a pulsar at the center of the Crab Nebula, precisely where the neutron star from the supernova should be located. Clearly, neutron stars and pulsars were the same, and the mystery of pulsars was solved.

ROBERT JASTROW
Mount Wilson Institute

See also ASTRONOMY; RADIO AND RADAR ASTRONOMY; STARS; TELESCOPES; UNIVERSE.

PUMICE. See ROCKS (Igneous Rock).

PUMPS

A pump is a machine that moves liquids and sometimes solids from one level to another and from one place to another. Pumps are very useful. They help bring water to homes and other buildings; they help provide water for irrigating crops; they make it easy to move oil, gasoline, chemicals, and waste out of industrial plants.

Pumps are among the oldest and most commonly used machines, and were used long ago by people in ancient Egypt, China, India, Greece, and Rome. Today pumps are the second most commonly used kind of industrial equipment. Electric motors rank first.

How Do Pumps Work?

Pumps move liquids by pressure or by suction, and sometimes by both methods, in the same way that you do when you sip a drink through a straw. As you suck through a straw, you pull some of the air out of it, which reduces the air pressure in the straw. This makes a space of lower pressure in the straw. The higher pressure on the surface of the drink pushes the liquid up into the straw to equalize the pressure, and the liquid flows into your mouth.

Air pressure is sometimes called **atmospheric pressure**. In 1643 the Italian scientist Evangelista Torricelli proved that air has weight. At sea level this weight is 14.7 pounds per square inch (1.036 kilograms per square centimeter).

A simple lift pump, like the old-fashioned suction pump, moves liquid with the help of this atmospheric pressure. The machinery of the pump is designed so that it can create a vacuum inside. Atmospheric pressure on the liquid outside pushes the liquid into the pump. Once the liquid is inside the pump and is in contact with the pumping machinery, the machinery pushes the liquid to higher levels.

Atmospheric pressure can hold water up to 34 feet (10 meters) high in a vertical pipe when the bottom of the pipe is in water and the top of the pipe is closed. Often, however, there is some leakage out of the pipe, and the vacuum created is not perfect. For this reason, suction pumps are not expected to lift a liquid more than about 25 feet (7.5 meters) high at sea level. If the liquid has to be lifted any higher, a pressure pump must be used.

Once in a while, air gets into the interior of a pump and can air-bind it, which prevents it from moving. It then needs to be **primed**—that is, the air in the pump needs to be removed. This is done by adding liquid to the pump or by using special priming machines. Some pumps are made in such a way that they are self-priming.

Kinds of Pumps

Pumps may be divided into several types, according to the ways in which liquids are moved by them. Positive displacement pumps move liquids by the action of a mechanical device in a tightly enclosed space. The device may move up and down, as in a piston pump, or by rotating, as in a gear pump. Turbomachinery pumps use rapidly rotating elements in a casing to set fluids in motion. Centrifugal and propeller pumps are also in this class.

How A Suction Pump Works

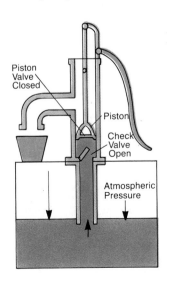
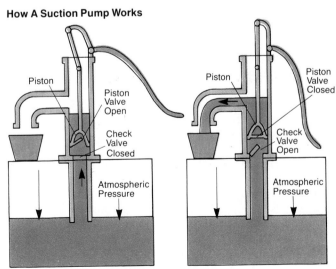

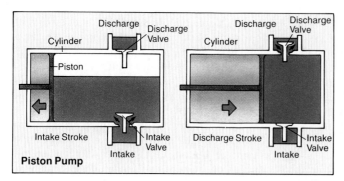

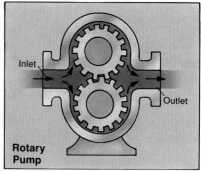

Piston Pump

Rotary Pump

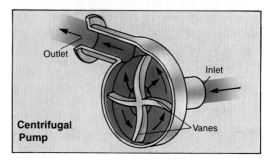

Centrifugal Pump

Piston Pumps. Piston pumps work by the up-and-down movement of a tightly fitting piston in a cylinder. When the piston moves one way, it sucks liquid into the cylinder through an opening called an intake port. On the return stroke it forces the liquid out through another opening called a discharge port. Valves control the flow of liquid into and out of the cylinder. A simple pump of this type is the hand-operated lift pump, which uses atmospheric pressure to move liquids. Fluids may also be moved in a piston pump by pressure applied to the piston. Fluid is discharged only on the return stroke, unless the pump is a double-acting one.

Rotary Pumps. In these pumps, rotating parts inside a close-fitting case cause a liquid to move because of the differences in pressure within the case. The parts may be two gears meshing together. As the gears unmesh, a partial vacuum is formed and liquid is drawn into the pump. On the side where the gears mesh, pressure forces the liquid out. In vane pumps the rotating part is located off center in the case. Liquids are forced out as the space between the vanes becomes smaller at the outlet side. Rotary pumps do not need valves, and they deliver a constant flow of liquid.

Centrifugal Pumps. Centrifugal force causes a rotating body to move away from the center of rotation. In a centrifugal pump, rapidly rotating elements such as vanes cause the fluid in the case to rotate. Centrifugal force pushes the fluid out of the discharge line. A vacuum is created inside the case as a result, and atmospheric pressure forces more fluid into the case. Centrifugal pumps are particularly useful for moving large flows of water against relatively low pressure.

Reviewed by IGOR J. KARASSIK
Consulting Engineer

PUNCTUATION

Ancient writers used few marks of punctuation. The words carved on ancient monuments are usually run together, and it is almost impossible to figure out their meaning. After the printing press was invented in the 1400's, type was set in sentences and paragraphs. Punctuation marks were used to help the reader understand the thoughts of the writer. Today punctuation marks are a necessary part of written communication.

▶**RULES FOR PUNCTUATION**

We must know the rules of punctuation and use them in our writing so that our meaning will be clear to the reader.

Period (.). The period is used after
(1) Sentences that are declarative (make a statement) or imperative (make a command).

The plane landed just before midnight.
Open the door, please.

(2) Many abbreviations.

Mr.	M.D.	Feb.
Rev.	A.M.	Ltd.
Jr.	vol.	Co.

(Many other examples are given in the article ABBREVIATIONS in Volume A.)

Question Mark (?). The question mark is used after an interrogative sentence.

Are you coming?

Exclamation Point (!). The exclamation point is used after a word, phrase, or sentence that expresses a sudden or strong emotion.

Oh! How dare you!

Comma (,). The comma is used to set off
(1) Nouns in direct address (the name of a person you are speaking to directly).

Dick, you are wanted on the telephone.

(2) An appositive (a word or phrase that identifies a noun or pronoun).

Mrs. Newman, the school principal, told me.

(3) Disconnected words, phrases, or clauses.

Yes, I'll do it for you.
Well, what do you think?
The news, to say the least, was a surprise.
He will, I believe, recover completely.

(4) Nonrestrictive phrases or clauses (information not essential to the meaning of the sentence).

Jimmy, who was making a last try, passed the other contestants.
The flag, as it floated in the breeze, was a sign of victory.

(5) Items in addresses and dates.

Edmonton, Alberta
October 12, 1980
Savannah, Georgia

(6) The salutation in a friendly letter and the complimentary close in all letters.

Dear Joan,
Sincerely yours,
Respectfully yours,

(7) Items in a series.

The three R's are reading, writing, and arithmetic.

(8) Adjectives that modify a noun individually. If the conjunction "and" can be put between the adjectives, a comma is used.

He was a brave, honest man.
(He was a brave and honest man.)

(9) Two independent clauses (clauses each containing a subject and a verb) joined by a co-ordinating conjunction (*and, but, or*).

I think he is wrong, but I cannot prove it.

(10) Adverbial clauses (clauses that modify the verb) at the beginning of a sentence.

If he can come next Thursday, he will.

(11) A direct quotation, to separate the speaker from what is said.

"That isn't possible," he declared.

A comma is used to clarify the meaning of a sentence that might be misread.

Soon after, the officer left.
To Mary, Jane was always right.

Semicolon (;). The semicolon is used
(1) To set off parts of a sentence that already contain commas.

They traveled all over the country, from Bangor, Maine, to Miami, Florida; from Chicago, Illinois, to Houston, Texas.

(2) To separate independent clauses in a compound sentence when they are not joined by a conjunction.

He did not go to the baseball game; he went swimming.

Colon (:). The colon is used
(1) After the salutation of a business letter.

Dear Dr. Brown:

(2) To introduce a list (three or more items).

He spoke four languages: French, German, Russian, and Chinese.

(3) To separate hour and minute figures in writing time.

The Boston train leaves at 10:35 P.M.

Dash (—). The dash is used
(1) To indicate a break in thought.

I'll help you—if you want help.

(2) Before a summary statement.

Food, clothing, shelter—these are the basic necessities.

Parentheses ( ). Parentheses are used to enclose an aside or an explanation.

She was just 18 (the legal age for voting).
He was (and still is) my friend.

Hyphen (-).   The hyphen is used

(1) To separate the syllables of a word that falls at the end of a line of writing and must be continued on the following line.

If you have any doubt, consult the schedule about the time of the train.

(2) To divide the parts of a compound word.

forty-five
brother-in-law

Apostrophe (').   The apostrophe is used

(1) To denote the possessive (ownership) case of nouns and indefinite pronouns.

The boy's coat was lost.
Boys' overcoats are on sale.
Everybody's business is nobody's business.

(2) To indicate that figures or letters have been left out.

The class of '64 held its reunion.
It isn't fair to the group.
I'll come with you.

(3) To form the plural of letters and figures.

Dot your *i*'s and cross your *t*'s.
Your 3's look like 8's.

Quotation Marks (" ").   Quotation marks are used

(1) To enclose a direct quotation (the exact words of a speaker).

"Are you ready?" she called.
"It will take less time," Tom's father said, "if you will help me."
A quotation within a quotation is enclosed in single quotation marks.
"Then," he continued, "we heard the cry 'Breakers ahead!' "
If a direct quotation consists of more than one paragraph, put quotation marks at the beginning of each paragraph and at the end of the last paragraph only.

(2) To enclose the title of a poem, a short story, a song, or an article if the title appears in a sentence.

Canada's national anthem is "O Canada."

Italics or Underlining.   Italics in printed matter are the same as underlining in writing or typescript. They are used

(1) To indicate the title of a book, play, motion picture, newspaper, or magazine if the title appears in a sentence.

The girl's favorite novel is *The Yearling*.

(2) To show the name of a ship or an airplane if the name appears in a sentence.

The *Queen Elizabeth 2* was one of the largest ocean liners.
Charles Lindbergh crossed the Atlantic Ocean in the *Spirit of St. Louis*.

(3) To indicate foreign words or phrases.

The Latin words *id est* means "that is."

Capitals.   Capitalize the following:

(1) The first word of every sentence.

The meeting began promptly.

(2) In many poems, the first word of a line.

It is an ancient Mariner,
And he stoppeth one of three.

(3) The first word of a direct quotation (unless the quotation is used as a part of your own sentence).

Patrick Henry cried, "Give me liberty, or give me death!"
The candidate called for a "new look in government."

(4) Proper nouns (names of particular persons, places, or things) and most adjectives derived from proper nouns.

Massachusetts	Sunday
Fourth of July	Fifth Avenue
Atlantic Ocean	June
Middle Ages	Red Cross
World War II	Protestant
House of Commons	Catholic
Council of Trent	Magna Carta
Supreme Court	European
King George V	Spanish

(5) Nouns and pronouns referring to the Deity (God) and sacred writings.

God	Bible
Allah	Old Testament
Torah	Great Spirit
Koran	Yahweh

(6) Titles used with proper names or in place of proper names.

Captain Jones	Her Majesty

(7) In literary titles, the first and last words and all other words except articles, coordinating conjunctions, and short prepositions.

The Wind in the Willows
A Child's Garden of Verses

(8) The words *North, South, East,* and *West* when they denote a recognized area.

The West is noted for its beautiful scenery and climate.

(9) Words denoting family relationship when used instead of the person's name or when used with the name (but not when a possessive pronoun is used).

Mother	my cousin
Uncle John	her father

(10) The pronoun I.
If you wait, I will get the book.

(11) The first word and all nouns in the salutation of a letter; the first word only in the complimentary close.

Dear Jack,	Very truly yours,
Dear Madam or Sir:	Sincerely,

(12) The first word of main topics and subtopics in an outline.

I. Means of promoting health
A. Balanced diet
B. Proper exercise
C. Adequate rest

Do not capitalize the following:

(1) Names of seasons—winter, spring, fall, summer—when used in a sentence.
It was a hot summer.

(2) Subjects of study, except languages, when used in a sentence.
I chose algebra and French.

(3) *North*, *south*, *east*, or *west* when referring to direction.
The plane was flying north.

Any writer, from a student doing homework to a country's president preparing a speech, must organize ideas and state them strongly and clearly. Punctuation is important. We should know how to use punctuation to help make our meaning clear.

MARY C. FOLEY
Author, *Language for Daily Use*

PUNIC WARS

Ancient Rome and Carthage, a city-state in North Africa, fought three wars with each other. They are known as the Punic Wars, from the Latin word for Phoenicians, an early people who founded Carthage. The conflicts resulted from competition between the two states for control of the island of Sicily and the western Mediterranean Sea. Rome was victorious in all three wars, the last of which resulted in the destruction of Carthage.

The First Punic War (264–241 B.C.) was fought mainly in Sicily. It was especially noteworthy because it saw the development of the Roman Navy. Neither side was able to win until the Romans succeeded in forcing the Carthaginians to the western part of Sicily and then defeated the Carthaginian fleet in a great naval battle. As a result of its defeat, Carthage was forced to give up the island and pay an enormous war tax.

The Second Punic War (218–201 B.C.) stemmed from Roman fears that Carthage, involved in the conquest of Spain, would use Spanish resources and soldiers to start a new war. Rome demanded that Carthage give up some of its Spanish territory. War broke out when Hannibal, the Carthaginian general in Spain, refused Rome's demands and crossed the Alps to invade Italy. For the next 16 years, Hannibal ravaged Roman territory and defeated the Romans in four major battles.

Rome, however, refused to surrender. In 202 B.C., Hannibal was forced to return to Africa to face a Roman army threatening Carthage. The Romans defeated Hannibal at Zama, west of the city, ending the war.

To keep Carthage in check, Rome deprived the city of its navy and its Spanish possessions. It also established a rival North African state called Numidia. The Third Punic War (149–146 B.C.) broke out when Carthage, angered over Numidian raids against its territory, attacked Rome's ally. The Romans followed the advice of a senator named Cato, who ended every speech with the words, "Carthage must be destroyed." They declared war on Carthage, which immediately surrendered. But the Carthaginians rebelled when they learned that Rome intended to force them from their city into a new one. After a difficult siege lasting three years, the Romans captured Carthage and destroyed it. It marked the end of Rome's most feared enemy.

Some 30 years later the Romans established their own colony on the site in what is now Tunisia. It eventually became the Roman city of Carthage, the leading city, after Rome itself, in the western half of the Roman Empire.

R. BRUCE HITCHNER
University of Virginia

See also HANNIBAL.

HAND PUPPET　　　　　**ROD PUPPET**　　　　　**SHADOW PUPPET**

PUPPETS AND MARIONETTES

A puppet is any animated figure that is directly controlled by a human being. A marionette is a puppet that is operated from above by strings attached to its body.

The origin of the puppet is still something of a mystery. Some historians think puppets were first made along the banks of the Ganges River in India. Others claim that the Egyptians were the first to invent puppets and marionettes. Well-preserved marionettes have been found among the relics of ancient Egyptian tombs. Chinese puppets and those of Japan and other Oriental countries also are a very old tradition, going back hundreds of years. The Greeks, too, according to the earliest accounts that have come down to us, had puppet theaters. Later, the Romans borrowed puppetry from the Greeks, as they did other art forms. Both Greek and Roman puppet shows were given in private homes, as well as in public places in the cities. Traveling shows gave performances on the road.

Every other country in Europe has had marionettes and puppets of one kind or another. Of them all, Italy is perhaps best known for its puppetry. In the Middle Ages, Italian showmen carried their *castelli dei burattini* (portable puppet theaters) to England, Germany, Spain, and France. These countries then adapted the shows to their own tastes.

At first the plays presented by the puppet theaters consisted of sacred scenes from the Old and New Testament, and stories of saints and martyrs. Then fables and comic characters and everyday situations were introduced. One of the most famous Italian puppets was a character called **Pulcinella**, a rogue and a merrymaker. When the Italian puppeteers took to traveling the highways and visiting the villages of France with their merry puppet shows, Pulcinella had his name changed to the French form, Polichinelle. In 1662 Polichinelle was brought to London. There his name was changed to Punch, and he was given a wife named Judy. Punch is a real fighter and triumphs over everybody, including the devil. Generations of audiences have delightedly watched bad old Punch batting Judy around and gaily whacking his way through life with his stick. Punch first appeared in America in the mid-1700's, much to the amusement of audiences in Philadelphia and New York.

Puppetry has been developed to a high art in the theater. Some puppet theaters are world famous, particularly the Central State Puppet Theater of Sergei Obraztsov in Moscow. Other well-known companies include the Lanchester Marionettes at Stratford-on-Avon, England; the Salzburg Marionette Theater of Hermann Aicher in Vienna, Austria; the Teatro del Nahuatl in Mexico City; and the Théâtre du Vrai Guignol in Paris. Through-

FINGER PUPPET

VENTRILOQUIST'S DUMMY

MARIONETTE

out Germany and Austria, **Hanswurst** and **Kasperl**, the traditional German puppet characters, continue to perform on many toy stages.

The Bunraku is the well-known puppet play of Japan. Puppeteers, dressed in black and working in full view of the audience, use rods to operate the figures, which are more than 1 meter, or about 4 feet, tall.

Television has made puppets very popular in the United States. **Howdy Doody**, **Kukla** and **Ollie**, the **Muppets**, and the Bil and Cora Baird puppets all became television favorites. Hand, or glove, puppets also became a special feature of several children's television programs, such as "Sesame Street" and "Captain Kangaroo."

▶ **KINDS OF PUPPETS**

There are six basic kinds of puppets.

The **hand puppet**, also known as the fist puppet, glove puppet, or guignol, is worn over the hand like a glove. The index finger is inserted in the neck, and the thumb and middle finger in the arms.

The **rod puppet**, sometimes called the stick puppet, is supported from below by a rod held in one hand, while the other hand operates rods attached to the puppet's hands. It is particularly popular in the Far East.

The **shadow puppet** is a form of rod puppet. As its name suggests, its shadow is cast on a cloth screen by a strong light from behind. In more elaborate shows the figures are made of translucent (light-passing) colored material, such as plastic or parchment, so that both color and shape are shown on the screen. Through special design and clever joining of body parts, delightful animation is worked by the attached rods.

The **finger puppet** gets its name from the use of the puppeteer's index and middle fingers as the puppet's legs. Shoes fit over the ends of these fingers, and the body is held in position by an elastic strap over the puppeteer's hand. For the stage, which is a regular tabletop, the puppeteer's arms may be disguised by long, black sleeves.

The **ventriloquist's dummy** is usually about one half adult size. Seated on the ventriloquist's knee, it is supported and animated by one hand through its back. The act consists of action and conversation between the dummy and the ventriloquist, who makes the dummy seem to talk.

The **marionette**, or string-operated puppet, is the most complicated of all types. It is the only kind of puppet that can be moved freely around the total stage area. Great skill and experience are necessary to make and operate the kind of marionette you probably have seen the professional puppeteers use. This kind requires 30 or more strings. There is a simpler marionette, however, which requires only seven or nine strings.

▶ HOW TO MAKE A HAND PUPPET

This is the simplest of all puppets to use. It is the one favored by some of the world's most famous puppeteers.

The Head

Carve the head and features simply from a material called **Styrofoam**. You can buy this at lumberyards, hobby stores, and some department stores. It is a light, porous plastic that can easily be carved with a sharp knife. For the puppet's neck make a cardboard cylinder 3 inches long that fits snugly down over the index finger of either hand. Make a hole in the base of the head and insert the cardboard neckpiece.

Cover the entire head and neck with three layers of papier-mâché, crisscrossed and pressed down firmly. Papier-mâché may be made of heavy brown paper torn in pieces about 1 inch wide and 6 inches long. Soak these pieces of paper in wheat paste (wallpaper paste), obtainable at a paint or hardware store. After the pieces have been soaked, remove them from the wheat paste, squeeze out excess paste, and apply them to the head. Refine the features of the head by final modeling of the papier-mâché.

Body

Outline the body foundation pattern on paper around the operator's hand and forearm. Allow ¾ inch extra at neck and sleeves and 1½ to 2 inches extra for the rest of the pattern. Cut two layers of heavy muslin from this pattern. Sew the two pieces together, leaving ⅜-inch seams. Turn the finished body foundation inside-out. Attach the head to the neck of the foundation with glue and cord. Sew felt or stuffed cloth hands, or glue carved hands, to the foundation sleeve ends. Costume the puppet over the foundation. Wigs can be made from felt, fur, hair, or yarn or can be modeled in papier-mâché and painted along with the rest of the head.

Operating the Hand Puppet

Rehearse in front of a mirror, always holding the puppet upright. Practice making the puppet express joy, sorrow, anger, and other emotions by bending and straightening the fingers. The human hand can be very expres-

HOW TO MAKE A HAND PUPPET

sive, and can be the puppet it controls. Try to develop the puppet's personality through a distinct style of action (fast or slow, graceful or jerky). Make the puppet appear to listen as well as talk, think, and have feelings. Make it handle objects. If you have a puppet on each hand, make them dance with each other, shake hands, fight, wrestle, and so on. Practice and imagination will make your puppet "come alive."

▶ THE HAND-PUPPET STAGE

You can make a simple stand-up or sit-down hand-puppet stage in a doorway by hanging a blanket on a rod just high enough to hide yourself from the audience. Or you can make a simple portable stage from a cardboard mattress container, obtainable from most furniture stores. Slit the back of the container down the middle and open the two halves at right angles to the front for side wings and supports. Cut out a stage opening the size and height from the floor you want. Attach a window shade for the front curtain and a black curtain at the back of the stage for a backdrop.

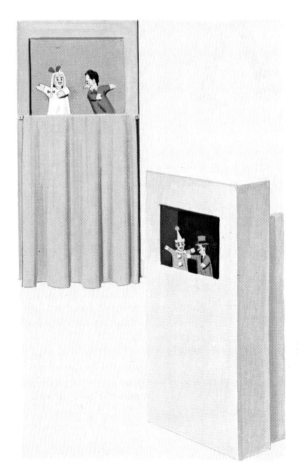

▶ HOW TO MAKE A MARIONETTE

The seven-string marionette will not be difficult for you to make, and it will be fun to learn to operate it.

Inexpensive stuffed cloth dolls or teddy bears make good marionettes, but you must do certain things to them for this purpose. Remove the arms and legs. Separate the arms at the elbows, and the legs at the knees and ankles. Remove some of the stuffing at these parts of the arms and legs to make them more limber. Then sew them back together loosely.

Take enough stuffing out of the stomach so that the doll bends easily at the waist, and stitch across. Do the same with the neck so that the head can turn and nod, and stitch across the neck. You can change the face of your doll by making new features with papier-mâché.

Weight the feet with pebbles or add wooden feet to your marionette to make it walk more firmly.

Stuffed cloth animals, too, can be made into marionettes by putting joints in the legs and weighting the feet so they will be steady on the stage.

Stringing the Marionette

Attach seven strings to the marionette—two to the hands, two to the knees, two to the sides of the head (above or behind the ears), and one to the back to make the marionette bend over.

Use black waxed thread or woven fishline about 3 feet (1 meter) long.

To manage those strings that make the marionette move, you need two controls. One is the main control, which can be cut from ¼-inch (6 millimeter) plywood, as shown in the diagram below, with holes bored for strings at

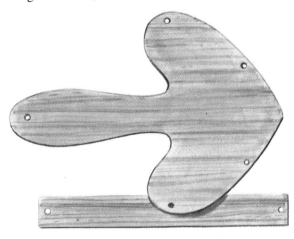

points indicated. This control works the back, head, and hands. The second control is a plywood crossboard with holes bored at both ends for the knee strings. After putting the strings through the holes in the controls, you can attach a bead to the end of each one or knot the string to keep it from slipping back through the hole.

Operating the Marionette

Hold the main control in the left hand and the leg bar in the right hand. Then feel the weight of the marionette by lifting it a few inches off the floor and setting it down again so it does not sag. Repeat this exercise to develop basic control. Next, without operating the leg bar, move the marionette from one part of the stage to another with careful timing and graceful motion. Then make the marionette sit and stand. Start moving the arms and hands. The hand string is continuous so that the hands may be moved separately or together—by pulling the right string only. If you want your marionette to move gracefully, you must learn to move the hand strings without jerks. Talk for your marionette, moving the hands and head meaningfully.

Walking is perhaps the most difficult thing to make a marionette do well. It requires much practice. First, keeping the marionette in place a few inches off the stage floor, move the leg bar so that the puppet's legs swing freely back and forth like pendulums. Walk the marionette in place, moving it slightly up and down with each step. Then start walking it around the stage.

Do not forget that only practice and more practice can teach you how to make your marionette do all the things you want it to in an almost natural manner.

The Marionette Stage

You can make a simple marionette stage in your home by using a doorway or archway. Cloth can be draped to hide you from your audience as you stand on the floor or a low table and work your marionette from behind a cloth backdrop fastened between two chairs or on a frame.

You will probably want to paint your backdrop. This is how to do it:

(1) Make on paper a small painted sketch of a scene.

(2) Stretch medium-weight unbleached muslin (a kind of cloth) on a wood frame for the backdrop.

(3) Copy your sketch on the muslin with chalk.

(4) Using packaged fabric dyes, obtainable at 10-cent stores, paint the backdrop over the chalk sketch. Use ordinary flat brushes.

There are many plays written for puppet performances, but most of them are too difficult for beginners. You can have fun creating your own simple play or adapting one from a fairy tale or nursery rhyme.

RUFUS ROSE
Rufus Rose Marionettes

"BUFFALO" BOB SMITH
Creator of Howdy Doody

See also VENTRILOQUISM.

PURIM

The festival of Purim is the most joyous of all Jewish holidays. It is a time of feasting, merrymaking, and thanksgiving, for it celebrates the rescue of the Jews of Persia many centuries ago from a plot to destroy them.

Purim is observed on the 14th day of the Hebrew month Adar, which falls in March or in the latter part of February. It is celebrated at a slightly different time during leap years. Purim, also called the Feast of Lots, is so named because the day chosen for the killing of the Jews was decided by chance, or lots. The Hebrew word for "lot" is *pur*.

The events of the Purim story, as told in the Book of Esther in the Bible, took place in Shushan (Susa), the capital city of Persia, during the reign of King Ahasuerus in the 5th century B.C. Haman, prime minister to King Ahasuerus, is the villain of the story. Queen Esther, the King's Jewish wife, is the heroine, and Mordecai, her cousin, is the hero.

Haman hated the Jews because Mordecai, one of their leaders, refused to bow down to him. Haman determined to punish Mordecai by destroying him and all the Jews in the kingdom. Haman aroused the King's anger by telling him that the Jews did not keep the King's laws. (King Ahasuerus did not know that his wife, Esther, was Jewish or that she was related to Mordecai.) Haman asked that the Jews be destroyed. The King consented.

Mordecai learned of the plan and asked Esther to plead with her husband for the lives of her people. Esther told the King about Haman's plot to kill the Jews. She begged Ahasuerus to save her people. From the court records, the King learned how Mordecai had once saved his life. Ahasuerus sent for Haman and asked how a man who pleased his King should be honored. Haman believed he was the man the King was thinking of. He advised that the man should be dressed in the King's robes and crown and should ride through the town on the King's horse. The King directed that this be done with Mordecai and that Haman be hanged on the gallows that Haman had prepared for Mordecai. The threatened massacre of the Jews turned into a victory.

Purim is celebrated in many ways. At the morning and evening services, the Book of Esther, called the *Megillah*, is read in the synagogue. Whenever the name of Haman is mentioned, a wave of noise sweeps over the congregation. The children are encouraged to take part in the uproar. They sound wooden rattles called groggers. The children as well as their elders enjoy the noisy change from the usual quiet behavior that marks the Jewish religious service.

In synagogues and other places people present plays and hold masquerade parties as part of the Purim celebration. The most popular costumes are those of Haman, Mordecai, and Queen Esther. Prizes are given for the best costumes. Gifts are exchanged by families and friends, and money and gifts are given to the poor. Purim banquets are held in homes, to which friends and neighbors are invited. Special cakes called *hamantaschen* are served. These are three-cornered cakes filled with poppy-seeds mixed with honey. The design for their shape is supposed to be that of the three-cornered hat that Haman wore when he was prime minister to Ahasuerus.

RABBI MORTIMER J. COHEN
Author, *Pathways Through the Bible*

The holiday of Purim is a time for merrymaking. Jewish children dress up as the main characters of the Book of Esther and participate in plays and carnivals. The beautiful Queen Esther (*at right*) and the wicked Haman (*left*) in his tri-cornered hat are the most popular character costumes.

PUSAN

Pusan is the chief seaport and the second largest city of the Republic of Korea (South Korea) and one of the leading ports of Asia. Its name, which means "pot [shaped] mountains," is derived from the surrounding mountains, which are shaped like Korean cooking pots.

Pusan is located on the southeastern tip of the Korean peninsula, facing the Korea Strait, which separates this part of the country from Japan. The city has an area of 167 square miles (432 square kilometers) and a population of more than 3.5 million. Pusan has the status of a special city, and its mayor, who is appointed by the president, has the rank of a government cabinet member.

Economic Importance. Pusan is a major industrial center as well as the nation's chief port. Its economic activities include shipbuilding and the manufacture of automobiles, textiles, shoes, machinery, chemicals, and a wide range of electronic goods. The city also serves as a base for the industry and commerce of surrounding Kyonsang Province and for much of the countryside beyond.

Places of Interest. Pusan has a variety of recreational and cultural attractions. Haeundae Beach is South Korea's most popular beach resort. Songdo (Song Island), an amusement area, and the Tongnae hot springs are other favorite spots. The nearby mountains are dotted with Buddhist temples; the largest, Pomosa, has many national cultural treasures. Pusan has two universities, Pusan National University and Dong-A University. The city is also the site of the United Nations cemetery, which contains the remains of many U.S. and allied soldiers killed in the Korean War of 1950–53.

History. The Pusan region has been continuously inhabited for some 3,000 years. Because of a fear of roving pirates, however, the Koreans for many centuries did not build their cities directly on the coast. Pusan first appears under its present name in 1368 as a port for rice shipments to Japan. It was opened to general foreign trade in 1876.

Pusan's beginnings as a major industrial city date from the period of Japanese colonial rule (1910–45). During the Korean War, it was the chief supply base for United Nations and South Korean forces fighting the Communist invasion from the North. For a time, the area known as the Pusan perimeter was the only part of South Korea still held by its defenders. Pusan also served as the temporary capital of the country, and its population was swelled by great numbers of refugees.

The growth of South Korea's economy following the war led to the development of other port cities. Nevertheless, Pusan still handles about half of the country's trade as well as providing much of its industrial output.

DAVID I. STEINBERG
Author, *Korea: Nexus of East Asia*

Pusan is the second largest city and the chief seaport of the Republic of Korea (South Korea). It is also one of the nation's most important industrial centers.

PUZZLES

A puzzle is a problem or device created to challenge your mind. People have always enjoyed solving puzzles. Oral riddles, the earliest known form of puzzles, are thought to have begun long ago with the development of language.

There are three broad classes of puzzles: riddles and word puzzles (see CROSSWORD PUZZLES and CHARADES in Volume C); mathematical puzzles (see NUMBER PUZZLES AND GAMES in Volume N); and mechanical puzzles, which are described below. Historical evidence tells us that all three classes of puzzles were present in the Middle East as far back as three to four thousand years ago.

Put-Together Puzzles

Put-together puzzles are solved by assembling or fitting the pieces together. The **jigsaw puzzle**, the most popular put-together puzzle, was invented around 1760 by the London mapmaker John Spilsbury as a way to teach geography to children. Another puzzle, the Chinese **Tangram**, has been popular since the 1800's. It uses seven pieces, called tans, that can be assembled in various ways to form silhouettes of people, animals, and objects.

Sam Loyd, America's greatest puzzle maker, designed thousands of puzzles in the late 1800's and the early 1900's. One of his best is the **Trick Mules Puzzle**, which has three rectangular pieces showing two riders and two mules. To solve the puzzle, a person must arrange the pieces (without bending or folding them) so that the two riders are riding at a fast pace. It sounds simple, but it is very difficult.

Take-Apart Puzzles

In a take-apart puzzle, the goal is to open the object, take the object apart, or find a secret compartment. Among the many take-apart puzzles are wooden balls with secret compartments, locks with hidden keyholes, and puzzle boxes with sliding panels. The object of the **Three Ring Puzzle** is to remove the rings without bending the bar running through them. Many kinds of products and events were advertised on this type of puzzle in the 1890's.

Interlocking Puzzles

Interlocking puzzles, which can be simple cubes or complex geometric shapes, are meant to be taken apart and then put back together. The three-dimensional wooden cross-shaped interlocking puzzles are called "burrs" because they resemble the seed burs of plants. In 1890, William Altekruse invented an interlocking burr puzzle that used twelve identical pieces. Stewart Coffin, a modern designer of interlocking puzzles, created a

---

PUZZLES TO MAKE AND SOLVE

Tangram:

Copy the seven tans shown below on a 5-by 8-inch index card. Cut them out and use them to form the five figures on the left.

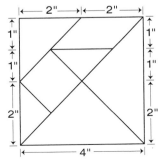

14-15 Puzzle:

Cut a $3\frac{1}{8}$ - by $3\frac{1}{8}$ -inch square hole in a piece of thick cardboard. Glue this piece onto another piece of cardboard that is the same size but without a hole. Write the numbers 1 through 15 on small pieces of paper and glue these to 15 pennies. Within the square hole, put the first 13 pennies in numerical order. Then place numbers 14 and 15 in reverse order, as shown. Now try to put all the pennies in numerical order by sliding them around within the square.

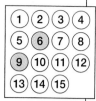
similar burr puzzle with 14 identical pieces in the 1970's.

Disentanglement Puzzles

The object of disentanglement puzzles is to remove parts such as rings or loops of string that are trapped within them. In the late 1800's, Sam Loyd used a loop of string fastened to a 6-inch-long stick to create the **Buttonhole Puzzle**. The object of this puzzle was to remove the string loop, which was fastened through the buttonhole, without cutting the string. One of Loyd's most successful puzzles, it was used as a promotional item for the New York Life Insurance Company.

Sequential Movement Puzzles

In sequential movement puzzles, pieces are moved around according to rules in order to reach a certain goal. The **Fifteen Puzzle**, a sliding block puzzle with 15 numbered blocks, appeared in 1880 and is still popular. In one version, the 14-15 Puzzle, the 15 blocks were placed in numerical order except for the last two, which were reversed. The challenge was to rearrange the blocks into the correct numerical order by sliding them around within a confined space.

Another famous, and very difficult, sequential movement puzzle is **Rubik's Cube**. In the 1980's, this cube became one of the most popular puzzles of all time. The cube initially has a different solid color on each of its six sides. The colors can be scrambled by twisting the cube in different directions. The object of the puzzle is to restore the colors as they appeared initially on each of the sides.

Dexterity Puzzles

Dexterity puzzles are solved through eye-hand coordination, and sometimes through logical thinking. **Cup and Ball** dexterity puzzles, in which a wooden ball is tossed in the air and caught in a cup or on the pointed end of a stick, have been popular for at least 400 years. A rolling-ball dexterity puzzle called **Pigs in Clover** was a huge success when it was introduced in 1889, and a modern version is still popular today. Anyone with enough patience and dexterity can solve it by rolling four marbles into the "pen" in the center of the circular maze.

Puzzle Jugs

Puzzle jugs were quite popular in Europe 400 years ago. The object of a **puzzle jug** is to drink from the container without spilling the contents through numerous holes. The secret is to find and use the hidden built-in tubes to suck the liquid as you would with a straw.

JERRY SLOCUM
Author, *The Puzzle Arcade* and
Puzzles Old & New

See also CHARADES; CROSSWORD PUZZLES; NUMBER PUZZLES AND GAMES; WORD GAMES.

PYLE, ERNIE. See JOURNALISM (Profiles).

PYRAMIDS. See EGYPTIAN ART AND ARCHITECTURE.

PYTHAGOREAN THEOREM. See GEOMETRY; MATHEMATICS, HISTORY OF.

DICTIONARY ENTRIES

The following list contains brief biographies and short entries on many different subjects. It can be used for quick reference. To find references to all the information in the encyclopedia on a particular subject, consult the Index.

Paca, William (1740–99), American Revolutionary leader, b. near Abington, Md. A signer of the Declaration of Independence, he was also a member (1774–79) of the Continental Congress, governor of Maryland (1782–85), and U.S. district judge for Maryland (1789–99).

Pacific States, three states of the United States—California, Oregon, and Washington—situated on the Pacific Ocean in the extreme western part of the nation. They are noted for their varied and magnificent scenery. They are also national leaders in agriculture, manufacturing, fishing, forestry, shipping, and tourism. Alaska (bordering the Pacific and Arctic oceans) and Hawaii (in the Pacific) are sometimes included as Pacific States.

Paderewski (pa-der-EF-skee), **Ignace Jan** (1860–1941), Polish concert pianist and patriot, b. Kurylowka, Poland. Paderewski was one of the best-known pianists of his time. He also worked tirelessly for Polish independence. When Poland gained independence after World War I, he served (1919) as the first prime minister of the Republic of Poland. After Germany invaded Poland in World War II, he was chosen president of the Polish parliament in exile (1940). He died in New York City and was buried in Arlington National Cemetery. In 1992 his remains were returned to Poland.

Paganini (pa-ga-NI-ni), **Niccolò** (1782–1840), Italian violinist and composer, b. Genoa. He made his debut in Genoa (1793) and later appeared throughout Europe. Widely acclaimed for his extraordinary virtuosity, he introduced new techniques of violin playing. He was also a guitarist and viola player. Among his compositions are 24 capriccios for unaccompanied violin, two violin concertos, and several sets of variations for violin. A theme from the *Capriccio in A minor* was used by Brahms, Rachmaninoff, and other composers for variation works.

Page, Ruth (1899–1991), American dancer and choreographer, b. Indianapolis, Ind. She was the leading dancer and the ballet director of the Chicago Opera Company in the 1930's and 1940's and performed in Europe and the Far East. She was ballet director of the Chicago Lyric Opera (1954–69) and choreographer and director for the Chicago Opera Ballet (1956–66). She choreographed many ballets adapted from the plots of operas, such as *Carmen* and *La Traviata.*

Paine, Robert Treat (1731–1814), American lawyer and statesman, b. Boston, Mass. A signer of the Declaration of Independence, he was also a member (1774–78) of the Continental Congress. Paine served as attorney general of Massachusetts (1777–90) and judge of the Massachusetts Supreme Court (1790–1804).

Paisley, Ian R. K. (1926–   ), Northern Ireland clergyman and political leader, b. Co. Armagh. A founder of the Free Presbyterian Church, he was elected to the British Parliament (1970) and is a former member (1970–72) of the Northern Ireland Parliament (Stormont). He was elected to the European Parliament (1979) and to the Second Northern Ireland Assembly (1982). An uncompromising Unionist, he has opposed any attempts to separate Northern Ireland from Britain and join it to the Republic of Ireland.

Palestine Liberation Organization (PLO), a political organization that seeks to form an independent nation for Palestinian Arabs in land controlled by Israel. Founded in 1964, it is an umbrella organization of various guerrilla groups. Yasir Arafat is chairman of its executive committee. In 1974 at Rabat, Morocco, Arab government leaders agreed that the PLO was the "sole legitimate representative of the Palestinian people." The PLO has used both terrorism and diplomacy in trying to achieve its aims. In 1993 the PLO signed an accord with Israel giving it self-rule in the Gaza Strip and the West Bank city of Jericho. Palestinians took control of the two areas in 1994.

Palmer, Alice Elvira Freeman (1855–1902), American educator, b. Colesville, N.Y. A pioneer of higher education for women, she was president of Wellesley College (1882–87) and dean of women at the University of Chicago (1892–95). She helped found the Association of Collegiate Alumnae (later the American Association of University Women).

Pan, in Greek mythology, god of woods and shepherds. He is often pictured as half-man and half-goat dancing with nymphs and playing the syrinx (shepherd's flute), a musical instrument made from reeds. It was believed that Pan frightened lonely travelers, and hence the word "panic" now means any sudden or groundless fear. His cult originated in Arcadia and spread throughout Greece. The Romans identified him with their god Faunus.

Panacea (pan-a-CE-a) ("all-healer"), in Greek mythology, goddess of health and daughter of Aesculapius, the god of medicine. With her sister, Hygeia (source of the word "hygiene"), she performed the temple rites and cared for the sacred serpents. The word "panacea" has come to mean a cure-all or single remedy for every disease.

Pan American Games, a series of athletic competitions held among Western Hemisphere nations. The Pan American Games are held every four years in the year preceding the Olympic Games. They were begun to encourage friendship among nations of the Western Hemisphere and to give amateur athletes experience in international competition. The ruling body of the games is the Pan American Sports Organization (PASO). Olympic committees from participating nations choose the athletes who will compete in the Pan American Games. The first Pan American Games were held in Buenos Aires in 1951.

Pan American Highway, an international system of highways extending nearly 17,000 miles (27,000 kilometers) south from Alaska to Chile. It is continuous except for an uncompleted stretch in the Darién Gap region in Panama and northwest Colombia. The system includes a highway network in the United States leading to the Mexican border. It then runs

Pan American Highway (continued)

through Mexico and Central America (this segment is known as the Inter-American Highway). Beyond the Darién Gap the Pan American Highway begins again in South America and continues south to Puerto Montt, Chile. Connecting and alternate routes extend the system eastward to Brazil. The highway was first proposed in 1923, and an agreement to complete it was signed in 1936 by all the American republics.

Panch'en Lama

(PON-chen LA-ma), is the title of a Tibetan Buddhist religious leader, second only to the Dalai Lama in importance. He is revered as an incarnation of the Amitabha Buddha. The first Panch'en Lama was designated in the 16th century.

Panhandle,

a geographical term to indicate a long thin strip of land (resembling the handle of a pan). These strips of land usually project from the main part of a territory or state. Panhandle areas in the United States are found in Texas, West Virginia, Alaska, Idaho, and Oklahoma.

Papal States,

former area of nearly 15,500 sq mi (about 40,000 sq km) with a population of more than 3,100,000, over which the pope had complete control. Located in central Italy, the papal states were founded in A.D. 754 and declared an independent monarchy in 1201. After 1870 the states became part of Italy.

Parable

(from Greek *parabole,* meaning "a comparison"), make-believe story that illustrates a moral or religious principle. Parables were told by the early rabbis and included in the Jewish Talmud and Midrash. The form was adopted by Jesus for his teachings.

Parents Without Partners

(PWP), an organization of single parents. Members of Parents Without Partners may be widows, widowers, divorced or separated parents, or those who are raising children alone for other reasons. Founded in 1957, the organization helps single parents solve the problems of raising children alone. It also works to make the idea of single parenthood generally accepted by society. Parents Without Partners has headquarters in Silver Spring, Md., and publishes a monthly magazine called *The Single Parent.*

Parks, Gordon

(1912–), American photographer, film director, journalist, and composer, b. Fort Scott, Kans. Parks was a photographer for *Life* magazine from 1948 to 1972. He published *The Learning Tree* (1963), *Born Black* (1971), *Moments Without Proper Names* (1975), and an autobiography, *A Choice of Weapons* (1966). He is the composer of numerous works for piano and wind instruments. He has also directed such movies as *Shaft, The Super Cops,* and *Leadbelly.*

Parnassus

(par-NAS-sus), a mountain in central Greece, north of the Gulf of Corinth, with an altitude of 8,026 ft (2,446 m). According to the ancient Greeks, Parnassus was sacred to Apollo, Dionysius, and the Muses. It has therefore become a symbol of inspiration for writers and artists.

Parrish, Maxfield

(1870–1966), American artist and illustrator, b. Philadelphia, Pa. He is noted for the design and color, especially a characteristic shade of blue, of his illustrations. Books he illustrated include *Arabian Nights Entertainments* and *Mother Goose in Prose.*

Partisans,

lightly armed guerrilla forces who undermine an enemy, usually in an occupied zone. Although such forces have existed throughout history, the term was popularized during World War II to describe the fighters in German-occupied areas of Europe, especially those in Yugoslavia under leadership of Marshal Tito. The term also refers to followers of a particular party or cause.

Pascal,

a computer language. Pascal was developed in the early 1970's as an educational language. It was designed to teach students about computer programming and computer science. It is named for Blaise Pascal, the French mathematician and philosopher of the 1600's who developed the first mechanical calculator.

Pasternak, Boris Leonidovich

(1890–1960), Russian poet, novelist, and translator, b. Moscow. He is best known for his epic novel *Dr. Zhivago.* The book was refused publication in the Soviet Union because of its anti-Communist views. It was published in the West in 1957. Pasternak was awarded the 1958 Nobel Prize for literature. When the Soviet government threatened to expel Pasternak from the Soviet Union, he refused the award. Pasternak's poetry collections include *Over the Barriers* (1917) and *My Sister Life* (1922). He also translated classical works from many languages into Russian. His autobiography is entitled *Safe Conduct* (1931).

Paton

(PAY-tuhn), **Alan Stewart** (1903–88), South African author, educator, and politician, b. Pietermaritzburg. He worked against South Africa's system of apartheid (racial separation) both in his writings and as founder and president of the multiracial Liberal Party (declared an illegal organization in 1968). Paton had been a teacher and principal of a reform school. But the success of his first novel, *Cry, the Beloved Country* (1948) led him to devote himself to writing. His other novels include *Too Late the Phalarope* (1953) and *Ah, But Your Land is Beautiful* (1981). Paton also wrote two autobiographical works, *Towards the Mountain* (1980) and *Journey Continued* (1988).

Patriarchs

(PAY-tri-arks), original rulers of a tribe or family. The name was used for the ancestral leaders of the Jewish people. Three ancient Jewish patriarchs were Abraham, Isaac, and Jacob. The title has been used since the 600's for the bishops of the five ancient sees (official local seat of a bishop) of Jerusalem, Antioch, Alexandria, Constantinople, and Rome. The Pope of the Roman Catholic Church is also known as the Patriarch of the West.

Patriots' Day,

a holiday celebrated in Maine and Massachusetts on the third Monday in April of each year. The holiday commemorates the battles of Lexington and Concord in the Revolutionary War.

Patroclus

(pa-TRO-clus), in Greek mythology, son of Menoetius and loyal friend of Achilles. Upon Achilles' refusal to fight because of a disagreement with Agamemnon, Patroclus put on Achilles' armor and led the Myrmidons in routing the Trojans. He was slain by Hector and avenged by Achilles, who in grief joined the fighting and took Hector's life.

Patti, Adelina

(Adela Juana Maria Patti) (1843–1919), Spanish-Italian coloratura soprano, b. Madrid, Spain. Following her New York debut in 1859, she appeared throughout

Europe, playing leading roles in operas of Rossini, Bellini, Donizetti, Gounod, and Verdi. She retired from opera in 1895, subsequently appearing in concerts.

Pauli (POW-li), **Wolfgang** (1900–58), Austrian physicist, b. Vienna. He worked on the theory and study of atomic particle behavior. Pauli received the 1945 Nobel Prize in physics for his development of the Pauli exclusion principle, which states that no two electrons in an atom can have the same quantum number. This principle has proved essential in the solving of problems of atomic structure and behavior. Pauli predicted the existence of neutrinos (detected 1956).

Paulist Fathers, Roman Catholic priests of the Missionary Society of St. Paul the Apostle, established in New York, N.Y., in 1858. The principal purpose of the society is to instruct non-Catholics in the Roman Catholic faith, chiefly in the United States.

Pavlova (PAV-lo-va), **Anna** (1885–1931), Russian ballet dancer, b. St. Petersburg. Trained at the Imperial Ballet School, St. Petersburg, she toured Europe and the United States from 1911. With her own company she performed throughout the Americas, Europe, the Orient, Australia, and New Zealand. Her greatest performances included leading roles in *Giselle, The Butterflies,* and *The Dying Swan* (created for her by Michel Fokine).

Paz, Octavio (1914–   ), Mexican writer, b. Mexico City. He was awarded the Nobel Prize for literature in 1990. Paz founded the literary review *Barandal* at age 17 and at 19 published his first book of poetry, *Forest Moon* (1933). In 1943 he received a Guggenheim fellowship that allowed him to travel and study in the United States. Paz entered Mexico's diplomatic service in 1945, serving as ambassador to India from 1962 to 1968. He also taught at several universities, including Harvard. Paz first won fame as a poet. "Sun Stone," a 584-line work structured after the Aztec calendar, is considered his most important poem. His essays were also highly praised, especially *The Labyrinth of Solitude* (1950). Other works include *Collected Poems, 1957–1987* (1987) and the essays *Alternating Current* (1967) and *One Earth, Four or Five Worlds* (1985).

Peale, Norman Vincent (1898–1993), American clergyman, b. Bowersville, Ohio. Ordained in 1922, he was minister of the Marble Collegiate Reformed Church in New York City from 1932 to his retirement in 1984. Through his sermons, newspaper columns, and television programs, he offered advice on the "art of living" and an upbeat religious message. He founded *Guideposts,* an inspirational magazine, and wrote *The Power of Positive Thinking.*

Peck, Gregory (1916–   ), American actor, b. La Jolla, Calif. He appeared in summer stock and on Broadway during the early 1940's. Some of his motion pictures are *Keys of the Kingdom, Twelve O'Clock High, Gentlemen's Agreement, The Man in the Gray Flannel Suit, Roman Holiday, The Guns of Navarone,* and *To Kill a Mockingbird* (for which he won the 1962 Oscar for best actor). In 1982, he made his television debut as Abraham Lincoln in the series *The Blue and the Gray.*

Pelias (PE-lias), in Greek mythology, a son of Poseidon and Tyro and half-brother of King Aeson of Iolcus. He seized the throne of Aeson and later was confronted by Jason, his nephew and the son of Aeson, who claimed the kingship. He refused to give up the throne until Jason returned with the Golden Fleece. Jason returned with the sorceress Medea. She persuaded Pelias' daughters to kill their father by falsely promising them that by killing him, they could restore him to life as a young man.

Pelion (or Pilion), a mountain in Thessaly, Greece. According to an ancient Greek legend, the Aloadae (giants) placed the mountain Pelion on top of Ossa, another mountain, in order to reach Olympus, the home of the gods. Pelion was the home of Chiron, the centaur (half-man and half-horse).

Peninsula, a land formation that is almost entirely surrounded by water. Any piece of land that juts out into a body of water may be called a peninsula. The Arabian Peninsula is the largest peninsula in the world. Other large peninsulas include the Iberian Peninsula (Spain and Portugal) and the Florida peninsula in the United States.

Penn, John (1740–88), American Revolutionary leader, b. Caroline County, Va. He was a member of the North Carolina provincial congress (1775) and the Second Continental Congress (1775–80), and a signer of the Declaration of Independence (1776). He was North Carolina's receiver of taxes under the Articles of Confederation (1784).

Pension, income received when a person retires or becomes disabled and cannot work. Pensions are provided by governments and private businesses, usually based on salary and number of years of service. Self-employed people sometimes set up their own pensions. The term "pension" originally referred to a gift from a sovereign for distinguished service.

Pepin III, the Short (714?–768), Frankish king (751–68). When his father, Charles Martel, died, Pepin assumed the Frankish throne and founded the Carolingian dynasty (751) after deposing Childeric III, the Merovingian king. He assisted Pope Stephen II by defeating King Aistulf of the Lombards and restoring territories, later incorporated into the Papal States, to the pope. He was the father of Charlemagne.

Perelman, S. J. (Sidney Joseph Perelman) (1904–79), American humorist, b. Brooklyn, N.Y. The topics of his satirical essays range from his own childhood to contemporary life in the United States. His essays were published in *The New Yorker* magazine beginning in 1931. Many were also published in collections such as *The Swiss Family Perelman* (1950), *Chicken Inspector No. 23* (1966), *Vinegar Puss* (1975), and *The Last Laugh* (1981). Perelman's screenplay for the film *Around the World in 80 Days* (1956) won an Academy Award.

Peres (perr-ess), **Shimon** (1923–   ), Israeli political leader, b. Wolozyn, Poland. Peres was elected to the Knesset (parliament) in 1959 and was appointed to several cabinet posts. He became minister of defense in 1974 and leader of the Labor Party in 1977. In 1984, Peres formed a national unity government with Likud, serving as prime minister until 1986, and as foreign minister from 1986 to 1988. Named foreign minister in a Labor-led government in 1992, he helped negotiate accords with the Palestine Liberation Organization (PLO) in 1993 and 1995. He succeeded Yitzhak Rabin as prime minister after Rabin's assassination in 1995 but was defeated in the 1996 election.

Perestroika (per-es-STROY-ka), Russian for "restructuring" or "rebuilding." The term was used by Soviet leader

Perestroika (continued)

Mikhail Gorbachev in his outline of reforms in 1987. It referred to the necessity of restructuring Soviet society and the economy to better meet the needs of the people. The economic reforms included measures to make state-run industries more competitive and efficient. But it failed to prevent the breakup of the Soviet Union in late 1991.

Pérez de Cuéllar (PEH-res de KWAY-yar), **Javier** (1920–), Peruvian diplomat and the secretary-general of the United Nations (1982–92), b. Lima. Before he was elected in 1981 to succeed Secretary-General Kurt Waldheim, Pérez de Cuéllar had held a number of diplomatic posts. He was Peru's ambassador to Switzerland (1964–66) and to the Soviet Union (1969–71). He headed his country's mission to the United Nations (1971–75) and then served as an under secretary-general for special political affairs (1979–81).

Peri (PAY-ri), **Jacopo** (1561–1633), Italian composer, b. Florence. He was a noted singer and musician of Florentine and Ferrara courts. With poet Ottavio Rinuccini (1562–1621), he wrote *Dafne*—the music of which is lost—generally considered to be the first true opera.

Perjury, a legal term meaning the act of lying under oath. Perjury committed in a court of law is a felony.

Perlman, Itzhak (1945–), Israeli violinist, b. Tel Aviv. Perlman's brilliant technique and expressiveness have made him one of the most widely praised violinists of the present day. Although he was disabled by polio at the age of 4 (and must use leg braces and crutches), he overcame the disability and began to perform by the age of 10. In 1958 he went to the United States, where he studied at the Juilliard School in New York City. He made his professional debut at Carnegie Hall in New York City in 1963. The next year he won the Leventritt Memorial Competition, which brought him engagements with leading orchestras. He has since performed in major cities throughout the world and has made many recordings.

Perón, Eva (María Eva Duarte de Perón) (1919–52), Argentinian political figure, b. Los Toldos, Argentina. An actress, she became Juan Perón's second wife in 1945 and helped her husband rise to the presidency in the following year. Without holding any official position, she became a powerful force in Argentinian politics. Popularly known as Evita, she was a stirring orator and won the devotion of the poor. She helped Argentinian women gain the right to vote, introduced educational reforms, and was involved in the government's welfare program. Her plans to run as vice president with Perón were blocked by the army, which opposed her.

Perrault, Charles (1628–1703), French poet and critic, b. Paris. He is best remembered for compiling the famous "Mother Goose" fairy tales. Perrault collected the traditional stories to entertain his children, retelling them in the simple and charming manner by which they are known today. The collection, known as *Tales of Mother Goose,* included *Cinderella, Little Red Riding Hood, Puss in Boots,* and *Sleeping Beauty.* During his own life, Perrault was famous as the author of the poem *The Century of Louis the Great* (1687). In it he maintained that the writers of his time were superior to those of the ancient world. This view sparked a controversy that raged for years in France.

Perry, Gaylord (1938–), American baseball player, b. Williamston, N.C. The only pitcher to win a Cy Young Award (1972, 1978) in each league. During his career (1962–83), Perry had a won-lost record of 314-265, an earned run average of 3.09, and 3,534 strikeouts. He later admitted to using the illegal spitball. Perry was elected to the Baseball Hall of Fame in 1991.

Pétain (pay-TAN), **Henri Philippe** (1856–1951), French general and political leader, b. Cauchy-a-la-Tour. After his successful defense of Verdun (1916) during World War I, he was made commander in chief of French armies (1917) and marshal of France (1918). He later served as minister of war (1934) and ambassador to Spain (1939). In World War II he was premier and later chief of state of the pro-fascist Vichy government of France (1940–44). He was sentenced to death for treason (1945) but the sentence was commuted. He died in prison.

Peterkin, Julia Mood (1880–1961), American writer, b. Laurens County, S.C. She wrote short stories and novels about black life on southern plantations. Her works include *Scarlet Sister Mary,* which was awarded the Pulitzer Prize (1929); *Green Thursday; Black April;* and *Roll, Jordan, Roll.*

Peterson, Esther Eggertsen (1906–), U.S. government official and consumer adviser, b. Provo, Utah. An advocate of equal opportunity for women, Peterson was active in labor unions in the 1940's and 1950's. From 1961 to 1969 she was assistant secretary of labor. During this time she headed the Women's Bureau of the Department of Labor and served on presidential committees on the status of women and on consumer interests. In the 1970's she worked as a consumer adviser in both private industry and government, and she headed the Consumer Affairs Council (1979–80).

Peter's Pence (Anglo-Saxon *Romefeot,* meaning "Rome-fee"), in the Middle Ages, a yearly tax of a penny per householder paid by peoples of several countries to the Catholic Church in Rome. Originating in England (787) under King Offa of Mercia, it spread to northern European countries in the 900's and 1000's. It was nullified in England (1534) under Henry VIII and disregarded in Europe after the Reformation. Presently (since 1860) the term refers to voluntary contributions of Roman Catholics sent by bishoprics to Rome, constituting part of the Vatican's income.

Peter the Hermit (Peter of Amiens) (1050?–1115), French monk, b. Amiens. An avid supporter of Pope Urban II's call (1096) for a crusade, he aroused popular enthusiasm and set out for Palestine with a group of followers. Most were killed by the Turks at Nicea (1096). Peter and the survivors joined the siege of Antioch (1097–98). Peter tried to desert but was caught and was present at Jerusalem's capture (1098).

Pewter, soft, silvery-gray metal with dull finish, composed chiefly of tin hardened with copper, antimony, bismuth, or lead. Originally made in ancient Rome and medieval Europe, it was widely used for utensils and housewares in the 1600's and 1700's in England, the Netherlands, and colonial North America.

Phaedra (FEE-druh), in Greek mythology, the daughter of Minos and Pasiphae and sister of Ariadne. She married Theseus and fell in love with his son Hippolytus. Enraged by his adamant rejection of her, she killed herself, falsely accusing Hippolytus of assaulting her. Believing her, Theseus with Poseidon's aid put his son to death.

Phaethon (PHAY-et-on), in Greek mythology, the son of Helios and Clymene. Exacting permission from Helios to drive the sun's chariot across the sky for a day, he was unable to control the horses. To prevent him from setting the world ablaze, Zeus killed Phaethon with a thunderbolt, and he plunged into the Eridanus (Po) river. His sisters, the Heliades, inconsolable at his death, were transformed into poplars, their tears perpetually turning into amber.

Pharisees, a Hebrew sect living in Judea in Palestine during the time of Jesus. The word Pharisees comes from the Aramaic language and means "separated ones." The Pharisees studied the first five books of the Old Testament (the Pentateuch) and were strict followers of the traditional oral law. They interpreted Jewish law to the people and formulated a set of strict rules for living. The New Testament tells that Jesus opposed the Pharisees' demands for rules beyond traditional Jewish law and called the Pharisees hypocrites (Matt. 23). Unlike the Sadducees, another group of Jewish scholars, the Pharisees believed in the resurrection of the dead, angels, and free will. Saul (St. Paul) was a Pharisee before he was converted to the Christian faith.

Philemon (phil-E-mon) **and Baucis** (BAU-cis), in Greek mythology, an aged couple of Phrygia. Despite their poverty, they offered hospitality to Zeus and Hermes, who, traveling through the country as humans, had been turned away at all other homes. The gods spared them from a deluge that covered the district, transformed their cottage into a temple, and made them priest and priestess. They desired to die together and so were turned into trees at the same moment.

Philip IV (Philip the Fair) (1268–1314), king of France (1285–1314) and son of Philip III, b. Fontainebleau. His dispute with Pope Boniface VIII resulted in the papal bulls *Clericis laicos* (1296), prohibiting taxation of clergy, and *Unam Sanctam* (1302), declaring the supremacy of papal authority. In retaliation, Philip had Boniface seized. Then he secured election of Pope Clement V, who ruled from Avignon, in France (1305-14). Philip's reign also was marked by centralized administration, curtailment of feudal rights, and persecution of Jews. Philip was called "the Fair" because he was said to be one of the most handsome men of his time.

Philip II (382–336 B.C.), king of Macedon and military commander. After becoming king (359 B.C.), he invaded the borderlands of the Greek city-states. The speeches of Demosthenes, warning Athens against him, were called Philippics—a word still used to indicate condemnation. By 338 B.C. he had conquered and unified Greece. He was chosen to lead Greek armies against Persia but was murdered before starting. He was succeeded by his son Alexander the Great.

Philistines (FIL-is-teens), an ancient people who established themselves in Canaan on the coast of Palestine in about the 1100's B.C. They developed a prosperous civilization and a strong military organization. The name "Palestine" is derived from Philistia, the region they controlled. The Philistines are known largely through the Old Testament. They warred almost continuously with the Israelites until they were defeated by King David. The most familiar biblical story of the period tells of the victory of young David over the Philistine Goliath. In modern times, the word "philistine" has been used as a term of

insult for a narrow-minded, ignorant person more concerned with material than cultural values.

Phobia (FO-bee-a), a very strong, irrational fear. Persons who are faced with these fears experience distressing symptoms such as heart palpitations, sweating, or a feeling of panic. There are dozens of recognized phobias, including claustrophobia, fear of closed or narrow places; agoraphobia, fear of open spaces; xenophobia, fear of strangers; nyctophobia, fear of the dark; and acrophobia, fear of height. Treatment usually involves helping the phobic person to gradually confront the feared object or situation.

Phoebe (PHE-be), in Greek mythology, a Titaness, wife of Coeus and grandmother of Artemis, goddess of the hunt, with whom Phoebe is often erroneously identified. In later writings she is identified with the moon goddess.

Phoenix, legendary bird of ancient Egypt, symbol of the rising and setting sun. A splendid red and gold bird, it burned itself to death in a pyre of spices after living about 500 years. It rose, reborn from the ashes, and flew from its native Arabia to the temple of the sun in Heliopolis, Egypt. For many religions the phoenix symbolizes rebirth.

Phosphorus, in Greek mythology, the morning star. The son of Eos, the goddess of dawn, and Astraeus, he is often represented as a youth holding a torch. The morning star is the single bright star in the dawn sky. It is known today to be the planet Venus.

Phrenology, study of the skull shape as indicating mental abilities and character traits. The theory that each bump on the skull indicates a special ability or characteristic was advanced by Franz Gall and Johann Spurzheim about 1810. Although rejected by many scientists the theory became popular in the 1800's, but was largely discredited by the early 1900's.

Phrygia (PHRIJ-ia), ancient country in central Asia Minor (now Turkey) inhabited by Indo-Europeans who crossed the Dardanelles from Europe in the 1200's B.C. Conquered by Lydians in the 600's B.C., they were subsequently ruled by Persia, Greece, and Rome. Phrygian legend and religion greatly influenced Greek mythology. Gordius and Midas were legendary Phrygian kings.

Physiognomy (phys-i-OG-nomy), theory that temperament and character can be judged by outward appearance, particularly facial features. Johann Kaspar Lavater (1741–1801) stimulated European interest in the theory. Criminologist Cesare Lombroso (1836–1909) tried to connect criminal behavior with physical traits. Some physiognomists claim ability to foretell the future from facial structure. The word "physiognomy" also refers to the characteristic expression of the face.

Piatigorsky (pi-at-i-GOR-ski), **Gregor** (1903–76), Russian-born American cellist, b. Yekaterinoslav (now Dnepropetrovsk). First cellist in the Berlin Philharmonic orchestra (1923–28), he appeared throughout Europe and the Americas in concert and chamber music performances, gaining wide acclaim for his virtuosity.

Pickett, George Edward (1825–75), Confederate general in the U.S. Civil War, b. Richmond, Va. After serving in the

Pickett, George Edward (continued)
Mexican War and in Texas (1849–56), he served on the North-west frontier (1856–61). Resigning from the U.S. Army at the outbreak of the Civil War (1861), he joined the Confederate forces and later was appointed major general in charge of a Virginia division (1862). He led the heroic but futile "Pickett's charge" at Gettysburg against Union forces (1863) and made a valiant stand at Five Forks, Virginia (1865).

Pieces of eight, Spanish coins used in the 1600's and 1700's and circulated in the American colonies, West Indies, and Europe. The coins, made of silver, were stamped with an "8" and valued at eight *reales* (Spanish monetary unit). The coin is frequently mentioned in pirate stories, such as *Treasure Island*.

Pied Piper of Hamelin, in German legend, magician who agreed to rid the rat-infested village of Hamelin of its vermin in return for a certain amount of money. Playing his magical pipe, he lured the rats away and into the Weser River, where they drowned. The townspeople, however, would not pay him, so the Pied Piper took up his pipe and enchanted all the children, who followed him and disappeared into Koppenberg hill. Browning's poem "The Pied Piper of Hamelin" tells this story.

Pierian (py-ER-ian) **spring,** sacred spring located in the ancient region of Macedonia called Pieria, where the Muses were first worshiped. The spring was believed to be the source of poetic inspiration.

Pierrot, a character in French pantomime. He is usually dressed as a clown, his face is painted white, and he wears a white blouse and pantaloons. The character originated in the Italian *Commedia dell'arte,* where he was called Pedrolino.

Pike, Zebulon Montgomery (1779–1813), American soldier, explorer, and discoverer of Pikes Peak in Colorado, b. Lamberton (now a part of Trenton), N.J. A lieutenant in the U.S. Army, in 1805 he led an expedition to trace the upper course of the Mississippi River. Later, on an expedition to explore the headwaters of the Red and Arkansas rivers and scout Spanish settlements in New Mexico, he discovered the mountain peak named in his honor. During the War of 1812 he was promoted to brigadier general. He was killed during an attack against the British in Canada.

Pilâtre de Rozier, Jean François (1754–85), French balloonist, b. Metz. He made the first aerial ascent (1783), in a balloon designed by the Montgolfier brothers, and crossed Paris in the first free balloon flight that same year. He developed and piloted a balloon that used hydrogen and hot-air sacs, but he was killed when the hydrogen exploded.

Pillars of Hercules, two promontories, or land projections, at the eastern end of the Strait of Gibraltar leading into the Mediterranean Sea. One is the Rock of Gibraltar and the other Mount Acho in Morocco. They were called Calpe and Abyla, respectively, in ancient times, and various legends offer explanations of their origin. One relates that the two masses were part of one mountain until Hercules broke through to get to the Mediterranean.

Pilobolus (pi-LAH-buh-lus) **Dance Theatre,** American dance company. Its athletic and experimental dance style combines elements of acrobatics, mime, and modern dance

movements. Pilobolus was founded in 1971 by Moses Pendleton and Jonathan Wolken, two undergraduates at Dartmouth College. Today Pilobolus is based in Washington, Conn. The company's notable works include *Monkshoods' Farewell* (1974), *Untitled* (1975), *Molly's Not Dead* (1978), *Day Two* (1982), and *Land 's Edge* (1986).

Pinkerton, Allan (1819–84), American detective, b. Glasgow, Scotland. He emigrated to the United States (1842). In Chicago, Ill., he set up (1850) his own detective agency (Pinkerton Agency), the first in the United States. He became nationally known when he solved the Adams Express robberies and, during the Civil War, planned President Lincoln's route to his inauguration (1861). He organized secret service and counterespionage activities in Washington, D.C. (1861–62).

Pinocchio (pin-O-kee-o), a wooden puppet who becomes a living boy in *The Adventures of Pinocchio,* by Carlo Collodi. First published in Italian as a story in a children's magazine and then as a book (1883), it has been translated into many languages. Pinocchio's nose grows longer every time he tells a lie, but at the end of the story, he reforms and gets his wish to become a real boy.

Pinter, Harold (1930–   ), British playwright, b. London. The word "Pinteresque" was coined to describe his highly original style, characterized by long pauses in the dialogue. His characters seek security but are afraid to communicate their true feelings. His first full-length play was *The Birthday Party* (1958). *The Caretaker* (1960), *The Homecoming* (1965), *Old Times* (1971), and *Betrayal* (1979) also won praise. Pinter has written screenplays for *The French Lieutenant's Woman* (1981) and other films, some based on his own plays.

Pinzón (peen-THONE) family, three Spanish brothers who accompanied Columbus on his first voyage (1492), b. Palos de la Frontera. Francisco Martín (1440?–93?) piloted the *Pinta,* and Martín Alonso (1440?–93) commanded it. The third brother, Vicente Yáñez (1460?–1524?), commanded the *Niña.* Martín parted from the other ships in November, 1492, and sighted Haiti. Vicente discovered the mouth of the Amazon (1500) and explored (with Juan Diaz de Solís) the coast of Yucatán (1506).

Pisano, Giovanni (1245?–1314?), Italian sculptor and architect, b. Pisa. Son of Nicola Pisano, he assisted (1265–68) his father on the pulpit of the Sienese cathedral. He was chief architect of the Cathedral of Siena and Cathedral of Pisa and builder of the Campo Santo in Pisa. His sculpture, which established the Italian Gothic style, includes the pulpits in the Sant' Andrea di Pistoia in Siena and in the Cathedral of Pisa.

Pisano, Nicola (or Niccolo) (1220?–84?), Italian sculptor and architect, b. Pisa. Pisano was an important pre-Renaissance sculptor. His works, in the Romanesque style, include the hexagonal pulpit in the baptistery at Pisa, the *Arca di San Domenico* at Bologna, and the octagonal pulpit in the Cathedral of Siena.

Pissarro (pi-SAR-ro), **Camille** (1830–1903), French impressionist painter, b. St. Thomas (now part of U.S. Virgin Islands). He moved to Paris in 1855. Inspired by Corot and Manet, he became a leading French impressionist, briefly turning to pointillism in the 1880's, and influenced the work of

Cézanne. His works, chiefly scenes of Paris and surrounding country, include *Boulevard Montmartre* and *Quais de la Seine.*

Pixies, small mischievous fairies or elves in the folklore of southwestern England, particularly Cornwall and Devon. It is said that they dance in the moonlight, play tricks on family members, and mislead travelers.

Plante (PLAHNT), **Jacques** (1929–86), Canadian ice hockey player, b. Shawinigan Falls, Que. One of the finest goalies in the history of the National Hockey League (NHL), Plante won or shared the Vezina Trophy as the league's top goalie a record seven times. In 1962, he became one of the few goalies in NHL history to win the Hart Trophy, given to the most valuable player. He is also remembered as the player who popularized the goalie mask. Plante played with the Montreal Canadiens for eleven seasons (1952–63). He also played for the New York Rangers, the St. Louis Blues, and the Toronto Maple Leafs. He was elected to the Hockey Hall of Fame in 1978.

Player piano (pianola), a mechanical, or self-playing, piano. The music is usually recorded on rolls of paper by means of punched holes. The roll of paper passes over a metal cylinder with holes in it corresponding to the keys of the piano. When holes in the paper line up with holes in the cylinder, streams of compressed air force the appropriate hammers of the piano to strike the piano strings. Player pianos were first developed in the late 1800's. They reached their greatest popularity in the 1920's, when sophisticated models could duplicate the performances of famous pianists. Coin-operated player pianos were known as nickelodeons.

Plebiscite (from the Latin *plebiscitum,* meaning "decree of the people"). In ancient Rome it denoted a decree decided upon by the *plebs,* or common people. Today a plebiscite usually refers to a vote by the people of a region or country to determine an important political matter, such as who shall rule them or how they should be ruled.

Pleiades (PLE-a-dese) (or Seven Sisters), (literally, "The Weepers"), in Greek mythology, the seven daughters of Atlas and Pleione who, either after death or during the flight from Orion, were transformed into stars. The sisters are identified with a group of faint stars in the constellation Taurus. The barely visible seventh star is said to represent either Electra, who moved to avoid seeing the fall of Troy, or Merope, who was ashamed of her marriage to a mortal. Alcyone, Celeno, Merope, Sterope, Taygeta, and Maia are the six other sisters.

Plummer, Christopher (1929–   ), Canadian actor, b. Toronto. A respected classical actor, Plummer began his professional career with the Canadian Repertory Theatre in Ottawa in 1950. During several seasons with the Stratford, Ontario, Shakespearean Festival, he played leading classical roles. In London and New York, he appeared in *The Lark, Becket, J. B.,* and other modern dramas. Plummer's many film roles include Captain von Trapp in *The Sound of Music* (1965), Pizarro in *The Royal Hunt of the Sun* (1969), and Kipling in *The Man Who Would Be King* (1975). His performance as Iago in *Othello* on Broadway in 1981 was highly praised.

Plutus, in Greek mythology, the personification of wealth. The son of Iasion and Demeter, he was said to have been blinded by Zeus so that he might bestow his gifts equally upon the good and bad. The word "plutocrat," meaning a person who exerts influence through wealth, is derived from Plutus' name.

Pogrom (from Russian, meaning "destruction"), organized attacking and killing of defenseless people, generally with the approval of government officials. The term "pogroms," first incorporated into English usage in 1905 when a series of such attacks were carried out by the reactionary Black Hundreds in Russia, has been applied especially to the massacre of Jews.

Politi, Leo (1908–96), American author and illustrator, b. Fresno, Calif. He spent much of his childhood in Italy, studying art at the Institute of Monza near Milan. His book *Song of the Swallows* was awarded the Caldecott Medal in 1950. His other books are *The Nicest Gift* (1973), *Three Stalks of Corn* (1976), and *Mr. Fong's Toy Shop* (1978).

Political asylum, refuge granted by a government to a citizen of a foreign country because of political activities which may make it dangerous for the person to return home.

Political science, social science concerned with the systematic study of government and the political organization and activities of a state. It includes such areas as political theory, political parties and groups, public opinion, and international relations. Originating in the writings of Plato and Aristotle, it was further developed by the English philosopher Thomas Hobbes (1588–1679), who formulated the social contract theory. Today it deals primarily with the acquisition and use of political power.

Polyhymnia (pol-ee-HIM-nia), a goddess in Greek mythology. She and her eight sisters, the daughters of Zeus and Mnemosyne, were the muses, or patrons of the arts and sciences. She presided over oratory and sacred song, and her symbol was the veil.

Pompadour (POM-pa-door), **Marquise de** (Jeanne Antoinette Poisson Lenormand d'Étoiles) (1721–64), favorite and powerful adviser of Louis XV of France, b. Paris. Introduced to the king at a ball (1744), she was installed by him at Versailles and given the estate of Pompadour. She then formulated the King's policies, both foreign and domestic. She shifted France's policy toward Austria from one of containment to one of alliance and thus brought on the calamitous Seven Years' War (1754–63).

Pons, Lily (Alice Joséphine Pons) (1904–76), French-born American opera singer, b. Cannes. A coloratura soprano, she was noted for her wide vocal range and seemingly effortless artistry. She made her operatic debut (1928) as Lakmé at the Mulhouse Municipal Opera, France, and her U.S. debut as Lucia with the Metropolitan Opera company (1931).

Ponselle (pon-SELL), **Rosa Melba** (Rosa Ponzillo) (1897–1981), American opera singer, b. Meriden, Conn. A noted soprano with a rich, dramatic voice, Ponselle first appeared with the Metropolitan Opera in 1918 as Leonora in *La Forza del Destino.* She made her London debut in *Norma* in 1929, and gained a reputation for her interpretations of roles in Italian operas. She retired as a performer in 1937. Later, she served for many years as artistic director of the Baltimore Opera.

Pontchartrain (PAHN-cher-train), **Lake,** a large, shallow lake in southeastern Louisiana, north of New Orleans. The Gulf Intracoastal Waterway crosses the lake and joins it to the Mississippi River at New Orleans by means of a canal. The lake receives part of the Mississippi's floodwaters through the Bonnet Carré Spillway. The Lake Pontchartrain Causeway, which extends 24 mi (39 km) over the lake, is the longest overwater highway in the world. The lake is filled with game fish, and it is a popular resort area.

Poor People's March (or Campaign), protest march on Washington, D.C., by representatives of the U.S. poor (May–June, 1968). First planned by Dr. Martin Luther King, Jr., leadership of the march passed to the Rev. Ralph Abernathy after King's assassination. The marchers were housed in a settlement of huts and tents called Resurrection City, set up near the Lincoln Memorial. For several days in late June, 50,000 people of all economic levels rallied in support of the poor.

Porter, Cole (1893–1964), American composer and lyricist, b. Peru, Ind. Educated at Yale University and Harvard Law School, Porter turned from law to music and wrote his first musical comedy, *See America First,* in 1916. His songs include "Begin the Beguine," "Night and Day," and "What Is This Thing Called Love?" Porter wrote many musical comedies, among them *Anything Goes; Kiss Me, Kate;* and *Can-Can;* and composed the music for several films, including *Silk Stockings* and *High Society.*

Porter, Eliot (1901–90), American photographer, b. Winnetka, Ill. A pioneer in color nature photography, Porter is noted for his "intimate landscapes," focusing on details like leaves and rock crevices. As a boy, he began photographing birds and other natural subjects. He attended Harvard University and in 1929 obtained an M.D. degree. But he gave up a medical career for photography when Alfred Stieglitz and other master photographers encouraged him in his hobby. Porter's many books, nearly all in color, include *In Wilderness Is the Preservation of the World* (1962), *Galapagos—The Flow of Wilderness* (1968), and *Birds of North America* (1972).

Porter, Gene Stratton (Geneva Grace Stratton) (1868–1924), American novelist and nature writer, b. Wabash, Ind. She wrote *Homing With the Birds* and other nature books, as well as the novel *Freckles.*

Potemkin (pot-YOM-kin), **Prince Gregori Aleksandrovich** (1739–91), Russian statesman, b. near Smolensk. A favorite of Empress Catherine II, he participated in the plot against Peter III that placed her on the throne. He was a distinguished fighter against the Turks and a primary influence on Catherine's policy. He was governor of Crimea (1783), built the arsenal of Kherson and the harbor of Sevastopol, ordered the construction of a fleet in the Black Sea, and commanded (1787–91) the Russian Army during the second Turkish War.

Powell, Lewis Franklin, Jr. (1907–   ), American jurist, b. Suffolk, Va. He received a law degree from Washington and Lee University in 1931. He practiced law in Richmond, Va., and was president of American Bar Association (1964–65) before being named to Supreme Court by President Nixon in 1972. He retired in 1987.

Praetorian (pre-TOR-ian) **Guard,** in ancient Rome, bodyguards of the emperor. A military force, organized by the Emperor Augustus, it grew so politically powerful that it could make or unmake emperors. The most flagrant of its deeds was the murder of Emperor Pertinax and public auctioning of the empire to Didius Julianus in A.D. 193. The guard was eventually suppressed by Constantine the Great in A.D. 312.

Prayer, Book of Common, official service book of the Church of England and the U.S. Episcopal Church. It was first issued in 1549 under Thomas Cranmer, archbishop of Canterbury, and revised in 1662. It contains prayers, rituals, and a calendar of holy days.

Prayer wheel, device used by Tibetan Buddhists (Lamaists) to aid in prayer. Barrel-shaped, it contains prayers or other sacred writings. Turning the wheel is a substitute for saying the prayers.

Premenstrual syndrome (PMS), a specific group of physical, mental, and emotional symptoms that are related to a woman's monthly menstrual cycle. One to two weeks before the start of each menstrual period, women with PMS experience symptoms that may include anxiety, depression, nervousness, anger, headaches, nausea, fluid retention, or insomnia. Though once thought to be a type of general depression, PMS is now recognized as a specific ailment related to monthly hormonal changes. Its exact cause is unknown, but its frequency increases with age and body weight. Treatments for PMS are varied. They include hormone or vitamin supplements, changes in diet, PMS support groups, and education about the effects of PMS on the body.

Preminger, Otto (1906–1986), American stage and film producer and director, b. Vienna, Austria. One of Europe's best-known producer-directors, he went to the United States in 1935 and, after directing several plays on Broadway, moved to Hollywood in 1943. His first success as a film director was *Laura* (1944), which is considered by some critics to be his best work. Preminger's other films include *The Moon is Blue* (1953), a comedy that challenged Hollywood's strict censorship rules; *Anatomy of a Murder* (1959); *Exodus* (1960); *Such Good Friends* (1971); and *The Human Factor* (1980).

Presidential Medal of Freedom, medal awarded by the president of the United States to honor civilians in peacetime. Given yearly to Americans (since 1963), the medal honors outstanding contributions in such areas as national security, world peace, and the arts.

Prester John (John the Priest), legendary Christian king and priest. He supposedly ruled over a fabulous kingdom in either Africa or Asia during the Middle Ages, and many legends sprang up about him. One story claims he had 70 kings as his slaves, and one account of his kingdom tells of ants that mined gold and of a magic herb that did away with demons.

Previn, André (1929–   ), American conductor, composer, and pianist, b. Berlin, Germany. Previn and his family went to the United States in 1938. He became a citizen in 1943. He became well known for the music he composed and arranged for many Hollywood films. The scores he arranged for the films *Gigi* (1958), *Porgy and Bess* (1959), *Irma La Douce* (1963), and *My Fair Lady* (1964) won Academy Awards. Previn was conductor of the Houston Symphony (1966–69), conductor of the London Symphony Orchestra (1968–79), and music director of the Pittsburgh Symphony Orchestra (1976–84). He served as music director of the Los Angeles Philharmonic (1984–89).

Priam (PRY-am), in Greek mythology, the king of Troy during the time of the Trojan War. Son of Laomedon and husband of Hecuba, he was the father of more than 60 children—among them Hector, Paris, Troilus, and Cassandra. When the Greeks entered Troy by ruse of the wooden horse, Priam was killed at Zeus's altar.

Priestley, J. B. (John Boynton Priestley) (1894–1984), English writer, b. Bradford, Yorkshire. An unusually prolific and varied writer, his novels (such as *The Good Companions, Bright Day, The Image Men*) and plays (*Dangerous Corner, Summer Day's Dream, The Glass Cage*) reflect his interest in expressionist forms, psychological themes, and social criticism. Priestley first wrote literary criticism at Cambridge University and published *The English Novel* in 1927. He also wrote mysteries (*An Inspector Calls*), social criticism (*The Edwardians*) and reminiscences (*Margin Released*).

Primus (PRI-mus), **Pearl** (1921–94), American dancer and choreographer, b. Trinidad, West Indies. Like Katherine Dunham, she was a student of anthropology who explored her African heritage in the world of dance. She made her New York concert debut in 1943, opened a school of dance in 1947, and often performed in Africa.

Printed circuit, electrical circuit whose parts are connected by metallic conductors that are printed or plated onto a plastic sheet. (In ordinary circuits the parts are connected by copper wires soldered from part to part.) Printed circuits are cheaper to make than soldered circuits, they save space and weight, and they are more reliable because there are no wires that can break.

Prisoner of war, person captured or interned by an enemy power during wartime. Most prisoners of war are members of armed forces, although some civilians are interned as prisoners. Various international agreements are designed to protect prisoners' rights. "Prisoner of war" is abbreviated POW.

Privy Council, a council originally chosen by the British monarch to conduct affairs of state. Today it is largely an honorary body. From the Middle Ages until the 1700's the Privy Council had considerable power. This declined after much of the monarch's power passed to the British Cabinet. Today each cabinet minister is also a member of the Privy Council.

Privy Seal, seal first used in conducting British rulers' private business and later for official business that did not call for the Great Seal. The Great Seal Act of 1848 simplified the use of the privy seal, and it is now primarily employed for documents that are later going to pass the Great Seal. The holder of the office of Lord Privy Seal is a member of the British cabinet.

Prix de Rome (pri d' ROM), **Grand,** scholarship given annually to French architects, engravers, musicians, painters, or sculptors. Awards are made through the supervision of Paris' École des Beaux Arts, and winners study at the French Academy in Rome. The Prix de Rome dates back to 1666.

Prodigal Son, in the New Testament (Luke 15:11–32), the repentant sinner in a parable related by Jesus. The story tells of a young man who leaves his father's house and squanders his inheritance. When he repents his wicked ways and returns home, his father rejoices and prepares a great feast. The phrase is still used to describe a wastrel who reforms.

Project HOPE (Health Opportunity for People Everywhere), a program that promotes better world health. Project HOPE trains medical personnel in developing countries in many parts of the world. Through the Institute for Health Policy Study, it conducts international conferences and other studies of health policy issues. From 1960 to 1973, the program sponsored the *S.S. Hope,* a hospital ship that conducted medical training missions in Asia, Africa, South America, and the Caribbean. Founded in 1958, the project is sponsored by the nonprofit People-to-People Health Foundation Inc. It has its headquarters in Millwood, Va., and publishes the *Hope News.*

Proportional Representation (P.R.), voting system designed to provide greater representation in governing bodies. Elections are based not on a simple majority but on a ratio of the total number of votes received by each candidate. Some form of the system is used in Norway, France, Italy, and other countries, as well as in a few American cities.

Protesilaus (pro-tes-il-A-us), in Greek mythology, the first soldier killed in the Trojan War. According to one legend, Protesilaus knew that the first man to land in Troy would meet this fate and thus knowingly gave his life. His wife, Laodamia, mourned so that the gods, it is said, allowed him to return and visit her for three hours.

Proteus (PRO-te-us), in Greek mythology, a sea-god who was able to change his shape. If, however, someone caught him and managed to hold him until he assumed his natural shape, Proteus would be forced to answer all questions. It was by this device, according to legend, that Menelaus discovered his way home from Troy.

Provensen, Alice (1918–) and **Martin** (1916–87), American writers and illustrators of children's books, b. Chicago, Ill. Both studied at the Art Institute of Chicago and the University of California. Their first joint effort was illustrating *The Fireside Book of Folk Songs* (1946). They illustrated several classics adapted for children, including *Shakespeare: Ten Great Plays* (1962). Jointly written and illustrated books include *An Owl and Three Pussycats* (1981), *Town and Country* (1985), and *The Glorious Flight: Across the Channel with Louis Bleriot* (1983), which won the Caldecott Medal.

Provost (PRO-vo), **Etienne** (1782?–1850), Canadian hunter and guide. He led several expeditions to the Rocky Mountain region and was for a while connected with the American Fur Company. In 1843 he accompanied James Audubon on a western trip. A city, valley, and river in Utah are named for him.

Ptolemy I (TOL-emy) (367?–284? B.C.), founder of the Ptolemaic dynasty in Egypt, b. Macedonia. After the death of Alexander the Great (323), Ptolemy won control of Egypt. He resigned (285) in favor of his son Ptolemy II after a reign of warfare and intrigue.

Purgatory (from the Latin *purgare,* meaning ''to cleanse''), in Christian belief, a state between heaven and hell for final purification. Some Christians believe that souls of those who die and are destined for heaven remain in purgatory until they have done penance for their last worldly sins. Their stay can be shortened by prayers of the living.

Putnam, Rufus (1738–1824), American military engineer and pioneer, b. Sutton, Mass. A self-taught geographer and mathematician, he served as engineer and rose to rank of brigadier general in the Continental Army. He was one of the founders of the Ohio Co. He established a settlement in Marietta, Ohio (1788), and became judge of the supreme court of the Northwest Territory (1790–96). He was U.S. surveyor general (1796–1803).

Pyramus (PIR-a-mus) **and Thisbe,** in Greek legend, Babylonian lovers. Forbidden by their parents to marry, they agree to run away and arrange to meet near a white mulberry bush. Thisbe, arriving first, is frightened away by a lioness. Pyramus finds her abandoned cloak, fears the lioness has devoured her, and kills himself. Thisbe returns and takes her life with Pyramus' sword. It is said that their blood colored the mulberries, making them red forever after. Shakespeare's *A Midsummer Night's Dream* has a parody of this legend.

Pyrrhus (PIR-rhus) (318?–272 B.C.), king of Epirus. A noted military tactician of his day, he went to Tarentum's aid against Rome. Although he defeated the Romans at Heraclea (280) and at Asculum (279), his losses were heavy and he was unable to effect a permanent peace. From his name comes the term "Pyrrhic victory," meaning a victory won at too great a cost.

Index

HOW TO USE THE DICTIONARY INDEX

See the beginning of the blue pages in Volume 1.

Pagodas (cont.)
    Shwe Dagon Pagoda (Rangoon, Burma) **B:**457
    picture(s) **O:**226
        Shwe Dagon Pagoda (Rangoon, Burma) **R:**151
Pago Pago (American Samoa) **U:**93
Pahang River (Malaysia) **M:**56
Pahari school (in Indian art) **I:**137
Pahlavi, Mohammed Reza *see* Mohammed Reza Pahlavi
Pahlavi, Reza Shah *see* Reza Shah Pahlavi
Pahlavi dynasty (of Iran) **I:**309–10
Pahoehoe (lava) **V:**382
Paige, Satchel (Leroy Robert Paige) (American baseball
      player) **B:**90
    picture(s) **B:**90
Pailes, William A. (American astronaut)
    picture(s) **S:**351
Pain
    anesthesia **A:**256–59; **S:**513
    hypnosis as an anesthetic **H:**313, 314
    medical history of a patient **M:**208d–208e
    narcotics as painkillers **N:**15
    reflex actions respond to pain **N:**116, 118
    tooth nerves **T:**43
    Why doesn't it hurt to cut your hair? **H:**5
Paine, Lewis (American abolitionist) **U:**16
Paine, Robert Treat (American lawyer and statesman) **P:**553
Paine, Thomas (English-born American writer) **P:**12–13
    American literature **A:**199
    founder of the United States **F:**392
    how Declaration of Independence was adopted **D:**59
    magazine publishing **M:**19
    Revolutionary War pamphlets **R:**202
Painkillers (drugs) **N:**15
Paint *see* Paints and pigments
Painted Desert (Arizona) **A:**404, 410
Painted-lady butterfly **B:**478; **H:**189
    picture(s) **B:**481
Painted turtles **T:**355–56
Painters (cats) *see* Mountain lions
Painters Eleven (Canadian artists) **C:**83
Painting **P:**14–32 *see also* the names of individual artists,
      such as Rembrandt, and art of specific countries, as
      Italy, art and architecture of
    Africa, art of **A:**75
    art of the artist **A:**438d–438e
    Audubon's birds **A:**491
    Australian aboriginal painters **A:**501
    baroque art **B:**63–68
    Byzantine **B:**493, 494
    Canada **C:**82, 83
    Dutch and Flemish art **D:**351–64
    Egyptian art in royal tombs **E:**116
    finger painting **F:**130–32
    folk art **F:**292–94
    French art **F:**424–32
    German art **G:**167–72
    Gothic art **G:**270
    Islamic art **I:**357–58
    miniatures of the Rajput school (India) **O:**225
    modern art **M:**386–96b
    oriental art **O:**222–29
    Renaissance art **R:**163–71
    Romanesque art **R:**295
    romanticism in art **R:**302–3
    Rome, art of **R:**319
    Spanish painting **S:**384, 385, 386, 387
    United States **U:**127
    watercolor **W:**58–61
    picture(s)
      American folk art **F:**292, 293
      cave paintings **P:**435, 436
Painting, industrial **P:**33–34
Painting, religious *see* Religious art
Painting with White Border (painting by Wassily Kandinsky)
    picture(s) **G:**172

Paint programs (computer graphics) **C:**481
Paints and pigments **P:**30, **32–34** *see also* Lacquers; Varnishes
    colors **C:**425–26
    effect on art of manufactured paints **P:**24, 27
    ink **I:**229
    lead **L:**93
    oil paints **P:**30
    pigments of prehistoric paintings **P:**15
    plastics **P:**329
    textiles **T:**143
    watercolor paints **W:**58
Pairing Off (card game) **C:**108
Paisley, Ian R. K. (Northern Ireland clergyman and political
      leader) **P:553**
Paiute (Indians of North America) **I:**182, 183, 186; **N:**128,
    134
Pakistan **P:**35–40a
    Afghanistan, relations with **A:**45
    Bangladesh **B:**50–51
    Bhutto, Benazir **B:**155b
    Bhutto, Zulfikar Ali **B:**155b
    ethnic groups in the United Kingdom **U:**56, 57
    India **I:**133, 134
    Karachi **K:**193
    Kashmir dispute **K:**198–99
    poverty **P:**419
    refugees **R:**137
    picture(s)
      flag **F:**233
      Hindu Kush **P:**38
      Islamabad **P:**39
      Karachi **P:**39
      Mohenjo-Daro **P:**40
      people **P:**35
      sugarcane field **P:**38
      village **P:**36
Palace Ladies Tuning the Lute (painting by Chou Fang)
    picture(s) **C:**274
Palace of Nations (United Nations)
    picture(s) **L:**95
Palace of the Governors (Santa Fe, New Mexico) **N:**188
Palaces
    Assyrian palaces **A:**371
    Islamic architecture **I:**357, 358
    Italian Renaissance architecture **A:**378
    Minoan architecture **A:**238, 372
    museums made from some palaces **M:**522
    Paris **P:**73–74
    Persian architecture **A:**242, 371–72
    Versailles **A:**379; **B:**66; **P:**74
    picture(s)
      King Minos' (Knossos, Crete) **A:**355
      Schönbrunn Palace (Vienna) **V:**332j
      Versailles **B:**66; **P:**76
Palais de Chaillot *see* Chaillot, Palais de
Palais Royal (Paris) **P:**73
Palau (island nation, Pacific Ocean) **P:**40b; **T:**115
    picture(s)
      flag **F:**242
      Kayangel atoll **P:**2
Palazzo Vecchio (palace in Florence, Italy) **F:**258
Palenque (Mexico) **M:**184
Paleocene epoch (in geology) **E:**25, 29
Pale of Settlement (Russian territory restricting Jews) **J:**109
Paleo-Indians (early inhabitants of the Americas) **I:**164–65
Paleolithic period *see* Old Stone Age
Paleontology (scientific study of fossils) **F:**380, 382, 383,
      387, 388–89 *see also* Fossils
    careers in biology **B:**197, 198
    earth science **E:**8
    Earth's history **E:**24
    evolution **E:**375
Paleozoic era (in geology) **E:**27–28; **F:**385–87
    prehistoric animals **P:**433
    table(s) **E:**25; **F:**384

Palestine (the Holy Land)   P:40c–43
  Arab-Israeli War (1967)   J:132
  Arabs   A:343, 346–47
  Ben-Gurion, David   B:142
  Christianity, history of   C:289
  Israel, history of   I:369, 375
  Jerusalem   J:78–82
  Jesus Christ   J:83–87
  Jewish immigration   J:110–11
  Jordan   J:132
  map at the time of Jesus Christ   J:84
  Syria   S:552
  World War I   W:275
  World War II in the Middle East   W:290
  Zionism   Z:379
Palestine Liberation Organization (PLO)   P:42, 43, **553**
  accord with Israel   A:467
  Israel's invasion of Lebanon   I:376
  Jordan   J:132
  Lebanon   L:122
Palestinian Arab refugees   I:375; P:42; R:137
  Jordan   J:129
  Lebanon   L:122, 123
Palestinian Arabs   see also Palestinian Arab refugees
  Kuwait   K:306
Palestinian Authority (Arab governing body in Palestine)   P:42
Palestrina, Giovanni Pierluigi da (Italian composer)   M:542;
    P:43
  choral music   C:283
  hymns   H:308
  Renaissance music   R:173–74
  vocal polyphony   I:410
Palettes (on which artists mix paints)
  decorated stoneware of ancient Egypt   D:70
Pali (language)   I:141
Palindromes (word games)   W:236
Palisades (on the Hudson River)   N:166
Palk Strait (Sri Lanka)   S:415
Palladian style (of architecture)   A:380–81; E:259
Palladio, Andrea (Italian architect)   A:380; R:170
  picture(s)
    Villa Rotunda   A:381
Palladium (element)   E:175
  jewelry   J:92
Pallas Athena   see Athena
Pallets (devices in timepieces)   C:369, 370
Pallium (Greek garment)   C:375
Palm (part of the hand)   F:79
Palm (tree)
  books made from leaves   B:320
  carnauba   B:378
  coconut palm   C:392
  Dahomey (Benin), chief crop of   D:4
  dates   D:41–42
  jungles   J:157
  Malaysia is world's leading producer of palm oil   M:57
  wax obtained from   W:76
  picture(s)
    coconut palm   T:302
Palma, Ricardo (Peruvian author)   L:70
Palmate compound leaves   L:113
  picture(s)   L:113
Palmate veins (of trees)   T:308
Palm civets (toddy cats) (animals)   G:94
  picture(s)   G:93
Palme, Olof (Swedish prime minister)   S:529
Palmer, Alice Elvira Freeman (American educator)   P:553
Palmer, Arnold (American golfer)   G:257, 258
  picture(s)   G:258
Palmer, Nathaniel (American sea captain)   A:295
Palmer, William J. (American railroad builder)   C:439
Palmer House (hotel, Chicago, Illinois)   H:259
Palmetto (tree)
  picture(s)
    Sabal palmetto is state tree of Florida and South

  Carolina   F:261; S:297
Palmetto State (nickname for South Carolina)   S:296, 297
Palm Sunday (religious holiday)   E:43; R:153, 284
  Roman Catholic Church observance of   R:292
Palmtop computers   see Hand-held computers
Palmyra (Syria)   S:551
  picture(s)
    ruins   A:463
Palo Alto (California)
  picture(s)
    conservation program   C:520
Palo Alto, Battle of (1846)   T:32
Palo Duro Canyon (Texas)   T:126, 132
Palomar, Mount (California)   see Mount Palomar Observatory
Palouse Hills (Washington)   W:16, 19, 22
Paloverde (tree)
  picture(s)
    state tree of Arizona   A:403
Palpation (medical examination by touch)   M:208h
Palsy, cerebral   see Cerebral palsy
Pamela: or Virtue Rewarded (novel by Richardson)   E:279;
    F:115
Pamir (Pamirs) (mountains of central Asia)   A:43–44
  Tajikistan   T:11
  picture(s)   T:10
Pampa (plains of South America)   S:277, 291
  Argentina   A:388, 390, 392
  prairies   P:426, 427, 428
  picture(s)   A:392; G:314
    prairies   P:429
Pampas ostriches   see Rheas
Pamunkey (Indians of North America)   I:178.
Pan (in Greek mythology)   G:363; P:553
Panacea (in Greek mythology)   P:553
Panama   P:44–49
  American military burial ground   N:31
  Balboa named it Darien   B:20
  Central America   C:172–75
  Cuna Indians   I:195
  life in Latin America   L:47–61
  national dance   D:30
  United States, relations with   J:123
  picture(s)
    flag   F:241
    Kuna Indians   N:294; P:45
    Panama City   P:47
    Panama Railroad   P:45
    sidewalk vendors   P:44
    U.S. troops   P:52
Panama, Isthmus of   P:44, 45, 49, 50
Panama Canal   P:49–51
  canal construction   C:88
  Caribbean Sea made a major waterway   C:112
  Eiffel, Alexandre Gustave   E:118
  Lesseps, Ferdinand de   L:157
  Panama, history of   P:48
  territorial expansion of the United States   T:114
  picture(s)
    locks   P:50
Panama Canal Area   P:51
Panama Canal Zone   P:51
  Roosevelt Corollary to the Monroe Doctrine   R:331
  territorial expansion of the United States   T:114
Panama City (capital of Panama)   P:46, 47
  picture(s)   P:47
Panama hats   E:68–69
Panama-Pacific International Exposition (San Francisco,
    California, 1915)   S:32
Pan American Day   H:154
Pan-American Exhibition (Buffalo, 1901)
  picture(s)   F:15
Pan American Games (series of athletic competitions held
    among Western Hemisphere nations)   P:553
Pan American Highway   P:553–54
Pan American Union   H:39

Pan Am flight 103 (airplane destroyed by bomb, 1988)   **T:**117
  picture(s)   **T:**117
Pancake Tuesday (religious holiday)   **R:**153
Panchatantra (fables from India)   **F:**3
Panch'en Lama (Tibetan Buddhist religious leader)   **P:**554;
  T:189, 191
Pancreas (gland)   **B:**288; **G:**227, 228
  Banting's findings on insulin extract   **B:**59
  diabetes   **D:**191
  digestive system   **B:**277; **D:**162
Pandas (animals)   **A:**452; **P:**52
  specialized diet   **M:**73; **Z:**385
  picture(s)   **E:**211; **P:**52; **Z:**384
Pandemic diseases
  worldwide influenza epidemic (1918)   **D:**195–96
Pandora (in Greek mythology)   **G:**364, 367
  picture(s)   **G:**367
Pandora (moon of Saturn)   **S:**56
Panel cartoons   **C:**127, 129
Panel discussions *see* Discussions
Panel paintings   **S:**384
Panfish
  baits for   **F:**213
Pangea (Pangaea) (prehistoric continent)   **G:**111, 113; **O:**16
  picture(s)   **G:**110
Pangolins (mammals)   **A:**283; **M:**74
  picture(s)   **M:**73
Panhandle (geographical term)   **P:**554
Panhandle State (nickname for West Virginia)   **W:**127
Panhard-Levassor (automobile)   **A:**540
Panhellenic festivals (in ancient Greece)   **G:**343
Panics and depressions *see* Depressions and recessions
Pankhurst, Emmeline Goulden (British suffragist)   **W:**215
  picture(s)   **W:**215
Panmunjom (South Korea)   **K:**304
Panniers (side bags for bicycles)   **C:**48
Panniers (skirt hoops)   **C:**377
Panning (for gold)   **G:**251
  gravity concentration of ores   **M:**233
Panning (in candy making)   **C:**96
Panoan (Native American language family)   **I:**197
Panoramas (curved pictures)   **D:**2
Panpipes (ancient musical instruments)   **O:**219
Pansy (flower)
  picture(s)   **G:**44
Pantaloon (clown)   **C:**386
Panthéon (Paris)   **P:**70, 71
Pantheon (temple in Rome, Italy)   **R:**305
  Roman civilization   **A:**232
  Roman engineers built domes   **A:**374
  picture(s)   **A:**232
Panthers (animals)   **F:**265; **L:**155
  picture(s)   **E:**210; **L:**155
Pantomimes (dramatic action without words) *see also* Charades
  charades   **C:**186–87
  clowns   **C:**386
  dance   **D:**24–25
  dance music   **D:**35
Pantothenic acid (a B-complex vitamin)   **V:**370c–370d
  table(s)   **V:**372
Panzer (armored) divisions (in World War II)   **W:**287
Papacy *see also* Popes
  emperors versus popes in Italy   **I:**388
  history of Roman Catholic Church   **R:**285
  Reformation was a nationalist movement   **C:**291–93
Papadopoulos, George (Greek president)   **G:**338
Papago (North American Indians) *see* O'o'dham
Papain (substance from papaya plant)
  used as a meat tenderizer   **M:**78
Papal Inquisition   **R:**286
Papal Line of Demarcation *see* Line of Demarcation
Papal Schism *see* Great Western Schism
Papal States (in central Italy)   **P:**554
  Italy, history of   **I:**389
  Renaissance, growth of city states during   **R:**157

Roman Catholic Church, history of the   **R:**285, 289;
  V:280, 281
Papandreou, Andreas (Greek political leader)   **G:**338
Papandreou, George (Greek prime minister)   **G:**338
Papaya (tropical fruit)   **M:**78
Papeete (capital of French Polynesia)   **P:**9
Paper   **P:**53–58
  bamboo used for making   **G:**318
  buttons made of paper   **B:**484
  Chinese invent   **B:**320
  communication, history of   **C:**463
  decoupage   **D:**80
  drawing, history of   **D:**313, 314
  drawing materials   **D:**306, 309, 310, 311
  gift wrapping   **G:**206–7
  How is paper recycled?   **P:**57
  illustration tradition   **I:**79
  inventions of communication   **I:**284
  Japanese houses   **H:**171
  Maine, industry in   **M:**50
  materials from plants   **P:**298
  New Hampshire, industry in   **N:**156
  origami   **O:**232–35
  paper money   **M:**413–14
  papier-mâché   **P:**58b–58c
  photographic printing paper   **P:**211
  Quebec production   **Q:**10
  rubbings   **R:**348b–349
  watercolor paper   **W:**58
  wax paper, invention of   **W:**76
Paperback books   **P:**58a
  children's literature   **C:**237
  history of   **B:**322
  illustration and illustrators   **I:**82
  publishing   **P:**524
Paper birch (tree)
  picture(s)   **T:**304
    state tree of New Hampshire   **N:**151
Paperboard   **P:**57
Paper chromatography   **E:**397
Paper Crane, The (book by Molly Bang)
  picture(s)   **C:**236
Paper mills   **P:**54
  picture(s)   **N:**138c; **P:**298
    automation   **A:**531
Paper money   **M:**413–14
  bank notes   **B:**53, 54
  dollar bills   **D:**258–59
  Engraving and Printing, Bureau of   **T:**294
Paper wasps
  picture(s)
    nest   **I:**246
Paper work *see* Papier-mâché
Papier-mâché   **P:**58b–58c
  early dolls made of   **D:**267
Papillae (structures on the tongue)   **B:**286
Papineau, Louis-Joseph (Canadian lawyer and politician)   **Q:**13
Paprika (spice)   **H:**114
  national spice of Hungary   **H:**284
  picture(s)   **H:**115
Papua New Guinea   **N:**149; **P:**58d–59
  Admiralty Islands   **I:**361; **P:**8
  Bismarck Archipelago   **P:**8
  Bougainville   **P:**8
  Buka   **P:**8
  New Britain   **P:**9
  New Ireland   **P:**10
  peace children   **I:**274
  picture(s)
    flag   **F:**242
    Melanesian boys   **P:**9
    open-pit copper mine   **P:**4
Papuans (a people of New Guinea)   **N:**148
Papyrus (plant)
  early writing material   **P:**57

Paris (cont.)
Olympic Games (1900, 1924) O:108, 109
Pompidou Center A:386a
theater T:160
town planning F:425
World War II F:419
map(s) P:75
picture(s) F:409
artificial pond with toy boats T:247
Bastille Day parade H:156
City of Science and Industry M:531
Eiffel Tower E:358
Louvre M:520
Notre Dame cathedral A:377
Pompidou Center F:432
sidewalk café C:314
Paris (in Greek mythology) G:368; T:316
Paris, Treaty of (1763)
British become masters of Saint Lawrence River S:14
French and Indian War F:465
French Canada ceded to England C:72; Q:14
Paris, Treaty of (1783) R:208; T:105–6; U:177
Adams, John A:13
Franklin's work F:457–58
Paris, Treaty of (1856) C:577
Paris, Treaty of (1898) P:187
Paris, Treaty of (1951, European Coal and Steel Community
agreement) E:369
Paris, University of U:219, 226
picture(s) U:225
Paris Bourse (stock exchange) S:456
Parishes (local units of government in Louisiana) L:299
Parisii (Gallic tribe) P:72
Paris International Exhibition (1878)
picture(s) F:14
Parison (conelike mass of glass) G:233
Paris Opera Ballet School B:26
Paris Opera House
picture(s) O:142; P:72
Paris Peace Conference (1919) W:281, 282–87
Paris peace talks (1968, Vietnam War) V:338
Parizeau, Jacques (Canadian political leader) Q:15
Park, Mungo (Scottish explorer) A:66; E:414
Parkas (hooded jackets worn by Eskimos) E:318–19
picture(s)
embroidered parka I:191
Park Chung Hee (South Korean general and political
leader) K:301
Parker, Charlie (American jazz saxophonist and
composer) J:61; K:189
picture(s) K:189
Parker, Ely S. (Seneca Iroquois) I:176
Parker, John (American patriot) R:198
Parker, John Palmer (American cattle rancher) H:56
Parker, Samuel (American inventor) L:111
Parker Brothers (game company) G:14, 21
Parker Dam (California–Arizona)
picture(s) D:19; R:241
Parking orbit (of a spacecraft) S:340e
Parkman, Francis (American historian) A:204
kinds of historical writing H:139
Parks P:76–77 *see also* Botanical gardens; National parks
(Canada); National Park System (of the United States);
Zoos; the names of parks, as Yellowstone; the places
of interest section in country, state, and city articles
amusement and theme parks P:79–80
Malawi's freshwater national park F:182
skateboard parks S:182
state parks *see* individual state articles
Parks, Gordon (American photographer, film director, journalist,
and composer) P:554
Parks, Rosa (American civil rights leader) A:79m, 130, 143;
C:330; N:28; S:115
picture(s) A:79n
Parkways, national *see* National parkways

Parliament, British P:83–84; U:68
Cromwell's Rump Parliament E:246
Gladstone's career G:225
impeachment process I:99
Long and Short Parliaments E:245–46
Magna Carta M:26
origin and present make-up E:240
parliament of the Middle Ages M:292
picture(s)
Houses of Parliament E:232, 340; L:288; U:55
Queen Elizabeth II presiding at opening
session G:274
Parliamentary procedure P:81–82
debates and discussions D:52–53
Parliament Hill (Ottawa) O:251–52
picture(s) O:250
Parliaments G:274, 276; P:83–84
British *see* Parliament, British
Canada C:77
Iceland's Althing was first democratic parliament I:36
prime minister P:458
Parlor games *see* Word games
Parmesan cheese C:195
Parmigianino (Parmigiano), Il (Italian painter) I:399
picture(s)
Madonna with the Long Neck (painting) I:399
Saint Thais (engraving) E:294
Parnassus (mountain in Greece) P:554
Parnell, Charles Stewart (Irish nationalist leader) I:324
Paro (Bhutan) B:155a
Parochial schools E:87
church-controlled colleges U:223
Parody (form of humor) H:280
Beerbohm, Sir Max E:288
folk music F:326
Parole C:576; P:481
aliens A:189
Parotid glands (found in front of the ear) D:197; G:226–27
Parr, Catherine (sixth wife of Henry VIII of England) H:108
Parrakeets *see* Parakeets
Parrish, Maxfield (American artist) P:554
Parris Island Marine Base (South Carolina) S:305
Parrot fever (disease) B:245; P:178–79
Parrotfish A:277; F:199
picture(s) F:201
Parrots P:85–86
endangered species B:244; E:209
flightless birds O:244
pet birds B:245–46; P:178–79
picture(s) P:85, 86
Amazon parrot P:178
gray parrot B:230
Parry (blocking movement in fencing) F:87
Parsifal (opera by Richard Wagner) O:160
Parsis (Parsees) (Indian followers of Zoroastrianism) Z:387
funeral customs F:493
religions of India R:152
Parsley (herb)
herbs and spices H:114
supposed medicinal powers F:281, 333
picture(s)
herbs and spices H:115
Parsons, Charles A. (English inventor) T:342
Partch, Harry (American composer) U:210
Parthenogenesis (development of unfertilized egg) E:101
Parthenon (temple in Athens, Greece) A:229, 230, 372–73
Doric style of Greek architecture G:351
Nashville (Tennessee) has a full-size reproduction T:79
Pericles P:152
relief sculpture G:350
picture(s) E:340; G:339
sculptures A:230
Parthians (ruling people of Persia) I:308; P:155, 156
Participles (verb forms) P:93

Particle accelerators (atom-smashing machines)
  vacuum used in **V:**264
Particleboard **F:**515; **W:**227
Particles, subatomic *see* Subatomic particles
Particulate matter (air pollutant) **A:**123
Parties **P:**87–91 *see also* Games
  etiquette **E:**339
  Halloween party **H:**14
  magic tricks **M:**23–25
  sugar-on-snow parties **M:**91
Parties, political *see* Political parties
Parti Québécois (Canadian political party) **C:**76; **P:**372; **Q:**13, 15
Partisans (guerrilla forces) **P:**554
  Yugoslavia **S:**125; **Y:**358
Partita (musical form) *see* Suite
Partnership (type of business) **B:**470–71
Parton, Dolly (American singer and songwriter) **C:**565; **T:**86
  picture(s) **C:**564; **T:**86
Parts of speech **P:**92–94
  grammar **G:**289–90
Parzival (romance by Wolfram von Eschenbach) **G:**176
Pascal (computer language) **P:**554
Pascal, Blaise (French mathematician and philosopher)
  computers, history of **C:**486
  discovered the principle of hydraulic systems **H:**297
  experiment with air pressure **E:**381
  France, literature of **F:**438
  invented an adding machine **O:**53
  number patterns **N:**381
  probability theory **M:**166–67
  vacuum experiments **V:**265
Pascal III (antipope) **R:**291
Pascal I, Saint (pope) **R:**290
Pascal II (pope) **R:**290
Pascal's Law (of liquid pressure) **H:**297
Pascal's triangle (mathematical lattice) **N:**381–83
Paschal (antipope) **R:**290
Pascoli, Giovanni (Italian poet) **I:**408
Pas de deux (in ballet) **B:**29
Pashto (language) *see* Pushtu
Pasillo (Latin American music) **L:**74
Pasolini, Pier Paolo (Italian film director and author) **I:**409
Pasqueflower
  picture(s)
    state flower of South Dakota **S:**313
Passaic River (New Jersey) **N:**167
Passamaquoddy Indians (of Maine) **I:**177; **M:**41, 51
Passed ball (in baseball) **B:**83
Passenger pigeons (extinct birds) **E:**209
Passenger ships **O:**30–33
Passenger trains **R:**80–81
Passing (in football) **F:**355–56
  picture(s) **F:**355
Passion (musical form) **M:**544
  choral music **C:**283
  development in baroque period **B:**70
Passion flower (state wildflower of Tennessee) **T:**78
Passion plays, medieval **G:**152; **P:**12
Passive immunity **I:**95
Passos, John Dos *see* Dos Passos, John
Passover (Jewish holiday) **P:**95–96
  Cup of Elijah **E:**189
  dietary precautions **J:**148
  Easter **E:**43, 44
  Jews' Exodus from Egypt **J:**103, 146b
  picture(s)
    Seder **P:**95
Passports **P:**96
  picture(s) **P:**96
Pastas (dried dough) **F:**336; **G:**281
  food of Italy **I:**382, 383
  food shopping **F:**349
Paste (type of adhesive) **G:**242
  collage making **C:**400–401

Pasteboard (used for printing playing cards) **C:**111
Pastels (artists' material) **D:**310; **P:**30
  picture(s) **D:**308
Pasternak, Boris Leonidovich (Russian novelist) **N:**363; **P:**554; **R:**380
  picture(s) **R:**379
Paste-up artists (people who prepare artwork for printing) **C:**458
Pasteur, Louis (French chemist) **P:**97–98
  advances in biological sciences **S:**73
  contributions to medicine **M:**208; **S:**513
  fermentation of wine **F:**90–91
  immune system **I:**98
  microbes, study of **M:**277–78
  signature reproduced **A:**527
  picture(s) **M:**278; **P:**97
Pasteurization (to kill micro-organisms) **M:**278; **P:**98
  food preservation **F:**342
  importance to medicine **M:**208
  milk, processing of **D:**9
  tuberculosis, protection against **D:**204
  picture(s) **F:**342
Pastoral nomads (desert people) **D:**128
Pastoral poetry (about country life) **E:**272
Pastoral prayer **P:**430
Pastukhov, Mount (Caucasus Mountains) **T:**59
"Pasture, The" (poem by Robert Frost) **F:**480
Pasture grasses **G:**317
Pastures
  feeding the dairy herd **D:**5–6
  grazing lands in national forests **N:**36
  pasture grasses **G:**317
  prairies **P:**427
Patagonia (plateau region of South America)
  Argentina **A:**392
  landforms of South America **S:**276, 280
  picture(s) **A:**391
    sheep ranch **P:**429
Patan (Nepal) **N:**109
Patasse, Ange-Felix (president of Central African Republic) **C:**171
Patch logging (of timber) **L:**324
Patchwork quilting **N:**101
Patella (kneecap) (bone of the leg) **S:**184
  diagram(s) **F:**79
Patent and Trademark Office (PTO) **C:**455
Patent Co-operation Treaty (1978) **P:**99
Patent leather **L:**110
Patent Office *see* United States Patent and Trademark Office
Patents **P:**99
  Edison's record number of **E:**70
  significant inventions and their patent dates **I:**281–83
Pater, Walter (English writer) **E:**284
Pater Noster *see* Lord's Prayer
Paterson (New Jersey) **N:**175, 178; **T:**146
Paterson, Andrew Barton (Banjo) (Australian bush balladist) **A:**500, 501
Paterson, Katherine (American author of children's books) **C:**235, 238
  picture(s)
    illustration by Donna Diamond for *Bridge to Terabithia* **C:**238
Paterson, William (American public official) **N:**179
Pathans *see* Pushtuns
Pathetic fallacy (figure of speech) **F:**122–23
Pathet Lao (rebel group of Laos) **L:**43
Pathfinder *see* Frémont, John Charles
Pathfinder, The (novel by James Fenimore Cooper) **C:**541
Pathogens (disease-producing organisms) **S:**33
  vectors **V:**284–85
Pathological anatomy **M:**206
Pathology (study of the nature of diseases) **B:**197; **H:**249; **M:**202
Patience (operetta by Gilbert and Sullivan) **G:**209
Pato (game) **A:**391

Paton, Alan Stewart (South African author, educator, and politician) **A:**76d; **P:554**
Patos, Lagoa dos (lake, Brazil) **L:**30
Patras (Greece) **G:**331
Patriarchal family **F:**43
Patriarchs (original rulers of a tribe or family) **P:554**
  Eastern Orthodox churches **E:**45
Patriarchy *see* Patriarchal family
Patricians (Roman social class) **P:**369; **R:**311, 313
Patrick, Saint (patron saint of Ireland) **P:100**
  Christianity, history of **C:**290
  converted the nation of Ireland **R:**284
  Fenian Cycle tales **I:**325
  Ireland, history of **I:**323
  Saint Patrick's Day **H:**152
  slavery **S:**196
  picture(s) **P:**100
Patriote, Le (Canadian theater group) **C:**66
Patriotic holidays **H:**154, 156–57
Patriotic songs *see* National anthems and patriotic songs
Patriot missile **M:**349
  picture(s) **M:**344, 346
Patriots (colonists critical of British rule) **R:**198
  political parties in colonial America **P:**370
Patriot's Day **D:**59; **P:554**
Patroclus (in Greek mythology) **P:554**
  Iliad, episodes in **I:**61
Patrol officers (police) **P:**363
Patrol ships and craft **U:**119
Patron (in Roman society) **R:**311
Patronage, political **C:**317 *see also* Spoils system
  power of the United States president over appointments and removals **P:**450, 453
Patronymic method (of name giving) **N:**5
Patroons (Dutch landowners in American colonies) **T:**175
Patsayev, Viktor I. (Soviet cosmonaut) **S:**346
Patternmaking
  clothing **C:**380, 381
  woodworking **W:**230
Patterns (in interior decorating) **I:**259
Patterns (learning tool) **L:**100
Patterns (of numbers) *see* Number patterns
Patterson, Floyd (American boxing champion) **B:**353
Patterson, Martha Johnson (acting first lady in Andrew Johnson's administration) **F:**172–73
Patterson, Percival (prime minister of Jamaica) **J:**19
Patterson, Thomas (Canadian businessman) **C:**66
Patti, Adelina (Spanish-Italian coloratura soprano) **P:554–55**
Patton, George S. (U.S. Army general) **P:**100; **W:**301
Patwin (Indians of North America) **I:**187
Patzcuaro, Lake (Mexico)
  picture(s) **N:**287
Paul, Alice (American reformer) **P:**101; **W:**212b, 213
  picture(s) **P:**101
Paul, Les (American guitar designer) **G:**412
Paul, Saint (apostle of Jesus Christ) **A:**329; **P:**101
  Christianity, history of **C:**286–87
  Pauline Epistles **B:**165
  Roman Catholic Church **R:**281
  picture(s) **P:**101
Paul, William Louis, Sr. (Native American politician and lawyer) **A:**157
Paul I, Saint (pope) **R:**290
Paul II (pope) **R:**291
Paul III (pope) **R:**291
Paul IV (pope) **R:**291
Paul V (pope) **R:**291
Paul VI (pope) **P:**102; **R:**291, 292–93
Pauli, Wolfgang (Austrian physicist) **P:**238, **555**
Pauline Epistles (in the New Testament) **B:**165; **C:**286; **P:**101
Pauling, Linus (American chemist) **O:**215; **P:**102; **S:**77
  picture(s) **P:**102
Paulist Fathers (Roman Catholic priests) **P:555**
Paulo Afonso Falls (Brazil) **W:**62, 63

Paul Revere (painting by Copley)
  picture(s) **U:**127
"Paul Revere's Ride" (poem by Longfellow)
  excerpt from **R:**192
Pausanias (Greek writer) **G:**359
Pavane (dance) **R:**173
Pavarotti, Luciano (Italian opera singer) **O:**141
Pavers (machines for mixing concrete) **R:**250
Pavese, Cesare (Italian novelist) **I:**409
Pavia (Italy) **I:**388
Pavlov, Ivan (Russian biologist) **P:103**
  learning **L:**98
  methods of studying behavior **P:**505–6
Pavlova, Anna (Russian ballet dancer) **P:555**
  ballet, history of **B:**29, 32
Pawcatuck River (Rhode Island–Connecticut) **R:**215
Pawhuska (Oklahoma) **O:**93
Pawnee (Indians of North America) **I:**180; **K:**186
  Kansas museum **K:**184
Pawtucket (Rhode Island) **R:**223
  textile industry **I:**223; **R:**218
Pax House (London, center for World Association of Girl Guides and Girl Scouts) **G:**219
Pax Romana (Roman Peace) (in Roman history) **R:**316, 317
Payload (objects carried by a rocket) **R:**255, 257
  warheads of missiles **M:**347–48
Payne, Cecilia (British-American astronomer) **A:**475
Payne-Aldrich Act (United States, 1909) **T:**4–5
Paysandú (Uruguay) **U:**240
Pay television **A:**29; **T:**49
Payton, Gary E. (American astronaut) **S:**350
Payton, Walter (American football player) **F:**363
  picture(s) **F:**363
Paz, Alonso de la (Guatemalan sculptor) **L:**64
Paz, Octavio (Mexican writer) **L:**71, 72; **M:**244; **P:555**
Paz Estenssoro, Victor (Bolivian political leader) **B:**310
Paz Zamora, Jaime (president of Bolivia) **B:**310
PBI (Polybenzimidazole) (manufactured fiber) **F:**111
PBX's *see* Private Branch Exchanges
PCB's *see* Polychlorinated biphenyls
PCP *see* Angel Dust
Peace: Burial at Sea (painting by Turner)
  picture(s) **T:**354
Peace Conference (Washington, D.C., 1861) **T:**368
Peace Corps **P:104**
  Kennedy administration **K:**209
Peace Garden State (nickname for North Dakota) **N:**322
Peace in our time (Chamberlain's announcement of Munich Pact, 1938) **W:**286
Peace movements **P:105–6** *see also* Disarmament
  Addams, Jane **A:**21
  international relations **I:**273–74
  Isaiah's call for peace **I:**345
  League of Nations **L:**94–95
  Nobel prizes **N:**266–68
  United Nations **U:**70–78
  Vietnam negotiations **V:**338
  What is a pacifist? **P:**106
Peace of God **F:**103
Peace River district (British Columbia) **A:**166; **B:**402, 405
Peach **P:107–8, 109** *see also* Plum
  picture(s)
    state flower of Delaware **D:**89
    sun drying of peaches **F:**339
Peach Festival (Japan) *see* Girls' Day
Peach State (nickname for Georgia) **G:**132, 133
Peachtree Street (Atlanta, Georgia) **A:**477; **G:**132
  picture(s)
    during Sherman's capture of Atlanta **C:**344
Peacock butterfly
  picture(s) **I:**230
Peacocks (birds)
  picture(s) **B:**215; **C:**426
Pea crabs (crustaceans) **C:**571; **M:**406
Peale, Anna Claypoole (American painter) **P:**110

Peale, Charles Willson (American painter)   **M:**133; **P:**110; **U:**127
picture(s)
    The Artist in His Museum (painting)   **P:**110
Peale, James (American painter)   **P:**110
Peale, Margaretta Angelica (American painter)   **P:**110
Peale, Norman Vincent (American clergyman)   **O:**73; **P:**555
Peale, Raphaelle (American painter)   **P:**110
picture(s)
    After the Bath (painting)   **P:**110
Peale, Rembrandt (American painter)   **P:**110
Peale, Rubens (American painter)   **P:**110
Peale, Sarah Miriam (American painter)   **P:**110
Peale, Titian Ramsay (American painter)   **P:**110
Peale family (of American artists)   **P:**110
Peanut butter   **P:**112
Peanut oil   **O:**76; **P:**112
Peanuts (comic strip)   **M:**339
picture(s)   **C:**129
Peanuts and peanut products   **P:**111–12
  Carver's work at Tuskegee Institute   **C:**130
  peanut butter, how to make   **P:**112
  peanut oil   **O:**76
  South American crop carried to Africa   **A:**99
  picture(s)   **A:**93
Pear   **P:**113
picture(s)
    orchard in Oregon   **O:**208
Pea Ridge, Battle of (1862, Civil War)   **A:**426, 428
Pea Ridge National Military Park (Arkansas)   **A:**424
Pearl danio (fish)   **F:**204
Pearl Harbor (United States naval base near Honolulu, Hawaii)   **H:**49, 59, 205
  aviation   **A:**564
  Japan   **J:**46
  World War II   **U:**196; **W:**292–93
  picture(s)
    World War II   **U:**195; **W:**293
Pearl Jam (American rock band)   **R:**262c
Pearl Mosque (Delhi, India)
picture(s)   **I:**139
Pearl of the Orient (nickname for Sri Lanka and Manila)   **M:**79; **S:**413
Pearl River (Louisiana–Mississippi)   **L:**303
Pearls   **P:**114–16
  early pearl diving methods   **U:**17
  How are artificial pearls made?   **P:**116
  Japan's cultured pearl industry   **J:**39
  jewelry   **J:**93
  organic gems   **G:**76
  oysters   **O:**289–90
  picture(s)
    jewelry   **J:**96
Pearly nautilus (mollusk)   **O:**293
  shells and shell collecting   **S:**149
Pearse, Pádhraic (Irish patriot)   **I:**324
Pearson, Hesketh (English biographer)   **E:**288
Pearson, Karl (English mathematician)   **S:**443
Pearson, Lester B. (prime minister of Canada)   **C:**76; **P:**116
Peary, Robert E. (American explorer)   **P:**117
  Arctic exploration   **A:**386d; **E:**416
Peas (vegetable)   **V:**292
  Mendel crossbred to prove genetic theories   **G:**79–81
  picture(s)
    leaves   **P:**305
    Mendel crossbred   **P:**299
Peasant dances   **D:**27
Peasants (farm workers on feudal manors)   **F:**102 *see also* Serfs
  Middle Ages, social classes of the   **M:**292
  Russia   **R:**365, 366; **U:**36, 50
  picture(s)   **F:**101, 103
    Russia   **R:**358
Peasants' Revolt (1381, in England)   **E:**241
"Pease Porridge Hot" (nursery rhyme)   **N:**415

Peat   **W:**147
  coal formation   **C:**388
  fuel   **F:**488, 489
  peat mosses   **G:**42; **M:**472, 473
  raw materials from plants   **P:**298
  picture(s)
    cutting turf   **I:**321; **P:**298
Pecan (tree)   **N:**434
  state tree of Texas   **T:**125
Peccaries (piglike mammals)   **P:**248
  hoofed mammals   **H:**211
  picture(s)   **H:**210
Peck (measure of volume)   **C:**532
Peck, Gregory (American actor)   **P:**555
Pecking orders (among birds)   **B:**222
Pecos (Indians of North America)   **I:**183
Pecos Bill (American folk hero story)   **G:**202
  excerpt from   **F:**319
Pecos River (New Mexico–Texas)   **N:**182–83; **T:**126
Pécs (Hungary)   **H:**286
Pectoral fins (of fish)   **F:**188; **S:**140
Pectoral muscle (in birds)   **B:**218
Peculiar galaxies   **U:**214
Peddlers (of goods)   **D:**118
Pediatrics (medical specialty)
  baby   **B:**3–4
  hospitals   **H:**247
  Taussig, Helen Brooke, and pediatric cardiology   **T:**24
Pedicel (part of ant's abdomen)   **A:**319
Pedigree (list of ancestors)
  dairy cattle breed associations   **D:**5
  stud books are records of Thoroughbred horses   **H:**231
Pedipalps (appendages of spiders)   **S:**402, 403, 406
Pedodontist (in dentistry)   **D:**115
Pedrarias Dávila (Pedro Arias de Avila) (Spanish colonial governor)   **B:**20
  De Soto a protégé of   **D:**138
Pedrell, Felipe (Spanish composer)   **S:**392d
Pedro I, Dom (emperor of Brazil)   **B:**384
  Portuguese royal family in Brazil   **P:**395
Pedro II, Dom (emperor of Brazil)   **B:**384
Peel, Sir Robert (British prime minister)   **P:**118, 368
Peele, George (English playwright)   **D:**298
Peelites (political followers of Sir Robert Peel)   **G:**225
Peer group (social group composed of members of equal standing)   **F:**39; **J:**169
Peer Gynt (play by Henrik Ibsen)   **I:**2
Pegasus (constellation)   **C:**526
Peg dolls   **D:**266
Peggy's Cove (Nova Scotia)   **N:**355
  picture(s)   **N:**352
Pegmatite dikes (rock masses)   **G:**70
Pegu (Burma)   **B:**457
P. E. I. *see* Prince Edward Island
Pei, I. M. (Chinese-American architect)   **P:**118; **U:**136
  East Building of the National Gallery of Art   **A:**386a; **N:**40
  Louvre's new entrance   **L:**317
  picture(s)   **I:**93
    East Building of the National Gallery of Art   **A:**386
    Louvre's new entrance   **L:**315
Peiping (China) *see* Beijing
Peipus, Lake (Estonia–Russia)   **E:**324
Pekin ducks   **P:**417
  picture(s)   **P:**416
Peking (China) *see* Beijing
Peking Opera   **T:**162
  picture(s)   **D:**295
Pelagic (water) environment (of the ocean)   **O:**23, 25
Pelagius I (pope)   **R:**290
Pelagius II (pope)   **R:**290
Pelé (Brazilian soccer player)   **P:**119
Peléean eruption (kind of volcanic eruption)   **V:**381
Pelham Bay Park (New York City)   **N:**231
Pelias (in Greek mythology)   **G:**367; **P:**555

Pelicans (birds) **B:**232; **P:119–20**
  "The Reason for the Pelican" (poem by Ciardi) **N:**275
  picture(s)
      brown pelicans **B:**223
      Florida **F:**264
      state bird of Louisiana **L:**299
Pelican State (nickname for Louisiana) **L:**299
Péligot, Eugène (French chemist) **U:**230
Pelion (Pilion) (mountain in Greece) **P:555**
Pella (Iowa)
  picture(s)
      19th-century lithograph of **C:**320
Pellagra (disease) **V:**370c
Pellan, Alfred (Canadian artist)
  picture(s)
      Végétaux Marins (painting) **C:**83
Pelléas et Mélisande (opera by Claude Debussy) **O:**160–61
Pellegra (nutrition-deficiency disease) **N:**429
Pellets (ammunition for guns) **G:**424
Pellicle (seed coat of a nut kernel) **N:**431
Peloponnesian War (431–404 B.C.) **A:**229–30; **G:**343–44;
      P:120a
  Pericles **P:**152
Peloponnesus (peninsula of Greece) **G:**332–33
Pelops (in Greek mythology) **G:**367
Pelota (jai alai ball) **J:**12
Pelton wheel (type of water turbine) **T:**341
Pelts (skins of fur-bearing animals) **F:**501, 502–4
Pelvic fins (of fish) **F:**188; **S:**140
Pelvis (hipbone) **S:**184
Pemba (island, Tanzania) **T:**17
Pemberton, John (American Civil War general) **C:**343
Pembina (North Dakota) **N:**334
PEMEX (Mexican petroleum agency) **M:**246
Pemmican (dried food)
  used by fur traders and Indians **I:**190
Penal colonies (of exiled criminals) **P:**481
  Australia **A:**515
  French Guiana **F:**466
  Siberia was formerly a Russian penal colony **S:**170
Penal Laws (imposed on Ireland) **I:**323, 324
Penance (sacrament of Roman Catholic Church) **R:**294
Penang (now **Pinang**) (Malaysia) **M:**58, 59
Pencil and paper games **G:**17
Pencils **P:143–44**
  drawing, history of **D:**316
  drawing materials **D:**306, 309
  What is the "lead" in a lead pencil? **L:**93
  picture(s) **D:**308
Pendants (jeweled ornaments) **J:**94
  picture(s) **J:**97
      Egyptian **D:**70
Pendentives (in architecture) **A:**375
  Byzantine architecture **B:**490
Penderecki, Krzysztof (Polish composer) **M:**548
Pendergast, Thomas J. (American politician) **T:**324
Pendleton Civil Service Act (United States, 1883) **C:**333;
      U:188–89
  Arthur, Chester Alan, signs into law **A:**439
Pendulum **C:**369, 371
  Galileo discovers laws governing **G:**5
  seismometer, used in a **E:**37
Penelope (in Greek mythology) **G:**369; **O:**51, 52
Peneus (Greek god) **G:**366
Penguins **P:120b–124**
  Antarctica **A:**293
  emperor penguin **B:**240
  flightless birds **O:**244
  picture(s) **A:**292
      Adelie penguins **H:**185
      emperor penguin **B:**232
      king penguin **B:**231
Penicillin (antibiotic) **A:**306, 307, 308, 310
  discovered by Fleming **F:**249
  fermentation process, new use of **F:**92

  genetic engineering, product of **G:**89
  how to grow a penicillium mold **A:**307
  medicine, history of **M:**208e
  rheumatic fever, treatment of **D:**200
  sac fungi produce penicillin **F:**497, 499, 500
  surgery, history of **S:**513
  picture(s) **F:**249
      Fleming's original culture **A:**307
Peninsula (land formation) **P:555**
Peninsular Ranges (California) **C:**20
Peninsular War (1808–1814) **N:**13; **S:**380
Penis (male anatomy) **B:**283; **R:**178, 179
  birth control **B:**248
  mammal reproduction **M:**68
Penitentiaries **P:**482
Penknives **P:**142
Penmanship *see* Handwriting
Penn, Irving (American photographer)
  picture(s)
      Man in White/Woman in Black, Morocco
      (photograph) **P:**206
Penn, John (American Revolutionary leader) **P:555**
Penn, William (English Quaker and founder of
      Pennsylvania) **P:125**, 138
  founding of Philadelphia **P:**180
  peace movements **P:**105
  proprietor of Delaware **D:**101–2
  Quaker rule of Pennsylvania **Q:**4
  thirteen American colonies **T:**176–77
Pennine Alps **A:**194b
Pennine Chain (England) **E:**233; **U:**61
Pennsbury Manor (home of William Penn) **C:**422
Pennsylvania **P:126–41**
  Civil War **C:**343
  colonial life in America **C:**411, 415, 419–20
  colonial sites you can visit today **C:**422
  farm life in colonial America **C:**413
  Gettysburg National Cemetery **N:**30
  Penn, William **P:**125
  petroleum, history of **P:**168
  Philadelphia **P:**180–81
  Pittsburgh **P:**266–67
  poverty in Appalachia **P:**419–20
  thirteen American colonies **T:**176–77
  United States, history of the **U:**175
  picture(s)
      Amish farmer **A:**89
      Bethlehem **C:**413
      Gettysburg National Cemetery **N:**30
      Gettysburg National Military Park **N:**52
      Johnstown Flood National Memorial **N:**52
Pennsylvania, University of **P:**130–31
Pennsylvania Dutch (German-speaking American
      colonists) **P:**130, 134; **T:**176
  folklore **F:**314
  fraktur documents **F:**293–94
  picture(s)
      folk art **D:**134; **F:**294
      "Welcome" sign **P:**138
Pennsylvania Hospital (Philadelphia) **H:**253
Pennsylvania Magazine **M:**19
Pennsylvanian period (in geology) **F:**386, 387
Pennsylvania Railroad **P:**140
Pennsylvania Society for Promoting the Abolition of Slavery **A:**6
Pennsylvania State University **P:**130
Pennsylvania system (of punishment) **P:**482
Pennsylvania Turnpike **P:**133
Penny Black (first postage stamp) **S:**420
Penny histories *see* Chapbooks
Penny papers (newspapers of 1800's) **J:**140; **N:**204
Penny Power (magazine) **C:**528
Pennyroyal (area of Kentucky) **K:**214
Penny system (of nail lengths) **N:**2
Pennywoodens *see* Peg dolls
Penobscot Indians (of Maine) **M:**41, 51

Pergamum (Asia Minor) L:172
Pergolesi, Giovanni Battista (Italian operatic composer) I:412
Peri, Jacopo (Italian composer) P:556
new music of the baroque era and the beginnings of
opera B:70; O:139
Pericles (Greek statesman) P:152
Athenian military leader A:230
oratory O:190
Peloponnesian War P:120a
picture(s)
statue G:343
Pericles (play by Shakespeare) S:136
Peridots (gemstones) see Olivines
Perigee (point of a satellite's orbit nearest Earth) S:365
moon's orbit M:446
Perihelion (point of a planet's orbit closest to the sun)
Mars M:105
Mercury R:143
solar system S:242
picture(s)
Mercury R:144
Periodicals see Magazines
Periodic table (of chemical elements) E:167–70
chemistry, history of C:209–10
definition C:204
Mendeleev's contribution to science S:74
valences and similar properties kept together C:202
Periodontal disease D:198
Periodontist (in dentistry) D:115
Periods (in geologic time scales) F:383; G:110
Periods (punctuation marks) P:540–41
Periods, menstrual see Menstruation
Periosteum (membrane around bone) B:274
Peripatetics (followers of Aristotle's philosophy) A:397
Peripheral nervous system (of the body) N:116–17, 118
Peripherals (input and output units of a computer) C:489,
490
telecommunications T:48
Periscopes (optical instruments) O:181
Perisphere (symbol of New York World's Fair, 1939)
picture(s) F:17
Perissodactyla (order of odd-toed hoofed mammals) H:208
horses and their relatives H:236
picture(s)
black rhinoceros as example M:73
Peristalsis (muscle contractions in digestion) D:161; S:461
Periwinkle (mollusk)
picture(s)
shell S:147
Periwinkle (plant) F:281
Perjury (legal term) P:556
Perkin, William Henry (English chemist) D:372
Perkins, Jacob (American inventor) R:134
Perkins, W. H. (English inventor) T:142
Perlman, Itzhak (Israeli violinist) I:371; P:556
Permafrost (permanently frozen subsoil) A:386b–386c; B:208
Alaska A:146
tundra T:331
Yukon and Northwest Territories (Canada) Y:360
Permalloy (alloy of iron and nickel) M:32
Permanent Commission on Human Rights (United
Nations) S:197
Permanent Court of Justice (The Hague) see International Court
of Justice
Permanent waves (in hairstyling) H:8
Permeability (of membranes) O:242–43
Permian period (in geology) E:25, 27
picture(s)
drifting continents G:112
table(s) F:384
Permineralization (fossilizing process) F:381
Permissions (in publishing) B:324
Perón, Eva (Argentinian political figure) A:395; P:556
picture(s) A:395
Perón, Isabel (president of Argentina) A:395

Perón, Juan (president of Argentina) A:395; F:64
picture(s) A:395
Peroration (conclusion of a speech) O:190
Perot, H. Ross (American businessman and presidential
candidate) B:469; C:367; T:139; U:205
Perov, Vasili (Russian painter) R:374
Peroxide (used in hair coloring) H:8
Perpendiculars (in geometry) G:121
Perpendicular style (in architecture) E:257
Perpetual calendar (for keeping track of time) C:15
Perrault, Charles (French poet and critic) P:556
France, literature of F:439
Mother Goose stories C:229; N:410
"Sleeping Beauty" F:27–29
Perrault, Claude (French architect) L:317
Perrot, Jules (French ballet dancer) B:27
history of the dance D:25–26
Perry (fermented pear juice) P:113
Perry, Gaylord (American baseball player) P:556
Perry, Matthew C. (American naval commander) P:152; R:225
Commodore Perry opens Japan's door J:44
Perry, Oliver Hazard (American naval officer) P:153; R:225
memorial in Ohio O:69
victory on Lake Erie M:270
War of 1812 W:9
picture(s) W:8
flag F:248
Perryville, Battle of (1862) K:226
Perse, Saint-John (French poet) F:442
Persecution
early Christians C:287, 288
witches W:209
Persephone (Proserpina) (Greek goddess) G:362, 363
Persepolis (ancient capital of Persia) A:371–72
ancient world, art of the A:242, 243; P:155
sculpture S:94
picture(s) A:227
sculpture P:154
Perseus (constellation) C:525
Perseus (hero in Greek mythology) G:365
picture(s) G:365
Pershing, John J. (American general) P:153
Persia, ancient I:308–9; P:154–57 see also Iran
Alexander the Great conquers A:178
ancient art A:242–43
ancient civilization A:227
architecture: dome, meaning of B:490
manuscript illustration I:357
New Year customs N:209
palaces A:371–72
Peloponnesian War P:120a
perfumes P:150
pottery P:408
relay system of postriders C:465
sculpture S:94
Zoroastrianism Z:387
picture(s)
manuscript illustration A:438c
relief sculpture from Susa T:143
Persian (Farsi) (language of Iranians) I:305; M:299
Persian cats C:138
picture(s) C:138
Persian Gulf
Asia's oil resources A:452
extreme temperatures A:453
pearls P:115
Persian Gulf War (1991) A:347, 466; P:158
Egypt, history of E:109
Iraq I:315, 316
Kurds K:305
Kuwait K:309
Middle East M:305
Organization of Petroleum Exporting Countries O:221
Powell, Colin P:421
United States, Armed Forces of the U:109, 115, 120,

123

United States, history of the   **U:**204
picture(s)
U.S. Army tank crews   **M:**305
Persian lamb (fur)   **F:**502; **N:**8; **T:**352
Persian melons   **M:**216
Persian rugs   **R:**355
picture(s)   **I:**306; **R:**354
Persian Wars (in the 5th century B.C.)   **G:**342–43
Persistence of Memory, The (painting by Salvador Dali)
picture(s)   **D:**13
Persistence of vision   **M:**478
Personal computer *see* Computer, personal
Personal ethics   **E:**329
Personality tests   **T:**118–19
Personality types (in psychology)   **J:**156; **P:**503
Personal names *see* Names
Personal pronouns   **P:**92
Personal property
disposed of by a testament (will)   **W:**174
Personification (figure of speech)   **F:**122–23
Perspective (illusion of depth in art)
ancient Greek art   **G:**349
Brunelleschi, Filippo   **I:**395; **R:**164
drawing   **D:**311–12
optical illusions   **O:**175
Pucelle, Jean   **F:**423
Perspiration (secretion to rid body of heat energy)   **E:**215
perspiring hands can cause gymnasts to slip   **G:**432
Perth (capital of Western Australia)   **A:**512, 514
Pertussis *see* Whooping cough
Peru   **P:**159–65
ancient textile weaving   **T:**143
Incas   **I:**107–10, 173
Indians, American   **I:**168, 170, 195–96
Latin-American art and architecture   **L:**63
life in Latin America   **L:**47–61
Lima   **L:**239
Pizarro, Francisco   **P:**268
San Martín, José de   **S:**36
tapestry designs   **T:**22
picture(s)
Andes   **A:**253
embroidered cloak   **N:**100
flag   **F:**239
Huascarán Valley citrus groves   **S:**290
Indians, American   **I:**163
Lima   **P:**165
Lima street vendors   **L:**239
Machu Picchu ruins   **A:**354; **S:**293; **W:**217
Peru (Humboldt) Current   **E:**19; **P:**163
climate of South America affected   **S:**279
Perugino, Pietro (Italian painter)
picture(s)
The Delivery of the Keys (painting)   **R:**281
Pesaro Madonna *see* Madonna with Saints and Members of the
Pesaro Family
Pescadores (islands in the Taiwan Strait)   **T:**8
Peshawar (Pakistan)   **P:**39–40
Peso (monetary unit)   **D:**257
Pest (section of Budapest)   **B:**422, 422a, 422b
Pestalozzi, Johann Heinrich (Swiss educational
reformer)   **E:**81–82; **K:**249
Pesticides   **H:**79; **P:**290–91 *see also* Insecticides
Carson, Rachel   **C:**121
environmental diseases   **D:**186
farm management   **F:**56–57
food chain affected by   **B:**244
food regulations and laws   **F:**346
household pest control   **H:**264
poisons found in the home   **P:**355
pollution by synthetic chemicals   **E:**299
water pollution   **W:**68
picture(s)
copper sulfate sprayed on grapes   **C:**205

Pests
ants   **A:**324
beetles   **B:**127
caterpillars   **B:**478
food spoilage   **F:**339
household pests   **H:**260–64
plant pests   **P:**286–91
rabbits in Australia   **A:**506
ticks   **T:**192
PET *see* Positron emission tomography
Pétain, Henri Philippe (French general and political
leader)   **P:**556
World Wars I and II in France   **F:**419; **W:**277, 289
Petals (of flowers)   **F:**282; **P:**306–7
Petasos (ancient Greek hat)   **H:**45
Petate (straw mat bed)   **L:**53–54
Petén (region of Guatemala)   **G:**396
Petén, Lake (Guatemala)   **L:**29
Peter, Saint (one of the 12 Apostles)   **P:**166
Apostles, The   **A:**328
Christianity, history of   **C:**286, 287
first pope   **R:**290
"rock" of the Roman Catholic Church   **R:**281–82
Vatican City and Saint Peter's Church   **V:**280–82
Peter I (czar of Russia) *see* Peter the Great
Peter III (emperor of Russia)   **C:**136
Peter I (king of Yugoslavia)   **Y:**358
Peter I and II (books of the New Testament)   **B:**166
Peter and the Wolf (musical composition by Sergei
Prokofiev)   **P:**485
Peterborough (New Hampshire)
first tax-supported library in the United States   **L:**175;
N:155
Peter Grimes (opera by Benjamin Britten)   **O:**161
Peterhof (summer palace, Saint Petersburg, Russia)
picture(s)   **S:**18b
Peterkin, Julia Mood (American writer)   **P:**556; **S:**309
Peter of Amiens *see* Peter the Hermit
Peter Pan (play by James M. Barrie)   **B:**73
excerpt from   **B:**73–74
Peter Piper (tongue twister)   **T:**225
Peter Rabbit, The Tale of (by Beatrix Potter)   **P:**405
picture(s)   **C:**239
Peters, Karl (German explorer)   **T:**19
Peters, Mike (American editorial cartoonist)   **C:**127
Petersburg (Virginia)
Civil War battle site   **C:**345
Peterson, Esther Eggertsen (U.S. government official and
consumer adviser)   **P:**556; **W:**212b
Peter's Pence   **P:**556
Peter the Great (Russian czar)   **P:**166; **R:**365, 377; **U:**45–46
Catherine I   **C:**136
Hermitage Museum began with his collections   **H:**116
higher education in Russia   **R:**358
Ivan V   **I:**414
Saint Petersburg founded by   **M:**468; **S:**18a–18b
westernization of architecture   **R:**372
Peter the Hermit (French monk)   **P:**556
First Crusade   **C:**588; **R:**286
Petherbridge, Margaret (American crossword puzzle
maker)   **C:**587
Petioles (of leaves)   **L:**112; **P:**306
Pétion, Alexandre Sabés (Haitian general and politician)   **H:**11
Petipa, Marius (French choreographer)   **B:**28–29; **D:**26
Petitcodiac River (New Brunswick)
tidal bore from Bay of Fundy   **N:**138; **T:**197
Petitgrain oil   **P:**64
Petition, freedom of *see* Freedom of petition
Petitioners (early English political party)   **P:**369
Petition of Right (1628)   **B:**184; **E:**245
Petitions (kind of prayer)   **P:**431
Petit Jean Mountain (Arkansas)
picture(s)   **A:**418
Petit jury *see* Trial (petit) jury
Petit mal (type of epilepsy)   **D:**192

Petit Piton (volcano, Saint Lucia) **S:**17
Petra (Jordan) **J:**131–32
Petrarch, Francesco (Italian poet) **I:**383, 406
  Renaissance humanism **R:**159, 160
Petrassi, Goffredo (Italian composer) **I:**412
Petrel (seabird)
  stormy petrel used as a torch **L:**231
  picture(s)
    Wilson's storm petrel **B:**240
Petrification (fossilizing process) **F:**381
Petrified Forest National Park (Arizona) **A:**410
Petrified wood
  evidence of ancient life **E:**374
  Petrified Forest (Flora, Mississippi) **M:**358
  picture(s) **F:**387
Petrochemicals (chemicals derived from petroleum or natural
    gas) **P:**174
  manufactured in Louisiana **L:**306
  Texas is largest producer **T:**129, 131
Petrodvorets (summer home of Peter the Great)
  picture(s) **F:**394
Petroglyphs (carved drawings on canyon walls) *see* Rock art
Petrograd (Russia) *see* Saint Petersburg
Petrol (fuel) *see* Gasoline
Petroleum and petroleum refining **P:**167–76
  Africa's resources **A:**49
  Alabama **A:**136
  Alaska **A:**144, 149, 151, 152, 158
  Arctic petroleum transported south by pipelines **A:**386d
  Asia's resources **A:**452
  Australia **A:**510
  automobiles' lubrication systems **A:**548
  Azerbaijan **A:**572
  Bahrain **B:**18, 19
  Brunei, Sultanate of **B:**415
  Canada's oil deposits and production **C:**59
  Colorado **C:**437
  desert countries, changes in **D:**127
  distillation process **D:**219
  Ecuador's leading industry **E:**67, 68
  energy supply **E:**219, 220–21
  engineering **E:**226
  Europe, oil resources of **E:**347
  fertilizer prices and the food supply **F:**351
  fertilizers **F:**98
  first aid for poisoning by petroleum products **P:**355
  gasoline a product of **G:**62
  geologists work for oil companies **G:**119
  Iraq's oil resources **I:**314
  Kansas **K:**178, 180, 183, 185
  kerosene derived from **K:**235
  Kuwait's oil reserves **K:**307, 309
  Libya **L:**189
  liquid fuels **F:**487, 490
  lubricants **L:**319
  Mexico **M:**245, 246
  Middle East **M:**303–4
  Montana **M:**435
  natural gas found just above petroleum deposits **N:**59
  natural resources, distribution of **N:**66
  North American mineral resources **N:**292
  North Sea deposits of oil and natural gas **U:**62, 64
  Norway **N:**347, 348
  ocean pollutant **E:**298–99; **W:**67–68
  oil spills **C:**518
  oil-well brine a source of iodine **I:**287
  Oklahoma **O:**84, 87
  Oman **O:**121
  Organization of Petroleum Exporting Countries **O:**221
  Persian Gulf War **P:**158
  poisonous petroleum products found in the home **P:**355
  protozoans help in exploration **P:**497
  Qatar **Q:**2, 3
  Russia **R:**362
  Saudi Arabia **S:**57, 58b

  seismic prospecting with explosives **E:**425
  Sudan **S:**479
  Texas **T:**124, 128, 140
  transportation industry **T:**291
  Tulsa (Oklahoma) **T:**330
  tundra **T:**331
  underwater oil well drilling **U:**25
  United Arab Emirates **U:**53
  Venezuela **V:**297, 299
  waxes made from **C:**94; **W:**76
  world distribution **W:**261
  world production **O:**221
  Wyoming **W:**331–32
  Yemen **Y:**349
  diagram(s)
    fractionating tower **P:**173
    rotary rig **P:**170
  map(s)
    world distribution **W:**263
  picture(s)
    Alberta oil sands recovery plant **A:**169
    Basra (Iraq) **B:**314
    Canada's oil deposits and production **C:**61
    Canadian refinery **P:**429
    Iranian workers **I:**307
    Libyan oil fields **A:**64
    Libyan refinery **S:**7
    Mexican refinery **M:**247
    oil pumps **N:**303; **U:**99
    oil refineries **A:**462; **M:**247, 303; **P:**173, 174; **U:**40
    oil rigs **A:**149; **E:**221, 304; **G:**102, 104; **I:**210;
      L:29; **M:**57; **N:**346; **O:**12; **P:**167; **T:**125
    Red Sea drilling **A:**347
    tanker unloading crude oil **F:**486
    Titusville (Pennsylvania) oil well **P:**140
Petroleum engineers **E:**226
Petroleum jelly **W:**76
Petronius (Roman writer) **L:**78
Petrosyan, Tigran (Armenian chess champion) **A:**431
Pets **P:**177–79
  birds **B:**245–47
  cats **C:**137–40
  dogs **D:**250, 251, 253–56
  farm birds as pets **B:**247
  fish as pets **F:**203–5
  gerbils **G:**410
  guinea pigs **G:**409
  hamsters **G:**409–10
  lizards and chameleons **L:**268
  nature, study of **N:**68
  parrots **P:**86
  turtles no longer popular pets **T:**357
Petticoat breeches (garments) **C:**377
Pettit, Bob (American basketball player) **B:**95j
  picture(s) **B:**95j
Petunia (plant)
  picture(s) **G:**28, 38, 48
Peul (African people) *see* Fulani
Pevsner, Antoine (Russian sculptor) **M:**392; **S:**104
  Gabo, Naum **G:**439
  picture(s)
    Developable Column **M:**393
Pewter (metal) **P:**556; **T:**207
  antiques and antique collecting **A:**316b
  knives, forks, and spoons **K:**285
Peyote cactus **C:**5
PGA *see* Professional Golfers' Association
Phaedra (in Greek mythology) **P:**556–57
Phaethon (in Greek mythology) **P:**557
Phagocytes (body cells) **I:**96
Phainopepla (desert bird)
  picture(s) **B:**237
Phalangers (marsupials) **M:**113
Phalanges (bones of the hands and feet) **S:**183, 184
  diagram(s) **F:**79, 80

Phalangist Party (Lebanese) L:122–23
Phalanx Close-in Weapons System U:120
Phantom of the Opera (musical by Lloyd Webber) M:559
Pharaohs (rulers of ancient Egypt) A:221, 223
   Egyptian tombs A:371
   Passover P:95
Pharisees (Hebrew sect in Judea) **P:557**
Pharmaceuticals *see* Drugs
Pharmacology (science of preparation, uses, and effects of
     drugs) D:333
   branch of biochemistry B:186
Pharmacopeia (list of drugs and drug formulas) D:334
Pharmacy (practice of preparing and selling
     medicines) D:332; H:249
   picture(s)
     17th-century pharmacy M:206
Pharos (lighthouse of Alexandria, Egypt) L:227
   one of the seven wonders of the ancient world W:219–20
Pharynx (of the body) B:278; D:161; L:328
Phase-contrast microscopes M:281
Phases (grains in alloys) A:191
Phases (of celestial bodies)
   Mercury M:232
   moon M:447
   observing Mercury and Venus P:279
   picture(s)
     moon M:448–49
Pheasant (game bird)
   picture(s)
     Lady Amherst's pheasant B:231
     ring-necked is state bird of South Dakota S:313
Phèdre (play by Jean Racine) D:299
Pheidippides (champion Athenian runner) O:105
Phenol (organic chemical) C:391
Phenol-formaldehyde (plastic) P:322
Phenylalanine (amino acid) D:198
Phenylketonuria (PKU) (disease) D:184, 198
   retardation, mental R:190
Pheromones (chemicals secreted by animals)
   ants A:318
   fish F:194
   insects I:235
Phi Beta Kappa (honor society) V:351
Phidias (Greek sculptor) G:350
   Greek civilization A:230
   statue of Zeus W:218
Philadelphia (Pennsylvania) P:126, 133, 138, 139, **180–81**
   colonial life in America C:419
   colonial sites you can visit today C:422
   fire fighting, history of F:145
   Franklin and the Library Company L:175
   Franklin's activities F:454–55
   Independence Hall I:113
   Liberty Bell L:170
   Revolutionary War R:203, 204
   signing of Declaration of Independence D:57
   United States mint established M:340
   picture(s) P:127
     Bank of the United States (building) B:52
     City Hall P:130
     Independence Hall P:131
     Liberty Bell P:127
Philadelphia Athletics (baseball team) B:91
Philadelphia Orchestra P:131
   diagram(s)
     orchestra seating plan O:196
   picture(s) O:192, 197
Philately *see* Stamps and stamp collecting
Philemon (book of the New Testament) B:165
Philemon and Baucis (in Greek mythology) **P:557**
Philharmonic Hall (Lincoln Center for the Performing Arts) *see*
     Avery Fisher Hall
Philip (antipope) R:290
Philip (prince of the United Kingdom of Great Britain and
     Northern Ireland, duke of Edinburgh) E:192

   picture(s) U:68
Philip (Metacomet) (Native American chief) I:202; M:149
Philip II (king of France, Philip Augustus) M:291
Philip IV (Philip the Fair) (king of France) **P:557**
   Roman Catholic Church in the Middle Ages M:291;
     R:287
Philip VI (king of France) F:413; H:281
Philip II (king of Macedon) **P:557**
   father of Alexander the Great A:177
Philip II (duke of Pomerania) D:261
Philip II (king of Spain) E:191; H:2; S:379
   attitude toward the Church R:288
   England and Elizabeth I E:243–44
   Netherlands, history of N:120d
   picture(s) S:380
Philip IV (king of Spain)
   Velázquez, Diego, was his court painter V:294
Philip V (king of Spain) C:72; S:380
Philip Augustus (king of France) L:316
Philip of Anjou *see* Philip V (king of Spain)
Philip of Bethsaida, Saint (one of the Apostles) A:328, 329
Philippe de Vitry (French composer) F:444
Philippi, Battle of (42 B.C.) A:495
Philippians (book of Bible) B:165
Philippics (forceful speeches)
   origin of the term O:190
Philippine mahogany *see* Lauan
Philippines P:182–88
   American occupation T:113
   Aquino, Corazon C. A:338
   dance D:32
   folk dance F:300, 303
   MacArthur, Douglas M:2
   Manila M:79
   McKinley accepts for the United States M:193
   Pershing, John J. P:153
   problem of lack of common language E:86
   Quezon, Manuel Q:18
   Spanish-American War S:393, 394
   Taft, William Howard, was governor T:4
   World War II W:293, 304–5
   picture(s)
     flag F:233
     girl A:455
     rice fields N:62; S:330
     stilt houses H:170; J:158
Philippine Sea O:46
Philipse Manor (farm, New York)
   picture(s) C:416
Philip the Good (Duke of Burgundy) D:365
Philistines (ancient people who established themselves in
     Canaan) P:40c, 557
   David and the Philistines D:43
   Jews, history of the J:103
Phillip, Arthur (British colonizer of Australia) A:515; E:413
Phillips, Wendell (American abolitionist)
   withdrew support from women's rights movement W:212a
Phillips Exeter Academy (New Hampshire) N:155
Phillips-head screws N:3
   screwdriver T:229
   picture(s) N:2
Philodendron (plant)
   picture(s) L:115
Philo Judaeus (Jewish historian) J:106
Philosopher's stone (mythical substance sought by
     alchemists) C:207
Philosophes (French writers) F:415, 467
Philosophy P:189–92
   ancient Greek philosophers A:231
   Aquinas, Saint Thomas A:338
   Aristotle A:396–97
   Confucius C:497
   Descartes, René D:123
   Dewey, John D:143
   ethics E:328–29

Piano (cont.)
Italy develops   I:411
keyboard instruments   K:239
Liszt's music for   L:257
MacDowell, Edward   M:3
orchestra seating plan   O:196
Rachmaninoff, Sergei   R:32
ragtime   J:57
recordings   R:123
romanticism in music   R:304
Schumann's music   G:187; S:59
stringed instuments   S:469
types of musical instruments   M:552
picture(s)
grand piano   K:239; M:552; P:240
Piano, Renzo (Italian architect)   A:386a
Pianola *see* Player piano
Piano rolls (recordings)   R:123
Piatigorsky, Gregor (Russian-born American cellist)   P:557
Piazza Minerva (Rome, Italy)   R:305
Piazza Navona (city square, Rome, Italy)   F:393–94
picture(s)   R:307
Piazzi, Giuseppe (Italian astonomer)   S:244
Pica (size of type)   T:370
Picadors (in bullfighting)   B:449
Picaresque (rogue) novels
Henry Fielding's *Tom Jones*   E:279–80
Spanish literature   S:390
Picasso, Pablo (Spanish-born painter of the French school)   P:243–44; S:387
art of the artist   A:438e
collage   C:400
drawing, history of   D:316
modern art   M:390
modern French art   F:431–32
modern Spanish art   S:387
painting in the 20th century   P:29–30
Picasso museum (Barcelona, Spain)   M:527
sculpture   S:103–4
worked with Braque   B:371
picture(s)
Child with a Dove (painting)   P:243
Demoiselles d'Avignon, Les (painting)   M:390
drawing of Manuel de Falla   S:392d
Girl Before a Mirror   A:438e
Girl with a Mandolin (painting)   D:136
Green Still Life (painting)   P:31
Guernica (mural)   S:387
Head of a Woman (sculpture)   S:104
ink drawing of two pigeons   D:316
portrait of Gertrude Stein   S:446
sculpture in Chicago   C:219
Three Musicians (painting)   P:243
Piccadilly Circus (London, England)   L:286–87
Piccard, Auguste (Swiss scientist, inventor, and explorer)   P:244
balloon ascents   B:36
bathyscaphe   E:418; O:42; U:20–21
Piccard, Jacques (Swiss scientist)   P:244
Piccolo (musical instrument)   M:553; W:183
picture(s)   M:553
Pick (used in playing a guitar)   G:411
Pick a card (trick)   T:1312
Pickering, Edward (American astronomer)   A:474
Picketing (labor union tactic)   L:8, 10
picture(s)   L:10
Pickett, George Edward (Confederate general in the U.S. Civil War)   P:557–58
Pickford, Mary (American actress and producer)   M:489, 491
Pickling (in steel production)   I:336
Pickling (of food)   F:344
olives   O:101
Pickup baler (farm machine)   F:58
Pick-up-sticks (game)   G:18

Pickup trucks
picture(s)   T:320
Pickwick Papers (book by Charles Dickens)   D:149
Picnics   O:264
picture(s)   U:96
Pictographs (pictograms) (early form of writing) *see* Picture writing
Pictographs (picture graphs) (style of graph)   G:310
Picts (early people of Scotland)   S:88
beginnings of English history   E:236
Picture books
Caldecott, Randolph   C:10
Caldecott Medal   C:11–12
children's book awards   C:240
children's literature   C:228, 237
list of   C:242–43
Picture editors (of magazines)   M:17
Picturephone *see* Video telephone
Pictures (works of art) *see* Cartoons; Engraving; Illustration and Illustrators; Painting; Photography; Posters
Picture tube (of a television set) *see* Cathode-ray tube
Picture writing   C:463; H:22 *see also* individual letters of the alphabet
alphabet   A:192
Chinese pictograms   B:320
development of languages   L:38
Pidgin (simplified form of English)   S:252
Piebald (horse marking)
picture(s)   H:238
Pieces of eight (Spanish coins)   P:558
Pie charts (circle graphs)   G:310–11; S:441–42
Pied coats (of dogs)   D:245–46
Piedmont glaciers   G:223
Alabama   A:132
Piedmont Region (eastern United States)   N:166, 285; P:128; S:298
Maryland   M:122, 124
Virginia   V:348, 349, 350, 352
Pied Piper of Hamelin   P:558
"Pied Piper of Hamelin, The" (poem by Robert Browning)
excerpt from   B:413
Piepowder Courts (England)   F:10
Pierce, Franklin (14th president of the United States)   N:162; P:245–47
Franklin Pierce Homestead   N:158
Hawthorne and Pierce   H:65
picture(s)   N:162; P:447
Pierce, Jane Means Appleton (wife of Franklin Pierce)   F:170; P:246, 247
picture(s)   F:171
Pierce, John Davis (American educator)   M:264
Pierce, Webb (American singer)   C:564
Pierian spring   P:558
Pierpont Morgan Library (New York City)   M:456
Pierre (capital of South Dakota)   S:324
picture(s)   S:325
Pierrot (character in French pantomime)   P:558
first Western clown to wear makeup   C:386
Piers (in construction) *see* Caissons
Piers Plowman (English poem)   E:269
Pies (baked goods)   B:388b
Pietà (sculpture by Michelangelo)   M:257; V:282
exhibited at New York World's Fair (1964–1965)   F:17
picture(s)   M:257
Piezoelectricity (of quartz crystals)   C:601; Q:5
forces, measurement of   F:365
Pig (number game)   N:394
Pigalle, Jean Baptiste (French sculptor)   S:101
Pigeons (birds)   B:242; O:244 *see also* Doves
carrier pigeons   C:466
operant conditioning   P:506–8
passenger pigeons are now extinct   B:244
pets   B:247; P:178–79
pigeon's milk   B:232

picture(s)
    homing pigeon **H:**193
    victoria crested pigeon **B:**230
Pig frogs **F:**477
Piggyback (freight hauling method) **R:**83; **T:**289
Pig iron **I:**332; **O:**217
Pig Latin (secret language) **C:**395
Pigments *see* Paints and pigments
Pigmies *see* Pygmies
Pignotti, Lorenzo (Italian fabulist) **F:**4
Pigpen cipher **C:**394–95
Pigs **P:**248
    hoofed mammals **H:**209, 211
    pigskin leather **L:**107
    raising pigs for market **M:**195–96
    world distribution **W:**266
    map(s)
        world distribution **W:**265
    picture(s) **M:**67, 374
        pig family **H:**210
Pigs, Bay of (Cuba)
    anti-Castro invasion attempt **C:**600; **K:**209
Pigs in Clover (puzzle) **P:**552
Pigskin leather **L:**107
Pigweed **W:**106
Pikas (animals of rabbit family) **R:**24
Pike (diving position) **D:**225
    picture(s) **D:**224
Pike (fish)
    picture(s) **F:**211
Pike, Zebulon Montgomery (American soldier) **P:**558
    exploration of the West **C:**442; **M:**338; **O:**273
Pikes Peak (Colorado)
    atmospheric pressure's effect on boiling point of a
        liquid **H:**91
    inspired the writing of "America the Beautiful" **N:**25
    picture(s) **C:**439
Pilar (Paraguay) **P:**65
Pilasters (in architecture) **B:**494
Pilate, Pontius (Roman governor of Judea) **J:**86
Pilâtre de Rozier, Jean François (French balloonist) **P:**558
    balloons and ballooning, history of **B:**34
Pilcomayo River (South America) **P:**63
Pile (of rugs and carpets) **R:**353, 354–55
Pileated woodpeckers (birds)
    picture(s)
        feet **B:**216
Pile drivers **B:**400
    picture(s) **B:**435
Pile fabrics **T:**142
Pile foundation (in construction) **B:**435
Pileus (ancient Roman hat) **H:**45
Pilgrimages
    Chaucer's *Canterbury Tales* **C:**191; **E:**270
    Crusades **C:**588–90
    holy places of Hindus **H:**130
    Muslims to Mecca **I:**353; **M:**199; **S:**58a
    picture(s)
        holy places of Hindus **H:**126, 129
        Muslims to Mecca **A:**344; **S:**58c
Pilgrim Pope (nickname for Paul VI) **P:**102
Pilgrims (Separatists from the Church of England) **P:**344–47
    colonial life in America **C:**409
    founders of Plymouth colony **T:**170–72
    Mayflower **M:**188
    Thanksgiving Day **T:**153–54
    picture(s)
        first Thanksgiving **T:**153
        founders of Plymouth colony **M:**146; **T:**167
Pilgrim's Progress (book by John Bunyan) **E:**276
    books for children **C:**229
    development of the novel **F:**115
Pili (bacterial structures) **B:**11
Pilion *see* Pelion
Pilipino (national language of the Philippines) **P:**182, 183

Pill (contraceptive) **B:**248
Pillar cranes (machines) **H:**146–47
Pillars (in architecture) *see* Columns
Pillars of Hercules **G:**204; **P:558**
Pillboxes (fortifications) **F:**379
Pillow Book, The (book by Sei Shonagon) **J:**41
Pillow lava **V:**382
Pilobolus Dance Theatre **P:558**
Pilon, Germain (French sculptor) **F:**424
Pilot, The (novel by James Fenimore Cooper) **C:**541
Pilotage (airplane navigation method) **A:**118
Piloting (navigational system) **N:**72–74
Pilots, airplane
    careers in aviation **A:**568–69
    training requirements **A:**567
Pilot snakes *see* Copperheads
Pilot whales (blackfish, potheads) **W:**149
    picture(s) **D:**275; **W:**150
Pilsen (Czechoslovakia) *see* Plzeň
Pilsudski, Józef (Polish statesman) **P:**361–62
Pima (Native Americans) *see* O'o'dham
Pima cotton **C:**560
Pimples **D:**187
Pina (plant fiber) **F:**109
Pinafore (operetta by Gilbert and Sullivan) *see* H.M.S. Pinafore
Pinang *see* Penang
Piñata (Latin-American Christmas custom) **C:**301; **L:**51–52
    Mexico **M:**243
Pinatubo, Mount (volcano, Philippines) **E:**15
    picture(s) **E:**15
Pinchback, Pickney Benton Stewart (American
    politician) **A:**79c
Pinchbeck (gold substitute) **J:**92
Pinch hitters (in baseball) **B:**80
Pinchincha, Battle of (1822) **E:**69
Pinchot, Gifford (American conservationist) **N:**32–33
    conservation program with Theodore Roosevelt **R:**331
    controversy with Taft **T:**5
Pinckney, Charles (American statesman,
    1757–1824) **S:**308–9, 311
Pinckney, Charles Cotesworth (American statesman,
    1746–1825) **S:**308
Pinckney, Elizabeth Lucas (West Indies-born American who
    initiated indigo culture) **S:**296, 308
Pinckney, Thomas (American statesman) **S:**308
Pinckney's Treaty (1795) **W:**44
Pincushion cacti **C:**5
Pindar (Greek poet) **G:**354
    Pindaric odes **O:**50
Pindus (mountain range in Greece) **G:**333
Pine (tree)
    Arizona has world's largest stand of ponderosa
        pines **A:**404
    bristlecone pine is oldest living thing **T:**300
    western white pine is state tree of Idaho **I:**49
    white pine was the most useful tree in the United
        States **L:**322
    picture(s)
        eastern white pine is provincial tree of Ontario **O:**124
        eastern white pine is state tree of Maine and
            Michigan **M:**37, 259
        loblolly pines **A:**133
        Mississippi's Piney Woods **M:**352
        Montana forest attacked by pine beetles **P:**286
        piñon pine is state tree of Nevada and New
            Mexico **N:**123, 181
        ponderosa pine is state tree of Montana **M:**429
        red pine is state tree of Minnesota **M:**327
        Scotch pine **P:**305
        seed **P:**307
        shortleaf is state tree of Arkansas **A:**417
        southern pine is state tree of Alabama **A:**131
        state tree of North Carolina **N:**307
        sugar pine **T:**301
        uses of the wood (white and yellow) and its

Pine (cont.)
        grain **W:**224
        western white pine is state tree of Idaho   **I:**47
        white pine   **T:**301
Pineal gland   **G:**228
Pineapple   **P:**249–50
    important crop to Hawaii   **H:**55–56
    pina fiber comes from leaves   **F:**109
    sign of welcome in colonial homes   **N:**98
    picture(s)   **H:**54; **P:**296, 529
Pine Barrens (New Jersey)   **N:**164, 166, 167, 172
Pine Bluff (Arkansas)   **A:**425
Pine Creek Gorge (Pennsylvania)   **P:**134
Piñeda, Alonso de (Spanish explorer)   **T:**137
Pine grosbeaks (birds)   **A:**277
Pine-knot torches   **L:**231
Pinel, Philippe (French doctor)   **M:**206
Pinelands National Reserve (New Jersey)   **N:**164, 172
Pinero, Arthur Wing (English dramatist)   **D:**301
Pine squirrels see Red squirrels
Pine-tree shillings (coins)   **M:**340
Pine Tree State (nickname for Maine)   **M:**36, 37
Piney Woods (Mississippi)   **M:**352, 353, 354
    picture(s)   **M:**352
Pinfeathers (immature feathers)   **P:**417
Ping-Pong see Table tennis
Pinhole camera   **E:**396
Pinion (smaller of a pair of gears)   **G:**65
Pink bollworm (insect)   **C:**561
Pinkerton, Allan (American detective)   **P:**558
Pinkney, Jerry (American illustrator of children's books)   **C:**235
    picture(s)   **C:**234
Pinna (part of the outer ear)   **E:**4
    picture(s)   **E:**5
Pinnate compound leaves   **L:**112
    picture(s)   **L:**113
Pinnate veins (of trees)   **T:**308
Pinnipeds (fin-footed mammals)
    fur seals   **F:**518
    sea lions   **S:**106
    seals   **S:**107–8
    walruses   **W:**6–7
    picture(s)
        hooded seal as example   **M:**71
Pinocchio (animated cartoon)   **M:**493
Pinocchio (wooden puppet who becomes a living boy)   **P:**558
Pinochet Ugarte, Augusto (Chilean military and political leader)   **C:**255
Pinocytosis (of animal cells)   **C:**161
Piñon (pine tree)
    picture(s)
        state tree of Nevada   **N:**123
        state tree of New Mexico   **N:**181
Pins
    jewelry   **J:**99
    picture(s)
        jewelry   **J:**98
Pinski, David (Yiddish playwright)   **Y:**351
Pint (measure of volume)   **C:**532; **W:**113, 115
Pinta (ship of Christopher Columbus)   **C:**446; **E:**406
Pinter, Harold (British playwright)   **D:**303; **E:**290; **P:**558
    picture(s)
        The Caretaker, scene from   **D:**303
Pinto (horse marking)
    picture(s)   **H:**238
Pinto da Costa, Manuel (president of São Tomé and Príncipe)   **S:**41
Pin tumbler cylinder locks   **L:**274–75, 276
Pinturicchio (Italian artist)
    picture(s)
        fresco of Virgin Mary and Christ Child   **M:**119
Pinworms   **D:**198–99
Pinyon see Piñon
Pinzón family   **P:**558

Pioneer (space probes)   **S:**340c, 360, 361
    Jupiter   **J:**159; **P:**279
    observatories in space   **O:**9
    search for life on other planets   **L:**211
    Venus   **V:**303a
Pioneer life   **C:**421; **P:**251–62
    in American literature   **A:**208; **R:**304
    Boone, Daniel   **B:**334–35
    Bowie knife, origin of   **B:**347
    Buffalo Bill   **B:**429
    cosmetics made at home   **C:**553
    Crockett, Davy   **C:**582
    Death Valley   **D:**131
    education: battle for the common school   **E:**83
    fur trade in North America   **F:**519–24
    gold discoveries   **G:**250–52
    guns and ammunition   **G:**415–22
    guns used for signal communication   **C:**467
    Montana   **M:**439
    Oklahoma "Sooners"   **O:**80
    overland trails   **O:**267–83
    Pony Express   **P:**383–84
    westward movement   **W:**140–44
Pioneers, The (novel by James Fenimore Cooper)   **C:**541
Pioneers' Town (state-sponsored camp, Budapest, Hungary)   **B:**422a
Pioneer Venus (space probe)   **S:**359, 360
Pipelines   **T:**289
    across Panama to relieve congestion in the canal   **P:**50
    Israel's water supply   **M:**302
    natural gas   **N:**60
    Trans-Alaska Pipeline   **A:**152, 158
    transporting petroleum products   **P:**172
    picture(s)
        in deserts of Saudi Arabia   **D:**126; **M:**301
        natural gas   **N:**58
Pipe organ   **O:**218–19
Piper Cub (airplane)   **A:**110, 111
Pipes (for conducting liquids, gases, or semisolids)
    plumbing   **P:**339–40
    seamless steel pipe   **I:**337
    valves   **V:**269–70
Pipes (for smoking)
    picture(s)   **I:**180
Pipes (vertical lava mass in which diamonds are usually found)   **D:**144, 145; **G:**70
Pipes of Pan see Panpipes
Pipestone National Monument (Minnesota)   **M:**334
Pipe welding   **P:**340
Pipil (Indians of Central America)   **E:**197
Pippin, Horace (American artist)
    picture(s)
        Mr. Prejudice   **A:**79m
Pippin, Scottie (American basketball player)
    picture(s)   **B:**95f
Piraeus (Greece)   **G:**331
    picture(s)   **M:**212
Pirandello, Luigi (Italian novelist and dramatist)   **D:**303; **I:**383, 409
Piranha (fish)   **F:**199
Pirarucu (fish)   **B:**380
Pirates and piracy   **P:**263–64 see also Vikings
    Caribbean Sea and islands   **C:**115
    Kidd, Captain William   **K:**241
    Laffite, Jean   **L:**23
    Ottoman corsairs   **O:**262
    picture(s)
        pirate makeup   **P:**338
Pirates of Penzance, The (operetta by Gilbert and Sullivan)   **G:**208–9; **M:**557
Pisa (Italy)
    picture(s)
        cathedral and leaning tower of   **C:**134; **I:**391
Pisac (Peru)
    picture(s)   **P:**159

Pisano, Giovanni (Italian sculptor and architect) **P:558**
  Italian sculpture of the later Middle Ages **I:**393
Pisano, Nicola (Niccolo) (Italian sculptor and architect) **P:558;**
  S:98, 100
  Italian sculpture of the later Middle Ages **I:**393
  picture(s)
    Baptistery of Pisa Cathedral pulpit **I:**393
Pisanosaurus (dinosaur) **D:**172
Piscataqua River (Maine–New Hampshire) **N:**152
Pisces (constellation) **C:**522
  picture(s) **C:**522
Pissarro, Camille (French painter) **P:558–59**
  impressionism in modern art **F:**430; **I:**103; **M:**387
Pistachio nuts **N:**434–35
Pistils (of flowers) **F:**282; **P:**307
Pistols (small guns) **G:**416
  duelists used **D:**346
Piston engines *see* Reciprocating engines
Piston rings (of the internal-combustion engine) **I:**264
Pistons (mechanical devices)
  airplane engines **A:**115
  automobile engines **A:**547
  brakes **A:**551
  hydraulic machines **H:**297–98, 299
  internal-combustion engines **E:**230; **I:**264
  jet engines compared to piston engines **J:**90
  piston engines **E:**229
  pneumatic tools **H:**300
  pumps **P:**540
  steam engines **S:**443
Pita (Greek bread) **B:**385
Pitcairn, John (British commander) **R:**198
Pitcairn Island (Pacific Ocean) **P:**10
  Bounty mutineers **B:**251
Pitch (in music) **M:**537–39, 541
  Africa, music of **A:**79
  range of the voice **V:**377
Pitch (of sound) **S:**258
  characteristic of the voice **S:**396
  voice disorders **S:**398
Pitch (sticky substance exuded from certain trees) **R:**184
Pitchblende (ore) **C:**601; **U:**230
Pitcher (in baseball) **B:**79–80
Pitcher, Molly (American heroine of Revolutionary War) **R:**206
Pitcher plants **P:**314
  picture(s) **W:**146
Pitching (movement of an airplane) **A:**113, 114
Pitch Lake (Trinidad and Tobago) **T:**315
Pith (of a woody stem) **W:**222
Pitman, Sir Isaac (English inventor of a shorthand
  system) **S:**160
Pitons (used in mountain climbing) **M:**500
Pitot-static tube (of an airspeed indicator) **A:**118
Pit quarry **Q:**4b
Pitt, William, Earl of Chatham (British statesman) **P:265**
  French and Indian War **F:**464
Pitt, William, the Younger (British statesman) **P:265**
  oratory **O:**191
  solution to England's trouble with Ireland **E:**252
  picture(s) **P:**459
Pitti Gallery (Florence, Italy) **M:**525
Pittsburgh (Pennsylvania) **P:**126, 133, **266–67**
  air pollution control **F:**291
  picture(s) **P:**135
    bridges **B:**395
    Carnegie Museum of Natural History **P:**134
Pittsburgh, University of **P:**266
Pituitary dwarfism *see* Dwarfism
Pituitary gland **B:**288; **G:**227, 228
  hormonal diseases **D:**184
  relation to the brain **B:**367
Pit vipers (poisonous snakes) **S:**212
  picture(s) **S:**214
Pius I, Saint (pope) **R:**290
Pius II (pope) **R:**291

Pius III (pope) **R:**291
Pius IV (pope) **R:**291
Pius V, Saint (pope) **O:**262; **R:**291
Pius VI (pope) **R:**291
Pius VII (pope) **R:**289, 291
Pius VIII (pope) **R:**291
Pius IX (pope) **R:**291
Pius X, Saint (pope) **R:**291, 292; **S:**18d
  Catholic hymns **H:**310
Pius XI (pope) **R:**291
  Lateran Treaty of 1929 **R:**292
Pius XII (pope) **P:268; R:**291, 292
  prayer **P:**431
Pivot joints (in the skeleton) **S:**184b
Pixel (computer term) **A:**298
  computer animation **A:**290
Pixies (mischievous fairies or elves) **P:559**
Pixii, Hippolyte (French instrument maker) **E:**154
Pizan, Christine de (French writer) **F:**436
Pizarro, Francisco (Spanish conqueror of Peru) **P:164, 268**
  conquest of the Incas **I:**110, 173
  Ecuador **E:**69
  exploration of the New World **E:**411
  married Huayna Capac's daughter **I:**195
Pizza (Italian food) **F:**336
  microbes' contribution to **M:**277
  unknown outside Naples before World War II **I:**382
Pizzicato (plucking the string of a musical instrument) **V:**345
PKU *see* Phenylketonuria
Place de la Concorde *see* Concorde, Place de la
Place des Arts (Montreal) **C:**67
Placekicking (in football)
  picture(s) **F:**356
Place names
  personal names derived from places **N:**4
Placenta (organ attached to uterus) **B:**2; **R:**179
Placental mammals **M:**69
  marsupials compared to **M:**114
Placentia (Newfoundland) **N:**145
Placer mining **M:**323
  gold **G:**251
Place Royale (Quebec City) **Q:**11
Placers (alluvial deposits containing minerals) **G:**248–49;
  O:217
Place settings *see* Table setting
Places of interest *see* the places of interest section of country,
  province, and state articles
Place value (in numeration systems) **N:**405
  arithmetic **A:**399
  decimal system **D:**56; **F:**400
Plague (disease) **D:**212 *see also* Bubonic plague
  outbreak in Saint Giles slums of London **L:**285
Plaice (fish) **H:**189
Plainchant *see* Plainsong
Plain City (book by Virginia Hamilton)
  picture(s) **C:**246
Plainclothes officers (in community police) **P:**363
Plains (stretches of flat land) **P:426–29** *see also* Great Plains
  tundra **T:**331
Plains Indians of North America **I:**179–82; **U:**188
  Indian Wars **I:**205
  museum in Browning (Montana) **M:**433
  music **M:**549
  White Buffalo Woman myth **M:**575
  picture(s) **I:**175
Plains of Abraham *see* Abraham, Plains of
Plainsong (plainchant) (musical form) **G:**183; **I:**410; **M:**542
  see also Gregorian chants
  development of musical notation **M:**539
  hymns **H:**310
Plaintiff (in law) **C:**566
Plamondon, Antoine Sébastien (Canadian artist)
  picture(s)
    Portrait of Soeur Saint-Alphonse (painting) **N:**42
Planar defects (in crystals) **M:**153

Planarians (worms)   **W:**312
　　diagram(s)
　　　nervous system   **B:**363
Planck, Max (German physicist)   **L:**225; **P:**231, 237
　　physics, history of   **P:**236
　　science in the 20th century   **S:**76
　　picture(s)   **P:**237
Plane geometry   **G:**120–21; **M:**157
Plane mirrors   **L:**212, 214
Plane projections (of maps)   **M:**97
Planers (tools)   **T:**232
　　preparing wood for furniture-making   **F:**515
　　sawmilling   **L:**326
　　woodworking   **W:**230
Planes (flat surfaces in design)   **D:**136
Planes (tools)   **T:**228–29, 234, 235
Planes, inclined (simple machines) *see* Inclined planes
Planetariums   **P:**269–73
　　make a carton planetarium   **E:**393
　　museums of astronomy   **M:**524
Planetary gears   **T:**280
Planetary nebulas (in astronomy)   **N:**96; **S:**431
Planetesimal theory (of origin of solar system)   **E:**23
　　may be why Uranus' axis is tilted   **U:**231
　　picture(s)   **E:**22
Planetoids *see* Asteroids
Plane trigonometry   **T:**312–13
Planets   **P:**275–82 *see also* Earth; the names of planets
　　astronomy, history of   **A:**471–73
　　comets, orbits of   **C:**452
　　discoveries of planets   **A:**472–73
　　Do planets exist beyond the solar system?   **P:**282
　　dust-cloud hypothesis of formation   **E:**22–23
　　formation   **S:**431
　　geology in the solar system   **G:**118–19
　　planetariums   **P:**269–73
　　planetoids (asteroids)   **S:**241, 244
　　radio astronomy studies   **R:**74
　　satellites   **S:**52
　　spacecraft tracking   **S:**340L
　　space probes   **S:**358–61
　　theories about the sun and planets   **S:**248–49
　　"wanderers" among constellations   **S:**78–79
　　What is the outermost planet in the solar system?   **N:**113
　　zodiac, planets seen in the belt of the   **S:**244
　　picture(s)
　　　relative sizes   **P:**280
Planet X hypothesis (of dinosaur extinction)   **D:**175
Plankton (drifting mass of small organisms)   **A:**181; **P:**283–85
　　crustaceans   **C:**591
　　ocean life   **O:**23–24
　　oceanographic studies   **O:**39
Planned Parenthood Federation of America   **B:**249
Planned Parenthood** v. **Casey (1992)   **W:**213
Planographic printing   **P:**302
Plan Overlord (invasion of France, World War II)   **W:**298
Plan position indicator (PPI) (of radar systems)   **R:**38
Plantagenet family (rulers of England)   **E:**244
Plantain (bananalike fruit)   **M:**78
　　picture(s)   **U:**7
Plantain (broad-leafed weed)
　　picture(s)   **W:**105
Plantar wart (skin disease)   **D:**205
Plantations
　　African American history   **A:**79e–79f
　　Brazilian fazendas   **B:**378
　　colonial America   **C:**414, 416; **H:**181
　　rubber   **R:**345–46
　　sugarcane and pineapple plantations in Hawaii   **H:**55–56
　　picture(s)
　　　colonial America   **C:**420
　　　slaves working in field   **U:**184
　　　tea plantation in Sri Lanka   **S:**414
Plant breeding *see* Breeding, plant

Plant defenses   **P:**316–17
　　weeds say "Hands off"   **W:**104, 106
Plant diseases *see also* the names of individual plants, as Corn
　　fungi   **F:**498, 499
　　vectors (carriers of diseases)   **V:**282–85
　　viruses in plants   **V:**367, 370a
Plante, Jacques (Canadian ice hockey player)   **P:559**
Plant enemies *see* Plant diseases; Plant pests
Planters (machines for sowing seed)   **F:**55, 60
　　picture(s)   **F:**56
Planting (of crops)   **F:**49, 55–56
　　gardens and gardening   **G:**30, 39–41
　　houseplants   **H:**265–69
　　vegetables   **V:**286–94
　　table(s)
　　　when, how and where to plant   **G:**49
Plant kingdom   **K:**253, 256; **L:**209; **P:**299
Plant pests (insects harmful to plants)   **P:**286–91
　　boll weevil   **C:**560–61
　　corn, enemies of   **C:**550
　　vectors (carriers of diseases)   **V:**284
　　weeds   **W:**104–6
Plant propagation   **P:**310
　　apple trees   **A:**332–33
　　gardens and gardening   **G:**40, 51
　　grapes and berries   **G:**298
　　grasses   **G:**316–17
　　houseplants   **H:**267
Plants   **P:**292–321 *see also* Botany; Vegetation; the names of
　　　plants, such as Corn; the natural resources section of
　　　continent, country, province, and state articles
　　acid rain's effects   **A:**10
　　Arctic region   **A:**386b, 386c
　　atmosphere, formation of   **E:**23
　　biological clocks   **L:**203–4, 207
　　bioluminescence   **B:**203
　　biomes   **B:**204, 205, 206, 208, 210
　　bogs   **W:**146–47
　　botanical gardens   **B:**342–43
　　botany   **B:**343
　　breeding *see* Breeding, plant
　　cactus   **C:**4–5
　　cave life   **C:**158
　　cell structure   **C:**160–61
　　climate and vegetation regions   **C:**364
　　coloration   **C:**427–28
　　defenses *see* Plant defenses
　　desert plants   **D:**124
　　diseases *see* Plant diseases
　　Do growing plants break up rocks?   **S:**235
　　dyes, sources of   **D:**369, 371
　　Earth, history of   **E:**24–29
　　Earth's geology affected by   **G:**117
　　ecology   **E:**53–55
　　ecosphere   **N:**63
　　endangered species   **E:**208–10
　　enemies *see* Plant diseases; Plant pests
　　evolution of   **E:**372–79; **F:**386–87
　　experiments in life sciences   **E:**383, 389–91
　　ferns   **F:**93–95
　　fertilizer elements, hunger signs for   **F:**96
　　first plants had no flowers   **F:**280
　　flowers   **F:**280–87
　　food chain producers   **L:**205
　　food plants *see* Plants, food
　　fossils   **F:**380–89
　　gardens and gardening   **G:**26–52
　　genetics   **G:**77–88
　　glands   **G:**226
　　grasses   **G:**314–19
　　houseplants   **H:**265–69
　　How big can a plant grow?   **P:**302
　　Humboldt's geographic findings on   **G:**99
　　jungle   **J:**157–58
　　kingdoms of living things   **K:**253, 256

Play (cont.)
   anthropological study **A:**303
   child development **C:**225, 226
   dogs need to play **D:**255
   dolphins' play **D:**278
   playgrounds **P:**77–78
   play-party games and folk dancing **D:**28
   toys **T:**247–51
Playa lakes (shallow lakes of brackish water) **D:**124; **O:**205
Playboy of the Western World, The (play by John Millington
      Synge) **I:**327
Play dough (modeling material) **C:**354
Player, Gary (South African golfer) **G:**259
   picture(s) **G:**259
Player piano (pianola) **P:**559
   piano rolls **R:**123
Playgrounds **P:**77–78
   kindergarten activities **K:**248
   picture(s)
      Holsteinsborg (Greenland) **G:**372
Playing cards *see* Card games
Play-party games
   dancing **D:**28
   songs **F:**326
Play production **P:**333–38; **T:**156–58
   puppets and marionettes **P:**547, 548
Plays *see* Drama
Playwrights (dramatists) (writers of plays) **T:**157
Plaza (public square in a city) **L:**57
Plaza de toros (bullfighting arena) **B:**449
Pleadings (in law) **C:**566
Plebeians (social class in ancient Rome) **P:**369; **R:**311, 313
Plebiscite **G:**276; **P:**559
Plectrum (used in playing a guitar) *see* Pick
Pledge of Allegiance (to the flag of the United States)
   saluting the flag **F:**246
Pléiade (French poets) **F:**437
Pleiades (in Greek mythology) **P:**559
Pleiades (star cluster) **N:**96
Pleiku (South Vietnam) **V:**337
Pleistocene epoch (in geology) **E:**25, 29
   Paleo-Indians **I:**164–65
   Pleistocene Ice Age **I:**10
   prehistoric people **P:**438–40
Plenty Coups (Crow Indian chief) **M:**441
Plenzdorf, Ulrich (German writer) **G:**182
Plessy v. *Ferguson* (Supreme Court ruling sets precedent for
      separate-but-equal facilities) **A:**79i; **C:**330; **S:**114
Pleura (membrane around the lung) **L:**328
Plexiglas *see* Lucite
Plexuses (networks of spinal nerves) **N:**116, 117
Pliers (tools) **T:**230
   picture(s) **T:**230
Plies (of a tire) **T:**209, 210
Plimoth Plantation (Massachusetts) **M:**144
Plinian eruption (kind of volcanic eruption) **V:**381
Pliny the Elder (Roman historian)
   account of the discovery of glass **G:**229
   died in Vesuvius' eruption **G:**108
   encyclopedia of natural sciences **E:**205
Pliny the Younger (Roman orator and writer) **L:**78
   early written account of a ghost **G:**199
Pliocene epoch (in geology) **E:**25, 29
Plique-à-jour (enameling technique) **E:**202
PLO *see* Palestine Liberation Organization
Ploesti oil fields (Romania) **R:**297
   picture(s) **R:**298
Plots (in fiction) **C:**478; **N:**358
Plotters (computer input devices) **C:**481
Plovdiv (Bulgaria) **B:**441
Plow-plant (once-over tillage) method (for planting
      seeds) **F:**55–56
Plows **F:**54
   agriculture, history of **A:**97, 98, 99, 100
   prairies developed by cultivation **P:**427–28

   preparing the soil for planting **F:**48–49
   picture(s) **C:**413
Plowshare (blade of a moldboard plow) **F:**54
Plucked instruments (in music) **M:**551
Plugs (lures for fishing) **F:**211
Plum **P:**108, 109
Plumage (feather coats of birds) **B:**214
Plumb bob (tool) **T:**234
Plumbing (piping system in a building) **P:**339–40
   origin of the word **L:**92; **P:**340
   picture(s)
      installing water pipes **B:**433
Plummer, Christopher (Canadian actor) **P:**559
   picture(s)
      in *Othello* **D:**298
Plurality (method of deciding an election) **E:**126
Plush (fabric) *see* Cut-pile fabric
Plutarch (Greek biographer) **G:**359
Pluto (planet) **P:**282, **341–44**
   astronomy, history of **A:**473
   Is Pluto really a planet? **P:**341
   not always the outermost planet **N:**113; **S:**241
   telescope makers, discoveries of **T:**61
Pluto (Roman god) *see* Hades
Plutonium (element) **E:**176; **U:**230
   breeder reactors **N:**370
   fission **F:**223
   nuclear weapons **N:**374
   radioactive wastes **N:**373
Plutonium dioxide **S:**363
Plutus (in Greek mythology) **P:**559
Plying (of yarn) **T:**141
Plymouth (Massachusetts) **P:**346, 347
   colonial sites you can visit today **C:**422
   places of interest in Massachusetts **M:**144
Plymouth Colony (in Massachusetts) **P:**344–47
   American colonies **M:**146; **T:**171–72
   colonial life in America **C:**409, 415
   King Philip's War **I:**202
   Mayflower **M:**188
   Thanksgiving Day **T:**153–54
   United States, history of the **U:**174
Plymouth Company (business company to colonize
      America) **T:**168, 170
Plymouth Rock (landing spot of Pilgrims) **P:**346
Plywood **W:**226–27
   furniture **F:**515
   need for better adhesives **G:**243
Plzeň (Czech Republic) **C:**609
PMS *see* Premenstrual syndrome
Pneumatic systems **H:**300
   tubes for mail delivery **P:**397
Pneumatic tires **A:**552; **T:**208, 209
Pneumatic trailers (for trucks) **T:**321
Pneumonia (infection of lungs) **D:**199; **L:**330
P-n junctions *see* Diodes
Po, Fernão do (Portuguese explorer who discovered
      Cameroon) **C:**40
Poaching (illegal hunting) **E:**209
Pocahontas (Native American princess) **I:**177; **J:**22, 23;
      V:356, 358
   Smith, John **S:**205
   picture(s) **I:**177
Pocatello (Idaho) **I:**51, 55
Pocket 110 cameras **P:**203
Pocket billiards *see* Pool
Pocket gophers (rodents) **R:**274
Pocket mice **R:**274
Pocket veto *see* Veto
Pocket watches
   picture(s) **W:**45
Pocono Mountains (Pennsylvania) **P:**129
Podgorica (capital of Montenegro, Yugoslavia) **M:**442; **Y:**357
Podkopayeva, Lilia (Ukrainian gymnast) **O:**120

Polarization (of light) L:223–24
   ants can sense polarized light A:319
Polarizing filters (in photography) P:205
Polarizing microscopes M:282
Polar night jet stream J:91
Polaroid Land Cameras P:216
Polar orbit (of space satellites) S:366
Polar regions see also Polar exploration
   Antarctica A:292–95
   Arctic A:386b–387
   climate C:364
   frigid zones Z:380
   glaciers G:221–25
   latitudes of North and South poles L:79
   longitudes of North and South poles L:80
   Mars, polar caps of M:108
   measuring depth of ice and snow I:6–7
   North America, climate of N:290
   picture(s)
      birds B:240
Polders (low land reclaimed from a body of water, in the
      Netherlands) N:120a
   picture(s) N:119
Polecats (related to weasels) O:258–59
   picture(s) O:258
Polenta (corn meal dish of Italy) I:383
Poles (for fishing) F:209
Poles, magnetic (in physics) M:28–29, 30
   electricity and magnetism E:140
   electric motors E:152
Poles, magnetic (of the Earth) E:11; G:437; R:49
Poles, telephone W:226
Pole vault (field event) T:257
   world record T:261
   picture(s) T:252, 256
Poliakoff, Stephen (English dramatist) D:303
Police P:363–68
   courts C:566–67
   crime and criminology C:575, 576
   crystallography used to identify poisons C:595
   local department helped by FBI F:76
   motorcycles, use of M:498
   Peel, Sir Robert P:118
   problems of law enforcement L:88
   radar used to catch speeding automobiles R:39
   Royal Canadian.Mounted Police C:79; P:368
   scuba diving squads S:187
   picture(s) M:512
      Royal Canadian Mounted Police N:295
Police (English rock group) R:262d
Police Athletic League (PAL) P:365
Police dogs D:241; P:365
Police procedural novel (type of fiction) M:565
Polichinelle (Italian puppet character) see Pulcinella
Policy Development, Office of (of the United States) P:451
Poliomyelitis (infantile paralysis) (virus disease) D:199
   Kenny, Elizabeth M:339
   Roosevelt, Franklin D., was victim of R:322–23
   vaccination V:260
   picture(s)
      polio virus V:362
Polis (city-state) see City-states
Polisario (Saharan independence group) M:461
Polish Corridor (created by Treaty of Versailles, after World War
      I) G:162; P:361
Polished rice R:229
Polishing see Grinding and polishing
Polish language P:357–58
   tongue twister used to catch German spies T:225–26
Polish Partitions (1772, 1793, 1795) P:361; U:11
Polish Rider, The (painting by Rembrandt van Rijn)
   picture(s) P:25
Polish United Workers' Party P:361
Politburo (governing body of Soviet Communist Party) U:44
Politi, Leo (American author and illustrator) P:559

Political action groups
   older people O:97
Political asylum P:559
Political cartoons see Cartoons, political
Political conventions see Conventions, political
Political economy see Economics
Political geography G:106
Political parties P:369–73 see also the government section of
      country articles; the names of parties
   beginnings of party system in England E:249, 253
   cartoon symbols C:127
   democratic right to choose D:106
   elections E:127–29
   Electoral College E:132
   government systems determined by G:274
   national nominating convention originated in Jackson's
      administration J:6
   organization in Congress U:168, 169
   parliaments P:83
   prime minister P:458
   Progressive (Bull Moose) formed by Theodore
      Roosevelt R:332
   state legislatures do business on party basis S:438
   United States, history of the U:178
   United States president is his party's leader P:453
   vice presidency of the United States V:326
   What was the Know-Nothing Party? F:128
Political platforms see Platforms, political
Political science (study of government and political
      organization) P:559
   international relations I:273–74
Political writing (United States) A:198–99
Polity (government by the many) G:273
Poliziano (Italian poet) I:406
Polk, James Knox (11th president of the United
      States) P:374–78
   Mexican War M:239b
   Monroe Doctrine M:427
   picture(s) P:446
Polk, Sarah Childress (wife of James K. Polk) F:169–70;
      P:374, 378
   picture(s) F:171
Polka (dance) D:30
Polk Doctrine (American foreign policy) P:377
Pollack (fish) F:217
Pollaiuolo, Antonio (Italian painter) I:396
Polled Hereford (breed of beef cattle) C:151
Pollen and pollination F:282, 284–86
   air pollution A:122
   bees B:117; H:202
   corn C:550
   flowers and seeds of plants P:308
   fossil pollen from Ice Ages I:14–15
   fruitgrowing F:483
   hay fever, cause of D:187
   reproduction P:310; R:177
   trees T:309–10
   use in dating archaeological sites A:361
Pollio, Vitruvius (Roman author) E:228
Polliwogs see Tadpoles
Pollock, Jackson (American painter) P:378
   action painting in modern art M:396b
   American painting in the 20th century P:31; U:134
   drawing, history of D:316
   surrealism's influence on S:518
   watercolor painting W:61
   picture(s)
      Number I (painting) M:396
      Number 3 (painting) D:133; U:134
      Reflection of the Big Dipper (painting) P:378
Polls (survey of people's opinions) see Opinion polls
Poll tax (fixed amount of money levied on citizens of a
      community) C:332
   Twenty-fourth Amendment U:160
   voting rights of African Americans A:79i

Pollution and pollutants see also Air pollution; Water pollution
air pollution   **A:**122–25; **E:**299–301
chemical industry   **C:**197
chemical poisoning of the environment endangers
   species   **E:**209
cities, problems of   **C:**321–22
detergents   **D:**141; **E:**297
energy sources, environmental problems of   **E:**219–20
environment, quality of   **E:**297–302
experiments and other science activities   **E:**398–99
fertilizers   **E:**297
food chain affected by   **B:**244
hazardous wastes   **H:**72–73
insecticides   **E:**299
national parks, challenges to   **N:**56
natural resources, how people affect   **N:**63, 66
noise   **N:**271
petroleum, environmental problems of   **P:**175–76
population explosion   **P:**396–97
sanitation, sewage, and refuse (solid waste)
   disposal   **E:**297–98, 301–2; **S:**33
steel industry   **I:**338
technology, effects of   **T:**41
water pollution   **E:**297–99; **W:**64–69
Pollux (star in Gemini constellation)   **C:**525
Polo (sport)   **P:379**
Afghanistan's form of polo   **A:**43
Polo, Marco (Venetian traveler)   **P:380**
brought back ice cream recipes   **I:**22
China   **C:**269
described Oriental cities   **C:**317
discovered source of spices   **H:**113
predecessor of the age of exploration   **E:**403–4
Venice, history of   **V:**301
   picture(s)
      miniature painting   **P:**380
Polonaise (dance of Poland)   **D:**30
Polonium (element)   **E:**176
discovered by the Curies   **C:**601
Polo ponies   **P:**379
Poltava, Battle of (1709)   **S:**529
Poltergeist (type of ghost)   **G:**200
Polyandry (family relationship)   **F:**44
Polybenzimidazole (manufactured fiber) see PBI
Polybius (Greek historian)   **G:**359; **H:**136
Polychaetes see Bristle worms
Polychlorinated biphenyls (PCB's) (toxic chemicals)
hazardous wastes   **H:**73
used as insulators in transformers   **T:**272
Polyclitus (sculptor)   **G:**350
Polyconic projections (of maps)   **M:**97
Polydectes (in Greek mythology)   **G:**365
Polyester (class of synthetic fibers)   **F:**111–12; **N:**437
   picture(s)
      micrograph of fibers   **F:**110
Polyethylene (plastic)   **P:**322
   diagram(s)
      molecule   **P:**325
Polygamy (form of marriage and family organization)   **F:**44
Polygnotus (Greek artist)   **G:**349
Polygonal numbers   **N:**386–88
Polygons (in geometry)   **G:**64, 121
Polygraph (lie detector)   **L:**193
Polygyny (family relationship)   **F:**44
Polyhedral viruses   **V:**362
Polyhedrons (in geometry)   **G:**123
Polyhymnia (in Greek mythology)   **P:559** see also Muses
Polymers and polymerization   **P:322**
chemical term defined   **C:**204
chemistry, history of   **C:**211
fibers   **F:**110, 111; **N:**440
petroleum refining   **P:**172
synthetic rubber   **R:**347–48a
Polynesia (Pacific islands)   **P:**3–4

Polynesian art
   picture(s)
      beaten barkcloth   **T:**141
Polynesians (Pacific islanders)   **P:**4–5
Hawaii   **H:**53–55
Maoris of New Zealand   **N:**235
Micronesia, Federated States of   **M:**280
Tonga   **T:**224
Western Samoa   **W:**124
   picture(s)
      Cook Island children   **P:**8
      Tahitian woman   **P:**10
Polyolefins (artificial fibers)   **F:**111
Polyphemus (one of the Cyclopes in Greek mythology)   **O:**51
Polyphony (in music)   **I:**410; **M:**541, 542
Africa, music of   **A:**79
baroque music   **B:**69
choral music   **C:**283
hymns   **H:**308
Leonin and Perotin (French composers)   **F:**444
Middle Ages   **M:**297
religious music   **G:**183
Polyplacophorans (mollusks)   **M:**407
Polypody (fern)   **F:**94
Polypropylene rope   **R:**334
Polyps (form of jellyfish and other coelenterates)   **J:**70–71,
   72, 73, 74–75
corals   **C:**547–48
Polytheism (belief in several gods)   **R:**146
Polytonality (in music)   **M:**398
Polyunsaturated fats   **N:**425
Polyurethane (synthetic rubber)   **R:**348a
foam used for furniture cushions   **U:**228
skateboard wheels   **S:**182
Polyvinylchloride (PVC)   **F:**214
Pomade (perfumed ointment)   **P:**151
Pomaks (Bulgarian-speaking Muslims)   **B:**440
Pomanders (bags or boxes containing fragrant
   substances)   **P:**150
jewelry   **J:**94
Pome fruits   **P:**113
Pomegranate (fruit)
Byzantine mosaics used designs of
   pomegranates   **B:**489–90
Pommel horse (in gymnastics)   **G:**432
   picture(s)   **G:**431
Pomo (Indians of North America)   **I:**186
Pompadour, Marquise de   **P:**559
Pomp and Circumstance marches (by Elgar)   **E:**188, 293
Pompeii (Italy)   **P:381**
Rome, art of   **P:**17; **R:**319
   picture(s)   **A:**355
      decorated wall   **I:**257
Pompey the Great (Roman statesman)   **C:**6; **R:**315–16
Pompidou, Georges Jean Raymond (French political leader)
election of 1969   **F:**420
Pompidou Center (Paris, France)   **A:**386a
   picture(s)   **F:**432
Pompion (colonial American name for pumpkin)   **C:**411
Ponape (Pacific island) see Pohnpei
Ponca (Indians of North America)   **I:**179
Ponca City (Oklahoma)   **O:**87
Ponce (Puerto Rico)   **P:**531
Ponce, Manuel M. (Mexican composer)   **L:**75
Ponce de León, Juan (Spanish explorer)   **P:382**
exploration of the new world   **E:**409
Florida   **F:**260, 271
tomb in Cathedral of San Juan Bautista (Puerto
   Rico)   **P:**531
   picture(s)
      exploration of the new world   **A:**87
Poncho (cloak or shawl worn in South America)
ruana is the Colombian poncho   **C:**404
Pond, Peter (American fur trader)   **A:**171

Ponderosa pine (tree)
    Arizona has world's largest stand **A:**404
    picture(s)
        state tree of Montana **M:**429
Ponds (small bodies of water)
    eutrophication **W:**65
    freezing of water **I:**3–4
    how to look at life in pond water through a
        microscope **M:**283
Ponies
    Chincoteague ponies **V:**354
    polo ponies **P:**379
    picture(s)
        ancient breeds of domestic horses **H:**237
        Chincoteague ponies **N:**55; **V:**348
Pons, Lily (French-born American opera singer) **P:**559
Ponselle, Rosa Melba (American opera singer) **P:**559
Pontchartrain, Lake (Louisiana) **P:**560
Pont du Gard (Roman aqueduct near Nîmes, France)
    picture(s) **E:**228; **R:**318
Ponte Milvio (bridge, Rome, Italy) **R:**306
Ponte Vecchio (bridge, Florence, Italy) **F:**258
Pontiac (chief of the Ottawa Indians) **I:**179; **P:**382
    Indian wars **I:**203–4; **O:**74
Pontiac's Rebellion (1763–1766) **I:**203–4; **P:**382
Pontian, Saint (pope) **R:**290
Pontic Mountains *see* Northern Anatolian Mountains
Pontil (rod used in shaping glass) **A:**316
Pontius Pilate *see* Pilate, Pontius
Pont Neuf (bridge, Paris, France) **F:**425
Pontoons (landing gear of seaplanes) **A:**114
Pony clubs **H:**227
Pony Express (mail service) **P:**383–84
    communication, history of **C:**466
    picture(s)
        stamp **S:**421
Poodle (dog) **D:**245, 251
Pooh (character in A. A. Milne's stories)
    picture(s) **M:**311
Pool (pocket billiards) **B:**179
Pool checkers (game) **C:**193
Poole, Elijah *see* Muhammad, Elijah
Poole, William Frederick (American librarian) **L:**180
Pool of London **L:**289
Pool of Water Lilies (painting by Monet)
    picture(s) **F:**430
Poopó, Lake (Bolivia) **L:**30
Poor *see* Poverty
Poor, John (American lawyer and railroad executive) **M:**49
Poor Henry (romance by Hartmann von Aue) **G:**176
Poorhouses (early form of public welfare) **S:**225
Poor laws (of England and the United States) **S:**225
Poor People's March (Campaign) (on Washington, D.C.) **P:**560
Poor Richard's Almanack (by Benjamin Franklin) **A:**198;
    F:454
    quoted on the importance of a nail **N:**3
    picture(s) **C:**418
Pop art **M:**396b; **P:**31–32; **U:**134
    Warhol, Andy **W:**7
Popayán (Colombia) **C:**403
Popcorn **C:**550
    recipe for popcorn balls **R:**116
Popé (Native American leader) **I:**183; **N:**192, 193
Pope, Albert (built first American bicycle) **B:**177
Pope, Alexander (English poet) **P:**384
    essays in poetry form **E:**322
    place in English literature **E:**277–78
    quotations from *An Essay on Criticism* **Q:**20
Pope, John (American Union general) **C:**341
Pope, John Russell (American architect) **N:**40; **W:**31
Popes (of Roman Catholic Church) **R:**290–91, 294
    forms of address **A:**22
    Gregory VII, Saint **G:**377
    Gregory XIII **G:**377
    Holy Roman Empire **H:**160–63

    infallibility **R:**289
    John XXIII **J:**114
    John Paul II **J:**115
    Leo XIII **L:**152
    Paul VI **P:**102
    Peter, Saint **P:**166
    Pius XII **P:**268
    power grows in Middle Ages **M:**294
    Ring of the Fisherman (seal ring of the pope) **J:**99
    Vatican City **V:**280–82
Popeye (comic strip) **C:**129
Popham colony (in Maine history) **M:**49
Popish Plot (1678) **P:**369 *see also* Oates, Titus
    against Charles II of England **E:**246
Poplar (tree)
    picture(s)
        uses of the wood and its grain **W:**224
Popocatepetl ("Smoking Mountain") (volcano, Mexico)
    picture(s) **M:**245
Popol Vuh (collection of Mayan myths) **G:**395; **L:**68; **M:**187,
    569
Popov, Leonid (Soviet cosmonaut) **S:**348
Popovich, Pavel Romanovich (Soviet cosmonaut) **S:**346
Poppy (flowering plant)
    medicine made from **F:**281
    opium poppy **N:**15
    source of morphine **D:**333
    picture(s) **G:**46
        golden poppy is state flower of California **C:**19
        yellow poppy **P:**318
Poppy seed **H:**114
Popular Front (in France) **F:**418–19
Popular music **M:**545; **R:**261
    compared to folk music **F:**321
    country music **C:**563–65
    rock music **R:**261–62d
    United States, music of the **U:**210
Popular sovereignty (in a democracy) **D:**106
Popular (squatter) sovereignty (in United States history)
    Douglas proposed **D:**288
    Kansas-Nebraska Act **K:**191; **L:**243
    Lincoln-Douglas debates **L:**244
Popular vote (for electors of the Electoral College) **E:**132
Population **P:**385–88 *see also* the facts and figures sections
        of continent, country, province, state, and city articles
    Africa **A:**54–55
    Asia **A:**454–55
    birth control **B:**249
    census **C:**167
    cities, densities in **C:**313–14
    continents' populations compared **C:**530
    distribution of world population **W:**263
    environment and population **E:**296–97
    Europe, density in **E:**350–51
    food supply **F:**350, 351
    genetic distribution **G:**87
    How is the U.S. population census taken? **C:**167
    immigration **I:**87–94
    natural resources, demands on **N:**65
    North America **N:**294–95, 298
    old age **O:**96–100
    people and the ecological balance **E:**55
    population geography **G:**106
    poverty as result of overpopulation **P:**420
    races, human **R:**28–31
    rapid growth is world problem **W:**269
    South America **S:**282
    United States, increases in **U:**96
    map(s)
        Africa, density in **A:**58
        Asia, density in **A:**456
        Australia's density **A:**503
        distribution of world population **W:**262
        North America, density in **N:**296
        South America **S:**280

United States, density in **U:**94
Population (in biology) **B:**196; **L:**204
Population cycles (in animals) **A:**286
Population density (number of people who live in an
area) **C:**313–14; **P:**385
diagram(s) **P:**388
Population explosion **E:**296–97; **P:**387
Mexico **M:**241
Population geography **G:**106
Populist Party (in the United States) **P:**372; **U:**188
Harrison's defeat in 1892 **H:**40
Pop-up books **B:**322
Pop Warner League Football (for children) **F:**361
Poquelin, Jean Baptiste *see* Molière
Porcelain **D:**71; **P:**407, 411–12
antiques **A:**316a
ceramics **C:**176, 177
coated steels **I:**337
Danish industry **D:**112
dolls made of **D:**267–68
Japanese art and architecture **J:**51
Korean celadon **K:**298–99
picture(s) **P:**410
Chinese plate **D:**71
Chinese vases **D:**69; **P:**409
Korean celadon **K:**300
Porcupines (rodents) **P:**389; **R:**275–76
quills **M:**74
picture(s) **P:**389; **R:**272
Pores (in the skin)
acne **D:**187
Porgy and Bess (folk opera by George Gershwin) **G:**190;
M:558; **O:**149
story of the opera **O:**161
picture(s) **M:**556; **O:**149
Po River (Italy) **I:**384, 385; **R:**245
tributaries rise in Alps **A:**194b
Pork (meat of hogs) **M:**196
tabooed by certain religions **F:**332
trichinosis from undercooked meat **D:**204
picture(s)
cuts of pork **M:**197
Pork-barrel bills (laws to win votes for politicians) **A:**439
Poromerics (type of plastic) **S:**159
Porphyry (rock) **R:**264
Porpoises (small whales) *see* Dolphins and porpoises
Por que fue sensible (aquatint by Goya) **G:**307
Port (left side of a boat or ship) **S:**11, 151
Porta, Giambattista della (Italian scientist) **C:**395
Portable life-support systems (for astronauts) **S:**340h, 343
Portable typewriters **T:**373
Portage la Prairie (Manitoba) **M:**85
Portages (paths connecting sections of a water route)
around Niagara Falls **N:**242
canoe camping **C:**49
canoe's weight important **C:**97
Grand Portage National Monument **M:**334
Portales, Diego (Chilean statesman) **C:**254
Port Antonio (Jamaica) **J:**18
Port-au-Prince (capital of Haiti) **H:**10
picture(s) **H:**9
Iron Market gate **C:**112
Port Chalmers (New Zealand) **N:**240
Portcullis (gate of a castle) **C:**131–32; **F:**377; **H:**178
Porter (type of beer) **B:**115
Porter, Cole (American composer and lyricist) **I:**157; **M:**558;
P:560
Porter, Edwin S. (American film producer) **M:**487–88
Porter, Eliot (American photographer) **P:**560
picture(s)
nature photograph **P:**199
Porter, Gene Stratton (American writer) **P:**560
Porter, Katherine Anne (American writer) **A:**212
Porter, William Sydney *see* Henry, O.
Portes Gil, Emilio (Mexican president) **M:**251

Port Étienne (Mauritania) *see* Nouadhibou
Portfolio assessments (of reading skills) *see* Authentic
assessments
Port-Gentil (Gabon) **G:**3
Port Harcourt (Nigeria) **N:**256–57
Porthos (one of *The Three Musketeers*) **D:**347–48
Portillo, José López *see* López Portillo, José
Portinari, Cândido (Brazilian artist) **B:**376
Port La Joie (now **Charlottetown**) (Prince Edward Island) **P:**466
Portland (Maine) **M:**41, 42, 43, 45, 48
picture(s) **M:**48
Wadsworth-Longfellow House **M:**44
Portland (Oregon) **O:**199, 209, 211; **P:**390
picture(s) **O:**208; **P:**390
public-transit bus **B:**464
Reed College **U:**222
Portland cement **B:**430; **C:**165
Michigan is a leading producer **M:**266
Portland Head Light (Maine) **M:**44
picture(s) **L:**228; **M:**44
Portland State University (Oregon) **O:**211
Port Louis (capital of Mauritius) **M:**181
Port Moresby (capital of Papua New Guinea) **P:**58d
Porto (Portugal) **P:**394
Pôrto Alegre (Brazil) **B:**383; **L:**30
Port of Spain (capital of Trinidad and Tobago) **T:**314
Portolá, Gaspar de (Spanish explorer) **C:**29
Porto-Novo (capital of Benin) **B:**143
Porto Rico *see* Puerto Rico
Portrait dolls **D:**270
Portrait of a Married Couple (painting by Hals)
picture(s) **D:**363; **N:**121
Portrait of Charles I Hunting (painting by van Dyck)
picture(s) **D:**361
Portrait of Madame X (painting by Sargent)
picture(s) **S:**41
Portrait of Soeur Saint-Alphonse (painting by Plamondon)
picture(s) **N:**42
Portrait of the Artist as a Young Man (novel by Joyce) **I:**327–28
Portrait of Two Young Men (painting by van Dyck)
picture(s) **V:**277
Portrait painting
Copley, John Singleton **U:**127
Dutch and Flemish art **B:**67; **D:**359
early American painters **U:**127
English painting **E:**260–61
folk art **F:**292–93
Gainsborough, Thomas **G:**4
Hals, Frans **H:**15
Holbein, Hans, the Younger **H:**148
mummy portraits **P:**17
Peale, Charles Willson **U:**127
Rembrandt's portraits **A:**438d; **R:**155–56
Reynolds, Sir Joshua **R:**210
Sargent, John Singer **S:**41
Stuart, Gilbert **R:**225; **U:**128
Van Dyck, Anthony **V:**277
Portrait photography **P:**218
picture(s)
lighting **P:**207
Portrait sculpture **S:**90, 96
Rome, art of **R:**319
picture(s)
Rome, art of **A:**438a
Port Royal (Nova Scotia) **C:**71; **T:**166
Ports *see* Harbors and ports
Port Said (Egypt) **E:**107; **S:**480, 481
Portsmouth (New Hampshire) **N:**159, 160
colonial sites you can visit today **C:**422
picture(s)
harbor **N:**157
Strawbery Banke **N:**158
Portsmouth, Treaty of (1905) **N:**159
Port Sudan (Sudan) **S:**479

Prado (museum, Madrid, Spain) **M:**15, 522; **P:**423–24
  picture(s) **P:**423
Praetorian Guard (in ancient Rome) **P:**560; **R:**316
  picture(s)
    relief carving **R:**316
Praetorius, Michael (German composer) **C:**118; **G:**184
Pragmatic Sanction (decree of Austria's Charles VI) **A:**524;
    H:3
Pragmatism (school of philosophy)
  Dewey, John **D:**143
  James, William **J:**21
Prague (Praha) (capital of Czech Republic) **C:**609, 610;
    P:425
  picture(s) **P:**425
    Hradčany Castle **C:**606
    outdoor café **C:**607
Prague Spring (in Czechoslovakian history) **C:**612
Praia (capital of Cape Verde) **C:**102
Prairie, The (novel by James Fenimore Cooper) **C:**541
Prairie crocus (flower)
  picture(s)
    provincial flower of Manitoba **M:**81
Prairie dogs (rodents) **R:**274
  poisoning of prairie dogs almost caused extinction of the
    black-footed ferret **E:**54
Prairie Hills (South Dakota) **S:**314
Prairie Home Companion, A (radio program) **M:**339
Prairie lily (flower)
  picture(s)
    provincial flower of Saskatchewan **S:**43
Prairie Provinces (Canadian provinces of Alberta, Manitoba,
    Saskatchewan) **A:**164–72; **C:**54; **M:**80–86; **S:**42–51
  Winnipeg **W:**190
Prairies **P:**426–29
  in American literature **A:**208
  Drift Prairie region of North Dakota **N:**322, 324
  grassland biomes **B:**205
  Indiana's protected prairie lands **I:**147
  Mississippi **M:**350
  North American soils **N:**291
  wildflowers **W:**171
Prairie schooners **P:**253–54
Prairie State (nickname for Illinois) **I:**62
Prairie style (of Frank Lloyd Wright) **W:**316
Prairie wolves *see* Coyotes
Praising Angels (tapestry) *see* Angeli Laudantes
Prajadhipok (king of Thailand) **T:**152
Prakrit (ancient language of India) **D:**296
Prandtauer, Jacob (Austrian architect) **G:**171
Prang, Louis (German-born American lithographer and
    engraver) **C:**298; **G:**375
Pranks (in American folk humor) **F:**317
Praseodymium (element) **E:**176
Praslin (island, Seychelles) **S:**129
Prather, Victor A., Jr. (American military balloonist) **B:**36
Pratolini, Vasco (Italian novelist) **I:**409
Pratt, Daniel (American manufacturer) **A:**142
Pravda (Russian newspaper) **N:**199
Praxiteles (Greek sculptor) **G:**350
Prayer **P:**430–31
  Engel v. *Vitale* and school prayer **S:**509
  grace **G:**445
  hymns **H:**306–12
  Islam **I:**352–53
  Judaism **J:**146a, 148
  litanies (ritual prayers) **E:**46
  public schools **F:**163
  Roman Catholic Church **R:**294
  saints **S:**18c
Prayer, Book of Common **P:**560
  Charles I **E:**245
  Henry VIII and the Church of England **E:**243
  selected prayers from **P:**430, 431
Prayer, The Lord's *see* Lord's Prayer
Prayer of Manasseh (apocryphal book of Bible) **B:**163

Prayer wheel (used by Tibetan Buddhists) **P:**560
Praying mantis (insect) *see* Mantis
Praying towns (of Massachusetts) **M:**148–49
Preakness horse race **H:**232
Precambrian Era (in geology) **E:**26; **F:**383, 385
  Archaeozoic Era **E:**25
  table(s) **F:**384
Precedent (in law) **C:**566
Precepts (rules of Roman Catholic Church) **R:**293
Precession (wobbling motion)
  Earth's movement **P:**271
  gyroscope **G:**436–37
Precincts (voting districts) **E:**129
Precious metals **E:**167
Precious stones
  aluminum compounds **A:**194c
  birthstones **G:**72
  carats **J:**92, 93
  gemstones **G:**68–76
  jewelry **J:**93
Precipitation (rain, snow, sleet, and hail) **R:**93–97 *see also*
    the climate section of continent, country, province, and
    state articles
  acid rain **A:**9–10
  Arctic region **A:**386c
  Australia **A:**505–6
  climate **C:**361–64
  clouds **C:**382–85
  drought **D:**328, 329
  fog **F:**290–91
  how rivers flow **R:**236–37
  Nebraska's extreme conditions **N:**85
  water cycle **W:**49
  weather, creation of **W:**81, 82, 83
  weather observations, making your own **W:**94
  world water resources **W:**257
  map(s)
    Africa **A:**50
    Asia **A:**448
    Australia **A:**509
    world patterns **W:**256
Precocial birds **B:**229
Precognition (kind of extrasensory perception) **E:**428
Pre-Columbian art (of Middle and South American Indian
    civilizations)
  ancient textile weaving in Peru **T:**143
  decorative arts **D:**72–73
  Peru **P:**164
  picture(s)
    Chimu woven tunic **T:**141
    embroidered Peruvian cloak **N:**100
    gold ornament of Colombia **C:**407
    Mayan sculpture **H:**199; **I:**170
    Moche funeral sculpture **I:**170
Predators
  in animal communities **L:**205–6
  cats are beasts of prey **C:**141–50
  marine organisms' food chain **O:**26
Predestination (in Calvinism) **C:**34
Predicate adjectives **P:**93
Pre-emption laws (for settlers of public lands) **P:**516, 517
Preening (of waterfowl) **D:**341
Prefabricated buildings **B:**438; **H:**171
  picture(s) **B:**438
Preferred stocks (those with priority in payment of
    dividends) **S:**454
Prefixes (additions at front of root parts of words) **W:**239
Pregnancy **M:**69
  AIDS can be passed to fetus **A:**100b
  baby **B:**2–3
  birth control (prevention of pregnancy) **B:**247–49
  child development **C:**223–24
  folic acid **V:**370c
  menstruation **M:**221, 222
  nutrition **N:**427

smoking, dangers of   H:76
teenagers   F:39
Prehensile tails
monkeys   M:421
opossums   M:114–15
Prehistoric animals   P:432–34
cats   C:142
dinosaurs   D:164–75
elephants   E:183
evolution   E:373–74, 375–76
fossils   F:380–89
marsupials   M:113
Prehistoric art   P:435–37
art as a record   A:438–38a
decorative arts   D:69–70
painting   P:14–15
sculpture   S:92–93
watercolor painting in caves   W:59
picture(s)
bison carving   A:438
Prehistoric people   P:438–42 *see also* Stone Age
Africa   A:65
agriculture, history of   A:97
archaeological evidence of   A:358–60
caves   C:157
cereal grains   G:286–87
chemistry, history of   C:206
clothing of   C:372
communication, history of   C:462–63
disabled people   D:176
domestication of the horse   H:237
etiquette, history of   E:337
fire and early people   F:141–42; H:94
grass and civilization   G:314
hunters and gatherers of food   F:329
Ice Age   I:12–13
magic used for curing disease   M:203
metallurgy, history of   M:236
numeration systems   N:403
physical anthropologists study   A:301
poetry in the dance   P:349
pottery   F:142; P:407
Southeast Asia, remains in   S:334
Stonehenge   S:462
technology, beginnings of   T:40
tools   T:232–33
toys   T:250
tunnel building   T:339
picture(s)
fossil skull   A:46
Stone Age lighting   L:231
Tollund man, head of   A:362
Prehistory (history before writing was invented)   A:349, 362
Prejudice
Hispanic Americans   H:133, 134, 135
racism   R:34–34a
segregation   S:113
Prelude (musical form)   M:546
Prelutsky, Jack (American poet)   C:235
"Jellyfish Stew"   N:274
Premadasa, Ranasinghe (Sri Lankan president)   S:416
Premature baby   B:2, 3
respiratory distress syndrome   L:330
vitamin E deficiency   V:370d
Premenstrual syndrome (PMS) (group of symptoms related to a woman's menstrual cycle)   P:558
managing menstruation   M:222
Premier *see* Prime minister
Preminger, Otto (American producer and director)   P:560
Premiums (insurance payments)   I:251
Premolars *see* Bicuspids
Přemysl family (rulers of Bohemia)   C:610
Prendergast, Maurice (American painter)   W:61
Preparators (in museums)   M:532
Preparatory drawings (in art)   D:313, 315

Preparatory schools   P:443–44
Connecticut   C:506
Prepositional phrases (in sentences)   P:94
Prepositions (words that relate a noun or pronoun to other words in sentences)   G:289; P:94
Pre-Raphaelite Brotherhood (group of 19th-century painters and poets)   E:263, 285
Rossetti, Dante Gabriel   R:338
Presbyopia (focusing disorder of the eye)   E:431
Presbyterian Church   C:293, 294; R:132
Church of Scotland   U:56
Knox, John   K:289
Presbyters (of the church)   C:287
Preschool *see* Nursery schools
Prescott (Arizona)   A:414
Prescott, Samuel (American patriot)   R:193
Prescott, William (American soldier)   R:200
Prescott, William Hickling (American historian)   A:204
types of historical writing   H:139
Prescription drugs   D:332
Preservation of American Antiquities, Act for (1906)   N:45
Preservation of food *see* Food preservation
Presidency of the United States   P:445–53 *see also* the names of presidents
Cabinet officers advise the president   C:2
candidate qualifications   E:128
Cleveland: one man, two presidents   C:357
commander in chief of armed forces   U:105
Congress and the Presidency   U:144
Electoral College   E:132
executive branch of the government   U:169–70
first ladies   F:164–80b
first to die in office was William Henry Harrison   H:43
forms of address   A:22
how many were lawyers   L:91
impeachment   I:99
libraries *see* Presidential libraries
naturalized citizens may not become president   C:326
New Hampshire primary election   N:150
presidential consideration of Congressional bills   U:166
Presidential Succession Act (1947)   V:328
Roosevelt re-elected for fourth term   R:326
three-time runners: Bryan   B:416; Clay   C:353
Twenty-fifth Amendment   U:160
Twenty-second Amendment   U:159
vice presidency of the United States   V:324–31
Washington's influence as first president   W:43–44
White House   W:164–67
Presidential governments   G:276
Presidential libraries
Dwight D. Eisenhower Library   K:181, 184
Franklin D. Roosevelt Library   N:214, 217
Gerald R. Ford Library   M:264
Harry S. Truman Library-Museum   M:370, 373
Herbert Hoover Presidential Library   I:298
John Fitzgerald Kennedy Library   M:141, 144
Lyndon B. Johnson Library   T:130
National Archives administers some   N:26
Rutherford B. Hayes Library   O:68
Presidential Medal of Freedom   D:67; P:560
Presidential Range (New Hampshire)   N:152
Presidential Succession Act (United States, 1947)   V:328
Presidential Unit Citation (American award)
picture(s)   D:66
President pro tempore (of the Senate)   U:169; V:325
President's Commission on the Status of Women   W:212b
President's Day (in the United States)   H:152
President's Foreign Intelligence Advisory Board (of the United States)   P:451
President's Intelligence Oversight Board (of the United States)   P:451
President's Own, The (Marine Corps band)   U:123
Presidents' wives *see* First ladies
Presley, Elvis (American entertainer)   R:262c
birthplace   M:358

Graceland T:82
　　Memphis was his home M:219
　　rock music R:262a
　　picture(s) M:518; R:262
　　　　birthplace M:358
Prespa, Lake (Greece–Macedonia) M:4
Press, freedom of the *see* Freedom of the press
Press agents *see* Public relations
Press associations *see* News services
Pressburg (Slovakia) *see* Bratislava
Pressed glass G:236
　　picture(s) G:235
Presses, hydraulic H:299; M:234
Presses, printing N:202; P:470–71, 474, 475–76, 477
　　picture(s) P:469
　　　　Franklin's press F:453
　　　　printing encyclopedias E:207
　　　　printing paper money D:259
Press forging (of metals) M:234
Pressing (extracting fats and oils from plant seeds or
　　pulp) O:78
Press release (document delivering information to a
　　newspaper) N:201
Pressure (in mechanics)
　　gases G:56–59
　　hydraulic systems H:297–99
　　ice melted by skates' pressure I:4
　　pneumatic systems H:300
Pressure, air (atmospheric) *see* Air pressure
Pressure cookers (for canning food) H:92
　　steaming food C:534
　　diagram(s) H:91
Pressure gradient force (in meteorology) W:184
Pressure points (for control of bleeding) F:159
　　picture(s) F:159
Pressure-sensitive tapes (adhesives) G:243
Pressure waves *see* Sound waves
Pressurized space suits *see* Space suits
Prester John (legendary Christian king and priest) P:560
Presto (musical term) M:541
Prestressed concrete C:166
Pretoria (administrative capital of South Africa) S:271, 272
Pretzels (food) B:388b
Prevailing winds (climatic control) C:362
Préval, René Garcia (Haitian president) H:12
Prevention of disease *see* Disease, prevention of
Preventive medicine D:210–13
　　cancer, prevention of C:93
　　circulatory system C:306
　　public health P:512–16
　　teeth, caring for T:44
Previn, André (American conductor, composer, and
　　pianist) P:560–61
Prévost, Antoine (Abbé Prévost) (French novelist) F:440
Prez, Josquin des *see* Josquin des Prez
Priam (in Greek mythology) P:561
　　Iliad, story of I:61
Pribilof Islands (Alaska) I:367; O:44
　　breeding territory of northern fur seals F:518
　　picture(s)
　　　　seals H:191
Price, Leontyne (American soprano) O:141
Price, Mark (American basketball player)
　　picture(s) B:95h
Price, Ray (American singer) C:564
Prices E:56–57, 61
　　farm prices A:91, 92; F:61–62
　　food shopping F:348
　　inflation and deflation of I:227–28
　　Nixon's wage-price freeze N:262e
　　retail pricing S:21
　　stock prices in depressions and recessions D:121, 122
　　Universal Price Code S:498
Price supports (for farm crops) F:61

Prickly pear (cactus) C:5
　　weed in Australia P:290
　　picture(s) L:112
Pride, Charlie (American singer) C:565
Prides (of lions) C:144
Priestley, J. B. (English writer) P:561
Priestley, Joseph (English scientist) P:454
　　picture(s) P:454
Priests M:293–94
Primary batteries B:103a–103b
Primary colors C:424–25; D:371
Primary elections E:128–29, 131
　　New Hampshire N:150
Primary products (raw materials) I:275
Primates (order of mammals) P:455–57
　　apes A:325–27
　　hands F:83–84
　　monkeys M:420–22
　　picture(s)
　　　　chimpanzee as example M:69
Primaticcio, Francesco (Italian artist) F:424; R:171
Primavera (Spring) (painting by Botticelli) P:20; U:3
　　picture(s) B:345
Prime (grade of meat) F:349
Prime meridian (Greenwich meridian) T:203
　　great circles on maps and globes M:96
　　Greenwich observatory G:374b
　　international date line I:270
　　latitude and longitude L:80
Prime minister (premier) P:458–59
　　Canada C:77, 78
　　Canada: forms of address A:22
　　England, history of E:249, 252
　　England, list of E:247
　　Gladstone's career G:225
　　parliaments P:83–84
　　Sri Lanka had first woman prime minister S:416
　　United Kingdom U:68
　　Walpole considered Britain's first prime minister W:5
Prime mover (energy source) E:133
Prime numbers N:385
Primer (explosive charge) E:423
Prime rate (lowest interest rate on loans) B:57
Primers (textbooks) E:81
　　etiquette, history of E:337
Prime time (on television) T:68
Priming (of pumps) P:539
Priming powder (for guns) G:415
Primitive art
　　folk art F:292–98
　　Metropolitan Museum of Art collection M:239a
　　as a record A:438–38a
　　sculpture S:92
Primitive people
　　art as a record A:438–38a
　　cultural anthropologists study A:301
　　dance celebrations D:22
　　law enforcement by folkways L:87
　　North American Indian beginnings I:164–65
　　religions R:145
　　superstition S:503
Primitive religion *see* Religion, primitive
Primo de Rivera, Miguel (Spanish political leader) S:381
Primroses (flowers)
　　picture(s) N:127
Primus, Pearl (American dancer and choreographer) P:561
Prince, The (political work) *see Principe, Il*
Prince Albert (Saskatchewan) S:49
Prince Albert National Park (Saskatchewan) S:47
Prince Edward Island (Canada) P:460–67
　　Canada's garden province C:52, 62
　　picture(s)
　　　　Green Gables P:465
Prince Edward Island National Park (Prince Edward
　　Island) P:465

Professional Bowlers Association **B:**350a
Professional football **F:**360, 364
Professional Golfers' Association (PGA) **G:**257, 258, 260
Professional Rodeo Cowboys Association (PRCA) **R:**277
Professions *see* Vocations
Profile Mountain (New Hampshire rock formation) *see* Cannon Mountain
Profiles in Courage (book by John F. Kennedy) **K:**210
Profit (in economics) **B:**471, 472, 473
Profit and loss statement *see* Income and expense statement
Profit motive (in economics)
    motive or aim of capitalism **C:**103
    percents, use of **P:**146
    product development **S:**20
Progesterone (hormone) **G:**228
Prognosis (in medicine) **C:**91
Programmed instruction **P:**483
    materials and methods in education **E:**89
Programming, computer *see* Computer programming
Program music **G:**187; **M:**547; **R:**304
Programs, television *see* Television programs
Progressive Conservative Party (in Canada) **C:**77
Progressive education **E:**88–89
    kindergarten and nursery schools **K:**249–50
Progressive Era (in United States history) **U:**190
Progressive Party (Bull Moose Party) (in the United States) **P:**372
    Roosevelt, Theodore **R:**332
    Truman wins in spite of third parties **T:**326
    Wilson wins because of third party **T:**6; **W:**178–79
    picture(s)
        symbol **P:**370
Prohibition (laws against alcoholic beverages) **P:**483–85
    Coolidge's administration **C:**539–40
    Eighteenth Amendment **U:**158
    Maryland's opposition **M:**134
    Twenty-first Amendment **U:**159
Prohibition Party (American history) **P:**484
Project Head Start **K:**248, 250
    compensatory education **E:**90
Project HOPE (Health Opportunity for People Everywhere) **P:**561
Projections (of maps) **M:**97
Projectors
    motion pictures **M:**479, 487
    planetariums **P:**270–72, 273
Projects *see also* Experiments and other science activities; How to; Indoor activities
    4-H club projects **F:**395–96
Prokaryotae (kingdom of living things) **B:**12; **F:**383; **K:**253, 258–59; **L:**209
    taxonomy **T:**27
    picture(s)
        antibiotics' effects on **A:**309
Prokofiev, Sergei (Russian composer) **P:**485; **R:**382
    opera **O:**148
Promessi sposi, I (The Betrothed) (novel by Alessandro Manzoni) **I:**408
Prometheus (in Greek mythology) **G:**363–64, 365; **M:**570
Prometheus (moon of Saturn) **S:**56
Promethium (element) **E:**176
Prominences (flames extending from the sun) **S:**495
    picture(s) **S:**492
"Promise" (poem by Paul Dunbar) **D:**349
Promised Land (Canaan) **M:**469
Promontory (Utah) **U:**252
Prompters (of plays) **P:**334
Pronghorn (hoofed mammal) **H:**217
    picture(s) **B:**206; **I:**47
Pronouns (words that take the place of nouns) **P:**92–93
Pronunciation **P:**486 *see also* individual letters of the alphabet
    English language **E:**267
    French compared to English **F:**435
    German language **G:**175
    Latin language **L:**76
    phonics **P:**194
    pronunciation guide to this encyclopedia **A:**590–91
    slang imitates sounds **S:**191
    some Greek words in everyday use **G:**353
    some Hawaiian words **H:**55
    speech **S:**395, 396
    speech disorders **S:**397
    vocabulary building, use in **V:**374
Proof (amount of alcohol in a beverage) **W:**161
Proof (in engraving and etching) **E:**294, 326
Proof (in printing) **P:**470
    linoleum-block printing **L:**251
Proof coins (struck for collectors) **C:**399
Proofreaders' marks **P:**487
Proofreading **B:**326, 330; **P:**487
    researching reports **R:**183
    spelling **S:**400
    picture(s) **E:**207
Propaganda **P:**488–89
    communication **C:**471
Propagation (of plants) *see* Plant propagation
Propane (gas, used as fuel) **F:**488
    hot-air balloons **B:**38
    picture(s)
        tanks **F:**488
Propellants (rocket fuels and oxidizers) **M:**344, 345; **R:**256, 257–58
Propellers
    airplanes **A:**39, 115, 116–17
    ocean liners, history of **O:**33
    screw propellers of ships **S:**156
Proper factors (of numbers) **N:**386
Proper fractions **F:**397
Proper nouns **P:**92
Properties (articles used in plays) *see* Props
Properties (chemical) **C:**199; **E:**167
Properties (of materials) **M:**151, 153–54
    metals **A:**190; **M:**233
Properties (of numbers) **N:**398–99
Property
    census **C:**167
    Communism, origins of **C:**472
    crimes against property **C:**574–75
    personal property disposed of by a testament (will) **W:**174
    real property **R:**112d–113
    Russia and private ownership of farm land **R:**363
Property insurance *see* Insurance, property
Property management (of real estate) **R:**113
Prophets (books of Bible, Old Testament) **B:**158–60
Prophets (in Islam) **I:**346
Prophets, Hebrew **J:**104–5
    Elijah **E:**189
    Isaiah **I:**345
    Jeremiah **J:**77
    Moses **M:**469
Prophets Mosque (Medina, Saudi Arabia)
    picture(s) **I:**347
Propodeum (part of ant's abdomen) **A:**319
Proportion (in art) **D:**134
    ancient Greek vases **G:**348
    architecture **A:**370
    Italian Renaissance architecture **A:**378
Proportion (in mathematics) **R:**107
Proportional Representation (P.R.) **P:**561
Proprietary hospitals **H:**252
Proprietor (of a business) **B:**470
Prop roots (of plants) **P:**303
Props (used in plays) **P:**337
    prop room backstage **T:**157
    picture(s) **P:**335, 336
Propulsion, jet *see* Jet propulsion
Propulsion system (in missiles) **M:**344–45
    rockets **R:**255–60
Pro Rodeo Hall of Champions (Colorado Springs, Colorado) **C:**438

picture(s) C:438
Proscenium stage T:156
picture(s) T:156
Prosecutor (in law) C:567; J:163
Prose Edda (book by Snorri Sturluson) N:277, 278, 279
Proserpina (Roman goddess) *see* Persephone
Pro set (formation in football) F:359
Prosimians (group of primates) P:455, 456
Prospecting (hunting for minerals) M:319–20, 324
gold G:251
for uranium with a Geiger counter G:67
Prosperity was just around the corner (slogan) H:224
Prosthodontist (in dentistry) D:115
Protactinium (element) E:176
Protectionism (in trade) I:276
Protective coloration A:283
amphibians A:214b
birds B:223
butterflies and moths B:478
fish F:200
frogs and toads F:477
insects use for protection I:243
molting of birds B:214
octopus O:292
optical illusion helps animals to survive O:175
shrimps S:167
tigers T:198
picture(s)
butterflies and moths B:479
Protective devices (of animals and plants) A:282–83
aardwolf H:305
amphibians A:214b–215
arachnids A:348
birds B:222–23
butterflies and moths B:478
cats, wild C:149
eel's body mucus E:97
frogs and toads F:477
hedgehogs' spines H:101, 102
insects I:243
leaves, special functions of L:117
lizards L:270–71
mammals' weapons for attack M:74
mollusks M:407
mustelids spray foul-smelling liquid O:257
olingos discharge foul-smelling secretion R:27
opossums play dead O:171
porcupines' quills P:389; R:276
skunks' chemical defense O:256; S:189
spiders S:405
turtles' shells T:356
picture(s)
insects I:242
Protective tariff T:23
Proteins
biochemistry, studies in B:187
biological classification determined by L:209
blood B:255, 257
body chemistry B:269, 292–93, 297–98; L:199
cotton meal is a source of C:561
digestion of B:277; D:161, 162–63
enzymes E:303
fibers F:108
gene splicing of bacteria G:90
genetics G:84–85
grain and grain products G:281, 282, 284
green tobacco leaves are a source of T:213
making of proteins B:297–98
milk has two kinds M:307
muscle cells contain special proteins B:275; M:519
nutrition N:423
soybeans S:337
viruses V:363, 364, 366
Proterozoic Eon (in geology) E:26
Protesilaus (in Greek mythology) P:561

Protestant Episcopal Church *see* Anglican Church
Protestantism P:490–94
baroque art, influence on B:64
Calvin, John C:34
Christianity, history of C:291–95
divorce D:230
English church under Henry VIII and Elizabeth I E:191, 242–43
forms of address for the clergy A:22
hymns H:308–10
Luther, Martin, led Reformation L:331
major denominations P:494
marriage rites W:101–2
prohibition P:484
Quakers Q:4–4a
Reformation R:130–33
Reformation spread standard form of German language G:175
reforms in the Roman Catholic Church R:288
Thirty Years' War T:179
Protest literature A:212
Proteus (in Greek mythology) P:561
Protist kingdom (group of one-celled organisms) K:253, 258; L:209; T:27
algae, classification of A:180
protozoans, classification of P:495
separating animals from plants A:264
Protoceratops (dinosaur) D:174
Protocol (kind of etiquette) E:337; T:296
Protons (atomic particles) A:485, 488; C:201, 202, 204
cosmic rays C:554, 555
elements E:166
ions and ionization I:287–89
nuclear energy N:366, 367
positive charges of electricity E:135
Proto-oncogene (genetic material) C:90, 91; V:369–70
Protoplasm (living matter)
cell structure C:160
Proto-science (term used for mythology) M:573
Protostars A:475
Prototypes (in automobile design) A:553
Protozoans (one-celled organisms) K:258; M:276; P:495–97
diseases caused by D:182–83
picture(s) A:265
Protozoologists (scientists who study protozoans) P:495
Protractor (mechanical drawing tool) M:200
geometry G:121
Proust, Marcel (French novelist) F:115, 442; N:361
Provençal (French dialect) F:433
Provence (region of France) F:404
Provensen, Alice and Martin (American writers and illustrators of children's books) C:240; P:561
picture(s)
illustration from *The Glorious Flight* C:247
Proverbs (book of the Old Testament) B:160
Proverbs (traditional sayings) P:498 *see also* Quotations
Africa, literature of A:76a, 76b
folklore F:311
Poor Richard's Almanack F:454
Providence (capital of Rhode Island) R:216–17, 219–20, 222, 225; U:174
founded by Roger Williams T:174; W:172
picture(s) R:221
Providence River (Rhode Island) R:215
Province House (Charlottetown, Prince Edward Island)
picture(s) P:467
Provincetown (Massachusetts) M:144
Pilgrims P:345; T:171
Provincetown Players (theatrical group) D:304; O:122; T:159
Provincial government (Canada) C:78–79
income tax I:111
libraries L:178
Provo (Utah) U:253–54
Provolone (Italian cheese) D:12
Provost, Etienne (Canadian hunter and guide) P:561

Proxima Centauri (star) S:429
Proximity fuses (of explosive shells) G:426
Proxmire, Edward William (American senator) U:139
Prudhoe Bay (Alaska) A:149, 152; T:331
Prunariu, Dumitru (Romanian cosmonaut) S:348
Prunes P:108
Pruning (of trees)
 apple trees A:332
 fruit trees F:483
 grape vines G:298
 stone fruit trees P:108
Prussia (former German state) G:160
 Berlin was its capital B:148
 Bismarck, Otto von B:250
 Franco-Prussian War F:452
 Frederick (kings) F:459–60
 Frederick William (kings) F:461
 Moltke, Helmuth von M:408
Prut River (Moldova–Romania) M:402
Przewalski's wild horse H:243–44
Przhevalski, Nikolai (Russian explorer) E:415
Psalms (book of the Old Testament) B:160
 Dead Sea Scrolls contain commentaries on D:47
 hymns H:306, 307, 308–9
 religious poems of King David D:43
 Twenty-third Psalm P:431
 picture(s)
  11th-century Psalter B:161
Psalter (Christian hymnal) H:307, 309
 picture(s)
  11th-century B:161
Psaltery (ancient stringed instrument) K:238
Pseudopods (fingerlike tubes of protoplasm) M:276; P:496
Pseudosuchia (ancestors of dinosaurs) D:168
Psittacosis (disease) see Parrot fever
Psoriasis (skin disease) D:199–200
PSR 1913 + 16 (binary star system) R:144
PSR B1257 + 12 (pulsar) P:282
Psychiatry M:225–28
 first reforms of treatment for mentally ill M:206
 Jung, Carl J:156
 mental health M:223, 225
Psychoanalysis M:208
 Freud, Sigmund F:474–75
 mental illness M:228
Psychological dependence (on narcotics) N:16, 17
Psychological time (change that is felt and experienced) T:204
Psychology P:499–511
 art of misdirection in magic M:23–24
 child development C:223–26
 crime, causes of C:575
 Do you remember everything you perceive? P:504
 dreaming D:317–18
 extrasensory perception E:427–28
 Freud, Sigmund F:473–75
 guidance counseling G:401–2
 hypnosis H:313–15
 illusion of motion in motion pictures M:478
 intelligence I:253–54
 Jung, Carl J:156
 learning L:98–106
 mental health M:223–25
 mental illness M:225–28
 Pavlov, Ivan P:103
 research in advertising A:34
 television, influence of T:71
 time, psychological T:204
 time management T:205–6
 What is an intelligence test? P:489
 What is instinct? P:506
 What is personality? P:503
 witchcraft beliefs W:209

Psychology, applied (in guidance counseling) G:401–2
Psychopharmacology (science dealing with effects of drugs on mental activity) M:228
Psychoses (forms of mental illness) M:227
Psychosomatic diseases D:186
 mental illness M:227
Psychotherapy (treatment for mentally ill persons) M:228
 narcotics addicts, treatment of N:17
Psychrometers (used to measure humidity) W:84
 how to make W:93
 picture(s) W:85
PT-109 (torpedo boat commanded by John F. Kennedy) K:206
Ptarmigans (birds) A:286
 picture(s)
  willow ptarmigan is state bird of Alaska A:145
PTA's see Parent-teacher associations
Pterodactyl (flying reptile)
 picture(s) D:168
Ptolemaic rulers of Egypt E:108
 Egyptian art and architecture of E:117
Ptolemaic system (of astronomy) A:471
 picture(s) A:472
Ptolemy (Ptolemacus), Claudius (Alexandrian astronomer and geographer) A:471; G:99; S:79
 history of map making M:98
 physics, history of P:233
 What and where are the Mountains of the Moon? A:61
Ptolemy I (founder of the Ptolemaic dynasty in Egypt) P:561
Ptyalin (digestive enzyme) B:296
P-type (positive type) semiconductor T:275
 diagram(s) T:274
Puberty (period of physical development during adolescence) A:23
Public accountants B:313
Public administration I:225
Public and Indian Housing, Office for H:270
Public assistance see Welfare, public
Public broadcasting (educational television) T:69
Public Debt, Bureau of the T:294
Public domain (of public lands) P:516–17
Public Enemy (motion picture, 1931) M:491
Public health P:512–16
 air pollution A:122–25; E:299–300
 ancient Rome's sanitation systems M:204
 cities, problems of C:321; U:236
 community helps to prevent disease D:211–13
 dentistry D:115
 environment, problems of the E:295–302
 fluoridation F:288–89
 food regulations and laws F:345–47
 hazardous wastes H:72–73
 health H:77
 hospital services H:253
 medical contributions of 19th century M:207–8
 mental retardation R:189–91
 noise pollution and control N:271
 nurses and nursing N:418–19
 Red Cross services R:126–27
 sanitation E:297–98, 301–2; S:33
 smoking is a health hazard S:207
 United Nations World Health Organization U:75
 vaccination required for travel V:261
 water pollution E:297–99; W:64–69
 water supply E:297–98
Public Health Service, United States P:512, 513–15
 Health and Human Services, United States Department of H:78–79
 smoking, efforts against S:207
Public houses (pubs) (taverns in the United Kingdom) U:58
 picture(s) U:58
Public housing
 New York City N:230
Public interest litigation L:90
Publicity (programs of public relations) P:518
 book publishing B:333

Pumps P:539–40
  air pressure experiments of Robert Boyle B:354
  fountains F:394
  heat pumps H:97
  hydraulic systems H:297, 299
  steam engines S:444
  vacuum, formation of V:263
Puna (plateau in Argentina) A:391
Punahou School (Honolulu, Hawaii) H:57
Puncak Jaya (highest point on New Guinea) N:148
Punch and Judy (puppet characters) P:544
Punchbowl (national cemetery, Hawaii) *see* National Memorial
    Cemetery of the Pacific
Punch card systems (for computers) C:486–87
  automation uses A:529
Punctuation P:540–43
Punic Wars (264–146 B.C.) **P:543**; R:314
  Hannibal H:26
Punishment
  colonial America C:417
  crime and criminology C:574–76
  early law enforcement L:88
  juvenile crime J:167–70
  law enforcement, steps in L:87, 88
  prisons P:480–82
  reformatories P:482
Punjab (state of India) I:127, 129, 134
Punjabis (people of Asia) P:35
  picture(s) P:35
Punk rock music R:262d
Puns (plays on words) H:279
  homonyms H:194
  jokes and riddles J:126
Punt (ancient civilization) E:400–401
Punt (in football) F:355–56
  picture(s) F:356
Punta, Cerro de (mountain, Puerto Rico) P:528
Punta del Este (Uruguay) U:240
Puntarenas (Costa Rica) C:557
Punty (iron rod used in glassmaking) G:229, 236
Pup, The (companion star to Sirius) S:429–30
Pupa (resting stage of insect cycles) I:232–33
  ants A:321
  bees B:119
  beetles B:127
  butterflies and moths B:476
  metamorphosis M:238
  protection of I:249
  picture(s)
    butterflies and moths B:477
Pupil (of the eye) B:275; E:430; M:208g
  lenses L:149
  picture(s)
    contracting and dilating M:518
Puppets and marionettes P:544–48
  Indonesian puppet plays I:207
  Japanese Bunraku J:32–33, 53
  Malay shadow plays M:55
  motion picture special effects M:484
  theater of China and Japan T:162
  three-dimensional animation A:289
Puppies D:252, 254–56
Puranas (Sanskrit literature) I:140
Purcell, Henry (English composer) E:292
  chamber music C:184
  opera in baroque period B:70
Purdue University (Indiana)
  picture(s) I:148
Purebred animals and plants
  cats C:137, 138, 139
  cattle D:5
  dog breeds D:247, 253
  genetic engineering G:88
Pure Food and Drug Act (United States, 1906) *see* Food and
    Drug Act, Federal

Purgatory (state between heaven and hell) P:562
Purges (in the Soviet Union under Stalin) C:473–74; U:50
Purging (self-induced vomiting) D:190
Purification of the Virgin Mary *see* Candlemas Day
Purim (Feast of Lots) (Jewish festival) J:146b; **P:549**
Puritan Revolution *see* Civil War, English
Puritans (in English and American colonial history)
  American literature A:197
  Calvin's teachings C:34
  Charles I clashes with the Puritans E:245
  Christmas carols outlawed by C:299
  colonial life in New England C:409, 417–18
  Connecticut settled by C:514
  Cromwell, Oliver C:585
  England, history of E:243
  Massachusetts Bay Colony T:172–73
  Reformation R:133
  relations with Plymouth Colony P:344, 347
  tax-supported schools E:80
Purkinje, Johannes (Czech scientist) S:73
Purl stitch (in knitting) K:279
Purple (color) C:429
Purple City *see* Forbidden City
Purple finch (bird)
  picture(s) B:238
Purple Heart (medal for bravery) D:65
  picture(s) D:66
Purple Sea (Finnish tapestry by Oili Maki)
  picture(s) T:22
Purple snail (mollusk)
  picture(s) S:147
Purple tube sponge
  picture(s) S:411
Purse seines (fishing nets) F:218
  picture(s) F:219
Purseweb spiders S:403
Pursuivants (assistants to heralds) H:110
Purvis, Robert (American abolitionist) A:6a
Pus (fluid in infected sores) D:208
Pusan (South Korea) K:298, 303; **P:550**
  picture(s) P:550
PUSH *see* Operation PUSH
Pusher prop (airplane engine) A:117
Pushkin (Russia)
  picture(s)
    palace R:373
Pushkin, Aleksander (Russian writer) D:300; N:360; R:377
Pushkin State Museum (Moscow, Russia) M:526
Pushtu (language) A:42
Pushtuns (Pathans) (a people of Afghanistan) A:42, 45; K:193
  Pakistan P:35
  picture(s) P:35
Push-ups (exercise) P:227
Push waves (of earthquakes) *see* P-waves
Pussy willows T:309–10
Putnam, Israel (American Revolutionary War officer) C:515;
    R:199
Putnam, Rufus (American military engineer and
    pioneer) **P:562**; W:141
Putter (golf club) G:254
Putting (in golf)
  picture(s) G:256
Put-together puzzles P:551
Puyallup (Indians of North America) I:188
Puzzle jugs P:552
Puzzles P:551–52
  crossword puzzles C:587–88
  early charades C:186
  mathematics in everyday life M:160
  number puzzles N:389–92, 394–95
  puzzle box in psychology P:504–5
  ring puzzle experiment P:510
PVC *see* Polyvinylchloride
P-waves (of earthquakes) E:14, 35–36, 37
Pyelonephritis (kidney disease) K:244

PHOTO CREDITS

The following list credits the sources of photos used in THE NEW BOOK OF KNOWLEDGE. Credits are listed, by page, photo by photo—left to right, top to bottom. Wherever appropriate, the name of the photographer has been listed with the source, the two being separated by a dash. When two or more photos by different photographers appear on one page, their credits are separated by semicolons.

P

2 © R. Stuart Cummings—Southern Stock Photo Agency; © Douglas Faulkner—Photo Researchers; © Lee Boltin.
3 © Photo Network; © Lee Boltin.
4 © Jack Fields—Photo Researchers; © David Austen—Woodfin Camp & Assoc.
5 © Lee Boltin
7 The Granger Collection; The Granger Collection.
8 © Jack Stein Grove—Tom Stack & Assoc.; © Jeffrey Aaronson—Network Aspen.
9 © Ian Steele—International Stock Photo; © Jeffrey Aaronson—Network Aspen.
10 © Timothy O'Keefe—Southern Stock Photo Agency; © Kal Muller—Woodfin Camp & Assoc.
14 Art Reference Bureau
16 Vatican Library, Rome—Art Reference Bureau; Giraudon—Louvre, Paris; Art Reference Bureau.
20 Art Reference Bureau
21 Louvre, Paris—Art Reference Bureau
22 The Metropolitan Museum of Art; Art Reference Bureau; Kunsthistorisches Museum, Vienna—Art Reference Bureau.
25 Frick Collection—New York; Pinacothek, Munich—Art Reference Bureau; Louvre, Paris—Art Reference Bureau.

26 National Gallery, London—Art Reference Bureau; Louvre, Paris—Art Reference Bureau.
27 Real Accademia de Belles Artes de San Fernando, Madrid—Art Reference Bureau; Art Reference Bureau.
28 The National Gallery, London—Art Reference Bureau; Louvre, Paris—Art Reference Bureau.
31 The Museum of Modern Art, N.Y.; The Museum of Modern Art, N.Y. photo—Marlborough-Gerson Gallery, N.Y.; Whitney Museum of American Art, N.Y.
33 The Sherwin-Williams Co.
35 © Arvind Garg—Gamma Liaison; © Fabry/Sipa—Leo de Wys; © Arvind Garg; © Arvind Garg—Gamma Liaison.
36 © Fabry/Sipa—Leo de Wys; © Bill Kaufman—Leo de Wys.
38 © Emil Muench—Photo Researchers; © J. Polleross—The Stock Market.
39 © Photo Researchers; © John Giordano—SABA.
40 The Bettmann Archive; © Paolo Koch—Photo Researchers
40a © Keystone—Sygma; © Charlyn Zlotnik—Woodfin Camp & Assoc.
40d © Raymond Dabolli—Sygma; © Maxim Clermont—Woodfin Camp & Assoc.; © Richard Nowitz.
41 UPI/Bettmann
43 © Jacques Langevin—Sygma

47 © Harvey Lloyd—The Stock Market; © Robert Frerck—Woodfin Camp & Assoc.
48 © Timothy Ross—Picture Group
50 © Robert Frerck—The Stock Market; © Harvey Lloyd—The Stock Market.
51 The Granger Collection
52 © Robert C. Simpson—Tom Stack & Assoc.
53 © J. Allan Cash LTD.
54 © Joe Sohm—The Stock Market; © Ulrich Zillmann—Okapia/Photo Researchers.
55 © Tommaso Guicciardini—Science Photo Library/Photo Researchers
56 © Ted Horowitz—The Stock Market
57 © Stephanie Maze—Woodfin Camp & Assoc.
58a © Robert W. Ginn—Unicorn Stock Photos
58b American Crafts Council
58d Alpha
60 United States Parachute Association
61 William E. Shapiro
62 Salmer
64 Luis Villota—The Stock Market
65 Abril—Gamma Liaison
68 J. Alex Langley—DPI
69 Francis Bannett—DPI
70 Rene Jacques
71 Bernard G. Silberstein—Rapho; Servicios Oficiales del Turismo Frances en Espana; Michel Cambazard.
72 Serrallier—Rapho Guillumette
73 Rene Jacques

74	Carle—Centra le Farbbild Agentus
76	Nicholas Foster—The Image Bank
77	Martin VanderWall—Leo de Wys
78	H. Armstrong Roberts
79	Melchior DiGiacomo—The Image Bank; H. Armstrong Roberts
80	Kahn Kurita—Gamma Liaison
84	Keystone
85	© William S. Peckover—Peter Arnold, Inc.; © Labat/Jacana—Photo Researchers; © Tom McHugh—Photo Researchers.
86	© Tom McHugh—Photo Researchers; © Gunter Ziesler—Peter Arnold, Inc.; © Steve Littlewood—Oxford Scientific Films/Animals Animals.
95	Ted Spiegel—Black Star
96	Robert Zuckerman
97	The Granger Collection
100	The Granger Collection
101	UPI/Bettmann Archive; The Granger Collection.
102	AP—Wide World Photos
103	The Granger Collection
104	C. Redenios—Peace Corps
107	Ministry of Agriculture, Paris
108–	Grant Heilman Photography
109	
110	Courtesy of the Pennsylvania Academy of the Fine Arts, Philadelphia. Gift of Mrs. Sarah Harrison (The Joseph Harrison, Jr. Collection); The Nelson-Atkins Museum of Art, Kansas City, Missouri (Purchase: Nelson Trust).
114	Cultured Pearl Associations of Japan and America; © Roudnitska—Gamma Liaison.
115	© James Pozarik—Gamma Liaison; © Claus Meyer—Black Star; © Christophe Loviny—Gamma Liaison.
117	UPI/Bettmann Newsphotos
118	© B. Bisson—Sygma
119	Syndication International
120	John Foster—U.S. Fish and Wildlife Service
120b	Philip Smith—National Audubon Society
122	L. G. Richards—Black Star
123	David Linton; David Linton; U.S. Navy.
125	John Warham; John Warham.
127	© Ed Wheeler—The Stock Market; © Kunio Owaki—The Stock Market; © J. Patton—H. Armstrong Roberts.
128	© H. Mark Weidman; © Isaac Geib—Grant Heilman Photography.
130	© J. Nettis—H. Armstrong Roberts; © Terry Wild Studio.
131	© James Blank—Root Resources
132	© Larry Lefever—Grant Heilman Photography
133	US STEEL; © Larry Lefever—Grant Heilman Photography.
134	© H. Mark Weidman; © H. Mark Weidman; © John A. Wee; © H. Mark Weidman.
135	© H. Mark Weidman
136	© Terry Wild Studio
138	Courtesy of the Pennsylvania Dutch Convention & Visitors Bureau, Lancaster, PA
139	The Granger Collection
140	The Granger Collection; The Bettmann Archive.
141	The Bettmann Archive
146	© Jon Levy/Gamma Liaison
147	© Peter Arnold, Inc.
148	© Ed Bock—The Stock Market
149	The Metropolitan Museum of Art, The Crosby Brown Collection of Musical Instruments, 1889.
154	© Superstock
155	Art Resource
156	© Bevilacqua—Salmer
157	The Bettmann Archive; The Granger Collection.
158	© P. Durand—Sygma
159	Allan Price—Taurus Photos
161	George Holton—Photo Researchers
163	Jerry Frank—DPI
164	Superstock
165	Manley Photo—Superstock
167	© Keith Wood/Tony Stone Images
169	© Joe Whyte/Photo Network
173	© Inga Spence/Tom Stack & Associates
174	Photo courtesy of Phillips Petroleum Company
175	© Michelle Barnes/Gamma Liaison
176	© Vanessa Vick/Photo Researchers, Inc.; © Greg Vaughn/Tom Stack & Associates.
177	Spectrum Colour Library; Hans Reinhard—Bruce Coleman Inc.
178	Picturepoint
179	Chapius—Atlas Photo
180	© Louis Goldman—Photo Researchers
181	© Bob Hahn—Taurus Photo
185	Howard F. Harper—Alpha
186	Robert Frerck—Odyssey Productions
193	© Craig Wells
195	Nipper is a trademark of RCA Corp.
196	© Dewitt Jones—Woodfin Camp & Assoc.
197	© World View/Bert Blokhuis—Science Photo Library/Photo Researchers
198	Andreas Feininger—Life magazine, © Time, Inc.
199	Gift of Eliot Porter in honor of David H. McCalpin—Courtesy of The Metropolitan Museum of Art New York; Peter Turner—The Image Bank; Ernst Haas.
200	Nikon
201	Art Resource
202	Richard Megna—Fundamental Photographs; Polaroid Corporation.
203	Kodak
204	Don Renner
206	© 1974 by Irving Penn—Courtesy of Vogue; Dorothea Lange Collection © The Oakland Collection, The City of Oakland, 1982.
207	Don Renner
208	Don Renner
209	Don Renner
212	Culver Pictures; New York Public Library.
213	Ansel Adams
214	Zimmerman—FPG International
215	Henri Cartier-Bresson—Magnum Photos; Margaret Bourke-White—Life magazine, © 1938, Time, Inc.
216	Philip Hyde
217	Philip Harrington; Ken McVey—After Image.
218	Hologram by Hart Perry—Collection of the Museum of Holography
219	John R. MacGregor—Peter Arnold, Inc.
220	Claude Nuridsany
222	Brian Brake—Photo Researchers
223	Glyn Cloyd
224	Stewart M. Green—Tom Stack & Assoc.; Southern Living—Photo Researchers; © Gary Brettnacher—Tony Stone Worldwide Ltd.
225	Phylane Norman—Nawrocki Stock Photo; T. Zimberoff—Sygma
226	Focus On Sports; Dorothy Tanous—Leo de Wys
227	Dorothy Tanous—Leo de Wys; Candee—Nawrocki Stock Photo
228	© CERN/P. Loiez/Science Photo Library/Photo Researchers
229	© Tony Stone Images; © Leonard Lessin—Peter Arnold, Inc.
230	© Peter Pearson—Tony Stone Images
232	© C. R. O'Dell—Rice University/NASA/Space Telescope Science Institute (all photos on page).
233	The Granger Collection
234	The Granger Collection
235	© Alfred Pasieka—Peter Arnold, Inc.
236	© Floyd Clark—Globe Photos; © Louise Parker—Courtesy, AIP Emilio Segre Visual Archives/American Institute.
237	© Science Photo Library/Photo Researchers; © AIP Emilio Segre Visual Archives—W. F. Meggers Collection/American Institute of Physics; © Paul Ehrenfast—AIP Niels Bohr Library—Jay M. Pasachoff.
238	© AIP Emilio Segre Visual Archives—Francis Simon Collection/American Institute of Physics; The Granger Collection; © Stanford University.
239	© 1984 Royal Observatory Edinburgh—Jay M. Pasachoff
240	Steinway & Sons
242	Steinway & Sons
243	Philadelphia Museum of Art, Gallatin Collection; © SPADEM Paris 1975, Courtesy of Lady Aberconway, Michael Holford Picture Library.
246	The Granger Collection
248	Comet Photo
266	© John A. Wee
269	Courtesy of the Reuben H. Fleet Space Theater; The Granger Collection.
270	Courtesy of Carl Zeiss, Inc.; © Hayden Planetarium.
271	Courtesy of Carl Zeiss, Inc.; Published with permission of Evans and Sutherland Computer Corporation.
272	© Mark E. Gibson; © Brian Sullivan—The American Museum of Natural History/Hayden Planetarium.
273	© Jim Schwabel—NE Stock Photo
274	Courtesy of the Discovery Place, Chapel Hill, North Carolina
275	JPL
285	Douglas P. Wilson
286	© Mickey Gibson—Animals Animals
287	© Patti Murray—Earth Scenes
288	© E. R. Degginger—Animals Animals
289	© Gilbert Grant—Photo Researchers
290	© Garry D. McMichael—Photo Researchers; © Holt Studios—Earth Scenes.
292	© David Muench
293	© Ray Coleman—Photo Researchers; © Willard Clay; © David Muench.
294	© J. Lotter—Tom Stack & Assoc.
295	© Martha Cooper—Peter Arnold, Inc.; The Granger Collection; © Robin Jane Solvang—Bruce Coleman Inc.
296	© David R. Frazier; © Ulrike Wlesch—Photo Researchers; © Thomas Kitchin—Tom Stack & Assoc.
297	© Alon Reininger—Photo Network; © Hans Reinhard—Bruce Coleman Inc.
298	© Adrian Baker—Leo de Wys; © Charles West—The Stock Market; © Lee L. Waldman—The Stock Market.
299	© Leslie Holzer—Science Source—Photo Researchers; © D. Goldberg—Sygma; © Hans Pfletschinger—Peter Arnold, Inc.
300	© Kenneth W. Fink—Photo Researchers
302	© S. J. Krasemann—Peter Arnold, Inc.; © John Mead—Science Photo Library—Photo Researchers.
306	© S. N. Nielsen—Bruce Coleman Inc.
307	© D. Cavagnaro—Peter Arnold, Inc.
308	© Peter Arnold—Peter Arnold, Inc.; © Dr. Jeremy Burgess—Science Photo Library/Photo Researchers.
310	© David R. Frzier
312	© Jack W. Dykinga—Bruce Coleman Inc.; © Dr. E. R. Degginger—Bruce Coleman Inc.
313	© Stephen Collins—Photo Researchers; © Lee Rentz—Bruce Coleman Inc.
314	© Ed Reschke—Peter Arnold, Inc.
315	© Ed Reschke—Peter Arnold, Inc.; © Ed Reschke—Peter Arnold, Inc.; © Nuridsany et Perennou—Photo Researchers.
316	© Matt Meadows—Peter Arnold, Inc.; © Willard Clay.
317	© Michael J. Balick—Peter Arnold, Inc.
318	© S. J. Krasemann—Peter Arnold, Inc.
320	© Willard Clay; © Willard Clay; © Wendell Metzen—Bruce Coleman Inc.
321	© Jim Nilsen—Tom Stack & Assoc.; © Willard Clay; © Willard Clay; © Willard Clay.
323	Avisun Corporation
324	Eastman Chemical Products
328	Shell Chemical Co.
329	Avisun Corporation
330	Art Reference Bureau
331	New York Zoological Society
332	New York Zoological Society
341	Courtesy of the Lowell Observatory
343	NASA—ESA
345	Courtesy of The New York Historical Society, New York City
348	Courtesy of The New York Historical Society, New York City
357	© Chris Niedenthal—Black Star
358	© Gamma Liaison; © Polska Agencja Interpress.
360	© Adam Tanner—Comstock; © Steve Leonard—Black Star.
362	© Adam Tanner—Comstock
363	© Ronnie Rauch—The Image Bank
364	© Richard Hutchings—Photo Researchers; Mick Hicks—Gamma Liaison; © Paul Katx—The Image Bank.
365	© Walter Bibikow—The Image Bank; © John V. A. F. Neal—Photo Researchers; © Yvonne Hemsey—Gamma Liaison.
367	Randy Taylor—Sygma; © Richard Wood—Taurus Photos; © Alvis Upitis—The Image Bank.
373	Courtesy, Democratic National Committee; Courtesy, Republican National Committee
376	The Granger Collection
377	
378	Stedelijk Museum, Amsterdam
379	© Jerry Cooke—Photo Researchers
380	The Granger Collection
381	© Ray Pfortner—Peter Arnold, Inc.
383	The Thomas Gilcrease Institute, Tulsa, Oklahoma
389	© John Cancalosi—Tom Stack & Assoc.
390	© C. Bruce Forster
391	© Paul Thompson—Photo Network
393	© Catherine Karnow—Woodfin Camp & Assoc.; © Gilles Bassignac—Gamma Liaison; ©